CRITICAL COMPANION TO

William Butler Yeats

CRITICAL COMPANION TO

William Butler Yeats

A Literary Reference to His Life and Work

DAVID A. ROSS

Facts On File
An imprint of Infobase Publishing

Facts On File, Inc.
An imprint of Infobase Publishing
132 West 31st Street
New York NY 10001

Library of Congress Cataloging-in-Publication Data
Ross, David A.
Critical companion to William Butler Yeats : a literary reference to his life and work / David A. Ross.
p. cm.
Includes bibliographical references and index.
ISBN 978-0-8160-5895-2 (acid-free paper) 1. Yeats, W. B. (William Butler), 1865–1939—Handbooks, manuals, etc. I. Title.
PR5906.R667 2009
821'.8—dc22   2008013642

Facts On File books are available at special discounts when purchased in bulk quantities for businesses, associations, institutions, or sales promotions. Please call our Special Sales Department in New York at (212) 967-8800 or (800) 322-8755.

You can find Facts On File on the World Wide Web at http://www.factsonfile.com

Text design adapted by Erika K. Arroyo
Cover design by Cathy Rincon

Printed in the United States of America

IBT Hermitage 10 9 8 7 6 5 4 3 2 1

This book is printed on acid-free paper.

CONTENTS

ABBREVIATIONS OF FREQUENTLY CITED TEXTS

AM Foster, R. F. *W. B. Yeats: A Life, I: The Apprentice Mage, 1865–1914.* Oxford and New York: Oxford University Press, 1997.

AP Foster, R. F. *W. B. Yeats: A Life, II: The Arch-Poet, 1915–1939.* Oxford and New York: Oxford University Press, 2003.

Aut. Yeats, W. B. *Autobiographies.* Edited by William H. O'Donnell and Douglas N. Archibald. Vol. 3, *The Collected Works of W. B. Yeats.* New York: Scribner, 1999.

AV Yeats, W. B. *A Vision.* London: Macmillan, 1981.

AV-1925 Yeats, W. B. *A Critical Edition of Yeats's A Vision (1925).* Edited by George Mills Harper and Walter Kelly Hood. London: Macmillan, 1978.

BG Saddlemyer, Ann. *Becoming George: The Life of Mrs W. B. Yeats.* Oxford and New York: Oxford University Press, 2002.

Biblio. Wade, Allan. *A Bibliography of the Writings of W. B. Yeats.* 3d ed. Revised and edited by Russell K. Alspach. London: Rupert Hart-Davis, 1968.

CCP Jeffares, A. Norman and A. S. Knowland. *A Commentary on the Collected Plays of W. B. Yeats.* London and Basingstoke: Macmillan Press, 1975.

CL1 Yeats, W. B. *The Collected Letters of W. B. Yeats.* Vol. 1. Edited by John Kelly and Eric Domville. Oxford: Clarendon Press, 1986.

CL2 Yeats, W. B. *The Collected Letters of W. B. Yeats.* Vol. 2. Edited by Warwick Gould, John Kelly, and Deirdre Toomey. Oxford: Clarendon Press, 1997.

CL3 Yeats, W. B. *The Collected Letters of W. B. Yeats.* Vol. 3. Edited by John Kelly and Ronald Schuchard. Oxford: Clarendon Press, 1994.

CL4 Yeats, W. B. *The Collected Letters of W. B. Yeats.* Vol. 4. Edited by John Kelly and Ronald Schuchard. Oxford: Clarendon Press, 2005.

E&I Yeats, W. B. *Essays and Introductions.* New York: Macmillan Company, 1961.

Expl. Yeats, W. B. *Explorations.* London: Macmillan & Co., 1962.

FF, BS, and WBY Yeats, W. B., Florence Farr, and Bernard Shaw. *Florence Farr, Bernard Shaw, and W. B. Yeats.* Edited by Clifford Bax. Shannon: Irish University Press, 1971.

GY Yeats, W. B., and Maud Gonne, *The Gonne-Yeats Letters 1893–1938.* Edited by Anna MacBride White and A. Norman Jeffares. Syracuse, N.Y.: Syracuse University Press, 1994.

I&R Mikhail, E. H., ed. *W. B. Yeats: Interviews and Recollections.* 2 vols. New York: Barnes & Noble Books, 1977.

IDM Yeats, W. B. *The Irish Dramatic Movement.* Edited by Mary FitzGerald and Richard J. Finneran. Vol. 8, *The Collected Works of W. B. Yeats.* New York: Scribner, 2003.

IY Ellmann, Richard. *The Identity of Yeats.* London: Faber and Faber, 1983.

JS&D Yeats, W. B. *John Sherman and Dhoya.* Edited by Richard J. Finneran. Vol. 12, *The Collected Works of W. B. Yeats.* New York: Macmillan Publishing Company, 1991.

LE Yeats, W. B. *Later Essays.* Edited by William H. O'Donnell. Vol. 5, *The Collected Works of W. B. Yeats.* New York: Charles Scribner's Sons, 1994.

Letters Yeats, W. B. *The Letters of W. B. Yeats.* Edited by Allan Wade. New York: Macmillan Company, 1955.

Letters to WBY&EP Gonne, Iseult. *Letters to W. B. Yeats and Ezra Pound from Iseult Gonne: a girl that knew all Dante once.* Edited by A. Norman Jeffares, Anna MacBride White, and Christina Bridgwater. Basingstoke and New York: Palgrave Macmillan, 2004.

LOP Yeats, W. B., and Dorothy Wellesley, *Letters on Poetry from W. B. Yeats to Dorothy Wellesley.* London and New York: Oxford University Press, 1964.

LTWBY Finneran, Richard J., George Mills Harper, and William M. Murphy, eds. *Letters to W. B. Yeats.* 2 vols. New York: Columbia University Press, 1977.

Mem. Yeats, W. B. *Memoirs.* Edited by Denis Donoghue. New York: Macmillan Company, 1973.

MM Ellmann, Richard. *Yeats: The Man and the Masks.* New York: E.P. Dutton & Co, 1973.

Myth. Yeats, W. B. *Mythologies.* London: Macmillan, 1982.

NCP Jeffares, A. Norman. *A New Commentary on the Poems of W. B. Yeats.* Stanford, Calif.: Stanford University Press, 1984.

P&I Yeats, W. B. *Prefaces and Introductions: Uncollected Prefaces and Introductions by Yeats to Works by Other Authors and to Anthologies Edited by Yeats.* Edited by William H. O'Donnell. Vol. 6, *The Collected Works of W. B. Yeats.* New York: Macmillan Publishing Company, 1989.

PF Murphy, William M. *Prodigal Father: The Life of John Butler Yeats (1839–1922).* Ithaca and London: Cornell University Press, 1978.

RG Unterecker, John. *A Reader's Guide to William Butler Yeats.* New York: Noonday Press, 1959.

SQ Gonne, Maud. *The Autobiography of Maud Gonne: A Servant of the Queen.* Edited by A. Norman Jeffares and Anna MacBride White. Chicago: University of Chicago Press, 1995.

SRV Yeats, W. B. *The Secret Rose, Stories by W. B. Yeats: A Variorum Edition.* Edited by Phillip L. Marcus, Warwick Gould, and Michael J. Sidnell. Ithaca and London: Cornell University Press, 1981.

SS Yeats, W. B. *The Senate Speeches of W. B. Yeats.* Edited by Donald R. Pearce. Bloomington: Indiana University Press, 1960.

UP1 Yeats, W. B. *Uncollected Prose by W. B. Yeats.* Vol. 1. Edited by John P. Frayne. New York: Columbia University Press, 1970.

UP2 Yeats, W. B. *Uncollected Prose by W. B. Yeats.* Vol. 2. Edited by John P. Frayne and Colton Johnson. New York: Columbia University Press, 1976.

VP Yeats, W. B. *The Variorum Edition of the Poems of W. B. Yeats.* Edited by Peter Allt and Russell K. Alspach. New York: Macmillan Company, 1968.

VPl Yeats, W. B. *The Variorum Edition of the Plays of W. B. Yeats.* Edited by Russell K. Alspach. New York: Macmillan Company, 1966.

WBY&TSM Yeats, W. B., and T. Sturge Moore. *W. B. Yeats and T. Sturge Moore: Their Correspondence 1901–1937.* Edited by Ursula Bridge. New York: Oxford University Press, 1953.

YC Kelly, John S. *A W. B. Yeats Chronology.* Basingstoke and New York: Palgrave Macmillan, 2003.

YD Conner, Lester I. *A Yeats Dictionary: Persons and Places in the Poetry of William Butler Yeats.* Syracuse, N.Y.: Syracuse University Press, 1998.

INTRODUCTION

The most difficult question to ask about any writer is what he or she has to teach us. The instinct *that* we are being taught does not easily translate into an understanding of *what* we are being taught. It is particularly difficult to find a transparent and consistent meaning in Yeats, who is more than usually protean and abundant as well as occasionally obscure. We must each find our own wisdom in Yeats, heeding those peculiar resonances that seem our own thought returned to us "with a certain alienated majesty," as Emerson has it. My own mind lingers, as if sensing clues to its own nature, on the paean to custom and ceremony that ends "A Prayer for my Daughter"; on Yeats's heart-sore beckoning to the honey-bees in "The Stare's Nest by my Window"; on the momentous arrival at self-absolution in "A Dialogue of Self and Soul"; on the empty saddle and darkening flood that grieve for civilization in "Coole and Ballylee, 1931"; and on any number of vatic pronouncements, the most mysterious and alluring of which is to be found in *Per Amica Silentia Lunae*: "I shall find the dark grow luminous, the void fruitful when I understand I have nothing, that the ringers in the tower have appointed for the hymen of the soul a passing bell."

Whatever meaning we extract from Yeats's work, Yeats himself reminds us what it means to be an artist of uncompromising conscience. From dreamy youth to blunt and sometimes brutal age, he toiled single-mindedly in pursuit of an ultimate intensity and integrity, determined to bring forth what he calls in "My Table" the "changeless work of art." He might have become the "smiling public man" so powerfully belied in "Among School Children" or succumbed to the easy solidity of politics—"the happiness that Shelley found when he tied a pamphlet to a fire balloon"; instead, he held to the precept that the poet must perpetually "climb to some waste room and find, forgotten there by youth, some bitter crust." Yeats also reminds us, in this age of, at best, modest self-witness, what it means to be an artist of reality-shifting aspiration. In "William Blake and the Imagination," Yeats calls his great mentor "a man crying out for a mythology, and trying to make one because he could not find one to his hand." Yeats, too, was a man crying out for a mythology and in the end went remarkably far in erecting against the mechanism of the modern universe a system of meaning that would free the soul from the drudgery of space and time, or that would, in his later conception, plunge the soul into the foul ditch of experience, there to find redemption in the ecstasy of its own defiance. To ask whether Yeats hits upon the truth of things is to miss the point. His body of thought is not a descriptive account but a symbolic act. It exemplifies the quest for meaning; exemplifies also the faith that there is meaning to be found. In all of this endeavor, Yeats reminds us what it means to be human and to be vast in one's humanity.

To enter the field of Yeats scholarship at this late date is an exercise in humility. In his preface to Lady Gregory's *Cuchulain of Muirthemne*, Yeats lights on the image of "swallows building their nests in the stone mouths of immense images."

The late-arriving scholar of Yeats might well regard himself as a swallow of this sort, belated and minor however busy. This book does not attempt to fight its way into the canonical discourse on Yeats. Its relatively humble aim is to provide the student and common reader with a general introduction to Yeats's life and work, and to serve as a staging ground for further reading, research, and discussion. Its chief recommendation is its relatively comprehensive scope, which allows a view of Yeats's thought in its full and intricate interconnection and makes clear certain unifying patterns.

This book requires little explanation. It contains individual entries on Yeats's work, influences, connections, activities, and contexts. Cross-referenced items are given in SMALL CAPITAL LETTERS on first reference within each entry, but not on subsequent reference within the same entry. I have tended to give birth and death dates for those mentioned in passing, but not for those accorded their own entries. I have omitted these dates where they are intrusive or easily ascertained. I have also given year of publication for published works, but not for works accorded their own entries. Again, I have omitted such dates where they are intrusive or beside the point. Parenthetical citations giving book title and page number are provided throughout for the reader's convenience. Where successive parenthetical notes refer to the same work, the title is dropped for concision's sake. Entries on Yeats's written work end with information about initial periodical publication and initial book publication. In cases where Yeats altered the title of a work, I have given information about initial publication under each title. This book contains much information on subjects not accorded their own entries. The terminal index is the best guide to what the book does and does not contain.

A work of this nature necessarily draws heavily on the work of others. The details of my debt are indicated in the bibliography at the end of this volume and in the brief essay on secondary sources that appears as Appendix 3. I would particularly like to mention Professors Harold Bloom and John Kelly, both of whom I was privileged to have as teachers. Their vast intellectual energy and diz-zying degrees of precise learning set a scholarly example that I cannot begin to follow. I would like also to mention Thomas Hodgson, instructor of philosophy at Philips Academy, Andover, who made logic, clarity, and intellectual honesty matters of conscience and first set me on the path of systematic thought. Beyond these teachers is the teacher of teachers, Yeats himself, whose equal we are not likely to see again. During the 10 years I have been a daily student of Yeats, bemused friends and family have asked whether I ever wearied of him. The answer was "no." There were times when I wearied of my own voice paraphrasing that which was constructed to resist paraphrase; there were times when I wearied of the humility forced on me by Yeats's intellect and the erudition of his commentators; but I have never for a moment wearied of Yeats's thought or work or the example of his life. Just as we can make our souls with "learned Italian things / And the proud stones of Greece," so we can make our souls with poems like "Meditations in Time of Civil War," "The Tower," "A Dialogue of Self and Soul," and "Byzantium." This has been my sustaining conviction.

There are only a few to thank, but these heartily and gratefully. Jeff Soloway, editor of this volume, guided the project with patience, knowledge, and common sense. Liz Forster and Patrick Casey of the Hugh Lane Gallery in Dublin answered my numerous questions and graciously assisted my quest for Yeats-related images. The staff of Fáilte Ireland's photographic library were equally helpful and gracious. Dean Ross, local historian and old-school gentleman, helped me locate the grave of Benjamin Purser in Gaffney, South Carolina, photographs of which were the price of reproducing Sarah Purser's portrait of Edward Martyn. My former student Stephen Ross, a gifted young scholar of Yeats and much else, helped me translate the sonnets by Ronsard upon which Yeats based "At the Abbey Theatre" and "When You are Old." My colleague Larry Goldberg and his wife, Raquel, have resolutely encouraged me in all my endeavors, as have my colleague Inger Brodey and her husband, Benjamin. Michael and Khoan Sullivan opened their home to my wife and me during our sojourn in Oxford. They taught us much about Chinese painting, but their devotion to each other was the great lesson of these years. I would finally like to thank my entire family, near and far, and in particular my mother, Jane Ross, whose perpetual readiness to help saw my household through a challenging period.

I dedicate this book to my wife and daughter. My wife was never more than a few feet from me as I wrote this book, while my infant daughter not infrequently nestled in my lap. The enterprise was arduous but never lonely. I say to my wife, as Yeats said to his, "how should I forget the wisdom that you brought, / The comfort that you made?"

PART I

Biography

William Butler Yeats
(1865–1939)

In his restless greatness, W. B. Yeats had many guises: SLIGO fledgling wonder-struck by the local fairy lore, boyish dreamer playing at being Byron's Manfred and SHELLEY's wandering poet, schoolboy Theosophist, acolyte of WILLIAM MORRIS, celebrant and would-be lover of "the loveliest woman born / Out of the mouth of Plenty's horn," initiate of secret societies and seeker of ghosts, exegete of WILLIAM BLAKE, collector of folklore and evangel of the Irish Renaissance, political activist and contrarian nationalist, plumed aesthete, symbolist and Parisian cultural tourist, fumbling Lothario, London man of letters, Dublin theatrical impresario, aristocrat in search of a lineage, proto-modernist (later arch-modernist), tower-ensconced mage, student of philosophy and geometer of reality, senator, European lion and NOBEL laureate, neo-Georgian sage, "last romantic," fascist fellow-traveler, "wild old wicked man," . . . and, finally, denizen of the "rag-and-bone shop of the heart." On the model of "The COMING OF WISDOM WITH TIME," however, Yeats's multifariousness had always an underlying unity. His myriad guises and activities were leaves swaying above a root that was the soul's war against the accidental, the abstract, and the modern, against all that would sheer the ancient flower of visionary comprehension and tragic joy. Bereaved of his Christianity after a boyhood encounter with an encyclopedia entry on sexual reproduction, Yeats spent the rest of his life in the thrall of an impulse to rediscover or re-create what he had lost: a reality of beautiful pattern and deepest meaning. It was not within Yeats's power to reverse "Bacon, Newton, Locke," but he did shift the order of things as only a few innovators of science and culture may do. With Marcel Proust, Thomas Mann, JAMES JOYCE, Franz Kafka, EZRA POUND, and T. S. ELIOT, he laid the foundation of modern literature; he fathered one of the world's great theaters; he initiated the revival of Irish culture and played no small part in securing Irish independence ("If it had not been for W. B. Yeats," declared Oliver St John Gogarty, "there would be no Irish Free State!");

William Butler Yeats, in late 1932 or early 1933, in New York. Photograph by Pirie MacDonald (1867–1942) *(Library of Congress)*

and he added to the world's legends the tale of his own ungratified if not exactly tragic love. More than this, he gave the world a mass of poetry that, through myriad shifts of style and emphasis, kept faith with the "rock-born, rock-wandering foot" of a fierce and beautiful muse, and belongs as much to the end of time as to the present moment. The abiding question is Yeats's own:

> What bonds no man could unbind,
> Being imagined within
> The labyrinth of the mind,
> What pursuing or fleeing,
> What wounds, what bloody press,
> Dragged into being
> This loveliness?

"YOUTH'S DREAMY LOAD": 1865–1886

William Butler Yeats was born in a modest suburban villa at 5 Sandymount Avenue, Dublin, Ireland, on June 13, 1865, to JOHN BUTLER YEATS and his wife of almost two years, the former Susan Mary Pollexfen. John Butler Yeats belonged to a reputable line of Protestant clergymen and landowners. His father, William Butler Yeats (1806–62), had been rector at Tullylish, where John Butler Yeats, the eldest of nine children, had been born in 1839. SUSAN YEATS, the third of 12 children, grew up amid her family's thriving shipping and milling concerns in Sligo, a bustling seaport overlooking Sligo Bay on the west coast of Ireland. After graduating from Trinity College, Dublin, John Butler Yeats studied law. He qualified as a barrister in January 1866, but the following year heeded a muse with whom he would always have problematic relations and decided to become a painter, moving the family to London and enrolling at Heatherley's Art School. He was a gifted portraitist whose studio was a perpetual symposium of brilliant conversation, but he lacked discipline and business sense, and the family slowly sank into permanent semi-penury. Susan Yeats, deep, grave, and quiet, was baffled by her husband's irresponsible ebullience, and the marriage became a mutual cross to bear. "I thought I would place myself under prison rule and learn all the virtues," John Butler Yeats later quipped (*PF* 37). William Butler was followed by five more children: Susan Mary "Lily" (1866–1949), Elizabeth Corbet "Lolly" (1868–1940), Robert Corbet (1870–73), John Butler "Jack" (1871–1957), and Jane Grace (1875–76). Yeats was fond of the placid Lily; frequently at odds with the fiery and stubborn Lolly; and oddly removed from the life of his brother, who went on to become a significant modern painter. Neither Yeats's work nor his letters take much notice of Jack. William M. Murphy observes that Jack, who lived apart from the family between the ages of eight and 16, "could never escape the feeling that his older brother regarded him as a person of no particular importance" (*Family Secrets* 270–271).

The family made its home at 23 Fitzroy Road, Regent's Park, London, from July 1867 to July 1873. During these years, however, the children and their mother spent months at a time in Sligo, their longest stay lasting from 1872 to 1874. They resided with Susan's parents at Merville, a large and handsome house befitting the family's commercial success. A bevy of well-meaning uncles, aunts, and cousins—Pollexfens and Middletons—surrounded the Yeats children in Sligo and nearby Rosses Point. There were dogs and ponies; gardens and lawns; rowing, sailing, and rambles. Middleton relations "took the nearest for friends" and brought Yeats to the local cottages, where he first heard the fairy stories that would later become so important to him (*Aut.* 48). Yeats was dreamy and imaginative, though late in learning to read and nothing of the prodigy. He received a haphazard early education, briefly attending "a dame-school kept by an old woman" and then receiving lessons in spelling and grammar from an old gentlewoman. Largely he shifted for himself with an encyclopedia he found in the library at Merville (54). For the rest of his life, Yeats associated Sligo with childhood happiness, with family stability and tradition, and with the folk-life of rural Ireland. When he speaks in "A PRAYER FOR MY DAUGHTER" of the importance of remaining "rooted in one dear perpetual place" it is undoubtedly his tenuous hold on Sligo that he has at least partially in mind.

In October 1874, the family reunited in London, living at 14 Edith Villas, North End, Fulham, while John Butler Yeats ineffectively plied his trade as a painter. London was a misery to Yeats, and he sometimes shed tears of longing for Sligo (58–59). He received sporadic lessons from his father and heard much literature read aloud, but his formal education did not begin until January 1877, when he enrolled at the Godolphin School in Hammersmith, a rough-and-tumble day school catering to "the sons of professional men who had failed or were at the outset of their career" (64). There Yeats remained until 1881. The school was true to its type, Yeats recalls in *AUTOBIOGRAPHIES*, "an obscene, bullying place, where a big boy would hit a small boy in the wind to see him double up, and where certain boys, too young for any emotion of sex, would sing the dirty songs of the street" (64). Yeats was teased for being Irish and lost nearly all of his numerous playground fistfights (59–63). If not happy at school, he was too detached and

SLIGO. 3272. W.L.

Sligo in the late 19th century *(National Library of Ireland)*

self-sufficient to be miserable. In the classroom, he was inconsistent and generally near the middle or bottom of his class (AM 25). Idleness was part of the problem; so too atrocious spelling (a deficiency Yeats would never outgrow) and an inability to discipline the excitement of his thought (*Aut.* 64–65). In the self-assessment of *Autobiographies,* he was simply "unfitted for school work" (64). Yeats's chief interest was natural history, and he was known in school as a collector of moths and butterflies (65, 69).

In spring 1879, the family moved to 8 Woodstock Road, BEDFORD PARK, the first of two sojourns in the progressive garden community popular with artists and writers, while Jack Yeats went to live with his grandparents in Sligo. The neighborhood was a picturesque embodiment of the aesthetic principles associated with William Morris. With its "peacock-blue doors" and wind-

ing streets, it struck Yeats as "a romantic excitement" (66). At this time John Butler Yeats's circle included the painters Edwin John Ellis (1848–1916) and John Trivett Nettleship (1841–1902), who had been his fellow students at art school. Yeats soaked up the artists' talk and became imprinted with his father's loose but passionately held philosophy, which accorded the arts absolute primacy and emphasized personality and intensity as the crucible of artistic creation.

In late 1881, strapped by the diminishing value of John Butler Yeats's inherited property, the family returned to Ireland. They resided at Balscaddan Cottage in Howth, a seaside village about 10 miles northeast of central Dublin, while Jack Yeats remained with his grandparents. John Butler Yeats rented a studio at 44 York Street, and his eldest son enrolled at the nearby Erasmus Smith High School, Harcourt Street. Each day father and son

Howth in the late 19th century. The Yeats family lived in the seaside village, some 10 miles northeast of Dublin, between 1881 and 1884. *(National Library of Ireland)*

commuted to Dublin by train, sharing breakfast and lunch in the studio (*W. B. Yeats* 32). Making these meals a tutorial in romantic aesthetics, the elder Yeats would read passages from plays and poems at their most passionate moment. The curriculum included Shakespeare, Byron, Shelley, and Keats (80–81). The following spring, the family moved to a house called Island View, which overlooked the harbor. Mrs. Yeats found a degree of happiness by the seaside at Howth, where she was sufficiently removed from the bafflements of the city. "When I think of her," Yeats writes in *Autobiographies*, "I almost always see her talking over a cup of tea in the kitchen with our servant, the fisherman's wife, on the only themes outside our house that seemed of interest—the fishing-people of Howth, or the pilots and fishing-people of Rosses Point" (78).

At the high school, Yeats was exposed to boys of his own stamp: JOHN EGLINTON, who later became a man of letters and a staff member at the National Library; Frederick James Gregg (1864–1927), who emigrated to New York in 1891 and became a journalist and friend to JOHN QUINN; and Charles Johnston (1867–1931), who collaborated in Yeats's early Theosophical activities and wound up marrying Madame Blavatsky's niece in 1888 (see *CL1* 101, 104). Yeats's academic doldrums continued, though he suffered no further bullying. Johnston remembers that Yeats "was strong in mathematics, especially Euclid, and he had a gift for chemistry, but he was no good at all at languages, whether ancient or modern. He just managed to stumble through his Homer, partly with his father's scholarly help, partly by aid of a bad translation" (*I&R*, I, 6). Yeats's worst subject was literature, for even Shakespeare was read "for his grammar exclusively" (*Aut.* 75). Even as he struggled academically, Yeats began to emerge as an unusual personality and nascent intellectual—even then, according to Johnston, he was a brilliant and tireless talker

(*I&R*, I, 7). For the moment, his passion remained natural history, and he "was hot for argument in refutation of Adam and Noah and the Seven Days" (*Aut.* 77). At the same time, Yeats had absorbed the poetry his father had read to him, and a new sensibility began to stir. As he carried his butterfly net about the cliffs of Howth, he would play at being the poet-mage of romantic myth. "I had many idols," Yeats recalls, "and as I climbed along the narrow ledge I was now Manfred on his glacier, and now Prince Athanase with his solitary lamp, but I soon chose Alastor for my chief of men and longed to share his melancholy, and maybe at last to disappear from everybody's sight as he disappeared drifting in a boat along some slow-moving river between great trees" (80).

In late 1883, Yeats left the high school, and John Butler Yeats took a new studio at 7 Stephen's Green (*PF* 135). In early 1884, under continuing financial pressure, the family moved from Howth to 10 Ashfield Terrace in the Dublin suburb of Terenure. As Yeats remembers, the house was a "villa where the red bricks were made pretentious and vulgar with streaks of slate colour," and the neighbors were an unpleasant lot suspicious of the artistic goings-on in their midst (*Aut.* 92–93). John Butler Yeats wanted his son to attend Trinity College as a matter of family tradition, but Yeats quietly worried that he would not be able to pass the admission examination (90). Less grandly, he enrolled in the Metropolitan School of Art in Kildare Street, where he remained from May 1884 until April 1886. Yeats blended comfortably enough with his misfit classmates and fell in with GEORGE RUSSELL (AE), an artist, poet, and mystic who was to be a lifelong—if frequently irritated—friend and collaborator in the work of the Irish Renaissance.

At this time, Yeats began to distance himself from his father. If John Butler Yeats was a romantic in his literary tastes and some of his aesthetic notions, he was also a genial humanist and Victorian positivist. "Sometimes I would try to argue with him," Yeats remembers in *Autobiographies*, "for I had come to think the philosophy of his fellow-artists and himself a misunderstanding created by Victorian science, and science I had grown to hate with a monkish

hate [. . .]. My father was painting many fine portraits, Dublin leaders of the bar, college notabilities, or chance comers whom he would paint for nothing if he liked their heads; but all displeased me. In my heart I thought that only beautiful things should be painted, and that only ancient things and the stuff of dreams were beautiful" (91–92). In opposition to "Victorian science," Yeats developed an uncompromising romanticism and esotericism. With Johnston, he began to explore A. P. Sinnett's *Esoteric Buddhism* (1883) and the doctrines of the THEOSOPHICAL SOCIETY. In June 1885, they founded a Hermetic Society for the discussion of such matters. The small group met in York Street and included Eglinton (97). Under the influence of Shelley's *Prometheus Unbound* (1820), Yeats held that "whatever the great poets had affirmed in their finest moments was the nearest we could come to an authoritative religion, and that their mythology, their spirits of water and wind, were but literal truth" (97). In April 1886, the Hermetic Society was succeeded by

Portrait of William Butler Yeats, ca. 1886, by John Butler Yeats *(Dublin City Gallery The Hugh Lane)*

the Dublin Lodge of the Theosophical Society, in which Yeats was more distantly involved.

Despite his prospective career as a painter, Yeats had begun to invent himself as a poet. He remembers in *Autobiographies*: "I had begun to write poetry in imitation of Shelley and of Edmund Spenser, play after play—for my father exalted dramatic poetry above all other kinds—and I invented fantastic and incoherent plots. My lines but seldom scanned, for I could not understand the prosody in the books, although there were many lines that taken by themselves had music" (81). His first composition, begun in 1882, was a dramatic poem about "a magician who sets up his throne in Asia, and expresses himself with Queen Mab-like heresy" (*W. B. Yeats* 43). Johnston remembers that his "first verses came forth out of a vast murmurous gloom of dreams, and were full of vague, enormous shapes of some supernatural forest" (*I&R*, I, 10). There rapidly followed a spate of promising verse, much of which appeared in the *DUBLIN UNIVERSITY REVIEW* and began the making of Yeats's reputation in Dublin. Yeats's more substantial contributions to the magazine were *The ISLAND OF STATUES* (April–July 1885), "Love and Death" (May 1885), *The SEEKER* (September 1885), an epilogue to *The Island of Statues* and *The Seeker* (October 1885, later "The SONG OF THE HAPPY SHEPHERD"), "The Two Titans. A Political Poem" (March 1886), and *MOSADA* (June 1886). In October 1886, he began "The WANDERINGS OF OISIN," the first poem to suggest the scale of his talent and ambition.

Far from being a solitary dreamer on the model of "Alastor" or his own *Seeker*, Yeats worked hard to find a place in the unsparing intellectual life of Dublin. He began to attend meetings of the CONTEMPORARY CLUB, which was, like the *Dublin University Review*, the brainchild of Charles Hubert Oldham (1860–1926), "a political economist and leader of a small group of intellectual Protestant Home Rulers in Trinity College," in Joseph Hone's description (*W. B. Yeats* 45). The club allowed Yeats to meet a host of writers, scholars, and politicians who in their different ways would set him thinking and cross paths with him in the future. The young scholar and poet Douglas Hyde (1860–1949) was a particular stimulation. His dream of reviving the

Gaelic language was not one Yeats could help further or undividedly endorse, but Hyde set Yeats an example of commitment to the national culture. Towering above all others in the stature of his pride and character was JOHN O'LEARY, an old Fenian just returned to Dublin after years of political exile. He urged Yeats to join the Young Ireland Society (of which he was president) and set Yeats on the path of Irish nationalism (*Aut.* 99–105). A devout collector, student, and defender of Irish literature, O'Leary insisted on the cultural dimension of Irish nationalism and thus alerted Yeats to the form his own nationalism would largely take. As Yeats wrote in 1889, "He, more clearly than any one, has seen that there is no fine nationality without literature, and seen the converse also, that there is no fine literature without nationality" (*Letters to the New Island* 12). Decades later, at the end of his life, Yeats continued to think of himself as a "nationalist of the school of John O'Leary" (*Letters* 920–921).

In the summer of 1885, Oldham introduced Yeats to the young poetess KATHARINE TYNAN, and he began to spend time at her family's dairy farm in Clondalkin, southwest of Dublin. She was to become Yeats's first female confidante and correspondent, as well as his first mature romantic interest. In *MEMOIRS*, Yeats admits to worrying that Tynan loved him and that he was duty-bound to marry her (*Mem.* 32). According to Tynan's sister, Yeats proposed and was rejected without heartbreak on either side (AM 72).

"THE CELTIC TWILIGHT": 1887–1903

Though Yeats had rapidly brought himself to the attention of intellectual Dublin, John Butler Yeats, seeking a wider field and more receptive market for his art, decided once again to try his luck in London. In May 1887, the family—with Jack soon to follow—established itself at 58 Eardley Crescent, South Kensington, a shabby little house that pleased no one. On August 11, Susan Yeats suffered the first of two strokes that would render her an invalid until her death in 1900. More happily, Yeats had, by June, renewed his acquaintance with William Morris, whom he had met in Dublin at a meeting of the Contemporary Club in April 1886.

Morris and his daughter, May (1862–1938), lived and worked at Kelmscott House in Hammersmith, and Yeats joined the circle of young admirers (George Bernard Shaw among them) who gathered there for suppers, French lessons (Yeats made little progress), and Sunday night lectures under the auspices of the Socialist League. Yeats was drawn to Morris's backward-looking aestheticism and under his influence briefly "turned Socialist," but he could not tolerate the materialism of Morris's followers, and he soon left the fold (*Aut.* 135–136). His sister Lily, on the other hand, joined the staff of Morris and Co. and worked as an embroideress under May Morris's direction from November 1888 to 1894.

In March 1888, the family moved to 3 Blenheim Road, Bedford Park, renting what Yeats called at the time a "fine roomy house" (*CL1* 56). Yeats's imagination was less struck by Bedford Park than it had been nine years earlier (*Aut.* 113) but he felt at home among the neighborhood artists and his father's friends. In addition to Ellis and Nettleship, these included the beautiful actress FLORENCE FARR, who would become an important collaborator in Yeats's poetic and dramatic experiments; Farr's brother-in-law, the painter Henry Mariott Paget (1856–1936); Frederick York Powell (1850–1904), professor of modern history at Oxford; and John Todhunter (1839–1916), physician, poet, playwright, and old college friend of John Butler Yeats. Stepping outside of the family circle, Yeats met W. E. Henley (1849–1903) in August 1888, and OSCAR WILDE at Henley's house in September. Like Morris, both men were models of self-command and force of personality, and Yeats often returned to them in his later ruminations. Henley had no trouble recognizing Yeats's talent and between 1889 and 1897 published a steady stream of his poems, essays, and stories in his journals the *Scots Observer* (later the *National Observer*) and the *New Review*. Despite being welcomed in these not insignificant circles, Yeats suffered pangs of homesickness for Ireland, as his poem "The LAKE ISLE OF INNISFREE"—sent in draft to Tynan in December 1888—attests (*CL1* 120–121; see also 231). Yeats celebrated Christmas day, 1888, with the Wilde family, an event vividly recollected in *Autobiographies* (127–129).

The topics that filled Yeats with "excitement" were increasingly esoteric, beyond both the sympathy and the understanding of John Butler Yeats. In May 1887, bearing an introduction from Charles Johnston, Yeats called on Helena Blavatsky (1831–91), spiritual leader and cofounder of the Theosophical Society (153–154). Yeats joined the esoteric section of the society in December 1888 and, affronted by the "abstraction" of the society's teachings, tried to push the society in the direction of magical experimentation (158–159). In November 1890, after a year of strained relations, Yeats published an article critical of the society magazine and was asked to resign (*CL1* 234–235). Yeats, however, had already jumped ship. On March 7, 1890, he had joined the HERMETIC ORDER OF THE GOLDEN DAWN, a Rosicrucian secret society whose charismatic cofounder and chief theoretician, MACGREGOR MATHERS, Yeats had met in the reading room at the British Museum (*Aut.* 159). In the elaborate ritual of the order, Yeats found a rich vein of symbolism to be mined in his poetry, and for the next three decades, through numerous schisms, he remained a committed initiate of the order. Supposing that his father had disparaged his "magical pursuits out of the immense depths of his ignorance," Yeats defended his occultism, with his usual bad spelling, in a July 1892 letter to O'Leary: "The mystical life is the centre of all that I do & all that I think & all that I write. It holds to my work the same relation that the philosophy of Godwin held to the work of Shelley & I have allways considered my self a voice of what I beleive to be a greater renaisance—the revolt of the soul against the intellect—now begining in the world" (*CL1* 303). Equally expressive of this "revolt" was Yeats and Ellis's four-year labor to produce *The Works of William Blake*, a three-volume edition of Blake's work complemented by elaborate critical and biographical apparatus. Published by Bernard Quaritch, London, in February 1893, the edition is famously eccentric in its scholarship, but it represents a thorough education in patterns of thought that would serve Yeats for the rest of his life.

On January 30, 1889, "the troubling" of Yeats's life began when MAUD GONNE called at 3 Blenheim Road with a letter of introduction from O'Leary

(*Mem.* 40). A political firebrand whose statuesque beauty Yeats would later compare to a "tightened bow" ("NO SECOND TROY"), Gonne was an incarnation of the romantic heroines Yeats had been imagining since boyhood, women who "loved in brief tragedy, or like the girl in [Shelley's] *The Revolt of Islam,* accompanied their lovers through all manner of wild places, lawless women without homes and without children" (*Aut.* 80). Despite initial denials (*CL1* 154), Yeats was immediately smitten, as he would remain in some sense for the rest of his life. He and Gonne dined each day of her nine-day stay in London. In the first of his many romantic offerings, Yeats proposed to write a play for her to act in Dublin and thus began to toil at *The COUNTESS CATHLEEN* (*Mem.* 40–41, 46–47). Gonne, in turn, stiffened Yeats's nationalism, though he remained nervously aware that her politics verged on fanaticism and resented her political commitment as his "one visible rival" (59, 63). They collaborated in politics throughout the 1890s, spearheading a scheme to found rural libraries, helping organize a protest of Queen Victoria's Diamond Jubilee, and helping organize the centennial commemoration of the 1798 rebellion. So too they collaborated in mystical activities. At Yeats's urging, Gonne joined the Golden Dawn on November 2, 1891 (*CL1* 266). She resigned in December 1894, put off by Masonic elements that she considered British, but Yeats and Gonne remained mystical intimates for years to come.

On August 3, 1891, Yeats asked Gonne to marry him. She rejected his proposal and hinted that there were reasons she could never marry (*Mem.* 46). Yeats did not receive a full explanation until December 1898, when Gonne confessed that she had been for many years the mistress of the French journalist Lucien Millevoye (1850–1918) and that she had mothered two children. A boy had been born on January 11, 1890, and had died on July 29 of the following year; a little girl had been born on August 6, 1894, and presently lived in France under the fiction that she was Gonne's niece (47, 132–134). This was ISEULT GONNE, destined to become a willowy beauty whom Yeats would woo with no more success than he had wooed her mother. Though devastated and emotionally depleted by these revelations, Yeats was not angry; on the contrary, he vowed to dedicate himself to Gonne's happiness and to content himself "with just that manner of love which she will give me abundantly" (*CL2* 320).

Yeats's literary endeavors had been inseparable from his cultural nationalism since he had fallen under the spell of O'Leary. His aspiration was to reestablish Ireland's hereditary mythology and to redeem the nation from the slough of modernity. In *Autobiographies,* Yeats recollects the question he put to himself as a young man: "Might I not, with health and good luck to aid me, create some new *Prometheus Unbound*; Patrick or Columcille, Oisin or Finn, in Prometheus' stead; and, instead of Caucasus, Cro-Patrick or Ben Bulben? Have not all races had their first unity from a mythology that marries them to rock and hill?" (166–167). As an imaginative writer, Yeats incorporated mythic, folkloric, and local elements in his work; as an editor and journalist, he championed the same, as well as attempted to rehabilitate the Anglo-Irish literary tradition of the 19th century. Simultaneously, he was a busy and increasingly influential cultural organizer. In 1892, he helped found the Irish Literary Society of London and the NATIONAL LITERARY SOCIETY of Dublin, both of which were dedicated to the advancement of Irish culture and letters.

Numerous works flowed from Yeats's pen during the late 1880s and early 1890s and cumulatively established him as a promising poet, playwright, and man of letters, as well as a gifted and industrious folklorist and a leading cultural figure in Ireland. His first collection of poems, *The Wanderings of Oisin and Other Poems,* appeared in January 1889. This was followed by *John Sherman and Dhoya* in November 1891 (see JOHN SHERMAN and "DHOYA"); *The Countess Kathleen and Various Legends and Lyrics* in September 1892; *The Celtic Twilight,* a book of Irish folklore, in December 1893; *The LAND OF HEART'S DESIRE* in April 1894; and his collected *Poems* in October 1895. *The Land of Heart's Desire* was successfully staged at the Avenue Theatre, London, in the spring of 1894, making it the first of Yeats's plays to be produced. Yeats further edited a number of volumes, including *Fairy and Folk Tales of the Irish Peasantry* in 1888; *Stories from Carleton* in August 1889; *Representative Irish Tales* in March 1891; *Irish Fairy Tales* in 1892; *The Works of William Blake* in February 1893; *The Poems of William Blake* in 1893; and *A Book of Irish Verse Selected from Modern Writers* in March 1895. The "early Yeats" is universally deprecated in favor of the "later Yeats," but this body of work, accepted on its own terms, is a significant achievement. Had he died in 1895, Yeats would doubtlessly impress posterity as something more than a rising London scribbler. He would not be mourned as Keats is mourned, but he would fascinate us as a queer and forceful talent.

In London, Yeats's Irish nationalism was increasingly complemented by a budding, French-influenced symbolism. His education in this regard was the RHYMERS' CLUB, a group of poets and writers who met from 1890 to 1896 at the Cheshire Cheese, a Fleet Street pub. The club's patron saints were Pater and Rossetti, and its tendencies were aesthetic and decadent. Of the group's dozen odd members, Yeats was particularly intrigued by the poets LIONEL JOHNSON and ARTHUR SYMONS, who became close friends. Johnson awakened Yeats to the aesthetic ideal of the "marmorean" (*Aut.* 185), while Symons, a scholar and translator of French literature, acted as cicerone as the monolingual Yeats attempted to learn something of Stéphane Mallarmé, VERLAINE, and Villiers de l'Isle-Adam. Prepped by Symons, Yeats visited PARIS for the first time in February 1894. He called on Verlaine in his tenement quarters and in the company of Gonne attended a five-hour performance of Villiers de l'Isle-Adam's symbolist drama *Axël*. He was never

Ye Olde Cheshire Cheese, the London pub that was home to the Rhymers' Club. Drawing by Frank Cox, ca. 1880 (*Guildhall Library, City of London*)

to forget one of the play's lines: "As for living, our servants will do that for us." In 1896, Symons became editor of the SAVOY, a brilliant but short-lived review. It was committed to advanced artistic notions and, under the art editorship of the notorious AUBREY BEARDSLEY, itself embodied a louche aestheticism. Yeats contributed poems and stories to the *Savoy* during its yearlong run, bringing to its pages the sumptuous visionary mysticism that marks his work of the mid- and late 1890s and has its perfect sobriquet in the adjective "dream-heavy" ("HE REMEMBERS FORGOTTEN BEAUTY"). This phase of Yeats's literary development is preserved in his three major publications of the period: *The Secret Rose*, a collection of stories published in April 1897; *The Wind Among the Reeds*, a collection of poems published in April 1899; and *The SHADOWY WATERS*, a verse drama published in December 1900.

In October 1895, Yeats finally left the family home. He briefly roomed with Symons at Fountain Court, the Temple, London, and then took a suite of rooms at 18 WOBURN BUILDINGS, a dingy edifice near St. Pancras Station that remained Yeats's home in London until 1919. The move to Woburn Buildings in February 1896 was in part motivated by the desire to consummate his relationship with Johnson's handsome cousin OLIVIA SHAKESPEAR, a 31-year-old novelist of modest talent unhappily married to a staid London solicitor. In April 1894, Yeats and Shakespear had attended a dinner celebrating the inaugural issue of the *Yellow Book* (the *Savoy's* predecessor as the bane of the bourgeoisie), and they had caught each other's eye. Johnson introduced them in June, and they began to see each other romantically (*Mem.* 72, 74). They considered eloping but decided to wait until Shakespear's aged mother died; in the meantime, they met "in railway carriages and at picture galleries and occasionally at her house" (85–86). After nearly a year of Platonic tenderness, Shakespear gently saw Yeats through the awkwardness of his first sexual experience (88). The affair ended in early 1897, when Yeats's ineradicable obsession with Gonne sent Shakespear "weeping away," as he puts it in "The LOVER MOURNS FOR THE LOSS OF LOVE" (see also *Mem.* 89). Genuinely fond of each

other, the erstwhile lovers resumed their friendship in 1900 and remained correspondents and confidantes until Shakespear died in 1938.

Augusta, Lady GREGORY, a middle-aged widow and Galway landowner, no less momentously entered Yeats's life in the summer of 1896. Hearing that Yeats and Symons were guests of her neighbor, the wealthy would-be playwright EDWARD MARTYN (*CL2* 47–49), she paid a visit and invited the three writers to lunch at her estate COOLE PARK (*Lady Gregory* 105). She saw more of Yeats in London that winter. Yeats was again Martyn's houseguest in the summer of 1897. Following a luncheon party at the home of another neighbor, Count Florimond de Basterot, Yeats and Lady Gregory secluded themselves in a quiet nook. The discussion turned to the theater, a subject that preoccupied Yeats, who had by this time written two plays of stature: *The Countess Cathleen* and *The Land of Heart's Desire*. "I said it was a pity we had no Irish theatre where such plays could be given," Lady Gregory recalled. "Mr. Yeats said that had always been a dream of his, but he had of late thought it an impossible one, for it could not at first pay its way, and there was no money to be found for such a thing in Ireland. We went on talking about it, and things seemed to grow possible as we talked, and before the end of the afternoon we had made our plan" (*Our Irish Theatre* 19). Before many days had passed, Yeats, Gregory, and Martyn had outlined a scheme to found an Irish theater. From this seed sprang the IRISH LITERARY THEATRE (1899–1901) and its successor institutions, the IRISH NATIONAL THEATRE SOCIETY and the ABBEY THEATRE. During the early years of the dramatic movement, Yeats did the administrative and organizational work of a company manager and shaped the fledgling movement's philosophy in the pages of its publications *Beltaine* (1899–1900, named for the ancient festival marking the arrival of summer), *Samhain* (1901–08, named for the ancient festival marking the arrival of winter), and *The Arrow* (1906–09). He also wrote a slew of plays. His early contributions to the movement's repertoire included *The Countess Cathleen* (first staged in May 1899), *DIARMUID AND GRANIA* (October 1901), *CATHLEEN NI HOULIHAN* (April 1902), *The POT OF BROTH*

Pastel rendering of Coole by W. B. Yeats, circa 1897 *(Fáilte Ireland)*

(October 1902), *The HOUR-GLASS* (March 1903), *The KING'S THRESHOLD* (October 1903), and *ON BAILE'S STRAND* (December 1904). Another play, *WHERE THERE IS NOTHING*, was produced by the London Stage Society in June 1904. As he readily acknowledged, Yeats had little instinct for the alchemy by which dramatic verse becomes drama. All the same, the best of these plays—*The Countess Cathleen, On Baile's Strand*—instance Yeats's profound gifts of language and thought.

On the brink of Gonne-related emotional collapse, Yeats began his 20-year string of summer sojourns at Coole Park in 1897 (*Aut.* 298; *Mem.* 125). Yeats and Lady Gregory collected folklore among the local cottages, and Yeats was restored to health by activity, diet, and open air. Before long, their friendship deepened into what may have been

the most important relationship of Yeats's entire life. Lady Gregory was indispensable in the work of both managing a theater and writing plays, but she was far more than a helpmate. In 1909, he would exalt her as "mother, friend, sister and brother," and credit her with bringing to his "wavering thoughts steadfast nobility" (*Aut.* 353; *Mem.* 160–161). Most fundamentally, she taught him by example what it meant to inherit and uphold a tradition.

Yeats's unusually long formative period ended in 1903 with the appearance of two watershed volumes: *Ideas of Good and Evil*, published by A. H. Bullen of London in May, and *In the Seven Woods*, published by the DUN EMER PRESS—the Yeats sisters' Morris-influenced venture—in August. A gorgeous, thick-woven arras of prose, *Ideas of Good and Evil* gathered essays that had appeared in periodicals over the previous eight years and brought to fruition the enterprise of the 1890s. *In the Seven Woods,* by contrast, pointed to the next phase of Yeats's development. The dream-heaviness of the "Celtic Twilight" had not entirely dissipated, but it contrasted with a new tautness and intensity. "IN THE SEVEN WOODS," "The FOLLY OF BEING COMFORTED," and "ADAM'S CURSE" were poems of the new type, as well as Yeats's first poems with the definite air of permanence. *On Baile's Strand,* the volume's lone play, instanced the "athletic joy" that was Yeats's new ideal, as well as initiated the dramatic cycle about the Irish hero CUCHULAIN that Yeats was to complete only upon his deathbed (CL3 577–578). In conjunction, the volumes placed Yeats at the threshold of greatness.

The era-ending thunderclap, however, was personal rather than artistic. Despite Gonne's revelations of 1898, Yeats had continued to court her, proposing marriage in February 1899 and again in 1900 (*New Biography* 112–113, 129). In February 1903, Yeats learned utterly to his surprise that in a matter of weeks she was to marry Major

John MacBride (1865–1916), a strapping military man revered by nationalists for his part against the British in the Boer War. Yeats received news of Gonne's engagement on February 7, just before giving a lecture. In "RECONCILIATION," he describes himself as deafened and blinded as if by lightning. Yeats attempted to dissuade Gonne in a series of desperate letters, but with no success (CL3 314–317; GY 164–168). Gonne married on February 21. The marriage was a fiasco from the start, but Yeats was not buoyed or appeased. The Blake- and Shelley-influenced romanticism that had served him since boyhood—a certain aspiring tendency of spirit—had been deeply shaken, and Yeats entered a long period of retrenchment epitomized by "LINES WRITTEN IN DEJECTION," which he began in 1916: "The holy centaurs of the hills are vanished; / I have nothing but the embittered sun. . . ."

"THE FINISHED MAN AMONG HIS ENEMIES": 1904–1917

In the years following Gonne's marriage, Yeats threw himself into practical life and wrote almost no verse. He sought to distract himself from disappointment but more fundamentally sought to correct his failure to win Gonne by transforming himself into the kind of "normal active man" represented by MacBride (*Aut.* 363; *Mem.* 181). To this end—coupled with the obvious financial motive—he departed on a 17-week tour of AMERICA in November 1903. He gave 64 lectures across the breadth of the country and earned a staggering $3,230.40 (CL3 467). He also solidified his friendship with John Quinn, a hard-charging New York lawyer and art collector temperamentally inclined to the doctrines of Nietzsche, in which he initiated Yeats (239, 313, 335). Yeats returned to Ireland somewhat changed—for the worse, as most of his family and acquaintances thought. The dreamy poet of the nineties was now a distant memory. Clad in a fur coat and grown a bit portly, Yeats had donned the mask of command and arrogance. In January 1906, Russell issued a rebuke: "There is probably not one of the younger people of whom you have not said some stinging and contemptuous remark. They may have been justified. But if you wish to lead a movement you can only do so

William Butler Yeats in 1902 *(Library of Congress)*

by silence on points which irritate you or by kindly suggestions to the people. A man without followers can do nothing and you have few or no friends in Dublin" (*CL4* 293; *LTWBY*, I, 153). Yeats was unapologetic in response: "I desire the love of very few people, my equals or my superiors. The love of the rest would be a bond & an intrusion" (*CL4* 290). After Yeats quarreled with Lolly over her management of the Dun Emer Press in the summer of 1906 (460, 463–467, 525–526), John Butler Yeats discerned and attempted to debunk the Nietzschean mask. "As you have dropped affection from the circle of your needs, have you also dropped love between man and woman?" he asked. "Is this the theory of the overman, if so, your demigodship is after all but a doctrinaire demi-godship. Your words are idle—and you are far more human than you think [. . .]. The men whom Nietzsche's theory fits are only great men of a sort, a sort of Yahoo great men. The struggle is how to get rid of them, they belong to the clumsy and brutal side of things [. . .]" (*Letters to his Son* 70).

Yeats's principal outlet was the Abbey Theatre, which opened its doors on December 27, 1904, with a performance of *On Baile's Strand* and Lady Gregory's *Spreading the News*. The theater occupied the hall of the old Mechanics' Institute on Abbey Street, Dublin, a building that had been leased and renovated with funds provided by ANNIE HORNIMAN, a British tea heiress and fellow member of the Golden Dawn. Yeats's first order of business was wresting the theater from those who conceived its mission as foremost political. He was not uncommitted to the nationalist cause, but he understood this cause as broadly cultural, and he understood that cultural rebirth depended on artistic freedom. "Even if what one defends be true," Yeats would later write in "J. M. Synge and the Ireland of his Time," "an attitude of defence, a continual apology, whatever the cause, makes the mind barren because it kills intellectual innocence; that delight in what is unforeseen, and in the mere spectacle of the world, the mere drifting hither and thither that must come before all true thought and emotion" (*E&I* 314). Purges, schisms, and reorganizations had been a soap operatic feature of the Irish dramatic movement since 1901, when the Irish

Literary Theatre dissolved. Having already shaken free of Martyn, GEORGE MOORE, Gonne, and Russell, Yeats continued his consolidation of power in 1905, when the Irish National Theatre Society became "The National Theatre Society Limited," a public limited company with the majority of shares allocated to Yeats, J. M. SYNGE, and Lady Gregory as members of a three-person executive committee. Yeats wrote to Quinn, on September 16, "I think we have seen the end of the democracy in the Theatre which was Russell's doing, for I go to Dublin at the end of the week to preside at a meeting summoned to abolish it. If all goes well Synge and Lady Gregory and myself will have everything in our hands [. . .]. It has been a long fight, but the change could not be made until the old method had discredited itself and until three or four people had got some sort of natural leadership" (*CL4* 178). Yeats's last fetter was Annie Horniman. Worn down by years of friction with all concerned, and recognizing that Yeats—whom she loved—was never to be hers, she bitterly withdrew from the Irish dramatic movement in 1910.

The battle for a politically independent "theatre of beauty" was fought not only backstage, but on the stage, and among the stalls, and in the newspapers. "Yeats found chauvinism and mob-spirit rising before him in a dozen shapes," writes Richard Ellmann, "now it was the actors, refusing to play Lady Gregory's *Twenty-Five* because they said it would stimulate emigration to America; now the audience objecting to Synge's *Shadow of the Glen* and then, more violently, to his *Playboy of the Western World*, for giving a picture of Ireland which was considered derogatory. Yeats fought every fight, sometimes by public speeches, sometimes by letters to newspapers and articles, sometimes by private persuasion, and with his supporters succeeded in stemming the tide. He became a terrible man in combat, who could compel by sheer force of personality [. . .]" (*MM* 176). Yeats met Synge in PARIS in December 1896 and famously sent him to learn his craft on the barren, windswept ARAN ISLANDS. Yeats discerned in Synge's integrity and solitude something that powerfully countervailed the contemporary culture, and he brought him into the theater movement in 1902. *The Playboy* controversy exploded on January 26, 1907, when the debut performance of the play incited a riot at the Abbey. The play's seven-day run was marked by disturbances, arrests, and public speeches, but Yeats steadfastly held his ground, refusing to apologize or compromise.

The controversy catalyzed Yeats's recoil against the middle class and deepened his embrace of the conservative and aristocratic values he found symbolized by Coole Park and expressed in the pages of Castiglione and Nietzsche. Yeats's aristocratic turn was reinforced in the spring of 1907 when he visited Italy—Florence, San Marino, Urbino, Pesaro, Ravenna, Rimini, Ferrara, and Venice—with Lady Gregory and her son ROBERT GREGORY, an aspiring artist. The physical vestiges of the Renaissance made a strong impression, as had Castiglione's *The Book of the Courtier,* which Lady Gregory had read to him in the summer of 1903 (*Yeats and Castiglione* 20). Yeats seized on the Renaissance as a model of cultural unity—action wed to reflection, heroism wed to artistry—and as an implicit reproach of middle-class modernity. Thereafter, the Renaissance became an important touchstone in poems like "The PEOPLE" and "To A WEALTHY MAN WHO PROMISED A SECOND SUBSCRIPTION TO THE DUBLIN MUNICIPAL GALLERY IF IT WERE PROVED THE PEOPLE WANTED PICTURES," and more obliquely in poems like "ANCESTRAL HOUSES," "AT GALWAY RACES," "IN MEMORY OF MAJOR ROBERT GREGORY," "MY HOUSE," "The TOWER," and "UPON A HOUSE SHAKEN BY THE "LAND AGITATION."

In December 1907, John Butler Yeats sailed for New York. What was supposed to have been a holiday with his daughter Lily became an emigration. Embarrassed by his continued improvidence, he spent the rest of his life in a lower-Manhattan boardinghouse under the semi-filial watch of John Quinn. He contributed the effervescence of his personality to the boardinghouse dining room, dispatched a steady stream of brilliant letters, and devoted himself to his art, but he found no more commercial success in New York than he had in Dublin. Yeats's attempts to bring his father home were unavailing, and their reunions were limited to Yeats's visits to New York in 1911, 1914, and 1920.

As a newly minted man of the world, Yeats did not disdain the casual affair. He had a brief fling with Florence Farr in 1905 and 1906 (CL4 112–113, 160, 327–328); he evidently resumed his intimacies for a time with Olivia Shakespear; and he enjoyed an unpretendingly carnal relationship with Mabel Dickinson—a "medical gymnast and masseuse" who occasionally acted at the Abbey—between 1908 and 1913 (AM 384). All the while, however, he remained obsessed by Gonne, whose marriage had decisively fallen apart, the birth of her son Sean MacBride, on January 26, 1904, notwithstanding. Gonne accused MacBride of drunkenness and jealousy, and she alleged that he had exposed himself to Iseult (CL4 7–8; GY 231–232). She filed for divorce in January 1905, and a French court granted a legal separation in the summer of 1906 (GY 232; for Yeats's account of the divorce saga, see CL4 *passim*). In July 1908, Yeats and Gonne renewed the "spiritual marriage" that had been their surrogate for actual marriage following Gonne's revelations of 1898 (GY 255–259). "Reconciliation" commemorates this phase of their relationship. The evidence indicates that in late 1908 or early 1909 Yeats and Gonne briefly became lovers, which is consistent with the sexually explicit reminiscence of "HIS MEMORIES" (AM 393). Despite their renewed intimacy, however, they remained divided by geography (she continued to reside in Paris), by religion (she had converted to Catholicism prior to her marriage), and by politics (her militancy had not abated); so too by Gonne's only partially dissolved marriage.

Yeats published no book of verse between 1903 and 1910, the most significant dry-spell of his career. He did, however, complete three plays, DEIRDRE, The UNICORN FROM THE STARS, and The GREEN HELMET, and revise much of his previous dramatic work. *Deirdre* is taut and suspenseful, but its psychological ironies do little to harness Yeats's fundamental powers as a romantic poet. *The Unicorn from the Stars* and *The Green Helmet* were in their different ways failed experiments, the former an unsuccessful attempt to rescue *Where There is Nothing,* the latter a "heroic farce" that spoke subtly to Yeats's profound disillusionment. The second in Yeats's dramatic cycle on Cuchulain, the play recognizes Cuchulain's heroic stature, but amid the scene of manic buffoonery his heroism lacks a worthy context and comes to seem pointlessly gestural. Undoubtedly, the play suggests Yeats's own sense of grievance and frustration, the thanklessness of his efforts on Ireland's behalf (a theme similarly manifest in "To a Shade"). In 1906, he began work on another misconceived drama, THE PLAYER QUEEN, which gave him so much trouble it was not to be performed until May 1919, and even then bore marks of its difficult gestation. Yeats fared better in prose. On December 15, 1907, the Dun Emer Press brought out *Discoveries,* a volume of brief and vigorous prose reflections. Yeats had become an unimpeachable prose stylist, and the volume was a splendid exhibition of craft.

In January 1907, Yeats began to plan an elegant eight-volume edition of his collected work to be published by A. H. Bullen, with the backing of a £1,500 guarantee from Annie Horniman (CL4 641–642). The edition appeared the following fall and winter as *The Collected Works in Verse & Prose of William Butler Yeats.* As Lytton Strachey wrote in an ambivalent unsigned review of the first two volumes, such an edition implicitly claimed for its author "a recognised and permanent place in the literature of a nation" (*Critical Heritage* 164). Yeats's ascension was further signaled in August 1910 when he received a Civil List Pension. Yeats could not afford to pass up the £150 annual stipend, but accepting such governmental largesse inevitably complicated his already rancorous relationship with Irish nationalists (*Letters* 544–545, 550).

Yeats's arrival as a modern (if not yet as a modernist) was announced by the publication of *The Green Helmet and Other Poems,* which the CUALA PRESS—successor to Dun Emer—brought out in December 1910. The volume included a sequence of wry, retrospective poems about Gonne, the most striking of which was "No Second Troy." The origin of her permanent myth can be pinpointed in the poem's great question: "What could have made her peaceful with a mind / That nobleness made simple as a fire, / With beauty like a tightened bow, a kind / That is not natural in an age like this, / Being high and solitary and most stern?" The "tightened bow"—an image of disciplined intensity, harnessed passion—might have done double duty as a symbol of Yeats's emerging aesthetic. The collection also displayed a new pugnacity and worldly orientation. Yeats polemically aired his aristocratic bent in poems like "Upon a Threatened House" (later "Upon a House shaken by the Land Agitation"), "These are the Clouds," and "At Galway Races," and he ground personal axes in poems like "Against Unworthy Praise," "The FASCINATION OF WHAT'S DIFFICULT," and "To a Poet, who would have me Praise certain Bad Poets, Imitators of His and Mine." When Macmillan published an expanded edition of the volume in October 1912, Yeats added a number of fine poems in the same vein, and one poem—"The COLD HEAVEN"—in a distinctly different vein. A poem of strange and unsettling intensity and massively compressed complexity, "The Cold Heaven" portended the visionary recommitment that would soon rejuvenate Yeats. The poem leapt beyond even poems like "No Second Troy" and "At Galway Races" and set the precedent for the impossible load-bearing of "LEDA AND THE SWAN" and "The SECOND COMING."

Yeats's modernism was either confirmed or inspired—notions vary—by his burgeoning friendship with EZRA POUND, a bumptious young American who arrived in London in August 1908 with the determination to meet Yeats, whom he regarded as the greatest living poet. In January 1909, Pound made the acquaintance of Shakespear and her daughter Dorothy (1886–1973), whom Pound would marry in 1914. In May, Shakespear brought Pound to meet Yeats at Woburn Buildings, and thereafter the two poets became increasingly enmeshed as friends and collaborators. In one of the most storied episodes of modernist legend, Yeats and Pound spent three winters—1913–14, 1915, 1915–16—secluded in Stone Cottage, a six-room house on the edge of Ashdown Forest in Sussex. As Yeats had trouble with his eyes, Pound served as paid secretary (*Letters* 584).

During the first winter at Stone Cottage, Pound translated Noh plays from the notes of the American Orientalist Ernest Fenollosa (1853–1908). Yeats immediately recognized the Noh as a precedent for the kind of spare, stylized drama toward which he had long and vaguely groped. Yeats explained his breakthrough in his introduction to Pound's 1916 volume of Noh translations *Certain Noble Plays of Japan*, crowing that with Fenollosa and Pound's help he had "invented a form of drama, distinguished, indirect, and symbolic, and having no need of mob or Press to pay its way—an aristocratic form" (*E&I* 221). Yeats's use of the word "invented" is well advised, for, as Hiro Ishibashi notes, Yeats undertook his Noh experiments "when there were less than twenty pieces available in English translation out of about 240 extant Noh plays (which can be acted), after seeing only some fragmentary amateur performances of *Noh*, never having seen a complete stage production, and never even having visited Japan" (*Yeats and the Noh* 151). Yeats's first attempt at Noh-influenced drama was AT THE HAWK'S WELL—the prefatory play of his Cuchulain cycle—which was first performed in Lady Cunard's London drawing room on April 2, 1916. The production featured the Japanese modern dancer Michio Ito and masks designed by Yeats's friend, the artist Edmund Dulac (1882–1953). Music, dance, and mask would remain integral components of Yeats's drama, while the Noh would remain his informing ideal, though he would depart from its only partially understood conventions in subtle but important ways.

Yeats's war upon the mores of the middle-class climaxed in the mighty salvo of *Poems Written in Discouragement*, 50 copies of which were published by the Cuala Press in October 1913. The slim volume included "To a Wealthy Man," "SEPTEMBER 1913," "TO A FRIEND WHOSE WORK HAS COME TO NOTHING," "Paudeen," and "To a Shade." The volume's mood of withering contempt was at once a belated reaction to the downfall of CHARLES STEWART PARNELL (which had finally come into symbolic focus) and a broadside in the ongoing battle to establish a gallery of modern art in Dublin. Lady Gregory's nephew HUGH LANE, an art dealer and collector, had promised his superb collection of modern French paintings to Dublin on the condition that the city build a suitable gallery. To Yeats's disgust, Lane's lofty gesture met with a petty response: municipal foot-dragging and the

insults of a public controversy. *Poems Written in Discouragement* was followed by an expanded volume, *Responsibilities: Poems and a Play*, which the Cuala Press published on May 25, 1914. Yeats's modernism—whether Pound-inspired or Pound-confirmed—was now on full display in a new tautness and topicality; in a new assertion of personality; in a sexual frankness and muscular belligerence that seemed to dispense firmly and finally with Victorian politesse. The volume brimmed with polemical and imaginative energy. In addition to the powerful poems that had appeared in *Poems Written in Discouragement*, highlights included "FALLEN MAJESTY" (another indelible homage to Gonne), "The Cold Heaven" (reprinted), and "The MAGI" (a foretaste of the apocalyptic metaphysics out of which Yeats would craft a bevy of later masterpieces). On March 20, 1916, the Cuala Press brought out *Reveries over Childhood and Youth*, the first installment of Yeats's memoirs.

Yeats's "middle period" ended with a flurry of drama, both political and personal. Unlike his fellow modernists, Yeats was oddly unconvulsed by World War I, evidently thinking it a European rather than an Irish affair. Only the deaths of Hugh Lane (a victim of the attack on the *Lusitania*) and Lady Gregory's son Robert (shot down over Italy in January 1918) shook him from his mood of detached disgust. The EASTER RISING of April 1916, on the other hand, seemed instantly to transform the very ground of Irish politics and culture and both appalled and electrified Yeats. He could not approve the imprudence of the rebellion, but nor could he fail to admire its extravagant courage. The rebellion confirmed Yeats's emergent preoccupations: questions about the agency and mechanism of historical change, anxieties about what seemed a dawning age of violence, a general sense that modernity had begun to spin out of control. His chief pronouncement on the rising was the complex and equivocal "EASTER 1916," whose refrain crystallized his one certainty: "All changed, changed utterly: / A terrible beauty is born."

By now well into middle age, Yeats was beginning to regret his bachelorhood. Vacationing at the Gonnes' seaside home in Normandy in the summer of 1916, he made a final, half-hearted bid for the hand of Maud Gonne, who had become a widow following the execution of MacBride for his part in the Easter Rising. Rebuffed yet again, he turned his attention to Iseult Gonne, a French-speaking beauty who had just turned 22. Yeats proposed late in the summer, but he made no more headway with daughter than with mother. His thwarted courtship and mood of defeated age yielded two fine poems, "MEN IMPROVE WITH THE YEARS" and "The LIVING BEAUTY." In late 1916, with the idea of founding a family upon some appropriately severe and symbolic spot, he began negotiations to purchase THOOR BALLYLEE, a stone tower and attached cottage in the neighborhood of Lady Gregory's Coole Park (*Letters* 615). After extensive renovations, the tower served until 1928 as a flood-prone summer home; even more, it became a chief poetic symbol, at once an image of hermetic solitude, transcendental aspiration, aristocratic strength, and historical decay.

Yeats revisited Normandy in the summer of 1917 and renewed his courtship of Iseult. He returned to London with the Gonne family in mid-September and received a final demurral from Iseult in a London tea shop. Determined at all costs to be married, he set his sights on Georgie Hyde-Lees, aged 25. She was an intellectually earnest product of upper-middle-class London and, from 1914, a fellow member of the Golden Dawn. Her mother, Nelly, had long moved in the same London circles as Olivia Shakespear. Widowed in 1909, Nelly married Shakespear's brother Harry Tucker in 1911. Shakespear was thus Georgie's step-aunt, while Dorothy Shakespear (Mrs. Ezra Pound) was Georgie's dear friend. Yeats and Georgie met in 1911, and he had long mulled the idea of proposing to her (*BG* 41, 80, 92–93). In his state of emotional exhaustion, as he told Lady Gregory, he was willing to settle for a "friendly serviceable woman" and Georgie—familiar, capable, intelligent, handsome without being unsettling—fit the bill (91). He proposed on September 26. Realizing that he remained smitten with Iseult, he suffered pangs of "wild misery" as the wedding approached (98). Despite Yeats's cold feet, the couple was married on October 20 at the Harrow Road Registry Office, London, with Nelly Tucker and Ezra Pound in attendance.

The couple began their marriage at the Ashdown Forest Hotel, near Stone Cottage. Tormented by the sense that he had betrayed both Iseult and George (as she was soon to rename herself), Yeats sunk into despair (*Letters* 633). In this condition, he wrote "OWEN AHERNE AND HIS DANCERS," which confesses the triangular nature of his feelings. George diagnosed not only the cause of her husband's malaise but the necessary corrective. Pretending to be in the grip of a controlling spirit, she took pen and paper and wrote that all was well with Iseult and that Yeats was right to marry (633). According to her later account, some genuine force seized her hand, and she continued writing (*BG* 102–103; *Unicorn* 253). Yeats's mood of despair was instantly displaced by feverish excitement. Determined to continue with the experiment, he instituted a laborious regimen of "automatic writing." The first four years of marriage saw 450 automatic writing sessions and produced 3,627 pages of preserved script, a mass of material teeming—whirling—with literary, historical, psychological, philosophical, and occult ideas (*AV-1925* xix–xxi). Between 1917 and 1925, Yeats sculpted this mass into A VISION.

"IN EXCITED REVERIE": 1918–1928

Marriage did not bring the settled domesticity that Yeats had wanted (or said he wanted). In the months following their marriage the Yeatses divided their time between Sussex and London. In January 1918, they moved to 45 Broad Street, OXFORD. They spent the following spring and summer in Ireland, while renovation of Thoor Ballylee proceeded, and in September made their first stay in the attached cottage. In October, they leased Maud Gonne's house at 73 Stephen's Green, and in December moved to 96 Stephen's Green, remaining until February 1919, when Yeats moved into the Stephen's Green Club and the pregnant George entered a nursing home. Anne Butler Yeats was born on February 26. By April, Yeats had begun "A Prayer for My Daughter," which wishes for Anne a life of gracious order, a life free of the "intellectual hatred" that had allegedly poisoned Gonne. The poem's emphasis on "custom" and "ceremony" reflects Yeats's deepening engagement with the Irish 18th century and signals a refinement of his aristocratic and conservative bent; the implicit Georgianism of the poem would remain a ground-note of Yeats's thought and poetry throughout the 1920s and 1930s. Following Anne's birth, the family moved to a rented house in Dundrum. In June, Yeats ended his long tenure in Woburn Buildings and the family arrived for the summer at Thoor Ballylee. In October 1919 the family moved into a house at 4 Broad Street, Oxford, where they were at a safe remove from the ANGLO-IRISH WAR, which began in January 1919 and ended in truce on July 11, 1921.

In January 1920, the Yeatses—sans baby— departed on a five-month lecture tour of North America. In New York, George Yeats and John Butler Yeats met and took an instant liking to each other. This would be Yeats's final visit with his father, who would die on February 3, 1922, deeply loved by all whom he had continuously exasperated. The Yeatses returned to Europe in June 1920 and resettled at 4 Broad Street in July. Their Oxford idyll involved occult research, visits to Lady Ottoline Morrell's nearby Garsington Manor, and awe-inspiring descents into the undergraduate culture of Oxford. Most dramatically, Yeats delivered a passionate attack upon the British campaign in Ireland at the Oxford Union on February 17, 1921. In general, Yeats played the part of resident literary celebrity and enjoyed himself. The Yeatses remained at Broad Street until April 1921, when they let the house as a money-saving measure and moved to Minchin's Cottage in Shillingford. In June, they moved to Cuttlebrook House in Thame, where Michael Butler Yeats was born on August 22. The family returned to Broad Street in the autumn.

Yeats had now entered into his full powers and had begun to reclaim the mantle of romantic vision that "Lines Written in Dejection" announces as lost. Henceforth, the run of his work would belong to the permanent legacy of Western literature. During the years just before and after his marriage Yeats published in rapid succession *Eight Poems* ("Form" at the Morland Press, April 1916), *Easter, 1916* (privately printed, late 1916), *The Wild Swans at Coole* (Cuala Press, November 1917),

Nine Poems (privately printed, October 1918), an expanded edition of *The Wild Swans at Coole* (Macmillan, March 1919), *Michael Robartes and the Dancer* (Cuala Press, February 1921), and *Seven Poems and a Fragment* (Cuala Press, June 1922). A spectacular display of copiousness that calls to mind Yeats's own image of the "abounding glittering jet," the volumes included a raft of instantly canonical poems. "The Wild Swans at Coole" ended Yeats's middle-period with culminating poignancy, while poems like "Easter 1916," "UNDER SATURN," and the intricate sequence "UPON A DYING LADY" demonstrated a deepening psychological and moral subtlety. The headiest development, however, was Yeats's return to the visionary mode of his youth, a renaissance that had been heralded by poems like "The Cold Heaven" and "The Magi." Gone was the dreaminess and vagueness of the 1890s. Yeats's visionary flights were now placed under the discipline of a thorough technical mastery and wed to a rigorous metaphysical conception, resulting in poetry that was as powerfully oracular, profoundly philosophical, and sternly beautiful as any in the language. Yeats's initial triumphs in this mode included "EGO DOMINUS TUUS" from the first edition of *The Wild Swans at Coole*; "The PHASES OF THE MOON" and "The DOUBLE VISION OF MICHAEL ROBARTES" from the second edition; "The Second Coming" from *Michael Robartes and the Dancer*; and "ALL SOULS' NIGHT" and "NINETEEN HUNDRED AND NINETEEN" (then titled "Thoughts upon the Present State of the World") from *Seven Poems and a Fragment*.

If Yeats's poetry had become a progress from triumph to triumph, his work in prose and drama was at the very least consistently arresting. Macmillan brought out PER AMICA SILENTIA LUNAE, a short philosophical treatise written in Yeats's most lapidary prose, on January 18, 1918. Though Yeats completed the treatise before his marriage, it heralded many of the themes of the automatic writing sessions and stands as a prolegomenon to the ideas of *A Vision*. Yeats's experiments in the Noh drama, meanwhile, were showcased in *Two Plays for Dancers*. Published by the Cuala Press in January 1919, the volume included The DREAMING OF THE BONES and The ONLY JEALOUSY OF EMER, the latter a further installment in his Cuchulain cycle as well as an attempt to interpret his lingering feelings for Maud, Iseult, and George. Macmillan brought out *Four Plays for Dancers* in October 1921, rounding out the contents of the earlier volume with *At the Hawk's Well* and CALVARY. Capping this spree, T. Werner Laurie published the second installment of Yeats's memoirs, *The Trembling of the Veil,* in October 1922. This was to be the core of what would eventually become *Autobiographies.*

In February 1922, the Yeatses arranged to lease 82 Merrion Square, a large and graceful Georgian house in one of Dublin's most distinguished neighborhoods (see AP 210). Meanwhile, the family decamped to Thoor Ballylee, where they would spend the summer while the IRISH CIVIL WAR flared across the countryside. Yeats supported the treaty that both ended the Anglo-Irish War and instigated the civil war, and he supported the new Free State government headed by William Cosgrave, all of which estranged him from Maud Gonne, whom Cosgrave's government was to imprison (*Letters* 697). In a mood of profound and sober reflection, with the human and historical comedy scrutable from his very door, Yeats began, in June, the seven-poem sequence "MEDITATIONS IN TIME OF CIVIL WAR," one of his greatest achievements. In late September, the family moved into the house at Merrion Square. The neighborhood suffered the occasional bomb blast, and on December 24, 1922, two bullets were fired through Yeats's window, but otherwise both family and house came through the war unscathed (696).

Before the year was out, Yeats's status as a dignitary of the new state was sealed by two honors. On December 7, President Cosgrave, acting on the recommendation of Yeats's old friend Oliver St. John Gogarty, appointed Yeats to a six-year term in the new Irish SENATE (SS 14–15). The position came with an annual salary of £360, which was no small sum to Yeats. As a senator, Yeats was at least theoretically a target of assassination, and his house was placed under guard (*Letters* 698). Later in the month, Trinity College presented him with an honorary doctorate, thus salving the old wounds and resentments that show in a poem like "The SCHOLARS." In the early days of his senatorial career,

Yeats devoted himself to work on *A Vision* during the mornings and attended to Senate business in the afternoons, making each day a juxtaposition of all but reverse universes (695). Yeats understood that he was a political neophyte and tended to keep a low profile, largely addressing himself to cultural and educational matters. As Joseph Hone notes, he "voted as a rule with a group of nominated Senators (peers, bankers, lawyers and business men), who expressed the views of that part of the Protestant and Unionist minority which wished to assist the new order" (*W. B. Yeats* 356). Yeats's most dramatic moment in the Senate came in June 1925, when he rose to defend the right to divorce and issued a passionate vindication of Ireland's Protestant minority (SS 89–102).

With Lily Yeats ailing, Cuala Industries moved from Churchtown to 82 Merrion Square in August 1923 (where it remained until it moved to a new showroom at 133 Lower Baggot Street in February 1925), and George Yeats assumed what would become a permanent creative and managerial role. That winter Yeats received the paramount honor of his career. On November 15, 1923, he became the first Irish author to win the Nobel Prize in literature. The honor inestimably added to Yeats's prestige and influence, and the financial windfall of roughly £7,500 was a godsend. Yeats used the money to relieve the debts of the Cuala Press, pay Lily's medical expenses, and furnish Merrion Square. The remainder later evaporated in inopportune investments (*Letters* 701–702; AP 415). In January 1924, the poet and his wife traveled to Stockholm to receive the prize. Yeats was delighted by the round of festivities and ceremonies that filled the eight-day stay, but even more he was impressed by what seemed a culture that had escaped the modern blight. Yeats recorded his impressions in "The Bounty of Sweden," at once a memoir of his Nobel activities and a vivid discourse on the ideal of unity of culture. The Cuala Press published "The Bounty of Sweden," along with Yeats's Nobel lecture "The Irish Dramatic Movement," in July 1925.

Now an honorary doctor, a senator, and a Nobel laureate, Yeats might have been expected to become the kind of "smiling public man" he describes in "AMONG SCHOOL CHILDREN." Far from sinking into self-satisfied celebrity, however, he became even more intensely creative and daringly speculative as the decade progressed. In July 1924, the Cuala Press brought out *The Cat and the Moon and Certain Poems*, which continued Yeats's torrent of creative achievement. In addition to "Meditations in Time of Civil War," the volume included "Leda and the Swan." Destined to become one of Yeats's most celebrated creations, the poem, like "The Second Coming," mythologizes the turning gyre of history and reduces its own myth to a single, searing concretion. In April 1925, Yeats at long last finished *A Vision*, which systematized the metaphysics that he and his wife had been exploring for years during their automatic writing sessions. T. Werner Laurie issued 600 copies to subscribers on January 15, 1926. The volume met with baffled silence. "*A Vision* reminds me of the stones I used to drop as a child in a certain very deep well," Yeats commented to Shakespear. "The splash is very far off and very faint" (*Letters* 712). Tireless in his determination to perfect his system, Yeats had returned to work on *A Vision* by April 1928 (739, 742). Working from cribs, Yeats further busied himself with translations of SOPHOCLES' *King Oedipus* and *Oedipus at Colonus*, striving for a language "bare, hard and natural like a saga" (720). The plays respectively debuted at the Abbey Theatre on December 7, 1926, and September 12, 1927.

Yeats's "communicators" had warned him to abstain from philosophical reading until he had completed *A Vision* (AV 12, 19). Now he was at liberty to plunge into the writings of the great philosophers. He read avidly if miscellaneously throughout the later 1920s in the attempt to confirm, contextualize, and better understand the doctrines of his own book. During the 1920s, Yeats struck up a lively philosophical exchange with the poet and artist T. STURGE MOORE, an old friend. His letters suggest the tenor of his reading: they mention Plato, Plotinus, George Berkeley, Hegel, Schopenhauer, Henry Adams, Bergson, Benedetto Croce, Bertrand Russell, G. E. Moore (Sturge Moore's brother), Giovanni Gentile, and Spengler, among other thinkers.

Yeats's intellectual bearings were shifting in other ways as well. Poems like "At Galway Races," "A Prayer for my Daughter," and "Upon a House shaken by the Land Agitation" had long indicated a predilection for the values and traditions of Ireland's landed class. By the mid-1920s, Yeats had more pointedly come to associate these values with the Protestant culture of Georgian Ireland and with the great figures of Georgian culture: JONATHAN SWIFT (1667–1745), Berkeley (1685–1753), Edmund Burke (1729–97), Oliver Goldsmith (1731–74), and Henry Grattan (1746–1820). Here was an example of passion wed to intellect and a confirmation of his own conservatism, which he epitomizes in his introduction to *The WORDS UPON THE WINDOW-PANE*: "the long-settled rule of powerful men, no great dogmatic structure, few great crowded streets, scattered unprogressive communities, much handiwork, wisdom wound into the roots of the grass" (*Expl.* 360; *VPl.* 965). Yeats's Georgianism was at its peak of enthusiasm during the later 1920s and early 1930s, providing a conceptual basis for a number of excellent poems ("BLOOD AND THE MOON," "IN MEMORY OF EVA GORE-BOOTH AND CON MARKIEWICZ," "PARNELL'S FUNERAL," "The SEVEN SAGES," "SWIFT'S EPITAPH") and for *The Words upon the Window-pane*, an intense foray into Swift's psychobiography.

If Yeats's imagination had never been more "excited, passionate, fantastical," as he wrote truly enough in "The Tower," his body was beginning to show wear and tear. In October 1927, he developed pneumonia exacerbated by what he called "general nervous breakdown," necessitating a winter abroad (*Letters* 730–733; AV 20). The Yeatses spent November in Algeciras and Seville, where Yeats continued to ail. On November 23, they relocated to Cannes; in February 1928, they proceeded to Rapallo, a seaside town just southeast of Genoa, and took rooms in a hotel. The primary attraction was Pound, who had resided in Rapallo since late 1924. In March, having decided to give up 82 Merrion Square on the assumption that Yeats could no longer withstand the Dublin winter, they took a five-year lease on an apartment at Via Americhe 12–8, which was still under construction and would

he following winter. Feeling bet-
ats was hard at work on A *Packet*
in introduction to the revised
. The Cuala Press published A
929, though the volume it was
appear until 1937. The Yeatses
in April 1928, sold 82 Merrion
moved into a flat at 42 Fitzwil-
1, in July (*Letters* 745). Yeats's
expired in September and he
appointment, regretting more
ss of income (745). Lady Greg-
been ailing since June 1923,
surgery for breast cancer. On
aret Gregory, Lady Gregory's
Coole Park to the Ministry of
ire. Lady Gregory managed to
but she suffered the indignity
from the ministry at £100 per
ournals, II, 180).

were years of transition and
y were also years of triumph.
ement of the 1920s culmi-
n published *The Tower* in
orating poetry from *October*
just 1927), *The Cat and the*
s *and a Fragment*, and fea-
iconic engraving of Thoor
Moore, the volume was
nism. The volume's slate
ded "All Souls' Night,"
," "Leda and the Swan,"
Civil War," "Nineteen
SAILING TO BYZANTIUM,"
e volume's minor poems
Yeats gloated to Shake-
is a great success, two
month, much the larg-
. .] When I get back to
erse again but no more
eading *The Tower* I was
, and long to live out of
e new vintage. Yet that
power and it is the best
rs 742). The book was
amazingly, he would go
ient.

"AN OLD MAN'S FRENZY": 1929–1939

Yeats ended 1928 as he began it, in Rapallo, with
Pound as his cantankerous but bracing daily companion. Rounding out the cenacle were the poet
Basil Bunting (1900–85) and the composer George
Antheil (1900–59), whom Yeats enlisted to compose the music for FIGHTING THE WAVES, a balletic
version of *The Only Jealousy of Emer* (761–762).
The Yeatses departed Rapallo in April 1929.
George returned to Fitzwilliam Square, while Yeats
stopped in London, where he saw old friends, made
the acquaintance of Wyndham Lewis (1882–1957),
and spent time with his brother. Yeats spent July at
Coole. His stay inspired the elegiac "COOLE PARK,
1929," which he began in August. He returned
to Dublin for the debut of *Fighting the Waves* at
the Abbey on August 13 and was delighted by the
performance. He told Shakespear, "Everyone here
is as convinced as I am that I have discovered a
new form by this combination of dance, speech
and music" (768). In October 1929, the Fountain
Press of New York brought out *The Winding Stair*,
another poetic *tour de force*. "In Memory of Eva
Gore-Booth and Con Markiewicz," "DEATH," "A
DIALOGUE OF SELF AND SOUL," "Oil and Blood,"
and the sequence "A WOMAN YOUNG AND OLD"
comprised the slim but commanding volume. "A
Dialogue of Self and Soul" was the crown jewel:
a magnificent compression of the most important
elements of his thought.

In November Yeats was once again ailing, this
time with a lung condition (770). The Yeatses
departed for Rapallo later in the month. Upon
arrival, Yeats suffered a significant breakdown,
involving "some sort of nervous collapse and a
temperature that rises to greet the setting sun"
(771). His affliction was diagnosed as Malta fever
(*WBY&TSM* 160). Yeats remained weak through
March and April, though the worst of the illness
had passed; he was well enough to return to Dublin
only in July 1930. Yeats's sickbed was a charac-
teristically vigorous one. He immersed himself in
the writings of Swift and came to feel an even
deeper bond with Georgian Ireland (*Letters* 773,
776). Yeats's months of reflection on Swift yielded
The Words upon the Window-pane. Finished in late
October 1930 (777), the play debuted at the Abbey

Theatre on November 17. Back in good health, Yeats passed late 1930 and early 1931 at work on a lengthy introduction to *The Words upon the Window-pane*; on a new play called The RESURRECTION; on the revised version of *A Vision*; and on an introduction to Joseph Hone and Mario Rossi's *Bishop Berkeley* (780–781). Having leased Hone's house in Killiney, about 10 miles south of Dublin, for the duration of the spring, Yeats busied himself with his usual social and business rounds. In May 1931, he returned to Oxford to receive an honorary doctorate.

In July, he arrived at Coole, where he would intermittently remain until May 1932, when Lady Gregory would finally succumb to cancer. During this long, plainly filial vigil, Yeats wrote "VACILLATION" (*Letters* 789–790) and "COOLE AND BALLYLEE, 1931." The latter poem, Yeats's final homage to the house that had been home and haven for more than 30 years, glimpses Lady Gregory in her moment of proud decline ("Sound of a stick upon the floor, a sound / From somebody that toils from chair to chair") and ends in elegiac self-summation ("We were the last romantics—chose for theme / Traditional sanctity and loveliness . . ."). Yeats was emotionally shattered by Lady Gregory's death. He told Rossi on June 6, "I have lost one who has been to me for nearly forty years my strength and my conscience" (796). He told H. J. C. Grierson on June 9, "Up till three months ago I had for a year or more written nothing but verse, then my imagination stopped and has showed no sign of moving since" (797). Not until April 1933 could Yeats report to Shakespear that he had returned to writing verse (808).

In May 1932, the Yeatses decided to give up 42 Fitzwilliam Square and move to Riversdale, a pleasant 18th-century cottage in Rathfarnham, a village just outside Dublin. "It has the most beautiful gardens I have seen round a small house, and all is well stocked," Yeats told Shakespear. "I shall step out from my study into the front garden—but as I write the words I know that I am heartbroken for Coole and its great woods" (795). The family moved in July, and by the end of the month Yeats could write to Shakespear in a less crestfallen mood: "At first I was unhappy, for every-

thing made me remember the great rooms and the great trees of Coole, my home for nearly forty years, but now that the pictures are up I feel more content. This little creeper-covered farm-house might be in a Calvert woodcut, and what could be more suitable for one's last decade?" (799). As the summer waned, Yeats found further distraction and consolation in a campaign to create an IRISH ACADEMY OF LETTERS (800–802). On October 21, 1932, Yeats departed for a three-month lecture tour of America to raise money for the new academy (803–804). Upon his return in January, he told Shakespear that he had "brought George about £700 and the Academy all the money it wants" for an array of literary awards (804).

Despite age, infirmity, and loss, Yeats continued to scale the heights as a poet. In November 1932, the Cuala Press published *Words for Music Perhaps*. The volume's bounty included "BYZANTIUM" (conceivably the pinnacle of Yeats's verse), "Vacillation" (an important elaboration of the ideas of "A Dialogue of Self and Soul"), "Coole Park, 1929," "Coole and Ballylee, 1931" (titled "Coole Park and Ballylee 1932"), "Swift's Epitaph" (a superb rendering of the Latin inscription that appears above Swift's tomb in St. Patrick's Cathedral), and "The Seven Sages" (an overt vindication of Georgianism). The volume ended with the long sequence "WORDS FOR MUSIC PERHAPS," whose primary persona, Crazy Jane, was one of Yeats's most

Yeats at Riversdale, Rathfarnham, County Dublin. Riversdale was the last of Yeats's Irish homes. (*Fáilte Ireland*)

vital creations and the avatar of a new scabrousness in his work.

In June 1933, Yeats received an honorary doctorate from Cambridge to complement his degrees from Trinity and Oxford (*Letters* 805, 811). During the spring and summer, he took a renewed interest in Irish politics, inspired by the emergence of the fascist "Blue Shirts" led by General Eoin O'Duffy (1892–1944). On July 13, he told Shakespear, "Politics are growing heroic. De Valera [who had come to power in the general election of February 1932] has forced political thought to face the most fundamental issues. A Fascist opposition is forming behind the scenes to be ready should some tragic situation develop. I find myself constantly urging the despotic rule of the educated classes as the only end to our troubles." He appended to his letter a distillation of *A Vision*'s political insight: "History is very simple—the rule of the many, then the rule of the few, day and night, night and day for ever, while in small disturbed nations day and night race" (811–812). O'Duffy called at Riversdale on July 17. Yeats's dispatch to Shakespear indicated second thoughts about fascist rule in Ireland: "Doubtless I shall hate it (though not so much as I hate Irish democracy) but it is September and we must not behave like the gay young sparks of May or June." It likewise indicated tempered enthusiasm for O'Duffy: "O'Duffy himself is autocratic, directing the movement from above down as if it were an army. I did not think him a great man though a pleasant one, but one never knows, his face and mind may harden or clarify" (812–813; see also 814). In August, the government successfully banned a mass demonstration of Blue Shirts in Dublin, after which the movement lost its head of steam, and O'Duffy accepted the leadership of the new Fine Gael party. Thereafter Yeats tended to distance himself (813–815, 820–821, 885). All the same, he saw fit to write the fascistic "Three Songs to the Same Tune" in November 1933 and publish it in February 1934. In a note to the poem in the December 1934 number of *Poetry*, Yeats avowed a politics of cultural unity and acknowledged that "marching men" would be required to see through his aim, but he disavowed the Blue Shirt movement and denied the partisan implications of his poem: "Because a friend [Der-mot MacManus] belonging to a political party wherewith I had once some loose associations, told me that it had, or was about to have, or might be persuaded to have, some such aim as mine, I wrote these songs. Finding that it neither would nor could, I increased their fantasy, their extravagance, their obscurity, that no party might sing them" (*VP* 837; see also 543–544). Yeats recanted more forcefully in "Parnell's Funeral." The second section of the poem, which appeared in October 1934, unfavorably contrasts O'Duffy—as well as de Valera and Cosgrave—with Parnell ("Their school a crowd, his master solitude").

Yeats was attracted by fascism's promise to undo the modern order, but this is not to say that he belonged to the school of Hitler. His model was Italian rather than German, and, like many during the 1920s, he construed Italian fascism as nothing more ominous than an ideology of vigorous traditionalism. Elizabeth Cullingford comments that Yeats "took the essentials of fascism to be order, hierarchy, discipline, devotion to culture, and the rule of the most educated" (*Yeats, Ireland and Fascism* 202). Essentially, Yeats longed for a restoration of the culture of Georgian Ireland, with its rich duality of peasant and noble bound—but not coerced—by ingrained traditions. In its Italian and Irish varieties, fascism briefly seemed a means to this end, a modern version of the "long-settled rule of powerful men" that he associated with the 18th century. When Nazism later came into view, he found it, like Soviet communism, a totalitarian vulgarity, an example of the "artificial unity which ends every civilization," as he told Ethel Mannin in December 1936 (*Letters* 869; see also AV 301–302). As a romantic and libertarian of the school of O'Leary, he reflexively rejected Nazism's program of propaganda, censorship, racism, and militarism. Cullingford ends her superbly lucid study of Yeats's politics with a judicious assessment: "Of all political stances [Yeats's] was probably closest to that of Burke's Old Whigs: an aristocratic liberalism that combined love of individual freedom with respect for the ties of the organic social group" (*Yeats, Ireland and Fascism* 235).

In September 1933, Macmillan brought out a new edition of *The Winding Stair* that encompassed the earlier edition as well as *Words for Music Perhaps*. The volume was an achievement to outscale and otherwise rival *The Tower*. Yeats had produced his second masterpiece of modernism. In November 1933, he began *The KING OF THE GREAT CLOCK TOWER*. He was further busy with the memoir of the Irish dramatic movement that would become *Dramatis Personae* (Cuala Press, December 1935) and with the revised edition of *A Vision* (*Letters* 819–820).

Yeats's marriage had for some time dwindled into affectionate complacency and practical partnership. During the mid- and later 1930s, Yeats found a compensating outlet in a host of new female friends and lovers. This romantic and sexual renaissance was in some sense catalyzed by the "Steinach operation" that Yeats underwent on April 5, 1934 (*Letters* 822; *AP* 496–500). Essentially a vasectomy, the surgery was touted as a rejuvenating procedure, and Yeats, whether for physical or psychosomatic reasons, was reinvigorated by it. The first of Yeats's love interests was the 27-year-old MARGOT RUDDOCK, a British actress and poet who introduced herself in the autumn of 1934. They met in London on October 4, and Yeats was soon addressing her as "my dearest" and "my love" (*Sweet Dancer* 24, 31). In late November, Yeats mentions being thrown into an "utter black gloom" by the fear that his "nervous inhibition" had not left him. The implication seems to be that Yeats had tried but failed to consummate the relationship (*Sweet Dancer* 30–31; *AP* 509). In his romantic excitement, Yeats began to rewrite *The King of the Great Clock Tower* as *A FULL MOON IN MARCH*, giving the queen a speaking part so Ruddock might act the role (*Sweet Dancer* 23). Yeats's second amour began in late December 1934, when Dr. Norman Haire (1892–1952), the obstetrician and gynecologist who had performed his Steinach operation and overseen his post-operative treatment, introduced him to Ethel Mannin (1900–84), a 34-year-old journalist, novelist, and advocate of sexual liberation. She recalls of their first meeting: "The occasion was an invitation to dinner at [Haire's] Harley Street house; I was to put on my most alluring evening dress and all my sex-appeal, for the famous poet to test out his rejuvenated reaction to an attractive young woman [. . .]" (*Young*

in the Twenties 67). The two soon became lovers, apparently with physical success (*AP* 510–513). George Yeats tolerated Yeats's scarcely concealed adultery, recognizing and generously accepting, as R. F. Foster writes, "his complexity, his insecurity, his romanticism, [and] his willfulness," as well as "his need for dignity and privacy" (513–514).

This heady phase was interrupted in January 1935, when Yeats suffered another bout of lung congestion. He was forced to take to his bed at Riversdale and remained convalescent until March (*Letters* 830–832). He relapsed in April and spent another month in bed. By mid-June he could report that he was well though unable to climb stairs without panting (835). Shaky health notwithstanding, Yeats was busy correcting proofs of *A Vision* and schooling himself to edit *The Oxford Book of Modern Verse* (833, 835). He welcomed the pretext to delve into contemporary verse, and he began a thorough review. His most exciting discovery was the verse of Lady DOROTHY WELLESLEY. Lady Ottoline Morrell was a friend of both poets and had no trouble bringing them together. On June 3, 1935, she drove Yeats to Penns in the Rocks, Wellesley's Sussex manor, for an overnight stay. In August, Yeats returned for a two-week visit with his daughter ("talented, gay and timid" as he told Wellesley in advance of their visit), and he made further visits in late October and early November (*Letters* 838; *LOP* 11). He and Wellesley spent much time discussing his anthology, and Yeats proposed that Wellesley prepare a volume of her selected poems, with an introduction by himself. The book was published in June 1936 as *Selections from the Poems of Dorothy Wellesley*. Romantically involved with BBC pioneer Hilda Matheson (1888–1940) from 1932, Wellesley was not among Yeats's lovers; rather, she and her house helped fill the void left by Lady Gregory and Coole (see *LOP* 38–39, 63).

On November 30, 1935, Yeats departed for Majorca with Shri Purohit Swami (1882–1941), an Indian monk to whom he had been introduced in June 1931 by T. Sturge Moore. Yeats had written introductions to the Swami's autobiography *An Indian Monk: His Life and Adventures* (Macmillan, November 1932) and to his translation of Bhagwan Shri Hamsa's *The Holy Mountain* (Faber and

Faber, September 1934). In Majorca, Yeats hoped to recover his health while collaborating with the Swami on a translation that was to be published by Faber and Faber in April 1937 as *The Ten Principal Upanishads*. Soon after arriving on December 12, Yeats added to his regimen by beginning *The Herne's Egg* (*Letters* 845–846; *LOP* 43–44). In January 1936, Yeats suffered a serious attack that made breathing "difficult and painful" (*Letters* 847; *LOP* 49). George Yeats rushed to his bedside, arriving on February 2. Yeats's convalescence was interrupted in mid-May by the early morning arrival of Ruddock, now in the grip of the psychosis that would require her permanent institutionalization in late 1937. Yeats gives a full account of the episode in a May letter to Shakespear (*Letters* 856) and in his introduction to Ruddock's *The Lemon Tree* (J.M. Dent & Sons, May 1937). In brief, Ruddock arrived unannounced in a state of suicidal mania (see "A Crazed Girl"). After borrowing clothes and money from the Swami, she fled to Barcelona, where she jumped out of a window and broke her knee. The British consul summoned Yeats to Barcelona, and he arranged for Ruddock to return to England with a nurse. Yeats was weak but essentially recovered by early April, and he and George departed for London on May 26.

Yeats visited Penns at the Rocks and made the social rounds in London before returning to Ireland in late June 1936. Though he had to be taken for his daily walk in a wheelchair (860, 862), he remained industrious, finishing *The Herne's Egg*, writing superb verse ("Lapis Lazuli," "To Dorothy Wellesley"), and correcting proofs of both *The Ten Principal Upanishads* and *A Vision*. On October 11, the BBC broadcast Yeats's talk "Modern Poetry," one of several BBC broadcasts in which Yeats was involved during the 1930s (see *Biblio.* 467–477 for a summary). *The Oxford Book of Modern Verse* appeared in November, prefaced by a substantial essay. The volume was greeted by "universal denunciation from both right and left," as Yeats told a correspondent, despite which "fifteen thousand have been sold in three months" (*Letters* 886). Without being in the least insincere, Yeats had loaded the anthology with the work of his friends. AE was represented by eight poems, Oliver

St. John Gogarty by 17, Wellesley by eight, Ruddock by seven, and Shri Purohit Swami by three (the same number as W. H. Auden).

During the first months of 1937, Yeats continued to correct proofs of *The Ten Principal Upanishads* and *A Vision*. In April, Edmund Dulac introduced Yeats to the journalist Edith Shackleton Heald (1885–1976), who was to be the last of his intimate female friends and lovers. Until Yeats's final departure for the Continent in November 1938, her house in Steyning, Sussex, would complement Penns in the Rocks as a country retreat. He busied himself also with radio broadcasts on April 22, July 3, and October 29, 1937, all three of which featured Ruddock as a reader (*Biblio.* 472–474). The revised version of *A Vision* finally appeared on October 7, 1937. Like the first edition, it elicited an uneasy mixture of admiration, consternation, and bafflement. Writing in the *Criterion*, Stephen Spender articulated the basic hesitation: "Like Blake, Mr. Yeats is prodigiously systematic, often illuminating, clear and even precise. The difficulty is, though, to discover on what plane he is being clear and to what he is consistent—where, in fact, his system, with its extensive philosophic claims, actually links up with reality" (*Critical Heritage* 402).

His health still fragile, Yeats departed for the south of France in January 1938, spending a month in Monte Carlo and Menton with Shackleton Heald. In early February, she went on to Paris, and George Yeats arrived to assume nursing and secretarial duties. The Yeatses moved to Cap-Martin on March 1 and returned to London on March 23. Yeats divided April and May between Penns in the Rocks, Steyning, and London, and finally returned to Ireland in June. On August 26, Yeats last saw Maud Gonne when she came to tea at Riversdale. Gonne remembered the afternoon in a 1945 letter to Mannin: "Politics had separated us for quite a long while, we got on each other's nerves over them & neither wanted to see the other, but at the last we had come together & the last time I saw him at Riversdale he was planning things we would do together when he returned—but he seemed to me so ill, I felt unhappy for I didn't think we would meet again in this life" (*GY* 453; see also *Scattering Branches* 25). By this time, Yeats understood that final preparations were in order. In August, he arranged to be buried in the church cemetery at Drumcliff, just north of Sligo, where his paternal great-grandfather had been rector from 1805 until his death in 1846, and he composed for himself a fitting epitaph: "Cast a cold eye / On life, on death. / Horseman, pass by!" (*Letters* 914). In October, Yeats received the news that Shakespear had died: she was the friend with whom Yeats had longest and most intimately shared himself (916).

Despite age and debility, Yeats had in reserve one last spree of inspired creativity, which lasted until his death. He was not wrong when he boasted to Shackleton Heald in March 1938, "My recent work has greater strangeness and I think greater intensity than anything I have done" (907). This was precisely the "old man's frenzy" to which he aspires in "An ACRE OF GRASS." Yeats's tumultuous swan song encompassed *New Poems* (Cuala Press, May 1938) and two posthumous volumes: *Last Poems and Two Plays* (Cuala Press, July 1939) and *ON THE BOILER* (Cuala Press, autumn 1939). *New Poems* was by turns salty in its display of tenacious vitality and lofty in its summarizing vision; it included, among much else, "The GYRES,"

Yeats's final resting place: the churchyard at Drumcliff, County Sligo, with Ben Bulben in the distance *(Fáilte Ireland)*

"Lapis Lazuli," the sexually explicit sequence on lady, lover, and chambermaid (see "The THREE BUSHES"), "An Acre of Grass," "BEAUTIFUL LOFTY THINGS," "The SPUR," and "The MUNICIPAL GALLERY REVISITED." Arguably an even stronger volume, *Last Poems and Two Plays* was rampant with competing final statements, representing some of Yeats's most ambitious and intricate verse. The volume's crowning achievements include "UNDER BEN BULBEN" (which ends with the words of Yeats's epitaph), "The STATUES," "NEWS FOR THE DELPHIC ORACLE," "LONG-LEGGED FLY," "A BRONZE HEAD," "The MAN AND THE ECHO," "The CIRCUS ANIMALS' DESERTION," and "POLITICS." "Beautiful Lofty Things," "A Bronze Head" and "The Circus Animals' Desertion"—perhaps also "Politics"—in their different ways take leave of Gonne: as she was his first great theme, so she was his last. The volume's plays, The DEATH OF CUCHULAIN and PURGATORY, were vigorous and unsettling finales. The former concluded the epochal cycle on Cuchulain with the hero's beheading at the hands of a blind beggar, while the latter, performed at the Abbey on August 10, 1938, amid a stir of religious controversy, wound the strands of Yeats's late thought—Georgianism, eugenics, modern degeneracy, life after death—into a final vision of existential horror (on the controversy, see *Letters* 913–915). Conceived in late 1937, *On the Boiler,* a prose meditation on culture and politics, was at once acute and rebarbative. In its eugenic emphasis and air of arrogant assertion, the book, as Yeats well understood, was an act of cultural pugilism. He told Mannin in December 1937, "I must lay aside the pleasant paths I have built up for years and seek the brutality, the ill breeding, the barbarism of truth" (903). His letters of the period repeatedly mention—perhaps with self-dramatizing relish—the likelihood that friends would turn on him (see 900–914).

In August 1938, Macmillan published *The Autobiography of William Butler Yeats,* which omitted the Nobel lecture but otherwise gave final form to Yeats's memoirs. The volume incorporated *Reveries over Childhood and Youth, The Trembling of the Veil, Dramatis Personae,* and *The Bounty of Sweden,* as well as extracts from the diaries of 1909–11.

Though an untrustworthy historical document and a bit of a motley assemblage, it is one of the signal memoirs of literary history. It is remarkable as a specimen of high prose, as an exercise in dauntless self-investigation and self-revelation, as a compendium of aesthetic and metaphysical reflection.

In late November 1938, the Yeatses departed for the south of France. They settled at the Hôtel Idéal-Séjour in Cap-Martin, where they had stayed the previous March. Amid the balmy weather and the quiet of the hotel—"perfect as ever"—Yeats exercised for the last time his vast ability, correcting proofs of *On the Boiler*, putting finishing touches on *The Death of Cuchulain*, and writing "Cuchulain Comforted" and "The Black Tower," his last poems (*LOP* 190–196). Michael Yeats paid a three-week visit before returning to Ireland on January 15, while Wellesley, Matheson, and the poet W. J. Turner (1884–1946), encamped in a nearby villa, regularly called during Yeats's last month. Sensing his approaching end, Yeats began to revolve the terms of his final comprehension. On December 23, he took his own measure in a letter to Mannin: "Am I a mystic?—no, I am a practical man. I have seen the raising of Lazarus and the loaves and fishes and have made the usual measurements, plummet line, spirit-level and have taken the temperature by pure mathematic" (921). He told Lady Elizabeth Pelham on January 4, "It seems to me that I have found what I wanted. When I try to put all into a phrase I say, 'Man can embody truth but he cannot know it.' I must embody it in the completion of my life. The abstract is not life and everywhere draws out its contradictions. You can refute Hegel but not the Saint or the Song of Sixpence. . . ." (922). Yeats's end came quickly. On January 24, he was too tired to join a farewell dinner for Turner and his wife; by January 26, it had become clear that he was dying. That night, as Wellesley records, he made final changes to *The Death of Cuchulain* and "Under Ben Bulben" (*LOP* 195). He passed into a coma on January 27 and died on January 28, 1939. He was buried on January 30 at the cemetery at Roquebrune. Due to the war, he was not interred in the Drumcliff churchyard until September 1948. With Ben Bulben majestic in the distance, Yeats's remains were borne with state ceremony to his final grave and laid beneath the great epitaph.

SOURCES

Elizabeth Cullingford, *Yeats, Ireland and Fascism*; Richard Ellmann, *Yeats: The Man and the Masks*; Richard J. Finneran, et al., eds., *Letters to W. B. Yeats* (vol. 1); R. F. Foster, *W. B. Yeats: A Life, I: The Apprentice Mage, II: The Arch-Poet*; Gregory, Lady, *Lady Gregory's Journals* (vol. 2, ed. Daniel J. Murphy), *Our Irish Theatre*; Stephen Gwynn, ed., *Scattering Branches: Tributes to the Memory of W. B. Yeats*; Joseph Hone, *W. B. Yeats*; Hiro Ishibashi, *Yeats and the Noh: Types of Japanese Beauty and Their Reflection in Yeats's Plays*; A. Norman Jeffares ed., *W. B. Yeats: The Critical Heritage, W. B. Yeats: A New Biography*; John S. Kelly, *A W. B. Yeats Chronology*; Mary Lou Kohfeldt, *Lady Gregory: The Woman behind the Irish Renaissance*; Ethel Mannin, *Young in the Twenties: A Chapter of Autobiography*; E. H. Mikhail, *W. B. Yeats: Interviews and Recollections* (vols. 1–2); Virginia Moore, *The Unicorn: William Butler Yeats' Search for Reality*; William M. Murphy, *Family Secrets: William Butler Yeats and His Relatives, Prodigal Father: The Life of John Butler Yeats (1839–1922)*; Ann Saddlemyer, *Becoming George: The Life of Mrs W. B. Yeats*; Corinna Salvadori, *Yeats and Castiglione: Poet and Courtier*; Allan Wade, *A Bibliography of the Writings of W. B. Yeats*; John Butler Yeats, *Letters to his Son W. B. Yeats and Others 1869–1922*; W. B. Yeats, *Ah, Sweet Dancer: W. B. Yeats and Margot Ruddock, Autobiographies, The Collected Letters of W. B. Yeats* (vols. 1–4), *A Critical Edition of Yeats's A Vision (1925), Essays and Introductions, Explorations, The Gonne-Yeats Letters 1893–1938, The Letters of W. B. Yeats, Letters on Poetry from W. B. Yeats to Dorothy Wellesley, Letters to the New Island, Memoirs, The Senate Speeches of W. B. Yeats, The Variorum Edition of the Plays of W. B. Yeats, The Variorum Edition of the Poems of W. B. Yeats, A Vision, W. B. Yeats and T. Sturge Moore: Their Correspondence 1901–1937.*

PART II

Yeats's Works

SELECTED POEMS

"Acre of Grass, An" (1938)

Like "A PRAYER FOR OLD AGE," "The SPUR," "WHY SHOULD NOT OLD MEN BE MAD," and "The Wild Old Wicked Man" (1938), "An Acre of Grass" defies the loss of emotional and intellectual intensity that putatively comes with old age. The scene is RIVERSDALE, an 18th-century farmhouse in the village of Rathfarnham that was Yeats's home from July 1932 until the end of his life. In a July 1932 letter, Yeats wrote to OLIVIA SHAKESPEAR, "I shall have a big old fruit garden all to myself—the study opens onto it and it is shut off from the flower garden and the croquet and tennis lawns and from the bowling green" (*Letters* 799; see also *AP* 446–447). This is presumably the acreage of the poem's title.

Having arrived at "life's end," Yeats takes stock of his diminished store: picture and book, an "acre of green grass / For air and exercise," a body no longer strong, the sleeplessness of age, lulled "temptation." Imagination and the mind continue to consume their "rag and bone" (a rehearsal of the famous imagery of "The CIRCUS ANIMALS' DESERTION"), but imagination is merely "loose," while the mind turns with the routine mechanism of a "mill." The truth cannot be bodied forth by the inertia of mental habit, but requires the visionary intensity that Yeats had attributed to Jonathan SWIFT in "BLOOD AND THE MOON" ("Swift beating on his breast in sibylline frenzy blind"). "Grant me an old man's frenzy," Yeats cries, hoping to remake himself as Shakespeare's Timon or Lear, or as WILLIAM BLAKE, who "beat upon the wall / Till Truth obeyed his call. . . ." In his introduction to *The Oxford Book of Modern Verse* (1936), Yeats reverts to a similar image as a metaphor of romantic resistance to human limitation: "The mischief began at the end of the seventeenth century when man became passive before a mechanized nature; that lasted to our own day with the exception of a brief period between Smart's *Song to David* and the death of Byron, wherein imprisoned man beat upon the door" (*LE* 194). Louis MacNeice comments that Timon and Lear "are chosen because in both of them passion was stronger than reason and in both of them disillusionment, anger, and hatred,

which would seem to lead to nihilism, lead actually to a most articulate assertion of human vitality and individuality," while Blake "remains what he had always been for Yeats, the champion of the soul, or rather of the humanly embodied soul, against mere abstract reason. In his contempt for those 'thoughts men think in the mind alone,' Yeats at the age of seventy was still more ready than in his youth to approve Blake's vindication of both God and the natural man and his attack on the rationalists [. . .]" (*Poetry of W. B. Yeats* 177–178).

In the final stanza, Michelangelo emerges, as he would even more prominently in "LONG-LEGGED FLY" and "UNDER BEN BULBEN," as a keystone of Yeats's thought. In Yeats's later understanding, Michelangelo (1475–1564) stands as an almost mythic incarnation of the *antithetical* type. In *A VISION*, Yeats asks "What if Christ and Oedipus or, to shift the names, Saint Catherine of Genoa and Michael Angelo, are the two scales of a balance, the two butt-ends of a seesaw? What if every two thousand and odd years something happens in the world to make one sacred, the other secular; one wise, the other foolish; one fair, the other foul; one divine, the other devilish?" (28–29). Not only was Michelangelo the consummate artist, but he was an artist who remained vigorously active and creative into old age. When he died at age 88, he was still hard at work as chief architect of St. Peter's Basilica. Yeats would have a mind like Michelangelo's, a mind grown powerful in its solitude, a mind that moves with equal command between the realms of heaven and earth, life and death, a mind unbowed by time.

Yeats's ambition to "shake the dead in their shrouds" recalls the final stanza of "ALL SOULS' NIGHT," while his desire for an "old man's eagle mind" shares the eagle imagery of "FRIENDS," "TO A WEALTHY MAN WHO PROMISED A SECOND SUBSCRIPTION TO THE DUBLIN MUNICIPAL GALLERY IF IT WERE PROVED THE PEOPLE WANTED PICTURES," and "UPON A HOUSE SHAKEN BY THE LAND AGITATION." The eagle suggests the keenness, strength, and lofty freedom of the aristocratic temper.

FIRST PUBLICATION: The *Atlantic Monthly* and the *London Mercury* (periodicals), April 1938. Reprinted in *New Poems*, The CUALA PRESS, Dublin, May 18, 1938.

BIBLIOGRAPHY

Foster, R. F. *W. B. Yeats: A Life, II: The Arch-Poet*; Mac-Neice, Louis. *The Poetry of W. B. Yeats*; Yeats, W. B. *Later Essays, The Letters of W. B. Yeats, A Vision*.

"Adam's Curse" (1902)

With "Adam's Curse" Yeats's mature STYLE begins to show itself. The fey lyricism of the early poems remains in evidence, but it is complemented by conversational and dramatic sinew. In addition, the entire poem has a dramatic complexity and tension not seen before, a development probably stimulated by Yeats's increasing immersion in the theater. The result is the first of Yeats's unquestionable master-pieces: a poem that moves with immense self-control through several voices and moods as it builds toward a climax both powerful and full of nuance. As T. S. ELIOT writes, "By the time of the volume of 1904 [*In the Seven Woods*] there is a development visible in a very lovely poem, The FOLLY OF BEING COMFORTED, and in *Adam's Curse*; something is coming through, and in beginning to speak as a particular man [Yeats] is beginning to speak for man" (*On Poetry and Poets* 300).

The poem recalls a crestfallen conversation between MAUD GONNE, her sister Kathleen Pilcher (1868–1919), and Yeats himself in May 1901 (*AM* 282). The setting was Kathleen's London home, where the Gonne family had congregated for a wedding (*SQ* 314–317). In her autobiography, *A Servant of the Queen* (1938), Gonne remembers the evening: "While we were still at dinner Willie Yeats arrived to see me and we all went into the drawing-room for coffee. Kathleen and I sat together on a big sofa amid piles of soft cushions. I was still in my dark clothes with the black veil I always wore when traveling instead of a hat, and we must have made a strange contrast. I saw Willie Yeats looking critically at me and he told Kathleen he liked her dress and that she was looking younger than ever. It was on that occasion Kathleen remarked that it was hard work being beautiful, which Willie turned into his poem *Adam's Curse*" (317). Yeats was not as "weary-hearted" as the poem's final lines sug-gest, however, for the next day he implored Gonne to marry him, promising that he could make her a beautiful life among artists and writers who would understand her (318).

The poem opens with a lament for the difficulty of the poet's lot. To achieve perfect yet seemingly spontaneous expression is harder than scrubbing floors or breaking stones, but the poet is neverthe-less considered an idler by the "noisy set / Of Bank-ers, schoolmasters, and clergymen / The martyrs call the world" (cf. *Aut.* 171). Kathleen points out that woman must similarly "labour to be beauti-ful," although "they do not talk of it at school" (a notion that anticipates "MICHAEL ROBARTES AND THE DANCER" and "TO A YOUNG BEAUTY"). Yeats agrees that there is no activity since the fall of Adam without its portion of labor. Even lovers must study the precedents set in old books, though, as he says, presumably thinking of his thwarted love for Gonne, "now it seems an idle trade enough." The three friends grow quiet "at the name of love" and gaze at the dying sunset and worn moon, images of the endless, melancholy round of days and nights that characterize the fallen world, conveyed in six lines remarkable for their subdued poignancy. In the final stanza Yeats recalls having a thought for Gonne's ears alone: that she was beautiful, and that he had striven to love her "in the old high way of love; / That it had all seemed happy, and yet we'd grown / As weary-hearted as that hollow moon." The poem thus ends on a note of futility, but futility that seems part of the beautiful, sad pat-tern of the universe.

Harold Bloom calls "Adam's Curse" one of "the undoubted poems of the language," and identifies it as a descendant of SHELLEY's conversational poems "Letter to Maria Gisborne," "Julian and Maddalo," "Rosalind and Helen," and the lyrics addressed to Jane Williams. "Like the Shelley of these poems," Bloom writes, "Yeats in *Adam's Curse* assumes the existence of a community of love, with its ease of common rhetoric, implicit code of external gesture, and, most vitally, ethos of limitation, including the dignity of failure" (*Yeats* 164, 166).

Always the most adept of Yeats's many lam-poonists, GEORGE MOORE found much to mock in Yeats's lachrymose tale of hard labor. In *Vale*

(1914), he recounts that a visitor had returned from COOLE PARK and told how "he had discovered the poet lying on a sofa in a shady corner, a plate of strawberries on his knee, and three or four adoring ladies serving him with cream and sugar, and how the poet, after wiping his hands on a napkin, had consented to recite some verses, and the verses he recited were these"—as punch line Moore quotes the self-pitying first stanza of "Adam's Curse" (*Hail and Farewell* 541).

FIRST PUBLICATION: The *Monthly Review* (periodical), December 1902. Reprinted in *In the Seven Woods: Being Poems Chiefly of the Irish Heroic Age*, The DUN EMER PRESS, Dundrum, August 1903.

BIBLIOGRAPHY

Bloom, Harold. *Yeats*; Eliot, T. S. *On Poetry and Poets*; Foster, R. F. *W. B. Yeats: A Life, I: The Apprentice Mage*; Gonne, Maud. *The Autobiography of Maud Gonne: A Servant of the Queen*; Moore, George. *Hail and Farewell*; Yeats, W. B. *Autobiographies*.

"After Long Silence" (1932)

See "WORDS FOR MUSIC PERHAPS."

"All Souls' Night" (1921, dated 1920)

Both the 1925 and 1937 editions of *A VISION* conclude with "All Souls' Night," and fittingly enough, for the poem pays homage to Yeats's fellow travelers on the esoteric path that led to the revelations of his chief philosophical work. Like "IN MEMORY OF MAJOR ROBERT GREGORY" and "The MUNICIPAL GALLERY REVISITED," the poem is an affectionate and generous necrology; like "The GREY ROCK," "IN MEMORY OF EVA GORE-BOOTH AND CON MARKIEWICZ," and "TO A SHADE," it communes with ghosts, as Yeats "calls up" the spirits of W. T. HORTON, FLORENCE FARR, and MACGREGOR MATHERS. All had belonged to the HERMETIC ORDER OF THE GOLDEN DAWN, and all had recently died, Horton in 1919, Farr in 1917, and Mathers in 1918. As Harold Bloom observes, "These are allied not only by their arcane obsessions, but as self-defeated questers, heroic failures of the peculiar variety epitomized by Browning's Childe Roland, archetype of the failed artist. [. . .] Horton, Florence Emery, and Mathers have the dignity of heroic failure, and the occultist's honorable death: Yeats's role is to hoard their recklessness, so as to make them into a poem" (*Yeats* 370). In "William Blake's Illustrations to the *Divine Comedy*" (1896), Yeats gets at the essential dynamic of their shared tragedy when he says that "he who half lives in eternity endures a rending of the structures of the mind, a crucifixion of the intellectual body" (*E&I* 128).

As the second stanza suggests, Yeats calls to these old friends in particular because he misses their intensity of esoteric conviction and their rootedness in his own occult tradition. Unlike most, they would have grasped and appreciated *A Vision* without necessarily endorsing its doctrines. In his dedication of the 1925 edition of *A Vision*, Yeats touches on the desire to commune with departed friends that likewise informs the poem: "It is a constant thought of mine that what we write is often a commendation of, or expostulation with, the friends of our youth, and that even if we survive all our friends we continue to prolong or to amend conversations that took place before our five-and-twentieth year" (*AV-1925* ix). The dedication cites both Horton and Farr as cherished collaborators of youth, while the recipient of the dedication—"Vestigia"—is Mathers's wife, Moina, sister of the French philosopher Henry Bergson (1859–1941).

From October 1919 to March 1922, Yeats and his family lived intermittently at 4 Broad Street, Oxford, opposite Balliol College. There Yeats conceived and composed "All Souls' Night," which Maurice Bowra calls "probably the finest poem ever written in Oxford" (*I&R*, II, 401). Playing on the latent eeriness of the crenellated, gargoyled university town, the poem opens as "the great Christ Church Bell"—the bell of Christ Church College—tolls midnight on All Souls' Eve. The occasion accounts for the poem's evocation of the dead, for in Catholic tradition All Souls' Day (November

2) is observed with prayers for the deliverance of souls in purgatory and visits to the graves of departed friends and family. Yeats has poured two glasses of bubbling muscatel. Not the wine, but the "wine-breath" is the properly ethereal sustenance of ghosts, as Yeats lectures with superbly impossible expertise (cf. the allusion to "the foam upon the cup" in "Poetry and Tradition," *E&I* 254). Hazard Adams infers from the second wine glass that Yeats keeps his midnight vigil with a companion, possibly GEORGE YEATS (*Book of Yeats's Vision* 152). More plausibly, Yeats has poured the second glass in expectation of a ghost, for it is a custom of All Souls' Day that food is left out for returning spirits. Yeats may have been attempting specifically to entice Farr, who wrote to JOHN QUINN in 1910 that she had adopted a diet consisting of "'muscatels' with only one big meal a day and 'snacks'" (*Florence Farr* 175). The "bubbling" of the wine, moreover, conjures the image of the proverbial witches' brew and hints at the tastes of an uncanny palate. Having a "marvelous thing" to communicate—the doctrines of *A Vision*—Yeats requires of his visitant a "mind that, if the cannon sound / From every quarter of the world, can stay / Wound in mind's pondering / As mummies in the mummy-cloth are wound. . . ." The ongoing ANGLO-IRISH WAR explains the distraction of "cannon." The enwound mummy signifies the ancient, the esoteric, and the eternal: a metaphor for the mind wound in its own pondering to the exclusion of the world. The mummy image also appears in the roughly contemporaneous "ON A PICTURE OF A BLACK CENTAUR BY EDMUND DULAC," there representing esoteric decadence in symbolic opposition to the wholesomeness of wine, and it recurs in "A BRONZE HEAD," "BYZANTIUM," "CONJUNCTIONS," and "VACILLATION."

The first of Yeats's revenants is Horton, a mystic, artist, and would-be poet with whom Yeats maintained a sometimes troubled friendship from the mid-1890s until Horton's death in 1919 (*W. B. Yeats and W. T. Horton* 3–4). Yeats could admire Horton's BLAKE- and BEARDSLEY-influenced drawings only with carefully worded qualification, and he actively discouraged his friend's attempts to write poetry (*CL3* 92). Yeats contributed a preface to Horton's *A Book of Images* (1898), a collection of mystically themed drawings. In 1903, Yeats published the revised preface as "SYMBOLISM IN PAINTING" (*E&I* 146–152), omitting all mention of Horton. Horton was shattered by the perceived slight. In 1917, he confessed to Yeats that the "blow" had permanently sapped his initiative (*CL3* 400; *W. B. Yeats and W. T. Horton* 132). Repeating the slight of "Symbolism in Painting," "All Souls' Night" entirely ignores Horton's artistic and poetic endeavors; instead it emphasizes the transcendent tenderness of his liaison with the journalist and historian Amy Audrey Locke (1881–1916), with whom Horton lived on a platonic basis from 1913 until her death following an operation for "ear and mastoid trouble" (*W. B. Yeats and W. T. Horton* 47–48). In his dedication to the 1925 edition of *A Vision*, Yeats writes that Horton "lived through that strange adventure, perhaps the strangest of all adventures—Platonic love. When he was a child his nurse said to him—'An Angel bent over your bed last night,' and in his seventeenth year he awoke to see the phantom of a beautiful woman at his bedside. Presently he gave himself up to all kinds of amorous adventures, until at last, in I think his fiftieth year but when he had still all his physical vigour, he thought 'I do not need women but God.' Then he and a very good, charming, young fellow-student fell in love with one another and though he could only keep down his passion with the most bitter struggle, they lived together platonically [. . .]. She died, and he survived her but a little time during which he saw her in apparition and attained through her certain of the traditional experiences of the saint" (*AV-1925* x). The poem's "slight companionable ghost" is evidently Locke seen "in apparition." Until Yeats revised it in 1933, the poem did not name Horton, but referred to "H——" or "X——." In his dedication of the 1925 edition of *A Vision*, Yeats also takes pains to preserve Horton's anonymity. George Mills Harper, who has closely examined Yeats's relationship with Horton, has no explanation for Yeats's seemingly unnecessary discretion (*W. B. Yeats and W. T. Horton* 73–74).

Yeats next conjures "Florence Emery," better known as Florence Farr (she married the actor Edward Emery in 1884; the couple separated in

1888 and divorced in 1895). An actress whose talent exceeded her success, Farr collaborated in Yeats's experiments with the psaltery (see "SPEAKING TO THE PSALTERY") and in the staging of his plays. She directed the 1894 production of *The LAND OF HEART'S DESIRE* and both directed and performed in the 1899 production of *The COUNTESS CATHLEEN*. According to George Yeats, Farr and Yeats had a "brief love affair," before Farr grew "bored" (*FF, BS, and WBY* 43; see also AM 290–291; MM 179). Yeats's introduction to the 1925 edition of *A Vision* clarifies the details of the fifth stanza of the poem. It tells how Farr "coming to her fiftieth year, dreading old age and fading beauty, had made a decision we all dreamt of at one time or another, and accepted a position as English teacher in a native school in Ceylon that she might study oriental thought, and had died there" (*AV-1925* ix–x). Before her death from breast cancer in 1917, as "All Souls' Night" has it, Farr came to the mystic realization that the soul is whirled about the circuit of the moon before finally plunging into the sun, there finding the reconciliation of "chance and choice" and sinking into "its own delight at last." The doctrine is attributed to "some learned Indian," presumably Ponnambalam Ramanathan (1851–1930), who founded the girl's college where Farr was principal and then bursar from 1912 until her death. Josephine Johnson, Farr's biographer, comments, "There is the opinion that Yeats wove himself into the character of Florence and that the learned Indian [mentioned in the poem] included the personalities of MOHINI MOHAN CHATTERJEE and Rabindranath Tagore. All is possible in the mind of a poet but the [sixth stanza] is written from the suggestion of Tamil verse Florence sent to Yeats during her years on the island and even, perhaps, from a suggestion by York Powell who in 1902 remarked that Florence played with her life as if it were a toy" (*Florence Farr* 189). At the same time, the doctrine of the stanza is clearly associable with Yeats's own most accustomed thought (see for example "The PHASES OF THE MOON" and "THERE"). Yeats specifically refers to the reconciliation of "chance and choice" in his note to CALVARY (*VPl.* 790–791), in "SOLOMON AND THE WITCH," and in *A Vision* (136). This

reconciliation signifies the collapse of antinomies that characterizes the 15th lunar phase, the phase of "complete beauty."

Yeats's final visitant is Mathers, the intellectual architect of the Golden Dawn and Yeats's mentor during the early years of his involvement with the group. Their falling out came in 1900 following one of the Golden Dawn's periodic schisms (see AM 231–232; CL2 523–524). *AUTOBIOGRAPHIES* elaborates the portrait of "All Souls' Night": "Mathers had much learning but little scholarship, much imagination and imperfect taste [. . .]. He was a necessary extravagance, and he had carried further than any one else a claim implicit in the romantic movement from the time of Shelley and of Goethe; and in body and in voice at least he was perfect; so might Faust have looked in his changeless aged youth" (162). The poem's seventh stanza includes one of Yeats's most straightforward statements of a perennial theme: "For meditations upon unknown thought / Make human intercourse grow less and less. . . ." This understanding, most obviously derived from the biographical example of BLAKE and Yeats's formative boyhood obsession with Shelley's "Alastor" (1816), begins its progress through Yeats's work in early poems such as "FERGUS AND THE DRUID" and "TO THE ROSE UPON THE ROOD OF TIME," and later manifests itself in poems like "The ROAD AT MY DOOR" and "The CHOICE." This understanding explains not only Mathers's descent into lonely eccentricity, but also the entire phenomenon of the "tragic generation," of which "All Souls' Night" is in part yet another consideration.

Changing his mind, in the end, Yeats decides that any ghost will do, as long as "his elements have grown so fine / The fume of muscatel / Can give his sharpened palate ecstasy. . . ." Yeats seeks, in short, a companion receptive to truths that are not empirical truths, the kind of "mummy truths" that belong to his own occult investigations, truths that the "living mock," being unable to process their mystery. The notion that the dead have access to truths beyond the comprehension of the living is consistent with "BLOOD AND THE MOON" ("wisdom is the property of the dead") and with a note to "The SECOND COMING" in which Yeats argues that the "subjective man"—to which type Horton, Farr, and Mathers belong—"reaches the narrow end of a gyre at death, for death is always [. . .] preceded by an intensification of the subjective life; and has a moment of revelation immediately after death [cf. "The COLD HEAVEN"], a revelation which they [i.e., the Judwalis] describe as his being carried into the presence of all his dead kindred, a moment whose objectivity is exactly equal to the subjectivity of death" (VP 824). The occultism of Horton, Farr, Mathers, and Yeats himself, it might be said, is the attempt to foreshadow in life the revelation of death, and in this sense the occult enterprise tends always to mingle with death, even to beckon to death, as explicitly in the case of Horton.

Yeats ends by defiantly affirming that he will hold to his own thought until he masters it and thus attains a vision of the place where the damned howl and the blessed dance. Such is the richness and ambition of the thought that winds him "in mind's wandering / As mummies in the mummy-cloth are wound" that he needs "no other thing." Yeats here reiterates the proud final lines of "I SEE PHANTOMS OF HATRED AND OF THE HEART'S FULLNESS AND OF THE COMING EMPTINESS" ("The half-read wisdom of daemonic images, / Suffice the ageing man as once the growing boy"), but the vision of himself mummified in the winding of his own thought has a darker cast. The winding of the mummy cloth metaphorizes the turning gyres that Yeats identifies in A Vision as the defining pattern of reality (see VP 823–825 for a brief account), but there is also the implication that Yeats enshrouds and entombs himself, just as, in their different ways, Horton, Farr, and Mathers deliberately estranged themselves from the common life (Yeats more explicitly embraces the tomb in "The LEADERS OF THE CROWD"). Yeats's enwinding mummy cloth is no innovation; in "Fergus and the Druid," first published in 1892, the Druid tells Fergus, "Take, if you must, this little bag of dreams; / Unloose the cord, and they will wrap you round."

FIRST PUBLICATION: The London Mercury (periodical), March 1921, and the New Republic (periodical), March 9, 1921. Reprinted in Seven Poems and a Fragment, The CUALA PRESS, Dundrum, June 1922.

BIBLIOGRAPHY

Adams, Hazard. The Book of Yeats's Vision: Romantic Modernism and Antithetical Tradition; Bloom, Harold. Yeats; Ellmann, Richard. Yeats: The Man and the Masks; Foster, R. F. W. B. Yeats: A Life, I: The Apprentice Mage; Harper, George Mills. W. B. Yeats and W. T. Horton; Horton, W. T. A Book of Images; Johnson, Josephine. Florence Farr: George Bernard Shaw's 'New Woman'; Mikhail, E. H., ed. W. B. Yeats: Interviews and Recollections (vol. 2); Yeats, W. B. Autobiographies, The Collected Letters of W. B. Yeats (vols. 2–3), A Critical Edition of Yeats's A Vision (1925), Essays and Introductions, Florence Farr, Bernard Shaw and W. B. Yeats, The Variorum Edition of the Plays of W. B. Yeats, The Variorum Edition of the Poems of W. B. Yeats, A Vision.

"All Things can Tempt me" (1909)

As "ADAM'S CURSE" contends that poetry is of all things the most laborious, "All Things can Tempt me" confesses that this labor is willingly shirked. Yeats enumerates the temptations to which he has fallen prey—a woman's face, and even worse, the "seeming needs" of "fool-driven" Ireland. "Now nothing but comes readier to the hand / Than this accustomed toil," Yeats adds, with slippery syntax, but seeming to mean that everything now comes readier to hand—is more welcome, more readily taken up—than poetry. When he was young, he demanded of the poet a heroic extravagance, but now, having lost faith in the legislating power of the romantic ego, he would choose to be "colder and dumber and deafer than a fish." The poem's conclusion strikes an unaccustomed note. As in "The COMING OF WISDOM WITH TIME" and "WORDS," Yeats's self-deflations typically involve an ironic insinuation of triumph. In this case, however, Yeats seems genuinely to throw over his own ambitions. At the very least, the poem hints at a creative or imaginative dejection that helps explain the long hiatus between the publication of In the Seven Woods (1903) and The Green Helmet and

Other Poems (1910), and the relative paucity of verse Yeats wrote during these years. Only "LINES WRITTEN IN DEJECTION" finds Yeats similarly lacking in rejuvenating reserves of imagination.

Yeats elaborates his susceptibility to distraction in AUTOBIOGRAPHIES. "It was many years before I understood that I had surrendered myself to the chief temptation of the artist, creation without toil," he writes, recollecting his busy involvement in the cultural and political movements of the 1890s. "Metrical composition is always very difficult to me, nothing is done upon the first day, not one rhyme is in its place; and when at last the rhymes begin to come, the first rough draft of a six-line stanza takes the whole day. At that time I had not formed a style, and sometimes a six-line stanza would take several days, and not seem finished even then; and I had not learnt, as I have now, to put it all out of my head before night, and so the last night was generally sleepless, and the last day a day of nervous strain. But now I had found the happiness that SHELLEY found when he tied a pamphlet to a fire balloon" (171). Yeats refers to Shelley's madcap scheme to disseminate his *Declaration of Rights*, a revolutionary pamphlet. Shelley memorialized the experiment in the sonnet "To a Balloon, laden with Knowledge" (1812).

FIRST PUBLICATION: The *English Review* (periodical), February 1909, under the title "Distraction." Reprinted in *The Green Helmet and Other Poems*, The CUALA PRESS, Churchtown, Dundrum, December 1910, under the sequence title "Momentary Thoughts" and the present title.

BIBLIOGRAPHY

Yeats, W. B. *Autobiographies*.

"Among School Children" (1927)

While he was member of the Irish SENATE, Yeats sat on a committee to examine the state of Irish schools and made education a particular concern. In a series of three levelheaded Senate speeches in the spring of 1926, he called for improved school buildings, improved hygiene, increased expenditure, closer government inspection, provision of school meals, and more vigorous efforts to educate the poor (*SS* 106–115). On March 21 and 22, 1926, Yeats inspected the Montessorian St. Otteran's School in Waterford, a "progressive convent school," as John Unterecker describes it (*RG* 191). Yeats reported delightedly to Lady GREGORY that the children's "literary work prose & verse was very remarkable," and that "the children were all clean & neat, & sometimes had embroidered little patterns of their own design on their dresses" (in the poem itself, the children's neatness rubs Yeats's ethic of reaction in the wrong way), and he again lauded the school in his March 26 Senate speech (*AP* 320–321; *SS* 111). GEORGE YEATS, on the other hand, was put off by what she felt to be the school's oppressive religious atmosphere, and she refused to return on the second day of the inspection. In a long, catty letter to the poet Thomas MacGreevy (1893–1967), she wrote that the nuns who ran the school "make one feel ashamed, ashamed of life and drinking and smoking" (*AP* 320–321; *BG* 320–321). Two months later, on May 26, Yeats began his great poem.

Like many of Yeats's later poems—"SAILING TO BYZANTIUM" and "The TOWER" for example—"Among School Children" has its point of departure in an ironic discrepancy between Yeats's old age (here conflated with his senatorial respectability) and his undiminished passion. The opening stanza sets the familiar theme. The return to the schoolroom, the inane smile (suggesting a vague analogy between Yeats and the "kind old nun"), the slippage into the role of mere ceremonial presence, all insinuate the "second childishness" of which Shakespeare speaks in *As You Like It*. The qualification "in the best modern way," however, represents Yeats at his most blatantly ironic (cf. the allusion to "our modern hope" in "EGO DOMINUS TUUS"). It discloses his resistance to the bland, conciliatory pose of "smiling public man" and anticipates the explosive reaction against the *mise en scène* of the schoolroom that forms the rest of the poem. As Hugh Kenner notes, the schoolroom is a catalogue of subtly inimical detail: the phrase "reading-books" connotes a "dead time's barbarous name for its books not fit to read," while the "history" studied at St. Otteran's was not Yeats's idea of history, excluding as it did "CUCHULAIN, Deirdre, the Morrigu, Queen Maeve, all the racial past" (*Colder Eye* 220). It might be added that cutting and sewing deliberately attempt to teach the middle-class industry and thrift that Yeats denounces in "SEPTEMBER 1913" and represent the kind of education in "useful things" that Paul Ruttledge denounces in *WHERE THERE IS NOTHING* (see VPl. 1068). Donald T. Torchiana less convincingly proposes the reverse interpretation that "the singing, ciphering, sewing, and reading Montessori children exemplify an education where mind and body are unified, where what a child senses, learns, and becomes are one" (*W. B. Yeats & Georgian Ireland* 323).

The second stanza begins a chain of reflection, bitter, esoteric, and passionate, that belies the façade of the "smiling public man." The children remind Yeats of a story MAUD GONNE once told of her youth: how a harsh reproof turned "some childish day to tragedy." "Ledaean body" casts Gonne in the habitual role of Helen, Leda's daughter. That she bends above a sinking fire, presumably in the act of stoking it, suggests her function within the complex of Yeats's aging imagination (cf. "The SPUR"). Gonne's penchant for tragedy keeps with her Helenic nature and sets her in opposition to the orderly, constructive—perhaps tamely domestic—milieu of the modern classroom. In contrast to his discomfort as an interloper in the classroom, Yeats recalls thrilling to Gonne's passionate remembrance, so much so that he felt that they "blent into a sphere," or else became the "yolk and white of the one shell." The metaphor alludes to Plato's *Symposium*, in which the playwright Aristophanes (died ca. 385 B.C.) explains that primordial man was spherical until Zeus divided him in two as one might "slice an egg with a hair," thus accounting for the perpetual human quest to find completion in another (*Collected Dialogues* 542–544). In the third stanza, Yeats conjures Gonne as she might have been as a girl, measuring her against the children of the classroom, for even "daughters of the Swan" (Helen and Clytemnestra were born of Leda after she was raped by Zeus in the form of a Swan) can share "something of every paddler's heritage." His

heart is driven wild, as in "FRIENDS" the thought of Gonne sends his heart surging with sweetness.

Concluding the meditation on Gonne, the fourth stanza considers her present image. As in "A PRAYER FOR MY DAUGHTER," with which the stanza shares the metaphors of meat and wind, Gonne has suffered the penalty for her perpetual confrontation with the world, and yet she remains a queen of the spirit. Her hollow cheek (answering the colored cheeks that Yeats observes in the previous stanza) recalls that of Dante in "Ego Dominus Tuus," and for all the toll of her error she seems as if fashioned by "Quattrocento finger" ("Da Vinci finger" in the version of the poem published in the *London Mercury*). The paradisiacal or visionary significance of the "Quattrocento" or 15th-century tradition in art is clarified in "HER VISION IN THE WOOD" and "UNDER BEN BULBEN" (lines 53–62). The latter poem has it that the Quattrocento put into paint gardens where everything resembles "forms that are or seem / When sleepers wake and yet still dream, / And when it's vanished still declare, / With only bed and bedstead there, / That heavens had opened." Thinking of Gonne in her youth, Yeats recalls his own once-proud though not quite Ledaean form, but chidingly reminds himself that it is "better to smile on all that smile." His resignation is less to old age than to the modern reality—the modern immunity to the tumult of beauty—represented by the schoolroom.

Yeats's reflections upon his own old age prompt the general reflection: What youthful mother would think her son, could she see him "with sixty or more winters upon his head," adequate compensation for "the pang of his birth, / Or the uncertainty of his setting forth?" (cf. the song that opens AT THE HAWK'S WELL). The obscure subordinate clauses of lines 33–36 are explained, albeit less clearly than they might be, by a note to the poem: "I have taken the 'honey of generation' from Porphyry's essay on 'The Cave of the Nymphs,' but find no warrant in Porphyry for considering it the 'drug' that destroys the 'recollection' of pre-natal freedom. He blamed a cup of oblivion given in the zodiacal sign of Cancer" (*VP* 828).

The allusions to "Plato's parable" and the Neoplatonist Porphyry (232/4–ca. 305) lead by association to Plato (ca. 429–347 B.C.), Aristotle (384–22 B.C.), and Pythagoras (sixth century B.C.), whose tendencies are objective, abstract, and systematic, as against the tragic passion represented by Gonne. On this basis, they are "Old clothes upon old sticks to scare a bird"; for all the immensity of their thought, they are scarecrows of "blear-eyed wisdom," just as Yeats has become—or seemingly become—"a comfortable kind of old scarecrow" in his guise of school inspector, of benevolently reasonable public man. Yeats decries the error of the intellect's subservience to reality in "The Tower" ("I mock Plotinus' thought / And cry in Plato's teeth, / Death and life were not / Till man made up the whole") and in A VISION he writes disparagingly that Aristotle and Plato "end creative system—to die into the truth is still to die—and [with them] formula begins. Yet even the truth into which Plato dies is a form of death, for when he separates the Eternal Ideas from Nature and shows them self-sustained he prepares the Christian desert and the Stoic suicide" (AV 271).

With cheekiness perhaps expressive of his philosophical qualms, Yeats frames Aristotle in the unseemly act of hiding the backside of his most famous pupil, the future Alexander the Great. *The Oxford English Dictionary* defines a *taws* as both a "whip for driving a spinning top" and an "instrument of family or school discipline, used in Scottish and many English schools, consisting of a leathern strap or thong, divided at the end into narrow strips." Yeats clearly intends the latter meaning (cf. "The Saint and the Hunchback" [1919]), but "plays" connotes the former. "Solider" may play on "soldier," thus collapsing the distinction between Aristotle and his worldly student. Pythagoras, meanwhile, is imagined fingering "upon a fiddle-stick," or violin bow; as an interjection, however, "fiddle-stick" exclaims the absurd or nonsensical. The repetition of "play" (lines 41 and 43) and the allusion to the taws evoke the schoolroom, returning the poem to its opening image. It may be that the children who "cipher" and "sing" continue the tradition of Pythagoras; or it may be, as Kenner asserts, that their play "perverts Pythagoras, who taught us how music is mathematically based, but whose *mathematik* was no more like shopkeepers'

ciphering than his *mousikē*, something sacred to the muse, was like mimicry of a sol-fa pitchpipe" (*Colder Eye* 220). The allusion to the philosopher's golden thighs, according to A. Norman Jeffares, is a borrowing from Thomas Taylor's translation of Iamblichus's *Life of Pythagoras* (NCP 254). Iamblichus (born ca. 250) was a Syrian Neoplatonist who had been a pupil of Porphyry. Richard Ellmann, on the other hand, traces the allusion to Diodorus Siculus, a Sicilian historian of the first century (IY 284). In a September 1926 letter to OLIVIA SHAKESPEAR, Yeats included a preliminary draft of this stanza and offered his own gloss on the significance of the three philosophers: "Here is a fragment of my last curse upon old age. It means that even the greatest men are owls, scarecrows, by the time their fame has come. Aristotle, remember, was Alexander's tutor, hence the taws (form of birch). [. . .]. Pythagoras made some measurement of the intervals between notes on a stretched string" (*Letters* 719). Following this cue, Richard Ellmann proposes that Yeats speaks of the "powerful theories of Plato, Aristotle, and Pythagoras, only to dismiss them because their theories, great as they were, proved powerless to avert the philosophers' own decrepitude and death" (IY 229). This reading, however, does not account for the element of lampoon, which hints at a doctrinal disagreement and connects the stanza with the rejection of Plato and Plotinus in "The Tower."

Nuns and mothers are instinctually wiser: they "worship images," as do poets and magicians. And yet the religious icon is no less heartbreaking than the image of the aged lover (Gonne) or the aged child (Yeats himself). Our desire exceeds the image, despite all that Yeats himself has said on its behalf. Suddenly gathering itself, the poem begins its leap into greatness with its cry to the "Presences"—the emanations of the ANIMA MUNDI—that inhere in the images that inspire our worship, whether the passionate worship of love, the pious worship of religion, or the affectionate worship of motherhood, and yet mock our enterprise by the example of their own eternity. To these "presences" Yeats commits his essential understanding, perhaps because they themselves embody or teach the reality of which he speaks. Yeats proposes not the abstraction of Plato,

Aristotle, and Pythagoras, but labor that is a "blossoming" or "dancing" of soul and body together, that yields a beauty arrived at joyously and spontaneously. Yeats's reaction against the "blear-eyed wisdom" continues a longstanding internal debate, the poles of which are marked by "The ROAD AT MY DOOR," which longs for release from the life-denial of the esoteric dream, and "I SEE PHANTOMS OF HATRED AND OF THE HEART'S FULLNESS AND OF THE COMING EMPTINESS," which reaffirms the esoteric dream. The poem culminates in lines as renowned as any Yeats wrote. The "blossoming" and "dancing" of line 57 are fully realized in the chestnut tree and the dancer, images of UNITY OF BEING whose secret Yeats would know, but cannot approach without falling into the language of multiplicity. The two questions of these lines are incorrectly put, for the tree is irreducible to leaf, blossom, or bole; the "body swayed to music" transcends the dichotomy of dancer and dance. These lines, however, achieve such passionate intensity of their own, such indissolubility of language and idea, that they answer even as they ask, and demonstrate the very thing they would know.

Ellmann reads in the poem's final stanza the terms of the Yeatsian paradise. He notes that the "location of 'where' is left in doubt, but not the body's right to be the soul's peer in whatever heaven there may be" (*IY* 50; see also 230). Elsewhere he describes the poem's culminating questions as an "apostrophe or secular adoration of the completed symbol of heavenly glory" (*MM* 252). Frank Kermode interprets the stanza as a triumph over the defeat articulated in "The LIVING BEAUTY" and posits the dancer as a reconception and revitalization of the aesthetic image in opposition to the lifeless stasis of bronze and marble. In the earlier poem, there is a "tormenting contrast between the images (signified by bronze and marble statuettes) and the living beauty," creating the need for an image in the spirit of the living beauty. "No static image will now serve," writes Kermode, "there must be movement, the different sort of life that a dancer has by comparison with the most perfect object of art. [. . .] The Image is to be all movement, yet with a kind of stillness" (*Romantic Image* 102). Kermode adds that the tree is "in a

sense necessary to the Dancer, since it so powerfully reinforces the idea of integrity—'root, shoot, blossom'—in the Image, and provides a traditional analogy in support of the Image's independent life" (123). The images of the tree and the dancer pervade Yeats's work, and have particularly crucial precedents in the laurel tree of "A Prayer for my Daughter" and the dancing girl in "The DOUBLE VISION OF MICHAEL ROBARTES."

FIRST PUBLICATION: The *Dial* and the *London Mercury* (periodicals), August 1927. Reprinted in *October Blast*, The CUALA PRESS, Dublin, August 1927.

BIBLIOGRAPHY

Ellmann, Richard. *Yeats: The Man and the Masks, The Identity of Yeats*; Foster, R. F. *W. B. Yeats: A Life, II: The Arch-Poet*; Jeffares, A. Norman. *A New Commentary on the Poems of W. B. Yeats*; Kenner, Hugh. *A Colder Eye: The Modern Irish Writers*; Kermode, Frank. *Romantic Image*; Plato, *The Collected Dialogues*; Saddlemyer, Ann. *Becoming George: The Life of Mrs W. B. Yeats*; Torchiana, Donald T. *W. B. Yeats & Georgian Ireland*; Unterecker, John. *A Reader's Guide to William Butler Yeats*; Yeats, W. B. *The Letters of W. B. Yeats, The Senate Speeches of W. B. Yeats, The Variorum Edition of the Plays of W. B. Yeats, The Variorum Edition of the Poems of W. B. Yeats, A Vision*.

"Ancestral Houses" (1923)

The "ancestral house" was for Yeats a perpetual symbol of tradition, ceremony, and aristocratic strength of character, and he managed to become a fixture in several such houses over the decades. His mainstays were Lady GREGORY's COOLE PARK in Galway; Lady Ottoline Morrell's Garsington Manor, a few miles southeast of OXFORD; and Lady DOROTHY WELLESLEY's Penns in the Rocks, near Withyham, Sussex (*AP* 530–533). The first of seven poems in the sequence "MEDITATIONS IN TIME OF CIVIL WAR," "Ancestral Houses" is generally thought to picture Garsington, but in Hugh Kenner's view its authentic if unstated subject is "a great Italian villa, and 'the greatest of mankind' are the men of the Renaissance" (*Colder Eye* 265). Whether Georgian or Florentine, Yeats's "violent bitter man" is clearly of a type with the Renaissance noblemen extolled, for example, in "TO A WEALTHY MAN WHO PROMISED A SECOND SUBSCRIPTION TO THE DUBLIN MUNICIPAL GALLERY IF IT WERE PROVED THE PEOPLE WANTED PICTURES." Much like COLERIDGE's "Kubla Khan" (1816) the poem ponders the sublimation by which violent passion becomes graceful form, and, going beyond "Kubla Khan," it wonders how graceful form can be sustained in the absence of violent passion. Shaping the poem are anxieties about the fate of his own house (cf. "MY DESCENDANTS" and "To be Carved on a Stone at Thoor Ballylee" [1921]) and the fate of Coole Park (eventually sold and demolished), but the poem also pertains, if obliquely, to the IRISH CIVIL WAR that is the overarching theme of the sequence, for it may be that nations are reared and tumbled just like houses, and by the same kind of "bitter and violent men."

"Ancestral Houses" opens with a vision of the ancestral house as an almost paradisiacal dispensation symbolized by the teeming, exuberant, perpetual energy of the fountain (cf. "The GIFT OF HARUN AL-RASHID," lines 94–95, and "The TOWER," line 125), an image most likely suggested by BLAKE (*E&I* 78, 113, 136) and SHELLEY (81–86). Doubtful that such a paradise could be anything but "mere dreams," Yeats reassures himself that Homer could have created only out of the same belief in the "abounding glittering jet." And yet he wonders whether "some marvellous empty sea-shell flung / Out of the obscure dark of the rich streams, / And not a fountain, were the symbol which / Shadows the inherited glory of the rich" (cf. the image of the shell in the prologue to *The ONLY JEALOUSY OF EMER*). Fountain and shell define what seem to be distinct creative or spiritual postures: outward and inward, activity and reverie, diffusion and accretion, spontaneity and deliberation. The one is allied to the "old nonchalance of the hand" ("EGO DOMINUS TUUS"), the other to the "labyrinth" of the self ("The PHASES OF THE MOON," line 55) or the "labyrinth of the mind" (*The Only Jealousy of Emer*, line 24). The

impossibility of deciding between the two terms ("now it seems") suggests that the aristocratic temper encompasses both ("now" does not indicate a shift in history or culture, but rather a shift in Yeats's wavering conception). The movement from fountain to shell makes an apt comparison with the movement from leaves to root in "The COMING OF WISDOM WITH TIME": both poems instance a retreat from the multiplicity of outward gesture. The shell's emphatic emptiness points toward the eventual ruin of the ancestral house, but also signifies the transcendence of everything merely personal and organic, everything merely human, and thus belongs to the same impulse or aspiration as the golden bird of "SAILING TO BYZANTIUM."

The poem's final three stanzas interrogate the dynamic by which such houses are created and sustained. "Some violent bitter man" calls in architect and artist, who are themselves "bitter and violent men," to create out of the energy of their own bitterness and violence a beauty that transcends its origins. But, Yeats wonders, can such houses and the traditions they represent endure when circumstance no longer demands the violence and bitterness that are the energy of creation? The problem is a practical one, as the kind of men who create are superseded by the kind of men who inherit (the nervous theme of "My Descendants"). Yeats may well have been thinking of Lady Gregory's son ROBERT GREGORY, whom he considered, for all the hyperbole of "IN MEMORY OF MAJOR ROBERT GREGORY," something less than a "violent bitter man." In a 1909 diary entry, Yeats touches on just the anxiety that informs "Ancestral Houses": "I thought of this house [Coole], slowly perfecting itself and the life within it in ever-increasing intensity of labour, and then of its probably sinking away through courteous incompetence, or rather sheer weakness of will, for ability has not failed in young Gregory. [. . .] Is it not always the tragedy of the great and the strong that they see before the end the small and the weak, in friendship or in enmity, pushing them from their place and marring what they have built, and doing one or the other in mere lightness of mind?" (*Mem.* 230). This brings Yeats to the great question of the poem, repeated in each of the poem's final two stanzas: What if violence and greatness are inextricable? What if the ceremonial beauty of the "ancestral house" exhausts our greatness as a function of exhausting our violence and our bitterness? The question seems to be rhetorical, suggesting the inevitability of decline.

Much of the poem's language and imagery is knit throughout the sequence. Stream and stone carry forward as crucial imagery in numerous instances; the "violent bitter man" anticipates the "man-at-arms" of "My House" and the soldiers of both "The Road at my Door" and "The Stare's Nest by my Window," as well as the culture of the sword implied in "My Table"; Juno and the peacock are redeployed in "My Table"; the "empty sea-shell" anticipates the "empty house of the stare" in "The Stare's Nest by my Window," while "the sweetness that all longed for night and day" is answered by the image of the honey-bee; "self-delight" recurs in "I see Phantoms of Hatred and of the Heart's Fullness and of the Coming Emptiness," and the "empty sea-shell" anticipates "the coming emptiness" of the latter poem's title.

The poem's startling amalgamation of violence and sweetness may have its point of departure in something remembered from the essay on Michelangelo in Walter Pater's *The Renaissance* (1873): "And to the true admirers of Michelangelo this is the true type of the Michelangelesque—sweetness and strength, pleasure with surprise, an energy of conception which seems at every moment about to break through all the conditions of comely form, recovering, touch by touch, a loveliness found usually only in the simplest natural things—*ex forti dulcedo* [from the strong, sweetness]" (57).

FIRST PUBLICATION: The *Dial* and the *London Mercury* (periodicals), January 1923. Reprinted in *The Cat and the Moon and Certain Poems*, The Cuala Press, Dublin, July 1924.

BIBLIOGRAPHY

Foster, R. F. *W. B. Yeats: A Life, II: The Arch-Poet*; Kenner, Hugh. *A Colder Eye: The Modern Irish Writers*; Pater, Walter. *The Renaissance: Studies in Art and Poetry*; W. B. Yeats, *Essays and Introductions, Memoirs*.

"Appointment, An" (1909)

Like "A Prayer on going into my House," "An Appointment" inveighs against the small-minded machinations of government in keeping with Yeats's burgeoning political conservatism. In the poem's tidy conceit, Yeats, being "out of heart with government," takes to the woods where he encounters a squirrel. He observes the squirrel's "proud, wayward" spirit, its whinny that sounds like laughter, its "fierce tooth and cleanly limb," and he reflects acerbically, "No government appointed him."

Though it stands well enough on its own terms, "An Appointment" stems from a minor controversy concerning Lady Gregory's nephew Hugh Lane, a prominent collector of modern art (see "To a Friend whose Work has come to Nothing," "To a Shade," and "To a Wealthy Man who promised a Second Subscription to the Dublin Municipal Gallery if it were proved the People wanted Pictures"). Originally titled "On the Appointment of Count Plunkett to the Curatorship of Dublin Museum, by Mr. T. W. Russell and Mr. Birrell, Hugh Lane being a candidate," the poem sardonically translates Yeats's outrage that Lane was passed over in favor of George Noble Plunkett (1851–1948) for the position of director of the National Museum of Science and Art (*CL4* 715; *Sir Hugh Lane* 75). Lady Gregory recalls that word of Plunkett's appointment arrived while Yeats was staying at Coole Park in mid-August 1907. Yeats "raged" over the news, as he considered it "one of the worst of crimes, that neglect to use the best man, the man of genius, in place of the timid obedient official," but he grew calmer after the sight of a squirrel in the woods "had given him a thought for some verses, the first he had ever written on any public event" (*Sir Hugh Lane* 75). Lane was "pleased, though a little puzzled, by the lines, that do but put in form of fantasy what another poet has called 'the difference between men of office and men of genius, between computed and uncomputed rank'" (75). As the poem's original title indicates, Yeats assumed that blame for the appointment belonged to the government officials T. W. Russell (1841–1920) and Augustine Birrell

(1850–1933). Lady Gregory later discovered that Birrell, who was chief secretary of Ireland at the time, had played no part in the decision (76).

Improbably enough, "An Appointment" is not Yeats's only poem upon a squirrel. In the defiantly minor poem "To a Squirrel at Kyle-na-no" (1917), Yeats asks the squirrel why he runs away, as Yeats wants only to scratch his head. The squirrel ("hushed and wise") also figures in "Life," which appeared in the February 1886 issue of the DUBLIN UNIVERSITY REVIEW but was not reprinted in Yeats's lifetime (see VP 686).

FIRST PUBLICATION: The *English Review* (periodical), February 1909, under the title "On a Recent Government Appointment in Ireland." Reprinted in *Responsibilities: Poems and a Play*, The CUALA PRESS, Churchtown, Dundrum, May 25, 1914, under the present title.

BIBLIOGRAPHY

Gregory, Lady. *Sir Hugh Lane: His Life and Legacy*; Yeats, W. B. *The Collected Letters of W. B. Yeats* (vol. 4), *The Variorum Edition of the Poems of W. B. Yeats*.

"Are You Content?" (1938)

COOLE PARK having taught him envy of family tradition, Yeats took pains to construct or affirm a family tradition for himself. In his "INTRODUCTORY RHYMES" to *Responsibilities* (1914), Yeats proudly enumerates a lineage of merchants, scholars, and soldiers who had embodied the "wasteful virtues"— a heroic nonchalance, an extravagance of personality. These ancestors were not high born, but their blood had come down to Yeats without having "passed through any huckster's loin." In both the "Introductory Rhymes" and "Are You Content?" Yeats addresses himself to these forebears as if answerable to their mute judgment. In both poems, Yeats is mistrustful of the abstraction of literature and uncertain that having served this abstraction he has done his part to uphold the family tradition. In comparison to horsemen, soldiers, and smugglers, or even in comparison to practical clergymen, Yeats finds himself—"whose virtues are the defini-

tions / Of the analytic mind," as he confesses in "The PEOPLE"—detached from the pulse of life.

In "Are You Content?" Yeats calls on his ancestors to judge what he has done, for only "eyes spiritualised by death can judge" ("wisdom is the property of the dead," Yeats writes in "BLOOD AND THE MOON"). He fears that in putting "what old loins have sent" at the service of literature he has traded deed for thought and betrayed the family tradition of natural force and manly vigor. Though he cannot judge his own merits, for his accomplishments, unlike those of his ancestors, are intangible and elusive, he confesses himself "not content." The second stanza calls the roll of the "half legendary men" against whom Yeats measures himself: his paternal great-grandfather the Rev. John Yeats (1774–1846), rector at Drumcliff, near SLIGO (cf. "Introductory Rhymes," "UNDER BEN BULBEN"); his paternal grandfather the Rev. William Butler Yeats (1806–62), rector at Tullyish, County Down, whose brother-in-law, Robert Corbet (d. 1870), was master of Sandymount Castle in Dublin, where JOHN BUTLER YEATS lived while attending Trinity College (*Early Memories* 56–60); his maternal grandfather WILLIAM POLLEXFEN; and his maternal great-grandfather William Middleton (1770–1832), the "smuggler." As Yeats tells in AUTOBIOGRAPHIES, Middleton attended to the sick after the great famine and died of the cholera he caught "from a man he carried in his arms into his own house" (43).

In the final stanza, Yeats weighs two courses as he comes to the end of his life. Sinking into comfortable senescence, he might become an old man "smiling at the sea." Then again he might embody in his own life what "Robert Browning meant / By an old hunter talking with Gods," an allusion to lines 323–324 of Browning's early poem "Pauline" (1833). A VISION clarifies the allusion to Browning, citing these same lines as a summarizing image of the man who belongs to the fourth lunar phase. Yeats says of this type, "He is full of practical wisdom, a wisdom of saws and proverbs, or founded upon concrete examples. He can see nothing beyond sense, but sense expands and contracts to meet his needs, and the needs of those who trust him. It is as though he woke suddenly out of sleep and thereupon saw more and remembered more than others. He has 'the wisdom of instinct', a wisdom perpetually excited by all those hopes and needs which concern his well-being or that of the race [. . .]" (110; for additional appropriations of Browning's lines, see *E&I* 409 or *LE* 110; *P&I* 127). In the context of "Are You Content?" the image of the hunter—practical, instinctual, natural—suggests the tradition of Yeats's forebears. Yeats, however, can only end with the reiteration of his discontent. As an artist, he must reject this tradition while suffering the tormenting desire to throw off his *antithetical* burden and embrace it. Poems like "The CHOICE," "The People," and "The ROAD AT MY DOOR" diagnose precisely the weight of this burden and the torment of this desire, while "A DIALOGUE OF SELF AND SOUL" achieves a momentary triumph over the alienation from life. Fittingly, each of the latter poem's last two stanzas begins with the declaration "I am content."

FIRST PUBLICATION: The *Atlantic Monthly* and the *London Mercury* (periodicals), April 1938. Reprinted in *New Poems*, The CUALA PRESS, Dublin, May 18, 1938.

BIBLIOGRAPHY

Yeats, John Butler. *Early Memories: Some Chapters of Autobiography*; Yeats, W. B. *Autobiographies, Essays and Introductions, Later Essays, Prefaces and Introductions, A Vision*.

"Arrow, The" (1903)

When "The Arrow" appeared in August 1903, MAUD GONNE was 36 years old. Yeats had predicted the decline of her beauty in earlier poems like "The Lover pleads with his Friend for Old Friends" (1897) and "WHEN YOU ARE OLD," but here, for the first time, though ever so tactfully, he notes a diminution. The poem thus initiates the kind of retrospective homage to Gonne's beauty that would become a staple in later poems like "BEAUTIFUL LOFTY THINGS," "BROKEN DREAMS," and "His Phoenix" (1916).

The pith of the eight-line poem is the claim that no man can know Gonne's beauty as it was

when she was "newly grown to be a woman, / Tall and noble but with face and bosom / Delicate in colour as apple blossom." The simile descends from Yeats's very first glimpse of Gonne when she called at BEDFORD PARK on January 30, 1889. In AUTOBIOGRAPHIES Yeats remembers that her "complexion was luminous, like that of apple-blossom through which the light falls, and I remember her standing that first day by a great heap of such blossoms in the window" (119–120; see also *Mem.* 40; *The Speckled Bird* 37, 40). The poem's penultimate line dutifully acknowledges the consolation of Gonne's mature beauty, but its final line explodes all mere decorum in a cry of frustrated connoisseurship. Gonne's mature beauty is "kinder"—softened, mellowed—but Yeats could "weep that the old is out of season." An idiom of the orchard or fruit stall, "out of season" plays on the prior allusion to the apple-blossom.

The poem's most challenging element is the image of the "arrow." In the first and second lines Yeats tells how a thought of Gonne's beauty came to him, and the poem—"this arrow, / Made out of a wild thought"—took form in his bones. The poem-as-arrow implies that the recollection of Gonne's youthful beauty pierces Yeats, but also that the poem's slight upon her mature beauty pierces Gonne (the frustrated lover's tweak of revenge). John Unterecker theorizes that the arrow is that of the "great archer" depicted in the final lines of "IN THE SEVEN WOODS," which immediately precedes "The Arrow" in Yeats's collected poems (RG 98). The fact that the two poems were not sequentially ordered in the first edition of *In the Seven Woods* (1903) hampers this theory, but it is certainly conceivable that Yeats intended "The Arrow" as an ironic counterpoint to "In the Seven Woods," the two poems contrasting Yeats's merely human arrows and the mythic, world-changing arrows let fly by the Great Archer.

As if repenting his own apostasy, Yeats retracts his criticism of Gonne's beauty in "The FOLLY OF BEING COMFORTED," which immediately follows "The Arrow" both in the first edition of *In the Seven Woods* and in the collected poems. In an impassioned reversal of opinion, Yeats cries, "O she had not these ways / When all the wild summer was in her gaze."

FIRST PUBLICATION: *In the Seven Woods: Being Poems Chiefly of the Irish Heroic Age*, The DUN EMER PRESS, Dundrum, August 1903.

BIBLIOGRAPHY

Unterecker, John. *A Reader's Guide to William Butler Yeats*; Yeats, W. B. *Autobiographies, Memoirs, The Speckled Bird*.

"At Algeciras—A Meditation upon Death" (1929, dated November 1928)

During the winter of 1927 Yeats suffered from "an exhausting cold" (*Letters* 730). Seeking a more salutary climate, he and his wife arrived in Spain on November 9. They spent five days at Algeciras, just west of Gibraltar, and then moved on to Seville, Cannes, and Rapallo, remaining abroad until April. As his condition worsened—he mentions "pneumonia and general nervous breakdown," and describes spitting blood—Yeats began to fear for his life (*Letters* 732–733; AV 20). On November 19, GEORGE YEATS wrote to Yeats's theatrical protégé Lennox Robinson (1886–1958), "WB of course is making his last will & testament at all hours of day and night, hurrying to finish a poem but has not been able to begin yet. 'Of course I shall never be able to go on with the autobio now . . .' etc etc. All poppycock. However in the same breath he talks of writing a poem on the herons at Algeciras 'in a few years time'" (AP 354). Yeats was as good as his word. He wrote "At Algeciras—A Meditation upon Death" the following November. Yeats was evidently captivated by the herons. While in Spain, he wrote of them to MAUD GONNE: "A multitude of white herons are beginning to roost among the dark branches of the trees just outside my windows. They fish in the Mediterranean on the other side of Gibraltar which is some ten miles off, & then fly home to the garden here for a night's sleep" (GY 443).

The poem's three stanzas seem mysteriously discrete but are subtly knit. The comings and goings of the "heron-billed pale cattle birds" allegorize the vacillation between life and death, sun and moon, objective and subjective. With the Strait of Gibraltar figured as a kind of Iberian Lethe, the birds, at nightfall, leave behind the sordidness of life, crossing the strait "to light"—a punning choice of verb, indicating the richness of the darkness—"In the rich midnight of the garden trees." The heavenward perch of the trees (referable to the symbol of the tower) and the paradisiacal implication of the garden suggest the transcendence that is the subjective or *antithetical* apotheosis (cf. the golden birds of "BYZANTIUM" and "SAILING TO BYZANTIUM"), though the dawn invariably dispels the night and signals another turn of the wheel. The birds' journey from the feeding and breeding ground of Morocco to the gardens of Spain parallels the journey of "Sailing to Byzantium," but this parallelism is tempered in "At Algeciras" by the willingness to "live it all again" that Yeats proclaims in "A DIALOGUE OF SELF AND SOUL," for the birds go forth to their Moroccan herds at daybreak—unlike "Sailing to Byzantium," "At Algeciras" implies no final escape from the "sensual music" of life. A note to CALVARY explains the symbolic implication of the birds within Yeats's larger system of thought: "Certain birds, especially as I see things, such lonely birds as the heron, hawk, eagle, and swan, are the natural symbols of subjectivity, especially when floating upon the wind alone or alighting upon some pool or river, while the beasts that run upon the ground, especially those that run in packs, are the natural symbols of objective man" (*VPl.* 789). That the birds are both "cattle birds" and "heron-billed" suggests the inescapable mutuality of objective and subjective, *primary* and *antithetical*, self and soul, that is the creative tension of reality.

Like the first stanza, the second is set at evening by the seashore. Yeats remembers as a boy gathering seashells at Rosses Point near SLIGO and showing them to an older friend whose approval he sought. The friend may have been George Middleton (b. 1847) or Henry Middleton (1862–1932), cousins whose company Yeats enjoyed on periodic visits to Rosses and Ballisodare, as he remembers in AUTOBIOGRAPHIES (48–49). "Newton's metaphor" alludes to a passage in Selig Brodetsky's (1888–1954) biography *Sir Isaac Newton* (1927). "I do not know what I may appear to the world," Brodetsky quotes Newton as saying, "but to myself I seem to have been only like a boy playing on the sea-shore, and diverting myself in now and then finding a smoother pebble or a prettier shell than ordinary, whilst the great ocean of truth lay all undiscovered before me" (153). Where Newton's shells belong to the abstraction of metaphor, Yeats's shells are "actual," are small tokens of reality and the joy of reality. At the same time, however, they are implicated in Yeats's larger pattern of shell symbolism. In poems like "ANCESTRAL HOUSES," "CRAZY JANE REPROVED," the prologue to The ONLY JEALOUSY OF EMER, "The SAD SHEPHERD," and "The SONG OF THE HAPPY SHEPHERD," Yeats equates the shell with the gyring or labyrinthine reality of the universe, and with the toil by which this reality is wrought or expressed. If the shell signifies "actuality," then, it simultaneously suggests the rich obscurity, the long labor, and the subtle art of this actuality.

The third stanza clarifies the implication of the second. As in boyhood Yeats had presented his older friend with the shell, so in adulthood he more wittingly presents "the Great Questioner" with an answer to the riddle represented by the shell. Again the scene is evening: The sun sets in a valedictory blaze and there is "an evening chill upon the air." The hour of waning life, however, is simultaneously the hour of fruition. Yeats bids his imagination run on "the Great Questioner"—apparently God himself, perhaps in his capacity as interrogator of the departed soul or else in his capacity as creator (to question, after all, is to toil at the construction of reality). "What He can question, what if questioned I / Can with a fitting confidence reply," Yeats concludes. The suggestion is that Yeats has completed the quest for esoteric understanding that he declares in the final lines of "ALL SOULS' NIGHT." "What if" lends these lines a mysterious weight, implying unspecified ramifications and the vague necessity of an adjustment in

the very order of things ("what if" is likewise the primary rhetorical device of "Ancestral Houses"). Yeats gives neither the divine question nor his own reply, for certain precious truths are not for the ears of "blasphemous men," as he avows in "EGO DOMINUS TUUS." There can be only the surmise that Yeats, having worked out the system of A VISION, has arrived at an ultimate knowledge whose image is the birds among the "rich midnight of the garden trees" and whose substance is the understanding that Robartes and Aherne deny to Yeats in "The PHASES OF THE MOON": that all things vacillate between the full and the dark.

FIRST PUBLICATION: A *Packet for Ezra Pound*, The CUALA PRESS, Dublin, August 1929, under the title "Meditations upon Death" (with the companion poem "MOHINI CHATTERJEE"). Reprinted in *Words for Music Perhaps*, The Cuala Press, Dublin, November 14, 1932, under the title "A Meditation written during Sickness at Algeciras." Reprinted in *The Winding Stair and Other Poems*, Macmillan and Co., London, September 19, 1933, under the present title.

BIBLIOGRAPHY

Brodetsky, Selig. *Sir Isaac Newton: A Brief Account of His Life and Work*; Foster, R. F. *W. B. Yeats: A Life, II: The Arch-Poet*; Unterecker, John. *A Reader's Guide to William Butler Yeats*; Yeats, W. B. *Autobiographies, The Gonne-Yeats Letters 1893–1938, The Letters of W. B. Yeats, The Variorum Edition of the Plays of W. B. Yeats, A Vision.*

"At Galway Races" (1909)

The chief philosophic statement of *The Green Helmet and Other Poems* (1910), "At Galway Races" intimates complex theories of culture, class, and history, all within a mere 16 lines. The poem opens with an image of the racecourse as the epitome of cultural health: All are united in a delight that is vital, spontaneous, and communal. "We, too, had good attendance once, / Hearers and hearteners of the work," Yeats adds wistfully. The inclusive "we" indicates himself and his fellow poets. Before "the merchant and the clerk" breathed their "timid breath" on the world, what is more, the poet had "horsemen for companions." The alliance between poet and horseman signifies the unity of imagination and will, beauty and strength, and corrects the contemporary disjunction between the artist and the man of action, whose sometimes acrimonious divorce is a function of their mutual decadence (cf. "ANCESTRAL HOUSES" and "TO A WEALTHY MAN WHO PROMISED A SECOND SUBSCRIPTION TO THE DUBLIN MUNICIPAL GALLERY IF IT WERE PROVED THE PEOPLE WANTED PICTURES" for examples of the desired symbiosis). The figure of the horseman dramatically reappears in "The GYRES" ("Those that Rocky Face holds dear, / Lovers of horses and of women") and in the final lines of "UNDER BEN BULBEN" ("Cast a cold eye / On life, on death. / Horseman, pass by!"), which became Yeats's epitaph. Signifying aristocratic élan, observance of tradition, subservience to a rigorous discipline, and life drawn from the "whole body," the horseman is the fit recipient of Yeats's final word. In his introduction to *The Oxford Book of Modern Verse* (1936), Yeats acknowledges that the horseman is an image of what "EGO DOMINUS TUUS" calls the "anti-self": "Irish by tradition and many ancestors, I love, though I have nothing to offer but the philosophy they deride, swashbucklers, horsemen, swift indifferent men [. . .]" (*LE* 187).

"Horsemen" further suggests both property and leisure, and demonstrates Yeats's increasing willingness to lionize the landed gentry in opposition to the middle classes, here unflatteringly represented by merchant and clerk (the assault on the middle classes would continue more witheringly in poems like "Paudeen" [1914], "SEPTEMBER 1913," "TO A SHADE," and "To a Wealthy Man"). The poem draws general inspiration from the milieu of Lady GREGORY's COOLE PARK, where Yeats probably composed it in the summer of 1908 (YC 121). In *AUTOBIOGRAPHIES*, Yeats mentions the rakish Richard Gregory (1761–1839) as the Gregory ancestor who most roused his interest, and asks, not incidentally, "Was it he or his father who had possessed the Arab horses, painted by Stubbs?" (292). Following in this tradition, Lady Gregory's husband, Sir William (1817–92), had

been a "prominent pillar of the English turf"—put another way, he was "forced to sell two thirds of the estate to pay his racing debts" (*Seventy Years* 22; *Lady Gregory* 50). ROBERT GREGORY, as "IN MEMORY OF MAJOR ROBERT GREGORY" commemorates, excelled both as a rider to hounds and as a jockey.

In its final lines, "At Galway Races" gives the first unmistakable hint of the cyclical conception of history and attendant lunar metaphor that would dominate so much of Yeats's later work and find its most systematic poetic expression in "The PHASES OF THE MOON." The world is not dead but sleeping and, upon a new moon, will wake into life, as the racecourse is alive; once again, the poet will "find hearteners among men / That ride upon horses."

FIRST PUBLICATION: The *English Review* (periodical), February 1909, under the title "Galway Races." Reprinted in *The Green Helmet and Other Poems*, The CUALA PRESS, Churchtown, Dundrum, December 1910, under the sequence title "Momentary Thoughts" and the present title.

BIBLIOGRAPHY

Gregory, Lady. *Seventy Years: Being the Autobiography of Lady Gregory*; Kelly, John S. *A W. B. Yeats Chronology*; Kohfeldt, Mary Lou. *Lady Gregory: The Woman behind the Irish Renaissance*; Yeats, W. B. *Autobiographies, Later Essays*.

"At the Abbey Theatre *(Imitated from Ronsard)*" (1912)

Like "The FASCINATION OF WHAT'S DIFFICULT," which also appears in the 1912 edition of *The Green Helmet and Other Poems*, "At the Abbey Theatre" is an animadversion on the aggravations and irritations of "theatre business." While the earlier poem complains about the difficulty of writing and managing, "At the Abbey Theatre" directs its spleen at the audience. Styled as an urgent request for advice, the poem lays before Craoibhín Aoibhin (as the ever-popular Douglas Hyde was known in Gaelic) the ABBEY THEATRE's dilemma: The audience complains with equal vehemence whether the material is "high and airy" or made of "common things." Yeats probably had in mind his own verse dramas, on the one hand, and J. M. SYNGE's *The Playboy of the Western World,* on the other. Yeats's most esoteric play, *The* SHADOWY WATERS, had been a spectacular flop in 1904 (AM 318), while the frank and earthy *Playboy* sparked riots in 1907. Yeats begs Hyde, who knows the Irish "to the bone," to impart "a new trick to please," to tell him whether there is some bridle with which to harness "this Proteus / That turns and changes like his draughty seas." In the poem's final two lines, Yeats abandons this mock solicitousness and with a surprising suddenness that is the poem's chief effect adopts the combative and imperious tone that equally characterizes "The Fascination of What's Difficult." Is there no solution, he asks in conclusion, revealing his true posture, but "when they mock us, that we mock again?" Yeats had already taken this approach, trading public mockery for public mockery following the disrupted performances of *The Playboy* (see *Expl.* 226–228; "ON THOSE THAT HATED 'THE PLAYBOY OF THE WESTERN WORLD', 1907"; *UP2* 348–355). The poem's characterization of Hyde as "the most popular of men" is ironic. As AUTOBIOGRAPHIES makes clear, Hyde's popularity was as much symptom of failure as mark of success. Mourning for "the great poet who died in his youth"—mourning for the poet that Hyde might have been—Yeats writes, "The Harps and Pepperpots got him and the Harps and Pepperpots kept him till he wrote in our common English [. . .] and took for his model the newspaper upon his breakfast-table, and became for no base reason beloved by multitudes who should never have heard his name till their schoolmasters showed it upon his tomb" (182).

Like "WHEN YOU ARE OLD," "At the Abbey Theatre" is modeled on a sonnet by Pierre de Ronsard (1524–85). In the poem, which first appeared in *La Continuation des Amours de Pierre de Ronsard* (1555), Ronsard addresses his fellow poet Pontus de Tyard (1521–1605) much as Yeats addresses Hyde:

Tyard, everyone said when I began
That I was too obscure for the common man:
Today, everyone says that I'm the reverse,
That I belie myself, writing low verse.
You, who have endured a like torment,
Tell me, please, how to proceed?
Tell me, if you know, how shall I appease
This headstrong monster, full of opinion?
When I'm high-flown, he won't read me,
When I'm common, he's full of scorn:
With which straitening bond, which nail, shall
    I hold
This monstrous Proteus who shifts with every
    blow?
Enough, enough, I take your point: let him talk,
And we'll mock him, as he mocks us.

Hyde responded to Yeats's poem in the January 1913 issue of the *Irish Review.* His "Answer to Mr. Yeats's Poem 'In the Abbey Theatre'" runs as follows:

Good friend, and old companion man-at-arms,
Who struck shrewd blows beside me long ago,
The Protean crowd perplexing you, I know
Shares common hopes with me, common
    alarms.
Therefore we fare together, and Circe's charms
On us are plied in vain. "Make friends not
    foes"
Is still our password, yet we too aim blows
When blows at us are aimed, and quick blood
    warms.

A narrower cult but broader art is mine,
Your wizard fingers strike a hundred strings
Bewildering with multitudinous things,
Whilst all our offerings are at one shrine.
Therefore we step together. Small the art
To keep one pace where men are one at heart.

Lester I. Conner notes that Hyde's name was more properly An Craoibhín Aoibhin, which is Gaelic for "delightful little branch." In Conner's phonetic rendering, the name is pronounced "en kre'ven e'vin" (*YD* 34–35).

FIRST PUBLICATION: *The Green Helmet and Other Poems,* Macmillan, New York, London, October 23, 1912.

BIBLIOGRAPHY

Conner, Lester I. *A Yeats Dictionary: Persons and Places in the Poetry of William Butler Yeats*; Foster, R. F. *W. B. Yeats: A Life, I: The Apprentice Mage*; Yeats, W. B. *Autobiographies, Explorations, Uncollected Prose by W. B. Yeats* (vol. 2).

FIRST PUBLICATION: The *New Statesman* (periodical), September 29, 1917. Reprinted in *The Wild Swans at Coole*, The CUALA PRESS, Churchtown, Dundrum, November 17, 1917.

BIBLIOGRAPHY

Yeats, W. B. *Autobiographies.*

"Balloon of the Mind, The" (1917)

A miracle of brevity, "The Balloon of the Mind" requires only four lines to reorder the central values of Yeats's early work. It affirms earthly discipline against transcendental or imaginative aspiration, or perhaps resorts to earthly discipline in compensation for the loss of imaginative inspiration. The poem plays on a single metaphorical image: the balloon of the mind "bellies and drags in the wind"; Yeats would bring it within the shed of the mind. That Yeats must *order* his hands to do his bidding suggests that his romantic instincts and his middle-aged scruples are at odds, with the latter firmly in command (the subjugation of the hands contrasts with "the old nonchalance of the hand" that Yeats mentions in "EGO DOMINUS TUUS"). Crucially, the balloon, even in its freedom, does not ascend, reflecting either Yeats's lost faith in the imagination as a transcendental vehicle or his sense of his own imaginative decline (cf. "LINES WRITTEN IN DEJECTION"). The very image of the balloon—bulbous, clumsy, wind blown—seems to denigrate the mind as a vehicle of transcendence. How different the "unmeasured mind" of "TO IRELAND IN THE COMING TIMES" or the "eagle mind" of "An ACRE OF GRASS." Yeats repeats the conceit of "The Balloon of the Mind" in AUTOBIOGRAPHIES. "I was unfitted for school work," he remembers of his youth, "and though I would often work well for weeks together, I had to give the whole evening to one lesson if I was to know it. My thoughts were a great excitement, but when I tried to do anything with them, it was like trying to pack a balloon into a shed in a high wind" (64–65).

"Beautiful Lofty Things" (1938)

In poems like "NO SECOND TROY" and "PARNELL'S FUNERAL," Yeats, no less than James JOYCE, conflates the mundane and the mythic as a means of writing on a simultaneously intimate and universal scale. In the Joycean manner, "Beautiful Lofty Things" finds the mythic element in the quotidian moment. The disproportion between the moment and its mythic overlay or heroic resonance is the essence of Joyce's and in this case Yeats's humane irony: the heroic is immanent in the least of our dramas. The poem bodies forth Yeats's "beautiful lofty things"—JOHN O'LEARY, JOHN BUTLER YEATS, Standish James O'Grady (1846–1928), Lady GREGORY, MAUD GONNE—in remembered tableaux of years earlier. In their proud strength and ardent personality, evident even in the chance moment, each bears the stamp of nobility and implicitly reproaches the rancorous mobbism that Yeats attributed to contemporary Ireland (cf. "Parnell's Funeral").

The train of remembrance begins with the "noble head" of O'Leary, the old Fenian who was a nationalist mentor and father-figure to Yeats during the 1880s. Yeats revered O'Leary as a last exemplar of "romantic Ireland" ("SEPTEMBER 1913") and a living reproach to everything small-minded in the nationalist politics of the present day. "Beautiful Lofty Things" frames O'Leary from the shoulders up, perhaps because O'Leary's "Roman virtue" tended to put Yeats in mind of an ancient bust or coin (*Aut.* 177; *Mem.* 42). Yeats's father had several times painted O'Leary's "noble head" (see *Yeats: Portrait of an Artistic Family*), which conceivably explains the subconscious logic of the poem's segue from O'Leary to the memory of John Butler Yeats defending J. M. SYNGE's *The Playboy of the Western World*. The play opened on January 26, 1907, to riot and protest. Never one to forego a polemical opportunity, Yeats presided over a public debate on the "freedom of the stage" at the ABBEY THEATRE on February 4 (for Yeats's comments see *Expl.* 226–228; *UP2* 348–355). John Butler Yeats took the stage and to cheers from the audience called Ireland "a land of saints." The audience turned on him when he added, devilishly, "a land of plaster saints" (*PF* 317; see also *Letters to his Son* 152; *W. B. Yeats* 220). Finally he took his seat amid an uproar.

John Butler Yeats's speech leads by association to another speech, this one delivered by O'Grady, a journalist and historian who made a lasting impression on Yeats. His history of ancient Ireland, consisting of *The Heroic Period* (1878) and *Cuculain and his Contemporaries* (1880), had an enormous influence on the younger generation that would lead the Irish Renaissance. These volumes, in Yeats's description, retell "the Irish heroic tales in romantic Carlylean prose" (*Aut.* 296). In AUTO-BIOGRAPHIES, Yeats sketches O'Grady as a man of the "passionate serving kind," in the phrase of "TO A SHADE," and pays this homage: "A Unionist in politics, a leader-writer on the *Daily Express*, the most Conservative paper in Ireland, hater of every form of democracy, he had given all his heart to the smaller Irish landowners, to whom he belonged, and with whom his childhood had been spent, and for them he wrote his books, and would soon rage over their failings in certain famous passages that many men would repeat to themselves like poets' rhymes. All round us people talked or wrote for victory's sake, and were hated for their victories—but here was a man whose rage was a swan-song over all that he had held most dear, and to whom for that very reason every Irish imaginative writer owed a portion of his soul" (183). "Beautiful Lofty Things" recollects O'Grady giving a speech toward the end of a dinner hosted by the *Daily Express* at the Shelbourne Hotel, Dublin, on May 11, 1899 (elaborately and comically rendered by GEORGE MOORE in chapter 4 of *Ave*; see also AM 211–212).

In *Autobiographies* Yeats gives a full account of the speech: "[O'Grady] was very drunk, but neither his voice nor his manner showed it. [. . .] He stood between two tables, touching one or the other for support, and said in a low penetrating voice: 'We have now a literary movement, it is not very important; it will be followed by a political movement, that will not be very important; then must come a military movement, that will be important indeed'. [. . .] Then O'Grady described the Boy Scout Act, which had just passed, urged the landlords of Ireland to avail themselves of that Act and drill the sons of their tenants—'paying but little attention to the age limit'—then, pointing to where he supposed England to be, they must bid them 'march to the conquest of that decadent nation'. I knew what was in his mind. England was decadent because, democratic and so without fixed principles, it had used Irish landlords, his own ancestors or living relatives, as its garrison, and later left them deserted among their enemies" (314–315).

O'Grady's fury at the fate of Irish landlords puts Yeats in mind of Lady Gregory, herself a landlord who fell upon hard times. A family connection—O'Grady was a second cousin of Lady Gregory's mother, Frances Persse—may also explain the transition (*Lady Gregory* 30). The poem remembers Lady Gregory imperturbably facing down one of the land crises that periodically shook COOLE PARK (cf. "UPON A HOUSE SHAKEN BY THE LAND AGITATION"). Embroiled with a tenant in a dispute over certain acres, Lady Gregory, as she tells in her journal, "showed him how easy it would be to shoot me through the unshuttered window if he wanted to use violence" (*Lady Gregory's Journals*, I, 337). The incident occurred on April 10, 1922, making Lady Gregory 70 rather than 80, as the poem has it. The "great ormolu table" is the writing desk that had belonged to Lady Gregory's husband, Sir William Gregory. She inherited it upon his death and had it shipped from the couple's London house to Coole (*Lady Gregory* 91; see also *Coole* 43).

As "FRIENDS" ends with a climactic recollection of Maud Gonne, so ends "Beautiful Lofty Things." The disproportion between the moment and its

Maud Gonne, circa 1901: "Pallas Athene in that straight back and arrogant head," as Yeats recalls in "Beautiful Lofty Things" *(Library of Congress)*

mythic or heroic implication is here at its most provocative. Merely waiting for a train—in her mere "straight back and arrogant head"—Gonne recalls "Pallas Athene" (cf. "A THOUGHT FROM PROPERTIUS"). The emphasis on back and head conjures the torso of a Greek statue, just as the emphasis on O'Leary's head may conjure coin or bust. T. R. Henn comments, "Yeats may have had in mind any one of a dozen different statues, but Phidias, to whom he refers so often, had made a head of Athena (Copenhagen) superbly arrogant, and the Lemnian Athena. Either could have fittingly expressed Maud Gonne's poise" (*Lonely Tower* 206–207). In *Autobiographies*, Yeats makes more explicit the association of Gonne with ancient sculpture, writing that if her "face, like the face of some Greek statue, showed little thought, her whole body seemed a masterwork of long labouring thought, as though a Scopas had measured and calculated, consorted with Egyptian sages, and mathematicians out of Babylon, that he might outface even Artemisia's sepulchral image with a living norm" (275). The image of Gonne waiting at the Howth train station specifically recollects an excursion of August 4, 1891 (YC 22). Yeats had proposed and Gonne had refused, mysteriously letting on that "there were reasons." The couple spent the next day "upon the cliff paths at Howth" before dining "at a little cottage near the Baily Lighthouse" where Gonne's childhood nurse lived (*Mem.* 46). The poem ends in elegy for the passing of a better age—"All the Olympians; a thing never known again"—a note that Yeats had struck previously in "COOLE PARK, 1929" and "COOLE AND BALLYLEE, 1931."

In "A CRAZED GIRL," which immediately follows in *New Poems* (1938) and in the standard edition of his collected poems, Yeats adds the actress and poet MARGOT RUDDOCK to his roster of "Beautiful Lofty Things" ("that girl I declare / A beautiful lofty thing"). "A Crazed Girl," however, does not or cannot invest Ruddock with enough weight to make her a plausible counterpart to the Olympians of "Beautiful Lofty Things."

FIRST PUBLICATION: *New Poems*, The CUALA PRESS, Dublin, May 18, 1938.

BIBLIOGRAPHY

Foster, R. F. *W. B. Yeats: A Life, I: The Apprentice Mage*; Gregory, Lady. *Coole, Lady Gregory's Journals* (vol. 1, ed. Daniel J. Murphy); Henn, T. R. *The Lonely Tower: Studies in the Poetry of W. B. Yeats*; Hone, Joseph. *W. B. Yeats*; Kelly, John S. *A W. B. Yeats Chronology*; Kohfeldt, Mary Lou. *Lady Gregory: The Woman behind the Irish Renaissance*; Moore, George. *Hail and Farewell*; Murphy, William M. *Prodigal Father: The Life of John Butler Yeats (1839–1922)*; Pyle, Hilary. *Yeats: Portrait of an Artistic Family*; Yeats, John Butler. *Letters to his Son W. B. Yeats and Others 1869–1922*; W. B. Yeats, *Autobiographies, Explorations, Memoirs, Uncollected Prose by W. B. Yeats* (vol. 2).

"Before the World was made" (1929)

See "A WOMAN YOUNG AND OLD."

"Blood and the Moon" (1929)

Like "ANCESTRAL HOUSES," "Blood and the Moon" is an excursus on the "bloody, arrogant power" by which men of fierce *antithetical* stamp sublimate what "BYZANTIUM" calls the "fury and the mire of human veins." In the poem's difficult conceptual scheme, the tower is both root and crown. Absorbing into itself the passions of the race, drenched in the blood of history, it aspires, though in the end futilely, to the enigmatic purity of the moon. Yeats wrote "Blood and the Moon," as well as "DEATH," in response to the assassination of KEVIN O'HIGGINS, vice president of the executive council and minister for justice and external affairs in the Free State government, and the one contemporary leader whom Yeats immensely admired (*VP* 831). To Yeats, O'Higgins typified the "bloody, arrogant power" by which humanity rears its towers, whether constructed by mason, philosopher, artist, or politician. In ON THE BOILER, Yeats adds O'Higgins's name to his roster of Irish heroes with the comment that "there is nothing too hard for such as these" (*Expl.* 442; *LE* 242).

"Blood and the Moon" begins as a formal blessing upon THOOR BALLYLEE in the spirit of "A PRAYER ON GOING INTO MY HOUSE" and "To be Carved on a Stone at Thoor Ballylee" (1921). Abruptly, however, the poem dispenses with the *primary* ritual of the blessing and plunges into the dynamics of *antithetical* aspiration, inclining to the dark idea, in Hazard Adams's words, that "antithetical power is violent in its moments of greatest creativity" (*Book of Yeats's Poems* 188). Yeats asserts the tower as the emblem of the *antithetical* impulse that utters and masters the primal energies of the race and more fundamentally of the blood. Thus conceived, the tower is a mocking rebuke of modernity, which in the description of "EGO

DOMINUS TUUS," has "lit upon the gentle, sensitive mind / And lost the old nonchalance of the hand." The accusation that the age is "half dead at the top" derives from Thoor Ballylee's ruined battlements and "waste room at the top" (*VP* 831). In "A DIALOGUE OF SELF AND SOUL" and "I SEE PHANTOMS OF HATRED AND OF THE HEART'S FULLNESS AND OF THE COMING EMPTINESS," this dilapidation metaphorizes the fate of the tower in an age either hostile or indifferent to the tower's *antithetical* aspiration, but here it suggests the aristocrats—leaders by birth or ability—who have betrayed their own tradition and abnegated the responsibilities of their elevation (cf. "IN MEMORY OF EVA GORE-BOOTH AND CON MARKIEWICZ" and "TO A WEALTHY MAN WHO PROMISED A SECOND SUBSCRIPTION TO THE DUBLIN MUNICIPAL GALLERY IF IT WERE PROVED THE PEOPLE WANTED PICTURES"). That these putative leaders are *half* dead suggests that they have neither the vigor of life nor the wisdom of death. O'Higgins was such a particularly grievous loss, in Yeats's view, because he was a rare exception to this half deadness.

The poem's second section posits the tower as the varying expression of a historically consistent impulse, citing the towers of Alexandria and Babylon and the tower image in the poetry of SHELLEY. Yeats specifically alludes to Shelley's *Prometheus Unbound* (IV, 99–104), but he was closely attentive to the image throughout Shelley (see "The PHILOSOPHY OF SHELLEY'S POETRY" and "The PHASES OF THE MOON"). Significantly, however, Yeats explicitly assigns his own tower not to the tradition of Shelley, as he might have done in his youth, but to the tradition of the Irish Georgians, Oliver Goldsmith (1728–74), JONATHAN SWIFT (dean of St. Patrick's Cathedral, Dublin), George Berkeley (1685–1753), and Edmund Burke (1729–97). Yeats's relatively late-arriving romance with the chief intellects of Georgian Ireland—also evidenced in "PARNELL'S FUNERAL," "The SEVEN SAGES," "SWIFT'S EPITAPH," "The TOWER," and *The WORDS UPON THE WINDOW-PANE*—allowed him to divorce his love of country from the mobbism he attributed to contemporary Ireland and wed it to a literary and intellectual tradition that accorded with his simultaneously romantic and conservative sensibility. In the conceptual scheme of "Blood and the Moon," Swift represents passionate integrity, Goldsmith sweetness, Burke tradition, and Berkeley human sovereignty. As Donald T. Torchiana observes, the image of Goldsmith "sipping at the honey-pot of his mind" retains "the vascular and sensual connotations" of Swift's "blood-sodden breast." Honey, meanwhile, recalls the bees of "THE STARE'S NEST BY MY WINDOW," which represent the richness of the unembittered mind, the mind free of intellectual hatred (*W. B. Yeats & Georgian Ireland* 275). Berkeley was presumably "God-appointed" when he became bishop of Cloyne in 1734. The unusual sobriquet may also acknowledge Berkeley as a bearer of metaphysical or divine truths. "Saeva indignatio"—"savage indignation"—quotes Swift's epitaph. The final two lines of the section seem to summarize the entire tradition pillared the four men: "The strength that gives our blood and state magnanimity of its own desire; / Everything that is not God consumed with intellectual fire." Strength—"bloody, arrogant power"—is the fundamental attribute. Out of strength comes the "magnanimity of desire" by which the body physical and the body politic transcend themselves in a blaze of "intellectual fire" that consumes "everything that is not God" ("SAILING TO BYZANTIUM" and "VACILLATION" envision similar baptismal fires).

The "purity of the unclouded moon" casts its light upon the floor of the tower, but reveals no stain of blood, despite the ancient violence of soldier, assassin, and executioner (cf. the "unspotted" sword of "A Dialogue of Self and Soul"). Hazard Adams writes: "Like some virgin goddess, the moon is pure, yet in that moonlight the 'blood of innocence' has frequently been shed. The moon's arrow suggests the wounding of the world with desire, yet the moon remains always pure, that desire never achieved" (*Book of Yeats's Poems* 189). Those who have shed no blood gather upon the stair and "clamour in drunken frenzy for the moon." These noisy petitioners apparently seek an expiation or communion that they have not earned and do not know how to pursue. Where Swift beats "on his breast in a sibylline frenzy blind"—rises to a tragic intensity that becomes oracular—these are merely clamorous and drunk (in the Yeatsian nomencla-

ture, "drunken frenzy" is equivocal, but "clamour," as in the third section of "NINETEEN HUNDRED AND NINETEEN," negatively connotes disorganized energy). In the final stanza of the poem, the moon and the tower are almost tenderly engaged. Butterflies and moths, gentle lunar emissaries, cling to the windows of the tower, as they seem to cling to the "moonlit skies." The aura of benediction finds support in "Tom O'Roughley" (1918), which associates the butterfly with wisdom, and in a note to "MEDITATIONS IN TIME OF CIVIL WAR," which associates the butterfly with "the crooked road of intuition" as against "the straight road of logic" (*VP* 827). T. R. Henn interprets the butterflies as human souls—presumably the souls of those butchered upon the tower's killing floor (*Lonely Tower* 132). Consistent with Henn's notion, Yeats unambiguously figures the soul as a butterfly in "Another Song of a Fool" (1919), in the concluding scene of *The HOUR-GLASS*, and in the juvenile play *Vivien and Time* (see *Desolate Reality* 28). He touches on the related folk belief in his headnote to "Ghosts" in *Fairy and Folk Tales of the Irish Peasantry* (*Fairy and Folk Tales of Ireland* 117–118; *P&I* 17; see also *VPl.* 643). Whether the moon descends by the creatures of its light, or the blood ascends by the souls of the departed, the tower seems graced, at last, by ethereal loveliness. Significantly, the windows are "glittering," a word that intimates the almost molecular wavering of reality in moments verging upon transcendence or transformation, as in "Ancestral Houses," "COOLE AND BALLYLEE, 1931," "DEMON AND BEAST," "LAPIS LAZULI," "The Tower," and "Vacillation."

Just as Yeats's *antithetical* reverie begins with an abrupt rejection of *primary* aspiration, so it ends with an abrupt rejection—or at least a complication—of *antithetical* aspiration. If the tower once symbolized a heroic if ruthless strength, it has come to symbolize the collapse of this strength amid the ruin of the modern nation. Unable to sustain the conviction that strength eventuates in the self-immolating transcendence of "intellectual fire," Yeats resigns himself to a fractured reality. He consigns "wisdom" to the dead, as in "ALL SOULS' NIGHT," "The LEADERS OF THE CROWD," and "The MOUNTAIN TOMB," though "Blood and the Moon" evidences nothing of the esoteric faith of these poems; he consigns "power" and its concomitant "stain of blood" to the living; and he consigns purity to the "visage of the moon / When it has looked in glory from a cloud" ("A MEMORY OF YOUTH" likewise ends with the benediction of the moon's sudden appearance from behind a cloud—an image of the moon's fickle but irresistible sovereignty). In Adams's gloss of these lines: "Antitheticality in life is impure though washed in moonlight, which produces only a frustrating desire, now fully identified with a violence actively produced by the moon's aloof purity. [. . .] Yet, as the poem ends, the poet, for all this, expresses his wondering devotion because of the very purity that generates violent desire" (*Book of Yeats's Poems* 190).

"Oil and Blood" (1929), which immediately follows in *The Winding Stair* (1929), explores a similar dichotomy in which blood is countervailed not by the moon, but by the "tombs of gold and lapis lazuli" and the "miraculous oil" exuded by the bodies of "holy men and women." The sanguinous motif continues in "Veronica's Napkin" (1932).

FIRST PUBLICATION: The *Exile* (periodical), Spring 1928. Reprinted in *The Winding Stair*, The Fountain Press, New York, October 1, 1929.

BIBLIOGRAPHY

Adams, Hazard. *The Book of Yeats's Poems*; Clark, David R. with Rosalind Clark, *W. B. Yeats and the Theatre of Desolate Reality* (expanded edition); Henn, T. R. *The Lonely Tower: Studies in the Poetry of W. B. Yeats*; Torchiana, Donald T. *W. B. Yeats & Georgian Ireland*; Yeats, W. B. *Explorations*, (ed.) *Fairy and Folk Tales of Ireland, Later Essays, Prefaces and Introductions, The Variorum Edition of the Plays of W. B. Yeats, The Variorum Edition of the Poems of W. B. Yeats*.

"Broken Dreams" (1917)

In *The Wild Swans at Coole* (1917) and in the collected edition of Yeats's poems, "Broken Dreams" is chief among an informal sequence of poems that takes up the theme of MAUD GONNE's middle age

(see "Memory" [1916], "HER PRAISE," "The PEOPLE," "His Phoenix" [1916], "A THOUGHT FROM PROPERTIUS," "A Deep-sworn Vow" [1917], and "PRESENCES"). A poem of immense tenderness and beauty, "Broken Dreams" has neither the wry humor of "Her Praise" and "His Phoenix," nor the rhetorical audacity of "FALLEN MAJESTY" and "NO SECOND TROY." In its deliberately transparent and unembellished language ("You are more beautiful than any one"), it seems to eschew the insincerity of the mask and to anticipate something of the renunciation of "The CIRCUS ANIMALS' DESERTION."

The opening two stanzas of the poem cover familiar ground. As in "Fallen Majesty" and "Her Praise," Gonne's youthful beauty has become the matter of half-forgotten legend, sustained only by the "vague memories" of those who were its witness. Gonne no longer leaves young men stunned and gaping, but perhaps "some old gaffer," having been saved on his deathbed by her prayers, has a blessing for her. Long cast as Helen of Troy, Gonne is at least momentarily restored to the role of the Countess Cathleen, saintly benefactress of the poor and the downtrodden, beloved by heaven (see *The COUNTESS CATHLEEN*). For Gonne's sake, Heaven has withheld its stroke of doom—that is, spared the old gaffer—"So great her portion in that peace you make / By merely walking in a room" (this a far cry from the Maud Gonne for whom there was no second Troy to burn). Perhaps too a young man will ask the old men to speak of "that lady / The poet stubborn with his passion sang us / When age might well have chilled his blood." Yeats's allusion to his own stubbornness echoes the central motif of "Her Praise" and "His Phoenix," in which this stubbornness is both exhibited and gently satirized.

In its third stanza, the poem suddenly modulates: magniloquence ("Heaven has put away the stroke of her doom," etc.) and contrivance ("From meagre girlhood's putting on / Burdensome beauty") gives way to limpid simplicity that seems the very language of intimacy and sincerity. Perhaps evoking his own mystical doctrine that the dead relive their lives in reverse (see the Goatherd's final speech in "Shepherd and Goatherd" [1919]), Yeats proclaims that "in the grave all, all, shall be renewed." There he will again see Gonne in "the first loveliness of womanhood." The ingeniously simple phrase "leaning or standing or walking," suggestive of comfortable physicality, contrasts with Gonne's religious exertions in the first stanza, and suggests that in the grave there will be a recovery of what might be called the innocence of the body.

In the fourth stanza, Yeats's reverence for Gonne's youthful beauty is belied by the revelation of a deeper sentiment and a fuller embrace. In a confession of love the more powerful for its subtlety and seeming unself-consciousness, Yeats's praise of Gonne's beauty suddenly shifts into the present tense ("You are more beautiful than any one"), giving the lie to his own talk of "vague memories" and intimating that beauty transcends the body. Correspondingly, Yeats's single cavil that Gonne's hands were not beautiful finds voice in the past tense ("had"), as if Gonne has put off all mere imperfection of the body even as she has grown old and grey (Gonne was then 50). Despite Gonne's imperfect hands, Yeats would alter nothing. The poem suddenly effloresces and loosens as it discovers the imagery of its highest emotion: Yeats urges Gonne not to "paddle to the wrist / In that mysterious, always brimming lake / Where those that have obeyed the holy law / Paddle and are perfect." In these lines there is at once radical revision of the Christian heaven mooted in the poem's opening stanza; an equation of Gonne with the undimmed graceful passion of the swans whose image opens the volume (see "The WILD SWANS AT COOLE"); and symbolic embrace of mortal imperfection against immortal perfection, the natural against the supernatural, in a continuation of an internal debate that stretches all the way back to "To THE ROSE UPON THE ROOD OF TIME" and "The WANDERINGS OF OISIN."

As the last stroke of mystic midnight dies (cf. "ALL SOULS' NIGHT"), the vision wanes, leaving only the reality of the solitary poet communing with "an image of air," turning in his mind "vague memories, nothing but memories." These lines carry forward the implication of the allusion to the "fervor" of Yeats's "youthful eyes" in line 25 and the implication of the poem generally: Beauty is not a phenomenon of the thing seen, but of the seer, whose passion constructs the image of its own desire.

FIRST PUBLICATION: The *Little Review* (periodical), June 1917. Reprinted in *The Wild Swans at Coole*, The CUALA PRESS, Churchtown, Dundrum, November 17, 1917.

"Bronze Head, A" (1939)

Like "THE MUNICIPAL GALLERY REVISITED," "A Bronze Head" has its pretext in the collection of the Municipal Gallery of Modern Art in Dublin, which had been founded by Lady GREGORY's nephew HUGH LANE. In this instance, Yeats departs on a dense and difficult reflection inspired by a bust of MAUD GONNE—a plaster cast painted bronze—that was the work of the young sculptor Laurence Campbell (*W. B. Yeats* 474). Gonne, unfortunately, left to posterity no comment on the poem that represents Yeats's most concerted attempt to encompass and explain her complexity.

Dispensing with all but the barest scene-setting, Yeats attributes to the bronze head the "empty eyeballs" that are a crucial motif in "THE DOUBLE VISION OF MICHAEL ROBARTES" and "The STATUES." Representing the transcendence of worldly curiosity and attachment, the motif of the empty eyeballs was inspired by the demeanor of ancient sculpture. "When I think of Rome," Yeats writes in A VISION, "I see always those heads with their world-considering eyes, and those bodies as conventional as the metaphors in a leading article, and compare in my imagination vague Grecian eyes gazing at nothing, Byzantine eyes of drilled ivory staring upon a vision, and those eyelids of China and of India, those veiled or half-veiled eyes weary of world and vision alike" (AV 277). Speaking of early Byzantium, Yeats adds that the ascetic has replaced the Greek athlete as a representative figure, "but all about him is an incredible splendour like that which we see pass under our closed eyelids as we lie between sleep and waking, no representation of a living world but the dream of a somnambulist. Even the drilled pupil of the eye, when the drill is in the hand of some Byzantine worker in ivory, undergoes a somnambulistic change, for its deep shadow among the faint lines of the tablet, its mechanical circle, where all else is rhythmical and flowing, give to Saint or Angel a look of some great bird staring at miracle" (280). Gonne—herself an ascetic of sorts, a saint of politics—shares the quality of seeming to stare at miracle; hence, the second line's slippage from "human" to "superhuman." Gonne's humanity—Yeats's old complaint—is consumed by the intensity of her vision or her hatred. This explains why "everything else"—body, emotion, personality—is "withered and mummy-dead." There is a similar reckoning of withered humanity in "AMONG SCHOOL CHILDREN" ("hollow of cheek") and in "IN MEMORY OF EVA GORE-BOOTH AND CON MARKIE-WICZ" ("withered old and skeleton-gaunt"). These lines can also be related to the ambivalent heroizing of "EASTER 1916" ("Too long a sacrifice / Can make a stone of the heart"); to the bitter account of Gonne in "FIRST LOVE" and "A PRAYER FOR MY DAUGHTER"; and most particularly to Yeats's diagnosis of Gonne's spiritual errancy in his journal: "Women, because the main event of their lives has been a giving of themselves, give themselves to an opinion as if [it] were some terrible stone doll. [. . .] They grow cruel, as if [in] defence of lover or child, and all this is done for something other than human life. At last the opinion becomes so much a part of them that it is as though a part of their flesh becomes, as it were, stone, and much of their being passes out of life. It was part of [Gonne's] power in the past that, though she made this surrender with her mind, she kept the sweetness of her voice and much humour, yet I cannot but fear for her" (*Aut.* 372–373; *Mem.* 192).

The question that ends the stanza echoes "The SECOND COMING" ("And what rough beast, its hour come round at last, / Slouches towards Bethlehem to be born?") and "The Statues" ("When Pearse summoned Cuchulain to his side, / What stalked through the Post Office?"). It implies, anticipating lines 22 and 23, that Gonne is possessed by some force or consciousness not entirely her own, by some "great tomb-haunter." The "tomb-haunter" is plausibly Gonne herself, for she had attempted to reincarnate her dead son Georges by conceiving a second child in her son's funeral vault (GY 23; *Mem.* 47–49, 133). But Yeats's wondering question and the mythologizing epithet "great" (cf. the

"Great Archer" of "IN THE SEVEN WOODS" and the "great enemy" of "HER FRIENDS BRING HER A CHRISTMAS TREE") equally suggest some inhuman mystic entity, some monstrous communicant of the tomb wisdom or "mummy truths" to which Yeats refers in poems like "ALL SOULS' NIGHT," "The LEADERS OF THE CROWD," and "The MOUNTAIN TOMB." The tomb-haunter seeks in the sky some answer to the "*Hysterica passio* of its own emptiness," but finds nothing to ease its restlessness and yearning. The paradoxical suggestion, possibly derived from the second stanza of SHELLEY's "Hymn to Intellectual Beauty" (1817), is that plumbing the tomb is an attempt—seemingly mistaken, as in Shelley—to sound out the skies, to discover, in the mysteries of death, the answering voice of a presiding divinity. The phrase "hysterica passio"—hysterical passion—is a favorite borrowing from *King Lear* (II, iv, 57). Yeats repeats the phrase in AUTOBIOG-RAPHIES (361), "PARNELL'S FUNERAL," and "ROSA ALCHEMICA," and in an August 5, 1936, letter to DOROTHY WELLESLEY (*LOP* 86).

In the second stanza, "great tomb-haunter" becomes "dark tomb-haunter" and the signification is squarely assigned to Gonne. As in "Among School Children" and "A Prayer for my Daughter," Yeats compares Gonne in her girlish splendor to the woman she became. Yeats can only wonder which guise is the truer one, or whether, following the philosopher J. M. E. McTaggart, her substance is composite, equally embodying the principles of life and death. In *The Nature of Existence* (1921), as Richard J. Finneran notes, McTaggart (1866–1925) proposes that "all substances are compound" (*The Poems* 682; cf. "MICHAEL ROBARTES AND THE DANCER," lines 44–48). John Crowe Ransom makes a subtle criticism of the allusion to McTaggart: "The most important aspect of Yeats's genius, I imagine, was his carefully nurtured gift for pure intrinsic particularity, for committing himself even in his 'noblest' moments to the image with absolutely local detail; a feat whose secret had been all but lost to English poetry. [. . .] But McTaggart is an unhappy particularity to rest the case on. Whatever the admirable Hegelian scholar may have meant to Yeats, he is not Pythagoras, and in fact he is defined for most of us by those footnotes that call his name in the academic treatises in ethics and metaphysics; in other words, as an item of the scientific rather than the poetic imagination" (*Yeats: Last Poems* 43). The same criticism might be levied against Yeats's invocation of the theologian Friedrich von Hügel (1852–1925) in "VACILLATION."

The third stanza recalls the concern that Yeats expresses in MEMOIRS ("I cannot but fear for her"). Even in her youthful beauty and gentleness, Gonne had possessed an unnerving "wildness," some tendency to destruction and self-destruction that plays out in Yeats's recurrent figuration of her as Helen (see "NO SECOND TROY" and "The SORROW OF LOVE"). At times Yeats thought that her soul had been shattered by a "vision of terror," which explains the imputation of both emptiness and longing in the first stanza. What constitutes and explains this "vision of terror," however, remains a mystery of Gonne's complex psychology and turbulent experience. Perhaps it was the death of her mother from tuberculosis in 1871, the recollection of which opens her autobiography, *A Servant of the Queen* (1938); perhaps it was something so inborn as to be ineffable. "Propinquity" describes Yeats's closeness to Gonne during the early 1890s; the allusion to "imagination" is obscure, but Yeats probably means that, in the profound tenderness of his love, he was capable of the pure empathy, the unmitigated realization of another's pain, that is the ultimate act of imagination. He, too, had "grown wild," caught up in the rhythms of her wildness and in his own concern, and had "wandered murmuring everywhere, 'My child, my child!'" in a display of ineffectual tenderness and longing to assist where assistance was impossible. Yeats's benediction in some sense responds to the religious crisis of the first stanza, and perhaps predicts Gonne's conversion to Catholicism insofar as the priest, addressed as "father," reciprocates by addressing the layperson as "my child." And yet this benediction does not begin to answer or allay the apocalyptic momentum of Gonne's emptiness.

At other times, awestruck by her unnatural intensity, Yeats thought Gonne "supernatural," as "though a sterner eye looked through her eye / On this foul world in its decline and fall; / On gangling stocks grown great, great stocks run dry. . . ." In F. A. C. Wilson's paraphrase, "Maud Gonne is possessed by an angel, which descants through her lips and with the terrible unsentimentality of heaven, on the degradation of spirit in the modern world" (*Yeats's Iconography* 291). The accusation of the world's decline reiterates the accusation of "The Statues" ("formless spawning fury") and "UNDER BEN BULBEN" ("Base-born products of base beds"), but in comparison to the general intricacy and imaginative ambition of the poem the eugenic theory implicit in these lines seems intellectually slack. Set in the naked light of prose in ON THE BOILER it seems even more unsatisfactory: "For now by our too much facility in this kind, in giving way for all to marry that will, too much liberty and indulgence in tolerating all sorts, there is a vast confusion of hereditary diseases, no family secure, no man almost free from some grievous infirmity or other" (*Expl.* 419; *LE* 228). In the poem's final line, Yeats wonders "what was left for massacre to save," thus casting Gonne as an apocalyptic avatar relatable to the sphinx of "The Second Coming" and reemphasizing her Helenic capacity for destruction.

"A Bronze Head" continues a long-established association of Gonne—statuesque, adamantine, classically beautiful—and the statue. In AUTOBIOGRAPHIES, Yeats extravagantly compares Gonne to the statue of Artemisia in the British Museum (274–275); in "BEAUTIFUL LOFTY THINGS" he envisions her as Pallas Athene sculpted in torso; and in *Memoirs*, he recounts a "double vision" in which Gonne "thought herself a great stone statue through which passed flame" and he felt himself "becoming flame and mounting up through and looking out of the eyes of a great stone Minerva" (134).

FIRST PUBLICATION: The *London Mercury* (periodical), March 1939, and the *New Republic*, March 22, 1939. Reprinted in *Last Poems and Two Plays*, The CUALA PRESS, Dublin, July 10, 1939.

BIBLIOGRAPHY

Hone, Joseph. *W. B. Yeats*; Stallworthy, John, ed. *Yeats: Last Poems*; Wilson, F. A. C. *Yeats's Iconography*; Yeats, W. B. *Autobiographies, Explorations, The Gonne-Yeats Letters 1893–1938, Later Essays,*

Letters on Poetry from W. B. Yeats to Dorothy Welles-ley, Memoirs, The Poems, A Vision.

"Byzantium"
(1932, dated 1930)

In its chiseled perfection of language, "Byzantium" is one of Yeats's indubitable masterpieces; in the lucidity of its agonized vista, it is his most ineluctable vision; in its comprehensive structure of idea, it is arguably his foremost statement. Helen Vendler calls the poem "Yeats's greatest single triumph," adding that in "Byzantium" the "sense of agonizing balance between opposites which was his primary poetic intuition receives its most acute rendering" (*Later Plays* 114). Yeats began the poem in the spring of 1930 while recovering from a months-long bout of Malta fever at Rapallo (*Expl.* 289). An April 30, 1930, diary entry records the germ of the poem: "Describe Byzantium as it is in the system towards the end of the first Christian millennium. A walking mummy. Flames at the street corners where the soul is purified, birds of hammered gold singing in the golden trees, in the harbour, offering their backs to the wailing dead that they may carry them to Paradise." Yeats adds, "These subjects have been in my head for some time, especially the last" (290). Yeats sent a draft of "Byzantium" to T. STURGE MOORE on October 4, 1930, and explained that the poem was prompted by Moore's criticism of "SAILING TO BYZANTIUM": "You objected to the last verse of *Sailing to Byzantium* because a bird made by a goldsmith was just as natural as anything else. That showed me that the idea needed exposition. Gongs were used in the Byzantine church" (*WBY&TSM* 164; for Moore's criticism, see 162). The late millennial setting of "Byzantium" importantly distinguishes it from "Sailing to Byzantium." Where the latter poem belongs to the unity of the sixth century (Phase 15 of the millennial cycle), the former finds in the apocalyptic disintegration of this unity the energy of a fiercer creation and more vexed salvation. This moment mattered particularly because it precedented the second Christian millennium as it likewise rounded to a rough close

(cf. "The SECOND COMING"). In the waning days of Byzantium, then, Yeats found the image of his own era and a context in which to play out his own metaphysics. Taking a different view, Vendler calls "Byzantium" Yeats's "most authoritative poetic word on Phase 15" (*Later Plays* 114).

The scene opens upon Byzantium. Night has fallen, but there is no sense of rest or resolution. The "images of day" recede, but they remain "unpurged"; the night cannot, as in the normal order of things, release the tension of the day. The "Emperor's drunken soldiery," like the unheeding falcon in "The Second Coming," at once implies social disorder and loose menace, while the implication of coarse revelry suggests the breakdown of the refinement pictured in the final stanza of "Sailing to Byzantium." The allusion to soldiers may also play on the memory of the ANGLO-IRISH WAR and the horror related in the first section of "NINETEEN HUNDRED AND NINETEEN" ("a drunken soldiery / Can leave the mother murdered at her door") and in "Reprisals" (*VP* 791). The sounds of the night likewise recede as the evening deepens into silence. The song of the "night-walkers"—prostitutes presumably, spiritual counterparts to the drunken soldiers—follows upon the echo of the "great cathedral gong" (cf. the second section of "Nineteen Hundred and Nineteen," in which the gong signifies Eastern or primal energy). The two "songs" signify the fundamental antithesis of all experience and reality, the opposition, in the terms of "A DIALOGUE OF SELF AND SOUL," between earth and heaven, sword and tower, ditch and stair, human and inhuman. The stanza's final four lines make explicit this tension in the very fabric of things: "A starlit or a moonlit dome disdains / All that man is, / All mere complexities, / The fury and the mire of human veins." Vendler comments, "The dome may be starlit (at Phase 1) or moonlit (at Phase 15); the perfect objective and the perfect subjective are alike independent of 'the fury and the mire of human veins'" (*Later Plays* 115; see also *Yeats* 384).

The second and third stanzas respectively represent the two means—the esoteric and the artistic—by which passion delivers humanity from the antitheses of mortality. In the second stanza, a figure neither man nor shade, neither living nor dead, but "superhuman," presents itself to the visionary eye. In explanation of the mystery of this transcendence, Yeats offers that "Hades' bobbin bound in mummy-cloth / May unwind the winding path. . . ." In this instance, "to unwind" means "to unspool" (in keeping with "bobbin") but also "to straighten"; it is to say that beyond living or natural confines the "winding path"—the vacillation treated in the first stanza—resolves into unity. In explanation of his own ability to summon such a figure, Yeats plays complicatedly upon the word "breath": "breathless mouths" may summon mouths with "no breath," that is, in moments of "excited reverie" ("A PRAYER FOR MY DAUGHTER") we are able to beckon to mysteries beyond life; as the third stanza of "Sailing to Byzantium" establishes, our own ecstasy is the medium of our communion with eternity. In its imagery of wound mummy-cloth the stanza echoes "ALL SOULS' NIGHT," and it may be that Yeats achieves something of the vision to which he commits himself in the final stanza of that poem ("Nothing can stay my glance / Until that glance run in the world's despite / To where the damned have howled away their hearts, / And where the blessed dance . . .").

The third stanza is counterpart to the second. As the second envisions neither man nor shade, but the image of the superhuman, so the third envisions neither bird nor "golden handiwork," but a "miracle" that belongs neither to life nor to art, though produced by the artist. The bird upon its "star-lit golden bough" can like the "cocks of Hades crow," which, remembering "MY TABLE" and "SOLOMON AND THE WITCH," figures the bird as an apocalyptic agent. In keeping with this agency, the bird can "by the moon embittered, scorn aloud / In glory of changeless metal / Common bird or petal / And all complexities of mire or blood." In its scorn of mire or blood, the bird is akin to the dome of the first stanza, but while the dome is "moonlit" the bird is "by the moon embittered": it rebels against the temporal cycle of the moon (or perhaps against everything that does not share in the purity of the moon) and refuses everything but its own perfection. Its scorn, conceivably, is the energy of its own apocalyptic annunciation.

The fourth stanza arrives at midnight, the witching hour, as in "All Souls' Night." The streets flicker with uncanny flames equatable with the "holy fire" postulated in the third stanza of "Sailing to Byzantium." The flames are begotten of themselves (cf. the "self-born mockers" of "AMONG SCHOOL CHILDREN") and thus belong entirely to the unity of their own energy or passion. The flames draw "blood-begotten spirits" as if irresistible in their intensity or in their promise of deliverance. In the purgatorial fire these spirits are shrived of "all complexities of fury," of everything that belongs to the order of nature ("Everything that is not God consumed with intellectual fire," Yeats writes in "BLOOD AND THE MOON"; "Look on that fire, salvation walks within," he writes in "VACILLATION"). Dance, trance, and flame, the triple metaphors of the stanza, are expressions of the same deepening into the unity of the self that is the essential rebirth and the essential salvation, a conception variously explored in the final stanza of "Among School Children," in the second section of "The DOUBLE VISION OF MICHAEL ROBARTES," in the second stanza of "MOHINI CHATTERJEE," and in the third stanza of "Sailing to Byzantium." The "agony of flame" cannot "singe a sleeve" because it is purely internal, a conflagration of the soul. Richard Ellmann draws attention to an unpublished note to A VISION that seems to flesh out the mysteries of the stanza: "At first we are subject to Destiny [. . .] but the point in the Zodiac where the whirl becomes a sphere once reached [cf. "CHOSEN"], we may escape from the constraint of our nature and from that of external things, entering upon a state where all fuel has become flame, where there is nothing but the state itself, nothing to constrain it or end it. We attain it always in the creation or enjoyment of a work of art, but that moment though eternal in the Daimon passes from us because it is not an attainment of our whole being. Philosophy has always explained its moment of moments in much the same way; nothing can be added to it, nothing taken away; that all progressions are full of illusion, that everything is born there like a ship in full sail" (IY 221).

Out of the fourth stanza's maelstrom of death and rebirth comes a vision of salvation inspired by Raphael's statue of "the Dolphin carrying one of the Holy Innocents to Heaven," as Yeats wrote to Moore on October 8, 1930 (*WBY&TSM* 165; see also *Lonely Tower* 247–248). Spirits straddle the dolphins in symbolic expression of their victory over mire and blood or perhaps in their sublimation of the energy of mire and blood (the dolphin similarly appears as the chariot of departed souls in "NEWS FOR THE DELPHIC ORACLE"). Inclining at the close to a conception of art as the organized expression of the transcendent agony described in the previous stanza, the poem shifts terms and ends with a declaration of aesthetic faith. The image of the dolphins breasting the flood metamorphoses into the image of imperial smithies breaking the flood, which is to say, disciplining and transcending the tumultuous accident of nature. The image of the imperial smithies—a slightly retrograde image out of "Sailing to Byzantium"—in turn gives way to the more acute epitomization of art in the image of the marble dancing floor breaking "bitter furies of complexity," which better encompasses the paradox of discipline and freedom, calculation and spontaneity, that is the mystery of all high expression. The poem's final lines, massive in their compression of idea, explain these furies of complexity as the infinite ramification of image by which the self-conscious mind or the world or the ANIMA MUNDI baffles and overwhelms the attempt at redemptive intensity. These furies have their image in that "dolphin-torn, that gong-tormented sea," an image that seems to encompass all of natural life. That the sea is "dolphin-torn" and "gong-tormented"—momentarily disturbed by our sexual or religious or artistic aspiration but not altered in its massive and inscrutable inertia—implies that the serene finality of "Sailing to Byzantium" is misplaced; that the struggle to "break the flood" is the impossibility by which we rouse ourselves to miracle.

FIRST PUBLICATION: *Words for Music Perhaps and Other Poems*, The CUALA PRESS, Dublin, November 14, 1932.

BIBLIOGRAPHY

Bloom, Harold. *Yeats*; Ellmann, Richard. *The Identity of Yeats*; Henn, T. R. *The Lonely Tower: Studies in the Poetry of W. B. Yeats*; Vendler, Helen Hennessy. *Yeats's Vision and the Later Plays*; Yeats, W. B. *Explorations, The Variorum Edition of the Poems of W. B. Yeats, W. B. Yeats and T. Sturge Moore: Their Correspondence 1901–1937.*

"Cat and the Moon, The" (1918)

Charming and yet rigorous, playful without being frivolous, "The Cat and the Moon" is the surprising coda to the weighty theorizing of "The PHASES OF THE MOON" and one of the few poems in Yeats's oeuvre that might appeal to a child. Even "A Cradle Song" (1890), with its angels "weary of trooping / With the whimpering dead," is an unlikely nursery favorite. The poem was inspired by Minnaloushe (spelling variable), the black Persian cat that belonged to ISEULT and MAUD GONNE. It had been born to a cat owned by Stephen MacKenna (1872–1934), whom Yeats venerated as the translator of Plotinus' *Enneads* (*Letters to WBY&EP* 189; *Sweet Dancer* 45). Yeats became acquainted with the cat while staying at Les Mouettes, the Gonnes' home in Colleville-sur-Mer, on the Normandy shore, during the summers of 1916 and 1917. In a letter written to T. STURGE MOORE during the summer of 1917, Yeats described the Gonnes' full menagerie: "I am living in a house with three and thirty singing birds [. . .]. There is also a Persian cat, a parrot, two dogs, two rabbits and two guinea-pigs and a Javanese cock which perches on Madame Gonne's chair" (*WBY&TSM* 28). Yeats recollects the cat in the prologue to PER AMICA SILENTIA LUNAE. Addressing Iseult, Yeats writes, "You will remember that afternoon in Calvados last summer when your black Persian 'Minoulooshe', who had walked behind us for a good mile, heard a wing flutter in a bramble-bush? For a long time we called him endearing names in vain. He seemed resolute to spend his night among the brambles. He had interrupted a conversation, often interrupted before, upon certain thoughts so long habitual that I may be permitted to call them my convictions. When I came back to London my mind ran again and again to those conversations and I could not rest till I had written out in this little book all that I had said or would have said. Read it some day when 'Minoulooshe' is asleep" (*LE* 1). Acknowledging the dedication, Iseult wrote to Yeats on June 6, 1917, "Minoulouche and I are very grateful and honoured to have our names in your book. He is a little familiar divinity and well at his place in an occult work, as for me I am wholly undeserving, but none the less proud" (*Letters to WBY&EP* 84).

The poem is an extract from the play *The* CAT AND THE MOON (dated 1917, published 1924). The first musician sings the first eight lines at the start of the play; the next eight lines at the middle of the play; and the final 12 lines at the close of the play. Yeats explains the poem and its relation to the play in the preface to the latter: "But as the populace might well alter out of all recognition, deprive of all apparent meaning, some philosophical thought or verse, I wrote a little poem where a cat is disturbed by the moon, and in the changing pupils of its eyes seems to repeat the movement of the moon's changes, and allowed myself as I wrote to think of the cat as the normal man and of the moon as the opposite he seeks perpetually, or as having any meaning I have conferred upon the moon elsewhere. Doubtless, too, when the lame man takes the saint upon his back [an allusion to the play] the normal man has become one with that opposite [. . .]" (*VPl.* 807; *Expl.* 402–403; see also *VPl.* 805).

The poem describes the cat, "nearest kin of the moon," creeping in the night, its "animal blood" troubled by the "pure cold light in the sky." There is something to be said against Yeats's construal of the cat as the "normal man." A restless night-wanderer like *Ille* in "EGO DOMINUS TUUS" or the "creatures of the full" in "The Phases of the Moon," the cat has the manner of the arch-subjective personality, the man "in whom the movement inward is stronger than the movement outward, the man who sees all reflected within himself," as Yeats writes in a note to "The SECOND COMING" (*VP* 824). In this case the moon is less the cat's opposite than its haunting self-image, as suggested by the correspondence between the cat's changing pupils and the changing moon; by the repeated suggestion that the cat and the moon are kindred; by the inescapability of the moon's almost pursuing presence; and by the converse association of the

dog with the objective personality in "SHE TURNS THE DOLLS' FACES TO THE WALL." On this reading, Minnaloushe is the thematic descendant of the parrot that "sways upon a tree, / Raging at his own image in the enamelled sea" in "The Indian to His Love" (1886). On the other hand, there is a definite opposition between the "animal blood" of the cat and the "pure cold light" of the moon; between the cat's blackness and the moon's glow; between the cat's creeping slink and the moon's sailing height.

"The Cat and the Moon" is intimately connected not only with "The Phases of the Moon" and "Ego Dominus Tuus," but also with "The DOUBLE VISION OF MICHAEL ROBARTES" (the three poems being the verse pillars of Yeats's post-marital metaphysics). In the latter poem, there is the repetition of numerous motifs: the spinning top, the moonlit eyeball, the dance (ecstatic in opposition to "courtly"), and feline subjectivity (the cat become a sphinx). Both poems might be described as assays upon the mystery of the moon's 15th phase ("The Cat and the Moon's" description of the moon as "sacred" seems to suggest the full moon). Minnaloushe initially resists the "immovable trance" that defines this phase (*AV* 136), wailing against the moon's sway, clinging to the natural order much as does Yeats in "TO THE ROSE UPON THE ROOD OF TIME." In the end, however, his eyes become synchronous with the moon (signified by the repetition of the adjective "changing" in the final two lines). It may be that this mysterious harmony signals the moment when, in the language of "The Phases of the Moon," the "soul begins to tremble into stillness / To die in the labyrinth of itself." Not incidentally, Yeats appends "The Cat and the Moon" to the third section of "The Tragic Generation" in AUTOBIOGRAPHIES. The poem punctuates an important discussion of UNITY OF BEING, which Yeats associates with the moon's 15th phase.

Yeats had toyed with the image of the moon-touched black cat long before he became acquainted with Minnaloushe or contemplated the doctrines of A VISION. In the early novella JOHN SHERMAN, the protagonist tells himself, "it would be a good thing to be a little black cat. To leap about in the moonlight and sleep in the sunlight, and catch flies, to have no hard tasks to do or hard decisions to come to, to be simple and full of animal spirits" (*JS&D* 32).

FIRST PUBLICATION: *Nine Poems*, privately printed by Clement Shorter, London, October 1918. Reprinted in *The Wild Swans at Coole*, Macmillan, London, New York, March 11, 1919.

BIBLIOGRAPHY

Gonne, Iseult. *Letters to W. B. Yeats and Ezra Pound from Iseult Gonne*; Yeats, W. B. *Ah, Sweet Dancer: W. B. Yeats and Margot Ruddock, Explorations, John Sherman and Dhoya, Later Essays, The Variorum Edition of the Plays of W. B. Yeats, The Variorum Edition of the Poems of W. B. Yeats, A Vision, W. B. Yeats and T. Sturge Moore: Their Correspondence 1901–1937.*

"Certain Artists bring her Dolls and Drawings" (1917)

The second of seven poems in the sequence "UPON A DYING LADY," "Certain Artists bring her Dolls and Drawings," like "HER COURTESY," tells of visiting the dying Mabel Beardsley (1871–1916) in the hospital on January 5, 1913. Yeats mentioned the dolls in a January 8 report on his visit to Lady GREGORY: "On a table near were four dolls dressed like people out of her brother's drawings. Women with loose trousers and boys that looked like women. Ricketts had made them, modelling the faces and sewing the clothes. They must have taken him days" (*Letters* 574). Beardsley's brother, AUBREY BEARDSLEY, was the arch-decadent illustrator who gave much of the character to the notorious journals the *Yellow Book* and the SAVOY during the 1890s; Charles Ricketts (1866–1931), a distinguished painter and stage designer, was one of Yeats's closest friends.

The poem is an exercise in carefully controlled rhetoric. Yeats requests that friends bring dolls or drawings to Beardsley's sickbed, but the magniloquent and commanding flourish of the opening line ("Bring where our Beauty lies") is immediately deflated by the broken rhythm of the second line, and further deflated by the warren of false starts and qualifications that follow ("or" four times, "maybe," "it may be"), lending the poem the air of a brave face that could not be sustained. The drawings might show "a friend's or an enemy's features," subtly suggesting the temper of Yeats and his circle: they are the passionate kind for whom enemies are a matter of course. Alternately the drawings might show Beardsley in a "silken dress / Cut in the Turkish fashion," or with her hair cut "like a boy's," details that chime with the allusion to rouge in "Her Courtesy" and inscribe an element of elegy for the aesthetic heyday of the 1890s. In the final two lines of the poem, Yeats declares in a suddenly wakened voice, "We have given the world our passion, / We have naught for death but toys." These lines might be read as defiant and dismissive, but more plausibly they are explanatory and apologetic. Having engaged so vigorously with life, Yeats and his circle have left nothing in reserve for the challenge of death. Their dolls and drawings and poems are mere toys, without the power to challenge or transcend (hence the deflation triggered in the poem's second line). Yeats's later work would be increasingly audacious in its attempt to respond to the ineluctability of death, to devise a means of resistance more concerted than the "toys" he mentions here. "DEATH," a commanding dismissal of death outright, is an obvious case in point.

FIRST PUBLICATION: The *Little Review* (periodical), August 1917, and the *New Statesman* (periodical), August 11, 1917. Reprinted in *The Wild Swans at Coole*, The CUALA PRESS, Churchtown, Dundrum, November 17, 1917.

BIBLIOGRAPHY

Yeats, W. B. *The Letters of W. B. Yeats.*

"Chambermaid's First Song, The" (1938)

See "The THREE BUSHES."

"Chambermaid's Second Song, The" (1938)

See "The THREE BUSHES."

"Choice, The" (1932)

"The Choice" first appeared as the penultimate stanza of "COOLE AND BALLYLEE, 1931" (then titled "Coole Park and Ballylee 1932"), but its ironies were unsuited to a poem of homage and twilit elegy, and Yeats published the stanza as a free-standing poem in *The Winding Stair and Other Poems* (1933). It presents starkly the opposition between life and art that had dominated Yeats's imagination from early in his career, a preoccupation traceable to the enormous boyhood influence of SHELLEY's "Alastor" (1816) (see *Aut.* 80). With esoteric or visionary propensities sometimes standing in for the artistic propensity, versions of the "choice" play out in youthful poems like "FERGUS AND THE DRUID," "TO THE ROSE UPON THE ROOD OF TIME," and "The WANDERINGS OF OISIN"; in plays like AT THE HAWK'S WELL ("I choose a pleasant life / Among indolent meadows; / Wisdom must live a bitter life"), The LAND OF HEART'S DESIRE, and The SHADOWY WATERS; in later masterpieces like "ALL SOULS' NIGHT" and "A DIALOGUE OF SELF AND SOUL"; and in the mythologization of the "tragic generation" in AUTOBIOGRAPHIES and "The GREY ROCK." To choose "perfection of the work" over "perfection of the life" is to embrace an impossible *antithetical* aspiration that leads to alienation from the natural and social worlds. Thus Fergus unlooses the Druid's bag of dreams and finds himself tangled in a web of sorrows; thus MACGREGOR MATHERS, as Yeats writes in "All Souls' Night," wound up crazed with loneliness, for "meditations upon unknown thought / Make human intercourse grow less and less; / They are neither paid nor praised"; thus Yeats himself felt the occasional stab of bitter regret, and could exclaim late in life, "Writing poisoned my youth! I could have been a happier man if I had stopped writing" (*I&R*, II, 201).

In "The Choice," the precise nature of this alienation is ambiguous. Refusal of the "heavenly mansion" suggests moral or religious damnation, while "raging in the dark" suggests the bitterness of solitude and failure (cf. "TO A FRIEND WHOSE WORK HAS COME TO NOTHING"). Sardonically aping the jaunty idioms and social curiosity that belong to the realm of life ("what's the news?"), Yeats recapitulates the grievances of those who renounce life. There is the "old perplexity" of the "empty purse" (cf. "The Grey Rock," lines 55–56); or it may be, reading this line differently, that the "old perplexity"—that which Fergus experiences upon loosening the Druid's bag of dreams or something like it—*results* in the "empty purse." So too the "day's vanity"—the conviction of achievement while in the throes of creation—dissipates in the "night's remorse." "Remorse," as Harold Bloom notes, is for Yeats, following BLAKE and Shelley, the "ultimate antagonist of the imagination" (*Yeats* 307). Only when we have cast out remorse, according to "A Dialogue of Self and Soul," do we experience the sweetness that allows us to laugh and, more significant from the perspective of the poet, to sing (on remorse, see also "The MUNICIPAL GALLERY REVISITED," "REMORSE FOR INTEMPERATE SPEECH," and "VACILLATION").

In the endless vacillation of Yeats's poetry, "The Choice" is counterweight to the preceding poem, "AT ALGECIRAS—A MEDITATION UPON DEATH," in which *antithetical* aspiration finds its image not in the "remorse" of the night but in the "rich midnight of the garden trees."

FIRST PUBLICATION: *Words for Music Perhaps and Other Poems*, The CUALA PRESS, Dublin, November 14, 1932, as the sixth stanza of "Coole Park and Ballylee 1932." Reprinted in *The Winding Stair and Other Poems*, Macmillan, London, September 19, 1933.

BIBLIOGRAPHY

Bloom, Harold. *Yeats*; Mikhail, E. H., ed. *W. B. Yeats: Interviews and Recollections* (vol. 2); Yeats, W. B. *Autobiographies.*

"Chosen" (1929)

See "A Woman Young and Old."

"Circus Animals' Desertion, The" (1939)

Yeats always believed that approaching death is foremost an invitation to self-summary and self-declaration, and his later poetry seeks concertedly for an epitaph that would express what he had been. "The Tower," superb as it is, arrived many years too early; "Under Ben Bulben" somewhat rambles and blusters, though it comes to a magnificent close; "Politics," which ends the collected poems, is charmingly humane but slight. Of the many poems that have the air of self-commemoration, "The Circus Animals' Desertion" seems most satisfactory and complete as a final statement. Despite its rhetoric of divestiture and disavowal, it is perfectly consistent with and beautifully states what had always been Yeats's most basic commitment to the "foul rag-and-bone shop of the heart." Oisin, Cathleen, and Cuchulain may have been masks, but even in the game of masks Yeats rehearsed the return to the place "where all the ladders start." Oisin's decision to return to Ireland after three centuries among the fairy isles was precisely such a return. "The Circus Animals' Desertion," indeed, merely restates the essential understanding "The Coming of Wisdom with Time," which Yeats wrote in 1909 (YC 128). "Reconciliation," written in 1908, similarly plays with the idea of divesting everything factitious, as does "Lines Written in Dejection," though in a mood of bereavement that represents Yeats at his least confident in his own deepest resources (121). There is a stirring of "The Circus Animals' Desertion" even in "To the Rose upon the Rood of Time," for what are worm and mouse and "heavy mortal hopes that toil and pass" except the root matter that "The Circus Animals' Desertion" would later charge with the provocative imagery of the shop and the slum? In this light, "The Circus Animals' Desertion" offers yet another mask—the mask of a new commitment to the heart about which there is very little that is new.

The first section of the poem, like the opening passages of "The Tower" and "Sailing to Byzantium," finds Yeats nursing the wound of age. He attempts to muster his "circus animals"—the spectacle of his many masks—but he can no longer command his accustomed resources and must be satisfied with the last resort that is the heart. This deprecation of the heart sets up a reversal of sentiment in the poem's final section, but not an exuberant reversal: the poem takes seriously the grimness of the self-reckoning by which we make an honest end.

"What can I but enumerate old themes?" Yeats asks at the start of the second section. The implication is that Yeats can do no better than recycle the themes of his early career. He possibly alludes to his ongoing work on the play The Death of Cuchulain, which he finished in his last weeks of life, ending a cycle of six plays on the legendary hero that he had begun in 1901 (Letters 921). Alternately, taking "old" to mean ancient or traditional rather than familiar or accustomed, the question implies that he can do no better than recycle the kind of folk themes that Oisin, Cathleen, and Cuchulain represent. On either reading, the question suggests that Yeats has become trapped in the habits of his own imagination, which themselves began in the insincere impulses of his youth. As "The Circus Animals' Desertion" has it, "The Wanderings of Oisin," begun in October 1886, was an elaborate pretense animated by the romantic or sexual longing of his young manhood (YC 8). The three islands of the boyhood poem were "vain" as symbols of an unrealizable desire for the infinite, as Yeats explained in an 1889 letter to Katharine Tynan: "There are three incompatable [sic] things which man is always seeking—infinite feeling, infinite battle, infinite repose—hence the three islands" (CL1 141).

The Countess Cathleen, begun in February 1889, was Yeats's first mature play (138, 142). It represents a "counter-truth" to "The Wanderings of Oisin," as it renounces rather than embraces the world. As Harold Bloom puts it, "the poem chooses what Yeats will later call Self over Soul, Oisin over Patrick, while the play chooses the countess over her poet-lover, responsibility over the dream, Soul or character over Self or personality" (*Yeats* 118). And yet the play was likewise a pretense: a projection of Yeats's romantic anxieties and a rationalization of his romantic frustration. Begun soon after Yeats and MAUD GONNE met in January 1889 (*Mem.* 41, 46–47), the play softens and sanctifies Gonne's self-sacrificial intensity, and this "dream"—the vision of the play—became a refuge from the more difficult and complicated reality of Gonne's personality.

The section's third stanza refers to ON BAILE'S STRAND (begun July 1901), the first of Yeats's plays on the subject of Cuchulain (*CL3* 88). The tale of Cuchulain, the Fool, and the Blind Man contained "Heart-mysteries" enough—difficult realities—but Yeats was again enchanted by the "dream" of the play: its vision of heroic intensity ("Character isolated by a deed") in which he could escape his own futile longings and the complexity of his own experience. "Players and painted stage took all my love," Yeats admits, "And not those things that they were emblems of."

"Whatever flames upon the night / Man's own resinous heart has fed," Yeats writes in "TWO SONGS FROM A PLAY," and "The Circus Animals' Desertion" shares this understanding. Oisin, Cathleen, and Cuchulain began in the heart, but tricked up its raw elements. These elements find their legitimate metaphor not in the frippery of the circus, but in the rough and elemental reality of urban refuse: kettle, bottle, can, iron, bone, rag, "that raving slut / Who keeps the till" ("raving" remembers "pity-crazed": the countess has her elemental image in the slut). His imagination failing in the end—departing the body almost as the soul does—Yeats can only "lie down where all the ladders start, / In the foul rag-and-bone shop of the heart." Gesturing toward the grave, these lines inscribe the same reluctant renunciation ("must") apparent in "Lines Written in Dejection" and connoted by "wither" in "The Coming of Wisdom with Time," but in this instance there is immense stoic dignity as Yeats accepts that he has come at last to what he calls in "MERU" the "desolation of reality." Bloom is incisive: "In 'VACILLATION' Yeats allows the heart the poetic honor of taking up the Self's

struggle against the soul, of making the claim for personality against character. 'The Circus Animals' Desertion' is something of a palinode in relation to 'Vacillation,' in that Yeats chooses the heart again, but without affection or respect for it. To be satisfied with one's heart as a poetic theme is to acknowledge what it pained Yeats to recognize, that his concern was not with the content of his poetic vision, as BLAKE's was, but with his relation as poet to his own vision, as WORDSWORTH's was, and SHELLEY's and Keats's also" (*Yeats* 457).

FIRST PUBLICATION: The *Atlantic Monthly* and the *London Mercury* (periodicals), January 1939. Reprinted in *Last Poems and Two Plays*, The CUALA PRESS, Dublin, July 10, 1939.

BIBLIOGRAPHY

Bloom, Harold. *Yeats*; Kelly, John S. A *W. B. Yeats Chronology*; Yeats, W. B. *The Collected Letters of W. B. Yeats* (vols. 1, 3), *The Letters of W. B. Yeats*, *Memoirs*.

"Closing Rhymes" to *Responsibilities* (1914)

Yeats opens *Responsibilities* (1914) on a note of apology (see "INTRODUCTORY RHYMES") and ends it on a note of mingled complaint and defiant solidarity with his own kind. From the "reed-throated whisperer"—ambiguously bird, spirit, and inward muse—Yeats surmises the existence of companions "beyond the fling of the dull ass's hoof." In John Unterecker's plausible interpretation, these companions are of the spirit world, "precisely those companions, those 'Old Fathers' he had invoked in the opening poem and the members of the Rhymers' Club he had invoked in 'The Grey Rock'" (*RG* 129). Such companions have their complement in the earthly realm. When summer arrives at Kyle-na-no (one of the "seven woods" of COOLE PARK), Yeats finds under the "ancient roof" of Lady GREGORY's manor house a "sterner conscience and a friendlier home." Girded by companions of his own high mettle, he can forgive the "wrong of wrongs": the "undreamt accidents" that have brought not

fame, a thing perished from the world, but notoriety, until all his "priceless things / Are but a post
the passing dogs defile."

As he acknowledges in line 6, Yeats borrows the
phrase "dull ass's hoof" from Ben Jonson (1572–
1637). The phrase appears in the epilogue to *The
Poetaster* (produced 1601): "There's something come
into my thought, / That must, and shall be sung, high,
and aloofe, / Safe from the wolves black jaw, and the
dull asses hoof." In "Pages from a Diary Written in
Nineteen Hundred and Thirty," Yeats attributes the
image of dogs defiling a post to Erasmus (*Expl.* 330).

Both "Introductory Rhymes" and "Closing
Rhymes" are meant as blows in Yeats's feud with
GEORGE MOORE, who had published an irreverent
account of the Irish Renaissance in the January and
February 1914 issues of the *English Review* and later
included this material in his memoir *Vale* (1914).
MAUD GONNE may have germinated the conceit of
the poem. In a January 1914 letter, having gotten
wind of Moore's article but not yet having read it,
Gonne wrote to Yeats that if she found herself "personally insulted" she would "dog whip" the author
(GY 334). Later in the month she wrote to Yeats,
who had apparently mentioned "Closing Rhymes"
in a letter of his own, "I am afraid [Moore's indis-
cretion] has given you a great deal of worry &
annoyance but if it has made you write a fine poem
that is some consolation. It is generally out of the
hard things in life that the best comes" (335).

FIRST PUBLICATION: The *New Statesman*
(periodical), February 7, 1914, under the title
"Notoriety." Reprinted in *Responsibilities: Poems and
a Play*, The CUALA PRESS, Churchtown, Dundrum,
May 25, 1914, without title.

BIBLIOGRAPHY

Unterecker, John. *A Reader's Guide to William Butler
Yeats*; W. B. Yeats, *Explorations*, *The Gonne-Yeats
Letters 1893–1938*.

(1910), "A Coat" complains of literary depreda-
tors. Yeats has made his song a coat covered with
"embroideries / Out of old mythologies / From heels
to throat," but the coat has been appropriated by
others who wear it as if it were their own. No matter, Yeats concludes, for "there's more enterprise /
In walking naked." A. Norman Jeffares speculates
that "A Coat," like "To a Poet," is directed against
the younger protégés of GEORGE RUSSELL (AE), and
specifically against Seumas O'Sullivan (1879–1958)
(*NCP* 127). Some of the rancor underlying these
poems is explained by the schisms of the ABBEY THE-
ATRE. Russell hints at these circumstances in a 1909
letter to JOHN QUINN: "W.B.Y. has made a great
many enemies among the younger writers in Dublin
and there are many, all members of the rival theatre
[the Theatre of Ireland] Seamus O'Sullivan, Colvin,
Stephens, Keohler & others. These are all friends of
mine and every Sunday evening they come to see
me. I know they feel bitterly to W.B.Y. but for this
I am not responsible" (AM 404; see also *Aut.* 331;
CL3 576–578; *CL4* 488; *Mem.* 222–223). Russell
was himself largely estranged from Yeats during the
years 1905–13, again as a result of theater quarrels.
Yeats's impulse to divest himself of the merely factitious recurs intermittently throughout his poetry. In
this respect "A Coat" bears comparison with "The
CIRCUS ANIMALS' DESERTION," "The COMING OF
WISDOM WITH TIME," and "RECONCILIATION."

FIRST PUBLICATION: *Poetry* (periodical),
May 1914. Reprinted in *Responsibilities: Poems and
a Play*, The CUALA PRESS, Churchtown, Dundrum,
May 25, 1914.

BIBLIOGRAPHY

Foster, R. F. *W. B. Yeats: A Life, I: The Apprentice
Mage*; Jeffares, A. Norman. *A New Commentary
on the Poems of W. B. Yeats*; Yeats, W. B. *Autobiographies, The Collected Letters of W. B. Yeats* (vols.
3–4), *Memoirs*.

"Coat, A" (1914)

Like "TO A POET, WHO WOULD HAVE ME PRAISE
CERTAIN BAD POETS, IMITATORS OF HIS AND MINE"

"Cold Heaven, The" (1912)

"The Cold Heaven" is perhaps the best wrought
poem of Yeats's middle period (the period marked

by *The Green Helmet and Other Poems* and *Responsibilities*) and one of the consummate achievements of Yeats's entire career. It is a tour de force in its reconciliation of spontaneous voice and metered verse; in its compression of emotion; in its discovery of a language so full of passionate gravity that it seems all but the natural language of existential petition. Even more than the run of Yeats's poems, "The Cold Heaven" resists paraphrase and reduction, due both to the perfection of its given form and to the idiosyncrasy of what seems to be its theology, and yet readers must attempt to translate its private mystery into some less glancing structure of idea.

The poem begins with a vision of the "cold and rook-delighting heaven," at once an image of the London sky in the drear of winter (the poem was written in late November 1912) and a revelation of the divine redoubt, in which ice seems to burn yet becomes "the more ice," betokening a passion unwed to the warmth of sentiment or the warmth of the body (YC 152). Yeats adverts to a similar conception of a transcendent cold in his essay "A General Introduction for my Work" (1937), writing that the heroines of Shakespeare, in the vision of their dying moments, become "God or Mother Goddess." In such moments the "supernatural is present, cold winds blow across our hands, upon our faces, the thermometer falls," and the actress must "be carried beyond feeling into the aboriginal ice" (E&I 523; LE 213–214). Yeats reiterates the longing for an intensity that reverses the organic in his hope for a poem as "cold and passionate as the dawn" ("The FISHERMAN") and in the snowbound settings of "LAPIS LAZULI" and "MERU." Amid the cold of the sky, the rooks are in their natural element, being *antithetical* spirits—wanton, indifferent, cruel, self-delighting, foreshadowing the reeling desert birds of "The SECOND COMING" (cf. VPl. 789).

Yeats's vision of the sky purges every "casual thought of that and this," everything out of keeping with the "aboriginal ice." Though the "hot blood of youth" has passed, Yeats is beset by lacerating memories of his failed love for MAUD GONNE. Taking "all the blame out of all sense and reason"—feeding with remorse the frenzy of

his heart—Yeats verges on some transcendental apotheosis. He cries, trembles, rocks to and fro, "riddled with light." What is this light? Perhaps an emanation of the world that opens at the far extremity of emotion—an intimation of heaven itself, but a heaven of withering judgment rather than sheltering comfort.

The poem ends with a haunted question, as do so many of Yeats's greatest poems, as for example "LEDA AND THE SWAN," "The Second Coming," and "The STATUES." Freed at last from "confusion of the death-bed," are our ghosts—our disincarnate souls—sent out "naked on the roads, as the books say, and stricken / By the injustice of the skies for punishment?" Yeats wants to know whether he has become a ghost or experienced that which ghosts experience: he seeks for a precedent in arcane lore by which to make sense of his own travail, as it were, upon the roads. The question implies that the moment of riddling light was a moment of death or was like a moment of death, and that Yeats, somehow unequal to the light, somehow unequal to the redemption of his own transcendental energy, finds himself in a kind of purgatory, a wanderer in a wasted realm that is a metaphor of his wasted love.

These lines long precede A VISION, but they seem anticipatory of it. *A Vision* theorizes two purgatorial modes: "In the *Dreaming Back*, the *Spirit* is compelled to live over and over again the events that had most moved it; there can be nothing new, but the old events stand forth in a light which is dim or bright according to the intensity of the passion that accompanied them. They occur in the order of their intensity or luminosity, the more intense first, and the painful are commonly the more intense, and repeat themselves again and again. In the *Return*, upon the other hand, the *Spirit* must live through past events in the order of their occurrence, because it is compelled by the *Celestial Body* to trace every passionate event to its cause until all are related and understood, turned into knowledge, made a part of itself" (226; see also AV-1925 226–227).

FIRST PUBLICATION: *The Green Helmet and Other Poems*, Macmillan, New York, London, October 23, 1912.

BIBLIOGRAPHY

Kelly, John S. *A W. B. Yeats Chronology*; Yeats, W. B. *A Critical Edition of Yeats's A Vision (1925), Essays and Introductions, Later Essays, A Variorum Edition of the Plays of W. B. Yeats, A Vision.*

"Coming of Wisdom with Time, The" (1910)

This four-line poem is one of Yeats's most straightforward and accessible in terms of language, and yet it is remarkably dense with ideas. The poem compresses to a pinhead what may be Yeats's most fundamental and pervasive conceptual understanding: that unity fragments into multiplicity and may be restored by a process of reaggregation or recuperation (see UNITY OF BEING). This, indeed, is Yeats's version of the fall—paradise lost and paradise regained. Over the course of his career Yeats applied this paradigm with equal readiness to history, metaphysics, and culture, and to the individual. In AUTOBIOGRAPHIES, he articulates this understanding in its historical dimension when he asks: "If Chaucer's personages had disengaged themselves from Chaucer's crowd, forgot their common goal and shrine, and after sundry magnifications became each in turn the centre of some Elizabethan play, and had after split into their elements and so given birth to romantic poetry, must I reverse the cinematograph?" (165–166). If Yeats can be said to have an overarching ambition it is to "reverse the cinematograph" in one sense or another.

"The Coming of Wisdom with Time" is a parable of the fall into multiplicity and the recuperation of unity in personal terms. The poem's opening line states the relation between the two conditions: "Though leaves are many, the root is one. . . ." The implication is that multiplicity, like the leaves, is a display of the merely evanescent and extrinsic, while unity, like the root, is permanent and fundamental, if obscure or hidden. Yeats elaborates this metaphorical scheme in the second and third lines—"Through all the lying days of my youth / I swayed my leaves and flowers in the sun. . . ."—and associates the leaves in their multiplicity with both youth and falsehood. Poems like "RECONCILIATION" and "The CIRCUS ANIMALS' DESERTION," in which Yeats derides his earlier work as gaudy spectacle only tenuously related to the truths of his heart, clarify the aspersion of "lying days." In the final line of the poem, Yeats declares his divestiture of everything factitious; having come into his maturity, he may now "wither into the truth." The verb "wither" subtly continues the pattern of metaphor, suggesting the withering of leaves in autumn and the return to the changeless unity of the root. It implies death but also the return to a deeper life.

The motif of divestiture recurs in "The COAT," and less obviously in "ALL THINGS CAN TEMPT ME" and "Reconciliation," while the leaf-root metaphor reemerges in the indelible final lines of "AMONG SCHOOL CHILDREN." In opposition to "The Coming of Wisdom with Time," however, "Among School Children" refuses to privilege the root over its leaves, and instead seeks reconciliation between the self and its outward forms.

FIRST PUBLICATION: *McClure's Magazine* (periodical), December 1910, under the title "Youth and Age." Reprinted in *The Green Helmet and Other Poems*, The CUALA PRESS, Churchtown, Dundrum, December 1910, under the sequence title "Momentary Thoughts" and the present title.

BIBLIOGRAPHY

Yeats, W. B. *Autobiographies.*

"Conjunctions" (1934)

See "SUPERNATURAL SONGS."

"Consolation" (1929)

See "A WOMAN YOUNG AND OLD."

"Coole and Ballylee, 1931" (1932)

The second of Yeats's homages to Lady GREGORY and COOLE PARK, "Coole and Ballylee, 1931" exceeds its predecessor "Coole Park, 1929," as Yeats himself thought (*Letters* 805–806). Where the first poem elegizes the great house and its mistress, the second poem swells into elegy for everything house and mistress stood for, and darkens, finally, into a vision of the tragedy of history itself. The gyres of history are not mentioned, but they turn beneath the poem's final, poignant stanza. In its ideal of permanence of place and "traditional sanctity and loveliness" the poem is cognate with "A PRAYER FOR MY DAUGHTER," but in its conviction that "all is changed" it belongs among "BLOOD AND THE MOON," "The NINETEENTH CENTURY AND AFTER," "The SEVEN SAGES," "Spilt Milk" (1932), and "THREE MOVEMENTS," though it surpasses in feeling and summarizing power all of these dark diagnoses of modernity. In a BBC radio broadcast of October 29, 1937, Yeats introduced the poem in his own terms: "From my twenty-seventh year until a few years ago all my public activities were associated with a famous country house in County Galway. In that house my dear friend, that woman of genius, Lady Gregory, gathered from time to time all men of talent, all profound men, in the intellectual life of modern Ireland. I have a house three or four miles from where her gate was, a mediaeval tower whose winding stair I am too old to climb. The river that passed my window sank into the earth in a round pool which the blind, or dark, poet Raftery called a cellar, then rose again and fell into a lake in Lady Gregory's park. The poem I am about to read was written shortly before Lady Gregory's death. It is typical of most of my recent poems, intricate in metaphor, the swan and water both emblems of the soul, not at all a dream, like my earlier poems, but a criticism of life" (*W. B. Yeats & Georgian Ireland* 327).

Ensconced at THOOR BALLYLEE, Yeats listens to the rushing of the stream beneath his window and in imagination follows its course as it runs for a mile, dips underground, rises in a "rocky place," and empties into the lake at Coole. "What's water but the generated soul?" Yeats asks, probably remembering Porphyry's (232/4–ca. 305) theory that "all souls come to be born because of water, and that 'even the generation of images in the mind is from water'" (*Myth.* 80), but perhaps also struck by the allegorical implications of the stream as it runs, submerges, spreads, and drops, just as man passes through youth, crisis, maturity, and death. Raftery is the Gaelic poet Anthony Raftery (1779–1835); as Yeats indicates in his radio comment, the epithet "dark" alludes to his blindness. Raftery likewise figures in "The TOWER" (associated with Homer, another sightless troubadour) and in much prose. "Dust hath closed Helen's Eye," an 1899 account of local lore, clarifies the allusion to Raftery's "cellar." Yeats quotes Raftery's verse—"And she said, 'Drink, Raftery, and a hundred welcomes, / There is a strong cellar in Ballylee"—and tells of meeting an old man who explained that "the strong cellar was the great hole where the river sunk underground" (*Myth.* 23).

The lake carries Yeats's thought to the surrounding wood, where he remembers standing amid dry sticks under a "wintry sun." Mirroring Yeats's mood, nature had "pulled her tragic buskin on"—a reference, as *The Oxford English Dictionary* tells us, to the "high thick-soled boot (*cothurnus*) worn by the actors in ancient Athenian tragedy" and "frequently contrasted with the 'sock' (*soccus*), or low shoe worn by comedians." To "put on the buskins," then, is to "assume a tragic style." The moment is full of passionate contradiction: even as woods and sun betoken death, the reaches of the lake are "glittering," a word that consistently carries transcendental implications in Yeats (see "ANCESTRAL HOUSES," "Blood and the Moon," "DEMON AND BEAST," "LAPIS LAZULI," and "VACILLATION"), while the flood, like the brimming cup in "ALL SOULS' NIGHT," suggests fullness, welling energy, pregnancy. As in "The WILD SWANS AT COOLE" and the third section of "NINETEEN HUNDRED AND NINETEEN," a swan suddenly takes flight. "Another emblem there!" Yeats cries, reminding that everything in the poem is emblematic, that the world itself, or everything that matters in the world, is a congeries of emblems whose source is the ANIMA MUNDI; or perhaps merely poking fun at his own relentless impulse to poeticize, even as the world wanes (cf. the reference to "the symbolic rose" in "MY HOUSE"). In this instance, the swan, as Yeats himself noted, symbolizes inspiration, but an inspiration both fleeting and susceptible (*W. B. Yeats* 429). The murderous "spot of ink" has its clue in a 1902 contribution to *Samhain*. Yeats asks, "Did not M. Tribulat Bonhomet discover that one spot of ink would kill a swan?" (*Expl.* 90; *IDM* 15). The allusion, as T. R. Henn explains, is to Villiers de l'Isle-Adam's novel *M. Triboulat Bonhomet* (1887); it may be, as Henn implies, that the "ink" signifies the writing process (*Lonely Tower* 138).

Yeats comes at last to the house where he had been a guest for more than 30 years. Much reduced by the breast cancer for which she first underwent surgery in 1923, Lady Gregory is the "last inheritor" (cf. "MY TABLE") who hobbles from chair to chair with the aid of a stick (parallel to the "dry sticks" of the wood: she too has come to the desiccation of winter). The two stanzas devoted to Coole compress the account given in AUTOBIOGRAPHIES ("Dramatis Personae," III). Here is the "inherited glory of the rich," in the phrase of "Ancestral Houses"—books, pictures, rooms, trees, and gardens, all bound by the traditions of the family and sustained over generations by clear eyes and firm hands ("alliances" says as much). Modernity, in contrast, knows nothing of the strength by which traditions are held together and made to endure ("We shift about—all that great glory spent—/ Like some poor Arab tribesman and his tent"). The emphasis on permanency of place—notable in both the first and last lines of the fifth stanza—is recurrent in Yeats (cf. "IN MEMORY OF ALFRED POLLEXFEN," "A Prayer for my Daughter," "UNDER SATURN"), not least because Yeats himself was so painfully rootless, an itinerant whose life was spent, the experiment at Thoor Ballylee excepted, in a succession of rented domiciles ("The LAKE ISLE OF INNISFREE" gives Yeats's sense of exile from his native SLIGO).

If the "we" of the penultimate stanza encompasses modern man in his impoverishment, the "we" of the ultimate stanza refers to the partnership of Yeats and Lady Gregory, and perhaps also of those who gathered about them and contributed

to their enterprise. "Coole Park, 1929" specifically mentions Douglas Hyde (1860–1949), J. M. SYNGE, John Shawe-Taylor (1866–1911), and HUGH LANE as sharers in the heyday of Coole. "We were the last romantics—chose for theme / Traditional sanctity and loveliness; / Whatever's written in what poets name / The book of the people" writes Yeats, in what may be his most clarion statement of purpose. The romantic tradition coming to an end may be that of the high romantic poets, chiefly BLAKE and SHELLEY, who dominated Yeats's youthful imagination, but more likely, as suggested by the combined resonance of tradition, sanctity, loveliness, and rootedness, he means the tradition that he had come to identify with the Irish Georgians lionized in "Blood and the Moon" and "The Seven Sages," and that he had epitomized in the former poem: "The strength that gives our blood and state magnanimity of its own desire; / Everything that is not God consumed with intellectual fire." The emphasis on the "book of the people" reiterates the understanding of "The Seven Sages" and looks forward to the understanding of "THE MUNICIPAL GALLERY REVISITED" that strength comes from "contact with the soil." The phrase "book of the people" fittingly comes from Raftery. In his essay "Literature and the Living Voice" (1906), Yeats writes that the "minstrel never dramatised anybody but himself. It was impossible, from the nature of the words the poet had put into his mouth, or that he had made for himself, that he should speak as another person. He will go no nearer to drama than we do in daily speech, and he will not allow you for any long time to forget himself. Our own Raftery will stop the tale to cry, 'This is what I, Raftery, wrote down in the book of the people'; or, 'I, myself, Raftery, went to bed without supper that night'" (*Expl.* 214–215; see also *AV* 170).

"But all is changed," Yeats continues, "that high horse riderless, / Though mounted in that saddle Homer rode / Where the swan drifts upon a darkening flood." As in "AT GALWAY RACES," "IN MEMORY OF MAJOR ROBERT GREGORY," and "UNDER BEN BULBEN," the horseman symbolizes the combination of passion, strength, and ceremony that Yeats attributes to the tradition that he and Lady Gregory bring to an end. That the horse is "mounted in that saddle Homer rode" suggests the idiosyncrasy of the word "romantic," for, as now becomes clear, Yeats has in mind nothing less than the "great song" ("The Nineteenth Century and After") of Western civilization itself, which is "romantic" only in the general sense that its essence is passionate and questing. The saddle, however, is empty: Homeric strength has given way. In a revision of the third stanza, the swan drifts upon "a darkening flood"— the swan a vision of twilit grace, an image of Coole and its traditions, of the West and its traditions, the flood a version of the "blood-dimmed tide" that signals the apocalypse in "The SECOND COMING." In an interview published in 1931, Yeats explained the historical conception that informs the poem's final stanza. "We are in our Hellenistic Age," Yeats told his interlocutor. "I think we have seen the best of European literature. We may have a Virgil ahead of us, but certainly not a Homer. The romantic age is over—and by romantic I mean the expression of personality and passion" (*I&R*, II, 200).

FIRST PUBLICATION: *Words for Music Perhaps and Other Poems*, The CUALA PRESS, Dublin, November 14, 1932, under the title "Coole Park and Ballylee 1932." Reprinted in *The Winding Stair and Other Poems*, Macmillan, London, September 19, 1933, under the title "Coole and Ballylee, 1931." Reprinted in *The Collected Poems of W. B. Yeats*, Macmillan, London, July 4, 1950, under the title "Coole Park and Ballylee, 1931" (the latter title is sometimes retained).

BIBLIOGRAPHY

Henn, T. R. *The Lonely Tower: Studies in the Poetry of W. B. Yeats*; Hone, Joseph. *W. B. Yeats*; Mikhail, E. H., ed. *W. B. Yeats: Interviews and Recollections* (vol. 2); Torchiana, Donald T. *W. B. Yeats & Georgian Ireland*; Yeats, W. B. *Autobiographies, Explorations, The Irish Dramatic Movement, The Letters of W. B. Yeats, Mythologies, A Vision.*

"Coole Park, 1929" (1931)

By 1929, both Lady GREGORY and her great manor house, COOLE PARK, were in their waning days.

Given as he was to premature elegy (see "The NEW FACES"), Yeats paid homage to the woman and to the house that had set him such a long and valuable example of "steadfast nobility" with a brace of handsome, bittersweet poems: "Coole Park, 1929" and "COOLE AND BALLYLEE, 1931" (*Mem.* 161). Yeats told OLIVIA SHAKESPEAR that he preferred the latter, but the former wound up with pride of place, first appearing as a preface to Lady Gregory's memoir *Coole*, published in 1931 by the CUALA PRESS (*Letters* 805–806).

A "swallow's flight," like the flight of the 59 swans in "The WILD SWANS AT COOLE," initiates a meditation on time and its bereavements. The hour is sunset, as in "The TOWER" and "Coole and Ballylee, 1931." Sycamore and lime-tree are wrapped in shade, though the "western cloud is luminous," signifying a splendor even in decline. Prompted by the hour of elegy, Yeats remembers the scholars and poets who gathered at Coole and "constructed there in nature's spite / For scholars and for poets after us, / Thoughts long knitted into a single thought, / A dance-like glory that those walls begot." The knitting of thought into a single thought and the ensuing "dance-like glory" (cf. "AMONG SCHOOL CHILDREN," "The DOUBLE VISION OF MICHAEL ROBARTES") intimate a flickering of the UNITY OF BEING that was for Yeats the highest of all dispensations.

The heyday of Coole comes back to Yeats in memories of those who gathered there: Douglas Hyde (1860–1949), J. M. SYNGE, John Shawe-Taylor (1866–1911), and HUGH LANE. Shawe-Taylor and Lane, Lady Gregory's nephews, were both casualties of World War I. Yeats remembers the former, a soldier and landowner, in a memorial essay of 1911 (*E&I* 343–345; see also *W. B. Yeats & Georgian Ireland* 44–57), and he elaborates on their impetuosity in a comment recorded by Lady Gregory: "[John's] action came from a power of calculation too rapid for the intellect to follow, like Hugh's in deciding on the authenticity of a picture. I, too, have occasionally had intuitions that surprised me afterwards by their wisdom, but had I been one of your nephews I would have acted upon them" (*Sir Hugh Lane* 67). The "one that ruffled in a manly pose / For all his timid heart" is Yeats himself, as he makes clear in AUTOBIOGRAPHIES: "A writer must die every day he lives, be reborn, as it is said in the Burial Service, an incorruptible self, that self opposite of all that he has named 'himself'. GEORGE MOORE, dreading the annihilation of an impersonal bleak realism, used life like a mediaeval ghost making a body for itself out of drifting dust and vapour; and have I not sung in describing guests at Coole—'There one that ruffled in a manly pose, For all his timid heart'—that one myself?" (336; see also *Between the Lines* 185–189).

If the poets and scholars came and went like the swallows, they were held in formation—a metaphorical variation on the knitting of thoughts "into a single thought"—by the character and will of Lady Gregory. As Harold Bloom observes, these lines reverse the opening image of "The SECOND COMING": the falcon *can* hear the falconer (*Yeats* 381). Whirling "upon a compass-point"—Lady Gregory herself, as John Stallworthy has it—they found "certainty upon the dreaming air, / The intellectual sweetness of those lines / That cut through time or cross it withershins" (*Between the Lines* 198). "Lines" refers to the geometry of the swallows in formation, as well as to the poetry that Yeats and others wrote at Coole ("passages" extends the pun). "Withershins," according to *The Oxford English Dictionary*, describes movement "in an anticlockwise direction" or "contrary to the apparent course of the sun (considered as unlucky or sinister)." Lady Gregory, then, presided over no mere country house idyll, but over a campaign, not unsuccesfully waged, against both nature ("in nature's spite") and time (cf. "The New Faces"). And yet, in the principal irony of the poem, the triumphs of Coole came like everything else to dispersal and ruin—Synge, Shawe-Taylor, and Lane dead prematurely; Lady Gregory grown old and infirm; Coole Park sold to the Ministry of Lands and Agriculture in April 1927. The transcendental moment, the poem wants to say, is eternal but not permanent. Its perfection is immutable, but its worldly scaffold is momentary like the coalescence of the swallows. As BLAKE wrote in an apothegm that Yeats liked to repeat, "The ruins of time build mansions in eternity" (*P&I* 88, 121; *UP2* 193).

The poem's final stanza is formally elegiac. Yeats begs traveler, scholar, and poet to halt amid the ruins of Coole and "dedicate—eyes bent upon the ground, / Back turned upon the brightness of the sun / And all the sensuality of the shade—/ A moment's memory to that laurelled head." An idiom of defiance or defense, "take your stand" suggests that Coole is to provide a rallying memory of "intellectual sweetness" in an age that has come to ruin like Coole itself ("Half dead at the top," as Yeats writes in "BLOOD AND THE MOON"), while the saplings rooting among the broken stone hint at the promise of rebirth. The allusion to sun and shade is the poem's most difficult detail. If sun and shade—or day and night, in the scheme of "A DIALOGUE OF SELF AND SOUL"—represent the fundamental antinomy in reality's war with itself, turning the back upon both is perhaps a gesture of homage to the transcendence of such antinomies—"the single thought"—once known at Coole. In John Unterecker's interpretation, the final stanza visualizes the ghosts of Lane, Shawe-Taylor, Hyde, Synge, and Yeats himself regathered to honor Lady Gregory; in this case, they turn their back upon both sun and shade as emblems of the reality that is no longer their own (*RG* 211). In draft, however, Yeats writes, "Here student, unknown traveller take your stand," which suggests that he did not have in mind the ghosts of Coole's heyday (*Between the Lines* 192, 195).

FIRST PUBLICATION: Lady Gregory, *Coole*, The CUALA PRESS, Dublin, 1931. Reprinted in *Words and Music Perhaps and Other Poems*, The Cuala Press, Dublin, November 14, 1932.

BIBLIOGRAPHY

Bloom, Harold. *Yeats*; Gregory, Lady. *Sir Hugh Lane: His Life and Legacy*; Stallworthy, John. *Between the Lines: Yeats's Poetry in the Making*; Torchiana, Donald T. *W. B. Yeats & Georgian Ireland*; Unterecker, John. *A Reader's Guide to William Butler Yeats*; Yeats, W. B. *Autobiographies, Essays and Introductions, The Letters of W. B. Yeats, Memoirs, Prefaces and Introductions, Uncollected Prose by W. B. Yeats* (vol. 2).

"Crazed Girl, A" (1937)

"A Crazed Girl" and its companion piece "Sweet Dancer" (1938) commemorate Yeats's brief but eventful fling with MARGOT RUDDOCK. Yeats met the 27-year-old Ruddock in October 1934 and immediately assumed the role of aesthetic mentor. The two maintained an artistic and romantic dalliance until the mentally unstable Ruddock was permanently institutionalized in late 1937.

Both poems revive the image of the dancing girl on the beach that Yeats had inaugurated years earlier in "TO A CHILD DANCING IN THE WIND," having been inspired by the sight of ISEULT GONNE dancing on the beach at Normandy (see *AV* 219–220). The image returned to Yeats after Ruddock gave an account of herself similarly dancing on the shore in the midst of her first nervous breakdown. As the story goes, Ruddock arrived unexpectedly in Majorca in May 1936, where Yeats was convalescing and translating the *Upanishads* with the Indian guru Shree Purohit Swami (1882–1941). Ruddock's account of her breakdown, included in her 1937 volume of poems *The Lemon Tree*, gives the essential background to both "A Crazed Girl" and "Sweet Dancer": "[. . .] I told Yeats that if I could not write a poem that would live I must die. He went through my poems but said I must work at each until it was perfect. I said, 'How can I made [sic] them perfect? I am too strong to die, too weak to live'. Then I thought that if I died my poems would live in my stead." While Yeats read her poems, Ruddock slipped outside unobserved. She continues, "I went slowly down to the shore through the rain; I thought, 'if I am to die something will help me', I stood on the rocks and could not go into the sea because there was so much in life I loved, then I was so happy at not having to die I danced" (*Sweet Dancer* 93). The next evening Ruddock departed for Barcelona where she tried to escape from a room in which she had been locked by well-meaning friends. She fell from a window and crashed through the roof of a barber's shop, breaking her knee. The next day she fled from the clinic where her knee had been treated and, hoping to return to Majorca, hid in the hold of boat (*Sweet Dancer* 96–97). Yeats gives a similar account of Ruddock's odyssey in a May 1936 letter to OLIVIA SHAKESPEAR and in his introduction to *The Lemon Tree* (*Letters* 856; *P&I* 186–190).

"A Crazed Girl," "Sweet Dancer," and "To a Child Dancing in the Wind" share the image of the dancer with more obviously major poems like "AMONG SCHOOL CHILDREN" and "The DOUBLE VISION OF MICHAEL ROBARTES." In all of these poems, the dancer signifies a centripetal unity of the self and an ecstasy that transcends body and mind. Embodying if only momentarily the spirit of the dancer, Ruddock belongs, as "A Crazed Girl" deliberately states, among the Olympians whom Yeats celebrates in the immediately preceding "BEAUTIFUL LOFTY THINGS."

FIRST PUBLICATION: Margot Ruddock, *The Lemon Tree*, J. M. Dent & Sons, London, May 1937, under the title "At Barcelona." Reprinted in *New Poems*, The CUALA PRESS, Dublin, May 18, 1938, under the present title.

BIBLIOGRAPHY

Yeats, W. B. *Ah, Sweet Dancer: W. B. Yeats and Margot Ruddock, The Letters of W. B. Yeats, Prefaces and Introductions, A Vision.*

"Crazy Jane and Jack the Journeyman" (1932)

See "WORDS FOR MUSIC PERHAPS."

"Crazy Jane and the Bishop" (1930)

See "WORDS FOR MUSIC PERHAPS."

"Crazy Jane grown Old looks at the Dancers" (1930)

See "WORDS FOR MUSIC PERHAPS."

"Crazy Jane on God" (1932)

See "Words for Music Perhaps."

"Crazy Jane on the Day of Judgment" (1932)

See "Words for Music Perhaps."

"Crazy Jane on the Mountain" (1939)

See "Words for Music Perhaps."

"Crazy Jane Reproved" (1930)

See "Words for Music Perhaps."

"Crazy Jane talks with the Bishop" (1933)

See "Words for Music Perhaps."

"Cuchulain's Fight with the Sea" (1892)

Yeats's earliest treatment of the legend of Cuchu-lain foreshadows perhaps his greatest treatment, the verse play On Baile's Strand. Like the more renowned play, "Cuchulain's Fight with the Sea" recounts Cuchulain's slaughter of a young challenger he belatedly discovers to be his own son. Much like Oedipus, he is overwhelmed by the cruel irony of his fate and becomes unhinged. In several significant respects, however, the play and the poem diverge. In the play it is Cuchulain's spurned lover Aoife rather than his jealous wife Emer who sends her son to smite Cuchulain. In the play, also, Cuchulain storms the sea as a matter of his own mad impulse, while in the poem he is impelled by the spells of Conchubar's druids, the high king fearing that Cuchulain will emerge from his trance to rave and slay the entire company. Additionally, Cuchulain's son is differently named. In the earlier versions of the poem (1892–1924) he is called Finmole; in later versions, he is called Cuchulain after his father ("Cuchulain I, mighty Cuchulain's son"), which lends itself to the irony that in killing his son Cuchulain destroys himself. In On Baile's Strand, he remains nameless.

In a note included in The Countess Kathleen and Various Legends and Lyrics, Yeats acknowledges that the poem is "founded on a West of Ireland legend" given in Jeremiah Curtin's 1890 volume Myth and Folk-Lore of Ireland (VP 799; on Curtin see CL1 269, 339). In its early incarnations the poem was called "The Death of Cuchullin," which follows Curtin's version of the tale in its clear implication that Cuchulain dies in the sea. Yeats's decision to change the poem's name to "Cuchulain's Fight with Sea" in 1925 was undoubtedly an attempt to achieve consistency with his dramatic cycle on the legend of Cuchulain, in which, following Lady Gregory's Cuchulain of Muirthemne (1902), Cuchulain emerges from the sea to fight another day. Birgit Bjersby additionally detects the influence of Samuel Ferguson's (1810–86) poem "Fergus Wry-Mouth," in which Fergus plunges into Loch Rury to fight the monster that disfigured his mouth and thereby jeopardized his rule, custom holding that the king must be physically unblemished (Interpretation of the Cuchulain Legend 25). Fergus fought beneath the waves for a day and night before emerging victorious over the monster, with his mouth restored.

Yeats may have found additional inspiration in Keats's Endymion (1818), in which Glaucus takes to the sea much as Cuchulain does: "And, with a blind voluptuous rage, I gave / Battle to the swollen billow-ridge, and drave / Large froth before me, while there yet remained / Hale strength, nor from my bones all marrow drained" (III, 611–614).

FIRST PUBLICATION: *United Ireland* (periodical), June 11, 1892, under the title "The Death of Cuchullin." Reprinted in *The Countess Kathleen and Various Legends and Lyrics*, T. Fisher Unwin, London, September 1892. Reprinted in *Early Poems and Stories*, Macmillan, London, September 22, 1925, under the title "Cuchulain's Fight with the Sea."

BIBLIOGRAPHY

Bjersby, Birgit. *The Interpretation of the Cuchulain Legend in the Works of W. B. Yeats*; Curtin, Jeremiah. *Myths and Folk-Lore of Ireland*; Yeats, W. B. *The Collected Letters of W. B. Yeats* (vol. 1), *The Variorum Edition of the Poems of W. B. Yeats*.

"Dancer at Cruachan and Cro-Patrick, The" (1932)

See "Words for Music Perhaps."

"Dawn, The" (1916)

Immediately following "Lines Written in Dejection" in Yeats's collected poems, "The Dawn" can be understood as an attempt to mediate between the competing claims of the moon (representing subjectivity, imagination) and the sun (representing objectivity, reality). Of this opposition, Yeats writes in his preface to Lady Gregory's *Gods and Fighting Men* (1904), "When we have drunk the cold cup of the moon's intoxication, we thirst for something beyond ourselves, and the mind flows outward to a natural immensity; but if we have drunk from the hot cup of the sun, our own fulness awakens, we desire little, for wherever one goes one's heart goes too; and if any ask what music is the sweetest, we can but answer, as Finn answered, 'What happens.' And yet the songs and stories that have come from either influence are a part, neither less than the other, of the pleasure that is the bride-bed of poetry" (*Expl.* 26; *P&I* 132).

Neither night nor day, the dawn represents a wavering moment in which the self momentarily escapes the poles of its possibility and exists as pure identity. The dawn is "ignorant" in the sense that it knows nothing beyond itself. In this respect it is opposed to the "old queen measuring a town / With the pin of a brooch" and the "withered" astronomers of "pedantic Babylon" who reduce the "careless planets in their courses" to mere sums. These are not creatures of the dawn, but of the day. The dawn "looks down" on them, a witness to their alien enterprises of measurement and calculation. Yeats would be like the ignorant and wanton dawn that "merely stood, rocking the glittering coach / Above the cloudy shoulders of the horses"—a reference to the equipage of Phoebus Apollo—for "no knowledge is worth a straw." The dawn's stasis ("merely stood") contrasts with the industry of the queen and the astronomers; so too it hints at a temporal transcendence that contrasts with their age ("old," "withered"). In its aspiration to cast off all mere intellect, the poem is associable with "All Things Can Tempt Me," in which Yeats declares his desire to be "Colder and dumber and deafer than a fish."

A. Norman Jeffares identifies the "old queen" as Emain and the town as Emain Macha (i.e., Armagh). In Jeffares's summary of the legend, "Emain, daughter of Hugh Roe, claimed to rule in her father's right after his death, and defeated his brother Dihorba in battle, married his brother Cimbaeth and captured Dihorba's five sons by a stratagem. She compelled the five princes to build her a palace" (*NCP* 151). In his *History of Ireland Critical and Philosophical* (1881), Standish James O'Grady (1846–1928) describes Emain marking the site of her palace with a pin (*NCP* 151; on O'Grady see "Beautiful Lofty Things").

"The Dawn" is closely related to "The Fisherman," in which Yeats declares his desire to write a poem "maybe as cold / And passionate as the dawn." Both poems were written in June 1914 (*YC* 174) and appeared in the February 1916 issue of *Poetry*. Both "The Dawn" and "The Fisherman" may in part call upon a memory Yeats describes in *Autobiographies*. While staying at Rosses Point as a boy (see Sligo), he had risen early to go boating with a cousin and another boy. Yeats napped in the boat and awoke toward dawn. "I had found again the windy light that moved me when a child," he recalls. "I persuaded myself that I had a passion for the dawn, and this passion, though mainly histrionic like a child's play, an ambitious game, had moments of sincerity. Years afterwards when I had finished *The WANDERINGS OF OISIN*, dissatisfied with its yellow and its dull green, with all that overcharged colour inherited from the romantic movement, I deliberately reshaped my style, deliberately sought out an impression as of cold light and tumbling clouds. I cast off traditional metaphors and loosened my rhythm, and recognizing that all the criticism of life known to me was alien and English, became as emotional as possible but with an emotion which I described to myself as cold" (86).

FIRST PUBLICATION: *Poetry* (periodical), February 1916. Reprinted in *Eight Poems*, "Form" at the Morland Press, London, April 1916 (see *Letters* 609–610), and in *The Wild Swans at Coole*, The CUALA PRESS, Churchtown, Dundrum, November 17, 1917.

BIBLIOGRAPHY

Jeffares, A. Norman. *A New Commentary on the Poems of W. B. Yeats*; Kelly, John S. *A W. B. Yeats Chronology*; Yeats, W. B. *Autobiographies, Explorations, The Letters of W. B. Yeats, Prefaces and Introductions*.

"Death" (1929)

In a 1933 note to *The Winding Stair and Other Poems*, Yeats writes that he was "roused" to write both "Death" and "BLOOD AND THE MOON" by the assassination of KEVIN O'HIGGINS (*VP* 831). The poem, however, transcends this personal and political context. It belongs to a lineage of poems extolling the "great man in his pride" (see "ANCESTRAL HOUSES," "TO A SHADE," "TO A WEALTHY MAN WHO PROMISED A SECOND SUBSCRIPTION TO THE DUBLIN MUNICIPAL GALLERY IF IT WERE PROVED THE PEOPLE WANTED PICTURES"), while its fierce existential defiance—the conviction of his own primacy with which the great man challenges the presumptuous emptiness of the universe—reiterates the insistence of "The TOWER" that "Death and life were not / Till man made up the whole, / Made lock, stock and barrel / Out of his bitter soul. . . ." Armed with this understanding, the great man transcends the vacillation between dread and hope and establishes his mastery of death itself. In their conviction that man creates death, both "Death" and "The Tower" fulfill the "supreme aim" that Yeats articulates in a July 26, 1935, letter to DOROTHY WELLESLEY: "To me the supreme aim is an act of faith and reason to make one rejoice in the midst of tragedy. An impossible aim; yet I think it true that nothing can injure us" (*Letters* 838; *LOP* 12).

In its 12 lines, "Death" proposes two subversions of mortality, both of which pervade Yeats's thought. First, there is the circularity of the universal pattern (see for example "AT GALWAY RACES" and "The PHASES OF THE MOON") according to which death is merely a phase in an endless recurrence (as Yeats writes in "UNDER BEN BULBEN," grave-diggers "but thrust their buried men / Back in the human mind again"). Second, there is the radical subjectivity that Yeats found confirmed in Berkeley (cf. "Blood and the Moon"), according to which "Man has created death." In Richard Ellmann's characterization of Yeats's defiant subjectivism, "Humanism rushes to the point of solipsism; rather than concede anything to the opposition, it erects man as not only the measure but also the creator of all things. Yeats utters his assertions in part because they are not acceptable, out of an obstinacy which he wants to be as mulish, and as heroic, as he can make it" (*IY* 225).

FIRST PUBLICATION: *The Winding Stair*, The Fountain Press, New York, October 1, 1929.

BIBLIOGRAPHY

Ellmann, Richard. *The Identity of Yeats*; Yeats, W. B. *The Letters of W. B. Yeats, Letters on Poetry from W. B. Yeats to Dorothy Wellesley, The Variorum Edition of the Poems of W. B. Yeats*.

"Death of the Hare, The" (1927)

See "A MAN YOUNG AND OLD."

"Delphic Oracle upon Plotinus, The" (1932)

See "WORDS FOR MUSIC PERHAPS."

"Demon and Beast" (1920)

"Demon and Beast" rehearses the conceptual structure that would find its definitive expression in "VACILLATION." As Yeats writes in the latter poem, "Between extremities / Man runs his course," and he finds reprieve from vacillation, from those "antinomies of day and night," only in sudden, startling moments of transcendent joy. "Demon and Beast" is the exploration of all that consists in such a moment. In moments of inexplicable grace, "crafty demon" and "loud beast"—an antithesis corresponding to soul and self, mind and body, *antithetical* and *primary*, "hatred" and "desire"—cease in their relentless struggle for mastery. There is a release that expresses itself in freedom and laughter, and in a sense of kinship with the lightly worn strength that is the demeanor of the Renaissance and the stamp of UNITY OF BEING.

As "Vacillation" stages its moment of joy in a tea shop as a means of emphasizing its unpredictable suddenness, "Demon and Beast" finds Yeats strolling through the halls of the National Gallery in Dublin. The pictures themselves seem to reflect his sense of benediction and unity. Where Yeats elsewhere must apologize to his forebears (see "INTRODUCTORY RHYMES" and "UNDER SATURN") he now feels welcomed. The Ormondes, from whom Yeats claimed distant descent, nod upon the wall. Luke Wadding (1588–1657), the Irish Franciscan who founded the College and Monastery of Saint Isadore in Rome, and Thomas Wentworth Strafford (1593–1641), lord lieutenant of Ireland from 1639, bid Yeats welcome as one of their own impassioned kind (YD 177–178, 191). Wadding's "glittering eyes" even amid death anticipate the "ancient, glittering eyes" of the Chinese sages in "LAPIS LAZULI": such eyes are the physical symbol of what, in "The GYRES," Yeats calls "tragic joy." Donald T. Torchi-

ana perceives the paintings as antinomies within the scheme of Irish history. In Yeats's moment of grace "personifications of the contending forces in Irish history seem to be resolved, understood, even blessed: Father Luke Wadding, a zealous partisan of the Gaelic Irish defeated at Kinsale; the Ormondes, great Anglo-Irish bearers of the Butler name; and the Earl of Strafford, who virtually enslaved Ireland to save an English crown" (*W. B. Yeats & Georgian Ireland* 297).

As liberation from the beast ("the loud beast ran") allows sympathetic communion with the highest men, so liberation from the demon ("being no more demoniac") allows sympathetic communion with the humblest beasts. In a reversal of the dispersion described in "The SECOND COMING" and "The WILD SWANS AT COOLE," Yeats describes a white gull (cf. the "white sea-bird" of the lovely prologue to The ONLY JEALOUSY OF EMER) as it descends in a spiral and takes its place by an "absurd / Portly green-pated bird" (cf. the "most ridiculous little bird" of "A MEMORY OF YOUTH"). Yeats's pleasure in this simplest spectacle of nature is a symptom of his release from the *antithetical* impulse that would spurn nature, as most obviously manifested in "SAILING TO BYZANTIUM." At the same time, the companionship between the two birds, the one allied with aspirant beauty (it wheels after its crumb), the other with content animality ("portly"), itself seems to symbolize the reconciliation of demon and beast. Significantly, the gull is described as "gyring down and perning there." If perning in the gyre signifies vacillation between antinomies in the poem's first stanza, it here suggests a centripetal withering into the unity of the self, as it does in "Sailing to Byzantium" and in "The DOUBLE VISION OF MICHAEL ROBARTES." Nature, then, encompasses both demon and beast and seemingly presides over the kind of graceful, effortless reconciliation that Yeats can sustain only in fleeting moments.

Yeats, however, cannot fully believe in the transcendence of the antinomy represented by "demon" and "beast." He is certain that "every natural victory"—as opposed to supernatural victory—belongs to one or to the other, and he wonders whether the sweetness of liberation from this duality is not a trick of delirious old age. Such hair-splitting is swept away in the exultant rush with which the poem ends. Yeats exclaims this sweetness as that which St. Anthony of Coma (ca. 251–356) knew as he and his followers fasted in "barren Thebaid," the territory surrounding Egyptian Thebes, or by the shore of Lake Mareotis, south of Alexandria. In contrast to these, the Caesars were all but impoverished, possessing nothing more than their thrones. The imagery of these lines derives, as A. Norman Jeffares notes, from the Rev. J. O. Hannay's *The Spirit and Origin of Christian Monasticism* and *The Wisdom of the Desert*, respectively published in 1903 and 1904 (*NCP* 200; on this desert monasticism, see also *Aut.* 238, 242; *E&I* 405; *LE* 108, 256; "UNDER BEN BULBEN").

FIRST PUBLICATION: The *Dial* (periodical), November 1920. Reprinted in *Michael Robartes and the Dancer*, The CUALA PRESS, Churchtown, Dundrum, February 1921.

BIBLIOGRAPHY

Conner, Lester I. *A Yeats Dictionary: Persons and Places in the Poetry of William Butler Yeats*; Jeffares, A. Norman. *A New Commentary on the Poems of W. B. Yeats*; Torchiana, Donald T. *W. B. Yeats & Georgian Ireland*; Yeats, W. B. *Autobiographies, Essays and Introductions, Later Essays*.

"Dialogue of Self and Soul, A" (1929)

"A Dialogue of Self and Soul" is one of Yeats's most flawlessly executed poems, fully the rival of more celebrated anthology pieces like "BYZANTIUM" and "SAILING TO BYZANTIUM." Harold Bloom does not go too far when he calls it one of "the language's glories" (*Yeats* 372). The poem returns to the essential confrontation of Yeats's entire thought, the dialogue of self and soul, out of which come the antinomies of the natural and the supernatural, the immanent and the transcendent, the active and the visionary, the *primary* and the *antithetical*, day and night, ditch and tower. In the words of a note to

"The SECOND COMING," the "human soul is always moving outward into the objective world or inward into itself; & this movement is double because the human soul would not be conscious were it not suspended between contraries, the greater the contrast the more intense the consciousness" (*VP* 824). "A Dialogue of Self and Soul" narrates precisely this movement and reaps precisely this reward of intense consciousness. If the soul tends to predominate in Yeats, here it is called to account and finally overwhelmed. In Bloom's précis, Yeats's "moral character or *primary* half summons his dominant personality or *antithetical*, questing half, to a judgment" (*Yeats* 373). In Yeats's own description, the poem "is a choice of rebirth rather than deliverance from birth," with the sword a "symbol of life" (*Letters* 729).

The Soul begins by summoning the Self—tellingly, the disincarnate *mind* of the Self—to the "winding ancient stair," emblematic of the "philosophical gyres" that are the pattern of reality, as Yeats tells in a note (*VP* 830–831). The winding stair is that which Dante mounts in "EGO DOMINUS TUUS" and that which Yeats mounts in "I SEE PHANTOMS OF HATRED AND OF THE HEART'S FULLNESS AND OF THE COMING EMPTINESS" and "MY HOUSE." The climb is the circuitous, dizzying labor by which the Soul, constantly thrown back upon itself, though never precisely as it was, attains the visionary vantage of the tower. The battlement is broken and crumbling, like the battlement of Yeats's own tower, THOOR BALLYLEE (*VP* 831; cf. "BLOOD AND THE MOON" and "I see Phantoms of Hatred"). Equally its ruin represents the *antithetical* tradition, which, as all but diagrammed in the final stanza of "My House," died into the life of its opposite and awaits rebirth with the coming of a new era. Upon the tower there is "breathless starlit air" and darkness: as in "ALL SOULS' NIGHT," "FERGUS AND THE DRUID," "The LEADERS OF THE CROWD," and "The MOUNTAIN TOMB," the visionary or esoteric propensity is antithetical to the warmth of life and the pulse of nature. Amid this darkness—inhuman, inscrutable, infinite, eternal—the soul finds an image of itself, but also loses itself. In answer, the Self offers as its own emblem Sato's Sword (see *Letters* 662). Here the sword is not the transcendental talisman described in "MY TABLE," though it remains immune to the spotting of the centuries; rather, it represents immersion in history (emphasized by the quadruple repetition of the temporal marker "still" and by the description of its embroidery as "old," "tattered," "faded") and the primacy of the material, the bodily, and the sexual. Where the soul summons the disincarnate "mind," the Self envisions the sword with tactile precision, appreciative of its rich objectivity. It is consecrated—a thing sacred—as a masterful work of the hand and as the heirloom of an ancient family. The sword rests upon the knees, thus reversing the previous stanza's emphasis on "mind," the lower extremities pitched against the upper. Significantly, it retains the sheen of a "looking-glass." In "THE TWO TREES," Yeats calls the looking-glass "the bitter glass" and "the glass of outer weariness," associating it with a lamentable self-consciousness and externality; elsewhere he associates it with a deplorable aesthetic naturalism (see E&I 404; Expl. 333; LE 108, 194, 200; AV 160). In "MICHAEL ROBARTES AND THE DANCER," however, the looking-glass signifies the antithetical triumph of the Self's absorption in its own beauty. In Bloom's needle-threading interpretation, the sword is emblematic "of the joyful and solipsistic creative energy that reduces all else to an image in a looking glass" (Yeats 374). Significantly again, the sword is wrapped in a "flowering, silken, old embroidery, torn / From some court-lady's dress . . ." (cf. Expl. 320). The silk-sheathed scabbard symbolizes the complementarity of female and male, of love and war, while the torn embroidery hints at some passionately violent or violently passionate moment: some embrace of life in its moment of highest intensity. The winding of the stair is answered by the winding of the embroidery, the one gyre opening upon the darkness of the sky, the other closing upon the brightness of the sword.

The poem's remaining stanzas follow the to-and-fro of an explicit debate. Reiterating "Sailing to Byzantium," the Soul argues that "love and war" belong to the prime of life, while the ripeness of age belongs to the labor of transcendence by which "ancestral night" delivers the earth-scorning soul from "the crime of death and birth." The Self upholds the sword against the tower, day against the night, and embraces the flowers of the scabbard in implicit opposition to the soul's scorn of the "earth." By a happy coincidence, the sword had been fashioned by "Montashigi"—Bishu Osafumé Motoshigé (1394–1428)—500 years earlier. Yeats makes opportunistic use of the sword's actual age, for 500 years is the span of the primary and antithetical tinctures that alternate within the millennial era. The period thus evokes the gyres of history described by the "geometry" of A VISION. Reasserting the sword, symbol of history embraced rather than transcended, the Self claims "as by a soldier's right" a "charter" to commit the crime of death and birth all over again. Consumed and stupefied by its own communion with the night—or "giving the Self up for lost," as Bloom has it (Yeats 374)—the Soul seems to abandon the argument. Its senses overwhelmed and its intellect shattered by its own fullness of mind, it can only stammer its vision of heaven, of resolved antinomies, of forgiveness (cf. "VACILLATION," section 1). The Soul's tongue is rendered a "stone," for poetry may not cross the threshold of heaven. As Yeats understood as early as "TO THE ROSE UPON THE ROOD OF TIME," the poet may strain but not sever his tether to the earth, thus differing from the saint, who "seeks not an eternal art, but his own eternity" (E&I 286). "A Dialogue of Self and Soul" is vastly more sophisticated than "TO THE ROSE UPON THE ROOD OF TIME" but essentially in agreement with it. Both poems witness the soul of the poet as it vacillates between necessary antitheses.

Transfiguring the motifs of blindness and the full basin, the Self asserts its own vision of a far more embattled salvation. The "living man," rendered blind by the vantage of his own incarnation, willingly drinks from the impurities of the ditch (the image descends from the same image in "ON A POLITICAL PRISONER," and from the image of the weasel's hole in "NINETEEN HUNDRED AND NINETEEN"). Thus he embraces the entire cycle of birth and death in defiance of everything he might be expected to "scorn": the "ignominy of boyhood," the pain and clumsiness of youth, the antagonisms of maturity, disfigurement of the self in the social mirror (the mirror recalls that of "The Two Trees"). The burden of life climaxes in the anguish of romance, which thinly veils, of course, the anguish of having failed to win MAUD GONNE. Wooing a "proud woman not kindred" of one's soul is, ironically, the "most fecund ditch of all," for it has bred so much of Yeats's poetry (cf. "WORDS"). The Self's soliloquy is a subtle structure of counterpoint. The Self declares that it forgives itself "the lot"; the Soul had maintained that only the dead are forgiven, apparently by some external agency. The Self describes the flow of sweetness within the breast; the Soul had described a filling of the brain—not a "flow" but an "overflow" whose source is, again, an external agency. The Self bursts into laughter and song; the Soul had been rendered mute. The Self is possessed by the conviction that it is blessed and that, suddenly free of the blindness of incarnation, everything it looks upon is blessed; the Soul had been rendered blind, unable to "look upon" anything. In the poem's chief irony, as Bloom puts it, "What the Self fights free of is everything in Yeats that has [been] mythologized at its expense" (*Yeats* 375). Versions of this same ecstatic liberation, seemingly driven by the *primary* impulse to embrace life, are to be found in "DEMON AND BEAST" and in "Vacillation."

The Self has the last word in "The Dialogue of Self and Soul," but the poem itself exists in dialogic relation with poems like "All Souls' Night" and "I see Phantoms of Hatred and of the Heart's Fullness and of the Coming Emptiness," which take the part of the esoteric flight against the existential embrace. To repeat the all-important understanding of Yeats's note to "The Second Coming," the "human soul would not be conscious were it not suspended between contraries, the greater the contrast the more intense the consciousness" (*VP* 824). In the final analysis, Yeats belongs to the party of neither the Soul nor the Self, but to the intense consciousness born of their contradiction. This explains an anecdote that for Yeats had the significance of an essential truth. In his diary of 1930, Yeats tells how he made "a certain girl see a vision of the Garden of Eden." She heard "the music of Paradise coming from the Tree of Life," and when he told her to put her ear against the tree, she found "that it was made by the continu-

ous clashing of swords" (*Expl.* 306; see also *Aut.* 209–210; *Myth.* 254, 259; *VPl.* 688, 703).

FIRST PUBLICATION: *The Winding Stair*, The Fountain Press, New York, October 1, 1929.

BIBLIOGRAPHY

Bloom, Harold. *Yeats*; Yeats, W. B. *Autobiographies, Essays and Introductions, Explorations, Later Essays, The Letters of W. B. Yeats, Mythologies, The Variorum Edition of the Plays of W. B. Yeats, The Variorum Edition of the Poems of W. B. Yeats, A Vision.*

"Dolls, The" (1914)

An anomaly among Yeats's poems, "The Dolls" seems to borrow its elements—the doll maker and his wife, the living dolls—from the world of fairy tale rather than from Irish legend, romantic tradition, or personal experience. At the same time, the poem begins to formalize Yeats's disdain of the organic, which would become a crucial element in late masterpieces like "BYZANTIUM" ("scorn aloud / In glory of changeless metal / Common bird or petal") and "SAILING TO BYZANTIUM" ("Once out of nature I shall never take / My bodily form from any natural thing"). In the poem's narrative, a child is born to a doll maker and his wife. The dolls of the house are revolted by the "noisy and filthy thing"; they bawl their disgust and complain of their "disgrace." In his sleep, the doll maker hears the dolls and stirs uncomfortably. His wife penitentially whispers in his ear, seemingly referring to the baby, "My dear, my dear, O dear, / It was an accident." Thus substance is set against flesh, art against life, design against accident, with Yeats's sympathies, as the wife's abject confession suggests, not entirely on the side of the baby. In a complicating detail, however, the jealously bawling doll disturbs the dollmaker's sleep much as the "noisy" baby might have done, suggesting a parallelism between actual progeny and artistic progeny. This parallelism is anticipated by the "INTRODUCTORY RHYMES" to *Responsibilities* (1914), in which Yeats apologizes to his forebears for having fathered books rather than children.

Yeats associated "The Dolls" with the contemporaneous poem "The MAGI," which also imagines a seat of unsympathetic inhuman judgment. "The fable for ["The Dolls"] came into my head while I was giving some lectures in Dublin," Yeats writes in a 1914 note. "I had noticed once again how all thought among us is frozen into 'something other than human life.' After I had made the poem, I looked up one day into the blue of the sky, and suddenly imagined, as if lost in the blue of the sky, stiff figures in procession. I remembered that they were the habitual image suggested by blue sky, and looking for a second fable called them 'The Magi,' complementary forms of those enraged dolls" (VP 820). A. Norman Jeffares associates the poem with a "parallel" passage in J. M. SYNGE's The Aran Islands (1907): "[Old Pat Dirane] talks usually in a mournful tone about his ill-health, and his death, which he feels to be approaching, yet he has occasional touches of humor [. . .]. Today a grotesque twopenny doll was lying on the floor near the old woman. He picked it up and examined it as if comparing it with her. Then he held it up: 'Is it you is after bringing that thing into the world,' he said, 'woman of the house?'" (Collected Plays and Poems and The Aran Islands 275; NCP 127).

FIRST PUBLICATION: Responsibilities: Poems and a Play, The CUALA PRESS, Churchtown, Dundrum, May 25, 1914.

BIBLIOGRAPHY

Jeffares, A. Norman. A New Commentary on the Poems of W. B. Yeats; Synge, J. M. Collected Plays and Poems and The Aran Islands; Yeats, W. B. The Variorum Edition of the Poems of W. B. Yeats.

"Double Vision of Michael Robartes, The" (1919)

With "EGO DOMINUS TUUS," and "The PHASES OF THE MOON," "The Double Vision of Michael Robartes" is one of three paramount philosophical statements in the 1919 edition of The Wild Swans at Coole. Together, the three poems hatch the vast and perplexing philosophy that would find full expression in A VISION. In a note dated 1922, Yeats says that he wrote these poems as a "text for exposition" (VP 821), by which he means as a vehicle for doctrine, but "The Double Vision of Michael Robartes" has an oracular immediacy that triumphs over the merely expository. In this respect, it is closer to "BYZANTIUM" than to "Ego Dominus Tuus" or "The Phases of the Moon," which are commentaries on visionary truths rather than visions proper. Michael Robartes, a persona introduced in the poems and stories of the 1890s (see "ROSA ALCHEMICA"), figures in all three poems as the archetype of the subjective personality, the man "in whom the movement inward is stronger than the movement outward, the man who sees all reflected within himself," as Yeats writes in a note to "The SECOND COMING," and as the purveyor of visionary comprehension (VP 824). In a note to The Wind Among the Reeds (1899), Yeats calls Robartes "the pride of the imagination brooding upon the greatness of its possessions, or the adoration of the Magi" (803). "The Double Vision of Michael Robartes" discloses the subjective experience of just this brooding. The "double vision" of the poem's title refers to Robartes's successive visions of the first lunar phase (section 1 of the poem) and the 15th lunar phase (section 2 of the poem), which amplify the haunting account of these key phases in "The Phases of the Moon" (see lines 104–116 for the first phase, lines 58–83 for the 15th phase).

The visionary locus is the "grey rock of Cashel" some 75 miles south of Dublin in County Tipperary (YD 25). The ancient seat of the kings of Munster, the rock is crowned by the hulking ruins of the 12th-century chapel of King Cormac McCarthy (the "ruined house" of line 68) as well as by the ruins of the 13th-century St. Patrick's Cathedral and the remains of a walled fortress. Richard Ellmann notes that the chapel's "present ruin is symbolic of the modern world in the same way that the 'half-dead' tower is symbolic of it in 'BLOOD AND THE MOON'" (IY 255). In its layering of ruins, the rock may also symbolize the cycle of birth and death, creation and destruction, that finds its governing image in the changes of the moon; and as a shrine of both

The Rock of Cashel, County Tipperary. The mount forms the visionary landscape of "The Double Vision of Michael Robartes": "On the grey rock of Cashel the mind's eye / Has called up the cold spirits that are born / When the old moon is vanished from the sky / And the new still hides her horn." *(Fáilte Ireland)*

church and crown, it may symbolize the duality of *primary* and *antithetical* tinctures epitomized by the first and 15th lunar phases (in Yeats's scheme, priest and saint belong to the *primary* tincture, while king and especially queen—in some instances at least— belong to the *antithetical* tincture).

Robartes sees first into the mysteries of the first lunar phase, when all is darkness and formlessness and man awaits his birth (when all is like "the dough before it is baked," in the language of "The Phases of the Moon"; when the "Pestle of the moon [. . .] pounds up all anew," in the language of "ON WOMAN"). The "blank eyes" of the mysterious agency of this creation suggest blindness born of the dark, but even more the "pitiless eyes" of the sphinx that slouches toward Bethlehem in "The SECOND COMING," eyes that never divagate from some inhuman, impersonal, inscrutable purpose. The ensuing lines—lines 7–16—are among the most difficult of

the poem. The speaker is Robartes himself. Though a type of the *antithetical* personality, Robartes seemingly feels some ancestral vestige of the compulsion by which man is born in the first phase, some vestige of the body's mastery over the soul that defines the *primary* tincture. He is constrained by his own limbs, which seem "wire-jointed" and "wooden," as if the limbs of a marionette. They in turn obey "some hidden magical breath," knowing neither good nor evil, so utterly dead that they feel no "Triumph that we obey"—that is, jaws and limbs feel no triumph that we obey the edicts of the body or perhaps the edicts of the hidden magical breath (in "The Phases of the Moon," Yeats speaks of the souls of the first phase not knowing "What's good or bad, or what it is to triumph / At the perfection of one's own obedience").

Robartes sees next into the mysteries of the 15th lunar phase. In this phase, as Yeats writes in *A Vision*, "All that the being has experienced as thought is visible to its eyes as a whole, and in this way it perceives, not as they are to others, but according to its own perception, all orders of existence," while "the body possesses the greatest possible beauty" (*AV* 136). In *A Vision*, Yeats calls the Sphinx an image of the "outward-looking mind, love and its lure" and Buddha an image of the "introspective knowledge of the mind's self-begotten unity," and he notes that these figures stand "like heraldic supporters guarding the mystery of the fifteenth phase" (207–208). Between these "heraldic supporters" dances the girl, whom Frank Kermode calls the "image of unified body and soul," the "perfect type" of the 15th phase, the "mysterious resolution between outward and inward"—between Sphinx and Buddha (*Romantic Image* 70–71). Ellmann's gloss has a similar emphasis: "The sphinx is the intellect, gazing on both known and unknown things; the Buddha is the heart, gazing on both loved and unloved things; and the dancing girl, most important of all, is primarily an image of art. She dances between them because art is neither intellectual nor emotional, but a balance of these qualities. The dancer [. . .] reconciles body and mind, dreaming and thinking [. . .] (*IY* 255). One of Yeats's most pervasive and vital motifs, as Kermode shows, the image of the dancing girl is referable to much else in Yeats's work. Among the most significant points of reference are the orgiastic dance that climaxes "Rosa Alchemica"; ISEULT GONNE dancing in "TO A CHILD DANCING IN THE WIND"; the queen dancing in *The* KING OF THE GREAT CLOCK TOWER; "Loie Fuller's Chinese dancers" in "NINETEEN HUNDRED AND NINETEEN"; the conflation of dancer and dance in the final stanza of "AMONG SCHOOL CHILDREN"; and the "complexities of fury" that die "into a dance / An agony of trance" in "BYZANTIUM."

All three figures—Sphinx, Buddha, dancing girl—have evaded the strictures of time and the finality of death. The mechanism of this transcendence is the infinitely dilated moment: "In contemplation had those three so wrought / Upon a moment, and so stretched it out / That they, time overthrown, / Were dead yet flesh and bone." This mechanism has a long lineage in romantic tradition

and a particularly crucial precedent in a passage from BLAKE's "Milton" that Yeats quoted habitually: "Every time, less than a pulsation of the artery / Is equal in its period & value to six thousand years; / For in this period the poet's work is done, & all the Great / Events of time start forth & are conceived in such a period, / Within a moment, a pulsation of the artery" ("Milton," I, pl. 28, lines 62–63, pl. 29, lines 1–3; for Yeats's appropriation of these lines see *E&I* 135, 172; *LE* 29; *UP2* 199; *AV* 24; see also "A Meditation in Time of War" [1920]). In *The* UNICORN FROM THE STARS, Yeats all but paraphrases Blake when he writes that "Events that are not begotten in joy are misbegotten and darken the world, and nothing is begotten in joy if the joy of a thousand years has not been crushed into a moment" (*VPl.* 688). Also germane is Walter Pater's *The Renaissance* (1873), a book sacred to the generation of the RHYMERS' CLUB. In his famous conclusion, Pater insists that the passing moment may be swollen into meaning by the impassioned aesthetic response.

"The Double Vision of Michael Robartes" ends with a reflection on the vanished vision. Robartes has seen at last the girl of his "unremembering nights," she who flies with the evanescence of his dreams and yet leaves the pulses quickened and mind undone as under the spell of Helen herself. The dancing girl is the achieved vision of the artist, but she is not entirely a creature culled from the depths of ANIMA MUNDI; she distinctly recalls both Iseult Gonne and MAUD GONNE, the former habitually figured as the dancing girl, the latter habitually figured as Helen (the question posed in "The CIRCUS ANIMALS' DESERTION"—"Those masterful images because complete / Grew in pure mind, but out of what began?"—seems pertinent here). In contrast with Sphinx, Buddha, and dancing girl, who have entered into the "agony of trance," Robartes remains mired in the folly of his desire, "caught between the pull / Of the dark moon and the full" (subject to "the circle of the moon / That pitches common things about," in the language of "Nineteen Hundred and Nineteen"). In gratitude for his vision, Robartes kisses a stone; this may be vague genuflection or it may be specific homage suggesting that "Cormac's ruined house" or its presiding spirits have in some sense "rewarded" him with the vision (in "CRAZY JANE ON THE MOUNTAIN," Crazy Jane kisses a stone after seeing a vision of CUCHULAIN and Emer). In Harold Bloom's final word, "Though no freer, [Robartes] is less ignorant; he has his reward. We see in him the man of *A Vision*, who can attain knowledge of process, but not freedom from the labyrinth process makes" (*Yeats* 20).

FIRST PUBLICATION: *The Wild Swans at Coole*, Macmillan, London, New York, March 11, 1919.

BIBLIOGRAPHY

Bloom, Harold. *Yeats*; Conner, Lester I. *A Yeats Dictionary: Persons and Places in the Poetry of William Butler Yeats*; Ellmann, Richard. *The Identity of Yeats*; Kermode, Frank. *Romantic Image*; Yeats, W. B. *Essays and Introductions, Later Essays, Uncollected Prose by W. B. Yeats* (vol. 2), *The Variorum Edition of the Plays of W. B. Yeats, The Variorum Edition of the Poems of W. B. Yeats, A Vision*.

"Easter 1916" (1920, dated September 25, 1916)

The EASTER RISING of 1916 catalyzed the final phase of the Irish struggle for independence and forced Yeats to recant the stinging assessment of "SEPTEMBER 1913" that "Romantic Ireland's dead and gone, / It's with O'LEARY in the grave." In the wake of the Easter Rising, Yeats decided that "September 1913" had come to sound "old-fashioned" (*VP* 820). "Easter 1916" is dated September 25, 1916, but a May 11 letter to Lady GREGORY, written 18 days after the rising began, contains its germ: "I am trying to write a poem on the men executed—'terrible beauty has been born again'" (*Letters* 613). Yeats writes in the same letter, "I had no idea that any public event could so deeply move me," and yet he remained ambivalent about the rising, as reflected in "Easter 1916," his principal public statement on the event. The poem's famous refrain may have been inspired by MAUD GONNE's remark in a May letter that the rebels "have raised the Irish cause again to a position of tragic dignity" (GY 372). Writing to Lady Gregory on May 11, Yeats credits Gonne with the comment that "tragic dignity has returned to Ireland" (613), which artistically elevates Gonne's actual comment and anticipates the language of his refrain.

The poem's opening lines—lines of "nerveless syntax onto which the great refrain will drop its iron portcullis," as Hugh Kenner puts it—have a penitential honesty (*Colder Eye* 228). Yeats confesses to just the kind of mockery he disparages in section five of "NINETEEN HUNDRED AND NINETEEN." He recalls occasionally bumping into the future martyrs of the rising as they came from "counter or desk" at the end of the workday. Even as he exchanged "polite meaningless words"—a phrase twice repeated, indicating the innocuous interchangeability of these encounters—Yeats nursed a "mocking tale or a gibe" to recount around the fire at his club. He may refer to the Arts Club, Upper Merrion Street, Dublin, a venue for dinner and discussion that was not, in Joseph Hone's estimate, "bookish or particularly intellectual" (*W. B. Yeats* 233–234; for Yeats at the Arts Club see *I&R*, I, 51–53). He may alternatively refer to the Stephen's Green Club (*New Biography* 215). The reference to "counter or desk" associates the prospective martyrs with the till-keeping middle class (the "nationalist petite bourgeoisie" in R. F. Foster's phrase) that Yeats had excoriated in "September 1913" and "Paudeen": hence his condescension (*AP* 59). Their emergence from "eighteenth-century houses" and their "vivid faces," however, hint at an unguessed spiritual continuity with the generation of Robert Emmet (1778–1803), Edward Fitzgerald (1763–98), and Wolfe Tone (1763–98). Yeats had been convinced that Dublin was a place "where motley is worn," but the rising exposed the magnitude of his misunderstanding: "All changed, changed utterly: / A terrible beauty is born."

The second stanza namelessly alludes to the leaders of the rising whom Yeats best knew, emphasizing the commonplace humanity out of which, by some miraculous alchemy, came the "terrible beauty" of the poem's refrain. As Kenner writes, Yeats "silhouettes anonymities, 'this woman,' 'this man,' 'this other' in part 2, against the sunburst of part 4, where names start forth and the poet-mage takes charge" (*Colder Eye* 229). The roster of the anonymous includes Constance Markiewicz (1868–1927) whose fall from youthful feminine grace into the shrillness of politics is recounted in "IN MEMORY OF EVA GORE-BOOTH AND CON MARKIEWICZ" and "ON A POLITICAL PRISONER." She was condemned to death for her part in the rising but her sentence was commuted to life imprisonment, and she was released from jail in 1917. There is Patrick Pearse (1879–1916), who founded the St. Enda's School for Boys in Dublin and proclaimed the birth of the Irish Republic from the steps of the General Post Office. Pearse rode "our wingèd horse"—Pegasus—in the sense that he couched the struggle for Irish independence in mythic and romantic terms. In a letter of May 1, 1916, to his sister Lolly, Yeats called Pearse a "man made dangerous by the Vertigo of Self Sacrifice," while EZRA POUND reported to JOHN QUINN Yeats's opinion that Pearse was "half-cracked" and suffering from "Emmet mania, same as some other lunatics think they are Napoleon or God" and that Pearse "wouldn't be happy until he was hanged" (*AP* 46). There is Thomas MacDonagh (1878–1916), a poet and playwright whom Yeats described in his 1909 diary as a "man with some literary faculty which will probably come to nothing through lack of culture and encouragement." He continues in terms that anticipate the critique of "Easter 1916": "In England this man would have become remarkable in some way, here he is being crushed by the mechanical logic and commonplace eloquence which give power to the most empty mind, because, being 'something other than human life', they have no use for distinguished feeling or individual thought. I mean that within his own mind this mechanical thought is crushing as with an iron roller all that is organic" (*Aut.* 360; *Mem.* 177–178; see also *CL4* 760, 782–784). Finally there is John MacBride (1865–1916), Maud Gonne's estranged husband. Though a "drunken vainglorious lout," MacBride is likewise "transformed utterly," a generous acknowledgment considering Yeats's hostility to the bluff military man who had bested him briefly but decisively in Gonne's affections. Pearse, MacDonagh, and Mac-

Patrick Pearse (1879–1916), ca. 1916. Pearse, who was executed as a leader of the Easter Rising, figures in a number of poems, including "Easter 1916" and "The Statues." *(Library of Congress)*

Bride were among 15 leaders of the rising executed by the British: Pearse and MacDonagh were shot on May 3, MacBride on May 5.

In its third stanza, "Easter 1916" contrasts the stoniness of hearts "with one purpose alone"—the stoniness of the single-minded political fanatic—with the "living stream": the supple, changing beauty of nature, the subtle shadings that make for poetry. More than this, such hearts "trouble" the living stream, which is to say, awaken the kind of inhuman destructive zeal exemplified by the Easter Rising. As R. F. Foster observes, these lines are implicitly addressed to Gonne and reiterate the plea, mooted six years earlier in the essay "J. M. SYNGE AND THE IRELAND OF HIS TIME," against "the morbid persistence of minds unsettled by some fixed idea" and all that "kills intellectual innocence; that delight in what is unforeseen, and in the mere spectacle of the world, the mere drifting hither and thither that must come before all true thought and emotion," against all that turns the "mind to stone" (*AP* 61–62; *E&I* 313–314). Yeats worked on the poem while staying at Les Mouettes, the Gonnes' home in Colleville-sur-Mer, on the Normandy shore, during the summer of 1916, and he unsuccessfully proposed to Gonne on July 1 (*YC* 186). In September 1916, Yeats read her the poem and implored her, in terms that echo his poem, "to forget the stone and its inner fire for the flashing, changing joy of life" (*AP* 62; *Scattering Branches* 32). This was a political and spiritual plea, but also a romantic plea, as Yeats knew he could succeed in his suit only by reconciling Gonne to the apolitical "flashing, changing joy of life."

In the final stanza, Yeats comes to the central spiritual and philosophical question of the poem. Is the sacrifice of the living heart ever justified? Or rather, as John O'Leary held, are there "things which a man should not do, perhaps even to save a nation" (*Aut.* 101, 178; *E&I* 247; *UP2* 36). As in "ON BEING ASKED FOR A WAR POEM," Yeats skirts the controversy of an answer by invoking the proper bounds of the poet's role, declaring it his part merely to "murmur name upon name, / As a mother names her child / When sleep at last has come / On limbs that had run wild." Yeats toys with the further metaphorization of death as nightfall, but not liking the romantic varnish of this—perhaps resisting something of the romantic varnish that had quickly come to surround the rising and especially its martyrs—Yeats reverts to the unvarnished reality of "death" and the matter-of-fact possibility that, after all, England might have kept its pledge to grant Ireland home rule as soon as the world war had come to an end. "And what if excess of love"—for Ireland—"Bewildered them till they died?" Yeats asks, but again retreats from the critical implication of his own question, and ends with a solemn martyrology that comported with popular sentiment. MacDonagh, MacBride, Pearse, and James Connolly (1870–1916) will be forever remembered wherever the green of Ireland is worn. The transition from motley to green epitomizes the poem's refrain: "All changed, changed utterly: / A terrible beauty is born."

Predictably, "Easter 1916" elicited a sharp rebuke from Gonne. "No I don't like your poem," she wrote on November 8, 1916, "it isn't worthy of you & above all it isn't worthy of the subject— Though it reflects your present state of mind perhaps, it isn't quite sincere enough for you who have studied philosophy & know something of history know quite well that sacrifice has never yet turned a heart to stone though it has immortalised many & through it alone mankind can rise to God. You recognise this in the line which was the original inspiration of your poem 'A terrible Beauty is born' but you let your present mood mar & confuse it till even some of the verses become unintelligible to many." Gonne also rejected the imputation that MacDonagh, Pearse, Connolly were "sterile fixed minds," insisting that "each served Ireland, which was their share of the world, the part they were in contact with, with varied faculties and vivid energy! those three were men of genius, with large comprehensive & speculative & active brains [. . .]. As for my husband he has entered Eternity by the great door of sacrifice which Christ opened & has therefore atoned for all [. . .]." She allows that the poem contains beautiful language but finds that it fails to be a "living thing which our race would treasure & repeat, such as a poet like you might have given to your nation & which would have avenged our material failure by its spiritual beauty" (*GY* 384–385). Harold Bloom perspicuously observes that the poem is highly uncharacteristic, as the visionary element ("A terrible beauty is born") is "not the strength of the poem, which excels in sober coloring of accurate moral description, a quality normally lacking in Yeats. *Easter 1916* is a model of sanity and proportion, and is genuinely Yeats's eighteenth-century poem [. . .]" (*Yeats* 314).

FIRST PUBLICATION: Privately printed by Clement Shorter, 1916 (25 copies). Reprinted in the *New Statesman* (periodical), October 23, 1920, and the *Dial* (periodical), November 1920. Reprinted in *Michael Robartes and the Dancer*, The CUALA PRESS, Churchtown, Dundrum, February 1921.

BIBLIOGRAPHY

Bloom, Harold. *Yeats*; Foster, R. F. *W. B. Yeats: A Life, II: The Arch-Poet*; Gwynn, Stephen, ed. *Scattering Branches: Tributes to the Memory of W. B. Yeats*;

Hone, Joseph. *W. B. Yeats*; Jeffares, A. Norman. *W. B. Yeats: A New Biography*; Kelly, John S. *A W. B. Yeats Chronology*; Kenner, Hugh. *A Colder Eye: The Modern Irish Writers*; Mikhail, E. H., ed. *Yeats: Interviews and Recollections* (vol. 1); W. B. Yeats, *Autobiographies, The Collected Letters of W. B. Yeats* (vol. 4), *Essays and Introductions, The Gonne-Yeats Letters 1893–1938, The Letters of W. B. Yeats, Memoirs, Uncollected Prose by W. B. Yeats* (vol. 2), *The Variorum Edition of the Poems of W. B. Yeats*.

"Ego Dominus Tuus" (1917)

"Ego Dominus Tuus" ("I am Thy Master") is one of Yeats's most ambitious and challenging poems. The title is drawn from the second section of Dante's *La Vita Nuova* (ca. 1292). The "Lord of Terrible Aspect"—the Spirit of Love—speaks the words of the title when he first appears before Dante (Yeats likewise refers to the scene in PER AMICA SILENTIA LUNAE; see *LE* 4). In "Ego Dominus Tuus," Yeats seeks a master of his own: the "mysterious one" who will reveal all that he would know.

"Ego Dominus Tuus" is the verse preamble to *Per Amica Silentia Lunae*, just as "The PHASES OF THE MOON" is the verse preamble to A VISION; together, the poems serve as an introduction to the esoteric philosophical system that Yeats developed during the late teens and early 1920s. Harold Bloom deftly summarizes: "The poem's theme, like the treatise, is mastery; of what sort is the poet's, and how does he attain to it? Where *Per Amica Silentia Lunae* gives a dual answer—from his anti-self, attained through self-annihilation, and from the ANIMA MUNDI, reached through vision—the poem gives a simpler but less imaginatively compelling reply. Mastery is the successful quest for the image, an image looking like oneself, but proving, of all imaginable things, to be the most unlike, or the anti-self" (*Yeats* 197). As Yeats explains in AUTOBIOGRAPHIES, the embrace of the anti-self or "mask" is the mechanism of UNITY OF BEING, the consummating rite of impassioned subjectivity, impossible and indeed abhorrent to those who "seek no image of desire, but await that which lies beyond their mind—unities not of the mind, but unities of Nature, unities of God—the man of science, the moralist, the humanitarian, the politician, Saint Simeon Stylites upon his pillar, Saint Anthony in his cavern, all whose preoccupation is to seem nothing; to hollow their hearts till they are void and without form, to summon a creator by revealing chaos, to become the lamp for another's wick and oil [. . .]" (200–201). "Ego Dominus Tuus" elaborates both the theory of the anti-self and the distinction between the two kinds of men.

The poem is a philosophical dialogue between *Hic* and *Ille*—"this" and "that," objective and subjective, *primary* and *antithetical*. As the owner of the tower—seemingly THOOR BALLYLEE—mentioned in the poem's opening lines, *Ille* is identifiable with Yeats, so much so that EZRA POUND jokingly dubbed the speakers of the poem "Hic and Willie" (*MM* 197). Yeats did not complete the purchase of Thoor Ballylee until June 1917, but "Ego Dominus Tuus" (dated December 1915 in *Per Amica*) suggests that he had set his sights on it much earlier. Like "The Phases of the Moon," "Ego Dominus Tuus" opens upon a scene inspired by Samuel Palmer's "The Lonely Tower," an illustration of Milton's "Il Penseroso" (1645). In Palmer's engraving, two lounging shepherds gaze at a dark tower in the distance, the lamp of midnight study emanating from its solitary window, the moon slight and low and yet mysteriously refulgent. Ille walks in the moonlight beneath his "wind-beaten tower" (whether habitually or presently is not clear). Enthralled by what Hic considers the "unconquerable delusion" of esoteric mastery, he traces in the sand magic shapes. As critics have noted, the scene descends from SHELLEY's *The Revolt of Islam* (1818). In his essay "The PHILOSOPHY OF SHELLEY'S POETRY" (1900), Yeats writes that "Shelley made his imprisoned Cythna become wise in all human wisdom through the contemplation of her own mind, and write out this wisdom upon the sands in 'signs' that were 'clear elemental shapes, whose smallest change' made 'a subtler language within language,' and were 'the key of truths which once were dimly taught in old Crotona'" (*E&I* 78; on sand writing, see also "The GIFT OF HARUN AL-RASHID"; *AV* 41; *AV-1925* xviii, 10–11).

The "wind-beaten tower" signifies transcendent labor in opposition to the leveling wind of inchoate nature and the vicissitudes of history. The contention of tower and wind recurs in "A PRAYER FOR MY DAUGHTER," and the leveling wind recurs in section 5 of "NINETEEN HUNDRED AND NINETEEN" (this imagery would seem to reverse that of Yeats's earliest poetry, in which the wind, emblematic of the storming Sidhe, was endowed with transcendent agency). From the tower comes the light of a lamp left burning beside "the open book / that Michael Robartes left. . . ." Robartes is a fictional alter ego representing the subjective personality, or the "pride of the imagination brooding upon the greatness of its possessions," as Yeats states in an 1899 note to *The Wind Among the Reeds* (VP 803). He appears in the poems and stories of the 1890s (see for example "ROSA ALCHEMICA") and found a second life as the mouthpiece of Yeats's mature philosophy (see "The DOUBLE VISION OF MICHAEL ROBARTES," "MICHAEL ROBARTES AND THE DANCER," "The Phases of the Moon"). The "open book" anticipates the elaborate framing device employed in the 1925 edition of *A Vision*, in which Yeats's philosophy is presented as a summary of a mystical book found by Robartes, the fanciful *Speculum Angelorum et Hominorum* of Giraldus (AV-1925 xxii).

A succinct exposition of the poem's argument follows Hic's scene-setting statement. Ille explains of his moonlit rambles, "By the help of an image / I call to my own opposite, summon all / That I have handled least, least looked upon," to which Hic answers, "And I would find myself and not an image." Summarizing much of Yeats's own disdain for the *primary* phase of history that characterizes modernity, Ille retorts that the desire to find oneself is the "modern hope," out of which comes the "gentle, sensitive mind" that no longer knows "the old nonchalance of the hand." Yeats means by the "nonchalance of the hand" artistry unencumbered by the crippling self-consciousness of modernity, artistry that derives from the "whole body" (*Aut.* 227). Corinna Salvadori identifies this "nonchalance" with Castiglione's concept of *sprezzatura*, which figured importantly in Yeats's thought from 1903 onward. Yeats usually renders *sprezzatura* as *recklessness*, following Thomas Hoby's 1561 transla-

tion of *The Book of the Courtier*, but, as Salvadori notes, he occasionally opts for *nonchalance*, following L. E. Opdycke's 1902 translation (*Yeats and Castiglione* 14, 84; see also *Letters* 857; *LOP* 63). Ille's retort echoes an important passage in *Per Amica Silentia Lunae*, underscoring Ille's association with Yeats himself: "Some years ago I began to believe that our culture, with its doctrine of sincerity and self-realisation, made us gentle and passive, and that the Middle Ages and the Renaissance were right to found theirs upon the imitation of Christ or of some classic hero. St Francis and Caesar Borgia made themselves over-mastering, creative persons by turning from the mirror to meditation upon a mask. When I had this thought I could see nothing else in life" (*LE* 10).

Hic rejoins with the example of Dante, who so "utterly found himself" that his "hollow face," more than any face but Christ's, came to dominate the Western imagination. Ille, rejecting this account, wonders instead whether Dante's cheeks were not hollowed by the "hunger for the apple on the bough / Most out of reach," and whether the Dante of popular imagination was the man "that Lapo and Guido knew," a reference to Lapo Gianni (ca. 1270–ca. 1330) and Guido Cavalcanti (ca. 1255–1300), both literary protégés of Dante and fellow practitioners of the *dolce stil nuovo*, or "sweet new style," which was marked by a spiritualized and idealized conception of romantic love. Ille speculates that Dante fashioned from his opposite a face that might have been a "stony face / Staring upon a Bedouin's horse-hair roof / From doored and windowed cliff, or half upturned / Among the coarse grass and the camel-dung." The "doored and windowed cliff" is a type of the ruling symbol of the tower, suggesting that Dante, like Yeats himself, belongs to the tradition of solitude and vision. The ruggedness and pitilessness of the Arabian scenery contrasts with the "gentle, sensitive mind" that typifies Western modernity. The half-upturned face evidently belongs to a toppled monument that once celebrated a conqueror or king, recalling Shelley's "Ozymandias" (1818), and comports with the invocation of the conquerors Achilles, Timor, and Babar as exemplars of triumphant subjectivity in "HER COURAGE." Whether in politics or literature or love, the essential thing is to set the "chisel to the hardest stone," to press beyond the natural limits of the self with such purity of commitment that everything unimpassioned burns away or withers away. Mocked and derided, exiled from his native Florence, Dante must climb the stair, which symbolizes the self's travail as it ascends into passionate solitude, while the tower itself symbolizes, among many other things, the consummation of this solitude. In his apotheosis he finds "the unpersuadable justice" that is the judgment of God (the "bitter bread" suggesting the host) and the "most exalted lady loved by a man." These are the symbols and the fruits of passionate solitude. In *Per Amica Silentia Lunae,* Yeats comments relevantly that Dante "celebrated the most pure lady poet ever sung and the Divine Justice, not merely because death took that lady and Florence banished her singer, but because he had to struggle in his own heart with his unjust anger and his lust," which is to say, that in these Dante found his opposite or anti-self (*LE* 7). Salvadori specifically associates the allusion to bread and stairs with *Paradiso,* Canto 17, in which Dante is warned: "You will come to learn how bitter as salt and stone / is the bread of others, how hard the way that goes / up and down stairs that never are your own" (*Yeats and Castiglione* 54; John Ciardi's translation).

Surely, Hic answers, there are artists of a different type, lovers of life, singers of happiness, who make "their art / Out of no tragic war." Ille insists that "those that love the world serve it in action, / Grow rich, popular of influence, / And should they paint or write, still it is action. . . ." Yeats may have been thinking of OSCAR WILDE, who, as he writes in *Autobiographies,* "could not endure the sedentary toil of creative art and so remained a man of action" (*Aut.* 130; see also 223; *LE* 182). Not incidentally, perhaps, the phrase "sedentary toil" recurs later in "Ego Dominus Tuus." In his greatest formulation of the fate that undid the "tragic generation," Yeats asks, "What portion in the world can the artist have / Who has awakened from the common dream / But dissipation and despair?" In contrast to "the common dream," upheld by the deceptions of the rhetorician and sentimentalist, art is "but a vision of reality." Hic cites John Keats

(1795–1821) as an example of the artist who sings his love of life, but Ille questions whether we know Keats any better than Dante. Keats's art may be happy, "but who knows his mind?" Ille unforgettably portrays Keats as a schoolboy with his "face and nose pressed to a sweet-shop window," the creator of "luxuriant song" out of the heartsickness of his poverty, illness, and ignorance (shades of "gaiety transfiguring all the dread," which Yeats would hit upon in "LAPIS LAZULI" as the mechanism of transcendence). Yeats reiterates this view of Keats in *Per Amica Silentia Lunae* (*LE* 6–7).

Recurring to his opening comments, Hic asks Ille, as if finally coming to the question that he had meant to ask all along, why he leaves the lamp burning beside Robartes's book (symbolizing occult study) and traces magical characters in the sand, for "a style is found by sedentary toil / And by the imitation of great masters." Ille answers that he seeks an "image" rather than a book, and that he calls to his mysterious opposite, his "anti-self," who shall disclose all that he seeks in a whisper, lest the birds "carry it away to blasphemous men." Ille's "image" is a descendant of the "symbol" that Yeats discusses in his early essays "The SYMBOLISM OF POETRY" and "MAGIC": no mere literary device, no mere garnishment of "style," but the "caller up of angels or of devils" from the depths of the "Great Memory" (*E&I* 50). Here the image conjures that which is most unlike the self, in the embrace of which the self transcends the mire of self-consciousness. These lines seem to remember that sacred book of Yeats's youth, Shelley's *Prometheus Unbound* (1820), which describes how the Magus Zoroaster met "his own image walking in the garden," with the explanation that "there are two worlds of life and death: / One that which thou beholdest, but the other / Is underneath the grave, where do inhabit / The shadows of all forms that think and live / Till death unite them. . . ." (I, 191–199).

Bloom's criticism of Ille's final speech—that it is too much "the expositional and doctrinal text," that it "expounds itself, as though the poet had become his own academy, his future critics"—is fair enough, though it is harder to credit his verdict that "Ego Dominus Tuus," though philosophically central, is "not one of Yeats's great poems" (*Yeats* 197, 204). Its philosophical provocations aside, the poem's portraits of Dante and Keats and its various *pensées* (on the modern mind, on the rhetorician and the sentimentalist) surely make it worthy of even the slimmest selection of Yeats's poetry.

FIRST PUBLICATION: *Poetry* (periodical), October 1917. Reprinted in *The Wild Swans at Coole*, The CUALA PRESS, Churchtown, Dundrum, November 17, 1917.

BIBLIOGRAPHY

Bloom, Harold. *Yeats*; Ellmann, Richard. *Yeats: The Man and the Masks*; Salvadori, Corinna. *Yeats and Castiglione: Poet and Courtier*; Yeats, W. B. *Autobiographies, A Critical Edition of Yeats's A Vision (1925), Essays and Introductions, Later Essays, The Letters of W. B. Yeats, Letters on Poetry from W. B. Yeats to Dorothy Wellesley, The Variorum Edition of the Poems of W. B. Yeats, A Vision*.

"Empty Cup, The" (1927)

See "A MAN YOUNG AND OLD."

"End of Day, The" (1917)

The fourth of seven poems in the sequence "UPON A DYING LADY," "The End of Day" is a brief postscript to "SHE TURNS THE DOLLS' FACES TO THE WALL." Both poems gently flout the Catholicism to which Mabel Beardsley (1871–1916) turned for spiritual comfort as she succumbed to cancer. The poem compares Beardsley to a child playing at the game of penance, "fantastical and wild," knowing that at the end of the day someone will call her into the house. In a letter of January 13, 1913, to Lady GREGORY, Yeats recounts a conversation with Beardsley that suggests what he may mean by her religious "play." "A palmist told me," she had told Yeats, "that when I was forty-two my life would take a turn for the better and now I shall spend my

forty-second year in heaven." She added, "O yes I shall go to heaven. Papists do'" (*Letters* 574). The poem's metaphor of childhood play (the word *play* appears four times in eight lines) echoes the doll motif in "CERTAIN ARTISTS BRING HER DOLLS AND DRAWINGS" and "She turns the Dolls' Faces to the Wall," and it may allude punningly to Beardsley's career as an actress.

FIRST PUBLICATION: The *Little Review* (periodical), August 1917, and the *New Statesman* (periodical), August 11, 1917. Reprinted in *The Wild Swans at Coole*, The CUALA PRESS, Churchtown, Dundrum, November 17, 1917.

BIBLIOGRAPHY

Yeats, W. B. *The Letters of W. B. Yeats*.

"Ephemera" (1887)

"Ephemera" is less well known than it might be. Written in 1884 (IY 287) and extensively revised for inclusion in Yeats's collected *Poems* of 1895, the poem narrates a conversation between lovers in the moment of their waning love. They stand hand in hand by the side of the lake, and the autumnal scenery seems to register the poignant melancholy of their loss. The woman strews her hair and bosom with dead leaves as if donning an ironic bridal garland. The man submits that they should not mourn for their tiredness, as other loves await them. As he says in the poem's final lines, "Before us lies eternity; our souls / Are love, and a continual farewell." Numerous critics have discerned in these lines an idea of reincarnation. This aspect of the poem, as Richard Ellmann notes, dates not from 1884, but from 1895 (IY 303; for the original version of the poem, see VP 79–81).

A thread of autobiography runs throughout Yeats's later love poems, but "Ephemera" is evidently a work of imagination. In 1884, the significant romantic involvements of Yeats's young manhood—KATHARINE TYNAN, MAUD GONNE, OLIVIA SHAKESPEAR—had not yet come into view. In addition to being lovely on its own terms,

"Ephemera" prefigures "ADAM'S CURSE," another elegiac conversation about fading love that echoes in the very framework of nature. As a lakeside meditation on the bereavements of time, "Ephemera" less overtly anticipates "The WILD SWANS AT COOLE." The "rabbit old and lame" that limps down the path is a homely anticipation of the "nine-and-fifty swans" that would spectacularly take flight several decades later.

FIRST PUBLICATION: *North & South* (periodical), February 26, 1887 (see YC 9). Reprinted in *The Wanderings of Oisin and Other Poems*, Kegan Paul, Trench & Co., London, January 1889.

BIBLIOGRAPHY

Ellmann, Richard. *The Identity of Yeats*; Kelly, John S. *A W. B. Yeats Chronology*; Yeats, W. B. A *Variorum Edition of the Poems of W. B. Yeats.*

"Fallen Majesty" (1912)

"Fallen Majesty" is one of the most extravagant of Yeats's many paeans to MAUD GONNE. As in "HER PRAISE," Yeats assumes the task of remembering, on behalf of forgetful later days, the splendor and majesty of Gonne's youthful beauty. In "Fallen Majesty," Yeats creates a dramatic context for his own act of memory, picturing himself, almost in the role of Aleel from The COUNTESS CATHLEEN, as "some last courtier at a gypsy camping-place / Babbling of fallen majesty. . . ." In the echoes of this simile, the poem encompasses not only the fallen majesty of Gonne, but the fallen majesty of Priam and King Lear, of all kings and queens whose passing marks the passing of an age, and it becomes something larger than it seems: a lament for the lapsarian tendency of the world itself. "Fallen Majesty" ends with an image as striking as any Yeats attached to Gonne. A crowd will gather and "not know it walks the very street / Whereon a thing once walked that seemed a burning cloud."

Gonne's electrifying presence as a political speaker during the 1890s explains the poem's allusion to the crowds that gathered if she "but showed her face." Yeats may have been remembering the political campaigns of 1897 and 1898, when Yeats and Gonne were much together in the effort to organize a protest of Queen Victoria's Jubilee and a national commemoration of the 1798 rebellion (for a detailed account see CL2 695–707). In those days, Yeats says in AUTOBIOGRAPHIES, Gonne's "power over crowds was at its height." He explains that there "was an element in her beauty that moved minds full of old Gaelic stories and poems, for she looked as though she lived in an ancient civilization where all superiorities whether of the mind or the body were a part of public ceremonial, were in some way the crowd's creation, as the entrance of the Pope into Saint Peter's is the crowd's creation. Her beauty, backed by her great stature, could instantly affect an assembly, and not, as often with our stage beauties, because obvious and florid, for it was incredibly distinguished [. . .]" (274–275).

In December 1912, Yeats submitted "Fallen Majesty," along with four other poems, to his friend and protégé EZRA POUND, then acting as "foreign correspondent" for *Poetry* magazine of Chicago. Pound took it upon himself to alter "Fallen Majesty," as well as "The MOUNTAIN TOMB" and "TO A CHILD DANCING IN THE WIND." In his most significant revision, Pound excised the weak qualifying phrase "as it were" from the final line of "Fallen Majesty," which originally read, "Once walked a thing that seemed, as it were, a burning cloud" (AM 475; IY 131; *Serious Character* 191). Yeats was at first "furious," but he recognized Pound's editorial wisdom and forgave his impudence (*Serious Character* 191).

FIRST PUBLICATION: *Poetry* (periodical), December 1912. Reprinted in *A Selection from the Poetry of W. B. Yeats*, Bernhard Tauchnitz, Leipzig, 1913, and in *Responsibilities: Poems and a Play*, The CUALA PRESS, Churchtown, Dundrum, May 25, 1914.

BIBLIOGRAPHY

Carpenter, Humphrey. A *Serious Character: The Life of Ezra Pound*; Ellmann, Richard. *The Identity of Yeats*; Foster, R. F. *W. B. Yeats: A Life, I: The Apprentice Mage*; Yeats, W. B. *Autobiographies, The Collected Letters of W. B. Yeats* (vol. 2).

"Fascination of What's Difficult, The" (1910)

As a poem like "NO SECOND TROY" introduces a new tautness of expression, "The Fascination of What's Difficult" introduces a new persona, that of the haughty and domineering man of the world. MAUD GONNE anticipated both the theme and the imperious tone of "The Fascination of What's Difficult" in a letter of June 26, 1908, to Yeats: "[The theater] is just as bad [as politics], or worse for it brings you among jealousies & petty quarrels & little animosities which you as a great writer should be above & apart from—It is because you vaguely feel this, that you are exasperated & often very unjust to our people—It is this exasperation that has made you take up old class prejudices which are unworthy of you, & makes you say cruel things which *sound* ungenerous—though you are never ungenerous really" (GY 256; see also 301). Gonne failed to understand that this emergent persona was less an accident than a conscious construction, a fulfillment of the "self-possession" that Yeats had been seeking since early manhood (*Aut.* 99).

The poem takes up precisely the concern that Gonne expresses: that the milieu of the theater is inappropriate for a lyric poet. Yeats admits that the "fascination of what's difficult"—writing plays—has dried the sap from his veins and rent "spontaneous joy" and "natural content" from his heart. Suddenly shifting into high metaphor, Yeats implicitly likens himself to Pegasus, the winged horse of Greek myth, which, despite its "holy blood" and gambols among the clouds of Olympus, must now "Shiver under the lash, strain, sweat and jolt / As though it dragged road metal." The sudden deflation of "road metal" predicts the rhetoric of quotidian squalor that Yeats would use so effectively in later poems like "The CIRCUS ANIMALS' DESERTION" ("Old kettles, old bottles, and a broken can, / Old iron, old bones, old rags"), "A DIALOGUE OF SELF AND SOUL" ("frog-spawn of a blind man's ditch"), and "The TOWER" ("battered kettle at the heel"). Prosodically, the effect of "road metal" is ingenious. The two words bring the line to a sudden jarring halt, forcing on the reader the unmistakable weight of the dragging load. Yeats ends the poem with a curse on all the messiness and frustration of "theater business," on "the day's war with every knave and dolt." He swears that he will "find the stable and pull out the bolt," thus freeing Pegasus from its demeaning confinement. As it happened, Yeats did no such thing. He remained an active playwright and theatrical impresario until the end of his days. The poem has a thematic counterpart in "AT THE ABBEY THEATRE," which likewise complains of theater business.

FIRST PUBLICATION: *The Green Helmet and Other Poems*, The CUALA PRESS, Churchtown, Dundrum, December 1910, under the sequence title "Momentary Thoughts" and the present title.

BIBLIOGRAPHY

Yeats, W. B. *Autobiographies*, *The Gonne-Yeats Letters 1893–1938*.

"Father and Child" (1929)

See "A WOMAN YOUNG AND OLD."

"Fergus and the Druid" (1892)

A 40-line dramatic dialogue between the two figures named in the poem's title, "Fergus and the Druid," like AT THE HAWK'S WELL and "TO THE ROSE UPON THE ROOD OF TIME," offers an ambivalent representation of the visionary or transcendental calling as both powerfully alluring and dangerously bereaving. While it offers liberation from the mundane world, it disintegrates the trappings of humanity in the process. As Harold Bloom observes, "The poem is an urgent warning made to Yeats's imagination by itself, but not one that he could heed" (*Yeats* 111). In the poem's simple but psychologically and philosophically central tale, Fergus, the king of Ulster, finally overtakes the Druid, whom he has been following all day. He tells the Druid that he has abandoned his throne, but that he still feels the crown upon his head, and that he would "Be no more a king / But learn the dreaming wisdom that is yours." The Druid asks the king to observe his "grey hair and hollow cheeks" (cf. Dante's "hollow face" in "Ego Dominus Tuus" and Maud Gonne's hollow cheeks in "Among School Children") and to observe his "hands that may not lift the sword." He tells Fergus, cautioningly, "No woman's loved me, no man sought my help." Such atrophy and alienation are the inevitable result of his "dreaming wisdom," a lesson that Yeats thoroughly absorbed as a youthful acolyte of Shelley's "Alastor" (1816) and inscribed in his early dramatic poem The Seeker (Aut. 80). Undaunted, Fergus prevails upon the Druid and receives a "bag of dreams." He unlooses the bag and in a moment passes through every grade of existence, from the "green drop in the surge" to the "king sitting upon a chair of gold." He becomes "nothing, knowing all" and finds himself enmeshed in "webs of sorrow." The burden of wisdom similarly plays out in "He thinks of his Past Greatness when a Part of the Constellations of Heaven," in which the wizard Mongan drinks "ale from the Country of the Young." Like Fergus, he passes through all the grades of experience and becomes irrevocably severed from the natural order.

A principal figure in the Red Branch or Ulster cycle of Irish legend, Fergus is a recurrent presence in Yeats's early work. He figures in the poems "The Old Age of Queen Maeve" (1903), "To the Rose upon the Rood of Time," "The Wanderings of Oisin" (III, line 89), and "Who Goes With Fergus?" (a lyric from The Countess Cathleen), and he is one of the main characters in the play Deirdre. In an 1899 note, Yeats gives a brief account of the king: "He married Nessa and [poet Sir Samuel Ferguson] makes him tell how she took him 'captive in a single look.' [. . .] Presently, because of his great love, he gave up his throne to Conchobar, her son by another, and lived out his days feasting, and fighting, and hunting" (VP 813).

FIRST PUBLICATION: The National Observer (periodical), May 21, 1892. Reprinted in The Countess Kathleen and Various Legends and Lyrics, T. Fisher Unwin, London, September 1892.

BIBLIOGRAPHY

Bloom, Harold. Yeats; Yeats, W. B. Autobiographies, The Variorum Edition of the Poems of W. B. Yeats.

"First Confession, A" (1929)

See "A Woman Young and Old."

"First Love" (1927)

See "A Man Young and Old."

"Fisherman, The" (1916)

In "To a Friend whose Work has come to Nothing," Yeats counsels Lady Gregory to turn from the disillusionments of society and secretly exult amid "a place of stone." In "The Fisherman," Yeats depicts something of this same exultant solitude, though the feverish complaint of the earlier poem has mellowed into a vision of quiet self-mastery. In a March 17, 1934, radio broadcast, Yeats introduced the poem in this way: "I had founded Irish literary societies, an Irish Theatre, I had become associated with the projects of others, I had met much unreasonable opposition. To overcome it I had to make my thoughts modern. Modern thought is not simple; I became argumentative, passionate, bitter; when I was very bitter I used to say to myself, 'I do not write for these people who attack everything that I value, not for those others who are lukewarm friends, I am writing for a man I have never seen.' I built up in my mind the picture of a man who lived in the country where I had lived, who fished in mountain streams where I had fished; I said to myself, 'I do not know whether he is born yet, but born or unborn it is for him I write.' I made this poem about him [. . .]" (UP2 498). T. R. Henn discerns in the fisherman something of J. M. Synge, who was "a keen fisherman and a great rambler in the Wicklow glens" (Lonely Tower 74). Henn adds that Yeats himself had little ability as a fisherman, and that "the fisherman was but another mask or compensation; to give a sense of wisdom, simplicity, the integrity of the lonely man, and maybe a certain aristocratic skill of hand and eye that could be related to the Renaissance tradition" (75).

The poem is an explanation of Yeats's evolving aesthetic commitments. In his mind's eye, he sees the fisherman as he takes to the hills at dawn. He wears "grey Connemara clothes," as if seamless in his relation to the grey hills. It is long since Yeats first conjured the "wise and simple man" in an almost involuntary reaction against his own attempt to write of the reality of contemporary Ireland: the hated living, the beloved dead (most likely an allusion to Synge, as Henn notes), the craven, the insolent, the knaves and mockers and demagogues, "the beating down of the wise / And great Art beaten down." This 12-line précis of the Irish rogue's gallery roils with the frustration of 30 years of hindered enterprise. Its informing memories undoubtedly include the attack on CHARLES STEWART PARNELL, the controversies surrounding *The COUNTESS CATHLEEN* and Synge's *In the Shadow of the Glen* and *The Playboy of the Western World,* the unchivalrous treatment of MAUD GONNE following her separation from her husband (see "Against Unworthy Praise"), the rebuff dealt to HUGH LANE, and the mocking tone of GEORGE MOORE's memoirs. "In scorn of this audience," Yeats had begun imagining the fisherman, a "man who does not exist / A man who is but a dream," and dedicated himself to creating in his image: "Before I am old / I shall have written him one / Poem maybe as cold / And passionate as the dawn." The decision to write for the fisherman rather than for the modern nation is the poem's essential discovery of commitment.

The association of passion, coldness, and the dawn is traceable to a boyhood memory that Yeats describes in *AUTOBIOGRAPHIES.* While staying at Rosses Point near Sligo, he had risen early to go boating with a cousin and another boy. Yeats napped in the boat and awoke toward dawn. "I had found again the windy light that moved me when a child," he recalls. "I persuaded myself that I had a passion for the dawn, and this passion, though mainly histrionic like a child's play, an ambitious

game, had moments of sincerity. Years afterwards when I had finished *The WANDERINGS OF OISIN,* dissatisfied with its yellow and its dull green, with all that overcharged colour inherited from the romantic movement, I deliberately reshaped my style, deliberately sought out an impression as of cold light and tumbling clouds" (86). In "A General Introduction for my Work" (1937), Yeats says that he borrowed the phrase "cold and passionate as the dawn" from one of JOHN BUTLER YEATS's letters, but the letter is untraced (*E&I* 523; *LE* 214, 415).

"The Fisherman" is sibling to "The DAWN," which likewise expresses the yearning for passionate simplicity and shares the symbol of the dawn. Both poems were written in June 1914 (YC 174) and appeared in the February 1916 issue of *Poetry.* Henn associates "The Fisherman" with "The Three Beggars" (1913), perceiving a kinship between the fisherman and the heron of the latter poem (*Lonely Tower* 92). A. Norman Jeffares associates "The Fisherman" with "AT GALWAY RACES," construing both poems as an attempt to conceptualize the ideal natural man (*NCP* 153). But this last underestimates the fisherman's beatific inscrutability and the transcendental implication of his mountain ascent. Arguably, the fisherman has less in common with the horsemen of "At Galway Races" than with the "two Chinamen" of "LAPIS LAZULI" and the hermits of "MERU." More subtly, the poem can be equated with "MY TABLE," both poems taking as their subjects that in the image of which they themselves would be written. Yeats returns to the fisherman in "The TOWER" and "WHY SHOULD NOT OLD MEN BE MAD?," employing the image with much the same resonance of solitude, pride, and integrity.

FIRST PUBLICATION: *Poetry* (periodical), February 1916. Reprinted in *Eight Poems,* Form, London, April 1916 (see *Letters* 609–610), and in *The Wild Swans at Coole,* The CUALA PRESS, Churchtown, Dundrum, November 17, 1917.

BIBLIOGRAPHY

Henn, T. R. *The Lonely Tower: Studies in the Poetry of W. B. Yeats*; Jeffares, A. Norman. *A New Commentary on the Poems of W. B. Yeats*; Kelly, John S. *A W. B. Yeats Chronology*; Yeats, W. B. *Autobiog-*

raphies, *Essays and Introductions*, *The Gonne-Yeats Letters 1893–1938*, *Later Essays*, *The Letters of W. B. Yeats*, *Uncollected Prose by W. B. Yeats* (vol. 2).

"Folly of Being Comforted, The" (1902)

"The Folly of Being Comforted" follows "The ARROW" both in the first edition of *In the Seven Woods* and in Yeats's collected poems. It not only defies the earlier poem's reservations about MAUD GONNE's mature beauty, but in its passionately mounting rhetoric utterly trumps the earlier and lesser poem, erasing all question of Gonne's lessening sway. Like "ADAM'S CURSE," "The Folly of Being Comforted" is a dialogue, suggesting, as John Unterecker theorizes, Yeats's increasing immersion in the theater (*RG* 99–109). "One that is ever kind"—Lady GREGORY, in her debut as a personage in Yeats's poetry—attempts to console Yeats in his maddening infatuation. She reminds him that Gonne's hair has begun to show signs of gray and that her eyes have begun to show "little shadows" (she was 35 when "The Folly of Being Comforted" appeared in print), and that he must have patience while Time makes "it easier to be wise." Yeats's heart erupts against these kindly intended words. He declares that "Time can but make her beauty over again," so great is her nobility, so clear the fire that "stirs about her." Directly contradicting the aspersion of "The Arrow," Yeats continues, "O she had not these ways / When all the wild summer was in her gaze," and ends in one of his great apostrophes: "O heart! O heart! if she'd but turn her head / You'd know the folly of being comforted."

FIRST PUBLICATION: The *Speaker* (periodical), January 11, 1902. Reprinted in *In the Seven Woods: Being Poems Chiefly of the Irish Heroic Age*, The DUN EMER PRESS, Dundrum, August 1903.

BIBLIOGRAPHY

Unterecker, John. *A Reader's Guide to William Butler Yeats*.

"Four Ages of Man, The" (1934)

See "SUPERNATURAL SONGS."

"Friends" (1912)

Yeats had a gift for making friends as well as for making enemies, and he never stinted in praise or affectionate memory of those he counted as friends. Setting a precedent of formal homage that would be carried to greater lengths in poems like "ALL SOULS' NIGHT" and "The MUNICIPAL GALLERY REVISITED," "Friends" praises three women who brought joy to Yeats's days: OLIVIA SHAKESPEAR, who was Yeats's mistress from early 1896 to March or April 1897 and thereafter remained a friend and confidante; Lady GREGORY, who had an unshakeable place in Yeats's life as both literary collaborator and in some manner surrogate mother (see *Aut.* 353); and MAUD GONNE, the eternal, maddening object of Yeats's desire. Yeats declares himself indebted to Shakespear for the years of unruffled affinity they have shared, a sentiment he reiterated upon her death in 1938, when he wrote, "For more than forty years she has been the centre of my life in London and during all that time we have never had a quarrel, sadness sometimes but never a difference" (*Letters* 916). Yeats declares himself indebted to Lady Gregory for having had the strength and understanding to unbind "youth's dreamy load," in effect liberating him to become both man and artist. In *AUTOBIOGRAPHIES*, Yeats offers a different and perhaps clearer formulation of this debt when he writes that Lady Gregory has brought to his "wavering thoughts steadfast nobility" (353). Yeats means that Lady Gregory helped him descend from the abstraction of his youth, setting him an example of tradition, decorum, and responsibility, and strengthening his impulse to engage the world. Yeats then turns to Gonne—inevitably the poem's culminating figure—but he is unsure what praise to give "her that took / All till my youth was gone, / With scarce a pitying look?" (note the pun on "gone"; Yeats repeats this trick in "HER PRAISE," "The LIVING BEAUTY," "RECONCILIATION," and "TO A YOUNG BEAUTY"). With unquestionable sexual insinuation, Yeats recounts lying wakeful at dawn for her sake, remembering her youthful beauty and the "eagle look"—proud, fierce, exultant—that remains, and shaking "from head to foot" with the sweetness that flows from his "heart's root" (Yeats repeats the phrase "eagle look" in The PLAYER QUEEN; see VPl. 733). This rush demonstrates the answer to the poem's chief question, "How could I praise that one?" Gonne brings misery in her train, but so too she vanquishes any counting of the "good and bad," exploding the hold of reason and objectivity and inspiring the ecstasy that allows Yeats's highest labor.

John Harwood argues, in contrast, that lines 4–9 refer to Lady Gregory and lines 10–16 to Shakespear. He explains: "A first and very different draft of the passage [lines 10–16] was sent to Lady Gregory by Yeats in January 1911 and ascribed to her, but the key phrase in the draft version is 'youth's bitter burden'—poverty—whereas the final version makes sense only in relation to Olivia Shakespear: 'youth's dreamy load' is the burden of Yeats's virginity. In the opening tribute to Lady Gregory [lines 1–9], the relation is between 'mind and delighted mind', whereas here the emphasis is on 'her hand', summoning for a moment the erotic imagery of the poems to Olivia in The Wind Among the Reeds: the 'lingering hand' in ['He Remembers Forgotten Beauty']" (Olivia Shakespear and W. B. Yeats 136). Arguing against Harwood's interpretation is Yeats's tendency to associate Lady Gregory with both strength and labor ("unbind" suggests something of this almost masculine strength), and his tendency to associate Shakespear with unruffled friendship, as in the letter quoted above. Moreover, Yeats elsewhere acknowledges Lady Gregory's integral part in his achievement in much the same terms as here. In AUTOBIOGRAPHIES, for example, Yeats writes, "I doubt I should have done much with my life but for her firmness and her care" (283).

FIRST PUBLICATION: The Green Helmet and Other Poems, Macmillan, New York, London, October 23, 1912.

BIBLIOGRAPHY

Harwood, John. Olivia Shakespear and W. B. Yeats: After Long Silence; Yeats, W. B. Autobiographies, The Letters of W. B. Yeats, The Variorum Edition of the Plays of W. B. Yeats.

"Friend's Illness, A" (1910)

In a mere seven lines, Yeats brings home the boundlessness of his regard for Lady GREGORY, his dearest friend and most important colleague, then taken dangerously ill though destined fully to recover. The poem's conceit is simple and yet remarkably unabashed: that the entire world is as nothing when weighed against a soul. According to biographer Mary Lou Kohfeldt, Lady Gregory suffered a cerebral hemorrhage on February 3, 1909, while at home at COOLE PARK (Lady Gregory 206). Yeats received word of his friend's collapse on the following day in Dublin. Writing in his journal on February 4, Yeats conveys the mood of alarmed love that almost immediately yielded "A Friend's Illness": "This morning I got a letter telling me of Lady Gregory's illness. I did not recognize her son's writing at first, and my mind wandered, I suppose because I am not well. I thought my mother was ill and that my sister was asking me to come at once: then I remembered that my mother died years ago and that more than kin was at stake. She has been to me mother, friend, sister and brother. I cannot realize the world without her—she brought to my wavering thoughts steadfast nobility. All day the thought of losing her is like a conflagration in the rafters. Friendship is all the house I have" (Aut. 353; Mem. 160–161). Yeats added on February 6, with perhaps some confusion about dates, "All Wednesday [probably Thursday, February 4] I heard Castiglione's phrase [from The Book of the Courtier] ringing in my memory, 'Never be it spoken without tears, the Duchess, too, is dead'. That slight phrase, which—coming where it did among the numbering of his dead—has often moved me till my eyes dimmed, and I felt all his sorrow as though one saw the worth of life fade for ever" (Aut. 353; Mem. 163). Yeats penned "A Friend's Illness" on February 5 and sent it to Lady

Gregory on February 8, with the explanation, "I mean by sickness and the scales that when one we love is ill we weigh them against a world without them" (*Seventy Years* 438). In response to this outpouring, Lady Gregory wrote in an undated letter that she was "glad of the illness" that brought Yeats closer to her (AM 398).

FIRST PUBLICATION: *The Green Helmet and Other Poems*, The CUALA PRESS, Churchtown, Dundrum, December 1910, under the sequence title "Momentary Thoughts" and the title "A Friend's Illness."

BIBLIOGRAPHY

Foster, R. F. *W. B. Yeats: A Life, I: The Apprentice Mage*; Gregory, Lady. *Seventy Years: Being the Autobiography of Lady Gregory*; Kohfeldt, Mary Lou. *Lady Gregory: The Woman behind the Irish Renaissance*; Yeats, W. B. *Autobiographies, Memoirs*.

"Friends of His Youth, The" (1926)

See "A MAN YOUNG AND OLD."

"From 'Oedipus at Colonus'" (1927)

See "A MAN YOUNG AND OLD."

"From the 'Antigone'" (1929)

See "A WOMAN YOUNG AND OLD."

"Gift of Harun Al-Rashid, The" (1924, dated 1923)

One of Yeats's longest poems at 193 lines, "The Gift of Harun Al-Rashid" commemorates in barely veiled terms Yeats's marriage and the experiments in automatic writing that soon followed and led to the doctrines of *A VISION* (see *Letters* 632–633). The poem is a pastiche of *The Arabian Nights*, which Yeats had read in the J. C. Mardrus–Powys Mathers translation of 1923 and admired enormously, placing it second to Shakespeare among the works that most moved him (*E&I* 447; *LE* 129; on the Mardrus-Mathers translation, see *AV-1925* xiii; *In Excited Reverie* 291; *Letters* 832). The poem elaborates the Arabism of "SOLOMON AND THE WITCH" and "Solomon to Sheba" (1918), which likewise commemorate Yeats's marriage. Yeats garbed his marriage poems in fictions of Arabia undoubtedly because the desert culture of the Middle East seemed severe, mysterious, and ancient, and thus in keeping with the wisdom conveyed by his wife. S. B. Bushrui further theorizes that his "choice of this Arabian background was to release his faculties from the inhibitions of the Irish cultural background and express more freely the theme of sexual love, before he was able to express it against his own Irish background" (*In Excited Reverie* 311). Furthermore, as Ann Saddlemyer notes, "Orientalism was in the air: GEORGE [YEATS] and Willy had known *The Arabian Nights* since childhood and were reintroduced by the evocative versions produced by Edmund Dulac and Laurence Housman; George had read much on the magic and astrology of Syrian religion; more recently [Frank Pearce] Sturm had lectured to the London THEOSOPHICAL SOCIETY on the philosophy of the Arabian alchemists; W. S. Blunt entertained his guests dressed in flowing Arab robes, and his wife Lady Ann had published *The Bedouin Tribes of the Euphrates*; James Elroy Flecker's *Hassan* was one of the theatrical successes of 1922" (BG 307; on Sturm [1879–1942] see 272–273; see also CL3 256; *Letters* 712, 781, 899; AV 69). It is also worth mentioning Charles Doughty's *Arabia Deserta* (1888), which Yeats and EZRA POUND read during their second winter's stay at Stone Cottage in 1915 (*Stone Cottage* 143–146).

"The Gift of Harun Al-Rashid" is a fantasy of Yeats's own devising, though it loosely borrows, as S. B. Bushrui notes, from the Mardrus-Mathers translation of "The Tale of Alā al-Dīn Abū Shāmāt (*In*

Excited Reverie 302). Harun al-Rashid (763/766–809) and Kusta ben Luka (ninth century) were genuine historical figures. Harun, the fifth caliph of the Abassid dynasty, ruled a vast Middle Eastern empire from his palatial seat in Baghdad. *The Arabian Nights*, in which he figures largely, made his court a byword of wealth and luxury. "We know Harun al Raschid through the *Arabian Nights* alone, and there he is the greatest of all traditional images of generosity and magnanimity," Yeats writes in ON THE BOILER, defending the caliph against the representation of him as a cruel tyrant in Flecker's play, which the ABBEY THEATRE had produced in June 1936. Oddly protective of Harun's reputation, Yeats lambasted the play as a historical "forgery" and a literary "impertinence" (*Expl.* 447–448; *LE* 246–247).

Kusta ben Luka—or Qustā ibn-Lūqā—was, writes Bushrui, "a translator of mathematical and philosophical works, and in addition had distinguished himself in medicine, philosophy, geometry, numbers and music. He mastered both Greek and Arabic, and the list of his original works and translations in the *Fihrist* [bibliography of Medieval Arabic texts] numbers thirty-four" (*In Excited Reverie* 301). In his introduction to the 1925 edition of *A Vision* Yeats describes Kusta as a "Christian Philosopher at the Court of Harun Al-Raschid," though he was apparently born after Harun's reign had come to an end; Bushrui cites 820 as his year of birth (*AV-1925* xix; *In Excited Reverie* 301). Yeats eventually acknowledged his mistake. In the 1937 edition of *A Vision*, he writes in the voice of John Aherne that "The Gift of Harun Al-Rashid" seems "to have got the dates wrong, for according to the story Robartes told my brother, the Founder of the Judwali Sect, Kusta ben Luka, was a young or youngish man when Harun Al-Rashid died. However, poetic licence may still exist" (*AV* 54). In a note to CALVARY, Yeats describes, in the voice of a "certain old Arab," Kusta ben Luka's teaching that all things should be divided "into Chance and Choice; one can think about the world and about man, or anything else until all has vanished but these two things, for they are indeed the first cause of the animate and inanimate world. They exist in God, for if they did not He would not have free-

dom, He would be bound by His own Choice. In God alone, indeed, can they be united, yet each be perfect and without limit or hindrance" (*VPl.* 790; cf. "ALL SOULS' NIGHT").

The poem presents a potentially disorienting warren of embedded narratives. Amid its own warren of embedded narratives, Yeats's 1924 note to the poem supplies a helpful précis. In the voice of Owen Aherne, Yeats explains that Harun celebrated the execution of his vizier Jaffer by taking a new bride. "Wishing to confer an equal happiness upon his friend," Yeats continues, "he chose a young bride for Kusta-ben-Luka. According to one tradition of the desert, she had, to the great surprise of her friends, fallen in love with the elderly philosopher, but according to another, Harun bought her from a passing merchant. Kusta, a Christian like the Caliph's own physician, had planned, one version of the story says, to end his days in a monastery at Nisibis, while another story has it that he was deep in a violent love-affair that he had arranged for himself. The only thing upon which there is general agreement is that he was warned by a dream to accept the gift of the Caliph, and that his wife, a few days after the marriage, began to talk in her sleep, and that she told him all those things which he had searched for vainly all his life in the great library of the Caliph, and in the conversation of wise men" (*VP* 828–829).

"The Gift of Harun al-Rashid" appeared in *English Life and The Illustrated Review* (January 1924), the *Dial* (June 1924), and *The Cat and the Moon and Certain Poems* (July 1924) before finding, under the title "Desert Geometry or The Gift of Harun Al-Raschid," what seems its natural place in the phantasmagoric framing apparatus of the 1925 edition of *A Vision*. Yeats struck the poem from the 1937 edition as part of a general purge. In his introduction, he explains that the first version of the book "fills me with shame. I had misinterpreted the geometry, and in my ignorance of philosophy failed to understand distinctions upon which the coherence of the whole depended, and as my wife was unwilling that her share should be known, and I to seem sole author, I had invented an unnatural story of an Arabian traveller which I must amend and find a place for some day because I was fool enough to write half a dozen poems that are unintelligible without it" (AV 19). The "unnatural story" refers to Michael Robartes' account of his activities in "Owen Aherne's" introduction to the 1925 edition.

FIRST PUBLICATION: *English Life and The Illustrated Review* (periodical), January 1924, under the title "The Gift of Haroun El Rashid." Reprinted in *The Cat and the Moon and Certain Poems*, The CUALA PRESS, Dublin, July 1924, under the title "The Gift of Harun-Al-Rashid." Reprinted in *A Vision*, privately printed by T. Werner Laurie, London, 1925, under the title "Desert Geometry or the Gift of Harun Al-Raschid." Reprinted in *The Tower*, Macmillan, London, February 14, 1928, under the present title.

BIBLIOGRAPHY

Jeffares, A. Norman, and K. G. W. Cross, eds. *In Excited Reverie: A Centenary Tribute to William Butler Yeats 1865–1939*; Longenbach, James. *Stone Cottage: Pound, Yeats, and Modernism*; Saddlemyer, Ann. *Becoming George: The Life of Mrs W. B. Yeats*; Yeats, W. B. *The Collected Letters of W. B. Yeats* (vol. 3), *A Critical Edition of Yeats's A Vision* (1925), *Essays and Introductions, Explorations, Later Essays, The Letters of W. B. Yeats, The Variorum Edition of the Plays of W. B. Yeats, The Variorum Edition of the Poems of W. B. Yeats, A Vision*.

"Girl's Song" (1930)

See "WORDS FOR MUSIC PERHAPS."

"Great Day, The" (1938)

"The Great Day," "Parnell," "What Was Lost," and "The Spur" appeared as a sequence under the title "Fragments" in the March 1938 issue of the *London Mercury*, and they have remained sequential in subsequent publications. Epigrammatic and mordant, the first three poems deride the revolutionary enthusiasm that suffused the intellectual culture of the 1930s, while "The Spur" defends the rage that informs the irony of these poems and "spurs" them into life. Yeats told DOROTHY WELLESLEY that the first three poems "give the essence" of his politics (*LOP* 123). "The Great Day" sends up a sarcastic cheer for political revolution, while observing that revolution changes merely the hand that holds the whip, one spiritual beggar replacing another. The problem, implicitly, is that modernity has rejected the nobility—the Renaissance virtue—that constitutes the conscience and instinct of a great ruling class ("TO A WEALTHY MAN WHO PROMISED A SECOND SUBSCRIPTION TO THE DUBLIN MUNICIPAL GALLERY IF IT WERE PROVED THE PEOPLE WANTED PICTURES" is a lecture on these virtues). The two lines of "Parnell" glimpse the character of the genuine leader, the man of "passionate serving kind," as Yeats puts it in "TO A SHADE." Like the great Georgians of "The SEVEN SAGES," CHARLES STEWART PARNELL walks the common road, signifying the wisdom that comes from closeness to life and the rejection of all abstraction. In place of utopian political fantasy, Parnell dispenses the bitter truth that the run of men will always know the hardness of life. According to Yeats, the poem is constructed upon "an actual saying of Parnell's" (*LOP* 123). "What Was Lost," the most complex of the three poems, grieves for Parnell as a lost king, with Yeats playing, as in "FALLEN MAJESTY," the role of the last courtier. The poem's final two lines return to the truth of the previous poem, acknowledging that for all the rise and fall of civilizations we merely "beat on the same small stone." In poems like "A DIALOGUE OF SELF AND SOUL," "The GYRES," "LAPIS LAZULI," and "VACILLATION" Yeats had blazed with "joy" in contemplation of the cycles that turn the world in tragic circles, but here there is mere stoic acknowledgment. "Rising and Setting" ostensibly refer to the sun, and more generally to the cyclic pattern of history, but the allusion to "Rising" may cynically pun on the EASTER RISING of 1916. The rising had struck Yeats as a regrettable repetition of previous failed rebellions, a confirmation that men indeed "always beat on the same small stone." The Rising may further have seemed an example of one beggar replacing—or trying to replace—another, for Yeats was at best ambivalent about the several Easter revolutionaries of his acquaintance.

If "What Was Lost" sings the wreckage of things, "The Spur" describes "lust and rage" as the mechanism of this song, especially in his old age. Yeats included a draft of "The Spur" in a December 11, 1936, letter to Ethel Mannin (1900–84), a novelist and journalist with whom he had a sexual relationship (on Mannin, see *AP* 510–515). The letter gives Yeats's "rage" an explicitly political character, suggesting the logic of "The Spur's" inclusion in the sequence. Yeats denied hatred of England ("Of course I don't hate the people of England, considering all I owe to Shakespeare, BLAKE, MORRIS—they are the one people I cannot hate") though he admitted hatred of "certain characteristics of modern England." Annotating his own ire, he inserted the four lines of "The Spur." The letter ends with a denunciation of the age that recalls "The Great Day": "I am alarmed at the growing moral cowardice of the world, as the old security disappears—people run in packs that they may get courage from one another and even sit at home and shiver" (*Letters* 872–873). Writing to Wellesley on December 4, 1936, Yeats also grew heated over politics, in this case the attempt to discredit Roger Casement (1864–1916), whose execution for his part in the Easter Rising was smoothed by the circulation of forged diaries that made him out to be homosexual. As he punctuated the letter to Mannin by quoting "The Spur," so he punctuated this letter by echoing it: "Forgive all this my dear but I have told you that my poetry all comes from rage or lust" (*Letters* 870–871; *LOP* 109).

FIRST PUBLICATION: The *London Mercury* (periodical), March 1938, under the title "Fragments" (with "Parnell," "What Was Lost" and "The Spur"). Reprinted, with its companion poems, in *New Poems*, The CUALA PRESS, Dublin, May 18, 1938.

BIBLIOGRAPHY

Foster, R. F. *W. B. Yeats: A Life, II: The Arch-Poet*; Yeats, W. B. *The Letters of W. B. Yeats, Letters on Poetry from W. B. Yeats to Dorothy Wellesley*.

"Grey Rock, The" (1913)

"The Grey Rock" is a long verse tale from Irish legend interspersed with apostrophes to the shades of Yeats's one-time companions in the RHYMERS' CLUB. Though it might appear at a distant remove from the 1890s, the tale allegorically celebrates those among Yeats's protégés who made it a "matter of conscience to turn from every kind of money-making" and set their store by "emotion which has no relation to any public interest" (*Aut.* 233). Unlike the warrior hero of the poem, these artists and writers spurned the solidities of the world in order to keep faith with ideals beyond the world.

The tale begins with a knotty preamble addressed to Yeats's "companions of the Cheshire Cheese," the London pub at which the Rhymers' Club met during the early 1890s. Yeats vouches for the tale as more likely to please the Rhymers than the "stories now in fashion," though they might think it a waste of breath to pretend "that there can be passion / That has more life in it than death," which suggests the Rhymers' unwholesome aestheticism (see *UP1* 248). The banter about Goban, brewer to the Sidhe, implies that for all their drinking the Rhymers imbibed nothing of the joy that comes from the wine of gods, and thus may feel removed from the poem. All the same, Yeats concludes, the "moral" of the story is theirs because it is his.

The tale proper opens with a tableau of the gods, drowsy with wine and meat, reposing at the table of their "great house at Slievenamon," a mountain in County Tipperary. Before them comes "one that was like woman made." As soon becomes clear, the woman is Aoife, not the warrior queen of Scotland, as in ON BAILE'S STRAND and The DEATH OF CUCHULAIN, but a version of the Irish goddess Aoibheal (*NCP* 104). In a passion, she urges them to mock and hound a man already dead and buried, "the worst of all dead men."

Interrupting his tale with a 28-line parenthesis addressed to the Rhymers, Yeats observes that even dreaming of this room would be enough to destroy the capacity for natural contentment, as happened to MAUD GONNE, who dreamed "when but a child / Of men and woman made like these," and came to despair of mortal marriage (in the event, Gonne did wind up marrying a "lout": Major John Mac-Bride, the "drunken, vainglorious lout" of "EASTER 1916"). The Rhymers presumably suffered a similar fate: They too had glimpsed some unachievable or inexpressible ideal and had gone to their destruction pining for the impossible. Yeats wonders whether the ghosts of his old "tavern comrades" have stood before the world's forgotten gods. They deserve such company, for in life they "kept the Muses' sterner laws" even to the death, never making poorer song that they "might have a heavier purse" or giving "loud service to a cause" that they "might have a troop of friends."

Parenthesis concluded, Aoife explains her outrage. There had been a great battle in which the invading Danes had been repulsed by an "unseen man" fighting among the Irish. Full of gratitude, Murrough, the Irish king's son, followed a trail of bloody footprints to the resting place of the invisible warrior and inquired of the thin air what friend had given "so fine a stroke." A young man suddenly materialized and revealed his secret: loving him and fearing his death, Aoife had fixed his shirt with a pin that hid him from sight. Seeing the wounds of Murrough, the young man was filled with shame. He removed the pin from his shirt, and that night died in battle. According to A. Norman Jeffares, Yeats here adapts the story of Dubhlaing O'Hartagan, who died fighting the Scandinavian invaders alongside Brian Boru, king of Munster, at the Battle of Clontarf, in 1014 (NCP 104; cf. Expl. 8; P&I 120).

Aoife bitterly complains that she had promised her beloved young man 200 years of life, and yet he had sacrificed all to the needs of his nation and to the esteem of his fellow men. In a frenzy of rage and despair, she throws herself on the ground and cries out, "Why are they faithless when their might / Is from the holy shades that rove / The grey rock and the windy light?" (on "windy light," see Aut. 86). And finally, "Why are the gods by men betrayed?" The gods smile indulgently and tip their cups, drenching her in Goban's wine. Instantaneously forgetting all that has passed, she stares at the gods in laughter.

Yeats ends with the "moral" intimated at the start of the poem. Unlike Aoife's beloved warrior,

who heeded the call of the world with a courage that lacked imagination, Yeats, in the spirit of the Rhymers, has kept faith with "that rock-born, rock-wandering foot"—that is, with Aoife, she who lives upon Craig Liath, the "grey rock," and with those of her kind (YD 8). This has meant falling out of repute with the "loud host before the sea, / That think sword-strokes were better meant / Than lover's music"—the clamorous nationalists of Dublin, caught up in the externalities of national affairs—but no matter as long as the "wandering foot's content."

Though inelegant in form and obscure in allusion, the poem is one of Yeats's strongest affirmations of the poet's freedom from obligation to "the noisy set / Of bankers, schoolmasters, and clergymen / The martyrs call the world" ("ADAM'S CURSE"). In this regard it is the conceptual descendant of a much earlier poem like "THE SECRET ROSE," which likewise preaches allegiance to forces beyond the world, and cognate with contemporary poems of social abnegation like "THE FISHERMAN" and "TO A FRIEND WHOSE WORK HAS COME TO NOTHING." The poem is further notable, as James Longenbach discerns, as an anticipation of one of modernism's chief devices: the juxtaposition of the modern and the mythic (Stone Cottage 167).

In its November 1913 issue, Poetry magazine named "The Grey Rock" the best poem to appear in its pages that year and awarded Yeats a £50 prize. Yeats accepted £10 with the intention of commissioning his friend T. STURGE MOORE to design a bookplate, but he asked that the remainder of the prize be given to a younger poet. Yeats wrote to the magazine's editor Harriet Monroe (1860–1936), "I vacillated a good deal until I thought of this solution, for it seemed to me so ungracious to refuse; but if I had accepted I should have been bothered by the image of some unknown needy young man in a garret" (Letters 584–585). The eventual recipient was EZRA POUND, who had insisted that Yeats receive the prize in the first place. Pound spent the money on two statuettes by Henri Gaudier-Brzeska (1891–1915) and a new typewriter (Selected Letters 27–28). In a review of Responsibilities in the May 1914 issue of Poetry, Pound said of the poem that had lined his pocket, "The Grey Rock is, I admit, obscure"—an ironic criticism from the future author of the *Cantos*—"but it outweighs this by a curious nobility, a nobility which is, to me at least, the very core of Mr. Yeats's production, the constant element in his writing" (*Literary Essays of Ezra Pound* 379).

FIRST PUBLICATION: The *British Review* and *Poetry* (periodicals), April 1913. Reprinted in *Responsibilities: Poems and a Play*, The CUALA PRESS, Churchtown, Dundrum, May 25, 1914.

BIBLIOGRAPHY

Conner, Lester I. *A Yeats Dictionary: Persons and Places in the Poetry of William Butler Yeats*; Jeffares, A. Norman. *A New Commentary on the Poems of W. B. Yeats*; Longenbach, James. *Stone Cottage: Pound, Yeats, and Modernism*; Pound, Ezra. *Literary Essays of Ezra Pound, Selected Letters of Ezra Pound, 1907–1941*; Yeats, W. B. *Autobiographies, Explorations, The Letters of W. B. Yeats, Memoirs, Prefaces and Introductions, Uncollected Prose by W. B. Yeats* (vol. 2).

"Gyres, The" (1938)

The tragic gaiety that "A DIALOGUE OF SELF AND SOUL," "LAPIS LAZULI," and "VACILLATION" extol is here an accomplished jubilance. Yeats unflinchingly embraces the ceaseless pattern of making and unmaking, doing and undoing, as the gyres of history "die each other's life, live each other's death" (AV 68, 197, 271), as represented by the figure of two interlocked gyres or cones, the vertex of the one centered on the base of the other (on the gyre, see AV 67–80). In this embrace, Yeats achieves something of the "Beatific Vision" he describes in a note to "The SECOND COMING": "The supreme religious act of [the Judwalis] faith is to fix the attention on the mathematical form of this movement until the whole past and future of humanity, or of an individual man, shall be present to the intellect as if it were accomplished in a single moment" (VP 824). With relevance to "The Gyres," Yeats goes on to describe the double movement of the interlocked gyres as it applies to human history. He theorizes that "the end of an age, which always

receives the revelation of the character of the next age, is represented by the coming of one gyre to its place of greatest expansion and of the other to that of its greatest contraction. At the present moment the life gyre is sweeping outward, unlike that before the birth of Christ which was narrowing, and has almost reached its greatest expansion. The revelation which approaches will however take its character from the contrary movement of the interior gyre. All our scientific, democratic, fact-accumulating, heterogeneous civilization belongs to the outward gyre and prepares not the continuance of itself but the revelation as in a lightning flash [. . .] of the civilization that must slowly take its place" (824–825). Yeats further distills this idea in a July 13, 1933, letter to OLIVIA SHAKESPEAR: "History is very simple—the rule of the many, then the rule of the few, day and night, night and day for ever, while in small disturbed nations day and night race" (*Letters* 812). "The Gyres" finds a source of "tragic joy" in the perpetual bereavement of the cycles of history, but it also takes less fraught joy in the promise of an age more congenial to Yeats's own *antithetical* sensibility.

The poem opens with a cry of excitement—"The gyres! the gyres!"—in response to the stirring of a new dispensation, and Yeats calls on "Old Rocky Face" to bear witness. The allusion to "Rocky Face" may be the most puzzling detail in Yeats's entire poetic *oeuvre*. The sphinx of "The Second Coming"—likewise an *antithetical* avatar—is a possible referent. Virginia Moore hypothesizes an allusion to BLAKE's Urizen. In *The First Book of Urizen*, as Moore points out, Urizen sleeps a "stony sleep" among rocks, "in chains of the mind locked up" (*Unicorn* 420). Both Harold Bloom and A. Norman Jeffares propose an allusion to Ahasuerus, the Wandering Jew of SHELLEY's *Queen Mab* (1813) and *Hellas* (1822), a mage-like figure who dominated Yeats's youthful imagination (NCP 359–361; *Yeats* 435; *Aut.* 151–153). In manuscript, Yeats refers to "Old Rocky Face" as "old cavern man" (*Yeats at Work* 145–146). This makes sense as an allusion to Ahasuerus, who, as Shelley writes, "dwells in a sea-cavern / 'Mid the Demonesi, less accessible / Than thou or God!" John Unterecker speculates that Yeats refers to the "Rocky Face of the moon which controls the gyres and which peers from the cavern of night" (*RG* 257). GEORGE YEATS's annotation of *New Poems* (1938) identifies Rocky Face as the Delphic Oracle that would more patently haunt "The DELPHIC ORACLE UPON PLOTINUS" and "NEWS FOR THE DELPHIC ORACLE" (*IY* 154; *Yeats at Work* 148). Whatever the case—and clearly Yeats was not intent on being transparent—Old Rocky Face is a type of the elemental power that eternally presides over the pattern of history.

Yeats directs the attention of Old Rocky Face to signs of the coalescing apocalypse. "Irrational streams of blood are staining earth" is a reiteration of "NINETEEN HUNDRED AND NINETEEN" and "The Second Coming," and of the sanguinary expectations evident in his letters of the period (see *Letters* 851). "Empedocles has thrown all things about," Yeats continues, which is to say that the gyres of history are in the process of reversing themselves. Empedocles (ca. 493–ca. 433 B.C.), a Greek philosopher, is for Yeats's purposes an ancestral theorist of the gyre; in *A VISION*, he writes that "Empedocles and Heraclitus thought that the universe had first one form and then its opposite in perpetual alternation [. . .]" (*AV* 246; see also 67–68). Speaking of his own era in the metaphors of antiquity, Yeats declares Hector once again dead and Troy once again in flames (cf. "TWO SONGS FROM A PLAY"). Yeats and those of his stamp watch and but "laugh in tragic joy," purging the bitterness of the scene in an embrace of its tragic intensity and its expression of the universal pattern. This is the joy of "A Dialogue of Self and Soul," "Lapis Lazuli," and "Vacillation." In "J. M. Synge and the Ireland of his Time" (1911), Yeats theorizes the nature of this joy: "There is in the creative joy an acceptance of what life brings, because we have understood the beauty of what it brings, or a hatred of death for what it takes away, which arouses within us, through some sympathy perhaps with all other men, an energy so noble, so powerful, that we laugh aloud and mock, in the terror or the sweetness of our exaltation, at death and oblivion" (*E&I* 322; see also *Expl.* 448–449; *LE* 247; *Letters* 838; *LOP* 12).

Echoing by turns "Nineteen Hundred and Nineteen" ("the nightmare / Rides upon sleep") and "BYZANTIUM" ("all complexities of mire or blood"),

Yeats cries "what matter" to the travesties of politics and the ignominy of the body and urges dry eyes at the passing of a "greater" and "more gracious time." Yeats may refer to the Georgian era and its legacy (cf. "IN MEMORY OF EVA GORE-BOOTH AND CON MARKIEWICZ"), or he may refer to the entire span of the European tradition (cf. "The NINETEENTH CENTURY AND AFTER"). Having arrived at the tragic understanding, he no longer pines, as he once did, for the revival of traditions in art now passed away. "For painted forms or boxes of make-up / In ancient tombs I sighed," he recalls in language that is carefully ambiguous. Are the painted forms and boxes of make-up to be found in ancient tombs, relics of dead artistic traditions, or does Yeats seek in ancient tombs, like SHELLEY in "Hymn to Intellectual Beauty" (1817), the key to wisdom and repossession? The poem's third stanza, in which a new *antithetical* dispensation rises from a broken sepulcher, accords with the former interpretation, while the tomb haunting of poems like "The LEADERS OF THE CROWD" and "ALL SOULS' NIGHT" sets a precedent for the latter. Against the temptations of remorse, the vatic voice—presumably the voice of Old Rocky Face—emanates from a cavern with the single command: "Rejoice!"

The third and final stanza of the poem cries again "what matter" as it contemplates the coarsening of conduct, work, and the soul itself, for the gyres will bring again an *antithetical* age, the return of those types dear to Rocky Face: lovers of horses (cf. "AT GALWAY RACES") and lovers of women (cf. "The TOWER," lines 105–120), those who live not in the abstraction of the mind but in the vitality of the "whole body" (*Aut.* 227; *E&I* 235). These shall disinter the "workman, noble and saint" from "marble of a broken sepulchre," or the "dark betwixt the polecat and the owl," or "any rich, dark nothing," which is to say, from the mysterious realm of death, night, and darkness, what Yeats in "A Dialogue of Self and Soul" calls "ancestral night," the "quarter where all thought is done," the darkness that is indistinguishable from the soul. The polecat and owl seem to indicate the antinomy of body and mind, *primary* and *antithetical*, following the suggestion of a note to CALVARY: "Certain birds, especially as I see things, such lonely birds as the heron, hawk, eagle, and swan, are the natural symbols of subjectivity, especially when floating upon the wind alone or alighting upon some pool or river, while the beasts that run upon the ground, especially those that run in packs, are the natural symbols of objective man" (VPl. 789). In due course, all things will run again on that "unfashionable gyre"—unfashionable because opposing the present gyre, or because *antithetical* solitude is always inimical to the masses (cf. "The Leaders of the Crowd").

FIRST PUBLICATION: *New Poems,* The CUALA PRESS, Dublin, May 18, 1938.

BIBLIOGRAPHY

Bloom, Harold. *Yeats;* Bradford, Curtis B. *Yeats at Work;* Ellmann, Richard. *The Identity of Yeats;* Jeffares, A. Norman. *A New Commentary on the Collected Poems of W. B. Yeats;* Moore, Virginia. *The Unicorn: William Butler Yeats' Search for Reality;* Unterecker, John. *A Reader's Guide to William Butler Yeats;* Yeats, W. B. *Autobiographies, Essays and Introductions, Explorations, Later Essays, The Letters of W. B. Yeats, Letters on Poetry from W. B. Yeats to Dorothy Wellesley, The Variorum Edition of the Plays of W. B. Yeats, The Variorum Edition of the Poems of W. B. Yeats, A Vision.*

"He and She" (1934)

See "SUPERNATURAL SONGS."

"He bids his Beloved be at Peace" (1896)

"He bids his Beloved be at Peace" is one of Yeats's most intense evocations of the spirits that both scathe and seduce the heart of man with their otherworldly beauty and force. Its evident counterparts are poems like "The HOSTING OF THE SIDHE" and "The UNAPPEASABLE HOST," but the underlying spiritual force is embodied differently, as Yeats explains in a note to the poem included in *The Wind Among the Reeds* (1899): "November, the old

beginning of winter, or of the victory of the Fomor, or powers of death, and dismay, and cold, and darkness, is associated by the Irish people with the horse-shaped Púcas, who are now mischievous spirits, but were once Fomorian divinities. I think that they may have some connection with the horses of Mannannan, who reigned over the country of the dead, where the Fomorian Tethra reigned also; and the horses of Mannannan, though they could cross the land as easily as the sea, are constantly associated with the waves" (VP 808; see also 795–796, 810; *Fairy and Folk Tales of Ireland* 87–98, 385). In the same note, Yeats explains the significance of the four compass points that so prominently inform the poem, attesting that he follows "much Irish and other mythology, and the magical tradition, in associating the North with night and sleep, and the East, the place of sunrise, with hope, and the South, the place of the sun when at its height, with passion and desire, and the West, the place of sunset, with fading and dreaming things" (808).

"He bids his Beloved be at Peace" describes the "Shadowy Horses"—the Púcas—as they bear down against the backdrop of the North's "creeping night," the East's "hidden joy," the West's "pale dew," and the South's "roses of crimson fire." In allusion to the spiritual meaning of the four compass points, Yeats cries, "O vanity of Sleep, Hope, Dream, endless Desire, / The Horses of Disaster plunge in the heavy clay. . . ." This is to say that humanity's delicate spiritual aspiration is trampled in the ferocious equine onslaught. "Plunge" and "clay"—the first term muscular, the second coarse—contrast with the ethereal play of light described in lines 3 through 6, but at the same time "clay" denotes the elemental matter of creation, as it does more evidently in the contemporaneous poem "The TRAVAIL OF PASSION." Imaginably, the "horses of disaster" are not merely plunging, but harrowing the furrows of life, preparing the ground for new creation. On this reading, the poem gestures toward the kind of creative apocalypse that Yeats would explore in later poems like "LEDA AND THE SWAN" and "The SECOND COMING," while the "horses of disaster" specifically herald the sphinx so famously imaged in the latter. Amid this onslaught, Yeats and his "beloved" take refuge in each other's arms, "drowning love's lonely hour in deep twilight of rest." Like "TO THE ROSE UPON THE ROOD OF TIME," these lines suggest Yeats's early ambivalence about embracing or acceding to transcendental energies that sever one from the natural world and the good of life. The contrast between the transcendental and the mundane is neatly figured in the opposing images of the horses' "tossing manes" and the woman's hair, which Yeats would have spread over his breast.

As Yeats acknowledges in MEMOIRS, these lines describe OLIVIA SHAKESPEAR (86). John Harwood cautions, however, that Yeats wrote the poem some months before he and Shakespear consummated their relationship and that it "would be unwise to assume that the image has a direct and literal origin in Yeats's experience with Olivia Shakespear, especially since the image [of the embowering hair, associated with Shakespear throughout *The Wind Among the Reeds*] was fully formed before Yeats ever set eyes on her" (*Olivia Shakespear and W. B. Yeats* 66). Harwood alludes to the hair imagery in "The Host of the Air," which was published in November 1893 as "The Stolen Bride." John Unterecker observes that in *The Wind Among the Reeds* hair supplants the ROSE as the "dominant" image of Yeats's verse, and he associates this emphasis on hair with a "growing sensuality that ultimately becomes the most characteristic element in [Yeats's] late verse" (RG 92).

In *The Wind Among the Reeds*, "He bids his Beloved be at Peace" is followed by "HE REPROVES THE CURLEW," which functions as an informal epilogue or antistrophe. The cry of the curlew reminds Yeats of the "long heavy hair" that was once shaken over his breast and rubs salt in the wound of his romantic loss.

FIRST PUBLICATION: The *SAVOY* (periodical), January 1896, under the sequence title "Two Love Poems" and the title "The Shadowy Horses" (paired with "The Travail of Passion"). Reprinted in *The Wind Among the Reeds*, Elkin Mathews, London, April 1899, under the title "Michael Robartes bids his Beloved be at Peace." Reprinted in *The Poetical Works of William B. Yeats* (vol. 1), Macmillan, New York, London, November 27, 1906, under the present title.

BIBLIOGRAPHY

Harwood, John. *Olivia Shakespear and W. B. Yeats: After Long Silence*; Unterecker, John. *A Reader's Guide to William Butler Yeats*; Yeats, W. B., ed. *Fairy and Folk Tales of Ireland, Memoirs, The Variorum Edition of the Poems of W. B. Yeats*.

"He gives his Beloved certain Rhymes" (1896)

Most critics identify the poem's "beloved" as Olivia SHAKESPEAR, Yeats's mistress from early 1896 to March or April 1897 and a lifelong friend (see for example AM 157; *Olivia Shakespear and W. B. Yeats* 71; *W. B. Yeats* 125). A. Norman Jeffares, however, identifies her as MAUD GONNE, an interestingly contrary surmise more consistent with the beloved's ability to make "all men's hearts . . . burn and beat" (*NCP* 58). As a public figure and a public speaker as well as a renowned beauty, Gonne is more plausibly described as the cynosure.

Each of the poem's two six-line stanzas opens with an allusion to the beloved fastening her hair. In the first stanza, this small act of creation, in which a lapidary perfection is so effortlessly achieved, contrasts with Yeats's laborious poetic efforts—"day out, day in"—to build a "sorrowful loveliness / Out of the battles of old times." In the second stanza, the small, indifferent gesture is enough to send all men's hearts burning and beating, and the stars themselves become content to light her passing feat. The poem does not much transcend conventional romantic hyperbole, but it does signal a nascent theme that would become increasingly important: the subtle inclination toward imperishable substance. Anticipating his later rhetoric of the "marmorean," Yeats alludes to the beloved's "pearl-pale hand" and urges her to "bind up every wandering tress" with a "golden pin," that is, to bring accident within a formal order of "golden handiwork" (in the phrase of "BYZANTIUM"). Yeats's mature aesthetic of stone and metal arguably traces its root to this crumb of innocuous romantic flattery.

The poem first appeared without title in the story "The Binding of the Hair" as a song sung by the severed head of the poet Aodh to queen Dectira (for the story, see *SRV* 177–181). Yeats again adopts the device of the song sung by the severed head in the late plays *The KING OF THE GREAT CLOCK TOWER* and *A FULL MOON IN MARCH*. In his commentary on the plays, Yeats acknowledges the precedent of the early story (*VPl.* 1010, 1311–1312).

FIRST PUBLICATION: The *SAVOY* (periodical), January 1896, untitled in the story "The Binding of the Hair." The story was reprinted in *The Secret Rose*, Lawrence & Bullen, London, April 1897. The poem was separately reprinted in *The Wind Among the Reeds*, Elkin Mathews, London, April 1899, under the title "Aedh gives his Beloved certain Rhymes." Reprinted in *The Poetical Works of William B. Yeats* (vol. 1), Macmillan, New York, London, November 27, 1906, under the present title.

BIBLIOGRAPHY

Foster, R. F. *W. B. Yeats: A Life, I: The Apprentice Mage*; Harwood, John. *Olivia Shakespear and W. B. Yeats: After Long Silence*; Hone, Joseph. *W. B. Yeats*; Jeffares, A. Norman. *A New Commentary on the Poems of W. B. Yeats*; Yeats, W. B. *The Secret Rose: A Variorum Edition, The Variorum Edition of the Plays of W. B. Yeats*.

"He hears the Cry of the Sedge" (1898)

"He hears the Cry of the Sedge" can be considered an elaboration of the final line of "HE REPROVES THE CURLEW: "There is enough evil in the crying of wind." In "He hears the Cry of the Sedge," the wind finds its voice as it passes through the sedge, and it speaks a terrible malediction: until the end of the world—when the "axle break / That keeps the stars in their round, / And hands hurl in the deep / The banners of East and West, / And the girdle of light is unbound"—Yeats will not sleep by the side of his beloved, presumably MAUD GONNE. Thus the wind militates against natural contentment, as it also does in "He reproves the Curlew," "HE THINKS OF HIS PAST GREATNESS WHEN A PART OF THE CONSTELLATIONS OF HEAVEN," and "The UNAPPEASABLE HOST" (in which the wind is associated with the Sidhe). In a note to the poem, Yeats explains that the "axle tree" stands for the "pole of the Heavens" that is often associated with the "Tree of Life" (*VP* 812; see also 177). John S. Kelly et al. usefully note of the poem's sixth and seventh lines that the symbolism of east and west was central to the ritual of the HERMETIC ORDER OF THE GOLDEN DAWN; most relevantly, the order's temple was "oriented between the Banner of the East, behind which is the altar, and the Banner of the West, behind which is the entrance" (*CL2* 297). Frank Hughes Murphy likewise makes an important observation: "The axle breaks of itself, suggesting a collapse of universal machinery that plunges all creation into chaos; but there are *hands* which hurl the banners of East and West into the deep, suggesting a guiding principle behind the destruction, one that must be presumed to outlive that terrible hour" (*Yeats's Early Poetry* 80). In Hughes's reading, the poem suggests not an apocalyptic end, but an apocalyptic renewal or transformation, after which Yeats may be eternally reunited with his beloved (79).

Gonne read "He hears the Cry of the Sedge," "HE THINKS OF THOSE WHO HAVE SPOKEN EVIL OF HIS BELOVED" and "The LOVER MOURNS FOR THE LOSS OF LOVE" in the May 1898 issue of the *Dome*. "I read over and over again your poem until I didn't need the book to read it, it is so beautiful," she enthused in a June 1898 letter, though whether she had in mind a specific poem or the entire sequence is not clear (*GY* 91).

FIRST PUBLICATION: The *Dome* (periodical), May 1898, under the sequence title "Aodh to Dectora. Three Songs" (paired with "He thinks of those who have Spoken Evil of his Beloved" and "The Lover mourns for the Loss of Love"). Reprinted in *The Wind Among the Reeds*, Elkin Mathews, London, April 1899, under the title "Aedh hears the Cry of the Sedge." Reprinted in *The Poetical Works of William B. Yeats* (vol. 1), Macmillan, New York, London, November 27, 1906, under the present title.

BIBLIOGRAPHY

Murphy, Frank Hughes. *Yeats's Early Poetry: The Quest for Reconciliation*; Yeats, W. B. *The Collected Letters of W. B. Yeats* (vol. 2), *The Gonne-Yeats Letters 1893–1938, The Variorum Edition of the Poems of W. B. Yeats.*

"Her Anxiety" (1930)

See "WORDS FOR MUSIC PERHAPS."

"Her Courage" (1917)

The sixth of seven poems in the sequence "UPON A DYING LADY," "Her Courage," like the first poem in the sequence, "HER COURTESY," celebrates Mabel Beardsley (1871–1916), then dying of cancer, as one of the high souls who "have lived in joy and laughed into the face of Death" (or, in the closely related language of "VACILLATION," as one of those who go "Proud, open-eyed and laughing to the tomb"). In seeming retort to the orthodox aspirations of "SHE TURNS THE DOLLS' FACES TO THE WALL" and "The END OF DAY," the poem envisions Beardsley joining upon her death those of kindred spirit at the "predestined dancing-place." The vision of the "dancing-place" harks back to Yeats's preoccupation with fairy lore during the 1890s (see for example "The STOLEN CHILD") and prompts him to apologize that he has "no speech but symbol, the pagan speech I made / Amid the dreams of youth. . . ." The inadequacy of Yeats's "pagan speech" would later become the theme of "The CIRCUS ANIMAL'S DESERTION," while the vision of the dead in the "predestined dancing-place" anticipates the final stanza of "ALL SOULS' NIGHT."

Yeats imagines Beardsley among a heterogeneous company of those who have given the world their passion, to borrow a phrase from "CERTAIN ARTISTS BRING HER DOLLS AND DRAWINGS." The denizens of the Yeatsian paradise include Grania (see *DIARMUID AND GRANIA*) and some "old cardinal" who "murmured of Giorgione at his latest breath." As an aesthete of Walter Pater's school—the last of this cultivated generation, perhaps—he contrasts with the presumptively philistine priest mentioned in "She turns the Dolls' Faces to the Wall." Giorgione (ca. 1478–ca. 1510) was one of the preeminent painters of the Italian Renaissance and a central enthusiasm of Pater's *Renaissance* (1873), a book whose influence on Yeats is recorded in the 26th and 27th lines of the "The PHASES OF THE MOON." In the scheme of A VISION Yeats assigns Giorgione to the 14th lunar phase, one of the two phases at which "the greatest human beauty becomes possible" (131). Achilles is the hero of *The Iliad*. Timor (1336–1405), known in the West as Tamburlaine or Tamerlaine, was a "Turkic conqueror of Islamic faith, chiefly remembered for the barbarity of his conquests from India and Russia to the Mediterranean Sea and for the cultural achievements of his dynasty" (*Encyclopaedia Britannica*). Babar (1483–1530) was "emperor (1526–30) and founder of the Mughal dynasty of India, a descendant of the Mongol conqueror Genghis Khan and also of Timur [i.e., Timor]. He was a military adventurer and soldier of distinction and a poet and diarist of genius, as well as a statesman" (*Encyclopedia Britannica*). A. Norman Jeffares tentatively identifies "Barhaim" as Bahram, the hunter of Edward Fitzgerald's *Rubáiyát of Omar Khayyam* (NCP 165).

These assorted heroes of the spirit have "lived in joy and laughed into the face of Death," fulfilling what Yeats, in a 1935 letter to DOROTHY WELLESLEY, calls the "supreme aim": achieving "an act of faith and reason to make one rejoice in the midst of tragedy" (*Letters* 838; *LOP* 12). In "J. M. Synge and the Ireland of his Time" (1912), Yeats theorizes the nature of this joy: "There is in the creative joy an acceptance of what life brings, because we have understood the beauty of what it brings, or a hatred of death for what it takes away, which arouses within us, through some sympathy perhaps with all other men, an energy so noble, so powerful, that we laugh aloud and mock, in the terror or the sweetness of our exaltation, at death and oblivion" (*E&I* 322). Numerous poems, including "DEATH," "The GYRES," and "LAPIS LAZULI," likewise take up the theme of heroic contempt or joy in the face of death.

FIRST PUBLICATION: The *Little Review* (periodical), August 1917, and the *New Statesman* (periodical), August 11, 1917. Reprinted in *The Wild Swans at Coole*, The CUALA PRESS, Churchtown, Dundrum, November 17, 1917.

BIBLIOGRAPHY

Jeffares, A. Norman. *A New Commentary on the Poems of W. B. Yeats*; Yeats, W. B. *Essays and Introductions*, *The Letters of W. B. Yeats*, *Letters on Poetry from W. B. Yeats to Dorothy Wellesley*, *A Vision*.

"Her Courtesy" (1917)

The first of seven poems in the sequence "UPON A DYING LADY," "Her Courtesy" recollects Yeats's first visit to the hospital, on January 5, 1913, to see Mabel Beardsley (1871–1916), then dying of cancer. The poem closely follows the account he gave in a January 8 letter to Lady GREGORY (*Letters* 574–575). Yeats was moved by this visit and deeply struck by Beardsley's dauntless spirit in the face of death. The eight-line poem lauds Beardsley's "courtesy," by which he means no mere manners, but an existential composure or dignity, an unwillingness to be rattled even by death (in "HER COURAGE," Yeats refers to those who "lived in joy and laughed into the face of Death"). Not wanting her visitors to be saddened by her condition, she gallantly musters her reserves of wit and humor, and yet the poem suggests that her spirits genuinely catch fire ("her eyes are laughter-lit"). Even on her deathbed she is capable of spontaneous joy. Beardsley's "laughter-lit eyes" anticipate the gaiety of Hamlet and Lear, and even more the "glittering eyes" of the "Chinamen" in "LAPIS LAZULI." The latter poem's great conceptual mechanism—"gaiety transfiguring all that dread"—may owe something to the memory of Beardsley laughing rather than weeping upon her deathbed. Beardsley's use of rouge is a telling detail. It suggests her composure as well as a certain instinctive defense of beauty even in the face of death; so too it evokes the artifice that defined the decadence of the 1890s. The embrace of artifice represented the attempt to subvert nature, and by

extension to subvert death as the intrinsic rule of nature, all of which sat well with Yeats at the time. The fascination with cosmetics and perfumes was the most obvious expression of this tendency; it is elaborated in Charles Baudelaire's "In Defense of Cosmetics," the sixth section of his essay "The Modern Painter" (1863); in Joris-Karl Huysmans's *Against Nature* (1884); and in Max Beerbohm's "A Defence of Cosmetics" (1894). Beerbohm's essay appeared in the *Yellow Book*, of which Mabel's brother AUBREY BEARDSLEY had been art editor.

The poem ends with a masterful complicating turn. Beardsley's defiant display reminds her visitors "of saints and of Petronius Arbiter." Petronius Arbiter is Gaius Petronius (first century A.D.), author of *The Satyricon*. As A. Norman Jeffares notes, Petronius is said to have served as "arbiter elegantiae," or director of the pleasures of the emperor Nero's court (*NCP* 164). The saints and Petronius represent seemingly reverse responses to the crisis of mortality—unworldly and worldly, ascetic and decadent, religious and hedonistic—but Beardsley embodies something of each and suggests their unlikely, underlying convergence of tragic dignity. The implication of the allusion to Petronius is clarified by a similar allusion in *The PLAYER QUEEN*: "Some will die like Cato, some like Cicero, some like Demosthenes, triumphing over death in sonorous eloquence, or, like Petronius Arbiter, will tell witty, scandalous tales [. . .]" (*VPl.* 746). In a February 4, 1905, letter to the *United Irishmen* in defense of J. M. SYNGE's *In the Shadow of the Glen* (1904), Yeats incidentally notes that Petronius's "identification with Arbiter Elegantarium is considered very uncertain by good scholars" (*UP2* 335).

FIRST PUBLICATION: The *Little Review* (periodical), August 1917, and the *New Statesman* (periodical), August 11, 1917. Reprinted in *The Wild Swans at Coole*, The CUALA PRESS, Churchtown, Dundrum, November 17, 1917.

BIBLIOGRAPHY

Jeffares, A. Norman. *A New Commentary on the Poems of W. B. Yeats*; Yeats, W. B. *The Letters of W. B. Yeats*, *Uncollected Prose by W. B. Yeats* (vol. 2), *The Variorum Edition of the Plays of W. B. Yeats*.

"Her Dream" (1930)

See "Words for Music Perhaps."

"He remembers Forgotten Beauty" (1896)

"He remembers Forgotten Beauty" is ostensibly a romantic paean to Olivia Shakespear, Yeats's mistress from early 1896 to March or April 1897, and yet in its emotional emphasis it is less a love poem than an evocation of past and future—on the one hand, a lost golden age of Pre-Raphaelite beauty, and on the other, the apocalypse that will eventually consummate this beauty. Its element of romance masks its deeper longing to conceive an order of being in opposition to modern reality. In this regard, it shares its matrix of emotion with a poem like "The Lake Isle of Innisfree" rather than with the many love poems that Yeats wrote to Maud Gonne.

Yeats tells his beloved that when he embraces her he presses his heart upon "the loveliness / That has long faded from the world," by which he means the stuff of traditional romance: jeweled crowns hurled into "shadowy pools" by kings, "love-tales" wrought in silk by dreaming ladies, roses and lilies born by ladies through "sacred corridors" fragrant with incense. This imagery is heavy-handed and formulaic in its Pre-Raphaelitism, but in the poem's final image of "swords" upon "iron knees" Yeats foreshadows something of the "hardness of outline" (Pound's phrase) that would begin to emerge in earnest in poems like "A Cold Heaven," "No Second Troy," and "The Magi" (*Literary Essays of Ezra Pound* 379). Yeats tells his beloved that when she sighs he hears "white Beauty" sighing for the "hours when all must fade like dew," even as her "high lonely mysteries" brood in half sleep, flame upon flame, deep upon deep, throne upon throne, "their swords upon their iron knees." The suggestion seems to be that Beauty's minions—ironclad warriors of the spirit, anticipatory of the brooding figures of "The Magi"—await an eventual apoca-lyptic awakening. Frank Hughes Murphy's gloss is reasonable: "The poem does not promise that Beauty's servants will rebuild the universe; conceivably Beauty prefers nothingness to a world of mere ugliness. But it seems more likely that Beauty, being a benevolent power sympathetic to the poet and the lover, will establish a new kingdom which will benefit both of them" (*Yeats's Early Poetry* 78).

FIRST PUBLICATION: The Savoy (periodical), July 1896, under the title "O'Sullivan Rua to Mary Lavell." Reprinted in *The Wind Among the Reeds*, Elkin Mathews, London, April 1899, under the title "Michael Robartes remembers Forgotten Beauty." Reprinted in *The Poetical Works of William B. Yeats* (vol. 1), Macmillan, New York, London, November 27, 1906, under the present title.

BIBLIOGRAPHY

Murphy, Frank Hughes. *Yeats's Early Poetry: The Quest for Reconciliation*; Pound, Ezra. *The Literary Essays of Ezra Pound.*

"He reproves the Curlew" (1896)

In *The Wind Among the Reeds* (1899), "He reproves the Curlew" follows "He bids his Beloved be at Peace," functioning as an informal epilogue or antistrophe. In "He bids his Beloved be at Peace," Yeats takes refuge from the plunging "Horses of Disaster" in the arms of his beloved, whom he elsewhere identifies as Olivia Shakespear (*Mem.* 86). He urges her to half close her eyes and let her hair fall over his breast in a "deep twilight of rest." In "He reproves the Curlew," Yeats urges the curlew to "cry no more in the air, / Or only to the water in the West," for its cry reminds him of the same "passion-dimmed eyes" and "long heavy hair" shaken upon his breast. Yeats complains, "There is enough evil in the crying of the wind." Both bird and wind suggest the desolation of Yeats's bereavement and ironically substitute for the plunging horses of disaster in the earlier poem. In "He hears the Cry of the Sedge," which appears later in *The Wind Among the Reeds*, Yeats specifies the "evil" implicit in the wind. As it passes through the sedge, the wind cries that he will not lie with his beloved until the end of the world. A similar message is delivered in "HE THINKS OF HIS PAST GREATNESS WHEN A PART OF THE CONSTELLATIONS OF HEAVEN."

FIRST PUBLICATION: The SAVOY (periodical), November 1896, under the sequence title "Windle-Straws" and the title "O'Sullivan Rua to the Curlew" (paired with "TO HIS HEART, BIDDING IT HAVE NO FEAR"). Reprinted in *The Wind Among the Reeds,* Elkin Mathews, London, April 1899, under the title "Hanrahan reproves the Curlew." Reprinted in *The Poetical Works of William B. Yeats* (vol. 1), Macmillan, New York, London, November 27, 1906, under the present title.

BIBLIOGRAPHY

Yeats, W. B. *Memoirs.*

"Her Friends bring her a Christmas Tree" (1917)

The final of seven poems in the sequence "UPON A DYING LADY," "Her Friends bring her a Christmas Tree" recollects the Christmas tree that decked the hospital room of Mabel Beardsley (1871–1916) when Yeats first visited her sickbed on January 5, 1913. "Beside her a Xmas tree with little toys containing sweets, which she gave us," Yeats wrote to Lady GREGORY on January 8. "Mr. Davis—Ricketts' patron—had brought it—I daresay it was Ricketts' idea. I will keep the little toy she gave me and I daresay she knew this" (*Letters* 574). Yeats refers to Sir Edmund Davis (1861–1939), the Australian-born mining magnate, and to Charles Ricketts (1866–1931), the distinguished painter and stage designer, one of Yeats's intimate friends.

The poem takes the form of an apology addressed to death itself ("great enemy"). It answers for the affront of the Christmas tree and Beardsley's continuing capacity for laughter, which have disrespectfully disturbed the solemnity of death's shadow. Yeats begs death to grant Beardsley a "little grace," asking, "What if a laughing eye / Have looked into your face? / It is about to die." The sup-

plication of these lines retreats from the passionate defiance of "HER COURTESY" and "HER COURAGE," and in particular recants the triumphant final line of the latter, in which Yeats extols those who "have lived in joy and laughed into the face of Death." The request for "a little grace" functions as an ironic commentary on the theme of penance and salvation in "SHE TURNS THE DOLLS' FACES TO THE WALL" and "The END OF DAY." Death, rather than God, is the presiding deity, at least in the hospital room. If "Her Friends bring her a Christmas Tree" is resigned to the supremacy of death, Yeats would later rededicate himself to the defiance of the "great enemy." In both "DEATH" and "The TOWER," to take only the most overt instances of this defiance, Yeats declares that man creates death and by implication governs it.

FIRST PUBLICATION: The *Little Review* (periodical), August 1917, and the *New Statesman* (periodical), August 11, 1917. Reprinted in *The Wild Swans at Coole,* The CUALA PRESS, Churchtown, Dundrum, November 17, 1917.

BIBLIOGRAPHY

Yeats, W. B. *The Letters of W. B. Yeats.*

"Her Praise" (1916)

A less tightly wound version of "FALLEN MAJESTY," "Her Praise" finds Yeats attempting to fan the dying flames of MAUD GONNE's legend. Though years have passed, Yeats remains as if in the first blush of love, pressing the praiseworthiness of his beloved on whoever is willing to listen. His victims in this case are EZRA POUND and his wife, Dorothy, with whom Yeats shared the six rooms of Stone Cottage in the winter of 1915. "I have gone about the house, gone up and down / As a man does who has published a new book, / Or a young girl dressed out in her new gown," Yeats writes of his quest for sympathetic ears, not sparing himself a certain gentle self-satire. The stuttering repetition of "gone" suggests the nervous excitement he continues to feel at the very thought of his beloved as well as inscribes a telltale pun (cf. "FRIENDS," "The LIVING

BEAUTY," "RECONCILIATION," and "TO A YOUNG BEAUTY"). Hook or crook having failed to turn the conversation to Gonne's praise, Yeats must seek the company of the poor, who devotedly remember Gonne's activism on their behalf during the 1890s. The poem's syntax and diction is unusually accessible, but John Unterecker draws attention to the poem's subtle complexity, noting the way it is unified "by echoing interwoven words (foremost, uppermost, foremost; praised, praise, praised, praise, praise; book, books; talk, talk, talk; name, name, name; new, new, new; old, old, old; young, young, young) and a complex pattern of internal rhymes and half-rhymes too intricate to reproduce without reproducing the entire text [. . .]" (RG 141). In the first edition of *The Wild Swans at Coole* as well as in Yeats's collected poems, "Her Praise" belongs to an informal sequence that grapples with the theme of Gonne's middle-age. It includes "Memory" (1916), "The PEOPLE," "His Phoenix" (1916), "A THOUGHT FROM PROPERTIUS," "BROKEN DREAMS," "A Deep-sworn Vow" (1917), and "PRESENCES."

FIRST PUBLICATION: *Poetry* (periodical), February 1916, under the title "The Thorn Tree." Reprinted in *Eight Poems*, "Form" at the Morland Press, April 1916 (see *Letters* 609–610), under the same title. Reprinted in *The Wild Swans at Coole*, The CUALA PRESS, Churchtown, Dundrum, November 17, 1917, under the present title.

BIBLIOGRAPHY

Unterecker, John. *A Reader's Guide to William Butler Yeats*; Yeats, W. B. *The Letters of W. B. Yeats.*

"Her Race" (1917)

The fifth of seven poems in the sequence titled "UPON A DYING LADY," "Her Race" lauds the dauntless spirit of Mabel Beardsley (1871–1916), sister of the arch-decadent illustrator AUBREY BEARDSLEY, famous for his contributions to the *Yellow Book* and the *SAVOY*. Yeats wrote the poem in February 1913 while Beardsley was hospitalized with the cancer that would eventually kill her. The poem's emphasis on "race" conforms to Yeats's preoccupation with lineage, but its specific cue may have been Aubrey's claim that he was a descendant of "the great Pitt," as Yeats recollects in AUTO-BIOGRAPHIES (253, 478). The Beardsleys' maternal grandfather was indeed named William Pitt, but there is no evidence that the great statesman William Pitt (1708–78) was a forebear.

Repeating the leitmotif of the entire sequence, the poem approvingly notes that Beardsley has "not grown uncivil" or bitter, as narrower natures might have done in the same circumstance. The phrase "not grown uncivil"—Latinate, measured in its double negative—implies something of the 18th-century decorum that was, for Yeats, the essence of aristocratic discipline, and suggests something of the tradition with which Yeats wants to associate Beardsley. Yeats attributes Beardsley's dignified display to the same pride he often attributes to Lady GREGORY: She knows herself to be a woman "No red and white of a face, / Or rank, raised from a common / Unreckonable race. . . ." The gist is that Beardsley draws a strengthening pride from the knowledge of her high lineage. The "red and white of a face" signifies roughness and perhaps exposure to the weather. At the same time, the phrase echoes and contrasts with the description of Beardsley with "rouge on the pallor of her face" in "HER COURTESY" and anticipates the allusions to death's face in "HER COURAGE" and "HER FRIENDS BRING HER A CHRISTMAS TREE" (by such repetitions Yeats knits his sequence into unity). Yeats ends, as he does so often, with a powerful rhetorical question: How should Beardsley's "heart fail her / Or sickness break her will / With her dead brother's valour / For an example still?" The question implies an entire theory of aristocratic tradition, valor begetting valor (note again the Latinate ring of the 18th century), the past indebting the present by its example. The salute to Aubrey Beardsley's "valour" takes account of both his quixotic tilt at late Victorian propriety and his ceaseless creative labor even as he suffered from tuberculosis. In MEMOIRS, Yeats elaborates on Beardsley's valor: "In Beardsley I found that noble courage that seems to me at times, whether in man or woman, the greatest of human faculties. I saw it in all he said and did, in the clear logic of speech and in [the] clean swift line of his art" (92).

FIRST PUBLICATION: The *Little Review* (periodical), August 1917, and the *New Statesman* (periodical), August 11, 1917. Reprinted in *The Wild Swans at Coole*, The CUALA PRESS, Churchtown, Dundrum, November 17, 1917.

BIBLIOGRAPHY

Yeats, W. B. *Autobiographies, Memoirs.*

"Her Triumph" (1929)

See "A WOMAN YOUNG AND OLD."

"Her Vision in the Wood" (1929)

See "A WOMAN YOUNG AND OLD."

"He thinks of his Past Greatness when a Part of the Constellations of Heaven" (1898)

"He thinks of his Past Greatness" complements "HE HEARS THE CRY OF THE SEDGE" and "HE REPROVES THE CURLEW," which appear earlier in *The Wind Among the Reeds* (1899). All three poems anguish in the cry of the wind, hearing in it a forlorn emptiness that reminds of the hopelessness of love. In "He thinks of his Past Greatness" and "He hears the Cry of the Sedge" the wind specifically prophecies that the narrator's head will never lie on the breast of his beloved, at least during his natural life.

While "He hears the Cry of the Sedge" and "He reproves the Curlew" seem to be consistent with Yeats's own voice, "He thinks of his Past Greatness" retains the trappings of its earliest incarnation as the lament of the wizard Mongan. Like Fergus in "FERGUS AND THE DRUID," the narrator has imbibed

mystical wisdom. Having come to know all things he finds himself severed from the natural world. In the completeness of his experience, he has been the mystic hazel-tree amid whose branches the stars themselves are hung (a version of the "axle-tree" of "He hears the Cry of the Sedge") and been the insignificant rush trodden under by horses. Finally he has become a man, a "hater of the wind," for the wind conveys the knowledge that he may not lie with his beloved "until he dies." As in "He hears the Cry of the Sedge," the word "until" is crucially ambiguous. It measures the hopeless span of life, but it also admits the possibility that death is an actuating condition, that romantic consummation will be possible *once he dies*. In the climactic final lines of the poem, the narrator cries out against the taunts of the natural world: "O beast of the wilderness, bird of the air, / Must I endure your amorous cries?" These lines deserve to be carefully noted as they anticipate both the opening stanza of "SAILING TO BYZANTIUM" and the rhetorical device of the terminal question that Yeats would later use to great effect in poems like "AMONG SCHOOL CHILDREN," "LEDA AND THE SWAN," and "The SECOND COMING."

The poem first appeared in the *Dome* accompanied by the following note: "Mongan, in the old Celtic poetry, is a famous wizard and king who remembers his passed lives. 'The Country of the Young' is a name in the Celtic poetry for the country of the gods and of the happy dead. The hazel tree was the Irish tree of Life or of Knowledge, and in Ireland it was doubtless, as elsewhere, the tree of the heavens. The Crooked Plough and the Pilot Star are translations of the Gaelic names of the Plough and the Pole Star" (*VP* 177). The "Plough," as *The Oxford English Dictionary* explains, is a "group of seven prominent stars [. . .] in the constellation of *Ursa Major*; also, that constellation as a whole."

FIRST PUBLICATION: The *Dome* (periodical), October 1898, under the title "Song of Mongan." Reprinted in *The Wind Among the Reeds*, Elkin Mathews, London, April 1899, under the title "Mongan thinks of his past Greatness." Reprinted in *The Poetical Works of William B. Yeats* (vol. 1), Macmillan, New York, London, November 27, 1906, under the present title.

BIBLIOGRAPHY

Yeats, W. B. *The Variorum Edition of the Poems of W. B. Yeats.*

"He thinks of those who have Spoken Evil of his Beloved" (1898)

This six-line poem is subtly out of place in the pages of *The Wind Among the Reeds* (1899). Where the volume tends to be languorous with a sensuous mysticism, "He thinks of those who have Spoken Evil of his Beloved" stirs with command and confrontation—a small but sure step toward the STYLE of later poems like "Against Unworthy Praise" (1910), "AT THE ABBEY THEATRE," "THE FASCINATION OF WHAT'S DIFFICULT," and "ON THOSE THAT HATED 'THE PLAYBOY OF THE WESTERN WORLD', 1907," and toward Yeats's emergence over the next decade as a putative man of action. The poem addresses MAUD GONNE, bidding her to "dream" about the great and proud, as against the rumor-mongers of contemporary Dublin. Yeats tells her to "weigh" his song with "the great and their pride," that is, to hear in it the voice of an older and better dispensation. Though made only from a "mouthful of air," it has the permanency that comes from greatness and pride, and, speaking to future generations, will turn against the present crop of slanderers and liars even their own grandchildren. This is to say that the poet is endowed with the power of defining reality, and that this power is not necessarily to be wielded gently or effacingly.

John S. Kelly et al. suggest that the poem is Yeats's response to public rumors concerning Gonne's relationship with the French politician and journalist Lucien Millevoye (CL2 315). On December 8, 1898—some eight months after the poem had been published in the *Dome*—Gonne confirmed the substance of these rumors, confessing to Yeats that she had been Millevoye's mistress and that she had borne him two children (CL2 314–315; Mem. 131–134). Following the scandal of

Gonne's separation from her husband, Major John MacBride (1865–1916), Yeats similarly came to her defense, lashing out at her detractors in the poem "Against Unworthy Praise" (1910).

In late June 1898, Gonne wrote to Yeats: "I read the Dome on the journey [from Dublin to London]. I read over & over again your poem until I didn't need the book to read it, it is so beautiful" (GY 91). Kelly et al. identify the "beautiful" poem as "He thinks of those who have Spoken Evil of his Beloved," but it seems equally possible that Gonne refers to "HE HEARS THE CRY OF THE SEDGE" or "The LOVER MOURNS FOR THE LOSS OF LOVE," which also appeared in the *Dome*, or to the sequence as a whole. "He hears the Cry of the Sedge" is perhaps the poem most aptly described as "beautiful."

FIRST PUBLICATION: The *Dome* (periodical), May 1898, under the sequence title "Aodh to Dectora. Three Songs" (paired with "He hears the Cry of the Sedge" and "The Lover mourns for the Loss of Love"). Reprinted in *The Wind Among the Reeds*, Elkin Mathews, London, April 1899, under the title "Aedh thinks of those who have Spoken Evil of his Beloved." Reprinted in *The Poetical Works of William B. Yeats* (vol. 1), Macmillan, New York, London, November 27, 1906, under the present title.

BIBLIOGRAPHY

Yeats, W. B. *The Collected Letters of W. B. Yeats* (vol. 2), *The Gonne-Yeats Letters 1893–1938*, *Memoirs*.

"He wishes for the Cloths of Heaven" (1899)

Like "A Poet to his Beloved" (1896), "He wishes for the Cloths of Heaven" takes as its theme its own status as a romantic offering. But where "A Poet to his Beloved," most likely addressed to OLIVIA SHAKESPEAR (see *Mem.* 86), comports itself with reasonable decorum ("I bring you with reverent hands / The books of my numberless dreams"), "He wishes for the Cloths of Heaven," most likely addressed to MAUD GONNE, wallows in an almost unctuous humility. Yeats wishes that he could lay under Gonne's feet the cloths of heaven, embroidered as they are with "golden and silver light, / The blue and the dim and the dark cloths / Of night and light and the half-light," but being poor, he has only his dreams. He ends with a plea for gentle treatment: "I have spread my dreams under your feet; / Tread softly because you tread on my dreams." According to biographer Joseph Hone, Yeats once commented during a lecture that "The Cap and Bells" (1894) is "the way to win a lady," while "He wishes for the Cloths of Heaven" is the way to lose one (*W. B. Yeats* 154). Yeats offers another and very different version of the sartorial metaphor in "A COAT."

FIRST PUBLICATION: *The Wind Among the Reeds*, Elkin Mathews, London, April 1899, under the title "Aedh wishes for the Cloths of Heaven." Reprinted in *The Poetical Works of William B. Yeats* (vol. 1), Macmillan, New York, London, November 27, 1906, under the present title.

BIBLIOGRAPHY

Hone, Joseph. *W. B. Yeats*; Yeats, W. B. *Memoirs*.

"He wishes his Beloved were Dead" (1898)

An odd and affecting romantic gambit addressed to MAUD GONNE, "He wishes his Beloved were Dead" conforms to its title, expressing a wish that Gonne were dead so her ghost might come and "murmur tender words" of forgiveness. Unlike the animate Gonne, whose will is that of the "wild birds," the ghost would not "rise and hasten away," as it would know its hair "was bound and wound / About the stars and moon and sun. . . ." (cf. "An IMAGE FROM A PAST LIFE"). This is not to suggest that the ghost would be bound in its place, but that its sense of intertwinement with the larger universe would mitigate its restlessness. The contrast between Gonne and her ghost functions as a subtle analysis of her temperament: Lacking a sense of her own intertwinement with the larger universe—lacking

religion, for all her later professions of Catholicism—Gonne cannot know the calm of possession or the comfort of rest. The poem opens and closes with the wish that Gonne were dead and buried, but in the second instance this wish is more softly and selflessly expressed. Yeats cries, "O would, beloved, that you lay, / Under the dock-leaves in the ground, / While lights were paling one by one," which envisions Gonne not merely dead but gently blanketed and gone to her rest. John Harwood, by contrast, detects in the poem a "barely concealed hostility," for having given up OLIVIA SHAKESPEAR Yeats had seen little of Gonne. According to Harwood, the poem "somewhat malevolently suggests that death might slow her down sufficiently to allow the poet to catch up" (*Olivia Shakespear and W. B. Yeats* 77).

FIRST PUBLICATION: The *Sketch* (periodical), February 9, 1898, under the title "Aodh to Dectora." Reprinted in *The Wind Among the Reeds*, Elkin Mathews, London, April 1899, under the title "Aedh wishes his Beloved were Dead." Reprinted in *The Poetical Works of William B. Yeats* (vol. 1), Macmillan, New York, London, November 27, 1906, under the present title.

BIBLIOGRAPHY

Harwood, John. *Olivia Shakespear and W. B. Yeats: After Long Silence*.

"His Bargain" (1930)

See "WORDS FOR MUSIC PERHAPS."

"His Confidence" (1930)

See "WORDS FOR MUSIC PERHAPS."

"His Memories" (1926)

See "A MAN YOUNG AND OLD."

"His Wildness" (1926)

See "A MAN YOUNG AND OLD."

"Hosting of the Sidhe, The" (1893)

"The powerful and wealthy," Yeats writes in an 1899 note to "The Hosting of the Sidhe," "called the gods of ancient Ireland the Tuatha De Danaan, or the Tribes of the goddess Danu, but the poor called them, and still sometimes call them, the Sidhe, from Aes Sidhe or Sluagh Sidhe, the people of the Faery Hills, as these words are usually explained. Sidhe is also Gaelic for wind, and certainly the Sidhe have much to do with the wind. They journey in whirling winds, the winds that were called the dance of the daughters of Herodias in the Middle Ages [. . .]. When the country people see the leaves whirling on the road they bless themselves, because they believe the Sidhe to be passing by. They are almost always said to wear no covering upon their heads, and to let their hair stream out; and the great among them, for they have great and simple, go much upon horseback. If any one becomes too much interested in them, and sees them over much, he loses all interest in ordinary things" (VP 800; see also CL4 774).

Like "The UNAPPEASABLE HOST," "The Hosting of the Sidhe" depicts the fairy troop in all their furious glory as they ride upon the winds from Knocknarea, a mountain just southwest of SLIGO, and "over the grave of Clooth-na-Bare," upon Slieve Daeane, a mountain just southeast of Sligo. "Clooth-na-Bare" is the "old woman of Bare," who, as Yeats tells in his folkloric piece "The Untiring Ones," went "all over the world seeking a lake deep enough to drown her faery life [i.e., her faery-granted immortality], of which she had grown weary, leaping from hill to lake and lake to hill, and setting up a cairn of stones wherever her feet lighted, until at last she found the deepest water in the world in the little Lough Ia [i.e., Loch Dagea], on the top of the Birds' Mountain [i.e., Slieve Dae-

Knocknarea, County Sligo, from which the fairy host storms down in "The Hosting of the Sidhe." *(Fáilte Ireland)*

ane] at Sligo" (*Myth.* 79). On the south side of the mountain is a megalithic monument associated with Clooth-na-Bare; this is what Yeats calls her grave (*Place Names* 22, 32; see also VP 801–802).

Caoilte tosses his "burning hair," and Niamh calls on all mere mortals to leave behind their mortal dreams and surrender to the passionate beauty of the fairy host. Even to look upon the host, as Niamh cries, is to lose forever one's capacity for natural contentment, a condition fully diagnosed in "The MAN WHO DREAMED OF FAERYLAND." As Yeats explains in his 1899 note, Caoilte was a mortal warrior who became a king among the Sidhe: "The great of the old times are among the Tribes of Danu [i.e. the Sidhe], and are kings and queens among them. Caolte [Yeats's spelling is variable] was a companion of Fiann; and years after his death he appeared to a king in a forest, and was a flaming man, that he might lead in the darkness" (VP 801). Niamh was a fairy princess of surpassing beauty. In the long poem "The WANDERINGS OF OISIN," she selects the mortal warrior Oisin as her lover and leads him away to Tir-na-nog, the realm of the fairies. She also figures in the poems "Alternative Song for the Severed Head in *The King of the Great Clock Tower*" (1934), "The CIRCUS ANIMALS' DESERTION," "The Danaan Quicken Tree" (1893), "The Lover asks Forgiveness because of his Many Moods" (1895), "NEWS FOR THE DELPHIC ORACLE," and "Under the Moon" (1901).

FIRST PUBLICATION: The *National Observer* (periodical), October 7, 1893, under the title "The Faery Host." Reprinted in THE CELTIC TWILIGHT, Lawrence and Bullen, London, December 1893, under the title "The Host." Reprinted in *The Wind Among the Reeds*, Elkin Mathews, London, April 1899, under the present title.

BIBLIOGRAPHY

McGarry, James P. *Place Names in the Writings of William Butler Yeats*; Yeats, W. B. *The Collected Letters of W. B. Yeats* (vol. 4), *Mythologies, The Variorum Edition of the Poems of W. B. Yeats*.

"Human Dignity" (1927)

See "A MAN YOUNG AND OLD."

"'I am of Ireland'" (1932)

See "WORDS FOR MUSIC PERHAPS."

"Image from a Past Life, An" (1920)

Michael Robartes and the Dancer (1921) includes a long note on the abstruse metaphysics underlying "An Image from a Past Life." The note attributes to Michael Robartes, Yeats's alter ego, comments that bear closely on the poem. "No lover, no husband has ever met in dreams the true image of wife or mistress," Yeats writes in the voice of Robartes.

"She who has perhaps filled his whole life with joy or disquiet cannot enter there. Her image can fill every moment of his waking life but only its counterfeit comes to him in sleep [. . .]. They are the forms of those whom he has loved in some past earthly life, chosen from *Spiritus Mundi* by the subconscious will, and through them, for they are not always hollow shades, the dead at whiles outface a living rival." Yeats adds in explanation of this phenomenon that souls "that are once linked by emotion never cease till the last drop of that emotion is exhausted [. . .] to affect one another, remaining always as it were in contact. Those whose past passions are unatoned seldom love living man or woman but only those loved long ago, of whom the living man or woman is but a brief symbol forgotten when some phase of some atonement is finished; but because in general the form does not pass into the memory, it is the moral being of the dead that is symbolised. [. . .] It is therefore only after full atonement or expiation, perhaps after many lives, that a natural deep satisfying love becomes possible [. . .]." In "Image from a Past Life," the "hovering thing" is a dream image belonging to the man, and yet it materializes before the woman; Yeats explains that "in moments of excitement images pass from one mind to another with extraordinary ease" (*VP* 822–823).

The poem itself, however, is no mere vehicle of doctrine. It has the pulse of living drama as its esoteric subtext plays out in a vignette of domestic jealousy and anxiety that undoubtedly has much to do with the difficulty of marrying a woman (GEORGE YEATS) who is not the woman one has been celebrating in poetry for 30 years (MAUD GONNE). In the 1890s, Yeats had adverted to the same difficulty in "The LOVER MOURNS FOR THE LOSS OF LOVE," telling how OLIVIA SHAKESPEAR saw the "image" of Gonne in his heart and went "weeping away." The poem's domestic interest is lent a chilling frisson by Gonne's figuration as something like a gothic succubus (a tradition Yeats more subtly mines in "PRESENCES"). R. F. Foster suggests that the "hovering thing" is not Maud Gonne but ISEULT GONNE (*AP* 191), to whom Yeats had proposed some two months before marrying George, while Ann Saddlemyer suggests that it represents Shakespear (*BG* 237), but "arrogant loveliness" seems particularly characteristic of

Maud Gonne (in the description of "No Second Troy," Gonne's beauty is "like a tightened bow, a kind / That is not natural in an age like this, / Being high and solitary and most stern"). Then too "Under Saturn," which immediately follows in *Michael Robartes and the Dancer* and Yeats's collected poems, resumes the theme of romantic ghosts, referring to a "lost love, inseparable from my thought / Because I have no other youth"—an unmistakable reference to Maud Gonne. The continuity between the two poems strongly suggests that in both cases the haunting presence is the elder Gonne.

The poem's language is poised gracefully between the ceremonial and the conversational ("relics of the idioms of the nineties with a new rhythmic pointing," in T. R. Henn's description) but its dramatic scenario is uncomplicated (*Lonely Tower* 61). A man and a woman—"He" and "She"—Yeats and Mrs. Yeats—find themselves amid a night charged with strangeness: "elaborate starlight" reflects on the dark stream, that which runs by Thoor Ballylee, pictured also in "Coole and Ballylee, 1931," "Ego Dominus Tuus," and "The Phases of the Moon." There is a scream from some "terrified, invisible beast or bird." The scream is an "image of poignant recollection," of the heart's torment, but is referable as well to the avian screams of annunciation or miracle in "Byzantium," "My Table," and "Solomon and the Witch" (which last immediately precedes "An Image from a Past Life" in *Michael Robartes and the Dancer* and in the collected poems). The woman places her hands over the man's eyes to conceal from him the vision of a "sweetheart from another life": a floating specter, "forced to linger / From vague distress / Or arrogant loveliness," who twirls "the starry eddies of her hair / Upon the paleness of a finger." The mention of "starry eddies" brings the image into relation with the physical scene, which the first stanza likewise describes in terms of starlight and eddies; she is no mere figment; the universe is somehow implicated in the conspiracy of her presence. The man reassures the woman that no image, though it might drive him mad with beauty, could make him anything except "fonder." The radical disproportion between madness and fondness gives the lie to his bland profession. Less than reassured, the

woman describes the specter as it sensually throws her arms above her head, either to flout her or to feel her hair as it "streams upon the wind," and the woman knows only that she fears the "hovering thing night brought me."

"He wishes his Beloved were Dead"—another poem of profound romantic ambivalence—represents Gonne with her hair similarly "bound and wound / About the stars and moon and sun. . . ." The motif, like the metaphorization of Gonne as Helen, reflects the sense that Gonne belongs to some larger pattern or reality, that her spirit is coextensive with a magnitude.

FIRST PUBLICATION: The *Nation* (periodical), November 6, 1920. Reprinted in *Michael Robartes and the Dancer*, The Cuala Press, Churchtown, Dundrum, February 1921.

BIBLIOGRAPHY

Foster, R. F. *W. B. Yeats: A Life, II: The Arch-Poet*; Henn, T. R. *The Lonely Tower: Studies in the Poetry of W. B. Yeats*; Saddlemyer, Ann. *Becoming George: The Life of Mrs W. B. Yeats*; Yeats, W. B. *A Variorum Edition of the Poems of W. B. Yeats*.

"In Memory of Alfred Pollexfen" (1917)

Alfred Pollexfen was the youngest of Yeats's seven maternal uncles (to go with five maternal aunts). He was born in 1854 and died in August 1916, leaving Yeats a legacy of £35 (*AP* 85). According to John S. Kelly et al., Pollexfen "worked for many years as a clerk in the offices of the family's Sligo Steam Navigation Company in Liverpool before returning to Sligo in 1910 to help run the family business" (*CL1* 3). In an August 14, 1916, letter to John Butler Yeats, Yeats's sister Lily (1866–1949) said of Alfred's last years in Sligo, "He had money and was no longer one of a great army of nobodies in Liverpool but had become 'Mr. Alfred' [cf. line 32] in a place where he was know[n] and which had known and respected his people before him" (*NCP* 162). The acknowledgment of Yeats's elegy aside, Alfred made little enough impression on his nephew. In AUTOBIOGRAPHIES, Yeats remembers only that the "youngest of my uncles was stout and humorous and had a tongue of leather over the keyhole of his door to keep the draught out [. . .]" (10). Yeats also recalls Alfred's eccentric anxiety about drafts in a letter to his father (*Letters* 533). Unsurprisingly, then, "In Memory of Alfred Pollexfen," despite its technical excellence, is somewhat bloodless and nerveless, arguably the least of Yeats's elegies written for friends and family. R. F. Foster calls it an "awkward elegy, studded with fine phrases in an uncertain and slightly banal catalogue" (AP 69). The poem, however, is only partially an elegy for Pollexfen. More broadly it elegizes the Pollexfen family and Yeats's connection to the places and personalities of his youth. It might also be said that the poem displays an unusual sympathy for those who have no claim upon heroism or greatness. Here is a version of the attention to "common things" of which Yeats had long ago spoken in "TO THE ROSE UPON THE ROOD OF TIME." Absent is what Giorgio Melchiori calls "that element of intellectual aristocratic pride which is the least appealing trait of Yeats's character as a man, and which, one suspects, he may partly have acquired through his frequentation of that arch-scorner, EZRA POUND" (*Whole Mystery of Art* 247).

Like "ALL SOULS' NIGHT" and "THE MUNICIPAL GALLERY REVISITED," the poem takes the form of a necrology in which Yeats invokes the dead one by one (the "banal catalogue" mentioned by Foster), beginning with his grandfather WILLIAM POLLEXFEN and his grandmother Elizabeth Pollexfen (1819–92), both dead for 25 years. There follows a brief tribute to Yeats's uncle GEORGE POLLEXFEN, a friend and fellow occultist. Yeats recalls of his funeral in 1910 that "Masons drove from miles away / To scatter the Acacia spray / Upon a melancholy man / Who had ended where his breath began." This seemingly innocuous recollection, says Foster, would be held against Yeats for the rest of his life by nationalist enemies like D. P. Moran (1869–1936) and Arthur Griffith (1871–1922), who considered Freemasonry a "secret Protestant conspiracy running Irish business life and leagued together in a specifically anti-Catholic alliance. The tactless boast about George's connections fuelled the campaign waged by pious nationalism to identify WBY with reactionary—even Orange—Protestantism" (AP 70). Yeats describes the funeral more fully in a September 29, 1910, letter to Lady GREGORY: "The funeral was very touching—the church full of the working people, Catholics who had never been in a Protestant church before, and the man next me crying all the time. [. . .] The Masons (there were 80 of them) had their own service and one by one threw acacia leaves into the grave with the traditional Masonic goodbye 'Alas my brother so mote it be'" (*Letters* 553).

The poem next pays its respects to the Pollexfens who lie "far from the customary skies" of Sligo, far from the local landmarks of the Mall (a promenade) and the grammar school, which Yeats calls "Eade's grammar school" after the headmaster William C. Eade (*Place Names* 44–45; *YD* 52). Yeats specifically mentions the sailor in the family, John Pollexfen (1845–1900), whose peripatetic life is rendered less heroic or romantic than merely itinerant (the deflation is orchestrated by the word "moping" and by the passive construction of the refrain, "But where is laid the sailor John . . ."). The question of family rootedness was a poignant and personal one for Yeats, who counted himself among the dislocated and footsore. "Friendship is all the house I have," he laments in his journal (*Aut.* 353; *Mem.* 161). The theme of rootedness recurs in "COOLE AND BALLYLEE, 1931," "A PRAYER FOR MY DAUGHTER" ("O may she live like some green laurel / Rooted in one dear perpetual place") and with specific reference to Sligo in "UNDER SATURN."

At last the poem arrives at Alfred Pollexfen, whose tale chimes with Lily Yeats's letter above. Having long been "a nobody in a great throng"—in Liverpool—Pollexfen, at age 50, returned to his native ground, where his name and his family were rooted in the common memory. Pollexfen thus escaped the fate of John and the many other wandering Pollexfens, as Yeats in some sense wished it were possible to do himself.

The poem ends with a turn from the biographical to the mystical or visionary, though in keeping with Pollexfen's stolidity the poem holds itself in check where it might otherwise have expanded into fuller beauty or larger meaning. Upon each death the women of the family have heard the cry of a "visionary white sea-bird," affirming that the unseen universe is somehow attuned even to the fate of the "nobody." The cry of the seabird was an established element of the family lore. In *Autobiographies*, Yeats says that the "sea-bird is the omen that announces the death or danger of a Pollexfen," and tells how Lily Yeats dreamt that she held "a wingless sea-bird in her arms" upon the death of their uncle William Middleton Pollexfen in 1913 (44). The image of the "visionary white sea-bird" is perhaps referable to the early poem "The White Birds" (1892), in which Yeats dreams that he and his beloved might be changed to "white birds on the wandering foam" and journey to "the numberless islands, and many a Danaan shore" where time and sorrow are unknown.

FIRST PUBLICATION: The *Little Review* (periodical), June 1917, under the title "In Memory." Reprinted in *The Wild Swans at Coole*, The CUALA PRESS, Churchtown, Dundrum, November 17, 1917, under the same title. Reprinted in *The Wild Swans at Coole*, Macmillan, London, New York, March 11, 1919, under the present title.

BIBLIOGRAPHY

Conner, Lester I. *A Yeats Dictionary: Persons and Places in the Poetry of William Butler Yeats*; Foster, R. F. *W. B. Yeats: A Life, II: The Arch-Poet*; Jeffares, A. Norman. *A New Commentary on the Poems of W. B. Yeats*; McGarry, James P. *Place Names in the Writings of William Butler Yeats*; Melchiori, Giorgio. *The Whole Mystery of Art: Pattern into Poetry in the Work of W. B. Yeats*; Yeats, W. B. *Autobiographies*, The Collected Letters of W. B. Yeats* (vol. 1), *The Letters of W. B. Yeats*, *Memoirs*.

"In Memory of Eva Gore-Booth and Con Markiewicz"
(1929, dated October 1927)

From October 1894 to May 1895 Yeats resided with his uncle GEORGE POLLEXFEN in SLIGO. In late

November and early December 1894, Yeats made two brief visits to nearby Lissadell (1830–35), the austere and elegant neoclassical manor of Sir Henry Gore-Booth (1843–1900), some three or four miles northwest of Sligo, on the northern shore of Sligo Bay. "My uncle had always had faith in my talent, but I think that now for the first time the few others that remained of my mother's people began to think I had not thrown away my life," Yeats recalls of his surprising social accession (*Mem.* 77). Though Yeats's maternal family had become wealthy as the owners of shipping and milling concerns, the Gore-Booths belonged to a yet more rarefied milieu. Yeats remembers glimpsing as a boy "the grey stone walls of Lissadell among its trees" and the sight of the beautiful Constance passing on horseback, but this world was not his own. "We were merchant people of the town," Yeats writes. "No matter how rich we grew, no matter how many thousands a year our mills or our ships brought in, we could never be 'county', nor indeed had we any desire to be so" (77–78). Yeats later forgot how he

Constance and Eva Gore-Booth at the opening of the Drumcliff Creamery in 1895 *(Joe McGowan)*

came to be invited to Lissadell, but he was enormously impressed by his first experience of a "great house" (Lady GREGORY's COOLE PARK was yet in his future), and he was particularly taken with Gore-Booth's daughters, Constance (1868–1927) and Eva (1870–1926). He remembers of his stay, "I was at once in closer sympathy with [Eva], whose delicate, gazelle-like beauty reflected a mind far more subtle and distinguished. Eva was for a couple of happy weeks my close friend, and I told her all of my unhappiness in love; indeed so close at once that I nearly said to her, as WILLIAM BLAKE said to Catherine Boucher, 'You pity me, there[fore] I love you.' 'But no,' I thought, 'this house would never accept so penniless a suitor,' and, besides, I was still deeply in love with that other [MAUD GONNE] and had but just written 'All Things Uncomely and Broken' [i.e., 'The LOVER TELLS OF THE ROSE IN HIS HEART']. I threw the Tarot, and when the Fool came up, which means that nothing at all would happen, I turned my mind away" (78–79). In a post-Lissadell letter to his sister Lily Yeats (1866–1949), Yeats gave an account of himself charming the Gore-Booth family with "old Irish stories" and collecting folklore from an "old tenant." He called the Gore-Booths a "very pleasant, kindly, inflamable family. Ever ready to take up new ideas & new things," and he described Lissadell as "an exceedingly impressive house inside with a great sitting room as high as a church & all things in good taste," while "outside it is grey square & bare yet set amid delightful grounds" (CL1 413–414, 418).

These memories remained with Yeats and formed the basis of the contrast between the idyllic garden of youth and the rancor of adulthood that structures "In Memory of Eva Gore-Booth and Con Markiewicz." The poem's opening lines recall the house as a vision of Georgian elegance and the two sisters in all their silken grace. On the evidence of the "gazelle-like beauty" attributed to her in Memoirs, Eva is the "gazelle." The metaphor of the veld might strain at its country-house context were its euphony not so precisely to the point. The idyll ends with a metaphorical decapitation—"raving autumn shears / Blossom from the summer's wreath"—that anticipates the allusion to Constance's death sentence in the following line. The concatenation of autumn

and summer, blossom and wreath, is redolent of TENNYSON's In Memoriam (1850), but where Tennyson's friend Arthur Hallam had died in body, the sisters die in spirit, victims of their own delusive modernity, apostates of the wisdom expressed in "MICHAEL ROBARTES AND THE DANCER" ("all beautiful women may / Live in uncomposite blessedness, / And lead us to the like—if they / Will banish every thought") and "A PRAYER FOR MY DAUGHTER" ("an intellectual hatred is the worst"). The latter poem, indeed, wishes for Anne Yeats (1919–2001) precisely the life that the Gore-Booth sisters had rejected. A nationalist firebrand, Constance fought with the Irish Citizen Army at St. Stephen's Green during the EASTER RISING. She was condemned to death, but her sentence was commuted to life imprisonment in deference to her sex, and she was released from jail in June 1917. Writing while Markiewicz was imprisoned, Yeats pondered his own accidental part in her predicament, speculating that he was "perhaps the first to give her any detailed account of one [MAUD GONNE] in imitation of whom, perhaps, she was to earn the life-sentence she is now serving" (Mem. 78). Markiewicz returned to prison four times between 1918 and 1923 while

Lissadell, County Sligo. "In Memory of Eva Gore-Booth and Con Markiewicz" recalls the great house: "The light of evening, Lissadell, / Great windows open to the south, / Two girls in silk kimonos, both / Beautiful, one a gazelle." *(Fáilte Ireland)*

The "great windows" of Lissadell, home of the Gore-Booth family (*Fáilte Ireland*)

serving as a member of the British Parliament, as minister of labor in the first and second Dáil Éireann, and as a member of the Free State Parliament from 1923 until her death (*Modern Ireland* 445). As the head of Cumann na mBan, a republican women's organization, Markiewicz opposed the treaty ending the ANGLO-IRISH WAR and supported the republican side during the IRISH CIVIL WAR. These post-1916 revolutionary involvements explain Yeats's description of her as "conspiring among the ignorant." He similarly writes of her in "EASTER 1916": "That woman's days were spent / In ignorant good-will, / Her nights in argument / Until her voice grew shrill." Eva, a minor poet and suffragette activist, dreamed of "some vague Utopia" and became, in her "skeleton-gaunt" old age, the image of her politics.

In the second stanza, Yeats addresses the shades of the sisters. Death having brought the revelatory refinement of consciousness that "ALL SOULS' NIGHT" and "BLOOD AND THE MOON" describe, they will at last realize "the folly of a fight / With a common wrong or right" ("too much business with the passing hour," in the phrase of "MY DESCENDANTS"). The "innocent and the beautiful" belong not to the rancor of politics, but to their own innocence and beauty, to a self-delight that verges on the transcendent and the Edenic, as the penultimate stanza of "A Prayer for my Daughter" theorizes. As their triumph in some sense belongs to the realm of eternity, their enemy—that which would undo their triumph—is time. In the final lines of the

poem, Yeats fantasizes the kind of violent assault upon the temporal order equally contemplated in "The LAMENTATION OF THE OLD PENSIONER" ("I spit into the face of Time / That has transfigured me"). His temporal rebellion grown practically dauntless, Yeats would burn up time itself: "Arise and bid me strike a match / And strike another till time catch. . . ."

Yeats repeats the request in the final line of the poem; in this instance, time remains the object of his scornful violence, but the "great gazebo"—an image of tinder all but awaiting the flame—is implicated in the fantasy of arson. In its connotations of graceful Georgianism and refined leisure, the gazebo, like Lissadell itself, represents the Anglo-Irish Ascendancy. Yeats increasingly identified with this class during the 1920s, and two years earlier had famously thundered in its defense on the floor of the SENATE: "We are one of the great stocks of Europe. We are the people of Burke; we are the people of Grattan; we are the people of SWIFT, the people of Emmet, the people of PARNELL. We have created the most of the modern literature of this country. We have created the best of its political intelligence" (SS 99). The political revolutions of the previous 10 years had overthrown the cultural and political leadership of this class, to Yeats's enormous dismay; in this light the class-betrayal of the Gore-Booth sisters perhaps seemed all the more deplorable and blameworthy. "They convicted us of guilt"—a senselessly circular formulation, embodying the illogic of "intellectual hatred"—encapsulates the repudiation of the Anglo-Irish Ascendancy by the newly ascendant Catholic middle-class. Prepared to immolate all that philistine modernity would degrade, Yeats would have the purified shades of the Gore-Booth sisters bid him strike the match. The gazebo, after all, is a hereditary possession, more theirs than his, and not to fall into the wrong hands.

In addition to her prominent place in "Easter 1916" and "In Memory of Eva Gore-Booth and Con Markiewicz," Constance Markiewicz is the "prisoner" of "ON A POLITICAL PRISONER," while Eva Gore-Booth is most likely the "Helen of social welfare" who climbs on a "wagonette to scream" in "WHY SHOULD NOT OLD MEN BE MAD?" Lissadell is passingly mentioned in "THE MAN WHO DREAMED OF FAERYLAND."

FIRST PUBLICATION: *The Winding Stair*, The Fountain Press, New York, October 1, 1929.

BIBLIOGRAPHY

Foster, R. F. *Modern Ireland, 1600–1972*; Yeats, W. B. *The Collected Letters of W. B. Yeats* (vol. 1), *Memoirs, The Senate Speeches of W. B. Yeats*.

"In Memory of Major Robert Gregory" (1918)

ROBERT GREGORY, the only child of Lady GREGORY and Sir William Gregory (1817–92), transferred from the 4th Connaught Rangers to the Royal Flying Corps in 1916. On January 23, 1918, Gregory's plane was shot down over Italy while he was returning from a mission behind enemy lines. Written in May and June 1918, "In Memory of Major Robert Gregory" was the second and most successful of Yeats's three immediate attempts to memorialize his friend's son. It followed "Shepherd and Goatherd" (1919), finished March 20, and preceded "An IRISH AIRMAN FORESEES HIS DEATH," begun June 30 (YC 198–200). Yeats wrote a fourth poem on Gregory's death, "Reprisals," in 1920, but Lady Gregory asked Yeats not to publish it, and it did not appear until 1948 (see VP 791). Given Yeats's uneasy relationship with Gregory and the supervising eye of Lady Gregory and Robert's widow Margaret, "In Memory of Major Robert Gregory" was an unlikely tour de force (AP 118, 126). Yeats considered it one his best poems (*Letters* 650), and Lady Gregory took comfort in the poem just as Yeats intended she should. "Yeats has written a beautiful poem in memory of [Robert]," she wrote to JOHN QUINN on June 18, 1918. "I am so grateful to him—it makes an extraordinary difference to me knowing my darling will be remembered" (*Lady Gregory* 255). Critics have agreed with these high assessments. Hugh Kenner calls "In Memory of Major Robert Gregory" Yeats's "first triumph" in his late "magisterial manner" (*Colder Eye* 235). Frank Kermode calls it a poem "worthy of much painful reading, perhaps the

first in which we hear the full range of the poet's voice; and with this heroic assurance of harmony goes an authentic mastery of design. After it, for twenty years, Yeats's poems, whenever he is using his whole range, are identifiable as the work of the master of the Gregory elegy" (*Romantic Image* 37). "In Memory of Major Robert Gregory" is particularly comparable to "ALL SOULS' NIGHT" and "The MUNICIPAL GALLERY REVISITED," which similarly invoke a procession of the dead and generously pause to give each ghost his due.

His family almost settled in the castle tower and adjacent cottage of THOOR BALLYLEE, Yeats reflects on the departed friends—"discoverers of forgotten truth" or "mere companions" of youth—who are unable to join them beside the fire and talk late into the night. In the poem's third and fourth stanzas, Yeats remembers LIONEL JOHNSON and J. M. SYNGE, who were in their different ways discoverers of "forgotten truth." Johnson shed the world in longing for "measureless consummation," while Synge chose "the living world for text" and at last, in a "desolate stony place," came upon "a race / Passionate and simple like his heart." Yeats alludes to the people of the ARAN ISLANDS. Synge lived on the islands intermittently between 1898 and 1902 and published his reflections in the 1907 travel memoir *The Aran Islands*.

Yeats next remembers his maternal uncle GEORGE POLLEXFEN (1839–1910), less a discoverer than a companion of youth. Like Robert Gregory, he had been a horseman (*Aut.* 84), but having become "sluggish and contemplative" he turned to astrology and came to consider "pure-bred horses" and "solid men," for all their passion, as the mere playthings of the stars. "Opposition, square, and trine," says A. Norman Jeffares, are "astrological terms for heavenly bodies, respectively separated by 180°, 90°, and 120°" (*NCP* 136). These lines implicitly object not to Pollexfen's habit of astrology, which Yeats of course shared, but to the denigration of passion as something less than a free and creative force.

In what might be considered a labored segue, Yeats acknowledges that he has grown accustomed to the absence of these old friends, but not to the idea that Gregory, his "dear friend's dear son, /

Aran Islanders. "In Memory of Major Robert Gregory" describes J. M. Synge, who lived among the islanders for a time, coming "Towards nightfall upon a race / Passionate and simple like his heart." *(Fáilte Ireland)*

Our Sidney and our perfect man, / Could share in that discourtesy of death," for the small wonders of the Galway countryside continue to remind of the man who loved them. Sir Philip Sidney (1554–86), poet and soldier, had likewise died in battle on the continent. If the comparison between Sidney and Gregory strains credulity, it is at least qualified by "our," which acknowledges the idiosyncrasy and subjectivity of affection, just as in the ninth stanza the ambiguity of the word "dreamed" exerts a subtle qualification. In the poem's eighth, ninth, and 10th stanzas, Yeats extols Gregory's prowess and daring as a horseman, his promise as a painter, and his expertise in domestic architecture. Gregory's rounded Renaissance virtue is chiseled in the thrice-repeated refrain, "Soldier, scholar, horsemen, he." Perhaps disingenuously, Yeats represents Gregory as having succeeded where Johnson, Synge, and Pollexfen had failed, for Gregory, like Sidney, had managed to reconcile the active and the contemplative impulses and had thus

attained a degree of UNITY OF BEING. The figure of the horseman recurs in Yeats's work as a symbol of this reconciliation, as in "AT GALWAY RACES," "THE GYRES," and "UNDER BEN BULBEN." In the 11th stanza the poem begins its closing modulation. Yeats places Gregory among those who blaze briefly and magnificently, asking, "What made us dream that he could comb grey hair?" Yeats's aborted autobiographical novel *The SPECKLED BIRD* employs the same conceit: a country lad says of Margaret (a fictionalized MAUD GONNE) that she "will never brush gray hairs." Yeats calls this a "common country phrase" (106, 132; see also *UP2* 170).

Yeats ends by confessing that he had set out to write a very different poem—a visionary poem in keeping with the bitter wind that shakes the shutter, the kind of poem exemplified by "All Souls' Night"—but the thought of Gregory's death took all his "heart for speech." The meaning of this apology is ambiguous. The overt suggestion is that Gregory's death displaced all other subject matter, that his death made impossible any flight of mere imagination and eloquence. And yet this flight, the channeling of the energy of the wind, as in "A PRAYER FOR MY DAUGHTER," is precisely what the stanzas devoted to Gregory, deliberate to the point of being inert in comparison to the lines on Johnson, Synge, and Pollexfen, might have benefited from. On this reading, the poem's final line becomes a veiled admission of failure: The thought of Gregory, whether prompted by sorrow or by obligation to Lady Gregory, has disrupted the mechanism of Yeats's most authentic poetry and unvoiced the poem that should have been.

FIRST PUBLICATION: The *English Review* (periodical), August 1918, under the title "In Memory of Robert Gregory." Reprinted in *The Wild Swans at Coole*, Macmillan, London, New York, March 11, 1919, under the present title.

BIBLIOGRAPHY

Foster, R. F. *W. B. Yeats: A Life, II: The Arch-Poet*; Jeffares, A. Norman. *A New Commentary on the Poems of W. B. Yeats*; Kelly, John S. *A W. B. Yeats Chronology*; Kenner, Hugh. *A Colder Eye: The Modern Irish Writers*; Kermode, Frank. *Romantic Image*; Kohfeldt, Mary Lou. *Lady Gregory: The Woman behind the Irish Renaissance*; W. B. Yeats, *Autobiographies, The Letters of W. B. Yeats, The Speckled Bird, Uncollected Prose by W. B. Yeats* (vol. 2), *The Variorum Edition of the Poems of W. B. Yeats*.

"In the Seven Woods" (1903, dated August 1902)

"In the Seven Woods," which opens the volume of the same name, rivals "ADAM'S CURSE" and "The FOLLY OF BEING COMFORTED" as the first masterpiece of Yeats's maturity. Confidently correcting the estrangement of "The LAKE ISLE OF INNISFREE," the poem shimmers with the energy of a natural world on the verge of some redemptive annunciation or birth. This represents Yeats in the full fledge of his mystic romanticism, and yet the poem remains grounded in a subtext of political frustration and shrewd self-examination. In its concrete

imagery and situation, "In the Seven Woods" begins the slow descent from the abstraction that characterized Yeats's poetry of the nineties and heralds an intensification of Yeats's already estimable poetic force. The poem's title refers to the "seven woods" of Lady GREGORY's estate, COOLE PARK. In his introductory lines to The SHADOWY WATERS (see VP 217–219), Yeats pays tribute to each of the woods, and tells how, walking among them, he dreamed that "beings happier than men" moved in the shadows, and how such intimations of an unseen Eden inspired him to write the story of Forgael and Dectora. Interrogating this invisible reality, Yeats asks, "Do our woods / And winds and ponds cover more quiet woods, / More shining winds, more star-glimmering ponds?" The woods have a similar liminal quality in "In the Seven Woods." They are of the world and yet stand on the threshold of a world beyond.

The poem's first nine lines consider the consolations of nature. Allayed by the sounds of pigeons and bees, Yeats is able to "put away / The unavailing outcries and the old bitterness / That empty the heart." That is, he is able to forget the cultural and political travail of modern Ireland. The heartbreaking symbol of this travail, for Yeats, is "Tara uprooted," an allusion to the recent excavation of the Hill of Tara, the seat of the ancient Irish kings in County Meath. As John S. Kelly et al. summarize the controversy, an Englishman named Groome contrived the peculiar theory that the Ark of the Covenant was buried beneath the hill, and he persuaded the owner of the land, Gustavus V. Briscoe, to allow him to excavate. There were legal challenges after digging began in May 1899, but these managed to halt the project only temporarily (CL3 208–209). In a June 24, 1902, letter to the *Times* of London, Douglas Hyde (1860–1949), GEORGE MOORE, and Yeats reported that they had recently visited the hill and found its "desecration" once again underway. Without hope of legal intervention, they could conclude only that Tara was "probably the most consecrated spot in Ireland, and its destruction will leave many bitter memories behind it" (CL3 208–209; UP2 294–295). In another galling development, Edward VII had been crowned on August 9, 1902. To a nationalist of Yeats's temperament, the affable playboy king's dominion over Ireland was likely even more objectionable than that of his mother, Queen Victoria, whom Yeats not unsympathetically cites as a representative figure of the 24th lunar phase in *A VISION* (169–172). "Tara uprooted" and the "new commonness upon the throne" have a clear relational logic, contrasting past greatness and present degeneracy, but even more the sudden transition from the unseated Irish kings to the newly seated British king suggests an implicit theme of usurpation. Yeats also may have concatenated Tara and Edward VII for a more personal reason. In August 1902, MAUD GONNE led a "children's excursion" to the ancient site and found that Briscoe had prepared the wood for a bonfire to celebrate the upcoming coronation of the king. As Gonne tells the tale in an August 12 letter to Yeats, "We felt it would serve a better purpose if burnt in honor of an Independent Ireland so lighted it & sang A Nation once again. The Constabulary didn't like it at all & danced & jumped with rage—they added greatly to the fun" (GY 156).

Despite the frustrations and humiliations of the age, Yeats declares himself "contented," but the opening line's contentment in nature has given way to the contentment of apocalyptic expectation, the violence implicit but unrealized in the "faint thunder" of the pigeons. Yeats rests assured in the knowledge that "Quiet" wanders among the pigeons and bees "laughing and eating her Wild heart," while "that Great Archer / Who but awaits His hour to shoot, still hangs / A cloudy quiver over Pairc-na-lee" ("calf field," one of the seven woods). The nature of this "Quiet" is intimated in Yeats's introductory lines to *The Shadow Waters*, in which he writes that "they that cleave / The waters of sleep can make a chattering tongue / Heavy like stone, their wisdom being half silence." It may be that "Quiet" personifies the silent wisdom of those "beings happier than men" and "immortal, mild, proud shadows" who "come from Eden on flying feet," and who make the Seven Woods their haunting ground. Or else "Quiet" may personify the silent intensity and unspoken rapture of nature (the introductory lines refer to the "green quiet" that uplifts the heart).

The allusion to the great archer is also obscure. John Unterecker associates it with Sagittarius, but

taken on its own terms it suggests some looming agent of apocalypse perhaps shaped in the clouds, some prefiguration of the annunciatory beast that would much later slouch toward Bethlehem in "The SECOND COMING" (RG 98). Further, the image is clearly related to Yeats's vision of a beautiful naked woman shooting an arrow at a star (for the definitive discussion of the vision of the archer, see CL2 658–663). The vision came to Yeats in response to his evocation of the "lunar power" on the night of August 14–15, 1896, while he was a guest at EDWARD MARTYN's Tulira Castle. Yeats recounted the experience in a letter to William Sharp (CL2 48), and later pondered the vision at some length in *AUTOBIOGRAPHIES* (280–282), *MEMOIRS* (100–101), and *PER AMICA SILENTIA LUNAE* (LE 14–15). Yeats related his vision to similar visions seen by others. The child of one of MACGREGOR MATHERS's occult pupils had seen a woman shooting an arrow into the sky and had been afraid that the woman had killed God, while the young ISEULT GONNE had seen a man shooting a gun at a star, though the star did not seem to mind dying as it "was so very old" (*Aut.* 281). With seeming relevance to "In the Seven Woods," Yeats asks, "Had some great event taken place in some world where myth is reality and had we seen some portion of it? One of my fellow-students quoted a Greek saying, 'Myths are the activities of the Daimons', or had we but seen in the memory of the race something believed thousands of years ago, or had somebody—I myself perhaps—but dreamed a fantastic dream which had come to those others by transference of thought?" (281). "In the Seven Woods" seems to embody the sense, implicit in Yeats's first question, of mythic reality behind the veneer of nature, or immanent within nature, waiting for the moment of conflation.

The image of the archer makes for a wry transition to "The ARROW," which follows in the collected poems, but it goes too far to suggest, as Unterecker does, that the archer of "In the Seven Woods" is "ready to unloose the arrow which comprises the second poem" (RG 98).

FIRST PUBLICATION: *In the Seven Woods: Being Poems Chiefly of the Irish Heroic Age*, The DUN EMER PRESS, Dundrum, August 1903.

BIBLIOGRAPHY

Unterecker, John. *A Reader's Guide to William Butler Yeats*; Yeats, W. B. *Autobiographies*, *The Collected Letters of W. B. Yeats* (vols. 2–3), *Later Essays*, *The Gonne-Yeats Letters 1893–1938*, *Memoirs*, *Uncollected Prose by W. B. Yeats* (vol. 2), *The Variorum Edition of the Poems of W. B. Yeats*, *A Vision*.

"Introductory Rhymes" to Responsibilities
(1914, dated January 1914)

Yeats opens his 1914 volume *Responsibilities* with an apology to his forebears. Having "come close on forty-nine" Yeats regrets that for "a barren passion's sake"—his doomed love for MAUD GONNE—he has no child, but only his literary achievement to "prove" the family blood. Framed by Yeats's words of apology is an apostrophe to various relatives—scholars, merchants, and soldiers—in whose example as men of action Yeats feels a reproach. A. Norman Jeffares identifies specific allusions to Jervis Yeats ("Old Dublin merchant"), d. 1712, a Dublin linen merchant (alternately Yeats may refer to Jervis Yeats's son or grandson, who followed in the family trade); to Yeats's paternal great-grandfather John Yeats ("Old country scholar"), 1774–1846, rector at Drumcliff, near SLIGO (cf. "ARE YOU CONTENT?," "UNDER BEN BULBEN," "UNDER SATURN"); to Yeats's maternal great-grandfather William Middleton ("Old merchant skipper"), 1770–1832, a shipping merchant (cf. "Are You Content?"); and to Yeats's maternal grandfather WILLIAM POLLEXFEN ("silent and fierce old man"), 1811–92, another shipping merchant (cf. "Are You Content?," "IN MEMORY OF ALFRED POLLEXFEN," "Under Saturn") (NCP 99–100). Yeats's tribute to his forebears might seem to contradict his aspersions on "the merchant and the clerk" in "AT GALWAY RACES," but clearly Yeats distinguishes between the merchants of yore, who were formidable men of robust personality, and the contemporary merchant, who breathes "on the world with timid breath" ("At Galway Races") and fumbles "in a greasy till" ("Sep-

tember 1913"). Despite the family's tradition of commerce, then, Yeats can boast that none in his family have passed through "huckster's loin."

Among the poem's several historical allusions, the most obscure is Yeats's description of the "old Dublin merchant" as "free of the ten and four." Jeffares explains that from 1783 to 1894, and possibly prior to this period, the family linen firm was exempt from the "six and ten percent tax" at the customhouse in Dublin (NCP 101). Robert Emmet (1778–1803) led an insurrection in Dublin on July 23, 1803. The insurrection was quelled and Emmet was executed on September 20. In AUTOBIOGRAPHIES, Yeats tells that John Yeats, as a friend of the failed insurrectionist, was "suspected and imprisoned though but for a few hours" (51). The Butler and Armstrong families had marital ties to the Yeats family. Yeats took particular pride in his connection to the Butlers, who had been the earls and dukes of Ormond, and Yeats would sometimes banter about being heir to the title (AM 435). The Battle of the Boyne—named for a river north of Dublin—was fought on July 1, 1690, between the forces of the deposed king James II and those of William III. The battle established William's control of Dublin and eastern Ireland.

Yeats intended "Introductory Rhymes" as a defiant response to GEORGE MOORE, who had published an irreverent account of the Irish Renaissance in the January and February 1914 issues of the *English Review* and later incorporated this material in his memoir *Vale* (1914). Gonne confirms the poem as a retort in a letter of January 1914: "As soon as I had read Moore's article I wrote to you saying there was nothing that needed answering as far as I am concerned & I think I agree with you that your poem is the best & most dignified answer you could give. The lines of that poem on your old sailor grandfather are particularly fine, at least Moore's scurrility has had that good result, it has made you write that poem" (GY 336). Moore had scathingly mocked Yeats's familial pretension, which explains the familial theme of "Introductory Rhymes." Moore recalled, for example, giving a talk in support of a picture exhibition organized by HUGH LANE, after which Yeats rose to comment: "When [Yeats] spoke the words, the middle classes, one would have thought that he was speaking against a personal foe, and we looked round asking each other with our eyes where on earth our Willie Yeats had picked up the strange belief that none but titled and carriage-folk could appreciate pictures. And we asked ourselves why our Willie Yeats should feel himself called upon to denounce his own class; millers and shipowners on one side, and on the other a portrait-painter of distinction; and we laughed, remembering AE's story, that one day whilst Yeats was crooning over his fire Yeats had said that if he had his rights he would be Duke of Ormonde. AE's answer was: I am afraid, Willie, you are overlooking your father—a detestable remark to make to a poet in search of an ancestry [. . .]" (*Hail and Farewell* 540). The "CLOSING RHYMES" to *Responsibilities* more sharply exact revenge for Moore's ribbing. Yeats describes his "priceless things" as "but a post the passing dogs defile."

FIRST PUBLICATION: *Responsibilities: Poems and a Play*, The CUALA PRESS, Churchtow, Dundrum, May 25, 1914, without title. Printed in *Responsibilities and Other Poems*, Macmillan, London, October 10, 1916, under the title "Introductory Rhymes" (given in list of contents).

BIBLIOGRAPHY

Foster, R. F. *W. B. Yeats: A Life, I: The Apprentice Mage*; Jeffares, A. Norman. *A New Commentary on the Poems of W. B. Yeats*; Moore, George. *Hail and Farewell*; Yeats, W. B. *Autobiographies, The Gonne-Yeats Letters 1893–1938*.

"Irish Airman Foresees his Death, An" (1919)

Yeats made four attempts to memorialize ROBERT GREGORY, the son of Lady GREGORY and Sir William Gregory (1817–92). A pilot in the Royal Flying Corps, he was shot down on January 23, 1918, while on a mission in Italy. Begun June 30, 1918, "An Irish Airman Foresees his Death" was the third of these attempts. It followed "Shepherd and Goatherd" (1919) and "IN MEMORY OF MAJOR ROBERT GREGORY" (the masterpiece of the sequence),

and preceded "Reprisals," sent to Lady Gregory in November 1920, but unpublished until 1948 (*YC* 198–200, 213; for "Reprisals" see *VP* 791).

In the 11th stanza of "In Memory of Major Robert Gregory," Yeats describes those whose ecstatic natures are realized in self-consuming conflagration. "An Irish Airman Foresees his Death" elaborates this conception, giving voice to Gregory's inner thought as he goes to the death that awaits him "among the clouds above." Gregory does not fight for his country. His country is "Kiltartan Cross," his countrymen "Kiltartan's poor." "Kiltartan" refers to a barony, parish, and village in Galway, "Kiltartan Cross" to a crossroads (*NCP* 138; *YD* 100). Gregory's allegiance is to the Irish countryside and to his own neighborhood, and not to the political abstraction of the United Kingdom, under whose flag he fights. If not for country, neither does he fight for law, duty, politics, or public acclaim, but rather in pursuit of the "lonely impulse of delight" that is to be found only in the clouds. This is to say that Gregory followed to his death the internal impulse of his own arch-subjective nature: the impulse to realize some solitary ecstasy, some inexpressible freedom. Past and future, the mere unfolding of days, are "waste of breath" when weighed in the balance with "this life, this death."

Yeats took up the question of Gregory's military motivation in a discussion of the poem in a July 3, 1937, radio broadcast: "Like many Protestant Irishmen he stood between two Nations. He said to me, 'I think I am going out of friendship.' Meaning, I suppose, that so many of his friends had gone. 'The English are not my people. My people are the people of Kiltartan.' [. . .] Presently his mother asked, 'Why has Robert joined?' I answered, 'I suppose he thought it his duty.' She said, 'It was his duty to stay here. He joined for the same reason I would have, had I been a young man. He could not keep out of it.' She was right. He was a born soldier. He said to Bernard Shaw shortly before his death, that he was never happy until he began to fight" (*W. B. Yeats & Georgian Ireland* 67–68; see also *Expl.* 309).

FIRST PUBLICATION: *The Wild Swans at Coole*, Macmillan, London, New York, March 11, 1919.

BIBLIOGRAPHY

Conner, Lester, I. A *Yeats Dictionary: Persons and Places in the Poetry of William Butler Yeats*; Jeffares, A. Norman. *A New Commentary on the Poems of W. B. Yeats*; Kelly, John S. A *W. B. Yeats Chronology*; Torchiana, Donald T. *W. B. Yeats & Georgian Ireland*; Yeats, W. B. *Explorations, The Variorum Edition of the Poems of W. B. Yeats*.

"I see Phantoms of Hatred and of the Heart's Fullness and of the Coming Emptiness" (1923, dated 1923)

The last of seven poems in "MEDITATIONS IN TIME OF CIVIL WAR," "I see Phantoms of Hatred," written in the "old, nostalgic alexandrines," as Louis MacNeice observes, is markedly at odds with the rest of the sequence: extravagant, visionary, and impassioned where the preceding poems tend to be tautly interrogative and meditative (*Poetry of W. B. Yeats* 153). Still, coherence is maintained to the last by the incorporation of many of the motifs and images of the sequence. Tower, stone, snow, river, moon, and sword recur, as does the dynamic of murder and reprisal; so too the sequence's underlying tension between action and vision, engagement and reverie, rises to final prominence and tentative resolution.

The poem opens much as "A PRAYER FOR MY DAUGHTER" and "The TOWER." Suspended halfway between heaven and earth, by the light of the moon, Yeats paces the battlements of THOOR BALLYLEE in a condition of visionary readiness. The mind begins to agitate beyond itself and "monstrous familiar images swim to the mind's eye." Yeats first sees "phantoms of hatred," which emblematize, presumably, the violence of the IRISH CIVIL WAR. The followers of Jacques Molay cry for vengeance upon his murderers, but they transmogrify into the kind of visionary parade of lost souls that Yeats had previously imagined in the story "Hanrahan's Vision" (see STORIES OF RED HANRAHAN). Full of their own rage, they bite randomly and reach for the embrace of nothing. Yeats feels himself nearly caught in their tumult, which suggests the lure of violence, of the mob, and more fundamentally the temptation to evade the burden of self-consciousness, all of which is implicit in "The ROAD AT MY DOOR." Jacques de Molay (1244–1314) was the last grand master of the Knights Templar, an order of knights founded in 1118 to secure lands and routes seized during the Crusades. In the summary of *The Encyclopedia Britannica*: "On Oct. 13, 1307, all the Templars in France, including Molay, were arrested and interrogated by command of Philip IV, who was intent on crushing the order and seizing its wealth. On Oct. 24, 1307, Molay, probably under torture, confessed that some of the charges brought against the order were true, but he rejected a charge of sodomy. He wrote to Templars throughout France, enjoining confession; but when the pope sent his own delegates to conduct the inquiries, Molay and many of his subjects retracted their statements, saying they had been exacted by torture. In November 1309 and in March 1310, Molay appealed for a personal judgment by the pope. But Clement decided to suppress the order (March 1312); and on March 18 or 19, 1314, a commission of three cardinals condemned Molay and other dignitaries of the order to perpetual imprisonment. On hearing this sentence, Molay again retracted his confession, and as a final punishment he was burned as a relapsed heretic by Philip IV's officers the same afternoon." In a note to "Meditations in Time of Civil War," Yeats explains that the cry for vengeance upon those who murdered Molay is a "fit symbol for those who labour for hatred, and so for sterility in various kinds. It is said to have been incorporated in the ritual of certain Masonic societies of the eighteenth century, and to have fed class hatred" (*VP* 827).

Yeats's vision of the "heart's fullness," by contrast, takes the form of beautiful ladies riding upon "magical unicorns." T. R. Henn and Giorgio Melchiori identify Gustave Moreau's painting *Ladies and Unicorns* as the specific inspiration of the poem's unicorn imagery (*Lonely Tower* 255;

Whole Mystery of Art 44–45, 70). While living at Riversdale during the 1930s, Yeats hung on his wall a reproduction of the painting (*Letters* 865). Yeats's poetry has little to do with unicorns, but the unicorn figures prominently in the plays *The PLAYER QUEEN, The UNICORN FROM THE STARS,* and *WHERE THERE IS NOTHING,* and in the story "The ADORATION OF THE MAGI" (for an exhaustive account of the unicorn in Yeats's work see *Whole Mystery of Art* 35–72). The ladies who ride upon the unicorns fulfill the feminine ideal of "uncomposite blessedness" that Michael Robartes articulates in "MICHAEL ROBARTES AND THE DANCER." Free from the intellectual abstraction represented by Babylonian astrology (cf. "The DAWN"), their minds have become pools where all sinks into unity, for only "stillness can remain when hearts are full / Of their own sweetness, bodies of their loveliness." The ascription of "sweetness" links the ladies to the redemptive activity of the honeybees of "The STARE'S NEST BY MY WINDOW." The ladies "close their musing eyes" in the recognition that all meaningful reality is inward, while the unicorns' eyelids are "half-closed," as if wavering between the realms of reality and dream. Yeats uses the phrase "half-closed eyelids" with related intention in "HER COURAGE" and "ROSA ALCHEMICA" (*Myth.* 277). The "aquamarine" of the unicorns' eyes is sufficiently explained by the sheer dazzle of the word, but it also counterpoints the pool of the ladies' minds. The unicorns' cloud-paleness, like the cloud-paleness of the rags pictured in the second stanza, suggests the imagination working upon the white mist that Yeats observes from the tower in the second line of the poem (by similar process of unconscious association, "rags" seems to yield "rage" in lines 11 and 27).

The vision of the "coming emptiness" materializes in the form of an "indifferent multitude" and then resolves more sharply into "brazen hawks" (whether or not the hawks constitute the multitude is not clear). Though it has different symbolic significance elsewhere—see for example "The Hawk" (1916) as well as the plays AT THE HAWK'S WELL and ON BAILE'S STRAND—the hawk here signifies blind rapine, mere animalism, and by extension the "logic-chopping" that is the modern rapine, the modern animalism. In his note to the poem, Yeats offers this gloss, quoting his own poem "Tom O'Roughley" (1918): "I suppose that I must have put hawks into the fourth stanza because I have a ring with a hawk and a butterfly upon it, to symbolize the straight road of logic, and so of mechanism, and the crooked road of intuition: 'For wisdom is a butterfly and not a gloomy bird of prey'" (*VP* 827). The hawk's "clanging wings"—metallic in token of its mechanism—have put out the moon, much as it is extinguished in "LINES WRITTEN IN DEJECTION." The "coming emptiness" figured by the hawk is the casually cruel future that seemed to Yeats already upon the world. As he writes in "NINETEEN HUNDRED AND NINETEEN," which follows both in *The Tower* (1928) and in the collected poems, "Now days are dragon-ridden, the nightmare / Rides upon sleep: a drunken soldiery / Can leave the mother, murdered at her door / To crawl in her own blood. . . ." Yeats asserts "the growing murderousness of the world" in *AUTOBIOGRAPHIES* (166) and elaborates in a 1936 letter to Ethel Mannin (1900–84): "[As] my sense of reality deepens, and I think it does with age, my horror at the cruelty of governments grows greater [. . .]. Communist, Fascist, nationalist, clerical, anti-clerical, all are responsible according to the number of their victims" (*Letters* 851).

In the final stanza of the poem, Yeats retreats from this reality to the chamber that "MY HOUSE" fixes as a locus of occult investigation. Yeats pauses on the stair—the stair of *antithetical* aspiration, in the scheme of "EGO DOMINUS TUUS"—and contemplates the worldly success—the hawkish predation—that he has foregone in pursuit of intangible mysteries (this same ruefulness is detectable in "ADAM'S CURSE" and "The CHOICE"). Throwing off the envy of "The Road at my Door," Yeats at the last affirms his most consistent identity, though not triumphantly, for his chosen course is too difficult to be celebrated: "The abstract joy, / The half-read wisdom of daemonic images, / Suffice the ageing man as once the growing boy." As in "My House," "daemonic" refers to the self's struggle to discover its own daemon or "opposite" or "anti-self," out of which comes revelation (see "Ego Dominus Tuus" for the fullest poetic expression of the doctrine of the self and anti-self). Richard Ellmann comments that these final lines "were probably written with WORDSWORTH's 'Ode on the Intimations of Immortality' in mind, and they illustrate the difference between the two poets. For Yeats claims no progression in philosophical insight from childhood to maturity; at neither period does the poet reflect calmly or with the 'philosophical mind'. Daemonic images are with him in old age as in boyhood. And the word 'suffice' has a peculiar Yeatsian irony about it: at no time in the poet's life have his images fully contented him, for his urge to action has always been thwarted by his stronger impulse to art. This latent 'horreur des lettres' is extremely un-Wordsworthian" (IY 223).

FIRST PUBLICATION: The *Dial* and the *London Mercury* (periodicals), January 1923. Reprinted in *The Cat and the Moon and Certain Poems*, The CUALA PRESS, Dublin, July 1924.

BIBLIOGRAPHY

Ellmann, Richard. *The Identity of Yeats*; Henn, T. R. *The Lonely Tower: Studies in the Poetry of W. B. Yeats*; MacNeice, Louis. *The Poetry of W. B. Yeats*; Melchiori, Giorgio. *The Whole Mystery of Art: Pattern into Poetry in the Work of W. B. Yeats*; Yeats, W. B. *Autobiographies, The Letters of W. B. Yeats, Mythologies, The Variorum Edition of the Poems of W. B. Yeats*.

"Lady's First Song, The" (1938)

See "The THREE BUSHES."

"Lady's Second Song, The" (1938)

See "The THREE BUSHES."

"Lady's Third Song, The" (1938)

See "The THREE BUSHES."

"Lake Isle of Innisfree, The" (1890)

In *AUTOBIOGRAPHIES*, Yeats describes this enchanting but also substantive and significant 12-line poem as "my first lyric with anything in its rhythm of my own music" (139). The myth-shrouded island amid the waters of Lough Gill near SLIGO had been part of Yeats's imaginative life since youth, bound up with dreams of romantic seclusion from the world and the example of Thoreau, as Yeats relates: "My father had read to me some passage out of *Walden*, and I planned to live some day in a cottage on a little island called Innisfree. [. . .] I thought that having conquered bodily desire and the inclination of my mind towards women and love, I should live, as Thoreau lived, seeking wisdom" (85). Years later Yeats came to write "Innisfree" as the result of a chance association. As variously recounted in *Autobiographies*, MEMOIRS, and JOHN SHERMAN, Yeats was wandering homesick down London's Fleet Street in December 1888 when he saw a fountain in a window display and was reminded of lake water and by association the Irish countryside (AM 79; *Aut.* 139; *JS&D* 57; *Mem.* 31). "The Lake Isle of Innisfree" elaborates this poignant moment of recognition and longing. The poem's refrain, "I will arise and go," fittingly derives from the parable of the prodigal son: "I will arise and go to my father" (Luke 15:18).

The poem's first eight lines declare a desire to take up a pastoral life in a lakeside cabin of "clay and wattles made" ("wattles": a weave of twigs and stakes used to side rural dwellings). Round the cabin are to be planted "nine bean-rows," a likely allusion to the "Bean-Field" chapter of *Walden*. The poem's final quatrain complicates Yeats's pastoral aspiration, however, by suddenly revealing his estrangement from the pastoral scene, which seems

Innisfree, Lough Gill, County Sligo. The small island inspired "The Lake Isle of Innisfree," which may be Yeats's best known and most beloved poem. *(Fáilte Ireland)*

to represent at once home, nation, and nature itself. Yeats hears "lake water lapping with low sounds by the shore" but only "in the deep heart's core" as he stands "on the roadway, or on the pavements grey." This sudden revelation of an unbridgeable distance suggests that the pastoral can be only a condition of the heart, at once compensatory and painful. In its suggestion of both loss and the frustrated desire for recuperation or restoration, the poem, suddenly transcending Thoreauvian pastiche, becomes a parable of the post-lapsarian condition.

"Innisfree" found an early and fervent admirer in Robert Louis Stevenson (1850–94). The novelist wrote from Samoa on April 14, 1894, to congratulate Yeats on the poem. "It is so quaint and airy, simple, artful, and eloquent to the heart," Stevenson enthused, adding that only Swinburne's poems and Meredith's "Love in the Valley" had equally captivated him (*Letters of Robert Louis Stevenson*, vol. 8, 262). Writing to Yeats's London mentor W. E. Henley (1849–1903) on July 15, Stevenson mentioned that "Innisfree" had "simply refused" to leave his memory (330). Yeats in turn sent a letter of thanks to Stevenson in which he said that "it

is the liking or disliking of one's fellow craftsmen, especially of those who have attained the perfect expression one does but grope for, which urges one to work on—else were it best to dream ones [sic] dreams in silence" (*CL1* 404; see also *CL4* 943). He graciously added that *Treasure Island* (1883) was "well nigh" the only book his seafaring grandfather, WILLIAM POLLEXFEN, was known to have read. "I wonder at the voice," he told Stevenson, "which while delighting the studious & cloistered spirits, can yet hush into admiration such as he, much as I wonder at that voice which stilled the waves of old."

The popularity of the poem, and especially the constant clamor to hear the poem recited, eventually began to wear on Yeats. "I confess I grow not a little jealous of the 'Lake Isle' which has put the noses of all my other children out of joint," Yeats told the future poet laureate Robert Bridges (1844–1930) on July 20, 1901 (*CL3* 90). In an October 4, 1907, letter to T. STURGE MOORE, Yeats referred to "that damned *Innisfree*" (*CL4* 741). DOROTHY WELLESLEY records that Yeats felt much the same irritation some three decades later: "I think that he hated all his early poems, and 'Innisfree' most of all. But one evening I begged him to read it. A look of tortured irritation came into his face, and continued there until the reading was over. I realized then that this particular poem was, generally speaking, the first one asked for. His later poems he was always willing to read, also those of other contemporary poets" (*LOP* 174).

Yeats sent an early version of the poem to KATH-ARINE TYNAN in a letter of December 21, 1888, with the comment that the poem had emerged from his work on *John Sherman*: "In my story I make one of the characters [i.e., Sherman] when ever he is in trouble long to go away and live alone on that Island—an old day dream of my own. Thinking over his feelings I made these verses about them" (*CL1* 120–121; see also *JS&D* 57).

FIRST PUBLICATION: The *National Observer* (periodical), December 13, 1890. Reprinted in *The Book of the Rhymers' Club*, Elkin Mathews, London, February 1892.

BIBLIOGRAPHY

Foster, R. F. *W. B. Yeats: A Life, I: The Apprentice Mage*; Stevenson, Robert Louis. *The Letters of Robert Louis Stevenson* (vol. 8); Yeats, W. B. *Autobiographies, The Collected Letters of W. B. Yeats* (vols. 1, 3–4), *John Sherman and Dhoya, Letters on Poetry from W. B. Yeats to Dorothy Wellesley, Memoirs.*

"Lamentation of the Old Pensioner, The" (1890)

More than any other poem in Yeats's oeuvre, "The Lamentation of the Old Pensioner" measures the extent of the poet's evolution in sensibility and STYLE. In its earliest version the poem conveys a vague melancholy having to do with the natural bereavements of age. In the almost completely rewritten version that appeared in the 1925 edition of *Early Poems and Stories*, this melancholy is supplanted by a tense amalgam of romantic regret, political disillusionment, and existential frustration, all of which culminates in the cry of rebellion that ends the revised poem: "I spit into the face of Time

/ That has transfigured me." To compare the first lines of the second stanza in original and revised form—"The road-side trees keep murmuring" and "Though lads are making pikes again"—is to compare manifestations of entirely different cosmologies (see *VP* 131–132). In its fierce resistance to the decline of old age, the final version of the poem anticipates late poems like "An ACRE OF GRASS," "A PRAYER FOR OLD AGE," "The SPUR," and "The Wild Old Wicked Man" (1938). As Peter Kuch writes, the pensioner is "now one with Crazy Jane, Tom the Lunatic, Ribh, several nameless religious beggars, and the raging, spitting Old Man who introduces Yeats's last play, The DEATH OF CUCHULAIN" (*Yeats and A.E.* 67).

In a note to the early versions of the poem, Yeats relates that the piece is "little more than a translation into verse of the very words of an old Wicklow peasant" (*VP* 799). In the 1891 prose piece "A Visionary," Yeats recounts the chance encounter between the "old Wicklow peasant" and GEORGE RUSSELL (AE) upon Two Rock Mountain near Dublin where both were roving late one night: "Both were unhappy: [Russell] because he had then first decided that art and poetry were not for him, and the old peasant because his life was ebbing out with no achievement remaining and no hope left him. The peasant was wandering in his mind with prolonged sorrow. Once he burst out with, 'God possesses the heavens—God possesses the heavens—but He covets the world'; and once he lamented that his old neighbours were gone, and that all had forgotten him: they used to draw a chair to the fire for him in every cabin, and now they said, 'Who is that old fellow there?' 'The fret' (Irish for doom) 'is over me,' he repeated, and then went on to talk once more of God and Heaven. More than once also he said, waving his arm towards the mountain, 'Only myself knows what happened under the thorn-tree forty years ago'; and as he said it the tears upon his face glistened in the moonlight" (*Myth.* 13–14). Yeats also comments on this incident in AUTOBIOGRAPHIES (202).

FIRST PUBLICATION: The *Scots Observer* (periodical), November 15, 1890, under the title "The Old Pensioner." Reprinted in *The Countess Kathleen and Various Legends and Lyrics*, T. Fisher

Unwin, London, September 1892, under the present title.

BIBLIOGRAPHY

Kuch, Peter. *Yeats and A.E.: 'The antagonism that unites dear friends'*; Yeats, W. B. *Autobiographies, Mythologies, The Variorum Edition of the Poems of W. B. Yeats.*

"Lapis Lazuli" (1938)

Yeats's late-arriving masterpiece has its blueprint in a letter of July 6, 1935, to DOROTHY WELLESLEY. He offers the opinion that "the true poetic movement of our time is towards some heroic discipline. People much occupied with morality always lose heroic ecstasy." In elaboration, he misquotes "Villanelle of the Poet's Road" by Ernest Dowson (1867–1900), a protégé from the days of the RHYMERS' CLUB: "Those who have it most often are those Dowson has described (I cannot find the poem but the lines run like this or something like this): 'Wine women and song / To us they belong / To us the bitter and gay.' 'Bitter and gay,' that is the heroic mood" (*Letters* 836–837; *LOP* 7). Toward the end of the letter, Yeats returns to the theme of the "heroic mood," associating it with a piece of sculpted lapis lazuli that had arrived two days earlier. The stone was a 70th birthday gift from Harry Clifton (1907–78), an aspiring poet from a wealthy landowning family and a friend of Yeats's Dublin crony Oliver St. John Gogarty (1878–1957) (*AP* 748). "Lapis Lazuli's" simple dedication—"For Harry Clifton"—reciprocates the kindness of the gift. Of the stone Yeats writes, "I notice that you have much lapis lazuli; someone has sent me a present of a great piece carved by some Chinese sculptor into the semblance of a mountain with temple, trees, paths and an ascetic and pupil about to climb the mountain. Ascetic, pupil, hard stone, eternal theme of the sensual east. The heroic cry in the midst of despair. But no, I am wrong, the east has its solutions always and therefore knows nothing of tragedy. It is we, not the east, that must raise the heroic cry" (*Letters* 837; *LOP* 8; see also

LOP 117–118). More than a year later the ideas of the letter transmogrified into the poem. Writing to Wellesley, Yeats called the poem, with justification, "almost the best I have made of recent years" (*Letters* 859; *LOP* 83). Embodying precisely the theme of the "heroic cry in the midst of tragedy," "Lapis Lazuli" belongs to a line of poems, including "DEATH," "A DIALOGUE OF SELF AND SOUL," "The GYRES," "HER COURAGE," "HER COURTESY," and "VACILLATION," that variously rehearse the cry of existential defiance.

"Lapis Lazuli" unfolds as a rejoinder to the shallow chatter of "hysterical women" (for variations on the theme of hysterical women, see *Aut.* 192; *E&I* 314). The dilettante immersion in the milieu of the arts suggests the woman of society, a type of the opinionated female ("everybody knows or else should know") whom Yeats denounces in "MICHAEL ROBARTES AND THE DANCER." Understanding nothing of the tragic-heroic temper, such women are impatient with the gaiety and inappositeness of the arts at a time when only "drastic" practical measures can save Europe from the destruction that would soon coalesce as World War II. "King Billy" refers to William III of England (1650–1702), who, as Lester I. Conner notes, "used 'bomb balls,' that is, artillery, against the Irish in the Battle of the Boyne in 1690." He adds that Yeats undoubtedly "intended King Billy to serve simultaneously as a reference to Kaiser Wilhelm II (1859–1941), whose planes and zeppelins bombed England in World War I" (*YD* 15). A. Norman Jeffares identifies "bomb-balls" as a specific allusion to the ballad "The Battle of the Boyne," which appeared in *Irish Minstrelsy* (1888), edited by H. Halliday Sparling. In the words of the song, "King James has pitched his tent between / The lines for to retire; / But King William threw his bomb-balls in / And set them all on fire" (*NCP* 363–364; *Yeats: Last Poems* 160).

Yeats's response to such women occupies the remainder of the poem. He rejects the attempt to evade the tragic pattern of life. This evasion is not only impossible, but misguided in principle, because it fails to recognize tragedy as the whetstone of the highest joy. Yeats invokes Hamlet, Lear, Ophelia, and Cordelia, Shakespeare's tragic fold. These do not weep, but in the moment of supreme calamity discover an intensity that erupts as a transcendental joy. In the moment when tragedy is "wrought to its uttermost," gaiety transfigures dread; there is "Black out; Heaven blazing into the head" (the fragmentary syntax of this line accords with the suddenness and immediacy of the experience). It is this moment, or some version of it, to which Yeats refers in "A Dialogue of Self and Soul" ("When such as I cast out remorse / So great a sweetness flows into the breast / We must laugh and we must sing, / We are blest by everything, / Everything we look upon is blest"); in "A General Introduction for my Work" (*E&I* 522–523; *LE* 213–214); in *Per Amica Silentia Lunae* (*LE* 31–32); in "Vacillation" ("While on the shop and street I gazed / My body of a sudden blazed; / And twenty minutes more or less / It seemed, so great my happiness, / That I was blesse'd and could bless"); and in an important note to *A Vision* (*IY* 221). *On The Boiler* contains the fullest and clearest explanation of the mechanics of this moment, in a passage that echoes the language and *dramatis personae* of "Lapis Lazuli": "No tragedy is legitimate unless it leads some great character to his final joy. Polonius may go out wretchedly, but I can hear the dance music in 'Absent thee from felicity awhile', or in Hamlet's speech over the dead Ophelia, and what of Cleopatra's last farewells, Lear's rage under the lightning, Oedipus sinking down at the story's end into an earth 'riven' by love? Some Frenchman has said that farce is the struggle against a ridiculous object, comedy against a movable object, tragedy against an immovable; and because the will, or energy, is greatest in tragedy, tragedy is the more noble; but I add that 'will or energy is eternal delight', and when its limit is reached it may become a pure, aimless joy, though the man, the shade, still mourns his lost object. It has, as it were, thrust up its arms towards those angels who have, as Villiers de l'Isle Adam quotes from St Thomas Aquinas, returned into themselves in an eternal moment" (*LE* 247).

Contradicting the fret of the "hysterical women," the third stanza stoically, even jauntily, observes that civilization has been perennially "put to the sword," populations sent fleeing, art and wisdom overthrown (cf. "Nineteen Hundred And Nineteen"). This is in the very nature of things, as symbolized by the precarious fragility that Yeats attributes to the works of Callimachus (fifth century B.C.), whom Yeats considered, with Phidias (cf. "Nineteen Hundred and Nineteen," "The Statues," "Under Ben Bulben"), one of the emblematic sculptors of ancient Greece. Callimachus revived the pure Ionic style, Yeats writes in *A Vision*, and "upon the only example of his work known to us, a marble chair, a Persian is represented, and may one not discover a Persian symbol in that bronze lamp, shaped like a palm, known to us by a description in Pausanias? But he was an archaistic workman, and those who set him to work brought back public life to an older form. One may see in masters and man a momentary dip into ebbing Asia" (*AV* 270; see also *E&I* 225). In his "dip into ebbing Asia," Callimachus heralds the three Chinamen of the next stanza. The work of Callimachus, a delicate and brief-lived apparition in stone, stands for all creation and all achievement. Like his "long lamp-chimney shaped like the stem / Of a slender palm," all things are prey to the violence of time, but are reborn by those whose gaiety has its paradoxical sanction in the tragic pattern of things.

With Coleridge's "Kubla Khan" (1816) an informing memory, the poem ends with a description of the mountain scene carved in the lapis lazuli given by Harry Clifton. The sculpture is subject to the evanescence described in the third stanza, but its scene is pregnant with the transfigured dread of the second stanza. Looking from their mountain redoubt upon "all the tragic scene" (echoes of the second stanza's theatrical motif), the Chinamen find a gaiety whose transcendental element—"Heaven blazing into the head," as the second stanza has it—is symbolized by their perch amid the sky and by their glittering eyes (cf. "Demon And Beast"). Unlike the women of the first stanza, who decry the political irrelevancy of the "fiddle-bow," the Chinamen attend to "mournful melodies" played by "accomplished fingers," finding in the melody the mood of tragedy that initiates the moment of transfiguration. The "long-legged bird" belongs to the *antithetical* aviary that includes heron, hawk, eagle, and swan, and symbolizes solitary aspiration (see *VPl.* 789). The longevity symbolized by the bird accords with the age of the Chinamen themselves and hints that "tragic joy" ("The Gyres") in some way cuts against the evanescence that the second stanza theorizes. That the slope is snow-covered is likewise significant, for, as Yeats writes in "A General Introduction for my Work," in the tragic moment "all must be cold." In this moment, the "supernatural is present, cold winds blow across our hands, upon our faces, the thermometer falls," and the imagination "must be carried beyond feeling into the aboriginal ice" (E&I 523; LE 213–214). "The FISHERMAN," "MERU," and the fourth section of "Vacillation" similarly suggest this association.

In Yeats's thought, as Richard Ellmann notes, Europe and Asia are generally more at variance than they seem to be here. "For the most part," writes Ellmann, Yeats "conceived of Asia as having the positive values of simplicity, naturalness, prescribed duties, and tradition, and the negative attributes of formlessness, vagueness, immensity, abstraction, asceticism, and submissiveness which helped to make it the matrix from which everything has come. Europe, on the other hand, stood for history, measurement, flesh, metaphor, concreteness, and aggressiveness. Christianity [. . .] was primarily Asiatic; Greek and Roman civilization, and the civilization of the Renaissance, were primarily European." Ellmann adds that Yeats "foresaw a dominantly Asiatic era to come with loathing. [. . .] He told Lady GREGORY that the god of the new age would be a Buddha or Sphinx, both of them Asiatic symbols, for as he had learned from Hegel, European civilization could not begin until Oedipus had destroyed the Asiatic sphinx which kept personality in bondage, and now the tables were to be turned, Oedipus himself to be destroyed" (IY 184–187; see also Lady Gregory's Journals, I, 600–601). Yeats makes a motif of East Asia not only in "Lapis Lazuli," but also in "Meru," "MY TABLE," "Nineteen Hundred and Nineteen" (II), and "Vacillation" (VI). In A Vision, he writes that the "Great Year"—that is, history itself—must be understood as "a marriage of symbolic Europe and symbolic Asia, the one begetting upon the other. When it commenced at its symbolic full moon in March—Christ or Christendom was begotten by the West upon the East. This begetting has been

followed by a spiritual predominance of Asia. After it must come an age begotten by the East upon the West that will take after its Mother in turn" (203; see also 270–271).

FIRST PUBLICATION: The London Mercury (periodical), March 1938. Reprinted in New Poems, The CUALA PRESS, Dublin, May 18, 1938.

BIBLIOGRAPHY

Conner, Lester I. A Yeats Dictionary: Persons and Places in the Poetry of William Butler Yeats; Ellmann, Richard. The Identity of Yeats; Foster, R. F. W. B. Yeats: A Life, II: The Arch-Poet; Gregory, Lady. Lady Gregory's Journals (vol. 1, ed. Daniel J. Murphy); Jeffares, A. Norman. A New Commentary on the Poems of W. B. Yeats; Stallworthy, John. ed., Yeats: Last Poems; Yeats, W. B. Autobiographies, Essays and Introductions, Later Essays, The Letters of W. B. Yeats, Letters on Poetry from W. B. Yeats to Dorothy Wellesley, The Variorum Edition of the Plays of W. B. Yeats, A Vision.

"Last Confession, A" (1929)

See "A WOMAN YOUNG AND OLD."

"Leaders of the Crowd, The" (1921)

Written in 1918 or 1919, "The Leaders of the Crowd" recoils against the baseness that Yeats attributed to Ireland's political culture since the death of CHARLES STEWART PARNELL in 1891. It thus belongs to the same genus as earlier poems like "ON THOSE THAT HATED 'THE PLAYBOY OF THE WESTERN WORLD', 1907," "SEPTEMBER 1913," "TO A FRIEND WHOSE WORK HAS COME TO NOTHING," and "TO A SHADE." These poems have their different emphases and gripes, but they share the sense that the political culture had become rancorous and low-minded and increasingly expressive of the middle-class sensibility that Yeats detested. Recalling the politics of the 1890s, Yeats gives the gist of his complaint in his essay "Poetry and Tradition" (1912): "Miss MAUD GONNE could still gather great crowds out of the slums by her beauty and sincerity, and speak to them of 'Mother Ireland with the crown of stars about her head'; but gradually the political movement she was associated with, finding it hard to build up any fine lasting thing, became content to attack little persons and little things. All movements are held together more by what they hate than by what they love, for love separates and individualises and quiets, but the nobler movements, the only movements on which literature can found itself, hate great and lasting things. All who have any old traditions have something of aristocracy, but we had opposing us from the first, though not strongly from the first, a type of mind which had been without influence in the generation of Grattan, and almost without it in that of Davis, and which has made a new nation out of Ireland, that was once old and full of memories" (*E&I* 249–250). "The Leaders of the Crowd" takes aim at this new type, but it is not clear whether it has in mind particular leaders. In *Michael Robartes and the Dancer* (1921), "The Leaders of the Crowd" immediately follows "ON A POLITICAL PRISONER," which deplores the bitterness, abstraction, and enmity that had consumed Constance Markiewicz (1868–1927). Anticipating the language of "The Leaders of the Crowd," it disparages Markiewicz as "blind and leader of the blind." "The Leaders of the Crowd" may elaborate the specific critique of Markiewicz and her allies, or it may refer generally to all those who fail to understand the spirit of JOHN O'LEARY's great apothegm: "There are things that a man must not do to save a nation" (*Aut.* 101, 178; *E&I* 247; *UP2* 36).

Against the false certainty, fantasy, and calumny that rule the crowd, Yeats upholds the "truth" whose symbol is the lamp of solitary study. The lamp is not political but occult. It is the lamp of "EGO DOMINUS TUUS" ("a lamp burns on beside the open book"), "MY HOUSE" ("his midnight candle glimmering"), and "The PHASES OF THE MOON" ("the lonely light that Samuel Palmer engraved"). The lamp has no part in the crude vigor of everyday life; it is "from the tomb," its light supernatural. Yeats here touches on his cardinal convictions that

wisdom is the "property of the dead" ("BLOOD AND THE MOON"), its truths "mummy truths" ("ALL SOULS' NIGHT"), the tomb itself a mystical space ("The MOUNTAIN TOMB," "Oil and Blood" [1929], "VACILLATION"). The cry that ends "To a Shade"— "Away, away! You are safer in the tomb"—urges not only refuge from the bruising vulgarity of contemporary politics, then, but conceivably also an embrace of the wisdom and solitude that were Parnell's natural element. As the leaders of the crowd *pull down* "established honour," so the "hysterica passio" of the mob *drags down* Parnell. In the service of the same polemic, Yeats also adopts the metaphor of the hunting pack in "To a Shade."

"PARNELL'S FUNERAL" applies the critique of "The Leaders of the Crowd" to a later generation of political leaders. Comparing Parnell to the chief politicians of the 1930s, Yeats comments, "Their school a crowd, his master solitude." The two poems also share an implicit metaphor of the stag being dragged down by the hunt.

FIRST PUBLICATION: *Michael Robartes and the Dancer*, The CUALA PRESS, Churchtown, Dundrum, February 1921.

BIBLIOGRAPHY

Yeats, W. B. *Autobiographies, Essays and Introductions, Uncollected Prose by W. B. Yeats* (vol. 2).

"Leda and the Swan" (1924)

Yeats's poems of apocalyptic annunciation can be arranged in historical sequence: "Leda and the Swan" announces the birth of the classical era that replaced the "Babylonian mathematical starlight"; "TWO SONGS FROM A PLAY" and "WISDOM" announce the birth of the Christian era that replaced the classical era; "The SECOND COMING" announces the birth of the *antithetical* era that will replace the Christian era. "Leda and the Swan" serves as epigraph to the "Dove or Swan" section of *A VISION*, which explains this historical progression. "I imagine the annunciation that founded Greece as made to Leda," Yeats writes, "remembering that they showed in a Spartan temple, strung up to the roof as a holy relic, an unhatched egg of hers; and that from one of her eggs came Love and from the other War. But all things are from antithesis, and when in my ignorance I try to imagine what older civilisation that annunciation rejected I can but see bird and woman blotting out some corner of the Babylonian mathematical starlight" (268). At the same time, Yeats speaks of the Ledaean annunciation as a parable of the present moment in a note to the poem: "I wrote Leda and the Swan because the editor of a political review [GEORGE RUSSELL, editor of the *Irish Statesman*] asked me for a poem. I thought, 'After the individualist, demagogic movement founded by Hobbes and popularized by the Encyclopaedists and the French Revolution, we have a soil so exhausted that it cannot grow that crop again for centuries.' Then I thought, 'Nothing is now possible but some movement from above preceded by some violent annunciation.' My fancy began to play with Leda and the Swan for metaphor, and I began this poem; but as I wrote, bird and lady took such possession of the scene that all politics went out of it, and my friend tells me that his 'conservative readers would misunderstand the poem'" (VP 828). Likewise, Lady GREGORY, while staying with Yeats at 82 Merrion Square in September 1923, recorded in her journal that Yeats had "talked of his long belief that the reign of democracy is over for the present, and in reaction there will be violent government from above, as now in Russia, and is beginning here. It is the thought of this force coming into the world that he is expressing in his Leda poem, not yet quite complete" (*Lady Gregory's Journals*, I, 477). In keeping with his historical understanding, Yeats titled the initial draft of the poem "Annunciation" (*Mem.* 272–275).

According to Greek myth, Zeus assumed the form of a swan and forced himself on Leda, queen of Sparta. She produced two eggs. According to the version of the myth to which Yeats subscribed, "Castor and Clytaemnestra broke the one shell, Helen and Pollux the other" (AV 51). Thus were set in motion the events that culminated in the fall of Troy ("The broken wall, the burning roof and tower / And Agamemnon dead"). "Leda and the Swan" is Yeats's most significant treatment of the myth, but it recurs in "The ADORATION OF

THE MAGI" (as revised in 1925), "AMONG SCHOOL CHILDREN," *The* HERNE'S EGG (*VPl.* 1016), "His Phoenix" (1916), "LULLABY," *The* PLAYER QUEEN (*VPl.* 744) and *A Vision* (51, 67, 268). That the myth became a preoccupation is unsurprising, as it teems with elements that play to the peculiarities of Yeats's imagination: the conflation of the sexual and the apocalyptic (see "SOLOMON AND THE WITCH"), the frisson of sexual violence (see "HIS MEMORIES"), and the mythic stature of Helen, whom Yeats perennially associated with MAUD GONNE. At the very center of the poem, of course, is the image of the swan, which appears in a preponderance of Yeats's greatest poems, including "Among School Children," "COOLE AND BALLYLEE, 1931," "NINETEEN HUNDRED AND NINETEEN," "The TOWER," and "The WILD SWANS AT COOLE." T. R. Henn characterizes the swan as an emblem of "power, phallic strength, purity, spirit and spirits (as all white birds), fidelity; fire and air (as the dove); the ineffable Godhead" (*Lonely Tower* 256). In a note to CALVARY, Yeats construes the swan this way: "Certain birds, especially as I see things, such lonely birds as the heron, hawk, eagle, and swan, are the natural symbols of subjectivity, especially when floating upon the wind alone or alighting upon some pool or river, while the beasts that run upon the ground, especially those that run in packs, are the natural symbols of objective man" (*VPl.* 789).

The poem itself is one of Yeats's signal achievements. It roils with the vast spiraling of the gyres of history, and yet the moment of violence is rendered in all its tactile immediacy and fluid sexuality: the concurrence of the eternal and the particular is flawless. The poem opens abruptly. We feel the shock of the "sudden blow" delivered from the air and recoil at the completeness of the god's descent into the animal: the predatory cunning of the dizzying cuff followed by the pounce, the unmincing emphasis on "webs" and "bill." We glimpse only a whirl of body parts—thighs, webs, nape, bill—in the commotion of the struggle. Clause by clause, the swan insinuates himself, distance closes in a progression from "caressed" to "caught" to "holds," from thigh and web, to nape and bill, to breast and breast, punctuated by the sudden transition to the active voice in the fourth line: The frenzy of struggle over, the swan is fully revealed, is fully in control.

If the god's full descent into the animal is the scandal of the first stanza, Leda's equivocal resistance is the scandal of the second. Her fingers are "terrified" but also "vague"; the swan, initially repellent as a creature of web and bill, is now a "feathered glory." Under the caresses that belong to the horror of the first stanza, her thighs are now "loosening." The rhetorical question of lines 7 and 8 renders the girl a mere "body" and frankly acknowledges her seduction with a possible pun on "laid": "And how can body, laid in that white rush, / But feel the strange heart beating where it lies?" The Swan's beating heart anticipates the allusion to the "brute blood of the air" in line 13, but is also referable to Christ's beating heart in The RESURRECTION (VPl. 929, 931) and to Dionysus's "beating heart" in "Two Songs from a Play." In a note to The Resurrection, Yeats attributes the motif to Sir William Crookes's Studies in Psychical Research, in which the author describes discovering a beating heart upon touching a "materialized form" (VPl. 935). In Yeats's several works of annunciation, the beating heart demonstrates that the divine is implicated in the passions of the world, and that the passions of the world are implicated in the divine; as Yeats writes in "RIBH DENOUNCES PATRICK," "Natural and supernatural with the self-same ring are wed." The terror comes from the realization that the universe is ruled not by some principle of reason or out of some lofty serenity, but by the same blood-sodden impulses that goad and bedevil man.

"A shudder in the loins": Yeats fiercely represses any suggestion of sentiment, maintaining the rebarbative strength of the poem. So too these lines exploit the ironic disproportion between the trifling spasm and the world-historical destiny that it initiates. Helen and Clytaemnestra are engendered upon Leda, but equally the fall of Troy ("broken wall," "burning roof and tower") and the murder of Clytaemnestra's husband Agamemnon are engendered upon the future. The poem ends not with a second rhetorical question, but with a genuine equivocation: "Did she put on his knowledge with his power / Before the indifferent beak could let her drop?" This is to raise the possibility that something of Zeus's power—something of his brute blood—has entered the human line, engendering the enormity of events that lie ahead. The question expresses an implicit anxiety that in the stream of human history knowledge and power are not necessarily coupled, that humanity lacks the lofty presence of mind to manage the energies of which it is the agent or vessel. This anxiety becomes a grim conviction in poems of historical dissolution like "Nineteen Hundred and Nineteen," "The Second Coming," and "The STARE'S NEST BY MY WINDOW." "Indifferent" reaffirms the terrifying, awe-inspiring, and infuriating aloofness of divinity, as well as the stark physicality of the act. Whatever the destiny he has engendered, Zeus is not above the accidents of the body and immediately subsides into what Thomas Whitaker calls "postcoital indifference" (Swan and Shadow 108). The adjective places a last check on the impulse to sentimentalize what Yeats wants to insist upon: that the forces that enact the pattern of the universe are not swayed by human sympathy or obligation, at least in an era of antithetical ascendancy.

FIRST PUBLICATION: The Dial (periodical), June 1924. Reprinted in The Cat and the Moon and Certain Poems, The CUALA PRESS, Dublin, July 1924.

BIBLIOGRAPHY

Gregory, Lady. Lady Gregory's Journals (vol. 1, ed. Daniel J. Murphy); Henn, T. R. The Lonely Tower: Studies in the Poetry of W. B. Yeats's; Whitaker, Thomas R. Swan and Shadow: Yeats's Dialogue with History; Yeats, W. B. Memoirs, The Variorum Edition of the Plays of W. B. Yeats, The Variorum Edition of the Poems of W. B. Yeats, A Vision.

"Lines Written in Dejection" (1917)

"Lines Written in Dejection" overtly belongs to a tradition of romantic self-lament most obviously marked by COLERIDGE's "Dejection: An Ode" (1802) and SHELLEY's "Stanzas written in Dejection—December 1818, Near Naples" (1824). As "The LIVING BEAUTY," "MEN IMPROVE WITH THE YEARS," "A Song," and "The WILD SWANS AT

COOLE" respond to the midlife ebb of the heart, so "Lines Written in Dejection," begun in September 1916, when Yeats was 51, responds to the ebb of the imagination, the loss of power to sustain a subjective reality in repudiation of the objective (YC 187). The poem pivots on an opposition between the feminine moon, which presides over the mind and the imagination, and the masculine sun, which presides over the body and the world. Gone are the "dark leopards of the moon," with their "round green eyes" and "long wavering bodies" (cf. "The CAT AND THE MOON"); the "wild witches," with their "angry tears"; the "holy centaurs of the hills." Banished is the "heroic mother moon." Having come to 50 years—note the surrender to the self-context of the temporal and the bodily—Yeats must endure the "embittered" and "timid" sun. The adjectives reflect Yeats's own condition, the particular symptoms of his fallenness from his own lunar nature; as it were, the sun is the symbol of Yeats's falseness to himself (on Yeats's allegiance to the moon, his status as a "moon man," see *Unicorn* 216–217). As its title indicates, "Lines Written in Dejection" expresses a mood rather than a permanent collapse or final admission of defeat. Yeats would soon reassert the authority and potency of the imagination with a vengeance. In "A PRAYER ON GOING INTO MY HOUSE," for example, Yeats insists that if he should dream "Sinbad the sailor's brought a painted chest, / Or image, from beyond the Loadstone Mountain, / That dream is a norm. . . ." It is precisely the loss of this ability to believe in one's dreams as a "norm" that "Lines Written in Dejection" laments.

FIRST PUBLICATION: *The Wild Swans at Coole*, The CUALA PRESS, Churchtown, Dundrum, November 17, 1917.

BIBLIOGRAPHY

Kelly, John S. A *W. B. Yeats Chronology*; Moore, Virginia. *The Unicorn: William Butler Yeats' Search for Reality.*

"Living Beauty, The" (1918)

"MEN IMPROVE WITH THE YEARS" stems from Yeats's first attempt to woo ISEULT GONNE in July and August 1916, while "The Living Beauty" stems from his second attempt in August 1917 (YC 194). The poems air much the same frustration: that the aging heart must content itself with aesthetic contemplation in lieu of the living embrace. Yeats bids his heart, spent and frozen, "draw content" from the beauty cast in bronze or hewn from marble, even though such beauty "when we have gone is gone again, / Being more indifferent to our solitude / Than 'twere an apparition" ("'twere" contracts the phrase "it were"). These lines suggest the inadequacy of objects that comfort only as long as they are beheld. Additionally they inscribe a pun on the word "gone." Read in this light, the phrase "when we have gone is gone again, / Being more indifferent to our solitude" encapsulates the fundamental romantic complaint of Yeats's entire life (there is the same pun in "FRIENDS," "HER PRAISE," "RECONCILIATION," and "TO A YOUNG BEAUTY"). In a concluding apostrophe to his own heart, Yeats declares that the "living beauty is for younger men: / We cannot pay its tribute of wild tears." These lines have a certain self-referential irony, as their anguish suggests an unextinguished capacity for "wild tears."

Frank Kermode identifies in "The Living Beauty" the germ of a crucial development in Yeats's poetic philosophy. "There is a tormenting contrast between [aesthetic] images (signified by the bronze and marble statuettes) and the living beauty," he observes. "And out of this contrast grows the need for a poetic image which will resemble the living beauty rather than the marble or bronze. No static symbol will now serve; there must be movement, the different sort of life that a dancer has by comparison with the most perfect object of art [. . .]. The Image is to be all movement, yet with a kind of stillness" (*Romantic Image* 102). Kermode perceives this development come to fruition in the final stanza of "AMONG SCHOOL CHILDREN."

"A Song" (1918), which immediately follows "The Living Beauty" in the 1919 edition of *The Wild Swans at Coole* and in the collected poems, and likewise dates from the summer of 1917, continues the lament for the guttering flame of the heart. Its refrain cries "*O who could have foretold / That the heart grows old?*" Yeats, of course, had long foretold that the heart grows old, first diagnosing the problem—what might be called the fundamental WORDSWORTHIAN or romantic problem—in "THE MEDITATION OF THE OLD FISHERMAN."

FIRST PUBLICATION: The *Little Review* (periodical), October 1918. Reprinted in *Nine Poems*, privately printed by Clement Shorter, London, October 1918, and in *The Wild Swans at Coole*, Macmillan, London, New York, March 11, 1919.

BIBLIOGRAPHY

Kermode, Frank. *Romantic Image*; Kelly, John S. *A W. B. Yeats Chronology*.

"Long-legged Fly" (1939)

The recognition of "Long-legged fly" is close to that of "The DOUBLE VISION OF MICHAEL ROBARTES," both being poems that ponder the mind as it outdances thought and enters into the silence and stillness of eternity. Both poems, additionally, have as their centerpiece the figure of the dancing girl. She reconciles, as Frank Kermode writes, "the division of soul and body, form and matter, life and death, artist and audience," and functions as a "type of the Fifteenth Phase"—the phase of "complete beauty"—in Yeats's scheme of lunar symbolism (*Romantic Image* 71–72; AV 135). Versions of the figure also appear in "AMONG SCHOOL CHILDREN," "A CRAZED GIRL," and "TO A CHILD DANCING IN THE WIND."

"Long-legged fly" draws together three provocatively disparate figures—Caesar, the anonymous dancing girl, and Michelangelo—as communicants of the same silence. The implication is that everything exalted in our humanity, whether world-historical or anonymous and transitory, participates in the same dynamic of meaning, and has the same kind of initiation in moments of unself-conscious reverie. This unself-consciousness is emphasized and rendered as a literal dissociation of mind and body by the poem's syntactic pattern. Not Caesar, but *a hand* props his head; not the dancer, but *her feet* practice the shuffle; not Michelangelo, but *his hand* "moves to and fro" (*Swan and Shadow* 121–122). In such moments, the body is freed of mind's

marionette strings and becomes an expression of the silence with which the mind communes.

The first stanza glimpses Caesar in his camp tent as he prepares his campaign of battle, his enterprise creative and civilizational rather than narrowly military or merely bloodthirsty. The second stanza glimpses the girl as she practices, in an unguarded moment, "a tinker shuffle / Picked up on a street." Adopting the voice of avuncular counsel he similarly trots out in "TO A YOUNG BEAUTY" and "Two Years Later" (see "To a Child Dancing in the Wind"), Yeats warns her to be more discrete, lest she incite the kind of conflagration that Helen did ("topless towers" are linked to Helen in "When Helen Lived" [1914]). The girl, like the girl in "The Double Vision of Michael Robartes" and "To a Child Dancing in the Wind," is most likely ISEULT GONNE as remembered in her younger days. Yeats gives the genesis of Iseult-as-dancing-girl in *A VISION*: "My imagination goes some years backward, and I remember a beautiful young girl singing at the edge of the sea in Normandy words and music of her own composition. She thought herself alone, stood barefooted between sea and sand; sang with lifted head of the civilisations that there had come and gone, ending every verse with the cry: 'O Lord, let something remain'" (219–220). T. R. Henn picks up on the detail that the girl has learned the tinker's dance in the street, and he associates it with the concluding lines of "The SEVEN SAGES," which insist that wisdom is learned upon the roads, and that it "comes of beggary" (*Lonely Tower* 86). The lines might also be associated with "Three Songs to the One Burden" (1939), which opens with the song of Mannion the "Roaring Tinker," and with *WHERE THERE IS NOTHING*, in which the hero, Paul Ruttledge, abandons his social station to join a clan of tinkers. He tells his scandalized acquaintances, "As I can't leap from cloud to cloud I want to wander from road to road," and he says of the roads themselves, "They are the serpent of eternity. I wonder they have never been worshipped. What are the stars beside them? They never meet one another. The roads are the only things that are infinite. They are all endless" (*VPl.* 1081). The concatenation of "street" and "tinker," then, amplifies on the implication of the dance and suggests a vagrant freedom and a footing of eternity. The third stanza envisions Michelangelo at work upon the ceiling of the Sistine Chapel. As in "MICHAEL ROBARTES AND THE DANCER" and "UNDER BEN BULBEN," Michelangelo weds the sacred and the profane, as do Caesar and the dancing girl in their different ways. Yeats instructs that "girls at puberty" should be kept out, lest they become excited, as does the "globe-trotting madam" in "Under Ben Bulben," by the image of Adam reclining in his masculine strength.

The poem's refrain—"Like a long-legged fly upon the stream / His mind moves upon silence"—suggests the individual mind moving gracefully and self-forgettingly upon the currents of a force or reality far larger that itself. Such silence is, perhaps, the subjective sensation of absorption in the ANIMA MUNDI. The imagery of fly and stream has also, perhaps, a certain spiritual connection to the scenes of mountain fishing that symbolize pride and solitude in "The FISHERMAN" and "The TOWER." The latter poem employs the "rod and fly" as a symbol of Yeats's youthful cleanliness of spirit (lines 9–11) and pictures "young upstanding men / Climbing the mountain side, / That under bursting dawn / They may drop a fly. . . " (lines 175–178).

FIRST PUBLICATION: The *London Mercury* (periodical), March 1939. Reprinted in *Last Poems and Two Plays*, The CUALA PRESS, Dublin, July 10, 1939.

BIBLIOGRAPHY

Henn, T. R. *The Lonely Tower: Studies in the Poetry of W. B. Yeats*; Kermode, Frank. *Romantic Image*; Whitaker, Thomas R. *Swan and Shadow: Yeats's Dialogue with History*; Yeats, W. B. *The Variorum Edition of the Plays of W. B. Yeats*, A Vision.

"Lover mourns for the Loss of Love, The" (1898)

A seven-line lyric addressed to MAUD GONNE, "The Lover mourns for the Loss of Love" tells of Yeats's continuing romantic bondage. Yeats writes that he had a "beautiful friend" and dreamed that

"the old despair"—his frustrated love for Gonne—would be allayed, but one day his beautiful friend looked into his heart and saw Gonne's image and went "weeping away." The poem is a nicely turned example of the argument *ad misericordiam*—the appeal to pity—but as Yeats was to say much later with reference to the war poets, "passive suffering is not a theme for poetry" (*LE* 199). The "beautiful friend" is OLIVIA SHAKESPEAR, who was Yeats's mistress from early 1896 to March or April 1897. In MEMOIRS, Yeats tells the unexpurgated story of this romance and recollects the specific incident that gave rise to "The Lover mourns for the Loss of Love." In February 1897, Gonne returned to London and invited him to dinner. "I dined with her and my trouble increased—she certainly had no thought of the mischief she was doing," Yeats recalls. "And at last one morning instead of reading much love poetry, as my way was to bring the right mood round, I wrote letters. My friend [Shakespear] found my mood did not answer hers and burst into tears. 'There is someone else in your heart,' she said. It was the breaking between us for many years" (89).

"He tells of a Valley full of Lovers" (1897) is a related parable of Gonne's injurious sway. Yeats's "lost love"—Gonne—emerges from a wood. Contradicting the exculpation of *Memoirs*, she moves "stealthily," as if predatory or mischievous. Yeats tells the women of the valley to cover the eyes of the young men, or else "remembering hers they will find no other face fair / Till all the valleys of the world have been withered away." Yeats returns to the sway of Gonne's beauty in "An IMAGE FROM A PAST LIFE," in which GEORGE YEATS plays the part of Shakespear. She does not go "weeping away," but she is haunted by Gonne all the same.

FIRST PUBLICATION: The *Dome* (periodical), May 1898, under the title "Aodh to Dectora. Three Songs" (with the companion poems "HE HEARS THE CRY OF THE SEDGE" and "HE THINKS OF THOSE WHO HAVE SPOKEN EVIL OF HIS BELOVED"). Reprinted in *The Wind Among the Reeds*, Elkin Mathews, London, April 1899, under the title "Aedh laments the Loss of Love." Reprinted in *The Poetical Works of William B. Yeats* (vol. 1), Macmillan, New York, London, November 27, 1906, under the present title.

BIBLIOGRAPHY

Yeats, W. B. *Later Essays, Memoirs.*

"Lover's Song, The" (1938)

See "The THREE BUSHES."

"Lover tells of the Rose in his Heart, The" (1892)

A paean to MAUD GONNE (*Mem.* 78), "The Lover tells of the Rose in his Heart" repudiates everything "uncomely and broken"—the "cry of a child by the roadway, the creak of a lumbering cart, / The heavy steps of the ploughmen"—as an affront to the image of Gonne that "blossoms a ROSE" in the depths of Yeats's heart. In the poem's second stanza, Yeats declares his intention to purge everything "unshapely" from the world, to refashion the world as a "casket of gold"—as a fit reliquary or tomb—for dreams of Gonne's image. In its reference to *dreams* of Gonne's image, the poem seems to suggest Yeats's uncertain or merely prospective possession of Gonne; it seems also to inscribe an awareness of its own activity of idealization. Yeats, meanwhile, would "sit on a green knoll apart," a mere observer of the refashioned world. The image suggests Yeats's inability to leave behind the natural world that he would repudiate and enter into the world—both golden and deathly—that he envisions. Here Yeats approaches a diagnosis of his own inability to win Gonne: he cannot make a sharp enough break with the natural world ("green knoll") to become one of her kind and credibly claim kinship. At the same time, the impulse to place Gonne's image within the casket of the refashioned world is the impulse to see her figuratively dead and buried. It links the poem to the more explicit expression of the same impulse in "HE WISHES HIS BELOVED WERE DEAD." Both poems fantasize Gonne's death out of desperation to escape the burden of a potentially self-destructive romantic anguish. Gonne aside, the poem's negation of the natural world, even as Yeats remains attached to it, represents a step toward the confidently transcendental vision of a late poem like "SAILING TO BYZANTIUM." Yeats's early impulse to remake the world as a "casket of gold" foretells his late impulse to take "such a form as Grecian goldsmiths make / Of hammered gold and gold enamelling. . . ."

FIRST PUBLICATION: The *National Observer* (periodical), November 12, 1892, under the title "The Rose in my Heart." Reprinted in *The Second Book of the Rhymers' Club*, Elkin Mathews & John Lane, London, Dodd, Mead & Company, New York, June 1894, under the same title. Reprinted in *The Wind Among the Reeds*, Elkin Mathews, London, April 1899, under the title "Aedh tells of the Rose in his Heart." Reprinted in *The Poetical Works of William B. Yeats* (vol. 1), Macmillan, New York, London, November 27, 1906, under the present title.

BIBLIOGRAPHY

Yeats, W. B. *Memoirs.*

"Love's Loneliness" (1930)

See "WORDS FOR MUSIC PERHAPS."

"Lullaby" (1931)

See "WORDS FOR MUSIC PERHAPS."

"Mad as the Mist and Snow" (1932)

See "WORDS FOR MUSIC PERHAPS."

"Magi, The" (1914)

"The Magi," a fierce and disturbing little poem, takes up the metaphysics of cyclic apocalypse that

Yeats had mooted in "AT GALWAY RACES," and that he would later raise to such impressive heights in poems like "LEDA AND THE SWAN" and "The SECOND COMING." "The Magi" is also thematically linked to "The COLD HEAVEN," which appears earlier in *Responsibilities* (1914). In "The Cold Heaven" Yeats is beset by "the injustice of the skies," while in "The Magi" he pierces the inscrutable sky and manages to apprehend something of its temper and motive. The phrases with which the poems respectively open—"Suddenly I saw" and "Now as at all times I can see"—suggest the poems' shared visionary propensity, as well as their different realizations of this propensity. If "The Cold Heaven" is a poem of failed or incomplete vision—the moment of riddling light comes and goes—"The Magi" is a poem of achieved vision. Yeats himself associated "The Magi" and "The DOLLS," which immediately follows in the pages of *Responsibilities*. As the magi yearn for a metaphysical birth, so the dolls deplore a physical birth. As Yeats explains in a 1914 note, "After I had made the poem ['The Dolls'], I looked up one day into the blue of the sky, and suddenly imagined, as if lost in the blue of the sky, stiff figures in procession. I remembered that they were the habitual image suggested by blue sky, and looking for a second fable called them 'The Magi,' complementary forms of those enraged dolls" (VP 820). "The Magi" is further associable with the much earlier poem "HE REMEMBERS FORGOTTEN BEAUTY," in which the "high lonely mysteries" of "white Beauty," their "swords upon their iron knees," brood "flame on flame, and deep on deep / Throne over throne. . . ." It may be that these same "high lonely mysteries" have been reborn in the form of the magi, though in the later poem they are less sentinels of a final peace than of an endless unrest, sentinels of the violent death and rebirth that is the savage pulse of the universe.

Like "He remembers Forgotten Beauty," "The Magi" pictures its warrior figures seated on high, terrible in their ceremony, "their ancient faces like rain-beaten stones." With "fixed eyes" they peer down "hoping to find once more, / Being by Calvary's turbulence unsatisfied, / The uncontrollable mystery on the bestial floor." This is to say that the death of Christ left the magi—almost vampirish in

their appetite for the energies of end and beginning—yearning for more of the same, for a renewal of the "uncontrollable mystery on the bestial floor," for some new birth in the manger, that all may come round again. In the pages of A VISION, Yeats explains the moment for which the magi wait and quotes his own poem to illustrate the point: "When the old *antithetical* becomes the new *primary*, moral feeling is changed into an organisation of experience which must in its turn seek a unity, the whole of experience. When the old *primary* becomes the new *antithetical*, the old realisation of an objective moral law is changed into a subconscious turbulent instinct. The world of rigid custom and law is broken up by 'the uncontrollable mystery upon the bestial floor'" (105). Yeats's poem intersects with the biblical tale of the three wise men or magi (see Matthew 2) only ironically and provocatively. Like their biblical counterparts, Yeats's magi look to the birth of Christ, though less with reverence and hope than with something like lust for the frenzy of apocalypse.

FIRST PUBLICATION: *Poetry* (periodical), May 1914, and the *New Statesman* (periodical), May 9, 1914. Reprinted in *Responsibilities: Poems and a Play*, The CUALA PRESS, Churchtown, Dundrum, May 25, 1914.

BIBLIOGRAPHY

Yeats, W. B. *The Variorum Edition of the Poems of W. B. Yeats, A Vision.*

"Man and the Echo, The" (1939)

In "To A FRIEND WHOSE WORK HAS COME TO NOTHING," Yeats urges Lady GREGORY to go to a "place of stone" and there be "secret and exult / Because of all things known / That is most difficult." In "The Man and the Echo" Yeats struggles with this very difficulty. He takes himself to a "place of stone" according to his own advice, but he finds it no easy thing to rise above the remorse to which he refers in "The CHOICE," "A DIALOGUE OF SELF AND SOUL," and "VACILLATION."

The "cleft that's christened Alt" refers to a glen on the south side of Knocknarea, a limestone mountain roughly three miles southwest of SLIGO. In *The Yeats Country*, Sheelah Kirby describes it as a "deep cleft in the hillside, about one mile long and only about thirty feet broad, bounded on each side by steep cliffs and overgrown with trees and shrubs. It was called by the old people the Alt, which is the Irish word for wooded glen, or cliff" (30). The cleft is a natural backdrop to Yeats's scene of self-reckoning, as it represents the duality of his aspiration and dejection. Its cold cleanliness of mountain rock recalls "The FISHERMAN," "The GREY ROCK," "ON A POLITICAL PRISONER," "To a Friend whose Work has come to Nothing," and "The TOWER," but the sunless pit indicates dejection amid the natural place of solitary exultation.

Yeats's remorse expresses itself in three questions, all having to do with the anxiety that his words have caused mischief or failed to prevent mischief, that is, having to do with the troublesome relation between literature and life. "Did that play of mine send out / Certain men the English shot?" Yeats asks. The play in question is CATHLEEN NI HOULIHAN, which debuted on April 2, 1902, at St. Teresa's Hall, Dublin, with MAUD GONNE in the role of Cathleen. Yeats wonders whether its mystic nationalism radicalized the younger generation and helped foment the EASTER RISING of 1916, which resulted in 16 executions. Stephen Gwynn's well-known comment in *Irish Literature and Drama in the English Language: A Short History* (1936) may have prompted Yeats's self-questioning: "But the effect of *Cathleen ni Houlihan* on me was that I went home asking myself if such plays should be produced unless one was prepared for people to go out to shoot and be shot. Yeats was not alone responsible; no doubt but Lady Gregory had helped him to get the peasant speech so perfect; but above all Miss Gonne's impersonation had stirred the audience as I have never seen another audience stirred" (159). In a memorial essay, Gonne herself concurs that Yeats helped foment the Easter Rising: "Without Yeats there would have been no Literary Revival in Ireland. Without the inspiration of that Revival and the glorification of beauty and heroic virtue, I

doubt if there would have been an Easter Week" (*Scattering Branches* 27).

Yeats next wonders whether he contributed to the mental breakdown of MARGOT RUDDOCK, a young actress and poet with whom he conducted an artistic and romantic dalliance from 1934 to 1937. His qualms may have to do with the rigorous artistic standard he tried to impose on her and with his blunt criticism of her work. "I do not like your recent poems," Yeats wrote in an April 1936 letter. "You do not work at your [technique] [. . .] you take the easiest course—leave out the rhymes or choose the most hackneyed rhymes, because— damn you—you are lazy" (*Sweet Dancer* 81). Ruddock felt crushed under the rigors of Yeats's criticism and complained as much in an April 1936 letter: "Do you know that you have made poetry, my solace and my joy, a bloody grind I hate! [. . .] I loathe poetry, I loathe working at it for given grammar and words (of which I have not enough), poetry should *not* be worked at. Scrub floors and sweat in offices but do not sweat at poetry which is spiritual sweat! And to make it physical sweat as well is to condemn it with all other earthly things" (88). Despite Yeats's sense of responsibility for Ruddock's breakdown, Roger McHugh's assessment seems fair: "Although Yeats and [Shree Purohit Swami], each in his own way, played an accidental part in the wastage of a beautiful and generous woman of undoubted talent, neither had any real responsibility for her fundamental misfortune; the seeds of her schizophrenia had been sown before they met her and grew their thorns just when she might have blossomed" (121). In a letter to the Swami, Yeats identifies this "accidental part," writing, "We put her out of relation with her habitual surroundings" (*BG* 258). Yeats may have meant by this that they unfitted her for anything except an artistic life that she was unequal to.

Completing his self-reckoning, Yeats wonders whether his "spoken words" could have "checked / That whereby a house lay wrecked." The house is COOLE PARK. Margaret Gregory, Lady GREGORY's daughter-in-law, inherited the house upon the death of ROBERT GREGORY, and sold it to the Ministry of Lands and Agriculture on April 1, 1927, with Lady Gregory acting as witness (*Lady Gregory*

290). It is not clear how Yeats's "spoken words" could have rescued the house. Perhaps he felt he had not done everything possible to counteract the political and cultural trends that gradually undid the Anglo-Irish Ascendancy, the Protestant landlord class to which Lady Gregory belonged. "Spoken," however, seems to imply a personal rather than a public or literary intercession. Perhaps he felt he had done too little to prevail on Margaret Gregory not to sell the house, or done too little to influence Robert Gregory's character. In MEMOIRS, Yeats explicitly links Coole's demise to Robert's character, imagining the house "sinking away through courteous incompetence, or rather sheer weakness of will, for ability has not failed in young Gregory" (230).

Yeats's dejected yearning for death is self-answered by the inner voice of resolution and wisdom in the man's second speech. The "spiritual intellect's great work" is not to shirk the burden of experience by finding refuge in death, but to expiate it in joy. This is what it means to clean "man's dirty slate." It is this expiation—this embrace of the self even in its worldly degradation—that Yeats dramatizes in the joyous cry of "A DIALOGUE OF SELF AND SOUL": "I am content to follow to its source / Every event in action or in thought; / Measure the lot; forgive myself the lot!" Yeats observes that in any case there is no release possible in "bodkin" (dagger) or "disease," because after death ("body gone") the body does not sleep, but wakes into self-questioning and self-judgment. Yeats alludes to the posthumous reality he describes in A VISION: "In the *Dreaming Back,* the *Spirit* is compelled to live over and over again the events that had most moved it; there can be nothing new, but the old events stand forth in a light which is dim or bright according to the intensity of the passion that accompanied them. [. . .] In the *Return,* upon the other hand, the *Spirit* must live through past events in the order of their occurrence, because it is compelled by the *Celestial Body* to trace every passionate event to its cause until all are related and understood, turned into knowledge, made a part of itself" (226; see also AV-1925 226–227). The soul "sinks at last into the night"—finds its permanent rest—only when "all's arranged in one clear view," or is brought into the unity of complete self-understanding and self-forgiveness.

"O Rocky Voice," Yeats calls out, referring to his own echo amid the rocks that is the poem's irregular refrain, but also conjuring the "Rocky Face" who is the vatic presence of "The GYRES," a mysterious personification of the elemental power that presides over the pattern of history. "Shall we in that great night rejoice?" Yeats asks of the voice. "What do we know but that we face / One another in this place?" Knowledge of the "great night" is the province of the dead. The living know only the entrapment within the self (symbolized by "the echo") and the irresolvable mystery of reality. Yeats's last question elicits no echo, has no answer, because the death cry of a rabbit gripped by the hawk or owl has distracted his thought: so all such questioning finds its revelation in death. As it were, the death of the rabbit—the reminder of the revelatory imminence of death—is the only answer attainable within the realm of life.

The poignancy of the rabbit in its death moment was embedded in Yeats's mind. "The DEATH OF THE HARE" employs the dead hare as metaphor for ISEULT GONNE's lost "wildness," and AUTOBIOGRAPHIES relates an incident that may have engendered the motif. While staying at Castle Dargan, the home of his cousin, the former Mary Middleton, Yeats "fished for pike [. . .] and shot at birds with a muzzle-loading pistol until somebody shot a rabbit and I heard it squeal. From that on I would kill nothing but the dumb fish" (74).

FIRST PUBLICATION: The *Atlantic Monthly* and the *London Mercury* (periodicals), January 1939, under the title "Man and the Echo." Reprinted in *Last Poems and Two Plays,* The CUALA PRESS, Dublin, July 10, 1939, under the present title.

BIBLIOGRAPHY

Gwynn, Stephen. *Irish Literature and Drama in the English Language: A Short History;* ed. *Scattering Branches: Tributes to the Memory of W. B. Yeats;* Kirby, Sheelah. *The Yeats Country: A Guide to the Sligo District and Other Places in the West of Ireland Associated with the Life and Work of W. B. Yeats;* Kohfeldt, Mary Lou. *Lady Gregory: The Woman behind the Irish Renaissance;* Saddlemyer, Ann.

Becoming George: The Life of Mrs W. B. Yeats; Yeats, W. B. *Ah, Sweet Dancer: W. B. Yeats and Margot Ruddock, Autobiographies, A Critical Edition of Yeats's A Vision (1925), Memoirs, A Vision.*

"Man who Dreamed of Faeryland, The" (1891)

"The Man who Dreamed of Faeryland" reiterates one of the most fundamental realizations of Yeats's early poetry: that the immortal fairy world and the mortal human world are locked in battle for the soul of man (see also "The Host of the Air" [1893], "The HOSTING OF THE SIDHE," *The LAND OF HEART'S DESIRE*, "The SONG OF WANDERING AENGUS," "The STOLEN CHILD," "The WANDERINGS OF OISIN"). The poem tells of a man from the neighborhood of SLIGO whose life is a restless tension between the competing claims of the two worlds. In the first stanza, the man stands amid a crowd at Drumahair (a town eight miles southwest of Sligo), his heart contemplating love. In the second, he wanders by the sands of Lissadell (the estate of the Gore-Booth family, northwest of Sligo), his mind running on money; in the third, he stands beside the well of Scanavin (near the village Collooney, south of Sligo), pondering vengeance against his mockers. He might have had satisfaction on all three counts, save for the mysterious voices that entice him with visions of the fairy realm. At Drumahair, he hears the fish at market sing of a "world-forgotten isle" where "Time can never mar a lover's vows." At Lissadell, he hears a lug-worm sing of a "gay, exulting, gentle race" who cease their dancing only to sup on wonderful fruit. By the well, he hears a lone knot-grass singing of a place where a "chosen race" rejoices unruffled by happenstance or accident. Each of these voices sap the man's healthy, natural impulses and stifle the realizable ambition with the unrealizable vision ("We come between him and the deed of his hand, / We come between him and the hope of his heart," as Niamh says in "The Hosting of the Sidhe" of those who look upon the fairy band). In the final stanza, the man has gone to his grave under the hill of Lug-

nagall (a townland at the foot of Cope's Mountain, northeast of Sligo), but even there he finds no rest, for the worms themselves cry of the divine summer that showers "upon the dancer by the dreamless wave." The poems ends with an almost taunting rhetorical question: "Why should those lovers that no lovers miss / Dream, until God burn Nature with a kiss?" The question suggests that the fairies, knowing consummate and perpetual love, have no impetus to dream, and in this they mock the inescapable yearning of the race of men. By 1931, Yeats had arrived at the opinion that "The Man who Dreamed of Faeryland" was a "bad poem," and he refused to read it even upon request (*I&R*, II, 399). Presumably its turgid folkloric mysticism was an embarrassing reminder of enthusiasms he had long outgrown.

FIRST PUBLICATION: The *National Observer* (periodical), February 7, 1891, under the title "A Man who Dreamed of Fairyland." Reprinted in *The Book of the Rhymers' Club*, Elkin Mathews, London, February 1892, under the same title. Reprinted in *The Countess Kathleen and Various Legends and Lyrics*, T. Fisher Unwin, London, September 1892, under the title "The Man who Dreamed of Fairyland." Reprinted in *Poems*, T. Fisher Unwin, London, October 1895, under the present title.

BIBLIOGRAPHY

Conner, Lester I. *A Yeats Dictionary: Persons and Places in the Poetry of William Butler Yeats*; Kirby, Sheelah. *The Yeats Country: A Guide to the Sligo District and Other Places in the West of Ireland Associated with the Life and Work of W. B. Yeats*; McGarry, James P. *Place Names in the Writings of William Butler Yeats*; Mikhail, E. H., ed., *W. B. Yeats: Interviews and Recollections* (vol. 2).

"Man Young and Old, A" (1926–1928, sequence)

Companion to "A WOMAN YOUNG AND OLD," "A Man Young and Old" is an 11-poem sequence consisting of "First Love," "Human Dignity," "The Mermaid," "The Death of the Hare," "The

Empty Cup," "His Memories," "The Friends of His Youth," "Summer and Spring," "The Secrets of the Old," "His Wildness," and "From 'Oedipus at Colonus,'" this last an excerpt from Yeats's translation of SOPHOCLES' play. Knit by numerous recurring motifs—moon, stone, tree, thorn, peacock—"A Man Young and Old," according to Yeats, concerns the "wild regrets, for youth and love, of an old man" (*Letters* 716). Informing these "regrets" are memories of MAUD GONNE, ISEULT GONNE, and OLIVIA SHAKESPEAR, the three love interests at the center of Yeats's poetic mythology.

"First Love," one of the most bitter of Yeats's poems of frustrated love, sets the tone of the entire sequence. While "NO SECOND TROY" in spite of itself venerates the sheer force of Gonne's destructive power, "First Love" records the damage. Like the disordering and destructive moon, she left Yeats crazed and dumbstruck (cf. "BLOOD AND THE MOON" and "The CAT AND THE MOON"). Yeats had frequently made flattery of his own abasement, as in "The FOLLY OF BEING COMFORTED," but in this instance the poem carries a genuinely negative charge. The allegation of stone-heartedness repeats the central conceit of "EASTER 1916" and echoes the analysis of Gonne's character in Yeats's journal of 1909: "Women, because the main event of their lives has been a giving of themselves, give themselves to an opinion as if [it] were some terrible stone doll. [. . .] They grow cruel, as if [in] defence of lover or child, and all this is done for something other than human life. At last the opinion becomes so much a part of them that it is as though a part of their flesh becomes, as it were, stone, and much of their being passes out of life. It was part of [Gonne's] power in the past that, though she made this surrender with her mind, she kept the sweetness of her voice and much humour, yet I cannot but fear for her" (*Aut.* 372–373; *Mem.* 192).

"Human Dignity" shuffles the terms of "First Love," with much the same implication of Yeats's abasement. The metaphor of the stone shifts from Gonne to Yeats, implying Yeats's sense of himself as splintered and cast off and beneath notice. "The broken tree" is the image of desolation, the "spreading laurel tree" of "A PRAYER FOR MY DAUGHTER" come to blight or planted in barren soil or riven by

lightning (like the tree in PURGATORY). The poem ends with perhaps unintended irony. Having written any number of poems publicizing the anguish of his love for Gonne, Yeats is unconvincing in the posture of one "dumb / From human dignity."

A. Norman Jeffares considers "The Mermaid" a parable of Yeats's affair with Olivia Shakespear in 1896 and 1897 (*NCP* 259). Certainly Shakespear "picked" Yeats as her own in a way that Gonne never did, though the mermaid clutching and dragging down her lover in her "cruel happiness" seems inconsistent with Shakespear's gentleness (cf. *Mem.* 88) and congeniality (cf. "FRIENDS"). "The Death of the Hare," on the other hand, clearly relates to Yeats's failed courtship of Iseult Gonne, with the younger Gonne metaphorized as the hare (cf. "Two Songs of a Fool," which establishes the hare metaphor). On this reading, the dead hare symbolizes Gonne in the unhappiness of her marriage to Francis Stuart (1902–2000), her youthful "wildness" lost (cf. "TO A CHILD DANCING IN THE WIND"). Asked about the poem in 1935, Yeats would say only that "the poem means that the lover may, while loving, feel sympathy with his beloved's dread of captivity" (*Letters* 840–841). The image of the dead hare recurs in "The MAN AND THE ECHO" and may derive from a trauma that Yeats recounts in *AUTOBIOGRAPHIES*: "I fished for pike at Castle Dargan and shot at birds with a muzzle-loading pistol until somebody shot a rabbit and I heard it squeal. From that on I would kill nothing but the dumb fish" (74).

Shakespear inarguably informs "The Empty Cup," as Yeats makes clear in a December 6, 1926, letter to Shakespear herself. The letter includes a draft of the poem and an illuminating explanation of its genesis: "I came upon two early photographs of you yesterday [. . .]. Who ever had a like profile?—a profile from a Sicilian coin. One looks back to one's youth as to [a] cup that a mad man dying of thirst left half tasted. I wonder if you feel like that" (*Letters* 721). Yeats had visited London in October and presumably seen Shakespear, explaining the poem's allusion to "October last" (*YC* 250). That the cup is now "dry as bone" suggests the wasted and lost opportunity of their love relationship (cf. "The LOVER MOURNS FOR THE LOSS OF LOVE").

In the bitterness of its complaint against age and sexual loss, "His Memories" is close to "The LAMENTATION OF THE OLD PENSIONER," but its unsettling edge of sexual brutality equally aligns it with "NEWS FOR THE DELPHIC ORACLE." Yeats's withered present is measured against the sexual consummation of December 1908 (AM 393–396; cf. "To A YOUNG GIRL"). Fully Helenic in her intensity, Maud Gonne lies in Yeats's arms and cries, ecstatically, or perhaps perversely, or perhaps sufferingly, "Strike me if I shriek." The evidence suggests that Yeats and Gonne did have a brief sexual relationship, but the seeming abandon of the poem's bedroom scene is incongruous with the "horror and terror of physical love" to which Gonne confesses in MEMOIRS, and perhaps also incongruous with Yeats's sexual timidity (134).

"The Friends of His Youth," "Summer and Spring," "The Secrets of the Old," and "His Wildness" depart from the direct autobiography of the preceding poems and predict the rustic puppet-play of "WORDS FOR MUSIC PERHAPS." Working further variations on the motif of the stone, "The Friends of His Youth" envisions Madge and Peter, the "friends" of the poem's title, descended into senile parody of youthful hope and achievement. The notion of the "stone doll" (see above) is brought forward again—Madge bears such a stone as if it were a child, literalizing the metaphor of the 1909 journal—while the previous poem's apparent "shriek" of sexual ecstasy is deflated as the "shriek" of mania. "Summer and Spring" fleshes out the triangular relations of the poems' storyline and measures the magnitude of the loss described in the previous poem. Both the narrator and his friend Peter find young love with Madge beneath an "old thorn-tree" that is yet capable of blossoming, either literally or figuratively, though its age and thorns foreshadow the "broken tree" of "Human Dignity." Though the narrator and Peter compete for Madge's affection, there is no sense of "heart's agony," as in "First Love" and "Human Dignity," but only youthful superabundance of life, of which even Peter's "murdering look" is a part. "The Secrets of the Old" proposes at least some compensation for the loss of this vernal intimacy and hopefulness: a certain shrewd wisdom, salty

candor, sated fascination. As they once exchanged the secrets of youth, the narrator and Madge now trade bedroom gossip and share a connoisseurship of the body. Margery is conceivably the narrator's wife; she joins Madge in a three-person "solitude," in an intimacy of secret-sharers (so Yeats shared his own sexual history with his wife). Alternately, Margery and Madge (both variants of Margaret) may be different personas belonging to the same woman: Margery the public face, Madge the private.

If the first nine poems of the sequence are shadowed by age, the 10th poem, "His Wildness," is shadowed by death. The narrator would "mount and sail" amid the "cloudy wrack," for the sensual passion, whether embodied in a local Peg or a world-historical Helen, has gone out of the world (as in "BEAUTIFUL LOFTY THINGS," the straight back is an emblem of Gonne). This is a personal bereavement—the natural loss and constriction wrought by time and death—but also a matter of historical declension: the age itself has rejected the joy of the body and the spontaneity of the passions. If "Easter 1916" informs the allusion to Gonne's heart of stone in "First Love," the political and historical implication of the sequence recurs in the charge that "some that stay" have "changed their silk for sack." As in "IN MEMORY OF EVA GOREBOOTH AND CON MARKIEWICZ," "ON A POLITICAL PRISONER," and "A Prayer for my Daughter," Yeats most likely has in mind the sackcloth of political fanaticism by which Gonne and the Gore-Booth sisters, in his estimation, had destroyed themselves. The second stanza of "His Wildness" acknowledges, however, that amid the equivocal Heaven of the first stanza there can be neither earthly consummation nor alleviation of earthly desire ("News for the Delphic Oracle" mocks the Delphic vision of Elysian ease on just these grounds). There can be only the same delusive and futile self-comfort that Peter and Madge devise for themselves in "The Friends of His Youth." The claim is that nothing, not even Heaven itself, can compensate for the loss of impassioned youth, what WORDSWORTH, attempting to cope with much the same sense of loss, calls the "splendour in the grass."

"From 'Oedipus at Colonus,'" a choral excerpt from Yeats's translation of Sophocles' play (see

VPl. 887), answers "His Wildness" and brings the sequence to a close on a note of characteristic stoic strength. Repudiating both vain desire and vain memory, it urges the "tragic joy"—the embrace of life even in its fleeting and contingent nature—that is the essence of Yeats's mature philosophy in poems like "A DIALOGUE OF SELF AND SOUL," "The GYRES," "LAPIS LAZULI," and "VACILLATION." In a March 13, 1927, letter to Shakespear, Yeats calls the last line of the poem "very bad Grecian but very good Elizabethan and so it must stay" (*Letters* 723).

FIRST PUBLICATION: "A Man Young and Old" first appeared as a sequence in *The Tower*, Macmillan, February, 14, 1928. "From 'Oedipus at Colonus'" appeared in *The Tower*, but not as part of "A Man Young and Old." It was appended to the sequence in *The Collected Poems*, Macmillan Company, New York, London, November 1933. "His Memories," "The Friends of His Youth," "Summer and Spring," and "His Wildness" first appeared in the *London Mercury* (periodical), April 1926, under the title "More Songs of an Old Countryman." "The Empty Cup" and "The Secrets of the Old" first appeared in the *London Mercury*, May 1927, under the title "Two Songs from the Old Countryman." "First Love," "Human Dignity," "The Mermaid," and "The Death of the Hare" first appeared in the *London Mercury*, May 1927, under the title "Four Songs from the Young Countryman." "First Love," "Human Dignity," "The Mermaid," and "The Death of the Hare" previously appeared in *October Blast*, The CUALA PRESS, Dublin, August, 1927, under the title "Young Countryman." "The Empty Cup," "His Memories," "The Friends of His Youth," "Summer and Spring," "The Secrets of the Old" and "His Wildness" previously appeared in *October Blast* under the title "Old Countryman."

BIBLIOGRAPHY

Foster, R. F. *W. B. Yeats: A Life, I: The Apprentice Mage*; Jeffares, A. Norman. *A New Commentary on the Poems of W. B. Yeats*; Kelly, John S. *A W. B. Yeats Chronology*; Yeats, W. B. *Autobiographies, The Letters of W. B. Yeats, Memoirs, The Variorum Edition of the Plays of W. B. Yeats*.

"Meditation of the Old Fisherman, The" (1886)

Yeats indicates the lapsarian trend of time in "The Meditation of the Old Fisherman," as well as in other early poems like "The LAMENTATION OF THE OLD PENSIONER," "The Old Men Admiring Themselves in the Water" (1903), and "The WANDERINGS OF OISIN." These poems conceive the elderly as the ravaged witnesses of the temporal travail and reveal Yeats's own temporal anguish and anxiety—this despite his youth. Yeats acknowledged this temperamental quirk when he observed to OLIVIA SHAKESPEAR in June 1932, "My first denunciation of old age I made in *The Wanderings of Usheen* (end of part 1) before I was twenty and the same denunciation comes in the last pages of the book" (*Letters* 798; the "book" is his collected poems, which was to be the first volume in an edition of his collected works). There is perhaps a wry allusion to the preoccupation of these early poems in the refrain of "A Song" (1918): *O who could have foretold / That the heart grows old?* The answer to the question is Yeats himself, who imagined precisely this loss 32 years earlier in "The Meditation of the Old Fisherman." That the "crack" lies in the subjectivity of the heart—not in the objective condition of the world—is suggested by the implausible nature of the fisherman's complaint: that the summers were once warmer, the waves gayer, the fish more plentiful (*creel*: a large wicker basket often used to carry fish), the women fairer. Yeats's mature poems of time and senescence—"An ACRE OF GRASS," "AMONG SCHOOL CHILDREN," "The LIVING BEAUTY," "MEN IMPROVE WITH THE YEARS," "A PRAYER FOR OLD AGE," "SAILING TO BYZANTIUM," "The SPUR," and "The TOWER," to name only a few—merely continue the meditation of boyhood in propria persona, the fisherman's lament now sanctioned by the experience of genuine years. In his notes to the poem, Yeats explains that the "Old Fisherman" was inspired by "a not very old fisherman at Rosses Point," who made similar comments one day while "out fishing in SLIGO Bay" (*VP* 844; see also 797). Rosses Point is a seaside village at the mouth of Sligo Harbor.

FIRST PUBLICATION: The *Irish Monthly* (periodical), October 1886. Reprinted in *Poems and Ballads of Young Ireland*, M. H. Gill and Son, Dublin, 1888, and in *The Wanderings of Oisin and Other Poems*, Kegan Paul, Trench & Co., London, January 1889.

BIBLIOGRAPHY

Yeats, W. B. *The Letters of W. B. Yeats*, *The Variorum Edition of the Poems of W. B. Yeats*.

"Meditations in Time of Civil War" (1923, sequence)

The seven immensely distinguished poems published under the heading "Meditations in Time of Civil War"—"ANCESTRAL HOUSES," "MY HOUSE," "MY TABLE," "MY DESCENDANTS," "The ROAD AT MY DOOR," "The STARE'S NEST BY MY WINDOW," and "I SEE PHANTOMS OF HATRED AND OF THE HEART'S FULLNESS AND OF THE COMING EMPTINESS"—take up themes of order and disorder, permanence and evanescence, advent and demise, action and meditation, that are relatable to the political moment without being reducible to it. As a whole, the sequence is one of Yeats's signal achievements. See also the IRISH CIVIL WAR.

FIRST PUBLICATION: The *Dial* and the *London Mercury* (periodicals), January 1923. Reprinted in *The Cat and the Moon and Certain Poems*, The CUALA PRESS, Dublin, July 1924.

"Meeting" (1929)

See "A WOMAN YOUNG AND OLD."

"Memory of Youth, A" (1912)

In its basic pattern—the vignette of faltering love in which the human crisis suddenly finds its own image in the symbol-language of nature—"A Mem-

ory of Youth" bears close comparison to "ADAM'S CURSE" and "EPHEMERA." The poem opens with the declaration that the "moments passed as at a play," suggesting Yeats's detachment from his performance in the part of earnest lover. He nonetheless deploys his considerable verbal resources in the attempt to sustain the waning moment of love, but all for naught: "A cloud blown from the cutthroat North / Suddenly hid Love's moon away." Reduced to silence, Yeats and his beloved, presumably MAUD GONNE, realize that "even the best of love must die" and would have been "savagely undone / Were it not that Love upon the cry / Of a most ridiculous little bird / Tore from the clouds his marvellous moon." The implication is that love is whimsical, arbitrary, miraculous, taking its cue, at least while in the mood, from the bright irrelevancy of the bird. There may be a temptation to relate the "most ridiculous little bird" to the parrot that "sways upon a tree, / Raging at his own image in the enamelled sea" in "The Indian to His Love" (1886), or to the golden birds of "BYZANTIUM" and "SAILING TO BYZANTIUM," or to the peacock who screams the apocalypse in "MY TABLE," but these comparisons should be made only with trepidation. The logic of the poem requires of the bird not a violent transcendental energy but a negligibility that demonstrates the capriciousness of love.

FIRST PUBLICATION: *Poetry* (periodical), December 1912, under the title "Love and the Bird." Reprinted in *Responsibilities: Poems and a Play*, The CUALA PRESS, Churchtown, Dundrum, May 25, 1914, under the present title.

"Men Improve with the Years" (1917)

"Men Improve with the Years" is one of several poems of the period that chronicle Yeats's fascination with ISEULT GONNE, whom he unsuccessfully courted (see also "The LIVING BEAUTY," "A Song" [1918], "TO A YOUNG BEAUTY," and "TO A YOUNG GIRL"). Like "The FOLLY OF BEING COMFORTED," it explores a strategy of romantic self-consolation only to discover its glaring inadequacy. With almost melodramatic self-deflation, Yeats presents himself as "worn out with dreams; / A weather-worn, marble triton / Among the streams. . . ." (the tritons were "a race of inferior sea-deities, or imaginary sea-monsters, of semi-human form," according to *The Oxford English Dictionary*). These lines ring with distant echoes of "FERGUS AND THE DRUID," in which the Druid likewise describes himself as having grown old with the burden of dreams; so too foreshadow Yeats's assumption of imperishable form in "SAILING TO BYZANTIUM," though the later poem's triumphant renunciation of the flesh would require an emotional revitalization that was not yet on the horizon. In the guise of the marble triton, Yeats looks upon Iseult's beauty with a detached aesthetic appreciation, as if he "had found in a book / A pictured beauty," and he declares himself delighted "to be but wise"—that is, delighted to be capable of such detached pleasure. His rhetoric suddenly flattening as it slips into bromide, Yeats unconvincingly or perhaps ironically offers that "men improve with the years." Just as Yeats refuses to accept specious consolation in "The Folly of Being Comforted," so he refuses to accept it in this instance. "And yet, and yet," he muses, "Is this my dream, or the truth?" Yeats's answer is an anguished admission of the inadequacy of anything less than the heart's passion: "O would that we had met / When I had my burning youth!" Like "The Living Beauty," the poem ends with an admission of defeated age. Yeats reiterates that he grows "old among dreams, / A weather-worn, marble triton, / Among the streams." As it happened, "Men Improve with the Years" proved a poor prophet of events. Yeats wrote the poem in July 1916; he proposed to Iseult in August 1916 and again in August 1917; he married George Hyde-Lees (see GEORGE YEATS) on October 20, 1917, and before long fathered two children (YC 186–187, 194–195).

FIRST PUBLICATION: The *Little Review* (periodical), June 1917. Reprinted in *The Wild Swans at Coole*, The CUALA PRESS, Churchtown, Dundrum, November 17, 1917.

BIBLIOGRAPHY

Kelly, John S. A *W. B. Yeats Chronology*.

"Mermaid, The" (1927)

See "A MAN YOUNG AND OLD."

"Meru" (1934)

See "SUPERNATURAL SONGS."

"Michael Robartes and the Dancer" (1920)

Following the brazenly obscure "DOUBLE VISION OF MICHAEL ROBARTES" in the collected poems, "Michael Robartes and the Dancer" provides a welcome leavening of parody. Robartes is no longer the kneeling visionary but the avuncular pedant, while the dancer who had "outdanced thought" and brought her body to perfection in the earlier poem is now the modern schoolgirl with ideas of her own. The climactic vision of the 15th phase of the lunar cycle has become a wry scene of domestic comedy that undoubtedly owes something to Yeats's conversations with ISEULT GONNE (perennially figured as the dancer, as in "TO A CHILD DANCING IN THE WIND," and the beneficiary of a comparable lecture in "TO A YOUNG BEAUTY"). According to GEORGE YEATS, Yeats explicitly associated "the lady" of the poem's opening lines with Iseult (*Lonely Tower* 249).

And yet the poem's argument—that thought is inimical to feminine beauty, that women should be educated according to the "heroic discipline of the looking-glass," that feminine beauty is the physical manifestation of UNITY OF BEING—recurs throughout Yeats's work in the most serious terms (*E&I* 270). In an April 21, 1889, letter to KATHARINE TYNAN, the sentiment of "Michael Robartes and the Dancer" is already present *in ovo*: "What poor delusiveness is all this 'higher education of women'. Men have set up a great mill, called examinations, to destroy the immagination [sic]. Why should women go through it, circumstance does not drive *them*. They come out with no repose no peacefulness—their minds no longer quiet gardens full of secluded paths and umbrage circled nooks, but loud as chaffering market places" (*CL1* 161). In "ADAM'S CURSE," Yeats extols MAUD GONNE's sister Kathleen Pilcher (1868–1919) as that "beautiful mild woman" who understands that "To be born woman is to know—/ Although they do not talk of it at school—/ That we must labour to be beautiful." In the sections of "Discoveries" (1907) titled "A Guitar Player" and "The Looking-Glass," Yeats compares a girl who plays the guitar and moves "freely" to her own music with a girl who has attended school, to the inevitable detriment of the latter. "I have just been talking to a girl with a shrill monotonous voice and an abrupt way of moving," Yeats writes. "She is fresh from school, where they have taught her history and geography whereby 'a soul can be discerned,' but what is the value of an education, or even in the long run of a science, that does not begin with the personality, the habitual self, and illustrate all by that?" (*E&I* 269). "ON WOMAN" gives thanks for the woman who "gives up all her mind" and never "quarrels with a thought / Because it is not her own." "IN MEMORY OF EVA GORE-BOOTH AND CON MARKIEWICZ" and "A PRAYER FOR MY DAUGHTER," by contrast, depict the fall from feminine simplicity into the ugly and withering discord of opinion. With Gonne's example in mind, Yeats prays that his daughter will come to "think opinions are accursed." "I SEE PHANTOMS OF HATRED AND OF THE HEART'S FULLNESS AND OF THE COMING EMPTINESS" envisions the fulfilled ideal: beautiful ladies riding upon unicorns, their minds "but a pool / Where even longing drowns under its own excess." He opines that "Nothing but stillness can remain when hearts are full / Of their own sweetness, bodies of their loveliness." In 1925, Yeats told the *Irish Times* that women had never created, nor had wanted to create, artistic masterpieces. "The reason was that women between the ages of 15 and 35, decently good-looking, got greater honour than was ever conferred on anybody, be he the greatest statesman or a man victorious in war. Why, then, should she toil for many years to produce a masterpiece?" Verging on the language of "Michael Robartes and the Dancer," Yeats added, "Looking into her glass, she saw a greater masterpiece than had ever been created in art or in sculpture" (*W. B. Yeats & Georgian Ireland* 211). In practice, however, Yeats was not the chauvinist that his rhetoric suggests. He struck what amounted to intellectual partnerships with Lady GREGORY and GEORGE YEATS; he maintained friendships on a thoroughly equal footing with any number of women (KATHARINE TYNAN, FLORENCE FARR, OLIVIA SHAKESPEAR, Lady Gregory, DOROTHY WELLESLEY, etc.); and he repeatedly rallied to the cause of women's rights as a senator (*Yeats, Ireland and Fascism* 177).

"Michael Robartes and the Dancer" opens with Robartes interpreting an altar piece whose primary source, according to George Yeats, is the "Saint George and the Dragon" attributed to the Venetian painter Paris Bordone (1500–71) and bequeathed to the National Gallery of Ireland by HUGH LANE. An additional inspiration may have been "St. George and the Dragon," an altar piece by Cosimo Tura (ca. 1430–95) that Yeats saw in the cathedral at Ferrara in 1907 (*Lonely Tower* 249). In Robartes's construal, the knight drives away the dragon that represents his lady's thought. But each night's work is undone as her thought "every morning rose again / And dug its claws and shrieked and fought." Undistracted by her own thought, she would have time to look "upon the glass / And on the instant would grow wise." Unflappable in her simplicity, the dancer summarizes, "You mean they argued." Robartes accepts her characterization, but warns that the looking-glass had better be taken seriously, for her lover will "turn green with rage / At all that is not pictured there." The dancer wants to know whether she might dispense with the discipline of the looking glass and instead go to college. Alluding to the scene in *The Iliad* in which Athena grabs Achilles' hair as he moves to slay Agamemnon (I, 197), Robartes tells the dancer to "pluck Athene by the hair," for no "mere book" can encompass the passionate reality of the goddess ("The PHASES OF THE MOON" and *The RESURRECTION* [*VPl.* 917] also allude to this scene). His point is that experience must be concrete, even tactile ("all must come to sight and touch"), in contrast to the abstraction of book learning. The dancer asks whether a beautiful woman can be learned like a man. Here, apparently, Yeats was unwilling to cross a political and domestic point of no return. Answering only indirectly, Robartes adduces the art of Paolo Veronese (1528–88) and Michelangelo (ca. 1475–1564) as evidence of the supremacy of the body and by implication the irrelevancy of what the dancer calls learning. The "lagoon" is a landmark of Venice, where Veronese did much of his work; Michelangelo's "Morning" and "Night" are statues in the Medici Chapel in Florence. In his 1924 manifesto, "To all Artists and Writers," Yeats amplifies on the resonance of these statues: "We proclaim Michaelangelo the most orthodox of men, because he set upon the tomb of the Medici 'Dawn' and 'Night,' vast forms shadowing the strength of antideluvian Patriarchs and the lust of the goat, the whole handiwork of God, even the abounding horn" (UP2 438).

The dancer says that she has heard there is "great danger in the body," but Robartes, nimbly parrying, points to the sacrament of communion, in which God is present not in his thought but in his body. "My wretched dragon is perplexed," says the dancer, who evidently retains her dry sense of humor amid Robartes's theoretical onslaught. Robartes cites a "Latin text" that gives the philosophy of his position: It shows that "blest souls are not composite, / And that all beautiful women may / Live in uncomposite blessedness," and that they may "lead us to the like" if they will only banish every thought but that of their own beauty. By "uncomposite blessedness" Robartes means Unity of Being, in which condition "All thought becomes an image and the soul / Becomes a body" ("The Phases of the Moon"). Emblematic of this triumph are the dancer in "The Double Vision of Michael Robartes," and Maud Gonne, at least as she was in the glory of her youth, when "her face, like the face of some Greek statue, showed little thought" and "her whole body seemed a master-work of long labouring thought, as though a Scopas had measured and calculated, consorted

with Egyptian sages, and mathematicians out of Babylon, that he might outface even Artemisia's sepulchral image with a living norm" (Aut. 275). Robartes's confidence in his "Latin text" contradicts his previous condemnation of mere bookish knowledge and touches on the poem's chief irony: Robartes understands everything while embodying nothing; the dancer, on the other hand, understands nothing, while arguably embodying a good deal. Not for nothing is she honored with the title of "dancer." "They say such different things at school," the dancer answers, in the poem's final word.

Throughout, the dancer's laconic part in the conversation is an ironic and comedic complication. It is not the dancer but Robartes who claws, shrieks, and fights ("I have principles to prove me right"), so much so that he fails to recognize the dancer's essential simplicity, which verges on the indifference of unity. The poem, then, is largely an exercise in self-ribbing. Yeats is all too aware, as he puts it in "The PEOPLE," that his "virtues are the definitions / Of the analytic mind," and that he "can neither close / The eye of the mind nor keep [his] tongue from speech." John Unterecker reads the poem differently: "Its strength lies, it seems to me, in a beautifully balanced ironic tension: Too stupid to realize that she does not need the sort of education she would have, the lady coyly rejects the only education that could possibly be of value to her" (RG 159).

FIRST PUBLICATION: The Dial (periodical), November 1920. Reprinted in Michael Robartes and the Dancer, The CUALA PRESS, Churchtown, Dundrum, February 1921.

BIBLIOGRAPHY

Cullingford, Elizabeth. Yeats, Ireland and Fascism; Henn, T. R. The Lonely Tower: Studies in the Poetry of W. B. Yeats; Torchiana, Donald T. W. B. Yeats & Georgian Ireland; John Unterecker, A Reader's Guide to William Butler Yeats; Yeats, W. B. Autobiographies, The Collected Letters of W. B. Yeats (vol. 1), Essays and Introductions, Uncollected Prose by W. B. Yeats (vol. 2), The Variorum Edition of the Plays of W. B. Yeats.

"Model for the Laureate, A" (1938)

"Politics, as the game is played to-day, are so much foul lying." So Yeats wrote to DOROTHY WELLESLEY on February 8, 1937 (*Letters* 880; *LOP* 126), and he reiterates the point in "The Old Stone Cross" (1938). Yeats had been from the start of his career profoundly ambivalent about politics, but ambivalence turned to bitter disillusionment in the 1930s, with his hopes for Ireland's spiritual rebirth having come to little or nothing; with collectivism ascendant both intellectually and politically; with World War II looming; and with men of "passionate serving kind" ("TO A SHADE") no longer even seated at the political table. "Model for the Laureate" gives Yeats's mood. Like the more famous "POLITICS," which closes Yeats's collected poems, it invokes the political in all its weight and state only to deflate it upon the barb of love. In the later poem politics is an inadequate, almost WORDSWORTHIAN compensation for the loss of young love; here it is a distraction from the fuller, more vital business to be transacted in the arms of a lover. Yeats quotes the poem in a letter of August 13, 1937, to Wellesley. Calling himself "as anarchic as a sparrow," he justifies the sentiment of the poem by quoting BLAKE ("Kings and Parliaments seem to me something other than human life") and Victor Hugo ("they are not worth one blade of grass that God gives for the nest of the linnet") (*LOP* 143). "A Model for the Laureate" may additionally remember the lofty recklessness of CHARLES STEWART PARNELL, who risked and ultimately lost his political position by pursuing an affair with a married woman.

The poem's first and second stanzas debunk pretensions to glory and power in general terms, but the third stanza has a more specific ax to grind. Yeats sent the poem to Wellesley on July 26, 1937, under the provisional title "A Marriage Ode," and the third stanza duly broaches King Edward VIII's decision to abdicate the throne in order to marry the American divorcee Wallis Simpson (the two were married on June 3, 1937). The stanza sees the "modern throne" as a congeries of corrupted and insincere patriotism ("Those cheers that can

be bought or sold"), feeble statesmanship ("That office fools have run"), and empty ceremony ("That waxen seal, that signature"), all of which the "muse" naturally finds rebarbative. Setting a "model for the laureate," Yeats celebrates not the throne, but the abandonment of the throne, and he implicitly extols Edward VIII as the kind of "decent man" who does *not* "keep his lover waiting." In a December 21, 1936, letter to Wellesley, Yeats was similarly approving. He mentions that "the ex-king's broadcast"—publicly announcing his abdication on December 11—was "moving, restrained & dignified" (*Letters* 874; *LOP* 113).

In his July 26 letter to Wellesley, Yeats said of his poem, "It is the kind of thing I would have written had I been made Laureate, which is perhaps why I was not made Laureate" (*LOP* 141). John Masefield became laureate upon the death of Robert Bridges in 1930 and served until his death in 1967. Yeats had been mentioned as the fitting successor to Bridges, for, as R. F. Foster notes, his "dominion citizenship made him eligible" for the laureateship (*AP* 404). Despite the prospect of an inevitable hullabaloo in Irish nationalist circles, Yeats was enticed by the honor, but in the end he welcomed Masefield's appointment. "He is an ideal Laureate from the point of view of a labour government," Yeats wrote to Lady GREGORY on May 25, 1930, "& I am more relieved [sic] than anything else, for I have no quality that could have moved the great mass of English readers & I would have had to postpone the new edition of 'A Vision' [. . .] not to hurt their feelings" (*AP* 405). Yeats and Masefield first met in November 1900 and remained close friends until Yeats's death (*CL2* 595–596; *I&R*, I, 44–47). Yeats dedicated The CAT AND THE MOON to Masefield in 1934 (see *VPl.* 792). Masefield in turn wrote a brief memoir, *Some Memories of W. B. Yeats*, which the CUALA PRESS published in 1940.

FIRST PUBLICATION: *New Poems*, The Cuala Press, Dublin, May 18, 1938.

BIBLIOGRAPHY

Foster, R. F. *W. B. Yeats: A Life, II: The Arch-Poet*; Mikhail, E. H., ed., *W. B. Yeats: Interviews and Recollections* (vol. 1); Yeats, W. B. *The Collected Letters of W. B. Yeats* (vol. 2), *The Letters of W. B. Yeats, Let-*

ters on Poetry from W. B. Yeats to Dorothy Wellesley, *The Variorum Edition of the Plays of W. B. Yeats.*

"Mohini Chatterjee" (1929, dated 1928)

The Bengali theosophist MOHINI CHATTERJEE, a protégé of Helena Blavatsky, arrived in Dublin in early 1886 to foment the mystic enthusiasm that had already taken hold among a small circle of young people, Yeats not least. He and several friends, including JOHN EGLINTON and GEORGE RUSSELL (AE), founded the Dublin Hermetic Society in June 1885 (*UP2* 121–122). This became the Dublin Theosophical Society in April 1886, though Yeats remained only an informal participant in the new organization (*AM* 47–48). In his essay "The Way of Wisdom" (1900), later titled "The Pathway" (1908), Yeats recounts that Chatterjee visited Dublin at the invitation of this small theosophical circle, and that he made his social debut at a meeting of "a certain club which still discusses everything with that leisure which is the compensation of unsuccessful countries" (*Early Essays* 289). The date was April 1886; the club was the CONTEMPORARY CLUB; the place was Charles Hubert Oldham's (1860–1926) rooms at Trinity College (*AM* 47). Chatterjee made a convincing Eastern holy man, and Yeats never forgot the experience of sitting at his feet. In "The Pathway" he remembers an especially resonant example of Chatterjee's conversation: "Somebody asked him if we should pray, but even prayer was too full of hope, of desire, of life, to have any part in that acquiescence that was his beginning of wisdom, and he answered that one should say, before sleeping: 'I have lived many lives. I have been a slave and a prince. Many a beloved has sat upon my knees, and I have sat upon the knees of many a beloved. Everything that has been shall be again.' Beautiful words, that I spoilt once by turning them into clumsy verse" (*Early Essays* 290). The "clumsy verse" was "Kanva on Himself" (*VP* 723) which Yeats included in *The Wanderings of Oisin and Other Poems* (1889) but never chose to reprint, and for good reason: The poem has the

PRE-RAPHAELITE mannerism of Yeats's earliest style. "Mohini Chatterjee" takes up the same memory of Chatterjee's conversation, as if to redeem the earlier poem's youthful deficiencies.

The poem's opening stanza quotes Chatterjee's teaching that desire and ambition are folly, for we eventually pass through all conceivable incarnations. This doctrine of reincarnation may have influenced "FERGUS AND THE DRUID" and "HE THINKS OF HIS PAST GREATNESS WHEN A PART OF THE CONSTELLATIONS OF HEAVEN." Both poems describe the passage through the panoply of incarnations; Yeats, however, perceives this passage as a threat to the integrity of the self ("But now I have grown nothing, knowing all") and emphasizes that it eventuates in sorrow and loss. As a romantic poet, Yeats could approach Eastern self-renunciation only with trepidation and anxiety.

The second stanza measures the intellectual distance Yeats had traveled in the decades since Chatterjee had made such an impression. Chatterjee proposes the eternal sequence of lives, but Yeats's language effects a subtle revision, suggesting the superimposition of lives ("grave is heaped on grave," "birth is heaped on birth") and by implication an all-encompassing simultaneity. This simultaneity does not share in the serene if vaguely wistful renunciation that Chatterjee counsels, but is fraught with sexual desire, apocalyptic violence, and driving purpose, with roiling, distinctly Western energies that, in the end, cannot be contained within the strictures of time. The "birth-hour and death-hour meet," which is less to say that life is reincarnated in life than that temporal distinctions collapse altogether, that linearity comes full circle in its own dissolution. As in "AMONG SCHOOL CHILDREN," "ALL SOULS' NIGHT," and "The DOUBLE VISION OF MICHAEL ROBARTES," the triumph over the heterogeneity of time finds its image in the self-consuming ecstasy of the dance.

FIRST PUBLICATION: *A Packet for Ezra Pound,* The CUALA PRESS, Dublin, August 1929, under the title "Meditations upon Death" (with the companion poem "AT ALGECIRAS—A MEDITATION UPON DEATH"). Reprinted in *Words for Music Perhaps and Other Poems,* The Cuala Press, Dublin, November 14, 1932, under the title "Mohini Chatterji."

Reprinted in *The Winding Stair and Others Poems*, Macmillan, London, September 19, 1933, under the present title.

BIBLIOGRAPHY

Foster, R. F. *W. B. Yeats: A Life, I: The Apprentice Mage*; Yeats, W. B. *Early Essays, Uncollected Prose by W. B. Yeats* (vol. 2), *The Variorum Edition of the Poems of W. B. Yeats*.

"Mother of God, The" (1932)

Like "The MAGI," *The RESURRECTION*, and "TWO SONGS FROM A PLAY" (the opening and closing songs of *The Resurrection*), "The Mother of God" reconceives Christ as a herald of apocalypse within Yeats's system of cyclic destruction and rebirth and shrouds him in the aura of supernatural terror that is for Yeats inseparable from the apocalyptic moment. It shares with "LEDA AND THE SWAN" a lurid fascination with the violence by which the new dispensation is begotten upon the world and with the terrible animal strength of the winged divinity (Zeus in the first instance, the archangel Gabriel in the second). Where "Leda and the Swan" unfolds in the violent rush of the act itself, however, "The Mother of God" is voiced as a postpartum complaint almost wry in the disjunction between its domestic context and its epochal subject matter. Yeats's note to *The Winding Stair and Other Poems* (1933) clarifies the opening stanza, which, departing from the biblical account, seems to conflate the Annunciation and the conception of Christ (cf. Luke 1:26–38). Yeats writes, "the words 'A fallen flare through the hollow of an ear' are, I am told, obscure. I had in my memory Byzantine mosaic pictures of the Annunciation, which show a line drawn from a star to the ear of the Virgin. She received the Word through the ear, a star fell, and a star was born" (*VP* 832). T. R. Henn pronounces himself stumped in the effort to identify any such mosaic and proposes two alternate sources: "One is the tempera drawing, BLAKE's 'Annunciation' (in which Gabriel stands with massive eagle wings on the left of the picture); and Ricketts' drawing

of which the title is 'Eros leaving Psyche'. Here the departing winged god stands beside the bed: the naked Psyche clutches his feet in the turmoil" (*Lonely Tower* 258). "Ricketts" is Charles Ricketts (1866–1931), an English artist and one of Yeats's close friends. "A Nativity" (1938), "A Stick of Incense" (1939), and "WISDOM" also treat the maternity of the virgin. All three poems stress the horror of the divine birth, while "A Nativity" repeats the reference to Mary's ear. Yeats was fond of the image of the hair standing on end. The image likewise turns up in *The HERNE'S EGG* (*VPl.* 1029, 1036), "PRESENCES," *The UNICORN FROM THE STARS* (687), and *The WORDS UPON THE WINDOW-PANE* (945).

FIRST PUBLICATION: *Words for Music Perhaps and Other Poems*, The CUALA PRESS, Dublin, November 14, 1932.

BIBLIOGRAPHY

Henn, T. R. *The Lonely Tower: Studies in the Poetry of W. B. Yeats*; W. B. Yeats, *The Variorum Edition of the Plays of W. B. Yeats*, *The Variorum Edition of the Poems of W. B. Yeats*.

"Mountain Tomb, The" (1912)

Echoing the sepulchral motif of the great poems "SEPTEMBER 1913" and "TO A SHADE," which appear earlier in *Responsibilities* (1914), "The Mountain Tomb" reprises the theme of loss and lapsed spirit, in a mystical rather than political key. Amid the topical and polemical poetry of Yeats's middle period, "The Mountain Tomb" oddly recalls the 1890s, when Yeats unabashedly mingled his poetic enterprise and his occult involvements.

The poem is a call to magical ritual and to ecstatic evocation of vision. Yeats summons his fellow congregants to some shrine or sanctuary in the vicinity of a cataract that "smokes upon the mountain side." The scene suggests the unconquered vitality of nature in opposition to spirit, and perhaps also, with a pun on "cataract," in keeping with the poem's ocular theme, a prevailing opacity of transcendental vision ("blinds" is another such pun). He exhorts them to dance, to gather roses, to kiss, to drink, for, as the refrain of the poem has it, "Our Father Rosicross is in his tomb." The dancing is not merely celebratory or funereal: "in vain, in vain" suggests that it is purposeful, which is to say, magical or ritualistic. The attempt is seemingly somehow to conjure or access the wisdom of Father Rosicross. The last of the poem's three stanzas confesses defeat. All is in vain, for the "cataract still cries," still testifies to the supremacy of nature. The "everlasting taper lights the gloom," but all wisdom remains shut in the "onyx eyes" of Father Rosicross, the stone eye symbolizing a vision that transcends the organic or natural world and therefore remains inaccessible (for related instances of the motif of the vacant eye see "A BRONZE HEAD," "THE DOUBLE VISION OF MICHAEL ROBARTES," "THE SECOND COMING," "THE STATUES," "UPON A HOUSE SHAKEN BY THE LAND AGITATION").

In his 1895 essay "The Body of the Father Christian Rosencrux," Yeats tells how the followers of Father Christian Rosencrux "wrapped his imperishable body in noble raiment and laid it under the house of their Order, in a tomb containing the symbols of all things in heaven and earth, and in the waters under the earth, and set about him inextinguishable magical lamps, which burnt on generation after generation, until other students of the Order came upon the tomb by chance." The entombed seer, according to Yeats, is a metaphor for the imagination, which in the modern age has been laid "in a great tomb of criticism, and had set over it inextinguishable magical lamps of wisdom and romance, and has been altogether so nobly housed and apparelled that we have forgotten that its wizard lips are closed, or but opened for the complaining of some melancholy and ghostly voice" (E&I 196). Yeats expresses his faith that "this age of criticism is about to pass, and an age of imagination, of emotion, of moods, of revelation, about to come in its place," but "The Mountain Tomb," written 17 years later, does not seem to share this confidence (197). The dancers are incapable of the necessary conviction or passion or abandon—their manhood lacks the requisite pride, in the language of the poem—and Father Rosicross remains imperturbably asleep.

The legend of Father Rosenkreuz is traceable to a 1614 volume called the *Fama Fraternitatis* (*Account of the Brotherhood*), which describes Rosenkreuz's travels throughout the Middle East in search of occult knowledge. Rosenkreuz was reputedly born in 1378 to a German family, but there is no evidence that he was other than an apocryphal personage (for a detailed account of Rosenkreuz, see *Unicorn* 150–157). As a member of the Rosicrucian HERMETIC ORDER OF THE GOLDEN DAWN, Yeats was intimately familiar with the Rosicrucian tradition and took from it one of his principal poetic symbols, the ROSE.

FIRST PUBLICATION: *Poetry* (periodical), December 1912. Reprinted in *A Selection from the Poetry of W. B. Yeats*, Bernhard Tauchnitz, Leipzig, 1913, and in *Responsibilities: Poems and a Play*, The CUALA PRESS, Churchtown, Dundrum, May 25, 1914.

BIBLIOGRAPHY

Moore, Virginia. *The Unicorn: William Butler Yeats' Search for Reality*; Yeats, W. B. *Essays and Introductions*.

"Municipal Gallery Revisited, The" (1937)

Conceived in the same bereaved spirit as "BEAUTIFUL LOFTY THINGS," "COOLE AND BALLYLEE, 1931," and "COOLE PARK, 1929," "The Municipal Gallery Revisited" is the last of Yeats's great eulogies on departed friends and a departed generation that had served the cause of "deep-rooted things," as Yeats here puts it. In a letter of September 5, 1937, to DOROTHY WELLESLEY, Yeats reported that he had just finished the poem and called it "perhaps the best poem I have written for some years." As Yeats told Wellesley, the poem had been "foreshadowed" by a speech he had given at a banquet sponsored by the IRISH ACADEMY OF LETTERS (*Letters* 897; *LOP* 144). The banquet was held on August 17 at the Dolphin Hotel in Dublin (*AP* 594). On the occasion a $6,000 subvention was made over to Yeats by "certain wealthy Irish Americans" who

Portrait of J. M. Synge by John Butler Yeats. Hugh Lane commissioned the painting in 1905. Yeats arrives at the painting in the final stanza of "The Municipal Gallery Revisited" and remarks on Synge's "grave deep face." *(Dublin City Gallery The Hugh Lane)*

wished to thank Yeats for his labor on behalf of Irish culture (*AP* 592–596; *VP* 839). Yeats told the gathering that a "good poem" was forming in his head "about the Ireland that we have all served, and the movement of which I have been a part," and that he comtemplated eventually sending the poem to his benefactors. He then recounted, in terms closely mirroring those of "The Municipal Gallery Revisited," his recent visit to the Municipal Gallery, and told of seeing "Ireland not as she is displayed in guide book or history, but, Ireland seen because of the magnificent vitality of her painters, in the glory of her passions. For the moment I could think of nothing but that Ireland: that great pictured song" (*VP* 839–840). Yeats eventually sent the 43 admirers who had contributed to the subvention a pamphlet, printed in December, that included his speech and two poems, "Dedication" (790) and "The Municipal Gallery Revisited" (*Biblio.* 192–193). The finished poem finds Yeats

wandering the galleries of the Municipal Gallery of Modern Art, Charlemont House, Parnell Square, Dublin (HUGH LANE founded the gallery at Clonmel House, Harcourt Street, in 1908; it is now called the Dublin City Gallery The Hugh Lane). Paintings of friends and acquaintances inspire a mood of nostalgic reflection that bursts into impassioned self-justification as Yeats arrives at the portraits of those who were his closest creative collaborators, Lady GREGORY and J. M. SYNGE.

Essentially prefatory, the first three stanzas light upon "the images of thirty years" and trace the mood of deepening reverie. In the first stanza, portraits of Roger Casement (1864–1916), Arthur Griffith (1872–1922), and KEVIN O'HIGGINS triangulate the political history of 20th-century Ireland. Casement was executed for his part in the EASTER RISING. Proceedings against him were smoothed by the circulation of forged diaries that made him out to be homosexual (cf. "The Ghost of Roger Casement" [1938] and "Roger Casement" [1937]; see also *Letters* 867–870, 880–884). Griffith was editor of the *United Irishman* (1889–1906), a founder of the Sinn Féin movement, and the first president of the Irish Free State. In *AUTOBIOGRAPHIES*, Yeats remembers him rallying to the defense of the controversial COUNTESS CATHLEEN. At the time an "enthusiastic anti-cleric," he "claimed to have brought 'a lot of men from the Quays and told them to applaud everything the Church would not like'" (309). Hostile to the unfettered and politically undependable aestheticism that was the essence of Yeats's cultural nationalism, Griffith later became a "slanderer of Lane and Synge" (309; on Yeats's various quarrels with Griffith see *AM* 327, 360–365; *CL4* 39; *Expl.* 114–118; *UP2* 306–308). In a letter of March 8, 1909, Yeats told Lady Gregory that he was writing a poem—"ON THOSE THAT HATED 'THE PLAYBOY OF THE WESTERN WORLD', 1907"—that denounced "Griffith and his like." He explained that, lacking "sanctity of the intellect," men of this stamp are able to renounce "external things" but not "envy, revenge, jealousy and so on" (*Letters* 525). Yeats took a more generous view when speaking in the Senate on March 14, 1923, on a bill to provide for Griffith's widow, sister, and children. Yeats acknowledged that he had been "deeply opposed" to Griffith "on matters connected with the Arts," but he lauded Griffith "as a man of the most enduring courage and the most steadfast will" who had managed to remain "thoroughly sane" while the rest of the country had gone "theory mad" (SS 35).

The image of the "revolutionary soldier kneeling to be blessed," like the "Abbot or Archbishop with an upraised hand / Blessing the Tricolour" (i.e., the Irish flag), is a detail from *The Blessing of the Colours* by Sir John Lavery (1856–1941). Arra M. Garab comments that the Lavery painting is a "metaphorical expression of Ireland's recent public character, where Church and State, revolutionary power and vested authority, form an unholy but popular alliance"; church and state further suggest "the two dominant elements which, when yoked together, within Yeats's lifetime toppled the Anglo-Irish Ascendancy" (*Last Poems* 185).

The second and third stanzas bring Yeats round to the Ireland of the arts—the Ireland that mattered most to him. The paintings of the first 10 lines are explicitly political, but in their passion conjure an Ireland that the "poets have imagined, terrible and gay." "Terrible" inevitably evokes the Ireland that Yeats himself had imagined in "EASTER 1916," while "gay" evokes the tragic joy of "A DIALOGUE OF SELF AND SOUL" and "LAPIS LAZULI." The lines are ambiguous: Yeats may want to suggest that the nation has fulfilled the dreams of the poets, or that the paintings merely repeat the dreams of the poets. Continuing the shift from political to aesthetic reflection, and thus approaching the terms of his own nationalism in opposition to the political nationalism of the first stanza, Yeats next comes upon the portrait of a woman, "Beautiful and gentle in her Venetian way," whom he had known 50 years earlier when he was a haunter of painters' studios. The third stanza continues the poem's emerging aesthetic emphasis, as it circles in upon Yeats's own life and touches the fringes of his own movement. Coming upon portraits of ROBERT GREGORY, Lane, and Hazel Lavery, Yeats is overwhelmed by the resurrection of his past upon the walls, and he can only "sink down" (foreshadowing the later allusion to his "mediaeval knees") under the weight of his emotion, his "covered eyes" hiding tears. Rob-

ert Gregory had been a painter of promise ("We dreamed that a great painter had been born / To cold Clare rock and Galway rock and thorn," as Yeats writes in his great elegy). Lane, Lady Gregory's nephew, had been a leading art collector as well as the founder of the Municipal Gallery. In the latter guise he is the "onlie begetter" of the paintings that have inspired the poem. As A. Norman Jeffares notes, the quoted phrase is from the dedication of Shakespeare's sonnets (*NCP* 400). Hazel Lavery (1880–1935) was the wife of the painter. It is perhaps merely a coincidence that Lavery and O'Higgins shared what R. F. Foster calls a "bedazzled and obsessive love-affair" (*AP* 343).

Gregory and Lane lead, by associations of family and artistic enterprise, to Mancini's portrait of

Portrait of Lady Gregory, 1907, by Antonio Mancini (1852–1930). Yeats writes in "The Municipal Gallery Revisited": "Mancini's portrait of Augusta Gregory, / 'Greatest since Rembrandt,' according to John Synge; / A great ebullient portrait certainly; / But where is the brush that could show anything / Of all that pride and that humility." *(Dublin City Gallery The Hugh Lane)*

Lady Gregory and thus to Yeats's true theme: the nobility that bound Lady Gregory, Synge, and himself, and made the basis of their artistic movement. Yeats speaks of Lady Gregory's pride and humility, and of the "deep-rooted things" upon which the traditions of COOLE PARK were founded. Yeats would bend his "mediaeval knees" in homage. As Ellmann notes, "he longs for no idol but for a principal of organization in which reverence and a sense of the fitness and orderliness of things will be possible" (*IY* 7). Though Coole had been sold in 1927 and would be demolished in 1941, Yeats does not weep. He understands that "No fox can foul the lair the badger swept," a metaphor that derives from Spenser, but also from the forests of Coole itself (cf. the introductory lines to *The SHADOWY WATERS*: "Dim Inchy wood, that hides badger and fox"). Yeats clarifies the image in his 1906 essay "Edmund Spenser": "At the end of a long beautiful passage [Spenser] laments that unworthy men should be in the dead Earl's place, and compares them to the fox—an unclean feeder—hiding in the lair 'the badger swept'" (*E&I* 359–360). Yeats refers to Spenser's poem "The Ruins of Time" (lines 216–217), which laments the death of the poet's patron, the Earl of Leicester. In John Unterecker's reading, Yeats "points up the implicit parallel between his own patroness Lady Gregory and Spenser's 'great Earl'" (*RG* 276). More generally, the image of the badger's neatly swept lair is consistent with the poem's larger themes of rootedness and contact with the earth. It reverses the foulness that Yeats more usually attributes to the burrow, hole, and ditch, as in "A DIALOGUE OF SELF AND SOUL" ("I am content to live it all again / And yet again, if it be life to pitch / Into the frog-spawn of a blind man's ditch"), "NINETEEN HUNDRED AND NINETEEN" ("weasels fighting in a hole"), "The Old Stone Cross" ("Because this age and the next age / Engender in the ditch"), "ON A POLITICAL PRISONER" ("Blind and leader of the blind / Drinking the foul ditch where they lie"), and *PURGATORY* ("a bastard that a pedlar got / Upon a tinker's daughter in a ditch"). In the sixth stanza, the strongest of the poem, Yeats articulates the aesthetic credo that is implicit in the fourth and fifth. As Yeats and his collaborators had demonstrated, only from

"contact with the soil" does art "Antaeus-like" grow strong. This is the "dream of the noble and the beggar-man," who, unlike the dreaded middle classes, have resisted the abstraction of modernity and upheld a form of wisdom deeper than logic or even thought ("wisdom comes of beggary," as Yeats writes in "The SEVEN SAGES").

The poem's final stanza acknowledges Synge as similarly "rooted"—so free of the modern abstraction that he could describe himself as "Forgetting human words." Yeats alludes to Synge's poem "Prelude" (1909), in which he writes that he "did but half remember human words, / In converse with the mountains, moors, and fens." Yeats likewise quotes Synge's phrase in his introduction to Oliver St John Gogarty's *Wild Apples* (*P&I* 173–174). In the famous final lines of "The Municipal Gallery Revisited," Yeats addresses himself to the judgment of his contemporaries or perhaps to the judgment of history and takes his stand not upon the achievement of his work, but upon the character of his friends and the national history traced in the "lineaments" of their faces. "Lineaments," for Yeats, connotes enduring outline or permanent shape that is itself the image of an inner life premised on permanent things, as against the vagaries of mood or emotion or the shallowness of the times. He suggests as much when he attributes to MAUD GONNE "the beauty of lineaments which BLAKE calls the highest beauty because it changes least from youth to age" (*Mem.* 40). He uses the word with similar significance in "FALLEN MAJESTY," "The GYRES," "His Phoenix" (1916), "MICHAEL ROBARTES AND THE DANCER" and "The STATUES." Effective as it may be, the poem's final couplet represents an unusually close approach to sentimentality or at least to conventional sentiment; a certain humidity creeps in, controverting the ideal of a poem "as cold / And passionate as the dawn" ("The FISHERMAN"). Undoubtedly Yeats felt himself to be saying only what was true. Virginia Moore makes the point: "The Sligo stable boy, the London athlete, GEORGE RUSSELL, KATHARINE TYNAN, Charles Johnston, FLORENCE FARR, ANNIE HORNIMAN, JOHN O'LEARY—great soul. . . . What wonderfully fortunate timing! Always when he needed them, friends came. Sensing potentialities in the

Charlemont House, an 18th-century town house in Parnell Square, Dublin, has been home to the Municipal Gallery of Modern Art since 1933. The gallery is now called the Dublin City Gallery The Hugh Lane. *(Dublin City Gallery The Hugh Lane)*

callow youth, they leaped to help: obscure ones and famous ones: they were with him in his setting out, and on his arrival" (*Unicorn* 415).

The poem refers in order to the following paintings: John Keating, *The Men of the West* ("ambush"); Lavery, *St. Patrick's Purgatory* ("pilgrims"), *The Court of Criminal Appeal* (Casement), portrait of Griffith, portrait of O'Higgins, *The Blessing of the Colours* ("soldier kneeling," "Abbot"); John Singer Sargent (1856–1925), portrait of Lady Charles Beresford; Charles Shannon (1863–1937), portrait of Robert Gregory; Sargent or Antonio Mancini (1852–1930), portrait of Hugh Lane (the gallery had two portraits of Lane in its collection); Lavery, *Hazel Lavery at Her Easel* ("living"), *"It is Finished"* ("dying": the artist's wife on her deathbed); Mancini, portrait of Lady Gregory; JOHN BUTLER YEATS, portrait of Synge (*Yeats at the Municipal Gallery*). The poem was not Yeats's first on the subject of the gallery. See also "To A SHADE" and

"TO A WEALTHY MAN WHO PROMISED A SECOND SUBSCRIPTION TO THE DUBLIN MUNICIPAL GALLERY IF IT WERE PROVED THE PEOPLE WANTED PICTURES." "DEMON AND BEAST" likewise finds Yeats meditating on pictures, but in this instance he roams the halls of the National Gallery in Dublin.

FIRST PUBLICATION: *A Speech and Two Poems*, privately printed, December 1937. Reprinted in *New Poems*, The CUALA PRESS, Dublin, May 18, 1938.

BIBLIOGRAPHY

Ellmann, Richard. *The Identity of Yeats*; Foster, R. F. *W. B. Yeats: A Life, I: The Apprentice Mage, II: The Arch-Poet*; Jeffares, A. Norman. *A New Commentary on the Poems of W. B. Yeats*; O'Connor, Patrick. Introduction, *Municipal Art Gallery*; Moore, Virginia. *The Unicorn: William Butler Yeats' Search for Reality*; Stallworthy, John, ed. *Yeats: Last Poems*; Synge, J. M. *Collected Plays and Poems and The Aran Islands*; Unterecker, John. *A Reader's Guide to William Butler Yeats*; Ussher, Arland. Introduction, *Yeats at the Municipal Gallery*; Wade, Allan. *A Bibliography of the Writings of W. B. Yeats*; Yeats, W. B. *Autobiographies, The Collected Letters of W. B. Yeats* (vol. 4), *Essays and Introductions, Explorations, The Letters of W. B. Yeats, Letters on Poetry from W. B. Yeats to Dorothy Wellesley, Memoirs, Prefaces and Introductions, The Senate Speeches of W. B. Yeats, Uncollected Prose by W. B. Yeats* (vol. 2), *The Variorum Edition of the Poems of W. B. Yeats*.

"My Descendants" (1923)

No sooner had Yeats ensured the continuation of his family line—Anne Butler Yeats was born in 1919, Michael Butler Yeats in 1921—than he began to worry about its decline. The anxiety undoubtedly stemmed from his unusually acute appreciation that it is in the nature of all things human to decline and fall ("Man is in love and loves what vanishes, / What more is there to say?" Yeats asks in "NINETEEN HUNDRED AND NINETEEN," summarizing his lapsarian conviction); perhaps the anxiety stemmed also from his long observation of the Gregory family line petering out for the reasons he interrogates in "ANCESTRAL HOUSES."

The fourth of seven poems in the sequence "MEDITATIONS IN TIME OF CIVIL WAR," "My Descendants" takes up the themes of tradition and inheritance mooted in "Ancestral Houses" and "MY TABLE," but its terms are intensely personal, picking up where "MY HOUSE" leaves off. As in "INTRODUCTORY RHYMES" to *Responsibilities* and "UNDER SATURN," Yeats is keenly aware of his family tradition and his responsibility to it. Having "inherited a vigorous mind," he must pass on the same vigor, and yet "life" does not accommodate this aspiration: in the poem's metaphor, the flower (perhaps the "symbolic rose" of "My House") is torn to petals, leaving the garden a patch of "common greenness." With a startling lack of parental sentimentality, Yeats turns the metaphor on his own children: What if they too "lose the flower," perhaps through "natural declension of the soul, / Through too much business with the passing hour, / Through too much play, or marriage with a fool?" "Too much business with the passing hour" repeats Yeats's oldest complaint against MAUD GONNE (see "A PRAYER FOR MY DAUGHTER"). "Too much play" may be aimed at ROBERT GREGORY (for Yeats's qualms, see *Mem.* 230), while "marriage with a fool" is almost certainly aimed at both MAUD GONNE (who disastrously married John MacBride in 1903) and ISEULT GONNE (who disastrously married Francis Stuart in 1920). In a 1932 letter to OLIVIA SHAKESPEAR, Yeats recalls that at the time of his marriage Stuart (1902–2000), though later a distinguished writer, had "seemed almost imbecile to his own relations," which makes specific sense of "fool" (*Letters* 800; see also "WHY SHOULD NOT OLD MEN BE MAD?" and Stuart's *Black List, Section H* 33). Yeats had experimented with the curse as a rhetorical device in "The FASCINATION OF WHAT'S DIFFICULT" and "A PRAYER ON GOING INTO MY HOUSE." Again with a startling lack of sentimentality, he here turns his power of malediction upon his own house. If his descendants should "lose the flower," he wishes that stair and tower should become a "roofless ruin that the owl / May build in the cracked masonry and cry / Her desolation to the desolate sky." The owl building in the masonry

foreshadows the bees of "THE STARE'S NEST BY MY WINDOW," the one symbolizing forlorn wisdom, the other rejuvenating life.

The final stanza resigns itself to the decline lamented in the first stanza by taking the largest philosophical perspective. The "Primum Mobile" or "Prime Mover"—that power that set the universe in motion—made the circle its governing motif. As Yeats first surmised in "AT GALWAY RACES" and fully theorized in "The PHASES OF THE MOON," everything travels the pattern of the circle, falling and rising and falling again. There is solace, Yeats here maintains, only in love and friendship. For friendship's sake, he chose a house in the neighborhood of Lady GREGORY's estate COOLE PARK; for love's sake, he renovated the house to please his wife GEORGE YEATS (who was 24 at the time of her marriage: a "girl" only from the vantage of Yeats's middle age). Whatever the delinquency of the family line, the "stones" of the tower will endure as a monument to friendship and love. "Stones" may indicate the tower intact or ruined, leaving it unclear whether the curse of the second stanza has been fulfilled.

FIRST PUBLICATION: The *Dial* and the *London Mercury* (periodicals), January 1923. Reprinted in *The Cat and the Moon and Certain Poems*, The CUALA PRESS, Dublin, July 1924.

BIBLIOGRAPHY

Stuart, Francis. *Black List, Section H*; Yeats, W. B. *The Letters of W. B. Yeats, Memoirs*.

"My House" (1923)

The second of seven poems in the sequence "MEDITATIONS IN TIME OF CIVIL WAR," "My House" personalizes the themes of "ANCESTRAL HOUSES," turning from ancestral houses in general to THOOR BALLYLEE, which Yeats hoped to make his own ancestral house. Where "Ancestral Houses" conceives the house as a majestic sublimation of Renaissance or Georgian strength, "My House" pictures Yeats's tower as roughly bucolic and bluntly occult, as it is in "EGO DOMINUS TUUS" and "The PHASES OF THE MOON." The "levelled lawns and gravelled ways" of "Ancestral Houses" give way to "an acre of stony ground"; peacock to "stilted water-hen"; gardens and terraces to bridge, tower, and farmhouse. Amid the stony ground rears the "symbolic rose," an extrusion less flamboyant than the "abounding glittering jet" of "Ancestral Houses." The self-conscious recognition that the rose is "symbolic" may sardonically comment on Yeats's early "rosolotry," in Richard Ellmann's phrase, but it may also be a sincere (if somewhat chastened) invocation of the ROSE and all that it represents in Yeats's symbolic system (IY 75). The rose's emergence from "stony ground" can be read as an emergence of mystic beauty from desolation ("stone" has this connotation in "COOLE PARK, 1929" and "EASTER 1916") or from austerity and integrity (this connotation in "Ancestral Houses," "CRAZY JANE ON THE MOUNTAIN," "The FISHERMAN," "The GREY ROCK," "TO A FRIEND WHOSE WORK HAS COME TO NOTHING," and "The TOWER").

A note to "The SECOND COMING" explains that the "human soul is always moving outward into the objective world or inward into itself" (VP 824). "My House" maps the latter movement, the pattern of the subjective man, the "man who sees all reflected within himself" (824). The poem winds in a tightening, ascending gyre, circumambulating the entire property before coiling in upon yard and tower and then, in the second stanza, venturing up the circular stairs to the "chamber arched with stone." The pattern continues within the chamber, as the poem narrows from ceiling to fireplace to "written page," which is symbolically the center of all that Yeats would do and found (Yeats brings the entire sequence of "Meditations in Time of Civil War" to a close with the affirmation of just such a written page: "The abstract joy, / The half-read wisdom of daemonic images, / Suffice the ageing man as once the growing boy"). In "Ego Dominus Tuus," Dante climbs the same stair, which symbolizes the burden and the exaltation of the subjective man ("MY DESCENDANTS" refers to the "laborious stair"). In Dante's case, this ascent ends in revelation; in "My House," it ends in the discovery of the implements of revelation, candle and book, that with which the Platonist of Milton's "Il Penseroso" (1645) toiled in the effort to shadow forth "How

the daemonic rage / Imagined everything" (Milton's Platonist is likewise invoked in "The Phases of the Moon"). By "daemonic rage," Yeats means the self's—or possibly the divine self's—struggle to discover its own daemon or "opposite" or "anti-self," out of which comes an *antithetical* and creative intensity; as Yeats writes in PER AMICA SILENTIA LUNAE, "man and Daemon feed the hunger in one another's hearts" (LE 11; see also Aut. 200–201; "Ego Dominus Tuus"). This "rage" is the mage's equivalent of the "violence" that is the constructive force of "Ancestral Houses." Both rage and violence signify the mind turning its cat-o'-nine-tails upon itself (to borrow from "The Phases of the Moon"), whipping itself into transcendent frenzy, a dynamic observable as early as "The Indian to his Love" (1886), which pictures a parrot swaying on a limb and raging at its own image in the sea. The "benighted travellers" who see the "midnight candle glimmering" allude to Samuel Palmer's engraving "The Lonely Tower," an illustration of "Il Penseroso" that Yeats cites in "The Phases of the Moon" ("The lonely light that Samuel Palmer engraved"). The engraving shows two travelers lounging in the moonlight as they take in the solitary glowing window of the distant tower.

The poem ends with a pairing of the two men who have "founded" at Thoor Ballylee. There is first a man-at-arms who fought some long, tragic rearguard action from the redoubt of the tower (the "rough men-at-arms" described in "The Tower," lines 81–88, are presumably his men). Yeats may have had in mind a scion of the de Burgo family, Normans who solidified their power during the 13th and 14th centuries by erecting 32 towers or castles in the district, including Thoor Ballylee. In their study of Thoor Ballylee, Mary Hanley and Liam Miller write, with relevance to "My House," that the de Burgo family remained Catholic despite the Reformation, and that "during the seventeenth and eighteenth centuries the Penal Laws effectively destroyed the power, wealth and influence of the family. Their lands passed into the ownership of Protestant settlers in the area, the Persses [Lady GREGORY was a Persse], the Lamberts, the Martyns [see EDWARD MARTYN] and the Gregorys" (*Thoor Ballylee* 10).

The second founder is Yeats himself, that his "bodily heirs may find, / To exalt a lonely mind, / Befitting emblems of adversity." The emphasis on meditative solitude accords with the aspersion on "too much business with the passing hour" in "My Descendants" and finds its reverse image in the "affable Irregular" of "The ROAD AT MY DOOR," whose simple humanity Yeats envies in a moment of self-doubt or self-weariness. "Emblems of adversity," meanwhile, echoes the allusion to "daemonic rage" and the sequence's general postulation of the tension of antithesis as a universal creative force. "Emblems of adversity" are tokens of this tension: reminders that the soul must, as Dante had done, set its "chisel to the hardest stone" ("Ego Dominus Tuus"). Yeats was wed to the notion that reality is structured in the image of interlocked gyres, the vertex of the one centered upon the base of the other, and that, in the phrase of Heraclitus, they "live each other's death, die each other's life" (*LE* 227, 234; *VPl.* 931, 934; *AV* 68, 197, 271). In this light, the soldier's "dwindling" men may metaphorize the dwindling of one gyre (the subjectivity of the Renaissance dying into the objectivity of the Enlightenment), and Yeats's advent the birth of another (the subjective age heralded in "The Second Coming").

FIRST PUBLICATION: The *Dial* and the *London Mercury* (periodicals), January 1923. Reprinted in *The Cat and the Moon and Certain Poems*, The CUALA PRESS, Dublin, July 1924.

BIBLIOGRAPHY

Ellmann, Richard. *The Identity of Yeats*; Hanley, Mary, and Liam Miller, *Thoor Ballylee: Home of William Butler Yeats*; Yeats, W. B. *Autobiographies, Later Essays, The Variorum Edition of the Plays of W. B. Yeats, The Variorum Edition of the Poems of W. B. Yeats, A Vision*.

"My Table" (1923)

"MY HOUSE" ends with an affirmation of the importance of "emblems of adversity." These are the talismans that "exalt a lonely mind." "My Table," which immediately follows "My House" in the seven-poem sequence "MEDITATIONS IN TIME OF CIVIL WAR," offers the example of just such an emblem: the ancient Japanese sword that was among Yeats's most cherished and poetically fecund possessions. The sword was a gift from Junzo Sato (b. 1897), a Japanese consular officer who introduced himself while Yeats was stopped in Portland, Oregon, on a speaking tour of AMERICA. The sword was the work of Bishu Osafumé Motoshigé (1394–1428), as Yeats mentions in "A DIALOGUE OF SELF AND SOUL." Yeats tells of the gift in a March 22, 1920, letter to his friend, the artist Edmund Dulac (1882–1953): "A rather wonderful thing happened the day before yesterday. A very distinguished looking Japanese came to see us. He had read my poetry when in Japan and had now just heard me lecture. He had something in his hand wrapped in embroidered silk. He said it was a present for me. He untied the silk cord that bound it and brought out a sword which had been for 500 years in his family. It had been made 550 years ago [ca. 1370] and he showed me the maker's name upon the hilt. I was greatly embarrassed at the thought of such a gift and went to fetch George [see GEORGE YEATS], thinking that we might find some way of refusing it. When she came I said 'But surely this ought always to remain in your family?' He answered 'My family have many swords.' But later he brought back my embarrassment by speaking of having given me 'his sword.' I had to accept it but I have written him a letter saying that I 'put him under a vow' to write and tell me when his first child is born—he is not yet married—that I may leave the sword back to his family in my will" (*Letters* 662). In gratitude, Yeats dedicated his play *The RESURRECTION* to Sato. Yeats bequeathed the sword to Sato's "eldest surviving or only son" as promised, but upon Yeats's death, George asked to keep the sword. "I did not present the sword with the intention of having it sent back to Japan," Sato responded. "I shall be very happy to give it to your son" (*BG* 570).

There is no mistake about the purpose of the sword's placement on Yeats's writing table: it is to moralize Yeats's days out of their aimlessness, that is, to provide Yeats with a perpetual reminder of what his art should be and what he should be as artist. The sword thus indicates the kind of art that Yeats aspired to: severe, adamantine, ancestral, wrought to timeless perfection. The sword is covered by a bit of "embroidered dress" (in "A Dialogue of Self and Soul," Yeats refers to "that flowering silken, old embroidery, torn / From some court-lady's dress. . . ."). In the context of "My Table," the embroidery offsets the sword's masculine strength, suggesting the interrelation of "violence" and "sweetness" that Yeats explores in "ANCESTRAL HOUSES." That Chaucer (born ca. 1340) had not drawn breath when the sword was forged indicates its impressive age, but more significantly emphasizes the sword's exemption from the heterogeneous modernity that begins to show itself, if only faintly, in Chaucer. In AUTOBIOGRAPHIES, Yeats recalls WILLIAM MORRIS cursing Chaucer "for destroying the English language with foreign words" (134). Elsewhere he adds that "Morris had never seemed to care greatly for any poet later than Chaucer and though I preferred Shakespeare to Chaucer I begrudged my own preference. Had not Europe shared one mind and heart, until both mind and heart began to break into fragments a little before Shakespeare's birth? Music and verse began to fall apart when Chaucer robbed verse of its speed that he might give it greater meditation [. . .]" (165). The sword belongs to an entirely different tradition than Chaucer does, but Yeats uses the sword's pre-Chaucerian origin to suggest the premodern unity of culture that made the sword possible.

In the lines that follow, the poem becomes difficult. The allusions to the moon are an unmistakable directive to correlate the poem with the theoretical system outlined in "The PHASES OF THE MOON" and A VISION. The sword is "curved like new moon" and "moon-luminous," and—no less significant—it lay in Sato's house for "five hundred years." The concatenation of "new moon" and "five hundred years" implies the 15th lunar phase within the millennial cycle, the phase of "complete beauty" and perfected artistic tradition, as epitomized by the Byzantium of "SAILING TO BYZANTIUM." The ensuing assertion that "if no change appears / No moon; only an aching heart / Conceives a changeless work of art" suggests that the sword, as the reification of the aching heart,

is empowered to overthrow the moon itself (the opening lines of "NINETEEN HUNDRED AND NINETEEN" are far less optimistic about the balance of power between the art object and time). Such moments are bound up with the particular magic of the 15th phase, when, as Yeats writes in "The Phases of the Moon," all is "fed with light and heaven is bare" (i.e., "no moon"). Underlying these lines is the same conceptual understanding that governs "Sailing to Byzantium": In the moment of annealing intensity (metaphorized as smithy or dance or forge), the soul assumes changeless form (the golden songbird of "Sailing to Byzantium") or manifests changeless form (Sato's sword), and time itself is brought to heel.

As both "Sailing to Byzantium" and "My Table" understand, however, the moment of consummation is the work of generations, as culture slowly rounds toward unity and tradition slowly wells toward apotheosis. The final 18 lines of "My Table" characterize the necessary tradition as conservative, reverent, selfless, and unself-conscious, effectively attributing to Japan a version of the craft tradition that Morris evokes in essays like "The Lesser Arts" (1882) and "Gothic Architecture" (1893). Yeats attributes much the same kind of tradition to Byzantium in A Vision: "The painter, the mosaic worker, the worker in gold and silver, the illuminator of sacred books, were almost impersonal, almost perhaps without the consciousness of individual design, absorbed in their subject-matter and that the vision of a whole people. They could copy out of old Gospel books those pictures that seemed as sacred as the text, and yet weave all into a vast design, the work of many that seemed the work of one, that made building, picture, pattern, metal-work of rail and lamp, seem but a single image [. . .]" (279–280). He envisions this kind of tradition as well in his description of the Stockholm City Hall in "The Bounty of Sweden" (Aut. 406–407).

At last the tradition culminates in the "most rich inheritor" whose heart aches with the longing of generations. With the advent of this inheritor—here Yeats veers sharply from the doctrines of Morris—the tradition becomes self-conscious ("waking wits"), aloof ("although a country's talk"), and transcendental ("Heaven's door"), in short, becomes the kind of *antithetical* romantic tradition with which Yeats identifies himself. So intense is the aching heart of the inheritor that the universe itself seems all but consumed in its apocalypse of desire ("SOLOMON AND THE WITCH" shares precisely this apocalyptic dynamic, though its desire is sexual rather than aesthetic). The apocalyptic moment is signaled by the scream of Juno's peacock (as by the crow of the cockerel in "Solomon and the Witch"), which makes a retroactive witticism of the bland allusions to goddess and peacock in the penultimate stanza of "Ancestral Houses." In Roman mythology, Juno is the wife of Jupiter and thus queen of the Gods. Her screaming peacock has no known literary source (*NCP* 227), but Yeats indicates its significance in *A Vision*: "A civilization is a struggle to keep self-control, and in this it is like some great tragic person, some Niobe who must display an almost superhuman will or the cry will not touch our sympathy. The loss of control over thought comes towards the end; first a sinking in upon the moral being, then the last surrender, the irrational cry, revelation—the scream of Juno's peacock" (*AV* 268). Niobe was a Theban queen of Greek mythology who boastfully compared her brood to that of the goddess Leto. Apollo and Artemis, Leto's only offspring, punished her hubris by slaying 12 of her 14 children. In pity, Zeus turned Niobe to stone, but even then she continued to weep (*Greek Myths* 258–259).

FIRST PUBLICATION: The *Dial* and the *London Mercury* (periodicals), January 1923. Reprinted in *The Cat and the Moon and Certain Poems*, The CUALA PRESS, Dublin, July 1924.

BIBLIOGRAPHY

Graves, Robert. *The Greek Myths*; Jeffares, A. Norman. *A New Commentary on the Poems of W. B. Yeats*; Saddlemyer, Ann. *Becoming George: The Life of Mrs W. B. Yeats*; Yeats, W. B. *Autobiographies*, *The Letters of W. B. Yeats*, *A Vision*.

"Needle's Eye, A" (1934)

See "SUPERNATURAL SONGS."

"Never Give all the Heart" (1905)

"Never Give all the Heart" is a word of advice from one whose romantic hopes have come to nothing. The informing disappointment was MAUD GONNE's marriage to John MacBride (1865–1916) on February 21, 1903, an event from which Yeats had not entirely recovered nearly a year later ("Never Give all the Heart" dates from December 1903, as does "OLD MEMORY," with which it might be paired; see *CL3* 483). Cynical and worldly, the poem represents Yeats at his farthest remove from the romanticism that was almost innate to his personality. Full of the remorse that is the romantic bane (see "REMORSE FOR INTEMPERATE SPEECH"), he wavers in his faith that the unbridled heart is the source of all meaning (cf. "TWO SONGS FROM A PLAY") and the path to all salvation. Yeats advises never giving all the heart, for "passionate women"—women of Gonne's type—have no interest in love that seems certain, even as they naively fail to recognize that love is never certain, that it "fades out from kiss to kiss." Such women will only "give their hearts up to the play." Whether "play" denotes a game or a drama, it suggests a charade of parts, a matching of wits, and the true lover, hampered by his own sincerity, can never hold his own. Yeats ends with a profession that validates the pessimism of the poem: "He that made this knows all the cost, / For he gave all his heart and lost." Yeats offers similar disheartened advice in "O Do Not Love Too Long" (1905).

FIRST PUBLICATION: *McLure's Magazine*, December 1905. Reprinted in *Poems, 1899–1905*, A. H. Bullen, London, Maunsel & Co., Dublin, October 1906.

BIBLIOGRAPHY

Yeats, W. B. *The Collected Letters of W. B. Yeats* (vol. 3).

"New Faces, The" (1922)

Though begun in late 1912, "The New Faces" was not published until 10 years later (*YC* 159). Mincing no words about Lady GREGORY's advancing years (she was then 60) and implicitly insulting her son, ROBERT GREGORY, the poem was not calculated to appeal to Yeats's dearest friend. Delicately, but for all that firmly, she had the poem put on ice. "The lines are very touching," she wrote to Yeats. "I have often thought our ghosts will haunt that path and our talk hang in the air—It is good to have a meeting place anyhow, in this place where so many children of our minds were born—You won't publish it just now will you? I think not" (*AM* 477). She similarly prevailed on Yeats to suppress "Reprisals" (*VP* 791), the fourth of his poems on the death of Robert Gregory. Though written in 1920, it did not appear until 1948.

Whatever its indelicacy, "The New Faces" is, like "COOLE PARK, 1929" and "COOLE AND BALLYLEE, 1931," a superb elegiac tribute to all that was accomplished under Lady Gregory's roof. Were Lady Gregory to predecease him, Yeats vows, he

Lady Gregory reposing under a catalpa tree at Coole Park, August 1927 (*Fáilte Ireland*)

would renounce COOLE PARK, where he and Lady Gregory had "wrought that shall break the teeth of Time" ("The LAMENTATION OF THE OLD PENSIONER" demonstrates a corresponding figurative violence: "I spit into the face of Time"). This is a prediction that their work will endure, but also an intimation of transcendental aspiration and metaphysical rebellion, a prediction that their work will somehow shatter the pattern of time (cf. "MY TABLE"). "Teeth," an ingenious usage, alludes to the internal mechanism of the clock as well as metaphorizes the devouring maw of time, resonating with the synecdochical emphasis on the "face" in the poem's title and in line 5. T. R. Henn, who discusses the poem's intricate play of vowel and consonantal values, notes the "explosive arrogant consonants" of this line (*Lonely Tower* 310).

The second stanza abandons what might seem the pouty resignation of the first. Yeats's "living feet" may relinquish the accustomed paths, but, after all, "night can outbalance day," an assertion weighted with meaning given the lunar-solar, subjective-objective opposition that imbues Yeats's thought (cf. "LINES WRITTEN IN DEJECTION"). Creatures of the night—of imagination, of inwardness—his ghost and that of Lady Gregory will "rove the garden gravel still," even in their shadowy state compacting more of life then those who come after. That Yeats and Lady Gregory rove not the garden but the "garden gravel" (premonitory of "ANCESTRAL HOUSES") suggests the consistent Yeatsian ideal of sweetness tempered by strength, even by roughness and violence. If the poem offended Lady Gregory's vanity, it must have equally offended her maternal affection, for "the living" could refer to none other than Robert Gregory, who inherited Coole upon coming of age in 1902 (for Yeats's misgivings about Gregory, see *Mem.* 230). The notion that the younger is unequal to the older generation equally informs poems like "Ancestral Houses," "BEAUTIFUL LOFTY THINGS," and "MY DESCENDANTS." The related notion of a general cultural decline is a pervasive conviction of Yeats's work (see for example "The NINETEENTH CENTURY AND AFTER").

FIRST PUBLICATION: *Seven Poems and a Fragment*, The CUALA PRESS, Dundrum, June 1922.

BIBLIOGRAPHY

Foster, R. F. *W. B. Yeats: A Life, I: The Apprentice Mage*; Henn, T. R. *The Lonely Tower: Studies in the Poetry of W. B. Yeats*; Kelly, John S. *A W. B. Yeats Chronology*; Yeats, W. B. *Memoirs, The Variorum Edition of the Poems of W. B. Yeats*.

"News for the Delphic Oracle" (1939)

Perhaps Yeats's fullest borrowing from COLERIDGE's "Kubla Khan"—"ANCESTRAL HOUSES" likewise shows this influence—"News for the Delphic Oracle" envisions the afterlife as a realm of Elysian contemplation before arriving, with sudden shocking candor, at a scene of pagan sexual frenzy that suggests the inescapable duality of experience, the necessary element of what "BYZANTIUM" dubs "the fury and the mire of human veins." In this respect "News for the Delphic Oracle" revises "The DELPHIC ORACLE UPON PLOTINUS," which envisions the same afterlife without overtly acknowledging its necessary relation to a reverse order, though the "salt blood" that blocks Plotinus's eyes at least hints at its existence.

Both "News for the Delphic Oracle" and "The Delphic Oracle upon Plotinus" extrapolate from Porphyry's *On the Life of Plotinus and the Arrangement of his Work*. This brief biographical account of the Neoplatonic philosopher appears as a preface in Stephen MacKenna's (1872–1934) monumental edition of Plotinus's *Enneads* (1917–30), which became a sacred book to Yeats during the 1920s. Porphyry (232/4–ca. 305) relates that after Plotinus died in A.D. 270 his disciple Amelius of Tuscany asked the oracle at Delphi where the soul of his master had gone. The oracle replied that Plotinus resided among the "heavenly consort" where "fragrant breezes play, where all is unison and winning tenderness and guileless joy, and the place is lavish of the nectar-streams the unfailing Gods bestow, with the blandishments of the Loves, and delicious airs, and tranquil sky: where Minos and Rhadamanthus dwell, great brethren of the golden race

of mighty Zeus; where dwell the just Aeacus, and Plato, consecrated power, and stately Pythagoras and all else that form the Choir of Immortal Love, that share their parentage with the most blessed spirits, there where the heart is ever lifted in joyous festival" (*Enneads* 16–17; see also *LE* 110–111). "The Delphic Oracle upon Plotinus" is relatively faithful to the account of the oracle, but "News for the Delphic Oracle" offers a corrective vision. According to the later poem, the land of the "heavenly consort" encompasses a more complicated reality in which the sacred and profane, the spiritual and the sensual, the contemplative and the violent, exist in some obscure but necessary duality, conceivably in a relation of repression or sublimation. This is the "news" of the poem's title. The notion that the higher impulses are wed or should be wed to the lower is a consistent emphasis of Yeats's later poetry, as in "An ACRE OF GRASS," "Ancestral Houses," "CRAZY JANE TALKS WITH THE BISHOP," "RIBH DENOUNCES PATRICK," "The SPUR," and the third section of "UNDER BEN BULBEN." The pronouncement of "The MUNICIPAL GALLERY REVISITED" that art grows strong only from contact with the soil embodies a related understanding.

The first section of "News for the Delphic Oracle" hews to the vision of "The Delphic Oracle upon Plotinus." In a mood of languorous repose that belies that passion of their lives, the luminaries of the ancient world enjoy a stately retirement amid the pastoral grass. "Codgers" suggest a comic senescence, while the reference to gold and silver in the first two lines, as F. A. C. Wilson notes, is an alchemical allusion, for "fused gold and silver, the solar and lunar principles indissolubly knit, is an alchemical emblem of perfection" (*Yeats and Tradition* 219). The "Choir of Immortal Love" includes Plotinus and Pythagoras (cf. "AMONG SCHOOL CHILDREN" and "The STATUES") following Porphyry's account, but also the Irish goddess Niamh (cf. "Alternative Song for the Severed Head in *The King of the Great Clock Tower*" [1934], "The Danaan Quicken Tree" [1893], "The HOSTING OF THE SIDHE," "The Lover asks Forgiveness because of his Many Moods" [1895], and "Under the Moon" [1901]) and her mortal lover Oisin (cf. "The CIRCUS ANIMALS' DESERTION"). As Yeats relates in

"The WANDERINGS OF OISIN," the legendary Irish hero spent 300 years in the Land of the Young as Niamh's consort before his yearning for the warrior life and the company of his old comrades prompted him to return to Ireland. Upon falling from his horse and touching his native ground despite Niamh's warning, he instantly became withered with the full span of his mortal years. Given his passionate unwillingness to forsake the mortal realm despite the seductions of immortal youth and the beauty of his bride, Oisin seems a particularly ironic Elysian. "News for the Delphic Oracle" specifically echoes the third book of "The Wanderings of Oisin," which tells how Oisin and Niamh succumbed to an enchanted sleep; when they were occasionally disturbed, they lifted their eyelids and "gazed on the grass with a sigh" (III, 100).

The second section theorizes the journey—analogous to the journey narrated in "SAILING TO BYZANTIUM"—by which the "Innocents" achieve their uninspired retirement. As in "Byzantium" and "The Delphic Oracle upon Plotinus," the dead are conveyed across the sea on the backs of dolphins, an ecstatic and even sexual transmigration inseparable from bodily intensity and immersion in the physical element, in comparison to which the Elysian state—post-coital, as Wilson has it—seems ironic or anticlimactic (*Yeats and Tradition* 220). Yeats derived the idea of dolphins as conveyors of the soul from Eugénie Strong's *Apotheosis and After Life* (1915), as many critics have noted (see *Letters* 668), and from Raphael's "statue of the Dolphin carrying one of the Holy Innocents to Heaven," as Yeats wrote to T. STURGE MOORE in a letter clarifying the meaning of "Byzantium" (*WBY&TSM* 165). Giorgio Melchiori notes that no such statue is attributed to Raphael, though there are "dolphins drawing Galatea's sea-chariot in Raphael's fresco of the myth of Galatea at the Farnesina in Rome" (to which Yeats seems to allude in "The REALISTS"), and there are "small representations in the fresco medallions of children and infant loves riding dolphins, in the grotesque decorations of Raphael's Loggia in the Vatican" (*Whole Mystery of Art* 213).

Upon this journey, the dead relive their deaths, in a version of the "Dreaming Back" that Yeats describes in *A VISION*: "In the *Dreaming Back*, the Spirit is compelled to live over and over again the events that had most moved it; there can be nothing new, but the old events stand forth in a light which is dim or bright according to the intensity of the passion that accompanied them. They occur in the order of their intensity or luminosity, the more intense first, and the painful are commonly the more intense, and repeat themselves again and again" (226; see also *AV-1925* 226–227). Alternatively, these lines may refer to the "Return"—the informing concept of "Shepherd and Goatherd" (1919)—in which "the *Spirit* must live through past events in the order of their occurrence, because it is compelled by the *Celestial Body* to trace every passionate event to its cause until all are related and understood, turned into knowledge, made a part of itself" (*AV* 226). Wilson draws attention to Thomas Taylor's translation of Porphyry's essay "The Caves of the Nymphs" as a possible inspiration. Porphyry explains Platonism's symbolism of the life cycle, which Wilson paraphrases this way: "Platonism symbolises the birth of the soul as its journey from the Isles of the Blessed in a celestial boat (the 'vehicle' in which the soul was thought to be contained); during life the soul is tossed about on the sea of emotion and passion; after death, living backwards through time, it recrosses the sea and returns to the island paradise from which it set out" (*Yeats and Tradition* 211). The ambiguity of the pronoun "their" in line 19 creates a difficulty. Do cries of the innocents or the waves "through their ancestral patterns dance"? The laughing ecstasy of the waves seems to identify them as the dancers, while the regressive dynamic of the dance ("through their ancestral patterns") suggests the process by which the innocents "dream back" or "return."

The third section of the poem peers beyond the circumscribed Elysian confines and exposes a scene of sexual violence that scandalizes the sighs and yawns of the first section and raises the essential philosophical question of the poem: What do the contrary worlds have to do with one another? What is the logic of their juxtaposition? The section's immediate inspiration, as T. R. Henn notes, is Poussin's "The Marriage of Peleus and Thetis," in the collection of the National Gallery of

Ireland (*Lonely Tower* 249; scholarly opinion later restored the painting to its original title, "Acis and Galatea"). In Greek mythology, Zeus chose Peleus, a mortal, to marry the Nereid Thetis. Zeus would have himself married Thetis, but, in Robert Graves's telling, he had been "discouraged by the Fates' prophecy that any son born to Thetis would become far more powerful than his father. He was also vexed that Thetis had rejected his advances, for her foster-mother Hera's sake, and therefore vowed that she should never marry an immortal." Having been advised that Thetis would resist marriage to a mortal, Peleus hid himself behind a bush of "myrtle-berries on the shores of a Thessalian islet, where Thetis often came, riding naked on a harnessed dolphin, to enjoy her midday sleep in the cave which this bush half screened. No sooner had she entered the cave and fallen asleep than Peleus seized hold of her. The struggle was silent and fierce. Thetis turned successively into fire, water, a lion, and a serpent; but Peleus had been warned what to expect, and he clung to her resolutely, even when she became an enormous slippery cuttle-fish and squirted ink at him [. . .]. Though burned, drenched, mauled, stung, and covered with sticky sepia ink, Peleus would not let her go and, in the end, she yielded and they lay locked in a passionate embrace" (*Greek Myths* 270–271). The opening lines of the poem's third section envision this scene, though it is not clear whether pre- or post-coitally. Peleus stares upon Thetis blinded by tears of love, and yet his love, more passionate than the vague satiety evoked in the first section, does not preclude violence, and is perhaps inseparable from the capacity for violence: this the lesson of "Ancestral Houses." Thetis's belly—the part of her that most coincides with the primality of nature, a child perhaps already conceived—listens to far off sounds. Reconceiving Coleridge's famous reference to "ancestral voices prophesying war," Thetis hears "intolerable music" emanating from the cavern of Pan. Though a god born of Hermes, the goat-legged Pan resided in Arcadia, where he tended his flocks and devoted himself to the art of seduction; his intolerable music contrasts with the presumable mellifluence of the Choir of Love. The poem's final four lines dissolve in a scrum of flashing limbs

as "nymphs and satyrs / Copulate in the foam," a scene of creative violence that repudiates the sighs of the first section and insists on the irremediable duality of existence.

In Wilson's Platonic interpretation, the second section shows "the path by which souls arrive at the Isles of the Blessed," and the third section shows "the road by which they return to the world" (*Yeats and Tradition* 222). Ellmann more convincingly construes the third section as completing the Yeatsian heaven in a way that acknowledges and satisfies "the whole man": "Neither the pagans of the first section nor the Christians of the second [associating "Innocents" with "the Church's first martyrs"] fulfill this need, although their aspirations can be included, along with a more sensual ideal, in Yeats's more ample paradise" (*IY* 285). This reading, however, does not sufficiently acknowledge the tension between the first and third sections, the implicit element of vacillation so pervasive in Yeats's poetry. In brief, the joke is upon Plotinus, who strove, as the oracle says in Porphyry's account, to "rise above the bitter waves of this blood-drenched life," only to arrive at an equally "blood-drenched" heaven (*Enneads* 16). Yeats scorns the Elysian sleepiness and its sentimentalities of love, believing, as his deepest conviction, that the "blood-drenched life" is not a bane to be transcended, but a source of energy to be embraced and channeled, and is thus inseparable from the perfection of paradise. Yeats had said as much in "Her Courage" and in his often repeated pronouncement that the music of paradise is the sound of clashing swords (*Aut.* 209–210; *Expl.* 306; *Myth.* 254, 259; *VPl.* 688, 703). In the end, "News for the Delphic" stages the same debate as "A Dialogue of Self and Soul" and the seventh section of "Vacillation," with the Choir of Love representing "Soul" and the nymphs and satyrs "Self." As the satire of the opening section suggests, "News for the Delphic Oracle" comes to the same conclusion as the earlier poems: The "blood-drenched life" is not to be thrown off or evaded. The closing lines of "Vacillation" closely coincide with the essential meaning of "News for the Delphic Oracle": "I—though heart might find relief / Did I become a Christian man and choose for my belief / What seems most welcome in the tomb—play a predestined heart. / Homer is my example and his unchristened heart."

FIRST PUBLICATION: The *London Mercury* (periodical), March 1939, and the *New Republic* (periodical), March 22, 1939. Reprinted in *Last Poems and Two Plays*, The CUALA PRESS, Dublin, July 10, 1939.

BIBLIOGRAPHY

Ellmann, Richard. *The Identity of Yeats*; Graves, Robert. *The Greek Myths*; Henn, T. R. *The Lonely Tower: Studies in the Poetry of W. B. Yeats*; Jeffares, A. Norman. *A New Commentary on the Poems of W. B. Yeats*; Melchiori, Giorgio. *The Whole Mystery of Art: Pattern into Poetry in the Work of W. B. Yeats*; Plotinus, *The Enneads*; Wilson, F. A. C. *W. B. Yeats and Tradition*; Yeats, W. B. *Autobiographies, A Critical Edition of Yeats's A Vision (1925), Explorations, Later Essays, The Letters of W. B. Yeats, Mythologies, The Variorum Edition of the Plays of W. B. Yeats, A Vision, W. B. Yeats and T. Sturge Moore: Their Correspondence 1901–1937*.

"Nineteen Hundred and Nineteen" (1921, dated 1919)

One of a handful of poems that attempt a grand synthesis of Yeatsian ideas—one thinks also of "BYZANTIUM," "A DIALOGUE OF SELF AND SOUL," "EGO DOMINUS TUUS," "MEDITATIONS IN TIME OF CIVIL WAR," "THE PHASES OF THE MOON," "THE TOWER," "VACILLATION"—"Nineteen Hundred and Nineteen" is the very definition of a major poem and a reasonable nominee as Yeats's magnum opus. It is a poem of apocalypse, and thus belongs to one of the earliest and deepest veins in Yeats's poetry, but Yeats had never before construed the apocalyptic moment with such dimensionality—not merely as the annunciation of a new dispensation, as in "LEDA AND THE SWAN," "MY TABLE," and "The SECOND COMING," but as a moment of anguished self-reckoning and world-reckoning, as an invitation to ponder the possibility of meaning within the grinding gyres of time. As Harold Bloom

writes, "*Nineteen Hundred and Nineteen* is a powerful antidote to such poems as *The Second Coming*, *Leda and the Swan*, and *The STATUES*, poems in which Yeats is a little too much at ease in his own system, a touch too secure in a superhuman posture as he contemplates the terrible annunciations made to men" (*Yeats* 362–363). In Yeats's own account, dispatched to OLIVIA SHAKESPEAR on April 9, 1921, the poems that constitute "Nineteen Hundred and Nineteen" are "not philosophical but simple and passionate, a lamentation over lost peace and lost hope" (*Letters* 668).

The poem's context is the ANGLO-IRISH WAR that began January 21, 1919, and ended in truce on July 11, 1921. Yeats apparently began "Nineteen Hundred and Nineteen" in 1919, but he did not finish until the spring or summer of 1921, with the war largely behind him (668). Like "Meditations in Time of Civil War," which it follows in *The Tower* (1928) and in the standard edition of Yeats's collected poems, "Nineteen Hundred and Nineteen" is preoccupied with the dynamics of permanence and evanescence, natural concerns in an era of convulsive change and destruction. Where the poems of "Meditations in Time of Civil War" in their different ways at least nod to the possibility of protection "from the circle of the moon," the opening section

The American dancer Loïe Fuller (1862–1928). In "Nineteen Hundred and Nineteen" Yeats remembers her "Chinese dancers" in a whirl of floating ribbon and associates the image with the whirl of "The Platonic Year." *(Library of Congress)*

of "Nineteen Hundred and Nineteen" sees only irony in the faith that flourished before the chastening of World War I. "Phidias' famous ivories" symbolize the fate of culture generally. They had seemed immutable in the miracle of their art, but nothing in the stream of time stands above fragility and susceptibility. Phidias, a Greek master-sculptor of the fifth century before Christ and a type of the supreme artist, was responsible for the statuary of the Parthenon (on Phidias, see also "The STATUES," "UNDER BEN BULBEN," AV 271). The "golden grasshoppers" were ornamental hairpins worn by fashionable Athenians, as Thucydides mentions in *The History of the Peloponnesian War* (NCP 230). In a subversion of "SAILING TO BYZANTIUM'S" fantasy of permanence—flesh finding permanence in the carapace of gold—they are midges of a moment for all their metallic perfection. In retrospect, such "ingenious lovely things" seem to have been mere "pretty toys," and in their innocent inconsequence they suggest the baubles—faith in law, progress, and peace—that were the playthings of Yeats's own generation during the halcyon late-Victorian days of "Home Rule expectations" and "Pax Britannica," in R. F. Foster's characterization (AP 194). As Yeats recalled of the turn of the century from the shattered vantage of 1924, "Everyone, certainly everyone who counted, everyone who influenced events believed that the world was growing better and better, and could not even help doing so owing to physical science and democratic politics, and that dream lasted for many years" (W. B. Yeats & Georgian Ireland 317; see also AP 265).

The transition to the present moment is sudden and startling: "Now days are dragon-ridden, the nightmare / Rides upon sleep. . . ." The dragon imagery comports with the observation, made in a July 11, 1919, letter to JOHN QUINN, that Ireland was "reeling back into the middle ages, without growing more picturesque" (Letters 658), while the oblique metaphorical suggestion of horses violently bearing down recalls the terrifying stampedes of early poems like "HE BIDS HIS BELOVED BE AT PEACE" and "The HOSTING OF THE SIDHE." The mother "murdered at her door" was Ellen Quinn, a young woman from Kiltartan, in the neighborhood of Lady GREGORY's COOLE PARK, who was

shot from a passing military lorry while standing at her front door with her baby in her arms (*Lady Gregory's Journals*, I, 197–200). The soldiers go "scot-free," possibly punning on the dress of the British forces. Bernard Krimm notes that the "Tans often wore Tam O'Shanters while the Auxiliary Division wore either this headgear or Glengarry caps"; alternatively, the pun may be directed at a "regular army unit stationed in the Gort area at the time, the Argyll and Sutherland Highlanders" (*Irish Free State* 4). For all the late-Victorian faith in peace and progress, the scene of horror suggests that in the end men are "but weasels fighting in a hole." For those who have risen above the illusion of permanence and the temptation of self-deceit—among whom Yeats clearly counts himself—there is the comfort that a world worthy of attention would distract from the higher claim of "ghostly solitude," a reaffirmation of the concluding stanza of "I SEE PHANTOMS OF HATRED AND OF THE HEART'S FULLNESS AND OF THE COMING EMPTINESS." In its own way, however, this too may be a "half-deceit," for the sixth stanza of the first section immediately descends from the rhetoric of the fifth stanza and continues to grope after "comfort." As if incapable of sustaining the previous stanza's stately renunciation, it returns with a kind of threadbare simplicity to the essential human dilemma that "Man is in love and loves what vanishes," and to the essential paradox that man himself, as "incendiary or bigot," destroys everything he most loves.

The poem's second section, faithful to the gleanings of Yeats's "ghostly solitude," finds a larger pattern in the details of destruction. The epitomizing image is not Phidias's famous ivories in their pretense of permanence, but Loïe Fuller's Chinese dancers. The wheels of the dance are evanescent, confessedly congruent with the "circle of the moon," and yet they shadow forth the Platonic Year, the greatest of governing cycles, with a circuit of 26,000 years (see AV 252). The terrible dragon of the fourth stanza becomes "a dragon of air," a momentary wisp of the universal inhalation and exhalation, a wind "furious" and "levelling" (as section five states) but so innate as to be beyond questioning or lamenting. "All men are dancers and their tread / Goes to the barbarous clangour of a gong," Yeats writes, hinting at the terrible ecstasy of the dance itself as the answer to his own earlier question, "But is there any comfort to be found?" The gong, which recurs in "Byzantium" and "The GYRES," symbolizes a savage energy that absorbs into itself—rather than attempts to transcend—the violence by which the world makes and unmakes itself. Yeats's own art would increasingly shed classical aspiration (as typified by "Sailing to Byzantium") and embrace the clangor of the gong (as typified by "Byzantium"). Fuller (1862–1928) was an American dancer popular in the Paris demimonde during the 1890s. ARTHUR SYMONS, a notorious haunter of dance halls and theaters, most likely brought her to Yeats's attention. In 1892, writing in the London newspaper the *Star*, Symons called Fuller's "serpentine dancing" the "sensation of the moment" and recommended it to connoisseurs "of what is curious, fanciful, and *fin de siècle* in dancing" (*Arthur Symons* 82–83). Frank Kermode, whose study *Romantic Image* adopts as its frontispiece an *art nouveau* drawing of Fuller by Thomas Theodor Heine, notes that she "performed at the Folies Bergère, in a great whirl of shining draperies, the scope of which she extended by manipulating sticks" (*Romantic Image* 85–86).

The third section, which Bloom calls "the poem's glory," expands on the man of "ghostly solitude" (*Yeats* 359). The world allows nothing as unequivocal as triumph, but the "solitary soul," like a swan, may achieve a desolate glory of pride and self-knowledge against the backdrop of "approaching night." Critical consensus identifies the "moralist or mythological poet" who "Compares the solitary soul to a swan" as SHELLEY. In "Prometheus Unbound," Asia declares, "My soul is an enchanted boat, / Which, like a sleeping swan, doth float / Upon the silver waves of thy sweet singing. . . ." (II, v, lines 72–74). The image may also recall the ascending swan of Shelley's "Alastor" (1816, lines 272–290), which presages "The WILD SWANS AT COOLE"; and T. STURGE MOORE's "The Dying Swan," to which Yeats attributes the swan imagery in "The Tower" (*VP* 826). Unlike the swan, a man "in his own secret meditation / Is lost amid the labyrinth that he has made / In art or politics"—a version of what Yeats calls "Hodos

Chameliontos" in AUTOBIOGRAPHIES (282–283), of the condition he metaphorizes as "the cold snows of a dream" in "The ROAD AT MY DOOR." Spurning the worldly orientation of art and politics even as practiced in meditative secrecy, Yeats cites "some Platonist"—Bloom suggests BLAKE, Jeffares suggests Thomas Taylor—who insists that "triumph can but mar our solitude" (*Yeats* 360–361; *NCP* 236). At this the swans leaps into the "desolate heaven": an image of the soul embracing the difficulty of its own world-defiant solitude. The image of the swan taking wing "can bring wildness, bring a rage / To end all things, to end / What my laborious life imagined, even / The half-imagined, the half-written page. . . ." These lines find their explanatory key in the concluding lines of "My Table." Both poems describe the aching heart come to such a pitch of intensity that it potentially becomes an apocalyptic energy, consuming even the artistic enterprise by which it was self-nurtured. Bloom assigns great weight to the subtle hedge of these lines ("*can* bring"): "The peculiar power of *Nineteen Hundred and Nineteen* is that Yeats persuades us that he feels the authentic strength of this temptation, this very personal and High Romantic apocalypse of the imagination, yet restrains himself from yielding to such temptation [. . .] for the sake of imagination, as the creative force divides against itself" (*Yeats* 362). That is, Yeats is torn between the welling apocalypse and the unfulfilled obligation of the half-written page. As Bloom writes, "it is his strength [*pace* Shelley] to persist until the page is fully imagined, fully written" (361). Consistent with Bloom's interpretation, the section ends not with the cry of Juno's peacock, as in "My Table," but with a return to the lament of the poem's first section, while the brief fourth section reiterates the weasel as the appropriate human image ("seven years ago," measured from the time of the poem's composition, places the moment of twilight innocence on the eve of World War I). This sudden retreat from the apocalyptic verge is precisely the persistence—the commitment to the half-written page—that Bloom indicates.

In an exasperated satire of the apocalyptic impulse that Yeats resists in the third section, the poem's fifth section urges yet more of the "weasel's twist, the weasel's tooth." Corrected for sarcasm,

Yeats's tirade acknowledges the leveling wind and the weasel's hole but condemns mockers of the "the great," "the wise," and "the good," mockers of those who have nobly toiled in solitude to rear impossible monuments against the erosive trend of time and the world. For all their simplicity of voice, these lines are full of careful cross-stitching. The "levelling wind"—an archetype of destructive force—connects to wind imagery both backward and forward, while its "shriek" (line 107) associates it with the shrieking mocker-weasels of section four. "Traffic" connects the mockers of section five with the incendiaries and bigots of section one, and the mockers' internecine turn in the fourth stanza recalls the infighting of the weasels in sections one and four. Throughout, Yeats conceives mockery as the human manifestation or realization of the leveling wind. The bitter memory of the treatment meted out to HUGH LANE, CHARLES STEWART PARNELL, and J. M. SYNGE, Yeats's martyrs of modern Irish culture, informs the indictment of mockery and mockers (see VP 818). To borrow the language of "TO A SHADE," these were men of "passionate serving kind" who had insults heaped upon them for their pains. Yeats himself felt the mob's open mockery during The COUNTESS CATHLEEN controversy (CL2 669–680) and in the pages of GEORGE MOORE's memoir of the Irish Renaissance Hail and Farewell ("all my priceless things / Are but a post the passing dogs defile," as he complained in the "CLOSING RHYMES" to Responsibilities). Yeats similarly confronts the baseness of mockery in poems like "AT THE ABBEY THEATRE," "ON THOSE THAT HATED 'THE PLAYBOY OF THE WESTERN WORLD', 1907," and the second of the "Three Songs to the Same Tune" (1934).

Section six opens with a subtle and difficult modulation. "Violence upon the roads" is more precisely defined as "violence of horses" (cf. "He bids his Beloved be at Peace"), but the horses become "wearied running round and round in their courses," wearied of the historical cycle (cf. "AT GALWAY RACES"), and, as if more spiritual than material, suddenly "break and vanish" in a sign of the gathering apocalypse. Yeats writes in a note to the poem, "The country people see at times certain apparitions whom they name now 'fallen angels,' now 'ancient inhabitants of the country,' and describe as riding at whiles 'with flowers upon the heads of the horses.' I have assumed [. . .] that these horsemen now that the times worsen, give way to worse" (VP 433). In their place comes a nightmarish procession much like the procession Yeats describes in the second stanza of "I see Phantoms of Hatred and of the Heart's Fullness and of the Coming Emptiness." Amid thunder and tumult, "Herodias' daughters have returned again"—"again" signifying the recurrence of the apocalyptic pattern. Herodias is a "witchqueen" of the middle ages (NCP 234). Her daughters, maddened and blinded, manifest themselves in the ghostly form of the "labyrinth of the wind," and in this belong to the lineage of the SIDHE, as Yeats states in a note to "The HOSTING OF THE SIDHE": "Sidhe is [. . .] Gaelic for wind, and certainly the Sidhe have much to do with the wind. They journey in whirling winds, the winds that were called the dance of the daughters of Herodias in the Middle Ages, Herodias doubtless taking the place of some old goddess. When old country people see the leaves whirling in the road, they bless themselves, because they believe the Sidhe to be passing by" (VP 800; see also CL4 774; UP2 69). The entire cluster of image and allusion may be indebted to Arthur Symons's poem "The Dance of the Daughters of Herodias" (1899). Though its point of departure is the biblical tale of Herodias and Salome, it anticipates the visionary and nightmarish spectacle of Yeats's poem: "I see a pale and windy multitude / Beaten about the air, as if the smoke / Of incense kindled into visible life / Shadowy and invisible presences; / And, in the cloudy darkness, I can see / The thin white feet of many women dancing, / And in their hands . . . I see it is the dance / Of the daughters of Herodias . . ." (Poems by Arthur Symons, II, 103).

There comes the stillness that is the brief equipoise between dispensations, and the "insolent fiend Robert Artisson," like the sphinx of "The Second Coming," lurches past on his embassy of annunciation (the sphinx slouches rather than lurches; its eyes are likewise blank; overhead, the same suggestion of shadow). In his note to the poem, Yeats describes Artisson as "an evil spirit much run after in Kilkenny at the start of the fourteenth century." He asks, "Are not those who travel in the whirling dust also in the Platonic Year?"—which is to say, subject to the cyclical pattern of the universe, due for a recurrent apocalyptic assignation with the world (*VP* 433). On the subject of Lady Alice Kyteler, A. Norman Jeffares quotes St. John D. Seymour's *Irish Witchcraft and Demonology* (1913). A member of a "good Anglo-Norman family," Kyteler was condemned as a witch on July 2, 1324, on charges that included keeping "a certain demon, an incubus, named Son of Art, or Robin son of Art, who had carnal knowledge of her, and from whom she admitted that she had received her wealth. This incubus made its appearance under various forms, sometimes as a cat, or as a hairy black dog, or in the likeness of a negro (Ethiops), accompanied by two others who were larger and taller than he, and of whom one carried an iron rod" (*NCP* 236). The peacock feathers and "red combs of her cocks" that Kyteler brings Artisson are sacrificial offerings, but equally they evoke the apocalyptic avian crowing of the end in "My Table" (peacock) and "SOLOMON AND THE WITCH" (cockerel). In Donald T. Torchiana's reading, the "seductive inversion of mistress and man" represents the inversion of modern Ireland as "honor and truth, law and public service, dim ideals from the aristocratic past" give way to "modern revolution" (*W. B. Yeats & Georgian Ireland* 318).

FIRST PUBLICATION: The *Dial* (periodical), September 1921, under the title "Thoughts upon the Present State of the World." Reprinted in *Seven Poems and a Fragment*, The CUALA PRESS, Dundrum, June 1922, under the same title. Reprinted in *The Tower*, Macmillan, February 14, 1928, under the present title.

BIBLIOGRAPHY

Beckson, Karl. *Arthur Symons: A Life*; Bloom, Harold. *Yeats*; Foster, R. F. *W. B. Yeats: A Life, II: The Arch-Poet*; Gregory, Lady. *Lady Gregory's Journals* (vol. 1, ed. Daniel J. Murphy); Jeffares, A. Norman. *A New Commentary on the Poems of W. B. Yeats*; Kermode, Frank. *Romantic Image*; Krimm, Bernard G. *W. B. Yeats and the Emergence of the Irish Free State, 1918–1939: Living in the Explosion*; Symons, Arthur. *Poems by Arthur Symons* (vol. 2); Torchiana, Donald T. *W. B. Yeats & Georgian Ireland*; Yeats, W. B. *The Collected Letters of W. B. Yeats* (vols. 2, 4), *The Letters of W. B. Yeats, Uncollected Prose by W. B. Yeats* (vol. 2), *The Variorum Edition of the Poems of W. B. Yeats, A Vision*.

"Nineteenth Century and After, The" (1932)

Yeats was consistent and pervasive in his revilement of an age that teaches children to "cut and sew, be neat in everything / In the best modern way" ("AMONG SCHOOL CHILDREN"); that is "half dead at the top" ("BLOOD AND THE MOON"); that has "lit upon the gentle, sensitive mind / And lost the old nonchalance of the hand" ("EGO DOMINUS TUUS"); that fumbles "in a greasy till" ("SEPTEMBER 1913"); that is overrun by "Whiggery" ("The SEVEN SAGES"). "The Nineteenth Century and After," a masterpiece of compression, is chief in an informal sequence of four poems, none longer than four lines, that mordantly elaborate this disaffection (see "Spilt Milk" [1932], "Statistics" [1932], and "THREE MOVEMENTS"; "Symbols" [1932] is similarly epigrammatic, but its intentions are less obviously polemical). Yeats included the poem in a letter of March 2, 1929, to OLIVIA SHAKESPEAR: "I have turned from Browning—to me a dangerous influence—to [WILLIAM] MORRIS and read through his *Defence of Guenevere* and some unfinished prose fragments with great wonder. I have come to fear the world's last great poetic period is over [the poem is inserted here]. The young do not feel like that—GEORGE [YEATS] does not, nor EZRA [POUND]—but men far off feel it—in Japan for instance" (*Letters* 759).

The four lines of "The Nineteenth Century and After" achieve an enormous plangency in their distant, despondent echo of the famous lines of Matthew Arnold's "Dover Beach" (1867), which describe the "melancholy, long, withdrawing roar" of the "Sea of Faith." In lines that most likely gave Yeats his central image of the pebbles under the receding wave, Arnold refers to the "grating roar / Of pebbles which the waves draw back, and fling, / At their return, up the high strand, / Begin, and cease, and then again begin, / With tremulous cadence slow, and bring / The eternal note of sadness in." Where Arnold seeks the arms of love as the last refuge of meaning, Yeats assumes the laconic, defeated voice of modernity and proposes a specious "delight" in the echoes of "the great song" that returns no more. "The great song"—its scale, power, and unity argued by the metaphor of the ocean—is nothing less than the tradition of Western culture and belief. The image of the "receding wave" lends the sequence a thematic unity; it looks back to the thinning liquid of "Spilt Milk" and forward both to the waning of "God's fire" in "Statistics" and to the "fish that lie gasping on the strand" in "Three Movements." The allusion to "God's fire," meanwhile, transfigures the allusion to "intellectual fire" in "Blood and the Moon."

Richard Ellmann notes that Yeats "wittily borrowed for his title the name of the review *The Nineteenth Century*, which had to change its name at the end of the century to *The Nineteenth Century and After*" (*IY* 266). In January 1898, the *Nineteenth Century* had published Yeats's "The Prisoners of the Gods," a long essay on Irish folklore (see *UP2* 74–87).

FIRST PUBLICATION: *Words for Music Perhaps and Other Poems*, The CUALA PRESS, Dublin, November 14, 1932.

BIBLIOGRAPHY

Ellmann, Richard. *The Identity of Yeats*; Yeats, W. B. *The Letters of W. B. Yeats, Uncollected Prose by W. B. Yeats* (vol. 2).

"No Second Troy" (1910)

As in "WORDS," the immediately preceding poem in *The Green Helmet and Other Poems* (under the title "The Consolation"), Yeats attempts to talk himself out of the temptation to blame MAUD GONNE for his perpetual romantic misery, and in the process constructs a poem that is faultlessly turned—itself a "tightened bow." EZRA POUND cites "No Second Troy" as the first indication of Yeats's mature

STYLE. In his review "The Later Yeats," Pound quotes the poem's last five lines and comments that "with the appearance of *The Green Helmet and Other Poems* one felt that the minor note—I use the word strictly in the musical sense—had gone or was going out of his poetry [. . .]. And since that time one has felt his work becoming gaunter, seeking greater hardness of outline" (*Literary Essays of Ezra Pound* 379).

The poem argues that Gonne, cast in the same heroic mold as Helen, could not have done otherwise than wreak havoc. Yeats asks, in the first of four rhetorical questions that constitute the poem's 12 lines, how she can be blamed for filling his days with misery, or for rousing an insurrectionary passion in "ignorant men." Yeats means to indicate the educated but narrowly political middle class that was prone to oppose his own sometimes wayward and obscure cultural nationalism; relevantly, Joseph Hone notes Yeats's aversion to "all the little semi-literary and semi-political clubs and societies out of which the Sinn Fein movement grew" (*NCP* 87; see also *Mem.* 57). The distinction between "little streets" and "the great" indicates Yeats's emerging commitment to aristocratic station, tradition, and élan that would become increasingly prominent in his work (see for example "UPON A HOUSE SHAKEN BY THE LAND AGITATION").

Yeats asks how Gonne could have brought peace with a mind that "nobleness made simple as a fire" and beauty "like a tightened bow, a kind / That is not natural in an age like this, / Being high and solitary and most stern?" That Gonne's beauty is out of phase with modernity—the spirit of the age being plebeian, practical, and sentimental—is a commonplace of Yeats's work. In AUTOBIOGRAPHIES, for example, he writes she "looked as though she lived in an ancient civilization where all superiorities whether of the mind or the body were a part of public ceremonial," and he goes on to describe her body as a seeming "master-work of long labouring thought, as though a Scopas had measured and calculated, consorted with Egyptian sages, and mathematicians out of Babylon [. . .]" (274–275). The "tightened bow," what is more, looks forward to the sword (see "MY TABLE") as an icon of the aesthetic that Yeats hoped to define and embody. Bow and sword share a severity and elegance that is a disciplined expression of violent or passionate impulse (the sword was ultimately a more apt symbol than the bow because of its immunity to time and its birth by purgatorial fire, another important motif, as in "BLOOD AND THE MOON," "SAILING TO BYZANTIUM," and "VACILLATION").

Yeats asks, finally, what else could Gonne have done "being what she is? / Was there another Troy for her to burn?" Richard Ellmann comments rightly, "The success of the poem comes partly from the poet's withholding the identification of his beloved with Helen until the last line, when it fairly explodes. Yeats manages this by basing the identification not merely on beauty, but also on destructive power, and thus shunning sentimentality." Ellmann adds that with this final question "the guilt of [Gonne's] actions is showered on her age. The poet attacks the Troy-less present for not being heroically inflammable" (IY 111–112). At the same time, the final question of the poem has a trace of wry humor, for Yeats's hyperbole, become practically boundless, begins to transform into a knowing confession of his own uxoriousness.

"No Second Troy" is Yeats's most striking invocation of Helen, but she reoccurs throughout his poetry as a figure of perpetual fascination, most often associated with Gonne. See also "HIS MEMORIES," "HIS WILDNESS," "LULLABY," "PEACE," "A PRAYER FOR MY DAUGHTER," "The SORROW OF LOVE," "Three Marching Songs" (1939), "The TOWER," "When Helen Lived" (1914), "WHY SHOULD NOT OLD MEN BE MAD?," and "A WOMAN HOMER SUNG."

FIRST PUBLICATION: *The Green Helmet and Other Poems*, The CUALA PRESS, Churchtown, Dundrum, December 1910, under the sequence title "Raymond Lully and his wife Pernella" and the present title.

BIBLIOGRAPHY

Ellmann, Richard. *The Identity of Yeats*; Jeffares, A. Norman. *A New Commentary on the Poems of W. B. Yeats*; Pound, Ezra. *The Literary Essays of Ezra Pound*; Yeats, W. B. *Autobiographies, Memoirs*.

"Old Memory" (1904)

"Old Memory" attempts to come to terms with the trauma of MAUD GONNE's unexpected marriage to John MacBride (1865–1916) on February 21, 1903. The marriage brought a crashing close to Yeats's epic courtship (at least for a time) and left Yeats emotionally shattered. Written in December 1903, while Yeats was traveling in AMERICA (CL3 483), "Old Memory" is a testament to one of the most disillusioned periods of Yeats's life.

Yeats instructs his thought—personified as a literal emissary—to carry a message to Gonne when the day's end awakens an old memory, presumably a memory of what existed between them before her marriage. Yeats's winged thought is to remind Gonne that her "strength, that is so lofty and fierce and kind, / It might call up a new age" is but "half hers," and by implication was not entirely hers to dispose of. Through the "long years of his youth"—since they first met on January 30, 1889—Yeats had "kneaded in the dough." Connoting as it does the raw stuff of later development, "dough" implies not only that Yeats had influenced Gonne's development, but that he had busied his hands with her very birth or at least with the birth of the mythology that had become inseparable from her persona (Yeats repeats the dough metaphor in "The PHASES OF THE MOON," again using it to suggest a state of primordial potential). Here the poem verges on the recognition, anticipatory of "The CIRCUS ANIMALS' DESERTION," that the Gonne of Yeats's poetry is a poetic construction as much as a living human being. After all this labor, Yeats continues, who would have thought that all would have come to naught, and that "dear words"—whether Yeats's or Gonne's—meant nothing.

But enough, Yeats says, stopping short his own rehearsal of woe, for "when we have blamed the wind we can blame love." He means that blaming love is as senseless as blaming the wind, both being forces of nature beyond design and control (there is much the same implication of love's caprice in "A MEMORY OF YOUTH"). More than this, though, the association of love with the wind lends the former something of the latter's empty loneliness and chill lament (cf. "He HEARS THE CRY OF THE SEDGE" and "He reproves the Curlew"). If there need be more, Yeats adds in conclusion, let there be nothing said that would be harshly spoken to "children that have strayed." The figuration of Gonne as a straying child comports with the allusion to wind and love, all being blamelessly wayward. Four days before her marriage Gonne joined the Catholic Church against Yeats's objections (see CL3 314–317; GY 164–167), which lends the verb "stray" an ironic resonance: no longer astray, Gonne, as Yeats would have it, has gone astray in some more fundamental way, betraying what he calls in one of his imploring letters "the religeon [sic] of free souls" (CL3 316; GY 164). With this final line of gentle reproof, Yeats absolves Gonne of all but losing her way and implies his own undiminished tenderness—the tenderness a parent feels for a child even as it strays (cf. "A Bronze Head": "I had grown wild / And wandered murmuring everywhere, 'My child, my child!'").

FIRST PUBLICATION: *Wayfarer's Love: Contributions from Living Poets*, ed. the Duchess of Sutherland, Archibald Constable & Co., London, October 1904 (on the anthology, see CL3 421–422, 494–495, 530). Reprinted in *Poems, 1899–1905*, A. H. Bullen, London, Maunsel & Co., Dublin, October 1906.

BIBLIOGRAPHY

Yeats, W. B. *The Collected Letters of W. B. Yeats* (vol. 3), *The Gonne-Yeats Letters 1893–1938*.

"Old Tom Again" (1932)

See "Words for Music Perhaps."

"On a Picture of a Black Centaur by Edmund Dulac" (1922)

From about 1912, the French-born artist, illustrator, set designer, and musician Edmund Dulac (1882–1953) was an artistic brother-in-arms and close friend to Yeats. Yeats's lover Ethel Mannin (1900–84) called Dulac "probably Yeats's greatest friend," though exception has to be made at the very least for Lady Gregory (I&R, II, 271; see also 313–316). Dulac's most important part in Yeats's tale was designing the costumes and masks for the debut production of At the Hawk's Well in 1916, an experiment in stylized drama that momentously reverberated for the duration of Yeats's career. Yeats indicates the importance of this collaboration in his essay "Certain Noble Plays of Japan" (1916): "I am writing with my imagination stirred by a visit to the studio of Mr. Dulac, the distinguished illustrator of the *Arabian Nights*. I saw there the mask and head-dress to be worn in a play of mine by the player who will speak the part of Cuchulain, and who, wearing this noble, half-Greek, half-Asiatic face, will appear perhaps like an image seen in reverie by some Orphic worshipper" (E&I 221; see also *Letters* 607–612). In gratitude for the artistic breakthrough of *At the Hawk's Well*, Yeats dedicated *The Winding Stair and Other Poems* (1933) to Dulac (see VP 831). Dulac additionally executed the portrait of "Giraldus" and the diagram of the "Great Wheel" that appear in A Vision (*Letters* 699–700).

The artist Cecil Salkeld (1910–72) provided Yeats's biographer Joseph Hone with an account of the genesis of "On a Picture of a Black Centaur by Edmund Dulac." In July 1920, Yeats visited Glenmalure, County Wicklow, where Maud Gonne and family were temporarily domiciled in a "primitive cottage" with Salkeld as guest (GY 405–407). On the morning after his arrival Yeats was preoccupied with a partially written poem. "Do you realize that eternity is not a long time but a *short* time?" Yeats asked Salkeld, suddenly interrupting their morning stroll. "I was thinking of those Ephesian topers," he continued, and by way of explanation produced a paper scratched with eight lines of poetry, indecipherable beyond the phrase "mummy wheat" (a phrase Yeats repeats in "Conjunctions"). That night Salkeld sat up late finishing a "water-colour picture of a weird centaur at the edge of a dark wood: in the foreground, in the shade of the wood, lay the seven Ephesian 'topers' in a drunken stupor, while far behind on a sunny distant desert plain elephants and the glory of a great army passed away into the distance." The following day Yeats examined the painting closely and critically. That evening he announced the completion of the poem: "When the ladies had withdrawn [after dinner], he produced a pigskin-covered brandy flask and a small beautifully written manuscript: 'Your picture made the thing clear', he said. 'I am going to dedicate the poem to you. I shall call it 'The Black Centaur'" (*W. B. Yeats* 330–332). Salkeld was "impressed and gratified," but Yeats reneged on his promise. The poem was published in *Seven Poems and Fragment* (1922) under the title "Suggested by a Picture of a Black Centaur," but appeared in *The Tower* (1928) as "On a Picture of a Black Centaur by Edmund Dulac." In T. R. Henn's account, backed by the authority of GEORGE YEATS, "the poem was started in relation to Dulac's picture but was altered to correspond to a picture of Cecil Salkeld's" (*Lonely Tower* 257).

The chief interpretive dilemma of the poem is the symbolic significance of the centaur. The memoir "Four Years," begun in the fall of 1920, several months after Yeats had completed "On a Picture of a Black Centaur," includes a remark that conceivably helps. Yeats recalls his youthful aesthetic theory that "all art should be a Centaur finding in the popular lore its back and its strong legs" (*AP* 177; *Aut.* 165). The centaur is thus allied with a vision of art free of all modern heterogeneity and decadence, strong from contact with the soil of the folk culture. Consistent with this metaphor, the centaur of the poem serves as an aesthetic guardian or standard-bearer. Yeats's work occupies "the black margin of the wood, / Even where horrible green parrots call and swing." The centaur has stamped it all into the mud. Yeats accepts that what "wholesome sun has ripened is wholesome food to eat, / And that alone," but nonetheless feels pained to be at the receiving end of this violence ("INTRODUCTORY RHYMES" to *Responsibilities* figures Yeats's poetry as his only progeny). In contrast to "wholesome food," Yeats's work has harvested mere "mummy wheat"—esoteric but dead, born not of the sun, but of the "mad abstract dark," under the unhealthy influ-

ence of the green parrots. The poem's distinction between the "wholesome sun" and the "mad abstract dark" is pervasive if variously expressed in Yeats's thought, as in poems like "The CHOICE," "I SEE PHANTOMS OF HATRED AND OF THE HEART'S FULLNESS AND OF THE COMING EMPTINESS," "The ROAD AT MY DOOR," "TO THE ROSE UPON THE ROOD OF TIME," and "WORDS." The *antithetical* artist chooses the "mad abstract dark," as Yeats had done, but at the risk of both life and art, for art requires—at least as it sometimes seemed to Yeats—a balanced footing, a sober engagement, an emotional flexibility, an ability and willingness to endure the mundane if only in order to write of it. This is the implicit moral of Yeats's account of the "tragic generation," which describes the human toll of the "mad abstract dark" (see AUTOBIOGRAPHIES). The parrots have a long lineage, beginning with the parrot of "The Indian to His Love" (1886), which "sways upon a tree, / Raging at his own image in the enamelled sea," and with the "painted birds" of "The WANDERINGS OF OISIN" (book I, lines 69–70, 180–187, 396–397, 416–420). Their *genus* is the *antithetical* bird consummately figured in "BYZANTIUM," "MY TABLE," and "SOLOMON AND THE WITCH." Here calling and swinging, they perhaps protest the centaur's action on behalf of the "wholesome sun."

In contrast to the "mummy wheat" of earlier days, Yeats now claims to bring "full-flavoured wine out of a barrel found / Where seven Ephesian topers slept and never knew / When Alexander's empire passed, they slept so sound." The "full-flavoured" wine mediates between "wholesome food" and "mummy wheat": it belongs with wheaten bread among the staffs of life, and yet it is suffused with religious and mystical associations, as in "ALL SOULS' NIGHT." The reference to "Ephesian topers"—i.e., drinkers, drunkards—has its explanation in Christian legend. The city of Ephesus was a commercial metropolis of Greek heritage on the west coast of Asia minor (now western Turkey). When it came under the anti-Christian persecution of the Roman emperor Decius in A.D. 250, seven young believers fled to a cave and miraculously fell into a centuries-long sleep, waking only when the cave was unsealed during the more accommodating reign of the Eastern Roman emperor Theodosius II (A.D. 408–50). Upon hearing the tale of the miracle, Theodosius's piety was aroused, and he had the sleepers, who expired after relating their tale, magnificently buried. Alexander the Great conquered Ephesus in 333 B.C.; his empire obviously "passed" long before the sleepers took to their cave. Yeats's transformation of the seven "sleepers" into the seven "topers" is mysterious. It apparently borrows from Salkeld's painting while reiterating the motif of Yeats's own poem "The Hour before Dawn" (1914), in which a cave-bound "sleeper" snoozes away the eons with the help of Goban's beer. In his only other reference to the Ephesian legend, Yeats reverts to the idea of "sleepers" rather than topers. On August 20, 1915, he sent his defense of political quiescence, "ON BEING ASKED FOR A WAR POEM," to Henry James (1843–1916), with the explanation that he planned to "keep the neighbourhood of the seven sleepers of Ephesus, hoping to catch their comfortable snores till bloody frivolity is over" (*Letters* 599–600).

Yeats invites the centaur to emulate the topers by stretching out his limbs and sleeping "a long Saturnian sleep." In this instance, "Saturnian" does not mean "saturnine" (see "UNDER SATURN"), but "pacific" or "untroubled," in reference to the mythic golden age under the rule of the Titan Saturn. Yeats relieves the centaur as sentinel against the "mad abstract dark," for, whatever the wayward abstraction of his "words," Yeats has loved the centaur better than his own soul. There is "none so fit"—i.e., as Yeats himself—to keep watch "upon those horrible green birds," perhaps because Yeats knows intimately their method of seduction, their lurid siren song.

As "On a Picture of a Black Centaur" seems to repudiate the *antithetical* impulse, so "LINES WRITTEN IN DEJECTION" grieves for its loss. The two poems represent Yeats at his farthest remove from his own nature as a man of the 17th lunar phase.

FIRST PUBLICATION: *Seven Poems and a Fragment*, The CUALA PRESS, Dundrum, June 1922, under the title "Suggested by a Picture of a Black Centaur." Reprinted in *The Tower*, Macmillan, London, February 14, 1928, under the present title.

BIBLIOGRAPHY

Foster, R. F. *W. B. Yeats: A Life, I: The Arch-Poet*; Henn, T. R. *The Lonely Tower: Studies in the Poetry of W. B. Yeats*; Hone, Joseph. *W. B. Yeats*; Mikhail, E. H., ed. *W. B. Yeats: Interviews and Recollections* (vol. 2); Yeats, W. B. *Autobiographies, Essays and Introductions, The Gonne-Yeats Letters 1893–1938, The Letters of W. B. Yeats, The Variorum Edition of the Poems of W. B. Yeats.*

"On a Political Prisoner" (1920)

"On a Political Prisoner" caps an informal sequence on the EASTER RISING that includes "EASTER 1916," "Sixteen Dead Men" (1920), and "The Rose Tree" (1920). Anticipating "IN MEMORY OF EVA GORE-BOOTH AND CON MARKIEWICZ" and reprising lines 17–23 of "Easter 1916," "On a Political Prisoner" contrasts Constance Markiewicz's middle age and youth as a commentary on the blighting effects of political fanaticism. The poem pictures Markiewicz (1868–1927) in her cell in Holloway Jail, London, where she was incarcerated from May 18, 1918, to March 10, 1919, on the pretext that she had been involved in the spurious "German Plot" (*Terrible Beauty* 184–197). Her cell was adjacent to that of MAUD GONNE, who had been arrested as part of the same general roundup. Referring to "On a Political Prisoner," Yeats wrote to his wife in 1918 that he was writing a poem "on Con to avoid writing one on Maud," though in "A PRAYER FOR MY DAUGHTER," begun in April 1919, Yeats would apply the same critique to her (NCP 195; YC 204). Markiewicz had not long before served 14 months in jail for her part in the Easter Rising. She was initially sentenced to death, but her sentence was commuted to life imprisonment due to her sex, and she was released as part of a general amnesty on June 18, 1917 (*Terrible Beauty* 151–171).

Yeats imagines that Markiewicz is visited by a "grey gull," symbol of feminine beauty (cf. the prefatory lines to The ONLY JEALOUSY OF EMER) and *antithetical* solitude (cf. the third section of

Constance Markiewicz (1868–1927), née Gore-Booth, in "the years before her mind / Became a bitter, an abstract thing. . . ." *(Library of Congress)*

"NINETEEN HUNDRED AND NINETEEN"). In a note to CALVARY, Yeats writes: "Certain birds, especially as I see things, such lonely birds as the heron, hawk, eagle, and swan, are the natural symbols of subjectivity, especially when floating upon the wind alone or alighting upon some pool or river, while the beasts that run upon the ground, especially those that run in packs, are the natural symbols of objective man" (VPl. 789). Yeats wonders whether the bird reminds her of what she had been "before her mind / Became a bitter, an abstract thing, / Her thought some popular enmity: / Blind and leader of the blind / Drinking the foul ditch where they lie?" As against this present reality, Yeats remembers Markiewicz—then Constance Gore-Booth—in the bloom of her youth, riding to a hunt in the neighborhood of Ben Bulben, a mountain a few miles to the east of Lissadell,

Markiewicz's family home (see SLIGO). Yeats also remembers Markiewicz as an equestrian in "Easter 1916" and, with reflections pertinent to "On a Political Prisoner," in MEMOIRS: "Con Gore-Booth all through my later boyhood had been romantic to me [. . .]. She had often passed me on horseback, going or coming from some hunt, and was acknowledged beauty of the county. I heard now and then [of] some tom-boyish feat or of her reckless riding, but the general impression was always that she was respected and admired. [. . .] She surprised me now at our first meeting by some small physical resemblance to Maud Gonne, though so much shorter and smaller, and by a very exact resemblance in voice. In later years her voice became shrill and high, but at the time I write of it was low and soft. I was perhaps the first to give her any detailed account of one [i.e., Gonne] in imitation of whom, perhaps, she was to earn the life-sentence she is now serving" (78).

In her youth, the poem continues, Markiewicz was "clean and sweet / Like any rock-bred, seaborne bird. . . ." "Rock-bred" has important resonance. In the Yeatsian scheme, rock, and especially mountain rock, connote purity of pride and solitude, as in "The FISHERMAN," "The GREY ROCK," "The MAN AND THE ECHO," "TO A FRIEND WHOSE WORK HAS COME TO NOTHING," and "The TOWER." The image of the sea, meanwhile, contrasts sharply with the image of the ditch in the second stanza, the one a sublime infinite bravely breasted by the solitary bird, the other a mere gutter. Yeats would embrace the ditch in expiation of his own humanity in "A DIALOGUE OF SELF AND SOUL," but the philosophical breakthrough of that poem waited some years in the future.

"The LEADERS OF THE CROWD," which follows "On a Political Prisoner" in both *Michael Robartes and the Dancer* (1921) and Yeats's collected poems, picks up on the aspersion of Markiewicz as "blind and leader of the blind" and elaborates on the incompatibility between the mobbism of politics and the solitude of the spiritual truth-seeker. Though she is not named in "The Leaders of the Crowd," Markiewicz was likely among the "leaders" whom the poem denounces. Moreover, the poem's motif of mendacity—"loose fantasy," "calumny"—

picks up on the punning phrase "where they lie" in "On a Political Prisoner."

FIRST PUBLICATION: *The Dial* (periodical), November 1920, and *The Nation* (periodical), November 13, 1920. Reprinted in *Michael Robartes and the Dancer*, The CUALA PRESS, Churchtown, Dundrum, February 1921.

BIBLIOGRAPHY

Jeffares, A. Norman. *A New Commentary on the Poems of W. B. Yeats*; Kelly, John S. *A W. B. Yeats Chronology*; Norman, Diana. *Terrible Beauty: A Life of Constance Markiewicz*; Yeats, W. B. *Memoirs, The Variorum Edition of the Plays of W. B. Yeats.*

"On being asked for a War Poem" (1916)

World War I was the defining event in the modernist consciousness, but Yeats managed to remain relatively aloof and unmoved. Giorgio Melchiori writes that World War I "was not the concern of an Irish nationalist—it was only another proof of the general disintegration. The EASTER RISING of 1916 came as a surprise to Yeats, a great shock: that *did* concern him, something new and unexpected, a revelation and a transformation of the world he knew. It was of course only his Irish world, but that again is typical: for Yeats the only things that mattered were his things: the universe at large of which he was always speaking was only a projection of his personal universe" (*Whole Mystery of Art* 63). That being said, Yeats was not without an opinion on the conflict. On February 18, 1915, Yeats wrote to Lady GREGORY, "I wonder if history will ever know at what man's door to lay the crime of this inexplicable war. I suppose, like most wars, it is at root a bagman's war, a sacrifice of the best for the worst. I feel strangely enough most for the young Germans who are now being killed. These spectacled, dreamy faces, or so I picture them, remind me more of men that I have known than the strong-bodied young English football players who pass my door at WOBURN BUILDINGS daily, marching in their khaki, or the positive-minded young Frenchmen" (*Seventy*

Years 521). Writing to JOHN QUINN on June 24, 1915, Yeats gave full vent to his disgusted disinterest, complaining that the war is "merely the most expensive outbreak of insolence and stupidity the world has ever seen, and I give it as little of my thought as I can. I went to my club this afternoon to look at the war news, but read Keats's Lamia instead" (*AP* 5). This sentiment undergirds "An IRISH AIRMAN FORESEES HIS DEATH," in which ROBERT GREGORY, who had enlisted in the Royal Flying Corps, is made to say, "Those that I fight I do not hate, / Those that I guard I do not love; / My country is Kiltartan Cross, / My countrymen Kiltartan's poor, / No likely end could bring them loss / Or leave them happier than before."

On August 20, 1915, Yeats sent "On being asked for a War Poem," then called "A Reason for Keeping Silent," to Henry James (1843–1916) for inclusion in *The Book of the Homeless* (1916), a literary anthology edited by Edith Wharton (1862–1937), proceeds from which were to benefit war refugees. Yeats commented to James, "It is the only thing I have written of the war or will write, so I hope it may not seem unfitting. I shall keep the neighbourhood of the seven sleepers of Ephesus, hoping to catch their comfortable snores till bloody frivolity is over" (*Letters* 600). The poem deftly parries the entire subject of the war: It is not an engagement but an explanation of principled disengagement. Poets had best remain silent "in times like these," for they have "no gift to set a statesman right"; they should meddle no further than the attempt to please a "young girl in the indolence of her youth, / Or an old man upon a winter's night." The "young girl" is most likely ISEULT GONNE, the iconic "young girl" of so many poems of the period (see "TO A YOUNG GIRL"). Yeats accuses her of "indolence" ("Has no one said those daring / Kind eyes should be more learn'd?") in "Two Years Later" (see "TO A CHILD DANCING IN THE WIND").

John Unterecker calls "On being asked for a War Poem" a "tongue-in-cheek" response to the request for a war poem (*RG* 143), but there is no reason to believe that Yeats intended the poem as anything except a serious statement, fully consistent with his lifelong insistence that art must be distilled of "impurities," by which he means everything topical, factual, and accidental (*Aut.*

148–149), including political and moral pleading. In his introduction to *The Oxford Book of Modern Verse* (1936), Yeats states his reservations about the kind of war poem that he himself was determined not to write: "I have a distaste for certain poems written in the midst of the great war [. . .]. The writers of these poems were invariably officers of exceptional courage and capacity, one a man constantly selected for dangerous work, all, I think, had the Military Cross; their letters are vivid and humorous, they were not without joy—for all skill is joyful—but felt bound, in the words of the best known, to plead the suffering of their men. [. . .] I have rejected these poems for the same reason that made [Matthew] Arnold withdraw his *Empedocles on Etna* from circulation; passive suffering is not a theme for poetry. In all the great tragedies, tragedy is a joy to the man who dies; in Greece the tragic chorus danced" (*LE* 199).

Elizabeth Cullingford discerns in Yeats's reticence a different rationale: "[Yeats's] attitude was not the result of indifference to human suffering, but deliberate Irish policy. Had he written a war poem it would have placed him on [John] Redmond's side in the recruiting controversy, and he had no desire to act as a propagandist for the Irish Parliamentary Party" (*Yeats, Ireland and Fascism* 86). Redmond, leader of the party, accepted British assurances that Ireland would be granted Home Rule following the war and urged his countrymen to fight on the British side overseas (*Modern Ireland* 472–473).

FIRST PUBLICATION: Edith Wharton, ed., *The Book of the Homeless*, Macmillan, London, March 1916, under the title "A Reason for Keeping Silent." Reprinted in *The Wild Swans at Coole*, The CUALA PRESS, Churchtown, Dundrum, November 17, 1917, under the present title.

BIBLIOGRAPHY

Cullingford, Elizabeth *Yeats, Ireland and Fascism*; Foster, R. F. *Modern Ireland, 1600–1972*, *W. B. Yeats: A Life, II: The Arch-Poet*; Gregory, Lady. *Seventy Years: Being the Autobiography of Lady Gregory*; Melchiori, Giorgio. *The Whole Mystery of Art: Pattern into Poetry in the Work of W. B. Yeats*; Unterecker, John. *A Reader's Guide to William Butler Yeats*; Yeats, W. B. *Autobiographies, Later Essays, The Letters of W. B. Yeats*.

"On hearing that the Students of our New University have joined the Agitation against Immoral Literature" (1912)

This four-line poem consists of a single rhetorical question. It asks, in effect, Where but here—meaning Ireland or Dublin—does "Pride and Truth" shake its sides—laugh uproariously—at the sight of youth restraining "reckless middle-age"? The question's barb depends on two inversions of the normal order: first, that "Pride and Truth" should "long to give themselves for wage," and second, that youth should be more timid than middle age. The allusion to "Pride and Truth" is obviously ironic; Yeats presumably has in mind the self-styled defenders of "Pride and Truth" that dominated the popular press. Undoubtedly, Yeats alludes to himself and Lady GREGORY when he refers to "reckless middle-age," for the ABBEY THEATRE, of which Yeats and Lady Gregory were the middle-aged directors, was then dogged by controversy. On March 12, 1912—less than a month before Yeats was to write "On hearing that the Students"—the Abbey players returned from a tour of AMERICA that had included the stateside debut of J. M. SYNGE's *The Playboy of the Western World* (YC 154–155). The play had sparked riots and had resulted in the arrest of the entire cast on charges of performing an "immoral and indecent" play (*Our Irish Theatre* 121). On March 5, 1912, Yeats wrote to his father, JOHN BUTLER YEATS, that the controversy in America had "re-acted powerfully" in Dublin and prompted attacks in the newspapers (*Letters* 568).

"On hearing that the Students" addresses the American controversy's spillover in Dublin. The specifics are indicated in the poem's original title in *The Green Helmet and Other Poems* (1912): "On hearing that the students of our new University have joined the Ancient Order of Hibernians and the Agitation against Immoral Literature." The new university, as Richard J. Finneran explains, is "University College Dublin, founded in 1854 as the Catholic University of Ireland; in 1908 it became one of the three Constituent Colleges of the National University of Ireland." It was considered "new" in contrast to Trinity College, Dublin, founded in 1591 (*The Poems* 636). The Ancient Order of Hibernians began as an Irish-American benevolent society founded in New York in 1836 (*Oxford Companion to Irish History*). R. F. Foster writes that the "aggressively Catholic organization" became influential throughout Ireland after a clerical ban on the order as a secret society was lifted in 1904. By 1912, "it was a force to be reckoned with in the south, where it was related closely to a contemporary wave of Catholic triumphalism" (*Modern Ireland* 432–443). The American branch of the Ancient Order of Hibernians participated in the agitation against the Abbey Theatre during its 1911–12 tour of America (*Our Irish Theatre* 128). In its disgust at the censorious and parochial culture of Dublin, "On hearing that the Students" is a natural companion to poems like "AT THE ABBEY THEATRE" and "ON THOSE THAT HATED 'THE PLAYBOY OF THE WESTERN WORLD', 1907."

FIRST PUBLICATION: *The Green Helmet and Other Poems*, Macmillan, New York, London, October 23, 1912, under the title "On hearing that the Students of our New University have joined the Ancient Order of Hibernians and the Agitation against Immoral Literature." Reprinted in *Later Poems*, Macmillan, London, November 3, 1922, under the present title.

BIBLIOGRAPHY

Connolly, S. J., ed., *The Oxford Companion to Irish History*; Foster, R. F. *Modern Ireland, 1600–1972*; Gregory, Lady. *Our Irish Theatre*; Kelly, John S. *A W. B. Yeats Chronology*; Yeats, W. B. *The Letters of W. B. Yeats, The Poems*.

"On those that hated 'The Playboy of the Western World', 1907" (1911)

"On those that hated" continues Yeats's campaign against the chauvinism and hypocrisy of the middle-class nationalists who had so often attempted to constrain cultural expression. Following in the pages of *Responsibilities* (1914) several poems that rail against those who had obstructed HUGH LANE's effort to establish a gallery of contemporary art in Dublin—"Paudeen" [1914], "TO A FRIEND WHOSE WORK HAS COME TO NOTHING," "TO A SHADE," and "TO A WEALTHY MAN WHO PROMISED A SECOND SUBSCRIPTION TO THE DUBLIN MUNICIPAL GALLERY IF IT WERE PROVED THE PEOPLE WANTED PICTURES"—"On those that hated" reverts to an earlier controversy with much the same root issues. In the most legendary contretemps of the Irish Renaissance, the ABBEY THEATRE's debut performances of J. M. SYNGE's play *The Playboy of the Western World* turned riotous as nationalists made a casus belli of the play's unsugared representation of the Irish peasantry. The play's chief offense was its alleged immodesty. As Lady GREGORY informed Yeats by telegram, the audience had broken up at the word "shift," that is, at the mention of feminine undergarments (*AM* 360). "On those that hated," a scorched earth campaign compressed into a mere six lines, charges the play's critics with a neurotic sexual obsession that manifests itself as hypocritical prudery. In the poem's devastating analogy, those who hated the *Playboy* are likened to the throngs of eunuchs who ran through the streets of hell to look upon "great Juan riding by," railing against him even as they stared, sweating, "upon his sinewy thigh." "Juan" (more usually "Don Juan") is the aristocratic seducer of women made famous in *El Burlador de Sevilla* by the Spanish playwright Tirso de Molina (ca. 1583–1648).

Yeats explains the logic of his analogy between those that hated the play and the eunuchs of hell in a March 1909 diary entry: "The root of it all [nationalist chauvinism] is that the political class in Ireland—the lower-middle class from whom the patriotic associations have drawn their journalists and their leaders for the last ten years—have suffered through the cultivation of hatred as the one energy of their movement, a deprivation which is the intellectual equivalent to a certain surgical operation. Hence the shrillness of their voices. They contemplate all creative power as the eunuchs contemplate Don Juan as he passes through Hell on the white horse" (*Aut.* 359; *Mem.* 176). In a March 8, 1909, letter to Lady GREGORY, Yeats mentions this diary entry and further illuminates the poem's animating idea: "I wound up my [diary] notes this morning with the sentence 'culture is the sanctity of the intellect.' I was thinking of men like Griffith and how they can renounce external things without [sanctity of the intellect] but not envy, revenge, jealousy and so on. I wrote a note a couple of days ago in which I compared Griffith and his like to the Eunuchs in Ricketts's picture watching Don Juan riding through Hell" (*Letters* 525). Yeats refers to Arthur Griffith (1872–1922), a founder of the Sinn Féin movement and later president of the Irish Free State (he is described "staring in hysterical pride" in "The MUNICIPAL GALLERY REVISITED"). A frequent adversary of Yeats's freethinking cultural nationalism, Griffith led the attack against both Synge's *In the Shadow of the Glenn* (see *Expl.* 114–123; *UP2* 306–308) and *The Playboy* (*AM* 363), believing, according to Yeats, that "literature should be subordinate to nationalism" (*Letters* 422). The painting is "Don Juan in Hell" (ca. 1908), by Yeats's close friend Charles Ricketts (1866–1931). It is reproduced in J. G. P. Delaney's *Charles Ricketts: A Biography* (1990).

In another diary entry—this one dated May 18, 1912—Yeats articulates the essentially Freudian understanding that feeds the poem's sexual theme: "When any part of human life has been left unexpressed, there is a hunger for its expression in large numbers of men, and if this expression is prevented artificially, the hunger becomes morbid, and if the educated do not become its voice, the ignorant will" (*Mem.* 265).

FIRST PUBLICATION: The *Irish Review* (periodical), December 1911, under the title "On those who Dislike the Playboy." Reprinted in *The Green Helmet and Other Poems*, Macmillan, New York, London, October 23, 1912, under the title "The Attack on the 'The Play Boy.'" Reprinted in *Later Poems*, Macmillan, March 26, 1922, under the present title.

BIBLIOGRAPHY

Delaney, J. G. P. *Charles Ricketts: A Biography*; Foster, R. F. *W. B. Yeats: A Life, I: The Apprentice Mage*; Yeats, W. B. *Autobiographies, Explorations, The Letters of W. B. Yeats, Memoirs, Uncollected Prose by W. B. Yeats* (vol. 2).

"On Woman" (1916)

Like "FRIENDS," "On Woman" begins in praise of women whose virtues—mildness, generosity, understanding—make for friendship and ease, but, as if in ironic self-refutation, the poem takes fire only with the evocation of a very different kind of woman: the woman whose beauty is "like a tightened bow" ("NO SECOND TROY"), who seems "a burning cloud" ("FALLEN MAJESTY"), who leaves one shaking "from head to foot" ("Friends"). Sheba is here the incarnation of the type, as is Helen of Troy in other poems, but the inevitable inspiration and model is MAUD GONNE. The distinction between the two types of women emerges in the second stanza. Solomon "grew wise / While talking with his queens," just as Yeats, according to "Friends," grew wise talking with OLIVIA SHAKESPEAR and Lady GREGORY. But Solomon could find no sufficient praise for Sheba, a mere "lass," when "she the iron wrought, or / When from the smithy fire / It shuddered in the water"—an elaborate metaphor of the sexual act, as brought home by the post-coital languor that ensues in the next four lines. John Unterecker refers to the poem's "new feats of frankness" (*RG* 139). Note especially the "harshness" of the couple's desire, which contrasts with the placidity of the women described in the first stanza and anticipates the frank sexual brutality of poems like "HIS MEMORIES," "LEDA AND THE SWAN," and "NEWS FOR THE DELPHIC ORACLE." In the 20-line sentence that is the poem's denouement, Yeats wishes God to grant—not in this life, but in a future life, once the "Pestle of the moon / That pounds up all anew" has brought round another birth—that which he had known during the crisis days of his love for Gonne: a passion great enough to leave him maddened, battered, distraught, "like Solomon / That Sheba led a dance." The poem iterates, then, Yeats's conviction that passion—even self-destructive passion—is the highest ambition and attainment. These lines are closely related to the final lines of "A DIALOGUE OF SELF AND SOUL," in which Yeats declares his willingness to plunge into the impure ditch of life, and into "that most fecund ditch of all, / The folly that man does / Or must suffer, if he woos / A proud woman not kindred of his soul." Among the poem's most pregnant details is the allusion to the "Pestle of the moon" that presides over the cycle of birth and death. The poem was completed May 25, 1914 (YC 174), making this allusion one of the first clear anticipations of the philosophical system that Yeats would fully unveil in "The PHASES OF THE MOON" and A VISION. It is noteworthy that Yeats, not yet having come into his full audacity, measures his words with the phrase "if the tale's true." Solomon and Sheba recur in "SOLOMON AND THE WITCH" and "Solomon to Sheba" (1918). Written later, these poems associate Sheba with GEORGE YEATS.

FIRST PUBLICATION: *Poetry* (periodical), February 1916. Reprinted in *Eight Poems*, "Form" at the Morland Press, London, April 1916 (see *Letters* 609–610), and in *The Wild Swans at Coole*, The CUALA PRESS, Churchtown, Dundrum, November 17, 1917.

BIBLIOGRAPHY

Kelly, John S. *A W. B. Yeats Chronology*; Unterecker, John. *A Reader's Guide to William Butler Yeats.*

"Owen Aherne and his Dancers" (1924)

Though not published until seven years later, Yeats wrote "Owen Aherne and his Dancers" in the days following his marriage (YC 195–196). The poem is Yeats's most revealing poetic account of the complications that beset his shifting romantic hopes (see also "Two Songs of a Fool" [1919]). Aherne is Yeats himself; the two dancers are ISEULT GONNE and GEORGE YEATS. Yeats had courted Iseult while staying at Les Mouettes, the Gonnes' home in Colleville-sur-Mer, on the Normandy shore, during the summers of 1916 and 1917. After Iseult rejected his proposal of marriage in August 1917,

Yeats proposed, with Iseult's blessing, to Georgie Hyde-Lees, whom he knew through her step-aunt OLIVIA SHAKESPEAR. The two married on October 20, 1917. Writing to Lady GREGORY on October 13, Yeats confessed that he was in an emotional tangle and that he had fallen into a "wild misery" upon fixing the marriage date. He explained, "I thought I loved Iseult & would love to my life's end and that I wrote the letter to Mrs Tucker [George's mother] to end by a kind of suicide an emotional strain that had become unendurable—my sheer bodily strength was worn out. Then I became a little happier remembering that I had two main thoughts when I wrote (1) that I might become unhappy through a long vain courtship [of Iseult] (2) that Iseult might become unhappy through accepting me out of mere kindness and gratitude. Then I spent most of yesterday with Iseult [. . .] & she was so noble & sweet & made me feel as well as know that neither of us could think of anything now but George's happiness that I became more content. This morning the storm has shifted & I think the marriage a great promise of happiness & tranquil work" (AP 100).

"Owen Aherne and his Dancers" repeats much of this internal debate. The first section of the poem, originally titled "The Lover Speaks," details Yeats's conflicted feelings for Iseult. Always the messengers of desolation (cf. "HE HEARS THE CRY OF THE SEDGE" and "HE REPROVES THE CURLEW"), the four winds visit the heart with longing, despair, pity, and fear. Yeats humbly confesses his fear—fear of hurting and of being hurt—and describes the heart going mad under the burden of its competing impulses. In the second section of the poem, originally titled "The Heart Replies," the heart denies the imputation of madness. It sent Yeats fleeing from Iseult not madly but deliberately, understanding that age may not mate with youth "so wildly bred," and that "cage bird" must mate with "cage bird." Calling his own heart a liar, Yeats gallantly denies that George is a creature of the cage, but his ambivalence is palpable. He accuses his heart of scheming to betray a "poor wretch" like himself, that is, to undo the prospective happiness of his marriage. "Wretch" is an unhappy word to be associated with a honeymoon, while "betray" implies not only treachery but also divulgence, the betrayable secret that Yeats's thoughts are "far away"—another unhappy honeymoon detail. The heart rightly ridicules Yeats's faint attempt at gallantry. It taunts that Yeats may say whatever he likes now that his tongue is past persuading Iseult to "mistake / Her childish gratitude for love. . . ." Always the repository of elemental truth, the locus of the essential man, the heart seems to speak what the self cannot admit: Yeats abandoned his suit not in madness and confusion, but generously and forlornly, in a moment when moral impulse and weakness of will had become fused.

A recurrent figure in Yeats's poems and stories, Aherne tends to represent the *primary* or *objective* personality, while Michael Robartes represents the *antithetical* or *subjective* personality (see *Book of Yeats's Vision* 39–57; see also *VP* 803, 821, 853). A VISION makes clear the distinction: "Aherne [. . .] was stout and sedentary-looking, bearded and dull of eye, but [Robartes] was lank, brown, muscular, clean-shaven, with an alert, ironical eye" (37). Further, Aherne is a "pious Catholic" who objects to Robartes's occultism but, lacking will, does whatever Robartes tells him (35). Yeats's adoption of Aherne as his poetic persona, then, tells a good deal about his sense of himself in this instance, and is the more revealing given that he adopts Robartes as his persona in two poems—"The DOUBLE VISION OF MICHAEL ROBARTES" and "MICHAEL ROBARTES AND THE DANCER"—that relate to his romantic interest in Iseult. In a note to CALVARY, Yeats observes that objective men, "however personally alone, are never alone in their thought, which is always developed in agreement or in conflict with the thought of others and always seeks the welfare of some cause or institution, while subjective men are the more lonely the more they are true to type, seeking always that which is unique or personal" (*VPl.* 789). Yeats's anguished solicitude for both Iseult and George suggests something of the objective man's tendency to "seek the welfare of some cause or institution" and accounts for his choice of mask. Yeats repeatedly figures Iseult as a dancer in token of her passionate spontaneity, as in "The Double Vision of Michael Robartes," "Michael Robartes and the Dancer," and "To A

CHILD DANCING IN THE WIND." George Yeats's figuration as one of Owen Aherne's "dancers," by contrast, seems another instance of the considerate bad faith that is a prominent theme of the poem.

FIRST PUBLICATION: The *Dial* (periodical), June 1924, under the titles "The Lover Speaks" (lines 1–12) and "The Heart Replies" (lines 13–24). Reprinted in *The Cat and the Moon and Certain Poems*, The CUALA PRESS, Dublin, 1924. Reprinted in *The Tower*, Macmillan and Co., London, February 14, 1928, under the present title.

BIBLIOGRAPHY

Adams, Hazard. *The Book of Yeats's Vision: Romantic Modernism and Antithetical Tradition*; Foster, R. F. *W. B. Yeats: A Life, II: The Arch-Poet*; Kelly, John S. *A W. B. Yeats Chronology*; Yeats, W. B. *The Variorum Edition of the Plays of W. B. Yeats*, The Variorum Edition of the Poems of W. B. Yeats, A Vision.*

"Parnell" (1938)

See "THE GREAT DAY."

"Parnell's Funeral" (1934)

"In the thirty years or so during which I have been reading Irish newspapers, three public controversies have stirred my imagination," Yeats writes in a note to *Responsibilities* (1914). "The first was the Parnell controversy. There were reasons to justify a man's joining either party, but there were none to justify, on one side or on the other, lying accusations forgetful of past service, a frenzy of detraction" (*VP* 818). Yeats never put behind him the scandal of adultery and divorce that brought down CHARLES STEWART PARNELL, leader of the Irish parliamentary party. He considered Parnell's downfall in 1890, followed by his death in 1891, no historical accident, but the confirmation of myth, for in the pattern of things the mob turns against the great man in its midst, out of fear, resentment, and leveling instinct. This is the pattern not only of Parnell, but of CUCHULAIN (see ON BAILE'S STRAND), HUGH LANE (see "To a SHADE"), KEVIN O'HIGGINS (see "DEATH"), and J. M. SYNGE (see "ON THOSE THAT HATED 'THE PLAYBOY OF THE WESTERN WORLD', 1907"). In the 1930s, more than 20 years after he had made Parnell the subject of "To a Shade," Yeats returned to the memory of the great man in a spate of poems. In addition to "Parnell's Funeral," there is "Parnell" (see "The GREAT DAY"), "Three Songs to the Same Tune" (1934), "Three Marching Songs" (1939), and "Come Gather Round Me, Parnellites" (1937). In Parnell, Yeats rediscovered a symbol of the personality, pride, and solitude that seemed to have gone out of Ireland.

"Parnell's Funeral"—Yeats's most involved exploration of the mythology that underpins his own preoccupation with Parnell—thinks back to Parnell's funeral at Glasnevin Cemetery in Dublin on October 11, 1891. That morning, as he tells in a note to the poem, Yeats had gone to Kingston Pier to meet MAUD GONNE on the early morning mail boat, and Parnell's body happened to arrive on the same boat (he died in Brighton). Yeats did not attend the funeral later in the day because, in his "sensitive and timid youth," he "hated crowds and what crowds implied" (cf. "The LEADERS OF THE CROWD"). Gonne was present and that evening brought news of the event (VP 834). "The Funeral is just over," Yeats wrote his sister Lily (1866–1949) on October 11. "The people are breathing fire & slaughter. The wreathes have such inscriptions as 'Murdered by the Priests' & a number of Wexford men were heard by man I know [sic] promising to remove a Bishop & seven priests before next sunday [sic]. Tomorrow will bring them cooler heads I doubt not" (CL1 265).

"Parnell's Funeral" opens on the scene of the funeral. Symbolizing its fundamental divergence from Parnell, the "crowd" is gathered under the tomb of "the Great Comedian," the nationalist parliamentarian Daniel O'Connell (1775–1847), whom Yeats contrasts with Parnell in AUTOBIOG-RAPHIES: "I had seen Ireland in my own time turn from the bragging rhetoric and gregarious humour of O'Connell's generation and school, and offer herself to the solitary and proud Parnell as to her anti-self, buskin followed hard on sock, and I. had

begun to hope, or to half hope, that we might be the first in Europe to seek unity [see UNITY OF BEING] as deliberately as it had been sought by theologian, poet, sculptor, architect, from the eleventh to the thirteenth century" (167–168). In MEMOIRS he writes that the "sense of form, whether that of Parnell or Grattan or Davis, of form in active life, has always been Protestant in Ireland. O'Connell, the one great Catholic figure, was form-less. The power of self-conquest, of elevation has been Protestant, and more or less a thing of class. All the tragedians were Protestant—O'Connell was a comedian. He had the gifts of the market place, of the clown at the fair" (213; see also I&R, I, 122; UP2 320). Above the funeral scene, "a brighter star shoots down," as reportedly occurred during the ceremony, despite the broad daylight. "I state a fact—it was witnessed by thousands," recalled Standish O'Grady, as quoted by Yeats in his note to the poem. "While his followers were committing Charles Parnell's remains to the earth, the sky was bright with strange lights and flames" (VP 834). Yeats associates this apparent sign written upon the heavens with apocalyptic annunciation and Par-nell with the sacrificial god whose death and birth reverse the gyres of history (cf. "The MAGI," The RESURRECTION, "TWO SONGS FROM A PLAY"). "I ask if the fall of a star may not upon occasion, sym-bolise an accepted sacrifice," he writes in his note (VP 834). The falling star is associable with the falling star that signals Christ's conception in both "The MOTHER OF GOD" and "A Nativity" (1938), while the "animal blood" of the crowd shudders with an instinctive sense of the uncanny, much as the Virgin Mary feels a "sudden chill" in her bones in "The Mother of God" and feels "terror-struck" in "A Nativity"; much as the Greek screams upon feeling Christ's beating heart in The Resurrection.

Yeats asks, "What is this sacrifice? Can someone there / Recall the Cretan barb that pierced a star?" The allusion is not an easy one. The search for an explanation begins with Yeats's evocation of a vision while a guest at EDWARD MARTYN's Tulira Castle in August 1896. Night after night Yeats attempted an "invocation of the moon." Finally he saw a galloping centaur and a few moments later "a naked woman of incredible beauty, standing upon a pedestal and shooting an arrow at a star" (*Aut.* 280; see also *CL2* 48, 658–663; *Mem.* 100–101; *LE* 14–15). As he relates in *Autobiographies*, Yeats relentlessly investigated the vision's meaning and the meaning of what seemed to be related visions: The child of a fellow member of the HERMETIC ORDER OF THE GOLDEN DAWN had seen a vision of a woman shooting an arrow into the sky and had feared that the arrow had killed God, while ISEULT GONNE had dreamed of a man with a gun shooting down a star and had then seen "the star lying in a cradle" (280–281). Yeats conjectured that the visions indicated the death of a god "in some world where myth is reality" or pictured some memory dredged from the ancient memory of the race or merely constituted a fantastic dream shared among minds. He learned from William Wynn Westcott (1848–1925), one of the founders of the Isis-Urania Temple of the Golden Dawn, however, that the visions corresponded to the symbolism of the Christian Cabbala: the centaur represented the elemental spirit, the woman represented "the divine spirit" of "the path Samekh," and the star represented the "golden heart" that is the "central point upon the cabbalistic Tree of Life" (281). Yeats annotated the account of the vision of the archer in *Autobiographies* with a long and muddled note that touches on many of the specific allusions of "Parnell's Funeral" (see *Aut.* 484–488). The gist of the note is that the goddess shoots her arrow at an embodiment of the cycle of death and rebirth, variously associated with the child-god, the heart, and the star, all of which the poem in turn associates with Parnell.

"An age is the reversal of an age": a pithy summary of Yeats's most fundamental tenet about history and the cosmic pattern that manifests itself in history. The present age reverses the age of Georgian Ireland whose epitomizing figures are Robert Emmet (1778–1803), Lord Edward Fitzgerald (1763–98), and Wolfe Tone (1763–98), all of whom, like Parnell, sacrificed themselves for Ireland. In those days, Irishmen (for this is presumably the "we" of line 18) "lived like men that watch a painted stage," implying that the age was suffused by the theatrical element of the rich personality, but also that it was prone to the artificial and the vicarious. Whatever its flaws, however, the "romantic Ireland" of the 18th cen-

tury ("SEPTEMBER 1913") was at least capable of venerating its heroes. The present age, by contrast, turns on its own heroes with an atavistic blood lust. Not the theatrical impulse of romantic self-immolation, but "popular rage, / *Hysterica passio* dragged this quarry down." "Hysterica passio"—"hysterical passion"—is a borrowing from *King Lear* (II, iv, line 57). Yeats repeats the phrase in *Autobiographies* (361; see also *Mem.* 179), "A BRONZE HEAD," and "ROSA ALCHEMICA," and in an August 5, 1936, letter to DOROTHY WELLESLEY (*LOP* 86). The implicit metaphor of these lines is the stag brought down by hounds, as Yeats makes clear in *Autobiographies*: "During the quarrel over Parnell's grave a quotation from Goethe ran through the papers, describing our Irish jealousy: 'The Irish seem to me like a pack of hounds, always dragging down some noble stag.' But I do not think we object to distinction for its own sake; if we kill the stag, it is that we may carry off his head and antlers" (244; see also 357; *Mem.* 163; "To a Shade"). Enacting some modern version of the ancient rite, the people played no part upon "a painted stage"—that is, were genuinely consumed by their own primitive frenzy—as they devoured Parnell's heart. As Yeats writes of the Parnell controversy in his note on the poem, "We had passed through an initiation like that of the Tibetan ascetic, who staggers half dead from a trance, where he has seen himself eaten alive and has not yet learned that the eater was himself" (*VP* 835).

Yeats would take upon himself Parnell's victimhood, and he defiantly invites the denunciations of Parnell's accusers as a kind of blast that would strip away everything adventitious. Taunting the crowd into its old frenzy, Yeats insists that "All that was said in Ireland is a lie / Bred out of the contagion of the throng, / Saving the rhyme rats hear before they die." These lines refer to *As You Like It*, in which Rosalind exclaims, "I was never so berhym'd since Pythagoras' time, that I was an Irish rat, which I can hardly remember" (III, ii, lines 176–178). According to his exegetes, Shakespeare refers to the notion that Irish enchanters could by their rhymes induce death in animals. Yeats thus seems to exempt the words of the poet from the contagion of lies, and perhaps as well to disparage his accusers as rodents. Figuratively flayed alive, Yeats is left with "nothing but the nothings that belong / To this bare soul," and he issues a final defiant boast: "let all men judge that can / Whether it be an animal or a man." Richard Ellmann observes that Yeats again and again "tries to tear off the polite, superficial part of himself," and he equates these lines with the famous final lines of "The CIRCUS ANIMALS' DESERTION" (MM 274–275). The theme of divestiture is implicit also in poems like "A COAT," "The COMING OF WISDOM WITH TIME," and "RECONCILIATION."

Emmet, Fitzgerald, and Tone are paralleled in the second section's reference to Eamon de Valera (1882–1975), William Thomas Cosgrave (1880–1965), and Eoin O'Duffy (1892–1944), all three leading figures in the politics of post-independence Ireland, all three, in Yeats's estimation, lesser men than Parnell. De Valera was a leader of the anti-Treaty forces during the IRISH CIVIL WAR. He later served as president of the executive council of the Irish Free State (1932–37), as prime minister (1937–48, 1951–54, 1957–59), and as president of the Irish Republic (1959–73). Cosgrave, a leader of the pro-Treaty forces during the Irish Civil War, was president of the executive council of the Irish Free State from 1922 to 1932. O'Duffy led the Army Comrades Association—the so-called Blueshirts, a short-lived fascist political movement—during 1933 and 1934, and was briefly the first president of the Fine Gael party that absorbed the Blueshirts (see *Letters* 811–815, 881, 885; *W. B. Yeats & Georgian Ireland* 156–165). O'Higgins, whom Yeats revered as a member of the heroic succession that included Parnell, was one of Cosgrave's chief lieutenants. He was assassinated on July 10, 1927, an event that reverberates in "BLOOD AND THE MOON" and "Death" (see *Expl.* 442; *Letters* 726–727). The gist of the lines on Cosgrave and O'Higgins is, as Bernard Krimm puts it, "that O'Higgins would be alive if Cosgrave had not been such a poor leader. If Cosgrave could not have won the Republicans over, the lines claim, at least he should have had the qualities to hold their violence in check" (*Free State* 171). Echoing "The Leaders of the Crowd," Yeats concludes, referring to Parnell as against his successors, "Their school a crowd, his master solitude; / Through JONATHAN SWIFT's dark grove he passed, and there / Plucked bitter wisdom that enriched his blood." Swift's "bitter wisdom" may refer to the wisdom of his political philosophy (see *Expl.* 351–353; *VPl.* 942), but more likely it refers to the wisdom that "comes of beggary," in the phrase of "The SEVEN SAGES," the wisdom of the tragic understanding irrespective of political forms. That Parnell "plucked wisdom" from "Swift's dark grove" breaks with the motif of blood ritual and intimates garden and orchard and the civilizational order of the 18th century. Thus higher men conduct themselves; thus they enrich their blood, take from one another, without bloodshed, without frenzy.

FIRST PUBLICATION: The *Spectator* (periodical), October 19, 1934, the first section under the title "A Parnellite at Parnell's Funeral," the second section under the title "Forty Years Later." The first section reprinted in *The King of the Great Clock Tower, Commentaries and Poems*, The CUALA PRESS, Dublin, December 14, 1934, under the title "A Parnellite at Parnell's Funeral"; the second reprinted in *A Full Moon in March*, Macmillan and Co., November 22, 1935, under the present title.

BIBLIOGRAPHY

Connolly, S. J., ed., *The Oxford Companion to Irish History*; Ellmann, Richard. *Yeats: The Man and the Masks*; Foster, R. F. *Modern Ireland, 1600–1972*; Krimm, Bernard G. *W. B. Yeats and the Emergence of the Irish Free State, 1918–1939: Living in the Explosion*; Mikhail, E. H., ed. *W. B. Yeats: Interviews and Recollections* (vol. 1); Torchiana, Donald T. *W. B. Yeats & Georgian Ireland*; Yeats, W. B. *Autobiographies, The Collected Letters of W. B. Yeats* (vols. 1–2), *Explorations, Later Essays, The Letters of W. B. Yeats, Letters on Poetry from W. B. Yeats to Dorothy Wellesley, Memoirs, Uncollected Prose by W. B. Yeats* (vol. 2), *The Variorum Edition of the Plays of W. B. Yeats, The Variorum Edition of the Poems of W. B. Yeats*.

"Parting" (1929)

See "A WOMAN YOUNG AND OLD."

"Peace" (1910)

In "The FOLLY OF BEING COMFORTED," Yeats passionately denies Lady GREGORY's suggestion that his longing for MAUD GONNE will diminish with the passage of time, for time only renews her beauty. "Peace," published seven years later, redacts much or all of this. In a mood of mellow age, Yeats is willing to acknowledge that Gonne is not impervious to the passage of time, and possibly—the poem is not definite—that there is a degree of comfort in this decline, just as Lady Gregory had promised.

The poem begins with an ambiguous sigh: "Ah, that Time could touch a form / That could show what Homer's age / Bred to be a hero's wage." Richard Ellmann suggests that these lines merely acknowledge and lament the ravaging power of time (*IY* 112). Differently read, however, "could" implies the *wish* that impotent time were able to touch Gonne's impervious form, in keeping with the sentiment of "The Folly of Being Comforted." The allusion to Homer—and implicitly to Helen—brings the poem into relation with "A WOMAN HOMER SUNG" and "NO SECOND TROY," which appear earlier in *The Green Helmet and Other Poems* (1910). Ellmann comments, "The word 'wage' calls attention to a feature of Homeric culture which a poet like TENNYSON would have euphemized" (112). Just so, this diction reflects Yeats's process of growth, his movement toward a remorseless and sometimes brutal rhetoric later on full display in poems like "BYZANTIUM" and "NEWS FOR THE DELPHIC ORACLE."

There follows a six-line intermezzo in which Yeats, as if recalling his part in the earlier conversation with Lady Gregory, quotes himself in praise of Gonne's beauty. Even were her life less of a "storm"—Yeats's perennial wish—painters would be drawn to her "noble lines," her "delicate high head, / All that sternness amid charm, / All that sweetness amid strength." The conflation of sweetness and strength is similarly made in "A Woman Homer Sung" and in "Against Unworthy Praise" (1910). This conflation conceivably derives from Walter Pater's essay on Michelangelo in *The Renaissance* (1873): "And to the true admirers of Michelangelo this is the true type of the Michelangelesque—sweetness and strength, pleasure with surprise, an energy of conception which seems at every moment about to break through all the conditions of comely form, recovering, touch by touch, a loveliness found usually only in the simplest natural things—*ex forti dulcedo* [from the strong, sweetness]" (57).

The final two lines of the poem retract the assertion—central to "The Folly of Being Comforted" and arguably implied in the first line here—that Gonne is impervious to the debasement of time: "Ah, but peace that comes at length, / Came when Time had touched her form." The question is whether the "peace" that comes with the passage of time belongs to Yeats or to Gonne herself. The former interpretation dovetails with the reasoning of "The Folly of Being Comforted," while the latter interpretation is supported by the earlier characterization of Gonne's life as a "storm," and thus lends the final lines a resolving logic.

Yeats wrote the poem in May 1910 while staying at Les Mouettes, Gonne's home in Colleville-sur-Mer, on the coast of Normandy. Yeats's journal includes a draft of the poem, but otherwise suggests little in the way of "peace": "Yesterday afternoon [. . .] Maud Gonne and I got into the old argument about *Sinn Féin* and its attack on SYNGE, and the general circumstances that surrounded the first split in the Theatre [see GY 176–178, 240–241]. I notice that this old quarrel is the one difference about which she feels strongly. I for this very reason let myself get drawn into it again and again, thinking to convince her at last that apart from wrongs and rights impossible to settle so long after, it was fundamental. I could not have done otherwise. My whole movement, my integrity as a man of letters, were alike involved" (*Mem.* 247).

FIRST PUBLICATION: *The Green Helmet and Other Poems*, The CUALA PRESS, Churchtown, Dundrum, December 1910, under the sequence title "Raymond Lully and his wife Pernella" and the present title.

BIBLIOGRAPHY

Ellmann, Richard. *The Identity of Yeats*; Pater, Walter. *The Renaissance: Studies in Art and Poetry*; Yeats, W. B. *The Gonne-Yeats Letters 1893–1938*, *Memoirs*.

"Peacock, The" (1914)

See "The WITCH."

"People, The" (1916)

In both *The Wild Swans at Coole* (1917) and Yeats's collected poems, "The People" belongs to a cluster of poems that takes up the theme of MAUD GONNE's middle age (see also "BROKEN DREAMS," "A Deep-sworn Vow" [1917], "HER PRAISE," "His Phoenix" [1916], "Memory" [1916], "PRESENCES," "A THOUGHT FROM PROPERTIUS"). In its complaint against "the people," however, the poem shares a misanthropic mood with the many poems rooted in the controversies surrounding J. M. SYNGE and HUGH LANE (see, among other poems, "AT THE ABBEY THEATRE," "The FISHERMAN," "ON THOSE THAT HATED 'THE PLAYBOY OF THE WESTERN WORLD', 1907," "SEPTEMBER 1913," "TO A FRIEND WHOSE WORK HAS COME TO NOTHING," "TO A SHADE," "TO A WEALTHY MAN WHO PROMISED A SECOND SUBSCRIPTION TO THE DUBLIN MUNICIPAL GALLERY IF IT WERE PROVED THE PEOPLE WANTED PICTURES").

Written in January 1915, the poem ostensibly records a conversation of 1906 ("after nine years"), but the allusions to Ferrara and Urbino, which Yeats visited in April and May 1907 with Lady GREGORY and ROBERT GREGORY, require a slightly adjusted chronology. The poem's clear source is an exchange of letters between Gonne and Yeats while the latter was traveling in Italy. Yeats had criticized the people for siding with Gonne's estranged husband, Major John MacBride (1865–1916), following the couple's separation in late 1904 and the divorce proceedings that began in 1905 (*CL4* 654). Gonne responded that the people, who see "only bald facts, & judge from them," were not to blame for turning against her, and that their objections both to herself and to Yeats were a "healthy sign" of their nationalism. "You who believe in the super man why do you grow indignant with the crowd because they don't think as you do, because their virtue is not your virtue, you should not want them

to think as you do. It would be a misfortune if the crowd began worrying over subtleties for it would be an end of action. I have a great belief in our people & would not for worlds see them change their ideals which I think are wonderfully right as far as they go [. . .]." This defense of the people enters directly in the poem, as does Gonne's excoriation of "the frauds who I had exposed, the publicans & drunkards I had driven out"—phrasing that Yeats imports almost intact (*GY* 240–241). Yeats's reading in Plutarch may have reinforced his sympathy with Gonne's position. On October 4, 1907, Yeats wrote to T. STURGE MOORE that "nothing is ever persecuted but the intellect, and the one thing Plutarch thought one should never complain of is the people. They are what they are, and it is our work to live our lives in their despite" (*CL4* 742).

A 37-line poem in the conversational style Yeats had introduced in "ADAM'S CURSE," "The People" opens with the familiar complaint that the "unmannerly town"—Dublin—heaps spite and defamation on its benefactors. In opposition to the squalid modernity of Dublin, Yeats, as in "To a Wealthy Man," invokes the nobility of Renaissance Italy. Instancing all he had forfeited for the people, he reminds that he might have chosen his home amid the "unperturbed and courtly images" of Ferrara or Urbino and had none for friend that "could not mix / Courtesy and passion" as did the nobles of the Renaissance (cf. *CL3* 118; *CL4* 683). "The Duchess" of these lines is Elisabetta Gonzaga of Urbino (1471–1526), about whom Yeats had learned in Baldesar Castiglione's *The Book of the Courtier* (1528). Castiglione's book, which Lady Gregory read to Yeats in the summer of 1903, ends with the arrival of dawn precisely as the poem describes (*Yeats and Castiglione* 20).

Characterized as a Phoenix—inextinguishable, transcendent—Gonne replies to Yeats much as in her 1907 letter. She too has been assailed by the local rogues and cheats, who "crawled from obscurity" only after her luck had changed (an allusion to her marital problems) and set upon her those she had served and even fed, and yet she has never once complained of the people. Gonne here implies a distinction stated more overtly in her letter between "the people" and "the wretched creatures who exploit the National cause for their own ends & divert the energy of the people, from the direct object" (GY 241).

With Yeats's chastened reply, the poem assumes philosophical complexity and enters into relation with "The DAWN" and "The FISHERMAN," which precede it in *The Wild Swans at Coole.* In her letter Gonne asserts an antithesis between action and subtlety of thought. Reiterating this antithesis, Yeats recognizes in Gonne's embrace of the people the purity of the mind unencumbered by subtlety and self-reflection, while he, "whose virtues are the definitions / Of the analytic mind," can neither "close the eye of the mind" nor keep his "tongue from speech," can never come to rest in any permanent relation or fixed conviction (cf. *Mem.* 252–255; *Myth.* 77). Yeats here touches on the bane that would find definitive expression in "BYZANTIUM's" allusion to "bitter furies of complexity." Yeats's heart leaps at Gonne's words, but he cannot emulate the simplicity of her passion (nor that of the Dawn or of the Fisherman). He was abashed then, and nine years later he remains abashed, his maddening lot that of the thinker perpetually "caught in the cold snows of a dream," in the phrase of "The ROAD AT MY DOOR."

In her autobiography *A Servant of the Queen* (1938), Gonne explains the difference between Yeats and herself in much that same terms as "The People": "I never indulged in self-analysis and often used to get impatient with Willie Yeats, who, like all writers, was terribly introspective and tried to make me so. 'I have no time to think of myself,' I told him which was literally true, for, unconsciously perhaps, I had redoubled work to avoid thought" (287). And in a memorial essay, she notes Yeats's discomfort with "the people": "Yeats's aloofness and his intolerance of mediocrity, a spiritual pride which is dangerous, tended to keep him apart from the first person of the National Trinity, the People [the 'Land' and the 'Spirit of Life' being the other two]. He hated crowds, I loved them" (*Scattering Branches* 27).

In March 1915, Gonne thanked Yeats for the sentiment of the poem. "To me you are too kind," she wrote. "You have often tried to defend & protect me with your art—& perhaps when we are dead I shall be known by those poems of yours—" (GY 356–357).

FIRST PUBLICATION: *Poetry* (periodical), February 1916, under the title "The Phoenix." Reprinted in *Eight Poems,* "Form" at the Morland Press, London, April 1916 (see *Letters* 609–610). Reprinted in *The Wild Swans at Coole,* The CUALA PRESS, Churchtown, Dundrum, November 17, 1917, under the present title.

BIBLIOGRAPHY

Gonne, Maud. *The Autobiography of Maud Gonne: A Servant of the Queen*; Gwynn, Stephen, ed. *Scattering Branches: Tributes to the Memory of W. B. Yeats*; Salvadori, Corinna. *Yeats and Castiglione: Poet and Courtier*; Yeats, W. B. *The Collected Letters of W. B. Yeats* (vols. 3–4), *The Gonne-Yeats Letters 1893–1938, The Letters of W. B. Yeats, Memoirs, Mythologies.*

"Phases of the Moon, The" (1919)

Where "EGO DOMINUS TUUS" expounds the doctrine of the anti-self, its philosophical counterpart, "The Phases of the Moon," provides a systematic exposition of the 28-phase lunar cycle that is the governing paradigm of both personality and history. In conjunction, the two poems provide a précis of the theories that Yeats elaborates in PER AMICA SILENTIA LUNAE and A VISION: Just as "Ego Dominus Tuus" appears as an introduction to *Per Amica,* "The Phases of the Moon" appears as an introduction to the "Great Wheel" section of A VISION. In AUTOBIOGRAPHIES, Yeats encapsulates the theory of the poem: "The bright part of the moon's disk, to adopt the symbolism of a certain poem ["The Phases of the Moon"], is subjective mind, and the dark, objective mind, and we have eight-and-twenty Phases for our classification of mankind, and of the movement of its thought. At the first phase—the night where there is no moonlight—all is objective, while when, upon the fifteenth night, the moon comes to the full, there is only subjective mind" (228; see also *VPl.* 566).

The Lonely Tower (1879) by Samuel Palmer (1805–1881). "The Phases of the Moon" finds a symbol of visionary toil in "the lonely light that Samuel Palmer engraved." *(Yale Center for British Art, Paul Mellon Collection)*

Like "Ego Dominus Tuus," "The Phases of the Moon" is a philosophical dialogue. "Ille" and "Hic" are superseded by Michael Robartes and Owen Aherne, but the duality of the *antithetical* and the *primary*, the subjective and the objective, is maintained. During the 1890s, Yeats introduced Robartes and Aherne in the stories "The ADORATION OF THE MAGI," "ROSA ALCHEMICA," and "The TABLES OF THE LAW," and he deployed Robartes as one of the chief personae in the poems of *The Wind Among the Reeds* (1899), characterizing him as "the pride of the imagination brooding upon the greatness of its possessions" (VP 803). Some 20 years later he resurrected the pair as personae in the "phantasmagoria" by which he attempted to explain his "philosophy of life and death" (821; see also 821–825, 853). In this guise, they figure in "The DOUBLE VISION OF MICHAEL ROBARTES,"

"MICHAEL ROBARTES AND THE DANCER," "OWEN AHERNE AND HIS DANCERS," and *A Vision*. As the supposed author of the introduction to the 1925 edition of *A Vision*, Aherne comments on "The Phases of the Moon": "On a walking tour in Connaught we passed THOOR BALLYLEE where Mr Yeats had settled for the summer, and words were spoken between us slightly resembling those in 'The Phases of the Moon,' and I noticed that as [Robartes's] friendship with me grew closer his animosity against Mr Yeats revived" (*AV-1925* xxi).

"The Phases of the Moon" opens on the same setting as "Ego Dominus Tuus." There is Yeats's tower, the stream, and the "dwindling and late-risen moon," which, as Hazard Adams reminds, represents "the late phases of an era, during which the primary attitude dominates" (*Book of Yeats's Vision* 60). Robartes and Aherne come upon the scene, dressed in "Connemara cloth" (cf. "The FISHERMAN"). Grown old and intimate, they are reminiscent of the fool and the blind man in ON BAILE'S STRAND and the lame beggar and the blind beggar in The CAT AND THE MOON: reverse types symbolic of the interlocked gyres that govern reality. A light from the tower shows Yeats deep in his studies. The sight elicits Robartes's scorn: Yeats has found "mere images" (that which Ille seeks), naively and perhaps even absurdly inspired by Milton's "Il Penseroso" (1645) and SHELLEY's "Prince Athanase" (1817), and by Samuel Palmer's (1805–81) engraving "The Lonely Tower," which illustrates "Il Penseroso." Yeats now "seeks in book or manuscript / What he shall never find" (in "Ego Dominus Tuus," ironically, Ille studies from a book "that Michael Robartes left"). The change in verb tense (intensified by "now") suggests that Yeats attempts to discover something beyond "mere images." Robartes's comments are obscure, but they conceivably depend on a distinction between the poetic or magical image (as Yeats explains in his essay "MAGIC," the two are the same) and an achieved philosophy of the kind A Vision purports to be, a distinction between glancing and systematic revelation. Robartes possesses this achieved philosophy, but he refuses to enlighten Yeats, miffed that Yeats wrote of him "in that extravagant style / He had learnt from Pater" and reported him to be dead. Robartes refers to "Rosa Alchemica," which ends with the sacking of Robartes's occult temple, and to "The Adoration of the Magi," which confirms that Robartes has died.

Aherne, however, begs Robartes to sing "the changes of the moon once more." There follows, with occasional childlike prompting from Aherne, a complete exposition of the moon's 28 phases, each of which is associated with a phase in the cycle of human personality. Robartes begins by telling of the passage from "the first crescent to the half" (Phases 2–8), in which "the dream / But summons to adventure and the man / Is always happy like a bird or a beast. . . ." These phases are colored by a simplicity not yet awakened to the tribulation of seeing through the "dream," not yet cognizant that adventure must be purchased with innocence. The passage "towards the full"—Phases 9–14—

entails the awakening into experience. Beauty and heroism are born, but at the cost of natural contentment. In its new self-consciousness, the mind lacerates the body as with a "cat-o'-nine tails." These are the phases of Achilles and Nietzsche, in which heroism is most overweening and precarious, barely able to control its own intensities: Athena must grab "Achilles by the hair" to keep him from slaying Agamemnon (Iliad, I, 197). In the 13th phase—the phrase of AUBREY BEARDS-LEY, Charles Baudelaire, and Ernest Dowson—the heroic impulse turns inward, and the soul begins to war with itself, while in the "frenzy of the fourteenth moon"—the phase of Giorgione, Keats, and "many beautiful women"—"the soul begins to tremble into stillness, / To die into the labyrinth of itself!" (AV 129–134). In A Vision, Yeats elaborates on the character of this phase: "Thought is disappearing into image; and in Keats, in some ways a perfect type, intellectual curiosity is at its weakest; there is scarcely an image, where his poetry is at its best, whose subjectivity has not been heightened by its use in many great poets, painters, sculptors, artificers. The being has almost reached the end of that elaboration of itself which has for its climax an absorption in time, where space can be but symbols or images in the mind" (134).

The 15th phase represents the full moon: the state of perfect subjectivity and complete beauty to which human life cannot attain (see 135–137). Of this mystical apotheosis "beyond the visible world," Robartes reports, "All thought becomes an image and the soul / Becomes a body. . . ." In this phase body and soul are too perfect to "lie in a cradle"—to suffer participation in the cycle of reincarnation—and too lonely "for the traffic of the world." Robartes and Aherne mull the mysterious dynamic of the 15th phase. Aherne says, "The song will have it"—the "song" that constitutes "The Phases of the Moon"—"That those that we have loved got their long fingers / From death, and wounds, or on Sinai's top, / Or from some bloody whip in their own hands." Long fingers seem to symbolize the beautiful body (cf. "BRO-KEN DREAMS," in which Yeats writes that MAUD GONNE's "small hands were not beautiful"). The suggestion of these lines is that bodily perfection comes only from some terrible trial of the soul or test of the self. Yeats's magnificent prologue to *The ONLY JEALOUSY OF EMER* inscribes a closely related conception: "What pursuing or fleeing, / What wounds, what bloody press, / Dragged into being / This loveliness?" (*VPl.* 531; *VP* 785). Also relevant is a note on *The Only Jealousy of Emer*: "Much that Robartes has written [*A Vision* is putatively derived from Robartes's papers] might be a commentary on Castiglione's saying that the physical beauty of woman is the spoil or monument of the victory of the soul, for physical beauty, only possible to subjective natures, is described as the result of emotional toil in past lives" (*VPl.* 566). Robartes's response to Aherne is telling: "The lover's heart knows that." Says Hazard Adams, "Robartes' answer suggests that Robartes does not consider that in any way his song conveys abstract or occult knowledge unless man has so alienated himself from his feelings that he cannot think with them" (*Book of Yeats's Vision* 63). The beautiful bodied run "from cradle to cradle"—pass through either the cycles of their own reincarnation or the cycles of the moon—until they entirely transcend "the loneliness of body and soul," the desolation of antinomy. The terror in their eyes, as Aherne says, signifies "memory or foreknowledge of the hour / When all is fed with light and heaven is bare" (cf. "The COLD HEAVEN"). Robartes adds that these "creatures of the full" wander the hills when the moon is full, frightening the country people. They are ghostly incarnations of their own inwardness. Aherne laughs at the thought of Yeats within the tower with "his sleepless candle and laborious pen," as if such a weird and beautiful transcendence could be achieved or understood by mere scholarship and rumination.

Robartes then speaks of the phases of the moon's wane, phases in which the soul "would be the world's servant" and takes "Upon the body and upon the soul / The coarseness of the drudge." At Phase 16, the "soul remembering its loneliness / Shudders in many cradles," while at Phases 17–22 the soul takes the form of "Reformer, merchant, statesman, learned man, / Dutiful husband, honest wife by turn," all deformed rather than beauti-

ful "because there is no deformity / But saves us from a dream." At Aherne's impatient prompting, Robartes skips to the description of Phase 1, in which souls are cast "beyond the verge" into darkness and cry to each other like bats, incarnations of pure body just as those of Phase 15 are incarnations of pure soul, without form or desire, though, as Aherne would have it, "set free." Aherne demands to hear of the "escape" that eventuates in the putative freedom of Phase 1. In the most cryptic lines in a cryptic poem, Robartes alludes to the last three phases, those of Hunchback (26), Saint (27), and Fool (28), and then seems to elaborate on the phase of the saint. "The up and down" suggests the interchange of Yeats's historical gyres, while "the wagon-wheel / Of beauty's cruelty and wisdom's chatter" suggests the lunar wheel itself: "beauty's cruelty" plausibly intimates the *antithetical* tincture, "wisdom's chatter" the *primary* (see *VPl.* 805). The linear path of the arrow in opposition to the cycles of history and personality marks this as in some sense the phase of escape or transcendence. In *Per Amica* Yeats offers a clarifying variation on this imagery of escape: "Only when we are saint or sage, and renounce Experience itself, can we, in imagery of the Christian Cabbala, leave the sudden lightning and the path of the serpent and become the bowman who aims his arrow at the centre of the sun" (*LE* 14–15). Adams comments, "It is clear that the phase of the saint is being described, but is there escape from the wheel? The bow is described as *once* being able to shoot an arrow out of the cyclic condition, but it is by no means clear that the archer escapes, only perhaps his thought" (*Book of Yeats's Vision* 64). The stipulation "once" may have to do with the historical decline that is one of Yeats's cardinal convictions: our scientific and mechanical age, though belonging to a *primary* era, begets the saint no more than the poet or the hero. Thomas Whitaker proposes, on the other hand, that "once" is self-referential: having become a poet, Yeats, "for the sake of his art," must remain bound to the cycles of experience (*Swan and Shadow* 68–69). This seems to assume that Yeats recognized in himself a potential saintliness that had to be repressed or denied. Yeats more likely agreed with his wife, who said upon GEORGE RUSSELL's death, "AE was the nearest to a saint you or I will ever meet. You are a better poet but no saint" (*Letters* 838).

The poem ends with Aherne mischievously proposing to ring the bell and mutter the lunar philosophy until Yeats should catch the phrase "Hunchback and Saint and Fool," which are words to "crack his wits" in the futile search for meaning. John Unterecker conceives this prospective encounter as the fulfillment of Ille's (that is, Yeats's) quest for his anti-self in "Ego Dominus Tuus." He ingeniously comments that Ille's "antics on the sand have, after all, succeeded in luring beneath the tower his anti-self Aherne, who, all unknowingly, revealed the secrets he delighted to think he had so successfully kept" (*RG* 153). In the end, his bed calling, Aherne laughs "to think that what seemed hard / Should be so simple," while a solitary bat circles overhead, emitting a "squeaky cry" that echoes Aherne's laughter. The slippage from man to bat recalls an earlier line—"They change their bodies at a word"—while the bat's cry echoes the batlike cries of the souls whom "the last servile crescent has set free," those who belong to Phase 1. The poem thus ends in the darkness with which the lunar cycle begins, all come full circle. Yeats, meanwhile, extinguishes his lamp in the tower overhead, signifying that his work is complete, or that it cannot be completed, or that he too must take to the bed that is the cradle of a new cycle.

FIRST PUBLICATION: *The Wild Swans at Coole*, Macmillan, London, New York, March 11, 1919.

BIBLIOGRAPHY

Adams, Hazard. *The Book of Yeats's Vision: Romantic Modernism and Antithetical Tradition*; Unterecker, John. *A Reader's Guide to William Butler Yeats*; Whitaker, Thomas R. *Swan and Shadow: Yeats's Dialogue with History*; Yeats, W. B. *Autobiographies, A Critical Edition of Yeats's A Vision (1925), Later Essays, The Letters of W. B. Yeats, The Variorum Edition of the Plays of W. B. Yeats, The Variorum Edition of the Poems of W. B. Yeats, A Vision*.

"Players ask for a Blessing on the Psalteries and on Themselves, The" (1903)

Desiring to reverse the divorce between poetry and the spoken word, Yeats and FLORENCE FARR asked the French-born musicologist Arnold Dolmetsch (1858–1940) to build them a "psaltery," a stringed instrument resembling a lyre. A final version of the instrument was complete by October 1901 (*CL3* 91). Yeats's essay on the psaltery experiments, "SPEAKING TO THE PSALTERY," ends with a vision of a "new art" of spoken poetry and imagines a future generation of troubadours who will "go here and there speaking their verses and their little stories wherever they can find a score or two of poetical-minded people in a big room, or a couple of poetical-minded friends sitting by the hearth, and poets will write them poems and little stories to the confounding of print and paper" (*E&I* 18–19). "The Players ask for a Blessing on the Psalteries and on Themselves" dramatizes this vision.

The poem's chief difficulty is determining whom the players address. In a June 3, 1902, letter to Dolmetsch, Yeats mentioned that he was writing a "Prayer to the Seven Archangels to bless the Seven Notes" and added that the prayer "is to be spoken first by two voices and then by one voice, then the other voice, & then two voices again" (*CL3* 195). This was a version of the poem that eventually became "The Players ask for a Blessing on the Psalteries and on Themselves," though it was apparently very different in its details. The poet and playwright Katharine Harris Bradley (1846–1914)—better known as "Michael Field," the pseudonym that she shared with her collaborator Edith Cooper—heard Yeats read a draft of the poem in June 1902 and recalls the archangels appearing in "shoes of the seven metals" (195). As it seems, then, the "masters of the glittering town" are the seven archangels and the "glittering town" is the heavenly city.

A choral exchange in three voices, the poem begins with the players asking in unison for a blessing on their hands, mouths, notes, and strings from the "masters of the glittering town." The players implore the masters to lay down the "shrilly trumpet," though "drunken with the flags that sway, / Over the ramparts and the towers, / And with the waving of your wings," which is to say, drunken with their own glory. The players' allusion to the "shrilly trumpet" suggests an opposition between their own art and the characteristic voice of both world and heavens—the one wavering, subtle, interior; the other blunt, clamorous, assertive. The players' rejection of the "shrilly trumpet" comports with "Speaking to the Psaltery," which describes art as a "monotony in external things for the sake of an interior variety, a sacrifice of gross effects to subtle effects, an asceticism of the imagination" (E&I 18). The players' allusion to the masters of the town waving their wings functions as an imagistic echo of the "flags that sway." These are images of the same vain fluttering, a kind of external ostentation that stands against the essential spirit of art (cf. the swaying leaves and flowers in "The COMING OF WISDOM WITH TIME").

The masters of the town, evidently, are not forthcoming with their blessing. The first player speculates that they "linger by the way," and he either sees or imagines one lingering by a wall, muttering to himself in dread of the "weight of mortal hours." "Leans" and "mutters" present an almost urban silhouette, vaguely and strangely aligning the wall with the "waste wall" Yeats would broach much later as an image of soulless modernity (see *Expl.* 377), while the anxious hesitation of the figure contrasts with the "proud and careless notes" of the musicians. He dreads the "weight of mortal hours" in the sense, perhaps, that he dreads descent into the human sphere. The second player offers a differing account, seeing or imagining that they hurry down "like plovers," a simile that seals the implication of fluttering vanity and lends a final point to the poem's critique.

The third voice calls to the "kinsmen of the Three in One"—seemingly the masters of the town as disciples of the Christian Trinity—to bless the hands that waken notes that "shall live on / When all this heavy history's done. . . ." However, the homely and fraternal epithet "kinsmen" jars with the prior description of the angels as "masters."

Plausibly, the players refer to themselves, with the suggestion that the artist, in the end, requires no blessing beyond his own. On this reading, "Three in One" might refer to the indissolubility of the musicians in the moment of their art or in the harmony of their music. More definitely, the players avow that the least scrap of true song endures no less than ramparts and towers. In its final lines, the poem subtly modulates: the exultant call for a blessing on "the hands that play" becomes an angst-ridden call for a blessing on the hands that "ebb away." The cry "our hands, our hands" is the mechanism of this angst, the repetition signaling an anguish that must become a cry. Thus the poem ends with the recognition that even the immortality of art fails to assuage the wound of the mortal artist, a dilemma that obsessed Yeats.

FIRST PUBLICATION: *In the Seven Woods: Being Poems Chiefly of the Irish Heroic Age*, The DUN EMER PRESS, Dundrum, August 1903.

BIBLIOGRAPHY

Yeats, W. B. *The Collected Letters of W. B. Yeats* (vol. 3), *Essays and Introductions, Explorations.*

"Politics" (1939)

Written in an era of rancorous ideology and looming war, Yeats's warmly human and well-loved poem throws over the political sphere as if it weighed nothing in the scale by which we measure the meaning and beauty of life, a theme he had previously mooted in "A MODEL FOR THE LAUREATE" and indeed had aired throughout his life despite his own sometimes active political involvements. In this regard, the poem can be read as an epilogue to the major political poem of Yeats's career, the skeptical and conflicted "EASTER 1916," and as an elaboration of the acute comment on the political mindset in "J. M. Synge and the Ireland of his Time" (1911): "Even if what one defends be true, an attitude of defence, a continual apology, whatever the cause, makes the mind barren because it kills intellectual innocence; that delight in what is unforeseen, and in the mere spectacle of the world, the mere drifting hither and thither that must come before all true thought and emotion" (*E&I* 314). This critique of the political mindset likewise informs "IN MEMORY OF EVA GORE-BOOTH AND CON MARKIEWICZ," "ON A POLITICAL PRISONER," and "A PRAYER FOR MY DAUGHTER," though the latter refers only generally to the curse of "intellectual hatred."

Yeats sent a draft of "Politics" to DOROTHY WELLESLEY on May 24, 1938, with this account: "There has been an article upon my work in the *Yale Review,* which is the only article on the subject which has not bored me for years. It commends me above other modern poets because my language is 'public'. [. . .] It goes on to say that, owing to my age and my relation to Ireland, I was unable to use this 'public' language on what it evidently considered the right public material, politics. The enclosed little poem is my reply. It is not a real incident, but a moment of meditation." In a postscript, Yeats adds, "In part my poem is a comment on——'s panic-stricken conversation" (redacted by Wellesley), and then cryptically, "No artesian well of the intellect can find the poetic theme" (*Letters* 908–909; *LOP* 163–165). Joseph Hone attributes the "panic-stricken conversation" to a guest whom Yeats had met while staying at Wellesley's Sussex house, Penns in the Rocks (*W. B. Yeats* 472).

The article that Yeats mentions is "Public Speech and Private Speech in Poetry" by the American poet Archibald MacLeish (1892–1982). The article, which appeared in the March 1938 number of the *Yale Review,* includes the quotation from Thomas Mann (1875–1955)—"In our time the destiny of man presents its meanings in political terms"—that serves as the poem's epigraph (*The Poems* 683). Mann's comment encapsulates the political preoccupation of the era, a preoccupation that Yeats considered an affront to the soul's autonomy, privacy, and mystery. Having been disappointed in his flirtation with the fascist Blueshirts, Yeats spurned this political preoccupation as well as the fanaticism that seemed to follow from it. In an April 8, 1936, letter to Ethel Mannin (1900–84), Yeats vilifies the entire murderous scene: "[As] my sense of reality deepens, and I think it does with age, my horror at the cruelty of governments grows greater [. . .]. Communist, Fascist, nationalist, clerical, anti-cleri-

cal, all are responsible according to the number of their victims. I have not been silent; I have used the only vehicle I possess—verse. If you have my poems by you, look up a poem called *The* SECOND COMING" (*Letters* 851).

By Yeats's instruction, "Politics" appeared as the final poem in *Last Poems and Two Plays* (1939), and it appears as the final poem in the standard edition of his collected poems (see *Yeats: Last Poems* 93–97). It brings the vast symphony of his poetic career to a close on a note of charming humanity and humility and with a final expression of the unfulfilled romantic desire that was for Yeats, in the language of "A DIALOGUE OF SELF AND SOUL," the "most fecund ditch of all."

FIRST PUBLICATION: The *Atlantic Monthly* and the *London Mercury* (periodicals) January 1939. Reprinted in *Last Poems and Two Plays,* The CUALA PRESS, Dublin, July 10, 1939.

BIBLIOGRAPHY

Hone, Joseph. *W. B. Yeats*; Stallworthy, John, ed. *Yeats: Last Poems*; Yeats, W. B. *Essays and Introductions, The Letters of W. B. Yeats, Letters on Poetry from W. B. Yeats to Dorothy Wellesley, The Poems.*

"Prayer for my Daughter, A" (1919, dated June 1919)

Yeats's daughter, Anne Butler Yeats, was born on February 26, 1919. By April Yeats had begun "A Prayer for my Daughter," a poem that has less to do with Anne Yeats in any specific sense than with Yeats's theories of femininity (cf. "IN MEMORY OF EVA GORE-BOOTH AND CON MARKIEWICZ" and "MICHAEL ROBARTES AND THE DANCER") and with his unresolved regret concerning MAUD GONNE. "A Prayer for My Daughter" employs the same stanza as "IN MEMORY OF MAJOR ROBERT GREGORY," a borrowing from Abraham Cowley's "On the Death of Mr. William Hervey" (1642), as Frank Kermode notes (*Romantic Image* 47; see also *Colder Eye* 233). The shared stanza underscores the poems' complementary attempts to envision masculine and feminine virtue brought to perfection.

"A Prayer for my Daughter" finds Yeats pacing in gloom and perturbation and prayer as the "haystack- and roof-levelling wind" pounds THOOR BALLYLEE. The wind tokens the modern apocalypse, as if the violent *antithetical* annunciation he envisions in the immediately preceding poem, "The SECOND COMING," had arrived. Yvor Winters writes with reference to "The Second Coming" that we "must face the fact that Yeats's attitude toward the beast is different from ours: we may find the beast terrifying, but Yeats finds him satisfying—he is Yeats's judgment upon all that we regard as civilized. Yeats approves of this kind of brutality" (*Poetry of W. B. Yeats* 10). The birth of his daughter, however, seems to have complicated Yeats's approval: his "excited reverie" is checked by a tender parental anxiety. Far from yearning for destruction, Yeats envisions custom and ceremony as a shield against it—as a means of checking and sublimating the frenzy of the wind (the "murderous innocence of the sea" is reborn as "innocence and beauty"), much as, in "ANCESTRAL HOUSES," the graceful Georgian estate sublimates the bitterness and violence of those who rear in stone.

In "Michael Robartes and the Dancer," Yeats writes that "all beautiful women may / Live in uncomposite blessedness / And lead us to the like—if they / Will banish every thought. . . ." Yeats's interest remains the condition of "uncomposite blessedness," but in "A Prayer for my Daughter" unreflecting beauty is less the mechanism than an even-tempered graciousness, a change in emphasis perhaps explained by the lessening influence of ISEULT GONNE and the deepening influence of GEORGE YEATS ("For how should I forget the wisdom that you brought, / The comfort that you made?" Yeats asks in "UNDER SATURN"). In the third and fourth stanzas, indeed, Yeats specifically warns against the kind of beauty that breeds obsession and stunts the impulses of "natural kindness" and "heart-revealing intimacy." Yeats cites the examples of Aphrodite and Helen, legendary beauties who were ill-fated or mismatched in love (Aphrodite's husband was the "bandy-leggèd smith" Hephaestus). Aphrodite's emergence from the sea brings her into metaphorical relation with the wind "bred on the Atlantic": both represent anarchic, destructive force, a "murderous inno-cence" ("innocence" in this case indicating the primal, the pure). Helen's implication in the violence of the sea hardly needs explanation: born of rape, she spawned the Trojan War (see "LEDA AND THE SWAN"). Inevitably Yeats has in mind Maud Gonne, whom he had so often figured as the second incarnation of Helen (see "NO SECOND TROY," "PEACE," "A WOMAN HOMER SUNG") and who likewise "had much trouble from a fool"—her estranged husband, John MacBride (1865–1916), a "drunken vainglorious lout," in the description of "EASTER 1916." Yeats's decades-long involvement with the Gonne women had taught him that such beauty tends to undo the "Horn of Plenty," an allusion to the nectar- and ambrosia-flowing cornucopia that Zeus received from Amalthea, the goat that had suckled him (*NCP* 206), but more generally a symbol of life's plenty, the kind of contentment that comes to those who live within the parameters of "the natural."

Reversing the dynamic of world-addling beauty, Yeats would have his daughter schooled in heart-winning courtesy. Thus learned she may become "a flourishing hidden tree," her thoughts like linnets "dispensing round / Their magnanimities of sound," her every activity undertaken in a spirit of merriment. "O may she live like some green laurel," Yeats cries, "Rooted in one dear perpetual place." The symbol of the tree finds its definitive expression here as well as in "AMONG SCHOOL CHILDREN," but Yeats had long recognized the tree as an image of sheltering beauty, rooted beneficence, and organic unity. In "THE TWO TREES," Yeats enjoins the young Gonne to gaze within her own heart, for the "holy tree is growing there; / From joy the holy branches start, / And all the trembling flowers they bear." Yeats's emphasis on the rootedness of the tree reflects his own sense of dislocation, the pained remembrance of his "child's vow sworn in vain / Never to leave that valley his fathers called their home" ("Under Saturn"). He hoped to correct this sense of dislocation by founding his family and his home upon the immovable monument of Thoor Ballylee. As he told John Masefield (1878–1967) in a May 1930 letter, "I have always wanted to live always in one place and have never managed it yet" (*AP* 400).

Having witnessed Gonne fall from youthful love-liness into middle-aged rancor—having witnessed her barter the Horn of Plenty and "every good / By quiet natures understood / For an old bellows full of angry wind"—Yeats above all else warns against "intellectual hatred" and the curse of "opinions" (for Gonne's "hatred" in full fury, see GY 167). In hope of reclaiming Gonne from the narrowness of her own purpose, he had made much the same plea in "Easter 1916" and in the essay "J. M. Synge and the Ireland of his Time" (1911). In the latter, Yeats contrasts "the morbid persistence of minds unset-tled by some fixed idea" with "intellectual inno-cence; that delight in what is unforeseen, and in the mere spectacle of the world, the mere drifting hither and thither that must come before all true thought and emotion" (E&I 313–314). In a Sep-tember 29, 1927, letter, Yeats told Gonne, "Today I have one settled conviction 'Create, draw a firm strong line & hate nothing whatever not even if he be your most cherished belief—Satan himself'. I hate many things but I do my best, & once some fifteen years ago, for I think one whole hour, I was free from hate. Like Faust I said 'stay moment' but in vain. I think it was the only happiness I have ever known" (GY 434).

Like the essay on Synge, "A Prayer for my Daughter" upholds innocence as the antidote to the barrenness of opinion: "all hatred driven hence, / The soul recovers radical innocence. . . ." ("radi-cal," from the Latin for "root," is obviously a word chosen carefully; Yeats differently conceives the recovery of "radical innocence" in "The COMING OF WISDOM WITH TIME"). Thus purified of hatred, the soul learns at last "that its own sweet will is Heav-en's will," and it becomes immune to the leveling wind (no longer the howling Atlantic gale, but the bellows of public opinion). The poem ends on its most beautiful note. Yeats wishes for his daughter a married home where all is "accustomed, ceremo-nious," and asks, in what can be considered the most succinct and yet encompassing statement of his own political and cultural conservatism, "How but in custom and in ceremony / Are innocence and beauty born? / Ceremony's a name for the rich horn, / And custom for the spreading laurel tree." Yeats, of course, had recently been a bridegroom,

but these lines can only be read as a final statement of the marriage portion he had promised Gonne, a final assay in an argument he had already lost.

FIRST PUBLICATION: *Poetry* (periodical), November 1919, and the *Irish Statesman* (peri-odical), November 8, 1919. Reprinted in *Michael Robartes and the Dancer*, The CUALA PRESS, Church-town, Dundrum, February 1921.

BIBLIOGRAPHY

Foster, R. F. *W. B. Yeats: A Life, II: The Arch-Poet*; Jeffares, A. Norman. *A New Commentary on the Poems of W. B. Yeats*; Kenner, Hugh. *A Colder Eye: The Modern Irish Writers*; Kermode, Frank. *Roman-tic Image*; Winters, Yvor. *The Poetry of W. B. Yeats*; Yeats, W. B. *Essays and Introductions, The Gonne-Yeats Letters 1893–1938*.

"Prayer for Old Age, A" (1934)

In the 1920s and even more in the 1930s, Yeats sloughed off the despondency of his middle years (cf. "LINES WRITTEN IN DEJECTION," "The LIVING BEAUTY," "MEN IMPROVE WITH THE YEARS," "The WILD SWANS AT COOLE") and mounted a vigorous campaign against the loss of emotional and intel-lectual intensity that he believed a part of old age. The stubborn refusal to go quietly into the dark explains his decision to undergo, on April 5, 1934, at the hands of Dr. Norman Haire, the so-called Steinach operation (see *Letters* 822). The opera-tion was merely a vasectomy, but it was believed to be both sexually and generally rejuvenating, and Yeats, whether for reasons physiological or psycho-logical, unquestionably found it so (AP 496–500). Yeats's geriatric unruliness became a pervasive theme of the 1930s in poems like "An ACRE OF GRASS," "The SPUR," "WHY SHOULD NOT OLD MEN BE MAD?," and "The Wild Old Wicked Man" (1938), and paraded itself in the sexual explicitness of "A MAN YOUNG AND OLD," "A WOMAN YOUNG AND OLD," "WORDS FOR MUSIC PERHAPS," and the sequence that begins with "The Lady's First Song" (see "The THREE BUSHES").

Published in November 1934, "A Prayer for Old Age" is characteristic of this late phase. Rejecting the transcendentalism of "SAILING TO BYZANTIUM," Yeats, in the spirit of "A DIALOGUE OF SELF AND SOUL" and "VACILLATION," affirms his commitment to the vitality of the body and the fullness of experience. Yeats begs God to preserve him from "those thoughts men think / In the mind alone," for "He that sings a lasting song / Thinks in a morrow-bone. . . ." This reiterates Yeats's recurrent denunciations of abstraction. In "Certain Noble Plays of Japan" (1916), he writes, for example, "We only believe in those thoughts which have been conceived not in the brain but in the whole body" (E&I 235). In AUTOBIOGRAPHIES, he commends in similar terms Bernardo Strozzi's (1581–1644) Portrait of a Venetian Gentleman, which he had seen in the National Gallery in Dublin: "Whatever thought broods in the dark eyes of that Venetian gentleman has drawn its life from his whole body; it feeds upon it as the flame feeds upon the candle—and should that thought be changed, his pose would change, his very cloak would rustle, for his whole body thinks" (227). The "marrow-bone" is the deepest strata of the body, beyond the sway of brain and heart, the bodily equivalent of the "soil" that Yeats extols in "The MUNICIPAL GALLERY REVISITED." It represents the body's attunement to itself and the repudiation of all abstraction and self-consciousness. In the poem's second and third stanzas, Yeats renounces both wisdom and praise, seeking instead the wanton energy—"life's own self-delight," in the phrase of "ANCESTRAL HOUSES"—that is the scandal of both intellect and society. Yeats would "seem," though he dies old, a "foolish, passionate man." John Unterecker notes the significance of the stipulation "seem": even as he strips away everything inconsistent with his own passionate simplicity, he constructs the inevitable mask (RG 245).

FIRST PUBLICATION: The Spectator (periodical), November 2, 1934, under the title "Old Age." Reprinted in the preface to The King of the Great Clock Tower, Commentaries and Poems, The CUALA PRESS, Dublin, December 14, 1934, without title. Reprinted in A Full Moon in March, Macmillan, November 22, 1935, under the present title.

BIBLIOGRAPHY

Foster, R. F. W. B. Yeats: A Life, II: The Arch-Poet; Unterecker, John. A Reader's Guide to William Butler Yeats; Yeats, W. B. Autobiographies, Essays and Introductions, The Letters of W. B. Yeats.

"Prayer on going into my House, A" (1918)

The "house" is Yeats's tower, THOOR BALLYLEE, which he purchased in June 1917. Yeats wrote the poem in April 1918, though he and his bride (see GEORGE YEATS) did not move into the adjoining cottage at Ballylee until September 1918 (YC 200). The 16-line poem condenses an entire philosophy of domesticity: the doctrine of the "house beautiful" learned at the feet of WILLIAM MORRIS and OSCAR WILDE as colored by the example of COOLE PARK and by Yeats's own aesthetic astringency.

Yeats asks God to bless the house on the condition that "all remain unspoiled." This surprising and perhaps off-putting conditionality is reiterated in "MY DESCENDANTS," in which Yeats calls for ruin upon the house should his descendants suffer "declension of the soul." By "unspoiled," Yeats means that the house should contain no furniture "not simple enough / For shepherd lads in Galilee," and that one should "handle nothing and set eyes on nothing / But what the great and passionate have used / Throughout so many varying centuries / We take it for the norm. . . ." (The conception of the house as a space of ordered tradition is definitively aired in the final stanza of "A PRAYER FOR MY DAUGHTER," in which Yeats expresses the hope that his daughter Anne will one day marry into a house where "all's accustomed, ceremonious"). Seemingly anxious that his prescriptions might impinge on the freedom and sovereignty of the imagination, Yeats issues a caveat that introduces a contrapuntal romanticism: should he dream that "Sinbad the sailor's brought a painted chest, / Or image, from beyond the Loadstone Mountain, / That dream is a norm. . . ." The allusion is to the tales of the Arabian Nights, which Yeats knew in both a child's edition of 1871 and in the four-volume edition of 1923 "rendered" and "collated" by Powys Mathers (*Descriptive Catalog* 40, 96; see also *Lonely Tower* 263–264). Yeats in effect declares the imagination's prerogative to legislate its own reality, as it were to deck the house with the stuff of dreams. "A Prayer on going into my House" thus rigorously and unapologetically balances the dual guises of conservative and romantic.

The poem ends in a lather of self-incitement, foretelling the "old man's frenzy" ("An ACRE OF GRASS") that would increasingly characterize Yeats's poetic persona. Should some "limb of the Devil" destroy the view by cutting down an ash or building a cottage "planned in a government office," Yeats calls upon God not only to "shorten his life," but also to "manacle his soul upon the Red Sea bottom." Yeats's gibe at government bureaucracy reiterates the conservative asperity of "An APPOINTMENT," while his curse concerning the Red Sea bottom is repeated in his "Letter to Michael's Schoolmaster" (*Expl.* 321). In the latter, Yeats sets out a provocatively reactionary program for his son's education ("Don't teach him one word of science, he can get all he wants in the newspapers and in any case it is no job for a gentleman") and consigns the teacher's soul to "the Red Sea bottom" if his strictures are not observed.

FIRST PUBLICATION: The *Little Review* (periodical), October 1918, and *Nine Poems*, privately printed by Clement Shorter, London, October 1918. Reprinted in *The Wild Swans at Coole*, Macmillan, London, New York, March 11, 1919.

BIBLIOGRAPHY

Henn, T. R. *The Lonely Tower: Studies in the Poetry of W. B. Yeats*; Kelly, John S. *A W. B. Yeats Chronology*; O'Shea, Edward. *A Descriptive Catalog of W. B. Yeats's Library*; Yeats, W. B. *Explorations*.

"Presences" (1917)

Associable with "FRIENDS" in its organizing allusion to three women, and to both "ALL SOULS' NIGHT"

and "An IMAGE FROM A PAST LIFE" in its theme of ghostly visitants, "Presences" flirts with the gothic tradition of the femme fatale or succubus before resolving in familiar homage to MAUD GONNE.

As in "All Souls' Night," the evening is alive with strange electricity. Since nightfall Yeats had dreamed of women climbing up his "creaking stair," laughing and rustling in their silks and lace. They had read all that he "had rhymed of that monstrous thing / Returned and yet unrequited love," and are perhaps the ghosts or the reified memories of past loves; or perhaps they are emanations of the unsettled conscience, manifestations of the "night's remorse" of which Yeats speaks in "The CHOICE." The phrase "that monstrous thing returned" has the propensity to slip in its meaning. Picking up on the slight sexual suggestion of "lace or silken stuff," it momentarily attaches itself to the women and lends them the faint air of chamber-haunting succubae. The women array themselves between the "great wood lectern and the fire" till Yeats can "hear their hearts beating." The flurry of imagery is resonant with meanings: The concatenation of wood and fire conveys the hint of conflagration, while the women's obtrusion between lectern and fire suggests the foiling of the light, the demand for attention, the disruption of Yeats's work. This less-than-transparent scene is perhaps referable to "The CIRCUS ANIMALS' DESERTION": "Players and painted stage took all my love, / And not those things that they were emblems of." Could it be that the women, having been mere emblems of "returned and yet unrequited love," appear to demand that their own beating hearts be heard? The beating hearts of the women anticipate Christ's beating heart in The RESURRECTION: Poem and play equally exploit the terrible incongruity of the ghostly and the vascular. In his introduction to *The Resurrection*, Yeats attributes the motif of the beating heart to an episode that Sir William Crookes (1832–1919) recounts in his *Researches in the Phenomena of Spiritualism* (1874): "After excluding every possibility of fraud, [Crookes] touched a materialised form and found the heart beating. I felt, though my intellect rejected what I read, the terror of the supernatural described by Job" (*VPl.* 935; see also *LE* 156). Yeats goes on to describe another supernatural instance whose elements of female visitation and supernatural horror may bear on "Presences": "Just before the war a much respected man of science entering a room in his own house found there two girl visitors—I have questioned all three—one lying asleep on the table, the other sitting on the end of the table screaming, the table floating in the air, and 'immediately vomited'" (*VPl.* 935).

The poem ends with a symbolic turn by which it seems suddenly to evade its own unease. The three women—one a harlot, one a child, one a queen—shed whatever individuality is suggested by their laughter, their timidity, and their wildness, and become eternal types—emblems—of lust, innocence, and pride. Despite this universal turn, the figures clearly have autobiographical correspondences. The child who "never looked upon man with desire" suggests ISEULT GONNE, to whom Yeats proposed marriage in both August 1916 and August 1917. She was 26 years old in November 1915, when Yeats began work on "Presences," and thus "a child" only figuratively or from the vantage of Yeats's middle age (YC 181). The suggestion of sexual innocence contradicts "TO A YOUNG GIRL," a poem of the same period, in which Yeats claims to know what makes her "heart beat so." The queen inevitably suggests Maud Gonne, whom Yeats figures as Helen in poems like "NO SECOND TROY," "PEACE," and "A WOMAN HOMER SUNG." "The Harlot" may reflect the needs of Yeats's symbolic scheme rather than any particular experience or person. A. Norman Jeffares plausibly conjectures that the allusion is to Mabel Dickinson (born 1875), with whom Yeats had an affair from 1908 to 1913. The affair ended in recrimination after a pregnancy scare; Yeats suspected that he had been the victim of a marriage ploy (*New Biography* 195–196; on Dickinson, see AM 383–385, 488–489). Yeats had no experience of actual "harlots," unlike many of his protégés of the 1890s. "In those days I was a convinced ascetic," he recalls in his 1936 radio broadcast on "Modern Poetry," "yet I envied Dowson his dissipated life. I thought it must be easy to think like Chaucer when you lived among those morbid, elegant, tragic women suggested by Dowson's poetry, painted and drawn by his friends Conder and BEARDSLEY" (LE 89).

"Presences" is Yeats's only poem set identifiably at WOBURN BUILDINGS. ROBERT GREGORY designed the "great wood lectern." It displayed the Kelmscott edition of *The Works of Geoffrey Chaucer* that Yeats received as a 40th birthday present from friends (CL4 166).

FIRST PUBLICATION: The *Little Review* (periodical), June 1917. Reprinted in *The Wild Swans at Coole*, The CUALA PRESS, Churchtown, Dundrum, November 17, 1917.

BIBLIOGRAPHY

Foster, R. F. *W. B. Yeats: A Life, I: The Apprentice Mage*; Jeffares, A. Norman. *W. B. Yeats: A New Biography*; Kelly, John S. *A W. B. Yeats Chronology*; Yeats, W. B. *The Collected Letters of W. B. Yeats* (vol. 4), *Later Essays, The Variorum Edition of the Plays of W. B. Yeats*.

"Realists, The" (1912)

"The Realists" is an eight-line exercise in ironic deadpan that belongs to the same genus as "The NINETEENTH CENTURY AND AFTER." The poem mouths the underlying logic of the school of aesthetic REALISM, thus laying bare its spiritual defeatism. In parody of his aesthetic adversaries, Yeats asks what is to be gained from books about "men that wive / In a dragon-guarded land" or from paintings of "the dolphin-drawn / Sea-nymphs in their pearly wagons," as these will only arouse a "hope to live" that had passed away with the dragons. In other words, these will arouse a hope that can no longer be fulfilled in the context of a material and scientific universe. The poem's evocation of books and paintings is probably not specific, but clearly Yeats has in mind the kind of art associated with PRE-RAPHAELITISM. The "hope to live" may refer to faith in the immortality of the soul; it may equally or alternatively refer to a longing for the lusty adventure—knightly exploits and the like—associated with days gone by. An image of sensual joy transcendently breasting the infinite, the dolphin significantly recurs in "BYZANTIUM" and "NEWS FOR THE DELPHIC ORACLE."

FIRST PUBLICATION: *Poetry* (periodical), December 1912. Reprinted in *Responsibilities: Poems and a Play,* The CUALA PRESS, Churchtown, Dundrum, May 25, 1914.

"Reconciliation" (1910)

According to R. F. Foster, Yeats visited MAUD GONNE in PARIS in June 1908 and the two renewed their "spiritual marriage" of 1898. In Foster's telling, "By the time he left on 25 June, their relationship had come nearer to a conventional resolution than ever before. He wrote in a notebook she gave him that though her new-found Catholicism prevented her remarrying, and 'the old dread of phisical [sic] love has awakened in her', she 'seems to love more than of old'" (AM 387). On July 26, Gonne sent Yeats a letter that makes plain the reawakening of more than friendly feelings between the two old friends. Describing her communion with Yeats on the astral plane, Gonne writes, "You had taken the form I think of a great serpent, but I am not quite sure. I only saw your face distinctly & as I looked into your eyes (as I did the day in Paris you asked me what I was thinking of) & your lips touched mine. We melted into one another till we formed only *one being, a being greater than ourselves* who felt all & knew all with double intensity [. . .]" (GY 257).

"Reconciliation," written in September 1908, marks this renewal of love. Like "NO SECOND TROY," the preceding poem in *The Green Helmet and Other Poems* (1910), "Reconciliation" begins on a note of blame and maneuvers toward exculpation. The poem's opening lines suggest that some may have blamed Gonne for depriving them of Yeats's verse. Yeats refers to his stunned attempt to get through a lecture after hearing the news of Gonne's marriage plans; on another reading, he may refer more generally to his poetic dry spell that lasted from 1903 to 1910. Richard Ellmann identifies the poem's specific allusion: "One night in February, 1903, [Yeats] went to give a lecture and just before he was to speak he was handed a letter in [Gonne's] familiar handwriting. Maud Gonne wrote, however, an unfamiliar message: she

had just married Major John MacBride in Paris. For a moment, 'the ears being deafened, the sight of the eyes blind / With lightning,' Yeats did not know what to do. Then he went through with his lecture, and afterwards members of the audience congratulated him on its excellence, but he could never remember a word of what he had said" (MM 159–160). R. F. Foster identifies the lecture as "The Future of Irish Drama," given on February 7 (AM 284). As Gonne was not married until February 21, the note undoubtedly informed Yeats of her engagement, not her marriage.

If Yeats was deafened and blinded—Ellmann quotes above the pertinent lines—upon learning that his dream of love had come to nothing, there were ramifications for his work as well. Yeats could find nothing "to make a song about but kings / Helmets, and swords, and half-forgotten things," all of which were "memories" of Gonne in her stately and severe beauty ("a kind that is not natural in an age like this," as Yeats puts it in "No Second Troy"). Yeats probably has in mind the plays of his middle years, ON BAILE'S STRAND (1903), *The* KING'S THRESHOLD (1904), and DEIRDRE (1907), although both *The King's Threshold* and *On Baile's Strand* were under way by the time of Gonne's engagement. More important than the specifics of the allusion, however, is Yeats's comprehension that heroic spectacle is the inadequate and perhaps even disingenuous expression of some deeper drama of the heart. As in "The CIRCUS ANIMALS' DESERTION," Yeats is alert to the forms of his own insincerity, revealing something of the vigilant self-consciousness that goes to the making of a great poet.

The poem's eighth line is its turning point. Once again restored to himself by Gonne's love, Yeats declares, "We'll out, for the world lives as long ago. . . ." Yeats means that that the world is once again endowed with the heroic glamour that had been the factitious theme (kings, helmets, swords) of his recent work. The locution "we'll out" is curious. Yeats may intend a contracted form of an idiom like "burst out" (i.e., in laughter) or "break out" (i.e., in tears). This interpretation chimes with the succeeding line, in which Yeats vows that he and Gonne, while in their "laughing, weeping fit," will "Hurl helmets, crowns, and swords into the pit." The dumping of these heroic accouterments is again reminiscent of "The Circus Animals' Desertion." It signifies Yeats's rejection of the factitious in favor of the real. As well as evoking a hellish abyss, "pit" signifies the seating area on the floor of a theater. In this light the lines more pointedly constitute a rejection of theatrical contrivance (*The Green Helmet and Other Poems* echoes this discontent with the theater in poems like "The FASCINATION OF WHAT'S DIFFICULT" and "AT THE ABBEY THEATRE," though the latter did not appear in the 1910 edition of the volume). This line of metaphor was bound to please Gonne, who had written Yeats a stern warning about over-immersion in the theater on the day following his departure from Paris: "The theatre is the millstone from which you must try to get free, or at least partially free [. . .]. You remember how for the *sake of Ireland,* I hated you in politics [. . .] because I always felt it took you from your writing & cheated Ireland of a greater gift than we could give her—& the theatre is just as bad, or worse for it brings you among jealousies & petty quarrels & little animosities which you as a great writer should be above & apart from" (GY 255–256).

The poem's final two lines instantly deflate the extravagant play of metaphor and emotion, thus enacting in earnest the poem's implicit program of putting off all insincerity, all mere stage dressing. Yeats pleads with Gonne, "But, dear, cling close to me; since you were gone, / My barren thoughts have chilled me to the bone." Revealingly, Yeats's plea for love is in the final analysis a plea for rescue from imaginative bankruptcy: even in the throes of love, the poet thinks first of his poem. Note the pun on "gone," an apparent trick Yeats repeats in "FRIENDS," "HER PRAISE," "The LIVING BEAUTY," and "TO A YOUNG BEAUTY."

FIRST PUBLICATION: *The Green Helmet and Other Poems,* The CUALA PRESS, Churchtown, Dundrum, December 1910, under the sequence title "Raymond Lully and his wife Pernella" and the present title.

BIBLIOGRAPHY

Ellmann, Richard. *Yeats: The Man and the Masks*; Foster, R. F. *W. B. Yeats: A Life, I: The Apprentice Mage*; Yeats, W. B. *The Gonne-Yeats Letters 1893–1938.*

"Remorse for Intemperate Speech" (1932, dated April 28, 1931)

If "VACILLATION" declares the victory of heart over soul ("Homer is my example and his unchristened heart"), "Remorse for Intemperate Speech" both deplores and implicitly celebrates the heart's unruly intensity, anticipating later poems of wild age like "The SPUR," "WHY SHOULD NOT OLD MEN BE MAD?," and "The Wild Old Wicked Man" (1938). The opening stanza recalls the 1890s, when Yeats was a bumptious neophyte of the literary societies and nationalist organizations. In AUTOBIOGRAPHIES, Yeats remembers the difficulty of checking his own intemperance: "I wished to become self-possessed, to be able to play with hostile minds as Hamlet played, to look in the lion's face, as it were, with unquivering eyelash. In Ireland harsh argument which had gone out of fashion in England was still the manner of our conversation [. . .]. I spoke easily and, I thought, well till some one was rude and then I would become silent or exaggerate my opinion to absurdity, or hesitate and grow confused, or be carried away myself by some party passion. I would spend hours afterwards going over my words and putting the wrong ones right" (99). ON THE BOILER includes a related reminiscence that shares the self-accusation of fanaticism with "Remorse for Intemperate Speech": "But it was not only with my father that I quarrelled, nor were economics the only theme. There was no dominant opinion I could accept. Then finding out that I [. . .] had become both boor and bore, I invented a patter, allowing myself an easy man's insincerity, and for honesty's sake a little malice, and now it seems that I can talk nothing else. But I think I have succeeded, and that none of my friends know that I am a fanatic" (*Expl.* 417; *LE* 226–227).

The second stanza alludes to Yeats's increasing immersion in the landed, titled world of Lady GREGORY, beginning in 1896. In this milieu "Fine manners, liberal speech / Turn hatred into sport," but Yeats's "fanatic heart" is irreclaimable: Its unruliness resists even this example of domestication or sublimation. The final stanza ascribes the "fanatic heart" to the peculiarities of Ireland, nation of "Great hatred / little room." The allusion takes account of Ireland's furious politics and perennial land agitation (see "UPON A HOUSE SHAKEN BY THE LAND AGITATION") and vaguely recollects "NINETEEN HUNDRED AND NINETEEN's" indelible image of "weasels fighting in a hole." The poem, in the end, is equivocal in its embrace of the "fanatic heart." "Maimed" chimes with the tentative critique of "EASTER 1916" ("Too long a sacrifice / Can make a stone of the heart"), but the penultimate and ultimate lines of "Remorse for Intemperate Speech" have the cadence of proud declaration, and Yeats generally identifies the heart's fanaticism with its creative energy. "Whatever flames upon the night / Man's own resinous heart has fed," as he expresses this notion in "TWO SONGS FROM A PLAY" (see also the second section of "PARNELL'S FUNERAL").

The theme of remorse—and in some cases the necessity to cast out remorse—is evident in numerous poems of Yeats's later period, including "The CHOICE," "A DIALOGUE OF SELF AND SOUL," "The MAN AND THE ECHO," "The MUNICIPAL GALLERY REVISITED," "Stream and Sun at Glendalough" (1932), and "Vacillation." In *Autobiographies* Yeats recalls of his early manhood, "For ten or twelve years more I suffered continual remorse, and only became content when my abstractions had composed themselves into picture and dramatization. My very remorse helped to spoil my early poetry, giving it an element of sentimentality through my refusal to permit it any share of an intellect which I considered impure" (163). Harold Bloom locates "the great original" of the romantic's "injunction to cast out remorse" in the eighth canto of SHELLEY's *The Revolt of Islam* (1818): "Reproach not thine own soul, but know thyself, / Nor hate another's crime, nor loathe thine own. / It is the dark idolatry of self, / Which, when our thoughts and actions once are gone, / Demands that man should weep, and bleed, and groan; / O vacant expiation! Be at rest—. / The past is Death's, the future is thine own; / And love and joy can make the foulest breast / A paradise of flowers, where peace might build her nest" (*Yeats* 376; see also 307). In his essay "The PHILOSOPHY OF SHELLEY'S POETRY," Yeats glosses these lines as follows: "[Shelley] even thought that

men might be immortal were they sinless, and his Cythna bids the sailors be without remorse, for all that live are stained as they are. It is thus, she says, that time marks men and their thoughts for the tomb" (*E&I* 70–71).

FIRST PUBLICATION: *Words for Music Perhaps and Other Poems*, The CUALA PRESS, Dublin, November 14, 1932.

BIBLIOGRAPHY
Bloom, Harold. *Yeats*; Yeats, W. B. *Autobiographies, Essays and Introductions, Explorations, Later Essays.*

"Results of Thought, The" (1932, dated August 1931)

Like "A WOMAN HOMER SUNG," "The Results of Thought" conceives the aesthetic enterprise as an attempt to transcend and redeem the degeneracy of nature, and more specifically salvage something of permanent beauty from the wreckage of old age. "The Results of Thought," however, is far more audacious in its aestheticism. It avows that art can dictate its own reality and supplant the defective reality of nature. In its underlying idea that art is the salvation of nature, the alchemical process by which nature assumes enduring form, "The Results of Thought" has its crucial antecedent in the second stanza of "A Woman Homer Sung" and its most important conceptual counterpart in "SAILING TO BYZANTIUM," though it differs significantly from both of these poems in tone and image.

As in "ALL SOULS' NIGHT" and "The Tragic Generation" (see AUTOBIOGRAPHIES), Yeats recalls friends and companions undone by their youths, "by that inhuman / Bitter glory wrecked." By "inhuman bitter glory" Yeats means the straining beyond natural limit that is both the bitterness and the glory of youth. "Acquaintance" and "companion" are generic references; the "dear brilliant woman" is surely Lady GREGORY (MAUD GONNE is never merely "dear"), though "inhuman bitter glory" carries *antithetical* connotations that do not normally apply to her. Yeats would later deploy the same idiom of wreckage in "The STATUES" to different effect: "We Irish, born into that ancient sect / But thrown upon this filthy modern tide /And by its formless spawning fury wrecked. . . ." The second stanza's diction—"toil" having explicitly occult significance in "The PHASES OF THE MOON," "summon" having supernatural connotations in "BYZANTIUM," "A DIALOGUE OF SELF AND SOUL," and "EGO DOMINUS TUUS"—decks Yeats in the robes of literary alchemist or conjuror of ghosts. Having long toiled to master the mysteries of his discipline, he can "straighten out" the ruin of the years, "summon back" the "wholesome strength" his friends knew in youth.

Like "The SECOND COMING," "The Statues," and "WHAT MAGIC DRUM?," "The Results of Thought" ends by wondering at its own vision of the monstrous, and ends all the more hair-raisingly for leaving its questions unanswered. The genuine shock of the poem is its rebarbative willingness to construe even friends in the monstrous imagery of age. These slouch to and fro like insensate beasts (compare their dull eyes to the thoughtless eyes of Robert Artisson in "NINETEEN HUNDRED AND NINETEEN"; Yeats knew that vacuity is itself monstrous). Wed to the reality of his own artistic vision, Yeats does not recognize the humanity much less the friendship of the slouching figures. In an inversion of art and life, they have become mere "images," supplanted by the reality that Yeats has summoned.

FIRST PUBLICATION: *Words for Music Perhaps and Other Poems*, The CUALA PRESS, Dublin, November 14, 1932.

"Ribh at the Tomb of Baile and Aillinn" (1934)

See "SUPERNATURAL SONGS."

"Ribh considers Christian Love insufficient" (1934)

See "SUPERNATURAL SONGS."

"Ribh denounces Patrick" (1934)

See "SUPERNATURAL SONGS."

"Ribh in Ecstasy" (1935)

See "SUPERNATURAL SONGS."

"Road at my Door, The" (1923)

"Between extremities / Man runs his course," Yeats writes in "VACILLATION." The poetic sequence "MEDITATIONS IN TIME OF CIVIL WAR" is similarly suspended between extremities. Where "ANCESTRAL HOUSES" urges the active passion of the imperious patron of the arts, "MY HOUSE" urges the visionary passion of the solitary mage (at least before gesturing toward reconciliation of the active and visionary in its final stanza). The fifth poem in the sequence, "The Road at My Door" swings in the direction of "Ancestral Houses," and thus sets up the final declaration of visionary propensity in "I SEE PHANTOMS OF HATRED AND OF THE HEART'S FULLNESS AND OF THE COMING EMPTINESS."

Unlike the preceding four poems in the sequence, "The Road at My Door" touches specifically on the IRISH CIVIL WAR in brief silhouettes of encounters with soldiers from both sides in the conflict. There is first the "affable Irregular"—a rebel against the provisional government of the newly created Irish Free State—who comes "cracking jokes of civil war / As though to die by gunshot were / The finest play under the sun." The epithet "Falstaffian"—a reference to Shakespeare's Sir John Falstaff, the jovial force of nature of *Henry IV* and *The Merry Wives of Windsor*—is appreciative of the soldier's vitality, but "comes cracking jokes," a barrage of un-Falstaffian consonants, insinuates a second thought. "Play" echoes the aspersion on "too much play" in "MY DESCENDANTS," and in its pun on the stage reiterates Yeats's ambivalence about a certain kind of romantic theatricality in poems like "The CIRCUS ANIMALS' DESERTION" and "PARNELL'S FUNERAL." Yeats accuses the soldier of insouciance, but insouciance bound up with what he calls in a letter to his sister Lolly Yeats "the Vertigo of Self Sacrifice"—a romantic death-craving that is the prime symptom of the nationalist fanaticism he questions in "EASTER 1916" (*AP* 46). A contingent of Free State soldiers next arrives, their partial uniform suggesting the rag-tag character of the entire war. Yeats complains of "the foul weather, hail and rain, / A pear-tree broken by the storm." This seemingly idle chatter has a symbolic gist: The broken pear tree is a token of the blasted countryside and in this respect anticipates the loosening wall and burned house of "The STARE'S NEST BY MY WINDOW," which immediately follows in the sequence (so too it foreshadows the "bare tree" of PURGATORY). Though Yeats supported the government, the scene may equally indicate a judicious policy of making nonpartisan small talk and sending soldiers on their way.

The poem's emotional and political detachment appears to be a mode of critique, but in the final stanza the poem reverses itself: what had seemed Yeats's skeptical humanism, reminiscent of his posture in "Easter 1916," is suddenly and surprisingly unmasked as saturnine envy. The "moor-hens" that were the living refutation of the stoniness of political fanaticism in "Easter 1916" here recur, with acute intertextual irony, as a mere tool of distraction from the envy the contemplative man feels for active men (notice that even Yeats's envy is couched *in his thought*). Yeats can only retire to his "chamber" (a word fraught with the occult associations established in "MY HOUSE") being "caught in the cold snows of a dream" ("snow" in contrast to the sun invoked in line 5). For Yeats, "cold" almost always has an *antithetical* or transcendental implication (cf. "The COLD HEAVEN," "The FISHERMAN," "LAPIS LAZULI," "MERU"), as it reverses the warmth by which the organic is mortally self-betrayed. "The dream," then, is the solitary, self-entangling toil of the poet-philosopher, the effort, as Yeats has it in "My House," to shadow forth "How the daemonic rage / Imagined everything." Yeats's reservations about this toil have a long pedigree, stretching all the way back

to "FERGUS AND THE DRUID," which conceives the "dreaming wisdom" of the druid as both irresistibly tempting and irreversibly estranging from everything natural and wholesome. Yeats is *caught* in his dream, just as Fergus is wrapped in "webs of sorrow" released from the Druid's "bag of dreams."

In "The PEOPLE," Yeats similarly posits himself as the contemplative man abashed in the presence of the active man, represented in this case by MAUD GONNE. Having lived not in thought but in deed, she is capable of "the purity of a natural force," while Yeats's own virtues are merely "the definitions / Of the analytic mind."

FIRST PUBLICATION: The *Dial* and the *London Mercury* (periodicals), January 1923. Reprinted in *The Cat and the Moon and Certain Poems*, The CUALA PRESS, Dublin, July 1924.

BIBLIOGRAPHY

Foster, R. F. *W. B. Yeats: A Life, II: The Arch-Poet.*

"Rose of Battle, The" (1892)

"The Rose of Battle" belongs to an informal sequence of early poems that revolves around the mystical symbol of the ROSE and includes "The Rose of Peace" (1892), "The Rose of the World" (1892), "The SECRET ROSE," and "To THE ROSE UPON THE ROOD OF TIME." A dense and obscure poem even by the standards of Yeats's mystical and visionary excursions—a "knotty problem of a poem," as Frank Hughes Murphy calls it—"The Rose of Battle" follows "To THE ROSE UPON THE ROOD OF TIME" in its central distinction between the comfort of the mundane and the burden of the visionary (*Yeats's Early Poetry* 56). In "The Rose of Battle," however, Yeats seems to abandon the attempt to mediate or balance the two poles of experience, implying instead that each person must accept unreservedly the calling intrinsic to their nature.

The poem envisions ships gathering in expectation of battle. With their "thought-woven sails" that "flap unfurled / Above the tide of hours," the ships suggest the welling of an apocalyptic moment in which eternity wars against time. There approaches a "band" with "spray-dabbled hair," some "hushed from fear," some "loud with hope." Yeats—or the voice that seems to speak for Yeats—calls to the gathered throng, urging them to turn if they can "from battles never done." Those who know the comforts of love may be spared the impending strife, though the logic of this exemption is expressed ambiguously: "Danger no refuge holds, and war no peace, / For him who hears love sing and never cease. . . ." The apparent meaning of these lines is that those mysteriously attuned to the song of love are in some sense saved and need not join in the impending battle as a spiritual rite of passage. Whether "love" implies a natural or supernatural condition of salvation is not clear, but "clean-swept hearth," like the worm and field-mouse of "To the Rose upon the Rood of Time," seems to evoke the comfort of the mundane. Those for whom love has made a "woven silence" have their opposite in the "sad, the lonely, the insatiable," those who seek more than the world naturally yields, those to whom "Old Night" tells something of her mystery. It is these who must "wage God's battles in the long grey ships," as if to expiate the longing in their "sad hearts."

In the poem's second stanza, Yeats addresses the mystic rose as a kindred thing likewise drawn by the ring of God's bell to "where the dim tides are hurled / Upon the wharves of sorrow. . . ." As if lending words of comfort, Yeats tells the rose that when the ships are at last defeated in fighting God's wars those who have striven shall no more hear the "little cry" of their own "sad hearts." These shall be free of the mortal compromise between life and death. The poem thus seems to end in recognition that it is not the lot of men to win such battles, merely to see them through and to be released at last from the sadness of their mortality.

FIRST PUBLICATION: *The Countess Kathleen and Various Legends and Lyrics*, T. Fisher Unwin, London, September 1892, under the title "They went forth to the Battle, but they always Fell." Reprinted in *Poems*, T. Fisher Unwin, London, October 1895, under the present title.

BIBLIOGRAPHY

Murphy, Frank Hughes. *Yeats's Early Poetry: The Quest for Reconciliation.*

"Sad Shepherd, The" (1886)

"Go gather by the humming sea / Some twisted, echo-harbouring shell, / And to its lips thy story tell, / And they thy comforters will be," counsels "The SONG OF THE HAPPY SHEPHERD." As if in response, "The Sad Shepherd" describes a sorrow-stricken man who seeks comfort in the stars, the sea, and the dewdrops, all to no avail. He returns to the shore and speaks his story into the "hollow, pearly heart" of a shell, hoping that the return of his "whispering words" will ease his "ancient burden." He softly sings into the shell, but the shell "Changed all he sang to inarticulate moan / Among her wildering whirls, forgetting him." The seeming contradiction between the two poems is perhaps none at all. The suggestion is that the shell answers in the spirit that we bring to it, and that "comfort"—release from the existential burden—must be an achievement of the self. Thus "The Sad Shepherd" substantiates "The Song of the Happy Shepherd's" root conviction that "there is no truth / Saving in thine own heart." In tandem the two poems set the terms for the existential triumph of a poem like "LAPIS LAZULI," which understands that transfiguring gaiety must be mustered from within.

FIRST PUBLICATION: The *DUBLIN UNIVERSITY REVIEW* (periodical), October 1886, under the title "Miserrimus." Reprinted in *The Wanderings of Oisin and Other Poems*, Kegan Paul, Trench & Co., London, January 1889, under the same title. Reprinted in *Poems*, T. Fisher Unwin, London, October 1895, under the present title.

"Sailing to Byzantium" (1927, dated 1927)

Yeats's two arch-canonical poems on the capital city of the Byzantine Empire, "Sailing to Byzantium" and "BYZANTIUM," are the exquisite crystallization of his persistent longing for spiritual redemption through the timelessness of art. Yeats equated the architecture of Byzantium during the reign of Justinian (527–65) with "the Sacred City in the Apocalypse of St. John" and conceived the city as the reification of the harmonies of the 15th lunar phase of the millennial cycle, the "phase of complete beauty" and UNITY OF BEING (AV 279, 135–137). Simultaneously, Byzantium belonged to the eighth phase of the 2,000-year era that began with the birth of Christ and represents what Hazard Adams calls "the supreme antithetical moment of a Millennium that belongs to a primary Era" (*Book of Yeats's Vision* 143). In *A VISION*, Byzantium is the pretext for Yeats's most vivid and comprehensive evocation of culture under the full moon. If given the chance to spend a month in the antique world, Yeats says, he would choose to visit Byzantium just before Justinian opened St. Sophia in 537 and closed the Platonic academy: "I think that in early Byzantium, maybe never before or since in recorded history, religious, aesthetic and practical life were one, that architect and artificers—though not, it may be, poets, for language had been the instrument of controversy and must have grown abstract—spoke to the multitude and the few alike. The painter, the mosaic worker, the worker in gold and silver, the illuminator of sacred books, were almost impersonal, almost perhaps without the consciousness of individual design, absorbed in their subject-matter and that the vision of a whole people. They could copy out of old Gospel books those pictures that seemed as sacred as the text, and yet weave all into a vast design, the work of many that seemed the work of one, that made building, picture, pattern, metalwork of rail and lamp, seem but a single image [. . .]" (279–280). "Sailing to Byzantium" is Yeats's most overt and audacious attempt to imagine himself reborn within the holy moonlight of the 15th lunar phase. As so often in Yeats, the template is the romantic quest of SHELLEY's "Alastor" (1816), but Yeats recognizes, as the Alastor-poet does not, that all journeys are metaphors of self-transformation or preparations for self-transformation. There is nothing to discover or embrace beyond the self's readiness, its welled intensity, its ability to imagine the terms of its new beginning. Byzantium, then, is less a place than a condition of triumph into which the imagination enters when it has finally thrown off all sense of its own limitation.

The poem opens with a valediction to the realm of "sensual music" that decisively severs the attachment so carefully preserved in "TO THE ROSE UPON THE ROOD OF TIME." For all the bluffness of the poem's opening gambit—"That is no country for old men"—the poem quickly assumes an immense pathos and complexity of motive. It is neither possible nor desirable to join in the sensual music of the natural world, and yet the vision of the young "in one another's arms," of the natural world in its summer revelry of birth, life, and death, is so irresistibly vibrant that Yeats half confesses to making a virtue of necessity. "Sensual music" and the "Birds in the trees . . . at their song" have their answering image in the following stanza and in the final lines of the poem, while the "salmon-falls" and "mackerel-crowded seas" await the transfiguration of the final lines of "Byzantium," in which the sea becomes the image of eternity and the dolphin the image of a breasting transcendence. "Caught" suggests that the cycle of birth and death has the aspect of a snare. It is precisely this capture that Yeats claims to have resisted or outgrown, tutored by the example of "Monuments of unageing intellect" (cf. "THE TOWER," lines 157–159).

In the second stanza, Yeats figures himself as a "tattered coat upon a stick," a version of the "comfortable kind of old scarecrow" imaged in "AMONG SCHOOL CHILDREN," a poem likewise dating from 1926. The self as scarecrow creates a deliberate contrast with the fleshiness depicted in the first stanza, and this emphatic decrepitude makes all the more surprising and dramatic the sudden revelation of reserves of imaginative energy and spiritual ambition. The vestments of decrepitude are incidental and can be thrown off: the soul need only "clap its hands and sing." Unlike the melodists of the first stanza, whose song is "sensual"—a matter of untutored bodily inspiration—the soul of the "aged man" sings the more ineluctably for having schooled itself in "monuments of its own magnificence." In the cross-texture of the poem, "monuments of its own magnificence" obviously modifies "monuments of unageing intellect." The suggestion seems to be that the soul contains within itself the image of what it might become, is itself the vessel of unageing intellect. Thus schooled—disciplined—

readied—Yeats has "sailed the seas and come / To the holy city of Byzantium," where the individual energy may achieve its climax by joining itself to a larger social and historical energy, an emphasis that explains Yeats's own attempts to wed himself to coterie, class, and nation. At the same time the journey to Byzantium is the geographical allegory of an approach to an internal threshold.

The poem's third stanza plunges into the maelstrom of purification and self-transformation. Yeats calls to the "sages standing in God's holy fire, / As in the gold mosaic of a wall. . . ." The simile suggests that the worldly realization of the holy fire, the closest correlative of its disciplined intensity, is the kind of art that belongs to an *antithetical* tradition come to greatness, as in Byzantium. Yeats would have the holy sages "perne in a gyre," which is to say, surround him, baffle him, gather him into the kind of centripetal unity of the self that he attributes to the dancer in "The DOUBLE VISION OF MICHAEL ROBARTES." It may be that as the sages "perne in a gyre" time itself is sped to transcendental stasis, again as in "The Double Vision of Michael Robartes" ("Mind moved yet seemed to stop / As 'twere a spinning-top"). It may also be that the gyre—the geometrical representation of the cycles of history and personality that are the gear-work of the philosophy of *A Vision* (see "The GYRES")—is invoked as a figure of ultimate reality. Yeats would have the sages consume his heart, which is "sick with desire / And fastened to a dying animal" (cf. "The Tower," lines 3–4). "Fastened," hinting at a metaphor of strap or harness, accentuates the inessential relation between inner and outer reality.

"God's holy fire" is the purgatorial fire so pervasive in Yeats's thought. The "holy fire" withers everything that is not of eternal spirit or substance, which explains the injunction of the soul to the heart in "VACILLATION," "Look on that fire, salvation walks within." Yeats touches on the same recognition in "BLOOD AND THE MOON," in which he speaks of "Everything that is not God consumed with intellectual fire," and in "MY TABLE," in which he equates the fire of the forge and the "aching heart" as crucibles of "changeless art." As the sword assumes eternal form by the intensity of fire in "My

Table," so the soul in "Sailing to Byzantium." The purgatorial fire also has inevitable associations with the "athanor," the furnace used by alchemists in their related attempt to transmute the perishable into imperishable, dross into gold. In "ROSA ALCHEMICA," Yeats explains, in terms relevant to "Sailing to Byzantium," that the doctrine of the alchemists was "no merely chemical phantasy, but a philosophy they applied to the world, to the elements and to man himself; and that they sought to fashion gold out of common metals merely as part of an universal transmutation of all things into some divine and imperishable substance [. . .]" (*Myth.* 267). The story ends in an ecstatic, reality-baffling dance, likewise joined by mosaical divinities, that anticipates the whirling, transcendental intensity by which the sages of "Sailing to Byzantium" gather Yeats into the "artifice of eternity." The purgatorial fire and the dance, then, are differing manifestations of the same transformational energy.

In the fourth stanza, Yeats imagines himself remade of just the "imperishable substance" that the alchemists sought, declaring, "Once out of nature I shall never take / My bodily form from any natural thing. . . ." Having "read somewhere that in the Emperor's palace at Byzantium was a tree made of gold and silver, and artificial birds that sang"—in fact having read this in Gibbon's *History of the Decline and Fall of the Roman Empire* and *The Cambridge Medieval History*—Yeats chooses to become a bird of hammered gold singing to "lords and ladies of Byzantium / Of what is past, or passing, or to come" (*VP* 825; *Between the Lines* 100). Thus he is at once freed from the decay of the body, the strictures of time, and the defilement of a popular audience, and a clean sweep is made of his most persistent grievances. The inspiration of these most famous lines has inevitably been the subject of much critical discussion. Keats's "Ode to a Nightingale" (1820) and SHELLEY's "To a Sky-Lark" (1820) are likely precedents. In both poems, the bird represents liberation, bodily and artistic, from the mire of mortality. George Bornstein notes as well an echo of Shelley's *Hellas* (1822), in which Hassan describes the sage Ahasuerus: "[From] his eye looks forth / A life of unconsumed thought which pierces / The present, and the past, and the to-come" (*Yeats and Shelley* 187; see lines 146–148). G. Wilson Knight instances the "enchanted" bird ("eyes of fire, his beak of gold, / All else of amethyst!") of COLERIDGE's 1817 play *Zapolya* (*Starlit Dome* 174–175, 310; in the play, see II, i, 65–80). T. R. Henn cites Marvell's "The Garden": "Casting the Bodies Vest aside, / My Soul into the Boughs does glide: / There like a Bird it sits and sings, / And, till prepared for longer flight / Waves in its Plumes the various light" (*Lonely Tower* 227). John Stallworthy draws attention to BLAKE's introduction to *Songs of Experience* (1794): 'Hear the voice of the bard, / Who present, past and future sees" (*Between the Lines* 99). Harold Bloom finds much the same substance in Blake's *Jerusalem* (written ca. 1804–07): "I see the past, present & future, existing all at once" (*Yeats* 348; see chapter I, plate 15). To this long list of possible influences might be added Shelley's *Queen Mab* (1813), in which the Fairy tells Ianthe, "Spirit, come! / This is thine high reward:—the past shall rise; / Thou shalt behold the present; I will teach / The secrets of the future" (II, 64–67).

The golden bird is also precedented in Yeats's own earliest work, indicating the long gestation of the image. In "The WANDERINGS OF OISIN," Yeats describes "painted birds" that keep "time with their bright wings and feet" as the "Immortals" sing of the ordeal of time. He describes also a "storm of birds in the Asian trees" that join the waves in murmuring "Unjust, unjust" at the spectacle of the world's evanescence (Book I, lines 416–420; see also lines 69–70, 180–187, 396–397). The birds of "Oisin" thus seem both to mark and to protest the passing of time. There are slews of related images in Yeats's subsequent work. Particularly relevant are "AT ALGECIRAS—A MEDITATION UPON DEATH," with its cattle-birds gathered in "the rich midnight of the garden trees"; "MY TABLE," which ends with the apocalyptic scream of Juno's peacock; THE SHADOWY WATERS, with its souls fleeing in the form of man-headed birds; and "SOLOMON AND THE WITCH," with its vatic cockerel. The image of the golden bird, violently *antithetical* rather than serenely transcendent, is reprised in "Byzantium."

Yeats's preoccupation with Byzantium was inspired, as A. Norman Jeffares notes, by W. G.

Holme's *The Age of Justinian and Theodora* (1905), O. M. Dalton's *Byzantine Art and Archeology* (1911), and Eugénie Strong's *Apotheosis and After Life: Three Lectures on Certain Phases of Art and Religion in the Roman Empire* (1915) (*NCP* 211; on the influence of *Apotheosis and After Life*, see *Whole Mystery of Art* 212). Yeats was also inspired by his exposure to Byzantine mosaics during his May 1907 visit to Ravenna with Lady GREGORY and ROBERT GREGORY and during his January 1925 visit to Monreale, Sicily, with EZRA POUND and his wife, Dorothy (*AM* 367–369; *AP* 279).

FIRST PUBLICATION: *October Blast*, The CUALA PRESS, Dublin, August 1927.

BIBLIOGRAPHY

Adams, Hazard. *The Book of Yeats's Vision: Romantic Modernism and Antithetical Tradition*; Bloom, Harold. *Yeats*; Bornstein, George. *Yeats and Shelley*; Foster, R. F. *W. B. Yeats: A Life, I: The Apprentice Mage, II: The Arch-Poet*; Henn, T. R. *The Lonely Tower: Studies in the Poetry of W. B. Yeats*; Jeffares, A. Norman. *A New Commentary on the Poems of W. B. Yeats*; Knight, G. Wilson. *The Starlit Dome: Studies in the Poetry of Vision*; Melchiori, Giorgio. *The Whole Mystery of Art: Pattern into Poetry in the Work of W. B. Yeats*; Stallworthy, John. *Between the Lines: Yeats's Poetry in the Making*; W. B. Yeats, *Mythologies, The Variorum Edition of the Poems of W. B. Yeats, A Vision*.

"Scholars, The" (1915)

Yeats was never on easy terms with the academy. JOHN BUTLER YEATS wanted his son to follow in the family tradition by attending Trinity College, Dublin, though he admitted that the college had done little enough for him and inspired none of his affection (*Early Memories* 68). Yeats feared he was not good enough in mathematics and classics to pass the entrance examination, and he refused to apply (*Aut.* 90). Yeats remained skeptical of the academy, considering it a milieu of dry cerebration and social conformity, unsympathetic if not openly hostile toward the ecstatic energies that give rise to poetry. As Yeats wrote in his preface to *A Book of Irish Verse Selected from Modern Writers* (1895), "Trinity College, which desires to be English, has been the mother of many verse writers and of few poets; and this can only be because she has set herself against the national genius, and taught her children to imitate alien styles and choose out alien themes, for it is not possible to believe that the educated Irishman alone is prosaic and uninventive" (*P&I* 109; see also *UP1* 231–234). Yeats reiterates his complaint against the culture of the university in several essays and letters, including "Dublin Scholasticism and Trinity College" (*UP1* 231–234), "Professor Dowden and Irish Literature" (346–349, 351–353), and "The Academic Class and the Agrarian Revolution" (*UP2* 148–152). Yeats's dim view of the university was borne out by John Butler Yeats's old friend EDWARD DOWDEN, who had become a professor of English literature at Trinity College in 1867. He had begun as a romantic figure with poetic aspirations, but by the end of his career, in Yeats's estimation, he had "turned Shakespeare into a British Benthamite, flattered SHELLEY but to hide his own growing lack of sympathy, abandoned for like reason that study of Goethe that should have been his life-work, and at last cared but for WORDSWORTH, the one great poet who, after brief blossom, was cut and sawn into planks of obvious utility" (*Aut.* 193). George Bornstein speculates that Yeats may have had Dowden specifically in mind when he wrote "The Scholars" (*Yeats and Shelley* 4). The poem may equally dredge up something of Dr. Barrett, a character in Charles Lever's novel *Charles O'Malley* (1841). In an excerpt from the novel that Yeats titled "Trinity College" and included in his anthology *Representative Irish Tales* (1891), Lever (1806–72) describes the diminutive, 70-year-old vice-provost in telling language: "His face was thin, pointed, and russet-coloured; his nose so aquiline as nearly to meet his projecting chin, and his small, gray eyes, red and bleary, peered beneath his well-worn cap with a glance of mingled fear and suspicion. His dress was a suit of the rustiest black, thread-bare, and patched in several places, while a pair of large brown slippers, far too big for his feet, imparted a sliding motion to his walk [. . .]." Having spent his entire life in the

university, Dr. Barret knows "absolutely nothing of the busy, active world that fussed and fumed so near him," and yet "a more profound scholar never graced the walls of the college." Further, he is a "distinguished Grecian" whose mind "never ceased acquiring" (*Representative Irish Tales* 294–295). The description of Dr. Barrett's slippers imparting a sliding motion to his walk may well have emerged from the labyrinth of memory in the description of Yeats's scholars wearing the carpet with their shuffling walk.

His animus softened by the need to boost his income, Yeats campaigned, albeit ambivalently, to succeed Dowden as professor of English literature at Trinity in 1910 and 1911, but in the end his hopes came to nothing (*AM* 429–431, 441; *Letters* 551, 555, 557). The possibility of a professorship recurred in 1913, but this opportunity likewise evaporated (*AM* 483–484). In later life, Yeats's came to view Trinity College as a symbol and preserve of the Georgian culture he so venerated, and he became more respectful and admiring (*W. B. Yeats & Georgian Ireland* 241). It most likely helped that Trinity conferred on him an honorary doctorate on December 20, 1922 (*AP* 224; *Letters* 694–695).

"The Scholars" is the honed poetic expression of Yeats's disdain for the culture of academia, with recent rebuffs at least partially informing the poem's bitter caricature. In terms straightforward enough to be powerfully polemical, it levies all of the old accusations: stolidity, conformity, and complacency. There is the additional accusation that academics live parasitically on the passions of authentic poets. The allusion to sleepless young men who versify "in love's despair / To flatter beauty's ignorant ear" is undoubtedly a wisp of autobiography that remembers his own thwarted but fecund courtship of MAUD GONNE (see "WORDS"). The poem ends with a devastating couplet: "Lord, what would they say, / Did their Catullus walk that way?" "Catullus" is Caius Valerious Catullus (ca. 84–ca. 54 B.C.). The Roman poet, who died before he was much older than 30, is known for his love lyrics. In his 1936 essay "Modern Poetry," Yeats remembers that the members of the RHYMERS' CLUB "tried to write like the poets of the Greek

Anthology, or like Catullus, or like the Jacobean Lyrists, men who wrote while poetry was still pure" (*LE* 92; see also 183). The lines on Catullus cut to what Yeats takes to be the essential paradox of the academic culture: It makes no effort to live in the spirit of what it ostensibly reveres.

FIRST PUBLICATION: *Catholic Anthology, 1914–1915*, Elkin Mathews, London, November 1915. Reprinted in *Poetry* (periodical), February 1916, and in *The Wild Swans at Coole*, The CUALA PRESS, Churchtown, Dundrum, November 17, 1917.

BIBLIOGRAPHY

Bornstein, George. *Yeats and Shelley*; Foster, R. F. W. B. *Yeats: A Life, I: The Apprentice Mage, II: The Arch-Poet*; Torchiana, Donald T. *W. B. Yeats & Georgian Ireland*; Yeats, John Butler. *Early Memories: Some Chapters of Autobiography*; Yeats, W. B. *Autobiographies, Later Essays, The Letters of W. B. Yeats, Prefaces and Introductions*, ed. *Representative Irish Tales, Uncollected Prose by W. B. Yeats* (vols. 1–2).

"Second Coming, The" (1920)

One of the most famous poems in the English language, "The Second Coming" is the definitive vision of the Yeatsian apocalypse. It incorporates and intensifies ideas of cyclic creation and destruction already articulated in poems like "The MAGI," "ON WOMAN," "THE PHASES OF THE MOON," and "SOLOMON AND THE WITCH," and more obliquely anticipated by "EASTER 1916" ("All changed, changed utterly: / A terrible beauty is born"). In its unsettling concatenation of images and startling revision of Christian doctrine, the poem finds the sufficient formula for genuine mythmaking and in this respect goes beyond a poem like "The Phases of the Moon," which, as Yeats admits, has the abstract quality of a "text for exposition" (*VP* 821).

The underlying "mathematical figure" of "The Second Coming," as Yeats states in a lengthy note to the poem, is the cone or gyre interlocked with its opposite, the vertex of the one centered upon the base of the other. This figure defines the relation not only between subjective and objective impulses within the individual, but also within the pattern of history. The end of an age, Yeats explains, "always receives the revelation of the character of the next age" and "is represented by the coming of one gyre to its place of greatest expansion and of the other to that of its greatest contraction. At the present moment the life gyre [i.e., the objective or *primary* impulse] is sweeping outward, unlike that before the birth of Christ which was narrowing, and has almost reached its greatest expansion. The revelation which approaches will however take its character from the contrary movement of the interior gyre [i.e., the subjective or *antithetical* impulse]. All our scientific, democratic, fact-accumulating, heterogeneous civilization belongs to the outward gyre and prepares not the continuance of itself but the revelation as in a lightning flash, though in a flash that will not strike only in one place, and will for a time be constantly repeated, of the civilization that must slowly take its place" (*VP* 824–825). In *A VISION*, Yeats expresses the idea more simply: "After an age of necessity, truth, goodness, mechanism, science, democracy, abstraction, peace, comes an age of freedom, fiction, evil, kindred, art, aristocracy, particularity, war" (52; see also 263, 277; *AV-1925* 210–215). In its first stanza, "The Second Coming" envisions just this "expansion" of the "life gyre" in the figure of the falcon circling in a widening gyre beyond the command of the falconer, an image that Yeats had rehearsed in the fine minor poem "The Hawk" (1916). The image reverses the beatific downward gyre of the white gull in "DEMON AND BEAST," such that the two poems in conjunction embody the double movement of the gyres as each dies into the life of the other. The image also reprises the central image of the "The WILD SWANS AT COOLE," the private bereavement of the earlier poem writ large as a symbol of universal dissolution, of anarchy "loosed upon the world," of the "blood-dimmed tide" drowning everywhere "the ceremony of innocence." This is something like the ceremony of innocence that Yeats wishes for his daughter in "A PRAYER FOR MY DAUGHTER," which immediately follows in *Michael Robartes and the Dancer* (1921) and in the collected poems.

In AUTOBIOGRAPHIES, Yeats recalls his conviction as a young man that the world had become "a bundle of fragments," but he admits that he did not foresee "the growing murderousness of the world" and quotes the first stanza of "The Second Coming" to emphasize the point (163–166). Yeats wrote "The Second Coming" in early January 1919 (YC 202); its sense of murderousness conceivably encompasses World War I, the EASTER RISING, and the Russian Revolution. The ANGLO-IRISH WAR, which has its great poem in "NINETEEN HUNDRED AND NINETEEN," was then brewing, but did not commence in earnest until January 21, 1919. Yeats specifically mentions Russia in a draft of the poem: "The Germans are . . . now to Russia come / Though every day some innocent has died" (*Between the Lines* 17). John Stallworthy notes that by "the end of July 1917 the Russian front had crumbled in face of the enemy. In October of that year the Bolsheviks brought off their revolution, and at the Treaty of Brest-Litovsk, on 3 March 1918, Lenin had surrendered to the Germans: Finland, Esthonia, Courland, Lithuania, and tracts of Russian Poland. The Germans had indeed come to Russia, and I think it not impossible that Yeats, with his reverence for the aristocratic virtues epitomized by Castiglione, had in mind the fate of the Russian Royal House, as he wrote: 'Though every day some innocent has died'" (*Between the Lines* 18–19; on the Russian royal family, see "CRAZY JANE ON THE MOUNTAIN"). In an April 8, 1936, letter to Ethel Mannin (1900–84), Yeats emphasized the political implications of the poem: "[As] my sense of reality deepens, and I think it does with age, my horror at the cruelty of governments grows greater [. . .]. Communist, Fascist, nationalist, clerical, anti-clerical, all are responsible according to the number of their victims. I have not been silent; I have used the only vehicle I possess—verse. If you have my poems by you, look up a poem called *The Second Coming*. It was written some sixteen or seventeen years ago and foretold what is happening" (*Letters* 851).

Whatever its political relevance, "The Second Coming" shares the understanding of *Autobiographies* that "the growing murderousness of the world" is a mere symptom of the culture's fall from UNITY OF BEING into the "bitter comedy" of self-division (165). Under these circumstances, the "best lack all conviction," being out of phase with their era and profoundly discouraged, while the worst are "full of passionate intensity." As many commentators have noted—for example, Bornstein, Henn, and Stallworthy—these lines closely follow SHELLEY's *Prometheus Unbound* (I, lines 625–628): "The good want power, but to weep barren tears. / The powerful goodness want: worse need for them. / The wise want love; and those who love want wisdom; / And all best things are thus confused to ill" (*Yeats and Shelley* 196; *Lonely Tower* 146; *Between the Lines* 23). The "passionate intensity" of "the worst" most likely has a personal as well as a global resonance, recollecting those who impeded and harassed HUGH LANE, J. M. SYNGE, and CHARLES STEWART PARNELL, and obstructed Yeats's own enterprise of Irish cultural renaissance.

The second stanza, echoing the desert scene in the final stanza of "Demon and Beast," stages the vision of destruction by which modernity is to be undone. Convinced that the "second coming" must be at hand, for the condition of the culture is unsustainable, Yeats sees "a vast image out of *Spiritus Mundi*," or the "world spirit," a version of the ANIMA MUNDI that is a central concept in Yeats's esoteric philosophy. In his notes to Lady GREGORY's *Visions and Beliefs in the West of Ireland* (1920), Yeats attributes the concept of the "spiritus mundi" to the Cambridge Platonist Henry More (1614–87) and describes it as a pervasive vital spirit that contains "all forms, so that the parents when a child is begotten, or a witch when the double is projected as a hare, but as it were, call upon the *Spiritus Mundi* for the form they need" (LE 271). In a note to "An IMAGE FROM A PAST LIFE," Yeats describes the *Spiritus Mundi* as a "general storehouse of images which have ceased to be a property of any personality or spirit" (VP 822). In this case, the mind's eye calls forth from the *Spiritus Mundi* a desert scene in which a "shape with lion body and the head of a man, / A gaze blank and pitiless as the sun, / Is moving its slow thighs," while above "reel shadows of the indignant desert birds," as if the noble, solitary falcon of the opening stanza has been reborn as its anti-self.

The image of the Sphinx had germinated for decades, inspired perhaps, as Harold Bloom and Stallworthy think, by Shelley's "Ozymandias," with its related vision: "Two vast and trunkless legs of stone / Stand in the desert . . . Near them, on the sand, / Half sunk a shattered visage lies . . ." (Yeats 319; Between the Lines 22–23). In Autobiographies, Yeats recalls an occult experiment that took place in 1890 or 1891 in which MacGregor Mathers induced a vision clearly anticipatory of the sphinx of "The Second Coming." Yeats saw "a desert and a black Titan raising himself up by his two hands from the middle of a heap of ancient ruins" (161). In his 1934 introduction to The Resurrection, Yeats's wonders, "Had I begun On Baile's Strand [in August 1901] or not when I began to imagine, as always at my left side just out of the range of the sight, a brazen winged beast that I associated with laughing ecstatic destruction?" (Expl. 393; VPl. 932). In a footnote, Yeats explicitly identifies the beast as that which "The Second Coming" describes. Giorgio Melchiori, meanwhile, associates the Sphinx with the apocalyptic unicorn that is a crucial motif in the plays The Player Queen, The Unicorn from the Stars, and Where There is Nothing, and in the story "The Adoration of the Magi." In Where There is Nothing, the Nietzschean iconoclast Paul Ruttledge envisions, as the symbol of his own destructive, messianic impulse, "a very terrible wild beast, with iron teeth and brazen claws that can root up spires and towers" (VPl. 1099). Thomas Whitaker discerns additional "symbolic ancestors" in "Blake's Orc awakening after eighteen centuries of sleep, the Black Pig visiting blissful destruction upon an exhausted world [see "The Valley of the Black Pig"], the uncontrollable mystery on the bestial floor [see "The Magi"] (Swan and Shadow 74).

The sphinx recurs far more complexly in "The Double Vision of Michael Robartes," where,

along with the Buddha, it flanks the dancing girl who embodies the transcendental stasis of the 15th lunar phase. In A Vision, Yeats calls the sphinx an image of the "outward-looking mind, love and its lure" and Buddha an image of the "introspective knowledge of the mind's self-begotten unity," and he notes that these figures stand "like heraldic supporters guarding the mystery of the fifteenth phase" (AV 207). The sphinx of "The Double Vision of Michael Robartes" seems a symbol of eternity rather than an agent of apocalypse, but it shares with the sphinx of "The Second Coming" its blank and pitiless stare, a motif likewise significant in poems as diverse as "A Bronze Head," "The Cat and the Moon," "The Phases of the Moon" (lines 84–88), "The Statues," and "Upon a House shaken by the Land Agitation," and indicating a vision of something beyond the world or an attunement to an invisible behest. In A Vision, Yeats, commenting on different traditions of statuary, hints at the significance of the blank eye: "When I think of Rome I see always those heads with their world-considering eyes, and those bodies as conventional as the metaphors in a leading article, and compare in my imagination vague Grecian eyes gazing at nothing, Byzantine eyes of drilled ivory staring upon a vision, and those eyelids of China and of India, those veiled or half-veiled eyes weary of world and vision alike" (275–277; see also 280).

In its chilling final lines, "The Second Coming" crossbreeds its dark cyclic vision with the traditional Christian mythos of the second coming (see Matthew 24) and revelation (see Revelation 13). Like some mutant Christ, the rough beast, "its hour come round at last," slouches toward Bethlehem to be born, not in initiation of a final heavenly peace, but in perpetuation of the violent revolutions of history and in annunciation of the birth of a new age, as in "The Magi" ("round" in this case has a literal signification). As Richard Ellmann writes, "The final intimation that the new god will be born in Bethlehem, which Christianity associates with passive infancy and the tenderness of maternal love, makes it brutishness particularly frightful" (IY 260). Yeats provides the relevant metaphysical framework in *A Vision*: "At the birth of Christ took place, and at the coming *antithetical* influx will take place, a change equivalent to the *interchange of the tinctures.* [. . .] The approaching *antithetical* influx and that particular *antithetical* dispensation for which the intellectual preparation has begun will reach its complete systematisation at that moment when, as I have already shown, the Great Year comes to its intellectual climax" (*AV* 262–263). Where the *primary* era of Christ is "dogmatic, levelling, unifying, feminine, humane, peace its means and end," the *antithetical* era of the beast will be "expressive, hierarchical, multiple, masculine, harsh, surgical" (263). Yeats punctuates the entire discussion by quoting "The Second Coming's" description of the sphinx, the physical and mythic symbol of the *"antithetical* influx" he describes. As to when this revelation was supposed to occur, Lady Gregory records in a journal entry of November 3, 1925, Yeats's prediction that the next revelation—that of "The Second Coming"—will come "perhaps not for another two hundred years" (*Lady Gregory's Journals*, I, 600–601).

Yeats explores similar ideas of annunciation in "LEDA AND THE SWAN," which also pictures the violent birth pangs of an *antithetical* age. As Giorgio Melchiori writes, Yeats considers the Trojan war that was set in motion by the rape of Leda, the birth of Christ, and "an indefinite event due to happen in our century"—the birth depicted in "The Second Coming"—to be the "three fundamental crises in world history, each of which reversed the established order and ushered in a new cycle of civilization" (*Whole Mystery of Art* 85).

FIRST PUBLICATION: The *Dial* (periodical), November 1920, and the *Nation* (periodical), November 6, 1920. Reprinted in *Michael Robartes and the Dancer*, The CUALA PRESS, Churchtown, Dundrum, February 1921.

BIBLIOGRAPHY

Bloom, Harold. *Yeats*; Bornstein, George. *Yeats and Shelley*; Ellmann, Richard. *The Identity of Yeats*; Lady Gregory. *Lady Gregory's Journals* (vol. 1, ed. Daniel J. Murphy); Henn, T. R. *The Lonely Tower: Studies in the Poetry of W. B. Yeats*; Kelly, John S. *A W. B. Yeats Chronology*; Melchiori, Giorgio. *The Whole Mystery of Art: Pattern into Poetry in the Work of W. B. Yeats*; Stallworthy, John. *Between the Lines: Yeats's Poetry in the Making*; Whitaker, Thomas R. *Swan and Shadow: Yeats's Dialogue with History*; Yeats, W. B. *Autobiographies, A Critical Edition of Yeats's A Vision (1925), Explorations, Later Essays, The Letters of W. B. Yeats, The Variorum Edition of the Plays of W. B. Yeats, The Variorum Edition of the Poems of W. B. Yeats, A Vision*.

"Secret Rose, The" (1896)

"The Secret Rose" joins "The ROSE OF BATTLE," "The Rose of Peace" (1892), "The Rose of the World" (1892), and "TO THE ROSE UPON THE ROOD OF TIME" as one of several early poems that invoke the symbol of the mystical ROSE. In the poem's opening lines, Yeats calls to the "far-off, most secret, and inviolate Rose" and asks that it enfold him in his "hour or hours" and admit him to the realm of sleep-touched beauty where those who sought the rose in "Holy Sepulchre" and "wine-vat" dwell beyond "the stir and tumult of defeated dreams." In plain terms, Yeats conceives the rose as a muse of transcendence. But in begging complete release or reprieve from the mundane world, he demonstrates nothing of the rich ambivalence that characterizes "To the Rose upon the Rood of Time," a poem far closer to his mature sensibility in its dialectical tension between natural and supernatural impulse.

The 21 lines that follow, explicated by Yeats himself in a long note to the poem (see *VP* 812–814), recount all those who are enfolded by the rose's "great leaves": the jeweled magi who attended Christ's birth (cf. "The MAGI"); the legendary Irish king Conchubar, who saw a vision of Christ's crucifixion and died in a frenzy of indignant rage (cf. DEIRDRE and ON BAILE'S STRAND), the legendary Irish hero CUCHULAIN, whom the goddess Fand seduced (see *The* ONLY JEALOUSY OF EMER and "Under the Moon" [1901]); the legendary Irish hero Caoilte, who madly drove the gods from their "liss" (lair, fort) after his fellows had been killed in the battle of Gabra (cf. "The HOSTING OF THE SIDHE"); the legendary Irish king Fergus, who abandoned his throne for love (see "FERGUS AND THE DRUID" and "WHO GOES WITH FERGUS?"); and, finally, a man who sold house and farm to go in pursuit of a "woman of so shining loveliness / That men threshed corn at midnight by a tress. . . ." As Yeats explains in his note, the allusion is to "The Red Pony," a tale in William Larminie's (1849–1900) *West Irish Folk Tales* (1894), a volume that Yeats glowingly reviewed in the June 1894 issue of the *Bookman* (see *UP1* 326–328). In Yeats's summary, the story tells of a young man who finds by the roadside a box containing a lock of hair so pure that it glows with light. The young man becomes a servant in the king's household and uses the miraculous lock to light his way in a dark stable. The king hears of the lock and sets his heart on the woman from whom it came. He sends the young man in search of the woman, and the young man winds up marrying her himself (*VP* 813–814; see also *UP2* 190).

In its embrace of these several dreaming, wayward figures, the rose as it were presides over and sanctifies their mutiny against the mundane or mortal world. Yeats likewise would be included in the embrace of the rose, as he announces in the last six lines of the poem. He too awaits the hour of the rose's "great wind of love and hate," which shall blow the stars about the sky. He asks—almost implores—in conclusion, "Surely thine hour has come, thy great wind blows, / Far-off, most secret, and inviolate Rose?" Frank Hughes Murphy characterizes Yeats's summons of the rose as an outright abandonment of "all faith in the heart's 'foul rag-and-bone shop,' the entire created world. In rejecting transient, earthly beauty because it is transient and all earthly things because they are imperfect, Yeats has fallen as far as he was ever to fall from the ambitious determination to reconcile the real and the ideal by unifying them" (*Yeats's Early Poetry* 82).

FIRST PUBLICATION: The *SAVOY* (periodical), September 1896, under the title "O' Sullivan Rua to the Secret Rose." Reprinted in *The Secret Rose*, Lawrence and Bullen, London, April 1897, under the title "To the Secret Rose." Reprinted in *The Wind Among the Reeds*, Elkin Mathews, London, April 1899, under the present title.

BIBLIOGRAPHY

Murphy, Frank Hughes. *Yeats's Early Poetry: The Quest for Reconciliation*; Yeats, W. B. *Uncollected Prose by W. B. Yeats* (vols. 1–2), *The Variorum Edition of the Poems of W. B. Yeats*.

"Secrets of the Old, The" (1927)

See "A MAN YOUNG AND OLD."

"September 1913" (1913)

"September 1913" elegizes both the Fenian hero JOHN O'LEARY, who died on March 16, 1907, and the national spirit that he represented. In 1885, O'Leary returned to Dublin after 20 years spent as a prisoner and political exile, and Yeats was immediately won over by the unself-conscious loftiness of his dignity and honesty. As Yeats writes in *AUTOBIOGRAPHIES*, O'Leary had "the moral genius that moves all young people." He was soon surrounded by a circle of young admirers that included MAUD GONNE, Douglas Hyde (1860–1949), the barrister John F. Taylor (1850–1902), KATHARINE TYNAN, and Yeats himself (100–101). Yeats's admiration for O'Leary was steeped in the sense that among the day's prominent figures "he alone had personality, a point of view not made for the crowd's sake, but for self-expression" (176). In his essay "Poetry and Tradition" (1908), Yeats refers to O'Leary's "romantic conception of Irish Nationality" and explains this conception as an "understanding of life and Nationality, built up by the generation of Grattan, which read Homer and Virgil, and by the generation of Davis, which had been pierced

Portrait of John O'Leary by John Butler Yeats. O'Leary's friends commissioned the painting in 1891. *(The National Gallery of Ireland)*

through by the idealism of Mazzini, and of the European revolutionists of the mid-century." Upon this conception, Yeats writes, he and LIONEL JOHNSON had "founded, as far as it was founded on anything but literature, our art and our Irish criticism" (*E&I* 246). It is this quality of personality wed to pride, dignity, and intellect that Yeats means to indicate when he speaks of "romantic Ireland" in "September 1913."

"September 1913" accuses the middle classes of a timidity and calculation that betrays the spirit of O'Leary and those of his stamp, a critique reiterated in poems like "AT GALWAY RACES" and "TO A WEALTHY MAN WHO PROMISED A SECOND SUBSCRIPTION TO THE DUBLIN MUNICIPAL GALLERY IF IT WERE PROVED THE PEOPLE WANTED PICTURES." In a note to *Responsibilities* (1914), Yeats summarizes the complaint against the middle class that all of these poems in their different ways articulate:

"Religious Ireland [. . .] thinks of divine things as a round of duties separated from life and not as an element that may be discovered in all circumstance and emotion, while political Ireland sees a good citizen but as a man who holds to certain opinions and not as a man of good will. Against all this we have but a few educated men and the remnants of an old traditional culture among the poor. Both were stronger forty years ago, before the rise of our new middle class which made its first public display during the nine years of the Parnellite split, showing how base at moments of excitement are minds without culture" (*VP* 819). Yeats learned at least something of this animus against the middle class from O'Leary himself. In his *Recollections of Fenians and Fenianism* (1896), O'Leary had written, in terms that foreshadow Yeats's own, "The middle class, I believe, in Ireland and elsewhere, to be distinctly the lowest class morally—that is, the class influenced by the lowest motives. The prudential virtues it has in abundance; but a regard for your own stomach and skin [. . .] is not the stuff out of which patriots are made" (I, 31). Elizabeth Cullingford calls this passage "the germ of Yeats's poetic denigration of the merchant and the clerk" (*Yeats, Ireland and Fascism* 5).

The first of the poem's four eight-line stanzas is as aggressively polemical as Yeats had yet dared to be. Addressing the middle classes directly, Yeats asks, "What need you, being come to sense, / But fumble in a greasy till / And add the halfpence to the pence / And prayer to shivering prayer, until / You have dried the marrow from the bone?" Commerce and religion, in these lines, are equally forms of unimaginative and venal obedience to an external discipline: They constitute the bulwark of "sense" that has thwarted passionate impulse and undone the nation. Shifting into a minor key, Yeats deflates this extravagant combative sarcasm with an almost sighing echo of popular sentiment—"For men were born to pray and save"—and then arrives, with a sudden, startling abandonment of irony, at the poem's great refrain: "Romantic Ireland's dead and gone, / It's with O'Leary in the grave."

The heroes of Ireland's long political struggle "were of a different kind," having no time to pray:

for them not the gestures of faith, but the actuality of martyrdom. And yet, Yeats asks, punning on the thriftiness mentioned in line six, what "could they save"? The inferable answer is that their sacrifice has gone for nothing, as it has not been answered in kind or perpetuated for all the clamor of nationalist sentiment. Was it for this—the hypocritical complacency of the middle class—that the "wild geese" took flight, for this that "Edward Fitzgerald died, / And Robert Emmet and Wolfe Tone, / All that delirium of the brave?" The "wild geese" were Irish soldiers who enlisted in foreign armies during the 18th century after Catholics were barred from serving in the Irish military (Catholics were readmitted to the military in 1793). Lord Edward Fitzgerald (1763–98), Wolfe Tone (1763–98), and Robert Emmet (1778–1803) are among Ireland's most celebrated nationalist heroes (cf. *Aut.* 276). Fitzgerald died of wounds suffered during his arrest as a participant in the rebellion of 1798; Tone committed suicide while imprisoned for his part in the same rebellion; Emmet was executed for his part in the failed insurrection of 1803. Yeats choice of the word *delirium*—a deliberate provocation—reproves the calculation of the middle classes with an ideal of reckless passion that scorns reason itself.

The poem's final stanza levels the undisguised charge of hypocrisy. For all its vaunted reverence for its national martyrs, middle-class Ireland would have nothing to do with such men if they were somehow brought before the present. The resurrected heroes would meet with the complaining cry that "some woman's yellow hair / Has maddened every mother's son. . . ." These lines may recollect Maud Gonne's seductive political sway during the 1890s. In *Autobiographies* Yeats remembers that "when men and woman did her bidding they did it not only because she was beautiful, but because that beauty suggested joy and freedom" (274). These lines may also allude to the sway of Cathleen ni Houlihan, the female personification of "romantic Ireland," who calls men from the comfort of the hearth to the sacrifice of the gallows, as in Yeats's play CATHLEEN NI HOULIHAN.

Originally subtitled "On reading much of the correspondence against the Art Gallery," "September 1913," like "TO A SHADE" and "To a Wealthy Man," was a broadside in the controversy that flared around HUGH LANE's attempt to establish a gallery of modern art in Dublin. As originally titled, the poem's meaning shifts slightly: where Fitzgerald, Tone, and Emmet heeded the call to battle, contemporary Ireland has failed to heed the call to an equivalent cultural battle. By implication, Lane, Lady GREGORY, and Yeats—advocates of the gallery—carry on the heroic nationalist endeavor of the 18th century, though on a different footing. The aspersion on middle-class penny counting, meanwhile, assumes a sharper polemical and topical edge in light of the ongoing effort to raise funds for the new gallery, and brings the poem into even closer relation with "To a Wealthy Man."

The EASTER RISING of 1916 forced Yeats to reconsider the premise of his poem. As he wrote in a note dated July 1916, "'Romantic Ireland's dead and gone' sounds old-fashioned now. It seemed true in 1913, but I did not foresee 1916. The late Dublin Rebellion, whatever one can say of its wisdom, will long be remembered for its heroism. 'They weighed so lightly what they gave,' and gave too in some cases without hope of success" (*VP* 820).

FIRST PUBLICATION: The *Irish Times*, September 8, 1913, under the title "Romance in Ireland (On reading much of the correspondence against the Art Gallery)." Reprinted in *Poems Written in Discouragement*, The CUALA PRESS, Dundrum, October 1913, under the present title.

BIBLIOGRAPHY

Cullingford, Elizabeth. *Yeats, Ireland and Fascism*; O'Leary, John. *Recollections of Fenians and Fenianism* (vol. 1); Yeats, W. B. *Autobiographies, Essays and Introductions, The Variorum Edition of the Poems of W. B. Yeats*.

"Seven Sages, The" (1932)

"We make out of the quarrel with others, rhetoric, but of the quarrel with ourselves, poetry," Yeats writes in PER AMICA SILENTIA LUNAE (*LE*

8). As much as any poem in Yeats's canon, "The Seven Sages," a seven-voice colloquy, is open to the charge of rhetoric. The poem argues for a reconstructed intellectual tradition with Edmund Burke (1729–97), Oliver Goldsmith (1728–74), George Berkeley (1685–1753), and JONATHAN SWIFT (1667–1745) as its pillars. Yeats champions the Irish Georgians as a corrective to the "Whiggery" of the modern age—the passionless rationalism that is the culprit in the four preceding poems, "Spilt Milk" (1932), "The NINETEENTH CENTURY AND AFTER," "Statistics" (1932), and "THREE MOVEMENTS." Yeats similarly extols the Irish Georgians in "BLOOD AND THE MOON," which is a headnote to all of these poems, and in his introduction to Joseph Hone and Mario M. Rossi's *Bishop Berkeley* (1931). In the latter, Yeats calls the litany of his heroes: "Berkeley with his belief in perception, that abstract ideas are mere words, Swift with his love of perfect nature, of the Houyhnhnms, his disbelief in Newton's system and every sort of machine, Goldsmith and his delight in the particulars of common life that shocked his contemporaries, Burke with his conviction that all states not grown slowly like a forest tree are tyrannies" (*E&I* 402; *LE* 107).

In "The Seven Sages," the first four voices recall, as cherished family tales, their great-grandfathers' and great-great-grandfathers' brushes with Burke, Goldsmith, Berkeley (Bishop of Cloyne from 1734 until his death), and "Stella," i.e., Esther Johnson (1681–1728), the pupil and Platonic intimate to whom Swift addressed his *Journal to Stella* (Yeats makes much of "Stella" in *The WORDS UPON THE WINDOW-PANE*). Henry Grattan (1746–1820), in whose house the first speaker's great-grandfather met Burke, was a nationalist parliamentarian whom Yeats similarly pairs with Burke in "The TOWER" as the twin embodiments of the Anglo-Irish tradition. The plain speech of Grattan's house, the allusion to the homely "pot-house bench" (i.e., tavern bench), the human foible of Berkeley's devotion to "tar-water" (see *E&I* 399; *Expl.* 324; *LE* 105), all imply rootedness in the life of the people. Such details suggest, in the formulation of Yeats's introduction to *Bishop Berkeley*, the "delight in the particulars of com-

mon life," and they have their ultimate explanation in "The MUNICIPAL GALLERY REVISITED": from contact with the soil, as "the noble and the beggar-man" understand, everything "Antaeus-like" grows strong.

"Whence came our thought?" asks the fifth voice. "From four great minds that hated Whiggery" answers the sixth. The fifth voice objects that Burke was himself a Whig in the literal sense that he belonged to the Whig Party that bestrode British politics during the 18th and 19th centuries. Broadly liberal without being in any sense radical, the Whigs were associated with parliamentary opposition to the power of the Crown, religious toleration, and economic and social reform. While probably unbothered by the particulars of this platform, Yeats perceived in the Whig mindset the baneful materialistic and democratic premises of the modern world view. The sixth voice duly responds that Whiggery was no mere party affiliation, but a state of mind: "A levelling, rancorous, rational sort of mind / That never looked out of the eye of a saint / Or out of drunkard's eye." "Saint" and "drunkard" build upon the earlier allusions to "the Bishop of Cloyne" and "pot-house bench." In opposition to the benevolent rationality of the Whig program, they represent the "zig-zag wantonness" that Yeats mentions in "Tom O'Roughley" (1918). The seventh voice interjects the essential accusation of the poem: "All's Whiggery now, / But we old men are massed against the world." Yeats would reprise this pose of wild, dissident age in numerous poems, most pronouncedly in "WHY SHOULD NOT OLD MEN BE MAD?"

Returning to the first voice, the poem offers, much like "Blood and the Moon," brief aperçus of the great Georgians. Burke set his "great melody" (cf. "The Nineteenth Century and After") against British colonial policy in America, Ireland, and India, and wrote his most famous work in opposition to the French Revolution. Goldsmith is remembered as the chronicler of roads and fields, beggars and cattle. In implicit explanation of Goldsmith's mildness, Yeats points out that, having died in 1774, he never saw the trefoil—i.e., clover—"stained with blood, / The avenging leaf those fields raised up against it." The allusion is to the insurrection of 1798 and to the long after-math of bloody violence between England and Ireland. As Donald T. Torchiana writes, the tre-foil "charges the sense with heraldic and national-ist significance in its emblematic blend of blood and shamrock" (*W. B. Yeats & Georgian Ireland* 277). The Fourth Voice offers that Swift's tomb (cf. "SWIFT'S EPITAPH") wears away this stain of blood by the uplifting example of its passionate dignity. Berkeley's is the voice of the provincial intellectual, which begins as the "rustle of a reed" and swells, as with the power of its own truth, into a "thunderclap." These lines, Torchiana says, are "meant to suggest the power of Berkeley's philoso-phy and growing influence in combating modern Whiggery" (252).

For schooling, says the seventh voice in con-clusion, the four great men "walked the roads / Mimicking what they heard, as children mimic; / They understood that wisdom comes of beggary." In his introduction to *Bishop Berkeley*, Yeats simi-larly associates his Georgian heroes with beggary. He observes that the "sense for what is permanent, as distinct from what is useful [. . .] comes from solitaries or from communities where the solitar-ies flourish, Indians with a begging-bowl, monks where their occupation is an adventure, men escaped out of machinery, improvident men that sit by the roadside and feel responsible for all that exists [. . .]." Though far from beggars themselves, the great Georgians belonged to such a community where "solitaries flourish"—the essentially premod-ern culture of 17th- and 18th-century Ireland—and "found in England the opposite that stung their own thought into expression and made it lucid" (*E&I* 401–402; *LE* 106–107). Anticipating the terms of "The Seven Sages," Yeats associates both itinerancy and drunkenness with spiritual wisdom in *WHERE THERE IS NOTHING*.

FIRST PUBLICATION: *Words for Music Per-haps and Other Poems*, The CUALA PRESS, Dublin, November 14, 1932.

BIBLIOGRAPHY

Torchiana, Donald T. *W. B. Yeats & Georgian Ireland*; Yeats, W. B. *Essays and Introduction, Explorations, Later Essays.*

"She turns the Dolls' Faces to the Wall" (1917)

The third of seven poems in the sequence "UPON A DYING LADY," "She turns the Dolls' Faces to the Wall," like "CERTAIN ARTISTS BRING HER DOLLS AND DRAWINGS," alludes to the dolls that Yeats's friend the artist Charles Ricketts (1866–1931) made for Mabel Beardsley (1871–1916) while she was hospitalized with the cancer that would even-tually take her life. Yeats mentioned the dolls in a January 8, 1913, letter to Lady GREGORY: "On a table near were four dolls dressed like people out of her brother's drawings. Women with loose trou-sers and boys that looked like women. Ricketts had made them, modelling the faces and sewing the clothes. They must have taken him days" (*Letters* 574). Beardsley's brother, AUBREY BEARDSLEY, was the arch-decadent illustrator who gave much of the character to the notorious journals the *Yellow Book* and the *SAVOY* during the 1890s.

As the preceding poems "HER COURTESY" and "Certain Artists bring her Dolls and Drawings" ruminate on defiant gaiety and artistic creation as responses to the ineluctability of death, "She turns the Dolls' Faces to the Wall" conversely ruminates on religious orthodoxy. The coming of a priest to say Mass prompts Beardsley to turn her dolls toward the wall, presumably on the girlish notion that the dolls are not communicants of the church and ought not to participate or witness; or perhaps worried that the decadent aesthetic of the dolls will offend the priest. The dolls include a Japa-nese lady, a Venetian lady (her "panniered skirt" copied from the Venetian painter Pietro Longhi, 1702–62), a meditative critic (cf. the Paterian car-dinal who murmurs of Giorgione in "HER COUR-AGE"), and "our Beauty with her Turkish trousers on." This last is the doll with "loose trousers" that Yeats mentioned in his letter to Lady Gregory. The phrase "our beauty," which in the preceding poem attaches to Beardsley, hints that the doll is mod-eled on her or that Yeats detected something of her in the doll.

The dolls are flush with personality and rich impulse, unlike the priest, who is motivated by a narrow self-importance ("the priest must have like every dog his day / Or keep us all awake with baying at the moon. . . ."). By associating him with the dog, Yeats identifies the priest as a man of objective nature; as he explains in a note to *Calvary*, "the beasts that run upon the ground, especially those that run in packs, are the natural symbols of objective man" (*VPl.* 789). As the moon signifies subjectivity in Yeats's symbolic scheme, the priest and the dog bay uncomprehendingly or antagonistically at their opposite. In "The CAT AND THE MOON," the image of the baying dog is reversed in the image of the slinking cat. Subjective in its nocturnal and solitary wandering, the cat finds in the moon a mysterious self-reflection rather than self-contrast. With the priest's arrival, Yeats and the dolls "being but the world were best away." That the dolls are described as "our dolls" links with them with Yeats and Ricketts, and with the values of artistic expression as against religious doctrine. The phrase "being but the world" sarcastically accedes to the priestly point of view, while echoing the penultimate line of "Certain Artists bring her Dolls and Drawings": "We have the given the world our passion. . . ."

Structurally if not philosophically, "She turns the Dolls' Faces to the Wall" bears comparison to "The DOLLS." In both poems the dolls are contrasted with an interloper who represents an antagonistic principle.

FIRST PUBLICATION: The *Little Review* (periodical), August 1917, and the *New Statesman*, August 11, 1917. Reprinted in *The Wild Swans at Coole*, The CUALA PRESS, Churchtown, Dundrum, November 17, 1917.

BIBLIOGRAPHY

Yeats, W. B. *The Collected Letters of W. B. Yeats*, The *Variorum Edition of the Plays of W. B. Yeats*.

"Solomon and the Witch"
(1921)

"It seems to me that true love is a discipline, and it needs so much wisdom that the love of Solomon and Sheba must have lasted, for all the silence of the Scriptures," Yeats wrote in his diary of 1909. "Each divines the secret self of the other, and refusing to believe in the mere daily self, creates a mirror where the lover or the beloved sees an image to copy in daily life; for love also creates the Mask" (*Aut.* 343; *Mem.* 144–145). The story of the king of Israel (ruled ca. 965–26 B.C.) and the queen of Sheba (a kingdom in western Arabia) remained with Yeats and yielded three poems—"ON WOMAN," "Solomon to Sheba" (1918), and "Solomon and the Witch"—that imagine the biblical figures as impassioned lovers. In the biblical tale, Sheba journeys to Jerusalem to test with "hard questions" the famous wisdom of Solomon. Dazzled by Solomon's "wisdom and prosperity," she gives the king a treasure of gold, spices, and precious stones, and then returns to her own kingdom. Solomon reciprocates—with a possible sexual suggestion—by giving "unto the queen of Sheba all her desire, whatsoever she asked, beside that which Solomon gave her of his royal bounty." According to legend, Sheba became one of Solomon's wives and bore him a son, Menilek, who founded the royal house of Abyssinia (1 Kings 10:1–13 and 2 Chronicles 9:1–12). All of this being said, S. B. Bushrui proposes that Yeats's notion of Solomon owes more to the *Arabian Nights* than to the Bible. In the Arabic tradition, according to Bushrui, Solomon is a "more glorious" version of Harun al-Rashid (see "The GIFT OF HARUN AL-RASHID") and is "represented as the wisest, richest, greatest, most virile and manly person within whom all opposites are reconciled, above all the reconciliation between the spiritual and the physical." With relevance to "Solomon and the Witch," the Arabic tradition holds that Solomon had "all birds, beasts and insects at his command; that he understood and spoke their language; and that he was lord and master over all the Djinn who feared and obeyed him—his power was supreme both in the natural and in the supernatural worlds" (*In Excited Reverie* 309–310). Yeats wrote "Solomon to Sheba" and "Solomon and the Witch" in the afterglow of his marriage, and the poems are generally thought to be tributes to his own conjugal bed. Yeats dubs Sheba "the witch," presumably, in recognition of GEORGE YEATS's mediumistic gifts.

"Solomon and the Witch," like "On Woman," instances the sexual candor that begins to mark Yeats's poetry during this period. Sheba recalls the amorous throes of the previous night, during which she "suddenly cried out in a strange tongue." Solomon, who in his wisdom understands the utterance of every man and beast, explains that the cockerel who "crowed out" the eternity of Eden "thought to have crowed it in again," being awakened by the conflation of "chance" and "choice" achieved by their lovemaking. As in "MY TABLE" (which shares the motif of the vatic bird), the suggestion is that passion brought to an ultimate intensity becomes an apocalyptic unity that compels a new historical dispensation or cycle. The world ends, as Solomon explains, speaking of chance and choice, "when these two things, / Though several, are a single light, / When oil and wick are burned in one . . . ." The crowing cock upon its "blossoming apple bough" belongs to a pervasive pattern of avian-apocalyptic imagery that extends from "The Indian to His Love" (1886) to "BYZANTIUM." It has a particularly close precedent in The KING's THRESHOLD, in which the poet Seanchan remembers long ago writing a poem about "the Garden in the East of the World, / And how spirits in the images of birds / Crowd in the branches of old Adam's crab-tree" (VPl. 303). "AN IMAGE FROM A PAST LIFE," which follows "Solomon and the Witch" in Michael Robartes and the Dancer (1921) and in the collected poems, resumes the motif of the vatic bird ("there comes that scream / From terrified, invisible beast or bird: / Image of poignant recollection").

According to A VISION, the conflation of chance and choice is a condition of the 15th lunar phase, the "phase of complete beauty," marked by the full moon. Yeats writes of this phase, "Now contemplation and desire, united into one, inhabit a world where every beloved image has bodily form, and every bodily form is loved. This love knows nothing of desire, for desire implies effort, and though there is still separation from the loved object, love accepts the separation as necessary to its own existence. [. . .] Chance and Choice have become interchangeable without losing their identity" (136). Yeats also adverts to chance and choice in "ALL SOULS' NIGHT," the epilogue to A Vision, describing FLORENCE FARR's discovery that the soul whirls about in the orbit of the moon until it "plunge into the sun; / And there, free and yet fast, / Being both Chance and Choice, / Forget its broken toys / And sink into its own delight at last." Consistent with the miraculous conflation of chance and choice, the moon that shines upon Solomon and Sheba is "wild" and "blessed," as, in "The CAT AND THE MOON," the moon is "sacred": all of these appellations indicate the full moon or the approach of the full moon.

In response to Solomon's abstruse disquisition, Sheba notes the obvious: far from being overthrown, the world remains as before. Solomon theorizes that the Cockerel found them "in the wrong," though "worth a crow," perhaps because "an image" was too strong or not strong enough. The gist is that all was not in exact harmony. Sheba observes the darkness and silence and emptiness of the "forbidden sacred grove" and the moon growing "wilder every minute." In an expostulation as surprisingly and winningly carnal as the more famous expostulation that ends "POLITICS," Sheba cries, "O! Solomon! let us try again."

FIRST PUBLICATION: Michael Robartes and the Dancer, The CUALA PRESS, Churchtown, Dundrum, February 1921.

BIBLIOGRAPHY

Jeffares, A. Norman, and K. G. W. Cross, eds. In Excited Reverie: A Centenary Tribute to William Butler Yeats 1865–1939; Yeats, W. B. Autobiographies, Memoirs, The Variorum Edition of the Plays of W. B. Yeats, A Vision.

"Song of the Happy Shepherd, The" (1885)

"The Song of the Happy Shepherd" was originally titled "An Epilogue. To 'The Island of Statues' and 'The Seeker' / Spoken by a Satyr, carrying a sea-shell" (VP 64). It was never included in the texts of The ISLAND OF STATUES or The SEEKER, however. Though it was published in Yeats's 20th year, the poem iterates themes that would become permanent elements of his mature work: a sense of cultural rupture, a repudiation of science and politics, an insistence that there is no truth save that discovered in one's own heart. These elements, moreover, are historicized in a pattern that faintly anticipates the later understanding of AUTOBIOGRAPHIES and A VISION. The poem suggests that history begins in happy dreams, shatters upon the "Grey Truth" promulgated by science, and recovers itself, though perhaps with some irremediable loss of innocence, by means of renewed dreams manifest in the language of poetry. In its emphasis on language as the crucial mechanism of recovery, the poem offers one of Yeats's most memorable and confident affirmations of the transcendental power of his own medium. "But O, sick children of the world," Yeats exclaims, "Of all the many changing things / In dreary dancing past us whirled, / To the cracked tune that Chronos sings, / Words alone are certain good." The poem goes so far as to speculate that the world itself is but a "sudden flaming word." In the poem's final lines (45–57), the Satyr-poet sings to a dead and buried fawn, urging it to "dream" once more. The poem thus ends with a ritual resurrection of the Arcadian world—or some version of it—effected by the power of artistic expression, and in this identifies and summarizes what would become Yeats's ruling aspiration. Hugh Kenner finds the "fingerprints" of Yeats's early reading everywhere in the poem. He detects the influence of Spenser, Marlowe, Milton, and Keats, and suggests Milton's "L'Allegro" (1645) and "Lycidas" (1638) as the poem's chief models (Colder Eye 72).

FIRST PUBLICATION: The DUBLIN UNIVERSITY REVIEW (periodical), October 1885, under the title, "An Epilogue. To 'The Island of Statues' and 'The Seeker' / Spoken by a Satyr, carrying a seashell." Reprinted in The Wanderings of Oisin and Other Poems, Kegan Paul, Trench & Co., London, 1889, under the title "Song of the Last Arcadian." Reprinted in Poems, T. Fisher Unwin, London, October, 1895, under the present title.

BIBLIOGRAPHY

Kenner, Hugh. A Colder Eye: The Modern Irish Writers; Yeats, W. B. The Variorum Edition of the Poems of W. B. Yeats.

"Song of Wandering Aengus, The" (1897)

"The Song of Wandering Aengus" reiterates the recurrent motif in Yeats's early work that the beckoning of the fairy world afflicts the human heart with unappeasable self-destructive longing (see also "The MAN WHO DREAMED OF FAERYLAND"). Though its trappings are Irish and folkloric, the poem articulates a version of the transcendental aspiration and frustration that is the conceptual tension of romanticism. Its most evident precursor, in terms of both theme and structure, is SHELLEY's "Alastor" (1816), a poem that dominated Yeats's boyhood consciousness (Aut. 80).

The poem is the self-told story of Aengus, here apparently a mere mortal though the detail of the hazel wand (see VP 807) obscurely associates him with his namesake, "the old Irish God of love and poetry and ecstasy" (Myth. 115) to whom Yeats's alludes in "He mourns for the change that has come upon him and his Beloved, and longs for the End of the World" (1897). Having been troubled by a fire in his head, Aengus took himself off to the hazel wood to do some fishing. He dangled a berry from a hazel wand and snared a "little silver trout." While he tended to the fire, the fish transformed into a "glimmering girl" who called his name and ran away, fading "into the brightening air." Ever since, he has been wandering in search of the girl. He envisions that, having found her, he will "walk among long dappled grass, / And pluck till time and times are done / The silver apples of the moon, / The golden apples of the sun."

In his notes to The Wind Among the Reeds, Yeats identifies the girl as one of the Sidhe, the "gods of ancient Ireland," and explains that if "any one becomes too much interested in them, and sees them over much, he loses all interest in ordinary things" (VP 806, 800; see also 804). With obvious relevancy to "The Song of Wandering Aengus," he adds that the Sidhe "can take all shapes, and those that are in the waters take often the shape of fish," and he mentions hearing from a Galway woman that there "are more of them in the sea than on the land, and they sometimes try to come over the side of the boat in the form of fishes, for they can take their choice shape." Frequently, as well, they take the shape of beautiful women (806).

The allusion to the "fire" in Aengus's head is both crucial and ambiguous. It conceivably suggests a transcendental propensity, restlessness, or readiness, and thus presages the more consummate image of "Heaven blazing into the head" in "LAPIS LAZULI." In the second stanza, Aengus goes to "blow the fire aflame," an ostensible reference to a campfire for the roasting of the fish, but, by an inevitable slippage, equally a reference to the fire in the head. The veiled suggestion seems to be that the call of the fairies allegorizes or reifies the fire in the head, that it is the heart calling to itself out of its own yearning and aspiration. The climactic image of Aengus plucking the silver apples of the moon and the golden apples of the sun is less an image of sexual consummation than of achieved transcendental aspiration. Aengus takes his place among the bounty of the stars, all earthly dispossession and deprivation having fallen away. The image is Edenic, but it resolves the biblical opposition between the garden and the apple. The garden is achieved not in opposition to transcendental aspiration, but as a function and fulfillment of it. The silver and gold of the apples is an important detail, for, as F. A. C. Wilson writes in a discussion of "NEWS FOR THE DELPHIC ORACLE," "fused gold and silver, the solar and lunar principles indissolubly knit, is an alchemical emblem of perfection" (*Yeats and Tradition* 219). A. Norman Jeffares detects a similar symbolic interplay of silver and gold, sun and moon, in "The Happy Townland" (1903), "HE WISHES FOR THE CLOTHS OF HEAVEN," "The Man who Dreamed of Faeryland," "THOSE DANCING DAYS ARE GONE," "The TOWER," and "Under the Round Tower" (1918) (*NCP* 35).

Many commentators associate the apple blossom in the fairy girl's hair with MAUD GONNE. In AUTOBIOGRAPHIES, Yeats remembers his first glimpse of Gonne and establishes her association with the apple blossom: "Her complexion was luminous, like that of apple-blossom through which the light falls, and I remember her standing that first day by a great heap of such blossoms in the window"

(120). Yeats's repeats the apple-blossom association in "The ARROW," in MEMOIRS (40), and in *The Speckled Bird* (37, 40). In "The Song of Wandering Aengus," however, the fairy girl is fey, slight, and retreating, none of which suggests the intensity and majesty of Gonne.

As Yeats mentions in his note, the poem was inspired by a "Greek folk song." Russell K. Alspach identifies the song as Lucy Garnett's translation of "The Three Fishes" in her *Greek Folk Poesy* (*VP* 806; *NCP* 52). Yeats unfavorably reviewed the volume in the October 1896 number of the *Bookman* (see *UP1* 409–412).

FIRST PUBLICATION: *The Sketch* (periodical), August 4, 1897, under the title "A Mad Song." Reprinted in *The Wind Among the Reeds*, Elkin Mathews, London, April 1899, under the present title.

BIBLIOGRAPHY

Jeffares, A. Norman. *A New Commentary on the Poems of W. B. Yeats*; Wilson, F. A. C. *W. B. Yeats and Tradition*; Yeats, W. B. *Autobiographies, Memoirs, Mythologies, The Speckled Bird, Uncollected Prose by W. B. Yeats* (vol. 1), *The Variorum Edition of the Poems of W. B. Yeats*.

"Sorrow of Love, The" (1892)

A dark and beautiful poem that treats the mythic advent of a girl equally reminiscent of MAUD GONNE and Helen of Troy, "The Sorrow of Love" underwent a particularly dramatic and successful transformation over the decades. The initial versions of the poem, with their gauzy veil of compound adjectives ("full round," "star-laden," "ever-singing," "curd-pale"), reveal the dying embers of Yeats's youthful PRE-RAPHAELITISM, while the final version of 1925 is tense with cold, climactic imagery and new complexities of destiny, prophesy, and strife. "The curd-pale moon, the white stars in the sky" eventually yields "A climbing moon upon an empty sky." By this alteration, typical of the entire revision, the passive becomes active, the decorative lean, and the empty pregnant. The evolution of the poem is discussed at length in John Stallworthy's *Between the Lines* (46–53; see also *Aut.* 321; *VP* 119–120).

In its final form, "The Sorrow of Love," like "LEDA AND THE SWAN" and "The SECOND COMING," conceives the world as intermittently subject to history-reversing annunciation. In its first stanza, the universe in the dual guise of animal particularity ("brawling of a sparrow") and abstract pattern ("brilliant moon") blots out "man's image and his cry"; in the second stanza, a girl arises who is "doomed like Odysseus and the labouring ships / And proud as Priam murdered with his peers"; in the third stanza both the natural and the heavenly worlds are mystically brought to heel by the advent of the girl: suddenly they can "but compose man's image and his cry." The girl's red lips connote the sensual, the passionate, and the sanguinary, and, being "mournful," seem to register their own fate, the tragic fate of all things that belong to the world, with its violence of ever-grinding historical gyres. There is a startling disproportion between the girl and the epic violence of the Trojan War, but they equally manifest doom and pride, the tragic tension whose intensity has a metaphysical significance. The suggestion is that in its most heightened moments humanity embodies forces that subdue and shape the universe itself.

Its metaphysics aside, "The Sorrow of Love" includes one of Yeats most memorable characterizations of Gonne as one who "seemed the greatness of the world in tears." On September 27, 1925, Yeats sent Gonne a copy of his *Early Poems and Stories*, which had been published five days earlier. He pointed out that some of the poems "have nothing of their old selves but the titles," and he told her that he was "especially pleased" with the revised version of "The Sorrow of Love." He added, "You may perhaps recognise the model for this particular portrait. I felt as I wrote that I recalled the exact expression of that time & that I had seen it at last as I could not when I was young & dimmed the window glass with my hot breath" (GY 431).

FIRST PUBLICATION: *The Countess Kathleen and Various Legends and Lyrics*, T. Fisher Unwin, London, September 1892.

BIBLIOGRAPHY

Stallworthy, John. *Between the Lines: Yeats Poetry in the Making*; Yeats, W. B. *Autobiographies*, *The Gonne-Yeats Letters 1893–1938*, *The Variorum Edition of the Poems of W. B. Yeats*.

"Spur, The" (1938)

See "THE GREAT DAY."

"Stare's Nest by my Window, The" (1923)

In the pattern of vacillation that structures the sequence "MEDITATIONS IN TIME OF CIVIL WAR," "The ROAD AT MY DOOR" finds its inevitable obverse in "The Stare's Nest by my Window." The former poem confesses a silent envy for the kind of active men who make war; the latter poem, in the spirit of "EASTER 1916," warns of the heart-deadening influence of fanaticism and looks to nature as the antidote to the morbidity and abstraction of politics. In the cross-weave of the sequence, "The Stare's Nest by my Window" is also referable to "ANCESTRAL HOUSES" and "MY DESCENDANTS," all three poems pondering the house as the symbolic intersection of the creative and destructive tendencies whose tension governs the world. As he calls upon the owl to preside over the desolation of his house in "My Descendants," Yeats here calls upon the honey-bee to preside over its rejuvenation.

"Declension of the soul" leads to ruin, the three poems equally hold. In "Ancestral Houses" and "My Descendants" this declension is a matter of lineal degeneration, but in "The Stare's Nest by my Window" its aspect is political and cultural, with the IRISH CIVIL WAR as specific catalyst. The wall, as Donald T. Torchiana writes, "becomes equivalent to the civil fabric or body politic rent by civil war," while the "raucous, strident character of the stare" figures "the screaming, abstraction-ridden politicians on both sides" who have been "sustained on base diets, the fantasies or grubby, fly-blown slogans of hatred" (*W. B. Yeats & Georgian Ireland* 315). As represented here, the war is scattered and pointless. "Somewhere a man is killed, or a house burned," writes Yeats. His weary vagueness compacts an entire commentary on the randomness and inscrutability of the war. In a travesty of "Ancestral Houses," the only thing reared in stone is a "barricade," while the dead soldier is "trundled down the road" as if in place of the brick or stone that is "trundled" in a better era (*trundle*: "To draw or push along on a wheel or wheels, as a wheelbarrow, vehicle, etc.," says *The Oxford English Dictionary*). Making clear the word's associations with the work of the mason, Yeats refers in *A VISION* to "stones as they are trundled down the road" (288).

"Easter 1916" provides the concise diagnosis that "Too long a sacrifice / Can make a stone of the heart," and "The Stare's Nest by my Window" essentially retains this formulation: "We had fed the heart on fantasies, / The heart's grown brutal from the fare; / More substance in our enmities / Than in our love. . . ." As "Easter 1916" finds its counter-symbol of natural impulse in moor-hen and moor-cock, "The Stare's Nest by my Window" adopts the honeybee. The bee builds in the very teeth of this destruction and decay, and serves as an image of nature at its most spontaneous, bountiful, and benign (cf. "IN THE SEVEN WOODS"). As the sword of "MY TABLE" moralizes the days out their aimlessness, so the bees may moralize away the rancor and morbid fixation of the political mindset (see the 1911 essay "J. M. Synge and the Ireland of his Times" for one of Yeats's most convincing expostulations against this rancor).

In a 1925 note to his NOBEL PRIZE lecture "The Irish Dramatic Movement," Yeats recalls writing "The Stare's Nest by my Window" during the chaos of the Civil War, and tells that the poem emerged out of "an overmastering desire not to grow unhappy or embittered, not to lose all sense of the beauty of nature. A stare (our West of Ireland name for a starling) had built in a hole beside my window and I made these verses out of the feeling of the moment." Yeats quotes the first two stanzas of "The Stare's Nest by my Window" and continues: "Presently a strange thing happened. I began to smell honey in places where honey could not be, at the end of a stone passage or at some windy turn of the road, and it came always with certain thoughts. When I got back to Dublin I was with angry people who argued over everything or were eager to know the exact facts: in the midst of the mood that makes realistic drama" (*Aut.* 522–523).

FIRST PUBLICATION: The *Dial* (periodical), January 1923, under the title "The Jay's Nest by my Window," and in the *London Mercury* (periodical), January 1923, under the present title. Reprinted in *The Cat and the Moon and Certain Poems*, The CUALA PRESS, Dublin, July 1924, under the present title.

BIBLIOGRAPHY

Torchiana, Donald T. *W. B. Yeats & Georgian Ireland*; Yeats, W. B. *Autobiographies, A Vision*.

"Statues, The" (1939, dated April 9, 1938)

One of the most dense, difficult, and obscurely grand of Yeats's poems, "The Statues" enlarges upon the West's discovery of "measurement" and the tradition of art and culture to which it gave rise, a development that Yeats similarly considers in AUTOBIOGRAPHIES (274–275); in his correspondence (*Letters* 921); in the prologue to *The ONLY JEALOUSY OF EMER*; in the fourth section of "UNDER BEN BULBEN"; and in *A VISION* (276). T. R. Henn conjectures that Yeats's preoccupation with measurement "derives from Blake's engraving 'The Ancient of Days' that hung at WOBURN BUILDINGS, in which God is measuring the world with compasses of lightning thrust down through the clouds" (*Lonely Tower* 326). A passage from ON THE BOILER echoes both the language and the idea of the poem and functions as an indispensable prose crib: "There are moments when I am certain that art must once again accept those Greek proportions which carry into plastic art the Pythagorean numbers, those faces which are divine because all there is empty and measured. Europe was not born when Greek galleys defeated the Persian hordes at Salamis, but when the Doric studios sent out those broad-backed marble statues against the multiform, vague, expressive Asiatic sea. They gave to the sexual instinct of Europe its goal, its fixed type" (*Expl.* 451; *LE* 249). Kathleen Raine provides an equally helpful general orientation: "From the same starting-point in 'half Asiatic' Greece, two great iconographies stem: the great primary and objective culture of the West, represented by the Renaissance, whose symbol for Yeats is the Sistine Chapel and especially Michelangelo's depiction of Adam, and culminating in the Renaissance prince Hamlet; and Buddhist iconography, stemming [. . .] from the Hellenistic influence which produced the Gandhara images of the Buddha, becoming ever more subjective as it moves from India to China. These are the contraries between which swing Yeats's gyres, the eternal contraries whose alternation will continue throughout history" (*Yeats the Initiate* 319–320).

"Pythagoras planned it," the poem opens, but what is "it"? Yeats presumably refers to the character of European sculpture, which manifests the "Pythagorean numbers" or mathematical ratios that Pythagoras (sixth century B.C.) discovered in the very fabric of the universe. Yeats alludes to Pythagoras's discovery in "AMONG SCHOOL CHILDREN": "World-famous golden-thighed Pythagoras / Fingered upon a fiddle-stick or strings / What a star sang and careless Muses heard. . . ." (see also *Letters* 719). Carrying "into plastic art the Pythagorean numbers" (in the language of *On the Boiler*), the Greek sculptors produced work that "lacked character"—individuality, personality, accident—but possessed some inscrutable congruency with the order of things, some beautiful rightness of proportion, that was enough to arrest the viewer and arouse the sexual passions of the young (cf. "Under Ben Bulben": "Michael Angelo left a proof / On the Sistine Chapel roof, / Where but half-awakened Adam / Can disturb globe-trotting Madam / Till her bowels are in heat . . ."). The second stanza proclaims the Greek sculptors even greater than Pythagoras because they gave flesh, and hence life, to what had been mere mathematical abstraction. It was these sculptors and not the Greek navy that defeated the "Persian hordes" at

Salamis in 480 B.C., who "put down / All Asiatic vague immensities" and won for Europe, as Yeats's writes in *A Vision*, its heyday of "Ionic elegance" and "Doric vigour" (268–273). Phidias (fifth century B.C.), according to *A Vision*, represents the apogee of this "deliberate turning away from all that is Eastern." In his work "Ionic and Doric influence unite" and "all is transformed by the full moon, and all abounds and flows" (270; on Phidias, see also "NINETEEN HUNDRED AND NINETEEN" and "Under Ben Bulben"). Phidias gave "women dreams and dreams their looking glass." That is, he formulated the proportions of the beautiful body, or as Yeats's expresses the point in *On the Boiler*, "gave to the sexual instinct of Europe its goal, its fixed type."

The poem's third stanza is one of the most elusive in Yeats's poetry. Yeats recognized the difficulty and gave a word of advice to Edith Shackleton Heald (1885–1976) in a letter of June 28, 1938: "In reading the third stanza remember the influence on modern sculpture and on the great seated Buddha of the sculptors who followed Alexander" (*Letters* 911). The reference to Alexander locates the stanza within the historical scheme of *A Vision* and associates it with the return of the Asiatic influence in the wake of his empire. Writes Yeats, "I identify the conquest of Alexander and the break-up of his kingdom, when Greek civilisation, formalised and codified, loses itself in Asia, with the beginning and end of the 22nd Phase, and his intention recorded by some historian to turn his arms westward shows that he is but a part of the impulse that creates Hellenised Rome and Asia." The empty eyeball of line 20 is likewise associated with Greece, presumably as it "loses itself in Asia": "When I think of Rome I see always those heads with their world-considering eyes, and those bodies as conventional as the metaphors in a leading article, and compare in my imagination vague Grecian eyes gazing at nothing, Byzantine eyes of drilled ivory staring upon a vision, and those eyelids of China and of India, those veiled or half-veiled eyes weary of world and vision alike" (*AV* 277). In "The DOUBLE VISION OF MICHAEL ROBARTES," likewise, the vacant eye is associated with the Buddha, symbolic of the East.

"One image crossed the many-headed" continues the pattern of obscurity. "Many-headed" echoes the "many-headed foam at Salamis" and refers to the waves of the sea. In Richard Ellmann's reasonable gloss, "the Greek sculptors' image of man followed Alexander's armies into India" (*IY* 189). Kathleen Raine more specifically discerns "an allusion to the Hellenic influence—and specifically the representation of Apollo—which, by way of the Gandhara school, gave rise to the typical icon of Buddha" (*Yeats the Initiate* 315). She notes that the "Hellenic influence on Buddhist sculpture was a discovery of the distinguished French authority, Albert Foucher, whose work *The Beginnings of Buddhist Art* [. . .] Yeats possessed" (315). The "image" announced in these lines is not Hamlet but is like the "fat dreamer" whom Hamlet replaced as the representative Western figure. In *Autobiographies* Yeats describes G. F. Watt's portrait of WILLIAM MORRIS (1870) and illuminates the historical understanding that informs the allusion. Yeats writes that Morris's "grave wide-open eyes" and "broad vigorous body" suggest "the dreamer of the Middle Ages," the "resolute European image that yet half remembers Buddha's motionless meditation, and has no trait in common with the wavering, lean image of hungry speculation, that cannot but because of certain famous Hamlets of our stage fill the mind's eye. Shakespeare himself foreshadowed a symbolic change, that is, a change in the whole temperament of the world, for though he called his Hamlet 'fat' and even 'scant of breath', he thrust between his fingers agile rapier and dagger" (132). Like the fat dreamer of the Middle Ages or the Buddha, then, the "image" knows that "knowledge increases unreality, that / Mirror on mirror mirrored is all the show," which echoes the understanding of *A Vision*: "Only one symbol exists, though the reflecting mirrors make many appear and all different" (240). In place of the "world-considering eyes" that characterized Rome (and presumably modernity), it exhibits "Empty eyeballs," the vague eyes of Greece that gaze at nothing, desiring nothing (240). The image and the idea of the stanza's final couplet recall "The SECOND COMING." In the apocalyptic moment, the Asian ascendancy represented by Buddha (see 207–208) dies into the life of a renewed West inferably represented by Grimalkin (i.e., a cat, as in *Macbeth*,

I, i, 9). Much like the Sphinx of the earlier poem, Grimalkin crawls toward "Buddha's emptiness" on an embassy of dethronement; alternately, it may be that Grimalkin crawls toward Buddha's emptiness in a gesture of submission.

The final stanza envisions another version of this apocalyptic reversal of gyre. As the Sphinx slouches towards Bethlehem, as Grimalkin crawls toward Buddha's emptiness, so Patrick Pearse "summoned CUCHULAIN to his side" and cast himself against the existing dispensation. Pearse (1879–1916), the most romantic figure of the 1916 EASTER RISING, stormed the post office in Dublin and proclaimed the Irish Republic from the steps. As Yeats explains in his letter to Edith Shackleton Heald, "Cuchulain is in the last stanza because Pearse and some of his followers had a cult of him. The Government has put a statue of Cuchulain in the rebuilt post office to commemorate this" (*Letters* 911). Implying that Pearse was the instrument of some larger pattern or force, Yeats asks, "What stalked through the Post Office?" (*The DEATH OF CUCHULAIN* closes with the same question: "What stood in the Post Office / With Pearse and Connolly?"). There follows an even more mysterious question: "What intellect, / What calculation, number, measurement, replied?" The implication is that Pearse entered into an obscure interchange or dialogue, presumably unsurmised or only dimly felt even by himself, with the pattern or pattern maker that Pythagoras had long before discovered.

The Irish, Yeats proposes in the poem's final five lines, are the inheritors of the ancient instinct for the eternal proportion, because Ireland has not fully succumbed to the debasement and disorder of modernity. Ireland has been "thrown upon this filthy modern tide / And by its formless spawning fury wrecked," but even so it maintains the instinct of Pythagoras and the classical sculptors for a deeper-lying reality. "Tide" establishes the poem's congruency with "The Second Coming," while "spawning," which is inextricable from the diction of "A DIALOGUE OF SELF AND SOUL," draws attention to "The Statues'" recantation of the earlier poem's unqualified embrace of life. The Irish continue to hear the call of the darkness that Yeats, in "A Dialogue of Self and Soul," equates with the "darkness of the soul" and terms "ancestral night." Within this darkness, they may trace the "lineaments of a plummet-measured face." Like the "boys and girls" of Pythagoras's day, they know such lineaments for the eternal pattern of beauty and instinctively offer themselves at its altar.

Harold Bloom, for one, is withering in his criticism of the poem, and in particular the poem's final stanza, finding in its zealous antimodernism tinged with the rhetoric of eugenics something essentially fascistic. "If lines four through six of this stanza began with 'We Germans' rather than 'We Irish,'" Bloom writes, "perhaps the critics would see the stanza more clearly for what it is, a disfigured and disfiguring emanation from hatred [. . .]. Pythagorean Fascism is a rather visionary variety of that blight, but is Fascism nevertheless" (*Yeats* 444). Elizabeth Cullingford comments, however, that "Yeats's version of eugenic theory owes little to ideas about breeding Aryan supermen, much to the Irish passion for breeding racehorses." Nevertheless, she admits, "Yeats was playing with theories which in other hands were to have terrible applications" (*Yeats, Ireland and Fascism* 229).

FIRST PUBLICATION: The *London Mercury* (periodical), March 1939. Reprinted in *Last Poems and Two Plays*, The CUALA PRESS, Dublin, July 10, 1939.

BIBLIOGRAPHY

Bloom, Harold. *Yeats*; Cullingford, Elizabeth. *Yeats, Ireland and Fascism*; Ellmann, Richard. *The Identity of Yeats*; Henn, T. R. *The Lonely Tower: Studies in the Poetry of W. B. Yeats*; Raine, Kathleen. *Yeats the Initiate: Essays on Certain Themes in the Work of W. B. Yeats*; Yeats, W. B. *Autobiographies, Explorations, Later Essays, The Letters of W. B. Yeats, The Variorum Edition of the Plays of W. B. Yeats, A Vision*.

"Stolen Child, The" (1886)

"The Stolen Child" is one of Yeats's numerous expansions on the theme of the fairies or Sidhe as tempters, seducers, and abductors (see, for exam-ple, "The Host of the Air" [1893], "The HOSTING OF THE SIDHE," "*The LAND OF HEART'S DESIRE*," "The MAN WHO DREAMED OF FAERYLAND," "The SONG OF WANDERING AENGUS," and "The WANDERINGS OF OISIN"). In "The Stolen Child," the fairies cajole a human child to join their ceaseless merriment amid "the waters and the wild," for the world is "more full of weeping" than the child can understand. Here as elsewhere Yeats registers ambivalence. To cross into the fairy world is to be liberated from the mortal and mundane, but also to be severed from one's own humanity. The stolen child, as Yeats writes, will "hear no more the lowing / Of the calves on the warm hillside / Or the kettle on the hob / Sing peace into his breast, / Or see the brown mice bob / Round and round the oatmeal-chest." The allusion to the "brown mice" echoes the allusion to the "field-mouse" in "TO THE ROSE UPON THE ROOD OF TIME," and suggests an analogy between the fairy world and the transcendental reality represented by the ROSE. Yeats powerfully feels the draw of the transcendental, but at this stage in his development, at least, he hesitates to untether himself, perhaps fearing the fate of the estranged poet-figures in COLERIDGE's "Kubla Khan" (1816) and SHELLEY's "Alastor" (1816). In a letter of March 14, 1888, to KATHARINE TYNAN, Yeats expresses a different reservation: "I have noticed some things about my poetry, I did not know before, in this process of correction [of *The Wanderings of Oisin and Other Poems*], for instance that it is almost all a flight into fairy land, from the real world, and a summons to that flight. The chorus to the "stollen child" [sic] sums it up—That is not the poetry of insight and knowledge but of longing and complaint—the cry of the heart against necessity. I hope some day to alter that and write poetry of insight and knowledge" (*CL1* 54–55). Here Yeats seems to point away from the transcendental enterprise altogether and to predict the restraint of the poetry of his middle period, typified by the volumes *The Green Helmet and Other Poems* (1910) and *Responsibilities: Poems and Play* (1914).

"The Stolen Child" hews both to the terrain and to the lore of SLIGO, where Yeats passed the happiest days of his childhood. Rosses Point is a village northwest of Sligo, on a promontory at the mouth of Sligo Harbour; Glen-Car is a valley northeast of Sligo, famous for its waterfall; Sleuth Wood (also known as Slish Wood) is a forest southeast of Sligo, on the south shore of Lough Gill. Yeats catalogues much of the local lore in his prose piece "Drumcliff and Rosses" (1889). Of particular relevance is his account of a "little promontory of sand and rocks and grass" at the northern corner of Rosses Point—a "mournful, haunted place"—where fairies like to poach unsuspecting human souls. "There is no more ready short-cut to the dim kingdom than this plovery headland," declares Yeats (*Myth.* 88). In a note to the poem Yeats similarly observes, "Further Rosses is a very noted fairy locality. There is here a little point of rocks where, if anyone falls asleep, there is danger of their waking silly, the fairies having carried off their souls" (*VP* 797).

FIRST PUBLICATION: The *Irish Monthly* (periodical), December 1886. Reprinted in *Poems and Ballads of Young Ireland*, M.H. Gill and Son, Dublin, February 25, 1889.

BIBLIOGRAPHY

Conner, Lester I. *A Yeats Dictionary: Persons and Places in the Poetry of William Butler Yeats*; Kirby, Sheelah. *The Yeats Country: A Guide to the Sligo District and Other Places in the West of Ireland Associated with the Life and Work of W. B. Yeats*; Yeats, W. B. *The Collected Letters of W. B. Yeats* (vol. 1), *Mythologies, The Variorum Edition of the Poems of W. B. Yeats*.

"Summer and Spring" (1926)

See "A MAN YOUNG AND OLD."

"Supernatural Songs" (1934–1935, sequence)

One of Yeats's principal statements on matters of the spirit, "Supernatural Songs" is a 12-poem sequence consisting of "Ribh at the Tomb of Baile and Aillinn," "Ribh denounces Patrick," "Ribh in Ecstasy," "There," "Ribh considers Christian Love insufficient," "He and She," "What Magic Drum?," "Whence had They come," "The Four Ages of Man," "Conjunctions," "A Needle's Eye," and "Meru." Virginia Moore observes that Yeats's "old transcendentalism, reinforced by the Hindus and the Chinese, sounds calm, sure, and, towards all that hugs the earth, defiant," and characterizes the sequence as an expression of "Yeats's all-but-final religious position" (*Unicorn* 358). Harold Bloom calls the sequence "intense and uneven," though he places "Ribh considers Christian Love insufficient" and "Meru" among Yeats's great poems (*Yeats* 411). T. R. Henn considers "Ribh at the Tomb of Baile and Aillinn" the pinnacle of the sequence and one of the pinnacles of Yeats's entire career. He concludes a brilliant exposition of the poem with an extravagant encomium: "It has a curious power of radiating new significances; a balanced symbolism set out cumulatively and logically, controlled and organized to its end. The fusion of religious and human love is an age-old theme; but the richness of suggestion, the tact and restraint, marks the poem as among the six perfect achievements of Yeats" (*Lonely Tower* 317).

Four of the poems are voiced by Ribh—pronounced "Reeve" or "Riv"—a figure of Yeats's own invention, whom Moore describes as a "Christianized Celtic hermit-magician" (*Yeats's Poems* 705; *YD* 158; *Unicorn* 83). Henn calls Ribh a "critic of early Christianity," but Moore argues that he "stands for true early Christianity; what he criticizes is Patrick's *later* Christianity" (*Lonely Tower* 314; *Unicorn* 452). In his preface to *A FULL MOON IN MARCH*, Yeats himself calls the "hermit Ribh" an "imaginary critic of St. Patrick. His Christianity, come perhaps from Egypt like much early Irish Christianity, echoes pre-Christian thought" (*VPl.* 1311). And in a commentary to "Supernatural Songs," Yeats writes, "Saint Patrick must have found in Ireland, for he was not its first missionary, men whose Christianity had come from Egypt, and retained characteristics of those older faiths that have become so important to our invention." He adds that he considers Ribh, "were it not for his ideas about the Trinity, an orthodox man" (*VP* 837–838). Yeats made no secret of his fascination with Egyptian hermetic Christianity, which, as Moore says, was "more esoteric and 'gnostic' than St. Patrick's Roman variety" (*Unicorn* 83). In several instances—AUTOBIOGRAPHIES (238, 242), "DEMON AND BEAST," an unadopted ending to his 1919 essay "If I were Four-and-Twenty (*LE* 256), "UNDER BEN BULBEN"—Yeats mentions the "Thebaid" (the territory surrounding Egyptian Thebes) and the "Mareotic Sea" (a saltwater lake south of Alexandria), where a community of hermits gathered around St. Anthony of Coma (ca. 251–356). Yeats finds in these desert communities a symbol of exultant and self-withering vision, and in St. Anthony a Christianized version of the poet of SHELLEY's "Alastor" (1816), the paradigmatic visionary quester. Ribh belongs to this tradition, uniting pre-Christian and Christian in a faith more "supernatural" than conventionally pious, though his elevation of bodily passion as a metaphysical principle is more Yeatsian than anything else. By contrast, St. Patrick (ca. 390–ca. 461), the patron saint of Ireland, represents the constrictions of orthodox or "later" Christianity. He serves as spiritual foil to the subjective man much as he does in "The WANDERINGS OF OISIN" and in the 1895 tale "The Old Men of the Twilight" (see *Myth.* 191–195).

In "Ribh at the Tomb of Baile and Aillinn"—rivaled only by "Meru" as the crowning achievement of the sequence—Yeats achieves a remarkably graceful and seamless reconciliation of the pagan and Christian traditions. Lady GREGORY recounts the legend of Baile and Aillinn in *Cuchulain of Muirthemne* (231–232), as does Yeats in "Baile and Aillinn," a 207-line poem that appears in *In the Seven Woods* (1903). The latter begins with an "argument" that summarizes the tragic tale: "Baile and Aillinn were lovers, but Aengus, the Master of Love, wishing them to be happy in his own land among the dead, told to each a story of the other's death, so that their hearts were broken and they died." "Ribh at the Tomb of Baile and Aillinn" continues the tale of the lovers beyond the grave. Explaining his unlikely presence at the tomb to a passerby, Ribh speaks "what none have heard": The lovers have been transfigured by the miracle of their deaths and have come together overhead in a

bodiless communion of light. Though lacking the grandness of Ribh's mystic architecture, "A LAST CONFESSION," the ninth poem in the sequence "A WOMAN YOUNG AND OLD," similarly imagines a coupling of naked souls. Underpinning both poems is Swedish mystic and theologian Emanuel Swedenborg's (1688–1772) notion that "the sexual intercourse of the angels is a conflagration of the whole being" (*Letters* 805; see also 807). Far from reviling the pagan tradition, as does St. Patrick in "The Wanderings of Oisin," Ribh reverently waits at the tomb of the lovers on the anniversary of their first embrace. With eyes made "aquiline" by spiritual discipline, he would receive their light as they couple in the darkness overhead, though Bloom observes, "the leaves of fallen nature somewhat break the light's circle" (*Yeats* 408). Within the circle of this light he reads his holy book, as if the pagan miracle illuminates the holiness of the Christian text and the Christian text explains the holiness of the pagan miracle. John Unterecker proposes that the "juncture of the apple and the yew" may have "in part symbolized this combination of traditions, the Biblical apple intertwined with the pagan yew," as well as the union of the dead lovers (*RG* 247). Henn, on the other hand, sees the apple and yew as "symbols of lover and the grave now left behind" (*Lonely Tower* 315). Overlaying both pagan and Christian traditions are possible occult implications. Ribh's traffic with dead spirits suggests this, as does the allusion to the "open book," which recalls the explicitly occult "open book" of "EGO DOMINUS TUUS." As Richard Ellmann quips, the holy book "is more likely to be *A Vision* than the Bible" (*IY* 281).

"Ribh denounces Patrick" (originally titled "Ribh prefers an Older Theology") continues the attempt to reconcile Christian and pagan traditions, though as Yeats suggests in his commentary on the sequence, Ribh is here at his most heterodox. Ribh denounces Patrick's Christianity as an "abstract Greek absurdity" and cites as particularly egregious the "masculine Trinity." Not Father, Son, and Holy Ghost, but man, woman, and child comprise the Trinity that patterns both the natural and the supernatural realms. As an "ephemeral fly begets, Godhead begets Godhead / For things below are copies, the Great Smaragdine Tablet said." This is to say that the sexual dynamic and the procreative urge govern the entire chain of being, making no distinction between mortal and immortal, physical and spiritual. "The Great Smaragdine Tablet" is the *Tabula Smaragdina*, an alchemical treatise published in 1541 and attributed to Hermes Trismegistus, a legendary Alexandrian philosopher who is said to have lived sometime during the first three centuries of the Christian era. Yeats likewise refers to Hermes' theory of natural and supernatural correspondence in his 1898 essay "SYMBOLISM IN PAINTING" (see *E&I* 146). It is typical of Yeats's subtlety that the reference to Hermes sustains the Trinitarian theme of the poem, "Trismegistus" meaning "thrice great." The difficult third stanza states that "all increase their kind," but passion inevitably sinks, "damped" by body and mind, that is, by the reassertion of nature. Nature may be momentarily transcended in the passion of the sexual act, but it coils itself even in the passionate embrace, like the serpent that renders momentary all Edenic manifestations. Nature is "juggling" perhaps in the sense that it encompasses the duality of body and mind, in contrast to the unity of passion or the self-identity of God. The fourth stanza elaborates on the coil of nature, which is the rival or negative element in the poem's theology. Nature's symbol is the "mirror-scalèd serpent," which represents multiplicity, or what Yeats calls in *Autobiographies* "Hodos Chameliontos," the Path of the Chameleon. The shifting play of the serpent's mirrored scales is the image of confusion, disorder, and self-consciousness. All who "run in couples"—all who beget—share in the ordered passion of the Trinity, but, lacking the perfection of the divine love, do not beget themselves, as "Godhead begets Godhead," and therefore lack complete self-identity and unity. The association of self-generation with divinity or miracle links these lines to "AMONG SCHOOL CHILDREN" ("self-born mockers of man's enterprise"), "BYZANTIUM" ("flame begotten of flame"), "VACILLATION" (section 2), and "OLD TOM AGAIN" ("Nor shall the self-begotten fail").

In "Ribh in Ecstasy," the hermit attributes his own incomprehensibility—perhaps the incomprehensibility of the previous poems—to the soul's discovery of its own "cause or ground" in the self-procreation of Godhead. In the condition of ecstasy, the self can neither stabilize nor organize its own language. As ecstasy wanes like the sexual spasm with which it is conflated, the "common round of day" resumes (a variation on the theme of the circle of light in "Ribh at the Tomb of Baile and Aillinn") and language returns to its mundane forms and comprehensible meanings.

As "Ribh in Ecstasy" envisions Godhead begetting Godhead upon Godhead in a pattern at once self-identical and circular, "There" envisions a divine point or heavenly realm where the circle rounds upon itself and enters into its own eternity, thus bringing the sequence's recurrent suggestion of circularity ("circle on the grass," "self-same ring," "coil in their embraces," "round of day") to an ultimate metaphysical realization. The image of the planets dropping into the sun has an antecedent in "ALL SOULS' NIGHT," which describes the soul as it follows the orbit of the moon until, sinking "into its own delight at last," it plunges into the sun.

"Ribh considers Christian Love Insufficient" shares the heterodoxy of "Ribh denounces Patrick." Both poems critique Christian doctrine as an insufficient expression of what Yeats likes to call the "whole man"—"blood, imagination, intellect, running together," in the characterization of "Discoveries" (*E&I* 266; see also 279; *Expl.* 303). "Why should I seek for love or study it?" Ribh asks. He indeed studies love in both "Ribh at the Tomb of Baile and Aillinn" and "Ribh denounces Patrick," but this does not preclude a tonic mood of hatred. Hatred, according to the poem's second stanza, frees the soul from "terror and deception," by which Yeats means the condition of remorse that "A DIALOGUE OF SELF AND SOUL" and "Vacillation" are so concerned to triumph over. Thus freed, the soul rids itself of "impurities," including the impurities of religion, for "thought," even of God, belongs to the intellect rather than to the soul; as a control informed Yeats during a 1933 automatic writing session, "We must hate all ideas concerning God that we possess, that, if we did not, absorption in God would be impossible" (*BG* 469). It is in this sense that "Hatred of God"—hatred of religious form and idea—"may bring the soul to

God." At midnight—the witching or miracle hour of "All Souls' Night," "Byzantium," and "CRAZY JANE AND THE BISHOP"—the soul finds its "bodily or mental furniture" most unendurable, and its hatred, its effort to brace and cleanse itself, collapses in a passionate recognition of reliance upon God's will and grace. These lines represent what may be Yeats's closest approach as a poet to an identifiable Christianity.

With "He and She," Ribh drops out of the sequence. As in "Ribh denounces Patrick" and "There," the pattern of reality is sexual and cyclical. Just as the moon perpetually flees the blinding light of the sun, so woman flees man. Her light "greater grows" the farther she flies (recalling the light-emitting angels of "Ribh at the Tomb of Baile and Aillinn"). This is to say that man desires most what he least can have. The final two lines of the poem—"All creation shivers / With that sweet cry"—suggests that the world participates in the same pattern or sympathetically witnesses the spectacle of pursuit. In either case, the pursuit is consistent with the natural order, as theorized in "Ribh denounces Patrick." In an August 28, 1934, letter to OLIVIA SHAKESPEAR, Yeats said of the poem, "It is of course my centric myth" (*Letters* 829).

"What Magic Drum?" invokes the child, the third element in Ribh's Trinity. Like "NEWS FOR THE DELPHIC ORACLE," the poem suggests that the civilized is perpetually threatened by the incursion of the savage. The repetition of masculine pronouns makes the poem's first stanza difficult to pin down. Seemingly, the stanza describes a father as he cradles his child. He "holds him from desire"—attempts to make himself still or calm—and stops his own breathing in order not to disturb the child's rest ("limbs" might belong either to father or to child, while "desire" alternatively might belong to the child). Father and child are bowered by "light-obliterating garden foliage" (cf. the foliage-broken light of "Ribh at the Tomb of Baile and Aillinn"), but beyond is the forest and the beating of a "magic drum." Like the "intolerable music" of "News for the Delphic Oracle" and the "gong" of "NINETEEN HUNDRED AND NINETEEN" and the "frenzied drum" of "A PRAYER FOR MY DAUGHTER," the drum is the disturbing voice of primal nature. The drum is

complemented by a vision of a beast that licks its young. Where the father "holds him from desire"—on one reading, puts off his own desire in order to tend the child—the beast's ministrations are sensual and even sexual: "Limb" and "belly," the words themselves soft and rounded, reoccur in the orgiastic climax of "News for the Delphic Oracle." This juxtaposition of man and beast, each tending to offspring, suggests an unsettling analogy. As much as he may indulge the idea of his own civility, man, no less than beast, belongs to the primal order of nature. His "desire" may be put off or repressed in moments of civility, but it only waits to return. Employing one of Yeats's most effective rhetorical devices, the poem ends, like "LEDA AND THE SWAN," "The MOTHER OF GOD," "The SECOND COMING," and "The STATUES," with questions that propagate their own mystery. "What from the forest came?" implies that the beast is no longer safely confined to the forest, that it has in some sense breached the cultivated garden-realm of civilization. "What beast has licked its young?" suggests, as in "The Second Coming" and "The Statues," the presence of a mysterious and unsettling incarnation. The poem asks in effect what force or energy expresses or enacts itself through the medium of nature.

"Whence had They come?" elaborates on the concluding question of "What Magic Drum?" and the mystery of incarnation. In their "sexual joy" boy and girl cry with voices not their own; the flagellant enacts a drama not his own. Like "What Magic Drum?," "Whence had They come" ends with the suggestion that the "sacred drama" of divinity enters the stream of history by mysterious incarnation, as in "Leda and the Swan" and "The Mother of God," and that world-transforming figures—in this instance Charlemagne—incarnate the divine agency.

"The Four Ages of Man" is the first of three epigrammatic poems that lead the sequence to the conclusion of "Meru." Writing on August 7, 1934, Yeats explained to Shakespear that the poem describes the "four ages of individual man, but they are also the four ages of civilization. [. . .] First age, *earth*, vegetative functions. Second age, *water*, blood, sex. Third age, *air*, breath, intellect. Fourth age, *fire,* soul, etc. In the first two the moon comes to the full—resurrection of Christ and Dionysus. Man becomes rational, no longer driven from below or above" (*Letters* 826; see also 823–825). The final couplet of the poem—"Now his wars with God begin; / At stroke of midnight God shall win"—recalls "Ribh considers Christian Love insufficient," in which God's victory, again at midnight, is the soul's submission.

Writing to Shakespear three weeks later, Yeats added an explanation of the cryptic astrology of "Conjunctions": "I was told, you may remember, that my two children would be Mars conjunctive Venus, Saturn conjunctive Jupiter respectively; and so they were—Anne the Mars-Venus personality. Then I was told that they would develop so that I could study in them the alternating dispensations, the Christian or objective, then the Antithetical or subjective. The Christian is the Mars-Venus—it is democratic. The Jupiter-Saturn civilization is born free among the most cultivated, out of tradition, out of rule" (*Letters* 828; see also *AV* 302). The poem, then, excitedly anticipates the *antithetical* civilization that will replace that Christian civilization (cf. "The Second Coming"). The new *antithetical* age will be rich in the "mummy wheat" that signifies esoteric and unnatural wisdom, as allusions to the mummy in "All Souls' Night," "Byzantium," and "On a Picture of a Black Centaur by Edmund Dulac" make clear. The present age, by contrast, is premised on the transformation of the sword into the cross, which is to say, on the sacrifice of the "whole man" upon the altar of religious order. The "goddess" (Venus) is joined to Mars in token of the astrological conjunction that signals this age, and she sighs upon his breast as if in recognition of its waning; "breast," meanwhile, plays on the imagery of "What Magic Drum?"

"A Needle's Eye" shares with "Whence had They come" a sense of some more fundamental reality from which the world emanates. The needle's eye itself—present also in "Cuchulain Comforted" (1939) and "Veronica's Napkin" (1932)—represents a conduit between the natural and supernatural realms, perhaps metaphorizing the birth canal or playing upon the biblical maxim that it is "easier for a camel to go through the eye of a needle, than for a rich man to enter into the kingdom of God" (Matthew 19; Mark 10; Luke 18). The notion that the unborn and the dead—witnessing spirits—goad and watch over the world is entrenched in Yeats's thought. It is intrinsic to his experiments in spiritism and mediumship, and loosely informs poems as disparate as "Introductory Rhymes" to *Responsibilities* and "The Magi."

A marvelous compression of an entire philosophy in sonnet form, "Meru" swerves from Ribh's Christian-Druidic supernaturalism and adopts the more characteristic posture of "Lapis Lazuli" and the sixth section of "Vacillation." As the poem theorizes, the illusion of civilization suffices man only so far; goaded by his own thought, he cannot cease in the restless work of civilization by which he hopes to come to the "desolation of reality." This is the condition of the absolute and the eternal, "desolate" because it sheds the "garment" of thought, the "bodily or mental furniture" mentioned in "Ribh considers Christian Love insufficient." But the hermits upon Meru and Everest, as Yeats envisions them, know better; they know that "day brings round the night" (cf. "He and She"), that the endless grinding of the historical gyres obliterates all contrivances of culture and erases even the mightiest empires ("Many ingenious lovely things are gone," Yeats writes in "Nineteen Hundred and Nineteen"). The hermits are kindred less to Ribh than to the Chinamen of "Lapis Lazuli," who stare with glittering eyes upon the tragic scene; to the great Lord of Chou of "Vacillation," who cries "Let all things pass away"; to the narrative voice of "Nineteen Hundred and Nineteen," which intones, "Man is in love and loves what vanishes / What more is there to say?"; and to the choral voice in Sophocles, which advocates "a gay goodnight and quickly turn away" (see "From 'Oedipus at Colonus'"). All of these mouthpieces belong to the mountain snow—the "aboriginal ice"—that Yeats associates with the tragic sensibility, and not to the circle of light in which Ribh reads his holy book (*E&I* 523; *LE* 214). The hermits have come into the desolation of reality, as their nakedness metaphorically suggests. Their wisdom is stoic and tragic rather than angel-illuminated, and yet not necessarily divorced from the supernatural. In the tragic moment, Yeats writes in a 1937 introduction to his work, "the thermometer falls" and the "supernatural is present" (*E&I* 523; *LE* 213).

The poem's striking Himalayan backdrop borrows from Yeats's reading in the religious literature of India. Meru is the name the *Mahābhārata* gives to Mount Kailās (elevation 22,030 feet) in the Himalayan range of Tibet. Yeats explains in his introduction to Bhagwan Shri Hamsa's *The Holy Mountain* (1934) that Indians, Chinese, and Mongols have ever since ancient times imagined the mountain as the dwelling place of their gods: "Thousands of Hindu, Tibetan and Chinese pilgrims, Vedāntic, or Buddhist, or of some older faith have encircled it, some bowing at every step, some falling prostrate, measuring the ground with their bodies; an outer ring for all, an inner and more perilous for those called by the priests to its greater penance. On another ring, higher yet, inaccessible to human feet, the Gods move in adoration. Still greater numbers have known it from the *Mahābhārata* or from the poetry of Kaliās [Indian poet of the fifth century], known that a tree covered with miraculous fruit rises from the lake at its foot, that sacred swans sing there, that the four great rivers of India rise there, with sands of gold, silver, emerald and ruby, that at certain seasons from the lake [. . .] springs a golden Phallos. Mānas Sarowar, the lake's full name, means 'The great intellectual Lake', and in this Mountain, this Lake, a dozen races find the birth-place of their Gods and of themselves. We too have learnt from Dante to imagine our Eden, or Earthly Paradise, upon a mountain, penitential rings upon the slope" (*E&I* 455; *LE* 143–144; see also *VPl.* 837).

FIRST PUBLICATION: "Supernatural Songs" first appeared as an eight-poem sequence—consisting of "Ribh at the Tomb of Baile and Aillinn," "Ribh prefers an Older Theology" (later "Ribh denounces Patrick"), "Ribh considers Christian Love insufficient," "He and She," "The Four Ages of Man," "Conjunctions," "A Needle's Eye," "Meru"—in the *London Mercury* and *Poetry* (periodicals), December 1934. The sequence was reprinted in *The King of the Great Clock Tower, Commentaries and Poems*, The CUALA PRESS, Dublin, December 14, 1934. The sequence in its present form, with "Ribh prefers an Older Theology"

retitled, first appeared in *A Full Moon in March*, Macmillan, London, November 22, 1935.

BIBLIOGRAPHY

Bloom, Harold. *Yeats*; Conner, Lester I. *A Yeats Dictionary: Persons and Places in the Poetry of William Butler Yeats*; Ellmann, Richard. *The Identity of Yeats*; Gregory, Lady. *Cuchulain of Muirthemne: The Story of the Men of the Red Branch of Ulster Arranged and Put into English by Lady Gregory*; Henn, T. R. *The Lonely Tower: Studies in the Poetry of W. B. Yeats*; Moore, Virginia. *The Unicorn: William Butler Yeats' Search for Reality*; Saddlemyer, Ann. *Becoming George: The Life of Mrs W. B. Yeats*; Unterecker, John. *A Reader's Guide to William Butler Yeats*; Yeats, W. B. *Autobiographies, Essays and Introductions, Explorations, Later Essays, The Letters of W. B. Yeats, Mythologies, The Variorum Edition of the Plays of W. B. Yeats, The Variorum Edition of the Poems of W. B. Yeats, Yeats's Poems, A Vision.*

"Swift's Epitaph" (1932)

Yeats's interest in JONATHAN SWIFT swelled almost to obsession during the late 1920s and early 1930s. In January 1929, Yeats wrote to T. STURGE MOORE from Rapallo: "For my first weeks here I read nothing but Swift but he became too exciting for my blood pressure and so after some sleeplessness I took, on my wife's advice, to detective stories again. Swift's *Epitaph* and Berkeley's *Commonplace Book* are the greatest works of modern Ireland" (*WBY&TSM* 141; see also 160). On April 7, 1930, Yeats opined to Lady GREGORY that Swift embodied "the last passion of the Renaissance" (*Letters* 773). On June 1, 1930, he reported to OLIVIA SHAKESPEAR that he was reading Swift constantly (776). On November 20, 1930, he declared to his future biographer Joseph Hone that he wanted "Protestant Ireland to base some vital part of its culture upon Burke, Swift, and Berkley" (779). Yeats's preoccupation with Swift also plays out in "BLOOD AND THE MOON" (which borrows its "Saeva Indignatio" from the epitaph), "The SEVEN SAGES," "PARNELL'S FUNERAL," and *The* WORDS UPON THE WINDOW-

PANE, the latter a full-bore attempt to grapple with the mysteries of Swift's life and personality.

Swift is buried in St. Patrick's Cathedral, Dublin, where he lies under "the greatest epitaph in history," as Yeats writes in *The Words upon the Window-pane* (*VPl.* 942). Yeats found in the epitaph a perfect expression of the passionate integrity and stoic disdain that comprise the aristocratic temper and function as Yeats's own mask in poems like "ANCESTRAL HOUSES," "Blood and the Moon," "DEATH," and "TO A WEALTHY MAN WHO PROMISED A SECOND SUBSCRIPTION TO THE DUBLIN MUNICIPAL GALLERY IF IT WERE PROVED THE PEOPLE WANTED PICTURES." In his preface to SYNGE's *Poems and Translations* (1909), Yeats theorizes the epitaph's resonance: "Now and then in history some man will speak a few simple sentences which never die, because his life gives them energy and meaning. They affect us as do the last words of Shakespeare's people, that gather up into themselves the energy of elaborate events, and they put strange meaning into half-forgotten things and accidents, like cries that reveal the combatants in some dim battle. Often a score of words will be enough [. . .]." Illustrating his point, Yeats asks, "And is not that epitaph Swift made in Latin for his own tomb more immortal than his pamphlets, perhaps than his great allegory?" (*E&I* 307–308).

Yeats masterfully translated the epitaph in September 1929, taking the liberty of introducing both the first line and the striking modifier "world-besotted." In *The Words upon the Window-pane*, Yeats pays himself a deserved compliment in the form of John Corbet's observation that the epitaph "is almost finer in English than in Latin" (*VPl.* 942). Swift's original is as follows: "*Hic* depositum est Corpus / IONATHAN SWIFT S.T.D / Hujus Ecclesiæ Cathedralis / Decani, / *Ubi* saeva Indignatio / Ulterius / Cor lacerare nequit. / Abi viator / Et imitare, si poteris, / Strenuum pro virili / Libertatis Vindicatorem" (*NCP* 291). Translated literally the epitaph reads: "Here lies the body of Jonathan Swift, Doctor of Divinity and Dean of this Cathedral Church, where savage indignation can no more lacerate his heart. Go, traveler, and imitate if you can one who strove with all his might to champion liberty" (*Jonathan Swift* 412).

In "Pages from a Diary Written in Nineteen Hundred and Thirty," Yeats denies a politically liberal reading of the epitaph's invocation of "human liberty," maintaining that "the liberty [Swift] served was that of intellect, not liberty for the masses but for those who could make it visible" (*Expl.* 315). In a February 14, 1932, letter to Hone, Yeats likewise attempted to qualify Swift's notion of "human liberty": "There was something not himself that Swift served. He called it 'freedom' but never defined it and thus has passion. Passion is to me the essential. I was educated upon Balzac and Shakespeare and cannot go beyond them. That passion is his charm" (*Letters* 791). In a 1933 letter to Mario M. Rossi, author of *Swift; or, The egotist* (1934), Yeats's elaborates his sense of Swift's "laceration": "When a [man] of Swift's sort is born into such dryness [i.e. the spiritual desiccation of his time], is he not in the Catholic sense of the word its *victim*? A French Catholic priest once told me of certain holy women. One was victim for a whole country, another for such and such a village. Is not Swift the human soul in that dryness, is not that his tragedy and his genius? Perhaps every historical phase may have its victims—its poisoned rat in a hole . . ." (819).

In a January 28, 1930, journal entry, Lady GREGORY records two early versions of Yeats's translation, both notably inferior to the final version. The less finished version reads: "Jonathan Swift is at the goal, / Savage indignation there / Cannot lacerate his soul, / Imitate him if you dare, / World estranged man for he / Saved human liberty" (*Lady Gregory's Journals*, II, 496).

FIRST PUBLICATION: The *Dublin Magazine* (periodical), October–December 1931, in the text of "The Words upon the Window Pane: A Commentary" (see *Expl.* 345–346; *VPl.* 958). Reprinted in *Words for Music Perhaps and Other Poems*, The CUALA PRESS, Dublin, November 14, 1932.

BIBLIOGRAPHY

Gregory, Lady. *Lady Gregory's Journals* (vol. 2, ed. Daniel J. Murphy); Jeffares, A. Norman. *A New Commentary on the Poems of W. B. Yeats*; David Nokes, *Jonathan Swift, A Hypocrite Reversed: A Critical Biography*; W. B. Yeats, *Essays and Introductions*,

Explorations, The Letters of W. B. Yeats, The Variorum Edition of the Plays of W. B. Yeats, W. B. Yeats and T. Sturge Moore: Their Correspondence 1901–1937.

"There" (1935)

See "SUPERNATURAL SONGS."

"Those Dancing Days are Gone" (1930)

See "WORDS FOR MUSIC PERHAPS."

"Thought from Propertius, A" (1917)

In *The Wild Swans at Coole* and the collected poems, "A Thought from Propertius" belongs to an informal sequence or cluster of poems whose subject is MAUD GONNE in middle age. It includes "BROKEN DREAMS," "A Deep-sworn Vow" (1917), "HER PRAISE," "His Phoenix" (1916), "The PEOPLE," and "PRESENCES." Where "Her Praise" and "His Phoenix" mildly parody Yeats's eagerness to extol Gonne's beauty, "A Thought from Propertius" takes up the mythic metaphorizing of "BEAUTIFUL LOFTY THINGS," "FALLEN MAJESTY," "NO SECOND TROY," "PEACE," "The SORROW OF LOVE," and "A WOMEN HOMER SUNG." In the poem's slender but resonant conceit, the nobility of Gonne's beauty is such that she might have "walked to the altar / Through the holy images / At Pallas Athene's side, / Or been fit spoil for a centaur / Drunk with the unmixed wine."

The poem seems a stock exercise in romantic hyperbole, but its terms are fraught with complications. The image of Gonne walking to the altar by the side of Pallas Athena is a riposte to the image of her walking to the altar by the side of Major John MacBride (the marriage, destined to be unhappy,

took place on February 21, 1903). The description of Gonne as fit spoil for a drunken centaur continues the vein of romantic hyperbole while imaginably taking an underhanded swipe at Mac-Bride (1865–1916), whom R. F. Foster describes as "red-haired, heavy-drinking, physically brave, rather inarticulate and utterly unmystical" (*AM* 284). In this context, "spoil" becomes a punning summary of the entire debacle of Gonne's marriage. Read differently, the centaur is the anti-self against which Yeats measures his own inadequacy. Where Yeats can only engage in the "definitions of the analytic mind," the centaur is full of unreflective passion and possesses the "purity of natural force" ("The People"). On this reading, the "unmixed wine" suggests itself as a symbol of the centaur's UNITY OF BEING.

"Propertius" is the Roman poet Sextus Propertius" (ca. 50–ca. 16 B.C.). A. Norman Jeffares suggests that "A Thought from Propertius" derives from the second poem in the second book of Propertius, a romantic paean that refers both to Athena ("tall and full her figure, and stately her walk, worthy the sister of Jove or like to Pallas") and to the centaur ("the Centaur's welcome spoil in the revel's midst") (*NCP* 158).

FIRST PUBLICATION: *The Wild Swans at Coole*, The CUALA PRESS, Churchtown, Dundrum, November 17, 1917.

BIBLIOGRAPHY

Foster, R. F. *W. B. Yeats: A Life, I: The Apprentice Mage*; Jeffares, A. Norman. *A New Commentary on the Poems of W. B. Yeats.*

"Three Bushes, The" (1937)

"I have [written] much curious love poetry of late which I would send you if I had a typist," Yeats wrote to Ethel Mannin (1900–84) on November 30, 1936. "There is a long ballad about a chaste lady who wishing to keep her lover sent her chambermaid to take her place in the dark. Besides the ballad, which I shall publish in my new *Broadsides* with music, and [sic] there are lyrics for the characters in it" (*Letters* 869). The ballad is "The Three Bushes," and the lyrics are the six short poems—"The Lady's First Song," "The Lady's Second Song," "The Lady's Third Song," "The Lover's Song," "The Chambermaid's First Song," and "The Chambermaid's Second Song"—that follow both in *New Poems* (1938) and in the collected poems. In a parenthetical subtitle, Yeats calls "The Three Bushes" an "incident from the 'Historia mei Temporis' of the Abbé Michel de Bourdeille" but this is fanciful. In a September 1936, letter, Yeats told DOROTHY WELLESLEY, "When we meet we will decide upon the name of the fourteenth or fifteenth [century] fabulist who made the original story" (*LOP* 95). Lester I. Conner notes the punning detail that "bourde is French for lie or fib" (*YD* 123). Yeats's poem, in fact, was based not on a 14th- or 15th-century source, but on a ballad written by Wellesley. Yeats appropriated her premise and rewrote the poem in his own manner. The correspondence between Yeats and Wellesley is much taken up with the collaboration (see *LOP* 64–83, 95–97, 102–108, 147–148).

The seven lyrics that accompany the ballad are remarkable for their concision and for the sexual candor that makes them among the most explicit poems that Yeats ever wrote. Wellesley herself objected to the "worm" as phallic metaphor in the Chambermaid's two songs, but Yeats defended it: "The 'worm' is right, its repulsiveness is right—so are the adjectives—'dull', 'limp', 'bare', all suggested by the naked body of the man, & taken with the worm by that body abject and helpless. All suggest her detachment, her 'cold breast', her motherlike prayer'" (*LOP* 108). Further, Yeats confessed that the poems' sexual wisdom was inspired by Wellesley herself: "My dear, my dear—when you crossed the room with that boyish movement, it was no man who looked at you, it was the woman in me. It seems that I can make a woman express herself as never before. I have looked out of her eyes. I have shared her desire" (*Letters* 868; *LOP* 108).

FIRST PUBLICATION: The *London Mercury* (periodical), January 1937. Reprinted in *A Broadside*, March 1937, and in *New Poems*, The CUALA PRESS, Dublin, May 18, 1938. "The Lady's First Song" and its companion pieces first appeared in *New Poems*.

BIBLIOGRAPHY

Conner, Lester I. *A Yeats Dictionary: Persons and Places in the Poetry of William Butler Yeats*; Yeats, W. B. *The Letters of W. B. Yeats, Letters on Poetry from W. B. Yeats to Dorothy Wellesley*.

"Three Movements" (1932)

The fourth in an informal sequence of epigrammatic poems that rail against the bankruptcy of modernity (see also "Spilt Milk" [1932], "The NINETEENTH CENTURY AND AFTER," and "Statistics" [1932]). "Three Movements" echoes the wave motif of "The Nineteenth Century and After" (and the related motif of thinning milk in "Spilt Milk"), with the suggestion that post-romantic fish—the fish that lie "gasping on the strand"—have been stranded by the receding wave that is, on the metaphor of "The Nineteenth Century and After," the "great song" of Western culture. That the "romantic fish swam in nets coming to the hand"—went voluntarily or naively to their own demise—suggests a certain insufficient visionary commitment. This line does not mean to impeach BLAKE or COLERIDGE, certainly, but it might point a finger at SHELLEY, TENNYSON, and WORDSWORTH, all of whom dabbled in "moral values that were not aesthetic values" (*Aut.* 242). In "COOLE AND BALLYLEE, 1931," Yeats identifies himself and those of his school as "the last romantics," which suggests his place in the historical scheme of "Three Movements." The poem paraphrases an unpublished passage from a diary entry of January 20, 1932: "The Passion in Shakespeare was a great fish in the sea, but from Goethe to the end of the Romantic movement the fish was in the net. It will soon be dead upon the shore" (*IY* 267).

FIRST PUBLICATION: *Words for Music Perhaps and Other Poems*, The CUALA PRESS, Dublin, November 14, 1932.

BIBLIOGRAPHY

Ellmann, Richard. *The Identity of Yeats*; Yeats, W. B. *Autobiographies*.

"Three Things" (1929)

See "WORDS FOR MUSIC PERHAPS."

"I. To a Child Dancing in the Wind"/ "II. Two Years Later" (1912, 1914)

ISEULT GONNE, the lovely French-born daughter of MAUD GONNE, makes her first appearance in Yeats's poetry with this brace of strong poems. Yeats wrote "To a Child Dancing in the Wind" while vacationing at Les Mouettes, the Gonnes' home in Normandy, in August 1912. It describes Iseult, then 18, dancing by the shore. The vision of innocence prompts a train of bitter reflection on the fall from innocence that lies ahead. Iseult, being young, knows nothing of the "fool's triumph," nor "love lost as soon as won," nor the "best labourer dead"—a litany of allusion that marks Yeats's own fall from innocence. These lines most likely allude to Major John MacBride's (1865–1916) successful courtship of Maud Gonne in 1903; to the futile rekindling of Yeats's romance with Maud Gonne in 1908 (see "RECONCILIATION"); and to the death of J. M. SYNGE in 1909. Yeats asks in closing, "What need have you to dread / The monstrous crying of wind?" These final lines echo the early poems of romantic despair "HE HEARS THE CRY OF THE SEDGE" and "HE REPROVES THE CURLEW." These complain of the wind, which, in its desolate cry, reminds of the tragedy at the heart of life. Implicitly, then, Yeats contrasts the romantic anguish of his own early years with Iseult's carefree joy. John Unterecker lauds the poem as "brilliantly versified" and calls attention to the "astonishing change of pace achieved by the suddenly introduced slow rhythm of the last line" (RG 126).

During the summer of 1916, four years after "To a Child Dancing in the Wind" had been published, the image of Gonne as the dancer on the beach continued to percolate. On July 9, Iseult wrote to Yeats from Normandy, "I am just come in from the shore, I never got such delight from running,

so much that feeling of 'wise delirium' [misquoting "SEPTEMBER 1913"]. I think that even you, to day would have wanted to run for more than mere exercise's sake" (Letters to WBY&EP 61). Yeats spent the latter part of the summer in Normandy and described Iseult in an August letter to Lady GREGORY: "To look at her dancing on the shore at the edge of the sea or coming in with her arms full of flowers you would think her the most joyous of creatures. And yet she is very unhappy—dying of self analysis" (AP 57). Yeats returned to the image of the dancing girl in the major poems "The DOUBLE VISION OF MICHAEL ROBARTES" and "LONG-LEGGED FLY," inferably with Iseult in mind. In the 1937 edition of A VISION, he reprises the specific image of Iseult dancing upon the beach, though in this instance the dance is fraught with tragic meaning: "My imagination goes some years backward, and I remember a beautiful young girl singing at the edge of the sea in Normandy words and music of her own composition. She thought herself alone, stood barefooted between sea and sand; sang with lifted head of the civilisations that there had come and gone, ending every verse with the cry: 'O Lord, let something remain'" (AV 220). The sight of MARGOT RUDDOCK dancing upon the Majorca shore in 1936 reignited the image of the solitary dancing girl and resulted in two poems, "Sweet Dancer" (1938) and "A CRAZED GIRL." Like "To a Child Dancing in the Wind," the latter poem is set against the background of the seashore.

Striking an avuncular pose in "Two Years Later," Yeats tries to warn Iseult to approach life more seriously and guardedly. Yeats asks whether no one has said that her "daring kind eyes should be more learned," which evidently touches on a long-standing gripe; in a 1907 letter, Maud Gonne had complained to Yeats that Iseult "is the despair of her governess & of the school where she goes every day, because of her laziness & because she will not learn what doesn't interest her. She is extraordinarily clever but won't work" (GY 240). Continuing platitudinously, Yeats reminds Iseult how the moths despair when they are burned. The prosaic sentiment and lifeless rhythm of these lines, coupled with the hackneyed image of the moth drawn to flame, suggests that Yeats is not much roused by his own argument, which, after all, cuts against the mythos of the "tragic generation" and the ingrained impulse of his own romanticism. Yeats adds that he could have warned her, but the old and young speak in different tongues.

Growing animated in the second stanza at the mere thought of Maud—a degree of wry self-understanding on display—Yeats exclaims that Iseult will wind up as her mother wound up, taking "whatever's offered" (a tart reference to Maud's misalliance with Major John MacBride), dreaming "that all the world's a friend," suffering, broken. However much he would warn and advise, being old, he speaks "a barbarous tongue." The self-ascription "barbarous" is the poem's complicating detail. Even as he urges caution in the sensible voice of middle age, Yeats asserts his own primal unruliness (perhaps the unruliness that comes with embittered age, as in "To a Child Dancing in the Wind" and most especially "WHY SHOULD NOT OLD MEN BE MAD?") and trumps the lesser intensity of Iseult's youthful recklessness (see "The NEW FACES" for a related trumping of the younger generation). In "NINETEEN HUNDRED AND NINETEEN," the adjective "barbarous" makes an important reappearance as the catchword of primal unruliness: "All men are dancers and their tread / Goes to the barbarous clangour of a gong." As events turned out, Yeats's concern for Iseult's future was well founded. In 1920 she married Francis Stuart (1902–2000), who would become a prominent writer; the marriage got off to the rockiest of starts and ended in separation (see GY 402–403).

FIRST PUBLICATION: "To a Child Dancing in the Wind" appeared in *Poetry* (periodical), December 1912, under the title "To a Child Dancing upon the Shore." Reprinted in *A Selection from the Poetry of W. B. Yeats*, Bernhard Tauchnitz, Leipzig, 1913, under the present title. "Two Years Later" appeared in *Poetry*, May 1914, under the title "To a Child Dancing in the Wind." The two poems appeared as the first and second parts of a single poem titled "To a Child Dancing in the Wind" in *Responsibilities: Poems and a Play*, The CUALA PRESS, Churchtown, Dundrum, May 25, 1914. The poems appeared in *Later Poems*, Macmillan, November 3, 1922, in their present form.

BIBLIOGRAPHY

Foster, R. F. *W. B. Yeats: A Life, II: The Arch-Poet*; Gonne, Iseult. *Letters to W. B. Yeats and Ezra Pound from Iseult Gonne*; Unterecker, John. *A Reader's Guide to William Butler Yeats*; Yeats, W. B. *The Gonne-Yeats's Letters 1893–1938, A Vision*.

"To a Friend whose Work has come to Nothing" (1913)

Like "SEPTEMBER 1913" and a "TO A SHADE," "To a Friend" bitterly rails against the modern middle class, which, in its sharp small-mindedness, invariably turns on those of higher motive and loftier sensibility. Lady GREGORY assumed that the "friend" mentioned in the poem's title was her nephew HUGH LANE, who was then embroiled in a messy campaign to establish a major gallery of modern art in Dublin (see "To a Shade" and "TO A WEALTHY MAN WHO PROMISED A SECOND SUBSCRIPTION TO THE DUBLIN MUNICIPAL GALLERY IF IT WERE PROVED THE PEOPLE WANTED PICTURES"). Yeats corrected this impression in a 1922 note, making clear that the poem is addressed to Lady Gregory herself (*VP* 819). The poem's context, however, evidently remains Lane's effort to establish his gallery. Lady Gregory was a prime abettor of the scheme.

Like "IN THE SEVEN WOODS," the poem counsels putting off the frustrating entanglements of the world and embracing an ecstatic solitude. Accept defeat, Yeats urges, for the "honor bred" cannot prevail against one who is unashamed even when caught in his own lies. This pessimistic stance was prompted by the groundswell of opposition to Lane's plan for a gallery that would have bridged the Liffey (see *Sir Hugh Lane* 84–109), while the imperturbable liar is William Martin Murphy (1844–1919), the wealthy newspaper proprietor who had marshaled middle-class opinion against the gallery proposal (Murphy receives an equal dose of comeuppance in "To a Shade," in which he is dubbed "old foul mouth"; see also *VP* 819–820). As he does so often, however, Yeats turns worldly defeat into spiritual victory. Bred to a "harder thing" than mere worldly triumph, Yeats urges Lady Gregory to turn away and "like a laughing string / Whereon mad fingers play / Amid a place of stone, / Be secret and exult, / Because of all things known / That is most difficult." Thus Yeats extols the revelry of the self in its abundance against the mere triumph of achieved ends that defines the "noisy set / Of bankers, schoolmasters, and clergymen / The martyrs call the world" ("ADAM'S CURSE"). The allusion to the "place of stone" conjures images of cairns and cromlechs and suggests the spiritual continuity between the ancient and the aristocrat. Both belong to traditions—to worlds—whose obedience lies beyond the practical and immediate.

FIRST PUBLICATION: *Poems Written in Discouragement*, The CUALA PRESS, Dundrum, October 1913.

BIBLIOGRAPHY

Gregory, Lady. *Sir Hugh Lane: His Life and Legacy*; Yeats, W. B. *The Variorum Edition of the Poems of W. B. Yeats.*

"To a Poet, who would have me Praise certain Bad Poets, Imitators of His and Mine" (1910)

This brief polemic is addressed to GEORGE RUSSELL (AE), who had gathered about himself a coterie of younger poets whom Yeats considered second-rate. In 1904, Russell edited *New Songs*, an anthology of poems by eight poets—Padraic Colum (1881–1972), Eva Gore-Booth (1870–1926), Thomas Keohler (1874–1942), Alice Milligan (1866–1953), Susan Mitchell (1866–1926), Seamas O'Sullivan (1879–1958), George Roberts (1873–1953), and Ella Young (1867–1956)—who belonged to his circle (*Myriad-Minded Man* 119). Yeats expresses his low estimate of Russell's acolytes in both "To a Poet" and "A COAT," and he more gently took exception in a long letter of April 1904 (CL3 576–578). In a September 1906 letter to KATHARINE TYNAN, Yeats grum-

bled that he does not care for "the people who imitate Russell or myself, that is to say Starkie (Seumas O'Sullivan) Keohler and Miss Young, or Roberts, and Miss Mitchell. This little group are always imitative and subjective and sentimental. They never see anything clearly or think anything clearly. [. . .] I do not think anything will come out of this group, because I do not feel any genuine inspiration amongst them, and they havn't [sic] as the more objective people have the inspiration of the Irish tradition. I once hoped a great deal from George Russell's influence, but I have come to think of it so far as it is a literary influence as opposed to everything I care for. He has the religious genius and it is the essence of the religious genius, I mean the genius of the religious teacher, to look upon all souls as equal. They are never equal in the eye of any craft, but Russell cannot bear anything that sets one man above another" (CL4 488). In *AUTOBIOGRAPHIES*, Yeats recalls his estrangement from this circle and the backbiting that ruled the day: "Five or six years earlier [AE] had published his lovely *Homeward; Songs by the Way* [1894], and because of those poems and what he was in himself, writers or would-be writers, among them James Stephens, who has all my admiration to-day, gathered at his house upon Sunday nights, making it a chief centre of literary life in Dublin. I was not friendly with that centre, considering it made up for the most part of 'barren rascals'—critics as Balzac saw critics. For the next few years it seemed to lead the opposition, not the violent attacks, but the sapping and mining" (331; see also *Mem.* 222–223).

FIRST PUBLICATION: *The Green Helmet and Other Poems*, The CUALA PRESS, Churchtown, Dundrum, December 1910, under the sequence title "Momentary Thoughts" and the title "To a Poet, who would have me Praise certain Bad Poets, Imitators of His and of Mine." Reprinted in *The Green Helmet and Other Poems*, R. Harold Paget, New York, under the same sequence title and the present title.

BIBLIOGRAPHY

Summerfield, Henry. *That Myriad-Minded Man: A Biography of George Russell, "A.E.," 1867–1935*;

Yeats, W. B. *Autobiographies*, *The Collected Letters of W. B. Yeats* (vols. 3–4), *Memoirs*.

"To a Shade" (1913, dated September 29, 1913)

"To a Shade" continues the lament for "romantic Ireland" that Yeats initiates in "SEPTEMBER 1913." As "September 1913" exalts JOHN O'LEARY as the embodiment of bygone pride and passion, so "To a Shade" exalts CHARLES STEWART PARNELL, who led the Irish delegation in Parliament before his adulterous affair with Katharine "Kitty" O'Shea (1845–1921) came to light in divorce proceedings and brought his political career crashing down. Parnell died a broken man in October 1891. In Yeats's account, his death inaugurated an era of partisan acrimony and small-minded propaganda, against which his own cultural movement was a reaction (see for example *Aut.* 191–193).

Yeats advises the shade of Parnell that if it should return to Dublin, whether to see the Parnell monument erected on O'Connell Street (cf. "Three Monuments" [1927]) or to take in the beautiful austerity of the sea, it should not tarry, for "they are at their old tricks again." The second stanza explains the latest travesty of parochial Dublin: A man of Parnell's own "passionate serving kind" has offered what would have given generations of Dubliners "loftier thought, / Sweeter emotion." But his efforts have been answered by insults and persecution, "the pack set" upon him by Parnell's enemy "old foul mouth." As in "TO A FRIEND WHOSE WORK HAS COME TO NOTHING" and "TO A WEALTHY MAN WHO PROMISED A SECOND SUBSCRIPTION TO THE DUBLIN MUNICIPAL GALLERY IF IT WERE PROVED THE PEOPLE WANTED PICTURES," Yeats alludes to HUGH LANE's attempt to establish a gallery of contemporary art in Dublin. Lane had promised his collection of impressionist paintings to the city provided that a suitable gallery be built to house them, but both the paintings and the condition attached to them met with derision in culturally conservative and nationalist circles, with wealthy newspaper pro-

Portrait of Hugh Lane, 1906, by John Singer Sargent (1856–1925). Lane was, in the words of "To a Shade," a man of "passionate serving kind." *(Dublin City Gallery The Hugh Lane)*

prietor William Martin Murphy (1844–1919)—"old foul mouth"—acting as ringleader. Murphy is invoked not only because of his role in the attack on Lane, but also, as Yeats's explains in a note to "To a Wealthy Man," because he had been "Mr. Healy's financial supporter in his attack upon Parnell" (*VP* 819). Yeats refers to Tim Healy (1855–1931), a member of Parliament who had been one of Parnell's most strenuous critics during the controversies of 1890 and 1891. The phrase "gentle blood" is a subtle provocation, implying that Dublin requires fine art as a corrective for its lack of breeding. In the poem's final stanza, pugnacity gives way to a fierce tenderness. Yeats urges Parnell's shade to "gather the Glasnevin coverlet" about its head, for Dublin is no more hospitable to men of passionate serving kind than in his own day, and he had experienced "enough of sorrow before death." Parnell is buried in Glasnevin Cemetery in Dublin (on his funeral, see *CL1* 265 and "PARNELL'S FUNERAL").

FIRST PUBLICATION: *Poems Written in Discouragement*, The CUALA PRESS, Dundrum, October 1913.

BIBLIOGRAPHY

Yeats, W. B. *Autobiographies, The Collected Letters of W. B. Yeats* (vol. 1), *The Variorum Edition of the Poems of W. B. Yeats*.

"To a Wealthy Man who promised a Second Subscription to the Dublin Municipal Gallery if it were proved the People wanted Pictures" (1913, dated December 1912)

"To a Wealthy Man" is one of several poems (see also "To a Friend whose Work has come to Nothing" and "To a Shade") that function as pugnacious blows in the controversy surrounding HUGH LANE's collection of impressionist paintings, which he had promised to Dublin on the condition that the city provide a suitable building to house them (see *Sir Hugh Lane* 84–109). The Dublin corporation committed £22,000 to the project, and a fund-raising campaign was initiated in late 1912 to cover the remaining cost of the proposed £45,000 gallery (AM 478–483; *Sir Hugh Lane* 90). Lady GREGORY recalls that the fund-raising was more difficult than anticipated: "The Dublin citizens had already accepted taxation for the building of a Gallery, and dwellers in the country, it may be, looked on such a building as a luxury for a well-to-do Dublin. And the few rich men in Ireland were also slow to help. Yeats, hearing that one of them had refused to add to what he had given at the first 'unless it could be proved the people wished for pictures,' wrote a vehement poem [. . .]" (*Sir Hugh Lane* 90–91). Yeats sent his verse polemic to Lane on January 1, 1913, with the explanation that it attempts to "meet the argument in Lady Ardilaun's letter to

somebody, her objection to giving because of Home Rule and Lloyd George, and still more to meet the general argument of people like Ardilaun that they not give unless there is a public demand." Yeats added the qualification, however, that the "wealthy man" to whom the poem is addressed "is of course an imaginary person" (*Letters* 573). Lord Ardilaun was Arthur Edward Guinness (1840–1915), of the famous brewing family. According to R. F. Foster, Ardilaun "showed a distinct lack of enthusiasm [for Lane's gallery], partly because one of the sites canvassed for the gallery was St Stephen's Green Park, donated to Dublin by his family, and [he] incensed the Lane-Gregory camp by remarking that there was little evidence of a public demand for a modern gallery" (AM 479).

"To a Wealthy Man" is a cutting lecture on the traditions and obligations of the aristocracy, and as such is more than a little cheekily flung in the face of an actual aristocrat. As Yeats has it, an aristocrat worthy of his position cares nothing for public opinion, but decrees and imposes out of the wealth of his own spirit. On this basis, Yeats rebukes his "wealthy man" for premising his subscription to the Dublin Municipal Gallery on the contributions of "Paudeen" and "Biddy"—archetypes of the Irish Catholic middle class—as if the "blind and ignorant town" knows best its own moral and spiritual good. Against this petty hair-splitting about the inclinations of "the people," Yeats's sets the examples of Ercole d'Este (1431–1505), duke of Ferrara, and Guidobaldo da Montefeltro (1472–1508), duke of Urbino, patrons of art and culture of whom Yeats had read in Castiglione's *The Book of the Courtier* (1528). Ercole cared nothing for the opinion of the "onion-sellers" when he sent his players to the marketplace to perform Plautus, the Roman dramatist (ca. 254–184 B.C.). Nor did Guidobaldo conduct a poll of the shepherds when he erected his palace, "a grammar school of courtesies / Where wit and beauty learned their trade / Upon Urbino's windy hill . . ." In the same spirit of indifference to public opinion, Cosimo de'Medici (1389–1464), upon being exiled to Venice in 1433, turned his attention to Michelozzo's "latest plan for the San Marco Library," that Italy might delight in art, logic, and law, renewing itself in the inspiration of ancient

Greece. Yeats refers to the architect Michelozzo di Bartolomeo (1396–1472), whom Cosimo commissioned to rebuild the monastery of San Marco in Florence. The highlight of the rebuilt monastery was the library. Finished in 1441, it is said to be the first library constructed in the spirit and style of the Renaissance.

The poem stumbles slightly in its final eight lines, putting none too gracefully what probably need not have been said, and ending on a note that smacks of the need to rhyme. The aristocrat must give what "the exultant heart calls good / That some new day may breed the best / Because you gave, not what they would, / But the right twigs for an eagle's nest!" (Yeats employs the same eagle and sun imagery to make a similar point in "UPON A HOUSE SHAKEN BY THE LAND AGITATION"). The chief problem may be that the slightness of the "twig" does not correspond to the kind of spiritual bounty and lofty open-handedness that Yeats is calling for.

In its disdain for "Paudeen" and "Biddy," the poem was bound to provoke hostility, especially as Dublin was ambivalent to begin with about both Lane's pictures and the condition attached to them. Something of this reception can be gleaned from Yeats's note to the poem in *Responsibilities: Poems and A Play*: "The first serious opposition [to the gallery] began in the *Irish Catholic*, the chief Dublin clerical paper, and Mr. William Murphy [. . .] a man of great influence, brought to its support a few days later his newspapers *The Evening Herald* and *The Irish Independent*, the most popular of Irish daily papers. He replied to my poem 'To a Wealthy Man' (I was thinking of a very different wealthy man) from what he described as 'Paudeen's point of view,' and 'Paudeen's point of view' it was. The enthusiasm for 'Sir Hugh Lane's Corots'—one paper spelled the name repeatedly 'Crot'—being but 'an exotic fashion,' waited 'some satirist like Gilbert' [i.e., William Gilbert, of Gilbert and Sullivan] who 'killed the aesthetic craze,' and as for the rest 'there were no greater humbugs in the world than art critics and so-called experts'" (VP 819–820).

FIRST PUBLICATION: *The Irish Times* (periodical), January 11, 1913, under the title, "The Gift," and the subtitle, "To a friend who promises a bigger subscription than his first to the Dublin Municipal Gallery if the amount collected proves that there is a considerable 'popular demand' for the pictures." Reprinted in *Poems Written in Discouragement*, The CUALA PRESS, Dundrum, October 1913, under the title, "To a Wealthy Man, who promised a Second Subscription if it were proved the People wanted Pictures." Reprinted in *Responsibilities: Poems and a Play*, The Cuala Press, Churchtown, Dundrum, May 25, 1914, under the present title.

BIBLIOGRAPHY

Foster, R. F. *W. B. Yeats: A Life, I: The Apprentice Mage*; Gregory, Lady. *Sir Hugh Lane: His Life and Legacy*; Yeats, W. B. *The Letters of W. B. Yeats*, *The Variorum Edition of the Poems of W. B. Yeats*.

"To a Young Beauty" (1918)

ISEULT GONNE was not only the object of Yeats's romantic desire, but also the frequent recipient of his avuncular advice, as in "Two Years Later" (see "TO A CHILD DANCING IN THE WIND") and "To a Young Beauty." The latter poem finds Yeats, by this time married to George Hyde-Lees (see GEORGE YEATS), rebuking the young Iseult, who had moved to London and taken a job at the School of Oriental Studies, for "keeping bohemian company," in A. Norman Jeffares's phrase (GY 43). This company included her coworker, the young poet and future novelist Iris Barry (1895–1969), with whom she shared a flat at 54 Beaufort Mansions in Chelsea, and Barry's lover Wyndham Lewis (1882–1957), the formidable writer and painter. In August the Yeatses arrived and removed Iseult to WOBURN BUILDINGS, which were then empty. On August 14, 1918, Yeats wrote to Lady GREGORY, "Maud Gonne has brought Iseult up in such a strange world that she is not shocked at what other girls are shocked at. As long as she herself lives & thinks rightly, she thinks nothing else matters. I am playing the stern uncle sent by her mother to carry off a foolish niece" (*Letters to WBY&EP* 135; on Barry, see 201).

In the straightforward opening stanza of the poem, Yeats urges Iseult to choose her "companions from the best," rather than from among every "Jack and Jill," the reversion to nursery rhyme suggesting his estimate of Iseult's circle and activities. In the less straightforward second stanza, Yeats encourages Iseult to take her "mirror for a school" (on the discipline of the mirror see "MICHAEL ROBARTES AND THE DANCER"). Therein she may learn the lesson of her own beauty and become "passionate" in the manner of the artist rather than "bountiful"—that is, childbearing, sexually active—in the manner of "more common beauties." The latter were "not born to keep in trim / With old Ezekiel's cherubim / But those of Beauvarlet." The allusion is to the French etcher and engraver Jacques-Firmin Beauvarlet (1731–97) whose cherubim ostensibly lack the visionary intensity of Ezekiel's, as in Ezek. 9:3, 10:2–19, 11:22, 28:16; 41:18 (NCP 143). In the 1890 essay "A Scholar Poet," Yeats styles Ezekiel as a forerunner of his own romantic transcendentalism, according to which poetry is "a direct message from the Most High." Ezekiel exemplified this mindset when he "lay upon his side and ate dung in order, as BLAKE says, to make men believe that there is an infinite in all things" (Letters to the New Island 102; for see also UP2 464; AV 179.).

In the poem's final stanza, Yeats acknowledges the burden of the devotion to beauty (much as in "ADAM'S CURSE" and "THE CHOICE"), yet he praises "the winters gone," punning mordantly on the family name. A figure of both the length and the character of his own experience, "winters" connotes age and hardship in contrast to the nursery rhyme patter of the first stanza, but also it evokes the "aboriginal ice" that Yeats associates with tragic intensity in his essay "A General Introduction for my Work" (E&I 523; LE 213), and in poems like "The COLD HEAVEN," "The FISHERMAN," "LAPIS LAZULI," and "MERU." These winters—the long exercise in self-discipline that is the life of the true artist—have an appropriately astringent reward: "There is not a fool can call me friend / And I may dine at journey's end / With Landor and with Donne." Having abided the stern dictate of the muses—having kept faith with the

"rock-born, rock-wandering foot" that he describes in "The GREY ROCK"—Yeats has earned the companionship of Walter Savage Landor (1775–1864) and John Donne (1572–1631), English poets who, unlike "every Jack and Jill," possess the passionate severity of the conquering mind. In PER AMICA SILENTIA LUNAE, he writes that Landor "topped us all in calm nobility when the pen was in his hand, as in the daily violence of his passion when he had laid it down," and he describes Landor as one who "lived loving and hating, ridiculous and unconquered, into extreme old age, all lost but the favour of his Muses" (LE 6, 16). In a 1912 letter, he writes of Donne's poetry that "the more precise and learned the thought the greater the beauty, the passion; the intricacy and subtleties of his imagination are the lengths and depths of the furrow made by his passion. His pedantry and his obscenity—the rock and the loam of his Eden—but make me the more certain that one who is but a man like us all has seen God" (Letters 570; see also Aut. 251).

FIRST PUBLICATION: Nine Poems, privately printed by Clement Shorter, London, October 1918. Reprinted in The Wild Swans at Coole, Macmillan, London, March 11, 1919.

BIBLIOGRAPHY

Gonne, Iseult. Letters to W. B. Yeats and Ezra Pound from Iseult Gonne; Jeffares, A. Norman. A New Commentary on the Poems of W. B. Yeats; Yeats, W. B. Autobiographies, Essays and Introductions, The Gonne-Yeats Letters 1893–1938, Later Essays, The Letters of W. B. Yeats, Letters to the New Island, Uncollected Prose by W. B. Yeats (vol. 2), A Vision.

"To a Young Girl" (1918)

While "The LIVING BEAUTY," "MEN IMPROVE WITH THE YEARS," and "A Song" (1918) stem from Yeats's unsuccessful courtship of Iseult Gonne in 1916 and 1917, "To a Young Girl," written in 1915 (YC 178), apparently stems from her teenage crush on him. As Yeats writes in a 1916 letter to Lady GREGORY, Iseult, four years earlier, had wished to marry him, and remained infatuated for the next two years (*AP* 57). A. Norman Jeffares reports that Iseult proposed to Yeats when she was 15 (circa 1909–1910) and was "refused because there was too much Mars in her horoscope" (*Man and Poet* 190). On the other hand, it may be that Yeats observes Iseult in the throes of some other crush. Whatever the case, the poem's structuring conceit is straightforward: Yeats understands what makes Iseult's "heart beat so," as his heart once beat in the same way for her mother, MAUD GONNE. The poem's psychological maneuvering, however, is less straigtforward. Despite its title, the poem is implicitly an appeal to Maud, whom Yeats still dreamed of marrying and to whom he proposed in July 1916. It provocatively reminds her that he had once set her "blood astir," with the implication that he might do so again. Yeats in all likelihood remembers 1908, when he and Gonne renewed their "spiritual marriage" of 10 years earlier (cf. "RECONCILIATION"). On July 26, 1908, Gonne sent Yeats a letter that describes her communion with him on the astral plane and indeed suggests a stirring of the blood: "You had taken the form I think of a great serpent, but I am not quite sure. I only saw your face distinctly & as I looked into your eyes (as I did the day in PARIS you asked me what I was thinking of) & your lips touched mine. We melted into one another till we formed only *one being, a being greater than ourselves* who felt all & knew all with double intensity [. . .]" (*GY* 257). "HIS MEMORIES" implies that Yeats's reconciliation with Gonne was at least briefly sexual.

FIRST PUBLICATION: The *Little Review* (periodical), October 1918. Reprinted in *Nine Poems*, privately printed by Clement Shorter, London, October 1918, and in *The Wild Swans at Coole*, Macmillan, London, March 11, 1919.

BIBLIOGRAPHY

Foster, R. F. *W. B. Yeats: A Life, II: The Arch-Poet*; Jeffares, A. Norman. *W. B. Yeats: Man and Poet*; Kelly, John S. *A W. B. Yeats Chronology*; Yeats, W. B. *The Gonne-Yeats Letters 1893–1938*.

"To Dorothy Wellesley" (1938)

The poet DOROTHY WELLESLEY was Yeats's principal intellectual confidante and correspondent from 1935 until his death. "To Dorothy Wellesley" christens her, perhaps speciously, as a poet of Yeats's own type: a dweller in the tower chamber (cf. "EGO DOMINUS TUUS," "I SEE PHANTOMS OF HATRED AND OF THE HEART'S FULLNESS AND OF THE COMING EMPTINESS," "MY HOUSE," "The PHASES OF THE MOON"), one who receives ghostly visitants (cf. "ALL SOULS' NIGHT," "PRESENCES"). Yeats sent the poem to Wellesley in a letter of August 1, 1936, and in an August 5 letter provided commentary: "I have never 'produced' a play in verse without showing the actors that the passion of the verse comes from the fact that the speakers are holding down violence or madness—'down Hysterica passio' [*King Lear,* II, iv, line 57]. All depends on the completeness of the holding down, on the stirring of the breast underneath. Even my poem 'To D. W.' should give this impression. The moon, the moonless night, the dark velvet, the sensual silence, the silent room and the violent bright furies. Without this conflict we have no passion only sentiment and thought." Yeats continues, "About the conflict in 'To D. W.', I did not plan it deliberately. That conflict is deep in my subconsciousness, perhaps in everybody's. I dream of clear water, perhaps two or three times (the moon of the poem), then come erotic dreams. Then for weeks perhaps I write poetry with sex for theme. Then comes the reversal—it came when I was young with some dream or some vision between waking and sleep with a flame in it. Then for weeks I get a symbolism like that in my Byzantium poem or in 'To D. W.' with flame for theme. [. . .] The water is sensation, peace, night, silence, indolence; the fire is passion, tension, day, music, energy" (*LOP* 86–87). Wellesley, in response, called the poem "very wonderful" (87).

Structured upon a double imperative—"stretch" and "climb"—the poem finds Yeats dispensing counsel, as he does in so many of his letters to Wellesley, who was 24 years his junior and by several orders of magnitude the lesser poet. Yeats urges Wellesley to stretch toward the "moonless midnight of the trees," and draw them close to her. These lines recall "AT ALGECIRAS—A MEDITATION UPON DEATH," with its birds that light in "the rich midnight of the garden trees," and even more "A DIALOGUE OF SELF AND SOUL," in which the advice to Wellesley finds its definitive form and metaphor: "Set all your mind upon the steep ascent, / Upon the broken, crumbling battlement, / Upon the breathless starlit air, / Upon the star that marks the hidden pole; / Fix every wandering thought upon / That quarter where all thought is done. . . ." Yeats, in short, urges Wellesley to fulfill her own nature as a poet of *antithetical* and transcendental stamp.

Being "rammed full / Of that most sensuous silence of the night"—that is, having followed the advice of the first stanza—Wellesley need only climb to her book-lined chamber ("chamber" having occult connotations, as in "My House") and await some version of the muse. Echoing "The SECOND COMING" ("And what rough beast, its hour come round at last, / Slouches towards Bethlehem to be born?") and "Presences" (in which a delegation of spectral women climb Yeats's "creaking stair"), the muse arrives as something fierce and unsettling. She represents neither "Content" (i.e., contentment) nor "satisfied Conscience"— the comfort and complacency of life reconciled to itself—but takes the form of the "Proud Furies each with her torch on high." The furies do not pursue and destroy the offender as in Greek myth (in this sense they are misrepresented by "ancient famous authors"), but they remain the enemies of settled comfort, troubling the mind with the example of their intensity and splendor.

The poem's obscure statement that "since the horizon's bought strange dogs are still" is illuminated by Wellesley in a March 4, 1936, letter. She mentions that she has "saved by twenty-four hours this little corner of Sussex from a town of scarlet bungalows" by buying "the lovely ridge" opposite Penns in the Rocks, her estate near Withyham in eastern Sussex (cf. "A PRAYER ON GOING INTO MY HOUSE"). In a note to her own letter, Wellesley admits that she cannot make sense of Yeats's line,

unless he "had the fantastic idea that after buying the few acres I evicted the people who lived on it, together with their dogs!" (*LOP* 53). The "Great Dane" is Wellesley's dog Brutus, who died in 1937. In a note to Yeats's brief letter of condolence, Wellesley mentions her "lasting joy" that her beloved dog had been included in Yeats's "majestic verse." She adds that the dog "himself had a great majesty, both of form and conduct, and Yeats had observed it. When he [Yeats] seemed too tired to reach a garden seat, the three of us would walk abreast, Yeats's hand and part of his great weight supported on my right shoulder, while my left hand and shoulder was supported by the great dog. I was always afraid of a landslide, but the great hound pacing slowly beside me never let me down. The seat was reached, the end achieved, and the tremendous Dane would settle down and turn into a piece of black and white marble until, our conversation ended, he would help us back again to the house" (*LOP* 145–146). Brutus, then, joins ISEULT GONNE's cat Minnaloushe (see "The CAT AND THE MOON") in Yeats's small but immortal menagerie of pets.

FIRST PUBLICATION: The *London Mercury* (periodical), March 1938, and the *Nation* (periodical), March 12, 1938, under the title "To a Friend." Reprinted in *New Poems*, The CUALA PRESS, Dublin, May 18, 1938, under the same title. Reprinted in *Last Poems & Plays*, Macmillan, London, January 1940, under the present title.

BIBLIOGRAPHY

Yeats, W. B. *Letters on Poetry from W. B. Yeats to Dorothy Wellesley.*

"To his Heart, bidding it have no Fear" (1896)

Though a mere seven lines, "To his Heart, bidding it have no Fear" attempts to quell the ambivalence of poems like "The Everlasting Voices" (1896), "HE BIDS HIS BELOVED BE AT PEACE," "The HOSTING OF THE SIDHE," and "TO THE ROSE UPON THE ROOD OF TIME," and to move toward a full commitment to the transcendental enterprise. Yeats instructs his "trembling heart" to remember the "wisdom out of the old days" that the "starry winds and the flame and the flood" should "cover over and hide" the heart that trembles before them, for the trembler has nothing to do with the "lonely, majestical multitude." Despite all such attempts to steady his nerves and commit himself to the ethereal "multitude," Yeats found richer matter in the heart's trembling, which he would later reconceive and philosophize as "vacillation" (see VP 824). A poem like "ALL SOULS' NIGHT," meanwhile, records the human cost of the transcendental enterprise and suggests why the heart trembles in the first place.

FIRST PUBLICATION: The SAVOY (periodical), November 1896, under the sequence title "Windle-Straws" and the title "Out of the Old Days" (paired with "HE REPROVES THE CURLEW"). Reprinted in The Wind Among the Reeds, Elkin Mathews, London, April 1899, under the title "To my Heart, bidding it have no Fear." Reprinted in Later Poems, Macmillan, London, November 3, 1922, under the present title.

"To Ireland in the Coming Times" (1892)

"To Ireland in the Coming Times" concludes Yeats's early collection The Countess Kathleen and Various Legends and Lyrics (1892), and brings to a close the section titled "The Rose" in Yeats's collected poems. This placement is careful and strategic, as "To Ireland in the Coming Times" attempts to explain and defend the preceding poems, especially against the allegation that in their extravagant mysticism they make no commitment to the nation.

Yeats opens the poem with the bald declaration that he would be counted among the national poets—those who sing to "sweeten Ireland's wrong"—however much his work is preoccupied with the spirit of eternal beauty (she of the "red-rose-bordered hem," an allusion to the mystical ROSE that the preceding poems take as their central symbol). In a subtle maneuver, Yeats draws

into relation his mystical concerns and his national aspirations, proclaiming his wish that Ireland break with the frenzied dance of time by brooding upon a "measured quietude" (cf. the "Quiet" of IN THE SEVEN WOODS"), which is to say by a disciplined absorption in the spirit of eternal beauty. Thus Yeats begins to evolve the cultural nationalism, premised on aesthetic and spiritual aspirations, that in coming years was so often to pit him against the explicitly political nationalism of the day.

Yeats reaffirms the nationalist aspect of his program in the second stanza, proclaiming that he stands with the likes of Thomas Davis (1814–45), James Clarence Mangan (1803–49), and Sir Samuel Ferguson (1810–86)—three of Ireland's most celebrated 19th-century poets and cultural nationalists—despite his inclination toward the mystical depths. The "elemental creatures," says Yeats, flee those of "unmeasured mind / To rant and rage in flood and wind," but they welcome those who tread "in measured ways" as fellow journeyers in pursuit of the "red-rose-bordered hem." "Measured" may indicate the discipline of occult study or metrical expression, the need for tradition and form even in the visionary enterprise; conceivably, it heralds the emphasis on "measurement" in AUTOBIOGRAPHIES (274–275); in the prologue to The ONLY JEALOUSY OF EMER; in "The STATUES"; in the fourth section of "UNDER BEN BULBEN"; and in A VISION (276). The stanza ends with an apostrophe to the fairies that dance under the moon and the exclamation "A Druid land, a Druid tune!" These lines equate the "elemental creatures" with the fairies and by extension with the essentially mystical and visionary tradition of Ireland. The pursuit of the "red-rose-bordered hem," then, abides by something deep within the national character and expresses a legitimate nationalism.

In the poem's third and final stanza, Yeats calls his work a testament to his love and dreams, conceivably suggesting his love of nation on the one hand, his dream of transcendence on the other. He declares that he writes for future generations even knowing that all things—both the mundane and the mystical—will eventually end in "truth's consuming ecstasy." His poetry will at least testify that his heart joined with the elemental creatures in pursuit of "the red-rose-bordered hem"—that his heart, in short, never swerved from its deepest calling.

FIRST PUBLICATION: *The Countess Kathleen and Various Legends and Lyrics*, T. Fisher Unwin, London, September 1892, under the title "Apologia Addressed to Ireland in the Coming Days." Reprinted in *Poems*, T. Fisher Unwin, London, October 1895, under the present title.

BIBLIOGRAPHY

Yeats, W. B. *Autobiographies, A Vision.*

"Tom at Cruachan" (1932)

See "WORDS FOR MUSIC PERHAPS."

"Tom the Lunatic" (1932)

See "WORDS FOR MUSIC PERHAPS."

"To the Rose upon the Rood of Time" (1892)

One of several early poems having to do with the mystical symbol of the ROSE, "To the Rose upon the Rood of Time," like "FERGUS AND THE DRUID" and "The WANDERINGS OF OISIN," represents a wavering uncertainty in Yeats's evolution toward a poetry of transcendence and vision, an uncertainty that he would never escape nor entirely desire to escape. The poem's agonized tension between the superhuman and human, the visionary and the mundane, anticipates the philosophical dialectic of poems like "A DIALOGUE OF SELF AND SOUL" and "VACILLATION," and establishes the paradigm of Yeats's deepest self-reckoning. In "To the Rose upon the Rood of Time," Yeats calls on the mystical rose to "come near, come near, come near" but begs also that it leave a "little space for the rose-breath to fill," worrying that once possessed

by the rose he will "no more hear common things that crave; / The weak worm hiding down in its small cave, / The field-mouse running by me in the grass. . . ." Yeats's fear that he will "learn to chaunt a tongue men do not know" (cf. "RIBH IN ECSTASY") gives the essence of his dilemma: to embrace the rose is to forsake the terms of a viable poetry, to become not only more than man but more than poet. If Yeats's commitment to his own humanity is ambivalent, his commitment to poetry is central and cardinal; he must preserve enough of his humanity to continue his calling. The image of the rose upon the cross is Rosicrucian. In a 1901 journal entry, Yeats recounts waking from a mystical dream and saying to himself that Father Rosy Cross "set the rose upon the cross and this by uniting religion and beauty, the spirit and nature—and the union of spirit and nature is magic" (*Unicorn* 168). By implication, the beams of the cross represent the union of antinomies, while the rose represents the efflorescence of their miraculous reconciliation. CUCHULAIN is a legendary hero in the Red Branch or Ulster cycle of Irish mythology, and the chief personage of Yeats's plays. Fergus is a legendary king of Ulster; he figures also in DEIRDRE, "Fergus and the Druid" and "WHO GOES WITH FERGUS?"

FIRST PUBLICATION: *The Countess Kathleen and Various Legends and Lyrics*, T. Fisher Unwin, London, September 1892.

BIBLIOGRAPHY

Moore, Virginia. *The Unicorn: William Butler Yeats' Search for Reality.*

"Tower, The" (1927, dated 1926)

As the ROSE is the chief symbol of Yeats's youth, so the tower is the chief symbol of his maturity, an emblem of both rootedness and transcendence, of the accretion of history and the purity of solitude. The tower—and more particularly THOOR BALLYLEE—figures in numerous poems from 1917 onward, but none with the summarizing stature of

"The Tower," a plausible contender as Yeats's chef d'oeuvre. Divided into three sections, the poem is at once a restive rumination upon age, a gathering of local history, and a last will and testament. Its unifying element is the "excited, passionate, fantastical imagination" as it recovers confidence in itself and emerges as the indomitable legislator of reality.

The poem's opening section revises the complaint aired in earlier poems like "The LIVING BEAUTY," "MEN IMPROVE WITH THE YEARS," and "A Song" (1918). In his middle-aged romantic disappointment and crisis of confidence, Yeats had lamented what seemed the terminal exhaustion of his own heart. "The Tower" reasserts the heart's passion but puzzles over the irony that the living heart is mocked by the dying body. This irony may be evaded by a retreat into the abstraction of philosophy, but it is precisely the consolation of the abstract that Yeats cannot allow himself and that the poem decries. "It seems," writes Yeats, repeating the lament of "The Living Beauty," "that I must bid the Muse go pack, / Choose Plato and Plotinus for a friend / Until imagination, ear and eye, / Can be content with argument and deal / In abstract things; or be derided by / A sort of battered kettle at the heel." These lines state a general dilemma, but they equally have a personal significance, for Yeats had begun an ambitious program of philosophical reading in the 1920s. In a letter of March 14, 1926, to T. STURGE MOORE, Yeats mentioned that he had read Plato and Plotinus every day for months, and that he had waited to begin this reading until after he had finished the first edition of A VISION in 1925, as his controls feared that if he came too much under the influence of academic philosophy he would "split up experience till it ceased to exist" (WBY&TSM 83; see also AV 12). Yeats now wonders whether this pallid triumph of the mind is the inevitable lot of the aged. The allusion to boyhood fishing expeditions upon Ben Bulben, a mountain just north of Yeats's native SLIGO, recalls "The FISHERMAN," which imagines the kind of man—powerful in his unself-consious integrity and bodily ease—least given to the abstraction of Plato and Plotinus, the kind of man that Yeats was himself until broken by the "sedentary trade" of poetry (lines 179–180).

Thoor Ballylee, County Galway. "I declare this tower is my symbol," Yeats writes in "Blood and the Moon." *(Fáilte Ireland)*

The second section of the poem finds Yeats pacing the battlements of Thoor Ballylee, as in "I SEE PHANTOMS OF HATRED AND OF THE HEART'S FULLNESS AND OF THE COMING EMPTINESS" and "A PRAYER FOR MY DAUGHTER." He beckons to those "images and memories" that he would question, in a version of the visionary parade of "ALL SOULS' NIGHT." The subsequent 12 stanzas conduct a historical tour of the neighborhood surrounding Thoor Ballylee. Yeats's note to the poem clarifies some of the detail: "The persons mentioned are associated by legend, story and tradition with the neighbourhood of Thoor Ballylee or Ballylee Castle, where the poem was written. Mrs. French lived at Peterswell in the eighteenth century and was related to Sir Jonah Barrington [1760–1834], who described the incident of the ears and the trouble that came of it [in *Personal Sketches of his own Time*]. The peasant beauty and the blind poet are Mary Hynes and Raftery, and the incident of the man drowned in Cloone Bog is recorded in my *Celtic Twilight*. Hanrahan's pursuit of the phantom hare and hounds is from my STORIES OF RED HANRAHAN. The ghosts have been seen at their game of dice in what is now my bedroom [cf. "MY HOUSE"], and the old bankrupt man lived about a hundred years ago. According to one legend he could only leave the Castle upon a Sunday because of his creditors, and according to another he hid in the secret passage" (VP 825; for Barrington's account of Mrs. French, see NCP 217–218).

Yeats's fullest account of Mary Hynes and Anthony Raftery (1779–1835), as well the tale of the drowned man, appear in his gathering of local lore "Dust hath closed Helen's Eye" (1899). Yeats ends the piece with a flourish, describing the local beauty and the blind poet who worshipped her as "perfect symbols of the sorrow of beauty and of the magnificence and penury of dreams"; in "The Tower" he equates them with Helen of Troy and Homer (Myth. 30). Yeats further mentions Hynes and Raftery in the 1899 essay "The Literary Movement in Ireland" (UP2 189–190); in the novel The SPECKLED BIRD (44, 156); and in his NOBEL PRIZE address, "The Irish Dramatic Movement" (Aut. 411). Lady Gregory, meanwhile, translates Raftery's poem in praise of Mary Hynes in her Kiltartan Poetry Book of 1918 (Yeats quotes this in "Dust hath closed Helen's Eye") and devotes to him the first chapter of her Poets and Dreamers (1903). Red Hanrahan's pursuit of the phantom hare is related in "Red Hanrahan" (1903), first collected in Stories of Red Hanrahan (Myth. 213–224). The story depicts the tribulations of the hedge schoolmaster Hanrahan. His sweetheart sends word that her mother has died and they may now marry. He means to leave at once, but a mysterious codger tempts him with cards. The cards become a hare and a pack of hounds. As if in a dream, Hanrahan follows the hunt out the door and across the countryside, eventually coming to a "very big shining house" where a woman of matchless queenly beauty awaits a hero to wake her from an enchanted torpor; but Hanrahan is abashed by the magnificence of the house and by the beauty of the woman, and he wakes the next morning in a field, never again to be a man entirely belonging to the visible world.

In this local procession—imperious patrician, peasant beauty, rustics smitten to madness, blind poet, rambling visionary, scandalous wastrel, "roughmen-at-arms" whose ghosts continue at their game of dice—Yeats finds a precedent of passion and personality that corroborates his own living heart and

exemplifies the tradition he would found upon and symbolize by the tower. Yeats asks whether they too raged against old age and finds his answer, presumably affirmative, "in those eyes / That are impatient to be gone. . . ." Yeats would have Hanrahan remain, however, for he has a further question for the "old lecher" who so thoroughly plumbed the mysteries of love in his later wanderings (on Hanrahan's lechery, see Myth. 239). MAUD GONNE never far from his mind, Yeats asks whether imagination dwells most upon the woman won or lost. The answer is never in doubt, and Yeats, in what amounts to his own confession of failure, compels Hanrahan to admit that he "turned aside / From a great labyrinth out of pride, / Cowardice, some silly over-subtle thought / Or anything called conscience once," and that the memory of this loss of nerve tortures him. The two questions with which the section ends have an important relationship: Yeats does not seek the answers he solicits, but rather insight into the dynamic by which the heart lacerates or spurs itself into renewed life (cf. "The SPUR"). Yeats probes, in effect, the heart's capacity to sustain itself by feeding on its own frenzy. The closing image of the eclipsed sun chimes with the earlier allusion to "day's declining beam" (line 21) and counterpoises allusions to the "livelong summer day" of youth (line 10) and to Hanrahan's careering "drunk or sober through the dawn" (line 58). The dawn symbolizes not merely youth and vigor in opposition to the "day's declining beam," but, as in "The DAWN" and "The Fisherman," a passion stripped of sentimentality and self-consciousness. The challenge is to cast out remorse and escape the sway of the sun altogether, a condition of beatitude whose image is the "Translunar Paradise" of the poem's third section.

Where the first and second sections of the poem are exasperated, interrogative, and restless, the third section introduces a new tone of confidence and decision ("I choose," "I declare," "I mock"), as if Yeats has drawn courage and resolution from the "images and memories" he has called from "ruin or from ancient trees." "It is time that I wrote my will," Yeats asserts, ready at last to stand upon his identity and reckon his possessions. He leaves his pride to "upstanding men" who "drop their cast at the side / Of dripping stone," not incidentally at dawn ("under bursting dawn" in the poem's penultimate stanza). Men such as these belong to the ideal type limned in "The Fisherman." So too they are fully fledged versions of Yeats himself as he cast his boyhood line upon Ben Bulben (lines 9–10), a self that Yeats has betrayed by long immersion in the abstractions of poetry (lines 179–180). This is the pride of the Anglo-Irish, the "people of Burke and Grattan / That gave, though free to refuse" (cf. "TO A SHADE"); so too it is the pride of the morning when "the headlong light is loose"; of the "fabulous horn" (cf. "A Prayer for my Daughter"); of "the sudden shower / When all streams are dry"; of that hour when the swan must "fix his eye / Upon a fading gleam" and sing his final song (cf. "COOLE AND BALLYLEE, 1931"). This spate of metaphor images the spontaneous brimming-over of passionate abundance. In his note to "The Tower," Yeats acknowledges that the description of the swan, perhaps the most perfect lines in a poem full of perfection, is a "theft" from T. Sturge Moore's poem "The Dying Swan," and yet a comparison of the two poems says more about Yeats's eminence than his thievery (VP 826; Moore's poem is included in both the note and in Yeats's 1936 edition of The Oxford Book of Modern Verse).

Yeats next declares his faith. Where Plato and Plotinus had seemed the inevitable companions of his senescence, Yeats now affronts them with the radically subjectivist conviction (likewise expressed in "DEATH" and more obliquely in "TWO SONGS FROM A PLAY") that "Death and life were not / Till man made up the whole, / Made lock, stock and barrel / Out of his bitter soul, / Aye, sun and moon and star, all. . . ." More than this, Yeats declares that "being dead, we rise, / Dream and so create / Translunar paradise." The crucial emphasis is that paradise is dreamt and created, a matter of imagination rather than metaphysics or theology. "Translunar" is at once richly evocative and obscure. According to The Oxford English Dictionary, the word is a synonym for "translunary" meaning "lying beyond or above the moon [. . .] etherial, insubstantial, visionary." In this unquestionably unorthodox context, it may signify the entire swathe of the heavens, "sun and moon and star," brought under the dominant image of the moon, which is associated at the full with

"complete beauty" (AV 135), with all that Yeats can surmise of transcendence. As "The PHASES OF THE MOON" has it, body and soul are "too perfect at the full to lie in a cradle / Too lonely for the traffic of the world: / Body and soul cast out and cast away / Beyond the visible world." Conceivably, "Translunar paradise" indicates just this realm beyond the visible world where the soul and body reside in their perfection. Yeats writes in "SAILING TO BYZANTIUM" that the soul has no "singing school but studying / Monuments of its own magnificence," and here again he emphasizes the tutelage of the high and the monumental. He has "prepared his peace"—passion having transcended even itself—with "learned Italian things" (perhaps Dante's Divine Comedy or Castiglione's Book of the Courtier, both central texts for Yeats); with the "proud stones of Greece" ("stones" implying architecture or sculpture; perhaps the Elgin Marbles, which Yeats saw regularly at the British Museum); with the imaginings of the poet and memories of love (that which troubled the day into darkness in the final stanza of the poem's second section). If the second section of the poem depicts passion frenziedly feeding upon itself, the third section depicts passion masterfully disciplined in the service of a "superhuman / Mirror-resembling dream," a self-legislated reality that reflects, as a mirror reflects, the substance of the "bitter soul." Significant is the transition from "heart" (line 2) to "soul" (lines 151 and 181). In Yeats's conceptualization, the soul might be defined as the heart brought to discipline, the heart reconstructed—forged, as "Sailing to Byzantium" has it—in the image of its own permanence.

The poem begins its closing strain with a seven-line stanza that functions as a complex cluster of metaphor. The daws (i.e., jackdaws or crows) construct their nest as Yeats his soul, gathering twigs as he gathers "learned Italian things" and "the proud stone of Greece." The daw warming her young balances the elegant demise of the swan and inscribes the promise of rebirth even as the poem segues toward death; so too it images Yeats's feeling of paternal responsibility for the next generation of "young upstanding men" mentioned in the next stanza. "Now shall I make my soul," Yeats declares, his faith in his own self-mastery now absolute. In a passage deleted from a radio broadcast aired by the BBC on September 8, 1931, Yeats similarly announced, "Now I am trying to write about the state of my soul, for it is right for an old man to make his soul, and some of my thoughts upon that subject I have put into a poem called 'Sailing to Byzantium'" (*Between the Lines* 96–97). As in "Sailing to Byzantium," Yeats here compels his soul to study in "learned school" until bodily decline and encroaching death "Seem but the clouds of the sky / When the horizon fades, / Or a bird's sleepy cry / Among the deepening shades"—not extinctions, but passing poignancies in the ongoing passion of life.

FIRST PUBLICATION: The *Criterion* (periodical), June 1927, and the *New Republic,* June 29, 1927. Reprinted in *October Blast,* The CUALA PRESS, Dublin, August 1927.

BIBLIOGRAPHY

Jeffares, A. Norman. *A New Commentary on the Poems of W. B. Yeats*; Stallworthy, John. *Between the Lines: Yeats's Poetry in the Making*; Yeats, W. B. *Autobiographies, Mythologies, The Speckled Bird, Uncollected Prose by W. B. Yeats* (vol. 2), *The Variorum Edition of the Poems of W. B. Yeats, A Vision, W. B. Yeats and T. Sturge Moore: Their Correspondence 1901–1937.*

"Travail of Passion, The" (1896)

"The Travail of Passion" epitomizes the lush mysticism, at once religious and decadent, that characterized the bulk of Yeats's poetry during the mid-1890s. Yeats imagines the "flaming lute-thronged angelic door" thrown open and "immortal passion" visiting itself in a breath upon "mortal clay" in a vision of Christ's incarnation, though not necessarily one to please the ecclesiastical authorities. The poem suddenly shifts to the scene of Christ's suffering as he makes his way to Calvary. Yeats writes in the voice of a grieved onlooker among other grieved onlookers that "our hearts" likewise endure the scourge, the thorns, the "bitter faces" of the mob, the "vinegar-heavy sponge," and the "flowers by Kedron stream," "Kedron"—alternately

"Cedron" and "Kidron"—is a brook that flows past Calvary and empties into the Dead Sea (see, for example, John 18:1). The poem's final three lines suggest Veronica wiping Christ's brow (the tale of Veronica's compassion is handed down by tradition, but not documented in Scripture), though the trappings of hair and perfume equally evoke the decadence of the nineties. "We will bend down and loosen our hair over you," says the speaker of the poem, "That it may drop faint perfume, and be heavy with dew, / Lilies of death-pale hope, roses of passionate dream." As Veronica is said to have given her kerchief and received it back marked with the image of Christ, so these lines envision both an offering and a benediction. The loosened hair sheds perfume even as it becomes heavy with dew, lilies, and roses, seemingly the result of caressing the divine body. The motif of loosened hair forming a sheltering bower relates the poem to "HE BIDS HIS BELOVED BE AT PEACE," "He tells of a Valley full of Lovers" (1897), and "HE REPROVES THE CURLEW," but in this case the hair preserves the divine against the mundane rather than preserves the mundane against the divine. The poem's title is not the least of its complexities. "Passion" conventionally refers to Christ's suffering and death (see Acts 1:3), but, as used both here and in poems like "A Poet to his Beloved" (1896) and "He reproves the Curlew," the word suggests the numinous, creative impulse of the universe. The "travail of passion," then, seems to indicate both the passion of Christ and the burden of embodying this impulse.

FIRST PUBLICATION: The *SAVOY* (periodical), January 1896, under the sequence title "Two Love Poems" and the title "The Travail of Passion" (paired with "He bids his Beloved be at Peace"). Reprinted in *The Wind Among the Reeds,* Elkin Mathews, London, April 1899, under the present title.

"Two Songs from a Play" (1927)

"Two Songs from a Play" is culled from *The RESURRECTION*: the first song opens the play, the second closes it. Like "LEDA AND THE SWAN" and "The

SECOND COMING," "Two Songs from a Play" concerns—even revels in—the process by which civilization reverses itself, by which, as Yeats writes in *The Resurrection*, quoting Heraclitus, "God and man die each other's life, live each other's death" (*VPl.* 931, 934). The play describes the violent shock as dispensation gives way to dispensation. In the streets of Jerusalem, the Greek god Dionysus is carried in funeral procession by his frenzied followers, signifying the end of the pagan era; meanwhile Christ is risen from his tomb, as if Dionysus reincarnate, signifying the start of the Christian era. The poem condenses this drama into a difficult philosophical statement.

Sir James Frazer's *Golden Bough* (1890–1915), according to Richard Ellmann, provides the "key" to the first stanza. Ellmann summarizes: "Dionysus, like Christ, was the child of a mortal and an immortal, of Persephone and Zeus. Because of the jealousy of Hera, the Titans tore him to pieces, but Athena snatched his heart from his body and bore it on her hand to Zeus. Then Zeus put the Titans to death and, according to one version, swallowed the heart and begat Dionysus afresh upon the mortal Semele" (*IY* 260). Thus Athena is the "staring virgin" of the poem. Her unseeing eyes recall the "blank and pitiless" gaze of the sphinx in "The Second Coming" and the immobile, moonlit eyeballs of the Buddha in "The DOUBLE VISION OF MICHAEL ROBARTES." In each instance the eye is trained on a reality or pattern lying behind the mere phenomena of the world. That Athena holds a "beating heart" signifies that death is merely transitional; so too it gives the stamp of blood to the abstraction of myth and affirms Yeats's conviction, manifest also in "Leda and the Swan" and "The MAGI," and theorized in "RIBH DENOUNCES PATRICK," that natural and supernatural share equally in the primal reality of the body. The motif of the beating heart recurs in *The Resurrection*: Christ's beating heart, the horrifying miracle of his incarnation, scandalizes the abstraction of the Greek (*VPl.* 929). Presiding over this apocalyptic drama, the Muses sing in celebration of the "Magnus Annus"—the Great Year—as it comes round again in one of its 2,000-year epicycles, as though "God's death were but a play." The muses are ecstatic because they sense in the

crisis a new eruption of drama and a new impetus of art. In their celebration of "God's death" they recall the "pale unsatisfied ones" of "The Magi," who likewise preside over and exult in the spilling of divine blood, though perhaps with darker, hungrier motive. The allusion to "God" in the capitalized singular enacts a slippage from Dionysus to Christ, underscoring the divine reincarnation that is the crucial theme of both poem and play.

In the second stanza, the aesthetic emphasis of the preceding lines is carried forward. The Argo's synecdochical reduction to *painted* prow (anticipating the allusion to the "painter's brush" in line 28) instructs that history attains permanence and meaning in the imaginings of art, and that, as the muses understand, the renewal of history has its greatest justification in the promise of new myths and epics, new fields of artistic expression. Numerous critics discern the stanza's inspiration in the fourth Eclogue of Virgil, which reads: "Yet shall some few traces of olden sin lurk behind, to call men to essay the sea in ships, to gird towns with walls, and to cleave the earth with furrows. A second Tiphys shall then arise, and a second Argo to carry chosen heroes; a second warfare, too, shall there be, and again shall a great Achilles be sent to Troy" (*NCP* 242). Yeats knew this passage well and refers to it in "The ADORATION OF THE MAGI" (*Myth.* 310); in "Discoveries" (*E&I* 290); in his 1904 essay "First Principles" (*Expl.* 150); in *The Resurrection* (*VPl.* 923, 925); and in the 1925 edition of *A VISION* (152). The stanza may also remember the final chorus of SHELLEY's *Hellas* (1822), which itself echoes the fourth Eclogue (see *Yeats and Shelley* 193–195).

Bestriding a world trembling with imminent collapse, the Roman Empire "stood appalled" (note the pun on the funereal "pall"), so stunned by the annunciation of the "fierce virgin and her Star" that it "dropped the reigns of peace and war." Yeats diagnoses precisely this moment of lost self-mastery in *A VISION*: "A civilization is a struggle to keep self-control, and in this it is like some great tragic person [. . .]. The loss of control over thought comes towards the end; first a sinking in upon the moral being, then the last surrender, the irrational cry, revelation—the scream of Juno's peacock" (268).

The "fierce virgin and her Star" present the chief difficulty in an immensely difficult poem. The virgin is Athena, but, as Ellmann notes, she is equally Astraea and Mary: "Yeats, delighted by cyclical rounds, was struck by the fact that both gods [Dionysus and Christ] had died and been reborn in March, when the sun was between the Ram and the Fish, and when the moon was beside the constellation Virgo, who carries the star Spica in her hand. Virgo is usually connected with Astraea, the last goddess to leave the world after the golden age; Virgil prophesied in the Fourth Eclogue that she would return and bring the golden age again, and the passage was commonly read in later centuries as a prophecy of the coming of Mary and Christ, the former as Virgo, the latter identified with Spica as the Star of Bethlehem" (IY 260). As Ellmann notes, then, the final lines of the stanza "daringly assert a parallelism and even identity between the three pairs, Astraea and Spica, Athena and Dionysus, and Mary and Christ [. . .]" (261).

As the first "song" concerns the death of Dionysus, the first stanza of the second song concerns the death (and, by implication, resurrection) of Christ. The "room" is the same depicted in *The Resurrection* (VPl. 905): the scene of the Last Supper, from which Christ emerged to suffer a final violence, to cast himself amid "Galilean turbulence." The "odour of blood" that accompanies Christ's death (represented in *The Resurrection* by the ecstatic frenzy of the Dionysian cultists and by the anti-Christian rampage of the "mob") ends the Greek culture of "Platonic tolerance" and "Doric discipline," represented in *The Resurrection* by the Greek guard, who says of the followers of Dionysus, "I cannot think all that self-surrender and self-abasement is Greek, despite the Greek name of its god," and who insists, offended by what might well be called the "odour of blood," that Jesus "never had a human body" (VPl. 917, 923; in "The STATUES," Yeats theorizes the birth of this "Doric discipline"). Thomas Whitaker remarks that the peculiar emphasis of "odour of blood" evokes the "spectacle of a sober and restrained culture maddened like some beast" (*Swan and Shadow* 106).

The phrase "fabulous, formless darkness" describes Christianity in the words of the Neopla-tonic philosopher Proclus (ca. 410/12–85). Yeats clarifies the meaning of the phrase in *A Vision*: "The world became Christian, 'that fabulous formless darkness', as it seemed to a philosopher of the fourth century, blotted out 'every beautiful thing', not through the conversion of crowds or general change of opinion, or through any pressure from below, for civilization was *antithetical* still, but by an act of power" (278). In *A VISION*, as well, Yeats provides a clue to the gnomic assertion that it was "Babylonian starlight" that brought in the "fabulous, formless darkness": "I imagine the annunciation that founded Greece as made to Leda [. . .]. But all things are from antithesis, and when in my ignorance I try to imagine what older civilisation that annunciation rejected I can but see bird and woman blotting out some corner of the Babylonian mathematical starlight" (268). "The DAWN" envisions just this culture of mathematical starlight, imagining the "withered men that saw / From their pedantic Babylon / The careless planets in their courses, / The stars fade out where the moon comes, / And took their tablets and did sums. . . ." Inferably, then, the Babylonian and Christian cultures, being abstract, impersonal, and scientific—being *primary* in opposition to the *antithetical* Greek culture—represent the same swing of the historical pendulum. In this sense the former heralds or introduces the latter. On the other hand, *A Vision* specifies that "mathematical starlight," defined as "Babylonian astrology," remained an element "in the friendships and antipathies of the Olympic gods" (268). The allusion to the Babylonian starlight "bringing in" Christianity, then, may merely indicate the Greek culture's demise in the birth of Christianity.

In opposition to the crushing determinism of the superhuman pattern that governs the poem's first three stanzas, the poem ends with a flourish of defiant humanism. Echoing "NINETEEN HUNDRED AND NINETEEN" ("Man is in love and loves what vanishes"), the poem acknowledges that the endless recurrence of the universe plays out as a tragedy of human bereavement and depletion, but in a sudden turn insists that "Whatever flames upon the night / Man's own resinous heart has fed," reconceiving the suggestion of wasting conflagration ("consumes") as defiant spectacle and offering perhaps Yeats's greatest image of the heart's transfiguration of its own tragedy. These lines look forward to "VACILLATION" ("From man's blood-sodden heart are sprung / Those branches of the night and day / Where the gaudy moon is hung") and comport with the radical subjectivism articulated in "DEATH" ("Man has created death") and "The TOWER" ("Death and life were not / Till man made up the whole"). The self-consuming dynamic of these lines, Whitaker notes (*Swan and Shadow* 23), is detectable also in "IN MEMORY OF MAJOR ROBERT GREGORY" ("Some burn damp faggots, others may consume / The entire combustible world in one small room") and in *AUTOBIOGRAPHIES*: "Our love-letters wear out our love; no school of painting outlasts its founders, every stroke of the brush exhausts the impulse, PRE-RAPHAELITISM had some twenty years; Impressionism thirty perhaps" (243). Yeats further takes up the idea in "HER ANXIETY" and in a 1929 letter to T. STURGE MOORE: "Sexual desire dies because every touch consumes the Myth, and yet a myth that cannot be so consumed becomes a spectre" (*WBY&TSM* 154).

FIRST PUBLICATION: The *Adelphi* (periodical), June 1927, as the opening and closing lines of *The Resurrection*. Reprinted in *October Blast*, The CUALA PRESS, Dublin, August 1927, under the present title.

BIBLIOGRAPHY

Bornstein, George. *Yeats and Shelley*; Ellmann, Richard. *The Identity of Yeats*; Jeffares, A. Norman. *A New Commentary on the Poems of W. B. Yeats*; Whitaker, Thomas R. *Swan and Shadow: Yeats's Dialogue with History*; Yeats, W. B. *Autobiographies, Essays and Introductions, Explorations, Mythologies, The Variorum Edition of the Plays of W. B. Yeats, A Vision, W. B. Yeats and T. Sturge Moore: Their Correspondence 1901–1937.*

"Two Trees, The" (1892)

"The Two Trees" is addressed to MAUD GONNE. According to Virginia Moore, it was Gonne's favorite among Yeats's poems, a revealing preference given that the poem deals directly with her own psychology (*Unicorn* 425). "The Two Trees" inscribes the nervous recognition that Gonne's mind hangs in the balance between "innocence" and "hatred," to borrow terms from "A PRAYER FOR MY DAUGHTER." The poem presents a plea for the rejection of self-consciousness, abstraction, and rancor, foreshadowing long in advance the prescriptions of "A Prayer for my Daughter" and rehearsing the symbol of the redemptive, life-giving tree that would reemerge in major poems like "AMONG SCHOOL CHILDREN" and "A Prayer for my Daughter." As late as 1909, Yeats's thought about Gonne continued to shadow the central dichotomy of "The Two Trees." He writes in MEMOIRS, referring to the kind of opinionated woman that Gonne epitomized, "They grow cruel, as if [in] defence of lover or child, and all this is done for something other than life. At last the opinion becomes so much a part of them that it is as though a part of their flesh becomes, as it were, stone, and much of their being passes out of life. It was part of [Gonne's] power in the past that, though she made this surrender with her mind, she kept the sweetness of her voice and much humour, yet I cannot but fear for her" (*Aut.* 372–373; *Mem.* 192). "The Two Trees" was the first of many such pleas for the sweetness of life in its unself-conscious blossom. Gonne remembers, for example, standing by the Normandy shore in September 1916 as Yeats read her "EASTER 1916" and implored her "to forget the stone and its inner fire for the flashing, changing joy of life" (*Scattering Branches* 32).

Among many other commentators, Moore identifies the "holy tree" of the heart with "the Cabalistic Tree of Life" (*Unicorn* 179). Richard Ellmann explains that the "Sephirotic tree has two aspects, one benign, the reverse side malign. On one side are the *Sephiroth*, on the other the dread *Qlippoth*. Since the Kabbalists consider man to be a microcosm, the double-natured tree is a picture both of the universe and of the human mind, whose faculties, even the lowest, can work for good or ill" (*IY* 76). The Tree of Life also figures, says Ellmann, in "HE HEARS THE CRY OF THE SEDGE," "HE THINKS OF

HIS PAST GREATNESS WHEN A PART OF THE CON-STELLATIONS OF HEAVEN," and "The Poet pleads with the Elemental Powers" (1892). Yeats explicitly comments on the Kabbalistic tree in "William Blake and his Illustrations to the *Divine Comedy*" (*E&I* 130); in "Discoveries" (272); and in a long note on the three poems Ellmann mentions (*VP* 811–812). In his essay on BLAKE's illustrations, Yeats articulates the tree's significance: "The kingdom that was passing was, [Blake] held, the kingdom of the Tree of Knowledge; the kingdom that was coming was the Kingdom of the Tree of Life: men who ate from the Tree of Knowledge wasted their days in anger against one another, and in taking one another captive in great nets; men who sought their food among the green leaves of the Tree of Life condemned none but the unimaginative and the idle, and those who forget that even love and death and old age are an imaginative art" (*E&I* 130).

For all its mooting of themes that would reoccur in more important contexts—the bane of self-consciousness, the antagonism between heart and mind—"The Two Trees" does not inaugurate the motif of the gyre, as it tantalizingly seems to do. The image of love and life "gyring" among "ignorant leafy ways" was the product of a late revision. Until 1929, line 15 read "Tossing and tossing to and fro," rather than "gyring, spiring to and fro" (*VP* 135). Frank Kermode comments on these anachronistic lines that in any case it "is not the gyres that are important here, but the emphatic 'ignorant'—this is the anti-intellectualist tree" (*Romantic Image* 120). The dream of "ignorance," by which Yeats means the transcendence of self-consciousness, similarly informs poems like "The DAWN," "The FISHERMAN," "MICHAEL ROBARTES AND THE DANCER" and "A Prayer for my Daughter." In "Michael Robartes and the Dancer," Yeats avows that "all beautiful women may / Live in uncomposite blessedness, / And lead us to the like—if they / Will banish every thought," and thus persists well into his maturity in the fundamental understanding of "The Two Trees."

FIRST PUBLICATION: *The Countess Kathleen and Various Legends and Lyrics*, T. Fisher Unwin, London, September 1892.

BIBLIOGRAPHY

Ellmann, Richard. *The Identity of Yeats*; Gwynn, Stephen, ed. *Scattering Branches: Tributes to the Memory of W. B. Yeats*; Kermode, Frank. *Romantic Image*; Moore, Virginia. *The Unicorn: William Butler Yeats' Search for Reality*; W. B. Yeats, *Autobiographies, Essays and Introductions, Memoirs, The Variorum Edition of the Poems of W. B. Yeats*.

"Two Years Later" (1914)

See "TO A CHILD DANCING IN THE WIND."

"Unappeasable Host, The" (1896)

"The Unappeasable Host" depicts the Sidhe as they lay siege, like a furious storm, to the heart of man. The opening lines of the poem envision the fairy children laughing and clapping in their cradles of gold. Meanwhile the poem's narrator—a woman, perhaps—clutches her own wailing child to her breast, sheltering it from the call that comes from the "narrow graves." The discrepancy between the children suggests the discrepancy between the fairy realm and the human realm: where the fairies sport in wanton high spirits, humans cringe in weakness and vulnerability. In the last six lines of the poem, Yeats marvelously realizes the desolate majesty of the fairy's beckoning call as it sweeps over the world in the form of wind. The winds "cry over the wandering sea" and "hover in the flaming West" and "beat the doors of Heaven" and finally "beat the doors of Hell," blowing there "many a whimpering ghost." In the end, the poem affirms this terrible beauty with a cry: "O heart the winds have shaken, the unappeasable host / Is comelier than candles at Mother Mary's feet." Implicitly the lines weigh the Catholicism of modern Ireland against the fairy lore of ancient Ireland and decide in favor of the latter. The candles, after all, are negligible in comparison to the sweeping wind of the fairies; so too they are distinctly vulnerable to the snuffing power of this wind. In this respect the poem urges nothing less than a revolution in reverence and belief.

"Danaan children" refers to the Sidhe. As Yeats explains in a note to *The Wind Among the Reeds* (1899), "The powerful and wealthy called the gods of ancient Ireland the Tuatha De Danaan, or the Tribes of the goddess Danu, but the poor called them, and still sometimes call them, the Sidhe, from Aes Sidhe or Sluagh Sidhe, the people of the Faery Hills, as these words are usually explained" (*VP* 800). In another note, Yeats writes that he uses the "wind as a symbol of vague desires and hopes, not merely because the Sidhe are in the wind, or because the wind bloweth as it listeth, but because wind and spirit and vague desire have been associated everywhere" (806). This seems to acknowledge the poem as a vision of the heart tormented by its own desire, and the Sidhe as an incarnation or a haunting epitome of what the heart might be, somehow freed of its own mortality or humanity. Yeats also depicts the onslaught of the Sidhe in "The HOSTING OF THE SIDHE," while in "HE BIDS HIS BELOVED BE AT PEACE" he depicts in similar terms the onslaught of the "horse-shaped Púcas, who are now mischievous spirits, but were once Fomorian divinities" (808; see also 796).

FIRST PUBLICATION: The SAVOY (periodical), April 1896, under the sequence title "Two Poems concerning Peasant Visionaries" and the title "A Cradle Song" (paired with "The VALLEY OF THE BLACK PIG"). Reprinted in *The Wind Among the Reeds*, Elkin Mathews, London, April 1899, under the title "A Cradle Song." Reprinted in *Selected Poems Lyrical and Narrative*, Macmillan, London, October 8, 1929, under the present title.

BIBLIOGRAPHY

Yeats, W. B. *The Variorum Edition of the Poems of W. B. Yeats.*

"Under Ben Bulben" (1939, dated September 4, 1938)

A medley of final wisdom and last advice culminating in the three lines of the great epitaph, "Under Ben Bulben" attempts what the third section of "The TOWER" more consummately achieves: a statement that completes Yeats's life and work. The poem lacks the flawless joinery of extended meditations like "MEDITATIONS IN TIME OF CIVIL WAR," "NINETEEN HUNDRED AND NINETEEN," "The Tower," and "VACILLATION"—Harold Bloom predicts that it will someday be seen as an edifice of "cant and rant"—but it has the directness of words spoken if not from the deathbed, than with the deathbed rapidly approaching (*Yeats* 325). An August 1938 letter to DOROTHY WELLESLEY indicates the genesis of the poem. Yeats told his confidante that he had been reading a book of essays about Rilke, and one of the essays, on Rilke's "ideas about death," had annoyed him (*Letters* 913; *LOP* 184; cf. *Letters* 916–917). The essay was "Rilke and the Conception of Death" by William Rose (1894–1961), in *Rainer Maria Rilke: Aspects of His Mind and Poetry*, edited by Rose and G. Craig Houston (*BG* 618). Yeats enclosed in his letter to Wellesley lines he had written in the margin of the book: "Draw rein; draw breath. / Cast a cold eye / On life, on death. / Horseman pass by." Within days Yeats had excised the first two lines and adopted the remaining three as his epitaph. As if shocked

Yeats's gravestone, Drumcliff, County Sligo. "Under Ben Bulben" ends with the great epitaph. *(Fáilte Ireland)*

into action by the realization that he had written the perfect epitaph for himself, he wrote to Ethel Mannin (1900–84) on August 22: "I am arranging my burial place. It will be in a little remote country churchyard in SLIGO, where my great grandfather [John Yeats, 1774–1846] was the clergyman a hundred years ago. Just my name and dates and these lines [quotes his epitaph]" (*Letters* 914). In September, Yeats visited Wellesley at Penns in the Rocks and presented her with a draft of "Under Ben Bulben" (*LOP* 184–188). He dictated final revisions of the poem upon his deathbed, changing the title from "His Convictions" to "Under Ben Bulben" (184–188). According to Wellesley, this was Yeats's final act of literary composition; the next morning he slipped into his "last coma" (195).

The poem's title, far more evocative than "His Convictions," refers to the flat-topped mountain immediately to the northeast of Drumcliff and roughly five miles to the north of Sligo, the port town that Yeats never ceased to regard as his native ground despite his decades-long absence (cf. "UNDER SATURN"). The title of the poem refers to Yeats's choice of burial place in the shadow of the mountain. It may also place Yeats's "convictions" in the shadow of the mountain, construed, as Yeats himself construed it, as a symbol of Irish myth, history, and soil, and as symbol of his own youth (cf. "The Tower"). In addition to "The Tower" and "Under Ben Bulben," the mountain figures in "Alternative Song for the Severed Head in *The King of the Great Clock Tower*" (1934), "ON A POLITICAL PRISONER" (which rehearses the phrase "Under Ben Bulben"), and "Towards Break of Day" (1920). The third act of *DIARMUID AND GRANIA* opens upon the "wooded slopes of Ben Bulben," and the mountain often crops up in the prose pieces collected in the 1893 volume *The Celtic Twilight* (see *Mythologies*).

The poem opens with the first of its several pieces of advice. We are to "swear by"—to abide by, to hold true to—the wisdom of the sages who gathered "Round the Mareotic Lake" (Lake Mareotis, south of Alexandria). To this place of retirement St. Anthony of Coma (ca. 251–356) and his followers came in the early years of the fourth century, seeking to devote themselves to ascetic contemplation (cf. *Aut.* 238, 242; "DEMON AND

BEAST"; *E&I* 405; *LE* 108, 256). In "The Witch of Atlas" (1820), SHELLEY describes his witch passing the lake (line 505). In Yeats's gloss, "When the Witch has passed in her boat from the caverned river, that is doubtless her own destiny, she passes along the Nile 'by Moeris and the Mareotid lakes,' and sees all human life shadowed upon its waters in shadows that 'never are erased but tremble ever' [. . .]" (*E&I* 85). The coupling of the Christian hermits and Shelley's witch-muse affirms the Mareotic Lake as a place of both *primary* wisdom and *antithetical* vision and lends a comprehensive authority to what follows. That the wisdom of the sages "set the cocks a-crow" implies a metaphysical reverberation: in both "MY TABLE" and "SOLOMON AND THE WITCH" the avian cry heralds the apocalyptic moment, the moment when passion, wrought to its uttermost, overwhelms the order of the world and forces a new dispensation. If not by the Mareotic sages, Yeats continues, then swear by the Sidhe, the fairy riders who were the terrifying visitants of early poems like "The HOSTING OF THE SIDHE" and "The UNAPPEASABLE HOST." In the "completeness of their passions won," the Christian sages and the Sidhe, whatever the religious incongruity of their pairing, equally speak the language of eternity. The remainder of the poem gives the "gist of what they mean."

Echoing the opening lines of "Vacillation"— "Between extremities / Man runs his course"—the second section conceives existence as a cycle of life and death that occurs between the eternities of race and soul. In a recurrence of the metaphysical pattern that finds its fullest expression in "A DIALOGUE OF SELF AND SOUL" and "Vacillation," these represent the *primary* and *antithetical* poles of experience, the soul's outward and inward movements (*VP* 824). Whatever the nature of our lives, however, our deaths return us to the "human mind," a version of the ANIMA MUNDI or *Spiritus Mundi*, where the soul finds a new form in preparation for rebirth within the world (cf. "DEATH," "MOHINI CHATTERJEE"). These lines versify a passage in ON THE BOILER in which Yeats charges that those who accept "the objective matter and space of popular science [. . .] compel denial of the immortality of the soul by hiding from the mass of the people that the grave-diggers have no place to bury us but in the human mind" (*Expl.* 436; *LE* 237).

The poem's third section theorizes the "completeness" of which the first section speaks. In the moment of violence—that is, in the moment of greatest intensity—man "completes his partial mind" and discovers his destiny. In this moment, everything adventitious and accidental falls away and he discovers, if only momentarily, the joy of UNITY OF BEING. Yeats was nuanced on the subject of violence: it variously represents the fullness of the spirit, as here (see also *AV* 52–53); the unruliness or indomitability of the passions, as in "The LAMENTATION OF THE OLD PENSIONER"; the impersonal and ineluctable agency of history, as in "LEDA AND THE SWAN" and "The SECOND COMING"; the aristocratic temper, as in "ANCESTRAL HOUSES" and "BLOOD AND THE MOON"; the abhorrent vacuity of modernity, as in "Nineteen Hundred and Nineteen" and "The Second Coming"; and the fruitful tension of antinomies, as in his repeated declaration that the music of paradise is made by the sound of clashing swords (*Aut.* 209–210; *Expl.* 306; *Myth.* 254. 259; *VPl.* 688, 703), or his declaration that "all noble things are the result of warfare" (*E&I* 321). Yeats himself had not a violent bone in his body. He yearns, then, for a mask, the embrace of his own opposite that "EGO DOMINUS TUUS" explains.

The section's opening lines refer to John Mitchel (1815–75), a revolutionary agitator and, in 1843, the founder of the *United Irishman*, an influential nationalist newspaper. Mitchel was convicted of treason and transported to Tasmania in 1848. He fled in 1853 and spent the next two decades working for the Irish cause in America. He returned to Ireland in 1875. Yeats generally admired Mitchel. In AUTOBIOGRAPHIES, he pays Mitchel the high compliment that his "influence comes mainly, though not altogether, from style, that also a form of power, an energy of life"; elsewhere he calls Mitchel "the only Young Ireland prose-writer who had a style at all" (*Aut.* 381, 172; for a full discussion of Yeats's thoughts on Mitchel, see *Yeats, Ireland and Fascism* 11–12). Mitchel's prayer for war appears in his *Jail Journal* (1854), which Yeats included in his list of the "Best Irish Books" in 1895 (*UPI* 382–387;

see also 356, 361). Hugh Kenner comments that Mitchel's prayer "had restated the old equation, England's difficulty, Ireland's opportunity," and notes that Yeats alters its spirit: "Mitchel's hopes were strategic. Yeats leads you to think they were adrenal" (*Colder Eye* 302). Yeats's approving quotation of Mitchel contradicts the tenor of his own war poems—"Nineteen Hundred and Nineteen," "ON BEING ASKED FOR A WAR POEM," "The STARE'S NEST BY MY WINDOW"—which are the reverse of martial, though "The ROAD AT MY DOOR" hints at the understanding of "Under Ben Bulben" that the "partial mind" completes itself in the bodily abandon of war; hence, Yeats's envy of the "brown Lieutenant and his men." Elizabeth Cullingford makes a useful distinction: "[Yeats's] philosophy sanctioned conflict, but not murder" (*Yeats, Ireland and Fascism* 124).

Violence provides the epiphany by which we know our work or choose our mate, as the final lines of the poem's third section have it; the fourth section picks up the allusion to work and turns to the problem of the artist. Yeats urges the poet and sculptor to keep watch over the "modish painter," reiterating his perpetual unease with the dilettante trend of modern art (cf. "TO A YOUNG BEAUTY"); the painter must follow the example of his "great forefathers" and—in an important summary of the artist's purpose—"Bring the soul of man to God." Arguing for the tradition that the modish painter would "shirk," Yeats invokes Egypt and Greece. These discovered, in their different ways, the art of "measurement," by which Yeats means the principles of proportion and balance that belong to *anima mundi* and pattern the world (cf. *Aut.* 275; *Letters* 921; "The STATUES"; *AV* 268–73). Phidias, a Greek master-sculptor of the fifth century before Christ whom Yeats likewise invokes in "Nineteen Hundred and Nineteen" and "The Statues," wed these principles to a vision of the organic, thus opening the way for Michelangelo (1475–1564), who brings to fullest expression the "profane perfection of mankind" (on Michelangelo, see also "LONG-LEGGED FLY" and "MICHAEL ROBARTES AND THE DANCER"). This profane perfection—this fully awakened human vigor—seems to emerge out of and transcend the daintier religious vision of the

"Quattrocento" (i.e., the 15th century). Michel-angelo's work on the frescoes of the Sistine Cha-pel ceiling, significantly, began in 1508 and ended in 1512, marking not the Quattrocento but the beginning of the Cinquecento. In the sequence of Yeats's account, however, Michelangelo precedes the Quattrocento; this places him at the center of the stanza and emphasizes the centrality and pin-nacle of his achievement.

The gyres of history unspooled this tradition to its end. The "greater dream" of the heavenly vision had gone (cf. "The NINETEENTH CENTURY AND AFTER"), but certain latecomers—Edward Calvert (1799–1883) and Richard Wilson (1714–82), BLAKE and Claude Lorrain (ca. 1605–82)—continued in the effort to prepare "a rest for the people of God," either upon a bed of mystic vision (Blake, Calvert) or upon a bed of natural beauty (Lorrain, Wilson). Calvert was the dis-ciple of Blake, just as Wilson was the disciple of Claude. The four painters, then, suggest the mindfulness of tradition that Yeats urges in the section's first stanza. "Palmer" is Samuel Palmer (1805–81), another disciple of Blake whose etch-ing "The Lonely Tower" figures in the opening lines of "The PHASES OF THE MOON" and provides an iconic vision of the mystic tower so important in Yeats's own imagery and symbolism. The phrase from Palmer is a quotation from A. H. Palmer's *The Life and Letters of Samuel Palmer* (1892), pages 15–16 (NCP 406). Yeats quotes Palmer's entire comment in his essay "William Blake and his Illustrations to the *Divine Comedy*" (1896). Speak-ing of Blake's illustration of Dr. Robert Thorn-ton's *Pastorals of Virgil* (1821), Palmer observes: "There is in all such a misty and dreamy glim-mer as penetrates and kindles the inmost soul and gives complete and unreserved delight, unlike the gaudy daylight of this world. They are like all this wonderful artist's work, the drawing aside of the fleshly curtain, and the glimpse which all the most holy, studious saints and sages have enjoyed, of the rest which remains to the people of God" (E&I 125). In his essay "Swedenborg, Mediums, and the Desolate Places" (1920), Yeats touches on the heavenly vision shared by Blake and his two disciples: always in Blake's "boys and girls walking

or dancing on smooth grass and in golden light, as in pastoral scenes cut upon wood or copper by his disciples Palmer and Calvert, one notices the peaceful Swedenborgian heaven" (*Expl.* 44; LE 56; on Calvert and Blake, see also E&I 149–150). Following the departing wisp of the "greater dream" in Calvert and Wilson, Blake and Claude, there was only "confusion," of which the "modish painter" is implicitly the agent and symbol.

In the poem's fifth section, Yeats urges the advice of the fourth section upon the younger gen-eration of Irish poets. They must eschew every-thing shallowly modern. This is familiar in Yeats's thought—it is roughly the advice he gives in "To a Young Beauty"—but the eugenic aspersion ("base-born products of base beds") is a late development and seems lazily simple in contrast to the intricate spiritual dialectic of the previous section. Yeats urges the aspiring poet to find his inspiration in those least tainted by modernity and least impli-cated in the middle-class counting of pence that he rails against in "SEPTEMBER 1913." Yeats's proces-sion of those with remembering hearts and heads includes peasants, "hard-riding country gentlemen" (cf. "AT GALWAY RACES," "IN MEMORY OF MAJOR ROBERT GREGORY"), monks, "porter drinkers" (cf. "A Drunken Man's Praise of Sobriety" [1938], "Three Songs to the One Burden" [1939], "The SEVEN SAGES"), and "lords and ladies gay." Yeats says here what "The MUNICIPAL GALLERY REVIS-ITED" had said somewhat more concisely and ele-gantly: that all grows strong from contact with the soil, and that this wisdom is the shared possession of the beggarman and the nobleman.

In the poem's sixth and final stanza, Yeats imag-ines himself already dead. Demonstrating his own mindfulness of tradition, he envisions his grave laid as instructed in the Drumcliff churchyard, some three or four miles north of Sligo, where his paternal great-grandfather, the Rev. John Yeats, had been rector from 1811 to 1846 (cf. "ARE YOU CONTENT?" and "INTRODUCTORY RHYMES" to *Responsibilities*). He descries his epitaph cut by "his command" (a final donning of the imperious and aristocratic mask) on "limestone quarried near the spot," symbolic of the immersion in the local or native soil that Yeats counsels in the previous section, and reminiscent of the emphasis on local materials in "To be Carved on a Stone at Thoor Ballylee" (1921). The epitaph itself inscribes the last of the poem's many injunctions: "Cast a cold eye / On life, on death. / Horseman, pass by!" The "cold eye" is congruent with the "derision" mentioned in "Death," and with the invocation of the cold as the barometer of disciplined passion in "The FISHERMAN" and "LAPIS LAZULI" (see also *E&I* 522–523; *LE* 213; *Letters* 837). The cold eye suggests the tragic vision that Yeats elaborates in the poem's second section and more fully in "Lapis Lazuli," the understanding that life and death are mere bagatelles, mere phases in an eternal recurrence, of no significance to one who comprehends and accepts the tragic pattern. "Horseman, pass by!" encourages the "cold eye," but also demonstrates Yeats's own "cold eye": his readiness to make little of his own grave and by implication his own death.

As Kenner notes, Yeats reverses the traditional sentiment of the Christian epitaph following the example of SWIFT (see "SWIFT'S EPITAPH"). "There was a collective voice the Christian dead used to assume," Kenner says, "Church Latin on a stone to bid travellers pause, in countless epitaphs that commenced, *Siste, viator.* 'Siste': stay, linger, ponder: Ponder on the fact of death. I have died, so shall you; be admonished. Thus, on many thousand stones, the voice of Christian death; and in 1745, Jonathan Swift's single voice presumed to defy that voice. *Abi, viator,* Swift says from his plaque in St. Patrick's, *et imitare si posteris:* . . . get moving, traveler, and imitate if you can. . . . Let the late Dean's savage indignation infect you, and like him perform public acts on behalf of fuller human life" (*Colder Eye* 339). Yeats's epitaph in these regards contrasts with the final stanza of "COOLE PARK, 1929," in which Yeats asks "traveler, scholar, poet" to pause in homage by the ruined remains of COOLE PARK and give "a moment's memory" to the "laurelled head" of Lady GREGORY.

The poem's burial instructions were eventually carried out, though not immediately upon Yeats's death. Yeats died at Roquebrune, France, on January 28, 1939. He remained interred in the Church of St. Pancras cemetery until the conclusion of World War II made it possible to transport his body

Ben Bulben, just north of Sligo. Yeats considered the mountain a symbol of Irish myth, history, and soil. *(Fáilte Ireland)*

to Ireland. On September 17, 1948, his body was interred in Drumcliff Churchyard under a stone engraved with the epitaph that closes "Under Ben Bulben" (*AP* 656–658). From the site of Yeats's grave, Ben Bulben is visible to the northeast.

FIRST PUBLICATION: The *Irish Independent,* and the *Irish Times* (periodicals), February 3, 1939. The *Irish Press,* February 3, 1939 (part VI only). Reprinted in *Last Poems and Two Plays,* The CUALA PRESS, Dublin, July 10, 1939.

BIBLIOGRAPHY

Bloom, Harold. *Yeats;* Cullingford, Elizabeth. *Yeats, Ireland and Fascism;* Foster, R. F. *W. B. Yeats: A Life, II: The Arch-Poet;* Jeffares, A. Norman. *A New Commentary on the Poems of W. B. Yeats;* Kenner, Hugh. *A Colder Eye: The Modern Irish Writers;* Saddlemyer, Ann. *Becoming George: The Life of Mrs W. B. Yeats;* Yeats, W. B. *Autobiographies, Essays and Introductions, Explorations, Later Essays, The Letters of W. B. Yeats, Letters on Poetry from W. B. Yeats to Dorothy Wellesley, Mythologies, Uncollected Prose by W. B. Yeats* (vol. 1), *The Variorum Edition of the Plays of W. B. Yeats, The Variorum Edition of the Poems of W. B. Yeats, A Vision.*

"Under Saturn" (1920, dated November 1919)

The theme of MAUD GONNE's lingering, marriage-disrupting presence, broached in "An IMAGE FROM A PAST LIFE," recurs if only to be dismissed in "UNDER SATURN," which immediately follows in *Michael Robartes and the Dancer* (1921) and in the collected poems. Addressing his wife, GEORGE YEATS, Yeats says that if he has become "saturnine" it is not because he pines for the "lost love" of Gonne, for he feels deeply the wisdom and comfort that marriage has brought. "Wisdom" takes account of George Yeats's benevolence and common sense (cf. *Letters* 634), but also her mediumistic gifts and her role in birthing the doctrines that would be systemized in A VISION. Yeats's doldrums instead have to do with the nagging of his conscience as he remembers his forebears: his maternal grandfather, WILLIAM POLLEXFEN; a Middleton "whose name you never heard," most likely his maternal grand-uncle William Middleton (1820–82), who had been William Pollexfen's business partner; and his paternal grandfather, the Reverend William Butler Yeats (1806–62). Yeats reminds his wife of an incident in which a laborer who had served the family shipping business accosted them near the SLIGO quay and cried, "You have come again, / And surely after twenty years it was time to come." Abashed, Yeats remembers "a child's vow sworn in vain / Never to leave that valley his fathers called their home." Despite this vow, Yeats had gradually lost hold of Sligo, which he regarded as his native soil and his spiritual home. In adulthood he lived the life of the literary cosmopolitan, residing in Dublin, Galway, OXFORD, and London, and making periodic continental and North American excursions.

Perhaps in reaction to the rootless experience of his later youth and adulthood, Yeats consistently emphasized the spiritual profit of remaining in "one dear perpetual place" ("A PRAYER FOR MY DAUGHTER") and deplored the modern tendency to "shift about" like "some poor Arab tribesman and his tent" ("COOLE AND BALLYLEE, 1931"). On this basis, he extolled the "noble and the beggar-man" ("The MUNICIPAL GALLERY REVISITED") in opposition to the migratory middle class. In "Discoveries," Yeats makes a quirky theology of the attachment to native soil: "I am orthodox and pray for a resurrection of the body, and am certain that a man should find his Holy Land where he first crept upon the floor, and that familiar woods and rivers should fade into symbol with so gradual a change that he may never discover, no, not even in ecstasy itself, that he is beyond space, and that time alone keeps him from Primum Mobile, Supernal Eden, Yellow Rose over all" (*E&I* 296). Fidelity to the native soil, a form of fidelity to the self in opposition to the flux of experience, underlies much of Yeats's aesthetic and explains his insistence that art find its school in the folk traditions and legends of the race or the nation. As Yeats expressed the point in "The Municipal Gallery Revisited," "John Synge, I and Augusta Gregory, thought / All that we did, all that we said or sang / Must come from contact with the soil, from that / Contact everything Antaeus-like grew strong."

FIRST PUBLICATION: *THE Dial* (periodical), November 1920. Reprinted in *Michael Robartes and the Dancer*, The CUALA PRESS, Churchtown, Dundrum, February 1921.

BIBLIOGRAPHY

Yeats, W. B. *Essays and Introductions, The Letters of W. B. Yeats.*

"Upon a Dying Lady" (1917, sequence)

The first of Yeats's experiments in formal poetic sequence, "Upon a Dying Lady" includes "HER COURTESY," "CERTAIN ARTISTS BRING HER DOLLS AND DRAWINGS," "SHE TURNS THE DOLLS' FACES TO THE WALL," "The END OF DAY," "HER RACE," "HER COURAGE," and "HER FRIENDS BRING HER A CHRISTMAS TREE." The seven poems take up the "strange charm" and "pathetic gaiety" of Mabel Beardsley, then hospitalized with the cancer of which she would die on May 8, 1916 (*Letters* 575). Beardsley was the sister of the arch-decadent illustrator AUBREY BEARDSLEY, whom Yeats had known during the mid-1890s when both were involved with the SAVOY. Yeats first met Aubrey Beardsley at a dinner at the New Lyric Club on January 22, 1896, to celebrate the launch of the *Savoy*, and he most likely met Mabel there as well (*CL2* 720; *I&R*, I, 28). The two lost touch, but when Yeats learned of Beardsley's illness in late 1912 he struck up the old acquaintance. R. F. Foster writes that the "old 1890s circle regrouped by her bedside; stories and jokes were passed around, along with memories of outrageous behaviour twenty years before. [. . .] The esoteric and sophisticated Beardsley circle, discussing sexual inversion and the Russian ballet, appealed to [Yeats] as an escape from Dublin spite and intrigue [. . .]" (*AM* 485–486).

Yeats wrote the seven poems included in "Upon a Dying Lady" between January 5 and February 18, 1913. During these weeks Yeats paid four visits to the hospital (*YC* 160–162). In a January 8 letter to Lady GREGORY, Yeats described his first visit on January 5. His account bears closely on the poetic sequence that began to germinate that very night:

> She was propped up on pillows with her cheeks I think a little rouged and looking very beautiful. Beside her a Xmas tree with little toys containing sweets, which she gave us. Mr. Davis—Ricketts' patron—had brought it—I daresay it was Ricketts' idea. I will keep the little toy she gave me and I daresay she knew this. On a table near were four dolls dressed like people out of her brother's drawings. Women with loose trousers and boys that looked like women. Ricketts had made them, modelling the faces and sewing the clothes. They must have taken him days. She had all her great lady airs and asked after my work and my health as if they were the most important things in the world to her. "A palmist told me," she said, "that when I was forty-two my life would take a turn for the better and now I shall spend my forty-second year in heaven" and then emphatically "O yes I shall go to heaven. Papists do." When I told her where Mrs. Emery was she said "How fine of her, but a girls' school! why she used to make even me blush!" Then she began telling improper stories

and inciting us (there were two men besides myself) to do the like. At moments she shook with laughter. [. . .] I lay awake most of the night with a poem in my head. I cannot overstate her strange charm—the pathetic gaiety. It was her brother but her brother was not I think loveable, only astounding and intrepid. (*Letters* 574–575)

Yeats refers to Sir Edmund Davis (1861–1939), the Australian-born mining magnate, and to Charles Ricketts (1866–1931), the distinguished painter and stage designer, one of Yeats's intimate friends. Mrs. Emery—Florence FARR—was then teaching in a girl's school in Ceylon where she too would die of cancer before many years were out. The rouge and "improper stories" figure in "Her Courtesy"; the dolls in "Certain Artists bring her Dolls and Drawings" and "She turns the Dolls' Faces to the Wall"; the Christmas tree in "Her Friends bring her a Christmas Tree"; the comparison to her brother in "Her Race." Yeats chose not to publish the sequence during the three years of Beardsley's decline, but he did send Beardsley drafts of the poems (*AM* 486).

FIRST PUBLICATION: The *Little Review* (periodical), August 1917, and the *New Statesman* (periodical), August 11, 1917. Reprinted in *The Wild Swans at Coole*, The CUALA PRESS, Churchtown, Dundrum, November 17, 1917.

BIBLIOGRAPHY

Foster, R. F. *W. B. Yeats: A Life, I: The Apprentice Mage*; Kelly, John S. *A W. B. Yeats Chronology*; Mikhail, E. H., ed. *W. B. Yeats: Interviews and Recollections* (vol. 1); Yeats, W. B. *The Collected Letters of W. B. Yeats* (vol. 2), *The Letters of W. B. Yeats*.

"Upon a House shaken by the Land Agitation" (1910)

The house in question is Lady GREGORY's Galway estate COOLE PARK, which was then being "shaken" by Ireland's decades-long struggle between landowners and tenants. The poem specifically responds to a dispute in which 15 tenants of the Gregory estate applied to the Land Court for a rent reduction. On July 30, 1909, the court approved the application and reduced the rent by roughly 20 percent (*Mem.* 226). Yeats, who was then a summer guest at Coole, set down a draft of the poem and summarized its idea in an August 7 journal entry: "Subject for poem. 'A Shaken House'. How should the world gain if this house failed, even though a hundred little houses were the better for it, for here power [has] gone forth or lingered, giving energy, precision; it gave to a far people beneficent rule [Lady Gregory's husband had been governor of Ceylon], and still under its roof living intellect is sweetened by old memories of its descent from far off? How should the world be better if the wren's nest flourish and the eagle's house is scattered?" Yeats adds, in homage to Coole, "This house has enriched my soul out of measure, because here life moves without restraint through spacious forms. Here there has been no compelled labour, no poverty-thwarted impulse" (225–226).

Like "No Second Troy" (which on similar grounds objects to "little streets" being hurled upon the "great"), the poem poses a series of rhetorical questions. Yeats loftily inquires how the world would be the better if great houses like Coole became "too ruinous / To breed the lidless eye that loves the sun," to breed the "sweet laughing eagle thoughts that grow / Where wings have memory of wings. . . ." The eagle's legendary capacity to stare directly into the sun, as if equal to the sun's blinding glory, explains the reference to "lidless eye," but this may also be considered a preliminary instance of the motif of the vacant stare so freighted with meaning in later poems like "A Bronze Head," "The Double Vision of Michael Robartes," "A Mountain Tomb," "The Second Coming," and "The Statues." As Frank Kermode argues, the vacant stare (or what he calls "the dead face") pervades the romantic and symbolist traditions, and represents the personality purified of the heterogeneous and accidental (see *Romantic Image* passim). The eagle, meanwhile, recurs as a symbol of the aristocratic or fiercely lofty spirit in "An Acre of Grass," "Friends," "Those Images" (1938), and "To a Wealthy Man who promised a Second

Subscription to the Dublin Municipal Gallery if it were proved the People wanted Pictures." Taking his cue from "Upon a House," Ezra Pound took to calling Yeats himself the "Eagle" (*Stone Cottage* 157).

In the poem's third and final rhetorical question, Yeats acknowledges the possibility that "mean roof-trees" would be sturdier for the fall of the great houses ("roof-trees" are the beams that uphold a roof). A deft synecdoche, the phrase indicates the tenant class by evoking both the rough cottages of the farmers and lives that aim at mere sturdiness, mere purchase on the physical world. The sturdiness of the roof-trees might be contrasted with the graceful gazebo of "In Memory of Eva Gore-Booth and Con Markiewicz" or Callimachus' "long lamp-chimney shaped like the stem / Of a slender palm" in "Lapis Lazuli," aristocratic forms that disdain sturdiness in favor of transcendent elegance. Even thus sturdied, however, the tenant class would never be able to attain "the gifts that govern men," or "gradual Time's last gift, a written speech / Wrought of high laughter, loveliness and ease." Both "beneficent rule" and superior literature, in other words, depend on the refinement inseparable from a leisured landowning class. Yeats would take up versions of this idea in later poems like "Coole and Ballylee, 1931," "Coole Park, 1929," and "A Prayer for my Daughter."

At the time of its publication, "Upon a House shaken by the Land Agitation" was Yeats's most strident statement of the increasingly conservative and aristocratic proclivities that so much peeved and bemused friends like Maud Gonne, George Moore, and George Russell (AE). Writing to John Quinn on March 20, 1911, Russell was mordant on the subject of "Upon a House": "I laughed over the 'Threatened House'. W.B.Y.'s affection for the aristocracy increases & he will slip into the reputation of Professor Mahaffy [J. P. Mahaffy, professor of ancient history at Trinity College] who never speaks without reference to 'his friend' the king, princess, duchess, duke, lord or whoever the rank may be. I think even the Peers would be amused over Yeats 'Threatened House'" (AM 435). R. F. Foster comments that the poem "necessarily read like a deliberate challenge to conventional nationalists, and symbolized how much he had distanced himself from their opinions since the death of [J. M.] SYNGE" (A 412).

FIRST PUBLICATION: McClure's Magazine, December 1910, under the title "To a Certain Country House in Time of Change." Reprinted in *The Green Helmet and Other Poems*, The CUALA PRESS, Churchtown, Dundrum, December 1910, under the sequence title "Momentary Thoughts" and the title "Upon a Threatened House." Reprinted in *The Green Helmet and Other Poems*, Macmillan, New York, London, October 23, 1912, under the present title.

BIBLIOGRAPHY

Foster, R. F. *W. B. Yeats: A Life, I: The Apprentice Mage*; Kermode, Frank. *The Romantic Image*; Longenbach, James. *Stone Cottage: Pound, Yeats, and Modernism*; Yeats, W. B. *Memoirs.*

"Vacillation" (1932, dated 1932)

The human soul, Yeats writes in a note to "The SECOND COMING," is "always moving outward into the objective world or inward into itself; & this movement is double because the human soul would not be conscious were it not suspended between contraries, the greater the contrast the more intense the consciousness" (VP 824). This double movement or "vacillation" between the poles of experience—*primary* and *antithetical*, objective and subjective, solar and lunar, self and soul—is among Yeats's fundamental intellectual instincts and seems almost inseparable from his personality. It is germinal in early poems like "FERGUS AND THE DRUID," "TO THE ROSE UPON THE ROOD OF TIME," and "The WANDERINGS OF OISIN," and it informs all of Yeats's mature psychological, historical, and metaphysical theorizing. He acknowledges as much in a letter of June 30, 1932, to OLIVIA SHAKESPEAR. "The swordsman throughout repudiates the saint," Yeats writes, summarizing the unifying thread of his life's work, "but not without vacillation." Quoting

from "Vacillation," he continues: "Is that perhaps the sole theme—Usheen and Patrick—'so get you gone Von Hügel though with blessings on your head'?" (Letters 798). Yeats similarly told GEORGE YEATS, "I have spent my life saying the same things in different ways. I denounced old age before I was twenty, and the swordsman throughout repudiates the saint—though with vacillation" (BG 620). One of Yeats's most ambitious and encompassing philosophical excursions, "Vacillation," originally titled "Wisdom" (Letters 788), ponders this pattern—and the mystery of release from this pattern—in a sequence of eight lyrics that are daringly various in form and tone and yet carefully tethered by the subtle pattern of idea.

The first stanza of the poem is Yeats's "system in little," as Virginia Moore calls it (Unicorn 404). "Between extremities / Man runs his course," Yeats states as his premise. The difficult point is the mechanism by which the pattern of vacillation between extremities is transcended. As in "BLOOD AND THE MOON" ("Everything that is not God consumed with intellectual fire"), "BYZANTIUM" ("An agony of flame that cannot singe a sleeve"), and "SAILING TO BYZANTIUM" ("O sages standing in God's holy fire"), Yeats equates the transcendental or purgatorial energy with fire. The "brand" or "flaming breath" destroys "All those antinomies / Of day and night"—of this Yeats is certain—but he is uncertain how this energy manifests itself in human experience. The body experiences this energy or the liberation provided by this energy as death, the heart as remorse. Yeats wonders, however, what room this leaves for joy, which he intuits as central to the transcendental dynamic. This intuition is close to the understanding of the final stanzas of "A DIALOGUE OF SELF AND SOUL" and the emphasis on tragic gaiety in "The GYRES" and "LAPIS LAZULI," and it finds much earlier precedent in *The UNICORN FROM THE STARS*, in which Yeats writes, "Events that are not begotten in joy are misbegotten and darken the world, and nothing is begotten in joy if the joy of a thousand years has not been crushed into a moment" (VPl. 688). All of this may remember the paean to joy in the fifth stanza of COLERIDGE's "Dejection: An Ode" (1802): "Joy, Lady! is the spirit and the power, /

Which wedding Nature to us gives in dower, / A new Earth and new Heaven. . . ."

Shifting from the reflective to the visionary voice, the poem's second section intensifies the conception of the first. The antinomies of the day and night—*primary* and *antithetical,* objective and subjective, in the language of A VISION—are figured as halves of a mystic tree, one abounding in verdure (cf. "A PRAYER FOR MY DAUGHTER"), the other glittering with flame. In "The Celtic Element in Literature" (1903), Yeats refers to the description of a similar tree in *The Mabinogian.* There one finds "the ancient worship of Nature and that troubled ecstasy before her" in the "beautiful passage about the burning tree, that has half its beauty from calling up a fancy of leaves so living and beautiful, they can be of no less living and beautiful a thing than flame," and he goes on to quote from Lady Charlotte Guest's 1877 translation: "They saw a tall tree by the side of the river, one half of which was in flames from the root to the top, and the other half was green and in full leaf" (*E&I* 176; cf. "The TWO TREES"). In Yeats's version of the mystic symbol, the tree's unalloyed "extremities" represent conditions of attainment or intensity that manifest themselves as an all-engulfing reality ("half is half and yet is all the scene"). Further, each represents a purity of condition that is expressed as the absolute self-identity of self-birth ("half and half consume what they renew"), as in "AMONG SCHOOL CHILDREN" ("O self-born mockers of man's enterprise") and "Byzantium" ("flame begotten of flame"). The final three lines of the stanza elaborately image the transcendental dynamic mooted in the first stanza. He who would escape the pattern of vacillation metaphorically hangs the image of Attis between that "staring fury" (the flaming tree) and the "blind lush leaf" (the verdurous tree), the former "staring" because visionary or straining after vision (cf. "TWO SONGS FROM A PLAY"), the latter "blind" because sunk in natural instinct or contentment (cf. "The CHAMBERMAID'S SECOND SONG" and "A Dialogue of Self and Soul"). The image of Attis, like the girl who dances between the Sphinx and Buddha in "The DOUBLE VISION OF MICHAEL ROBARTES," renders the energy of vacillation as a redemptive unity. As Richard Ellmann writes, "To hang the image

of Attis between the two sides of the tree was to give up one's hopes for normal experience and to become one with the god, thereby achieving a reconcilement of the antinomies" (*IY* 273). In a September 6, 1921, letter to T. STURGE MOORE, Yeats called the "Tree with Mask hanging on the trunk" one of his "main symbols" (*WBY&TSM* 38).

Sir James Frazer's *Golden Bough* (1890–1915), which Yeats read and thoroughly absorbed during the 1890s, clarifies the allusion to Attis. In one version of the Phrygian and later Roman legend, Attis was a shepherd boy loved by Cybele, queen of the gods (in other versions he was her son). In a fit of jealousy, she afflicted him with madness, and he died after castrating himself. At the repentant goddess's request, Zeus allowed Attis's spirit to pass into the pine-tree beneath which he unmanned himself. In the Roman tradition, votaries celebrated the springtime festival of Attis and Cybele by hanging Attis in effigy upon the trunk of a pine-tree (the specific allusion of the poem). On March 22 of each year, in Frazer's description of these rites, "a pine-tree was cut in the woods and brought into the sanctuary of Cybele, where it was treated as a great divinity. The duty of carrying the sacred tree was entrusted to a guild of Tree-bearers. The trunk was swathed like a corpse with woollen bands and decked with wreaths of violets, for violets were said to have sprung from the blood of Attis [. . .] and the effigy of a young man, doubtless Attis himself, was tied to the middle of the stem." On the following day, says Frazer, "Stirred by the wild barbaric music of clashing cymbals, rumbling drums, droning horns, and screaming flutes, the inferior clergy whirled about in the dance with waggling heads and streaming hair, until, rapt into a frenzy of excitement and insensible to pain, they gashed their bodies with potsherds or slashed them with knives in order to bespatter the altar and the sacred tree with their flowing blood" (*Golden Bough,* IV, I, 267–268). This scene of ecstasy—reminiscent of the ecstatic dance of "Byzantium," "The Double Vision of Michael Robartes," "NINETEEN HUNDRED AND NINETEEN," and "ROSA ALCHEMICA"—touches, perhaps, what Yeats means by "joy," and explains the invocation of Attis. As Yeats writes, the votary of Attis "May not know what he knows"—that is, may not be able to explain the transcendental dynamic—but knows the joy that is its enabling condition.

The third section of the poem repeats the internal structure of the first two sections. Consistent with the extremity of day and with the abounding foliage of the mystic tree, one should attend to practical ambition, though even the pursuit of wealth is marked by the pattern of vacillation, for solar gold has its complement in lunar silver, and the two combined are, as F. A. C. Wilson notes, an alchemical symbol of perfection (*Yeats and Tradition* 219). And yet, however sound the desire to prosper, "women dote upon an idle man / Although their children need a rich estate," a point illustrated by the adventures of Red Hanrahan. John Unterecker draws the conclusion that "man must live in both of the areas in which he vacillates" (*RG* 221), must embody both the *primary* engagement with the world and the *antithetical* rejection of the world. The ensuing stanza returns to the image of the divided tree and envisions an escape from the "Lethean foliage" of vacillation in the deepening purpose and strengthening faculties of age (cf. "The COMING OF WISDOM WITH TIME," which adopts foliage as an image of youthful vacillation or perhaps merely youthful caprice). Yeats urges the need to prepare for death, to remake the soul in the image of a redemptive unity or ecstasy. In keeping with the existential defiance of "DEATH," "A Dialogue of Self and Soul," "The Gyres," "HER COURAGE," "HER COURTESY," and "Lapis Lazuli," Yeats insists that in this effort we must abstain from all work of "intellect or faith" that is "not suited for such men as come / Proud, open-eyed and laughing to the tomb."

This tragic gaiety is the fullest casting out of remorse, and there follows in the poem's fourth section, as in the final stanza of "A Dialogue of Self and Soul," an access of joy, a consciousness of salvation, that is the transcendental condition. Associating the verb "blazed" with the motif of fire in the second section, one is tempted to place this moment of joy within the pattern of vacillation, but it may also be associated with the "flaming breath" of the first section, in which case, in keeping with its aspect of religious ecstasy, it represents the moment of release. Aged 50—with 10 years' labor of preparation behind him—Yeats sits "a solitary man, / In a crowded London shop." The contrast between Yeats's solitude and the society of the shop signals the subjective and objective antinomies between which man vacillates, as do, in the same way, the open book and the empty cup in the following line. The "open book" has occult connotations, as in the opening lines of both "EGO DOMINUS TUUS" and "The PHASES OF THE MOON," while the cup has both bodily and social connotations. The antinomy of book and cup resolves in the image of the "marble table-top," which recalls the "marbles of the dancing floor" that "break bitter furies of complexity" in "Byzantium" (Yeats habitually associates marble, in its reconciliation of eternal substance and organic form, with the transcendence of antinomies).

The table-top dialectic of the first stanza primes for the release of the second. Yeats's body suddenly blazes with happiness. Echoing the final lines of "A Dialogue of Self and Soul," he is filled with the conviction that he is blessed and can be blessed. This is the "moment of moments" Yeats describes in an unpublished note to *A Vision*: "At first we are subject to Destiny [. . .] but the point in the Zodiac where the whirl becomes a sphere once reached, we may escape from the constraint of our nature and from that of external things, entering upon a state where all fuel has become flame, where there is nothing but the state itself, nothing to constrain it or end it. We attain it always in the creation or enjoyment of a work of art, but that moment though eternal in the Daimon passes from us because it is not an attainment of our whole being. Philosophy has always explained its moment of moments in much the same way; nothing can be added to it, nothing taken away; that all progressions are full of illusion, that everything is born there like a ship in full sail" (*IY* 221). In PER AMICA SILENTIA LUNAE, Yeats likewise describes the "moment of moments" and, as in "Vacillation," sets the scene in a restaurant, suggesting that both prose and poem draw on a specific memory: "At certain moments, always unforeseen, I become happy, most commonly when at hazard I have opened some book of verse. Sometimes it is my own verse when, instead of discovering new technical flaws, I read with all the excitement of the first writing. Perhaps I am sitting in some crowded restaurant, the open book beside me, or closed, my excitement having over-brimmed the page. I look at the strangers near as if I had known them all my life, and it seems strange that I cannot speak to them: everything fills me with affection, I have no longer any fears or any needs; I do not even remember that this happy mood must come to an end. It seems as if the vehicle had suddenly grown pure and far extended and so luminous that the images from ANIMA MUNDI, embodied there and drunk with that sweetness, would, like a country drunkard who has thrown a wisp into his own thatch, burn up time" (*LE* 31; see also *GY* 434; *Letters* 785).

It is an important stipulation of the note to *A Vision* quoted above that the moment "passes from us because it is not an attainment of our whole being." Just so, the fifth section of "Vacillation" plunges the poem back into the pattern of antinomy. The joy of the first and fourth sections is answered by the weight of remorse mentioned in the first, while the escape from "Lethean foliage" of the third section becomes here a distracted indifference to the antinomies of day and night as they play out in the sunlit summer sky and the moonlit winter field. Beset by the sense of responsibility and the pangs of conscience, Yeats cannot "look thereon," cannot plunge even into the vacillation of everyday life. The first section weighs the possibility that remorse is a manifestation of the "brand" or "flaming breath" that comes to destroy the antinomies of day and night, but the section's hesitation is here validated: Remorse is an abdication rather than a victory. On this basis, "A MUNICIPAL GALLERY REVISITED" praises KEVIN O'HIGGINS, a late addition to Yeats's pantheon of heroes, as "a soul incapable of remorse or rest."

As an antidote to the remorse of the previous section, the sixth section variously pictures the tragic dignity and gaiety of the third section. In both the new-mown field of ancient China and the toppled towers of Babylon and Nineveh, Yeats finds images of the evanescence that our joy must embrace if we are to go "Proud, open-eyed and laughing to the tomb." An apostle of this joy, the

"great lord of Chou" cries "Let all things pass away," reversing the cry of the differently tempered ISEULT GONNE in *A Vision*: "O Lord, let something remain" (220). The Lord of Chou is Ji Dan, who served the early Western Chou dynasty as prime minister during the 12th century B.C. He is popularly known as "Chou Gong" or "Lord of Chou" (incidentally, the epigraph to *Responsibilities* is mistaken: it is Ji Dan rather than the "Prince of Chang"—the king Ji served—about whom Confucius fails to dream in *The Analects*). As a Chinese sage of the mountain snows, the Lord of Chou anticipates the three Chinamen of "Lapis Lazuli" who stare with gay eyes from their mountain perch upon "all the tragic scene," and the holy men of "MERU" who know that "day brings round the night" in an endless cycle of eclipse. Like the sage, the conqueror has joyously abandoned himself to the cycles that whirl out the towers of Babylon or Nineveh and whirl in the "milk-white asses" drawing their homely carts; the asses are "milk-white" because unstained by the heroic violence—the "bloody arrogant power," in the phrase of "Blood and the Moon"—by which great civilizations rise and fall. The final stanza elaborately metaphorizes the dynamic of human creation, rooting it in the heart's passion ("From man's blood-sodden heart are sprung / Those branches of the night and day / Where the gaudy moon is hung"), as does "Two Songs from a Play" ("Whatever flames upon the night / Man's own resinous heart has fed"). The moon, like the image of Attis similarly hung amid the branches of night and day, may represent the transcendence of antinomies; alternately, it may represent the ultimate alignment of the artistic enterprise with the dispensation of the night. "Song" epitomizes the creative impulse, but paradoxically finds its strength—its deepest theme—in the embrace of evanescence; its beauty is a "tragic joy," premised on the understanding that all beauty, including its own, fleets and goes.

With its motif of fire, the seventh section recalls the dichotomy of the second section and the apotheosis of the fourth ("My body of a sudden blazed"). More generally, it recalls, indeed continues, the abstract philosophical exchange of "A Dialogue of Self and Soul," with the lines of debate essentially unchanged, though "the Heart" has replaced "the Self" as the interlocutor of "the Soul." As in "A Dialogue of Self and Soul," the Soul aspires to a reality above or beyond the appearances of the world (seeks deliverance from the "crime of death and birth" in the language of the earlier poem), but the Heart objects that art, our most instinctive calling, is necessarily rooted in the mundane (this the surprisingly disciplined early understanding of "To the Rose upon the Rood of Time"). Persisting in its transcendentalism, the Soul points to Isaiah's divine epiphany and absolution by fire as the realization of all human desire, as an indisputable and unanswerable glory. This refers to the biblical episode in which Isaiah tells of seeing the throne of the Lord. Being a man of "unclean lips" who dwelled "in the midst of a people of unclean lips," he feared that he was "undone." One of the seraphim, however, descended with a coal from the altar of God and laid it upon Isaiah's mouth, saying, "Lo, this hath touched thy lips; and thine iniquity is taken away, and thy sin purged" (Isaiah 6:1–7). The Heart deplores the idea of being "struck dumb"—being deprived of a "theme," of the human complexity that gives substance to art—in the "simplicity of fire." "Look on that fire, salvation walks within," commands the Soul, echoing, in its conception of the transcendental or purgatorial fire, "Blood and the Moon," "Byzantium," and "Sailing to Byzantium." *Per Amica Silentia Lunae* theorizes precisely this dichotomy between human complexity and fire: "There are two realities, the terrestrial and the condition of fire. All power is from the terrestrial condition, for there all opposites meet and there only is the extreme of choice possible, full freedom. And there the heterogeneous is, and evil, for evil is the strain one upon another of opposites; but in the condition of fire is all music and all rest" (*LE* 25). Having the final word, as does the Self in "A Dialogue of Self and Soul," the Heart rejoins with the example of Homer, type and epitome of all artists, who had no "theme" but "original sin." This may allude to Homer's vision of human nature as mutinous and unruly, or more specifically to the elopement of Helen and Paris, which set in motion the Trojan War and constituted antiquity's version of "original sin."

Yeats included a draft of the seventh section in a January 3, 1932, letter to Olivia Shakespear. His commentary aligns the antinomies of day and night, foliage and fire, Heart and Soul, with the more familiar and intuitive antinomies of saint and hero, comedy and tragedy. It also provides a helpful explanatory key to the poem's difficult final section, which it clearly outlines. "I feel that this is the choice of the saint (St Theresa's ecstasy, Gandhi's smiling face): comedy; and the heroic choice: Tragedy (Dante, Don Quixote)," writes Yeats. "Live Tragically but be not deceived (not the fool's Tragedy). Yet I accept all the miracles. Why should not the old embalmers come back as ghosts and bestow upon the saint all the care once bestowed upon Rameses? Why should I doubt the tale that when St Theresa's tomb was opened in the middle of the nineteenth century the still undecayed body dripped with fragrant oil? I shall be a sinful man to the end, and think upon my death-bed of all the nights I wasted in my youth" (*Letters* 790).

The final stanza of the poem reconceives the debate between the Soul and the Heart as a choice between the religious renunciation and the profane embrace of the world. As in "A Dialogue of Self and Soul," Yeats, in the end, chooses to drink from the impure ditch of life. "Von Hügel" is Baron Friedrich von Hügel (1852–1925), Catholic theologian and author of *The Mystical Element of Religion, as Studied in St. Catherine of Genoa and Her Friends* (1908). Yeats must "part" ways with von Hügel, though not unsympathetically, for he himself accepts the Christian miracles and mysteries surrounding the body of St. Teresa (1515–82), which "lies undecayed in tomb, / Bathed in miraculous oil, sweet odours from it come, / Healing from its lettered slab" (cf. "Oil and Blood" [1929]; on St. Teresa's body, see also *WBY&TSM* 121–122). Echoing his letter to Shakespear, Yeats speculates that the "self-same hands" that had "eternalized the body of a modern saint" (i.e., Teresa) had once "scooped out Pharaoh's mummy." The implication is that these transhistorical hands are eternal rather than human, or that in this work human hands are guided by an eternal agency. Yeats's heart "might find relief" in Christianity, but such is not his "predestined part" (the heart is a "singer born," as the preceding stanza has it). The final lines of "COOLE AND BALLYLEE, 1931" affirm Homer as the patriarch of the romantic or *antithetical* lineage in which Yeats places himself. In "Vacillation," Yeats again commits himself to the example of Homer and "his unchristened heart," but the emphasis on Homer's "heart," already established as a symbol of the *primary*, suggests a more complicated interplay of tinctures. Tellingly uncertain about what Scripture has said, Yeats offers as the heart's image the "lion and the honeycomb," symbol of strength wed to sweetness, violence to love. In the Bible, Samson slays a lion and returns to find its carcass filled with bees and honey, of which he eats (Judges 14:8–9), but the images of lion and honeycomb are self-sufficient and hardly require biblical explanation. Yeats concludes "Vacillation," one of his longest and most ambitious poems, on a charmingly blithe and affable note, suggesting his own ease with the outcome of the poem's internal debate: "So get you gone, Von Hügel, though with a blessing on your head." The blessing is a gesture of amity that signifies the interdependence of antinomies, but also, with both the fifth section of the poem and "A Dialogue of Self and Soul" in mind, an affirmation that Yeats has cast out remorse. In embracing the pattern of vacillation, Yeats transcends it and achieves the very blessedness he has renounced. Is this an *antithetical* victory or a *primary* victory? Virginia Moore holds that in "Vacillation" the *antithetical* serves the *primary*; it might equally be said that the *antithetical* and *primary* serve each other, and that joy is reducible to neither (*Unicorn* 405–406).

FIRST PUBLICATION: *Words for Music Perhaps and Other Poems*, The CUALA PRESS, Dublin, November 14, 1932, with sections titled as follows: 1. "What is Joy." 2. "The Burning Tree" (including sections 2 and 3 in subsequent printings); 3. "Happiness" (section 4 in subsequent printings); 4. "Conscience" (section 5 in subsequent printings); 5. "Conquerors" (section 6 in subsequent printings); 6. "A Dialogue" (section 7 in subsequent printings); 7. "Von Hügel" (section 8 in subsequent printings). Reprinted in *The Winding Stair*, Macmillan, London, September 19, 1933, in its present form.

BIBLIOGRAPHY

Ellmann, Richard. *The Identity of* Yeats; Frazer, James George. *The Golden Bough: A Study in Magic and Religion* (1915 edition, Part 4, vol. 1); Moore, Virginia. *The Unicorn: William Butler Yeats' Search for Reality*; Saddlemyer, Ann. *Becoming George: The Life of Mrs W. B. Yeats*; Unterecker, John. *A Reader's Guide to William Butler Yeats*; Wilson, F. A. C. *W. B. Yeats and Tradition*; Yeats, W. B. *Essays and Introductions, The Gonne-Yeats Letters 1893–1938, Later Essays, The Letters of W. B. Yeats, The Variorum Edition of the Plays of W. B. Yeats, The Variorum Edition of the Poems of W. B. Yeats, A Vision, W. B. Yeats and T. Sturge Moore: Their Correspondence 1901–1937*.

"Valley of the Black Pig, The" (1896)

"The Valley of the Black Pig" tells of the legendary battle in which Ireland's enemies—manifest in the form of the black pig—will finally be routed. "The Irish peasantry have for generations comforted themselves, in their misfortunes, with visions of a great battle, to be fought in a mysterious valley called, 'The Valley of the Black Pig,' and to break at last the power of their enemies," Yeats explains in a note that appeared with the poem upon its first publication in the SAVOY (VP 161). In *The Wind Among the Reeds* (1899), Yeats included a second note that expands on the meaning of this battle. Drawing on Sir James Frazer's *The Golden Bough* (1890–1915), Yeats describes the pig as a version of a universal mythological tendency. The pig is one not only with the boar that kills Diarmuid (see DIARMUID AND GRANIA), but also with "the cutty black sow" of "Welsh November rhymes"; the boar that kills Adonis; the boar that kills Attis; and the "pig embodiment of Typhon" (809). Yeats explains that the pig "seems to have been originally a genius of the corn, and, seemingly because the too great power of their divinity makes divine things dangerous to mortals, its flesh was forbidden to many eastern nations; but as the meaning of the prohibition was forgotten, abhorrence took the place of reverence, pigs and boars grew into types of evil, and were described as the enemies of the very gods they once typified [. . .]. The Pig would, therefore, become the Black Pig, a type of cold and of winter that awake in November, the old beginning of winter, to do battle with the summer, and with the fruit and leaves, and finally, as I suggest; and as I believe, for the purposes of poetry; of the darkness that will at last destroy the gods and the world" (809). Yeats goes on to suggest that the battle of the Black Pig is associable with many of the battles of Irish legend, and that "all of these battles are one, the battle of all things with shadowy decay" (810; see also *Myth.* 111). Yeats also adverts to the legend of the black pig in "He mourns for the Change that has come upon him and his Beloved, and longs for the End of the World" (1897), in which the narrator wishes that "the Boar without bristles had come from the West / And had rooted the sun and moon and stars out of the sky / And lay in the darkness, grunting, and turning to his rest."

In many ways, Yeats's lengthy annotation of "The Valley of the Black Pig" is more intriguing than the poem, which does not manage fully to dramatize the energy or scale of the apocalyptic battle, and in this respect falls short of the example set by "HE BIDS HIS BELOVED BE AT PEACE," with its irresistible plunging rhythm. Narrated in the voice of a "peasant visionary," as its original sequence title indicates, "The Valley of the Black Pig" describes, in the first four of its eight lines, a dream-awakened spectacle of battle—hurtling spears, fallen horsemen, the cries of "perishing armies." In its final four lines, the poem becomes more enigmatic. The peasant declares that he and his kind—those who "still labour by the cromlech on the shore, / The grey cairn on the hill," that is, those of the ancient unworldly peasant temper—have grown weary of the "world's empires" and "bow down to you, / Master of the still stars and of the flaming door" (according to *The Oxford English Dictionary*, a cromlech is a "structure of prehistoric age consisting of a large flat or flattish unhewn stone resting horizontally on three or more stones set upright"; a cairn is a "pyramid of rough stones, raised for a memorial or mark of some kind"). The "flaming door," like the "flaming lute-thronged angelic door" of "The

TRAVAIL OF PASSION," suggests transcendental passage to another, higher realm. The peasant visionary may address as "Master of the still stars and of the flaming door" that which vanquishes the black pig and restores the world to the fold of the divine and the eternal; alternately, he may address the black pig itself, conceived and revered, as it was in ancient times, as a divinity in its own right. The latter interpretation explains the emphasis of "still" in the poem's fifth line: The peasant visionary upholds the ancient ways, and by implication the ancient religion that Yeats describes in his note.

In AUTOBIOGRAPHIES, Yeats attributes the poem at least in part to the influence of his occult mentor MACGREGOR MATHERS. Yeats writes that Mathers "began to foresee changes in the world, announcing in 1893 or 1894 the imminence of immense wars" and that in 1895 or 1896 he began to learn ambulance work in anticipation of the cataclysm. Yeats wonders whether "some talk of his" was the unconscious inspiration for "The Valley of the Black Pig" (257).

FIRST PUBLICATION: The *Savoy* (periodical), April 1896, under the sequence title "Two Poems concerning Peasant Visionaries" and the present title (paired with "The UNAPPEASABLE HOST"). Reprinted in *The Wind Among the Reeds*, Elkin Mathews, London, April 1899, under the present title.

BIBLIOGRAPHY

Yeats, W. B. *Autobiographies, Mythologies, The Variorum Edition of the Poems of W. B. Yeats.*

"Wanderings of Oisin, The" (1889)

Yeats began "The Wanderings of Oisin" (pronounced ush' een) in October 1886, when he was 21 (*YD* 136). It was the longest poem (915 lines) that he would ever write and the first poem to suggest the magnitude of his talent. It suggested too the extent of his ambition. As he remembers in AUTOBIOGRAPHIES, he had hoped to create a new sacred book that would re-consecrate Irish myth and nationhood and restore unity of culture: "Might I not, with health and good luck to aid me, create some new *Prometheus Unbound*; Patrick or Columcille, Oisin or Finn, in Prometheus' stead; and, instead of Caucasus, Cro-Patrick or Ben Bulben? Have not all races had their first unity from a mythology that marries them to rock and hill? We had in Ireland imaginative stories, which the uneducated classes knew and even sang, and might we not make those stories current among the educated classes [. . .] and at last, it might be, so deepen the political passion of the nation that all, artist and poet, craftsman and day-labourer would accept a common design?" (166–167).

Critics and friends praised the poem upon its publication, and Yeats felt the novice author's natural delight in a first success (*CL1* 157). EDWARD DOWDEN, W. E. Henley (1849–1903), and WILLIAM MORRIS were among the notables who applauded the young poet's effort (*CL1* 128, 132, 142, 145, 152; *Mem.* 21). A September 1888 letter to KATHARINE TYNAN registers Yeats's excitement at his own achievement, but also his penchant for shrewd self-evaluation and for reflection upon the psychology of his own artistry: "[The second part of the poem] is the most inspired but the least artistic of the three. The last has most art. Because I was in complete solitude—no one near me but old and reticent people—when I wrote it. It was the greatest effort of all my things. When I had finished I brought it round to read to my uncle GEORGE POLLEXFEN, and could hardly read so collapsed I was. My voice quite broken. It really was a kind of a vision it beset me day and night. Not that I ever wrote more than a few lines in a day. But those few lines took me hours. And all the rest of the time, I walked about the roads thinking of it [. . .] With the other parts I am much disappointed—they seem only shadows of what I saw. But the third must have got itself expressed—it kept me from my sleep too long. Yet the second part is more deep and poetic. It is not inspiration that exhausts one, but art. The first parts I felt. I saw the second. Yet there too perhaps only shaddows [sic] have got them selves [sic] onto paper" (*CL1* 98). Despite the poem's augury of greatness in its depth of theme and vibrancy of detail, Yeats's

discontent with its language only grew. In *Autobiographies*, he writes that he was "dissatisfied with its yellow and its dull green, with all that overcharged colour inherited from the romantic movement" and deliberately attempted to change his style, seeking out "an impression as of cold light and tumbling clouds." Upon finishing the poem he found his style "too elaborate, too ornamental," and "thought for some weeks of sleeping upon a board" (86, 279–280). Restlessly unhappy with the poem in its original form, Yeats altered almost every line of the original over subsequent decades (see *VP* 1–63; on Yeats's continual fiddling with the spelling of the poem's proper names, see *Colder Eye* 116).

The poem's source material is various. In a 1912 note to the poem, Yeats mentions "the Middle Irish dialogues of Saint Patrick and Oisin and a certain Gaelic poem of the last century" (*VP* 793). In a letter to the *Spectator*, he more specifically divulged his source material: "The first few pages are developed from a most beautiful old poem written by one of the numerous half-forgotten Gaelic poets who lived in Ireland in the last century. In the quarrels between the saint and the blind warrior, I have used suggestions from various ballad Dialogues of Oisin and Patrick, published by the Ossianic Society. The pages dealing with the three islands [. . .] are wholly my own, having no further root in tradition than the Irish peasant's notion that *Tir-u-au-oge* (the Country of the Young) is made up of three phantom islands" (*CL1* 176–177). John Kelly and Eric Domville, in their meticulous annotation of Yeats's letters, provide further detail: "WBY took much of his material from the *Transactions of the Ossianic Society* (1854–63), in vol. I of which is an account of the Battle of Gabhra, translated by Nicholas O'Kearney; vol. III contains Standish O'Grady's translation of 'The Lament of Oisin after the Fenians', and John O'Daly's rendering of the 'Dialogues of Oisin and Patrick' appears in vol. V. The eighteenth-century poem was Michael Comyn's 'The Lay of Oisin in the Land of Youth', published in vol. IV of the *Transactions*" (*CL1* 176). A. Norman Jeffares adds that Yeats "may have drawn on descriptions of paradises met in accounts by Charles Henry Foote, Crofton Croker and Gerald Griffin of various underwater and island paradises, and later included some of these in *Fairy and Folk Tales of the Irish Peasantry* (1888) and *Representative Irish Tales* (1891)" (*New Biography* 39). And yet, as Harold Bloom notes, the poem is less Irish than arch-romantic, belonging to the tradition of internalized quest-romance marked by Spenser, Milton, BLAKE, WORDSWORTH, SHELLEY, and Keats, among others (*Yeats* 83–92).

Yeats dedicated "The Wanderings of Oisin" to the painter and poet Edwin John Ellis (1848–1916), an old friend of JOHN BUTLER YEATS with whom Yeats coedited *The Works of William Blake* (1893). Ellis particularly admired the poem (*CL1* 50), and Yeats recognized in Ellis a kindred spirit and mentor. As Yeats recalls in MEMOIRS, "I owe to my discussions with this man, who was very sane and yet I think always on the border of insanity, certain doctrines about the Divine Vision and the nature of God which have protected me for the search for living experience, and owe to him perhaps my mastery of verse. [. . .] I had still the intellectual habits of a provincial, and fixed my imagination on great work to the neglect of detail—my *Wanderings of Oisin* were but the first of a whole *Légende des Siècles*, and so on—but I learned for the first time that I might find perfect self-expression in the management of a cadence. He complained that 'Shy in the doorway' in one of my early poems ["To an Isle in the Water"] was abominable, because 'Shyin' was the name of a Chinaman, and though I did not alter the line I acquired a more delicate attention to sound" (30–31; see also *Aut.* 143–147). The poem's epigraph comments on Oisin's stubborn affection for the Fenians, but the attribution to "Tulka" is mysterious. The Czech painter Josef Tulka (b. 1846) is one possible source of the quotation; the Swedenborgian writer Charles Augustus Tulk (1786–1849) is another (*The Poems* 683–684; *NCP* 429).

The narrative of the poem unfolds as Oisin, from the vantage of his old age, relates the adventures of his life to Saint Patrick (ca. 390–ca. 461), who had brought Christianity to druidic Ireland, as Yeats tells in his 1895 story "The Old Men of the Twilight" (see *Myth.* 191–195). In the embedded narrative of the poem, Oisin and his fellow Fenians come upon the beautiful fairy princess Niamh. Having heard tales of Oisin's deeds as warrior and poet and fallen in love, she has come to bring him away with her. He immediately falls into a "desperate gulf of love," and the two ride over the sea until they come to the "Island of Dancing," where the inhabitants dance and revel in mockery of "Time and Fate and Chance." Oisin indulges in the hunt and in the pleasures of the bed. After 100 years, he finds a spear washed upon the shore and suddenly longs to return to his warrior comrades and the life of mortal men. Yielding to Oisin's sorrow, Niamh bridles her horse and conveys her lover across the sea to the "Isle of Many Fears." There Oisin finds a lady chained in the vast hall of the sea god Manannan. He frees her and confronts her captor, a shape-changing and ever-renewing demon. For another hundred years, he fights the demon on every fourth day, feasting with the ladies between battles. One day the sea washes up a beech bough, and Oisin, remembering that he had once stood with Finn under an old beech tree, is again filled with longing for Ireland. Yielding to his sorrow once more, Niamh brings Oisin to the "Island of Forgetfulness," which is inhabited by slumbering giants of great beauty, with hands like the claws of birds. Round them lie battle arms. Weary of war, they had gripped the soporific bell-branch and fallen into eternal slumber. Oisin tries to rouse the sleepers, but he himself falls asleep and dreams of the Fenians. After 100 years, the "ancient sadness of man" begins to move in his bosom, and he wakes with the resolution to revisit his native land. Hoping Oisin will return to the fairy realm after assuaging his homesickness, Niamh agrees to let him go. She warns, however, that if his foot so much as brushes the earth he will be lost to her forever.

Oisin returns to Ireland only to discover the Fenians dead and the people physically and spiritually enfeebled by Christianity, which has arrived in his absence. Leaning from his saddle to toss a bag of sand after disgustedly observing two rustics struggle with it, Oisin falls to the ground and immediately grows old with the 300 years that are his true span. The rustics bring him to a church, where he meets Patrick. Recognizing Patrick as an "old man surrounded by dreams"—a type of the sage, though in the end a false sage—Oisin asks after his old comrades. Patrick describes them suffering the tortures of Christian damnation. Oisin declares that he will go to them, and together they will war upon the demons and sweep them from hell. Patrick rebukes Oisin for the "demon love" of his youth and for his "godless and passionate age," but Oisin is unbowed; he will "dwell in the house of the Fenians, be they in flames or at feast."

In a February 6, 1889, letter to Katharine Tynan, Yeats elaborated on the meaning of the three islands that are the foundation of the poem's symbolic scheme: "There are three incompatable [sic] things which man is always seeking—infinite feeling, infinite battle, infinite repose—hence the three islands" (CL1 141). "The CIRCUS ANIMALS' DESERTION," which reflects somewhat satirically on "The Wanderings of Oisin," similarly refers to "three enchanted islands, allegorical dreams, / Vain gaiety, vain battle, vain repose." In a 1934 introduction to The RESURRECTION, Yeats explains that he was drawn to the legend of Oisin because he found its element of perpetual longing for the infinite—represented by the restless movement from island to island—a perfect corrective to the Victorian "myth" of progress, to which he had a rebellious aversion in his youth. "How hard it was to refrain from pointing out that Oisin after old age, its illumination half accepted, half rejected, would pass in death over another sea to another island," he says (VPl. 932). In "NEWS FOR THE DELPHIC ORACLE," which he wrote some 50 years after "The Wanderings of Oisin," Yeats imagines Oisin and Niamh ensconced among the immortals on just such "another island"—ironically so, for Elysian release is precisely what Oisin cannot abide in the earlier poem.

The final exchange between Oisin and Patrick—as Yeats rightly implies in his letter of September 1888 to Tynan—is the poem's triumph. Having the dialogical structure that Yeats would employ in "A DIALOGUE OF SELF AND SOUL" and "VACILLATION," it comes to much the same conclusion as these late masterpieces, that the impassioned embrace of life (the way of the hero, the warrior) is both the highest defiance and the only redemption, as it embraces and exalts what in any

case cannot be evaded: the tragedy of human existence, or what "The Wanderings of Oisin" calls "Time and Fate and Chance." The final section of "Vacillation" more or less paraphrases Oisin's essential sentiment: "I—though heart might find relief did I become a Christian man and choose for my belief / What seems most welcome in the tomb—play a predestined part. / Homer is my example and his unchristened heart." Yeats himself links "The Wanderings of Oisin" and "Vacillation" in an important letter of July 8, 1932, to OLIVIA SHAKESPEAR: "My first denunciation of old age I made in The Wanderings of Usheen (end of part I) before I was twenty and the same denunciation comes in the last pages of the book [i.e., of the collected poems]. The swordsman throughout repudiates the saint, but not without vacillation. Is that perhaps the sole theme—Usheen and Patrick—'so get you gone Von Hügel though with blessings on your head'?" (Letters 798). Also foreshadowing an important element in Yeats's later work are the "storm of birds in the Asian trees" that murmur "Unjust, unjust" at the passage of time (I, lines 418–422). As John Unterecker notes, Yeats "had already begun to work out in these sketchy images of immortal 'painted birds' not only the pattern of that significant parrot of 'The Indian to His Love' which rages 'at his own image in the enamelled sea' but as well the outline of the great, symbolic golden bird of 'SAILING TO BYZANTIUM' who, free from sensual music and the limits of flesh, sings undying song" (RG 51). Even more, perhaps, the birds of The Wanderings of Oisin presage the world-affronted bird of "BYZANTIUM."

Yeats's note to the poem explains many of the allusions to Irish figures, events, and places. The bell-branch, for example, was a "legendary branch whose shaking cast all men into a gentle sleep"; the Fenians were the "great military order of which Finn was chief"; Gabhra was "the great battle in which the power of the Fenians was broken." For Yeats's complete annotation, see The Variorum Edition of the Poems of W. B. Yeats, pages 794–796.

In addition to "The Circus Animals' Desertion" and "News for the Delphic Oracle," Niamh figures in "Alternative Song for the Severed Head in The

King of the Great Clock Tower" (1934), "The Dan-aan Quicken Tree" (1893), "The HOSTING OF THE SIDHE," "The Lover asks Forgiveness because of his Many Moods" (1895), and "Under the Moon" (1901), while Patrick is central to "SUPERNATURAL SONGS."

FIRST PUBLICATION: *The Wanderings of Oisin and Other Poems*, Kegan Paul, Trench & Co., London, January 1889.

BIBLIOGRAPHY

Bloom, Harold. *Yeats*; Conner, Lester I. *A Yeats Dictionary: Persons and Places in the Poetry of William Butler Yeats*; Jeffares, A. Norman. *A New Commentary on the Poems of W. B. Yeats, W. B. Yeats: A New Biography*; Kenner, Hugh. *A Colder Eye: The Modern Irish Writers*; Unterecker, John. *A Reader's Guide to William Butler Yeats*; Yeats, W. B. *Autobiographies, The Collected Letters of W. B. Yeats* (vol. 1), *The Letters of W. B. Yeats, Memoirs, Mythologies, The Poems, The Variorum Edition of the Plays of W. B. Yeats, The Variorum Edition of the Poems of W. B. Yeats*.

"What Magic Drum?" (1935)

See "SUPERNATURAL SONGS."

"What Was Lost" (1938)

See "THE GREAT DAY."

"Wheel, The" (1922)

Presumably on good authority, Joseph Hone records that "The Wheel" is "exceptional among [Yeats's] poems in that it was written on the instant of thought. His wife and he were on Euston platform half an hour before the Irish mail train was due to start. He disappeared suddenly and came back in good time for the train with the poem as it stands written out on a sheet of Euston Hotel notepaper" (*W. B. Yeats* 365). The eight-line poem observes the constant desire for change of season with the explanation that "what disturbs our blood / Is but its longing for the tomb." Yeats was on less than fond terms with death, as in their different ways poems like "DEATH" and "SAILING TO BYZANTIUM" demonstrate; the "longing for the tomb" in this case signifies less a readiness for a final surcease, than a transcendental desire to escape the "wheels" of history and the brutal buffeting of time. Yeats's conception of the "tomb," meanwhile, is versatile and not reflexively synonymous with death. In "The MOUNTAIN TOMB," Father Rosicross sleeps in his tomb not the sleep of death, but, as it seems, of continuing wisdom. "The LEADERS OF THE CROWD" identifies the tomb as the locus of occult wisdom. "TO A SHADE" urges the roving ghost of PARNELL to return to the refuge of the tomb (see also "CRAZY JANE AND THE BISHOP," with its refrain "All find safety in the tomb"). "VACILLATION" observes that "the body of Saint Teresa lies undecayed in tomb, / Bathed in miraculous oil, sweet odours from it come, / Healing from its lettered slab." In the grip of the same subject, Yeats wrote to T. STURGE MOORE: "By the bye, please don't quote him [Moore's brother, the philosopher G. E. Moore] again till you have asked him this question: 'How do you account for the fact that when the Tomb of St. Theresa was opened her body exuded miraculous oil and smelt of violets?' If he cannot account for such primary facts he knows nothing" (*WBY&TSM* 121–122). "The CAT AND THE MOON" similarly refers to a disturbance of the blood ("Black Minnaloushe stared at the moon, / For, wander and wail as he would, / The pure cold light in the sky / Troubled his animal blood"). The moon ("pure," "sacred") and the tomb equally stand beyond the wheel of time and awaken a restive desire. This restiveness tellingly registers in the blood, which, in its *circulation*, is the least instance of the universal pattern.

FIRST PUBLICATION: *Seven Poems and a Fragment*, The CUALA PRESS, Dundrum, June 1922.

BIBLIOGRAPHY

Hone, Joseph. *W. B. Yeats*; Yeats, W. B. *W. B. Yeats and T. Sturge Moore: Their Correspondence 1901–1937*.

"Whence had They come?" (1935)

See "SUPERNATURAL SONGS."

"When You are Old" (1892)

"When You are Old" was written in October 1891 during a period when Yeats's relationship with MAUD GONNE hung in the balance (YC 23). Gonne's two-year-old son Georges by the French journalist and politician Lucien Millevoye (1850–1918) died of meningitis in France on August 31, and she arrived in Dublin on October 21 in a state of emotional collapse (AM 92, 115–117; Mem. 47–48). In her grief, Gonne drew closer to Yeats, participating in his occult experiments and joining the HERMETIC ORDER OF THE GOLDEN DAWN (CL1 266). In Memoirs, Yeats writes of these weeks, "She had come [to] have need of me, as it seemed, and I had no doubt that need would become love, that it was already coming so. I had even as I watched her a sense of cruelty, as though I were a hunter taking captive some beautiful wild creature" (Mem. 49). "When You are Old" was perhaps a salvo in this campaign, a reminder of the wistful, solitary old age that awaits those who let slip the chance at love. The poem pictures Gonne "old and grey and full of sleep" as she takes from the shelf "this book" (presumably the book that was to become The Countess Kathleen and Various Legends and Lyrics). Yeats imagines her dreaming of her many admirers, some false, some true, but particularly remembering the "one man"—Yeats himself—who embraced her sorrow as well as her beauty, and murmuring to herself a little sadly how "Love fled / And paced upon the mountains overhead / And hid his face amid a crowd of stars." The final lines seem to figure Yeats himself in his romantic heartbreak: agitated and abashed, and yet, in the magnitude of his feeling, at one with the magnitude of the universe. The poem thus draws a gently admonitory contrast between Gonne and Yeats. Having spurned love, she has waned into shrunken domesticity—she

can only "murmur," can muster only a "little" sadness—while he has kept faith with the grandeur of the heavens. The contrast is crystallized in the disjunction between the "glowing bars" (i.e., grate railings) of Gonne's hearth and the "crowd of stars" amid which love hides its head.

Like "AT THE ABBEY THEATRE," "When You are Old" is based on a sonnet by Pierre de Ronsard (1524–85). Ronsard's poem, which first appeared in Le Second Livre des Sonnets pour Hélène (1578), may be translated thus:

> When you are old, sitting by the fire,
> Stitching and unstitching by the evening candle,
> You will sing my words and marvel,
> "Ronsard made poems of me when I was beautiful."
> There'll be no maid, finished with work
> And already half asleep, to hear
> And stir at the sound of my verse
> And praise your immortal name.
> Beneath the earth, a boneless phantom
> Amid the myrtle shade, I'll take my rest.
> You'll stand before the hearth, crouched with age,
> Regretting my love and your proud disdain.
> Live, if you hear me, wait not for tomorrow:
> Gather today the roses of life.

FIRST PUBLICATION: The Countess Kathleen and Various Legends and Lyrics, T. Fisher Unwin, London, September 1892.

BIBLIOGRAPHY

Foster, R. F. W. B. Yeats: A Life, I: The Apprentice Mage; Kelly, John S. A W. B. Yeats Chronology; Yeats, W. B. The Collected Letters of W. B. Yeats (vol. 1), Memoirs.

"White Birds, The" (1892)

A. Norman Jeffares relates the genesis of "The White Birds" as MAUD GONNE related it to him. The story goes that Gonne and Yeats were walking one afternoon on the cliffs at Howth at the mouth of Dublin Bay when two seagulls flew overhead and out to sea. Gonne remarked that of all birds she would choose to be a seagull, and three days later Yeats sent a poem inspired by her offhand comment (Man and Poet 68).

The date of the excursion was August 4, 1891, the day after Yeats's first fruitless proposal of marriage (YC 22). In MEMOIRS Yeats recollects the day without mentioning the poem's moment of conception: "We spent the next day upon the cliff paths at Howth and dined at a little cottage near the Baily Lighthouse, where her old nurse lived, and I overheard the old nurse asking if we were engaged to be married. At the day's end I found I had spent ten shillings, which seemed to me a very great sum" (46). He recollects this day as well in "BEAUTIFUL LOFTY THINGS."

The poem expresses a desperate escapist desire that is hardly surprising given Yeats's quashed marital hopes. Yeats dreams that he and Gonne might become white birds and depart to the "numberless islands of the Danaan shore" where time would forget them. "Danaan" refers to the Tuatha De Danaan, the gods of ancient Ireland, also known as the Sidhe (VP 800). In an 1892 note to the poem, Yeats explains that the "birds of fairyland are white as snow" and that the "Danaan shore" is "Tier-nan-oge, or fairyland" (799). Upon this shore, the lovers would find refuge from the "sadness" of the temporal world, as symbolized by the fleeting meteor and the evening star, and from the "weariness" of mortal love, as symbolized by those "dreamers" the ROSE and the lily.

"The White Birds" might be charged with lacking Yeats's accustomed vigor and audacity. Unlike its infinitely more sophisticated descendant "SAILING TO BYZANTIUM," the poem fantasizes a condition of transcendence without undertaking the struggle to imagine a mechanism or energy of transcendence. Yeats diagnosed the problem that the poem epitomizes in an 1888 letter to KATHARINE TYNAN: "I have noticed some things about my poetry [. . .] for instance that it is almost all a flight into fairy land, from the real world, and a summons to that flight. The chorus to ["The STOLEN CHILD"] sums it up—That is not the poetry of insight and knowledge but of longing and complaint—the cry of the heart against necessity. I hope some day to alter that and write poetry of insight and knowledge" (CL1 54–55).

FIRST PUBLICATION: The National Observer (periodical), May 7, 1892. Reprinted in The Countess Kathleen and Various Legends and Lyrics, T. Fisher Unwin, London, September 1892.

BIBLIOGRAPHY

Jeffares, A. Norman. W. B. Yeats: Man and Poet; Kelly, John S. A W. B. Yeats Chronology; Yeats, W. B. The Collected Letters of W. B. Yeats (vol. 1), Memoirs, The Variorum Edition of the Poems of W. B. Yeats.

"Who Goes with Fergus?" (1892)

A 12-line lyric of gossamer delicacy and beauty, the poem originally appeared in the second scene of Yeats's play THE COUNTESS CATHLEEN (see VPl. 52, 54, 65). The 1912 edition of Poems extracts "Who Goes with Fergus?" from the play and presents it as a freestanding poem (Biblio. 106–107). The poem beckons "young man" and "maid" to follow the legendary king Fergus of Ulster in his self-chosen exile (see "FERGUS AND THE DRUID" and "The SECRET ROSE") amid the "deep wood's woven shade." The poem urges them away with the admonition to "brood on hopes and fear no more," and "no more turn aside and brood / Upon love's bitter mystery. . . ." The poem ends by apotheosizing Fergus, who, as it were by mystical power of imagination, "rules the white breast of the dim sea / And all dishevelled wandering stars." The poem is enshrined as a recurring motif in JAMES JOYCE's Ulysses (1922). Having sung the poem to his dying mother, Stephen Dedalus is haunted by the phrase "love's bitter mystery" (see 1.239–264, 3.445, 15.4190, 15.4932–4933). T. S. ELIOT, for his part, places the poem among the few of Yeats's early poems that are "as perfect of their kind as anything in the language" (On Poetry and Poets 298).

FIRST PUBLICATION: The Countess Kathleen and Various Legends and Lyrics, T. Fisher Unwin, London, September 1892. Reprinted as a freestanding poem in Poems, T. Fisher Unwin, London, September 1912.

BIBLIOGRAPHY

Eliot, T. S. On Poetry and Poets; Joyce, James. Ulysses; Wade, Allan. A Bibliography of the Writings of W. B. Yeats; Yeats, W. B. The Variorum Edition of the Plays of W. B. Yeats.

"Why should not Old Men be Mad?" (1939)

Like "To a Child Dancing in the Wind," "Why should not Old Men be Mad?" explores the disjunction between the unknowing innocence of youth and the bitter knowledge of age. If "To a Child Dancing in the Wind" is vaguely wistful and envious, "Why should not Old Men be Mad?" revels in the energy of a wild grief or rage that is bound up, as in "An Acre of Grass" and "The Spur," with creative energy. Otherwise the poems have much the same complaint. As "To a Child Dancing in the Wind" recites the exactions of experience in the form of "the fool's triumph" (probably a reference to Major John MacBride's successful courtship of Maud Gonne in 1903), "love lost as soon as won" (probably a reference to Yeats's intermittent romance with Gonne), and "the best labourer dead / And all the sheaves to bind" (a reference to J. M. Synge), so "Why should not Old Men be Mad?" has its litany of disillusionments. Donald T. Torchiana proposes that the fly-fisherman turned drunken journalist is Robert Maire Smyllie (1894–1954), editor of the *Irish Times* from 1934. Hugh Oram, in his history of the Irish newspaper, says that Smyllie "had the reputation of being able to drink more than virtually any other journalist in Dublin, yet he had a remarkable capacity of concealment" (*Newspaper Book* 185). It was Smyllie, then an assistant editor at the *Irish Times*, who relayed to Yeats the news that he had won the Nobel Prize in 1922 (*I&R*, II, 323–324). "Smyllie himself," says Torchiana, "seems to have recognized the intent of Yeats's couplets, since he had little good to say thereafter of Yeats or even of his son Michael" (*W. B. Yeats & Georgian Ireland* 353). "The Fisherman" and "The Tower" employ the fisherman as a symbol of a cleanly pride and solitude, suggesting that the youthful fly-fisherman of "Why should not Old Men be Mad?" emerges out of Yeats's own symbolism at least as much as actual life. Iseult Gonne is the girl who knew all Dante only to "bear children to a dunce." In 1920, she entered into a disastrous marriage with the writer Francis Stuart (1902–2000) (GY 402–407). In a July 25, 1932,

letter to Lady Gregory, Yeats mentions that at the time of his marriage Stuart had "seemed almost imbecile to his own relations," though Yeats had since come to recognize his talent and predicted that with a little luck he would become "our great writer" (*Letters* 800; on Stuart's "imbecility," see also *Black List, Section H* 33). Stuart clearly considered this a gibe at his own expense, for in his poem "Remembering Yeats" (1988) he asks, "And why—though why not—had he called me a dunce?" The Stuarts' children Dolores, Ian, and Katherine, were born in 1921, 1926, and 1931 (*Letters to WBY&EP* xvii–xviii). Eva Gore-Booth (1870–1926), a suffragette activist, is probably the Helen who climbs upon a wagonette to scream of "social welfare." In "In Memory of Eva Gore-Booth and Con Markiewicz," Yeats writes of Gore-Booth, "I know not what the younger dreams—/ Some vague Utopia—and she seems, / When withered old and skeleton-gaunt, / An image of such politics." Constance Markiewicz (1868–1927), a nationalist organizer and politician (see "Easter 1916" and "To a Political Prisoner") is also a plausible model for the screaming Helen of the poem, as is Maud Gonne. In *Memoirs*, Yeats writes that Markiewicz's voice had become "shrill and high" with age (79), while he habitually associated Gonne with Helen, as in "No Second Troy," "The Sorrow of Love," and "A Woman Homer Sung."

Turning to general principles, Yeats observes that some think it a "matter of course that chance / Should starve good men and bad advance," that men should be broken by life. Young men know nothing of such things, but when they master the wisdom that "old books tell"—the same wisdom that "observant old men" know from the length of their experience—they will know why old men are mad. The wisdom that "old books tell" is that "no better can be had"—i.e., no better "finish" or outcome—than the thwarting of promise described in the poem. Yeats probably did not have in mind a specific "old book," but his translation of Sophocles' *Oedipus at Colonus* propounds just this bitter wisdom: "Never to have lived is best, ancient writers say; / Never to have drawn the breath of life, never to have looked into the eye of day; / The second best's a gay goodnight and quickly turn away"

(*VPl* 887; *VP* 459). Poems like "The GYRES," "LAPIS LAZULI," and "MERU" propose ecstatic resignation in response to the "tragic scene" of life, but "Why Should not Old Men be Mad?" represents Yeats's indignation at its most raw and inconsolable.

FIRST PUBLICATION: *On the Boiler*, The CUALA PRESS, Dublin, autumn 1939, without title. Reprinted in *Last Poems & Plays*, Macmillan, London, January 1940, under the present title.

BIBLIOGRAPHY

Gonne, Iseult. *Letters to W. B. Yeats's and Ezra Pound from Iseult Gonne*; Mikhail, E. H., ed. *W. B. Yeats: Interviews and Recollections* (vol. 2); Oram, Hugh. *The Newspaper Book: A History of Newspapers in Ireland, 1649–1983*; Stuart, Francis. *Black List, Section H*; Torchiana, Donald T. *W. B. Yeats & Georgian Ireland*; Yeats, W. B. *The Gonne-Yeats Letters 1893–1938*, *The Letters of W. B. Yeats*, *Memoirs*, *The Variorum Edition of the Plays of W. B. Yeats*, *The Variorum Edition of the Poems of W. B. Yeats*.

"Wild Swans at Coole, The" (1917)

Commencing with a graceful flourish the volume bearing its name, "The Wild Swans at Coole" inaugurates Yeats's final phase, in which, his labor come to fruition, he seems effortlessly to assume the voice of the ages. And yet "The Wild Swans at Coole" is a poem of depressed self-reflection, as Yeats measures his own attrition against the triumph implicit in the flight of the swans. Written in October 1916 following unsuccessful marriage proposals to both MAUD GONNE (July 1) and ISEULT GONNE (ca. August 12), the poem finds Yeats sweeping the ashes of his heart, much as in "ADAM'S CURSE," which likewise reads in the beauty of the natural world a parable of the heart's weariness (*YC* 186–187). As Harold Bloom observes, the animating crisis of the poem is not romantic rejection, but Yeats's unimpassioned response to romantic rejection, the troubled suspicion that the heart has lost its capacity to feel deeply (*Yeats* 191). Hugh Kenner expresses the dilemma this way: "It is the High Romantic complaint; Poetry, it says, is the mind's joyous gift of leaping to meet immediate experience: a gift the young have by birthright: but men grow old. Yeats knows he is older now than ever a Romantic poet was who made a poem worth reading" (*Colder Eye* 261). Yeats airs the same "complaint" more overtly in "The LIVING BEAUTY," "MEN IMPROVE WITH THE YEARS," and "A Song" (1918). As it happened, unanticipated emotional renewal arrived the following year in the form of marriage to Georgie Hyde-Lees (see GEORGE YEATS) and the occult experimentation that led to A VISION.

The poem begins with a tender evocation of the scenery surrounding Lady GREGORY's estate, COOLE PARK, which had long been Yeats's spiritual home and for long summer stretches his actual home. A crisp autumnal beauty is settled on trees, paths, lake, and sky, as Yeats relates in lines almost entirely drained of affect. Kenner argues that these lines embody "the flattest syntax [Yeats] could manage" and enact a "whole theory of poetic deterioration, whereby [. . .] abstraction overtakes you when age has drained the energy that made metaphors once" (*Colder Eye* 261). Yeats counts 59 swans upon the lake, and he cannot but reflect that it has been 19 years since he first made his count: thus opens the poem's movement of elegiac retrospection. The swans suddenly "scatter wheeling in great broken rings," an image of circling flight that Yeats would later rehabilitate with different intentions in "DEMON AND BEAST" and "The SECOND COMING"; the specific image of the swan taking flight, meanwhile, would recur in the third section of "NINETEEN HUNDRED AND NINETEEN." Yeats painfully acknowledges that "all's changed"—in his own heart—since he first witnessed the magnificent spectacle of the swans taking to the sky. In the fourth stanza, Yeats's vague soreness of heart finds its diagnosis in the image of the swans as they paddle and climb "lover by lover." Their serene self-delight attests that their "hearts have not grown old," that "passion or conquest, wander where they will, / Attend upon them still," in contrast to Yeats himself. In the poem's final stanza, Yeats watches the swans "drift on the still water" (an image that recurs in the final lines of "COOLE AND BALLYLEE,

1931" and in the third section of "The TOWER"), calling them "mysterious, beautiful"—mysterious inferably because he cannot comprehend the secret of their self-mastery. The poem ends in a second bereavement: Yeats wonders where the swans will have gone when he wakes one day "to find that they have flown away," suggesting that even vicarious passion is fugitive for the aging romantic poet. And yet, as Kenner argues, there is a Yeats present who is "superior to the enervated Yeats in the poem," a Yeats who "can supply at need such powerful words as make the swans 'scatter wheeling in great broken rings / Upon their clamorous wings.' And who is this superior Yeats? We shall be taught to call him the anti-self, master of 'all / That I have handled least, least looked upon' ['EGO DOMINUS TUUS'], someone precisely un-natural, a poet reconstituted by intent contrivance of the relics of a poet who has aged away" (262).

Bloom proposes WORDSWORTH's "Tintern Abbey" (1798) and SHELLEY's "Alastor" (1816) as the poem's crucial precursors. "Wordsworth both longs for and does not desire the raptures of an earlier phase, when he later returns to a crucially remembered landscape," Bloom writes. "Judiciously he balances loss and gain, the means of balance being the compensatory imagination, with its deeper autumnal music and sober coloring rising to take the place of a fled ecstasy" (Yeats 191). "The Wild Swans at Coole" is less willing to strike this balance or make the best of loss, for Yeats's transcendental aspirations are undoubtedly fiercer than Wordsworth's, but it can at least be said that the two poems stage a similar self-confrontation between present self and past self using a scene of familiar beauty as a frame of reference. Shelley's "Alastor" is more specific in its influence, lending the central image of the swan as "an emblem of the subjective quest, but the quest realized as he, the Poet, never can realize it, precisely because his greater powers cannot be fulfilled by the inadequate context of nature [. . .]. Yeats too sees in the swan his antithetical quest fulfilled, but his regret is that for him the passionate or outward-bound aspect of the quest is forever over" (192; for the swan in "Alastor," see lines 274–290). Kenner, on the other hand, locates the poem's ancestry in

Keats's "Ode to a Nightingale" (1819), Shelley's "To a Skylark" (1820), and Wordsworth's "To the Cuckoo" (1807), noting how consistently "Romantic élan rhymed with the flight of some bird," He also cites COLERIDGE's "Dejection: An Ode" (1802) and Wordsworth's "Ode: Intimations of Immortality" (1807) as seminal formulations of the romantic "theory of poetic deterioration" (Colder Eye 261).

FIRST PUBLICATION: The Little Review (periodical), June 1917. Reprinted in The Wild Swans at Coole, The CUALA PRESS, Churchtown, Dundrum, November 17, 1917.

BIBLIOGRAPHY

Bloom, Harold. Yeats; Kelly, John S. A W. B. Yeats Chronology; Kenner, Hugh. A Colder Eye: The Modern Irish Writers.

"Wisdom" (1927)

Continuing the biblical revisionism of "TWO SONGS FROM A PLAY" (which precedes it in the 1928 edition of The Tower), and preambling the epochal birth-moment of "LEDA AND THE SWAN" (which follows in The Tower), "Wisdom" brazenly offers an "amended" gospel. Christianity did not find itself in the humble manger, but in the high-aesthetic forms of Byzantine and medieval art: so far so good. Lines eight through 15 begin the plunge into obscurity. Yeats seems to reimagine the Virgin Mary in keeping with the sumptuousness of the art tradition that grew up around her and in Yeats's heterodox view justifies her. She is dressed and throned as a queen (according to The Oxford English Dictionary, "chryselephantine" refers to gold and ivory, and specifically to "statues overlaid with gold and ivory, such as the Olympian Zeus and Athene Parthenos of Phidias"). She stitches at a "purple hoarded" that her son "might be nobly breeched / In starry towers of Babylon / Noah's freshet never reached." Here Mary seems to foresee Christ as the latest in the ancient line of Babylonian astronomer-kings (cf. "The DAWN" and "Two Songs from a Play": "The Babylonian starlight brought / A fabulous, formless darkness in," i.e., brought in Christianity). That Noah's flood never reached these towers suggests their dizzying transcendental height and exemption from history, perhaps even from the divine will (with the implication that Mary fails to understand the shift in *tincture* heralded by her son; she envisions him as a magus of an *antithetical* wisdom). "King Abundance got Him on / Innocence; and Wisdom He"—that is, God begat Christ on Mary. Her "innocence" is sexual, of course, but is also explained by her misunderstanding of the kind of king she is about to bear. "Wisdom He" identifies Christ as the incarnation or fulfillment of Wisdom. "That cognomen"—i.e., "Wisdom"—"sounded best," Yeats explains. What seems at first a flippant demythologization, however, winds up preparing for an even fiercer mythologization. The purpose of the "cognomen" was not to contrive or advertise Christ's wisdom, but to conceal, as too offputting, too terrifying—as not fit for public consumption—the "wild infancy" that "drove horror from His Mother's breast." As in "The Magi," "The Mother of God," and "A Nativity" (1938), Yeats conceives the Christian arrival, like all such history-reversing arrivals, as necessarily violent and terrible (cf. "Leda and the Swan" and "The Second Coming"). It is a detail worth pondering, however, that Christ's "wild infancy" drives away rather than induces his mother's horror. It may be that Mary's initial horror has been replaced by some larger realization or resignation, or that exposure to the supernatural shattered her humanity (Yeats's fear in "To the Rose upon the Rood of Time") and rendered her a type of the "staring virgin" mentioned in "Two Songs from a Play."

FIRST PUBLICATION: *October Blast*, The Cuala Press, Dublin, August 1927.

"Witch, The (I.)"/Peacock, The (II.)" (1914)

As a suite, the two poems descant on the inconsequence of mere riches. In "The Witch," Yeats compresses his critique to a pinhead of potent metaphor: scrambling for riches is like bedding with a "foul witch" and, once "drained dry," being brought to the chamber where lies despairing "one long sought." The poem is notable for its sexual flagrance, an element that would become increasingly prominent in the work to come. The poem was even saltier in draft, referring not to a "foul witch" but to a "stale bitch" (*Man and Poet* 120; *Stone Cottage* 57). In "The Peacock," a more involved poem, Yeats elaborates on the meaninglessness of mere riches to one who has "made a great peacock / With the pride of his eye," which is to say, to the genuine artist, who begets luxuriance from the pride of his own nature. His "whim"—his artistic impulse—does not depend on wealth, but takes its nourishment from the "stone-beaten, stone-grey, / And desolate Three Rock. . . ." Yeats refers to Three Rock Mountain, a "1,763-foot promontory south of Dublin," with "magnificent views of Dublin Bay, the Hill of Howth, and the inland ranges" (YD 183). Yeats may have had in mind the inspiration of the view, but more probably the inspiration of the rock itself—adamant, ancient, and severe, scorning all sentimentality and evanescence. In "The Grey Rock," Yeats similarly concatenates the artistic impulse with the desolation of mountain rock, proposing that all human might is "from the holy shades that rove / The grey rock and the windy light," and avowing that he has kept faith with the "rock-born, rock-wandering foot" of the goddess Aoife, who in this context is a type of the muse. "The Peacock" concludes that whether the true artist lives or dies amid the "wet rocks and heather," his "ghost will be gay, / Adding feather to feather / For the pride of his eye." The implication is that artistic creation, unlike mere wealth creation, is an act of transcendent joy, unbounded by life and death.

Humphrey Carpenter, Ezra Pound's biographer, speculates that Yeats borrowed the image of the peacock from a dinner given on January 18, 1914, by the poet Wilfred Scawen Blunt (1840–1922) for a delegation of admirers. In addition to Yeats, attendees included Richard Aldington (1892–1962), F. S. Flint (1885–1960), T. Sturge Moore, Victor Plarr (1863–1929), and Pound. Carpenter quotes Blunt's granddaughter in recollection of the elaborate dish that was the meal's centerpiece: "Regarding the roasted peacock—The one appearing in full plumage was in fact the skin of the whole bird arranged over a dummy to look realistic—the roasted bird followed on a separate dish" (*Serious Character* 229). Hugh Kenner has an entirely different explanation of the peacock image: "His own eyes being troublesome, [Yeats] had brought Pound [to STONE COTTAGE] to read, and they were likely sampling the Pennells' *Life of Whistler*, where on page 301 we find the master's tart appraisal of riches ('It is better to live on bread and cheese and paint beautiful things than to live like Dives and paint potboilers') and five pages later his proposal for a 'great peacock ten feet high'" (*Colder Eye* 77; *Dives*—Latin, "rich"—is the name sometimes given to the man of wealth mentioned in Luke 16: 19–31). Kenner notes that the peacock "was to have gone on a stairhead panel of the new (1892) Boston library" but it was never executed (77). Blunt's dinner may have put peacock on the brain, but Kenner's theory makes more sense of the poem. In Canto 83 (1948), Pound recalls Yeats laboring at "The Peacock" at Stone Cottage and transliterates some of his overheard verbal experimentation:

> . . . I recalled the noise in the chimney
> as it were the wind in the chimney
>   but was in reality Uncle William
> downstairs composing
> that had made a great Peeeeacock
>   in the proide ov his oiye
>   had made a great peeeeeeecock in the . . .
> made a great peacock
>   in the proide of his oyyee
>
> proide ov his oy-ee
> as indeed he had, and perdurable
>
> a great peacock aere perennius ["more enduring than bronze," Horace, *Odes*, III, 30]

Yeats's choice of the peacock as an epitomizing art object may foreshadow the abundance of avian imagery that would soon emerge in his own poems. As Pound suggests, Yeats made his own great peacock in the pride of his eye, whether one thinks of "BYZANTIUM," "NINETEEN HUNDRED AND NINETEEN," "SAILING TO BYZANTIUM," "SOLOMON AND THE WITCH," or "The WILD SWANS AT COOLE." The peacock specifically figures in "ANCESTRAL HOUSES," "HIS WILDNESS," and "MY TABLE."

FIRST PUBLICATION: *Poetry* (periodical), May 1914. Reprinted in *Responsibilities: Poems and a Play*, The CUALA PRESS, Churchtown, Dundrum, May 25, 1914.

BIBLIOGRAPHY

Carpenter, Humphrey. *A Serious Character: The Life of Ezra Pound*; Conner, Lester I. *A Yeats Dictionary: Persons and Places in the Poetry of W. B. Yeats*; Jeffares, A. Norman. *W. B. Yeats: Man and Poet*; Kenner, Hugh. *A Colder Eye: The Modern Irish Writers*; Longenbach, James. *Stone Cottage: Pound, Yeats, and Modernism*; Terrell, Carroll F. *A Companion to The Cantos of Ezra Pound*.

"Woman Homer Sung, A" (1910)

Yeats published no book of new verse between 1903 and 1910, but with "A Woman Homer Sung," the second poem in *The Green Helmet and Other Poems*, he picked up where he had left off seven years earlier, both ruing and mythologizing MAUD GONNE. Yeats opens the 21-line poem by wryly recalling the tormenting jealousy of his youth: if any man approached Gonne, Yeats "shook with hate and fear," but if any man failed to acknowledge her beauty, it was "bitter wrong." Thus racked with conflicting passion, Yeats "wrote and wrought," and now, having become gray—Yeats was 45 in 1910—he dreams that his work is sufficiently consummate that future generations will be able to say that he "shadowed in a glass / What thing her body was." In the last of the poem's three stanzas, Yeats's recalls Gonne in the splendor of her youth. Like "a woman Homer sung" she was full of fire, sweetness, and pride, so much so that "life and letters seem / But an heroic dream." This final turn reverses the previous stanza's implication that art is able to "shadow in a glass" the glories of life. The phrase "life and letters" connotes the standard Victorian biography—that is, the attempt to mirror the reality of a human life. In Gonne's case, this attempt must remain a "heroic dream," for she exceeds any mere simulacrum. This recognition retroactively accounts for the verb *dream* in the second stanza, with its implication of fantasy and delusion. The "woman Homer sung" is Helen of Troy, whose beauty, like that of Gonne, was at once miraculous and dooming. The poem's admission of artistic impotence or limitation is echoed in "WORDS," the poem that immediately follows in *The Green Helmet and Other Poems* (under the title "The Consolation"), while the association between Helen and Gonne recurs in "NO SECOND TROY" and "PEACE," which appear later in the volume, and in "The SORROW OF LOVE."

FIRST PUBLICATION: *The Green Helmet and Other Poems*, The CUALA PRESS, Churchtown, Dundrum, December 1910, under the sequence title "Raymond Lully and his wife Pernella" and the present title.

"Woman Young and Old, A" (1929, sequence)

"A Woman Young and Old" consists of "Father and Child," "Before the World was made," "A First Confession," "Her Triumph," "Consolation," "Chosen," "Parting," "Her Vision in the Wood," "A Last Confession," "Meeting," and "From the 'Antigone.'" In June 1927, Yeats told OLIVIA SHAKESPEAR that he was writing the sequence to balance "A MAN YOUNG AND OLD" (*Letters* 725). The sequences not only balance each other—each consisting of 11 poems, each ending with a translation from SOPHOCLES—but they complicatedly interlace in a mutual borrowing of themes and motifs that makes each an excellent commentary on the other. Both sequences are wrenched by the curse of time, the conundrum of loss, and the urgency of both physical and metaphysical desire; at the same time, they differ in their respective attempts to embody something characteristic of masculinity and femininity. Yeats began "A Woman Young and Old" in May 1926, while he was in the middle of writing "A Man Young and Old," but the sequences did not appear side by side, as they might have to

good effect, in *The Tower* (1928). In a 1933 note to *The Winding Stairs and Other Poems*, Yeats writes that "A Woman Young and Old" was omitted from *The Tower* for reasons that he cannot recall (*VP* 831). The explanation is that the New York printer and publisher William Edwin Rudge (1876–1931) had offered Yeats the windfall sum of £300 (£400, according to Joseph Hone) for "six months' use of sixteen or so pages of verse" (*Letters* 728–729; *W. B. Yeats* 394–395). Yeats completed his end of the bargain by providing "A Woman Young and Old," as well as "BLOOD AND THE MOON," "DEATH," "A DIALOGUE OF SELF AND SOUL," "IN MEMORY OF EVA GORE-BOOTH AND CON MARKIEWICZ," and "Oil and Blood," all of which appeared in the 1929 edition of *The Winding Stair* published by Rudge's Fountain Press (*Biblio.* 164–165).

"Father and Child," based on a 1926 exchange between George and Anne Yeats, opens the sequence with a vignette of female desire in its earliest and most rudimentary form (*BG* 363). Whether seriously or facetiously, the father invokes the authority of conventional opinion, but this weighs nothing against the beauty of a young man's hair and the coldness of a "March wind" in his eyes. Yeats alludes to the same coldness in AUTOBIOGRAPHIES (86), "The FISHERMAN," "A General Introduction for my Work" (*E&I* 522–523; *LE* 213), and elsewhere. A metaphor for passion free of sentiment, free of the loose and the accidental, it signifies everything the girl desires by uncorrupted instinct and everything the father fails to understand or cannot feel through lost or dulled instinct. "Before the World was made" is evidently set a few years later, for the girl dabbles with cosmetics and has a "beloved." The unreflective instinct of childhood has given way to the sentimental aspiration of late adolescence or young womanhood. The girl would be loved not bodily but spiritually—loved for what she was "before the world was made"—and yet she retains a mischievous willingness to use her spiritual aspiration as moral cover. If she uses makeup, it is only because she seeks the face she had "before the world was made"; if she casts a roving eye on other men, she would have her beloved concern himself with only that aspect of her that existed "before the world was made."

"A First Confession" finds the spiritual self losing its battle with the bodily self, the "better self" succumbing to the impulses of the coquette, all of which is rendered with a candid self-knowledge that suggests once again a leap in years. On its face, the third stanza is the most enigmatic of the entire sequence. Yeats's note provides the crucial clue: "I have symbolised a woman's love as the struggle of the darkness to keep the sun from rising from its earthly bed" (VP 830). "Brightness that I pull back / From the Zodiac" thus refers to the sun as the symbol of the masculine principle (perhaps to a specific man figured as the sun), to which the woman puts her question: "Why those questioning eyes / That are fixed upon me?" "Those questioning eyes" suggests a certain masculine comprehension of female wiles. The stanza's closing question—"What can they do but shun me / If empty night replies?"—is a self-justification: It suggests that coquetry is a necessary mask, that the primal reality of the feminine principle has a terrifying mysteriousness that must be concealed. Coquetry, then, is not a matter of arousing physical attraction but of negating metaphysical antipathy. Equating the "empty night" of female desire with the "ancestral night" of "A Dialogue of Self and Soul," one can map the female-male antithesis of "A First Confession" onto the more fundamental antithesis of "soul" and "self." The emptiness of the night indicates something unself-conscious or instinctual within the woman, something that exists beyond sentiment, personality, and knowledge, and that disconcertingly verges on the inhuman or impersonal.

"Her Triumph" finds the woman the captive of her own dissembling or coquetry, that which her "better self disowns," here metaphorized as a dragon (cf. "MICHAEL ROBARTES AND THE DANCER"). The woman does the bidding of the dragon not because she is compelled, but because, as against her younger self in "Before the World was made" and "A First Confession," she cannot conceive another or a better master. Love, however, arrives as a questing hero to set her free, and now she and her beloved "stare" (cf. "TWO SONGS FROM A PLAY") in astonishment at the sea, symbol of the enormity and power of love itself, while a "miraculous strange bird" shrieks at them

(shriek picks up a central motif of "A Man Young and Old"; see also "Her Vision in the Wood"). On the one hand, the bird recalls the "ridiculous little bird" of "A MEMORY OF YOUTH"—a kind of feathered cupid—upon whose cry Love tears "from the clouds his marvellous moon"; but on the other hand, the stridency of shrieks and the aggressive thrust of the preposition at place the bird upon the same bough as the apocalyptic and nature-scorning avians of "BYZANTIUM," "The Indian to His Love" (1886), "MY TABLE," "SOLOMON AND THE WITCH," and "The WANDERINGS OF OISIN." Does nature offer a benediction or a malediction, or does it merely register, as in "Solomon and the Witch," some essential shift in the order of things?

"Consolation" sets the consolation of the body against the wisdom of the sages, the kind of stoic wisdom, presumably, with which "A Man Young and Old" concludes: "Never to have lived is best, ancient writers say; / Never to have drawn the breath of life, never to have looked into the eye of day; / The second best's a gay goodnight and quickly turn away." The woman shares the sage's belief in the crime of birth, but finds in the tragic circumstance of life the desperate impetus of her passion, and in the throes of this passion "the crime can be forgot" (cf. "A Dialogue of Self and Soul").

"Chosen," the central and finest poem of the sequence, is closely allied to the final stanza of "A First Confession," taking up again the male-female opposition between day and night. "The lot of love is chosen," as the woman has learned "Struggling for an image on the track / Of the whirling Zodiac." In the chasing orbits of moon and sun, night and dark, the Zodiac indicates the interplay of masculine and feminine. As the masculine sun sets and rises ("horror of daybreak"), so love entails the joy of possession and the pain of dispossession ("love's bitter-sweet," in the phrase of "Her Vision in the Wood"). In the midst of this perpetual hello and good-bye, however, there is an eternal moment ("Eternity is not a long time but a short time" Yeats once remarked) in which heart is joined to heart and both "drift on the miraculous stream" where the "Zodiac is changed into a sphere," symbol not of restless cycle but eternal self-presence and completion (*W. B. Yeats* 331). Yeats's 1928 note on these lines is clarifying: "I have symbolised a woman's love as the struggle of the darkness to keep the sun from rising from its earthly bed. In the last stanza of The Choice I change the symbol to that of the souls of man and woman ascending through the Zodiac. In some Neoplatonist or Hermatist—whose name I forget—the whorl changes into a sphere at one of the points where the Milky Way crosses the Zodiac" (*VP* 830). In a 1933 note, Yeats specifies that the "learned astrologer" of the poem is Macrobius (fifth century), and that the relevant passage is from Macrobius's commentary on Cicero's *Dream of Scipio*: ". . . when the sun is in Aquarius, we sacrifice to the Shades, for it is in the sign inimical to human life; and from thence the meeting-place of Zodiac and Milky Way, the descending soul by its defluction is drawn out of the spherical, the sole divine form, into the cone" (831; for a detailed discussion of Yeats's Platonic and Neoplatonic sources, see *Yeats and Tradition* 205–211). The *Dream of Scipio* is an epilogue to Cicero's *On the State* (54–51 B.C.), in which, writes Michael Grant, Scipio Aemilianus is "shown the heavenly habitation of great souls" (*Greek and Latin Authors* 94).

With a nod to *Romeo and Juliet*, as critics have widely noted, "Parting" replays "the struggle of the darkness to keep the sun from rising from its earthly bed" as a bedroom tussle, while recasting the shrieking bird of "Her Triumph" as herald of both night and day; as dual or undecidable emblem of both female subjectivity and male objectivity. The bird may in fact sing in the dawn—the man can be trusted on such matters of fact presumably—but the woman is undaunted by mere matters of fact. The man trails off inconsequentially; the woman has the last word—an irresistibly alluring last word—and thus carries the argument. The victory is a victory of female sexuality, to be sure, but even more basically it is a victory of the self-legislating or *antithetical* imagination.

"Her Vision in the Wood" departs in circumstance, tone, and form from the rest of the sequence. Joseph Hone calls it "Dantesque in its somber magnificence" (*W. B. Yeats* 437). So too it departs

from the condition of youth. The poem locates the woman in a visionary wood, where she rages at the realization that she is "too old for a man's love." Imagining that she can assuage a "greater with a lesser pang" and wanting to know that her withered veins are not empty, she draws her own blood with her nail (foreshadowed by the spurious laceration of "A First Confession"). There appears a visionary procession (cf. MOHINI CHATTERJEE) bearing upon a litter a man fatally wounded by some beast (cf. DIARMUID AND GRANIA). He is "all blood and mire," a phrase Yeats would slightly adjust and famously redeploy in "Byzantium." The poem ends with the suggestion of mysterious transference. Both "victim" and "torturer" of the woman's heart, the man bears the wound that the woman inflicted on herself (not incidentally, this complicates the pronounced theme of masculine victimization in "A Man Young and Old": the woman, after all, is neither heartless nor unsuffering).

Like "HIS WILDNESS," the penultimate poem of "A Man Young and Old," "A Last Confession" envisions the earthly drama of desire and love continuing even beyond life. The woman confesses that she drew most pleasure from a "lively lad" to whom she gave herself merely bodily, as beast gives to beast (cf. "The LADY'S FIRST SONG"), while love brought her only misery. When the soul throws off the body, however, it shall find its counterpart, and the two souls shall "cling so tight, / There's not a bird of day that dare / Extinguish that delight," a reference to the disobliging bird of "Parting." Tellingly, the soul's communion finds its metaphors in the pleasure of the body, for the Heavenly hope, as so often in Yeats, is not to transcend but to reenact in purer or higher form the drama of life. Yeats likewise, and far more beautifully, depicts the coupling of unencumbered souls in "RIBH AT THE TOMB OF BAILE AND AILLINN," the first poem in the sequence "SUPERNATURAL SONGS."

"Meeting" ironically contrasts with the communion of "Her Vision in the Wood" and "A Last Confession." Man and woman meet not as tragically wound-connected spirits, nor as liberated souls, but as cantankerous codgers who happen upon one another, perhaps upon the road, symbol of time and accident, locus of bitter reality (cf. "The FRIENDS OF

HIS YOUTH," the seventh poem of "A Man Young and Old"; also "The SEVEN SAGES"). Old lovers as it seems, they displace onto one another the bitterness of their age and the resentment of their parted ways. Though the poem has the generalized air of parable, "Each hating what the other loved" may have its explanation in the estrangement of Yeats and MAUD GONNE, who as the years passed found it increasingly difficult to ignore the incompatibility of their politics and temperaments. The "beggarly habiliment" of the final lines might refer to the "cloak and hood" of age (thus upholding the body in its youthful beauty) or to the "clothes" of bodily existence that "A Last Confession" mentions (thus upholding the soul in its eternal beauty). Both "A Last Confession" and "Meeting," in any case, share the metaphysical premise of "Before the World was made" that bodily reality is a mere vestment that is ideally discarded.

As "A Man Young and Old" ends with Yeats's translation of lines from Sophocles' *Oedipus at Colonus*, so "A Woman Young and Old" ends with his translation of lines from his *Antigone*. As the former poem counsels stoic resignation, so the latter poem counsels existential rebellion, however futile in the end. These, indeed, are the poles of Yeats's own response to the "crime of being born" ("Consolation"), marked, for example, by "UNDER BEN BULBEN" ("Cast a cold eye / On life, on death") and by "The LAMENTATION OF THE OLD PENSIONER" ("I spit into the face of Time").

FIRST PUBLICATION: *The Winding Stair*, Fountain Press, New York, October 1, 1929. "Chosen" was originally titled "The Choice." It appeared under its present title in *The Winding Stairs and Other Poems*, Macmillan, London, September 19, 1933.

BIBLIOGRAPHY

Grant, Michael. *Greek and Latin Authors: 800 B.C.–A.D. 1000*; Hone, Joseph. *W. B. Yeats*; Saddlemyer, Ann. *Becoming George: The Life of Mrs W. B. Yeats*; Wade, Allan. *A Bibliography of the Writings of W. B. Yeats*; Wilson, F. A. C. *W. B. Yeats and Tradition*; Yeats, W. B. *Essays and Introductions, Later Essays, The Letters of W. B. Yeats, The Variorum Edition of the Poems of W. B. Yeats*.

"Words" (1910)

From 1910 to 1933 "Words" was titled "The Consolation," but the indicated consolation is fraught with irony. Yeats tells of the realization that his "darling," the inevitable MAUD GONNE, fails to understand what he has done or what he would do in the "blind bitter land" of Ireland. These lines allude to a long-existing tension between Yeats's own freethinking cultural nationalism and Gonne's militant political nationalism, which resulted in bitter disagreements and quarrels (see, for example, GY 176–178). This impasse fills Yeats with despair, but his despondency is alleviated by remembering that so much of his work—his ceaseless effort to make words obey his call—has been motivated by the desire to explain himself to Gonne. Had she understood him, Yeats asks, with an evident sexual double meaning, "who can say / What would have shaken from the sieve?" Lacking the challenge of her incomprehension, he might "have thrown poor words away / And been content to live." Here Yeats anticipates the dichotomy of "The CHOICE," according to which the "intellect of man" must choose between perfection of the life and perfection of the work. The crux of Yeats's consolation is that his vain pursuit of Gonne—his unanswered love, his broken life—has resulted in perfection of the work. Yeats echoes the self-understanding of "Words" in "A DIALOGUE OF SELF AND SOUL," calling his catastrophic love for Gonne "that most fecund ditch of all," and declaring his willingness "to live it all again." A reader with a psychological bent might well ask whether Yeats's epic passion was not animated all along by the ulterior purpose of poetic creation. For her own part, Gonne clearly understood her role in helping to shake words from the sieve of Yeats's mind. "The world should thank me for not marrying you," she once told Yeats, fully grasping the relation between his romantic discontentment and his poetic achievement (SQ 319). Drafts of the poem are included in MEMOIRS (141–144).

FIRST PUBLICATION: *The Green Helmet and Other Poems*, The CUALA PRESS, Churchtown, Dundrum, December 1910, under the sequence title "Raymond Lully and his wife Pernella" and the title "The Consolation." Reprinted in *The Collected Poems of W. B. Yeats*, Macmillan Company, New York, November 14, 1933, under the present title.

BIBLIOGRAPHY

Gonne, Maud. *The Autobiography of Maud Gonne: A Servant of the Queen*; Yeats, W. B. *The Gonne-Yeats Letters 1893–1938, Memoirs.*

"Words for Music Perhaps"
(1929–33, sequence)

"They walked the roads / Mimicking what they heard, as children mimic; / They understood that wisdom comes of beggary," writes Yeats in "The SEVEN SAGES," referring to the great Irish Georgians. As if attempting to capture the spirit of the roads and the wisdom of beggary, Yeats evolved a new (but far from exclusive) style during the late 1920s and 1930s that was spare and vigorous, scabrous and balladic, philosophical without being theoretical or willfully obscure, unafraid of the traditional refrain. It washed its hands entirely of what Hugh Kenner calls the "Yeats of *ottiva rima* and lofty composure" (*Colder Eye* 315). "Words for Music Perhaps" epitomizes this development. Consisting of 25 relatively short poems, it is the longest sequence of Yeats's career and yet it is impeccably terse. Yeats began the sequence in early February 1929 (YC 263) and sent a progress report to OLIVIA SHAKESPEAR in March: "I am writing *Twelve poems for music*—have done three of them (and two other poems)—no[t] so much that they may be sung as that I may define their kind of emotion to myself. I want them to be all emotion and all impersonal. One of the three I have written is my best lyric for some years I think. They are the opposite of my recent work and all praise of joyous life, though in the best of them ["Three Things"] it is a dry bone on the shore that sings the praise" (*Letters* 758). While correcting proofs of the sequence for republication in *The Winding Stair and Other Poems* in August 1933, Yeats shed additional light on the impetus of the sequence: "'Crazy Jane' poems (the origin of some of these you know)

and the little group of love poems that follow ['A WOMAN YOUNG AND OLD'] are, I think, exciting and strange. Sexual abstinence fed their fire—I was ill and yet full of desire. They sometimes came out of the greatest mental excitement I am capable of" (814). The individual poems of the sequence may appear slight relative to the Yeats of "ottiva rima and lofty composure," but each has numerous combinatory possibilities, and the entire sequence forms an immensely complex network of shifting and displaced meaning. Yeats is not as a matter of course given credit for this aspect of his genius, but he was a master of making poems talk among themselves.

Crazy Jane, the chief personage of the sequence, is perhaps the best known and most distinctive of all Yeats's poetic masks. Yeats had contemplated such a persona for some 30 years. In a 1904 note to *The POT OF BROTH*, he writes that he had borrowed a tune in the play from "an old woman known as Cracked Mary, who wanders about the plain of Aidhne [in Galway], and who sometimes sees unearthly riders on white horses coming through stony fields to her hovel door in the night time" (*VPl.* 254). Evidently, Crazy Jane is an amalgam of this "Cracked Mary" and another "Cracked Mary" then living in the neighborhood of Lady GREGORY's COOLE PARK. Ann Saddlemyer identifies the latter as one Mrs. Cusack. According to GEORGE YEATS, "she was a bit touched in the head. But it was a head full of amusing, often obscene stories about things she'd see on her rambles. I used to seek her out and get her to tell them to me. Then I'd go home and tell W. B. [. . .] He loved them. He asked me to get as many as I could for him. And so I saw a good deal of Cracked Mary at that time" (BG 176–177). Yeats adopted the name Crazy Jane only after trying on Cracked Mary. "Crazy Jane and the Bishop," "Crazy Jane Reproved," and "Crazy Jane grown old looks at the Dancers" were originally poems about Cracked Mary (*Biblio.* 170–171), and Yeats wrote another poem, "Cracked Mary's Vision," which he intended to include in *Words for Music Perhaps* before deciding that its refrain, "May the devil take King George," was an ungracious jab at George V (1865–1936), who was then seriously ill (AP 386; IY 101–102). According to

A. Norman Jeffares, Yeats changed the name of his protagonist "in case some of her relatives should object to her somewhat outspoken comments on life as Yeats reproduced them" (*Man and Poet* 256). In a November 1931 letter to Shakespear, Yeats acknowledged Mrs. Cusack as his literary model and recounted her antics: "Crazy Jane is more or less founded upon an old woman who lives in a little cottage near Gort. She loves her flower-garden—she has just sent Lady Gregory some flowers in spite of the season—and [has] an amazing power of audacious speech. One of her great performances is a description of how the meanness of a Gort shopkeeper's wife over the price of a glass of porter made her so despair of the human race that she got drunk. The incidents of that drunkenness are of an epic magnificence. She is the local satirist and a really terrible one" (*Letters* 785–786).

In Yeats's hands, Crazy Jane becomes something more than a ribald local character. She is a type of the wise fool, sharp-tongued and slatternly but also deeply seeing and understanding. Richard Ellmann comments, "Crazy Jane, because of her name, could speak with all the prerogatives of the Elizabethan fool without, of course, being crazy at all." He adds that Crazy Jane "is not so wild as she appears, or as Yeats pretended," and that, far from being cracked or crazy, there is a Yeatsian sophistication in her conception of love "as a conflict of opposites but also as an escape from them to unity, wholeness, or, to use a word which she would not have used, to beatitude" (*MM* 268). As Oisin and Ribh denounce St. Patrick in "The Wanderings of Oisin" and "Supernatural Songs," respectively, so Crazy Jane denounces her nemesis the Bishop. As different as the legendary hero, the Christian-druidic hermit, and the rural Irish termagant seem to be, they are equally believers in the wholeness of the body and the fullness of the personality, and in consequence enemies of the Christianity that Ribh calls an "abstract Greek absurdity." The aged Oisin and the hermit Ribh are voluntary social exiles, while Jane, who rails at the conventions of respectable society from the social periphery, is an outcast. None of these has a place in a society that is affronted by passions that belong to what Yeats's elsewhere calls the "whole man" (*E&I* 266).

The first seven poems of "Words for Music Perhaps"—"Crazy Jane and the Bishop," "Crazy Jane Reproved," "Crazy Jane on the Day of Judgment," "Crazy Jane and Jack the Journeyman," "Crazy Jane on God," "Crazy Jane talks with the Bishop," "Crazy Jane grown old looks at the Dancers"—are explicitly poems of Crazy Jane. "Crazy Jane and the Bishop" gives the essentials of Jane's tale. In her youth, she had loved Jack the Journeyman. As a "journeyman"—a craftsman with no settled employment or establishment—he is a creature of the road, that is, of lived bodily experience, in keeping with the notion of "The Seven Sages." In those long-past days, the bishop was not even a parish priest. His later ascent implies the willingness to pander and self-aggrandize, and the poem witnesses this penchant in embryo. Making a public show of his own virtue, he drove Jack from the neighborhood, pronouncing with a Bible in his fist that he and Jane "lived like beast and beast." Now grown old, Jane meets Jack's ghost beneath the "blasted oak" and upon the stroke of midnight, the witching hour, calls down curses on the bishop's head. The parenthetical refrain "All find safety in the tomb" seems the voice of disembodied wisdom, the vatic voice, whispering of a final reconciliation of antitheses represented by the "solid man" and the "coxcomb," by the Bishop and Jane, much as the same voice whispers "All things remain in God" in "Crazy Jane on God."

"Crazy Jane Reproved" continues the admonition of the bishop. It warns against the rough play of the sexually vigorous journeyman, but in terms that are more likely to entice than repel the lusty Jane. The bishop's assumption that Jane shares his own faint-heartedness is the poem's implicit comedy. Taking a lurid, sweaty interest in such matters, the bishop interprets the thunderstorm as a sexual sundering of the heavens ("Heaven yawns"), and draws the conclusion that Europa "played the fool / That changed a lover for a bull." The vaginal suggestion of the shell answers the phallic suggestion of the "birch-tree" in the previous poem and evokes the divine love-play. It is this that made "the joints of Heaven crack." The bishop offers the moral never to "hang your heart upon / A roaring, ranting journeyman," inferably because one's own joints may be similarly cracked. The refrain—"Fol de rol, fol de rol"—underscores the nonsense of this admonition, at least from Crazy Jane's perspective.

"Crazy Jane on the Day of Judgment" affirms that love must be a movement of the "whole body and soul," while acknowledging that, in the sub-eternal sphere, it can be only a fragmentary and partial experience. In "Crazy Jane and Jack the Journeyman," Jane's doctrine of the body is taken to an extreme of heterodoxy. She pities the "lonely ghost" that goes to God and will herself "leap into the light lost / In my mother's womb." Yeats may allude to the process of "dreaming back" that he describes in "Shepherd and Goatherd" (1919), which envisions a return to the cradle if not the womb. Yeats's account of the "dreaming back" in A VISION is consistent with the poem's emphasis on light: "In the *Dreaming Back,* the *Spirit* is compelled to live over and over again the events that had most moved it; there can be nothing new, but the old events stand forth in a light which is dim or bright according to the intensity of the passion that accompanied them" (226; see also AV-1925 226–227). Were Jane to be left unburied, however, her ghost would walk the road with Jack, so thoroughly did the skein of love bind them in life. Even in death, she refuses to surrender the vigor of life, untempted even by the promise of Heaven. By the instinct of her body, as it were, Crazy Jane rejects the abstraction of the Bishop's Christianity, much as Ribh rejects the abstraction of St. Patrick's Christianity ("an abstract Greek absurdity" as Ribh calls it in "RIBH DENOUNCES PATRICK").

"Crazy Jane on God" rescues God from the emptiness of this abstraction, finding divinity manifested in the ebb and flow of sexual experience; in battle or in mystic vision of battle (the banners are ambiguously located in the sky; the battle is over, but conceivably replays itself as ghostly memory); and in occult miracle. Crazy Jane's vision of battle is illuminated by a passage in PER AMICA SILENTIA LUNAE in which Yeats alludes to a similar vision of "ancient armies fighting above bones or ashes" and explains that we "carry to ANIMA MUNDI our memory, and that memory is for a time our external world; and all passionate moments recur again and again, for passion desires its own recurrence more

than any event, and whatever there is of corresponding complacency or remorse is our beginning of judgement [. . .]" (LE 24). Likewise, Crazy Jane's vision of the ruined house "suddenly lit up" can be related to the introduction to The WORDS UPON THE WINDOW-PANE. Among a litany of miraculous or supernatural occurrences, Yeats mentions a house "suddenly lit up" and makes the point that "Crazy Jane on God" makes implicitly: "All about us there seems to start up a precise inexplicable teeming life, and the earth becomes once more, not in rhetorical metaphor, but in reality, sacred" (Expl. 369; VPl. 970). As many critics have noted, the "house" of both the poem and the introduction is Castle Dargan in County SLIGO, where Yeats's cousin, the former Mary Middleton, lived with her husband, the "brawling squireen" John Robert Ormsby (Aut. 73–74). Yeats mentions the castle in The KING OF THE GREAT CLOCK TOWER ("O, but I saw a solemn sight; / *Said the rambling, shambling travelling-man;* / Castle Dargan's ruin all lit, / Lovely ladies dancing in it") and depicts it as the miraculously lit house in PURGATORY (VPl. 1003, 1048). The poem's refrain—"All things remain in God"—suggests a parallelism between God and the ANIMA MUNDI and makes Crazy Jane, if not a Neoplatonist of Yeats's own stamp, then at least an instinctive sharer of his basic idea.

If not the best poem in the sequence, "Crazy Jane talks with the Bishop" is the most striking and arguably the most philosophically central. The Bishop and Jane meet on the road. He urges her to abandon her aging body and enter a "heavenly mansion." Jane replies with a crucial statement of principle: "Fair and foul are near of kin, / And fair needs foul. . . ." This idea pervades Yeats's poetry from the early "TO THE ROSE UPON THE ROOD OF TIME" to the late "NEWS FOR THE DELPHIC ORACLE" and compresses the philosophical complexity of late masterpieces like "A DIALOGUE OF SELF AND SOUL" and "VACILLATION." Continuing her point, Jane travesties the Bishop's heavenly mansion in the most notorious of her utterances: "But Love has pitched his mansion in / The place of excrement; / For nothing can be sole or whole / That has not been rent." The shift from the heavenly to the sexual mansion is sufficiently heterodox, but the "kinship" between the sexual and the excremental, the whole and the rent—what the Christian would call good and evil—is even more fundamentally subversive, as it embraces both terms as the inextricable duality that patterns the richness of the universe. Jane's defense of the "rent" specifically retorts to the Bishop's concerns in "Crazy Jane Reproved."

"Crazy Jane grown old looks at the Dancers" stemmed from a dream. In a March 1929 letter to Shakespear, Yeats related its substance: "Last night I saw in a dream strange ragged excited people singing in a crowd. The most visible were a man and woman who were I think dancing. The man was swinging round his head a weight at the end of a rope or leather thong, and I knew that he did not know whether he would strike her dead or not, and both had their eyes fixed on each other, and both sang their love for one another. I suppose it was BLAKE's old thought 'sexual love is founded upon spiritual hate'—I will probably find I have written it in a poem in a few days [. . .]" (*Letters* 758). In the context of the Crazy Jane sequence, the poem reiterates the emphasis that "fair and foul"—in this case, love and hate—are "near of kin." Crazy Jane considers the distinction between love and hate inessential; what matters is the intensity of the dance.

"Girl's Song" initiates seven poems—balancing the seven preceding poems on Crazy Jane—that are conceivably voiced by the young man and woman of "Crazy Jane grown old looks at the Dancers." Abandoning Crazy Jane, the sequence becomes more introspective and wryly aware of the human comedy—closer in tone to "A MAN YOUNG AND OLD" and "A Woman Young and Old." "Girl's Song" and "Young Man's Song" trade reflections on the aging of lovers. The girl wonders whether the essential self is young or old, while the young man is obliged by his own romantic idealism to believe that the essential self preexists the world and the clutches of time (as believes the girl in "BEFORE THE WORLD WAS MADE," the second poem of "A Woman Young and Old"). "No withered crone I saw / Before the world was made," declares the young man. In "Crazy Jane talks with the Bishop," by contrast, the bishop not only sees the withered

crone, but sees her with cruel and unsentimental clarity ("Those breasts are flat and fallen now . . ."). "Her Anxiety" and "His Confidence" continue the previous two poems' dialectic of cynicism and idealism. "Her Anxiety" all but paraphrases the more significant "TWO SONGS FROM A PLAY" ("Everything that man esteems / Endures a moment or a day. / Love's pleasure drives his love away") as the girl proclaims the self-consuming nature of love. The refrain, "*Prove that I lie*," makes reason the arbiter of truth, as if taunting the previous poem's faith in the heart. "His Confidence" affirms "undying love" despite the wrinkles that come of defending one's beloved; despite a heart broken in two as it strikes to bring love forth from a "desolate source." These lines undoubtedly remember Yeats's own romantic anguish as the would-be lover of MAUD GONNE. The allusion to "wrongs" most likely recalls rumors of her irregular lifestyle during the late 1890s (see *Mem.* 132) and the hostile reaction to her divorce proceedings against her popular husband, Major John MacBride (1865–1916) in 1905. Yeats's chivalry played out in two poems: "HE THINKS OF THOSE WHO HAVE SPOKEN EVIL OF HIS BELOVED" and "Against Unworthy Praise" (1910). The allusion to the "desolate source" recalls the countess's self-description, equally relevant to Gonne, in *The COUNTESS CATHLEEN*: ". . . not you / But I am the empty pitcher."

With "Love's Loneliness," the dramatic or narrative structure of the sequence becomes less pronounced, though "Love's Loneliness," "Her Dream," and "His Bargain" arguably continue the dialectic of the previous poems as man and woman advance in age and sophistication. "Love's Loneliness" is a prayer for ancestral succor in the loneliness and dread of love. In its appeal to "old fathers," it recalls the "INTRODUCTORY RHYMES" to *Responsibilities* and "ARE YOU CONTENT?" "Her Dream" answers the previous poem's mood of shadow and thorn, efflorescing in a vision of love as a heavenly canopy. The poem turns on the allusion to "Berenice's burning hair," to which Yeats also alludes in "Veronica's Napkin" (1932). Lester I. Conner explains that "Berenice II of Cyrene (d. 217 B.C.) was the wife of Ptolemy III. When her husband departed on an expedition to Syria from

Egypt, Berenice made a votive offering of a lock of her hair for her husband's safe return. The lock disappeared mysteriously and became, according to legend, [the constellation Coma Berenices]" (*YD* 14–15). Berenice's hair overspreading the night is referable to the "coal-black hair" of "Crazy Jane grown old looks at the Dancers," as well as to much else in Yeats: the "burning hair" of Caoilte in "THE HOSTING OF THE SIDHE"; the embowering hair that recurs in the poems of *The Wind Among the Reeds* (see, for example, "HE BIDS HIS BELOVED BE AT PEACE" and "HE REPROVES THE CURLEW"); and the "starry eddies" of hair that stream upon the wind in "An IMAGE FROM A PAST LIFE." Much like "A FRIEND'S ILLNESS" and "POLITICS," "His Bargain" lightly weighs the universal against the particular, the entire world against the flash of feeling. The male speaker dismisses the spindle of time upon which eternity unwinds itself, having made a "bargain"—that is, having dedicated himself—to the winding of his love's hair. In an example of the sardonic cross talk of the sequence, the poem responds to "Crazy Jane grown old looks at the Dancers," in which the young man "wound" his love's hair as if to strangle her, and to "Her Dream," in which the woman dreams of sheering the very locks with which the man has made his bargain.

"Three Things" and "Lullaby" form a dyad on the comforts of the female body. The former poem elaborates the anxiety of bodily decline mooted in "Girl's Song" and "Young Man's Song." It also continues the bone motif introduced in "Crazy Jane and Jack the Journeyman" and "Young Man's Song," and reprises the image of the wave-worn bone upon the shore introduced in "The Collar-Bone of a Hare" (1917), though with different meaning and intention. The bone—that of a woman—calls on death to "give three things back," for she wants again to experience the distinct forms of sensual fulfillment that belong to mother, lover, and wife. In the ambiguous third stanza, the woman meets or perhaps wakes beside her husband or at least her "rightful man"; they evidently couple (then or later) and the woman stretches and yawns in sexual satiety (stretching and yawning have explicitly sexual connotations in "ON WOMAN"). The poem's poignancy derives from the discrepancy between the

richness of life and the desiccation of death, and from the irrepressible and inexpugnable element of life that remains in the bone's unembittered song, justifying the young man in his claim that "She would as bravely show / Did all the fabric fade" ("Young Man's Song"). "Lullaby," as Yeats told Shakespear in March 1929, is the song of a mother to her child (*Letters* 760). Taking its cue from the first stanza of "Three Things," "Lullaby" sings the comforts of the maternal breast. Making no sharp distinction between the maternal body and the sexual body, the mother promises sleep such as Paris, Tristram, and Zeus knew in their lovers' arms. The poem's second stanza refers to the love potion inadvertently swallowed by Tristram and Isolde in Sir Thomas Malory's *Le Morte d'Arthur* (1485). The allusion to "roe" and "doe" implies, conceivably, that the love-stricken Tristram had lost interest in the hunt. The third stanza refers to the river Eurotas in Sparta. Espying Leda bathing in the river, Zeus descends in the form of a swan and rapes the Spartan queen, thus begetting Helen and initiating the events of the poem's first stanza. In "LEDA AND THE SWAN," the sated god drops the woman from its "indifferent beak," but "Lullaby," dauntless in its idea of female beneficence, imagines the god gathered into Leda's "protecting care." Zeus's rape of Leda echoes his abduction of Europa in "Crazy Jane Reproved." In both instances, Zeus majestically assumes animal form, challenging the bishop's aspersion on the coupling of beasts in "Crazy Jane and the Bishop." Beasts and gods, Yeats want to say, are not so obviously antithetical; as Jane expresses the same notion in "Crazy Jane talks with the Bishop," "Fair and foul are near of kin."

"After Long Silence" (a splendid reversion to the Yeats of "lofty composure") and "Mad as the Mist and Snow" are the only poems in the sequence seemingly written in Yeats's own voice. "After Long Silence" addresses Shakespear. "All other lovers being estranged or dead" gives the hint; as does the allusion to "Art and Song," the subject of so much correspondence between them; as does an October 1933 letter to Shakespear in which Yeats quotes the final lines of the poem and asks whether she remembers the "autumn evenings" before he departed for Rapallo (*Letters* 815; see also 772).

Yeats's left for Italy on November 21, 1929, and he wrote the poem in late November or early December, presumably as a token of whatever memories and reflections were jogged on those autumn evenings. The poem has the air of midnight wisdom and lonely conclave notable in esoteric poems like "ALL SOULS' NIGHT," "EGO DOMINUS TUUS," and "The PHASES OF THE MOON" (the "lamplight" recalls the explicitly occult lamps of "Ego Dominus Tuus" and "The LEADERS OF THE CROWD"). In this instance, wisdom involves a natural rather than supernatural transcendence of the body. "Bodily decrepitude" frees and vitalizes the mind, as the surging repetition of "descant and yet again descant" demonstrates. The point applies to Yeats as well as to Crazy Jane, who is equally but differently wise in her bodily decrepitude. The poem, however, does not denigrate the body as merely obstructive and malign (as does the Bishop), nor does it privilege the wisdom that compensates for the body's decline (as does "SAILING TO BYZANTIUM" in a complex perversion of Wordsworthianism [see WILLIAM WORDSWORTH]). The interpolation of love in the final line leaves the poem balanced between its opposed terms—wisdom and love, decrepitude and ignorance—as if wed to life in all its phases.

As "After Long Silence" addresses Shakespear, "Mad as the Mist and Snow" possibly addresses GEORGE RUSSELL (AE), who was Yeats's oldest friend and protégé. The two poets met as students at the Metropolitan School of Art in 1884, when both were indeed "unlettered lads." Unterecker alternately proposes EZRA POUND as Yeats's guest, reasoning that the poem was written in Rapallo, where Pound lived (RG 233). By the time Yeats met Pound in 1909, however, neither was "unlettered" and Yeats was most certainly not a "lad." Like "After Long Silence," "Mad as the Mist and Snow" opens on an esoteric scene of elderly wisdom burning the midnight lamp, with the expectation, deriving from COLERIDGE's "Dejection: An Ode" (1802), that the wind of the first lines will provide the energy of some mounting flight or vision, as in "IN MEMORY OF MAJOR ROBERT GREGORY" and "A PRAYER FOR MY DAUGHTER." But in this instance the wind moves Yeats to reflection rather than vision. The wind's swirling confusion seems

to prompt by association the observation that the world ("everything outside us") is "Mad as the mist and snow," especially in comparison to the mental keenness of Yeats and his confabulator. The second and third stanzas function as qualifications, as Yeats realizes that his implicit distinction between keenness and madness is unsatisfactory. The madness of the mist and snow represents the helter-skelter of the world—"Hodos Chameliontos" as Yeats calls it in AUTOBIOGRAPHIES—but also the impetuousness and energy of youth (second stanza) and the austere passion of the great artist or thinker (third stanza). As applied to Cicero and Homer in the final stanza, madness connotes not confusion but inspired frenzy and defiant energy, as it does in the Crazy Jane poems and in "Why should not Old Men be Mad?" This is the frenzy that Yeats explicitly courts in "An ACRE OF GRASS" and "The SPUR." The vagrant energy of "madness" is qualified, however, by the snow and the cold, which connote disciplined passion, stoic wisdom, and tragic joy. In the final instance of the refrain, "mist and snow" shifts into relation with the "aboriginal ice" of "A General Introduction for my Work" (E&I 523; LE 213) and with the snows of "LAPIS LAZULI," "MERU," and "Vacillation" (section VI).

The refrain of "Mad as the Mist and Snow" prefaces the sequence's final phase, in which "Tom the Lunatic" emerges as a masculine counterpart to Crazy Jane. He is not named in "Those Dancing Days are Gone" and "'I am of Ireland,'" but presumably he figures in these poems. In "Those Dancing Days are Gone," an old man sings of time's ruin with a rapturous sense of self-expansion and unity conveyed by the refrain. Like the Chinamen of "Lapis Lazuli," though unequal to the stillness of their self-possession, he has attained the condition of tragic joy. As Yeats writes in a note to *The Winding Stair and Other Poems* (1933), "'I am of Ireland'" was "developed from three or four lines of an Irish fourteenth-century dance song somebody repeated to me a few years ago" (VP 830). Richard Ellmann identifies Frank O'Connor (1903–66) as the "somebody" who introduced Yeats to the song (IY 280). In Yeats's rendition, a "solitary man" hears the call of the mystical female voice. This is the call of Ireland, as in CATHLEEN NI HOULIHAN, but also the fairy call, as in early poems like "The Hosting of the Sidhe," *The Land of Heart's Desire*, "The Song of Wandering Aengus," "The Unappeasable Host," and "The Wanderings of Oisin." The man hesitates, as it is getting late ("time runs on"), but then considers the imperfection of the earthly dance ("The fiddlers are all thumbs," etc.). He cocks a "malicious eye" and repeats that "time runs on," this time with a different and more significant meaning: struck by the banality of the mundane, he suddenly looks forward to the destructive course of time (hence "malicious"). Jogged by his own mention of the trumpet, he may more specifically look forward to the Day of Judgment (introduced as a motif in "Crazy Jane on the Day of Judgment").

"The Dancer at Cruachan and Cro-Patrick" envisions a dancer ecstatically celebrating "One that is perfect or at peace." The speaker of the poem is an "Irish saint," as clarified by Yeats's introduction to Shri Purohit Swami's *An Indian Monk: His Life and Adventures* (1932). There Yeats refers to "those Irish monks who made innumerable poems about bird and beast, and spread the doctrine that Christ was the most beautiful of men. Some Irish saint, whose name I have forgotten, sang 'There is one among the beasts that is perfect, one among the fish, one perfect among men'" (*E&I* 431; *LE* 133; see also *E&I* 291). The saint and the lunatic, however, are clearly paired by the dance and by the locale of Cruachan (see "Tom at Cruachan") as figures of the same type: celebrants of the wholeness of the body and world. If its perspective is Christian, the poem represents a sharp revision of the Bishop's Christianity. While the Bishop denigrates the body and the natural world in "Crazy Jane and the Bishop," the dancer celebrates both. The pairing of Cruachan and Cro-Patrick, moreover, suggests the dancer's reconciliation of paganism and Christianity in the manner of Ribh. Cruachan is a hill in County Roscommon said to be the ancient seat of the kings and queens of Connacht and the burial place of Queen Maeve; as Yeats gives its name, the hill is pronounced "kro'ken" (*YD* 40; *Place Names* 38–39). Cro-Patrick is a mountain in County Mayo where St. Patrick (ca. 390–ca. 461) is said to have prayed and fasted, and from its summit to have cast out the snakes of Ireland (*YD* 39–40; *Place Names* 38). Cruachan has pagan connotations, then, while Cro-Patrick has Christian connotations.

"Tom the Lunatic" explains the theology behind the dancer's religious ecstasy. In a vision of doubt or despair, Tom sees nature extinguished and his fellow vagabonds and roisterers in the death shroud. Quickly recovering his spiritual composure, he reaffirms his faith that every man and beast exists in the unchanging eye of God (cf. "Crazy Jane on God"). The pairing of mare and stallion, cock and hen (the cock, as T. R. Henn observes, possesses "the gift of unwearied vitality in copulation"), and the emphasis on the "vigour" of the blood, suggest that God's eye brings into being not the abstract reality of the Bishop, but the pulsing, lusting world of Crazy Jane (*Lonely Tower* 237). "Tom at Cruachan" places Tom on the storied hill, and thus identifies him with the celebrant of "The Dancer at Cruachan and Cro-Patrick." Carrying forward the image of stallion and mare from the previous poem, it places the eternal and temporal on a footing of equality and mutual dependence. By structural analogy, it affirms Crazy Jane's conviction that "Fair and foul are near of kin, / And fair needs foul" and disavows the bishop's antithesis of "heavenly mansion" and "foul sty." "Old Tom Again" shares with "Tom the Lunatic" and "Tom at Cruachan" the conviction that the world reposes and originates in the divine. In its metaphor of the wind-blown ship, which picks up the allusion to sailors in "Crazy Jane Reproved," the poem asserts that the world emerges from "perfection" and remains driven by something of this perfection. "Nor shall the self-begotten fail" further suggests that the world drives toward some purpose, the fulfillment of some task at which it is theoretically possible to fail. "Self-begotten" suggests divine agency, for Yeats recurrently associates self-generation with divinity or miracle, as in "Among School Children" ("self-born mockers of man's enterprise") and "Byzantium" ("flames begotten of flame"). In a marvelous gesture of confidence, the poem calls "fantastic" not those who believe in the power of such divinity, but those who believe in the material bounds of birth and death represented by "Building-yard and stormy shore, / Winding-sheet and swaddling-clothes."

"The Delphic Oracle upon Plotinus," like "News for the Delphic Oracle," derives from a passage in Porphyry's (232/4–ca. 305) biographical essay *On the Life of Plotinus and the Arrangement of his Work.* After Plotinus died in A.D. 270, his disciple, Amelius of Tuscany, asked the oracle at Delphi where the soul of his master had gone. The oracle replied that Plotinus resided "where fragrant breezes play, where all is unison and winning tenderness and guileless joy, and the place is lavish of the nectar-streams the unfailing Gods bestow, with the blandishments of the Loves, and delicious airs, and tranquil sky: where Minos and Rhadamanthus dwell, great brethren of the golden race of mighty Zeus; where dwell the Just Aeacus, and Plato, consecrated power, and stately Pythagoras and all else that form the Choir of Immortal Love, that share their parentage with the most blessed spirits, there where the heart is ever lifted in joyous festival" (*Enneads* 16–17). The sons of Europa and Zeus, Minos and Rhadamanthus hark back to "Crazy Jane Reproved"; they were made judges of the souls of the dead in recognition of their virtuous lives (*Greek Myths* 121). In its shift from rustic Ireland to ancient Greece, from Crazy Jane and Tom the Lunatic to the sages of ancient philosophy, "The Delphic Oracle upon Plotinus" is a startling conclusion to a sequence otherwise relatively consistent in tone and matter. Like many poems in "Word for Music Perhaps," it responds to the poem that precedes it. In this instance the sailing "out of perfection" in "Old Tom Again" becomes a sailing—or a swimming—toward perfection. The "salt blood" that blocks the eyes of Plotinus is the complicating detail. It is part of the obscuring veil of time to which "Crazy Jane on the Day of Judgment" refers, but it also represents the pulse and vigor of the body in which the entire sequence finds the substance of its religion. It does not go too far to see an implicit analogy between the great sages and the likes of Jane and Tom. In one way or another, all of these ponderers of the human condition struggle amid the buffetings of the sea, richly immersed in their own experience, goaded by a vision of something beyond.

In 1938, Yeats wrote a final poem in the voice of Crazy Jane, "Crazy Jane on the Mountain," which first appeared untitled in ON THE BOILER (see *LE* 243). Uncharacteristically alluding to the world of affairs, Crazy Jane leaves off cursing the Bishop and derides George V for passively allowing his "cousins"—Czar Nicholas II and his family—to be murdered by the Bolsheviks in 1918 (for Yeats's reaction to this event, see *Expl.* 442–443; *LE* 242–243; *LOP* 171–172). The poem implicitly compares the limp will and murderous banality of the modern world ("the best lack all conviction" in the words of "The SECOND COMING") to the fierce purity of the ancients represented by CUCHULAIN and Emer, whom Crazy Jane sees pass in mystic procession. She kisses the stone in homage to the legendary figures (cf. the penultimate stanza of "The DOUBLE VISION OF MICHAEL ROBARTES"), for the stone is of their nature, and she weeps in the dirt for all that has been lost.

FIRST PUBLICATION: "Words for Music Perhaps" first appeared as a sequence in *Words for Music Perhaps and Other Poems,* The CUALA PRESS, Dublin, November 14, 1932. It did not include "Crazy Jane Talks with the Bishop," which was inserted as the sixth poem when the sequence was republished in *The Winding Stair and Other Poems,* Macmillan, London, September 19, 1933. "Three Things" previously appeared in the *New Republic* (periodical), October 2, 1929, and in *Three Things,* Faber and Faber, London, October 9, 1929. "Girl's Song," "Young Man's Song," "Her Dream," "His Bargain," "Her Anxiety," "His Confidence," and "Love's Loneliness" previously appeared in the *New Republic,* October 22, 1930. "Those Dancing Days are Gone" (under the title "A Song for Music"), "Love's Loneliness," "Her Dream," "His Bargain," "Crazy Jane grown old looks at the Dancers" (under the title "Crazy Jane and the Dancers"), "Crazy Jane and the Bishop," and "Crazy Jane Reproved" previously appeared in the *London Mercury* (periodical), November, 1930. "Those Dancing Days are Gone" (under the title "A Song for Music"), "Crazy Jane and the Bishop" (under the title "Cracked Mary and the Bishop"), "Crazy Jane grown old looks at the Dancers" (under the title "Cracked Mary and the Dancers"), and "Crazy Jane Reproved (under the title "Cracked Mary Reproved") previously appeared in the *New Republic,* November 12, 1930.

"Lullaby" previously appeared in *The New Keep-sake*, Cobden-Sanderson, London, November 1931 (anthology).

BIBLIOGRAPHY

Conner, Lester I. *A Yeats Dictionary: Persons and Places in the Poetry of William Butler Yeats*; Ellmann, Richard. *The Identity of Yeats*, *Yeats: The Man and the Masks*; Foster, R. F. *W. B. Yeats: A Life, II: The Arch-Poet*; Graves, Robert. *The Greek Myths*; Henn, T. R. *The Lonely Tower: Studies in the Poetry of W. B. Yeats*; Jeffares, A. Norman. *W. B. Yeats: Man and Poet*; Kelly, John S. *A W. B. Yeats Chronology*; Kenner, Hugh. *A Colder Eye: The Modern Irish Writers*; McGarry, James P. *Place Names in the Writings of William Butler Yeats*; Plotinus, *The Enneads*; Saddle-myer, Ann. *Becoming George: The Life of Mrs W. B. Yeats*; Unterecker, John. *A Reader's Guide to William Butler Yeats*; Wade, Allan. *A Bibliography of the Writings of W. B. Yeats*; Yeats, W. B. *Autobiographies*, *A Critical Edition of Yeats's A Vision (1925)*, *Essays and Introductions*, *Explorations*, *Later Essays*, *The Letters of W. B. Yeats*, *Letters on Poetry from W. B. Yeats to Dorothy Wellesley*, *The Variorum Edition of the Plays of W. B. Yeats*, *The Variorum Edition of the Poems of W. B. Yeats*, *A Vision*.

"Young Man's Song"

See "WORDS FOR MUSIC PERHAPS."

THE COMPLETE PLAYS
AND DRAMATIC POEMS

At the Hawk's Well (1917)

This one-act play, which tells of the youthful CUCH-ULAIN's disastrous quest for immortality, is notable in several respects: as Yeats's first experiment with the mask as a central device of his drama (a "mask will enable me to substitute for the face of some commonplace player, or for that face repainted to suit his own vulgar fancy, the fine invention of a sculptor"); as his first thoroughgoing homage to the Japanese Noh drama; and as his first exercise in creating a drama for performance in the well-heeled drawing room in keeping with his middle-aged turn toward ideals of aristocratic tradition and ceremony (*E&I* 226). In "Certain Noble Plays of Japan," an introduction to EZRA POUND's transla-tions of Noh drama from the notes of the American Orientalist Ernest Fenollosa (1853–1908), Yeats trumpets the breakthrough of *At the Hawk's Well*: "I have written a little play that can be played in a room for so little money that forty or fifty readers of poetry can pay the price. There will be no scenery, for three musicians, whose seeming sunburned faces will, I hope, suggest that they have wandered from village to village in some country of our dreams, can describe place and weather, and at moments action and accompany it all by drum and gong or flute and dulcimer. Instead of the players working themselves into a violence of passion indecorous in our sitting-room, the music, the beauty of form and voice all come to climax in pantomimic dance." Yeats was moved to boast, "I have invented a form of drama, distinguished, indirect, and symbolic, and having no need of mob or Press to pay its way—an aristocratic form" (221). A letter to JOHN QUINN written on the morning of the play's debut fur-ther elaborates the rationale of the drawing-room ethic: "I hope to create a form of drama which may delight the best minds of my time, and all the more because it can pay its expenses without the others [i.e. without a public audience]. If when the play is perfectly performed (musicians are the devil) Bal-four and Sargent and Ricketts and STURGE MOORE and [Augustus] John and the Prime Minister and a few pretty ladies will come to see it, I shall have a success that would have pleased SOPHOCLES. No press, no photographs in the papers, no crowd. I

shall be happier than Sophocles. I shall be as lucky as a Japanese dramatic poet at the Court of the Shogun" (*Letters* 610; see also *VPl.* 415–419).

In conformity with Yeats's newly articulated principles, *At the Hawk's Well* was first performed on April 2, 1916, at 20 Cavendish Square, the Lon-don home of Lady "Emerald" Cunard. Two days later it was performed at 8 Chesterfield Gardens, the home of Lady Islington, to benefit the Union for Women and Girls, which provided dinners for factory girls and munitions workers (*AP* 40; *VPl.* 416). Attendees of the latter performance included Queen Alexandra, Princess Victoria, the grand duchess George of Russia, the princess of Monaco, the ranee of Sarawak, the Spanish ambassador, Margot Asquith, the duchess of Marlborough, and Lady Randolph Churchill, as well as T. S. ELIOT and Ezra Pound (*AP* 39; *YC* 184). The perfor-mances featured music for bamboo pipes, zither, drums, and gong composed by the artist Edmund Dulac (1882–1953), who performed on drums and gong (*AP* 38). The versatile Dulac also created the simple stage props and masks (see *VPl.* 416, 1305). In "Certain Noble Plays of Japan" Yeats calls Dulac's mask of Cuchulain a "noble, half-Greek, half-Asiatic face" that will make its wearer seem "like an image seen in reverie by some Orphic wor-shipper" (*E&I* 221), and in his letter to Quinn he compares it to an "archaic Greek statue" (*Letters* 610). Further adding to the production's modernist exoticism, the Japanese dancer Michio Ito, whom Lady Cunard had introduced as a London drawing room attraction and brought to Yeats's attention, danced in the role of the Guardian of the Well. A "disciple of Nijinsky and the *Ballet Russe*" who had studied dance in Paris and Germany, Ito was as removed from the authentic Noh drama as were Yeats and Pound themselves (*AP* 38–39; *Stone Cot-tage* 198–201). "Rather than bringing an authentic understanding of the Noh to Pound and Yeats," James Longenbach comments, "Itow confirmed their own Western expectations, making Yeats's *At the Hawk's Well* possible" (*Stone Cottage* 200). In "Certain Noble Plays of Japan," Yeats recounts that he had seen Ito dance in a studio, in a draw-ing room, and on a small, well-lit stage, but only in the studio and drawing room, in natural light, did Yeats perceive in Ito the "tragic image" that his imagination had long sought: "There, where no studied lighting, no stage-picture made an artificial world, he was able, as he rose from the floor, where he had been sitting cross-legged, or as he threw out an arm, to recede from us into some more powerful life. Because that separation was achieved by human means alone, he receded but to inhabit as it were the deeps of the mind" (*E&I* 224).

At the Hawk's Well belongs to a group of Noh-inspired plays that also includes The DREAMING OF THE BONES, The ONLY JEALOUSY OF EMER, and CALVARY. The plays were published as *Four Plays for Dancers* in 1921 and continue to appear under this heading in Yeats's collected plays. David R. Clark calls these plays the "anti-self" of naturalistic drama (*Desolate Reality* 122). *At the Hawk's Well* also belongs to a sequence of plays about the life of Cuchulain. In narrative order, the sequence consists of *At The Hawk's Well*, The GREEN HELMET, ON BAILE'S STRAND, The *Only Jealousy of Emer* (rewritten as FIGHTING THE WAVES), and The DEATH OF CUCHULAIN. The play initiates many of the sequence's themes and plot elements. In particular, it introduces Aoife (pronounced ee' fa), who later becomes Cuchulain's lover and the mother of his son, and it establishes the curse that comes to fruition in *On Baile's Strand* (*YD* 8). Reg Skene describes the play as an "initiation ceremony in which Cuchulain accepts his hawk nature, his tragic destiny and the heroic commitment on which that destiny is based" (*Cuchulain Plays* 143).

More broadly, the play belongs to a category of plays and poems that explore the human cost of *antithetical* aspiration, the desire for something more than the comforts of house and hearth, cows and dogs and children (as the final song of *At the Hawk's Well* styles the life of natural contentment). Albeit in the ignorance and arrogance of youth, Cuchulain chooses the self-withering path of the transcendental seeker and accordingly suffers the curse of Fergus in "FERGUS AND THE DRUID," of the wanderer in "The MAN WHO DREAMED OF FAERYLAND," of Mongan in "HE THINKS OF HIS PAST GREATNESS WHEN A PART OF THE CONSTELLATIONS OF HEAVEN," of MACGREGOR MATHERS in "ALL SOULS' NIGHT"—the fate that Yeats himself eschews in "TO THE ROSE UPON THE ROOD OF TIME." Unlike Fergus, Cuchulain is a man of action in no danger of losing touch with himself or the world, but, having gazed into the "unmoistened eyes" of the Woman of the Sidhe, he can know nothing further of natural contentment. MAUD GONNE inevitably informs Yeats's conception of the Woman of the Sidhe, the merest sight of whom is enough to vex an entire life. Gonne surmised her own entwinement with the hawk after Yeats sent her a précis of the play in 1916: "I did not feel at all surprised when you told me about the Hawk influence—I always knew it in a vague way that you & I are both connected with a hawk. It has been my symbol which I designated in a certain occult work—& I think it has been in several of the visions we have had together [. . .]" (*GY* 370). The play's premise of the hawk-guarded mountain may have been inspired by Ben Bulben, a mountain just north of SLIGO that was "famous for hawks" (*Myth.* 88, 90).

According to Birgit Bjersby, the plot of *At the Hawk's Well* has no precedent in the legends of Cuchulain (*Interpretation of the Cuchulain Legend* 39). She proposes the Irish legend of Connla's Well as a plausible inspiration, and mentions as possible sources the chapter titled "Nuts of Knowledge" in Standish James O'Grady's *History of Ireland* (vol. 1, 1878); William Carleton's tale "Tubber Derg, or The Red Well," which Yeats included in his 1889 volume *Stories from Carleton*; and GEORGE RUSSELL's (AE) poem "Connla's Well," which Yeats included in his 1895 volume *A Book of Irish Verse Selected from Modern Writers* and commends in his 1897 article "Three Irish Poets" (*UP2* 71–72). Bjersby notes that the motif of the pilgrimage to a well guarded by a "venerable figure" closely corresponds to a vision of Connla's Well that Yeats and his fellow initiates of the HERMETIC ORDER OF THE GOLDEN DAWN evoked (*Interpretation of the Cuchulain Legend* 42–44; see also MM 123–125). J. M. SYNGE's play *The Well of the Saints*, a tale involving a fountain of youth, may also have lent itself to Yeats's imagination, according to Bjersby. Harold Bloom, on the other hand, discerns the influence of WILLIAM MORRIS's prose romance *The Well at the World's End* (1896), which Yeats reviewed (*UP1*

418) and mentions in "The Happiest of the Poets," his 1903 essay on Morris (*Yeats* 294–296; see also *Interpretation of the Cuchulain Legend* 44). Yeats reprises the theme of the miraculous well in the play The CAT AND THE MOON.

DRAMATIS PERSONAE: Three Musicians (their faces made up to resemble masks); The Guardian of the Well (with face made up to resemble a mask); An Old Man (wearing a mask); A Young Man (wearing a mask).

FIRST PERFORMANCE: 20 Cavendish Square, London, April 2, 1916 (see above).

FIRST PUBLICATION: *Harper's Bazaar* (periodical), March 1917. Reprinted in *The Wild Swans At Coole*, CUALA PRESS, Churchtown, Dundrum, November 17, 1917.

SYNOPSIS

The scene is laid in the "Irish Heroic Age." A bare stage fronts a patterned screen, with gong and zither to the rear. Three musicians enter and unfold a black cloth embroidered with the image of a hawk. Singing, they call to the mind's eye a "man climbing up to a place / The salt sea wind has swept bare." The Guardian of the Well, a girl, enters and crouches beside a blue cloth representing the well. The musicians fold the black cloth while describing, in alternations of song and speech, the windswept, withered, twilit mountainside; the guardian's weariness with the task of keeping the well free of leaves; and the approach of a bent old man. He scolds the Guardian for her silence and complains that the Sidhe might have chosen a more companionable guardian. He is struck by an unusual quality in her silence and observes that she had the same "glassy look about the eyes / Last time it happened." Cuchulain, a young man in golden attire, enters. He has come from "an ancient house beyond the sea" in search of a well said to impart immortal life. The Old Man points to the well, but Cuchulain sees no water. The Old Man asks mockingly, "And do you think so great a gift is found / By no more toil than spreading out a sail, / And climbing a steep hill?" He has waited 50 years for the "secret moment," known only to the "holy shades / That dance upon the desolate mountain," when the immortalizing waters fleetingly material-

ize. Fancying himself lucky in all things, Cuchulain pledges to wait. The Old Man orders him away, insisting that the place belongs only to himself, the Guardian, and the "deceivers of men" (i.e., the Sidhe). Cuchulain is taken aback by the Old Man's enmity toward the dancers whom "all others bless." The Old Man tells how the dancers have cheated him: Three times he has awoken from a sudden sleep to find the stones wet.

The Guardian gives the cry of the hawk. Cuchulain scans the sky for the "great gray hawk" that had attacked him as he climbed to the well, but he sees nothing. The cry was not from a hawk, says the Old Man, but from the Woman of the Sidhe, the "mountain witch, the unappeasable shadow" who is "always flitting upon this mountain-side, / To allure or destroy." All who gaze "in her unmoistened eyes" are cursed: one is doomed in love, or one's children are killed, or one goes mad and kills one's own children—a foreshadowing of *On Baile's Strand*. The Guardian again cries like a hawk. The Old Man realizes that the Woman of the Sidhe possesses her body. Her shivering signals the coming of the water. Fearful that Cuchulain will take what is rightfully his, he orders him away; after bickering they agree to share the water. Cuchulain makes the mistake of glancing at the Guardian and attracting her notice. She rises and throws off her cloak; her dress suggests the plumage of a hawk. The Old Man covers his head, unable to bear her eyes, which are "not of this world," but Cuchulain, unafraid, vows to sit by the well until he has grown immortal like herself. The Guardian begins to dance in the manner of a hawk. The Old Man sinks into sleep, while Cuchulain falls under the spell of the dance. Maddened, he staggers to his feet and tauntingly cries, "Run where you will, Grey Bird, you shall be perched upon my wrist." The First Musician hears water splash. Cuchulain indifferently turns to look and follows the Guardian offstage. The Old Man creeps to the well only to find the stones wet and the basin empty. Cuchulain returns having lost sight of the Guardian and recovered his senses. The Old Man cries in exasperation that Cuchulain has been lured from the fountain at the crucial moment. He warns Cuchulain that the Woman of the Sidhe has summoned the warrior queen Aoife and her troop to take his life. Full of heroic spirit, the young man goes to the fight. As they unfold and refold the cloth, the musicians praise domesticity in opposition to the "obscurity of strife" and "bitter life" of unnatural aspiration.

BIBLIOGRAPHY

Bjersby, Birgit. *The Interpretation of the Cuchulain Legend in the Works of W. B. Yeats*; Bloom, Harold. *Yeats*; Clark, David R., with Rosalind Clark, *W. B. Yeats and the Theatre of Desolate Reality*; Conner, Lester I. *A Yeats Dictionary: Persons and Places in the Poetry of William Butler Yeats*; Ellmann, Richard. *Yeats: The Man and the Masks*; Foster, R. F. *W. B. Yeats: A Life, II: The Arch-Poet*; Kelley, John S. *A W. B. Yeats Chronology*; Longenbach, James. *Stone Cottage: Pound, Yeats, and Modernism*; Skene, Reg. *The Cuchulain Plays of W. B. Yeats: A Study*; Yeats, W. B. *Essays and Introductions, The Gonne-Yeats Letters 1893–1938, The Letters of W. B. Yeats, Mythologies, Uncollected Prose by W. B. Yeats* (vols. 1–2), *The Variorum Edition of the Plays of W. B. Yeats*.

Calvary (1921)

Like T. S. ELIOT's "The Journey of the Magi" (1927), *Calvary* is an ironic consideration of the resentment aroused by the burden of the Christian message. In Yeats's conception, this message impinges on the freedom and self-sufficiency of the world and the world naturally tries to throw off its new yoke (*VPl.* 789). Lazarus and Judas betray Christ not because they doubt his divinity, but because they are convinced of it. They object to any order, divine or otherwise, external to their own motives, while the Roman guards find an ironic satisfaction in the wanton play of a universe governed (or ungoverned) by chance. In a note to *Four Plays for Dancers* (1921), Yeats comments that Lazarus and Judas are "types of that intellectual despair" that lay beyond Christ's sympathy, while the Roman soldiers represent "a form of objectivity that lay beyond His help" (790).

Lazarus and Judas, however, represent opposite poles—the one subjective, the other objective—of the deicidal impulse (this explains away what might otherwise seem the redundancy of the two figures). Lazarus opposes Christ in fidelity to his own dreaming wisdom. His image is the heron—content with his own "savage heart," absorbed by his own image in the water, crazed by the full moon—of which the musicians sing. In his note to the play, Yeats explains this avian symbolism and heralds the doctrines of *A VISION*: "[Such] lonely birds as the heron, hawk, eagle, and swan, are the natural symbols of subjectivity, especially when floating upon the wind alone or alighting upon some pool or river, while the beasts that run upon the ground, especially those that run in packs, are the natural symbols of objective man. Objective men, however personally alone, are never alone in their thought, which is always developed in agreement or in conflict with the thought of others and always seeks the welfare of some cause or institution, while subjective men are the more lonely the more they are true to type, seeking always that which is unique or personal. I have used my bird-symbolism in these songs to increase the objective loneliness of Christ by contrasting it with a loneliness, opposite in kind, that unlike His can be, whether joyous or sorrowful, sufficient to itself. I have surrounded Him with images of those He cannot save, not only with birds, who have served neither God nor Caesar, and await none or for a different savior, but with Lazarus and Judas and the Roman soldiers for whom He has died in vain" (*VPl.* 790; on the origins of this important note in GEORGE YEATS's automatic script, see *Making of Yeats's 'A Vision'*, II, 400). Anticipating this formulation, the 1895 story "The Old Men of the Twilight" (*Myth.* 191–195) similarly opposes the subjectivity of the heron and the objectivity of Christianity, while *The KING'S THRESHOLD* and *WHERE THERE IS NOTHING* associate the arch-subjective figures of Seanchan the Bard and Paul Ruttledge with the image of the crane in the moonlight (*VPl.* 263, 1152).

Lazarus, meanwhile, is a realization of the personality type belonging to Phase 26 of the lunar cycle, the phase of the "Hunchback." As Yeats postulates in *A Vision*, the deformity that marks a man of this phase "may be of any kind, great or little, for it is but symbolised in the hump that thwarts what seems the ambition of a Caesar or of an Achilles." Such a man "commits crimes, not because he wants to [. . .] but because he wants to feel certain that he can; and he is full of malice because, finding no impulse but in his own ambition, he is made jealous by the impulse of others. He is all emphasis, and the greater that emphasis the more does he show himself incapable of emotion, the more does he display his sterility. If he live amid a theologically minded people, his greatest temptation may be to defy God, to become a Judas, who betrays, not for thirty pieces of silver, but that he may call himself creator" (177–178).

Calvary's plot device derives from OSCAR WILDE's story "The Doer of Good" (1894). In AUTOBIOGRAPHIES, Yeats recalls the substance of the story as an actor friend first relayed it to him: "Christ came from a white plain to a purple city, and as He passed through the first street He heard voices overhead, and saw a young man lying drunk upon a window-sill. 'Why do you waste your soul in drunkenness?' He said. 'Lord, I was a leper and You healed me, what else can I do?' A little further through the town He saw a young man following a harlot, and said, 'Why do you dissolve your soul in debauchery?' and the young man answered, 'Lord, I was blind, and You healed me, what else can I do?' At last in the middle of the city He saw an old man crouching, weeping upon the ground, and when He asked why he wept, the old man answered, "Lord, I was dead, and You raised me into life, what else can I do but weep?"" (224). Yeats adds that the published version of the story was ruined by the "verbal decoration" characteristic of the era and that its "terrible beauty" returns to him only when he remembers the words of the actor.

The play belongs to a group of plays inspired by the Japanese Noh drama that includes AT THE HAWK'S WELL, The DREAMING OF THE BONES, and The ONLY JEALOUSY OF EMER. They were published as *Four Plays for Dancers* in 1921 and continue to appear under this heading in Yeats's collected plays. In keeping with Noh convention, the plays employ masks and extremely simple stage settings, making them suitable for performance "in a drawing-room or in a studio" (*VPl*. 566). In his 1916 essay "Certain Noble Plays of Japan," an introduction to Pound's

volume of translations, Yeats boasted, "I have invented a form of drama, distinguished, indirect, and symbolic, and having no need of mob or Press to pay its way—an aristocratic form" (*E&I* 221).

DRAMATIS PERSONAE: Three Musicians, their faces made up to resemble masks; Christ, wearing a mask; Lazarus, wearing a mask; Judas, wearing a mask; Three Roman Soldiers, their faces masked or made up to resemble masks.

FIRST PERFORMANCE: The play was not performed during Yeats's lifetime.

FIRST PUBLICATION: *Four Plays for Dancers*, Macmillan, London, October 28, 1921.

SYNOPSIS

The three musicians fold and unfold the ceremonial cloth as they sing of the "moon-crazed heron" entranced by its own reflection in the stream, with the refrain that "God has not died for the white heron." The First Musician narrates as Christ enters carrying a cross. It is Good Friday, the day "whereon Christ dreams His passion through." Christ ascends Calvary "as a dreamer climbs," while the "cross that but exists because He Dreams it, / Shortens His breath and wears away His strength." A surly crowd mocks his pretensions to divinity. Lazarus enters, and the crowd shrinks from him, terrified by his "deathly" face. Lazarus announces that he is the man who has died and been resurrected by Christ. Aggrieved to have been woken from the comfort of his death, to have been dragged like a rabbit from its hole, Lazarus rebukes Christ for blinding "with light the solitude / That death has made. . . ." He bids Christ to Calvary and departs in search of a tomb amid the "desert places where there is nothing / But howling wind and solitary birds." Martha and "the three Marys" gather around Christ, showering him with tears and cleaning his feet with their hair. Upon the entry of Judas all flee as though in terror. Judas unashamedly announces himself as Christ's betrayer. Christ is puzzled that Judas should doubt his divinity after witnessing his miracles. Judas responds that he recognized Christ's divinity from the first. His treachery was an attempt to free himself from his divine power: "I could not bear to think you had but to whistle / And I must do. . . ." Having committed the ultimate sin, Judas revels in his existential self-liberation: "And now / Is there a secret left I do not know / Knowing that if a man betrays a God / He is the stronger of the two?" Christ counters that his treachery "was decreed that hour / When the foundations of the world were laid." His treachery may have been fated, says Judas, but it was not fated that he, Judas, should be the betrayer, nor that he should do the deed for "thirty pieces and no more, no less, / And neither with a nod nor a sent message, / But with a kiss upon your cheek." Judas holds up the cross while Christ stands before it as if crucified. Three Roman soldiers enter. They are disciples of chance, old gamblers who amiably exempt themselves from the intentionality of Christ's order, desiring nothing from Christ beyond the amusement of dicing for his cloak once he is dead. The Second Soldier tells Christ, "Whatever happens is the best, we say, / So that it's unexpected," while the First Soldier tells him, "They say you're good and that you made the world, / But it's no matter." The Soldiers dance the "dance of the dice-throwers," in which they quarrel and settle the dispute by throwing dice and join "hand to hand and wheel about the cross." The Roman Soldier says that Christ would know this dance if he were the "God of dice" but "he is not that God." Genuinely horrified by what amounts to a vision of his own negation, Christ cries out "My Father, why hast Thou forsaken Me?" The Musicians fold and unfold the cloth as they sing of the sea-bird, ger-eagle, and cygnet, each sufficient to itself. As their refrain has it, "God has not appeared to the birds."

BIBLIOGRAPHY

Harper, George Mills. *The Making of Yeats's 'A Vision': A Study of the Automatic Script* (vol. 2); W. B. Yeats, *Autobiographies, Essays and Introductions, Mythologies, The Variorum Edition of the Plays of W. B. Yeats, A Vision.*

Cat and the Moon, The (1924)

This one-act comedy tells the story of two beggars, one blind, one lame, who visit a sacred well in order to be cured of their debilities. It did not appear in print until 1924, though it was dated 1917 in its first edition. As Yeats explains in a note to *The Cat and the Moon and Certain Poems* (1924), the play was originally intended for inclusion in *Four Plays for Dancers* (1921), but he judged that it was "in a different mood" and decided to omit it from the volume, which wound up including the more overtly Noh-influenced plays AT THE HAWK'S WELL, The DREAMING OF THE BONES, The ONLY JEALOUSY OF EMER, and CALVARY (VPl. 805). In 1934, the play appeared in *Wheels and Butterflies*, a second volume of "Plays for Dancers," and it continues to appear under the heading of "Wheels and Butterflies" in some editions of Yeats's collected plays (see for example *Plays*).

The play harks back to the peasant comedy of *The POT OF BROTH*, but its humor is complicated by an interspersion of symbolism related to the philosophy of "The PHASES OF THE MOON" and *A VISION*. As Yeats writes in his 1924 note, "Minnaloushe and the Moon were perhaps—it all grows faint to me—an exposition of man's relation to what I called the Antithetical Tincture, and when the Saint mounts upon the back of the Lame Beggar he personifies a certain great spiritual event which may take place when Primary Tincture, as I have called it, supersedes Antithetical [. . .]" (VPl. 805). By "antithetical tincture" and "primary tincture," Yeats means opposing modes of being that respectively represent revelry in the self and subservience to the world (the *antithetical* tincture is described in "The Phases of the Moon," lines 31–100, the *primary* in lines 100–116; see also *A Vision*). In the play, the Blind Beggar represents the *antithetical* tincture, while the Lame Beggar, clearly ascendant in his new blessedness, represents the *primary*. The climactic *primary* phases of the lunar cycle (phases 26, 27, and 28) entail a "great spiritual event" in the sense that Hunchback, Saint, and Fool approach absorption in God (see VPl. 807; "The Phases of the Moon," lines 119–123).

The play includes three songs about the cat "Minnaloushe," whose "animal blood" is troubled by the "pure cold light of the moon." These songs appear as a single poem, "The Cat and the Moon," in *Nine Poems* (1918) and in *The Wild Swans at*

Coole (1919). In a note to *Wheels and Butterflies* (1934), Yeats writes that he allowed himself "to think of the cat as the normal man and of the moon as the opposite he seeks perpetually, or as having any meaning I have conferred upon the moon elsewhere. Doubtless, too, when the lame man takes the saint upon his back, the normal man has become one with that opposite [. . .]" (*VPl.* 807). Minnaloushe was no poetic contrivance, but a family pet belonging to ISEULT GONNE. A lover of names for their own sake—one thinks of Beauvarlet, Callimachus, MOHINI CHATTERJEE, Empedocles, Guidobaldo, Petronius Arbiter, Montashigi—Yeats could hardly have resisted mentioning such a fancifully endowed cat. Minnaloushe also figures in the prologue to PER AMICA SILENTIA LUNAE. The gamboling cat had disrupted a certain conversation between himself and Iseult, Yeats remembers, and upon returning from Normandy to London he felt the need to set down all that he "had said or would have said" (*LE* 1).

"The holy well of Saint Colman," as the Blind Beggar calls it, was a local landmark not far from THOOR BALLYLEE and COOLE PARK. According to James P. McGarry, the well "is in the townland of Corker in Kiltartan where the Saint was born and was placed under an ash tree by his mother. She was in hiding at the time and wanted to baptise the child, but there was no water nearby. However, a fountain miraculously gushed forth under the shelter of the tree" (*Place Names* 78). The *Catholic Encyclopedia* (1913–14) relates that St. Colman (ca. 560–632) "lived for many years as a hermit in Arranmore, where he built two churches, both forming the present group of ruins at Kilmurvy. Thence he sought greater seclusion in the woods of Burren, in 592, and at length, in 610, founded a monastery, which became the centre of the tribal Diocese of Aidhne, practically coextensive with the present See of Kilmacduagh" (Vol. 4, 114). Yeats elaborates on the well in his introduction to *Wheels and Butterflies*: "A couple of miles as the crow flies from my Galway house is a blessed well. Some thirty years ago the Gaelic League organised some kind of procession or 'pattern' there, somebody else put a roof over it, somebody else was cured of a lame leg or a blind eye or the falling

sickness. There are many offerings at the well-side left by sufferers; I seem to remember bits of cloth torn perhaps from a dress, hairpins, and little pious pictures. The tradition is that centuries ago a blind man and a lame man dreamed that somewhere in Ireland a well would cure them and set out to find it, the lame man on the blind man's back" (*VPl.* 806–807; see also 279, 805).

Lending the play an element of playful malice, the Blind Beggar's tale of the "holy man in the big house at Laban" who knocks about the roads with an "old lecher from the county of Mayo" caricatures GEORGE MOORE and EDWARD MARTYN, who were, as Yeats writes in AUTOBIOGRAPHIES, "in certain characteristics typical peasants, the peasant sinner, peasant saint" (300; see also *VPl.* 808). Moore's family had been landowners in Mayo; as Yeats explains in *Autobiographies*, Laban is a townland (in Galway) where Martyn went to chapel (300). The Blind Beggar points to these mismatched companions as evidence that "the bigger the sinner the better pleased is the saint." It may be that the Blind Beggar and the Lame Beggar are themselves to some extent caricatures of Moore and Martyn. Yeats undoubtedly sought a degree of revenge for the flippant portrayal of himself and Lady GREGORY in *Vale* (1914), the final volume of Moore's memoir *Hail and Farewell*.

DRAMATIS PERSONAE: A Blind Beggar; a Lame Beggar; Three Musicians. Their faces are made up to resemble masks.

FIRST PERFORMANCE: Produced by the Dublin Drama League at the ABBEY THEATRE, Dublin, May 9 and 10, 1926.

FIRST PUBLICATION: The *Criterion* (periodical) and the *Dial* (periodical) July 1924. Reprinted in *The Cat and the Moon and Certain Poems*, CUALA PRESS, Dublin, July 1924.

SYNOPSIS

The scene is laid on a bare stage before a patterned screen showing St. Colman's Well. The three musicians, with zither, drum, and flute, sit to the rear. The First Musician sings of Minnaloushe (see above). The Blind Beggar enters with the Lame Beggar on his back. The Blind Beggar counts the paces, having been told that it was just over 1,000 paces to the holy well of Saint Colman. At 1,009 paces, the well has not come into view. The Blind Beggar accuses the Lame Beggar of losing the way; the Lame Beggar accuses the Blind Beggar of taking short strides. Continuing, the beggars circle the stage while the First Musician sings again of Minnaloushe. The beggars stop at the ash tree that marks the well. They have come to be cured of their maladies. Having second thoughts, the Blind Beggar remarks that blindness is a great advantage to a beggar, but the Lame Beggar reminds him of the disadvantages. They poach only half as much as they could otherwise; furthermore—in a satire of *primary* moral reasoning—"poor men" often steal from him and thus expose themselves to the perils of purgatory. The Lame Beggar hopes to see the saint himself, a "grander thing" than having his legs restored, and he worries that they are "without an Ave or a Paternoster to put before the prayer or after the prayer." The Blind Beggar suggests that the saint would be better pleased if they did not know a prayer. "What pleasure can he have in all that holy company kneeling at his well on holidays and Sunday, and they as innocent maybe as himself?" he asks. The Blind Beggar reminds him of the holy man in the big house at Laban. He knocks about with an old lecher who tells his sins as the holy man tries to "head him off and quiet him down that he may quit telling them." The Blind Beggar proposes that the holy man "wouldn't have him different, no, not if he was to get all Ireland," for the "bigger the sinner the better pleased is the saint." The Lame Beggar reiterates that the saint "has a great liking maybe for Latin," and the Blind Beggar, out of patience, tries to hit him with his stick.

The beggars immediately kneel as the First Musician intones in the voice of the saint, "Will you be cured or will you be blessed?" The Blind Beggar chooses to be cured. The saint pleads with him to reconsider: "I am a saint and lonely. Will you become blessed and stay blind and we will be together always?" Apologetically, the Blind Beggar persists in his desire to be cured, as he is continuously robbed. The Lame Beggar claims that "it's all in his head" and complains that the Blind Beggar has nagged him all day, suspecting that he stole his sheep. The Blind Beggar explains that the other's

sheepskin coat put the idea into his head, though he admits that his sheep was black, while the Lame Beggar says his coat is white. The First Musician then asks the Lame Beggar whether he would be cured or blessed. The Lame Beggar wants to know whether there is really a book of the blessed, and whether his name would appear in the book. The Lame Beggar decides it would be an even "grander thing" to have his name in the book than to have the use of his legs and decides to be blessed. The First Musician proclaims the Blind Beggar cured and the Lame Beggar blessed. No longer blind, the Beggar glances over the scene, but does not see the saint. The Lame Beggar says that he is directly before them. The Blind Beggar sees that the Lame Beggar's coat is black after all. Ignoring the Lame Beggar's new state of blessedness, he delivers a beating (in the form of a dance) and exits. The Lame Beggar must stop him before he rouses the country against him. The First Musician climbs upon his back (or says he has done so—no such stage direction is given). Miraculously, the Lame Beggar feels no weight. The First Musician commands the Lame Beggar to bless the road by dancing. The Lame Beggar dances, clumsily at first and then nimbly. He exits dancing. The First Musician again sings of Minnaloushe, who "lifts to the changing moon / His changing eyes."

BIBLIOGRAPHY

Herbermann, Charles G., et al., eds. *The Catholic Encyclopedia: An International Work of Reference on the Constitution, Doctrine, Discipline, and History of the Catholic Church*; McGarry, James P. *Place Names in the Writings of William Butler Yeats*; Yeats, W. B. *Autobiographies, Later Essays, The Plays, The Variorum Edition of the Plays of W. B. Yeats*.

Cathleen ni Houlihan (1902)

One of Yeats's most overtly nationalistic statements, *Cathleen ni Houlihan* is a version of *The LAND OF HEART'S DESIRE* in which the hearth-shattering call of Mother Ireland substitutes for the hearth-shattering call of the fairy world. Both plays emphasize the small-mindedness of rural life and dramatize the allure of some more ardent possibility. In a *Samhain* article of 1903, Yeats cannot conceal his worry that the play crosses the line that distinguishes art from propaganda, and he somewhat hair-splittingly tries to exonerate himself: "I am a Nationalist, and certain of my intimate friends have made Irish politics the business of their lives, and this made certain thoughts habitual with me, and an accident made these thoughts take fire in such a way that I could give them dramatic expression. I had a very vivid dream one night, and I made *Cathleen ni Houlihan* out of this dream. But if some external necessity had forced me to write nothing but drama with an obviously patriotic intention, instead of letting my work shape itself under the casual impulses of dreams and daily thoughts, I would have lost, in a short time, the power to write movingly upon any theme" (*Expl.* 116; *IDM* 33; see also *Expl.* 199; *IDM* 92; on Yeats's dream, see *VPl.* 232). In a 1904 memorandum he provided to Horace Plunkett (who not incidentally was assisting the ABBEY THEATRE with its patent application), Yeats denied that *Cathleen ni Houlihan* "is a political play of a propagandist kind," but his tone is defensive: "I took a piece of human life, thoughts that men had felt, hopes they had died for, and I put this into what I believe to be sincere dramatic form. I have never written a play to advocate any kind of opinion and I think that such a play would be necessarily bad art, or at any rate a very humble kind of art. At the same time I feel that I have no right to exclude for myself or for others, any of the passionate material of drama" (*CL3* 623). All the same, Yeats was not above invoking the play to bolster his credibility in nationalist circles. At the public debate on J. M. SYNGE's *Playboy of the Western World* held on February 4, 1907, Yeats attempted to outflank his adversaries by declaring at the outset, "The author of *Cathleen ni Houlihan* addresses you." Mary Colum recalls that the audience "forgot its antagonism for a few moments and Yeats got his cheers" (*W. B. Yeats* 220). The writer Stephen Gwynn, for one, came away asking himself whether "such plays should be produced unless one was prepared for people to go out to shoot and be shot" (*Irish Literature and Drama* 159). George

Bernard Shaw had much the same reaction, telling Lady GREGORY, "When I see that play I feel it might lead a man to do something foolish" (*Seventy Years* 444). Toward the end of his life, Yeats had his own pangs of anxiety on this count, asking in "The MAN AND THE ECHO," "Did that play of mine send out / Certain men the English shot?"

In *AUTOBIOGRAPHIES*, Yeats asserts that *Cathleen ni Houlihan* was the first Irish play in which "dialect was not used with an exclusively comic intention," and he acknowledges that Lady Gregory helped him render the speech of the country people (*Aut.* 332; see also *VPl.* 232). Gregory evidently considered herself the primary author of the play and bore a certain quiet grudge that her contribution was not fully acknowledged. On July 18, 1925, she entered in her diary: "I see in a list of Yeats plays *Unicorn* as before and *Pot of Broth* now—put as 'written with Lady Gregory.' Rather hard on me not giving my name with *Kathleen ni Houlihan* that I wrote all but all of" (*Lady Gregory's Journals*, II, 28; see also 13, 527). R. F. Foster observes that the play "bears the hallmark of the other plays Gregory came to write. It is straightforward, rather heavy-handed, reliant on predictable dramatic by-play, and—for all its mechanical construction—dramatically very powerful. It is also directly propagandistic, on the lines of the article 'Felons of Our Land', which she had published in the *Cornhill* the year before" (*AM* 249).

With its rousing patriotic theme and accessible language, *Cathleen ni Houlihan* was bound to be popular. Following the play's initial three-day run, Yeats wrote to Lady Gregory that the play had elicited "continual applause" and that crowds had been turned away at the doors each night (*CL3* 167). In 1925, speaking of his plays to Lady Gregory, Yeats said, "I have never made one in sympathy with my audience except *Kathleen ni Houlihan*. And that was you and a dream" (*Lady Gregory's Journals*, II, 13). When Yeats visited Stockholm to receive the NOBEL PRIZE in 1923, it was *Cathleen ni Houlihan* that was performed in his honor (*Aut.* 407–408).

In the play's debut production, MAUD GONNE (who as a young woman had contemplated an acting career) performed the role of Cathleen with what Yeats called "weird power" (*Aut.* 332; *CL3*

167). In 1908 he remembered that Gonne "played very finely, and her great height made Cathleen seem a divine being fallen into our mortal infirmity" (*VPl*. 233). Yeats may be suspected of exaggerating the "weird power" of Gonne, but Gwynn concurs that her "impersonation had stirred the audience as I have never seen another audience stirred," and William Fay (1872–1947), who co-directed the play and acted the part of Peter Gillane, remembers Gonne as the "living embodiment of Kathleen" (*Irish Literature and Drama* 159; *Abbey Theatre: Interviews and Recollections* 16). Yeats had desperately wanted Gonne to play the role of Cathleen, which she had in some sense inspired. But as she recalls in her autobiography (1938), Gonne had sworn off acting as a distraction from her political work. In the end they struck a bargain: Gonne agreed to perform on the condition that the play be produced under the auspices of Inghinidhe na hÉireann ("Daughters of Ireland"), the nationalist woman's organization that she had founded in 1900 (*SQ* 176–7; see also *GY* 176–8). When the play opened, Gonne's biographer reports, "the banner of Inghinidhe—a golden sunburst on a blue background—was displayed in all its glory" (*Maud Gonne* 73).

The play is set against the backdrop of the Insurrection of 1798. It alludes to the French expeditionary force under General Humbert that landed at Killala, a seaside village in north Mayo, on August 22, 1798. The French enlisted approximately 3,000 local volunteers and defeated government forces at Castlebar, but they were forced to surrender on September 8. The government accepted the French surrender but massacred some 2,000 of the Irish volunteers (*Oxford Companion to Irish History* 251–252).

Yeats also takes up the theme of *Cathleen ni Houlihan* in his story "Hanrahan and Cathleen, the Daughter of Houlihan" (see STORIES OF RED HANRAHAN) and in his poem "Red Hanrahan's Song about Ireland" (an extract from the story). In 1945, according to A. Norman Jeffares, Gonne declared this her favorite among Yeats's poems (*New Biography* 88). Something of the theme reemerges in "SEPTEMBER 1913": "Yet could we turn the years again, / And call those exiles as they were / In all

their loneliness and pain, / You'd cry, 'Some woman's yellow hair / Has maddened every mother's son. . . .'"

DRAMATIS PERSONAE: Peter Gillane; Michael Gillane, his son, going to be married; Patrick Gillane, a lad of 12, Michael's brother; Bridget Gillane, Peter's wife; Delia Cahel, engaged to Michael; the Poor Old Woman; neighbors.

FIRST PERFORMANCE: Produced by W. G. Fay's Irish National Dramatic Company at St. Teresa's Hall, Dublin, April 2, 1902.

FIRST PUBLICATION: *Samhain* (periodical), October 1902. Reprinted in *Cathleen ni Hoolihan*, A. H. Bullen, London, October 1902. Yeats altered the spelling from "Hoolihan" to "Houlihan" when he reprinted the play in *The Hour-Glass, Cathleen Ni Houlihan, The Pot of Broth: Being Volume Two of Plays for an Irish Theatre*, A.H. Bullen, London, March 1904.

SYNOPSIS

The scene is a cottage near Killala in 1798. Bridget unwraps a parcel while Peter and Patrick relax by the fire. There is cheering in the distance; the family wonders whether there is a hurling match. The parcel laid open, Peter and Bridget remark on the fineness of Michael's wedding clothes: the family has come up in the world. Patrick notices an old woman who comes down the road and turns toward a neighboring property. He recalls gossip about a "strange woman that goes through the country whatever time there's war or trouble coming." Michael returns to the cottage with Delia's dowry of 100 pounds. Peter plans to use the money, for which he bargained aggressively, to expand the farm. The family congratulates itself on the excellent match. Delia is beautiful and of good family, and she has not claimed any of the dowry for her own use. They again hear the mysterious cheering and send Patrick to investigate. Michael spots the same old woman coming toward the house. She enters and announces that she has long traveled the roads. The family asks what set her wandering. Allegorizing the essential political grievance of Ireland, she answers that strangers have overrun her house and stolen her "four beautiful green fields"

The old woman sings of yellow-haired Donough, who went to the gallows for love of her. Many have died for her, she says, and there are "some that will die to-morrow." Nervously suspecting that the woman is from "beyond the world," Bridget urges Peter to give her a "few pence or a shilling itself" to "bring her on her way." Reluctantly he offers a shilling, but the old woman does not want mere silver. "If any would give me help he must give me himself, he must give me all," she says. "Good friends" are gathering to reclaim her house and fields, and she must go to welcome them. Michael offers to accompany her, but Bridget, mindful of the wedding on the next day, scolds him for forgetting his responsibilities. The old woman identifies herself as "Cathleen, the daughter of Houlihan," a name that Peter believes he once heard in a song. Michael asks what help he can give. Those who help her, she warns, risk health, home, and life, though for all that they will "think they are well paid." As she exits, she can be heard singing from outside that those who help her shall be remembered forever. Michael is entranced. Bridget says that he "has the look of a man that has got the touch" and tries to recall his attention to the wedding clothes. Michael can only ask, "What wedding are you talking of?" They hear cheering once more. Delia, Patrick, and neighbors burst into the cottage. Patrick excitedly announces that French ships have arrived in the bay and that the boys of the town are rushing down the hillside to join the cause. Delia begs Michael not to leave, but he hears the old woman's voice outside and rushes from the cottage. Peter asks Patrick whether he had seen an old woman on the path. Patrick says that he had seen only a "young girl, and she had the walk of a queen."

BIBLIOGRAPHY

Connolly, S. J., ed. *The Oxford Companion to Irish History*; Foster, R. F. *W. B. Yeats: A Life, I: The Apprentice Mage*; Gonne, Maud. *The Autobiography of Maud Gonne: A Servant of the Queen*; Gregory, Lady. *Lady Gregory's Journals* (vol. 2, ed. Daniel J. Murphy), *Seventy Years: Being the Autobiography of Lady Gregory*; Gwynn, Stephen. *Irish Literature and Drama in the English Language: A Short History*; Hone, Joseph. *W. B. Yeats*; Jeffares, A. Norman. *W. B. Yeats: A New Biography*; Mikhail, E. H., ed. *The Abbey Theatre: Interviews and Recollections*; Ward, Margaret. *Maud Gonne: A Life*; Yeats, W. B. *Autobiographies, The Collected Letters of W. B. Yeats* (vol. 3), *Explorations, The Gonne-Yeats Letters 1893–1938, The Irish Dramatic Movement, The Variorum Edition of the Plays of W. B. Yeats*.

Countess Cathleen, The (1892)

Yeats's impassioned poetic drama was the first play staged by the IRISH LITERARY THEATRE and thus can be considered the inaugural play of the Irish dramatic movement. The play presents a version of the Faustian bargain in which the peasants of a rural neighborhood barter their souls for food during a period of famine; the compassionate Countess Cathleen then barters her own soul in order to redeem theirs. The play, as Yeats writes in his 1934 introduction to *Letters to the New Island*, began as a reaction against the examples of SHELLEY's *The Cenci* and TENNYSON's *Becket*, which were "deliberately oratorical; instead of creating drama in the mood of 'The Lotos-Eaters' or of *Epipsychidion* they had tried to escape their characteristics, had thought of the theatre as outside the general movement of literature." In the attempt to restore drama to literature, Yeats set himself the task of writing *The Countess Cathleen* while "avoiding every oratorical phrase or cadence" (*Letters to the New Island* 3–4; see also VPl. 212). David R. Clark observes in the play a broader attempt "to settle the relative claims of art, love, patriotism, and belief; to find a way of uniting these by fusing Irish paganism, traditional Christianity and an aesthetic faith in the occult symbols of artist mystics; and thus to present a united front to materialism" (*Desolate Reality* 129).

The play is based on a story by the Irish author John Augustus O'Shea (1839–1905) that appeared in the *Shamrock*, a weekly journal of Irish history, literature, and the arts, on October 6, 1867. As Yeats attests, O'Shea's story had been "drifting about the Irish Press ever since" (CL2 539, 653–654; VPl. 170). Yeats reprinted the story in his

Fairy and Folk Tales of the Irish Peasantry (1888) on the assumption that it was indigenous to Irish folklore, though he acknowledged that he had been unable "to find out the original source" (*Fairy and Folk Tales of Ireland* 211). In September 1892, after Yeats's play had appeared in print, O'Shea revealed in a letter to a London newspaper that his tale was merely a translation of a French story set in Ireland—"Les Marchands d'âmes" by Léo Lespés (1815–75)—and that he had taken the liberty of renaming the heroine, Ketty O'Donnor, after himself (*CL2* 653–654). Yeats reprints "Les Marchands d'âmes," which first appeared in Lespé's *Les Matinées de Timothée Trim* (Paris, 1865), in his notes to the play (see *VPl.* 170–173).

Yeats began the play in February 1889 soon after meeting MAUD GONNE. She was looking for a "play that she could act in Dublin," and Yeats desperately wanted to please her (*Mem.* 41; see also *CL1* 142, 145, 148, 154). Though the proposed collaboration never came to be, Yeats dedicated the play to Gonne, "at whose suggestion it was planned out and begun some three years ago" (*VPl.* 2). Yeats recalls telling Gonne after reading her the play for the first time that he had "come to understand the tale of a woman selling her soul to buy food for a starving people as a symbol of all souls who lose their peace, or their fineness, or any beauty of the spirit in political service, but chiefly of her soul that had seemed so incapable of rest" (*Mem.* 47). Yeats reiterates the association between the countess and Gonne in "The CIRCUS ANIMALS' DESERTION," in which (on one reading) he describes the play as a comforting dream of Gonne softened into saintliness. At the very least, the countess takes account of Gonne's heroic stature and her bond with the peasantry (see "HER PRAISE" and "The PEOPLE"). Cathleen's tender dismissal of the lovesick poet Aleel thus assumes an obvious autobiographical dimension. In this light, one of the play's most interesting (and possibly self-serving) details is Cathleen's explanation of the couple's emotional impasse: "not you / But I am the empty pitcher."

Already possessing a germinal notion of what he would later call "antinomies," Yeats conceived the play as the converse of his poem "The WANDERINGS OF OISIN," which he had published three years

earlier. The play, Yeats wrote in his introduction to *The Countess Kathleen and Various Legends and Lyrics* (1892), "is an attempt to mingle personal thought and feeling with the beliefs and customs of Christian Ireland; whereas the longest poem in my earlier book [i.e., "Oisin"] endeavoured to set forth the impress left on my imagination by the Pre-Christian cycle of legends. The Christian cycle being mainly concerned with contending moods and moral motives needed, I thought, a dramatic vehicle. The tumultuous and heroic Pagan cycle, on the other hand, having to do with vast and shadowy activities and with great impersonal emotions, expressed itself naturally—or so I imagined—in epic and epic-lyric measures" (*VPl.* 1288).

Yeats was initially delighted with the play as both written (*CL1* 172) and staged (*CL2* 409, 412). Later he took a dimmer view. In AUTOBIOGRAPHIES he writes that the play "was ill-constructed, the dialogue turning aside at the lure of word or metaphor, very different, I hope, from the play as it is to-day after many alterations, every alteration tested by performance. It was not, nor is it now, more than a piece of tapestry. The Countess sells her soul, but she is not transformed. If I were to think out that scene to-day, she would, the moment her hand has signed, burst into loud laughter, mock at all she has held holy, horrify the peasants in the midst of their temptations. Nothing satisfied me but FLORENCE FARR's performance in the part of Aleel [in the debut production]. Dublin talked of it for years, and after five-and-thirty years I keep among my unforgettable memories the sense of coming disaster she put into the words: '. . . but now / Two grey horned owls hooted above our heads'" (309–310).

Yeats's revised the play even more thoroughly than was his custom, and could announce to LIONEL JOHNSON in January 1895 that he had "rewritten" the play (*CL1* 433). Yeats, in fact, wrote five distinct versions of the play, which respectively appeared in print in 1892, 1895, 1901, 1912, and 1919; it was the third version of the play that famously initiated the Irish Literary Theatre in 1899 (*Yeats the Playwright* 12–15). The trend of these revisions, as Clark observes, involved "the progressive reduction of the number of characters; the fusing of characters whose functions may be combined; the growing tendency to portray, not human inconsistency and idiosyncrasy, but passionate types; the growing prominence of Aleel [. . .]; the addition of the love scenes between Aleel and the Countess in order to motivate Aleel's centrality and to shift the whole center of the play from the traditional and outer toward the private and inner; the alteration of the final scene from supernaturalism based on naturalism to an elaborate and vague angelic show in which the objective world dissolves" (*Desolate Reality* 131). Peter Ure observes that the Countess began to some degree as a *persona* of Yeats himself but eventually became "much more like a heroic mask modelled from Maud Gonne's noble lineaments," and that the play gradually moved toward "some symbolic adumbration of Yeats's notions about Maud Gonne and about beautiful women who betray themselves by climbing on wagonettes to scream" (*Yeats the Playwright* 21). Aleel, meanwhile, evolved into "a complete and successful symbol of the subjective life," heralding the poet-lover-dreamers of Yeats's later verse and drama (24–25). In Yeats's own summary, the play began as a moral question as to whether a soul may "sacrifice itself for a good end," but in the process of revision philosophy gradually gave way to the expression of character (*Aut.* 346; *Mem.* 150). Whatever its lingering imperfections, the final version of the play has a grave beauty in places, as for example in Oona's closing lamentation that the "years like great black oxen tread the world, / And God the herdsman goads them on behind, / And I am broken by their passing feet."

The depiction of starving peasants bartering their souls for food aroused a storm of protest on both religious and nationalist grounds when the play was first produced by the Irish Literary Theatre in 1899 (for a comprehensive summary of the controversy, see *CL2* 669–674). EDWARD MARTYN, a scrupulous Catholic and one of the infant theater's founders, was so alarmed by the play's theology that he considered withdrawing his support for the venture. Yeats was able to reassure him only by having the play vetted by two respected ecclesiasts (*Aut.* 308–309; *CL2* 377–391; *Mem.* 119–120). Much of the controversy was stirred up by Frank Hugh O'Donnell (1848–1916), an editor

and former member of Parliament who penned an overheated pamphlet in rebuttal of the play titled *Souls for Gold! Pseudo-Celtic Drama in Dublin* (on O'Donnell, see *CL2* 707–712). "What a contemptible Ireland is the Ireland of Mr. W. B. Yeats's neo-Celtic fantastications!" O'Donnell howled in a representative passage. "Not an Irish man or woman in 'five-score baronies' to prefer Faith and Honour to a full belly in the Devil's Kitchen" (*CL2* 679; see also 408; for the full pamphlet, see 674–680). Cardinal Michael Logue (1839–1924)—"a dull, pious old man," according to Yeats—meanwhile penned a letter to the *Daily Nation* in which he admitted that he had not read the play but all the same admonished that "an Irish Catholic audience which could patiently sit out such a play must have sadly degenerated, both in religion and patriotism" (*Aut.* 308; *Mem.* 120; *CL2* 410–411). Responding in kind, Yeats reprimanded the cardinal for his "reckless indignation," which he called "part of that carelessness and indifference which the older generation in Ireland has too often shown in the discussion of intellectual issues" (*CL2* 410).

Fearing a riot, Yeats requested the presence of police on opening night (*Aut.* 309), but in the end there were mere interruptions and catcalls. On the following day, the *Freeman's Journal* gave an account of the ruction: "An audience of between 400 and 500 assembled to witness the presentation of *The Countess Cathleen*. A small organised knot of less than a dozen disorderly boys, who evidently mistook the whole moral significance of the play, cast ridicule upon themselves by hissing the demons under the impression that they were hissing the poet. But the audience, representative of every section of educated opinion in Dublin, was most enthusiastic, recalling the actors and the author again and again and cheering loudly" (*Ireland's Abbey Theatre* 9). Yeats presents his own account in *Autobiographies*: "Every disturbance was drowned by cheers. Arthur Griffith, afterwards slanderer of LANE and SYNGE, founder of the Sinn Fein Movement, first President of the Irish Free State, and at that time an enthusiastic anti-cleric, claimed to have brought 'a lot of men from the Quays and told them to applaud everything the Church would not like'. I did not want my play turned into an anti-clerical demonstration, and decided from the general feeling of discomfort when an evil peasant in my first act trampled upon a Catholic shrine that the disturbances were in part my own fault. In using what I considered traditional symbols I forgot that in Ireland they are not symbols but realities. But the attacks in the main, like those upon Synge and O'Casey, came from the public ignorance of literary method" (309). JAMES JOYCE attended the play's debut and vividly re-created the scene in *A Portrait of the Artist as a Young Man* (1916):

> [Stephen Dedalus] was alone at the side of the balcony, looking out of jaded eyes at the culture of Dublin in the stalls and at the tawdry scene-cloths and human dolls framed by the garish lamps of the stage. A burly policeman sweated behind him and seemed at every moment about to act. The catcalls and hisses and mocking cries ran in rude gusts round the hall from his scattered fellowstudents.
> —A libel on Ireland!
> —Made in Germany!
> —Blasphemy!
> —We never sold our faith!
> —No Irish woman ever did it!
> —We want no amateur atheists.
> —We want no budding Buddhists. (226)

On the following day, in Richard Ellmann's telling, several of Joyce's friends at University College, Dublin, "composed a letter of protest to the *Freeman's Journal* [published May 10], and it was left on a table in the college the next morning so that all who wished might sign it. Joyce was asked and refused" (*James Joyce* 67). Joyce later made lines from the play a motif of *Ulysses* (see "WHO GOES WITH FERGUS?").

In addition to inaugurating the Irish theatrical movement, the play and attendant controversy gave face to the cultural and religious opposition that would become not only a permanent hindrance but also a fecund theme for Yeats (see for example "The FISHERMAN," "ON THOSE THAT HATED 'THE PLAYBOY OF THE WESTERN WORLD', 1907," "TO A FRIEND WHOSE WORK HAS COME TO NOTHING," "TO A SHADE"). J. M. Synge's *In the Shadow of the Glenn* in 1903 (see AM 294–300)

and *The Playboy of the Western World* in 1907 (357–367) provoked further installments of the same fundamental dispute between an aestheticism divorced from politics and a Catholic nationalism wed to politics.

DRAMATIS PERSONAE: Shemus Rua, a peasant; Mary, his wife; Teigue, his son; Aleel, a poet; the Countess Cathleen; Oona, her foster-mother; two demons disguised as merchants; peasants, servants, angelical beings.

FIRST PERFORMANCE: Produced by the Irish Literary Theatre in the Antient Concert Rooms, Dublin, May 8, 1899. A copyright performance of the play was given at the Athenaeum Theatre, London, on May 6, 1892 (CL1 293, 295).

FIRST PUBLICATION: *The Countess Kathleen and Various Legends and Lyrics*, T. Fisher Unwin, London, September 1892. Yeats altered the spelling from "Kathleen" to "Cathleen" when he reprinted the play in *Poems*, T. Fisher Unwin, London, October 1895.

SYNOPSIS

Scene 1

The scene—which should "have the effect of missal painting"—is laid in a cottage in "old times." Mary and Teigue discuss the uncanny omens of recent days. Teigue, a boy of about 14, stands at the door and sees two owls with human faces. Mary cries, "Mother of God, defend us!" but Teigue wonders the good of praying when, as his father says, "God and the Mother of God have dropped asleep." Shemus returns to the cottage. He has spent the day foraging in the woods and begging by the road, but he has nothing to show for it. In nearby cottages he has seen the dead bodies of the starved. Cathleen, Oona, and Aleel arrive, having lost their way. Anguished by the family's poverty, Cathleen offers the little money she has left after a day of almsgiving and tells the family they shall have more if they come to her the next day. Cathleen and Oona depart for the castle, led by Mary. Disgruntled to have received so little from the countess and misanthropic in his poverty, Shemus summons the devils of the woods, proposing to "share and share alike." Mary pleads with him, but he cuffs her into silence. Two figures dressed as Eastern merchants enter, unroll a blanket on the floor, and lay out money from their purses. They present themselves as travelers "for the Master of all merchants" and offer to purchase the souls of Shemus, Teigue, and Mary. As part of the bargain, Shemus and Teigue must alert the entire neighborhood that the merchants are buying souls. Shemus and Teigue depart on this errand with a bag of money to prove their tale. Mary jeers at the merchants ("You shall at last dry like dry leaves and hang / Nailed like dead vermin to the doors of God") and then faints.

Scene 2

Cathleen, Oona, and Aleel rest in a wood, with a view of Cathleen's castle in the distance. Aleel tries to cheer the melancholy countess with stories and songs of Queen Maeve, while trading barbs with the stern and pious nurse. Cathleen's steward brings the news that peasants have invaded the garden and stolen a cartload of cabbage. Moved rather than angered, Cathleen quotes a learned theologian who holds that "starving men may take what's necessary, / And yet be sinless." Shemus and Teigue stumble upon the party, beside themselves with delight that something as insubstantial and useless as the soul has "grown a marketable thing." Horrified, Cathleen pledges to buy back their souls for 20 times the money, but Shemus and Teigue refuse to be helped, for "souls—if there are souls—/ But keep the flesh out of its merriment." Shemus and Teigue scamper away, and Cathleen orders Aleel and Oona to bring them back. Cathleen instructs her steward to sell all but her house and use the funds to purchase "herds of cattle" and "ships of meal." Aleel and Oona return. The poet has tussled with Shemus and Teigue and suffered a slight knife wound. Cathleen vows to make her home a refuge till the "walls burst and the roof fall on us" and to have nothing of her own.

Scene 3

The countess kneels before an altar in the oratory of her castle; she rises and goes into the hall. Aleel approaches and begs her to fly from castle until the "evil days are done," for an angel with "birds about his head"—or perhaps an "old god" as Cathleen thinks—came to him in a dream and warned that death awaits her. Cathleen is tempted by the vision of a enchanted idyll in Aleel's company, but she recalls her duty and vows that she will remain and pray until her heart has "grown to Heaven like a tree, and there / Rustled its leaves, till Heaven has saved my people." With due reticence, Aleel confesses his love. Cathleen acknowledges that poets are worthier than kings or queens, but insists that earthly love is not in her nature. She tells Aleel, "not you, / But I am the empty pitcher." She tenderly banishes the poet from her court with a kiss upon the forehead and returns to the oratory, where she falls asleep. The merchants sneak into the hall and rob the treasury. Rather than flee with the bags of treasure, they hatch a scheme to secure for the countess's soul. They wake her and present themselves as ordinary merchants. They bring spurious news that her cattle agent has fallen sick and her grain ships lie becalmed, and that only her pledged wealth keeps the peasants from bartering their souls. They speculate that her own soul would be worth "five hundred thousand crowns and more," before fleeing at the sound of voices and feet. Oona announces that the treasury has been robbed. The porter recollects that two owls whispering in human voices had passed.

Scene 4

A wood near the castle, as in scene 2. Four peasants pass, pondering the glittering beauty of gold. The two merchants silently follow. Aleel enters and admonishes his heart to be still, for its "sorrowful love can never be told."

Scene 5

Mary lies unconscious on her bed, surrounded by candles. The merchants congratulate themselves on their ruse: Word has spread that Cathleen has failed to bring relief, though her ships and cattle are actually within three days of arrival. Shemus and Teigue enter with a crowd of peasants. Shemus contemptuously exhibits his wife as one who "mocked" his masters and suffered the consequences. She would eat no food bought with their money, and tried to live on "nettles, dock, and dandelion." The merchants bargain for the souls of the peasants, but do not offer full price, as each soul is flawed by some petty sin. Aleel enters. He would part with his soul for nothing, being tired of it, but the merchants tell him that his soul belongs to Cathleen and he cannot give away what is not his. A relatively virtuous old woman receives 1,000 crowns for her soul, but screams in pain as she takes up the money. The peasants become afraid and demand the return of their souls. Cathleen enters and offers her soul for 500,000 crowns and the release of the souls that have already been sold. The merchants accept these terms but acknowledge that her sacrifice has already moved the peasants' hearts and effected the release of their souls. Cathleen signs her name and departs to disburse money among the peasants. The second merchant envisions years of vigil as they await Cathleen's death, but the first merchant says that her heart began to break when she signed her soul away, and that death is already upon her. He hears the "brazen door of hell move on its hinges, / And the eternal revelry float hither / To hearten us." Aleel perceives the open door as well and names the devil's minions—the traitors and malefactors of Irish legend—as they come forth. The peasants return with the unconscious countess and report that as they carried her they were beset by a terrible storm. Cathleen stirs, cries that the storm is dragging her away, and bids farewell to Oona and Aleel. She dies amid the blessings of the peasants. Aleel execrates "Time and Fate and Change" and longs for the "great hour" when they "shall plunge headlong through bottomless space." He sees angels and devils clashing in the air. There is darkness and then a "visionary light." All seem suddenly upon a mountain, at the feet of a legion of armed angels. Aleel seizes an angel and demands to know the fate of Cathleen. The angel says that "Mary of the seven times wounded heart / Has kissed her lips, and the long blessed hair / Has fallen on her face," with the explanation that "The Light of Lights / Looks always on the motive, not the deed / The Shadow of Shadows on the deed alone."

BIBLIOGRAPHY

Clark, David R., with Rosalind Clark. *W. B. Yeats and the Theatre of Desolate Reality* (expanded edition); Ellmann, Richard. *James Joyce*; Foster, R. F. *W. B. Yeats: A Life, I: The Apprentice Mage*; Joyce, James. *A Portrait of the Artist as a Young Man*; Robinson, Lennox. *Ireland's Abbey Theatre: A History, 1899–1951*; Ure, Peter. *Yeats the Playwright: A Commentary on the Character and Design in the Major Plays*; Yeats, W. B. *Autobiographies, The Collected Letters of W. B. Yeats* (vols. 1–2), (ed.) *Fairy and Folk Tales of Ireland, Letters to the New Island, Memoirs, The Variorum Edition of the Plays of W. B. Yeats*.

Death of Cuchulain, The (1939)

"I am writing a play on the death of CUCHULAIN, an episode or two from the old epic," Yeats told Ethel Mannin (1900–84) in October 1938. "My 'private philosophy' is there but there must be no sign of it; all must be like an old faery tale. It guides me to certain conclusions and gives me precision but I do not write it. To me all things are made of the conflict of two states of consciousness, beings or persons which die each other's life, live each other's death. This is true of life and death themselves" (*Letters* 917–918). Two days before he died, Yeats was busy with revisions to what had become *The Death of Cuchulain*, his last play and, with "UNDER BEN BULBEN," the last work to come under his pen (*Letters* 921–922; *LOP* 195). In the weeks before his death, Yeats read a draft of the play to DOROTHY WELLESLEY, who had come to visit him on his sickbed in Cap-Martin, France. "He was half sitting up on his bed, much excited," Wellesley recalls. "Almost his first words were: 'I want to read you my new play.' And this he did. In spite of the confusion of a much corrected manuscript, he read with great fire. [. . .] I was much moved, aware that it was in some sense a premonition of his own death, though I did not know it was to come so soon" (*LOP* 192).

The play brings to an ironical but not necessarily bitter end Yeats's dramatic sequence on the life and adventures of Cuchulain that he had begun nearly 40 years earlier. Arranged in narrative order, the sequence consists of AT THE HAWK'S WELL, *The* GREEN HELMET, ON BAILE'S STRAND, *The* ONLY JEALOUSY OF EMER (rewritten as FIGHTING

THE WAVES), and *The Death of Cuchulain*. Peter Ure calls it the "most majestically designed and the most perfect" of Yeats's plays on Cuchulain, and he credits Yeats with contriving "more explicitly than ever before, and with a bold disregard for the timider realisms which it is not absurd to compare with the methods of Shakespeare's last plays, the acting out of the ironies attendant upon the hero's nature and fate" (*Yeats the Playwright* 82). Helen Vendler, on the other hand, objects to the play's "obscurity and confusion," and can only consider it a "tentative final statement" rather than a "finished piece of work" (*Later Plays* 247). The play indeed has the occasional imperfections of a draft—a certain slackness in the dialogue between Eithne and Cuchulain, the clumsy pretext by which Aoife makes way for the Blind Man—but in its waning moments it rises to the valedictory occasion, ending with the beautiful and macabre spectacle of Emer dancing about the symbol of her husband's severed head, and with a final shaft of poetry in Yeats's most astringent late style.

In a December 1938 letter to Edith Shackleton Heald (1885–1976), Yeats mentioned that he had written a related lyric (*Letters* 921; see also *LOP* 193). The poem is the ironically titled "Cuchulain Comforted" (1939), which describes Cuchulain's arrival among the shades. "Convicted cowards all," the shades would have Cuchulain put off his arms and don a shroud as they do. The implication is that the hero must stand alone, beset by the mob, even in death, a theme shared with "ON THOSE THAT HATED 'THE PLAYBOY OF THE WESTERN WORLD', 1907."

DRAMATIS PERSONAE: Cuchulain; Eithne Inguba; Aoife; Emer; the Morrigu, goddess of war; an old man; a blind man; a servant; singer, piper and drummer.

FIRST PERFORMANCE: Produced by Austin Clarke's Lyric Theatre at the ABBEY THEATRE, Dublin, August 2, 1949.

FIRST PUBLICATION: *Last Poems and Two Plays*, The CUALA PRESS, Dublin, July 10, 1939.

SYNOPSIS

The scene is laid on a bare stage. A very old man "looking like something out of mythology"—a proxy for Yeats himself in his guise of wild age—opens the play with a lengthy harangue on the vileness of the modern age. The Old Man asserts that the play was written for an audience of only 50 or 100 like-minded people (in keeping with the principles of the new drama Yeats had announced in "Certain Noble Plays of Japan" [*E&I* 221–222] and in his preface to *At the Hawk's Well* [*VPl.* 415–417]). A larger audience, he says, would perforce include "people who are educating themselves out of the Book Societies and the like, sciolists all [i.e., dilettantes, smatterers], pickpockets and opinionated bitches." The Old Man says he had wanted the play to be full of dance, because "where there are no words there is less to spoil," but the age being what it is, he had not been able to find a suitably tragic dancer. He says that he "could have got such a dancer once, but she has gone; the tragic-comedian dancer, the tragic dancer, upon the same neck love and loathing, life and death." This pays tribute to Ninette de Valois (1898–2001), who had directed the Abbey Theatre's short-lived school of ballet and performed in productions of *Fighting the Waves* and *The KING OF THE GREAT CLOCK TOWER*. Disgusted, he cries, "I spit upon the dancers painted by Degas."

Eithne Inguba, Cuchulain's mistress, has come from Emer, his wife. She bears the message that he must take up arms even if it means his death, for "Connacht ruffians" led by Queen Maeve have burned his house at Muirthemne. Cuchulain, however, has already begun preparations for battle. He notices that Eithne Inguba holds a letter, but she does not know how it got into her hand. It contains Emer's actual message: His forces are outnumbered and he is not to strike until the following morning, when Conall Caernach will come with a "great host." Cuchulain prefers Eithne's "unwritten words" and pledges himself and his "handful" to the fight whatever the odds. The Morrigu enters, visible only to Eithne Inguba. A goddess with the head of a crow, she touches her black wing to Eithne's shoulder and suddenly Eithne understands what has happened. Maeve, once Cuchulain's lover, entranced her and sent her to deliver the false message. Cuchulain accuses her of trying to have him killed so she can take up with a younger man and in her excitement having forgotten the letter in her hand. Though innocent, she scorns Cuchulain for forgiving her perceived treachery. She takes this display of weakness as a sign that he is about to die. She declares that she will have herself murdered by his servants so her shade may greet his and "prove it no traitor." Cuchulain declares "I make the truth!" but heroic self-sanction has degenerated into mere rhetoric; in the next moment he authorizes his servant to test Eithne's veracity by giving her poppy juice. He instructs his servant to protect her life as if it were his own—another sign of his softened mettle—and that in the event of his death she is to be given to Conall Caernach, who is reputed to be a good lover.

The stage darkens and lights again, revealing Cuchulain with six mortal wounds. The warrior queen Aoife, who had been Cuchulain's lover (cf. *At the Hawk's Well* and *On Baile's Strand*), enters to take his life. Cuchulain asks to be tied to a stone so he may die on his feet. He recognizes Aoife, now an old woman, as she assists him. He assumes she was let through the ranks of Maeve's army because she has the right to kill him in vengeance for the death of their son (see *On Baile's Strand*), but she corrects him: His dead horse had sprung from a pool and made three circles about him, and none but she had dared approach. She binds his hands, fearing that his strength may return "when the time comes," though Cuchulain urges her not to spoil her beautiful veil. She asks about the death of their son and Cuchulain briefly relates the tale (see *On Baile's Strand*). She in turn recalls the battle that brought them together. He took her sword and threw her to the ground. That night she went in search of her conqueror and conceived a son. She hides as a man approaches, assuming he will flee when he finds himself alone with Cuchulain. It is the Blind Man, last seen in *On Baile's Strand*. He says that he accidentally wandered into Maeve's tent and was offered 12 pennies to bring Cuchulain's head; Cuchulain thinks 12 pennies good enough reason to take a man's life. He sees floating before him "a soft feathery shape," which is his soul's first shape and the shape he will have when he is dead (cf. *The Shadowy Waters*, in which departed souls likewise take the forms of birds). The Blind Man

asks whether he is ready. Cuchulain senses that the floating shape is about to sing.

The curtain falls and opens upon the Morrigu, who stands with a parallelogram, representing Cuchulain's head. Six further parallelograms, arranged near the backcloth, represent the six men who delivered the mortal wounds. The Morrigu describes each: one was a youthful looking man, another Maeve's latest lover, two were her valiant sons, two were of no account, creeping in only as Cuchulain was weakening. The Morrigu exits, leaving the head of Cuchulain. Emer enters, dancing as if raging at the heads of the six assailants. She seems about to prostrate herself before the head of Cuchulain when she hears a "few faint bird notes." The stage darkens slowly and there is music "of some Irish fair." The stage brightens to reveal three musicians in ragged street clothes. The street singer sings the words of the harlot to the beggar man. In a trysting place of her own mind or vision, she has lain with the ancient heroes, and she wonders what forces incarnate themselves in the pattern of history—the same question Yeats ponders in poems such as "A Bronze Head," "The Mother of God," "The Second Coming," "The Statues," "What Magic Drum?," and "Whence had They Come?" The mythic immanence, she proposes, is not remote, but startlingly active and present. Paraphrasing "The Statues," she asks, "What stood in the Post Office / With Pearse and Connolly?" (see Easter Rising). Cuchulain "seemed" to have been in the post office, as the rebels, it may be, wrought some ineffable and intangible presence into the image of their fantasy and desire. In a June 1938 letter to Shackleton Heald, Yeats explained "The Statues" in terms pertinent to the closely related final lines of *The Death of Cuchulain*: "Cuchulain is in the last stanza because Pearse and some of his followers had a cult of him. The Government has put a statue of Cuchulain [by Oliver Sheppard] in the rebuilt post office to commemorate this" (*Letters* 911).

BIBLIOGRAPHY

Ure, Peter. *Yeats the Playwright: A Commentary on the Character and Design in the Major Plays*; Vendler, Helen Hennessy. *Yeats's Vision and the Later Plays*;

Yeats, W. B. *Essays and Introductions*, *The Letters of W. B. Yeats*, *Letters on Poetry from W. B. Yeats to Dorothy Wellesley*, *The Variorum Edition of the Plays of W. B. Yeats*.

Deirdre (1907)

Though it predates Yeats's mature turn to modernist astringency and Noh-influenced minimalism, *Deirdre* remains a compelling piece. Set in a small house beset by shadowy assailants and surrounded by an enemy wood, the play is a remorselessly tightening construct of physical and metaphysical entrapment whose representative image is the net in which Naoise is finally caught. In this aspect the play recalls and validates Yeats's theory of tragedy: "Some Frenchman has said that farce is the struggle against a ridiculous object, comedy against a movable object, tragedy against an immovable; and because the will, or energy, is greatest in tragedy, tragedy is the more noble; but I add that 'will or energy is eternal delight', and when its limit is reached it may become a pure, aimless joy, though the man, the shade, still mourns his lost object" (*LE* 247; see also 213–214). Deirdre's final words—"Now strike the wire, and sing to it a while, / Knowing that all is happy . . ."—instance this "pure, aimless joy." In a November 1906 letter to FLORENCE FARR, Yeats extolled the play as "most powerful and even sensational" (*CL4* 518–519). Following the play's November debut at the ABBEY THEATRE, he told KATHARINE TYNAN that he considered it his best play, and he boasted that "the last half of it holds the audience in as strong a grip as does *Kathleen ni Houlihan*" (526). T. STURGE MOORE, for one, agreed with Yeats's estimate. In a fulsome and excited letter of congratulations, he told Yeats that if "adequately rendered" the play would "produce the effect of a religious mystery by the perfection of its seclusion from the world and the rare distinction of its self-decreed limitations." Furthermore, he detected in Yeats's verse a "new simplicity" (*WBY&TSM* 11).

The play tells of the young beauty Deirdre, who elopes with her lover, King Naoise (pronounced "Neesh-e," according to Yeats), only to be lured back into the clutches of her spurned suitor, the aged King Conchubar (pronounced "Conohar"), under the pretense that her betrayal has been forgiven. In a 1906 note to the play, Yeats describes Deirdre as "the Irish Helen, and Naisi her Paris, and Concobar her Menelaus" (*VPl.* 389; elsewhere Yeats calls Diarmuid and Grania "the Irish Paris and Helen"; see *UP2* 496). Fergus, who rounds out the play's central figures, is nothing like the world-spurning pursuer of "dreaming wisdom" Yeats depicts in "FERGUS AND THE DRUID"; here, as in the "old poems," he is a "mixture of chivalry and folly" who has been "tricked into abdicating his throne by Conchubar" (*VPl.* 389).

The play adapts an episode in the Red Branch cycle of Irish mythology that Yeats calls perhaps "the most famous of all Irish legends." It is based on Lady GREGORY's version of the tale in her 1902 volume *Cuchulain of Muirthemne* (389, 1284). Yeats considered Lady Gregory's the "best version," and he had taken an almost proprietary interest in its composition (see *CL3* 136, 141, 144–145). Yeats particularly urged Lady Gregory to incorporate something of Deirdre's children (which his play does not). "Deirdre is the normal, compassionate, wise house wife lifted into immortality by beauty & tragedy," he wrote in January 1902. "Her fealing [sic] for her lover is the fealing of the house wife for the man of the house. She would have been less beautiful, considering her type if she had not been fruitful" (144). Lady Gregory, in turn, helped Yeats with the composition of his play. In the 1930s, he told DOROTHY WELLESLEY that Lady Gregory had written the end of *Deirdre* on his "fundamental mass" (*LOP* 46).

Among the architects of the Irish Renaissance, not only Lady Gregory and Yeats but also GEORGE RUSSELL (AE) and J. M. SYNGE interpreted the legend of Deirdre. AE's *Deirdre* debuted on April 2, 1902, on a bill with Yeats's CATHLEEN NI HOULIHAN. Yeats at first hated the play as "superficial & sentimental," but he gradually warmed to it during performance (*CL3* 166–167). In AUTOBIOGRAPHIES, he calls the play a protest against his own *DIARMUID AND GRANIA*, which had "made men out of heroes," and dismissively comments that, although well constructed, "all its male characters resembled Lord TENNYSON's King Arthur" (331). Synge's *Deirdre of the Sorrows*, which might have been a "world-famous masterpiece," according to Yeats, was left unfinished upon his death on March 24, 1909 (325). The play was "pieced together," as R. F. Foster puts it, by Yeats, Lady Gregory, and Synge's fiancé, Molly Allgood (1887–1952), for performance on January 13, 1910, at the Abbey Theatre (AM 403).

DRAMATIS PERSONAE: Musicians; Fergus, an old man; Naoise, a young king; Deirdre, his queen; a dark-faced messenger; Conchubar, the old king of Ulad, who is still strong and vigorous; a dark-faced executioner.

FIRST PERFORMANCE: Produced by the National Theatre Society Ltd. (see IRISH NATIONAL THEATRE SOCIETY) at the Abbey Theatre, Dublin, November 24, 1906.

FIRST PUBLICATION: *The Poetical Works of William B. Yeats in Two Volumes*, Macmillan, New York, London, July 8, 1907.

SYNOPSIS

The scene is laid in a rough guest-house in a wood. Two women with musical instruments crouch by the fire. Having reconnoitered, the First Musician enters and informs the others that they have happened upon a house for travelers belonging to King Conchubar, and that the woods are those where Queen Deirdre was raised. She relates that some dozen years ago the king discovered a beautiful child being reared in the woods by an old witch. As the child grew into womanhood he became enamored. A month before Conchubar and Deirdre were at last to be married, the young king Naoise carried her off. The First Musician bids the others closer that she "may whisper the secrets of a king." She has come from Conchubar's house, where there are preparations for a festivity—but before she can say more she is interrupted by Fergus's arrival. Garrulous and benevolent, he explains that his diplomacy has convinced Conchubar to forgive Deirdre and Naoise, who are soon to cross this very threshold. The musicians doubt that an old man's jealousy can be so easily allayed. Fergus explains that the "need for some young, famous, popular man

/ To lead the troops, the murmur of the crowd, / And his own natural impulse, urged him to it." Dark and barbaric-looking men gather outside. The First Musician recognizes them as the kind of men whom "kings will gather for a murderous task," but Fergus smiles at her fears and imagines that they are merely foreign merchants. The First Musician tries to warn Fergus of the "murderous purpose" she ascertained while in Conchubar's house, but he will not hear the king slandered.

Deirdre and Naoise arrive. Deirdre is disheveled and pale. Naoise chides her for being afraid, but he himself wonders that there is no one to welcome them. Fergus assures them that the king sent no messenger only because he plans to come himself. Deirdre remains anxious, but Naoise affirms that the king "cannot break his faith." Naoise and Fergus go in search of a royal messenger, leaving the women alone. Deirdre confesses her fear that "love drowned and floating is but hate; / And that a king who hates sleeps ill at night / Till he has killed; and that, though the day laughs, / We shall be dead at cock-crow." The First Musician hints that the king plans to kill Naoise, and to claim her as his own. Deirdre begs her to tell what she knows. In Conchubar's house the First Musician saw a bridal bed with love-inducing stones wrested from the hearts and brains of Libyan dragons sewn into its embroidery. Deirdre summons Naoise. Even at the risk of death he is unwilling to break his pledge of trust to Conchubar, and she realizes that he too has had a premonition of death. Changing tactics suddenly, Deirdre declares that she has made herself beautiful in order to rouse Conchubar's desire, but that she "might change round again / Were we aboard our ship and on the sea." Naoise agrees to depart, but Fergus calls him a fool for heeding "crafty words." Changing tactics again, she asks Naoise whether they were not born to wander, to abide upon "windy summits." Fergus argues that their flight would unravel the peace that has been so laboriously established, and in any case they could not escape.

Deirdre proposes to disfigure herself, but Naoise commands her to "leave the gods' handiwork unblotched, and wait / For their decision, our decision is past." A messenger arrives: Fergus and Deirdre are summoned to the court, not so the "traitor that bore off the Queen." Finally acknowledging the king's betrayal, Fergus goes to muster allies who can convey the couple to their ships. Naoise proposes to hold off the king's soldiers as long as possible and then give Deirdre a "cleanly death" with his own blade, but he changes his mind: "What need is there / For all that ostentation at my setting?" They agree to await death in the calmness of love and resignation. They play chess while the musicians sing, but Deirdre cannot contain herself; kneeling at Naoise's feet, she recalls the first night of their love and implores "that old vehement, bewildering kiss." Conchubar appears at the door, but then disappears as Naoise fetches his spear and shield; full of disdain at the king's cowardice, Naoise goes in pursuit. Deirdre, meanwhile, takes a knife from the First Musician so she may "strike a blow for Naoise, / If Conchubar call the Libyans to his aid." Conchubar and his men enter, dragging Naoise in a net. The king pledges to release Naoise if Deirdre will enter his house of her own free will and show the people that he has "not taken her by force and guile." Deirdre agrees to this bargain, but Naoise would not have her buy his life with her body. Deirdre kneels before Conchubar and begs for his mercy. Unseen by her Naoise is gagged and dragged behind the curtain. The executioner emerges from behind the curtain with a bloody sword. Deirdre would throw herself upon Naoise, but checks herself. Adopting the role of the changeable female, she agrees to be Conchubar's queen only on the condition that she may lay out Naoise's body. Conchubar succumbs to her wiles and cajolery, and finally permits her to go behind the curtain. Fergus arrives with an army of "a thousand reaping-hooks and scythes" and demands the release of Naoise. Conchubar announces that he has arrived too late and bids the curtain be drawn. Naoise is dead—so too Deirdre. Outside there are shouts for Conchubar's death. The dark-faced men draw their swords and encircle the king. He waves them away superbly: "I have no need of weapons, / There's not a traitor that dare stop my way. / Howl, if you will; but I, being King, did right / In choosing her most fitting to be Queen, / And letting no boy lover take the sway."

BIBLIOGRAPHY

Foster, R. F. *W. B. Yeats: A Life, I: The Apprentice Mage*; Yeats, W. B. *Autobiographies, The Collected Letters of W. B. Yeats* (vols. 3–4), *Later Essays, Letters on Poetry from W. B. Yeats to Dorothy Wellesley, Uncollected Prose by W. B. Yeats* (vol. 2), *The Variorum Edition of the Plays of W. B. Yeats's, W. B. Yeats and T. Sturge Moore: Their Correspondence 1901–1937.*

Diarmuid and Grania (written 1899–1901, published 1951)

Yeats's first theatrical adaptation of material from Irish heroic legend was not published during his lifetime and with good reason. Though it has moments of dramatic intensity, the play is messily sprawling, overly intricate, and long-winded. Furthermore, in the words of novelist Violet Martin (1862–1915), it offers "a strange mix of saga and modern French situations" (AM 251). This incongruity is explained by the fact that the play was a collaboration between Yeats and GEORGE MOORE, an unlikely pairing given Moore's pedigree as a naturalist in the tradition of Émile Zola. In *Ave* (1911), the first installment of his autobiographical epic *Hail and Farewell*, Moore remembers that the seed of the collaboration was his incidental query as to whether Yeats knew the legend of Diarmuid and Grania: "He began to tell it to me in its many variants, surprising me with unexpected dramatic situations, at first sight contradictory and incoherent, but on closer scrutiny revealing a psychology in germ which it would interest me to unfold. A wonderful hour of literature that was, flowering into a resolution to write an heroic play together" (*Hail and Farewell* 203). The enterprise was governed by a "compact" according to which Yeats had jurisdiction over language and Moore over plot construction, but even so, there was much argument (see *Aut.* 322; CL2 460–461, 585–586). Both men left tart accounts of this collaboration, Moore in *Ave*, Yeats in AUTOBIOGRAPHIES. As proof that "two such literary lunatics" as Yeats and himself existed contemporaneously in Ireland, Moore recalls Yeats's plan for achieving a convincing Irish vernacular: Moore would write the play in French, Taidgh O'Donoghue (1874–1949) would translate the text into Irish, Lady GREGORY would translate the text back into English, and Yeats himself would provide final stylistic touches—like a *chef des sauces* applying gravy, as Moore's metaphor has it (*Hail and Farewell* 246–255, 312). Moore writes that he preserved his aborted manuscript in French to remind him "what a damned fool a clever man like Yeats can be when he is in the mood to be a fool" (255). For his part, Yeats gripes, "Because Moore thought that all drama should be about possible people set in their appropriate surroundings, because he was fundamentally a realist [. . .] he required many dull, numb words. But he put them in more often than not because had no feeling for words in themselves, none for their historical associations. He insisted for days upon calling the Fianna 'soldiers'" (*Aut.* 322).

The IRISH LITERARY THEATRE presented the play at the Gaiety Theatre, Dublin, on October 2, 1901—the first and only production during Yeats's lifetime. The play provoked objections on aesthetic grounds, moral grounds (having to do with Grania's infidelity), and political grounds (having to do with its production by a British company). Theater diarist Joseph Holloway (1861–1944) judged it a "beautiful piece full of weird suggestiveness, but lacking here and there in dramatic action." The "lackadaisical manner and eternal attitudinising" of Mrs. Benson in the role of Grania and the "erratic" lighting did not help matters. His verdict was "favourable if not enthusiastic" (*Joseph Holloway's Abbey Theatre* 14). In *Autobiographies*, Yeats fuzzily remembers the play as an opening-night success that unaccountably fizzled: "Theatre managers must have thought it failed, or that the newspapers' comments had taken freshness from it, for the London managers who had admired it in MS. were silent. Yet it did not seem to fail; when MAUD GONNE and I got into our cab to go to some supper party after the performance, the crowd from the gallery wanted to take the horse out of the cab and drag us there, but Maud Gonne, weary of public demonstrations, refused. What was it like? York Powell, Scandinavian scholar, historian, an impres-

sionable man, preferred it to Ibsen's *Vikings at Helgeland*. I do not know. I have but a draft of some unfinished scenes, and of the performance I can but recall Benson's athletic dignity [as Diarmuid] in one scene and the notes of the horn in Elgar's dirge over the dead Diarmuid" (326–327). More than likely, "the crowd from the gallery" had been stirred not by *Diarmuid and Grania*, but by the play that followed, Douglas Hyde's *Casadh an tSugain* (*The Twisting of the Rope*), which the Keating branch of the Gaelic League performed in Gaelic to great acclaim. Lennox Robinson recounts, "If the reception given to *Diarmuid and Grania* was lukewarm—when not definitely hostile—Dr. Hyde's play went with a swing from start to finish, thanks to its excellent plot and the author's [. . .] exuberant acting. Of course such ultra-Irish papers, the *Leader*, for instance, rejoiced in the Gaelic play's success in contrast to the English-acted one" (*Ireland's Abbey Theatre* 22).

In an introduction to the play upon its first publication in 1951, William Becker notes that the play was nearly lost to posterity. Following the play's first and only production in 1901, the "few complete typescripts used by the actors disappeared, leaving only a stack of haphazard manuscript notes and incomplete drafts among Yeats's private papers. Thus until the discovery of the typescript on which the present version is based, the play was commonly thought to be lost. This typescript [. . .] seems to have been Moore's and was given to its present owner by Lady Cunard shortly before her death" (*VPl.* 1169).

Yeats first dealt with the legend of Diarmuid and Grania in his early poem "A Faery Song" (1891), a song sung by the fairies over the lovers' grave. He also alludes to the legend in "HER COURAGE." In a note to "The VALLEY OF THE BLACK PIG," Yeats associates the apocalyptic black pig of his poem with the boar that kills Diarmuid. Yeats explains that the pig "seems to have been originally a genius of the corn, and, seemingly because the too great power of their divinity makes divine things dangerous to mortals, its flesh was forbidden to many eastern nations; but as the meaning of the prohibition was forgotten, abhorrence took the place of reverence, pigs and boars grew into types of evil, and were described as the enemies of the very gods they once typified [. . .]. The Pig would, therefore, become the Black Pig, a type of cold and of winter that awake in November, the old beginning of winter, to do battle with the summer, and with the fruit and leaves, and finally, as I suggest; and as I believe, for the purposes of poetry; of the darkness that will at last destroy the gods and the world" (VP 809–811).

Becker mentions that Lady Gregory provided the synopsis of the legend from which Yeats and Moore worked, though, as Moore tells, she objected to the project from the start, fearing that Moore's influence "might break up the mould" of Yeats's mind (VPl. 1169; *Hail and Farewell* 203–206). She later included a version of the tale, which derives from the Finn or "white" cycle of Irish mythology, in her *Gods and Fighting Men* (1904).

DRAMATIS PERSONAE: King Cormac, the high king; Finn MacCoole, the chief of the Fianna; Diarmuid, Goll, Usheen, Caoelte (his chief men); Conan the Bald, one of the Fianna; Niall, a head servant; Fergus, Fathna, Griffan (spearmen); Grania, the king's daughter; Laban, a druidess; an old man; a boy; a young man; a shepherd; the four troops of the Fianna; serving men.

FIRST PERFORMANCE: The Gaiety Theatre, Dublin, October 21, 1901. The play was produced by the F.R. Benson Company for the Irish Literary Theatre.

FIRST PUBLICATION: The *Dublin Magazine* (periodical), April–June 1951.

SYNOPSIS

Act 1

The scene is the banquet hall in Tara. As they lay the table for the wedding feast of Finn and Grania, Niall tells the boy of the Fianna. Finn's father, Cool, drew a thousand men from each kingdom and created an army to defend against foreign invaders. There has been strife between the Fianna and the high king since Cool's day—he himself died while warring against Cormac's father—but the wedding should mend relations. Grania and Laban enter. Grania refuses to marry Finn. He is too old for her, and further she has had an epiphany of love: "The mist was hanging on the brow of

the hill, and something seemed to be moving over the world and to come out of the mist. It was beautiful, mother." Grania has not told her father of her change of heart because she would miss the chance to see the Fianna. "So that you might pick a man who would carry you away," accuses Laban. She laments Cormac's refusal to heed her prophesies of "flights and battles, ruin on ruin." Laban describes the principal Fianna and at last comes to Diarmuid: "It is said of him that he will not be remembered for deeds of arms but as a true lover, and that he will die young." Grania's interest is aroused, for Laban has prophesied that one no older than herself will carry her away. It was for such a man that she looked into the mist, and she begs Laban to help them elope. Laban reluctantly agrees to bewitch the ale at the wedding feast. Cormac enters. Grania declares that she does not want to marry as "kings and queens marry," and Cormac suspects that she has set her heart on "some boy." Grania slyly pledges, "I shall wed this night him who is the chief man among them in my eyes."

The Fianna enter. Declaring the "bride price" on the threshold, Finn swears to defend Cormac's kingdom. Grania startles Diarmuid by taking him aside and telling him that she will be "wedded and bedded" unless someone carries her away. Grania asks to serve the ale one last time. Laban places a spell on the ale and instructs Grania to serve all save Caoelte, Usheen, and Diarmuid. The guests begin to grow sleepy. Conan tells the "pleasant story" of the death of Diarmuid. The story goes that Diarmuid was "put out to foster" with a shepherd. Jealous that the shepherd's son was more beautiful than his own, Diarmuid's father killed the boy. With a druidic hazel stick the shepherd turned his second son into a black boar that would some day emerge from the woods to ravage Ireland and kill Diarmuid. The Fianna fall asleep. Grania reveals her love for Diarmuid and her plan to escape with him. They fall into one another's arms, but Diarmuid remembers his position. Should he break his oath to Finn, "the earth would send famine, the corn would wither, the Fianna would be divided, an enemy would come." Grania retorts with Laban's prophecy that they will flee and "be happy under green boughs and become wise in all woodland wisdom." Finally, Grania appeals to his obligation to help a woman in distress. Diarmuid cannot refuse to help, but he will not break His oath to Finn: His sword shall protect Grania by day and lie between them by night. Grania and Diarmuid depart for the woods; Usheen and Caoelte agree to tell Finn that they have headed toward the sea.

Act 2

Cormac and Laban have journeyed to Diarmuid's rustic house, their first visit in the seven years since the wedding feast. Cormac bewails that the Fianna are divided, that foreign galleys are on the shore, that the pursuit of Diarmuid and Grania will begin again. He has given Diarmuid a kingdom, but, as he warned on the previous night, he cannot defend him against either Finn or foreign invaders. Cormac has brought the Fianna in the hope that Diarmuid would return to them, but Diarmuid has ordered the Fianna to leave his valley. Cormac takes comfort that Grania is well loved, but she confesses that "in this valley love has become terrible and we are sometimes afraid of one another." Diarmuid enters and refuses to reconsider his defiance. To Grania's sorrow, Cormac departs to inform the Fianna of his stance. Diarmuid suspects a ruse; further, he has become attached to the pastoral life. He realizes, however, that Grania is restless and bored, and he worries that her love is dwindling. She says that she will better love him after he rejoins the Fianna and comes to her with the "reek of battle" upon him.

A shepherd with a hazel stick briefly appears in the doorway. Diarmuid follows as if entranced, feeling himself bidden to leave the valley and rejoin the Fianna. Diarmuid, Cormac, and the Fianna enter. Diarmuid and Grania graciously welcome the guests. Usheen proposes that Finn and Diarmuid bind themselves by blood. They fill a cup with their blood and drink. Conan enters with news of a great beast. The others rush outside; Finn and Grania remain. Finn says that the beast must be the boar of which he has heard talk. Grania is alarmed, but she admits that she has grown weary of the valley, and that she had schemed to bring him because she desired to see him in his greatness. Diarmuid interrupts, his suspicion and jealousy aroused. The others enter. Finn taunts Diarmuid

for leaving the hunt to keep his eye on him. Conan taunts that Diarmuid remembered his tale and fled upon realizing that the beast was a boar. Diarmuid and Finn draw their swords. The Fianna come between them, cautioning that he "who raises his hand against the blood bond raises his hand against the gods." Conan proposes that Finn and Diarmuid should each hunt the boar with Grania as prize. Finn admits that he loves Grania and accuses Diarmuid of using the "old tale" to evade the challenge of the hunt. Finn calls his men to the hunt, "let him who will stay behind." They exit. Grania and Cormac bar the door, but Diarmuid recognizes his fate and exits with his spear. Grania weeps. If she still loves him, Cormac says, she must bring him back. She follows in pursuit.

Act 3

Diarmuid sleeps under a tree on the slope of Ben Bulben. Two peasants talk of the wild, stormy night. The young man has seen two armies in battle and Diarmuid's dead grandfather amid the fleeing host, seen also the god Aonghus—Diarmuid's protector, according to the old man—driving the wild boar that the Fianna hunt. Grania enters, having pursued Diarmuid all night. She implores him to return, for she has dreamed that she was seated with Finn, and Diarmuid's shield was hung among the shields of the slain. Diarmuid cries, "Ah, foolish gods, can you find nothing better than the dreams of an unfaithful wife to vex and shake my will." Grania swears her love, but Diarmuid, wavering between love and heartbroken madness, threatens to kill her. She begs for death, but he drives her away and goes after the boar. Caoelte and Usheen enter, followed by Diarmuid. They urge him to quit the hunt for the beast, which is not mortal. Undeterred, Diarmuid heads in the direction of screams and sounds of battle. The Fianna enter, disoriented, exhausted, cold, and afraid. Finn rouses them, and they continue the search for the boar. Finn returns with Grania, whom he has found unguarded. She begs him to kill the boar and save Diarmuid. He asks, "If I kill the boar, will you belong to me?" She answers ambiguously, "Not because you kill the boar." He says that Diarmuid's death has been foretold and he can do nothing. There is a cry. Finn rushes to the sound and returns with the wounded Diarmuid. He cries for the water that might save him, but when he sees that Finn and Grania have been together he pours it away and dies. There is news that the boar has been killed. The Fianna enter. Grania commands them to mourn, and each vows a tribute to Diarmuid. Conan says, "Grania makes great mourning for Diarmuid, but her welcome to Finn shall be greater."

BIBLIOGRAPHY

Foster, R. F. *W. B. Yeats: A Life, I: The Apprentice Mage*; Holloway, Joseph. *Joseph Holloway's Abbey Theatre: A Selection from His Unpublished Journal Impressions of a Dublin Playgoer*; Moore, George. *Hail and Farewell*; Robinson, Lennox. *Ireland's Abbey Theatre: A History, 1899–1951*; Yeats, W. B. *Autobiographies, The Collected Letters of W. B. Yeats* (vol. 2), *The Variorum Edition of the Plays of W. B. Yeats, The Variorum Edition of the Poems of W. B. Yeats.*

Dreaming of the Bones, The (1919)

A thoroughly successful synthesis of high poetry, obscure occult theory, and compelling drama, this one-act play is set in the days following the EASTER RISING. While waiting upon a desolate mountain for a boat that is to smuggle him from the shore of County Clare to the nearby ARAN ISLANDS, a young rebel is visited by the shades of the 12th-century lovers Diarmuid and Dervorgilla (the former not to be confused with the legendary protagonist of Yeats's play DIARMUID AND GRANIA). Jeffares and Knowland summarize the history of the accursed couple: "Historically, Diarmuid Mac-Murrough, king of Leinster, had carried off in 1152 Dervorgilla, daughter of the King of Meath, and wife of Tegernan O'Rourke. He appealed for help to Henry II of England, who gave him an army under Strongbow (Richard Fitzgilbert de Clare, Earl of Pembroke, ca. 1130–76) in order to regain the kingdom of Leinster, from which he had been banished. Dervorgilla, having outlived O'Rourke,

Diarmuid, Henry and Strongbow, is said to have died at the abbey of Mellefont, near Drogheda in 1193, aged eighty-five" (CCP 157–158). In Yeats's telling, the shades of the couple suffer a terrible penance for the crime of ushering in a foreign invasion: They may look upon one another but never touch. Their release depends on the forgiveness of one of their own race, but the young rebel, steadfastly nationalistic, refuses to oblige them. Here, as in poems like "EASTER 1916," "ON A POLITICAL PRISONER," and "IN MEMORY OF EVA GORE-BOOTH AND CON MARKIEWICZ," Yeats explores the insufficiency of politics as a response to life. A creature of politics, the young rebel can grasp only the treachery of Diarmuid and Dervorgilla; their enormity of spirit and the tragic beauty of their penance are lost upon him. As Harold Bloom notes, "Though the young revolutionary has fought in the Post Office, it is the ghostly lovers who wear heroic masks, for the soldier lacks imagination [. . .]. When the lovers dance before him, they offer the soldier his supreme chance to cast out fanaticism and hatred, but though he almost yields, he ends in an ugly obduracy, cursing the temptation." Bloom adds that Yeats had seen a similar hatred "disfigure MAUD GONNE, and other women of surpassing excellence, and in his more visionary and redemptive moods he understood such hatred as a blight upon Ireland" (*Yeats* 308).

Yeats previously treated the historical episode of Diarmuid and Dervorgilla in his 1905 story "Hanrahan's Vision" (see STORIES OF RED HANRAHAN). The story anticipates the rough outline of the play, but it entirely lacks the play's political dimension. In the story, Red Hanrahan sees a visionary procession of lovers. Dervorgilla explains the different species of lover in the procession and briefly relates her own history. In this version of the tale, the couple's essential error is not political but subtly emotional: "It was but the blossom of the man and of the woman we loved in one another, and so when we died there was no lasting unbreakable quiet about us, and the bitterness of the battles we brought into Ireland turned to our own punishment" (*Myth.* 251). The story ends with Hanrahan—amply endowed with the imagination that the young rebel lacks—screaming in terror.

The Dreaming of the Bones belongs to a group of plays that includes At the Hawk's Well, *The* Only Jealousy of Emer, and Calvary. *The Dreaming of the Bones* and *The Only Jealousy* were published as *Two Plays for Dancers* in 1919; all four plays were published as *Four Plays for Dancers* in 1921. In keeping with the conventions of the Japanese Noh drama, the plays employ masks and extremely simple stage settings, making them suitable for performance in a drawing-room or studio (see *E&I* 221–222; *VPl.* 415–419, 566). At the same time, *The Dreaming of the Bones* anticipates *The* Words upon the Window-pane and Purgatory, which in related fashion take up the penitential dream-life of departed spirits. The play's basic idea, Yeats writes in a note, "is derived from the world-wide belief that the dead dream back, for a certain time, through the more personal thoughts and deeds of life. The wicked, according to Cornelius Agrippa, dream themselves to be consumed by flames and persecuted by demons; and there is precisely the same thought in a Japanese 'Noh' play, where a spirit, advised by a Buddhist priest she has met upon the road, seeks to escape from the flames by ceasing to believe in the dream. The lovers in my play have lost themselves in a different but still self-created winding of the labyrinth of conscience" (*VPl.* 777). Yeats gives his mature formulation of the "dreaming back" in A Vision: "In the *Dreaming Back*, the *Spirit* is compelled to live over and over again the events that had most moved it; there can be nothing new, but the old events stand forth in a light which is dim or bright according to the intensity of the passion that accompanied them. They occur in the order of their intensity or luminosity, the more intense first, and the painful are commonly the more intense, and repeat themselves again and again" (226; see also *AV-1925* 226–227).

DRAMATIS PERSONAE: Three Musicians, their faces made up to resemble masks; a young man; a stranger, wearing a mask; a young girl, wearing a mask.

FIRST PERFORMANCE: Produced by the National Theatre Society Ltd. (see the Irish National Theatre Society) at the Abbey Theatre, Dublin, December 6, 1931.

FIRST PUBLICATION: *The Little Review* (periodical), January 1919. Reprinted in *Two Plays for Dancers*, The Cuala Press, Churchtown, Dundrum, January 1919.

SYNOPSIS

The scene is set on a bare stage backed by a curtain showing a pattern of mountain and sky. Two musicians play upon their instruments or fold and unfold a ceremonial cloth while the First Musician sings of the "dizzy dreams" that spring from the "dry bones of the dead" and walk the night. Reverting to speech, the First Musician describes the scene: It is the hour before dawn; the moon is covered, darkening the little village and the road to the Abbey of Corcomroe; the birds cry their loneliness. A young man carrying a lantern approaches in the rustic garb of a fisherman from the Aran Islands. The Young Man enters, praying in Irish. The Stranger and the Young Girl follow, dressed in the costumes of past times. Raising his lantern, the Young Man nervously asks who creeps through the dark. The Stranger inquires what he has to fear, and the Young Girl blows out his lantern, which the Young Man takes to be the action of the wind. Without his lantern, the Young Man has no choice but to place himself in the hands of the passing couple. The Stranger asks whether he has fought in Dublin, and the Young Man answers that he was at the Post Office, and that he will be shot if captured (cf. "The Statues" and the final song of *The* Death of Cuchulain). He tells them his plan of escape: He is to lie on the mountain and keep watch for an "Aran coracle" that is to arrive at daybreak (and take him to the islands). The Stranger offers to act as guide. Knowing the terrain, he can keep him from the eyes of living men, though he cannot "answer for the dead." He explains that on certain days, in the hour before daybreak, the mountain is haunted. Some of these penitential shades "for an old scruple must hang spitted / Upon the swaying tops of lofty trees; / Some are consumed in fire, some withered up / By hail and sleet out of the wintry North, / And some but live through their old lives again." The Young Man says that he does not fear the "invisible tumult / Of the fantastic conscience," but those who can jail or shoot him.

The three figures circle the stage as the First Musician narrates their progress. Surveying the scene from the mountaintop, the Young Man asks whether "there is no house / Famous for sanctity or architectural beauty / In Clare or Kerry, or in all wide Connacht, / The enemy has not unroofed?" In explanation of the destruction, the Stranger points out the burial place of Donough O'Brien (one of a "group of nobles who invited the Scots to invade Thomond and take it from the King. After their defeat Donough escaped from the battlefield of Athenry but fell in 1317 near the Abbey of Corcomroe"; CCP 162). Such self-serving men, says the Young Man, made Ireland weak. He curses O'Brien and his kind. He asks whether the shades who do penance upon the mountaintop come from the abbey graveyard. The Young Girl says that those buried in the graveyard were but common sinners, "no callers-in of the alien from oversea." They mix "in a brief dream-battle above their bones; / Or make one drove; or drift in amity; / Or in the hurry of the heavenly round / Forget their earthly names." The shades upon the mountaintop, by contrast, wander alone, being accursed. The Young Man conjectures that these are "angry ghosts / Who wander in a willful solitude," but the Young Girl answers that they "have no thought but love." Their penance being the heartbreak of their incomplete union, they may join eyes but not lips. When head is bent to head, or hand slips into hand, the "memory of their crime flows up between / And drives them apart." The Young Man wonders what "passionate sin" could demand such terrible and unending penance. The Young Girl answers that those of whom she speaks committed no mere passionate sin. She tells of one whose husband overthrew her lover in battle. He, "being blind / And bitter and bitterly in love," brought a foreign army from across the sea and sold his country into slavery. They will remain accursed until some member of their own race forgives them. The Young Man guesses that she speaks of Diarmuid and Dervorgilla, "who brought the Norman in," and hopes they shall never be forgiven. The three figures again make a circle around the stage, indicating their ascent to the mountain summit. From there they see the Aran Islands, the Connemara Hills, and Galway, which are strewn with ruin. The Young Man observes that the country would have been "most beautiful" like "any old admired Italian town," but for the couple they would have him pardon.

The Stranger and Young Girl begin to dance and gaze on each other with passionate eyes. "Seven hundred years our lips have never met," says the Young Girl. The Young Man realizes that he beholds Diarmuid and Dervorgilla, and describes their dance: The two are engulfed in one another; they cover their eyes as though their hearts had been suddenly broken; they drift from rock to rock; they raise their hands as though "to snatch the sleep / That lingers always in the abyss of the sky / Though they can never reach it." Finally, a cloud floats over the mountain and they are "swept away." The Stranger and the Young Girl exit to the relief of the Young Man, who had almost yielded to the "terrible temptation of the place" and forgiven them. The musicians unfold and fold the cloth while singing of the "music of a lost kingdom" carried by the wind.

BIBLIOGRAPHY

Bloom, Harold. *Yeats*; Jeffares, A. Norman, and A. S. Knowland, *A Commentary on the Collected Plays of W. B. Yeats*; Yeats, W. B. *A Critical Edition of Yeats A Vision (1925)*, *Essays and Introductions*, *Mythologies*, *The Variorum Edition of the Plays of W. B. Yeats*, *A Vision*.

Fighting the Waves (1934)

In a preface included in *Wheels and Butterflies* (1934), Yeats illuminates his decision to rewrite *The Only Jealousy of Emer* as an avant-garde ballet: "I wrote *The Only Jealousy of Emer* for performance in a private house or studio, considering it, for reasons which I have explained, unsuited to a public stage. Then somebody put it on a public stage in Holland and Hildo van Krop made his powerful masks. Because the dramatist who can collaborate with a great sculptor is lucky, I rewrote the play not only to fit it for such a stage but to free it from abstraction and confusion. I have retold the story in prose which I have tried to make very simple, and left imaginative suggestion to dancers, singers, musicians" (*Expl.* 370; *VPl.* 567). The Dutch production debuted in Amsterdam on April 2, 1922. Yeats borrowed the masks designed by Krop (1884–1970) for the play's debut production at the ABBEY THEATRE in August 1929, and he dedicated the play to Krop upon its publication in *Wheels and Butterflies* (*The Abbey* 141; see also *Letters* 765, 768; *VPl.* 567).

Lending further avant-garde frisson to the Abbey's production, EZRA POUND's American protégé George Antheil (1900–59) composed the score. As always, Yeats was eager to ally himself with the "new school," and he wrote excitedly to Lady GREGORY in March 1929 about the young composer: "Antheil is here [Rapallo] and has started on a musical setting for a trilogy consisting of *The Hawk's Well* [see AT THE HAWK'S WELL], ON BAILE'S STRAND and the new version of *The Only Jealousy of Emer* which I call *Fighting the Waves*. If he persists, and he is at present enthusiastic, it means a performance in Vienna in the autumn. He has a great name there since his setting of *Oedipus* a few months ago. He is a revolutionary musician—there was a riot of almost Abbey intensity over some music of his in America. [. . .] He is about 28 and looks 18 and has a face of indescribable innocence. His wife, a first violinist from somewhere or other, look equally young and innocent. Both are persons of impulse and he may or he may not get through his month of toil upon the three plays" (760). *Fighting the Waves* was produced as planned, but the three plays about CUCHULAIN were not presented as a trilogy; nor did Antheil complete more than the one score (*Bad Boy* 228). Yeats found Antheil's score "heroic and barbaric and strange" (*Letters* 761–762; see also *VPl.* 567), though Joseph Holloway (1861–1944) judged that the "steam whistle of a merry-go-round discourses heavenly music by comparison" (*The Abbey* 141). Rounding out the experiment was the ballerina Ninette de Valois (1898–2001)—born in County Wicklow as Edris Stannis—who performed in the role of Fand (and later as the queen in *The KING OF THE*

GREAT CLOCK TOWER). In ON THE BOILER Yeats remembers her performance as one of the haunting moments of his theatrical career (*Expl.* 416; *LE* 226), and in the prologue to *The DEATH OF CUCHULAIN* he extols her as the antithesis of the dancers painted by Degas: a tragic dancer whose type has since disappeared.

Yeats considered the opening performance of the play a thorough triumph. He told OLIVIA SHAKESPEAR on August 24, 1929, that *Fighting the Waves* has been "my greatest success on the stage since *Kathleen-ni-Houlihan* [see CATHLEEN NI HOULIHAN], and its production was a great event here, the politician[s] and the governor general and the American minister present—the masks by the Dutchman Krop magnificent and Antheil's music. Everyone here is as convinced as I am that I have discovered a new form by this combination of dance, speech and music. The dancing of the goddess [Fand] in her abstract almost nonrepresentative mask was extraordinarily exciting" (*Letters* 767–768).

Fighting the Waves largely adheres to the language and plot of *The Only Jealousy of Emer*. The most significant alteration is the excision of the dialogue between the Ghost of Cuchulain and the Woman of the Sidhe as she attempts to seduce him. In the revised play, the struggle between the two unfolds as a mute dance. For a synopsis, see *The Only Jealousy of Emer*.

DRAMATIS PERSONAE: Three Musicians; Cuchulain; the ghost of Cuchulain; Emer; Eithne Inguba; the figure of Cuchulain; the woman of the Sidhe.

FIRST PERFORMANCE: Produced by the National Theatre Society (see IRISH NATIONAL THEATRE SOCIETY) at the Abbey Theatre, Dublin, August 13, 1929.

FIRST PUBLICATION: *Wheels and Butterflies*, Macmillan, London, November 13, 1934.

BIBLIOGRAPHY

Antheil, George. *Bad Boy of Music*; Hunt, Hugh. *The Abbey: Ireland's National Theatre, 1904–1978*; Yeats, W. B. *Explorations, Later Essays, The Letters of W. B. Yeats, The Variorum Edition of the Plays of W. B. Yeats.*

Full Moon in March, A (1935)

Unhappy with The KING OF THE GREAT CLOCK TOWER even in its second incarnation as a verse play (see *Letters* 830), Yeats immediately proceeded to rewrite it as *A Full Moon in March*. In the final event, the two verse plays made their first print appearances back to back in the 1935 collection *A Full Moon in March* (the prose version of *The King of the Great Clock Tower* had appeared the year before). In a November 1934 letter to MARGOT RUDDOCK, Yeats explained the decision to re-create the earlier play: "I am rewriting *The King of the Great Clock Tower*, giving the Queen a speaking part, that you may act it. I have so arranged it that you can give place to a dancer (quite easy as you will both wear masks). The old version of the play is bad because abstract and incoherent. This version is poignant and simple—lyrical dialogue all simple. It takes years to get my plays right" (*Sweet Dancer* 23; see also 46). In a preface to *A Full Moon in March*, Yeats gives a different explanation: "In *The King of the Great Clock Tower* there are three characters, King, Queen and Stroller, and that is a character too many; reduced to the essentials, Queen and Stroller, the fable should have greater intensity. I started afresh and called the new version *A Full Moon in March*" (*VPl.* 1311–1312). On the motif of the severed head, see the entry on *The King of the Great Clock Tower*.

Yeats alludes to the "full moon in March" with a range of astrological, historical, and philosophical meanings in mind. In *A VISION*, he offers a dense disquisition that serves as a useful footnote to the play: "Caesar was killed on the 15th day of March, the month of victims and of saviours. Two years before, he had instituted our solar Julian Year, and in a few generations the discovery of the body of Attis among the reeds would be commemorated upon that day, though, before 'Ides' lost its first meaning, the ceremony needed a full moon or the fifteenth day of a lunar March. Even Easter, which the rest of Christendom commemorated on the first full moon after the Vernal Equinox, would sometimes be commemorated by Christians living under the influence of the Julian Year upon the day before the fifteenth day of the solar March. It

seemed as if the magical character of the full moon was transferred to a day and night where the moon had as it were a merely legal or official existence" (245; see also 196–197; 203). In the 1925 edition of *A Vision*, the "full moon in March" emphatically represents the mystical moment of historical transition, the moment of the birth and death of gods: "Did the great victims of Antiquity, Christ, Cæsar, Socrates—Love, Justice, Truth—die under the first full Moon after the vernal equinox? Christ did, as the date of Easter shows; Cæsar did,—beware the Ides of March—and the sentence upon Socrates was pronounced when the Sacred Ship sailed for what recent research considers a March Festival at Delos, the renewal of Apollo and the Earth. Did that Festival begin at the new Moon, and the Moon show all but full on the Piræus when the Ship put in to port, and was it full when Socrates drank the Hemlock? When I write these words, and recall the place of the precessional Sun, should there not be a stirring in the roots of my hair?" (*AV-1925* 163–164). In *THE RESURRECTION*, the "full moon in March" has a similar significance. The Greek observes Dionysian worshippers ecstatically parading through the streets following Christ's death and comments, "Three days after the full moon, a full moon in March, they sing the death of the god and pray for his resurrection" (*VPl.* 915).

DRAMATIS PERSONAE: First attendant; second attendant; the queen; the swineherd.

FIRST PERFORMANCE: The play was not staged in Yeats's lifetime.

FIRST PUBLICATION: *Poetry* (periodical), March 1935. Reprinted in *A Full Moon in March*, Macmillan, London, November 22, 1935.

SYNOPSIS

The curtain rises on the two attendants, an elderly woman and a young man, who stand before an inner curtain. As the Second Attendant sings of the indifferent power of love, which makes no distinction between "crown of gold" and "dung of swine," they part the inner curtain to reveal the Queen. In a moment the Swineherd enters. He has heard that the Queen will marry the man who sings best. The Queen corrects him: She will marry whomever "best sings his passion." She punishes some for the impudence of presenting themselves, but she permits the Swineherd's song, despite his foul appearance and his admission of madness. The Swineherd has heard that the Queen can be won only at a "full moon in March," and he observes that there is such a moon. The Queen warns that she is "cruel as the winter of virginity" (cf. *Aut.* 247), and that she has killed and maimed singers who displeased her; as she has taken an unaccountable liking to him, she urges him to leave while he can. The Swineherd seems not to hear; he has been imagining their marriage night "from the first touch and kiss." His fearlessness reminds the Queen of what a lover once told her: God alone looks upon her without fear. The Swineherd offers: "Desiring cruelty, he made you cruel. / I shall embrace body and cruelty, / Desiring both as though I had made both." The Queen asks whether, like all her suitors, he proposes to flatter her beauty. When he first heard her name, says the Swineherd, he rolled in the dung of swine and laughed—he knows nothing of beauty and cares nothing for kingdoms. The Queen consents to abandon her throne and house should his song move her, but she wants to know what she will gain. The Swineherd answers, "A song—the night of love, / An ignorant forest and the dung of swine." Turning to her court in a suddenly changed mood, the Queen declares that she allowed the Swineherd to prolong his "complexities of insult" only so she might punish his audacity with no question of injustice. The Queen tells him to pray for he will be momentarily beheaded. This reminds the Swineherd of a story about a woman covered in blood, a drop of which "entered her womb and there begat a child." Seemingly entranced, the Queen echoes his words, with the added detail that the blood comes from a severed head. Recovering herself, the Queen orders the Swineherd removed from her sight. She turns her back to the audience and slowly removes her veil.

The attendants close the inner curtain upon the scene and tell of an "ancient Irish Queen" who put her lover's head on a stake (a reference to the story of Aodh and Dectira, which Yeats recounts in "The Binding of the Hair"). They reopen the curtain to reveal the unveiled Queen with the Swineherd's severed head in her hands. Speaking

for the Queen, the First Attendant sings, "Great my love before you came, / Greater when I loved in shame, / Greatest when there broke from me / Storm of virgin cruelty." The Queen dances, laying the head upon the throne. Speaking for the head, the Second Attendant sings of Jack and Jill. In this version of the nursery rhyme, Jill murders Jack and hangs "his heart beyond the hill, / A-twinkle in the sky. / A *full moon in March.*" As she dances, the Queen takes up the head, kisses it, and slowly sinks as she presses it to her breast. The attendants close the inner curtain. The Second attendant asks why "those holy, haughty feet descend / From emblematic niches. . . ." He speaks seemingly at once of the moon and of the Queen—the Queen as emblem or personification of the moon. "What do they seek for? Why must they descend?" The First Attendant answers, "For desecration and the lover's night." The supernatural, this is to say, yearns for the impurity of the natural, seeks the tension of antinomy that is the creative energy of reality. In *The Only Jealousy of Emer*, the goddess Fand expresses a similar supernatural insufficiency: "Because I long I am not complete./ . . . When your mouth and my mouth meet / All my round shall be complete / Imagining all its circles run . . ." (*VPl.* 551, 555). As Crazy Jane theorizes in "Crazy Jane and the Bishop," "Fair and foul are near of kin, / And fair needs foul."

BIBLIOGRAPHY

Yeats, W. B. *Ah, Sweet Dancer: W. B. Yeats and Margot Ruddock, Autobiographies, A Critical Edition of Yeats A Vision (1925), The Letters of W. B. Yeats, The Variorum Edition of the Plays of W. B. Yeats, A Vision.*

Green Helmet, The (1910)

The second play in Yeats's dramatic sequence on the life and adventures of CUCHULAIN, *The Green Helmet* tells of the mythical Irish hero's return from Scotland and his rise to preeminence among the local kings (arranged in narrative order, the sequence consists of AT THE HAWK'S WELL, *The*

Green Helmet, ON BAILE'S STRAND, *The* ONLY JEALOUSY OF EMER, and *The* DEATH OF CUCHU-LAIN). The play is largely based on the chapters titled "The Feast of Bricriu" and "The Championship of Ulster" in Lady GREGORY's *Cuchulain of Muirthemne* (1902), a popular and influential rendering of the legendary hero's life and adventures for which Yeats wrote the introduction (*Interpretation of the Cuchulain Legend 32; VPl. 454*). Lady Gregory was more often than not an unacknowledged partner in Yeats's playwriting, but, as Yeats stipulates in his preface to *Plays in Prose and Verse* (1922), the *Green Helmet* and *The* PLAYER QUEEN were alone among all his plays wholly his own (*VPl. 1306*).

Subtitled "An Heroic Farce," the play largely departs from the high-heroic tone that characterizes the other plays in the sequence, though it reiterates many of the sequence's common themes, most especially the hero's defining quality of tragic joy ("the laughing lip that shall not turn from laughing, whatever rise or fall") and his inevitable ill-use by the mob (a theme that pervades Yeats's work; see especially his representations of HUGH LANE, CHARLES STEWART PARNELL, and J. M. SYNGE). Robert Welch, historian of the ABBEY THEATRE, proposes that the plays' theme of "heroism isolated by a selfless act when others fail in nerve and honour" allegorizes Yeats's own travails as a would-be hero of the theater: "The squabbling for precedence and the faithless caving in of Cuchulain's comrades when issued with an unremitting challenge reflects Yeats's experiences in the Abbey through the past years: Miss [ANNIE] HORNIMAN's demands, [GEORGE] RUSSELL's two-facedness, the Fays' estrangement, the howling of the nationalist press, the condescension of the British. Naturally enough, the Red Man gives the green helmet, symbol of authority, to Cuchulain" (*Abbey Theatre* 53–54).

The Green Helmet was Yeats's second effort to dramatize the middle episode in his Cuchulain cycle. His first attempt, the prose play *The Golden Helmet*, was performed March 19, 1908, at the Abbey Theatre, and published later that year both as an eponymous volume and as part of Yeats's collected works (*Biblio. 85, 89*).

DRAMATIS PERSONAE: Laegaire (pronounced "Leary," according to Yeats); Conall; Cuchulain; Red Man, a spirit; Emer; Laegaire's wife; Laeg, Cuchulain's chariot-driver; stable boys and scullions; black men; etc.

FIRST PERFORMANCE: Produced by the National Theatre Society Ltd. (see IRISH NATIONAL THEATRE SOCIETY) at the Abbey Theatre, Dublin, February 10, 1910.

FIRST PUBLICATION: *The Green Helmet and Other Poems*, The CUALA PRESS, Churchtown, Dundrum, December 1910.

SYNOPSIS

The scene is laid in a log house fronting rocks and a moonlit sea visible through the two rear windows. Laegaire thinks he has seen through the window a "cat-headed man out of Connacht," but Conall insists that he has killed them all, cutting off a hundred heads and stealing their treasure. Laegaire believes he hears the voice of Cuchulain, but Conall reminds him that Cuchulain is in Scotland (see ON BAILE'S STRAND). Laegaire wishes he would come home, for his young wife Emer "spreads her tail like a peacock" and antagonizes the other women. Conall spots a man in a long green cloak. In a panic, Laegaire and Conall try to block the entrance of what they take to be a "shape-changer," but the man pushes his way into the room. Laegaire urges the man to continue on to the big house, which is luckier. The man jokingly wonders that the flagon is full and the cups empty, and they recognize him as Cuchulain. They urge him to return to Scotland, for the country has become unlucky, and the house has "fallen on shame and disgrace." Soon after Cuchulain left, Conall relates, there appeared a "wide, high man" with a "red foxy cloak" who became drunk and proposed a game: He would allow someone to chop off his head if he might then be allowed to chop off theirs. Conall was annoyed by the Red Man's laughter and chopped off his head. The head fell to the ground and continued to laugh; then the body took up the head and disappeared into the sea. Worried that the episode would make them laughingstocks, Conall and Laegaire swore to keep it a secret. Twelve months later the Red Man returned with his head in place once more. He demanded "his debt and his right" and threatened that the land would be "disgraced" if they failed to uphold the agreement. Conall and Laegaire remained silent. The Red Man promised to return in another 12 months, and the period had elapsed that very day.

They hear a splash from the shore. Before the men can put their backs to the door, a tall red-headed, red-cloaked man with a great sword in his hand stands on the threshold. Cuchulain jeers at him, threatening an old-fashioned punch if the sword be useless. The Red Man declares himself the "kindest of all Shape-Changers" and denies that the game had been in earnest. As proof of his goodwill, he brings the gift of a green helmet to be given to the bravest of them. He lays the helmet on the ground and exits. Laegaire and Conall immediately begin to argue over who deserves the helmet. Cuchulain settles the dispute: They will share the helmet by filling it with drink and passing it around. Suddenly there is the din of the charioteers, scullions, and stable boys arguing and attempting to silence each other with horns. The boys rush in, each touting the superior heroism of his own master. The argument had arisen after the Red Man stopped by the hall and told them of the helmet. Cuchulain explains that the helmet will be handed round, but an argument immediately erupts as to who shall have the first drink. Cuchulain shouts that the Red Man brought the helmet to stir up quarrels and that they have fallen into the trap. As Cuchulain attempts to disperse the crowd, the heroes' wives are heard arguing over the merits of their husbands. They arrive at the door wrestling with one another, each wanting to enter first. Cuchulain puts his spear across the door and commands the others to break holes in the wall so the wives may enter simultaneously. The wives enter, but they continue to bicker. Cuchulain takes the helmet and throws it into the sea, to the outrage of all. The wives rush at each other with daggers. Cuchulain forces them back, and Conall and Laegaire draw their swords upon Cuchulain. There is utter tumult. Three black hands reach through the windows and put out the torches; moving forms pass by the window. Moonlight gradually fills the house, revealing the Red Man and two black cat-headed men. One carries the helmet, one the sword. The

Red Man has come to demand his debt. Cuchulain offers his own head. Emer keens and implores and finally tries to take her own life. Cuchulain seizes her dagger and asks, "Would you stay the great barnacle-goose / When its eyes are turned to the sea and its beak to the salt of the air?" Cuchulain kneels before the Red Man. He is not beheaded, but crowned with the helmet. The Red Man calls himself the "rector" of the land. Age after age he sifts it, seeking a man who strikes his fancy to be its champion. He chooses the "heart that grows no bitterer although betrayed by all; / The hand that loves to scatter; the life like a gambler's throw. . . ."

BIBLIOGRAPHY

Bjersby, Birgit. *The Interpretation of the Cuchulain Legend in the Works of W. B. Yeats*; Wade, Allan. *A Bibliography of the Writings of W. B. Yeats*; Welch, Robert. *The Abbey Theatre, 1899–1999*; Yeats, W. B. *The Variorum Edition of the Plays of W. B. Yeats*.

Herne's Egg, The (1938)

"I have a three-act tragic-comedy in my head to write in Majorca," Yeats told DOROTHY WELLESLEY in November 1935. He predicted that it would be "as wild a play as PLAYER QUEEN, as amusing but more tragedy and philosophic depth" (*Letters* 843; *LOP* 40). Writing to Ethel Mannin (1900–84) the following month, he called the play "the strangest wildest thing I have ever written" and reported that for the past three months he had possessed "more vigour of style" than he had for years (*Letters* 845). The play wound up running to a longish six scenes rather than three acts, but it turned out to be as "wild" as advertised. So much so that when Yeats submitted the play to the ABBEY THEATRE it so "disturbed" the board that he withdrew it. As Yeats explained to Mannin in February 1938, a member of the board "had decided that the seven ravishers of the heroine are the seven sacraments" (904–905). The recalcitrant member was the government representative Richard Hayes (1878–1958), a devout Catholic who later became director of the National Library (*The Abbey* 161; *AP* 465). Yeats wrote to

Wellesley in December 1936 that he was "greatly relieved" by the withdrawal of the play, being "no longer fit for riots" (*Letters* 871; *LOP* 110). This was at best a partial truth. Frank O'Connor (1903–66), a member of the board and a supporter of the play, remembers that Yeats was "bitterly hurt at the rejection of his beautiful play by a gang of nobodies" (*I&R*, II, 343). According to O'Connor, Yeats himself had made the point about the sacraments to board member F. R. Higgins (1896–1941). Higgins had relayed Yeats's statement to Hayes, and Hayes had threatened to resign if the play were produced. Higgins himself had opposed the play, and Ernest Blythe (1899–1975) had supported the play only because it was "so obscure that no one would notice it was obscene" (II, 343–344).

The play draws on oddly paired sources: Samuel Ferguson's epic poem "Congal" (1872)—a version of the Irish legendary tale *The Battle of Mag Rath*—and Balzac's novel *Seraphita* (1834). From the former comes the rudiments of the subplot involving Congal and Aedh; from the latter, the rudiments of the subplot involving the Great Herne and Attracta (see *VPl.* 1311; *Plays* 916; *W. B. Yeats and Tradition* 102–111). For all that, the play is an idiosyncratic product of Yeats's own imagination, uniting motifs that run throughout his work. The Great Herne at once recalls the heron of CALVARY and the hawk of AT THE HAWK'S WELL; Attracta recalls a long lineage of moon- or god-possessed women, as for example the queen in A FULL MOON IN MARCH and MAUD GONNE in "A BRONZE HEAD"; the sexual congress between the Herne and Attracta recalls "LEDA AND THE SWAN"; the ironic parallelism between hero and fool recalls ON BAILE'S STRAND; the fool as executioner recalls The DEATH OF CUCHULAIN; the braying of the donkey recalls *The Player Queen*; the crucial symbolism of the full moon derives from the philosophy of A VISION and has a clear dramatic antecedent in *A Full Moon in March*. The theme of reincarnation is familiar in poems like "DEATH," "EPHEMERA," and "MOHINI CHATTERJEE." In *The Herne's Egg*, Yeats reprised the theme under the stimulus of Shri Purohit Swami (1882–1941), with whom he was busy translating the *Upanishads* in Majorca. Yeats told Wellesley in December 1935:

"Shri Purohit Swami is with me, and the play is his philosophy in a fable, or mine confirmed by him" (*Letters* 844; *LOP* 42).

The aesthetic and philosophical success of the play has been disputed by many of its most prominent critics. R. F. Foster calls the play "incoherent" (*AP* 612). Harold Bloom calls it "a monument to the mounting confusion and systematic inhumanity of the last phase of Yeats" and dismisses it as "unequivocally rancid," though he acknowledges that there is "lasting power in it, the strength of a great imagination misused" (*Yeats* 422, 424). Helen Vendler calls it "essentially a rather arid and contrived piece of theatrical writing" (*Later Plays* 160). F. A. C. Wilson takes the play very seriously indeed and provides an extensive exegesis, but acknowledges that it is "quite unapproachable without a knowledge of the whole body of Yeats's symbolism" (*W. B. Yeats and Tradition* 101).

DRAMATIS PERSONAE: Congal, king of Connaught; Aedh, king of Tara; Corney, Attracta's servant; Mike, Pat, Malachi, Mathias, James, John, Connaught soldiers; Attracta, a priestess; Kate, Agnes, Mary, friends of Attracta; soldiers of Tara; a fool.

FIRST PERFORMANCE: Produced by Austin Clarke's Lyric Theatre Company at the Abbey Theatre, Dublin, October 29, 1950.

FIRST PUBLICATION: *The Herne's Egg: A Stage Play*, Macmillan, London, January 21, 1938.

SYNOPSIS

Scene 1

Amid mist and rock, soldiers clash, while the backcloth shows a herne perched high above. The battle shifts off stage, leaving only the two kings, Congal and Aedh. Old friends fighting their 50th battle against one another, they agree to take a rest and fall into easy conversation. They have fought all day, so well matched are their armies. Each king has lost 25 men and been wounded on the shoulder.

Scene 2

The battleground is deserted. Corney enters with a donkey (a "donkey on wheels, like a child's toy, but life-size," according to the stage directions); Congal and his soldiers follow. Congal has learned of a

great "hernery" nearby belonging to the prophet-
ess Attracta. He orders his men to bring back eggs.
"Manners!' cries Mike. Congal agrees to ask for
the eggs if Corney will tell him how to summon
Attracta. There is a flute carved from a herne's thigh
on a nearby rock. He says that "The Great Herne's
Feather" will summon her "if she has a mind to
come," and he plays the song. Congal's men go in
search of eggs. Attracta enters. Congal tells her that
peace has been made, and that he wants to present a
gift of eggs at Tara, where he and his men are to dine
that night. Attracta says that only women "betrothed
or married to the Herne" may eat or handle the
eggs. Congal calls her mad, and offers that women
"thrown into despair / By the winter of their virginity
/ Take its abominable snow" and make an "image of
god or bird or beast / To feed their sensuality. . . ."
Congal judges an "old campaigner" to be the cure
for "everything that woman dreams," but Mike holds
that no fewer than seven men will serve the purpose.
Attracta says that "there is no happiness but the
Great Herne." Congal considers her in no position to
know, but Attracta says that as the betrothed of the
Great Herne she knows "what may be known." She
burns "not in the flesh but in the mind," though the
time will come when she will be laid on the "blazing
bed" and the bird will take her maidenhead. Corney
and the soldiers lead in the donkey laden with eggs.
Attracta places a curse on Congal: He shall become
a fool and die at the hands of a fool. He considers this
but a natural fate for an old warrior; unperturbed, he
exits with his men. Kate, Agnes, and Mary enter
timidly, with a gift of cream, butter, and eggs, wanting Attracta to help them find husbands. Attracta
promises that they will marry as soon as she herself
marries, and her nuptials will be very soon, perhaps
that very night. The sound of the flute is heard: The
Herne calls her. Attracta's eyes become glassy and
her limbs stiff. Mary has twice seen her in this condition: like a marionette in unpracticed hands, she will
move stiffly for a few minutes and then take leave in
long dancing leaps as the god remembers his skill.
Attracta fulfills Mary's prediction. The girls dispute
whether the god and his bride will couple in "blue-
black midnight," where sun, moon, and stars are
extinguished and "no woman has gone," or "in the
blazing heart of the sun."

Scene 3

Congal and his men, along with Corney and the
donkey, arrive at the gates of Tara. A great bird—
the Great Herne himself, according to Corney—
circles overhead. Congal orders his man to bring
it down with stones, but none can hit it. The bird
swoops low and the men attack it with their swords,
but again to no avail. It disappears behind the wall
of Tara. As the soldiers place their arms in a basket carried by Aedh's servants, Corney sings "The
Great Herne's Feather," putting Congal's "teeth on
edge."

Scene 4

Congal enters the empty banquet hall drunkenly
shouting that he has been insulted and calling
on his men to grab whatever will make a handy
weapon. He exits to one side as Aedh, in a similar
rage, enters from the other. Congal returns with two
table legs. Every other man at table had received a
herne's egg, but Congal had received a common
hen's egg. He challenges Aedh to a duel with the
table legs. Aedh alleges that the hen's egg was part
of Congal's own plot to draw him into a fight with
an unfamiliar weapon, but all the same he is willing
to fight. The fight moves off stage. Congal returns,
the fight won; he has killed Aedh with a blow to
the head. The insult had to be answered, but he
regrets Aedh's death, for against one another they
had been able to fight like gentlemen. Congal wonders whether the curse is at work. As if in her sleep,
Attracta enters carrying a herne's egg. It was she
who made the fatal substitution of the eggs. The
king resolves to avenge himself on the Great Herne
by assaulting his bride—seven of them will "handle,
penetrate, and possess her, / And do her a great
good by that action, / Melting out the virgin snow,
/ And that snow image, the Great Herne. . . ." He
takes the herne's egg and lays it upon the ground.
As the men toss their caps at the egg to decide who
will take her first, Attracta sings that "no lesser
life, man, bird or beast, / Can make unblessed what
a beast made blessed, / Can make impure what a
beast made pure."

Scene 5

Attracta and Corney stand before the gate of Tara.
They prepare to carry away the unbroken herne's

eggs, for "such eggs are holy." Congal and his men enter. Misinterpreting the scene, Congal congratulates Attracta on being "no more a herne's bride," but a "sensible woman" who turns her thoughts to "the cupboard and the larder." He adds that the seven men who held her in their arms wish her good luck. Attracta says that it was the Herne who came to her and that she had lain beside him as his "pure bride." Congal scoffs. All seven men swear that they did as they pledged to do. Attracta implores the Great Herne to declare her pure. There is thunder and all except Attracta and Congal kneel. Three of Congal's men deny their wrongdoing. Attracta says that the Great Herne knows "every man's deed" and will meet out a "most memorable punishment": in their next incarnations the six men will be "pushed down a step or two" and become cat, rat, bat, dog, wolf, or goose. She calls on the Great Herne to confirm her words and there is another peel of thunder. Congal sinks to his knees. She tells him that he will die upon the holy mountain of Slieve Fuadh [in County Armagh] when the moon is next full. Terrified into submission, Congal says that he will come.

Scene 6

Congal arrives at the mountaintop where he finds Tom Fool. He has heard that Congal is to die by the hand of a fool, and he hopes to win "great glory" as well as some pennies by doing the deed himself. He has cleared an area in which to fight, and appropriated pot, lid, and spit from Widow Rooney's kitchen to serve as helmet, shield, and sword. Congal reveals his identity. He has lost his sword, but considers it just as well to fight with his hands. They exit. Attracta and Corney enter, leading the donkey. Attracta repeats a stanza from her earlier song (see scene 4). They exit as Congal and Tom return. The king carries pot, lid, and spit. Having survived the encounter with the fool, he supposes there must be some other fool on the mountain. Tom exhorts him to kill his rival, Johnny from Meath, should he present himself as a challenger. Congal promises to do so. He borrows the spear to check its sharpness and thrusts at the king, slightly wounding him. Congal senses fate turning against him. He imagines

having to defend himself against fool after fool as he becomes ever more "moon-crazed, moon-blind." He reasons that he can elude the Great Herne's curse, and thus deny him victory, by taking his own life. It occurs to him, however, that he himself may be a fool, in which case his death would fulfill the curse. Tom assures him that he is no fool, for fools are chased by dogs. The king falls on the spit and the fool exits. Attracta and Corney enter. Congal fears that the Great Herne will turn him into a beast in his next life, and he pleads for Attracta's protection. Attracta agrees to help if "his shape is not yet fixed upon." Congal cries that he has defeated the Great Herne and dies. Attracta commands Corney to "lie and beget" with her while Congal's body is still warm. It is the will of the Herne, whose instruments they are. Being pure spirit, the Herne begets only his own image in the mirror of her spirit; the present business requires the imperfection of a man. The donkey brays. He has broken loose and coupled with another donkey. Attracta had hoped to "give a human form to Congal," but she is too late: He will be reborn as a donkey.

BIBLIOGRAPHY

Bloom, Harold. *Yeats*; Foster, R. F. *W. B. Yeats: A Life, I: The Arch-Poet*; Hunt, Hugh. *The Abbey: Ireland's National Theatre, 1904–1978*; Mikhail, E. H., ed. *W. B. Yeats: Interviews and Recollections* (vol. 2); Vendler, Helen Hennessy. *Yeats's Vision and the Later Plays*; Wilson, F. A. C. *W. B. Yeats and Tradition*; Yeats, W. B. *The Letters of W. B. Yeats, Letters on Poetry from W. B. Yeats to Dorothy Wellesley, The Plays, The Variorum Edition of the Plays of W. B. Yeats*.

Hour-Glass, The (prose version 1903, verse version 1913)

"SYNGE's work, the work of Lady GREGORY, my own CATHLEEN NI HOULIHAN and my *Hour-Glass* in its prose form, are characteristic of our first ambition," Yeats said of the Irish dramatic movement in his

NOBEL PRIZE lecture. "They bring the imagination and speech of the country, all that poetical tradition descended from the Middle Ages, to the people of the town" (*Aut.* 417). The play is one of Yeats's most plainspoken protests against the aridity of scientific materialism and academicism (cf. "The SCHOLARS"), and one of his closest approaches to religious orthodoxy; otherwise, it is relatively unremarkable—sturdily constructed upon its simple basis, but lacking Yeats's usual heights of language and complexity of idea.

The play closely follows Lady Wilde's tale "The Priest's Soul," which appears in the first volume of her *Ancient Legends of Ireland* (1887) and in Yeats's anthology *Fairy and Folk Tales of the Irish Peasantry* (1888). Yeats again reprinted the story in the notes to *The Hour-Glass* included in the fourth volume of *The Collected Works in Verse & Prose of William Butler Yeats* (1908; see *VPl.* 640–644).

Yeats wrote two versions of the play, the first in prose, the second—which he began as early as January 1903 but did not finish until 1913—partially in verse (*CL3* 294–295, 313, 561). In a preface to the second version, Yeats explains that he had always been ashamed by the sight of the wise man prostrating himself before the fool. "My own meanings had vanished and I saw before me a cowardly person who seemed to cry out 'the wisdom of the world is foolishness' and to understand the words not as may a scholar and a gentleman but as do ignorant preachers. I began a revision of the words from the moment when the play converted a music hall singer and sent him to mass and to confession; but no revision of words could change the effect of the Wise Man down on his knees before the Fool; so last year I changed action and all" (*VPl.* 577, 645–646). Despite this change of style, the versions share the same general structure of idea and plot and retain common language. Yeats by no means changed "all."

Yeats first alluded to the play in an April 1902 letter to Lady Gregory: "I have a plan for a little religeous [sic] play in one act with quite as striking a plot as 'Kathleen' [i.e., THE COUNTESS CATHLEEN]—It cannot offend anybody & may propitiate Holy Church" (*CL3* 174). His desire to set things right with the church remembers the ruckus cre-

ated by the allegedly blasphemous and unpatriotic *Countess Cathleen* three years earlier. As it turned out, *The Hour-Glass*'s apparent gesture toward orthodox religion left some members of the audience "with afterthoughts [that] were sometimes a little hostile," as Yeats commented in a December 1903 letter to Frank Fay (1870–1931), who had played the fool in the debut production. "Some of them felt that because I had written it, it must of necessity contain some hidden heresy, while others, finding it impossible to believe that I really thought those things, supposed I had written it out of a mere archaistic emotion and that it was therefore a mere literary experiment" (501; see also 348). This suspicion has some basis: Like many of Yeats's poems, the play draws on the mystical and supernatural resonance of Catholicism without in the least acknowledging the authority or the specific teachings of the church.

Yeats was delighted by the debut production of the play. Fay had evidently understood Yeats's conception of the fool (see 219–220) for his performance in the role was "beautiful, wise and subtle" (413). In March 1903, Yeats reported to JOHN QUINN that the production had been the first in which his ideas had been thoroughly carried out: "The actors were dressed in purple with little bits of green here & there, & the back ground [sic] was made of green sacking. The effect was even more telling than I had expected. Everything seemed remote, naïve spiritual [sic], & the attention, liberated from irrelevant distractions, was occupied as it cannot be on an ordinary stage with what was said & done" (333). T. STURGE MOORE designed the sets and ROBERT GREGORY the costumes, following Yeats's instructions. Hugh Hunt comments that the influence of set designer Gordon Craig (1872–1966) was already evident in the play's simple and evocative scenery (*The Abbey* 42). Yeats became a fervent and lifelong admirer of Craig after seeing his production of Purcell's *Dido and Aeneas* and *The Masque of Love* in 1901 (*CL3* 157–160). The two became active collaborators in 1910, when Craig designed screens for a revival of *The Hour-Glass* played at the ABBEY THEATRE, January 13–15, 1911 (see *Letters* 554–555; *UP2* 393–394; *VPl.* 644–645).

DRAMATIS PERSONAE: A Wise Man; Bridget, his wife; Teigue, a fool; angel; children and pupils.

FIRST PERFORMANCE: Prose version: Produced by the IRISH NATIONAL THEATRE SOCIETY at Molesworth Hall, Dublin, March 14, 1903. Verse version: Produced by the National Theatre Society Ltd. (see Irish National Theatre Society) at the Abbey Theatre, Dublin, November 21, 1912.

FIRST PUBLICATION: Prose version: the *North American Review* (periodical), September 1903. Reprinted in *The Hour-Glass*, William Heinemann, London, 1903 (12 copies only) and in *The Hour-Glass and Other Plays*, Macmillan, London, New York, January 13, 1904. Verse version: *The Mask* (periodical), April 1913. Reprinted in *The Hour Glass*, The CUALA PRESS, Churchtown, Dundrum, January 1914 (50 copies only) and in *Responsibilities: Poems and a Play*, The Cuala Press, Churchtown, Dundrum, May 25, 1914.

SYNOPSIS (VERSE VERSION)

The Wise Man's five pupils are to select a lesson for their daily tutorial. The fourth pupil has been instructed in a dream to challenge the atheism of the Wise Man, but the first pupil objects. Teigue arrives, begging for pennies. The pupils make him kneel and place a book on his back. Wary of choosing foolishly and displeasing their teacher, they decide to select a random passage for study. They draw a curtain and enter their master's study. They have selected a passage written by a beggar upon the walls of Babylon. It tells of "two countries, one visible and one invisible," each the reverse of the other. The Wise Man calls the passage nonsense and will have nothing to do with it. As it was written by a beggar, he huffs, they might ask a beggar what it means. Teigue declares that everybody in the world knows what it means, and that he himself has heard the lambs bleating in the invisible world. The Wise Man explains that the passage refers to a "spiritual kingdom that cannot be seen or known till the faculties, whereby we master the kingdom of this world, wither away like green things in winter." He calls this "the most mischievous thought that ever passed out of a man's mouth," though he admits that were it true it would "alter every-

thing," and that—here becoming troubled—he has twice dreamed of it. The pupils exit, and the Wise Man is almost lost in the recollection of his dream. Teigue's renewed requests for a penny recall him. Teigue remarks on the changed character of the countryside: There is the sound of snoring at the break of day where once there was the sound of ringing bells, young men playing cards where once they climbed the hill to the blessed well, friars drinking wine and obeying their wives where once they fasted and served the poor—all due to the Wise Man's teaching. The Wise Man notices that Teigue carries a pair of shears. He offers four pennies for an explanation. Teigue says that each night men lay great black nets to catch the feet of angels, and each morning before dawn he releases the angels. The two argue about the existence of angels, and the Wise Man admits he is haunted by an inexplicable notion of a "crisis of the spirit wherein we get new sight."

The fool creeps away, and an Angel appears. He tells the Wise Man that he will die and be damned as soon as his hour-glass empties, for no soul has crossed the threshold of heaven since he opened his school. The Wise Man pleads that his doubt followed naturally from the suffering and hardship of the world, but the Angel answers, "What's dearth and death and sickness to the soul / That knows no virtue but itself?" The Angel offers a gleam of hope: if within the hour he can find a single soul willing to profess belief he may pass through the purgatorial fire and come to his peace. The Angel departs and the pupils and fool return. The Wise Man attempts to elicit a profession of belief, insisting that an angel had stood upon the very spot, but the pupils assume they are being tested and parry his arguments. They push forward the fourth pupil, whom they teasingly accuse of true belief. The pupil maintains, however, that he had defended religion only to "make them argue." The Wise Man dismisses them and summons his wife. A simple, domestic woman, she affirms that a "good wife only believes in what her husband tells her." He next calls his children. Like the pupils, they are stubbornly faithful to his own skeptical teachings. The fool returns, but the wise man is again disappointed; the fool, perversely, refuses to say a thing. He exits only to return a moment later, having met the Angel upon the threshold and been told to answer whatever questions are put to him. The Wise Man, however, has come to his moment of realization and self-reckoning. He commands the fool to remain silent, crying "May God's will prevail upon the instant, / Although His will be my eternal pain." With the final cry that "all that we have done's undone, / Our speculation but as the wind," he dies. The Angel enters with a casket. The Fool observes a white butterfly emerge from the dead man's mouth. He catches it in his hands and puts it into the Angel's casket so it may be released in the garden of paradise.

BIBLIOGRAPHY

Hunt, Hugh. *The Abbey: Ireland's National Theatre, 1904–1978*; W. B. Yeats. *Autobiographies, The Collected Letters of W. B. Yeats* (vol. 3), *The Letters of W. B. Yeats, Uncollected Prose by W. B. Yeats* (vol. 2), *The Variorum Edition of the Plays of W. B. Yeats.*

Island of Statues, The (1885)

Subtitled "An Arcadian Faery Tale," *The Island of Statues* was Yeats's first published work. He conceived the play, like TIME AND THE WITCH VIVIEN, as a dramatic vehicle for his distant cousin LAURA ARMSTRONG, who was to have played the Enchantress, but the play "soon grew beyond the scope of drawing room acting" (*CLI* 155). In AUTOBIOGRAPHIES, Yeats characterizes the piece as an "Arcadian play in imitation of Edmund Spenser," and he recalls having to read it "to a gathering of critics who were to decide whether it was worthy of publication in the College magazine" (98). Yeats must have acquitted himself well enough, for excerpts from the play—two fairy songs from act 2, scene 3—appeared in the March 1885 issue of the DUBLIN UNIVERSITY REVIEW, and the entire play began a serial appearance in the April issue. In a September 1888 letter to KATHARINE TYNAN, Yeats assessed the play and the mindset that produced it: "I am sure the Island is good of its kind. I was then living a quite harmonius [sic] poetic life. Never thinking out of my depth. Always harmonius narrow, calm. Taking small interest in people but most ardently moved by the more minute kinds of natural beauty. [. . .] Every thing done then was quite passionless" (*CL1* 98).

In an August 1889 letter to GEORGE RUSSELL (AE), Yeats mentioned that he would have liked to have included the entire play in *The Wanderings of Oisin and Other Poems* (1889), but the volume would have become too long (143). The volume did include "The Cloak, the Boat, and the Shoes," a version of "Voices," one of the lyrics from the play he had published in the March 1885 number of the *Dublin University Review*. Yeats chose not to include *The Island of Statues* in his collected works, and the play was not republished until the appearance of *The Variorum Edition of the Poems of W. B. Yeats* in 1957. He did, however, canonize "The Cloak, the Boat, and the Shoes" and "The SONG OF THE HAPPY SHEPHERD," an "epilogue" to *The Island of Statues* and The SEEKER that was first published in the October 1885 issue of the *Dublin University Review*. In a 1937 radio broadcast Yeats explained that he had preserved the two poems not because he liked them, but because certain friends had liked them (*UP2* 509).

The play powerfully appealed to MAUD GONNE, for one, and it may have led her to Yeats's doorstep. Writing to Tynan on January 31, 1889, Yeats described Gonne's initial visit to BEDFORD PARK: "Miss Gone [. . .] was here yesterday with introduction from the Olearys [see JOHN O'LEARY] she says she cried over 'Island of Statues' fragment but altogether favoured the Enchantress and hated Nachina" (134). AE admired the play as well and saw to it that selections were published in the December 1899 issue of the *Irish Homestead* (*LTWBY*, I, 65). The contemporary critic Hugh Kenner finds the play—"long, symbolical, SHELLEYAN"—full of promise: "This first time he scatters rhymes headlong, 'a poisèd lily,' 'a cellar chilly,' a gifted schoolboy's shards of sparkling glass. Yet how gifted! Whatever we make of the plan, he completed it, his joy in the pulse, in the rhymes, in the very inversions refracted everywhere [. . .]. Parts are better than parts of [Keats's] *Endymion*, and four 1885 issues of the *Dublin University Review*

contained proof that co-linguists of the aging TEN-
NYSON might yet once more own a poet" (*Colder Eye*
128). At the very least the play introduces themes
and motifs that foreshadow Yeats's maturity: the
cruelty of goddess or queen (both Naschina and
the Enchantress herald elements of this type, epitomized by the queen of *A FULL MOON IN MARCH*),
the alchemical inversion of the perishable and the
imperishable (the lure of the imperishable explains
Gonne's unsettling approval of the Enchantress),
the "burthen of the infinite" (as the Enchantress
calls it), the apocalyptic sway of the moon.

DRAMATIS PERSONAE: Naschina, shepherdess; Colin, shepherd; Thernot, shepherd; Almintor,
a hunter; Antonio, his page; Enchantress of the
Island; a company of the sleepers of the Isle.

FIRST PUBLICATION: *The Dublin University
Review* (periodical), April–July, 1885. Reprinted in
The Variorum Edition of the Poems of W. B. Yeats,
Macmillan, New York, October 29, 1957.

SYNOPSIS

Act 1, scene 1

Thernot summons Naschina from her cottage.
Colin enters and likewise summons her. They
engage in competing serenades. Naschina scolds
them for their "busy tumults." The bickering shepherds are sent scurrying by the sound of a horn and
a flying arrow, which they take to be advance warning of robbers. The culprits turn out to be Almintor
and Antonio, neighborhood hunters, who enter in
pursuit of a heron. Almintor immediately becomes
amorous, but his flattery reduces Naschina to tears.
She grieves that there is no man in Arcady who
"sustains his soul in courage or in might." The
kind of man she could love would not bring her
trinkets, as do Arcadian men, but prove his devotion by going in quest of battle with dragons and
enchanters.

Act 1, scene 2

Almintor and Antonio make their way through a
remote forest valley upon a quest of the type to
impress Naschina. There is a small island upon the
lake where lives a great Enchantress. She keeps
watch over the "goblin flower of joy," possession
of which brings truth, wisdom, and "long years of

youth / Beyond a mortal's years." The many who
have ventured onto the island seeking the flower
have been "changed for ever into moon-white
stone." A fairy voice—that which "sang around the
tree" as Eve fell into sin—beckons them to follow.

Act 1, scene 3

Amid the "immovable figures of those who have
failed in their quest," fairy voices banter. Almintor
enters, having been conveyed to the island on a
winged boat. Unsure how to proceed, he decides
to shoot an arrow from a pinnacle and trust the
gods to guide it to the magic flower. He exits. A
fairy voice commands a goblin servant to "pilot the
course of his arrow's deceit." The arrow falls and
Almintor reenters. He plucks the nearest flower
and turns to stone.

Act 2, scene 1

Naschina commiserates with Antonio. She has
passed a "weary week" and shed many tears since
Almintor left. She asks again to hear how he
departed in the living boat that flapped its wings
across the lake like "some wild drake." She decides
to dress herself as a shepherd boy and go in search
of him. She exits. Colin and Thernot enter, still
bickering over Naschina, but hesitant to fight.
Naschina reenters. Antonio introduces her as
Guarimond, a shepherd boy grief-stricken by the
loss of a beloved sheep. "More grief is mine," says
Colin. He explains that both he and Thernot love
Naschina and asks whether they must fight for her.
She says, "There is no way but that ye fight I wis, /
If *her* ye love." They unhappily resign themselves to
the battle. Concerned that she may have instigated
some mischief, Naschina asks if they are likely to
carry out their plan. Antonio assures her that this
is unthinkable.

Act 2, scene 2

Naschina and Antonio make their way through a
remote part of the forest. They come to the shore
of the lake, from which they can see the Enchantress's island. Once again, the fairy boat, a "huddling
blackness," draws near. Naschina and Antonio exit,
and Antonio reenters alone, deeply affected by the
sight of Naschina disappearing into the "mists of
evening." Colin and Thernot enter with swords.

Antonio's amusement fades as the duel unfolds in earnest. Thernot is wounded. Antonio tries to intervene. As the shepherds clash, Antonio hears the "wild horns" that "told Almintor's end," and he supposes that Naschina's end has come as well. He tells the shepherds to heed "the dirge of her ye love," but the fight continues.

Act 2, scene 3

The disguised Naschina enters with the beautiful Enchantress. Naschina entreats the Enchantress to lead her to the "statued place." The Enchantress partially opens a gate to reveal the statues, some bending, some holding withered flowers. Naschina would find the enchanted flower and rescue her "sad hunter-friend," but the Enchantress blocks her way. Only a shepherdess "long years foretold" can discover the flower, and she can claim the flower only if something willingly dies for her. In any case, the Enchantress would cast a spell upon her as soon as she set foot on the island, for she herself would die if the flower were plucked. Naschina asks the Enchantress to send out a cry that "one shall die, unless one die for her," claiming merely to be curious whether "anything will stir / For such a call." In exchange for a kiss from the handsome youth, the Enchantress dispatches her spirits to raise the cry. The Enchantress, meanwhile, attempts to woo Naschina. A fairy voice reports that it has delivered the cry, and that "one alone of all would hark, / A man who by a dead man stood," with a bloody rapier in his hand. A second voice tells of seeing below a shepherd boy swimming toward the island with a sword clenched in his teeth. Upon hearing the cry, he let himself sink. Realizing that Colin and Thernot are dead for her sake—it is not clear which has allowed himself to drown—Naschina reveals that she is the prophesied shepherdess. She commands the Enchantress to bring the flower, for she has become the more powerful. The Enchantress points to a "scarlet bloom" within a "cloven rock." She warns Naschina that having assumed this new power she will outlive her "amorous happy time" and her soul will suffer the "burthen of the infinite." Feeling the "warmth of life" chilling within her, the Enchantress exits to die. Naschina follows and reenters, having seen the Enchantress

fade and vanish. She opens the gate and places the flower upon the lips of Almintor, waking him. She wakes the other sleepers. Spellbound since ancient days, they inquire about Aeneas, Arthur, Pan, and the Trojan War. The sleepers pledge to remain on the island with Naschina—still in shepherd's costume—as their king, but she defers to Almintor, who names her queen. Under the rising moon, Almintor and the other sleepers cast long shadows, but Naschina stands shadowless.

BIBLIOGRAPHY

Finneran, Richard J., et al., eds. *Letters to W. B. Yeats* (vol. 1); Kenner, Hugh. *A Colder Eye: The Modern Irish Writers;* W. B. Yeats, *Autobiographies, The Collected Letters of W. B. Yeats* (vol. 1), *Uncollected Prose by W. B. Yeats* (vol. 2).

King of the Great Clock Tower, The (1934, verse version 1935)

Yeats finished a prose-and-verse version of the play in January 1934 and it was produced in July at the ABBEY THEATRE on a bill with *The RESURRECTION* (YC 286). Concluding that "prose dialogue is as unpopular among my studious friends as dialogue in verse among actors and playgoers," he rewrote the dialogue in verse (*VPl.* 1311). Still dissatisfied, he rewrote the play entirely as *A FULL MOON IN MARCH,* and the two plays appeared back to back in the 1935 volume of the same name. In a November 1934 letter to MARGOT RUDDOCK, Yeats accounted for his decision to transform *The King of the Great Clock Tower* into *A Full Moon in March:* "I am rewriting *The King of the Great Clock Tower,* giving the Queen a speaking part, that you may act it. I have so arranged it that you can give place to a dancer (quite easy as you will both wear masks). The old version of the play is bad because abstract and incoherent. This version is poignant and simple—lyrical dialogue all simple. It takes years to get my plays right" (*Sweet Dancer* 23; see also 46; *Letters* 830). In a preface to *A Full Moon in March,* Yeats gives a different explanation: "In *The King of* the *Great Clock Tower* there are three characters, King, Queen and Stroller, and that is a character too many; reduced to the essentials, Queen and Stroller, the fable should have greater intensity. I started afresh and called the new version *A Full Moon in March*" (*VPl.* 1311–1312).

During a visit to Rapallo in June 1934, Yeats asked EZRA POUND to read *The King of the Great Clock Tower* in draft. Pound's denunciation of the play as "putrid" precipitated an uncharacteristic crisis of confidence. Much like "Panurge consulting oracles as to whether he should get married and rejecting all that did not confirm his own desire," Yeats sought and received encouragement from several protégés belonging to his "own school" (*VPl.* 1310–1311). In July, he was vindicated by an article in the *Sunday Times* entitled "Two New Plays by W. B. Yeats" (*Plays* 909). The following month he instructed OLIVIA SHAKESPEAR to forward a cutting of the article to Pound (her son-in-law) in order to "confound him. He may have been right to condemn it as poetry but he condemned it as drama. It has turned out the most popular of my dance plays" (*Letters* 827).

The King of the Great Clock Tower continues the experiment in Noh-influenced drama that had begun nearly 20 years earlier in AT THE HAWK'S WELL. As Yeats remarks in his 1934 commentary on the play: "FIGHTING THE WAVES and the present play so far imitate the Japanese model that they climax in a dance, substitute suggestion for representation, but like the Japanese plays themselves they are stage plays" (*VPl.* 1009). In the play's debut production, ballerina Ninette de Valois (1898–2001)—who had directed the Abbey Theatre's short-lived school of ballet (1927–33) and performed in *Fighting the Waves*—played the part of the queen. The second version of *The King of the Great Clock Tower* is dedicated to her, with "pardon for covering her expressive face with a mask."

Like CALVARY, *The King of the Great Clock Tower* dramatizes the distinction between the *primary* and *antithetical* tinctures, opposing modes of being that respectively represent subservience to the world and revelry in the self (see A VISION). The King, whose proclivities are public and political, manifests the *primary* tincture, while the Queen and the

Stroller, whose proclivities are private and poetic, manifest the *antithetical* tincture. The King's gesture of subservience to the Queen at the end of the play suggests, however, that he instinctively understands that his own mode has been eclipsed in the moment of miracle. The clock tower is a crucial motif of the play, a totem of the *primary* tincture, representing mechanism, order, and sequence. Countering the implication of the clock tower are the allusions to the possibility of temporal transcendence that suffuse the talk of the Stroller and the songs of the attendants. The Queen, meanwhile, belongs to a thematic lineage that loosely includes Mallarmé's Hérodiade (see *Aut.* 247), the "staring virgin" of "TWO SONGS FROM A PLAY," Attracta in "The HERNE'S EGG," and MAUD GONNE as figured in "A BRONZE HEAD": She is the virgin staring upon miracle, at once a muse and an icon demanding sacrifice—the cruel divinity of the artistic process. In Thomas Whitaker's description, she is the "frigid lunar Queen" who "descends from her absolute realm to enter a slaying and fructifying union with the temporal—with the hero, poet, or other manifestation of the solar cycle, who must die to create" (*Swan and Shadow* 284).

Bernard Krimm, on the other hand, interprets the play as a political allegory, associating the clock tower with Big Ben and the British government, and the beheading of the Stroller with the executions that followed the EASTER RISING of 1916. "Against the king of this clock tower," Krimm comments, "the red-bearded Stroller found himself pitted, just as the Irish patriots found themselves pitted against the might of Westminster. [. . .] With the ultimate victory of the Stroller over the King of the Great Clock Tower [. . .] Yeats invites us to see the superiority of Irish thought over English philosophy as well as the ultimate victory of Irish political sacrifice" (*Irish Free State* 212–215).

The motif of the severed head dominates both *The King of the Great Clock Tower* and *A Full Moon in March*. It descends from Yeats's story "The Binding of the Hair," which appeared in the January 1896 number of the SAVOY (see SRV 177–181), and recurs also in *The GREEN HELMET* and *The DEATH OF CUCHULAIN*. In his 1934 commentary on *The King of the Great Clock Tower*, Yeats observes that the "dance with the severed head, suggests the central idea of WILDE's *Salome* [1893]. Wilde took it from Heine, who has somewhere described Salome in hell throwing into the air the head of John the Baptist. Heine may have found it in some Jewish religious legend for it is part of the old ritual of the year: the mother goddess and the slain god. In the first edition of *The Secret Rose* [1897] there is a story ["The Binding of the Hair"] based on some old Gaelic legend. A certain man swears to sing the praise of a certain woman, his head is cut off and the head sings. A poem of mine called, 'HE GIVES HIS BELOVED CERTAIN RHYMES' was the song of the head. In attempting to put that story into a dance play I found that I had gone close to Salome's dance in Wilde's play. But in his play the dance is before the head is cut off" (*VPl.* 1010; see also 1311–1312; *Letters* 826–827). Appended at the end of the play is an alternate version of the song sung by the severed head; it appears in Yeats's collected poems as "Alternative Song for the Severed Head in *The King of the Great Clock Tower.*"

DRAMATIS PERSONAE: First attendant; second attendant; the King, the Queen; the Stroller.

FIRST PERFORMANCE: Produced by the National Theatre Society Ltd. (see the IRISH NATIONAL THEATRE SOCIETY) at the Abbey Theatre, Dublin, July 30, 1934.

FIRST PUBLICATION: *Life and Letters* (periodical), November 1934. Reprinted in *The King of the Great Clock Tower, Commentaries and Poems,* The CUALA PRESS, Dublin, December 14, 1934. The version in verse first appeared in *A Full Moon in March,* Macmillan, London, November 22, 1935.

SYNOPSIS (VERSE VERSION)

The stage curtain rises. As they sing of the timelessness of "Tir-nan-oge," the Celtic fairy world, two attendants part an inner curtain and reveal the King and Queen upon thrones. The King insists that the Queen must finally reveal her country, name, and family, as it has been a year since she ascended in mystery to the throne. The Queen remains impassive. The first attendant admits the Stroller. A poet and a fool, he has been singing the Queen's beauty since he first heard of it. Now he has come to see her for himself. The King asks whether he has no wife or mistress to sing of. He says that he had a wife, but the image of the Queen made her seem "fat, slow, thick of the limbs, / In all her movements like a Michaelmas goose." He demands to see the Queen, and the King, amazed by his audacity, acknowledges her at his side. The Stroller judges her neither "so red, nor white, nor full in the breast" as he had imagined, but no matter as long as he proclaims her the most beautiful. The King orders him to be gone, but the Stroller has sworn before a simpleton he met in a tavern that the Queen would dance for him. The gods had appeared and approved of what he had sworn, and they had prophesized that the Queen would kiss his mouth "on stroke of midnight when the old year dies." The King orders him beheaded. Undaunted, the Stroller declares that the Queen must dance; grateful, he must sing; grateful in her turn, the Queen must kiss him. The King offers to spare the Stroller if the Queen will break her silence, but she remains impassive. The King issues the death sentence and commands the queen to "laugh, dance or sing"—anything that will break the trance of her staring eyes. As if in the voice of the Queen, the second attendant sings of the sexual opposition between man and woman: the man assaults, the woman consumes. The King receives the head of the Stroller and mockingly commands it to sing. The Queen begins to dance. She takes up the Stroller's head. As if in the voice of the head, the first attendant sings of the "marvel" when "the dead and living kiss." The second attendant strikes the gong, indicating the tolling of midnight. At the last stroke the Queen kisses the Stroller's lips. The King draws his sword to strike her, but instead kneels and lays his sword at her feet. The attendants close the inner curtain as they sing of a discussion between the rambling man and the "wicked, crooked, hawthorn tree" as to whether "lovely things" are subject to the passage of time.

BIBLIOGRAPHY

Krimm, Bernard G. *W. B. Yeats and the Emergence of the Irish Free State, 1918–1939: Living in the Explosion*; Whitaker, Thomas R. *Swan and Shadow: Yeats's Dialogue with History*; Yeats, W. B. *Ah, Sweet Dancer: W. B. Yeats and Margot Ruddock, Autobiog-*

raphies, *The Letters of W. B. Yeats, The Plays, The Secret Rose: A Variorum Edition, The Variorum Edition of the Plays of W. B. Yeats.*

King's Threshold, The (1904)

The play tells the tale of the poet Seanchan (pronounced "Shanahan"). Stripped of his seat on the council of state, he undertakes a hunger strike in order to restore the ancient prerogative of the poet (*CL3* 413). A. Norman Jeffares and A. S. Knowland note that the play has possible roots in a medley of source material. They cite "Seanchan the Bard and the King of the Cats," Lady Wilde's rendering of the tale in *Ancient Legends of Ireland* (1887); *Sancan the Bard,* a play written 10 years earlier by Yeats's friend and BLAKE collaborator Edwin Ellis (1848–1916); and "Immtheacht na Tromdaimhe," a Middle Irish tale that had been reprinted in the Transactions of the Ossianic Society (*CCP* 43; see also *VPl.* 314–315, 526, 1283–1284; on Ellis's play, see *Yeats the Playwright* 32–34). As Yeats points out in a 1903 installment of *Samhain,* however, his version of the story is told "from the poet's point of view, and not, like the old story-tellers, from the king's" (*Expl.* 102–103; *IDM* 23; see also *VPl.* 313, 315, 1283–1284). It thus becomes a vehicle for a distinctly romantic complaint about the increasingly marginal place of the poet in modern society, a version of SHELLEY's complaint in "A Defence of Poetry" (written 1821) that the "poets have been challenged to resign the civic crown to reasoners and mechanists" (paragraph 32). Yeats hints at the contemporary Irish version of this conflict in a 1906 note to the play: "[*The King's Threshold*] was written when our Society [the IRISH NATIONAL THEATRE SOCIETY] was having a hard fight for the recognition of pure art in a community of which one half was buried in the practical affairs of life, and the other half in politics and a propagandist patriotism" (*VPl.* 315).

As a sustained argument for the prerogatives of "pure art" and the spiritual preeminence of the poet, the play naturally flew in the face of nationalist opinion. The provocation was compounded by J. M. SYNGE's *In the Shadow of the Glen,* with which *The King's Threshold* shared a bill in October 1903. "These two plays," writes Robert Welch, "seemed to turn aside from any form of Irish civic responsibility. *The King's Threshold,* with the hauteur of its hunger-striking poet, disdaining duty and the pressure to conform, was bad enough; but Synge's play, with its (then) shockingly frank depiction of adultery, greed, and moral cowardice amongst Irish country people, was seen as a calculated insult" (*Abbey Theatre* 25). MAUD GONNE, as well as the actors Dudley Digges and Máire T. Quinn, duly resigned from the Irish National Theatre Society and made a show of walking out of Molesworth Hall on opening night (*The Abbey* 49–50; *CL3* 428–429, 436; *GY* 173–178).

The most significant of Yeats's many revisions of the play came in 1922 (on the evolution of the play, see *Yeats the Playwright* 34–39). In earlier versions of the play Seanchan reconciles with the king, but in the revised version he withers and dies the martyr's death, much as his romantic-visionary counterpart Paul Ruttledge dies in WHERE THERE IS NOTHING. In a prologue to the original version of the play, spoken by an old man, Yeats justifies the reconciliation between poet and king: "Some think it would be a finer tale if Seanchan had died at the end of it, and the king had the guilt at his door, for that might have served the poet's cause better in the end. But that is not true, for if he that is in the story but a shadow and an image of poetry had not risen up from the death that threatened him, the ending would not have been true and joyful enough to be put into the voices of players and proclaimed in the mouths of trumpets, and poetry would have been badly served" (*VPl.* 313). In his notes to *Plays in Prose and Verse* (1922), Yeats in turn justifies the revised ending: "I have given the play the tragic end I would have given it at the first, had not a friend advised me to 'write comedy and have a few happy moments in the theatre.' My friend meant that tragic emotion, depending as it does upon gradually deepening reverie, is so fragile, that it is shattered by a wrong movement or cadence, or even by a light in the wrong place" (316). Numerous commentators have drawn a connection between the revised ending and the case of Terence MacSwiney (1879–1920), the lord mayor of Cork, who died following a 74-day hunger strike while imprisoned in Britain for possessing a Royal Irish Constabulary cipher. Yeats disavowed this connection in 1922, noting that when he wrote the play "neither suffragette nor patriot had adopted the hunger strike, nor had the hunger strike been used anywhere, so far as I know, as a political weapon" (*VPl.* 315), but in a September 1920 letter he told Lennox Robinson (1886–1958) that he was rewriting the play in case "the Mayor of Cork may make it tragically appropriate" (*AP* 182; see also *Irish Free State* 23–32).

The debut production brought ANNIE HORNIMAN, later to bankroll the ABBEY THEATRE, into the Irish dramatic movement as an inexperienced but determined costume designer, and—far more important—as financier. Máire Nic Shiubhlaigh (1888–1959), who played the part of Fedelm, remembers that Horniman "came to Dublin about the summer of 1903, took rooms in a large hotel, imported bales of the most expensive dress materials, engaged a team of English theatrical costumiers, and began fitting us out [. . .]" (*Abbey: Interviews and Recollections* 42). Yeats was lukewarm about Horniman's costumes, but he predicted—not without ulterior motive perhaps—that she would eventually come into her own (*CL3* 528).

The play is dedicated to Frank Fay (1870–1931) for his "beautiful speaking in the character of Seanchan." In an August 1903 letter, Yeats predicted great things for his performance: "I am afraid you will have an exhausting part in Seanchan, but you will find plenty to act and the best dramatic verse I have written to speak. Your brother [William Fay] told me that he meant to cast you as Seanchan, and I am very glad of it. I have long wanted to see you with some part which would give you the highest opportunities. Your playing of the Fool in the HOURGLASS was beautiful, wise and subtle, but such a part can never express anyone's whole nature. It has to be created more or less from without. Your performance of Seanchan will I believe establish all our fames" (413).

DRAMATIS PERSONAE: King Guaire; Seanchan; his pupils; the mayor of Kinvara; two cripples; Brian, an old servant; the lord high chamberlain; a soldier; a monk; court ladies; two princesses; Fedelm.

FIRST PERFORMANCE: Produced by the IRISH NATIONAL THEATRE SOCIETY at Molesworth Hall, Dublin, October 8, 1903.

FIRST PUBLICATION: Printed in New York for private circulation (see *Biblio.* 71–72), and then in *The King's Threshold and On Baile's Strand: Being Volume Three of Plays for an Irish Theatre*, A. H. Bullen, London, March 1904.

SYNOPSIS

There is a table laden with food before the king's palace; Seanchan lies on the steps surrounded by his pupils. The king has summoned the musicians and poets of the land to save Seanchan, who refuses to eat or drink that he might die according to the old custom that a man who starves on another's threshold forever disgraces it. The king explains that he removed Seanchan from the council of the state because his courtiers objected to a mere man of letters seated among them. Seanchan had "pleaded for the poets' right, / Established at the establishment of the world," but the king had insisted that it was the "men who ruled the world, / And not the men who sang it, who should sit / Where there was the most honour." His reputation suffering and yet unable to give way without damaging the authority of the throne, the king asks the students to persuade their master to abandon his protest. When he learns the nature of the disagreement, the oldest pupil chides Seanchan for overreacting. The pupil speaks so much like a courtier that Seanchan puts an old lesson to him. He asks why poetry is honoured. The pupil answers that poets hung "Images of the life that was in Eden / About the child-bed of the world, that it, / Looking upon those images, might bear / Triumphant children." Seanchan asks how these images should be guarded. Like the most precious treasures of legend, the pupil answers. The youngest pupil throws himself at the poet's feet and asks what will become of him without his master. Seanchan answers that the poets had but promised him their "sorrow," and then proclaims a gospel of tragic joy: "And I would have all know that when all falls / In ruin, poetry calls out in joy, / Being the scattering hand, the bursting pod, / The victim's joy among the holy flame, / God's laughter at the shattering of the world. / And now that joy laughs out, and weeps and burns / On these bare steps." Thwarted, the pupils decide to beg the king to reverse his decision.

The mayor of Kinvara, the two cripples, and Brian enter. In a comically bumbling and pompous speech, the mayor implores the poet to do the "reasonable" thing and give way in a matter of "mere sentiment," especially as he may upset the king's intention to give Kinvara—Seanchan's hometown—new grazing land. Seanchan replies in scorn. The mayor reminds Seanchan of the cattle that died the previous winter for lack of grass. Brian, the cripples, and the mayor argue about the respective rights of poet and king, with the mayor adopting the position of unthinking loyalty. Brian and the cripples finally seize the mayor and give him a drubbing as he shouts for help. The chamberlain arrives in a dudgeon. The cripples slink away, and the chamberlain shoves the mayor and Brian from the steps with his staff. The mayor bows and grovels on his way out, and promises to bring Seanchan's fiancé.

The monk and soldier emerge from the palace as the court ladies peep from behind the palace curtain. The chamberlain asks them to do whatever they can. The monk has spoken "too many homilies wherein / The wanton imagination of the poets / has been condemned" to play the role of flatterer, while the soldier simply declares "good riddance." The girls prevail on the soldier, though they themselves have been loud against Seanchan; they complain that there is no more music for dancing and that they have been pelted by stones while on the road. The soldier rudely presses meat on the poet. Seanchan calls the soldier the "King's Dog" and tells him to crouch down and wag his tail. The soldier draws his sword, but the chamberlain steps in. Trying a new gambit, he claims to be something of a poet himself. Therefore poetry has its representative on the council. Seanchan answers that he should then cry aloud that the poet has invented the very reality of the king and court: has consecrated the crown; christened gold and silver as precious; emboldened the soldier by "commending wasteful virtues"; inspired royal finery with tales of enchanted kings. The monk would go to the king and console him. Seanchan calls him near and

whisperingly asks whether his God that was once so wild has learned to "eat bread / From the King's hand, and perch upon his finger." Losing patience, the girls depart to see a hurley match. Knowing what draws them, Seanchan calls out bitterly that the poet's love songs have bred their desire. The two young princesses come from the palace with food. Seanchan takes the hand of one. He recalls that her mother had once been taken in hand and blessed by a leper, and he would know whether he is being served from contaminated hands. All about him are lepers, he cries, and he flings the content of the cup in their faces. All flee as he staggers and looks up at the moon, seeing it as a leper blessing all with leprosy.

Fedelm enters. She begs Seanchan to come away and be married, but Seanchan is absorbed in a vision of the stars marrying the earth and begetting a great race. She promises to bring him to a smooth lawn where he and his pupils can sing poems under an apple tree. He knows the place and unfolds a vision of the garden of Eden. Fedelm offers bread soaked in wine; he is about to accept it when he remembers himself and rebukes her for tempting him. Fedelm proffers her white arms and soft neck as "better than the brown earth," but Seanchan in a sudden rage casts her away as a traitor; just as suddenly he realizes what he has done and embraces her with the words, "If I had eaten when you bid me, sweetheart, / The kiss of multitudes in times to come / Had been the poorer." All else having failed, the king enters to offer bread with his own hands. Seanchan refuses to eat. The king, "all king again," commands his courtiers to lead in the pupils with halters around their necks. They will be killed if Seanchan does not relent. The king tells the pupils to beg for their lives, but they urge Seanchan to uphold the poet's right. Seanchan rises with a sudden resurgence of strength. He declares that he will outface even the leprous moon, and that when he and his pupils are dead they should be laid uncovered on some windy hill so that "mankind and that leper there may know / Dead faces laugh." These are his last words. The oldest pupil cries that "some strange triumphant thought / So filled his heart with joy that it has burst / Being grown too mighty for our frailty. . . ." The youngest pupil calls upon the "long-throated swans upon the waves of time" to sing loudly and wake the great race "beyond the wall of the world," but the oldest pupil corrects him: "Not what it leaves behind it in the light / But what it carries with it to the dark / Exalts the soul; nor song nor trumpet-blast / Can call up races from the worsening world / To mend the wrong and mar the solitude / Of the great shade we follow to the tomb."

BIBLIOGRAPHY

Foster, R. F. *W. B. Yeats: A Life, II: The Arch-Poet*; Hunt, Hugh. *The Abbey: Ireland's National Theatre, 1904–1978*; Jeffares, A. Norman, and A. S. Knowland. *A Commentary on the Collected Plays of W. B. Yeats*; Krimm, Bernard G. *W. B. Yeats and the Emergence of the Irish Free State, 1918–1939: Living in the Explosion*; Mikhail, E. H., ed. *The Abbey Theatre: Interviews and Recollections*; Ure, Peter. *Yeats the Playwright: A Commentary on the Character and Design in the Major Plays*; Wade, Allan. *A Bibliography of the Writings of W. B. Yeats*; Welch, Robert. *The Abbey Theatre, 1899–1999*; Yeats, W. B. *The Collected Letters of W. B. Yeats* (vol. 3), *Explorations, The Gonne-Yeats Letters 1893–1938, The Irish Dramatic Movement, The Variorum Edition of the Plays of W. B. Yeats*.

Land of Heart's Desire, The
(1894)

Unlike *The ISLAND OF STATUES* and *The COUNTESS CATHLEEN, The Land of Heart's Desire* is less dramatic poetry than poetic drama: a play to be acted rather than read or recited on stage. It thus marked an important development in Yeats's career as a playwright. It was, not coincidentally, the first of his plays to be professionally performed, and it was well received during its six-week run at the Avenue Theatre in London, in a production secretly financed by ANNIE HORNIMAN and directed by FLORENCE FARR, to whom the play is dedicated. The play shared a bill with John Todhunter's *A Comedy of Sighs* and then with George Bernard

Shaw's more successful *Arms and the Man* (see *Aut.* 219–222; *CL1* 385–386; *Mem.* 74). In bringing together Yeats, Shaw, and Horniman, the program represented not only a landmark of modern drama, but in some sense the commencement of the Irish dramatic movement. Yeats, who had been diligently writing plays for some 12 years, reveled in finally seeing one of his plays performed. GEORGE MOORE gives a silhouette of Yeats in the flush of his first dramatic success: "His play neither pleased nor displeased; it struck me as an inoffensive trifle, but himself had provoked a violent antipathy as he strode to and forth at the back of the dress circle, a long black cloak drooping from his shoulders, a soft black sombrero on his head, a voluminous black silk tie flowing from his collar, loose black trousers dragging untidily over his long, heavy feet—a man of such excessive appearance that I could not do otherwise—could I?—than to mistake him for an Irish parody of the poetry that I had seen all my life strutting its rhythmic way in the alleys of the Luxembourg Gardens, preening its rhymes by the fountains, excessive in habit and gait" (*Hail and Farewell* 78–79).

The play tells of a young and restless bride lured from home to the land of the fairies. It is associable with a number of early poems that ponder the competing claims of the human and fairy realms, as for example "The Host of the Air" (1893), "The HOSTING OF THE SIDHE," "The MAN WHO DREAMED OF FAERYLAND," "The STOLEN CHILD," "The UNAPPEASABLE HOST," "The WANDERINGS OF OISIN," and "The WHITE BIRDS." In terms of dramatic structure, it closely resembles CATHLEEN NI HOULIHAN, in which the national call substitutes for the fairy call (see *VPl.* 235). In MEMOIRS, Yeats explains the play as an allegory of his frustrated romance with MAUD GONNE: "I began to write *The Land of Heart's Desire* to supply the niece [Dorothy Paget] of a new friend, Miss Florence Farr, with a part, and put into it my own despair. I could not tell why Maud Gonne had turned from me unless she had done so from some vague desire for some impossible life, for some unvarying excitement like that of the heroine of my play" (72–73).

In a 1938 letter, Yeats revealed that the names Hart and Bruin remember names "common in the village of Rosses at Rosses Point, SLIGO. There were pilots and innkeepers of the name of Bruin and probably also of the name Hart, though in the case of the Harts my memory is more vague [. . .]. My memory is that about half the village were called Bruin" (*Letters* 908). The play is set in Kilmacowen, which is about four and half miles southwest of Yeats's native Sligo. James P. McGarry explains that Kilmacowen is a townland, and not a "barony" as Yeats writes in his headnote to the play (*Place Names* 59).

DRAMATIS PERSONAE: Maureen Bruin; Bridget Bruin, his wife; Shawn Bruin, his son; Mary Bruin, his daughter-in-law; Father Hart; a faery child.

FIRST PERFORMANCE: The Avenue Theatre, London, March 29, 1894.

FIRST PUBLICATION: *The Land of Heart's Desire*, T. Fisher Unwin, London, April 1894.

SYNOPSIS

The scene is laid in a cottage in Kilmacowen on May Eve during some "remote time." Father Hart sits with the family. Bridget complains that instead of cleaning the dinner pots Mary has been bent over an old book. Written by Maureen's grandfather, a dreaming impractical man, the book has lain in the thatch for 50 years. Father Hart asks what the book is about. Mary answers that she is reading how Princess Edain heard a voice calling her one May Eve and followed until she came to the Land of Faery, a realm of eternal youth and high spirits. Father Hart warns that Edain was misled by "some wrecked angel" and urges Mary to resign herself to the "little round of deeds and days" ordained by God. Maureen recommends that they place a branch of "blessed quicken wood" over the door for luck, as faeries steal newly married brides on May Eve. Mary hangs the branch, but, as she reports, a faery child "ran up out of the wind" and made off with it. Mary hears a knock at the door; she answers and then returns to fetch milk for the visitor, a "little queer old woman dressed in green." Bridget exclaims, "The Good people beg for milk and fire / Upon May Eve—woe to the house that gives, / For they have power upon it for a year." Father Hart promises that the cross hanging on

the wall will protect them. Maureen tells Mary to put away her "dreams of discontent," and reminds her of the stocking full of guineas and the hundred acres that she will eventually inherit. Mary again answers the door. She retrieves a piece of turf from the fire to give a "little queer old man" seeking a light for his pipe. Bridget declares that Mary, idle and fine at the best of times, is no longer fit to be a wife. Mary replies that she does not care whether she gives the house into the power of the faeries and calls out: "Faeries, come take me out of this dull world, / For I would ride with you upon the wind, / (Run on the top of the dishevelled tide,) / And dance upon the mountains like a flame." Afraid of losing his bride, Shawn affirms his love and recalls Mary to herself.

A child is heard singing of the wind that withers the lonely heart. Maureen brings in a child of entrancing beauty. Bridget surmises that she is high born. The child is about to dance when she sees the crucifix on the wall and shrieks. Half-entranced, Father Hart removes the cross to another room. The child dances and again sings of the "lonely of heart." Mary hears invisible pipes and "other small steps beating upon the floor." The child says she is older than even the ancient eagle-cock, and the family finally grasps that she is not of this world. Shawn tries to grab her, but the removal of the cross has made her invulnerable, as if surrounded by a glass wall. The Faery embraces Mary and calls her away to the Land of Heart's Desire. Father Hart urges her to remember her duties. The Faery counters that she will grow "like the rest; / Bear children, cook, and bend above the churn, / And wrangle over butter, fowl, and eggs, / Until at last, grown old and bitter of tongue, / You're crouching there and shivering at the grave." Father Hart claims Mary in "the Name of One crucified," but the Faery claims her in the name of her own heart. Shawn holds out his arms and vows his love—Mary is torn—her resistance to the Faery seems to weaken—she collapses, dead. Outside the faery voices sing.

BIBLIOGRAPHY

McGarry, James P. *Place Names in the Writings of William Butler Yeats*; Moore, George. *Hail and Farewell*;

Yeats, W. B. *Autobiographies, The Collected Letters of W. B. Yeats* (vol. 1); *The Letters of W. B. Yeats, Memoirs, The Variorum Edition of the Plays of W. B. Yeats.*

Mosada (1886)

Yeats's early play concerns a young Moorish girl, Mosada, who is arrested by the Spanish Inquisition. Unbeknownst to her, Gomez, her departed lover, has become a leader of the Inquisition. In the play's tragic denouement, the girl ingests poison, and the two lovers realize each other's identity only as her life slips away (for the play, see *VP* 689–704). Written in 1884, the play was published in the DUB-LIN UNIVERSITY REVIEW in June 1886 and privately printed by Sealy, Bryers, and Walker, Dublin, most likely in October (*Biblio.* 19), making it the first of Yeats's books. The edition of 100 copies was issued to subscribers drummed up by JOHN BUTLER YEATS and EDWARD DOWDEN, and the few extant copies are now a valuable rarity (*W. B. Yeats* 49; *Biblio.* 20). The volume's frontispiece featured a sketch of the poet by the elder Yeats (for the sketch, see *AP* 40), a bit of self-promotion that rightly made Yeats nervous. "There was to have been a picture of some incident in the play but my father was too much of a portrait painter not to do this instead," Yeats wrote on the frontispiece in JOHN QUINN's copy of the book. "I was alarmed at the impudence of putting a portrait in my first book, but my father was full of ancient & modern instances" (*AP* 40; *Biblio.* 19). John Butler Yeats presented a copy of the volume "with some emphasis" to Gerard Manley Hopkins when he came to call at his Stephen's Green studio. Hopkins commented to Coventry Patmore that he did not think much of *Mosada* (nor of "The Two Titans"), and vindicated Yeats on the matter of the frontispiece: "For a young man's pamphlet this was something too much, but you will understand a father's feeling" (*MM* 49; *PF* 146). Yeats subsequently included the play in *The Wanderings of Oisin and Other Poems* (1889) and then struck it from his canon.

DRAMATIS PERSONAE: Mosada, a Moorish lady; Ebremar, a monk; Cola, a lame boy; monks and inquisitors.

FIRST PUBLICATION: The *Dublin University Review* (periodical), June 1886. Reprinted in *Mosada. A Dramatic Poem*, Sealy, Bryers, and Walker, Dublin, October 1886.

SYNOPSIS

Scene 1

Mosada is alone in a "little Moorish room." She pines for her lover Gomez, who had stopped in her village three years earlier. He had arrived in the springtime and departed in the autumn, unable to accept his own love for an infidel. Cola enters. Mosada has summoned the seer to conjure a vision of Gomez, but he objects that the great monk Ebremar has denounced such conjuring. She peers into the cloud of burning herbs herself, but she sees nothing. She implores Cola to try; he in turn implores her to let the vision sleep. Mosada beckons a once-great enchantress from her sleep upon a far isle. They feel the presence of phantoms, and Mosada, ecstatic, declares herself "Eastern-hearted once again," upon which the officers of the Inquisition burst into the room and arrest her as a practitioner of magic. Cola begs to be forgiven. He has betrayed her under threat of damnation. The soldiers tauntingly allude to the stake. Distraught, for the inquisitors had promised that Mosada would not be harmed, Cola begs the officers to arrest him in her place. As she stoops to kiss her friend, Mosada calls her arrest Allah's will.

Scene II

Monks and inquisitors are gathered in the building of the Inquisition in Granada. All bow to Ebremar as he enters. The First Inquisitor pleads for Mosada's life, but Ebremar, "bright-eyed" and "hollow-cheeked" from fasting, is unyielding. He dismisses the others and importunes God to fill him with "rage" so he may destroy the heathen and "shake the sullen kings / Upon their thrones."

Scene III

Alone in her dungeon, Mosada hears carpenters building "circling seats" from which the churchmen will view her immolation. She decides that she will not be "of that pale company whose feet / Ere long shall falter through the noisy square. . . ." She sucks a drop of poison from her ring and grows weak, crying out in her extremity for Gomez. Ebremar enters and starts upon recognizing the apparently sleeping girl as his own Mosada. He kneels and covers her with kisses. He tells her they shall escape through a secret passage and flee to a boat waiting on the river. Her mind wandering, she grieves for their lost love and imagines herself once again on the mountaintop watching him disappear into the mist. The monk and inquisitors enter to find Mosada dead. Ebremar is pale and the "flame that shone within his eyes but now / Has flickered and gone out." He quickly recovers his severity, however, and would see the other prisoners before they go to the stake.

BIBLIOGRAPHY

Ellmann, Richard. *Yeats: The Man and the Masks*; Foster, R. F. *W. B. Yeats: A Life, I: The Apprentice Mage*; Joseph Hone, *W. B. Yeats*; Murphy, William M. *Prodigal Father: The Life of John Butler Yeats (1839–1922)*; Wade, Allan. *A Bibliography of the Writings of W. B. Yeats*; Yeats, W. B. *A Variorum Edition of the Poems of W. B. Yeats*.

On Baile's Strand (1903)

The inaugural play of the ABBEY THEATRE, *On Baile's Strand* recounts the plight of the legendary Irish hero CUCHULAIN, who slays a young champion and afterward discovers that he has killed the son he had always wanted (an event foreshadowed in AT THE HAWK'S WELL). Stricken with grief to the point of madness, he plunges into the sea to slay the waves. The play was particularly fit to christen the new theater, as it made good Yeats's longstanding contention that a national drama must go to school in ancient myth and legend, must avail itself of the "accumulated beauty of the ages," following the examples of Wagner in Germany and Ibsen in Norway (*UP2* 131; see LITERARY IDEALS IN IRELAND for Yeats's part in the debate about the ingredients of national drama). It was also fit to christen the new theater as the most accomplished play Yeats had yet written, and, in revised form, perhaps the most generally sound play he would ever write (on Yeats's revisions, see *VPl.* 526).

The play opened on a bill with Lady GREGORY's *Spreading the News* and Yeats's CATHLEEN NI HOULIHAN. "All three plays were completely successful," recorded Joseph Holloway (1861–1944), "and the audience dispersed delighted; and the opening night of the Abbey Theatre must be written down a great big success." (*Joseph Holloway's Abbey Theatre* 51; see also *CL3* 690–691). Yeats responded to loud calls for the author of *On Baile's Strand* with a curtain speech. According to the *Freeman's Journal*, Yeats "did not disguise the pleasure that the reception of the play gave him" and expressed "his thanks to the audience, and his thanks to the lady to whose spirit and generosity the Society owes its new home [ANNIE HORNIMAN]. Authors, he said, must be free to choose their own way; but in their pilgrimage towards beauty and truth they require companions by the way" (*Ireland's Abbey Theatre* 47). Heading the cast were Frank Fay (1870–1931) as Cuchulain and William Fay (1872–1947) as the fool. In ON THE BOILER, Yeats reflects that he has had "greater luck than any other modern English-speaking dramatist," for he has "aimed at tragic ecstasy" and occasionally seen it played in his own work and in the work of friends. The moments that may well haunt him on his deathbed include "William Fay at the end of *On Baile's Strand*" (*Expl.* 416; *LE* 226). In 1906, Yeats dedicated the play to Fay "because of the beautiful phantasy of his playing in the character of the fool."

The play is largely based on the chapter titled "The Only Son of Aoife" in Lady GREGORY's *Cuchulain of Muirthemne* (1902), a popular and influential rendering of the ancient hero's life and adventures for which Yeats wrote the introduction (*Interpretation of the Cuchulain Legend* 27). The play was the first written of Yeats's six plays about Cuchulain. Arranged in narrative order, the sequence consists of *At The Hawk's Well*, *The* GREEN HELMET, *On Baile's Strand*, *The* ONLY JEALOUSY OF EMER (rewritten as FIGHTING THE WAVES), and *The* DEATH OF CUCHULAIN. In his diaries of the Abbey Theatre, Holloway records a conversation in which Yeats mentioned that he wrote *On Baile's Strand* with CHARLES STEWART PARNELL in mind. "People who do aught for Ireland," Holloway recalls Yeats saying, "ever and always have to fight the waves in the end" (*Joseph Holloway's Abbey Theatre* 58). The comment is unsurprising; in Yeats's characteristic representation, both Cuchulain and Parnell are types of the tragic hero whose passionate intensity provokes the mistrust and resentment of lesser men (see "To a Shade").

"Cuchulain's Fight with the Sea" (1892) likewise depicts the hero's slaughter of his own son and descent into madness, but with significant discrepancies. In the poem, the jealous Emer rather than the spurned Aoife sends her son to smite Cuchulain, while Cuchulain is driven into the sea by the spells of Conchubar's druids, for the high king fears that Cuchulain, deranged with grief, will slay the entire company.

DRAMATIS PERSONAE: A Fool; a Blind Man; Cuchulain, king of Muirthemne; Conchubar, high king of Uladh; a young man, son of Cuchulain; kings and singing women.

FIRST PERFORMANCE: Produced by the Irish National Theatre Society at the Abbey Theatre, Dublin, December 27, 1904.

FIRST PUBLICATION: *In the Seven Woods: Being Poems Chiefly of the Irish Heroic Age*, The Dun Emer Press, Dundrum, August 1903.

SYNOPSIS

The Fool and Blind Man enter an assembly house near the sea. The Blind Man feels the legs of a throne and guesses that Conchubar, the powerful high king, has come to impose an oath of loyalty on Cuchulain. As their stolen fowl cooks, he tells of overhearing three wounded sentinels. A young man with red hair had come ashore and refused to give his name. He had killed one sentinel and sent the other three fleeing. Having been in Scotland, the Blind Man recognizes the young man as the son of Aoife, the fierce Scottish queen, "the great woman-fighter Cuchulain got the mastery over in the North." In her house, he remembers, there was a red-haired boy whom she was training to defeat Cuchulain. The Blind Man knows but will not reveal the identity of the boy's father.

The Blind Man and Fool exit as the kings enter. Cuchulain refuses to pledge himself as Conchubar's "bondsman" merely because "a youngster out of Aoife's country / Has found the shore

ill-guarded." He has long defended Conchubar's throne, and he asks whether he must now swear obedience as if he "were some cattle-raising king." Conchubar replies that his children worry that when they inherit the throne they will be at the mercy of a man "nobody can buy or bid or bind." Cuchulain charges that his children's bones lack "pith" and "marrow," which Conchubar interprets as the jealousy of a childless man. Cuchulain calls it lucky that there is no "pallid ghost or mockery of a man" to desecrate his halls, but Conchubar knows better; he has heard him cry in his sleep, "I have no son." Cuchulain would leave neither house nor name to a son unable to meet him in battle. Conchubar chides Cuchulain for being so particular, and for thinking Aoife, that "fierce woman of the camp," alone worthy of bearing him a son. Cuchulain bristles at Conchubar's faint irony and lauds Aoife's wild beauty and strength. Though childless, she was fit to bear kings. Now, as Conchubar reminds him, she wars against the kingdom and grows ever stronger. There is no wonder in this, says Cuchulain, for love is but "a brief forgiveness between opposites." Kings, dancers, musicians, and women wait outside to learn the outcome of the conference. Cuchulain is done with negotiation and calls for dancing in the wood. The kings unanimously urge him to pledge obedience. They have become sedate and domestic, Cuchulain realizes, while he remains wild. Disheartened, he agrees to pledge his loyalty and submits to a ritual of fire and song.

As the ritual culminates, the young man enters. He has come from Aoife's country to challenge Cuchulain. He refuses to give his name, though he is nobly born. Impressed, Cuchulain agrees to fight. He notices the young man's resemblance to Aoife and decides to make a companion of him. The kings want to accept the challenge themselves, but Cuchulain declares that no man shall take up a challenge that he has declined, and that whoever would fight the young man must fight him. With such as this for his son, Cuchulain says, he would scatter his enemies "like water from a dish." Conchubar cries that he will not stand for such a friendship, that Cuchulain has been maddened by witchcraft. Cuchulain seizes Conchubar, and then suddenly checks himself, persuaded that he has been bewitched after all. He turns on the young man, calling "Out, out! I say, for now it's sword on sword!"

The three women who led the ritual are alone. One sees in a bowl of ashes an augury of Cuchulain's death. Wailing and lamenting, they exit to witness the "quenching of this greatness." The Fool drags in the Blind Man and complains that he has eaten the entire fowl. Cuchulain enters with the boast that there is no witchcraft that he cannot break. He wipes blood from his sword. The Blind Man asks if he has killed the young man. Cuchulain answers only that the young man had "thought to have saved himself with witchcraft." The Fool blurts out that the Blind Man knew him in Scotland and that he had been reared to defeat Cuchulain. Cuchulain demands the name of his mother. The Blind Man is too frightened to tell, but the Fool reveals that he had been Aoife's son. Cuchulain demands to know the father. The Blind Man refuses to tell, but the Fool has heard the Blind Man say that her only lover had been the one man who had bested her in combat. Cuchulain trembles violently. The Blind Man says, "It is his own son he has slain." Cuchulain remembers the part played by Conchubar and demands to know where the king has fled. The Fool watches from the door and describes the scene: Cuchulain approaches Conchubar, but then plunges into the sea to fight the waves. On every wave, the Blind Man says, he sees the crown of Conchubar. The Fool reports that people are running from their houses to see—that the waves have mastered him. The Blind Man leads the Fool away to loot the abandoned houses.

BIBLIOGRAPHY

Bjersby, Birgit. *The Interpretation of the Cuchulain Legend in the Works of W. B. Yeats*; Holloway, Joseph. *Joseph Holloway's Abbey Theatre: A Selection from His Unpublished Journal* Impressions of a Dublin Playgoer; Robinson, Lennox. *Ireland's Abbey Theatre: A History, 1899–1951*; Yeats, W. B. *Explorations, The Collected Letters of W. B. Yeats* (vol. 3), *Later Essays, Uncollected Prose by W. B. Yeats* (vol. 2), *The Variorum Edition of the Plays of W. B. Yeats*.

Only Jealousy of Emer, The (1919)

The Only Jealousy of Emer begins in the immediate aftermath of the calamity that ends ON BAILE'S STRAND. CUCHULAIN has washed up on the shore after having killed his son and plunged into the sea. He is alive, but a god of the Sidhe possesses his body and will restore his spirit only on the condition that Emer renounce her dearest hope: that her husband will grow weary of women and adventure and pass his last years by her side. The play derives from an Irish saga of the Middle Ages called *The Sickbed of Cuchulain and the Only Jealousy of Emer* (for a summary, see *Interpretation of the Cuchulain Legend* 45–46), but its more immediate influence is the chapter titled "The Only Jealousy of Emer" in Lady GREGORY's *Cuchulain of Muirthemne* (1902).

The Only Jealousy of Emer is the fourth play in Yeats's dramatic sequence on the life of Cuchulain. Arranged in narrative order, the sequence consists of AT THE HAWK'S WELL, *The* GREEN HELMET, *On Baile's Strand, The Only Jealousy of Emer*, and *The* DEATH OF CUCHULAIN. Yeats rewrote *The Only Jealousy of Emer* as FIGHTING THE WAVES, a spare version of the same story incorporating dance and music. The play also belongs to a group that includes *At the Hawk's Well, The* DREAMING OF THE BONES, and CALVARY. These were published as *Four Plays for Dancers* (1921) and continue to be presented under that heading in some versions of Yeats's collected plays. In keeping with the conventions of the Japanese Noh drama, the plays for dancers employ masks and extremely simple stage settings, making them suitable for performance "in a drawing-room or in a studio" (*VPl.* 566).

As Yeats well understood, the play's love triangle has an autobiographical dimension in which Cuchulain represents Yeats himself, Emer represents GEORGE YEATS, Eithne represents ISEULT GONNE, and the goddess Fand represents MAUD GONNE (for a summary of the characters' multiple and complex significations, see *Making of Yeats's 'A Vision'*, I, 150). On this basis, Helen Vendler associates the play with "An IMAGE FROM A PAST LIFE" and "UNDER SATURN," both of which "are about the persistence of the image of Maud Gonne in Yeats's mind even after his marriage" (*Later Plays* 218). If Fand is a symbolic representation of Maud Gonne, she is also, as the play stipulates, a manifestation of the hawk goddess whom Cuchulain encounters in *At the Hawk's Well* (see VPl. 553, 555). It is a striking consistency that Gonne had associated herself with the hawk goddess of the earlier play (see GY 370).

The play opens with a 28-line song that, for sheer limpid loveliness, belongs with Yeats's best poetry. It ponders the turbulent, submerged, and long-laboring forces that give birth to "a woman's beauty"; in this regard, it might be considered the obverse of "IN MEMORY OF EVA GORE-BOOTH AND CON MARKIEWICZ," which considers the forces that degrade a woman's beauty. In its conception of measurement as an imposition of order, it bears comparison with "The STATUES"; in its notion of feminine delicacy thrown up by "vast troubled waters"—in its implicit dynamic of sublimation—it bears comparison with "ANCESTRAL HOUSES." It was printed as "A Woman's Beauty is like a White Frail Bird" in *Selected Poems* (1929), but it was not included in later editions of Yeats's collected poems.

DRAMATIS PERSONAE: Three musicians, their faces made up to resemble masks; the Ghost of Cuchulain, masked; the figure of Cuchulain, masked; Emer and Eithne Inguba, masked, or their faces made up to resemble masks; the Woman of the Sidhe, masked.

FIRST PERFORMANCE: Amsterdam, April 2, 1922 (in translation). Produced by the Dublin Drama League at the ABBEY THEATRE, Dublin, May 9, 1926.

FIRST PUBLICATION: *Poetry* (periodical), January, 1919. Reprinted in *Two Plays for Dancers*, The CUALA PRESS, Churchtown, Dundrum, January 1919.

SYNOPSIS

The musicians enter with a folded black cloth. As the cloth is unfolded and folded again, the first musician sings of the beauty of women (see above). The folded cloth reveals Cuchulain on a curtained bed. An identically dressed and masked figure crouches at the front of the stage. Emer, Cuchulain's wife,

sits by the bedside. She calls Eithne Inguba, his mistress, to the bedside, but the younger woman, having wronged the queen, hesitates. Emer assures her that only they who have loved Cuchulain have the right to watch over the sickbed. Emer confirms that Cuchulain is alive, but she suspects that an "image has been put into his place / A sea-borne log bewitched into his likeness. . . ." Eithne urges Emer to call Cuchulain's name, but Emer admits that she long ago lost sway over Cuchulain. Prodded by Emer, Eithne calls to Cuchulain and kisses the lying figure. She is startled to feel some "some evil thing." The figure stirs and introduces himself as Bricriu, "maker of discord among gods and men," come from the court of Manannan, god of the sea. He parts the curtain and declares that everything Cuchulain loves must flee the sight of his face. Eithne duly flees, while Emer remains. Undeterred by this proof of her diminished place, she demands the return of her husband. The god will free Cuchulain if Emer renounces her hope to be once again "the apple of his eye." Emer has but two precious things, hope and memory, and she refuses. Bricriu taunts that her hope will come to nothing in any case: Cuchulain will "die of wounds and toil / On some fare shore or mountain, a strange woman / Beside his mattress."

He touches her eyes and reveals the crouching ghost of Cuchulain. A Woman of the Sidhe enters in mask and garments like the metalwork of an idol. The goddess dances seductively about the ghost of Cuchulain and sheds a glow like moonlight "upon the fifteenth night" [see A VISION]. Cuchulain is pained by memories of Emer in her "happy youth / Before her man had broken troth," and realizes that the goddess is the same he encountered as a young man at the hawk's well [see *At the Hawk's Well*]. The goddess invites him to kiss her, thereby erasing all memories and staying time itself. Cuchulain moves to kiss her but turns away with the cry "O Emer, Emer!" The goddess reminds Cuchulain that in life he had valued "every slut" above Emer. As if desperate to escape the bitterness of his memories, Cuchulain cries "Your mouth, your mouth!" and follows the goddess offstage. Bricriu tells Emer that he has come to thwart Fand [as he names the goddess] and that she has only a moment to save

Cuchulain. Emer renounces her husband's love, and the figure of Cuchulain sinks back upon the bed. Eithne at once returns to the bedside. She observes that Cuchulain stirs and boasts that she has "won him from the sea." Cuchulain asks Eithne to hold him in her arms, for he has been "in some strange place" and he is afraid. The musicians sing of the "bitter reward / Of many a tragic tomb" as they once more unfold and fold the cloth.

BIBLIOGRAPHY

Bjersby, Birgit. *The Interpretation of the Cuchulain Legend in the Works of W. B. Yeats*; Harper, George Mills. *The Making of Yeats's 'A Vision': A Study of the Automatic Script* (vols. 1–2); Vendler, Helen Hennessy. *Yeats's Vision and the Later Plays*; Yeats, W. B. *The Gonne-Yeats Letters 1893–1938, The Variorum Edition of the Plays of W. B. Yeats.*

Player Queen, The (1922)

Part fairy tale, part court farce, and part philosophical rigmarole, *The Player Queen* is out of keeping with the tenor of Yeats's later plays, as it eschews both Irish subject matter and the influence of the Japanese Noh drama. Part of the explanation is that Yeats began work on the play as early as 1906 (YC 104), and that even in its much revised final version it bears the hallmarks of the earlier period (for the play's genesis, see *Letters* 511–513). The play's incessant talk of the unicorn as apocalyptic avatar, for example, suggests a common origin with WHERE THERE IS NOTHING and *The* UNICORN FROM THE STARS, published in 1902 and 1908 respectively. In a note to *Plays in Prose and Verse* (1922), Yeats describes the play's protracted and laborious gestation: "I began in, I think, 1907, a verse tragedy, but at that time the thought I have set forth in PER AMICA SILENTIA LUNAE was coming into my head, and I found examples of it everywhere. I wasted the best working months of several years in an attempt to write a poetical play where every character became an example of the finding or not finding of what I have called the Antithetical Self; and because passion and

not thought makes tragedy, what I made had neither simplicity nor life. I knew precisely what was wrong and yet could neither escape from thought nor give up my play. At last it came into my head all of a sudden that I could get rid of the play if I turned it into a farce; and never did I do anything so easily, for I think that I wrote the present play in about a month [. . .] (*VPl.* 761; see also 933). Yeats explains also that the play is not set in Ireland—his only play not so set—because he wanted to accommodate stage screens designed by Gordon Craig (1872–1966): "My *dramatis personae* have no nationality because Mr. Craig's screens, where every line must suggest some mathematical proportion, where all is phantastic, incredible, and luminous, have no nationality" (761; see also 1306; on Craig's stage design, see *Letters* 555; *Noble Drama* 49–52; UP2 392–394).

In its final incarnation, the play is a lively, ambitious, and chaotic variation on the gutter-to-gown theme of so many fairy tales. During a violent uprising, the actress Decima changes costume with the queen of an anonymous kingdom. Passionate and commanding where the queen is nunnish and weak, Decima permanently assumes the throne after winning the hearts of the people, while the rightful queen gladly disappears to a convent. The play's most interesting suggestion is that Decima, like the unicorn with which she is associated, is an avatar of a new historical phase in which Christianity is routed by a more passionate dispensation of beauty and cruelty. In this respect, the play is related not only to *Where There is Nothing* and *The Unicorn from the Stars*, but also to poems of apocalyptic annunciation like "LEDA AND THE SWAN" and "The SECOND COMING." Helen Vendler finds the play's essential preoccupation the relationship between muse (Decima), poet (Septimus), and "unknown divinity of inspiration" (unicorn), and she discerns in this "Yeatsian Trinity" the crux of more successful later plays like A FULL MOON IN MARCH, *The* KING OF THE GREAT CLOCK TOWER, and *The* HERNE'S EGG (*Later Plays* 138).

DRAMATIS PERSONAE: Decima, Septimus, Nona, the queen, the prime minister, the bishop, the stage manager, the tapster, an old beggar, old men, old women, citizens, countrymen, players, etc.

FIRST PERFORMANCE: Produced by the Incorporated Stage Society at King's Hall, Covent Garden, London, May, 25, 1919. Presented by the National Theatre Society Ltd. (see the IRISH NATIONAL THEATRE SOCIETY) at the ABBEY THEATRE, Dublin, December 9, 1919.

FIRST PUBLICATION: *The Dial* (periodical), November 1922, and *Plays in Prose and Verse*, Macmillan, London, November 3, 1922.

SYNOPSIS

Scene 1

Two old men lean from windows and discuss the "mischief" that has beset the city. Septimus, "a handsome man of thirty-five," staggers drunkenly and bangs on doors. Haranguing the roused neighborhood, he divulges piecemeal his tale of woe. He is a poet and dramatist. His wife, an actress, is supposed to play in the royal castle at noon, but she has run away. The talk turns to the city's political crisis. The queen has been secluded during the seven years since her father died. Some believe she is a witch, others a holy woman. There is a lively debate. One looks forward to her death so the prime minister may assume power. Another relates that she was spied coupling with a "great white unicorn." The crowd exits, but returns in fear after meeting the old beggar on a side street. He has aroused superstitious terror ever since he signaled the king's death by braying like a donkey. All but Septimus flee as the old beggar enters. Septimus nurses his grievances, but the beggar says only "I want straw," and the two head toward the castle.

Scene 2

In the throne room, the prime minister accuses the players of sabotaging their production of "The Tragical History of Noah's Deluge" in order to put on "some dull, poetical thing, full of long speeches." Nona pleads that Decima, who was to play Noah's wife, has disappeared, having been heard to say she "would drown rather than play a woman older than thirty." Decima peeks from her hiding place under the throne. The prime minister, full of bluster, commands the players to find the actress. The queen enters. The prime minister has instructed her to show herself before the angry crowd gathered outside the castle. Inspired by Holy Saint Octema, she is ready for martyrdom. The prime minister, however, has a plan to mollify the crowd. They exit. Nona sets down wine and lobster and retreats to the rear. Decima emerges for the food, but Nona will let her eat only if she agrees to perform. Decima believes she is meant for a "great queen's part." Nona retorts that she was "born in a ditch" and points out that Septimus will go to prison if there is no play. Decima deems a spell in prison just the thing to remind him of his "beautiful cruel wife" and enhance her beauty in his eyes. Appalled, Nona threatens to play the role, but Decima reminds her that Septimus has pledged to perform only with her. Nona insinuatingly suggests that he would break his oath for her sake. A jealous spat erupts. Decima pulls Septimus's love poems from her bodice. "They have lain upon your heart, but they were made upon my shoulder," Nona says. The players enter dressed as beasts. Nona announces that she will play Noah's wife. Decima proclaims herself "dead sick" of Septimus and glad to be rid of both man and part. Wavering between exuberance and hysteria, she dances with the beasts while singing of selecting one or another as her new mate.

Still drunk, Septimus enters and proclaims "the end of the Christian Era, the coming of a New Dispensation, that of the New Adam, that of the Unicorn." He laments, however, that the unicorn is "chaste," that "he hesitates, he hesitates." He reports that a mob with pitchforks and burning wisps is heading to the palace and that the players should prepare to die. Septimus plans his final words; he will rail against the unicorn for its chastity and bid him "trample mankind to death and beget a new race." The stage manager has an escape plan and leads the players out. Nona makes a bundle of the players' costumes and ties it to Septimus's back as he speaks of the unicorn: "Man is nothing till he is united to an image. Now the Unicorn is both an image and beast; that is why he alone can be the new Adam." Nona tries to lead him away, but Decima has locked the gate. She demands that Septimus swear to expel Nona from the company. Nona urges him to swear, but Septimus is not the kind of "rascally sober man" to swear falsely. Nona snatches the key and flees. Singing of the unicorn and moving slowly in order not to seem afraid, Septimus follows her out. The old beggar enters. He feels the itch that signals a new dispensation and exits in search of straw. Decima is about to kill herself with a pair of scissors when the queen enters and implores her not to sin. Decima proposes that they trade identities so the queen may escape. "I shall die whatever you do," she pleads, "and if only I could wear that gold brocade and those gold slippers for one moment, it would not be so hard to die." They change clothes and the queen departs for a convent.

Decima assumes the throne as a crowd gathers outside the palace. The bishop reports that her decision to marry the prime minister has ended the political crisis. The prime minister enters with hurried self-justifications, but the sight of Decima on the throne arrests him. She addresses the crowd: "I am Queen. I know what it is to be Queen." Amid cheers, she vows to take a husband of common blood. Septimus tells the prime minister that the queen is his wife, but the prime minister understands that the crowd is "mad after her pretty face" and that there is nothing to be done: The crown has changed heads. The bray of the donkey is heard and the beggar is dragged in. The bishop denounces him as an impostor. The prime minister, who knows better, sentences him to be hanged. Determined to wed Decima, he calls for the banishment of Septimus and his players. Decima would have them dance before they depart. The new queen takes up the mask of Noah's sister and says of Decima, "She was a bad, headstrong, cruel woman, and seeks destruction somewhere and with some man she knows nothing of; such a woman they tell me that this mask would well become, this foolish, smiling face!"

BIBLIOGRAPHY

Kelly, John S. *A W. B. Yeats Chronology*; Miller, Liam. *The Noble Drama of W. B. Yeats*; Vendler, Helen Hennessy. *Yeats's Vision and the Later Plays*; Yeats, W. B. *The Letters of W. B. Yeats, Uncollected Prose by W. B. Yeats* (vol. 2), *The Variorum Edition of the Plays of W. B. Yeats*.

Pot of Broth, The (1903)

This one-act play is Yeats's closest approach to the kind of "little comedies of country life" that Lady GREGORY specialized in (*LE* 47), and indeed it was written with more than a little of her assistance, as Yeats explains in a note to *Plays in Prose and Verse* (1922): "I hardly know how much of the play is my work, for Lady Gregory helped me as she has helped me in every play of mine where there is dialect, and sometimes where there is not. In those first years of the Theatre we all helped one another with plots, ideas, and dialogue, but certainly I was the most indebted as I had no mastery of speech that purported to be of real life. This play may be more Lady Gregory's than mine, for I remember once urging her to include it in her own work, and her refusing to do so. The dialect, unlike that of CATHLEEN NI HOULIHAN, which was written about the same date, has not, I think, the right temper, being gay, mercurial, and suggestive of rapid speech. Probably we were still under the influence of the Irish novelists, who never escaped, even when they had grown up amid country speech, from the dialect of Dublin" (*VPl.* 254; see also 1296; *Aut.* 332). The play has a neat farcical logic, but it is emotionally and intellectually negligible in comparison to the bulk of Yeats's dramatic work. Yeats judged it a "trivial, unambitious retelling of an old folk-tale," though he considered it an instructive experiment in the representation of country dialect (*Aut.* 332–333). When it was played in 1902, the innocuous little play, as Joseph Hone writes, "pleased all" (*W. B. Yeats* 178).

DRAMATIS PERSONAE: John Coneely, an elderly man; Sibby Coneely, a young or middle-aged woman; a tramp.

FIRST PERFORMANCE: Produced by the Irish National Dramatic Company (see the IRISH NATIONAL THEATRE SOCIETY) at the Antient Concert Rooms, Dublin, October 30, 1902.

FIRST PUBLICATION: *The Gael* (periodical), September 1903. Reprinted in *The Hour-Glass and Other Plays*, Macmillan, London, New York, January 13, 1904.

SYNOPSIS

In the kitchen of a cottage the table is laden with meat and vegetables. The tramp enters and looks about, finding two empty pots, a bottle of milk, and a locked chest. He sniffs at the keyhole and detects whiskey. There is a commotion outside as Sibby and John chase an escaped hen. Catching the name "Sibby," the tramp realizes he is in the house of Sibby Coneely, famous for her niggardliness. Down to his last crust of bread and facing a long walk to the nearest town, he takes inventory of his pockets: a pipe, a handkerchief, a knife handle, and a stone he picked up to throw at a yelping dog. He bemoans that his wits, which had once been a sufficient guard against hunger, have been dulled by hardship. Hearing the cackle of the hen, the tramp conceives a plan. Outside, John and Sibby have caught the hen for the priest's dinner.

John greets the tramp with surprise and rummages in the chest to find him something to eat. Sibby enters with a chicken. A niggard indeed, she grudges having to serve the priest even an old hen past laying. Averse to serving bacon—presumably a luxury item—she rationalizes that the "genteel" are not greedy for meat like "potato-diggers or harvest men," and that it will do even better to serve the old ham bone she has been saving. She notices the tramp and tells him that they have nothing for him. The tramp corrects her: He does not desire to receive, but to give. He presents the stone, which is "better than beef and mutton, and currant cakes, and sacks of flour." Sibby asks what the stone is for, but the tramp says that those who gave it to him would not like him to divulge the secret. Sibby asks John whether he thinks the tramp has friends among the Sidhe. The tramp reveals that the stone can produce a pot of broth. Intrigued, Sibby offers him pot and water. He asks for a bit of herb "for fear the enchantment might slip away from it." None being in the house, he makes do by grabbing some cabbage and onion.

Dropping the ham bone into the pot, the tramp tells how his greyhound followed a hare through the furze and came upon on old man. The old man promised him the stone if he would call off his dog, vowing that it would make not only broth, but also stirabout [porridge], poteen [whiskey], and wine.

In order to maintain the luck of the charm, the tramp says, he must color the water, and he grabs a handful of meal. Since the stone came into Catholic hands it spoils all meat on Fridays, but on every other day—and here he grabs the hen by way of demonstration—it cooks meat nicely. The tramp takes the chicken out of the pot. Sibby and the tramp taste the soup. Sibby would give anything for the stone. The tramp refuses to part with it, ponders trading it for a pot, and finally presents it as a gift for their kindness. He then claims the chicken and the bottle of whiskey, which, under the circumstances, they surely would not begrudge him. John follows him out and returns having shaken the hand of a "very gifted man."

BIBLIOGRAPHY

Hone, Joseph. *W. B. Yeats*; Yeats, W. B. *Autobiographies, Later Essays, The Variorum Edition of the Plays of W. B. Yeats.*

Purgatory (1939)

This one-act play follows the example of *The Words upon the Window-pane* and *The Dreaming of the Bones*, which are likewise purgatorial visions. The most theoretically explicit of the three plays, *Purgatory* airs Yeats's conviction that troubled spirits must revisit their greatest crisis and perpetually reenact the fateful experience. In his curtain speech following the play's debut in August 1938, Yeats stated unequivocally, "I have put nothing into the play because it seemed picturesque; I have put there my own conviction about this world and the next" (*Letters* 913; *LOP* 184). Yeats explains the underlying theory of the play in *A Vision*: "In the *Dreaming Back*, the *Spirit* is compelled to live over and over again the events that had most moved it; there can be nothing new, but the old events stand forth in a light which is dim or bright according to the intensity of the passion that accompanied them. They occur in the order of their intensity or luminosity, the more intense first, and the painful are commonly the more intense, and repeat themselves again and again. In the

Return, upon the other hand, the *Spirit* must live through past events in the order of their occurrence, because it is compelled by the *Celestial Body* to trace every passionate event to its cause until all are related and understood, turned into knowledge, made a part of itself" (226; see also *AV-1925* 226–227).

Where *The Words upon the Window-pane* uses the device of psychic reenactment to dramatize decisive moments in the life of Jonathan SWIFT, *Purgatory* uses it to dramatize the decline of a "great house," and more generally to elegize the crumbling culture of Ascendancy Ireland. In this respect, the play is of a piece with poems like "COOLE AND BALLYLEE, 1931," "COOLE PARK, 1929," and "UPON A HOUSE SHAKEN BY THE LAND AGITATION." The embedded tale of the house's decline makes no specific reference, but the august tradition of the house—ancestral residence of "Magistrates, colonels, members of Parliament, / Captains and Governors, and long ago / Men that had fought at Aughrim and the Boyne"—is inferably patterned on Lady GREGORY'S COOLE PARK, which Yeats similarly describes in *AUTOBIOGRAPHIES* (see 291–292).

As supernaturally lit up in the night, the house recalls on Castle Dargan in County SLIGO, where Yeats's cousin, the former Mary Middleton, lived with her husband, the "brawling squireen" John Robert Ormsby (*Aut.* 73–74). Yeats refers to the miraculously lit castle in *The KING OF THE GREAT CLOCK TOWER*: "O, but I saw a solemn sight; / *Said the rambling, shambling travelling-man;* / Castle Dargan's ruin all lit, / Lovely ladies dancing in it" (*VPl.* 1003). Without mentioning Castle Dargan by name, he repeats the image of the living ruin in "CRAZY JANE ON GOD," in "The Curse of Cromwell" (1937), and in his introduction to *The Words upon the Window-pane* (*Expl.* 369; *VPl.* 970). The play's theme of mésalliance most likely derives from an episode in the history of the castle. As James P. McGarry notes, there is "the true story of a Miss Ormsby of Castledargan who eloped with a groom. They married and lived happily on a small farm in the townland of Glenn, between Collooney and Coolaney where their descendants still reside. The play is obviously based on this story" (*Place Names* 27–28). Joseph Hone, on the other hand, draws

attention to a ghost story that Yeats had been told by his friend the artist Charles Ricketts (1866–1931) at one of the latter's "Friday evenings" (*W. B. Yeats* 287–288), while R. F. Foster points to the decline of the St. George family, whose dilapidated Galway estate, Tyrone House, was not far from Coole Park and THOOR BALLYLEE (*AP* 618).

In a 1938 interview printed in the *Irish Independent*, Yeats discussed the cultural and historical anxiety at the heart of the play: "In my play, a spirit suffers because of its share, when alive, in the destruction of an honoured house; that destruction is taking place all over Ireland to-day. Sometimes it is the result of poverty, but more often because a new individualistic generation has lost interest in the ancient sanctities. I know of old houses, old pictures, old furniture that have been sold without apparent regret. In some few cases a house has been destroyed by a mésalliance. I have founded my play on this exceptional case, partly because of my interest in certain problems of eugenics, partly because it enables me to depict more vividly than would otherwise be possible the tragedy of the house. In Germany there is special legislation to enable old families to go on living where their fathers lived. The problem is not Irish, but European, though it is perhaps more acute here than elsewhere" (*W. B. Yeats & Georgian Ireland* 357–358). Yeats's "interest in certain problems of eugenics" (see ON THE BOILER) manifests itself in *Purgatory* in the familial decline that follows from union with a groom in the grandparental generation and union with a tinker's daughter in the parental generation. The inheritor of this doubly tainted blood—the "Boy"—is a mere ruffian, incapable of understanding much less revering "the ancient sanctities." Yeats expresses similar anxieties about the tendency toward familial decline and domestic collapse in poems like "ANCESTRAL HOUSES" and "MY DESCENDENTS," and similar bitterness about Ireland's cultural decline in "The STATUES": "We Irish, born into that ancient sect / But thrown upon this filthy modern tide / And by its formless spawning fury wrecked / Climb to our proper dark. . . ."

Purgatory debuted on August 10, 1938, as part of a two-week festival honoring the history of the ABBEY THEATRE. Yeats's curtain speech was his final public foray. Hugh Hunt writes that when "the familiar white-haired figure walked onto the stage, no longer as upright as in former days, a wave of emotion seemed to sweep through the audience, for the Festival was a salute to the theatre he had inspired, and *Purgatory* was his farewell to Ireland" (*The Abbey* 163). Yeats told Edith Shackleton Heald (1885–1976) on August 15: "My play has been a sensational success so far as the audience went. I have never seen a more excited house. [. . .] But I have had this before. The trouble is outside. The press or the clerics get to work—the tribal dance and the drums. This time the trouble is theological. As always I have to remain silent and see my work travestied because I will not use up my fragile energies on impermanent writing" (*Letters* 913–914; on the theological controversy, see *AP* 628; *W. B. Yeats* 476). Anne Butler Yeats (1919–2001) designed the sets for *Purgatory* and for a revival of ON BAILE'S STRAND that played on August 11. Yeats told Shackleton Heald that his daughter's work had been greatly admired (*Letters* 914).

DRAMATIS PERSONAE: A boy, an old man.

FIRST PERFORMANCE: Produced by the National Theatre Society Ltd. (see IRISH NATIONAL THEATRE SOCIETY) at the Abbey Theatre, Dublin, August 10, 1938.

FIRST PUBLICATION: *Last Poems and Two Plays,* The CUALA PRESS, Dublin, July 10, 1939.

SYNOPSIS

An old man and his son pass a ruined house and tree. The old man points out that the house is not as empty as it looks, but contains the "souls in Purgatory that come back / To habitations and familiar spots." The boy takes him to be out of his wits again. The old man continues that the souls of those in purgatory relive their transgressions until they come to know the consequences of what they have done. Only when the consequences have run their course does the dream come to an end. The house had once been part of a great estate belonging to his mother's family. She married a groom and died giving birth to himself. Her mother had never spoken to her again, and she was right, according to the old man, for the groom later sold the estate's trees to pay his gambling debts and keep himself in horses, drink, and women. The boy asks, "What's right and wrong? / My grand-dad got the girl and the money." The old man calls it a "capital offense" to destroy a house in which so many "great men, grew up, married, died." When the old man had been 16—the same age as the boy—his father drunkenly set the house on fire. Amid the flames, he stabbed his father with the knife he now uses to eat. He was suspected of the murder and fled to become an itinerant peddler.

The old man hears the sound of hoofs and cries, "Beat! Beat! / This night is the anniversary / Of my mother's wedding night, / Or of the night wherein I was begotten." He sees a ghostly reenactment of the fateful night. His father approaches with a whiskey bottle. He has stayed late "bragging and drinking in the public house." A window is lit, showing a young girl, though the boy sees only an "empty gap in the wall." The old man's father dismounts. His mother lets him into the house. They ascend to her chamber. The old man calls out, "Do not let him touch you! It is not true / That drunken men cannot beget, / And if he touch he must beget / And you must bear his murderer." Nothing can prevent fate from playing itself out, he reminds himself. He notices that the boy has rummaged in the pack for money and now tries to slip away. They struggle and the boy threatens to kill the old man, just as the old man had killed his own father. A window is lit, showing a man pouring whiskey. The boy is suddenly able to perceive the ghostly drama: He calls the figure a "dead, living, murdered man" and covers his eyes in horror. The old man stabs the boy, with the bemused observation, "My father and my son on the same jack-knife!" The stage darkens; the tree alone is illuminated. The old man deems the tree an emblem of his mother's purified soul. In ending the family line, he believes he has ended the chain of consequences following from his mother's transgression and liberated her soul from its recurring dream. As he cleans the knife, he hears the sound of hoofs once again. He realizes that he has been mistaken, that her mind cannot escape its dream. "Twice a murderer, and all for nothing," he laments. He calls out to God, "Release my mother's soul from its dream! / Mankind can do no more.

Appease / The misery of the living and the remorse of the dead."

BIBLIOGRAPHY

Foster, R. F. *W. B. Yeats: A Life, II: The Arch-Poet*; Hone, Joseph. *W. B. Yeats*; Hunt, Hugh. *The Abbey: Ireland's National Theatre, 1904–1978*; McGarry, James P. *Place Names in the Writings of William Butler Yeats*; Torchiana, Donald T. *W. B. Yeats & Georgian Ireland*; Yeats, W. B. *Autobiographies, A Critical Edition of Yeats's A Vision (1925), Explorations, The Letters of W. B. Yeats, Letters on Poetry from W. B. Yeats to Dorothy Wellesley, The Variorum Edition of the Plays of W. B. Yeats, A Vision*.

Resurrection, The (1927)

Taking up the story of Christ where CALVARY leaves off, *The Resurrection* tells of the days following the crucifixion. Violent mobs are on the hunt for Christians, the followers of Dionysus ecstatically parade in the streets, and rumors of Christ's resurrection have begun to spread. Amid this tumult, a Greek, a Hebrew, and a Syrian stand guard over the endangered apostles. As Helen Vendler puts it, the Hebrew is *'l'homme moyen sensuel*, rather glad that Christ has turned out to be human after all, because it would have been so troublesome to have to take a real Messiah into account; the Greek is the dispassionate intellectual, observing with analytical interest the Dionysian ceremonies in the streets; the Syrian is the believer in mystery [. . .]" (*Later Plays* 179). As they bicker, speculate, and philosophize, they dramatize the anxieties and complexities of the moment marked by Christ's death and rebirth, in which, as the Syrian says, the circle begins again.

The "circle" is at once the 1,000-year "millennium" and the 2,000-year "era" that Yeats describes in A VISION. Additionally, it may be the "Great Year" itself. Yeats gives this account of the geometry underlying the play in his introduction: "Ptolemy thought the precession of the equinoxes moved at the rate of a degree every hundred years, and that somewhere about the time of Christ and

Caesar the equinoctial sun had returned to its original place in the constellations, completing and recommencing the thirty-six thousand years, or three hundred and sixty incarnations of a hundred years apiece, of Plato's Man of Ur [. . .]. Whatever [the length of the Great Year], it divided, and so did every unit whose multiple it was, into waxing and waning, day and night, or summer and winter. There was everywhere a conflict like that of my play between two principles or 'elemental forms of the mind,' each 'living the other's life, dying the other's death'" (*VPl.* 933–934; *Expl.* 395–396; see also "The Great Year of the Ancients" in *A Vision*). In *A Vision*, Yeats calls this moment of death-in-birth and birth-in-death the *interchange of the tinctures*, and, in terms relevant to *The Resurrection*, describes the specific nature of the transition marked by Christ: "Before the birth of Christ religion and vitality were polytheistic, *antithetical*, and to this the philosophers opposed their *primary*, secular thought. Plato thinks all things into Unity and is the 'First Christian'. At the birth of Christ religious life becomes *primary*, secular life *antithetical*—man gives to Caesar the things that are Caesar's. A *primary* dispensation looking beyond itself towards a transcendent power is dogmatic, levelling, unifying, feminine, humane, peace its means and end; an *antithetical* dispensation obeys imminent power, is expressive, hierarchical, multiple, masculine, harsh, surgical" (262–263). In different ways, seemingly, the Greek and Hebrew belong to the *antithetical* dispensation (with which Yeats tended to sympathize in spite of himself), but they embody the decadence of its dying moments. Unlike Lazarus and Judas in *Calvary*, they lack the rebellious strength to reject Christ even in his divinity, and they wind up unmanned by a reality which they cannot understand and to which they cannot genuinely accommodate themselves. In its theme of apocalyptic annunciation *The Resurrection* is affiliated with "LEDA AND THE SWAN" and "The SECOND COMING," which respectively dramatize the birth of the historical dispensations that precede and succeed the Christian dispensation. It also contributes to an ongoing meditation on the birth and death of Christ that includes, in addition to *Calvary*, poems such as "The MAGI," "The

MOTHER OF GOD," "A Nativity" (1938), "A Stick of Incense" (1939), and "WISDOM."

In his introduction, Yeats accounts for the play's element of supernatural terror: "Years ago I read Sir William Crookes' *Studies in Psychical Research.* After excluding every possibility of fraud, he touched a materialised form and found the heart beating. I felt, though my intellect rejected what I read, the terror of the supernatural described by Job. Just before the war a much respected man of science entering a room in his own house found there two girl visitors—I have questioned all three—one lying asleep on the table, the other sitting on the end of the table screaming, the table floating in the air, and 'immediately vomited.' I took from the beating heart, from my momentary terror, from the shock of the man of science, the central situation of my play: the young man touching the heart of the phantom and screaming" (*VPl.* 935; see also *LE* 156). The book by Sir William Crookes (1832–1919) is *Researches in the Phenomena of Spiritualism* (1874). Yeats also employs the motif of the beating heart in "PRESENCES."

The Resurrection is dedicated to Junzo Sato. Then a Japanese consular officer, Sato introduced himself and made a present of an ancestral sword while Yeats was stopped in Portland, Oregon, in March 1920 (see *Letters* 662). Yeats commemorates the sword in "A DIALOGUE OF SELF AND SOUL," "Symbols" (1932), and "MY TABLE," the latter a poem of apocalypse that obliquely connects Sato's sword to the themes of *The Resurrection.*

The play's opening and closing songs appeared as "TWO SONGS FROM A PLAY" in *October Blast* (1927) and in *The Tower* (1928), and the poem was subsequently included in Yeats's collected poems. It is among Yeats's densest and most difficult statements, summarizing in 32 lines much of his philosophy of history. With the prologue to *The ONLY JEALOUSY OF EMER,* the poem is arguably the most significant verse to emerge from Yeats's drama.

DRAMATIS PERSONAE: The Hebrew, the Greek, the Syrian, Christ, three musicians.

FIRST PERFORMANCE: Produced by the National Theatre Society Ltd. (see IRISH NATIONAL THEATRE SOCIETY) at the ABBEY THEATRE, Dublin, July 30, 1934.

FIRST PUBLICATION: *The Adelphi* (periodical), June 1927. Reprinted in *Stories of Michael Robartes and His Friends: An Extract from a Record Made by His Friends: and a Play in Prose,* The CUALA PRESS, Dublin, March 1932.

SYNOPSIS

As they unfold and fold the ceremonial curtain, the three musicians sing of the apocalyptic moment in which the "staring virgin" (Pallas Athene) tears the heart from the body of "holy Dionysus," symbolizing the dynamic of divine death and resurrection. The Greek has been to ask a rabbi about the ruckus in the streets. According to the rabbi, the followers of Dionysus have been parading in a frenzy so terrifying that even the "mob" has left them alone—or, the Greek adds ironically, the mob had been "so busy hunting Christians it had time for nothing else." The Hebrew says the mob can be held off long enough to allow the 11 apostles [those who remain following the suicide of Judas] to "escape over the roofs." He will defend the stairs; when he is killed, the Greek can take over his position. The Hebrew asks where the Syrian has gone. The Greek answers that he has sent him on an errand.

The apostles are gathered in the inner room. The Greek confides that the apostles "do not know what to think. When Jesus was taken they could no longer believe him the Messiah. We can find consolation, but for the Eleven it was always complete light or complete darkness." The Greek glances out the window at the three crosses upon Calvary. To the shock of the Hebrew, he laughs at the scene. "We Greeks understand these things," he explains. "No god has ever been buried; no god has ever suffered. Christ only seemed to be born, only seemed to eat, seemed to sleep, seemed to walk, seemed to die." The Greek boasts that he shall prove this. The Hebrew inclines to the idea that Christ was merely a man, though "the best man who ever lived." In a state of exhaustion, perhaps, he came to think himself the Messiah because "of all destinies it seemed the most terrible." The Greek reveals the nature of his proof: He has sent the Syrian to confirm that the tomb is empty. The Hebrew admits that he is glad that Christ was not the Messiah, for one "had to give up all worldly knowledge, all ambition, do nothing of one's own will." Rattles and drums draw the Greek to the window. The followers of Dionysus—men dressed as women so they may attain "in worship a woman's self-abandonment"—carry an effigy of the dead god. They have cut themselves with knives, in imitation of the murder of the god, while a man and a woman couple in the street. The Greek calls them "the most ignorant and excitable class of Asiatic Greeks, the dregs of the population." He cannot consider such "self-surrender and self-abasement" properly Greek. In the Greek tradition, man and god remain separate; man "does not surrender his soul," but maintains his privacy.

The Syrian enters and demands to speak to the apostles at once. On his way to the tomb he met Mary, the mother of Jesus, and the other Galilean women. They had been to the tomb and found it empty. A "man all shining" had stood in the door and proclaimed Christ's resurrection, and then Christ himself had appeared. The Hebrew refuses to let the Syrian disturb the apostles with "the dreams of women." The Greek does not doubt that the tomb is empty, but he says there must be better proof before bringing the matter to the apostles. He adds his belief that Jesus will eventually pass through the walls like the phantom he has always been and speak to the apostles himself. The Syrian insists that Christ is no phantom, noting that the stone before his tomb had been rolled back. The Hebrew suggests that Christ's followers stole the body to make it seem that Christ had arisen. Exasperated, the Syrian asks, paraphrasing the song that opens the play, "What matter if it contradicts all human knowledge?—another Argo seeks another fleece, another Troy is sacked." The Syrian laughs at the very idea of human knowledge. He asks, "What if there is always something that lies outside knowledge, outside order? What if at the moment when knowledge and order seem complete that something appears?"

Again at the window, the Greek reports that the Dionysian worshippers dance outside and proclaim that their god has arisen. He wonders why they have stopped to stare at the house. Christ—wearing a stylized mask—enters. The Hebrew shrinks in terror, but the Greek is neither surprised nor afraid. He reassures the Hebrew that the phantom "has been crucified and buried, but only in semblance, and is among us once more." He gestures as if passing his hand through Christ to show that he is a mere phantom, but he feels his beating heart and screams in terror. Christ passes into the inner room. The Syrian looks and tells what he sees: Christ stands among the apostles and shows the wound in his side. The Greek cries, "O Athens, Alexandria, Rome, something has come to destroy you! The heart of a phantom is beating. Man has begun to die! Your words are clear at last, O Heraclitus. God and man die each other's life, live each other's death." As they unfold and fold the ceremonial curtain, the musicians sing again of the new dispensation: "Odour of blood when Christ was slain / Made all Platonic tolerance vain / And vain all Doric discipline."

BIBLIOGRAPHY

Vendler, Helen Hennessy. *Yeats's Vision and the Later Plays*; Yeats, W. B. *Explorations, The Letters of W. B. Yeats, The Variorum Edition of the Plays of W. B. Yeats, A Vision.*

Seeker, The (1885)

Subtitled "A Dramatic Poem—in Two Scenes," the 81-line drama is perhaps Yeats's most undisguised version of SHELLEY's "Alastor" (1816), a poem inextricable from the most basic patterns of Yeats's thought (see *Aut.* 80). *The Seeker* tells of an old knight who has sacrificed the normal satisfactions of life to follow the beckoning of a mysterious voice, only to learn in his dying moments that the voice is that of the bearded hag Infamy. Like Shelley's wandering hero, the knight is guilty of shirking his social responsibilities and abandoning his social role. "Infamy"—debasement in the eyes of others—is the result of his delusive quest, suggesting that the social dimension may be evaded but not finally escaped. Yeats would dispense with such Shelleyan social scruples in poems like "FERGUS AND THE DRUID" and "TO THE ROSE UPON THE ROOD OF TIME," though these poems remain trepidatious about the estrangement that is the cost of the visionary calling. Yeats published the poem in the *DUBLIN UNIVERSITY REVIEW* and in *The Wanderings of Oisin and Other Poems* (1889), but he subsequently struck it from his collected work (for the poem, see *VP* 681–685). He did, however, preserve "The SONG OF THE HAPPY SHEPHERD," an "epilogue" to both *The ISLAND OF STATUES* and *The Seeker.*

FIRST PUBLICATION: *The Dublin University Review* (periodical), September 1885. Reprinted in *The Wanderings of Oisin and Other Poems*, Kegan Paul, Trench, & Co., London, January 1889.

SYNOPSIS

Scene 1

Three shepherds sit by a fire in a woodland valley. An old knight enters. A voice has summoned him to the shepherds' land after "three score years of dream-led wandering" and now his wandering shall at last end. He asks them the way to "the long-lost forest of the sprite." The shepherds beg him not to go there, for there goblin snakes sing and all die who enter. The old knight ignores their warning and continues on his way.

Scene 2

The knight comes to a ruined palace and finds a motionless figure. The knight bows before the figure, whose words "through fourscore" years have filled his "echoing heart." It was this figure that called him forth from the dance and made him a "coward in the field." The knight cries "Speak! Speak!" but the figure is silent. The knight asks himself in dismay, "Were all my wandering days of no avail, / Untouched of human joy or human love?" He feels life ebbing from him and begs to see the figure's face. A light reveals a bearded witch. "What thing art thou?" asks the distraught knight. "I sought thee not." The figure answers, "Men call me Infamy. / I know not what I am." The knight grieves for all he sacrificed in pursuit of the voice. The figure holds up a mirror to the knight, seeming to suggest that the infamy is his own, that he beholds himself. The knight falls. "What, lover, die before our lips have met?" asks the figure. The knight cries in his last moment, "Again, the voice! the voice!"

BIBLIOGRAPHY

Yeats, W. B. *Autobiographies, The Variorum Edition of the Poems of W. B. Yeats.*

Shadowy Waters, The (1900)

The Shadowy Waters is a consummate example of the transcendental quest central to romanticism as well as a crucial anticipation of the sea-journey that Yeats would bring to thematic fruition in "SAILING TO BYZANTIUM." The play—Yeats's "eternal work-in-progress," as R. F. Foster calls it—was early conceived, long nurtured, and much revised, resulting in a textual history as confusing as any in Yeats's corpus (AM 174). In AUTOBIOGRAPHIES, Yeats recollects that he started work on the play as early as 1885: "Once when staying with my uncle at Rosses Point, where he went for certain months of the year, I called upon a cousin towards midnight and asked him to get his yacht out, for I wanted to find what sea-birds began to stir before dawn. [...] I had wanted the birds' cries for the poem that became fifteen years afterwards *The Shadowy Waters*, and it had been full of observation had I been able to write it when I first planned it" (85–86; see also *VPl.* 340). Yeats first mentioned the play in a March 1894 letter to JOHN O'LEARY, calling it a "wild mystical thing carefully arranged to be an insult to the regular theatre goer who is hated by both of us" (CL1 384). Under the influence of ARTHUR SYMONS's translations of Mallarmé (see *Aut.* 247), he labored throughout the 1890s and finally published the play—or more accurately, the dramatic poem—in the *North American Review* in May 1900 (for this version, see *VP* 745–769). He brought the play out in book form in December, accompanied by a prologue (beginning "I walked among the Seven Woods of Coole") that had previously appeared in the December 1, 1900, number of the *Speaker* (for the prologue, see *VP* 217–218, 745–746). This version of the play powerfully moved MAUD GONNE, who was in some sense the intended recipient of its romantic and occult plea. She wrote in a letter of December 1900, "Oh it is beautiful, more beautiful even than I remembered it [. . .]. It is perhaps the most beautiful thing you have ever written, & yet while I write this I feel that is treason to the Secret Rose & to the other poems" (GY 138). GEORGE RUSSELL (AE) likewise wrote in December 1900 to congratulate Yeats. In light of its exquisite archaism, he proposed that *The Shadowy Waters* "should have been printed faintly on dim twilight coloured paper and bound in skins with golden symbolism of stars and sybils and Druidic emblems," and that "a nineteenth century person in this hideous world ought not to read it until he has cast aside his modern clothes and put on an ancient robe, and found out somewhere an old hall in a castle hung round with mementos of a thousand years ago to read it in" (*LTWBY*, I, 75).

The IRISH NATIONAL THEATRE SOCIETY staged this version of *The Shadowy Waters* at Molesworth Hall in January 1904. The production met with a baleful response despite the play's authentic and haunting PRE-RAPHAELITE beauty. J. M. SYNGE called it "the most DISTRESSING failure the mind can imagine,—a half empty room, with growling men and tittering females" (AM 318; see also CL3 540). Joseph Holloway (1861–1944), that inveterate and commonsensical theatergoer, commented that the piece "fairly mystified the audience by the uncanny monotony of its strange incomprehensibleness, until a peculiar, not wholly disagreeable dreariness filled the minds of all who listened to the strange music of the chanted words. What it was all about was hard to say, but the atmosphere of the poet was caught by the interpreters in a way that compelled attention, despite the depression conjured by the poet's weird imaginings" (*Joseph Holloway's Abbey Theatre* 32). Yeats himself admitted that the performance "pleased a few friends, though it must have bewildered and bored the greater portion of the audience" (*VPl*. 340).

Unwilling to relent, Yeats revised the play for publication in the 1906 volume *Poems 1899–1905* (for this version, see VP 217–252). In a letter of July 15, 1905, to FLORENCE FARR, Yeats explained the logic of his latest revision: "I am [. . .] getting rid of needless symbols, making the people answer each other, and making the ground work simple and intelligible. I find I am enriching the

poetry and the character of Forgael greatly in the process. I shall make it as strong a play as *The KING'S THRESHOLD* and perhaps put it in rehearsal in Dublin again. I am surprised [sic] at the badness of a great deal of it in its present form. The performance [at the Abbey on July 5] has enabled me to see the play with a fresh eye" (CL4 133; see also 134–135). In September, he told JOHN QUINN that the "very temper of the thing is different. It is full of homely phrases and of the idiom of daily speech. I have made the sailors rough as sailors should be, characterised all the people more or less, and yet not lost any of my lyrical moments. It has become a simple passionate play, or at any rate it has a simple passionate story for the common sight-seer though it keep something back for instructed eyes" (CL4 179). This version of the play was performed at the ABBEY THEATRE on December 8, 1906, with scenery designed by ROBERT GREGORY (*VPl*. 340–342; *UP2* 430). Realizing that even this latest version of the poem was not an entirely viable performance piece, he rewrote it again, resulting in the so-called acting version of 1907 (see *VPl*. 317–343). The latter version, with some further amendment, is included in editions of Yeats's collected plays. Of Yeats's many revisions, Harold Bloom provides this assessment: "[I] find a progressive imaginative loss with each fresh version of *The Shadowy Waters*. A dramatic gain is continuous, and the 'acting version' is certainly more actable than what came before. But *The Shadowy Waters* is more effective as poem than as play anyway, and more effective in 1900 than in its two principal later versions. After 1903 (Maud Gonne's marriage) Yeats was too bitter in his revisions not to violate the spirit of *The Shadowy Waters*. The middle Yeats was hardly the right custodian of the culmination of the vision of the early Yeats, and *The Shadowy Waters* suffered for it" (*Yeats* 136).

Yeats remarks in a 1907 note that *The Shadowy Waters* and *The LAND OF HEART'S DESIRE* contain "a good deal of incidental Irish folklore and mythology but are not founded on any particular story" (*VPl*. 1283). Though *The Shadowy Waters* is an original tale, Yeats evidently drew the names of his characters from Standish O'Grady's *History of Ireland* (1878–80), in which Dectora is CUCHULAIN's mother and Forgael is Emer's father (*W. B. Yeats and Irish Folklore* 27).

DRAMATIS PERSONAE: Forgael, Aibric, sailors, Dectora.

FIRST PERFORMANCE: Presented by the Irish National Theatre Society at Molesworth Hall, Dublin, January 14, 1904.

FIRST PUBLICATION: The *North American Review* (periodical), May 1900. Reprinted as *The Shadowy Waters*, Hodder and Stoughton, London, December 1900.

SYNOPSIS
("ACTING VERSION")

On the deck of a ship, Forgael sleeps while Aibric mans the tiller. The sailors complain of the long journey through the "waste places of the great sea," the lack of plunder, and the dwindling supplies. Suspecting that Forgael is mad, they plot to kill him. They put their conspiracy to Aibric, but he scoffs at the idea of betraying Forgael, his master since youth. Forgael stirs and the sailors exit. He asks whether Aibric has seen his "pilots," the birds that are the souls of the departed. Aibric is convinced that Forgael is being lured to his death. He knows their promises—that he will be led to "some Ever-living woman"—but such hopes are folly. He urges Forgael to find some mortal woman and live like other men, free of "impossible dreams." Forgael insists that earthly love cannot be absolute. He admits that he can "see nothing plain," yet sometimes a torch is lit within his head, and then "all that is impossible is certain."

The sailors spy a ship in the mist. On the deck, a king and queen kiss. Aibric orders an attack. Forgael remains at the tiller, watching as the souls of the battle dead assume the form of birds and hover about the ship. The sailors return with Dectora, who demands satisfaction for the death of her husband and wishes that the storm that had drowned her ships and the "treasures of nine conquered nations" had drowned her as well. Forgael avows that even if he were to let her sail homeward "a wave so huge / It had washed among the stars and put them out" would return her to where she stood now. She wonders whether he is mad. He denies that he is mad, if it be not mad to hear mes-

sages from "lasting watchers." Promising "love in their immortal fashion," the watchers have caught them both in their net and given him the "old harp of the nine spells" so that none might take her from him. Dectora denies that she, "the daughter and granddaughter of a king," can be compelled to share anyone's bed. Forgael swears that he will not kiss her until her lips have called him her beloved. As she mounts the bulwark to throw herself into the sea, Forgael merely folds his arms, for she cannot "leap out of the golden net."

The sailors intercede, promising to bear her home if she will pardon them. Dectora pledges a "golden galley full of fruit" to whomever kills Forgael. Forgael plays upon the harp and the sailors depart in a trance. Forgael plays on, baffling Dectora into the belief that he is the one she laments. The birds overhead assault him with their "railing and reproach and mockery" because he has won her love by magic. He answers that he is impelled by the Ever-living. Dectora fawns lovingly on Forgael, but he is stung by remorse and confesses that he has deceived her. Dectora does not care how her love was won, now that her body "has begun to dream" and Forgael has "grown to be a burning coal / In the imagination and intellect." Forgael weeps that he has nothing to give her but "desolate waters and a battered ship," but she would have the world emptied of all except the meeting of their lips. Forgael sees the "ash-grey" birds as they fly into the west. They beckon them to follow to the "country at the end of the world / Where no child's born but to outlive the moon."

The sailors and Aibric return, having discovered an immense treasure in Dectora's ship. Aibric pleads with Forgael to sail for home. Forgael is determined to continue his journey. Aibric warns Dectora that she goes to her death. Dectora begs Forgael to carry her to some "familiar place" where they may be contented in their love, but Forgael cannot deny the call of the birds. Forgael entreats Dectora to let the sailors bring her home, but she refuses. As the two ships part, she exults that she and Forgael will be alone forever. She places her crown upon his head and covers him with her hair. Forgael cries, "Beloved, having dragged the net about us, / And knitted mesh to mesh, we grow immortal; / And that old harp awakens of itself / To cry aloud to the grey birds, and dreams, / That have had dreams for father, live in us."

BIBLIOGRAPHY

Bloom, Harold. *Yeats*; Finneran, Richard J., et al., eds. *Letters to W. B. Yeats* (vol. 1); Foster, R. F. *W. B. Yeats: A Life, I: The Apprentice Mage*; Holloway, Joseph. *Joseph Holloway's Abbey Theatre: A Selection from His Unpublished Journal Impressions of a Dublin Playgoer*; Thuente, Mary Helen. *W. B. Yeats and Irish Folklore*; Yeats, W. B. *Autobiographies, The Collected Letters of W. B. Yeats* (vols. 1, 3–4), *The Gonne-Yeats Letters 1893–1938, Uncollected Prose by W. B. Yeats* (vol. 2), *The Variorum Edition of the Plays of W. B. Yeats, The Variorum Edition of the Poems of W. B. Yeats*.

Sophocles' 'King Oedipus' (1928)

See Part III, SOPHOCLES.

Sophocles' 'Oedipus at Colonus' (1934)

See Part III, SOPHOCLES.

Time and the Witch Vivien (1889)

Time and the Witch Vivien is a revised fragment from Yeats's unpublished two-act play *Vivien and Time*, which he wrote between the fall of 1882 and January 1884 (*Desolate Reality* 67; *CL1* 129). It initiates one of Yeats's most enduring themes: the battle against time itself. Under the cover of her own persiflage, Vivien attempts one of the most naked gambits of temporal rebellion in an oeuvre full of such gambits. As stated in a twice-repeated stage direction, Vivien "lays the hour-glass on its side," but to no avail, for Time "rights it again." Seen in this aspect, the dramatic fragment, slight as it is, heralds later monuments like "The DOUBLE VISION OF MICHAEL ROBARTES" ("In contemplation had those three so wrought / Upon a moment, and so stretched it out / That they, time overthrown, / Were dead yet flesh and bone") and "SAILING TO BYZANTIUM," as well as the powerful punctuating line in the later version of "The LAMENTATION OF THE OLD PENSIONER" ("I spit into the face of Time") and the punning defiance of "THE NEW FACES" ("we wrought that shall break the teeth of Time"). Yeats modeled his headstrong heroine on his cousin, the beautiful, red-haired LAURA ARMSTRONG, on whom Yeats had an adolescent crush (see *Aut.* 87–88; *CL1* 154–155). According to Richard Ellmann, *Vivien and Time* was "rehearsed and possibly presented by Yeats and a group of his friends at the home of a Judge Wright on Howth," with Laura playing the role of Vivien (*MM* 35). Yeats included *Time and the Witch Vivien* in *The Wanderings of Oisin and Other Poems* (1889), but otherwise chose not to reprint the extract.

Time and the Witch Vivien appears in *The Variorum Edition of the Poems of W. B. Yeats* (see 720–722). *Vivien and Time* appears in full in David R. Clark's *W. B. Yeats and the Theatre of Desolate Reality* (see 23–48). Clark comments that *Vivien and Time* "shows us Yeats as he was before Ireland and the occult possessed him" (6). He finds in the early play the genesis of numerous themes and images central to Yeats's mature work, and he proposes TENNYSON's "Merlin and Vivien" as the play's most obvious inspiration (71–74).

DRAMATIS PERSONAE: Vivien, Time.

FIRST PUBLICATION: THE WANDERINGS OF OISIN AND OTHER POEMS, Kegan Paul, Trench, and Co., London, January 1889.

SYNOPSIS

In a marble-flagged and pillared room, Vivien peers into a fountain and congratulates herself on her beauty and her "power in spells and secret rites." She senses some "fierce magician" approaching, but hears only the "wavering steps" of an old man. Time enters in the guise of an old peddler carrying scythe, hour-glass, and black bag. Vivien asks him to sit, but he neither rests nor sits. She asks what his bag contains. He responds, "Grey hairs and crutches, crutches and grey hairs, / Mansions of memories and mellow thoughts / Where dwell the minds of old men having peace. . . ." Vivien wants none of these. He suggests she may buy them some day, but she cries "Never!" She offhandedly lays the hour-glass on its side, and Time turns it right side up. She offers to buy the hour-glass, but it is not for sale. Vivien has heard that the old man is a "gambler and a player / At chances and at moments with mankind," and offers to roll dice for the hour-glass. Time throws double sixes. Vivien alleges that "Time always plays / With loaded dice" and calls for a game of chess. Time agrees to play, but for new stakes. Victorious, Vivien will triumph in her "many plots"; defeated, she will die. Time quickly checks Vivien's king. Her position desperate, she cries—perhaps punning on the literary implication of "plots"—"I have such plots—/ Such war plots, peace plots, love plots—every side; / I cannot go into the bloodless land / Among the whimpering ghosts." Time calls checkmate. Vivien dies.

BIBLIOGRAPHY

Clark, David R., with Rosalind Clark. *W. B. Yeats and the Theatre of Desolate Reality*; Ellmann, Richard. *Yeats: The Man and the Masks*; Yeats, W. B. *Autobiographies, The Collected Letters of W. B. Yeats* (vol. 1), *The Variorum Edition of the Poems of W. B. Yeats*.

Unicorn from the Stars, The (1908)

Dissatisfied with the theological parable WHERE THERE IS NOTHING (1902)—a "crude play with some dramatic force" (*VPl.* 933)—Yeats rewrote the story in 1907 as *The Unicorn from the Stars*, retaining the core idea of a religious visionary who raises a revolt against the soulless constrictions of modern society, but simplifying the plot and transforming much of the language and char-

acterization. The five-act sprawl of the earlier play is thus brought under tighter control, but breadth and intensity of emotion are lost. The most significant revision concerns the nature of the protagonist. Where Paul Ruttledge is a commanding and messianic romantic hero, Martin Hearne is a visionary naïf, not quite sure of his own powers or purpose. In a note to *The Unicorn from the Stars*, Yeats explains that he had come "to dislike a central character so arid and so dominating. We cannot sympathize with a man who sets his anger at once lightly and confidently to overthrow the order of the world; but our hearts can go out to him, as I think, if he speak with some humility, so far as his daily self carries him, out of a cloudy light of vision" (712). So too Yeats brought his play into line with his countercampaign against the kind of narrow-minded nationalist politics that had pitted itself against J. M. SYNGE's *The Playboy of the Western World* in January 1907. It does not go too far to construe Hearne as a version of Synge himself. The beggars would make him a mere tool of their political ambitions, and they turn on him acrimoniously—nearly violently—when he remains faithful to his spiritual vision. Throughout Yeats's work, beggary symbolizes spiritual wisdom—"the poor, they have nothing, and so they can see Heaven as we cannot," as Martin expresses the characteristic notion—but here the beggars more closely reflect the spiritual pettiness that Yeats tends to ascribe to the middle class (670).

In another important revision, *The Unicorn from the Stars* refines and magnifies the apocalyptic imagery of *Where There is Nothing*. In the earlier play, Paul imagines a "very terrible beast, with iron teeth and brazen claws that can root up spires and towers." He calls the beast "Laughter, the mightiest of the enemies of God" (1099; see also 1163, 932). Later in the play, he experiences a vision in which a troop of white angels calls on him to preach his gospel of world destruction, while the white unicorns they ride upon trample "the ground as though the world were already falling in pieces" (1132). In *The Unicorn from the Stars*, Yeats amalgamates "beast" and unicorn, reimagining the latter as an apocalyptic juggernaut that tramples that world beneath its hooves and making it the central image of the play. This conception of the unicorn is likewise central to *The* PLAYER QUEEN and foreshadows the slouching beast of "The SECOND COMING." In *The Unicorn from the Stars,* Father John remembers being told by a French monk that the unicorn represents "virginal strength, a rushing, lasting, tireless strength" (*VPl.* 660). In 1920, Yeats told his sister Lolly (1868–1940) that the unicorn of the play's title "is a private symbol belonging to my mystical order" and that it represents the soul (*Letters* 662). This characterization seems inappropriate to *The Unicorn from the Stars* and *The Player Queen,* though in keeping with the bookplate showing a unicorn leaping from a lightning-riven tower that T. STURGE MOORE designed for GEORGE YEATS IN 1918 (*WBY&TSM* 33–35). Yeats's "mystical order" was the HERMETIC ORDER OF THE GOLDEN DAWN. In its system of ritual, those in the third grade of adeptship bore the title of *Monocris* (or *Monoceros*) *de Astris,* or "Unicorn from the Stars" (*Unicorn* 146; *Whole Mystery of Art* 47). A. Norman Jeffares calls it a "temporary title, assumed upon completion of the Practicus Grade" (*New Biography* 132). In the play, Martin's description of trampling unicorns reminds Father John of the Latin phrase, though he cannot remember where he heard it (*VPl.* 659).

Yeats wrote *The Unicorn from the Stars,* like *Where There is Nothing,* in close collaboration with Lady GREGORY, and indeed considered the play as much hers as his own. As published in 1908, the play was credited both to Yeats and to Lady Gregory (*Biblio.* 84–85, 87–88). In a note to the play, Yeats explains, "I began [. . .] to dictate the play to Lady Gregory, but since I had last worked with her, her knowledge of the stage and her mastery of dialogue had so increased that my imagination could not go neck to neck with hers. I found myself, too, with an old difficulty, that my words flow freely alone when my people speak in verse, or in words that are like those we put into verse; and so after an attempt to work alone I gave my scheme to her. The result is a play almost wholly hers in handiwork, which I can yet read [. . .] and recognize thoughts, a point of view, an artistic aim which seem a part of my world" (*VPl.* 712; see also 713, 1296, 1306, 1309; *Aut.* 334; *Letters* 503).

R. F. Foster reports that the play was an "utter flop" when first performed at the ABBEY THEATRE in November 1907. One newspaper critic wrote, not without cause, "The whole thing is an essay, a sermon, a preaching [. . .]. A few days of it would kill the Abbey Theatre, and naturally" (*AM* 374). Joseph Holloway (1861–1944), diarist and Abbey regular, judged the play "strange and dramatically ineffective." He records that the play was "presented before a thin house (mostly of friends of the dramatists), and greeted with laughter in the wrong places. The audience was mystified during the first act as nothing was explained to them. They got an inkling in Act II, but it was not until Act III that any real interest was taken in the piece" (*Joseph Holloway's Abbey Theatre* 96).

DRAMATIS PERSONAE: Father John; Thomas Hearne, a coachbuilder; Andrew Hearne, his brother; Martin Hearne, his nephew; beggars (Johnny Bocach, Paudeen, Biddy Lally, Nanny).

FIRST PERFORMANCE: Produced by the National Theatre Society Ltd. (see IRISH NATIONAL THEATRE SOCIETY) at the Abbey Theatre, Dublin, November 21, 1907.

FIRST PUBLICATION: *The Unicorn from the Stars* (by Yeats and Lady Gregory), Macmillan, New York, January 15, 1908 (copyright edition). Reprinted in *The Unicorn from the Stars and Other Plays* (by Yeats and Lady Gregory), Macmillan, New York, May 13, 1908.

SYNOPSIS

Act 1

Father John enters a coachbuilder's shop. He has been praying over the entranced Martin. Thomas says that Martin used to fall asleep and wake with stories of white horses and angels, and that he cured him with a "few strokes of the rod." Father John reminds him that Martin's dreams set him building the golden coach, which the lord lieutenant has purchased. Father John exits to continue his prayer. Thomas and Andrew discuss Martin's illness—Thomas holding that "there is no such thing as a trance"—and exit to resume their work. Father John enters with Martin, who complains of being revived. In his dream, he had been beset by white horses with white shining riders. They had carried him to a garden, where the horses had changed into unicorns. They had crushed the grapes and trampled the wheat, and wine had flowed all about. Martin wants to know how to return. Father John warns against the "life of vision," but Martin cannot bear to contemplate life as a coachbuilder, "seeing nothing but common things" and doing "some foolish work." Thomas and Andrew return; Father John goes to pray. Martin does not expect them to believe what he has seen, but Andrew confesses that he too has had "very queer dreams." Thomas boasts, "You had, till I cured you, taking you in hand and binding you to the hours of the clock." Thomas recommends a regimen of work on the unfinished coach. Martin defends his freedom of mind and soul, and vows to leave with whatever money he has not spent on the coach. Thomas tosses him a bag of coins. Trying to restore calm, Andrew ushers Thomas out of the room. He confides to Martin that he too has visions and that for 20 years he has been slipping out of the house at night. Johnny Bocach calls for alms at the window. He climbs inside looking for something to grab. As Andrew seizes him, he shouts "Destruction on us all!" Martin recognizes the words of his dream. He has been commanded to "destroy, to overthrow all that comes between us and God." He believes the poor will understand his message. Andrew pledges to help him. Martin tells Johnny to gather his people, as they "have a great thing to do."

Act 2

Martin sets a table in the workshop; he is expecting a large gathering. Father John confesses that he too has dreamed of the world destroyed and in consequence has been banished to his present "lonely parish" where he can do no harm. Martin welcomes a gaggle of drunken beggars. He calls for paint to make a banner showing the unicorn, under which he plans to rally the "lawbreakers, the tinkers, the sievemakers, the sheepstealers." The beggars take Martin for a nationalist rabble-rouser who is going to set the unicorn against the English lion. Martin pays Biddy, a fortune-teller, to tell him "where it is best to begin and what will happen in the end." She sees smoke and burning, which he interprets as a directive to "bring men once more to the wild-

ness of the clean green earth," but Johnny takes to mean that they must destroy the "big houses and the towns" and reclaim the fields for the "ancient race." She next sees a gallows and an old priest. Martin takes this to mean that they must destroy law and church and restore men to the ancient ways that made them "hard and strong." Johnny interprets these as symbols of English law and the Protestant church. Thomas brings the news that the entire town is drunk. Martin proclaims that one begins to live only when one has "put work away" and recalls that in the paradise of his vision the shining people spent their days in a "dance bred of the secret frenzy of their hearts, or a battle where the sword made a sound that was like laughter." Martin arrives at an important summary of his philosophy: "Events that are not begotten in joy are misbegotten and darken the world, and nothing is begotten in joy if the joy of a thousand years has not been crushed into a moment." Thomas threatens them all with jail. The beggars seize him, but Martin orders them to let him go, for "the moment has come to begin the war." Entirely misunderstanding the nature of this war, Johnny cries, "Up with the Unicorn and destroy the Lion!" Martin orders them to make a pyre of the golden coach. He says, "We will destroy all that can perish! It is only the soul than can suffer no injury. The soul of man is of the imperishable substance of the stars!"—and throws a wisp of fire onto the heap.

Act 3

Nanny and Biddy squat in a rocky place before dawn, with rich articles strewn about. Martin lies nearby as if dead. Nancy congratulates Paudeen on the success of their raid, which ended in the torching of two "big houses." They credit Martin's spirit and daring. Johnny and Paudeen lament the fall of "so good a leader" in the fight against the British. Johnny says, "If he had held out and held up, it is my belief he would have freed Ireland!" Andrew enters and reports that the village has come to a standstill and that the landowners are "up against him." He asks after Martin. Nanny believes that he is dead, but Father John, summoned by Andrew, reports that he is in a trance. They urge him to wake Martin, but he fears that the mystical command might be interrupted and confused a second time. Johnny tries to touch a piece of lighted sod to Martin's feet, but Father John dashes it away. "I will not give in to leave him swooning there and the country waiting for him to awake!" cries Johnny. Martin stirs, mumbling of "sweet marvellous music" louder even than the trampling of the unicorns: "It is certainly the music of paradise. Ah, now I hear, now I understand. It is the continual clashing of swords!" Johnny misconstrues this as a call to fight the British. Martin realizes that his war against church and state has been mistaken, for the "battle we have to fight is fought out in our own mind." Johnny and Paudeen denounce Martin as a traitor. Martin sees a vision of a thousand white unicorns bearing riders with drawn swords. Thomas brings news that Martin is to be arrested. As constables arrive, Martin expresses his final understanding of his own visions: "That is the joy of Heaven, continual battle. I thought the battle was here, and that the joy was to be found here on earth, that all one had to do was to bring again the old wild earth of the stories—but no, it is not here; we shall not come to that joy, that battle, till we have put out the senses, everything that can be seen and handled, as I put out this candle. We must put out the whole world as I put out this candle. [. . .] Where there is nothing, where there is nothing—there is God!" The beggars and constables tussle. Amid the struggle, Martin is shot and killed. Thomas laments the strangeness of the world, while Andrew reflects that it is best to "keep to yourself the thing that you know, and to do in quiet the thing you want to do."

BIBLIOGRAPHY

Foster, R. F. *W. B. Yeats: A Life, I: The Apprentice Mage*; Holloway, Joseph. *Joseph Holloway's Abbey Theatre: A Selection from His Unpublished Journal* Impressions of a Dublin Playgoer; Jeffares, A. Norman. *W. B. Yeats: A New Biography*; Melchiori, Giorgio. *The Whole Mystery of Art: Pattern into Poetry in the Work of W. B. Yeats*; Moore, Virginia. *The Unicorn: William Butler Yeats' Search for Reality*; Wade, Allan. *A Bibliography of the Writings of W. B. Yeats*; Yeats, W. B. *Autobiographies*, *The Letters of W. B. Yeats*, *The Variorum Edition of the Plays of W. B. Yeats*, *W. B. Yeats and T. Sturge Moore: Their Correspondence 1901–1937*.

Where There is Nothing (1902)

Yeats's longest play is also one of his most philosophically ambitious: It presents a fully fledged theological conception in which divine communion is achieved in the joy of a destructive or antinomian freedom. "Where there is nothing there is God," Paul Ruttledge says, summarizing the play's idea of divinity as an apocalyptic negation of everything social and material, everything fixed by "Law and Number." Yeats had first employed this phrase in an 1896 story titled "Where there is Nothing, there is God" (*Myth.* 185) and he would repeat the phrase in *The Unicorn from the Stars* (*VPl.* 709). The play began as a prospective collaboration with George Moore, but when Moore withdrew from the Irish Literary Theatre the project fell apart and the two writers turned to squabbling over ownership of the play's ideas and plot elements. Moore, who wanted to novelize the tale, went so far as to threaten a legal injunction against Yeats (see *Aut.* 333–334; *CL3* 228, 238–239, 244; *UP2* 299; *VPl.* 712–714). Despite Moore's threats, Yeats went forward with the play, completing a draft in September 1902. In the attempt to preempt Moore, Yeats rushed his version of the story into print as a "special supplement" to the *United Irishman* on November 1, accompanied by the essay "The Freedom of the Theatre" (see *UP2* 297–299). Yeats told Allan Wade that he had taken this course because "he knew Moore would not dare to issue an injunction against a Nationalist newspaper for fear of getting his windows broken" (*Biblio.* 60; see also *Aut.* 334). In addition, John Quinn did Yeats the favor of printing the play at his own expense in New York in order to secure the American copyright (*CL3* 238–239; *LTWBY*, I, 104–106). In *Autobiographies*, Yeats writes that he and Moore "were never cordial again," and he accepts his fair share of the blame: "Had I abandoned my plot and made him write the novel, he might have put beside *Muslin* and *The Lake* a third masterpiece, but I was young, vain, self-righteous, and bent on proving myself a man of action" (334). Yeats wrote the play with the editorial and secretarial assistance of Douglas Hyde (1860–1949) and Lady Gregory (*Aut.* 334; *Letters* 503; *VPl.* 712–713, 1296, 1306,

1309). Yeats dedicated the play to Lady Gregory in gratitude for her help, calling the play in part her own (*VPl.* 1292, 232).

The result of this messy and rushed gestation was a play Yeats almost immediately judged an artistic failure (see *Aut.* 334; *CL3* 391; *VPl.* 712–713, 933, 1296). From the perspective of 1908, the play seemed "hurried and oratorical, with events cast into the plot because they seemed lively or amusing in themselves, and not because they grew out of the characters and the plot; and I came to dislike a central character so arid and so dominating" (*VPl.* 712). He was also uneasy about the play on moral and religious grounds. In "The Freedom of the Theatre," he defends it at once defiantly and apprehensively: "I have put my stick into so many beehives that I feel a little anxious. Someone is sure to say I have written a mischievous attack upon the Law, upon Church and State, upon Sobriety, upon Custom and even upon the Sun in his strength. I have some reason to expect this, for ingenious theatre-goers [. . .] have found my poor little 'LAND OF HEART'S DESIRE' to be both clerical and anticlerical; and when 'The COUNTESS CATHLEEN' was acted, the opinions of my demons were said to be my own opinions [. . .]" (*UP2* 297). In the essay's conclusion, Yeats rejects the very notion that art has nonaesthetic obligations: "In 'Where There is Nothing,' Paul, because he is a seeker after God, desires the destruction of all things. So far as I am a dramatist, so far as I have made these people alive, I watch them with wonder and pity, and I do not even ask myself were they right to go upon that journey" (298–299). Joseph Hone has it that the play could not be presented in Dublin for the obvious religious reasons (*W. B. Yeats* 186); in consequence, it was first produced in London by the Incorporated Stage Society (on the society, see *CL3* 721–725; *CL4* 1024–1025). In 1907, Yeats's second thoughts got the best of him and he rewrote the play as *The Unicorn from the Stars*, again in close collaboration with Lady Gregory.

Though sprawling and formless, *Where There is Nothing* is aggressively philosophical and intellectually arresting. Numerous commentators have cited BLAKE and Nietzsche as the dominant influences upon the play's thought, and Yeats mentions in *Autobiographies* the influence of Tolstoy (334). His joyous destructive zeal aside, Paul Ruttledge's basic lineaments are the prophetic and transcendental impulses inseparable from the romantic conception. In this regard, he is distantly related to Forgael, the vision-wasted wanderer of *The SHADOWY WATERS,* and to the visionary abandoners of home in CATHLEEN NI HOULIHAN and *The Land of Heart's Desire.* Writing to Quinn in February 1903, Yeats compared Paul to WILLIAM MORRIS, whom he described as "too absorbed and busy to give much of himself to persons" (*CL3* 312). As an apostle of tragic joy and an avatar of apocalypse, Paul predicts much in Yeats's later thought. He is in some sense ancestor to the Yeats who declares "Bid me strike a match and blow" in IN MEMORY OF EVA GORE-BOOTH AND CON MARKIEWICZ"; who envisions "Everything that is not God consumed with intellectual fire" in "BLOOD AND THE MOON"; who declares "We that look on but laugh in tragic joy" in "The GYRES"; who takes grim pleasure in the destruction promised by the slouching beast of "The SECOND COMING."

DRAMATIC PERSONAE: Paul Ruttledge, a country gentleman; Thomas Ruttledge, his brother; Mrs. Thomas Ruttledge; magistrates (Mr. Dowler, Mr. Algie, Colonel Lawley, Mr. Joyce); Mr. Green, a stipendiary magistrate; tinkers (Sabina Silver, Molly the Scold, Charlie Ward, Paddy Cockfight, Tommy the Song, Johneen, etc.); friars (Father Jerome, Father Aloysius, Father Colman, Father Bartley); other friars, and a crowd of countrymen.

FIRST PERFORMANCE: Produced by the Incorporated Stage Society at the Royal Court Theatre, London, June 26, 1904.

FIRST PUBLICATION: The *United Irishman,* supplement, November 1, 1902. Privately printed by John Quinn for copyright purposes (see *Biblio.* 60–61). Reprinted in *Where There is Nothing,* A. H. Bullen, London, May 1903.

SYNOPSIS

Act 1

Paul tends to his yard. Thomas and Mrs. Ruttledge, who have made a comfortable home in Paul's house, urge him to join the local magistrates who have gathered for lunch, but he has no interest in conventionalities. Father Jerome appears at the gate and mentions that the local school is going to put up new buildings and begin teaching technical skills. Paul points to the magistrates as examples of the trend toward "useful things" and complains that people "have forgotten their freedom." Concerned, Father Jerome asks whether Paul's old dreams or visions have recurred. Paul admits that he sometimes dreams of pulling down his house, sometimes the entire world. Jerome urges him to speak with his superior, but Paul no longer knows whether he is a Christian. Paul and Jerome exit. The tinkers Charlie Ward and Johneen enter, plying their trade. Charlie compares himself to the crows. Struck by this image of wayward freedom, Paul instantly decides to leave home. He offers to trade clothes with Charlie. They exit to the potting shed as the others enter. Paul enters in rustic dress and announces that he is going to join the tinkers. There is shocked protest. Mr. Green opines that Paul, like Rousseau, "has some idea of going back to the dark ages," and asks, "Do you want to lose all the world has gained since then?" Paul answers, "What has it gained? I am among those who think that sin and death came into the world the day Newton eat the apple. I know you are going to tell me he only saw it fall. Never mind, it is all the same thing."

Act 2

In the tinkers' roadside camp, Paul receives a soldering lesson from Charlie, meets the other tinkers, and hears of the tinkers' hardships. Paul says that he is sick of lighted rooms and welcomes the dark: "Yes, I think that is what I want. The dark, where there is nothing that is anything, and nobody that is anybody; one can be free there, where there is nothing." Paul proposes to bind himself to the tinkers by marriage. Charlie calls over Sabina Silver, and she accepts Paul's proposal. A priest approaches on the road. Paul suggests they marry immediately, but Charlie insists they marry in the tinker way by jumping over the "budget" (i.e., the pouch in which the tinker carries his tools). The priest turns out to be Jerome, who is astonished to find Paul among the tinkers. Paul explains that he seeks "endless battle" against the world, that he pursues "Laughter, the mightiest of the enemies of God." Jerome urges Paul in the name of God to return to his old life, but the tinkers drive him off with threats and

hexes. Paul proposes a wedding celebration. He orders "all the public-houses thrown open and free drinks going for a week." Paul takes Sabina's hand and they leap over the budget.

Act 3

Paul and the tinkers lounge in a farm shed, exhausted by a week of wedding revelry. The magistrates, including Thomas Ruttledge, arrive in a mood of outraged propriety and demand to be let in. The whole countryside is drunk; Mr. Dowler's butler has been missing for two days; not a stroke of work has been done in a week. They have wired Dublin requesting police; they are due on the four o'clock train. Thomas begs Paul to come home. Mr. Green demands that Paul stop the flow of free drink. Paul says that Heaven itself is a place of idleness. Mr. Green says that the world could not go on without work, and Paul wonders why the world should go on: "Let us send messengers everywhere to tell the people to stop working, and then the world may come to an end." Thinking Paul mad, the justices attempt to leave, but Paul orders the tinkers to detain them. As the justices intend to put the tinkers on trial, he will put them on trial instead. They are tied up. "They say they are living like Christians," Paul begins. "Let us see." As a soldier, Colonel Lawley has not turned the other cheek; as a rich man, Mr. Dowler clings to his property; as a judge, Mr. Green upholds the others in their breaking of Christ's law. Johneen announces that the soldiers' train has arrived. All flee except Paul. He grants his wealth to Thomas and takes his leave, expecting never to see him again.

Act. 4

The tinkers deposit Paul, who is injured, at the monastery door. Wanted for their misdeeds, they have no choice but to ring the bell and leave him in the care of the monks. The scene shifts to the crypt under the monastery church. Five years have passed since Paul entered the monastery; he has become a friar. A year before he had gone into a trance; when he awoke he had preached meditation as a way of getting "out of time into eternity." Once again, Paul has gone into a trance. His followers dance before him, as Paul has instructed them to do. The superior enters and halts the blasphemous dance. The friars scurry away. The superior decrees that Paul may no longer preach. He exits. Aloysius and Jerome help Paul to a chair, and Aloysius goes in search of Paul's followers. Paul relates his trance vision. He was attacked by beasts representing the "part of mankind that is not human; the part that builds up the things that keep the soul from God." These were scattered by a bright light shed by a host of laughing angels riding unicorns. They called upon him to preach. Jerome asks Paul to submit to the orders of the superior, but Paul has received "other orders." Forlorn, Jerome exits with the news that Paul will not obey. Meanwhile, Paul's disciples have entered. Paul considers them ready to hear the truth and unfolds the spiritual history of man. Life began in simplicity and communion with nature, in the knowledge that "the green Earth was the Love of God and that all Life was the Will of God," but animal spirits crept from their holes and began to whisper, and men created laws, which were "the first mouthful of the apple." They next built houses and towns, and then churches, which restrict the holiness of creation to a few spots only. Paul concludes, "We must destroy the World; we must destroy everything that has Law and Number, for where there is nothing, there is God." These lessons, Paul says, he learned from Jesus Christ, who "made a terrible joy, and sent it to overturn governments, and all settled order." The superior enters. He expels Paul from the monastery and threatens with damnation any monk who follows him. Several kneel in obedience; several gather about Paul. He removes his habit and declares that as he has pulled down his house, he will pull down the world.

Act 5

Amid ecclesiastical ruins, Aloysius tells Colman that there is almost no food left. They have come to realize that Paul's message—that the kingdom of heaven is within—is too abstruse for the people. Aloysius proposes that they expand their movement by teaching youngsters basket weaving. Paul enters with Charlie Ward, who recalls fondly the week of mass drunkenness of years earlier. As he once made the people drunk on liquor, Paul says, he now rolls out a new barrel from a cellar under the earth. Colman moots the basket weaving plan:

not only would it popularize their cause, but the baskets could be sold and a grant could be procured from the Technical Board. Eventually workshops and "good houses" might be built, and "some little place" for prayer. Paul scorns the plan as putting up everything he would tear down. Charlie invites Paul to rejoin the tinkers, but Aloysius proposes that they gather the tinkers, tramps, and beggars into a great army. Paul sees it at once: "We could march on the towns, and we could break up all settled order; we could bring back the old joyful, dangerous, individual life." Paul rejects his own vision, however, remembering that "we cannot destroy the world with armies, it is inside our minds that it must be destroyed, it must be consumed in a moment inside our minds." Bartley enters out of breath; the people are coming up the road with stones and sticks. Paul chooses to wait for them. He calls death "the last adventure, the first perfect joy, for at death the soul comes into possession of itself, and returns to the joy that made it." Aloysius would stay with him, but Colman drags him away. The mob rushes in, decrying Paul as heretic and witch. They leave him lying on the ground and go in search of others. Aloysius and Colman creep back, see Paul wounded, and flee again at the sound of voices. Charlie and Sabina enter and bend over Paul. He cries out, "O plunge me into the wine barrel, into the wine barrel of God." He dies, leaving Sabina swaying and keening.

BIBLIOGRAPHY

Finneran, Richard, et al., eds. *Letters to W. B. Yeats* (vol. 1); Hone, Joseph. *W. B. Yeats*; Wade, Allan. *A Bibliography of the Writings of W. B. Yeats*; Yeats, W. B. *Autobiographies, The Collected Letters of W. B. Yeats* (vols. 3–4), *The Letters of W. B. Yeats, Mythologies, Uncollected Prose by W. B. Yeats* (vol. 2), *The Variorum Edition of the Plays of W. B. Yeats*.

Words upon the Window-pane, The (1934)

This one-act play is a dramatically thin pretext for an emotionally intense deliberation on the life and character of JONATHAN SWIFT (on Swift, see "BLOOD AND THE MOON," "PARNELL'S FUNERAL," "The SEVEN SAGES," and "SWIFT'S EPITAPH"). Yeats wrote the play in September and October 1930 (*Letters* 777), while he was immersed in the writings of Swift (773, 776). The play crowned his discovery of Irish Georgianism as a tradition by which he might validate his own reaction against the "Whiggery" that he considered the evil genius of the modern age ("The Seven Sages"). His introduction to the play adverts to this hunt for an intellectual heritage: "I collect materials for my thought and work, for some identification of my beliefs with the nation itself, I seek an image of the modern mind's discovery of itself, of its own permanent form, in that one Irish century that escaped from darkness and confusion" (*Expl.* 344–345; *VPl.* 957–958). At the same time, the play chronicles the instability and decline of this tradition, as symbolized by the degeneration of the country retreat into a common lodging house and by the middle-class philistinism of the guests at the séance. Rome has given way to AMERICA, Belfast, and London, the rule of intellect has given way to the rule of democracy, passionate intensity has given way to frittering small-mindedness. Swift's worst fears, clearly, have been realized. David R. Clark calls the theme of the play "enforced loss": "The house is decayed; some of the sitters have lost loved ones; the medium is impoverished; the séance is a failure; the spirits lose the chance to speak, the sitters the chance to hear; Vanessa loses Swift; Stella loses money at cards as well as health and life; Swift loses Stella, his reason, his friends, his appearance; the world loses a great moment of its history; Mrs. Henderson is tired out; a china saucer is shattered" (*Desolate Reality* 229).

The play's framing device is a Dublin séance in which the crisis moments in Swift's romantic relationships with "Stella" and "Vanessa" are played out by their spirits before the assembled guests. "Stella" was the pet name of Esther Johnson (1681–1728), "Vanessa" the pet name of Hester Vanhomrigh (1690–1723), younger women with whom Swift had romantic but evidently platonic relationships. Swift met Stella in 1689, when he became secretary to Sir William Temple and went to live at Moor Park, Sir William's estate in Surrey. Stella was the eight-year-old daughter of the housekeeper. She had been to some extent adopted as a member of the household, and there were rumors—never substantiated—that she was Sir William's daughter (*Jonathan Swift* 18–19). Swift gave the young girl lessons, and the two became fond of each other. In 1701, Swift invited Stella and her companion Rebecca Dingley, who were by then employed in the house of Sir William's sister, to join him in Dublin (58–60). They remained in Dublin for the rest of their lives, providing Swift with a surrogate family and an ersatz household. Yeats wrote his *Journal to Stella* between 1710 and 1713, while in England. Biographer David Nokes calls it the most "obvious symbol of [Swift's] determination to retain his connection with Dublin. [. . .] Every day, night and morning, usually while still in bed, Swift would cover the pages with his tiny writing, pouring out all the news of the day, mingled with riddles and puns, admonitions and anecdotes, hopes and fears, all in a teasing tone, half lover-like, half avuncular" (117). The theory that Swift and Stella secretly married in 1716 has long been aired, but this is a matter of speculation and circumstantial evidence (217–218).

In contrast to the soft and yielding Stella, Vanessa was headstrong, impulsive, clever, and altogether more difficult to manage. Swift met her while he was in London in 1708 (78). When he returned two years later, the Vanhomrighs, downwardly mobile Dublin émigrés of Dutch extraction, made a place for him in their family circle (154–166). Swift's relationship with Vanessa, according to Nokes, began "as practically an exact counterpart of that with Stella. What could be more agreeable than, having established the precise kind of domicile that he favoured with [Stella] in Dublin, to find its mirror-image here in London? Like Esther Johnson, Hester Vanhomrigh was a sickly fatherless girl; like her she was surrounded by other females" (159). Vanessa declared her love in 1712, but Swift, emotionally constricted and in some sense committed to Stella, put her off, as Yeats depicts in his play (161). The relationship inconclusively and painfully dragged on until Vanessa's death in 1723.

The play's title recalls certain lines of doggerel—"Mary Kilpatrick—very young / Ugly face and pleasant tongue"—that had been etched upon a glass window in a house at Glasnevin, about a mile from the center of Dublin (*Letters* 891). The house had since become the family home of the physician and poet Oliver St John Gogarty (1878–1957), one of Yeats's close friends, and Yeats had been a guest there in October 1909 (*Gogarty* 13, 44–45). Household lore held that Swift had visited the house and left the bantering lines behind. According to Ulick O'Connor, Gogarty's biographer, the lines address a servant girl (*Gogarty* 13). In 1937, however, Yeats excitedly informed Gogarty that Mary Kilpatrick was apparently "the sister of the Earl of Ossory," who had "married the second Lord Holland and died of consumption beloved by everybody in 1778" (*Letters* 891). In the play, "the words upon the window-pane" are transformed into lines from a poem by Stella.

In November 1930, Yeats began a long introduction to the play (see *Explorations* 343–369 or *VPl.* 957–970) that was intended, in conjunction with the three other introductions that appear in *Wheels and Butterflies* (1934), to lay out a scheme of intellectual nationalism (*Letters* 779). The introduction is one of Yeats's several indispensable statements on "that one Irish century that escaped from darkness and confusion," when "UNITY OF BEING was still possible though somewhat over-rationalised and abstract, more diagram than body" (*VPl.* 958, 964). It argues that Swift foresaw the spiritual and cultural ruin of the coming democratic age and attempted a hopeless rearguard action in defense of a vision of civilization founded on "the long settled rule of powerful men, no great dogmatic structure, few great crowded streets, scattered unprogressive communities, much handiwork, wisdom wound into the roots of the grass" (965). It also addresses the mystery of Swift's unwillingness to draw closer either to Stella or to Vanessa. After considering various explanations—physical defect, dread of passing on his incipient madness, syphilis, a shared parent in Sir William Temple—Yeats judges the matter an irresolvable mystery (965–966). As in his play, however, he circumspectly proposes that the "intellect of Swift's age, persuaded that the mechanicians mocked by Gulliver would prevail, that its moment of freedom could not last, so dreaded the historic process that it became in the half-mad mind of Swift a dread of parentage" (967).

Like *The* DREAMING OF THE BONES and PURGATORY, *The Words upon the Window-pane* is a purgatorial vision of the soul attempting to free itself from the imprisonment of its past. Yeats explains the play's informing theory in *A* VISION: "In the *Dreaming Back*, the *Spirit* is compelled to live over and over again the events that had most moved it; there can be nothing new, but the old events stand forth in a light which is dim or bright according to the intensity of the passion that accompanied them. They occur in the order of their intensity or luminosity, the more intense first, and the painful are commonly the more intense, and repeat themselves again and again. In the *Return*, upon the other hand, the *Spirit* must live through past events in the order of their occurrence, because it is compelled by the *Celestial Body* to trace every passionate event to its cause until all are related and understood, turned into knowledge, made a part of itself" (226; see also *AV-1925* 226–227). Peter Ure suggests that Stella's spirit is absent from the séance because it "has long ago proceeded to some purer stage of the discarnate life" (*Yeats the Playwright* 100–101).

The play is generally regarded as one of Yeats's best. It is also—and perhaps not coincidentally—one of his least characteristic. It is unusually accessible in a number of regards: It dispenses with Yeats's sometimes dense verse in favor of conversational prose; it embraces a degree of melodrama; it comports with the modern predilection for the psychological case study and with the Freudian emphasis on sexual psychology. Hugh Hunt calls it Yeats's "only realistic play," while Clark observes more subtly that "the devices of modern realism—showing forth a supernatural event—are used to discredit the world-view they imply" (*The Abbey* 141; *Desolate Reality* 123). Following the play's debut in November 1930, Yeats told OLIVIA SHAKESPEAR that the play had been "a much greater success" than he had hoped, and that it had been "beautifully acted" (*Letters* 779).

DRAMATIS PERSONAE: Dr. Trench, Miss Mackenna, John Corbet, Cornelius Patterson, Abraham Johnson, Mrs. Mallet, Mrs. Henderson.

FIRST PEFORMANCE: Produced by the National Theatre Society Ltd. (see IRISH NATIONAL THEATRE SOCIETY) at the ABBEY THEATRE, Dublin, November 17, 1930.

FIRST PUBLICATION: *The Words upon the Window Pane: A Play in One Act, with Notes upon the Play and its Subject,* The CUALA PRESS, Dublin, April 1934.

SYNOPSIS

The scene is laid in the common room of a Dublin lodging-house. Miss Mackenna leads in John Corbet and Dr. Trench, who have arrived for a séance. Mrs. Henderson, the medium, rests upstairs. Corbet hopes she will not mind his skepticism. Trench assures him that everyone must find out the truth for himself but tells him not to expect too much, as a "hostile influence" disturbed the last séance. Corbet is impressed by the room. Trench says that the house had once been a country house belonging to friends of Stella (see above). He shows Corbet a window-pane on which lines from one of Stella's poems have been cut, possibly by Stella herself. Corbet knows the lines: They are from a poem Stella wrote for Swift's 54th birthday, one of her three surviving poems, "enough to prove her a better poet than Swift." Corbet, a student at Cambridge, explains that Swift and Stella are the subjects of his doctoral essay, which argues that "in Swift's day men of intellect reached the height of their power—the greatest position they ever attained in society and the State, that everything great in Ireland and in our character, in what remains of our architecture, comes from that day; that we have kept its seal longer than England." Trench calls Swift's a "tragic life," and mentions "the great Ministers that were his friends, banished and broken." Corbet says that the tragedy of Swift's life went deeper than mere political setbacks: "His ideal order was the Roman Senate, his ideal men Brutus and Cato. Such an order and such men had seemed possible once more, but the movement passed and he foresaw the ruin to come, Democracy, Rousseau, the French Revolution; that is why

he hated the common run of men,—'I hate lawyers, I hate doctors,' he said, 'though I love Dr. So-and-so and Judge So-and so'—that is why he wrote *Gulliver,* that is why he wore out his brain, that is why he felt *saeva indignatio* [savage indignation], that is why he sleeps under the greatest epitaph in history" (see "Swift's Epitaph"). Meanwhile, the other guests have arrived. Mr. Johnson hopes the evil influence can be driven away so he can communicate with the American evangelist Dwight Lyman Moody (1837–99). Mrs. Mallet, who wants advice from her departed husband about opening a teashop in Folkestone, seconds his hope. She complains that two obstreperous spirits ruined the previous two séances. Such spirits are not evil, according to Dr. Trench, but tormented. It is their purgatorial condition to believe they are still living and to repeat over and over again some "passionate or tragic" event of their past lives. Such spirits often visit the house where the event occurred.

Miss Mackenna and Mrs. Henderson enter and all take their places about the table. Mrs. Henderson falls asleep and begins to speak in the voice of her control, a little girl named Lulu. Lulu sees a young lady dressed as for "a fancy dress party." She says the "bad old man"—one of the spoiling spirits from the previous séance—has returned. Mrs. Henderson alternates between the voices of a man and a woman. The man asks, "How dare you write to her? How dare you ask if we were married?" He reproaches the lady for ingratitude and reminds her of the many times he forsook state business to read Plutarch with her, teaching her to think not as Hester Vanhomrigh but as Cato or Brutus. Corbet recognizes the voices: Swift addresses Vanessa. Vanessa begs Swift to marry her if he is not already married to Stella, as he claims not to be, but Swift says there is something in his blood that must not be passed on to a child. Vanessa guesses he is speaking of a tendency to madness. Her own blood, she says, will counteract whatever is unhealthy in his. Swift refuses to add another "to the healthy rascaldom and knavery of the world." Vanessa places his hands upon her breast and urges him to resist the lure of solitude. Swift tries to flee. Mrs. Henderson, possessed by the spirit of Swift, beats upon the locked door of the room and sinks in exhaustion. Mrs. Mallet leads her back to her chair. She continues in Swift's voice. Swift calls out to Stella. He asks whether she regrets having no children or husband, but only a "cross and ageing man for friend." Attempting to comfort himself, Swift recites from the poem that appears on the window-pane. It attests that love founded on the soul rather than on the flesh prolongs youthful looks. Swift reads on. The final stanzas assuage his fear of solitude; they describe how Swift's example will help Stella bear with dignity the sorrow of his death, but only for a day, for she will immediately follow him to the grave. Swift cries out that she will long outlive him, and he is comforted that she will be the one to close his eyes.

All exit except Mrs. Henderson and Corbet. Unconvinced by the séance, he prefers to consider Mrs. Henderson "an accomplished actress and scholar." Speaking scholar to scholar, as it were, he theorizes that Swift represented "the intellect of his epoch, that arrogant intellect free at last from superstition," and that he dreaded the future, foreseeing the collapse of this intellect with the coming of the democratic age. He asks her, "Did he refuse to beget children because of that dread? Was Swift mad? Or was it the intellect itself that was mad?" Mrs. Henderson asks whether he refers to the spirit of the "dirty old man," for she had seen him, dirty and diseased. In his old age, Corbet confirms, Swift was lonely and neglected, Stella having died and his friends having deserted him. Dr. Trench calls from the door and Corbet departs. Mrs. Henderson lapses into Swift's voice. He cannot count on his fingers the number of great ministers who were his friends but are now gone. He cries, "Perish the day on which I was born!" [Job 3:3].

BIBLIOGRAPHY

Clark, David R., with Rosalind Clark. *W. B. Yeats and the Theatre of Desolate Reality*; Hunt, Hugh. *The Abbey: Ireland's National Theatre, 1904–1978*; Nokes, David. *Jonathan Swift, A Hypocrite Reversed: A Critical Biography*; O'Connor, Ulick. *Oliver St John Gogarty: A Poet and His Times*; Ure, Peter. *Yeats the Playwright: A Commentary on Character and Design in the Major Plays*; Yeats, W. B. *A Critical Edition of Yeats's A Vision (1925)*, *Explorations*, *The Letters of W. B. Yeats*, *The Variorum Edition of the Plays of W. B. Yeats*, *A Vision*.

Selected Fiction and Prose

"Adoration of the Magi, The" (1897)

"The Adoration of the Magi" follows "ROSA ALCHEMICA" and "The TABLES OF THE LAW" and completes Yeats's trilogy of early stories about Michael Robartes and Owen Aherne. So too it completes the eccentric theology of "The Tables of the Law," and like that story ends with the unnamed narrator—seemingly an imprecise version of Yeats himself—clinging in terror to the forms of religious orthodoxy. Both stories vacillate between this orthodoxy and a heretical conception of ecstatic communion and revelation in a pattern that Yeats rehearses with somewhat different emphasis in "TO THE ROSE UPON THE ROOD OF TIME" and "VACILLATION," among other poems. The logic of Yeats's hesitation is encapsulated by the words that Aherne speaks in "The Tables of the Law": "I have lost my soul because I have looked out of the eyes of the angels" (*Myth.* 306).

Though too much a "text for exposition" (*VP* 821) entirely to succeed as fiction, "The Adoration of the Magi" is notable as an early expression of the apocalyptic dynamic—historical dispensations succeeding each other in an ever-recurring turbulence of death and birth—that would resurface in *A Vision* and in numerous later poems, including "LEDA AND THE SWAN" "The MAGI," "The SECOND COMING," and "TWO SONGS FROM A PLAY" (it should be noted that the story's seemingly anticipatory allusion to Leda is the result of a 1925 revision). In his introduction to *The RESURRECTION,* Yeats acknowledges the story's importance in the evolution of his thought: "Presently Oisin and his islands faded and the sort of images that come into *Rosa Alchemica* and *The Adoration of the Magi* took their place. Our civilization was about to reverse itself, or some new civilization about to be born from all that our age had rejected, from all that my stories symbolised as a harlot, and take after its mother; because we had worshipped a single god it would worship many [. . .]"(*Expl.* 393; *VPl.* 932). Giorgio Melchiori dismisses the story as merely "a psychological document" with "all the naiveté and the absurdity of most documents of this kind" but

notes its interest "as a further proof that the conception of the decay and birth of civilizations was already in Yeats's mind at this time, and two of its poles, or points of crisis (the Christian nativity and the present century) were as clear to him then as they were to be at the time of writing 'The Second Coming'" (*Whole Mystery of Art* 82–83).

Like "Rosa Alchemica," the story opens with an unexpected knock on the door. The narrator admits three brothers from the ARAN ISLANDS. The weather-beaten wanderers tell a strange story. Michael Robartes had arrived long ago in a fishing boat and "told them of the coming again of the gods and the ancient things" (*Myth.* 309). Years later the oldest of the brothers heard a voice over the water announce Robartes's death (in "The PHASES OF THE MOON," Robartes complains that Yeats had erroneously reported his death). Soon after, the second-oldest brother fell asleep over Virgil's Fifth Eclogue and spoke in a strange voice that summoned them to PARIS "where a dying woman would give them secret names and thereby so transform the world that another Leda would open her knees to the swan, another Achilles beleaguer Troy" (310; cf. "Leda and the Swan" and "Two Songs from a Play"). The men were mysteriously guided to the bedside of a dying prostitute. Upon their arrival, she shrieked as if in childbirth and fell into a death-like sleep. Suddenly the second-oldest man crowed like a cock (cf. "MY TABLE" and "SOLOMON AND THE WITCH"). Speaking in the voice of "Hermes the Shepherd of the Dead," he explained that the woman had given birth to an apocalyptic unicorn that "was gone from the room wellnigh upon the instant" of its birth (312; on the unicorn, see *Whole Mystery of Art* 35–72). Restored to himself, he told of having witnessed the biblical nativity scene. A cock had crowed and "a man with wings on his heels swept up through the air, and as he passed me, cried out, 'Foolish old men, you had once all the wisdom of the stars'" (*Myth.* 313). The youngest interpreted this to mean that "when people are good the world likes them and takes possession of them, and so eternity comes through people who are not good or who have been forgotten. Perhaps Christianity was good and the world liked it, so now it is going away and the Immortals are beginning to awake" (313–314). Having laid their parchments on the floor and prepared their pens, the brothers awaited the revelation of the "secret names," but the dying prostitute murmured only obscure "names of endearment": "Hard sweetness," "Dear bitterness," "O solitude," "O terror," and the name a symbolist painter she had known. The narrator fears that the old men were themselves "immortal demons" sent to mislead him with an "untrue story," and he has since striven to lose himself "among the prayers and the sorrows of the multitude" (315).

In a 1909 diary entry, Yeats envisioned changes to the story that were never implemented: "I see clearly that when I rewrite *The Adoration of the Magi* the message given to the old men must be a series of seemingly arbitrary commands: A year of silence, certain rules of diet, and so on. Without the arbitrary there cannot be religion, because there cannot be the last sacrifice, that of the spirit. The old men should refuse to record the message on hearing that it contains not wisdom but the supernaturally sanctioned arbitrary, the commanded pose that makes all definite. The tree has to die before it can be made into a cross" (*Aut.* 344; *Mem.* 147).

FIRST PUBLICATION: *The Tables of the Law. The Adoration of the Magi*, privately printed, June 1897. According to Allan Wade: "Although described as 'privately printed,' copies of this book were advertised in some of Lawrence and Bullen's catalogues for sale at five shillings each" (*Biblio.* 43). In a 1925 note, Yeats explains that "The Tables of the Law" and "The Adoration of the Magi" were "intended to be part of *The Secret Rose* [1897], but the publisher, A. H. Bullen, took a distaste to them and asked me to leave them out, and then after the book was published liked them and put them into a little volume by themselves" (*Myth.* 1).

BIBLIOGRAPHY

Melchiori, Giorgio. *The Whole Mystery of Art: Pattern into Poetry in the Work of W. B. Yeats*; Wade, Allan. *A Bibliography of the Writings of W. B. Yeats*; Yeats, W. B. *Autobiographies, Explorations, Memoirs, Mythologies, The Variorum Edition of the Plays of W. B. Yeats, The Variorum Edition of the Poems of W. B. Yeats*.

"At Stratford-on-Avon" (1901)

Yeats's most comprehensive statement on William Shakespeare was the fruit of his experience at the annual Shakespeare festival at Stratford-on-Avon, April 22–27, 1901. In attendance as the paid correspondent of the *Speaker*, Yeats saw F. R. Benson's company perform *King John, Richard II*, the second part of *Henry IV, Henry V*, the second part of *Henry VI*, and *Richard III* (*E&I* 96). From his room at the Shakespeare Hotel, Yeats wrote to Lady GREGORY on April 25, "It is delightful seeing the plays in an atmosphere of enthusiasm & in this beautiful place. The theatre is a charming gothic red brick building in a garden with a river flowing by its walls. It is thronged every night—indeed [sic] they had to get me a kitchen chair to sit on the night I came. I see a good deal of the Company & would see more but I am very busy. [. . .] I am working in the library of the Shakespeare Institute which is attached to the theatre & [the librarian] has given up to me his private room. But for a half hour or so for lunch I am here all day, from 10 to six when I dine & dress for the theatre. I feal [sic] that I am getting deeper into Shakespeare'[s] mystery than ever before [. . .]" (*CL3* 61–62). During this week as well, Yeats arranged for the production of his own play, DIARMUID AND GRANIA, which Benson wound up staging the following October at the Gaiety Theatre in Dublin (61).

"At Stratford-on-Avon" opens in praise of the festival's sincerity and integrity, which stands in stark contrast to the commercial entertainment of London. "Surely a bitter hatred of London is becoming a mark of those that love the arts, and all that have this hatred should help anything that looks like a beginning of a centre of art elsewhere," Yeats writes, undoubtedly thinking of his own attempts to initiate a literary theater in Ireland (*E&I* 98). Yeats's only reservations concern the "half-round" shape of the theater at Stratford and the "naturalistic scene-painting" that accommodates the half-round theater's varied sight lines. Such "flashy landscape-painting," Yeats argues in an anticipation of his own stage experiments at the

ABBEY THEATRE, should be replaced by "decorative scene-painting," which "would not overwhelm, as our naturalistic scenery does, the idealistic art of the poet" (99–100).

Slipping into the main current of his essay, Yeats considers Shakespeare's Victorian critics, JOHN BUTLER YEATS's college friend EDWARD DOWDEN, author of *Shakspere: A Critical Study of his Mind & Art* (1875), chief among them. Yeats charges that an ingrained utilitarianism made it impossible for them to understand "that a man's business may at times be revelation, and not reformation." With "efficiency in action" as their criterion, they could not comprehend characters like Coriolanus, Hamlet, Timon, and Richard II as anything except cautionary examples, and Shakespearean criticism became a "vulgar worshipper of success." Though he admits that these characters changed "many things for the worse," Yeats calls them "greater in the Divine Hierarchies" than the likes of Fortinbras, Aufidius, and Henry V (103). Alluding to Richard II, Yeats continues, "To suppose that Shakespeare preferred the men who deposed his king is to suppose that Shakespeare judged men with the eyes of a Municipal Councillor weighing the merits of a Town Clerk" (105). Shakespeare, indeed, saw in Richard the "defeat that awaits all, whether they be artist or saint, who find themselves where men ask of them a rough energy and have nothing to give but some contemplative virtue, whether lyrical fantasy, or sweetness of temper, or dreamy dignity, or love of God, or love of His creatures" (106). Naturally, Dowden revered Richard's temperamental opposite, Henry V, whom he considered the representative Anglo-Saxon and "the model Shakespeare held up before England" (104). That Shakespeare intended the bluff and coarse-nerved Henry as a type of his ideal man Yeats does not believe for a moment, holding instead that in the eyes of the bard he was akin to "some handsome spirited horse" (109). The comparison between Richard and Henry anticipates Yeats's later distinction between *antithetical* and *primary* men (see *A VISION*) and the essential division within his own plays between *antithetical* figures like CUCHULAIN and Seanchan and *primary* figures like Conchubar

and King Guaire (see ON BAILE'S STRAND and *The KING'S THRESHOLD*).

It strikes Yeats in closing that Shakespeare's history plays have the "extravagant and superhuman" quality of Greek myth. He speculates that had the Renaissance not brought in "the stories of other lands," English history might have become the basis of a national mythology on the order of the Greek, and English literature might have had the "simplicity and unity of Greek literature," for "no man, even though he be Shakespeare, can write perfectly when his web is woven of threads that have been spun in many lands" (109). On the other hand, such foreign stories would have found no ear but for the "sinking down of popular imagination, the dying out of traditional fantasy, the ebbing out of the energy of race" (109–110).

Yeats's quarrel with Dowden—aired also in *AUTOBIOGRAPHIES*—repeats his father's ancient quarrel with Dowden on the same subject. In an 1874 exchange of letters, the elder Yeats rejected Dowden's preference for Henry IV over Richard, charging Dowden with "a sort of splenetic morality that would be fitter in the mouth of the old gardener" and fulminating against "a most damnable heresy—worship of success" (*PF* 97). In comparison to his usurper, Richard had a "more mounting spirit, his disdain was nobler, his mirth more joyous, his happiness had a more untiring wing" (99). In the copy of the 1908 edition of *Ideas of Good and Evil* he presented to JOHN QUINN, Yeats *fils* wrote, "I think the best of these Essays is that on Shakespeare. It is a family exasperation with the Dowden point of view, which rather filled Dublin in my youth. There is a good deal of my father in it, though nothing is just as he would have put it" (*Biblio.* 90).

FIRST PUBLICATION: The *Speaker* (periodical), May 11 and 18, 1901. Reprinted in *Ideas of Good and Evil*, A. H. Bullen, London, May 1903.

BIBLIOGRAPHY

Murphy, William M. *Prodigal Father: The Life of John Butler Yeats (1839–1922)*; Wade, Allan. *A Bibliography of the Writings of W. B. Yeats*; Yeats, W. B. *Autobiographies, The Collected Letters of W. B. Yeats* (vol. 3), *Essays and Introductions*.

Autobiographies (1916–1935)

A gathering of autobiographical pieces published between 1916 and 1935 with Yeats's NOBEL PRIZE lecture and 96 journal entries (most dating from 1909) rounding out the exposition, *Autobiographies* belies its ad hoc character and stands as one of the great literary memoirs of the 20th century, a masterpiece of style and self-reflection to rival *The Education of Henry Adams*, Virginia Woolf's diaries, and Nabokov's *Speak, Memory*. It is, further, Yeats's chief prose document, more central, in the end, than *A VISION*. It includes a carefully shaped account of youth, adolescence, and young manhood, remembrances of the political and artistic milieus in which Yeats moved, vivid silhouettes and astute psychological analysis of fellow-travelers, historical, cultural, and philosophical meditation largely premised on the notions of Unity of Culture and UNITY OF BEING, all set in prose of immense grave poise. The volume is particularly valuable for the light it sheds on Yeats's creative work. Though it establishes nothing like a sharp or complete factual outline, it sets the creative work in a tellingly selective context of personal history. Even more important, it is a sourcebook of ideas, dispositions, and patterns that inform the creative work—the primacy of passion and personality, the insufficiency of scientific reason, the despoliation of politics, the eternal antagonism of the mob, the estrangement suffered by those who seek "pure beauty" (242), the cycling of history and culture through phases of greater and lesser unity, aristocratic tradition as an image of the ordered culture and the ordered soul.

Autobiographies consists of "Reveries over Childhood and Youth" (1916); "The Trembling of the Veil," which in turn consists of "Four Years: 1887–1891" (1921), "Ireland after Parnell" (1922), "Hodos Chameliontos" (1922), "The Tragic Generation" (1922), and "The Stirring of the Bones" (1922); "Dramatis Personae: 1896–1902" (1935); "Estrangement: Extracts from A Diary Kept in 1909" (1926); "The Death of Synge" (1928); "The Bounty of Sweden" (1924); and "The Irish Dramatic Movement: A Lecture delivered to the Royal Academy of Sweden" (1924). *The Autobiography*

of William Butler Yeats (Macmillan, 1938) omitted the Nobel Prize lecture, but otherwise collected Yeats's autobiographical writings in final form. *Autobiographies* (Macmillan, 1955) restored the lecture and revived the title Yeats had given his autobiographical writings in 1926. This is the text that has become standard (for a full discussion, see *Aut.* 13–16). In 1915 and 1916, Yeats additionally wrote a rough draft of a memoir of the late 1880s and 1890s. "Containing much that is not for publication now if ever," as he wrote on the envelope containing the manuscript, it appeared in 1972 as *MEMOIRS*, along with the text of all 252 entries in Yeats's journal. Much of this material is more stylishly if less frankly treated in "The Trembling of the Veil" and "Dramatis Personae."

Not least, *Autobiographies* is a brilliant work of psychological portraiture and what might be called psycho-metaphysical portraiture (Yeats's fascinating, counter-Freudian attempt—not unsuccessful—to use his evolving metaphysical system as a tool of psychological analysis and human taxonomy). The text turns its eye on AUBREY BEARDSLEY, Helena Blavatsky (see THEOSOPHICAL SOCIETY), EDWARD DOWDEN, Ernest Dowson (1867–1900), Edwin Ellis (1848–1916), FLORENCE FARR, MAUD GONNE, Lady GREGORY, W. E. Henley (1849–1903), Douglas Hyde (1860–1949), LIONEL JOHNSON, EDWARD MARTYN, MACGREGOR MATHERS, GEORGE MOORE, WILLIAM MORRIS, Standish James O'Grady (1846–1928), JOHN O'LEARY, GEORGE POLLEXFEN, GEORGE RUSSELL (AE), George Bernard Shaw (1856–1950), ARTHUR SYMONS, J. M. SYNGE, OSCAR WILDE, and JOHN BUTLER YEATS.

As was inevitable, Yeats ruffled certain feathers. OLIVIA SHAKESPEAR took exception to Yeats's portrayal of her cousin Lionel Johnson in an excerpt from *The Trembling of the Veil* published in the *London Mercury* (*Letters* 685), and Mathers's widow, Moina, strenuously objected to the representation of her husband. Writing to Yeats in 1924, she denounced *The Trembling of the Veil* as an "awful book" and called the account of Mathers a "caricature portrait" (*LTWBY*, II, 447–448, 451). Yeats mollified her by making slight revisions and dedicating the 1925 edition of *A VISION* to her. Yeats worried about John Butler Yeats's reaction to *Rev-*

eries over Childhood and Youth, and especially about his reaction to the unflattering depiction of his old friend Dowden as a poet fallen into the desuetude of academia (*Letters* 602–603). In the event, Yeats's father declared that the book "promises to be among the classics forever" (*LTWBY,* II, 334). Symons similarly assessed *The Trembling of the Veil* as "an absolute masterpiece: far & away the best thing [Yeats] has ever done" (*Arthur Symons* 304).

BIBLIOGRAPHY

Beckson, Karl. *Arthur Symons: A Life*; Finneran, Richard J., et al., eds. *Letters to W. B. Yeats* (vol. 2); Yeats, W. B. *Autobiographies, The Letters of W. B. Yeats.*

"Autumn of the Body, The" (1898)

A companion piece to "The SYMBOLISM OF POETRY," "The Autumn of the Body" is one of Yeats's most unrestrained statements against the literature "of outward things" and one of his closest approaches to the decadent sensibility. Yeats observes that writers all over Europe are struggling "against the picturesque and declamatory way of writing, against that 'externality' which a time of scientific and political thought has brought into literature" (*E&I* 189). He places in the vanguard of this movement the symbolist writers Philippe-Auguste Villiers de l'Isle-Adam (1838–89) and Maurice Maeterlinck (1862–1949) and praises with extravagant Paterian metaphor the spiritual beauty of their work. He observes that there has been "a like change in England" and that a "new poetry" is throwing off the influence of the early SHELLEY, TENNYSON, Browning, and Swinburne, whose work "tried to absorb into itself the science and politics, the philosophy and morality of its time" (190). Dante Gabriel Rossetti (1828–82), Andrew Lang (1844–1912), Edmund Gosse (1849–1928), Austin Dobson (1840–1921), and Robert Bridges (1844–1930) exemplify this revolution in sensibility, and even more so English painting, which "began to cast out things, as they are seen by minds plunged in the labor of life, so much before French painting that ideal art is sometimes called

English art upon the Continent." These "faint lights and faint colours and faint outlines and faint energies" are dismissed by many as mere "decadence," but Yeats, believing that the arts "lie dreaming of things to come," chooses to call this faintness "the autumn of the body" (191). In light of these developments, Yeats wonders whether man is about to ascend "the stairway he has been descending from the first days." In literature, this descent is traceable in the work of Homer, Virgil, Dante, and Shakespeare, each more than the last preoccupied with outward things. With Goethe, WORDSWORTH, and Browning, poetry became altogether a criticism of life and an interpretation of "things as they are" (192). Having "wooed and won the world," Yeats writes, man has become weary, but the arts are "about to take upon their shoulders the burdens that have fallen from the shoulders of priests" and effect a rejuvenation of the spirit. Yeats ends with the surmise that poets will discover once again how to tell the story of Odysseus so that it becomes "the signature or symbol of a mood of the divine imagination" (193).

The essay was Yeats's concluding salvo in a public debate that played itself out in the pages of the Dublin *Daily Express* during the autumn and winter of 1898. The full newspaper exchange, with contributions from Yeats, JOHN EGLINTON, GEORGE RUSSELL (AE), and William Larminie (1849–1900), is collected in the 1899 anthology LITERARY IDEALS IN IRELAND.

FIRST PUBLICATION: The Dublin *Daily Express,* December 3, 1898, under the title "The Autumn of the Flesh." Reprinted in *Literary Ideals in Ireland,* T. Fisher Unwin, London, May 1899, and in *Ideas of Good and Evil,* A. H. Bullen, London, May 1903.

BIBLIOGRAPHY

Yeats, W. B. *Essays and Introductions.*

"Dhoya" (1891)

A tale of mythic Ireland, "Dhoya" was Yeats's first attempt to write fiction. In September 1887, not long after finishing the short story, Yeats assessed "Dhoya" in fair terms: "somewhat over dreamy and florid but quite readible [sic] any way" (*CL1* 36). In MEMOIRS, he recalls the story's genesis: "I was greatly troubled because I was making no money. [. . .] My father suggested that I should write a story and, partly in London and partly in SLIGO, where I stayed with my uncle GEORGE POLLEXFEN, I wrote *Dhoya*, a fantastic tale of the heroic age. My father was dissatisfied and said he meant a story with real people, and I began JOHN SHERMAN, putting into it my memory of Sligo and my longing for it" (*Mem.* 31). Yeats wrote "Dhoya" in late August or early September of 1887 (*CL1* 33, 36). He submitted the story to the *Gael*, but it is unknown whether the story was published (43). "Dhoya" languished until March 1891, when T. Fisher Unwin accepted *John Sherman* for publication in the "Pseudonym Library" (247). In June, Yeats reported to JOHN O'LEARY that "Dhoya" was to be added to the volume, and the two stories were published in November as *John Sherman and Dhoya* (250–251). Yeats was identified only by the pseudonym "Ganconagh"—an "old little Irish spirit"—but chafed at the condition of anonymity (*JS&D* 93–94). "If you will kindly review it & say that it is mine I shall be well pleased," he wrote to a prospective reviewer. "People are given to thinking I can only write of the fantastical & wild & this book has to do so far as the long story is concerned with very ordinary persons & events—This is why I want it to be known as mine [. . .]" (*CL1* 268). As "Dhoya" includes verses that Yeats had already published as "Girl's Song" in *The Wanderings of Oisin and Other Poems* (1889), the pseudonym, in any case, was likely to be "pretty transparent," as Yeats told KATHARINE TYNAN (*CL1* 253; see also 248, 268; for the poem, see *VP* 723). Yeats republished the stories with minor revisions in 1908, but thereafter excluded them from his canon (*JS&D* xxvii–i).

The tale concerns love between mortal and immortal, a theme that finds more significant expression in the contemporaneous "WANDERINGS OF OISIN." The protagonist is Dhoya, a giant who has slaved since childhood at the oar of a Fomorian galley (in a note to *The Wanderings of Oisin and Other Poems*, Yeats calls the Fomorians "the gods of night and death and cold"; they were "misshapen and had now the heads of goats and bulls, and now but one leg, and one arm that came out of the middle of their breasts" [*VP* 795]). Terrified by Dhoya's bouts of reckless fury, the Fomorians strand him on the shore of the Bay of Ballah (as Yeats specifies in his preface to *John Sherman and Dhoya*, Ballah is Sligo in all but name). Dhoya finds a cavern in which to live. As the years pass, his bouts of fury intensify. While asleep he sometimes feels a mysterious touch. Fearing evil spirits, he makes an offering to the moon, only to scatter his pyre in a rage. He hears a voice call him and glimpses a beautiful woman. He pursues her, but longing gives way to "supernatural fear" and he hurries back to his cavern (*JS & D* 85). He finds the woman waiting and his possessions neatly arranged. She flings her arms around him and cries that she has forsaken the fairy world, for only "the changing, and moody, and angry, and weary can love" (86). The "strangely-wedded ones" pass many days in happy seclusion. One day Dhoya encounters a fairy who demands the return of the "most beautiful of our bands" (87). The two battle for a full night. Dhoya grips the fairy's throat, and the fairy fades into thin air. Some time later, the fairy reappears at the mouth of the cavern and challenges Dhoya to a game of chess. Enraged at the sight of his enemy, Dhoya agrees to stake his bride against the fairy's life. Dhoya promptly loses, and the two fairies fade to nothingness. Dhoya raves like a wild beast for a night and a day before leaping upon a wild horse and charging off a thousand-foot cliff "into the Western sea" (92).

Mary Helen Thuente notes that "the basic situation of a man who marries a fairy bride and then loses her to a fairy husband in a chess game derives from an old Irish tale in *The Book of the Dun Cow*" (*W. B. Yeats and Irish Folklore* 28). Yeats's poem "The Two Kings" (1913) is another version of the old tale. In the juvenile drama "TIME AND THE WITCH VIVIEN," the heroine Vivien stakes her life on the outcome of a chess game with Time. Like Dhoya, she quickly loses to her supernatural opponent.

FIRST PUBLICATION: *John Sherman and Dhoya*, T. Fisher Unwin, London, November 1891.

BIBLIOGRAPHY

Thuente, Mary Helen. *W. B. Yeats and Irish Folklore*; Yeats, W. B. *The Collected Letters of W. B. Yeats* (vol. 1), *John Sherman and Dhoya*, *Memoirs*, *The Variorum Edition of the Poems of W. B. Yeats*.

John Sherman (1891)

John Sherman, a novelette, was Yeats's first attempt to write an extended work of fiction. He followed with an attempt at a novel—the aborted SPECKLED BIRD—before abandoning the experiment for good. The story is simple, lucid, and neatly constructed, but at the same time cautious; it augurs little of Yeats's stylistic genius or philosophical and psychological ambition, in this differing from "The WANDERINGS OF OISIN," another major undertaking of the late 1880s. This restraint was not accidental or unself-conscious. The difficulty, Yeats told JOHN O'LEARY in October 1888, is "to keep the characters from turning into eastern symbolic monsters of some sort which would be a curious thing to happen to a curate and a young man from the country" (*CL1* 104). In a December 1891 letter to KATHARINE TYNAN, Yeats called attention to his protagonist as a carefully drawn "Irish type" and acknowledged his ambition to be recognized as "an Irish novelist not as an English or cosmopolitan [sic] one choosing Ireland as a background." Sherman, he explained, belongs "to the small gentry who in the West at any rate love their native places without perhaps loving Ireland. They do not travell [sic] & are shut off from England by the whole breadth of Ireland with the result that they are forced to make their native town their world. I remember when we were children how intense our devotion was to all things in SLIGO & still see in my mother the old feeling" (275).

Yeats describes the genesis of the story in MEMOIRS: "I was greatly troubled because I was making no money. [. . .] My father suggested that I should write a story and, partly in London and partly in SLIGO, where I stayed with my uncle GEORGE POLLEXFEN, I wrote DHOYA, a fantastic tale of the heroic age. My father was dissatisfied and said he

meant a story with real people, and I began *John Sherman*, putting into it my memory of Sligo and my longing for it. While writing it I was going along the Strand and, passing a shop window where there was a little ball kept dancing by a jet of water, I remembered waters about Sligo and was moved to a sudden emotion that shaped itself into 'The LAKE ISLE OF INNISFREE'" (*Mem.* 31; see also *CL1* 120–121). The protagonist John Sherman is too drifting and lackadaisical to be confused with Yeats himself, but Sherman's longing for Ballah directly translates Yeats's longing for Sligo. Like Yeats, Sherman dreams of retiring to Innisfree and building there "a wooden hut" for himself (*JS&D* 57). In a November 1888 letter to O'Leary, Yeats went so far as to describe the "motif" of the story as "hatred of London" (*CL1* 110).

In March 1891, Yeats told Tynan that *John Sherman* contained more of himself than any of his previous work (245–246). Autobiographical correspondences indeed abound. Ballah is unmistakably Sligo, as Yeats confirms in his 1907 preface (*JS&D* 1). As A. Norman Jeffares notes, the differences between the Sherman and Howard families mirror the divide between the Yeats and Pollexfen families, while Sherman himself resembles Yeats's cousin Henry Middleton (1862–1932), and Sherman's shipping firm clearly fictionalizes the Pollexfens' Sligo Steam Navigation Company (*New Biography* 63; on Middleton, see "Three Songs to the One Burden"). Mrs. Sherman—a "spare, delicate-featured woman, with somewhat thin lips tightly closed as with silent people, and eyes at once gentle and distrustful, tempering the hardness of the lips"—distinctly resembles SUSAN YEATS, the poet's mother (*JS&D* 12). Margaret Leland recalls Yeats's distant cousin LAURA ARMSTRONG, who also inspired the character of Vivien in Yeats's juvenile drama TIME AND THE WITCH VIVIEN (see *CL1* 154–155). William Howard is at least partially modeled on the Reverend John Dowden (1840–1910), brother of EDWARD DOWDEN and an old friend of JOHN BUTLER YEATS. William M. Murphy describes John Dowden as, like Howard, "attached to the Holy—if not quite Roman Catholic Church"; again like Howard, Dowden was briefly a curate in Sligo, where he was suspect for his "high church" tendencies (*PF* 44–45). Most revealing and significant is the resemblance between Mary Carton and Tynan, Yeats's chief correspondent and closest literary protégé during the late 1880s. In MEMOIRS, Yeats remembers wondering whether Tynan was in love with him and whether it was his duty to marry her; according to Tynan's sister, Yeats in fact proposed (*AM* 72–73; *Mem.* 32). The relationship between Sherman and Mary is likewise balanced uncertainly between genuine friendship and a not entirely reciprocal romantic attraction.

Yeats contemplated *John Sherman* as early as September 1887 (*CL1* 36). In April 1888 he was reading up on the 18th century, the era in which the story was originally set (59). By early May he had transferred the story to the present day and begun writing. He reported to Tynan: "I also am writing a short story—it goes on fairly well the style quite sane and the theme modern, more character than plot in it" (67). In a June letter to Tynan, Yeats worried that the story would wind up in his "multiplying boxes of unsaleable MSS—work to[o] strange at one moment and to[o] incoherent the next for any first class Magazine and too ambitious for local papers. Yet I dont [sic] know that it is ambition for I have no wish but to write a saleable story" (71). In March 1891, T. Fisher Unwin accepted the story for publication in its "Pseudonym Library." In June, Yeats reported to O'Leary that "Dhoya" was to be added to the volume, and the two stories were duly published in November as *John Sherman and Dhoya* (247, 250–251). Yeats adopted the pseudonym "Ganconagh"—an "old little Irish spirit"—but did not relish the condition of anonymity (*JS&D* 93–94). "If you will kindly review it & say that it is mine I shall be well pleased," he told a prospective reviewer. "People are given to thinking I can only write of the fantastical & wild & this book has to do so far as the long story is concerned with very ordinary persons & events—This is why I want it to be known as mine" (*CL1* 268; see also 248, 253). Yeats republished the stories with minor revisions in 1908, but thereafter excluded them from his canon (*JS&D* xxvii–i).

The story is indeed both "sane" and "modern." It concerns the eponymous hero John Sherman, age "almost thirty," who dwells modestly with his mother in Ballah, an Irish country town. Studiously without a profession, Sherman spends his time puttering in the garden, dipping into books, walking, hunting, and fishing. His friend and confidante is Mary Carton, daughter of the old rector. They are comfortably paired rather than passionately attracted, and the town matchmakers have long given up on them. When his uncle offers him £100 a year to join his ship-broking firm in London, Sherman takes Mary's responsible advice and accepts the position. Sherman, his mother, and their aged servant move to a rented house in Hammersmith. There ensue three uneventful years of office work. Sherman occasionally calls on the Lelands, the well-to-do wife and pretty daughter of a deceased ship-broker who had been a client of his uncle. Margaret Leland is flighty and flirtatious, willful and self-dramatizing. Inevitably Sherman falls in love with her. He hesitates to propose, understanding that to marry her would be "to separate himself from the old life he loved so well," until one day he finds scattered about a park bench scraps of a letter from Margaret to a friend in which she melodramatically laments that she is "falling in love again" (32). Recognizing himself in the letter, Sherman proposes that night. His new fiancé attempts to "improve" his stolid country ways by taking him to the theater, opera, and parties. Meanwhile Sherman cannot bring himself to tell Mary of his engagement. When she sees Mary's picture in a photograph book, Margaret bristles and insists that he write at once. He decides to tell Mary in person. She nearly faints upon hearing the news. He realizes that he and Mary love one another, but he lacks the energy and resolve to change course. He returns to London, bound in "one of those dangerous moments when the sense of personal identity is shaken, when one's past and present seem about to dissolve partnership" (47).

Sherman becomes moody and withdrawn and longs for Ballah. He invites his old friend the Rev. William Howard to spend the autumn in London. Howard is a "High Church curate"—a "clerical coxcomb" to his enemies—with a "habit of getting his mind possessed with some strange opinion, or what seemed so to his parishioners, and of preaching it while the notion lasted in the most startling way" (52–53). Having recently lost his parish, he accepts Sherman's invitation. Sherman encourages an attachment between Howard and Margaret, surmising that each will be susceptible to the superficial charms of the other. Howard confesses himself "hopelessly in love" and Sherman releases Margaret. He returns to Ballah and proposes to Mary, but she, to his bewilderment, castigates him—"You have done no duty that came to you. You have tired of everything you should cling to; and now you have come to this little town because here is idleness and irresponsibility"—and declares an end to their friendship (74). Sherman spends the night walking the countryside and toward dawn passes the rectory where Mary lives. He finds her by the gate. She realizes that she has been proud and foolish, and that it is enough that he loves her. She looks "upon him whom she loved as full of a helplessness that needed protection, a reverberation of the feeling of the mother for the child at the breast" (78).

FIRST PUBLICATION: *John Sherman and Dhoya*, T. Fisher Unwin, London, November 1891.

BIBLIOGRAPHY

Foster, R. F. *W. B. Yeats; A Life, I: The Apprentice Mage*; Jeffares, A. Norman. *W. B. Yeats: A New Biography*; Murphy, William M. *Prodigal Father: The Life of John Butler Yeats (1839–1922)*; Yeats, W. B. *Autobiographies, The Collected Letters of W. B. Yeats* (vol. 1), *John Sherman and Dhoya, Memoirs*.

letters

Yeats was a prolific correspondent, leaving behind some 10,000 known letters spanning the years 1876 to 1939. "Yesterday I wrote 17, and today—it is 12:30—I have already reached that number," Yeats told MARGOT RUDDOCK in July 1935, giving some idea of his copious correspondence (*Sweet Dancer* 41). Yeats's letters occasionally shine with the style and intellectual daring of his published work, but in the main their value is biographical and historical. Taken together, they provide a nearly day-by-day account of Yeats's whereabouts, connections, and activities, and make palpable the texture of his everyday life; so too they serve as an indispensable record of the cultural life of Ireland and literary London. Perhaps surprisingly, given that Yeats was such a painstaking writer and obsessive reviser, the letters are truly letters rather than literary set pieces sent through the mail, and they bear all the marks of rapid and unpremeditated composition. In Kelly and Domville's description, they are "nearly always untidy, mostly undated, misspelt and badly punctuated" (*CL1* xl). Yeats's spelling, indeed, seems at times a matter of wildly errant guesswork. In an April 1929 letter to T. STURGE MOORE, he explains his chronic inability: "I cannot spell today. I find I do not know what words contain repeated letters and what words do not. It is a matter of nerves with me. If I get out a dictionary I will have to look up too many words" (*WBY&TSM* 154).

The definitive edition of the letters is the massive and meticulously annotated *Collected Letters of W. B. Yeats*, published by Oxford University Press under the general editorship of John S. Kelly. Four volumes have been published to date (2008); the completed edition, which will include Yeats's every known letter, is expected to run to 12 or more volumes. This edition is gradually outmoding *The Letters of W. B. Yeats*, which was edited by Allan Wade and has been the standard edition of Yeats's letters since its publication in 1954. In addition to the above, Yeats's correspondence—both to and from—has been collected in numerous volumes, including the following: Katharine Tynan, *Twenty-Five Years: Reminiscences* (1913), *The Middle Years* (1916); *Passages from the Letters of John Butler Yeats* (1917—recipients not specified); *Further Letters of John Butler Yeats* (1920—recipients not specified); *Some Passages from the Letters of AE to W. B. Yeats* (1936); *Letters on Poetry from W. B. Yeats to Dorothy Wellesley* (1940); *Florence Farr, Bernard Shaw and W. B. Yeats* (1941); John Butler Yeats, *Letters to his Son W. B. Yeats and Others, 1869–1922* (1944); *Some Letters from W. B. Yeats to John O'Leary and his Sister* (1953); *Letters to Katharine Tynan* (1953); *W. B. Yeats and T. Sturge Moore: Their Correspondence 1901–1937* (1953); *Letters from AE* (1961); *Yeats and Patrick McCartan, a Fenian friendship* (1965); *Ah, Sweet Dancer: W. B. Yeats and Margot Ruddock*

(1970); *Some Letters of John M. Synge to Lady Gregory and W. B. Yeats* (1971); *The Correspondence of Robert Bridges and W. B. Yeats* (1977); *Letters to W. B. Yeats*, vols. 1–2 (1977); *W. B. Yeats and W. T. Horton: The Record of an Occult Friendship* (1979); *Theatre Business: The Correspondence of the First Abbey Theatre Directors: William Butler Yeats, Lady Gregory and J. M. Synge* (1982); *The Letters of John Quinn to William Butler Yeats* (1983); *The Collected Letters of John Millington Synge* (1983–84); *The Gonne-Yeats Letters 1893–1938: Always Your Friend* (1992); Arthur Symons, *Letters to W. B. Yeats, 1892–1902* (1989); and *Letters to W. B. Yeats and Ezra Pound from Iseult Gonne: a girl that knew all Dante once* (2003).

BIBLIOGRAPHY

Yeats, W. B. *Ah, Sweet Dancer: W. B. Yeats and Margot Ruddock, The Collected Letters of W. B. Yeats* (vol. 1), *W. B. Yeats and T. Sturge Moore: Their Correspondence 1901–1937.*

Literary Ideals in Ireland (1899)

This slim volume collects nine essays—three by Yeats, three by JOHN EGLINTON, two by GEORGE RUSSELL (AE) and one by William Larminie (1849–1900)—that originally appeared in answer to one another in the pages of the Dublin *Daily Express* during the fall and winter of 1898. At the time, Yeats described himself as "deep in a controversy about symbolism in poetry." Yeats *argued* for symbolism in poetry, but more accurately the controversy sprang from a disagreement about the kind of literature that might express and unify a nation (CL2 307). This became a general argument about what literature should be. Writing to JOHN BUTLER YEATS in early November, Yeats suggested that he deliberately contrived the controversy to "excite general interest in Irish legends & in the Irish literary attitude in Dublin this month, as a preliminary to the publication of our dramatic project in December" (282). The "dramatic project" was the formation of the IRISH LITERARY THEATRE, which

Yeats announced in the *Daily Express* on January 12, 1899 (338). In JOHN QUINN's copy of *Literary Ideals in Ireland*, Yeats said of the controversy, on the other hand, "This was a stirring row while it lasted and we were all very angry" (*Biblio.* 286).

The debate grew out of Eglinton's "What should be the Subjects of a National Drama?," which appeared on September 17. A librarian and man of letters immortalized in JOYCE's *Ulysses* (1922), Eglinton asserts that ancient legends "obstinately refuse to be taken up out of their old environment and be transplanted into the world of modern sympathies," and that a national drama or literature "must spring from a native interest in life and its problems and a strong capacity for life among the people" (*Literary Ideals* 11, 13). Yeats rose to this bait on September 24, appending to an article on the poet Nora Hopper (1871–1906) a note in which he cites Ibsen and Wagner as evidence that a "national drama" may be rooted in ancient myth and legend (17). Eglinton retorted with a second article also titled "What should be the Subjects of a National Drama?" This appeared on October 8 (it was retitled "National Drama and Contemporary Life" in *Literary Ideals in Ireland*). Eglinton grants that legends can be the stuff of contemporary art, but they must be molded by the spirit of the times. Finn and CUCHULAIN, he says, "must be expected to take up on their broad shoulders something of the weariness and fret of our age, if only to show how lightly they may be carried [. . .]" (24). Eglinton commends the example of WORDSWORTH, who "confers upon common things the radiance of the imagination," in opposition to the modern poet, who "does not feel the facts of life enough, but seeks in art an escape from them" (26–27).

The allusion to Wordsworth, one of Yeats's *bêtes noires*, fanned the flames of dispute, and Yeats responded on October 29 with "John Eglinton and Spiritual Art," an assault on art that functions as a "criticism of life" (36). Yeats denounces this as "the poetry of the utilitarian and the rhetorician and the sentimentalist and the popular journalist and the popular preacher" in contrast to the poetry of the "seer," who seeks to "express great passions that are not in nature." Yeats predicts that a renewal of faith will "liberate the arts from 'their age' and from life, and leave them more and more free to lose themselves in beauty, and to busy themselves, like all the great poetry of the past and like religions of all times, with 'old faiths, myths, dreams,' the accumulated beauty of the age" (35–36). Eglinton's final, somewhat scattered contribution to the debate, "Mr. Yeats and Popular Poetry," appeared on November 5. On the defensive, Eglinton reiterates that an ancient legend comes down to us "in a certain form, the form in which it has spontaneously clothed itself, and which fits it as the body fits the soul," and it can only have new life when something of the author's age and personality is added to it (41). More provocatively, he proposes that inventions like the steam engine, the dynamo, and the kinematograph comprise the true poetry of the age, and he reaffirms his admiration of Wordsworth.

AE weighed in with "Literary Ideals in Ireland" on November 12, restating the terms of the debate more clearly than either Eglinton or Yeats had done, and arguing on the side of Yeats that ancient ideals, embodying as they do something of the eternal, are as contemporary as "electrical science" (51–52). Yeats told Lady GREGORY on November 13 that AE and Eglinton had argued these matters until 2 A.M. on the evening of November 11–12 and that Eglinton had gone "away in a huff," which raised Yeats's hopes that he would reply in print (CL2 299–300).

The next to enter the fray was Larminie, "a fine folklorist & bad but wildly eccentric poet," in Yeats's estimation (302; on Larminie, see also 268; *UP1* 228–230; 326–328). His "Legends as Material for Literature," which appeared on November 19, comes down somewhere between the positions of Eglinton and Yeats. Spurning the "cold-blooded languor" of contemporary aesthetes, he insists that "great results" come only from vital ideas and urges engagement with the world, but on the semi-transcendental grounds that "[k]nowledge of life and its facts is simply a knowledge of the behaviour of spirits immersed in matter under varied conditions" (*Literary Ideals* 60–64). Yeats's final contribution to the debate was "The Autumn of the Flesh," which appeared on December 3 (see "The AUTUMN OF THE BODY"). Itself beautifully

and provocatively languorous, the essay describes the arts retreating from outward things in an "ever more arduous search for an almost disembodied ecstasy" (75). The debate came to a close on December 10 with AE's eloquent "Nationality and Cosmopolitanism in Literature," which repudiates the cosmopolitanism of modern European literature (Goethe, Balzac, Tolstoy) in favor of the kind of truly national tradition (exemplified by the arts of ancient Egypt and Greece) that creates the soul of a nation (81). Yeats wrote a further installment in the debate, but it did not appear in print (for the piece, see *CL2* 294–298). Kelly et al. speculate that the essay languished because *Daily Express* editor T. P. Gill (1858–1931) wanted to bring other contributors into the controversy (294). This piece became the germ of Yeats's essay "The SYMBOLISM OF POETRY."

In *AUTOBIOGRAPHIES*, Yeats remembers the *Daily Express*' brief heyday as the organ of the Irish renaissance: "Horace Plunkett had bought the *Daily Express*. Under T. P. Gill, an ex-Parnellite Member and London journalist, it expounded Plunkett's agricultural policy, avoiding all that might excite passion. [. . .] When it wrote of a Protestant and of a Catholic Archbishop, old subscribers withdrew because the first, being the only true Archbishop, required no prefix. New subscribers bought little but the Friday number, which reviewed books, avoided contemporary politics, but contained articles that made people say: 'Something is going to happen'. In its correspondence column, controversies were fought out that are still remembered" (313–314; see also *UP2* 162). In November 1899, the paper passed into unionist hands and immediately abandoned the Irish movement (see *CL2* 455, 470–471, 714).

FIRST PUBLICATION: The *Daily Express* (periodical), September 17–December 10, 1899. Reprinted in *Literary Ideals in Ireland*, T. Fisher Unwin, London, May 1899.

BIBLIOGRAPHY

Wade, Allan. *A Bibliography of the Writings of W. B. Yeats*; Yeats, W. B. *Autobiographies, The Collected Letters of W. B. Yeats* (vol. 2), *Literary Ideals in Ireland, Uncollected Prose by W. B. Yeats* (vols. 1–2).

"Magic" (1901)

Yeats understood that his poetry required a reality in which the soul predominates over the body and the timeless predominates over the temporal. During his late teenage years he began the work of articulating the reality of such a universe, turning against Victorian science, which he had "grown to hate with a monkish hate," and embracing the occult in its place (*Aut.* 92). Writing to JOHN O'LEARY in July 1892, Yeats defended his occultism as an inextricable element in his intellectual enterprise: "The mystical life is the centre of all that I do & all that I think & all that I write. It holds to my work the same relation that the philosophy of Godwin held to the work SHELLEY & I have all-ways considered my self a voice of what I beleive [sic] to be a greater renaisance [sic]—the revolt of the soul against the intellect—now beginning in the world" (*CL1* 303). Yeats's occultism led him to the THEOSOPHICAL SOCIETY and the HERMETIC ORDER OF THE GOLDEN DAWN, and spawned much of the imagery and idea of his poetry from start to finish. "Magic" is Yeats's principal public defense of his early involvement in the occult and the most comprehensive explanation of his early mystical philosophy.

The essay opens with a declaration of belief in "the evocation of spirits," in "the power of creating magical illusions," and in "the visions of truth in the depths of the mind when the eyes are closed." Three metaphysical premises underlie this belief: "(1) That the borders of our mind are ever shifting, and that many minds can flow into one another, as it were, and create or reveal a single mind, a single energy. (2) That the borders of our memories are as shifting, and that our memories are a part of one great memory, the memory of Nature herself. (3) That this great mind and great memory can be evoked by symbols" (on the "great memory" see also ANIMA MUNDI). The modern world, Yeats says, has assumed "a certain evil, a certain ugliness, that comes from the slow perishing through the centuries of a quality of mind that made this belief and its evidences common over the world" (*E&I* 28). Attempting to prove his point, Yeats recalls at length an evening of magical experimentation at the home of MACGREGOR MATHERS and his wife,

Moina, in 1890 or 1891. The three evoked strange and rambling visions, each largely seeing as the others saw. Yeats goes on to describe other paranormal experiences. While visiting PARIS in 1898, he imagined his arm in a sling just as he passed a servant setting the table. He went for a newspaper and returned to find that the girl had alarmed the house with news that he had injured his arm (for another version of this anecdote see *Aut.* 259). On another occasion, he considered sending a note to a "fellow student" but hesitated. He later learned that he had seemed to appear to this friend and deliver the message in person. Yeats repeats this anecdote in MEMOIRS and reveals that the "fellow student" was MAUD GONNE (87).

Demonstrating that his belief in magic would not have been exceptional in earlier times, Yeats quotes Joseph Glanvill's tale of the "scholar-gipsy" from chapter 20 of *The Vanity of Dogmatizing* (1661), which Matthew Arnold reworked in his famous poem of 1853. Glanvill's tale concerns a student who leaves OXFORD for lack of funds. He joins a band of gypsies and learns their magical lore. Meeting some of his old schoolfellows, he demonstrates his magical power by leaving them to themselves for a while and returning with a full report of their conversation. He explains that by "power of imagination" he had dictated the conversation to them. Whether or not angels and devils exist within us or without, says Yeats, we must admit that "invisible beings, far-wandering influences, shapes that may have floated from a hermit of the wilderness, brood over council-chambers and studies and battlefields," nor can we be certain that a great world-changing passion "did not begin in the mind of some shepherd boy, lighting up his eyes for a moment before it ran upon its way" (41; Yeats repeats this striking notion in "The SYMBOLISM OF POETRY"; see 158). Such influences still abide, but are less powerful than they were, for the modern city has destroyed the "passive meditative life" and modern education has "made our souls less sensitive" (41). "Savages" by contrast—whether Laplanders or Irish peasants—"live always on the edges of vision" (42). The modern writer, Yeats says, is counterpart to those ancients who "sat for hours imagining themselves to be stocks and stones and beasts of the wood, till the images were so vivid that the passers-by became but a part of the imagination of the dreamer, and wept or laughed or ran away as he would have them," while poetry and music arose from the "sounds the enchanters made to help their imagination to enchant" and to reveal the "transitory mind made out of many minds" (43). The "transitory mind" was most often the "genius" of the family or tribe, but when the enchanter became sufficiently "mighty-souled" he unlocked nothing less than the "genius of the world" (44).

The underlying reality of the "one mind" or the "Great Memory" explains the otherwise inexplicable repetitions of image and pattern that unite the myths and visions of the world. Symbols, according to Yeats, draw upon this underlying reality and are "the greatest of all powers whether they are used consciously by the masters of magic, or half unconsciously by their successors, the poet, the musician and the artist" (49). He adds, "Whatever the passions of man have gathered about, becomes a symbol in the Great Memory, and in the hands of him who has the secret it is a worker of wonders, a caller-up of angels or of devils" (50). Yeats worries that he has revealed too much and possibly aroused the resentment of the beings who may watch over "the ancient secret," but whatever the risk, he affirms in the end, "we must cry out that imagination is always seeking to remake the world according to the impulses and the patterns in that Great Mind, and that Great Memory" (52).

FIRST PUBLICATION: The *Monthly Review* (periodical), September 1901. Reprinted in *Ideas of Good and Evil*, A. H. Bullen, London, May 1903.

BIBLIOGRAPHY

Yeats, W. B. *Autobiographies, The Collected Letters of W. B. Yeats* (vol. 1), *Essays and Introductions, Memoirs*.

Memoirs (1972)

Yeats's unpolished and long unpublished memoir of his young manhood, begun in 1915 and laid aside in 1917, is not the masterpiece of style nor the philosophical and psychological tour de force that his assembled AUTOBIOGRAPHIES turned out to be, but its frankness, especially concerning sexual and romantic matters, makes it a valuable document. Yeats recognized that he had been indiscreet and wrote on the envelope in which he placed the manuscript, "Private. A first rough draft of Memoirs made in 1916–17 and containing much that is not for publication now if ever" (*Mem*. 19; see also *Letters* 603). Yeats conceived the memoir as a sequel to the first of his autobiographical accounts, *Reveries over Childhood and Youth*, which the CUALA PRESS brought out in March 1916. Sticking to relatively unvarnished recollection, he attempts to tell the story of his life from roughly 1887 to "1896 or thereabouts," though in fact the jumbled chronology of the tale extends as far forward as 1899 (*Mem*. 19). Yeats returned to these years in both *The Trembling of the Veil* (1922) and *Dramatis Personae* (1935), retelling the story of his early manhood with more discretion and style. These accounts were eventually canonized in *Autobiographies*, while the account of 1915–17 languished until 1972, when Macmillan brought out *Memoirs*. Edited and annotated by Denis Donoghue, the volume includes the memoir (134 pages as paginated) and the full text of Yeats's journal, which spans the years 1908 to 1930, though the majority of entries were made in 1909 and 1910. Portions of this journal—96 of 252 total entries—appear also in *Autobiographies* (see "Estrangement" and "The Death of Synge").

The memoir presents a portrait of the artist as an incomplete young man, full of amorphous passion but not yet grown into his mature aspiration or ability (*Mem*. 63). The Yeats of these pages wavers between bravado and timidity, between the quest for manly self-possession and the subtlety of mind that made such self-possession impossible. If it lacks all but flashes of Yeats's high style, the memoir is bravely vulnerable and seems to represent a rare lowering of masks. Yeats goes so far as to relate the circumstances of his first self-induced orgasm (so that "some young man of talent" might be spared the shame that he had felt), and he tells of his "continual struggle against an experience that almost invariably left [him] with exhausted nerves" and a sense of self-loathing (71–72; see also 125). This is Yeats at his farthest remove from the assertive public voice and vatic confidence of so many of the poems—a genuine instance of the circus animals' desertion.

Most valuable, because unique and directly relevant to the poems of the 1890s, is Yeats's account of his affair with OLIVIA SHAKESPEAR (discretely veiled as "Diana Vernon"). Yeats describes the slow progress of his affair with the beautiful married novelist and his impotence from "nervous excitement" when the time finally came to consummate the relationship. Though explicit, Yeats's account is far from tawdry, touched as it is by undiminished affection and by self-deprecating honesty. Also important is the finale in which Yeats remembers Maud Gonne's revelation of her secret life in PARIS—of her years as the mistress of the Boulangist journalist Lucien Millevoye (1850–1918), of her dead son, Georges (whom Yeats had thought adopted), of her daughter, ISEULT GONNE, of her "horror and terror of physical love" (134). Yeats describes a sexually tinged "double vision" that came to himself and to Gonne ("She thought herself a great stone statue through which passed flame, and I felt myself becoming flame and mounting up through and looking out of the eyes of a great stone Minerva") but the climax is a false one. Lady GREGORY urged Yeats not to leave Gonne until he had received a promise of marriage, but Yeats was not made of such steadfast stuff, and he brings the memoir to a close with a confession of his own inadequacy: "No, I am too exhausted; I can do no more."

Such self-invaded privacies aside, the memoir includes meaty accounts of WILLIAM MORRIS; OSCAR WILDE and his downfall; Helena Blavatsky (1831–91) and the THEOSOPHICAL SOCIETY; MACGREGOR MATHERS, in both London and Paris; Edwin Ellis (1848–1916), with whom Yeats edited *The Works of William Blake* (1893); KATHARINE TYNAN, whom Yeats thought of marrying; LIONEL JOHNSON and the RHYMERS' CLUB; W. E. Henley (1849–1903), the poet and editor whose *Scots Observer* and *National Observer* published a good deal of Yeats's early work; the founding and early initiatives of the Irish Literary Society of London and the NATIONAL LITERARY SOCIETY; JOHN O'LEARY and his "disciple" J. F. Taylor (1850–1902), the barrister; Douglas Hyde (1860–1949); Charles Hubert Oldham (1860–1926), founder of the CONTEMPORARY CLUB; the initiative of the NEW IRISH LIBRARY; GEORGE POLLEXFEN; Yeats's early visit to Lissadell, home of the Gore-Booth family; the founding and brief embattled career of the *SAVOY*, with descants on its leading lights ARTHUR SYMONS, AUBREY BEARDSLEY, and Ernest Dowson (1867–1900); Yeats's first visit to EDWARD MARTYN's Tulira Castle; Yeats's first visit to COOLE PARK and the burgeoning of his friendship with Lady Gregory; Yeats's visit to Paris in 1896, where he met J. M. SYNGE; Yeats's part in organizing the commemoration of the 100th anniversary of the rebellion of 1798; the protest of Queen Victoria's Diamond Jubilee; the founding of the IRISH LITERARY THEATRE; and the religious opposition to *The COUNTESS CATHLEEN*.

FIRST PUBLICATION: *Memoirs*, Macmillan, London, 1972.

BIBLIOGRAPHY

Yeats, W. B. *The Letters of W. B. Yeats, Memoirs.*

On the Boiler (1939)

Yeats's last major work of prose exemplifies what "An ACRE OF GRASS" calls "an old man's frenzy." A slim prose treatise that reflects on the degeneracy of contemporary culture ("that hell wherein we suffer"), *On the Boiler* represents Yeats at his most noxious from the contemporary perspective: contemptuous of the middle class and the representative democracy that gave it power, dangerously invested in eugenic theory, looking forward to class war as the only means of reordering society, by turns cranky and arrogant. On the other hand, *On the Boiler* is a brilliant and bracing polemic: muscularly written, full of personality, dense with ideas. Donald T. Torchiana calls the book "the expression of a lifetime" in its emphasis on "able men, a unified Ireland, a country based on the soil, the intellectual and literary contributions of famous men" (*W. B. Yeats & Georgian Ireland* 343).

Writing to DOROTHY WELLESLEY in November 1937, Yeats envisioned *On the Boiler* as a biannual prose miscellany on the model of John Ruskin's *Fors Clavigera* (1871–84), a series of 96 pamphlets in which the great critic had railed against the Victorian age. "It will be an amusing thing to do—I shall curse my enemies and bless my friends," Yeats told Wellesley. "My enemies will hit back, and that will give me the joy of answering them" (*Letters* 900; *LOP* 148). The following month he told Ethel Mannin (1900–84) that he planned to "lay aside the pleasant paths I have built up for years and seek the brutality, the ill breeding, the barbarism of truth" (903). With more self-dramatization than genuine worry, perhaps, Yeats predicted ruptures and ostracism. In December 1937, he fretted to Wellesley that he would lose friends if he were able "to get on to paper the passion that is in my head" (902). In February 1938, he told Mannin that writing *On the Boiler* had "meant a long exploration of my convictions, or instincts, and at first I had black moods of depression, thinking you and one or two other friends would turn against me. Certainly no party will be helped by what I say, and no class" (904). In June, he wrote to MAUD GONNE, "Perhaps you will hate me for it. For the first time I am saying what I believe about Irish and European politics. I wonder how many friends I will have left" (910). In August, he fretted in a letter to Mannin, "Half my friends may never speak to me when it comes out" (914).

In the event, Yeats did not live to experience the furor he claimed to fear. The CUALA PRESS published the 48-page volume posthumously in the autumn of 1939. It included a short preface, prose reflections divided by loose theme into six sections ("The Name," "Preliminaries," "To-morrow's Revolution," "Private Thoughts," "Ireland after the Revolution," "Other Matters"), and the play PURGATORY, an appropriately anguished tale of familial and cultural decline that had appeared some months earlier in *Last Poems and Two Plays*. Interspersed were three untitled poems appearing in print for the first time. In *Last Poems & Plays* (1940) these poems were titled "WHY SHOULD NOT OLD MEN BE MAD?" (which gives the spirit of the entire enterprise), "Crazy Jane on the Mountain"

(see "WORDS FOR MUSIC PERHAPS"), and "The Statesman's Holiday." Yeats began a second installment of *On the Boiler*, but died before making more than a start (*Letters* 921). George Yeats told Richard Ellmann that the second installment was to have been a fulmination "against all institutional religions" (*Second Puberty*). Conor Cruise O'Brien comments that it was probably fortunate for Yeats's future reputation "that he died in January 1939 before the political momentum of his last years could carry him any farther than *On the Boiler*" (*In Excited Reverie* 273).

As he explains in "The Name," Yeats gleaned the title *On the Boiler* from a youthful memory. Wandering about the SLIGO quays, he had seen a painted notice announcing that "the great McCoy"—a "mad ship's carpenter," he later learned—would speak on the "old boiler." Yeats knew the boiler; it was "very big, very high, the top far out of reach, and all red rust" (*LE* 220). Like McCoy, Yeats would hold forth figuratively if not literally from the old boiler, a scabrous and scandalous prophet of the public thoroughfares.

"To-morrow's Revolution" is the book's most notable section, because it covers entirely new ground, and shockingly so. For the first time, Yeats publicly expounds his eugenic theories and makes the case for a government policy that would "limit the families of the unintelligent classes" (232). This represents Yeats's closest approach to fascism as conceived on the Continent, but Yeats makes a crucial distinction. While the "Fascist countries" share his conviction that "civilisation has reached a crisis, and found their eloquence upon that knowledge," they "put quantity before quality" and "offer bounties for the seventh, eighth or ninth baby, and accelerate degeneration" (230). Yeats desires not the swelling of national population and power, but the refinement of national "mother-wit" and the empowerment of those in possession of this mother-wit. Though he recognizes that there are occasionally "clever men born among dunces, and dunces among clever men," he accepts that intelligence is generally consistent with class and holds that "sooner or later we must limit the families of the unintelligent classes" (*LE* 232). Whatever its moral and political merits, the discussion is indispensable background to the eugenic motif in "The STATUES" ("formless spawning fury"), "Three Songs to the One Burden" ("The common breeds the common, / A lout begets a lout," "Throw likely couples into bed / And knock the others down"), and "UNDER BEN BULBEN" ("Base-born products of base beds").

"Private Thoughts" contains a deft evocation of the culture's attainment and fall from UNITY OF BEING ("mother-wit expressed in its perfection") and perhaps Yeats's most honed repudiation of the scientific worldview, in which he argues, thought-provokingly and counterfascistically, that the scientific objectification of the world makes "possible the stimulation and condonation of revolutionary massacre and the multiplication of murderous weapons by substituting for the old humanity with its unique irreplaceable individuals something that can be chopped and measured like a piece of cheese" (237). "Ireland after the Revolution" sets down what Yeats called in a letter "a policy for young Ireland" (*Letters* 901). Yeats calls for an educational program that excludes everything "but Greek, Gaelic, mathematics, and perhaps one modern language" (*LE* 239). He dismisses Latin as "a language of the Greco-Roman decadence" (239), as he does in the like-minded "Letter to Michael's Schoolmaster" (*Expl.* 320–321), and he holds that "English, history, and geography and those pleasant easy things which are the most important of all should be taught by father and mother, ancestral tradition, and the child's own reading [. . .]" (*LE* 241). Yeats would also have Ireland bolster its military and unify itself by war ("Desire some just war, that big house and hovel, college and public house, civil servant—his Gaelic certificate in his pocket—and international bridge-playing woman, may know that they belong to one nation"); distance itself from English political culture, which is characterized by a dispassionate abstraction inimical to Ireland's own "ancient, cold, explosive detonating impartiality"; and adopt a shared religion based on "some new argument that death is but passing from one room into another, for lacking that there can be no great lasting quality" (241–243). "Other Matters" touches on the contemporary arts of Ireland. If there is an implicit binding

moral or standard of judgment to be found in the section's miscellany, it comes in section four: "The arts are all the bridal chambers of joy. No tragedy is legitimate unless it leads some great character to his final joy" (247).

On the Boiler is reprinted, with certain omissions, in *Explorations* (1962). It is reprinted in full in *Later Essays* (1994).

FIRST PUBLICATION: *On the Boiler*, The Cuala Press, Dublin, autumn, 1939.

BIBLIOGRAPHY

Ellmann, Richard. *W. B. Yeats's Second Puberty: A lecture delivered at the Library of Congress on April 2, 1984*; Jeffares, A. Norman, and K. G. W. Cross, eds. *In Excited Reverie: A Centenary Tribute to W. B. Yeats, 1865–1939*; Torchiana, Donald T. *W. B. Yeats & Georgian Ireland*; Yeats, W. B. *Explorations, Later Essays, The Letters of W. B. Yeats, Letters on Poetry from W. B. Yeats to Dorothy Wellesley*.

Per Amica Silentia Lunae (1918)

Per Amica Silentia Lunae is an initial foray into the occult philosophizing that would ramify as the weird and massive architecture of A VISION. It is also a small but resplendent monument of English prose, its language gnomic and in Yeats's own word "marmorean," having shed, like baby fat, the sensuous swelling subordination and passionate momentum of Yeats's early prose (*LE* 7). It is, as Harold Bloom writes, "a masterpiece in the tradition of the marmoreal reverie, worthy to stand beside Browne's *Urn Burial* and *Garden of Cyrus* or most of Pater. Except for the AUTOBIOGRAPHIES, it is Yeats's great achievement in prose, a book to be read and reread, unlike *A Vision*, which we are compelled to study, but so frequently with regret" (*Yeats* 179). The epigrammatic beauty of the volume is captured in what may be the most striking of *Per Amica*'s many striking professions: "I shall find the dark grow luminous, the void fruitful when I understand I have nothing, that the ringers in the tower have appointed for the hymen of the soul a passing bell" (9). T. R. Henn demurs, however, contending that the "rhythms of Pater" lend the language of *Per Amica* "a certain stilted quality, almost as of parody" (*In Excited Reverie* 106).

The book's title—as Yeats translated it, "Through the Friendly Silences of the Moon" (*LE* 293)—derives from the second book of Virgil's *Aeneid,* in which the Greek ships emerge from hiding and make for Troy, which has been laid open by the ruse of the wooden horse. In Robert Fitzgerald's translation of the pertinent passage: "The Argive fleet, / Drawn up in line abreast, left Tenedos / Through the aloof moon's friendly stillnesses / And made for the familiar shore" (*Aeniad* 42). What Yeats meant by the title is obscure. He may have seen himself laying open philosophical or spiritual gates as the Greeks laid open a physical gate, his enterprise blessed or illuminated by the moon that figures so largely in his emerging philosophy. In *Per Amica,* Yeats gives only an obscure hint at his intention. He describes how he had tried to bring his mind close to the minds of poets, peasants, mediums, and monks, those who had not lost access to the "general mind," and concludes, "[I] have put myself to school where all things are seen: *A Tenedo Tacitae per Amica Silentia Lunae*" (*LE* 16).

Per Amica commences with an affectionate prologue addressed to Iseult Gonne, whom Yeats had lingering hopes of marrying. As Yeats relates, *Per Amica* germinated in certain conversations with Iseult while he vacationed at Les Mouettes, the Gonnes' seaside house at Colleville-sur-Mer, in Calvados, Normandy, in the summer of 1916. He recalls that the Gonnes' cat Minnaloushe (see "The Cat and the Moon") interrupted one such conversation, "often interrupted before, upon certain thoughts so long habitual that I may be permitted to call them my convictions. When I came to back to London"—in late August 1916—"my mind ran again and again to those conversations and I could not rest till I had written out in this little book all that I had said or would have said" (1). Iseult was flattered by the prologue and wrote to Yeats on June 6, 1917, "Minnaloushe and I are very grateful and honoured to have our names in your book. He is a little familiar divinity and well at his place in an occult work, as for me I am wholly undeserv-

ing, but none the less proud" (*Letters to WBY&EP* 84). Serving as preamble, "Ego Dominus Tuus," a difficult and oracular dialogue that had previously appeared in *The Wild Swans at Coole* (1917), broaches crucial themes of *Per Amica*: the quest for self-apotheosis by the discovery of the "anti-self," that which is most unlike ourselves; Dante and Keats as emblematic seekers of the anti-self; art as the "vision of reality," as against the delusions of the sentimentalist and the rhetorician; the modern passivity and gentleness that have replaced the instinct for the *antithetical* quest.

Per Amica proper is divided into two complementary sections: "Anima Hominis" (the soul of man) and "anima mundi" (the soul of the world). The former sets down the mysterious dynamic of self and antiself. It calls the antiself the "Daemon" and defines its relation to the mask: "[The] Daemon comes not as like to like but seeking its own opposite, for man and Daemon feed the hunger in one another's hearts. Because the ghost [i.e., the Daemon] is simple, the man heterogeneous and confused, they are but knit together when the man has found a mask whose lineaments permit the expression of all the man most lacks, and it may be dreads, and of that only" (*LE* 11). Because the Daemon "would ever set us to the hardest work among those not impossible"—that which reverses the nature of the self—man and Daemon exist in a state of perpetual warfare (11; see also 28). The mask represents the self's dream of its own reborn reality, the form to which it aspires. The quest for the mask is the "quarrel with ourselves" (8) that defines the true poet, as well as the hero and the saint; it is not an escape from reality, but an expression of the "passion for reality," for reality, in Yeats's understanding, is realizable only by the most difficult of possible forms of self-transcendence. The mask is not achieved once and for all time, but must be perpetually renewed in the tumult of passion. Embittered by the perpetual forfeiture of comfort and complacency, the mask-seeker, like Dante in "Ego Dominus Tuus," must "climb to some waste room and find, forgotten there by youth, some bitter crust" (16).

Section XI of "Anima Hominis" notably anticipates the doctrine of the historical gyre, which would be central to the "desert geometry" of *A Vision* (*AV*-1925 xxi). In the key passage, Yeats notes "the winding movement of nature," and opines parenthetically, "I do not doubt those heaving circles, those winding arcs, whether in one man's life or in that of an age, are mathematical, and that some in the world, or beyond the world, have foreknown the event and pricked upon the calendar the life-span of a Christ, a Buddha, a Napoleon: that every movement, in feeling or in thought, prepares in the dark by its own increasing clarity and confidence its own executioner" (14). In *A Vision* Yeats tells that the spirit who visited his wife's pen soon after their marriage had this passage in mind. "I had made a distinction," Yeats recounts, "between the perfection that is from a man's combat with himself and that which is from a combat with circumstance [perhaps "Anima Hominis," V], and upon this simple distinction he built up an elaborate classification of men according to their more or less complete expression of one type or the other. He supported his classification by a series of geometrical symbols and put these symbols in an order that answered the question in my essay [i.e., *Per Amica*] as to whether some prophet could not prick upon the calendar the birth of a Napoleon or a Christ" (*AV* 8–9).

"Anima mundi" develops the concept of a world-soul that had been present in Yeats's thought since he had spoken of a "great memory" in his turn-of-the-century essays "The Philosophy of Shelley's Poetry" and "Magic" (see ANIMA MUNDI). Guided by the Neoplatonism of Henry More (1614–87), Yeats holds that the individual soul exists in relation to the world soul and shares in its shapes and forms; in his own words, "our animal spirits or vehicles are but as it were a condensation of the vehicle of *anima mundi*, and give substance to its images in the faint materialisation of our common thought [. . .]" (*LE* 21). This universal underlying reality of the *anima mundi* explains the phenomena of spiritism: evocation of universal images, shared memory, mediumship, prevision, ghostly reenactments of past events (cf. "Crazy Jane on God"), ghostly visitation. The strictures of time and space, as Yeats has it, are merely epiphenomenal; the eternity of *anima mundi* is the fundamental reality, and

spiritism merely recognizes the evidence of its commerce with the world.

In a brief epilogue addressed to Iseult, Yeats recalls Paris during the 1890s. In those days, reality seemed "full of the trembling of the veil of the temple" (in the phrase of Mallarmé, from which Yeats later took the title of his second installment of memoirs), as if on the verge of some mystic annunciation or revelation. Comparing the poets of the 1890s to the later French poets, Paul Louis Charles Claudel (1868–1955), Francis Jammes (1868–1938), and Charles Pierre Piguy (1873–1914), all of whom turned from the "magic soul" to nation and church, Yeats asks in conclusion, "Have not my thoughts run through a like round, though I have not found my tradition in the Catholic Church, which was not the church of my childhood, but where the tradition is, as I believe, more universal and more ancient?" (*LE* 33). Implying the movement of his thought toward something even more basic than church and nation, Yeats reiterates the pattern of "The Coming of Wisdom with Time."

If Yeats's specific theories are idiosyncratic, his root notions never veer so far from instinct and tradition that they become solipsistic and simply bizarre. An anonymous reviewer of *Per Amica* concludes sagely, "And yet, with it all, Mr. Yeats is a poet, as moonlight is beautiful. The beauty that we see is the only thing common between his mind and ours. There may not be sense to us, but there is music; and in that there is a common language, though we cannot translate it into words" (*Critical Heritage* 210).

FIRST PUBLICATION: *Per Amica Silentia Lunae*, Macmillan, London, New York, January 18, 1918.

BIBLIOGRAPHY

Bloom, Harold. *Yeats*; Gonne, Iseult. *Letters to W. B. Yeats and Ezra Pound from Iseult Gonne*; Jeffares, A. Norman, ed. *W. B. Yeats: The Critical Heritage*; Jeffares, A. Norman, and K. G. W. Cross, eds. *In Excited Reverie: A Centenary Tribute to William Butler Yeats, 1865–1939*; W. B. Yeats, *A Critical Edition of Yeats's A Vision (1925)*, *Later Essays*, *A Vision*.

"Philosophy of Shelley's Poetry, The" (1900–1903)

Begun in July 1899 (see *CL2* 433), this relatively long essay is Yeats's most comprehensive discussion of SHELLEY, who was, with BLAKE, the most important of his early poetic and philosophical influences. In the first section of the essay, "His Ruling Ideas," Yeats remembers his early reverence for *Prometheus Unbound* (1820), which he took to be "among the sacred books of the world" (cf. *Aut.* 95, 166, 246–247), and objects to the view of a "learned scholar"—EDWARD DOWDEN, author of the two-volume *Life of Percy Bysshe Shelley* (1886)—that it is merely "Godwin's *Political Justice* put into rhyme, and that Shelley was a crude revolutionist, and believed that the overturning of kings and priests would regenerate mankind" (*E&I* 65–6; cf. *CL1* 303). Attempting to establish the contrary view that Shelley's thought is "full of subtlety," Yeats presents a long medley of quotations from Shelley's work and concludes that Shelley had "reawakened in himself the age of faith" (*E&I* 77). The second section of the essay, "His Ruling Symbols," moots the notion, also taken up in "MAGIC" and "The SYMBOLISM OF POETRY," that "our little memories are but a part of some great Memory," and that "the great Memory is also a dwelling-house of symbols, of images that are living souls" (79; cf. ANIMA MUNDI). As one deeply given to the state of reverie, Shelley "could hardly have helped perceiving that an image that has transcended particular time and place becomes a symbol, passes beyond death, as it were, and becomes a living soul" (80). In light of this metaphysical conception Yeats examines several of the recurring symbols of Shelley's poetry: cave, river, tower, morning and evening star, moon, and sun. This discussion has a double interest given Yeats's appropriation of tower, moon, and sun as ruling symbols in his own work, and his not infrequent invocation of cave (see, for example, "The GYRES" and "NEWS FOR THE DELPHIC ORACLE") and river or stream (see, for example, the third section of "The TOWER"). Yeats concludes with a memorable characterization of the two poets who meant the

most to him: "In ancient times, it seems to me that Blake, who for all his protest was glad to be alive, and ever spoke of his gladness, would have worshipped in some chapel of the Sun, but that Shelley, who hated life because he sought 'more in life than any understood,' would have wandered, lost in a ceaseless reverie, in some chapel of the Star of infinite desire" (94).

FIRST PUBLICATION: "His Ruling Ideas" first appeared in the *Dome*, May–July 1900, under the title "The Philosophy of Shelley's Poetry." The full essay first appeared in *Ideas of Good and Evil*, A. H. Bullen, London, May 1903.

BIBLIOGRAPHY

Yeats, W. B. *Autobiographies*, *The Collected Letters of W. B. Yeats* (vols. 1–2), *Essays and Introductions*.

"Prometheus Unbound" (1933)

In his 1903 essay, "The PHILOSOPHY OF SHELLEY'S POETRY," Yeats ranks SHELLEY's phantasmagoric versa drama *Prometheus Unbound* (1820) "among the sacred books of the world" (see also *Aut.* 95, 166, 246–247). In his later essay on the poem, Yeats expresses a certain interpretative frustration. Like so many critics before and after him, he wonders at the enigma of Demogorgon, who names himself "Eternity" and ascends to unseat the tyrant Jupiter. The inclusion of this grim and inscrutable deus ex machina, Yeats charges, renders the plot "incoherent, its interpretation impossible" (*LE* 119; *E&I* 420). He asks why Demogorgon, whose function is beneficent, bears "so terrible a shape," and why Shelley, in contrast to BLAKE, is "terrified of the Last Day like a Victorian child" (*LE* 119; *E&I* 420). Yeats sees the nightmarish representation of Demogorgon as part of a larger morbidity that infects and undermines Shelley's work. Yeats explains this taint with the intriguing insight that "Shelley was not a mystic, his system of thought was constructed by his logical faculty to satisfy desire, not a symbolic revelation received after the suspension of all desire" (*LE* 120; *E&I*

421–422). An "unconverted man though certainly a visionary," Shelley lacked the "radiating light" of those whose minds are visited by divinity. He was thus prey to "sadness and disquiet" (*LE* 121; *E&I* 423). Yeats concludes with a consideration of Shelley's influence on his own generation, recollecting the tremendous vogue for Shelley during the years of his early manhood. He mentions that during "middle life" he had looked back and found that "[Shelley] and not BLAKE, whom I had studied more and with more approval, had shaped my life, and when I thought of the tumultuous and often tragic lives of friends or acquaintances I attributed to his direct or indirect influence their Jacobin frenzies, their brown demons" (*LE* 122; *E&I* 424–425).

Harold Bloom theorizes the ambivalence of Yeats's essay: "The old Yeats wrote of his disappointment with 'Prometheus,' of its failure to satisfy *in him* his expectations of its religion-making power. But his expectations were at fault and his impatience with Demogorgon unjustified. [. . .] Yeats expected what Shelley *on mythmaking principle* refused to give. The point of scene iv, Act II [in which Demogorgon evades Asia's questions about the nature of God] is that it refuses to put itself to us as Scripture—it precisely does not want to be 'a holy book.' [Shelley's essay 'A Defence of Poetry'] knows all about the hardening of poetry into religion, and 'Prometheus' knows what the *Defence* knows. Blake is what Yeats wanted, and in the final phase took. Blake offers *a* myth in place of religion—a contrapuntal myth which can fulfill all the functions of religion. Shelley is fiercely tentative—he gives us not a myth but only a fully conscious exemplification of the experiment of mythmaking" (*Shelley's Mythmaking* 123–124).

FIRST PUBLICATION: The *Spectator* (periodical), March 17, 1933. Reprinted in *Essays 1931 to 1936*, The CUALA PRESS, Dublin, December 14, 1937.

BIBLIOGRAPHY

Bloom, Harold. *Shelley's Mythmaking*; Yeats, W. B. *Essays and Introductions, Later Essays*.

"Rosa Alchemica" (1896)

Yeats's most successful work of fiction, the short story "Rosa Alchemica" merits the praise that MAUD GONNE showered on it in a letter of 1897: "I wanted often to write & tell you how much I love your book The Secret Rose, it is what I like best of all your work. [. . .] I have read it all through & go back & read some of it many times, especially Rosa Alchemica. That is what I think I like the best. The language is so lovely, it is like some wonderful eastern jewel. One never tires of it—it must be heavenly to be able to express one's thoughts like that—" (GY 70). GEORGE RUSSELL (AE) was also full of praise: "The *Rosa Alchemica* is a most wonderful piece of prose. Everything in it thought and word are so rich that they seem the gathering in the temple of the mind of thousands of pilgrim rays returning and leaving there their many experiences" (*Letters from AE* 19).

In AUTOBIOGRAPHIES, Yeats acknowledges the story's indebtedness to Villiers de l'Isle-Adam (1838–89) and Walter Pater (1839–94), while in "The PHASES OF THE MOON" Michael Robartes complains that Yeats had written of him "in that extravagant style / He had learnt from Pater" (*Aut.* 247). Yeats had seen Villiers de l'Isle-Adam's *Axël* performed in PARIS in February 1894 and had puzzled through the text in French (*Aut.* 246; *LE* 32–33; *P&I* 156–158; *UP1* 320–325). From Villiers de l'Isle-Adam Yeats borrows something of mood, setting, and character; from Pater, as Robartes alleges, something of his style. The opening section of "Rosa Alchemica" additionally seems to borrow from the hyper-refined domesticity of Des Esseintes, the antihero of Joris-Karl Huysman's arch-decadent novel *Against Nature* (1884), which Yeats would have found mentioned in OSCAR WILDE's *The Picture of Dorian Gray* (1890) and in ARTHUR SYMONS's essay "The Decadent Movement in Literature" (1893).

The story fleshes out the figure of Michael Robartes, in whose voice Yeats narrates three poems of the mid-1890s: "Michael Robartes bids his Beloved be at Peace," "Michael Robartes remembers Forgotten Beauty," and "Michael Robartes asks Forgiveness because of his many Moods" (Yeats revised these titles in 1906: see "HE BIDS HIS BELOVED BE AT PEACE," "HE REMEMBERS FORGOTTEN BEAUTY," and "The Lover asks Forgiveness because of his Many Moods"). In a note to these poems in *The Wind Among the Reeds* (1899), Yeats calls Robartes "the pride of the imagination brooding upon the greatness of its possessions, or the adoration of the Magi" (*VP* 803). If he is a mere "principle of the mind" in these poems, "Rosa Alchemica" introduces him as an archetype of the occult quester (803). In 1897, Yeats told Lady GREGORY that he had modeled Robartes on Russell, to whom he dedicated *The Secret Rose* in 1897 (see *CL2* 59–60) and to whom the trilogy of occult stories composed of "Rosa Alchemica," "The TABLES OF THE LAW," and "The ADORATION OF THE MAGI" remains dedicated (see Gould and Toomey, eds., *Mythologies* 366–367). Upon meeting Russell, Lady Gregory was relieved to find little resemblance between the "gentle quiet man" and the fictive Robartes, whom Yeats describes as having "wild red hair, fierce eyes, sensitive, tremulous lips and rough clothes" and looking "something between a debauchee, a saint, and a peasant" (*Lady Gregory's Diaries 1892–1902* 149–150; *Myth.* 271). Robartes is more plausibly modeled on MACGREGOR MATHERS, the charismatic and eccentric conceptual architect of the HERMETIC ORDER OF THE GOLDEN DAWN.

If resplendent in its jeweled prose, "Rosa Alchemica" is simple enough in outline. The narrator is unnamed, but he is inferably Owen Aherne, Robartes's crony in "The Phases of the Moon" and elsewhere (see AV 54–55). Aherne has secluded himself in a Dublin house where he devotes himself to alchemical research and aesthetic contemplation. Robartes, whom Aherne knew 10 years earlier when both had been students in Paris, arrives unannounced and invites him to join his Order of the Alchemical Rose. Aherne declines, as he had in Paris, but falls into a visionary trance induced by Robartes's Syrian incense or by some power belonging to Robartes himself. He wakens having "been with eternal things" and agrees to join the order. Aherne and Robartes travel by train to the west of Ireland and come to the Temple of the Alchemical Rose upon "the very end of a dilapidated and almost deserted pier" (*Myth.* 280). Left alone to prepare for his initiation ceremony, Aherne reads of the founding of the order upon the principle of "spiritual alchemy," by which the soul distills itself until it becomes immortal (284). Aherne is led to a circular room in which the initiation ceremony takes the form of an ecstatic communal dance. He again falls into a visionary trance. The mosaic ROSE upon the ceiling seems to descend and its petals to become divinities. Realizing that the "immortal august woman" with whom he dances is drinking up his soul "as an ox drinks up a wayside pool," the narrator collapses in a faint (290). He wakes at dawn amid sleepers sprawled on the dance floor, the spell of the previous night now worn off and the room revealed in its shabbiness. The narrator hears angry villagers attempting to break into the temple. Unable to wake Robartes, he flees the building and escapes along the shore, beset by "voices of exultation and lamentation" that ring in the air over his head. Looking back on this misadventure, he confesses that at times he still seems to hear these voices, but guards himself with rosary and prayer.

In its concatenation of alchemy, fire, dance, trance, and Byzantine mosaic, as Giorgio Melchiori notes, the story anticipates both "BYZANTIUM" and "SAILING TO BYZANTIUM" (*Whole Mystery of Art* 218–225). Melchiori writes in reference to the latter poem, "The sages, vague hieratical figures descending with a winding circular movement from a mosaic background, cannot help reminding us of those mysterious divinities coming down from the mosaic in the ceiling of the circular room in 'Rosa Alchemica'" (223). So too it anticipates the figure of the dancer with whom Yeats associates transcendental unity in poems like "AMONG SCHOOL CHILDREN," "LONG-LEGGED FLY," and "The DOUBLE VISION OF MICHAEL ROBARTES."

The tale of Robartes and Aherne continues in "The Tables of the Law" and "The Adoration of the Magi," which follow "Rosa Alchemica" in an informal trilogy, though they did not appear in the same volume until 1908 (*Biblio.* 90–91; see also Gould and Toomey, eds., *Mythologies* li–ii). In a 1925 note,

Yeats explains that "The Tables of the Law" and "The Adoration of the Magi" were "intended to be part of *The Secret Rose* [1897], but the publisher, A. H. Bullen, took a distaste to them and asked me to leave them out, and then after the book was published liked them and put them into a little volume by themselves" (*Myth.* 1). Yeats considered all three stories "preliminary studies" for *The SPECKLED BIRD*. As it turned out, the stories assumed an important place in Yeats's canon while the novel floundered and was eventually aborted (*CL2* 63).

Yeats's occult aspirations revived in the years following his marriage and he took a renewed interest in Robartes and Aherne, who had languished since the 1890s. They figure prominently in the later poems "The Double Vision of Michael Robartes," "EGO DOMINUS TUUS," "MICHAEL ROBARTES AND THE DANCER," "OWEN AHERNE AND HIS DANCERS," and "The Phases of the Moon"; in notes to "The Double Vision of Michael Robartes," "The GIFT OF HARUN AL-RASHID," "An IMAGE FROM A PAST LIFE," "Michael Robartes and the Dancer," "The Phases of the Moon," and "The SECOND COMING" (see VP 820–825, 828–830); in notes to CALVARY, *The DREAMING OF THE BONES*, and *The ONLY JEALOUSY OF EMER* (*VPl.* 789–791, 777–779, 566); in prefaces to *The Wild Swans at Coole* and *Michael Robartes and the Dancer* (VP 852–853); and in the fictional framing apparatus of *A VISION* (see both the 1925 and 1937 editions).

FIRST PUBLICATION: *The SAVOY* (periodical), April 1896. Reprinted in *The Secret Rose*, Lawrence & Bullen, London, April 1897.

BIBLIOGRAPHY

Gregory, Lady. *Lady Gregory's Diaries, 1892–1902*; Melchiori, Giorgio. *The Whole Mystery of Art: Pattern into Poetry in the Work of W. B. Yeats*; Russell, George (AE). *Letters from AE*; Wade, Allan. *A Bibliography of the Writings of W. B. Yeats*; Yeats, W. B. *Autobiographies*, *The Collected Letters of W. B. Yeats* (vol. 2), *The Gonne-Yeats Letters 1893–1938*, *Later Essays*, *Mythologies*, *Mythologies* (eds. Warwick Gould and Deirdre Toomey), *Prefaces and Introductions*, *Uncollected Prose by W. B. Yeats* (vol. 1), *The Variorum Edition of the Plays of W. B. Yeats*, *The Variorum Edition of the Poems of W. B. Yeats*, *A Vision*.

"Speaking to the Psaltery" (1902)

On February 26, 1901, Yeats and FLORENCE FARR, who had already begun to experiment with chanted verse (CL2 597; CL3 21, 35), attended a concert performance by Arnold Dolmetsch (1858–1940), a French-born musicologist and luthier who was working to revive interest in early English music and instrumentation (CL3 68). Yeats saw the chance to fulfill his dream of reintegrating music and poetry and prevailed on Dolmetsch to build him a "psaltery," a stringed instrument reminiscent of a lyre. The idea was that poetry could be chanted to the accompaniment of such an instrument. In John Kelly and Ronald Schuchard's description, the instrument was made of satinwood and "had 26 alternating strings of fine steel and twisted brass arranged an octave apart so that the octave could be played with one finger" (91). Completed in October 1901 after much experimentation, the instrument wound up costing £10 rather than £4, and both Yeats and Farr had to scramble to raise funds. "Speaking to the Psaltery," published in May 1902, was evidently a contribution to this fund-raising effort (91, 121). On June 10, 1902, Yeats gave a lecture on "Speaking to Musical Notes" at Clifford's Inn Hall, London, in order to raise funds for the construction of six additional psalteries, which were to be less elaborate and less expensive, at £2.10s.0d each (181, 194, 253). The lecture featured Farr's first public performance on the instrument. Yeats, Farr, and Dolmetsch experimented with the psaltery throughout 1901 and 1902, and Yeats gave additional lectures on the subject at Clifford's Inn Hall on May 5 ("Recording the Music of Speech"), May 12 ("Heroic Folk Literature"), and May 29, 1903 ("Poetry and the Living Voice") (YC 87). In July 1901, Yeats told the future poet laureate Robert Bridges (1844–1930), "I shall be altogether content if we can perfect this art for I have never felt that reading was better than an error, a part of the fall into the flesh, a mouthful of the apple" (CL3 92). In the ensuing years, Yeats and Farr periodically took to the stage to demonstrate their new art. They gave their last performance in 1911 (CL4 885).

The chief testament to this season of experimentation is "Speaking to the Psaltery," in which Yeats argues for the restoration of the ancient relation between poetry and music. The essay begins with an evocation of Farr reciting to the accompaniment of the psaltery—not singing, but speaking "to a notation as definite as that of song, using the instrument, which murmured sweetly and faintly, to give her the changing notes" (*E&I* 13). Yeats explains that he has dreamed since boyhood that poetry might again be a communal art, as it had been in the days of Homer, when "wild-eyed men" spoke to "murmuring wires" while "audiences in many-coloured robes listened, hushed and excited" (14). Such a hope led Yeats and GEORGE RUSSELL (AE) to consider the music of their own verse. They discovered that they composed "to notes that could be written down" and "turned into something like a Gregorian hymn if one sang them in the ordinary way" (14). Yeats had some of his verse rendered in musical notation by a friend; he brought the notation to Farr, and she gave the words "a new quality by the beauty of her voice." They continued to experiment, but it was only after Dolmetsch constructed the psaltery, which was capable of expressing "all the chromatic intervals within the range of the speaking voice," that they found their way (16). In place of the "intonation that copies the accidental surface of life," Yeats foresees, with the help of the psaltery, a "new art" based on subtleties of rhythm that are the "glimmer, the fragrance, the spirit of all intense literature," and he ventures to imagine troubadours who will "go here and there speaking their verses and their little stories wherever they can find a score or two of poetical-minded people in a big room, or a couple of poetical-minded friends sitting by the hearth, and poets will write them poems and little stories to the confounding of print and paper" (18–19). In the service of this vision, Yeats pledges that he will write his longer poems for the stage and his shorter poems for the psaltery, provided some "strong angel" keeps him to his good intentions (20). This emphasis on speech explains Yeats's immersion in the theater, while his envisioned audience of "poetical-minded friends sitting by the hearth" predicts the embrace

of Japanese Noh drama that he announces in "Certain Noble Plays of Japan" (1916) and in his notes to AT THE HAWK'S WELL (*VPl.* 415–419).

Yeats additionally describes his experiments with the psaltery in a note to *The* KING OF THE GREAT CLOCK TOWER (*VPl.* 1008–1009).

FIRST PUBLICATION: The *Monthly Review* (periodical), May 1902. Reprinted in *Ideas of Good and Evil*, A. H. Bullen, London, May 1903. Parts 4 and 5 (the latter by Farr) first appeared in *The Collected Works in Verse and Prose of William Butler Yeats* (vol. 3), Shakespeare Head Press, Stratford-on-Avon, October 1908, and were appended to "Speaking to the Psaltery" in *Essays*, Macmillan, London, May 6, 1924 (see *Biblio.* 144).

BIBLIOGRAPHY

Kelly, John S. *A W. B. Yeats Chronology*; Wade, Allan. *A Bibliography of the Writings of W. B. Yeats*; Yeats, W. B. *The Collected Letters of W. B. Yeats* (vols. 2–4), *Essays and Introductions*, *The Variorum Edition of the Plays of W. B. Yeats*.

Speckled Bird, The (1941)

Of all Yeats's major literary endeavors, only *The Speckled Bird*, an 80-odd-page fragment of a novel, is a decided failure. It freely borrows from Yeats's life and thus has an intrinsic autobiographical interest, but the plot—such as it is—is stilted, and Yeats's prose, by which he extricates himself from many another scrape, does not begin to approach the sumptuousness of roughly contemporaneous stories like "The ADORATION OF THE MAGI," "ROSA ALCHEMICA," and "The TABLES OF THE LAW." Yeats's error, it may be, was to belie his own temperament and aesthetic impulses by attempting a novel in the realistic mode of his friend GEORGE MOORE, to whom he turned for plot advice, with the corresponding necessity of muting the poetry of his prose and the energy of his vision (*CL2* 538–539). In AUTOBIOGRAPHIES, Yeats theorizes the nature of his troubles: "I was in poor health, the strain of youth had been greater than it commonly is [. . .] and I had lost myself besides, as I had done periodically for years, upon Hodos Chameliontos ["The Path of the Chameleon," connoting multiplicity rather than unity]. The first time was in my eighteenth or nineteenth year, when I tried to create a more multitudinous dramatic form, and now I had got there through a novel that I could neither write nor cease to write which had Hodos Chameliontos for its theme. My chief person was to see all the modern visionary sects pass before his bewildered eyes, as Flaubert's Saint Anthony saw the Christian sects, and I was as helpless to create artistic, as my chief person to create philosophic, order. It was not that I do not love order, or that I lack capacity for it, but that—and not in the arts and in thought only—I outrun my strength. It is not so much that I choose too many elements, as that the possible unities themselves seem without number [. . .]. Perhaps fifty years ago I had been in less trouble, but what can one do when the age itself has come to Hodos Chameliontos?" (282–283).

Only *The* PLAYER QUEEN and *The* SHADOWY WATERS brought as much vexation as *The Speckled Bird*. He began work on the novel in 1896 under contract to Lawrence & Bullen. He was to receive the generous sum of £105, half to be advanced in weekly installments, half to be paid upon publication, as well as royalties of 20 percent on copies sold after the first 2,500 (*CL2* 67, 556–557). His letters regularly reported that the novel—the "miserable novel," as he called it—progressed "but slowly" (*CL2* 77, 104, 108, 249, 426, 572; *CL3* 80, 82). In 1901, with Yeats still lost upon Hodos Chameliontos, Bullen agreed to publish *Ideas of Good and Evil* in lieu of *The Speckled Bird* (*CL3* 138). In a 1900 letter to William Robertson Nicholl (1851–1923), literary adviser to Hodder & Stoughton, which was negotiating for the rights to his catalogue, Yeats confessed (before thinking better of the passage and crossing it out), "I had never done a novel of any length & had no knowledge of what I was in for. I went away & wrote till the £50 were exhausted & then found I was in such a tangle that I had to start afresh" (*CL2* 193, 556–557). Yeats abandoned the project in 1902 or 1903 after writing four widely varying drafts (1897, 1897–98,

1900, and 1902). The unfinished novel languished for decades before scholars began the process of disinterring it. Excerpts appeared in the March 1941 number of *The Bell* and in the summer 1955 number of *Irish Writing*. In 1973 and 1974, the CUALA PRESS published a handsome two-volume edition of the "final" version edited by William H. O'Donnell. There followed—all edited by O'Donnell—*The Literatim Transcription of the Manuscripts of William Butler Yeats's The Speckled Bird* in 1976; a reader's edition, collecting all four versions, in 1976; and a revised and meticulously annotated edition of the same in 2003.

The novel's title derives from Jeremiah 12:9. Walking by the sea, the young hero Michael Hearne notices an owl harassed by smaller birds and thinks to himself, "That is what the Bible means when it says: 'Mine Inheritance is as the speckled bird, all the birds of the heavens are against it'" (4). Michael is presumably another such "speckled bird." In the "final" version of the novel, Michael passes a lonely youth with his distracted painter-landlord father John Hearne (patterned on JOHN BUTLER YEATS) in a house on the coast of Galway. Like Yeats himself, Michael has a yearning, dreaming nature. A series of accidental enchantments—the *Mabinogion* and the *Morte d'Arthur*, the fairy tales told by the local peasants, a painting of the Virgin Mary he finds in the attic—comprise his essential education, and he takes to fasting in order to see visions. Alarmed, John Hearne brings his son, aged 15, to PARIS. At the home of Henderson, a friend from his father's painting days, Michael meets Samuel Maclagan (patterned on MACGREGOR MATHERS) and Margaret Henderson (patterned on MAUD GONNE). Michael falls desperately in love with Margaret, but she will not marry him, having promised her mother that she would marry a Catholic and recognizing that Michael will always be married to his dreams. Distraught, Michael flees to London. Collaborating with Maclagan, he devotes himself to founding a mystical order that is to "bring back the gods," much like the "Celtic Mystical Order" at which Yeats labored for many years (see *CL2* 663–669; *Mem.* 123–125).

Michael anticipates that Margaret will one day join the order as its queen, but about a year later Harriet St. George (modeled on OLIVIA SHAKESPEAR) arrives with a message from Margaret. She has married a Captain Peters of Galway, and, unhappy, she begs him to come. Michael is stunned, just as Yeats had been when he learned in December 1898 of Gonne's relationship with Lucien Millevoye (*CL2* 314–315; *Mem.* 131–134), and as he would be again in February 1903 when he learned she planned to marry John MacBride (*CL3* 314–317). Michael immediately departs for Galway. He takes a room at an inn near the Peters's house and meets Margaret clandestinely in a nearby valley. He begs her to flee with him. She admits to loving him, but with a sisterly love; meeting him again, however, she succumbs to her misery and agrees to flee to France. Michael departs to make plans. He returns to the valley, and Harriet informs him that Margaret is pregnant and must remain true to her marriage.

The story ends 10 years later. Michael has joined Maclagan in Paris, the latter exiled following a split in his mystical society (events paralleling the 1900 schism in the HERMETIC ORDER OF THE GOLDEN DAWN). Michael tells how for a time he met Margaret among the hills, but eventually returned to London and for two or three years kept up a love affair with Harriet. In one of the novel's more revealing passages, Yeats clearly alludes to his own affair with Shakespear: "[Michael] knew that he had not even a shadow of love for this new friend, but this in itself attracted him to her; he would not put what he was quite determined could always be no more than a shadow in the place of a substance. This woman seemed so friendly and unexacting that he thought she would understand and demand nothing that he could not give [. . .]" (80).

FIRST PUBLICATION: Extracts were published in *The Bell* (periodical), March 1941, and *Irish Writing* (periodical), Summer, 1955.

BIBLIOGRAPHY

Yeats, W. B. *Autobiographies, The Collected Letters of W. B. Yeats* (vols. 2–3), *Memoirs, The Speckled Bird* (2003).

Stories of Red Hanrahan (1892–1903)

The tale of Red Hanrahan, "hedge schoolmaster" turned visionary wanderer, unfolds in a sequence of six short stories: "Red Hanrahan," "The Twisting of the Rope," "Hanrahan and Cathleen, the Daughter of Houlihan," "Red Hanrahan's Curse," "Hanrahan's Vision," and "The Death of Hanrahan." The latter five stories debuted in various periodicals during the early and mid-1890s and appeared with a story called "The Book of the Great Dhoul and Hanrahan the Red" in *The Secret Rose*, which Lawrence & Bullen published in April 1897 (for "The Book of the Great Dhoul and Hanrahan the Red," see *SRV* 184–197). Having made sweeping revisions in 1903 and 1904 with the help of Lady GREGORY and swapped "The Book of the Great Dhoul and Hanrahan the Red" for "Red Hanrahan" (which first appeared in 1903), Yeats republished the sequence as *Stories of Red Hanrahan*, which the DUN EMER PRESS brought out in May 1905. From 1913 onward, the stories appeared in anthologies of Yeats's prose under the section title "Stories of Red Hanrahan" and they remain under this section title in *Mythologies* (1959). In June 1905, Yeats inscribed this elucidation in JOHN QUINN's copy of *Stories of Red Hanrahan*: "Red Hanrahan is an imaginary name—I saw it over a shop, or rather part of it over a shop in a Galway village—but there were many poets like him in the eighteenth century in Ireland. I wrote these stories first in literary English but I could not get any sense of the village life with the words. Now, however, Lady Gregory has helped me, & I think the stories have the emotion of folklore. They are but half mine now, & often her beautiful idiom is the better half" (*Biblio.* 74).

Yeats based his schoolmaster-poet-visionary on Owen Rua O'Sullivan (1748–84) and William Dall O'Heffernan (1720–60), Munster peasant poets of whom he had read in John O'Daly and Edward Walsh's *Reliques of Irish Jacobite Poetry* (1844) and in Walsh's *Irish Popular Songs* (1847) (*W. B. Yeats and Irish Folklore* 198–199). Making this derivation explicit, Yeats's early versions of the Hanrahan stories identify the protagonist as Owen O'Sullivan and O'Sullivan the Red (*W. B. Yeats and Irish Folklore* 199; for early versions of the Hanrahan tales, see *VSR*). Yeats first mentions O'Sullivan in his 1889 essay "Popular Ballad Poetry of Ireland," calling him "pious and profligate" (*UP1* 149). In his introduction to *A Book of Irish Verse Selected from Modern Writers* (1895), Yeats remembers O'Sullivan and O'Heffernan as among the 18th-century poets whose "songs had made the people, crushed by the disasters of the Boyne and Aughrim, remember their ancient greatness" (*Book of Irish Verse* xvii; *P&I* 102). Like Hanrahan, O'Sullivan had been a hedge school master. Hedge schools, in Gould and Toomey's helpful account, "developed in the seventeenth-century to provide paid but unlicensed education for Catholic children. They continued after the repeal of the Penal Laws (which had effectively proscribed Catholic education in Ireland), only declining with the advent of free National Schools in 1831. Hedge schools were so termed for being usually held in the open air, or in temporary structures, as teaching by Catholics was illegal; in winter, when teaching was impossible, the hedge schoolmaster became an itinerant, relying on local hospitality" (Gould and Toomey, eds., *Mythologies* 343). Yeats's principal source of information about hedge schools was the novelist and short story writer William Carleton (1794–1869), who had been both hedge student and hedge master. Yeats included Carleton's "Hedge School" in his 1889 volume *Stories from Carleton.* In "Popular Ballad Poetry of Ireland," Yeats writes that the hedge schoolmaster, "with his zeal for learning, and his efforts, not often successful, to do creative work, was a not uninteresting forerunner of the modern man of letters" (*UP1* 149).

"Red Hanrahan" introduces the hero as a semi-respectable rural schoolmaster: a "tall, strong, red-haired young man" with his "little inkpot hanging from his neck by a chain, and his big Virgil and his primer in the skirt of his coat." Hanrahan is summoned to a barn where local men lounge on Samhain Eve, a festival marking the start of winter and, as Thuente writes, "celebrated as a night when fairies were especially active" (*W. B. Yeats and Irish Folklore* 203). One of the men has a message from

Mary Lavelle, Hanrahan's sweetheart; her mother has died and Hanrahan must hurry to her so they can be married. He prepares to depart immediately, but an "old mountainy man" lures him into a game of cards. The cards—"Spades and Diamonds, Courage and Power; Clubs and Hearts, Knowledge and Pleasure," as the old man says—become a hare and a pack of hounds. As if in a dream, Hanrahan follows the chase out the door and across the countryside, eventually coming to a "very big shining house" on Slieve Echtge ("a range of mountains stretching from Loughrea in County Galway to near Lough Derg on the Shannon in County Clare" [*Place Names* 45]). There four old women keep guard, each holding an object that corresponds to one of the suits in the deck of cards: a cauldron for pleasure, a stone for power, a spear for courage, and a sword for knowledge. Thuente discerns also a correspondence to "the four treasures of the Tuatha De Danann, the gods of ancient Ireland: the Cauldron of the Dagda, the Stone of Destiny, the Spear of Lug and the Sword of Nuada." She observes that Yeats "carefully links contemporary fairy legends with ancient Irish mythology" (*W. B. Yeats and Irish Folklore* 204; see also *IY* 29). Under this guard, a woman of perfect queenly beauty awaits a hero to free her from an enchanted torpor. Abashed by the magnificence of the house and the beauty of the woman, Hanrahan cannot find his tongue. He wakes the next morning in a field, never again to be a man entirely belonging to the mundane world. After a year spent dazedly wandering, he recalls Mary's summons. He finds her house empty and learns that she has married and gone "looking for work in London or Liverpool or some big place."

"The Twisting of the Rope" portrays Hanrahan well advanced in his estrangement from the mundane world. He has become a bedraggled wandering poet, both revered and feared by the local people, who believe he half belongs to the Sidhe. He comes to a door where there is fiddling and dancing. He joins the party and captivates Oona, the attractive daughter of the house. He coaxes her to come away with him to the "high hollow townland" beyond the reach of death (cf. *The* LAND OF HEART'S DESIRE). Oona's mother is afraid to have Hanrahan put out and so resorts to a trick. She asks him to twist a rope of hay. Showing off his skill at rope twisting, he backs himself into the road and she bolts the door against him.

"Hanrahan and Cathleen, the Daughter of Houlihan" tells how Hanrahan stopped for a time in the home of two woman, Margaret Rooney and Mary Gillis, and how the "bocachs [i.e., tramps] and blind men and fiddlers" would gather each night to hear him sing and recite. One night, thinking of "Ireland and the weight of grief that is on her," he sings of "Cathleen, the daughter of Houlihan" (cf. CATH-LEEN NI HOULIHAN), and the entire room falls into tears. The song is reprinted as "Red Hanrahan's Song about Ireland" in Yeats's collected poems.

"Red Hanrahan's Curse" finds Hanrahan with a small cabin and a few students. A young woman asks him to put a curse on her elderly fiancé, whom she calls as old as Hanrahan himself. Hanrahan suddenly feels the weight of his years, and he writes a song that curses everything old—himself, eagle, yew, pike, the old men of the neighborhood. He sends his students to sing the song where they will. The next day the old men come with sticks. They burn his cabin and Hanrahan "must go wandering again."

"Hanrahan's Vision" is the most lavishly styled of the Hanrahan stories. Hanrahan is upon Ben Bulben when he sees the vision of the story's title. A flutter of ROSE leaves turns into a procession of beautiful young men and women. Shadowy arms reach out of the mist without being able to grasp those that pass, and whirling in a train behind them are the Sidhe. He then sees a second procession of lovers "with heart-shaped mirrors" instead of hearts, each "looking on their own faces in one another's mirrors"; and then a procession of women with "wild beckoning arms" and bodies that are "but shadows without life." As in *The DREAMING OF THE BONES*, Dervorgilla and Diarmuid appear. They explain that those who had passed first were great lovers from legendary times; these had sought a "beauty that is as lasting as the night and the stars" and are thus preserved from "the warring and the perishing." Those who had passed second were lovers whose love was all self-triumph and vanity. Those who had passed third were women who desired nothing except to be loved. Unhappier than all of these are Dervorgilla and Diarmuid themselves. Having

"brought the Norman into Ireland" (cf. *The Dreaming of the Bones*), they are cursed to appear in each other's eyes as bodies long moldered in the earth. At this Hanrahan can only scream in terror.

"The Death of Hanrahan" finds Hanrahan old and beaten down and again wandering near Slieve Echtge, where had had seen the "shining house" of the queenly beauty years earlier. Here he meets the withered beggar Winny Byrne, who never ceases her cry "I am beautiful, I am beautiful." After a fall leaves him shaken and ill, he comes to her cabin and sees inside the four old women of "Red Hanrahan." Winny finds him and helps him to bed. As he declines, he hears voices and music in the rafters. As the moment of extremity approaches, Winny suddenly appears young and beautiful and embraces him with the words, "I am one of the lasting people, of the lasting unwearied Voices, that make my dwelling in the broken and the dying, and those that have lost their wits; and I came looking for you, and you are mine until the whole world is burned out like a candle that is spent." Looking about, Hanrahan sees that "the house was crowded with pale shadowy hands, and that every hand was holding what was sometimes like a wisp lighted for a marriage, and sometimes like a tall white candle for the dead."

Additionally, Hanrahan is one of the "person-ages" who recur as symbolic personae in the poems collected in *The Wind Among the Reeds* (1899). In a note to the volume, Yeats characterizes Hanrahan as "fire blown by the wind" and as "the simplicity of an imagination too changeable to gather perma-nent possessions, or the adoration of the shepherds" (VP 803). Sometimes under the name "O'Sullivan Rua" (see the discussion of Owen Rua O'Sullivan above), Hanrahan figures in many poems of the mid-1890s, including "He tells of the Perfect Beauty" and "A Poet to his Beloved," printed together under the title "O'Sullivan the Red to Mary Lavell" in the *Senate*, March 1896, and in *United Ireland*, April 4, 1896; "He REMEMBERS FOR-GOTTEN BEAUTY," titled "O'Sullivan Rua to Mary Lavell" in the *SAVOY*, July 1896; "He REPROVES THE CURLEW," titled "O'Sullivan Rua to the Curlew" in the *Savoy*, November 1896, and "Hanrahan reproves the Curlew" in *The Wind Among the Reeds*; "The Lover speaks to the Hearers of his Songs in

Coming Days," titled "Hanrahan speaks to the Hearers of his Songs in Coming Days" in *The Wind Among the Reeds*; "Maid Quiet," titled "O'Sullivan the Red upon his Wanderings" in the *New Review*, August 1897, and "Hanrahan laments because of his Wanderings" in *The Wind Among the Reeds*; and "The SECRET ROSE," titled "O'Sullivan Rua to the Secret Rose" in the *Savoy*, September 1896. Hanrahan is scarcer in the later poems. He is mentioned in "Alternative Song for the Severed Head in *The King of the Great Clock Tower*" (1934) and is revived with great significance in "The TOWER."

FIRST PUBLICATION: "Red Hanrahan" first appeared in the *Independent Review*, December 1903. "The Twisting of the Rope" first appeared in the *National Observer*, December 24, 1892. "Hanrahan and Cathleen, the Daughter of Houlihan" first appeared (under the title "Kathleen-Ny-Hoolihan") in the *National Observer*, August 4, 1894. "Red Hanrahan's Curse" first appeared (under the title "The Curse of O'Sullivan the Red upon Old Age") in the *National Observer*, September 29, 1894. "Hanrahan's Vision" first appeared (under the title "The Vision of O'Sullivan the Red") in the *New Review*, April 1896. "The Death of Hanrahan" first appeared (under the title "The Death of O'Sullivan the Red") in the *New Review*, December 1896.

BIBLIOGRAPHY

Ellmann, Richard. *The Identity of Yeats*; Thuente, Mary Helen. *W. B. Yeats and Irish Folklore*; McGarry, James P. *Place Names in the Writings of William Butler Yeats*; Wade, Allan. *A Bibliography of the Writings of W. B. Yeats*; Yeats, W. B., ed. *A Book of Irish Verse Selected from Modern Writers, Mythologies* (eds. Warwick Gould and Deirdre Toomey), *Prefaces and Introductions, The Secret Rose: A Variorum Edition, Uncollected Prose by W. B. Yeats* (vol. 1).

"Symbolism in Painting" (1898)

Emerging from the same moment and mindset as the "The SYMBOLISM OF POETRY," the essay extends Yeats's philosophy of symbolism to painting, a field he knew something about, having attended art school and spent much time in the studio of his father, JOHN BUTLER YEATS. Yeats begins by distinguishing between symbolism and allegory, the former being a wavering expression of vision or imagination, the latter a fixed system of correspondence (see the related discussion in section 4 of "The Symbolism of Poetry"). Yeats illustrates his point by contrasting Michelangelo's statue of a horned Moses in the church of San Pietro in Vinculi (located in Rome) and Tintoretto's painting *Origin of the Milky Way* (ca. 1577): "A hundred generations might write out what seemed the meaning of the one, and they would write different meanings, for no symbol tells all its meaning to any generation; but when you have said, 'That woman there is Juno, and the milk out of her breast is making the Milky Way,' you have told the meaning of the other, and the fine painting, which has added so much irrelevant beauty, has not told it better." As against mere "story-telling" and "portraiture," Yeats affirms the symbol as a talisman that "entangles, in complex colours and forms, a part of the Divine Essence" (*E&I* 148). Religious and visionary people see the same kind of symbols in their trances because "religious and visionary thought is thought about perfection and the way to perfection; and symbols are the only things free enough from all bonds to speak of perfection" (149). Yeats then gives examples of artists who have adopted the symbolic mode: Wagner, Keats, BLAKE, Edward Calvert (1799–1883), Dante Gabriel Rossetti (1828–82), Philippe-Auguste Villiers de l'Isle-Adam (1838–89), AUBREY BEARDSLEY, Charles Ricketts (1866–1931), Charles Shannon (1863–1937), James McNeill Whistler (1834–1903), Maurice Maeterlinck (1862–1949), and PAUL VERLAINE, all of whom, unlike their Christian forebears, accept "all symbolisms [. . .] all the Divine Intellect, its anger and its pity, its waking and its sleep, its love and its lust, for the substance of their art" (149). Yeats makes a further distinction between those like Keats and Calvert, who do not bring their symbols into some larger system of relation, and writers like Blake and Wagner, who set their symbols in the "great procession" (149–150). Though his veneration for those of the latter type is palpable,

Yeats admits such do not necessarily make the best artists, because the imagination is "too great to be bounded by a picture or a song," and because "so august a beauty moves before the mind that they forget the things which move before the eyes" (150; cf. "TO THE ROSE UPON THE ROOD OF TIME"). Having closed his eyes but a moment before and seen a blue-robed company that swept by in a blinding light, Yeats asks whether such a vision is a reflection of eternal reality in the "vegetable glass of nature" (Blake's phrase) or a "momentary dream." To answer, Yeats says in conclusion, "is to take sides in the only controversy in which it is greatly worth taking sides, and in the only controversy which may never be decided" (152).

"Symbolism in Painting" first appeared as the introduction to W. T. HORTON's A *Book of Images* (1898). Yeats cut the section dealing with Horton's own work when he reprinted the essay in *Ideas of Good and Evil* (1903). Horton was devastated by the omission, as he explained to Yeats in a letter of March 30, 1917: "The other evening I was at STURGE MOORE's shewing [sic] some of my drawings & he asked me how it was I was not publishing my drawings. I answered that somehow I lost all initiative after finishing a drawing—suddenly I realized what had originally caused this strange apathy & I told him—that it was ever since you dealt me that blow with reference to the introduction, in my 'Book of Images,' reprinted with no mention of me at all in your 'Ideas of Good & Evil.' I have never really got over that for it led many to think my work was of no further account in your eyes, or that I'd done something that made me no longer fit to be mentioned by you, or that I no longer drew, or was dead" (*W. B. Yeats and W. T. Horton* 132; see also CL2 184; CL3 400).

FIRST PUBLICATION: Untitled in W. T. Horton, *A Book of Images*, The Unicorn Press, London, March 1898. Reprinted as "Symbolism in Painting" in *Ideas of Good and Evil*, A. H. Bullen, London, May 1903 (the first two sections only).

BIBLIOGRAPHY

Harper, George Mills. *W. B. Yeats and W. T. Horton: A Record of an Occult Friendship*; Horton, W. T. A *Book of Images*; Yeats, W. B. *The Collected Letters of W. B. Yeats* (vols. 2–3), *Essays and Introductions*.

"Symbolism of Poetry, The" (1900)

Complementing "SYMBOLISM IN PAINTING" and "The AUTUMN OF THE BODY," the essay is a central statement of Yeats's early philosophy of literature and a testament to his eager appropriation of French symbolism. Yeats begins by defending the necessity of a philosophy of art in opposition to those of journalistic mentality who insist that art is unpremeditated and spontaneous. The quest for such a philosophy, Yeats explains, leads artists to the "inspiration of early times," and now writers "have begun to dwell upon the element of evocation, of suggestion, upon what we call the symbolism in great writers" (E&I 155). Yeats explains that all sounds, colors, and forms, either "because of their preordained energies or because of long association," evoke precise emotional response, or as he otherwise puts it, "call down among us certain disembodied powers, whose footsteps over our hearts we call emotions" (156–157). As expression becomes more perfect, so "the emotion, the power, the god it calls among us" becomes more powerful, and even a little lyric may eventually exert intangible but profound influence on the world (157–158). When he ponders even the most momentous wars and religious movements, Yeats says, he is never sure that "it has not all happened because of something that a boy piped in Thessaly" (158; Yeats airs the same notion in "MAGIC"; see 41). In this ceaseless shaping of the forms that channel the most potent energies, poets, artists, and musicians are "continually making and unmaking mankind," a notion that hews closely to SHELLEY's famous exaltation of poets as the "unacknowledged legislators of the World" in "A Defence of Poetry" (157). The purpose of rhythm, meanwhile, is to induce the kind of trance in which "the mind liberated from the pressure of the will is unfolded in symbols" (159).

Yeats proceeds to distinguish between two types of symbol: the emotional, which evokes the emotions alone, and the intellectual, which evokes ideas or some intermixture of ideas and emotions, and constitutes what is usually meant by the word "symbol." Yeats gives "a rushy pool in the moonlight" as an example of the former, the moon itself as an example of the latter, for the moon belongs to a larger order of meaning that encompasses "divine people, and things that have shaken off our mortality, the tower of ivory, the queen of waters, the shining stag among enchanted woods, the white hare sitting upon the hilltop [. . .]" (160–162). Yeats gets at the distinction in another way by citing Shakespeare as master of the emotional symbol, Dante as master of the intellectual symbol. Turning his attention to later eras, Yeats mentions Gérard de Nerval (1808–55), Maurice Maeterlink (1862–1949), and Philippe-Auguste Villiers de l'Isle-Adam (1838–89) as writers who have turned to intellectual symbols, thus foreshadowing "the new sacred book, of which all the arts, as somebody has said, are beginning to dream" (162). Yeats ends by asking what kind of poetry would follow from a general embrace of symbolism. His answer, running some 400 words, rivals the extravagant eloquence of Pater, whose influence is palpable; the crux is that poetry would cast out "those energetic rhythms, as of a man running, which are the invention of the will with its eyes always on something to be done or undone; and we would seek out those wavering, meditative, organic rhythms, which are the embodiment of the imagination, that neither desires nor hates, because it has done with time, and only wishes to gaze upon some reality, some beauty [. . .]" (164).

"The Symbolism of Poetry" had its germ in an unpublished letter that Yeats sent to the Dublin *Daily Express* in November 1898 (CL2 294–298). The letter was part of an ongoing debate in the pages of the *Daily Express* sparked by JOHN EGLINTON's article "What should be the Subjects of a National Drama?" The full newspaper exchange, with contributions from Yeats, Eglinton, GEORGE RUSSELL (AE), and William Larminie (1849–1900), is collected in the 1899 anthology LITERARY IDEALS IN IRELAND.

FIRST PUBLICATION: The *Dome* (periodical), April 1900. Reprinted in *Ideas of Good and Evil*, A. H. Bullen, London, May 1903.

BIBLIOGRAPHY
Yeats, W. B. *The Collected Letters of W. B. Yeats* (vol. 2), *Essays and Introductions*.

"Tables of the Law, The" (1897)

One of three early tales of Michael Robartes and Owen Aherne, "The Tables of the Law" follows "ROSA ALCHEMICA" and precedes "The ADORATION OF THE MAGI" in narrative order. Lacking the prismatic splendor of "Rosa Alchemica" or the mythic potency of "The Adoration of the Magi," "The Tables of the Law" might be considered the least of the three stories. Yeats himself thought little of either "The Tables of the Law" or "The Adoration of the Magi"; in JOHN QUINN's copy of the 1897 volume that contained both stories Yeats wrote, "The portrait which is by my father, & the Latin which is by LIONEL JOHNSON, are the only things which are worth anything in this little book" (*Biblio.* 43). JAMES JOYCE, on the other hand, thought highly of the tales and called "The Adoration of the Magi" a "story which one of the great Russians might have written" (*Critical Writings* 71). When Joyce met Yeats for the first time he told him how much he admired the stories and urged him to reprint them (*My Brother's Keeper* 180). In his brief prefatory note to the 1904 edition of *The Tables of the Law* and *The Adoration of the Magi*, Yeats acknowledged Joyce's prodding: "I do not think I should have reprinted them had I not met a young man in Ireland the other day who liked them very much and nothing else at all that I have written" (*Critical Writings* 71; Gould and Toomey, eds., *Mythologies* li). Though it may be a "text for exposition" more than a story proper, "The Tables of the Law" redeems itself by the subtlety and intensity of its heretical vision, and in this respect anticipates, for example, "SUPERNATURAL SONGS" (VP 821).

"The Tables of the Law" tells of two encounters between Owen Aherne and an unnamed narrator (evidently a version of Yeats himself) who had known Aherne years earlier when both had been students in PARIS and members of a small circle devoted to alchemy and mysticism. Over dinner, the narrator, seeing a chance to satisfy an old curiosity, asks why Aherne never became a cleric of the Catholic Church. In explanation, Aherne leads the narrator to his private chapel and shows him, upon the altar, an ornate bronze box containing the lone surviving copy of *Liber inducens in Evangelium aeternum*, a "secret book" written by the 12th-century abbot Joachim of Flora and passed down from generation to generation (on Joachim, see Gould and Toomey, eds., *Mythologies* 403–406). Aherne describes the heretical doctrines of the book, which displace the commandments of the Father and Son with those of the Holy Spirit. In Aherne's encapsulation, Joachim secretly taught that certain men "were elected, not to live, but to reveal that hidden substance of God which is colour and music and softness and a sweet odour; and that these have no father but the Holy Spirit. Just as poets and painters and musicians labour at their works, building them with lawless and lawful things alike, so long as they embody the beauty that is beyond the grave, these children of the Holy Spirit labour at their moments with eyes upon the shining substance on which Time has heaped the refuse of creation; for the world only exists to be a tale in the ears of coming generations; and terror and content, birth and death, love and hatred, and the fruit of the Tree, are but instruments for that supreme art which is to win us from life and gather us into eternity like doves into their dove-cots" (*Myth.* 300–301). Growing excited, Aherne announces that he shall travel the world and upon his return write his own "secret law" upon the empty ivory tablets with which he has replaced the tablets bearing the biblical commandments; and that he will gather pupils "that they may discover their law in the study of my law, and the Kingdom of the Holy Spirit be more widely and firmly established" (301). Upon returning to Aherne's house a few days later the narrator finds him departed.

Ten years later the narrator glimpses Aherne along the Dublin quays and attempts unsuccessfully to follow him; he makes inquiries and knocks on Aherne's door, but to no avail. Weeks later he glimpses Aherne again and follows him home.

Aherne reluctantly admits him to the house, now covered in dust and cobwebs, and shows him the ivory tablets, which have been finely engraved in Latin. Aherne confesses that the philosophy of Joachim has been his ruin, for he has realized that man can enter the heart of God only by sin and repentance. "It may be," he says, "that the angels who have hearts of the Divine Ecstasy, and bodies of the Divine Intellect, need nothing but a thirst for the immortal element, in hope, in desire, in dreams; but we whose hearts perish every moment, and whose bodies melt away like a sigh, must bow and obey!" (305). The retreat into orthodoxy, however, is no longer possible: "I have seen the whole, and how can I come again to believe that a part is the whole? I have lost my soul because I have looked out of the eyes of the angels" (306). The narrator then sees a vision of purple-robed figures who hover about Aherne and sigh over his sorrow, and he hears a voice cry, "He has charged even his angels with folly, and they also bow and obey; but let your heart mingle with our hearts, which are wrought of divine ecstasy, and your body with our bodies, which are wrought of divine intellect" (306). The narrator is full of terror, perceiving the robed figures as tempters who would dissolve all that bound him to "spiritual and social order" and leave his soul "naked and shivering among the winds that blow from beyond this world and from beyond the stars." He flees the house, and never again dares to pass it in the street, though he believes Aherne to "have been driven into some distant country by the spirits whose name is legion, and whose throne is in the indefinite abyss, and whom he obeys and cannot see" (307).

FIRST PUBLICATION: The SAVOY (periodical), November 1896. Reprinted in *The Tables of the Law. The Adoration of the Magi*, privately printed, June 1897. According to Allan Wade: "Although described as 'privately printed,' copies of this book were advertised in some of Lawrence and Bullen's catalogues for sale at five shillings each" (*Biblio.* 43). In a 1925 note, Yeats explains that "The Tables of the Law" and "The Adoration of the Magi" were "intended to be part of *The Secret Rose* [1897], but the publisher, A. H. Bullen, took a distaste to them and asked me to leave them out, and then after the book was published liked them and put them into a little volume by themselves" (*Myth.* 1).

BIBLIOGRAPHY

Joyce, James. *The Critical Writings*; Joyce, Stanislaus. *My Brother's Keeper: James Joyce's Early Years*; Wade, Allan. *A Bibliography of the Writings of W. B. Yeats*; Yeats, W. B. *Mythologies, Mythologies* (eds. Warwick Gould and Deirdre Toomey), *The Variorum Edition of the Poems of W. B. Yeats*.

Vision, A (1925, 1937)

First published in 1925 and extensively revised for republication in 1937, Yeats's only extended philosophical work, like JAMES JOYCE's *Finnegans Wake* and EZRA POUND's *Cantos*, exemplifies modernism's willingness to test the limits of comprehensibility in pursuit of an all-encompassing vision. *A Vision* is full of idiosyncratic terminology, but its more basic difficulty is that, in the tradition of high modernist experiment, it baffles our settled habits of interpretation and forces us to ponder the mystery not only of what it says but of *what it is*. Are we to take seriously its putative coherence or to make what use we can of its sometimes brilliant, sometimes maddening parts and pieces? Are we to extract from the husk of its system an implicit poetry? Is its system the essence of its poetry? Does it shed light on the world or merely on Yeats? What light does it shed on the poems and plays? Are its junctures of impenetrable obscurity strategic or botched? How to evaluate the epistemological status of a system allegedly communicated by spirits? Are its putative truths figurative or literal? These are but a few of the questions to which there are no easy answers. Yeats himself was coy about the status of his system. In a June 1925 letter to his young friend L. A. G. Strong (1896–1958), he spoke of *A Vision* as a "form of science for the study of human nature" (*Letters* 709), but in his introduction to the 1937 edition—dated "November 23rd 1928, and later"—he is less staunch about the "science" of it: "Some will ask whether I believe in the actual

existence of my circuits of sun and moon. [. . .] To such a question I can but answer that if sometimes, overwhelmed by miracle as all men must be when in the midst of it, I have taken such periods literally, my reason has soon recovered; and now that the system stands out clearly in my imagination I regard them as stylistic arrangements of experience comparable to the cubes in the drawing of Wyndham Lewis and to the ovoids in the sculpture of Brancusi. They have helped me to hold in a single thought reality and justice" (*AV* 24–25). Writing to OLIVIA SHAKESPEAR in February 1931, Yeats professed to have constructed a "myth" and observed in his own defense that "one can believe in a myth—one only assents to philosophy" (*Letters* 781).

A Vision's status as a record of supernatural revelation is complicated—perhaps belied—by its clear emergence from Yeats's most habitual patterns of thought. A. Norman Jeffares suggests that this distinction between *antithetical* and *primary* may ultimately trace to the familial distinction between Pollexfen and Yeats upon which JOHN BUTLER YEATS loved to mull (*New Biography* 206–207). "The SONG OF THE HAPPY SHEPHERD" (1885) heralds *A Vision*'s conception of alternating *antithetical* and *primary* eras ("Of old the world on dreaming fed; / Grey Truth is now her painted toy"). "The WANDERINGS OF OISIN" (1889) explicitly renders this an alternation between pagan and Christian eras, as well as introduces *A Vision*'s distinction between subjective and objective men in the figures of Oisin and Patrick. "TO THE ROSE UPON THE ROOD OF TIME" (1892) locates the same divide within the single breast and thus predicts *A Vision*'s conviction that the "individual soul," no less than human history, oscillates between *antithetical* and *primary* (*AV* 89). The poems and stories of the 1890s introduce Michael Robartes and Owen Aherne as opposite personality types and forerunners of the distinction between subjective and objective men (see, for example, "The ADORATION OF THE MAGI," "ROSA ALCHEMICA," and "The TABLES OF THE LAW"). They reappear with much the same significance in the framing material of both the 1925 and 1937 editions of *A Vision*. Yeats had clearly formalized both the distinction between *antithetical* and *primary* and the cyclic theory of history by August 1908, when he began to write "AT GALWAY RACES," a poem obviously pregnant with the doctrines of *A Vision* (YC 121–122).

As Thomas R. Whitaker argues, Yeats's conceptualization of history as a cycle of alternating eras has numerous precedents in his early reading. There are related conceptions in A. P. Sinnett's *Esoteric Buddhism* (1883), which describes "the ebbing and flowing of the tide wave of humanity, and the great wheel which begins in Nirvana or the 'subjective side of Nature,' cycles through the 'objective side of Nature' under the impulse of Karma and of Tanka [. . .] and finally returns to its Source" (23–24); in THEOSOPHICAL doctrine, according to which "all evolution results from the conflict between the individuality of Lucifer (which Yeats would later call *antithetical*) and the transcendence of Christ (which he would call *primary*)" (24); in what were for Yeats basic poetic texts like BLAKE's prophetic books, Byron's *Childe Harold's Pilgrimage*, SHELLEY's *Hellas*, and Arnold's "Dover Beach" (25, 29); in the thought of Thomas Carlyle and followers such as John Ruskin, WILLIAM MORRIS, Standish James O'Grady (1846–1928), Edward Carpenter (1844–1929), and JOHN EGLINTON (30); and in Arthur Hallam's essay "On Some of the Characteristics of Modern Poetry and on the Lyrical Poems of Alfred Tennyson" (1831), which "argued that the '*objective* amelioration' brought by modern machinery would cause a 'decrease of *subjective* power' as the 'higher feelings' were absorbed into the 'palpable interests of ordinary life'" (31; on Hallam's essay, see *Aut.* 358, 361; *E&I* 347–349; *UP1* 276–277; *UP2* 34, 88–89, 130). In *A Vision*, Yeats mentions Empedocles, Heraclitus, Plato, Swedenborg, and Blake as forerunners of his philosophy of the gyre, while his correspondent Dr. Frank Pearce Sturm had sent him pertinent passages in Thomas Aquinas, John Dee (1527–1608), Macrobius (ca. fifth century), and "an unknown mediaeval writer" (*AV* 67–72; *AV-1925* xi–xii). Among contemporary writers who influenced or concurred in his theory of history, Yeats mentions Austrian art critic Josef Strzygowski (1862–1941), German explorer and ethnologist Leo Frobenius (1873–1938), American historian and philosopher Henry Adams (1838–1918), British Egyptologist Flinders Petrie (1853–1942), and German philosopher Oswald Spengler (1880–1936) (257–262; see also *Swan and Shadow* 82–84). Nietzsche's conception of the "eternal recurrence" and his distinction between "Dionysian" and "Apollonian" (roughly congruent with the distinction between *antithetical* and *primary*) were another likely influence (see *AV* 299; *CL3* 372).

Yeats may have been encouraged in his presiding motifs of wheel and gyre by his long immersion in the HERMETIC ORDER OF THE GOLDEN DAWN. The group's rituals, Virginia Moore quips, were "as full of wheels as a watch shop" (*Unicorn* 263; see also 274–277). Also rooted in Yeats's occult activities was the postulation of moon and sun as symbolic metaphysical poles, the former *antithetical,* the latter *primary.* This conception is germinal in the 1897 poem "The SONG OF WANDERING AENGUS," which itself translates occult sources and the ritual of the Golden Dawn. In an 1898 notebook, Yeats stated simply and presciently, "Solar vision objective. Moon vision subjective" (*Unicorn* 265). He makes a comparable distinction between sun and moon in "The PHILOSOPHY OF SHELLEY's POETRY" (*E&I* 91–95) and in an 1904 analysis of Conchubar and CUCHULAIN that he sent to Frank Fay (1870–1931), who was to play the latter in the debut performance of ON BAILE'S STRAND (*CL3* 527). "ON WOMAN" (1916) establishes the moon as the presiding deity of apocalyptic shifts in what *A Vision* calls "tincture," while "LINES WRITTEN IN DEJECTION" (1917) in effect formalizes the symbolic opposition between moon and sun.

A Vision's apocalyptic dynamic has countless potential sources in religious, occult, mythological, and poetic traditions. It is perhaps most basically rooted in the Bible; in Shelley's *Prometheus Unbound* (1820), which was Yeats's "sacred book" as a youth (*Aut.* 95; *E&I* 65); and in Irish legends like that of the Black Pig (see *VP* 808–811). In Yeats's own work, the apocalyptic is an obvious keynote from the 1890s onward, as in "HE HEARS THE CRY OF THE SEDGE," "He mourns for the Change that has come upon him and his Beloved, and longs for the End of the World" (1897), "HE REMEMBERS FORGOTTEN BEAUTY," "He tells of a Valley full of Lovers"

(1897), "He tells of the Perfect Beauty" (1896), "IN THE SEVEN WOODS," "The Moods" (1897), "The ROSE OF BATTLE," "The SECRET ROSE," "The VALLEY OF THE BLACK PIG," and WHERE THERE IS NOTHING. A mature poem of apocalypse like "The SECOND COMING" merely aligns this old expectancy with Yeats's emergent philosophic framework.

Most proximately, *A Vision* builds on the ideas of PER AMICA SILENTIA LUNAE, a brief and beautifully "marmorean" philosophical treatise that appeared in January 1918. It introduced several concepts—daimon, mask, antiself—that recur in *A Vision*, and it groped toward the conception of the historical gyre. In the key passage, Yeats notes "the winding movement of nature," and opines parenthetically, "I do not doubt those heaving circles, those winding arcs, whether in one man's life or in that of an age, are mathematical, and that some in the world, or beyond the world, have foreknown the event and pricked upon the calendar the life-span of a Christ, a Buddha, a Napoleon: that every movement, in feeling or in thought, prepares in the dark by its own increasing clarity and confidence its own executioner" (*LE* 14).

In the leap from *Per Amica* to *A Vision*, the story takes a strange turn. While honeymooning in October 1917, Yeats fell into a "great gloom" (*Letters* 633). GEORGE YEATS tried to mend the situation by a display of "automatic writing." As if channeling spirits, she scribbled the reassurance that ISEULT GONNE was "well at heart" and that marriage had been the right decision (633). In the middle of what began as a harmless ruse, George felt her hand genuinely gripped by a controlling force and continued to write (*BG* 102–103; *Unicorn* 253). In the 1937 edition of *A Vision*, Yeats revealed the secret of these circumstances against his wife's wishes: "On the afternoon of October 24th 1917, four days after my marriage, my wife surprised me by attempting automatic writing. What came in disjointed sentences, in almost illegible writing, was so exciting, sometimes so profound, that I persuaded her to give an hour or two day after day to the unknown writer, and after some half-dozen such hours offered to spend what remained of life explaining and piecing together those scattered sentences. 'No,' was the answer, 'we have come to give you metaphors for

poetry'" (8). George Yeats told Richard Ellmann that Yeats's insistence on candor "provoked the most painful quarrel, perhaps the only serious one of their marriage" (*Yeats's Second Puberty*).

Within two weeks of their marriage, as Ann Saddlemyer writes, the newlyweds "began to look upon George's script as an ongoing record of revelation which should be properly annotated and preserved" (*BG* 105). It was the usual arrangement that Yeats asked questions and George, in a state of hypnotic trance, translated responses from various controls or "instructors." The first three years of the marriage were feverishly busy; over the first seven years, 450 automatic writing sessions yielded 3,627 preserved pages of script, while George's "philosophical sleeps" yielded another 270 pages (*AV-1925* xix–xxi). In *A Vision*, Yeats recalls the inception of the book's doctrines in the automatic writing sessions. At first taking his theme from *Per Amica*, the "unknown writer" began with Yeats's distinction "between the perfection that is from a man's combat with himself and that which is from a combat with circumstance, and upon this simple distinction he built up an elaborate classification of men according to their more or less complete expression of one type or the other. He supported his classification by a series of geometrical symbols and put these symbols in an order that answered the question [in *Per Amica*] as to whether some prophet could not prick upon the calendar the birth of a Napoleon or a Christ. A system of symbolism, strange to my wife and to myself, certainly awaited expression, and when I asked how long that would take I was told years" (8–9).

By January 1918, Yeats had begun *A Vision*, which he provisionally called *The Discoveries of Michael Robartes* (*Letters* 644). Yeats wrote to Lady GREGORY on January 4, "A very profound, very exciting mystical philosophy—which seems the fulfillment of many dreams and prophecies—is coming in strange ways to George and myself. [. . .] It is coming into my work a great deal and makes me feel that for the first time I understand human life. I am writing it all out in a series of dialogues about a supposed medieval book, the *Speculum Angelorum et Hominum* by Giraldus, and a sect of Arabs called the Judwalis (diagrammatists)." He added,

"I live with a strange sense of revelation and never know what the day will bring. You will be astonished at the change in my work, at its intricate passion" (643–644; on the origin of Giraldus in the automatic script, see *Making of Yeats's 'A Vision'*, II, 213). Yeats later abandoned the dialogue format and transformed this material into the fanciful framing device of the 1925 edition of *A Vision*, which was duly subtitled "An Explanation of Life Founded upon the Writings of Giraldus and upon Certain Doctrines Attributed to Kusta Ben Luka." Yeats labored on *A Vision* for another seven years, though giving advance notice of its doctrines in poems like "The CAT AND THE MOON" (1918), "The DOUBLE VISION OF MICHAEL ROBARTES" (1919), "The PHASES OF THE MOON" (1919), "Shepherd and Goatherd" (1919), "DEMON AND BEAST" (1920), "The Second Coming" (1920), and "MY TABLE" (1923); in plays like CALVARY (1921) and *The CAT AND THE MOON* (1924); and in prose works like *The Trembling of the Veil* (1921–22) and "The Bounty of Sweden" (1924).

T. Werner Laurie of London finally published *A Vision*—the first and only publication of the 1925 text during Yeats's lifetime—in an edition of 600 numbered and signed copies (*Biblio.* 151–153). It was issued to subscribers on January 15, 1926, and met with a deafening silence, as Yeats complained to Shakespear in March 1926: "*A Vision* reminds me of the stones I used to drop as a child into a certain very deep well. The splash is very far off and very faint. Not a review except one by AE—either the publisher has sold the review copies or the editors have—and no response of any kind except from a very learned doctor in the North of England who sends me profound and curious extracts from ancient philosophies on the subject of gyres. A few men here are reading me, so I may found an Irish heresy" (*Letters* 712). The learned doctor was Frank Pearce Sturm (1879–1942), a surgeon, poet, and mystic whom Yeats had known since 1902 and with whom he had previously corresponded (see AV 69; CL3 256). Yeats later described him as one of *A Vision*'s few "very devoted readers" and yet later wrote that much of the 1937 edition was intended for him alone (*Letters* 781, 899). The review by AE (see GEORGE RUSSELL), deeply respectful if unsure of its footing, appeared in the *Irish Statesman* on February 13, 1926. AE acknowledges the extraordinary complexity, beauty, and scope of *A Vision*, but he is unable to judge whether it will join Blake's prophetic books as an inscrutable masterpiece or ultimately come to seem Yeats's "greatest erring from the way of his natural genius" (*Critical Heritage* 272). AE raises at least one question that would nag at *A Vision*: the extent to which the foreordination of its cycles is compatible with free will (269–270).

By April 1928, Yeats was at work on "the final version" of *A Vision*, which he expected to complete the following year (*Letters* 739, 742). As it happened, the new edition, a sweeping transformation, did not appear until October 1937, when Macmillan brought out the revised work in an edition of 1,500 copies (*Biblio.* 191–192). In his introduction to the new edition, Yeats confesses that, excepting only the sections titled "The Twenty-Eight Embodiments" and "Dove or Swan," the 1925 edition fills him with shame. "I had misinterpreted the geometry," he admits, "and in my ignorance of philosophy failed to understand distinctions upon which the coherence of the whole depended, and as my wife was unwilling that her share should be known, and I to seem sole author, I had invented an unnatural story of an Arabian traveller which I must amend and find a place for some day because I was fool enough to write half a dozen poems that are unintelligible without it" (AV 19).

The 1937 edition reprises "The Phases of the Moon" (as prologue), "The Twenty-Eight Embodiments" (lightly revised and retitled "The Twenty-Eight Incarnations"), "Dove or Swan" (lightly revised and truncated, with "LEDA AND THE SWAN" retained as its first section), and "ALL SOULS' NIGHT" (as epilogue), but otherwise reorders, rewrites, and amplifies upon the earlier edition. Its front matter abandons both the dedication to "Vestigia" (i.e., Moina Mathers) and the two pieces fancifully attributed to Owen Aherne: first, the introduction recounting Michael Robartes's discovery of the doctrines of *A Vision* in the fictitious *Speculum Angelorum et Hominorum* ("Mirror of Angels and Men") and in the traditions of the equally fictitious Judwalis tribe of Arabia, and second, "The Dance of the Four Royal Persons," which tells how the philosopher Kusta ben Luka converted the Arabian caliph to the truths of the "Great Wheel" (cf. "The Gift of Harun Al-Rashid," which appears in the 1925 edition as Book II, Section 1). Replacing these are "A Packet for Ezra Pound" (first published by the Cuala Press in 1929, and here functioning as a relatively conventional introduction) and a new story of Michael Robartes and Owen Aherne, much in the manner of the stories of the 1890s. The story embeds several symbolic narrations as Robartes's pupils tell their stories and Robartes himself recounts his discovery of the *Speculum* in a Viennese tenement and his sojourn among the Judwalis. Robartes then presents his followers with the "lost egg of Leda" (cf. "Leda and the Swan"), which he intends to bury in the desert, where it will seed a new *antithetical* era to be born of warfare (cf. "The Second Coming"). *A Vision*, it might be said, attempts to explain the metaphysics by which such reversals are woven into the very pattern of reality.

The 1937 edition divides technical discussion into five books: (1) "The Great Wheel" (consisting of "The Principal Symbol," "Examination of the Wheel," and "The Twenty-Eight Incarnations"), (2) "The Completed Symbol," (3) "The Soul in Judgment," (4) "The Great Year of the Ancients," and (5) "Dove or Swan." This neat superstructure, however, conceals teeming complexity and pockets of befuddling oracular mystery. In his review of the 1925 edition, Russell acknowledges being "unable in a brief space to give the slightest idea" of *A Vision*'s technical complexity, for "almost any of its crammed pages would need a volume to elucidate its meanings" (*Critical Heritage* 272). Virginia Moore offers with only a little less alarm that to "comment on every detail would take three books" (*Unicorn* 261). Helen Vendler encapsulates the dilemma: "There are two dangers involved in trying to explain *A Vision*: one is the risk of being swamped by detail, in an effort toward fidelity; the other is the temptation to ignore important details in order to make some schematization work" (*Later Plays* 48). *A Vision*'s basic lines can be roughly sketched, but only on the understanding that there is far more to say in all instances; that Yeats does not answer all questions; that all is open to inter-

pretation and to debate. Vendler's second danger is the pertinent one.

In "The Great Wheel," Yeats introduces his central intuition that reality is a tension of opposed forces whose image is two interlocked "gyres," "vortexes," or "cones," the vertex of one centered upon the base of the other, each dying into the life of the other. Yeats associates one gyre with objectivity or what he calls the *primary tincture,* and the other gyre with "subjectivity" or what he calls the *antithetical tincture.* The tinctures are nothing less than the defining poles of human reality; from the shifting proportions of their influence all human manifestations derive their essential character. The *primary tincture* is characterized by externality and factuality, while the *antithetical tincture* expresses "our inner world of desire and imagination" (*AV* 73). Put even more succinctly: "The *primary* is that which serves, the *antithetical* is that which creates" (85). In a note to *Calvary*, Yeats observes that objective men, "however personally alone, are never alone in their thought, which is always developed in agreement or in conflict with the thought of others and always seeks the welfare of some cause or institution, while subjective men are the more lonely the more they are true to type, seeking always that which is unique or personal" (*VPl.* 789). Culturally and historically, Yeats associates the *primary tincture* with "necessity, truth, goodness, mechanism, science, democracy, abstraction, peace," while he associates the *antithetical tincture* with "freedom, fiction, evil, kindred, art, aristocracy, particularity, war" (*AV* 52). He reiterates that a "*primary* dispensation looking beyond itself towards a transcendent power is dogmatic, levelling, unifying, feminine, humane, peace its means and end; an *antithetical* dispensation obeys imminent power, is expressive, hierarchical, multiple, masculine, harsh, surgical" (263; see also 277).

Yeats further introduces *Four Faculties* consisting of two pairs of opposed terms: *Will* and *Mask, Creative Mind* and *Body of Fate,* with *Mask* and *Creative Mind* further subdivided into "True" and "False." Yeats describes *Will* and *Mask* "as the will and its object, or the Is and the Ought (or that which should be)," and *Creative Mind* and *Body* of Fate "as thought and its object, or the Knower and the Known." *Will* and *Mask* "are lunar or *antithetical* or natural," while *Creative Mind* and *Body of Fate* are "solar or *primary* or reasonable" (73). The *Faculties* can be represented, Yeats writes, "by two opposing cones so drawn that the *Will* of the one is the *Mask* of the other, the *Creative Mind* of the one the *Body of Fate* of the other," which is to say that *Will* and *Mask* are inversions of each other, as are *Creative Mind* and *Body of Fate* (73). These opposing cones—rendered as triangles in Yeats's diagrams—can be superimposed on the cones of the *tinctures,* creating a full map of being. *Will* and *Creative Mind* mark the angles of one hypotenuse; *Mask* and *Body of Fate* mark the angles of the other; *Will* is opposite to *Mask* and *Creative Mind* opposite to *Body of Fate* (77). The *Four Faculties,* moreover, are related to the *Daimon* or antiself discussed in "The Completed Symbol," as well as in *Per Amica* and "Ego Dominus Tuus." Yeats calls the *Four Faculties* "the result of the four memories of the *Daimon* or ultimate self." A person's "*Body of Fate,* the series of events forced upon him from without, is shaped out of the *Daimon's* memory of the events of his past incarnations; his *Mask* or object of desire or idea of the good, out of its memory of the moments of exaltation in his past lives; his *Will* or normal ego out of its memory of all the events of his present life, whether consciously remembered or not; his *Creative Mind* from its memory of ideas—or universals—displayed by actual men in past lives, or their spirits between lives" (83). Yeats somewhat clarifies the exceedingly difficult scheme of the *Four Faculties* by a metaphor from the commedia dell'arte: "The stage-manager, or *Daimon,* offers his actor an inherited scenario, the *Body of Fate,* and a *Mask* or rôle as unlike as possible to his natural ego or *Will,* and leaves him to improvise through his *Creative Mind* the dialogue and details of the plot. He must discover or reveal a being which only exists with extreme effort, when his muscles are as it were all taut and all his energies active. But this is *antithetical* man. For *primary* man I go to the *Commedia dell' Arte* in its decline. The *Will* is weak and cannot create a rôle, and so, if it transform itself, does so after an accepted pattern, some traditional clown or pantaloon" (84).

Yeats extrapolates the figure of a circle from the four points of intersection between the two interlocked gyres of the tinctures (79–80), and this he associates with the 28 phases of the moon (cf. "The Phases of the Moon," which introduces A *Vision*). The point at which the vertex of the *antithetical* gyre meets the base of the *primary* gyre represents Phase 1, the phase of complete objectivity, the phase of the moonless night. The point at which the vertex of the *primary* gyre meets the base of the *antithetical* gyre represents Phase 15, the phase of complete subjectivity, the phase of the full moon. Phase 1 and Phase 15, as Yeats stipulates, "are not human incarnations because human life is impossible without strife between the *tinctures*" (79). At these phases there occurs what Yeats calls the "interchange of the tinctures," according to which "those thoughts, emotions, energies, which were *primary* before Phase 15 or Phase 1 are *antithetical* after, those that were *antithetical* are *primary*" (89). Phase 8 initiates the struggle to find personality and begins the *antithetical* phases of the lunar cycle (phases in which the moon is more bright than dark), while Phase 22 initiates the struggle to lose personality and begins the *primary* phases (phases in which the moon is more dark than bright). As Yeats has it, all people, cultures, and eras belong to one or another phase of the moon, according to the place of the *Will* upon the lunar wheel (73, 79). A man is assigned to Phase 17, for example, because his *Will* belongs to Phase 17. *Mask, Creative Mind,* and *Body of Fate* follow from the phase of the *Will* according to the geometry of the interlocked gyres as superimposed upon the lunar wheel. As the two bases rotate, their vertices determine the phases of the *Four Faculties.* If, for example, *Will* is at Phase 17—Yeats's own phase—*Mask* is at Phase 3, *Creative Mind* is at Phase 13, and *Body of Fate* is at Phase 27 (*Book of Yeats's Vision* 78). Furthermore, every phase is "in itself a wheel," and the individual soul turns, as it were, upon its own axis. Yeats comments that the "individual soul is awakened by a violent oscillation (one thinks of Verlaine oscillating between the church and the brothel) until it sinks in on that Whole where the contraries are united, the antinomies resolved" (AV 89). Poems like "A Dialogue of Self and Soul," "To the

Rose upon the Rood of Time," and "Vacillation" document precisely this pattern of oscillation, while the second section of "A Dialogue of
Self and Soul" and the fourth section of "Vacillation" intimate the moment of resolved antinomy.

In the subsection titled "The Twenty-Eight
Incarnations," Yeats characterizes each lunar
phase and gives examples of men and women of
each phase, in effect providing a complete table
of human nature. Vendler remarks that "Yeats's
classification becomes nearly a new morality, with
a sinless prototype [marked by Phase 15] and varying degrees of approach to that prototype, as we
are shown a whole and perfect being surrounded
by a group of incomplete aspirants to his perfection. The wording of the descriptions of the early
phases leaves no doubt that those phases are stages
in progress toward Phase 15, and that subjectivity
and personality are the great goals" (*Later Plays*
27). Yeats's placement of his own friends is intriguing in its revelation of his genuine sense of them.
Aubrey Beardsley and Ernest Dowson, cronies of the 1890s, are assigned to Phase 13 (with
Baudelaire), Oscar Wilde to 19 (with Byron and
Gabriele d'Annunzio), George Bernard Shaw and
George Moore to 21 (with Lamarck and H. G.
Wells), J. M. Synge to 23 (with Rembrandt), Lady
Gregory to 24 (with Queen Victoria and John
Galsworthy), and George Russell (AE) to 25 (with
Cardinal Newman, Luther, Calvin, and George
Herbert). In his review of the 1925 edition, Russell pronounces himself "a little uncomfortable"
with some of his "fellow-prisoners" in Phase 25,
and he speculates that Yeats's designations are not
without a certain "impish humour"; he had particularly in mind the dismissive lumping of Moore
and Shaw with the prosaic Wells (*Critical Heritage* 271). Lady Gregory likewise complained in
her journal, "[Yeats] had told me my division, 24,
was 'a very good one', but I don't know that I like
being classed [. . .] with Queen Victoria!! So do
we appear to our friends. But I don't think she
could have written *Seven Short Plays*" (*Lady Gregory's Journals*, II, 45). Equally revealing is Yeats's
placement of the writers who mattered most to
him. Nietzsche is assigned to Phase 12, Keats to
14 (with Giorgione and "many beautiful women"),

Blake to 16 (with Rabelais, Aretino, Paracelsus,
and "some beautiful women"), Dante, Shelley, and
Walter Savage Landor to 17, Goethe and Matthew
Arnold to 18, Shakespeare and Balzac to 20 (with
Napoleon). Though he does not say so in *A Vision*,
Yeats considered himself a man of Phase 17, the
phase of "*Daimonic* Man" in which Unity of Being
and "consequent expression of *Daimonic* thought"
is most easy (*Making of Yeats's 'A Vision'*, II, 116).
At this phase, true *Mask* is "simplification through
intensity," while false mask is "dispersal" (see AV
90–92, 140–145). As a man of Phase 17, Yeats
was nestled with telling symbolism between Maud
Gonne at Phase 16 and George Yeats at Phase 18
(*Making of Yeats's 'A Vision'*, II, 116).

In "The Completed Symbol"—easily the most
bewildering of *A Vision*'s five books—Yeats complicates his already complicated scheme by introducing the *Four Principles—Husk, Passionate Body,
Spirit,* and *Celestial Body*—to complement the *Four
Faculties.* The *Faculties,* Yeats explains, "are man's
voluntary and acquired powers and their objects;
the *Principles* are the innate ground of the *Faculties,*
and must act upon one another in the same way"
(AV 187). *Spirit* and *Celestial Body* (like *Creative
Mind* and *Body of Fate*) are "mind and its object,"
while *Husk* and *Passionate Body* (like *Will* and *Mask*)
are "sense and the object of sense" (187–188). As
the interlocked gyres of the *Faculties* are mapped
onto the 28 phases of the lunar cycle divided, so the
interlocked gyres of the *Principles* are mapped onto
the 12 months of the solar cycle (188). As the *Four
Faculties* relate to human nature, the *Four Principles*
relate to *Daimonic* nature: The *Husk* represents "the
Daimon's hunger to make apparent to itself certain
Daimons, and the organs of sense are that hunger
made visible"; the *Passionate Body* is "the sum of
those *Daimons*"; the *Spirit* is "the *Daimon's* knowledge, for in the *Spirit* it knows all other *Daimons*
as the Divine Ideas in their unity"; *Celestial Body*
is the achieved condition of this unity—speaking
of the Daimons, Yeats says simply, "They are one
in the *Celestial Body*" (189). Attempting to make
sense of this, Hazard Adams comments that the
"Daimon is a symbol of our own pure being, but,
of course, since our state is antinomial, it is seen
symbolically as other and opposite to us and driven

as we are by desire" (*Book of Yeats's Vision* 101). While the *Faculties* apply only to life, the *Principles* apply both to life and to the period "between lives": "At death consciousness passes from *Husk* to *Spirit*; *Husk* and *Passionate Body* are said to *disappear* [. . .] and *Spirit* turns from *Passionate Body* and clings to *Celestial Body* until they are one and there is only *Spirit*; pure mind, containing within itself pure truth, that which depends only upon itself: as in the *primary* phases, *Creative Mind* clings to *Body of Fate* until mind deprived of its obstacle can create no more and nothing is left but 'the spirits at one', unrelated facts and aimless mind, the burning out that awaits all voluntary effort" (188–189). The *Faculties* and *Principles*, as this indicates, are not distinct but interactive, and the shifting combinations of the two wheels bear on human life in specific ways—emotion, for example, is "formed by *Will*, acted upon by *Mask* and *Celestial Body*, or by *Mask* and *Passionate Body*" (195).

Crucially, Yeats stipulates that his metaphysics of the *Daimonic* plane is a construct of the imperfect human perspective, an allegory of the inexpressible. The "ultimate reality" is the "phaseless sphere" or "Thirteenth Cone" (193; see also 240, 247). This reflects the "eternal instant" of the *Daimon*, which is "unintelligible to all bound to the antinomies" (193). Later Yeats speaks of the Thirteenth Cone as that "cycle which may deliver us from the twelve cycles of time and space." It contains "all souls that have been set free and every *Daimon* and *Ghostly Self*" (the name given to the *Daimon* when it inhabits the phaseless sphere) and in some sense propagates the mundane world. Yeats says only that "spiritual *influx* is from its circumference, animate life from its centre" (193; 210–211). At the same time, our actions, whether "lived in life, or remembered in death, are the food and drink of the *Spirits* of the *Thirteenth Cone*, that which gives them separation and solidity" (230). In general outline, at least, the "thirteenth cone" represents transcendent reality in what is after all a recognizable dualism between heaven and earth, eternity and time; insofar as it is emanative, it resembles Yeats's accustomed conception of the ANIMA MUNDI. In his 1930 diary Yeats clarifies both the idea of the Thirteenth Cone and its religious connotation: "Berke-

ley in the *Commonplace Book* thought that 'we perceive' and are passive whereas God creates in perceiving. He creates what we perceive. I substitute for God the Thirteenth Cone, the Thirteenth Cone therefore creates our perceptions—all the visible world—as held in common by our wheel" (*Expl.* 320). Further, the *Thirteenth Cone* interpolates an incalculable element in Yeats's otherwise calculable system and thus preserves the possibility (or perhaps merely semblance) of free will. The particulars of history, Yeats writes in the penultimate paragraph of *A Vision*, "are the work of the *Thirteenth Cone* or cycle which is in every man and called by every man his freedom. Doubtless, for it can do all things and knows all things, it knows what it will do with its own freedom but it has kept the secret" (302).

Extending Yeats's analysis of the realm of the dead, "The Soul in Judgment" charts the passage from death to rebirth. Those who regard it as "bizarre at best and silly at worst," writes Hazard Adams, might keep in mind that it continues "a literary and folk tradition gradually eroded in the West by primary thought," and that "to carry it on as Yeats does is a deliberate gesture of defiance against modern positivism and its negation of antithetical, poetic tradition." Adams characterizes "The Soul in Judgment" as an expression of "antithetical desire" rather than "an expression of primary belief (or disbelief)," which is to say that it not only ignores but deliberately rejects the normal bases of knowledge and criteria of validity (*Book of Yeats's Vision* 110). Evidently harboring reservations of his own, Yeats writes in his "Introduction" that "The Soul in Judgment" is "the most unfinished" of *A Vision*'s five books (AV 23).

With disconcerting assurance and specificity, "The Soul in Judgment" describes the six states between death and birth. These correspond to the six solar months between Aries and Libra, and to the *primary* phases (22 through 28) of the lunar cycle (223). The first state is *The Vision of the Blood Kindred*, which entails the "vision of all those bound to us through *Husk* or *Passionate Body*" (223). Yeats gives the impression that the *Meditation* is the second state, but the subsequent identification of the *Return* as the second state means that in some way it must be encompassed by or related to *The Vision of the Blood Kindred*. It entails the *Spirit*'s "first vision and understanding of the *Celestial Body*" (223). The second state is evidently the *Return*, which, confusingly, seems to have three components of its own: the *Return* proper, the *Dreaming Back*, and the *Phantasmagoria*. In the *Return*, "the *Spirit* must live through past events in the order of their occurrence, because it is compelled by the *Celestial Body* to trace every passionate event to its cause until all are related and understood" (226). In the *Dreaming Back*, "the *Spirit* is compelled to live over and over again the events that had most moved it" (226). In both the *Return* and the *Dreaming Back*, the *Spirit*, assisted by *Teaching Spirits* (or *Spirits* of the *Thirteenth Cone*), "may not merely dream through the consequences of its acts but amend them, bringing this or that to the attention of the living" (228). The *Return* and the *Dreaming Back* presumably inform the purgatorial phenomena of "Shepherd and Goatherd" (1919) and PURGATORY. In the *Phantasmagoria*—which is likewise assisted by *Teaching Spirits*—the "physical and moral life is completed" as a means of exhausting emotion (230). All three states of the *Return* involve the *Spirit* coming to terms with the life that it has left behind, as a means of preparation for a new life. In the third state, called the *Shiftings*, the *Spirit* is "purified of good and evil" by a reversal of the moral disposition that defined it during life: "In so far as the man did good without knowing evil, or evil without knowing good, his nature is reversed until that knowledge is obtained" (231). The fourth state, called *Marriage* (or the *Beatitude*), is a state of "equilibrium" in which good and evil "vanish into the whole" (232). In the fifth state, called *Purification*, memory vanishes and the *Husk* and *Passionate Body* are re-created anew. The *Spirit*, meanwhile, becomes "self-shaping, self-moving, plastic to itself," and must discover "its own aim," conceived as a form of perfection (233–234). In the final state of *Foreknowledge*, the *Spirit*'s form of perfection becomes the basis of its new incarnation, but the *Spirit* cannot be reborn until "the vision of that life is completed and accepted" (234).

"The Great Year of the Ancients" and "Dove or Swan" provide relief from the suffocating close-ness of "The Completed Symbol" and "The Soul in Judgment." They leave behind the metaphysical system-building of earlier chapters and find room for expansion in the attempt to reconcile the figure of the interlocked gyres with the pattern of history and culture. On this more accustomed footing, Yeats displays the prose craft and cultural insight—an instinct for implicit narrative and pattern, for symbolic detail, for the relation between art and world-conception—that are the familiar elements of his genius. In "The Great Year of the Ancients," Yeats places his cyclic conception of history in an intellectual lineage that begins with the thought of Anaximander, Empedocles, Heraclitus, Plato, Plotinus, and Proclus, and in the ancients' realization that the rotation of the zodiacal constellations inscribe a "great year" or "Platonic year" measured variously. Ptolemy and later Thomas Taylor fixed its period at 36,000 years, while Yeats endorses a corrected period of 26,000 years (252). Further, Ptolemy, following Plotinus, held that "the stars did not themselves affect human destiny but were pointers which enabled us to calculate the condition of the universe at any particular moment and therefore its effect on the individual life" (252–253). His wife's automatic script led Yeats to much the same conclusion. His specific realization was that the interlocked cones of the *tinctures* can be mapped onto the Great Year, and that history itself is an oscillation between *primary* and *antithetical* civilization, a great passage through the 28 phases of the moon.

"Dove or Swan," a mosaic of vivid silhouettes and daring generalizations, is the most accessible and compelling book of *A Vision*. Less concerned with the currents of politics than with art and thought, the discussion is a brilliant exercise in synecdoche as centuries are epitomized in the image of this or that altarpiece or stained-glass window, all reduced to vivid artifacts, to microcosmic images. There is no attempt to marshal facts and figures, nor even the attempt at inductive argument by repetition of example. Here again there is, in Hazard Adam's words, "a deliberate gesture of defiance against modern positivism" (*Book of Yeats's Vision* 110). This might be termed *antithetical* historiography; its object, to borrow from Yeats's comment on

Dante as historian in "J. M. Synge and the Ireland of his Time" (1911), is not to add to our "knowledge" but to our "being" (*E&I* 340). Yeats hints at a similar understanding in AUTOBIOGRAPHIES when he approvingly recalls Frederick York Powell's (1850–1904) notion that history is "a memory of men who were amusing or exciting to think about" (116). If contemporary historians—*primary* by training and inclination—will inevitably quibble or even wholly object, the casual reader is likely to be compelled in spite of himself by the dazzle of Yeats's rhetoric and the flight of his synthetic imagination. Further, "Dove or Swan" is an indispensable companion to Yeats's creative work. As a comprehensive if radically concise interpretation of Western history, it is a font of contexts and hints, and a consistently useful tool for the triangulation of poetic difficulty.

Expanding on the discussion of "The Great Year of the Ancients," "Dove or Swan" presents a chronological narrative of Western history in its movement through the lunar phases of the 2,000-year cycle and the 1,000-year epicycle, and its corresponding oscillation between the *tinctures*. The narrative begins with the "annunciation" made to Leda and traces the full circuit of the classical era (2000 B.C. to A.D. 1). It then takes up the ensuing circuit of the Christian era, which begins with the birth of Christ (A.D. 1) and continues to the present day (Phase 22 of the Christian era). The title of the book derives from the initiating moments of the Christian and classical eras. Representing the *primary* tincture, "dove" alludes to the many artistic depictions of the annunciation made to Mary in which the Holy Spirit descends in the form of the bird (see Luke 1:26–38). Representing the *antithetical* tincture, "swan" alludes to the rape of Leda (see "Leda and the Swan," which introduces "Dove or Swan").

Complicating Yeats's cyclic model, the 2,000-year "era" overlaps with the 1,000-year "millennium," so that an *antithetical* phase of civilization may be contained within a larger *primary* era (the Italian Renaissance is thus circumstanced) and *vice versa*. According to Yeats's geometry, Phase 28 of each millennium is Phase 1 or 15 of the encompassing era, while Phase 15 of each millennium is

Phase 8 or 22 of the encompassing era (267). The era itself is half of a 4,000-year cycle whose 15th phase—in the case of the present cycle, the age of Christ—comes "at a period of war or trouble" (263, 268). None of this is to say, however, that people passively or automatically embody their civilization's historical phase. Individuals may be more or less in accord with the historical phase in which they find themselves, just as civilizations may be more or less in accord with their encompassing eras. Yeats himself was a man of *antithetical* nature engaged in active and self-conscious rebellion against an increasingly *primary* age, as were Blake and Nietzsche (AV 299).

There is further an interchange between East and West, Asia and Europe, respectively representing what Whitaker calls "*primary* transcendence" and "*antithetical* immanence" (*Swan and Shadow* 84). A revolution of the "Great Year," according to Yeats, "must be thought of as the marriage of symbolic Europe and symbolic Asia, the one begetting upon the other. When it commenced at its symbolic full moon in March—Christ or Christendom was begotten by the West upon the East. This begetting has been followed by a spiritual predominance of Asia. After it must come an age begotten by the East upon the West that will take after its Mother in turn" (203). Yeats specifies the trend of civilization at various points beneath the millennial full moon: Phidian Greece was "westward-moving" (after Alexander "Greek civilization, formalized and codified, loses itself in Asia"); Byzantium was "eastward-moving"; the European Renaissance "westward-moving" (270–271). Among Yeats's poems, "The STATUES" explicitly addresses this pattern of alternation between East and West.

Each shift in era involves an *interchange of the tinctures* that is marked by apocalyptic "annunciation" or "revelation," moments of world-changing turmoil from which Yeats wrung a good deal of his best poetry. The classical era had its natal horror in the rape of Leda (see "Leda and the Swan") and the Christian era in the birth of Christ (see "The MAGI," "The MOTHER OF GOD," *The RESURRECTION*, "TWO SONGS FROM A PLAY"). Yeats envisions the birth of the next era—an *antithetical* era in answer to the *primary* era of Christianity—in "The

Second Coming" (see also *AV-1925* 213–215). In *A Vision*'s most vivid pronouncement upon the apocalyptic dynamics of history, Yeats describes a civilization as "a struggle to keep self-control, and in this it is like some great tragic person, some Niobe who must display an almost superhuman will or the cry will not touch our sympathy. The loss of control over thought comes towards the end; first a sinking in upon the moral being, then the last surrender, the irrational cry, revelation—the scream of Juno's peacock" (268; cf. *Aut.* 356: "All civilization is held together by the suggestions of an invisible hypnotist—by artificially created illusions"). The scream of Juno's peacock recurs in "My Table," a poem closely aligned with the lunar and apocalyptic theories of *A Vision*.

Yeats's narrative inevitably dwells upon historical moments that correspond to the climactic lunar phases. As a devotee of Unity of Being, he lingers in veneration upon Byzantium in the age of Justinian (circa A.D. 550), and upon Italy in the age of Botticelli, Crivelli, Mantegna, and da Vinci (circa 1450–1550). These civilizations represent phases 8 and 22 of the *primary* Christian era, but they belong to Phase 15—the supreme *antithetical* phase—of their respective millennial cycles and manifest the "Unity of Culture" that Yeats mentions repeatedly in *Autobiographies* (214–215, 229, 268, 273). Yeats's description of Byzantium at its zenith is his fullest evocation of culture under the glow of the full moon, and as such represents that toward which all of his cultural theorizing, propagandizing, and organizing yearns, however remotely. Were he granted a month in antiquity, he says, he would "spend it in Byzantium a little before Justinian opened St. Sophia and closed the Academy of Plato." There he might find "in some little wine-shop some philosophical worker in mosaic who could answer all my questions, the supernatural descending nearer to him than to Plotinus even, for the pride of his delicate skill would make what was an instrument of power to princes and clerics, a murderous madness in the mob, show as a lovely flexible presence like that of a perfect human body." He summarizes that in "early Byzantium, maybe never before or since in recorded history, religious, aesthetic and practical life were one, that architect and artificers—though

not, it may be, poets, for language had been the instrument of controversy and must have grown abstract—spoke to the multitude and the few alike. The painter, the mosaic worker, the worker in gold and silver, the illuminator of sacred books, were almost impersonal, almost perhaps without the consciousness of individual design, absorbed in their subject-matter and that the vision of a whole people" (279–280). This describes nothing less than a condition of cultural beatitude—a world traditional, communal, religious, aesthetic, coherent—as against the "bundle of fragments" that is the modern world (*Aut.* 163; cf. Yeats's panegyric upon the Stockholm City Hall, *Aut.* 406–407). "SAILING TO BYZANTIUM" is Yeats's poetic monument to Byzantium in its lunar glory. "BYZANTIUM" is sometimes ascribed to this moment as well, but Yeats associated it with "the end of the first Christian millennium," and the poem itself is consistent with the "Asiatic and anarchic Europe" of the "last quarter" that he describes in *A Vision* (*Expl.* 290; *AV* 283).

The Italian Renaissance embodied a similar unity ("Intellect and emotion, *primary* curiosity and the *antithetical* dream, are for the moment one") but its triumph was more precarious and embattled. Representing not only the 15th phase of the millennium but also the 22nd phase of the Christian era, it belonged to the "fading circle" of Christendom and to the trend of fragmentation that begins with the "rebirth of the secular intellect in the eleventh century" (293). Indeed, the Renaissance is the product of this fragmentation. It saw "the breaking of the Christian synthesis," just as the age of Phidias—likewise a concatenation of 15th and 22nd phases—saw "the breaking of Greek traditional faith" (291; cf. 270–271). This moment of dissolution was simultaneously a moment of freedom in which the reconciliation of paganism and Christianity became suddenly possible. This reconciliation meant to Pope Julius II (1443–1513) that "Greek and Roman Antiquity were as sacred as that of Judea, and like it 'a vestibule of Christianity,'" and "meant to the mind of Dürer—a visitor to Venice during the movement of the gyre—that the human norm, discovered from the measurement of ancient statues, was God's first handiwork, that 'perfectly proportioned human body' which had seemed to Dante Unity of Being symbolised" (291). Liberated by this reconciliation, the great artists of the day—Sandro Botticelli (1444/5–1510), Carlo Crivelli (ca. 1430–94), Andrea Mantegna (1430/1–1506), and Leonardo da Vinci (1452–1519)—made the immediately preceding school of Masaccio (1401–ca. 1428) "seem heavy and common by something we may call intellectual beauty or compare perhaps to that kind of bodily beauty which Castiglione called 'the spoil or monument of the victory of the soul'" (292–293). Born in 1475, Michelangelo, whom Yeats mentions in "An ACRE OF GRASS," "LONG-LEGGED FLY," "MICHAEL ROBARTES AND THE DANCER," and "UNDER BEN BULBEN," is more vital, exultant, and sexual than his immediate predecessors, a figure of the 16th rather than the 15th millennial phase (293–294).

Unlike the 1937 edition, the 1925 edition allows itself to peer prophetically into the future. Yeats notes the incipience of Phase 23 in his own day, citing as representative figures Pound, ELIOT, Joyce, and Luigi Pirandello (1867–1936), who "eliminate from metaphor the poet's phantasy and substitute a strangeness discovered by historical or contemporary research or who break up the logical processes of thought by flooding them with associated ideas or words that seem to drift into the mind by chance" (*AV-1925* 211–212). Envisioning the concluding phases of the Christian era and the birth of a new *antithetical* era, he foresees "new races, as it were, seeking domination, a world resembling but for its immensity that of the Greek tribes—each with its own Daimon or ancestral hero—the brood of Leda, War and Love; history grown symbolic, the biography changed into a myth" (214). More darkly, he recognizes that the *antithetical* impulse "may grow a fanaticism and a terror, and at its first outsetting oppress the ignorant—even the innocent—as Christianity oppressed the wise [. . .]" (215).

BIBLIOGRAPHY

Adams, Hazard. *The Book of Yeats's Vision: Romantic Modernism and Antithetical Tradition*; Ellmann, Richard. *W. B. Yeats's Second Puberty: A lecture delivered at the Library of Congress on April 2, 1984*; Gregory, Lady. *Lady Gregory's Journals* (vol. 2, ed. Daniel J. Murphy); Harper, George Mills. *The Making of Yeats's 'A Vision': A Study of the Automatic Script* (vols. 1–2); Jeffares, A. Norman (ed.), *W. B. Yeats: The Critical Heritage*, *W. B. Yeats: A New Biography*; Kelly, John S. *A W. B. Yeats Chronology*; Moore, Virginia. *The Unicorn: William Butler Yeats' Search for Reality*; Saddlemyer, Ann. *Becoming George: The Life of Mrs W. B. Yeats*; Vendler, Helen Hennessy. *Yeats's Vision and the Later Plays*; Wade, Allan. *A Bibliography of the Writings of W. B. Yeats*; Whitaker, Thomas R. *Swan and Shadow: Yeats's Dialogue with History*; Yeats, W. B. *Autobiographies*, *The Collected Letters of W. B. Yeats* (vol. 3), *A Critical Edition of Yeats's A Vision (1925)*, *Essays and Introductions*, *Explorations*, *Later Essays*, *The Letters of W. B. Yeats*, *Uncollected Prose by W. B. Yeats* (vols. 1–2), *The Variorum Edition of the Plays of W. B. Yeats*, *The Variorum Edition of the Poems of W. B. Yeats*, *A Vision*.

PART III

People, Places, and Ideas

Abbey Theatre   The founding of the Abbey Theatre in 1904 marked the arrival of the Irish dramatic movement that Yeats, Lady GREGORY, and
EDWARD MARTYN had launched five years earlier,
lending it an undeniable solidity and institutional
standing in the local culture of Dublin and the
larger culture of Ireland. In an irony not lost on
anyone, the Abbey Theatre came to life through
the largesse of ANNIE HORNIMAN, a British tea
heiress with a particular aversion to the politics of
Irish nationalism. In October 1903, flush with the
excitement of having designed the costumes for the
IRISH NATIONAL THEATRE SOCIETY's production of
The KING'S THRESHOLD, Horniman offered to provide a building for the society's use. By April 1904,
the matter had been settled. Horniman acquired
a £170-per-year lease to the Mechanics' Institute
building on Abbey Street and an adjoining morgue
on Marlborough Street with the intention of ren-
ovating the facility and providing it cost-free to
the society (*CL3* 572–573). Playwright and Abbey
director Lennox Robinson gives the history of the
building: "A theatre, the old Theatre Royal Opera
House in Abbey Street, built in 1820, had been
burned down some years later. The Mechanics'
Institute, then situate in Capel Street, acquired
the site and built on it their new premises. As
well as a small concert-hall, there was a lending-
library, a reading-room and a chemical laboratory.
The Institute wanted to change the concert-hall
into a theatre for letting purposes, but theatres in
Ireland require a Patent from the Lord Lieutenant. Such Patents are, naturally, opposed by rival
theatres and the Mechanics' did not obtain one.

The Abbey Theatre, Dublin, in 1949 *(Fáilte Ireland)*

The concert-hall, therefore, could only be used for short sketches or vaudeville shows not lasting more than twenty minutes." According to Robinson, the property became "practically derelict" after the fire department demanded alterations that the institute could not afford (*Ireland's Abbey Theatre* 42).

Horniman spent between £1,300 and £3,000—accounts vary—on initial renovations to the property, which were designed by the architect and tireless theater-diarist Joseph Holloway (1861–1944). The renovations primarily involved joining the two buildings to create a second entrance on Marlborough Street, adding dressing rooms, and rebuilding the stage. The finished stage was 40 feet wide and 16 feet 4 inches deep, curtain line to back wall; the depth was considered unsatisfactory, but a public lane to the rear of the theater prevented expansion. The renovated theater sat 178 in the stalls, 186 in the pit, and 198 in the balcony (*CL3* 695). Actress Máire Nic Shiubhlaigh (1888–1959) remembers that for the players, "emerging from the out-of-the-way Molesworth Hall, with memories of our earlier appearances in Camden Street still vivid, it was wonderful to be able to play in a real theatre at last. We had a 'greenroom'—a sort of common room where we could meet and wait between the acts of plays—a stage, which, even if it was not very big, was reasonably well equipped, and we had a more or less draught-proof auditorium that would not offend those people who were used to the comforts of the bigger theatres. We could at least be sure that there would never again be murmurs about hard chairs and cold breezes" (*Abbey Theatre: Interviews and Recollections* 45). The new theater was an expression not only of the burgeoning Irish dramatic movement but also of Irish arts and crafts, as Yeats suggests in the 1904 installment of *Samhain* (1901–8), the magazine of the Irish theater movement: "The work of decoration and alteration has been done by Irishmen, and everything, with the exception of some few things that are not made here, or not of a good enough quality, has been manufactured in Ireland. The stained glass in the entrance hall is the work of Miss Sarah Purser and her apprentices, the large copper mirror-frames are from the new metal works at Youghal, and the pictures of some of our players are by an Irish Art-ist" (*Expl.* 124; *IDM* 40). The Irish artist was John Butler Yeats, the poet's father, whose fine portraits of the theater's leading figures—Frank Fay (1870–1931), William Fay (1872–1947), Horniman, Douglas Hyde (1860–1949), George Russell (AE), Máire Nic Shiubhlaigh—were displayed in the lobby and green room (*CL3* 695). Horniman purchased adjacent properties in 1905 and 1907, thus providing space for the construction of six dressing rooms and numerous workrooms (*CL3* 695–696; *Ireland's Abbey Theatre* 43).

On December 27, 1904, before a full house, the Abbey's curtain rose for the first time. The bill featured Yeats's On Baile's Strand and Cathleen Ni Houlihan, and Lady Gregory's *Spreading the News* (*Our Irish Theatre* 36). Yeats took to the stage following the performance. "We will be able to be courageous," he proclaimed, "and can take as our mottoes those written over the three gates of the City of Love by Edmund Spenser—over the first gate was, 'Be bold!', over the second, 'Be Bold, Be Bold! And evermore be bold!', and over the third, 'Be Bold! And Yet Be Not Too Bold!'" (*The Abbey* 62).

Relations with Horniman steadily soured over the next several years. In 1910, she sold the society the lease to the theater for £1,000 and retired from the Irish dramatic movement. In August 1925, the government agreed to provide the Abbey, then nearly bankrupt, with an annual subsidy (£850 to start), making it Ireland's official "national theater" (136). As Robinson remembers, "After eight years (1916–24) of increasing poverty the Theatre was now able to pay its players salaries somewhat appropriate to their merits, it was able to replenish its shabby wardrobe and to build new scenery" (*Ireland's Abbey Theatre* 126–127). In November 1926, an experimental and teaching theater, the Peacock, opened in a renovated space that included a 100-seat auditorium, a café, a scene dock, and dressing rooms. The new theater was home to the Abbey School of Acting and to the short-lived Abbey School of Ballet. The ballet school opened in 1927 and closed in 1933 (*The Abbey* 137–138). Its director, the Irish-born ballerina Ninette de Valois (1898–2001), was instrumental in bringing to the stage Yeats's "Plays for Dancers," and she is duly lauded in the speech that opens THE DEATH OF CUCHULAIN.

In the early morning of July 18, 1951, a rich chapter in the history of both Irish and modern drama came to an end when a fire broke out and irreparably damaged the stage area and dressing rooms of the original Abbey building. It was a small mercy that the Abbey's collection of pictures was undamaged. The Abbey troupe performed in the Rupert Guinness Memorial Hall and the Queen's Theatre for the next 15 years. On July 18, 1966— 15 years to the day after the catastrophic fire—a new Abbey Theatre, seating 628, opened on the site of the original building. The new Peacock Theatre, seating 157, opened the following July (*The Abbey* 195–200). The theater's foundation stone, laid by President Eamon de Valera on September 3, 1963, bore the names of Frank Fay, William Fay, Lady Gregory, J. M. SYNGE, and Yeats (*The Abbey Theatre* 174).

Bibliography

Foster, R. F. *W. B. Yeats: A Life, I: The Apprentice Mage*; Gregory, Lady. *Our Irish Theatre*; Hunt, Hugh. *The Abbey: Ireland's National Theatre, 1904–1979*; Mikhail, E. H. ed. *The Abbey Theatre: Interviews and Recollections*; Ritschel, Nelson O'Ceallaigh. *Productions of the Irish Theatre Movement, 1899–1916: A Checklist*; Robinson, Lennox. *Ireland's Abbey Theatre: A History, 1899–1951*; Welch, Robert. *The Abbey Theatre, 1899–1999*; Yeats, W. B. *The Collected Letters of W. B. Yeats* (vol. 3), *Explorations*, *The Irish Dramatic Movement*.

AE   See RUSSELL, GEORGE.

America   Yeats made five visits to America: four grueling lecture tours that took him the breadth and width of the country, and a briefer northeastern swing with the ABBEY THEATRE. The tours had multiple purposes, allowing Yeats to expand his reading audience, to drum up publicity for the Irish literary movement, to earn substantial fees, and to visit with his friend JOHN QUINN and with his father, JOHN BUTLER YEATS (who lived a life of expatriate semi-vagabondage in New York from 1907 until his death in 1922).

Yeats's first visit (November 11, 1903, to March 9, 1904) took him to New York, New Haven, Boston, Hartford, Philadelphia (with EZRA POUND in attendance), Montreal, Washington, St. Louis, Indianapolis, Chicago, St. Paul, San Francisco, Madison, Toronto, Baltimore, and lesser points in between (*AM* 305). The 17-week tour, entailing 64 lectures hosted by colleges and literary societies, garnered Yeats $3,230.40 (*CL3* 467). Putting this sum in perspective, R. F. Foster notes that in the two months following his tour Yeats earned only £2.13s.0d (*AM* 314). Highlights of the trip included making the acquaintance of Harvard philosopher William James (*CL3* 509) and President Theodore Roosevelt. Yeats lunched with the Roosevelt family in Washington, D.C., on December 28. The author and diplomat Maurice Egan (1852–1924) recalls a pricelessly incongruous moment. President Roosevelt, speaking of the balance of power in Europe, inadvertently referred to "the little peoples," upon which Yeats, who had been silent, snapped to attention. Egan recounts the exchange that followed: "'Sure,' he said, 'you'll find the little people all over Ireland. Every old man that's raked the hay in the meadow has seen one of the little people. I have seen some of them myself.' Mr. Roosevelt looked as if he had been struck suddenly by a thunderbolt. I had presence of mind enough to ask: 'What are the little people like?' 'They're not like the little insignificant English fairies,' Yeats said contemptuously. 'They're over seven feet high; they're the old gods come back again!' 'My Heavens,' said Roosevelt *sotto voce*; the children were delighted evidently. But Yeats subsided into silence, in contemplation of the sweetness and strength of the Irish fairies" (*CL3* 500; *Recollections* 210–211). His own seeming distraction notwithstanding, Yeats wrote to his theatrical colleague Frank Fay (1870–1931) that he had found Roosevelt "extraordinarily well informed about our whole movement—indeed, one of the best read men I have met" (*CL3* 500).

Though inevitably wearied by his long tour, Yeats responded enthusiastically to the way of things in the United States. Upon returning to England, he told the *Daily Chronicle* that he had been amazed by the "entire lack of intolerance" he had found in America. "While I was there I got papers from

Ireland telling me of the difficulties at home over the Irish University question," Yeats said. "Now, at the Catholic University of Notre Dame, in Indiana, where all the professors are priests, I found about 100 Nonconformists, and I was told that a Jew had just carried off the prize in Christian doctrine! This problem, as others, America has solved very efficiently" (520). His chief statement on his experiences is the article "America and the Arts" (1905), in which he compliments America's "vivid life where everything is more intense than elsewhere—a thirst for money, for ideas, for power, beyond our understanding," but wonders why America has not produced a higher standard of art (UP2 339, 341–342; for additional impressions of America see 308–310). In an emphatic aside, Yeats sings the praises of American women, whom he found "imaginative, impulsive, and curious about ideas," unlike their British counterparts. He mentions the "great joy" he felt in speaking before so many "fair heads that are learning and yet not unlearning life, about the queens of old Irish romance who were fitted to be the perfect mistress and the perfect wife, and yet when the need called for it to carry a bow through the wilderness" (341; see also CL3 482).

Yeats's subsequent lecture tours in 1914 (February 7 to April 2), 1920 (January 24 to May 29), and 1932–33 (October 26 to January 22) followed a similar pattern. Yeats made the 1920 tour in the company of his wife, GEORGE YEATS. The visit turned out to be Yeats's final reunion with his father, who died in 1922. Happily, John Butler Yeats was delighted with his daughter-in-law, whom he found unpretentious and engagingly salty. He wrote to his daughter Lily that George possessed "no vast depths," but "endless kindness and sympathy and I fancy a lot of practical talent" (PF 507). George, in turn, was charmed by her impish and irrepressible father-in-law, and she visited him on most days while Yeats lectured out of town (507). The tour occasioned at least one event that would have important reverberations in Yeats's work. In Portland, Oregon, the Japanese consular officer Junzo Sato (b. 1897) introduced himself and presented Yeats with a 500-year-old sword that had descended through the generations of his family (see Letters 662). The sword became a central symbol in two of Yeats's most important poems, "A DIALOGUE OF SELF AND SOUL" and "MY TABLE." In gratitude for the unexpected gift, Yeats dedicated to Sato his play The RESURRECTION.

In 1911, Yeats and Lady GREGORY led the Abbey Theatre on its first visit to America. The tour extended from September to March, but Yeats remained for less than a month (September 21 to October 18), executing a preemptive lecture campaign in defense of J. M. SYNGE's The Playboy of the Western World, which was the centerpiece of the Abbey's traveling repertoire (AM 445). Irish-American opposition nonetheless mounted. The United Irish Societies of New York went so far as to publish a pledge to "drive the vile thing from the stage" (Our Irish Theatre 102). The play opened quietly enough at the Plymouth Theatre in Boston on October 16, but potatoes were hurled at the stage during a performance at the Maxine Elliot Theatre in New York on November 27, and the first act had to be played over again because of the noise. Yeats's old acquaintance Theodore Roosevelt, at Lady Gregory's invitation, attended the performance on the following night in the attempt to discourage any further trouble (this was not to be the end of Roosevelt's assistance; he published a complimentary article on the Abbey Theatre in the December 16 number of the Outlook; see Our Irish Theatre 245). The company successfully finished its weeklong run in New York, but had no such luck in Philadelphia. On January 18, following disrupted performances on the two previous nights, 11 members of the company were arrested on charges of performing "lascivious, sacrilegious, obscene or indecent plays" (Our Irish Theatre 231). Quinn, an eminent lawyer, rushed from New York to defend the players in court. He delivered, in his own phrase, "a knock-out blow" and the case was soon dismissed (124). Despite this prickly reception, the company achieved a good deal, holding its ground against Irish-American touchiness and establishing its reputation in America.

Bibliography

Egan, Maurice Francis. *Recollections of a Happy Life*; Foster, R. F. *W. B. Yeats: A Life, I: The Apprentice Mage*; Gregory, Lady. *Our Irish Theatre*; Kelly, John

S. *A W. B. Yeats Chronology*; Murphy, William M. *Prodigal Father: The Life of John Butler Yeats (1839–1922)*; Yeats, W. B. *The Collected Letters of W. B. Yeats* (vol. 3), *The Letters of W. B. Yeats, Uncollected Prose by W. B. Yeats* (vol. 2).

Anglo-Irish War Political backdrop to "NINE-TEEN HUNDRED AND NINETEEN" and "Reprisals" (1948), the Anglo-Irish War, sometimes called the Irish War of Independence, effectively ended British rule in the 26 counties of southern Ireland. The war began January 21, 1919, and ended in truce on July 11, 1921. "Broadly speaking," F. S. L. Lyons summarizes, "the hostilities fell into three phases. During the first of these, which occupied virtually the whole of 1919 and the early months of 1920, patterns of events emerged only very slowly and incidents, though numerous, were mostly on a small scale. The second phase, filling the latter part of 1920, saw the British counter-measures taking shape and terror and counter-terror reaching a crescendo with the fearful blows struck by both sides in November and December. The final phase occupied the first six months of 1921 and although overshadowed by the long-awaited truce in July of that year, it witnessed the systematic exploitation by the Irish flying columns of the tactics of ambush, the development of guerilla war *à l'outrance*" (*Ireland Since the Famine* 409–410). In the final tally of Irish casualties, 752 soldiers and civilians were killed and 866 were wounded (415). On December 6, 1921, representatives of the British and Irish governments signed the peace treaty that led both to the establishment of the Irish Free State and to the IRISH CIVIL WAR.

During the years of the war Yeats intermittently resided in OXFORD, but he was minutely attentive to affairs in Ireland. Lady GREGORY, who remained at COOLE PARK, kept Yeats informed of local developments. In the most haunting and abhorrent local incident, Ellen Quinn, the wife of a neighborhood farmer well known to Lady Gregory, was shot from a passing military lorry while she held her baby in her arms, a tragedy that Yeats would resurrect in "Nineteen Hundred and Nineteen" (lines 26–28) as an emblem of modern barbarity (*Lady Gregory's Journals*, I,

197). At a meeting of the Oxford Union on February 17, 1921, Yeats denounced the tactics of the Black and Tans, who were brutally prosecuting the British military campaign, though he likewise distanced himself from Sinn Féin (*W. B. Yeats* 333–334; *AP* 188). Yeats's comments were edged by elegy for a loftier age: "Gladstone! Salisbury! Asquith! They were Victorians. I am a Victorian. They knew the meaning of the words 'Truth' and 'honour' and 'Justice.' But you do not know the meaning of them. You do not understand the language I speak so I will sit down" (*AP* 188).

Though it ended in effective Irish independence, the war tended to put Yeats in the saturnine, philosophical mood that colors "Nineteen Hundred and Nineteen," and perhaps the more so as it came on the heels of World War I, which Yeats had witnessed with detached disgust. Civilization itself seemed convulsed in a terrible death spasm, a sense that informs both "Nineteen Hundred and Nineteen" and "The SECOND COMING." Writing to JOHN QUINN on July 11, 1919, Yeats observed, "We are reeling back into the middle ages, without growing more picturesque" (*Letters* 658). On March 29, 1921, he told GEORGE RUSSELL (AE), "I have little hope: something we will get [i.e. some political accommodation from the British] but not enough to set things right. I have little hope of the future anywhere. I think all the old systematic idealisms are dead and are forced to death by sheer mathematics. The world is like the schools of painting which exhaust any technical method in a few years. We have to discover a new force and till it is discovered mere hungers and futilities will reign" (666).

Bibliography
Foster, R. F. *W. B. Yeats: A Life, II: The Arch-Poet*; Gregory, Lady. *Lady Gregory's Journals* (vol. 1, ed. Daniel J. Murphy); Hone, Joseph. *W. B. Yeats*; Lyons, F. S. L. *Ireland Since the Famine*; Yeats, W. B. *The Letters of W. B. Yeats*.

anima mundi One of the fundamental concepts of Yeats's metaphysical thought, *anima mundi* ("world soul" or "soul of the world") is a repository of archetypal images and emotions from which issue the permanent forms of the world. The artist and the magician have the gift of access to the *anima mundi* and cull from its depths the symbols that pattern their work and the culture of the world. Yeats's most substantive references to the *anima mundi* are to be found in the section of PER AMICA SILENTIA LUNAE titled "anima mundi" (*LE* 16–33) and in the 1925 edition of A VISION. In the latter, Yeats defines the *anima mundi* as the "receptacle of emotional images when purified from whatever unites them to one man rather than to another" (*AV-1925* 176).

Yeats attributes the concept of the "world soul" to the writings of Plotinus (see *AV-1925* 176) and to the English Neoplatonic philosopher Henry More (1614–87). In AUTOBIOGRAPHIES, Yeats recalls being amazed by the repetition of certain archetypal images and knowing himself "face to face with the anima mundi described by Platonic philosophers, and more especially in modern times by Henry More, which has a memory independent of embodied individual memories, though they constantly enrich it with their images and their thoughts" (210; see also 212). Yeats is thinking of *The Immortality of the Soul* (1659), in which More defines the "Spirit of Nature" as a "substance incorporeal, but without Sense and Animadversion, pervading the whole Matter of the Universe, and exercising a Plastical power therein according to the sundry predispositions and occasions in the parts it works upon, raising such Phaenomena in the World, by directing the parts of the Matter and their Motion, as cannot be resolved into mere Mechanical powers" (bk. III, ch. XII, sect. 1; see also *LE* 22).

Seemingly interchangeable with the *anima mundi* is the *spiritus mundi* ("world spirit"), which Yeats defines as "a general storehouse of images which have ceased to be a property of any personality or spirit" (*VP* 822). This concept, too, Yeats explicitly credits to More. In his notes to Lady GREGORY's *Visions and Beliefs in the West of Ireland* (1920), for example, Yeats mentions Cornelius Agrippa's conception of the air as a "vital spirit passing through all beings giving life and substance to all things," and adds, "Henry More is more precise and philosophical and believes that

this air which he calls *Spiritus Mundi* contains all forms, so that the parents when a child is begotten, or a witch when the double is projected as a hare, but as it were, call upon the *Spiritus Mundi* for the form they need" (*LE* 271). Once again, Yeats alludes to *The Immortality of the Soul* (see bk. III, ch. VI, sect. 7).

Anticipating the notion of the *anima mundi*, Yeats speaks of a "great memory" in his 1900 essay "The PHILOSOPHY OF SHELLEY'S POETRY" and in his 1901 essay "MAGIC." In the latter, Yeats posits the great memory as the foundation of his belief in magic and enumerates three elemental doctrines: "(1) That the borders of our mind are ever shifting, and that many minds can flow into one another, as it were, and create or reveal a single mind, a single energy. (2) That the borders of our memories are as shifting, and that our memories are a part of one great memory, the memory of Nature herself. (3) That this great mind and great memory can be evoked by symbols" (*E&I* 28). Later in the essay, Yeats crucially stipulates that the relationship between the mind and the great memory is reciprocal: "Whatever the passions of man have gathered about, becomes a symbol in the Great Memory, and in the hands of him who has the secret it is a worker of wonders, a caller-up of angels or of devils" (50).

Variations on the notion of a "general storehouse" are discernible in poems like "BEFORE THE WORLD WAS MADE," "CRAZY JANE ON GOD," "Paudeen" (1913), and "UNDER BEN BULBEN" (lines 21–24), but Yeats only twice invokes *anima mundi* as a formal conception. In "The SECOND COMING," Yeats refers to the apocalyptic sphinx as "a vast image out of *Spiritus Mundi*." In "The TOWER," he calls before his mind's eye "certain men-at-arms" whose "images, in the Great Memory stored, / Come with loud cry and panting breast / To break upon a sleeper's rest / While their great wooden dice beat on the board" (lines 85–89).

Bibliography

More, Henry. *The Immortality of the Soul*; Yeats, W. B. *Autobiographies, A Critical Edition of Yeats's A Vision (1925), Essays and Introductions, Later Essays, The Variorum Edition of the Poems of W. B. Yeats.*

Aran Islands   Thirty miles west of Galway Bay soar the immense limestone cliffs of the sparsely populated, Gaelic-speaking Aran Islands. The islands consist of Inishmore ("Large Island"), Inishmaan ("Middle Island"), and Inisheer ("South Island"), which together comprehend a mere 18 square miles. The islands figured prominently in Yeats's imagination from early in his career, representing a rural life untainted by the self-consciousness and heterogeneity of modern Europe. Yeats made his first and only visit to the islands August 5 to 7, 1896, in the company of EDWARD MARTYN, Martin Morris (1867–1927), and ARTHUR SYMONS (*CL2* 47). Some accounts include GEORGE MOORE in the party (see for example *Arthur Symons* 145; *Speckled Bird* 200). The excursionists set sail from Cashla Bay on the Galway coast in a large "hooker" or single-masted fishing boat and four hours later made land. They visited both Inishmore and Inishmaan, taking in various ruins and soliciting fairy stories from the natives, but rough weather prevented them from landing on Inisheer. Symons's description of the trip, "The Isles of Aran," appeared the following December in the *SAVOY*, and later in *Cites and Sea-Coasts and Islands* (1918). Symons writes that upon the party's return to the mainland he felt as if he had "stepped out of some strange, half-magical, almost real dream," which gives the tenor of the visit (*Cities and Sea-Coasts* 302). Yeats made the trip with the particular purpose of gathering impressions for his novel *The* SPECKLED BIRD, the earliest version of which is partially set on the islands (*CL2* 47, 63; *Speckled Bird* 82–94). Both Symons and Yeats recall meeting upon Inishmaan an old man who told them, "If any gentleman has done a crime, we'll hide him. There was a gentleman that killed his father, and I had him in my own house six months till he got away to America" (*Aut.* 262; *Cities and Sea-Coasts* 323). The tale may have informed Yeats's play *The* DREAMING OF THE BONES, in which a young rebel has arranged an escape to the Aran Islands in the aftermath of the EASTER RISING.

The most far-reaching consequence of Yeats's trip was his notion upon first meeting J. M. SYNGE on December 21, 1896, at the Hôtel Corneille in Paris, that the 25-year-old writer would benefit from his own visit to the islands. As Yeats tells the story, Synge was writing "morbid and melancholy verse" under French influence. "He told me that he had learned Irish at Trinity College," Yeats remembers, "so I urged him to go to the Aran Islands and find a life that had never been expressed in literature, instead of a life where all had been expressed. I did not divine his genius, but I felt he needed something to take him out of his morbidity and melancholy. Perhaps I would have given the advice to any young Irish writer who knew Irish, for I had been that summer upon Inishmaan and Inishmore, and was full of the subject. [. . .] Over a year was to pass before he took my advice and settled for a while in an Aran cottage, and became happy, having escaped at last, as he wrote, 'from the squalor of the poor and the nullity of the rich'" (*Aut.* 262–263; see also *E&I* 299, 325; *Mem.* 104–105). Synge lived on the islands intermittently between 1898 and 1902 and recorded his experiences in the memoir *The Aran Islands* (1907). The experience touched the entirety of his art, as Yeats suggests in his essay "J. M. Synge and the Ireland of his Time" (1911): "As I read *The Aran Islands* right through for the first time since he showed it me in manuscript, I come to understand how much knowledge of the real life of Ireland went to the creation of a world which is yet as fantastic as the Spain of Cervantes. Here is the story of *The Playboy*, of *The Shadow of the Glen*; here is the ghost on horseback and the finding of the young man's body of *Riders to the Sea*, numberless ways of speech and vehement pictures that had seemed to owe nothing to observation, and all to some overflowing of himself, or to some mere necessity of dramatic construction" (*E&I* 326). Most notably, Synge extrapolated *The Playboy of the Western World* (1907) from the tale about the patricide who had found shelter on the islands, which he had heard just as Yeats had, possibly from the same old man (*Aut.* 416; *E&I* 337–338).

In Yeats's own mythology, the Aran Islanders represent ancient instinct and ancient pattern uncorrupted by the baleful influence of modernity. In *Autobiographies*, Yeats imagines an Aran Islander wandering into the Luxembourg Gallery and "turning bewildered from Impressionist or

Killeaney Harbour, Inishmore, Aran Islands. Yeats visited the islands in 1896 and ever after opposed their desolate beauty and ancient folkways to the decadence of the modern world. *(Fáilte Ireland)*

Post-Impressionist, but lingering at Moreau's *Jason*, to study in mute astonishment the elaborate background, where there are so many jewels, so much wrought stone and moulded bronze. Had not lover promised mistress in his own island song, 'A ship with a gold and silver mast, gloves of the skin of a fish, and shoes of the skin of a bird, and a suit of the dearest silk in Ireland'?" (248).

Bibliography

Beckson, Karl. *Arthur Symons: A Life*; Symons, Arthur. *Cities and Sea-Coasts and Islands*; Yeats, W. B. *Autobiographies, The Collected Letters of W. B. Yeats* (vol. 2), *Essays and Introductions, Memoirs, The Speckled Bird*.

Armstrong, Laura (born 1862) Yeats's distant cousin, a passionate and pretty redhead, was the model for the enchantresses in The ISLAND OF STATUES and TIME AND THE WITCH VIVIEN, and for the character Margaret Leland in JOHN SHERMAN (CL1 155). In AUTOBIOGRAPHIES, Yeats remembers seeing Armstrong for the first time as she drove a pony-carriage up a hill at Howth (in 1882, according to R. F. Foster) and soon falling in love, despite the fact that she was three years older and already engaged. He describes her in retrospect as a "wild creature, a fine mimic, and given to bursts of religion," and recalls that he wrote her some "bad poems" (AM 34; *Aut.* 87–88). Writing to Katharine TYNAN on March 21, 1889, Yeats offered his fullest comment on Armstrong in the process of denying his attraction to his new acquaintance MAUD GONNE: "As for the rest [Gonne] had a borrowed interest, reminding me of Laura Armstrong without Laura's wild dash of half insane genius. Laura is to me always a pleasent [sic] memory she woke me from the metallic sleep of science and set me writing my first play. Do not mistake me she is only as a myth and a symbol. Will you forgive me having talked of her—She interests me far more than Miss Gonne does and yet is only as a myth and a symbol. [. . .] 'Time and the Witch Vivien' was written for her to act. 'The Island of Statues' was begun with the same notion though it soon grew beyond the scope of drawing room acting. The part of the enchantress in both poems was written for her. She used to sign her letters Vivien" (*CL1* 154–155). Armstrong married and divorced a Dublin solicitor and later, as rumor had it, married a Welsh gardener (*CL1* 155; *PF* 568–569).

Bibliography

Foster, R. F. *W. B. Yeats: A Life, I: The Apprentice Mage*; Murphy, William M. *Prodigal Father: The Life of John Butler Yeats (1839–1922)*; Yeats, W. B. *Autobiographies, The Collected Letters of W. B. Yeats* (vol. 1).

Beardsley, Aubrey Vincent (1872–1898) One of the most colorful casualties of Yeats's "tragic generation," Beardsley meteorically rose to fame and infamy during the 1890s as art editor and chief illustrator of the *Yellow Book* and the SAVOY, the short-lived but immensely influential organs of the interrelated aesthetic and decadent movements. He grew up in straitened conditions, his father the wastrel son of a well-to-do jeweler, his mother a sometime governess and piano teacher who was very much devoted to her precociously literate and artistic son. Between debilitating bouts of the tuberculosis that plagued him from age seven, Beardsley attended Hamilton Lodge, a boarding school near Brighton, and, with financial assistance from his maternal grandfather, the Brighton Grammar School. In 1888, at aged 16, Beardsley became a clerk in London, working first in the office of a surveyor and then in the office of the Guardian Fire and Life company (*Beardsley* 19). In his spare time, he read voraciously and honed his obvious talent for drawing, absorbing the influences of PRE-RAPHAELITISM, James McNeill Whistler (1834–1903), and Joris-Karl Huysmans (1848–1907), whose novel *Against Nature* (1884) was the "breviary of decadence," in ARTHUR SYMONS's phrase. In July 1891, Beardsley audaciously presented himself and his portfolio at the door of Edward Burne-Jones (1833–

98). The renowned Pre-Raphaelite painter was dazzled by Beardsley's drawings and encouraged him to pursue a career in art. The following summer, the bookseller Frederick Evans put him in touch with the publisher J. M. Dent, and he was hired to illustrate an edition of *Le Morte d'Arthur* (35–39). Bolstered by a £500 bequest from a great-aunt and the assignment from Dent, Beardsley abandoned his career as a clerk toward the end of the summer in 1892 and launched his career as a professional illustrator (32, 39).

In June 1893, Beardsley's ascent began in earnest when the publisher John Lane hired him to illustrate the English translation of Oscar Wilde's play *Salomé* (57). The edition was a succès de scandale, and Beardsley, for better and for worse, would be thereafter associated with Wilde (whom he intensely disliked) and the decadent school. Beardsley, then, was the obvious choice as art editor of John Lane's

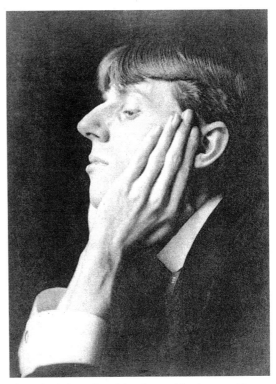

The artist Aubrey Beardsley, bane of the bourgeoisie, ca. 1895. Photograph by Frederick H. Evans (1853–1943) *(Library of Congress)*

new quarterly the *Yellow Book*, which went on sale on April 15, 1894. It was yet another succès de scandale, and Beardsley became a celebrity. Wilde had nothing to do with the *Yellow Book*, Beardsley having blackballed him, but rumor mistakenly had it that when he was arrested on morals charges on April 5, 1895, he made his way to the Bow Street police station with the *Yellow Book* under his arm; the volume was actually a French novel, but the mob that gathered to throw stones through the window of Lane's offices was not interested in fine distinctions (122). Beardsley, already associated with Wilde in the public mind, was dimissed as a placatory gesture (*Mem.* 90). As Yeats writes, "the moment had come to get rid of unpopular persons" (*Aut.* 249). Beardsley's next venture was the *Savoy*, which was intended, in Stanley Weintraub's words, "to pick up the discarded banners left by the retreat of *The Yellow Book* into respectability" (*Beardsley* 133). The publisher Leonard Smithers (1861–1907) enlisted Symons as editor of the prospective quarterly. In Yeats's telling, "Symons made two conditions: that Smithers should drop his secret trade in lascivious books, and appoint Aubrey Beardsley, whom Symons had I think never met, art editor. Both conditions were accepted, and we began a warfare on the British public at a time when we had all against us" (*Mem* 90; see also *Aut.* 248).

In the spring of 1894, Beardsley designed the poster for a bill of plays at the Avenue Theatre, London, that included Yeats's *The* LAND OF HEART'S DESIRE. Beardsley's design—showing a darkly sensual, richly maned woman peering from behind a transparent curtain—later appeared on the title page of the first edition of the play, published by T. Fisher Unwin in April 1894 (*CLI* 388–389; for a reproduction of the cover, see *Biblo.* 31). Liam Miller suggests that the poster was a lasting inspiration to Yeats; he discerns in Beardsley's woman an anticipation of Yeats's doctrine of the mask and a foreshadowing of the kind of cruel muse or goddess he would depict in later plays like *The* ONLY JEALOUSY OF EMER, *The* KING OF THE GREAT CLOCK TOWER, and *A* FULL MOON IN MARCH (*Noble Drama* 15). Yeats and Beardsley, then, almost certainly had at least a glancing familiarity with each other by April 16, 1894,

when both attended the inaugural dinner of the *Yellow Book* at the Hotel d'Italia in Soho. It was at this dinner that Yeats first laid eyes on OLIVIA SHAKESPEAR, who was to become his mistress and lifelong friend (*Olivia Shakespear and W. B. Yeats* 30–32; *Mem.* 72). According to Max Beerbohm, however, Yeats did not meet Beardsley (nor his sister Mabel) until January 22, 1896, when a dinner was held at the New Lyric Club to celebrate the inaugural issue of the *Savoy*. Beerbohm recalls Yeats chewing Beardsley's ear with a learned disquisition on the "lore and rites of Diabolism," to which Beardsley was "too polite not to go on saying at intervals, in his hard, quick voice, 'Oh really? How perfectly entrancing!' and 'Oh really? How perfectly sweet!'" (*I&R*, I, 28–29).

Though Yeats and Beardsley were never close friends, Beardsley figures prominently in the account of the period Yeats gives in AUTOBIOGRAPHIES (see 248–255; see also *Mem.* 90–92). In his most ambitious observation, Yeats writes of Beardsley, "He was in my Lunar metaphor a man of the thirteenth Phase, his nature on the edge of UNITY OF BEING, the understanding of that Unity by the intellect his one overmastering purpose [. . .] and so being all subjective he would take upon himself not the consequences but the knowledge of sin. I surrender myself to the wild thought that by so doing he enabled persons who had never heard his name to recover innocence. [. . .] I see in his fat women and shadowy pathetic girls, his horrible children, half child, half embryo, in all the lascivious monstrous imagery of the privately published designs, the phantasms that from the beginning have defied the scourge and the hair shirt" (*Aut.* 254). In MEMOIRS, Yeats lauds Beardsley as the "first satirist of the soul English art has produced" and notes his "icy passion for all reality" (92).

Shadowed by tuberculosis his entire life, Beardsley finally died of the disease in 1898, shortly after he converted to Catholicism. Beardsley was to have illustrated a proposed edition of Yeats's play *The* SHADOWY WATERS. Illness, however, prevented him from completing all but a single drawing, which has since been lost (*CL2* 61; *Nobel Drama* 22–23). When MABEL BEARDSLEY (1871–1916) was hospitalized with cancer in 1913, Yeats wrote a lovely and intricate poetic sequence titled "UPON A DYING LADY." The fifth poem of the sequence, "HER RACE," ends with the question, "And how should her heart fail her / Or sickness break her will / With her dead brother's valour / For an example still?"

Bibliography

Harwood, John. *Olivia Shakespear and W. B. Yeats: After Long Silence*; Mikhail, E. H., ed. *W. B. Yeats: Interviews and Recollections* (vol. 1); Miller, Liam. *The Noble Drama of W. B. Yeats*; Wade, Allan. *A Bibliography of the Writings of W. B. Yeats*; Weintraub, Stanley. *Beardsley: A Biography*; W. B. Yeats, *Autobiographies, The Collected Letters of W. B. Yeats* (vols. 1–2), *Memoirs.*

Beardsley, Mabel (1871–1916)   See "UPON A DYING LADY."

Bedford Park   Situated about six miles southwest of downtown London, Bedford Park was the first of England's "garden suburbs." The attempt was to provide "a self-contained community of comfortable, moderately priced yet attractive houses for the middle classes" (*Early Community* 9). Construction began in 1876, and by 1883 the estate had largely taken shape, its 113 acres encompassing 490 houses, clubhouse, church, inn, school of art, and several stores. In 1884, rival schools were instituted, one strictly secular, the other Christian. Lively designs by E. W. Godwin, Norman Shaw, and others in the eclectic redbrick Queen Anne style lent the development an air of aestheticism, and Bedford Park quickly became associated with the aesthetic movement, then at its height. In Yeats's description, Bedford Park seemed to represent the "PRE-RAPHAELITE movement at last affecting life" (*Aut.* 113). Bedford Park's physical

A view of Bedford Park by John Nash, from a portfolio of nine lithographs titled "Bedford Park 1882" and published by Vincent Brooks, Day and Son, 1882. *(Guildhall Library, City of London)*

appeal, in combination with its communal atmosphere, moderate cost, and proximity to the city, soon attracted a bevy of writers and painters to the community, including painter, set designer, and illustrator Henry Marriott Paget (1856–1936); historian Frederick York Powell (1850–1904); physician, playwright, and poet John Todhunter (1839–1916); and JOHN BUTLER YEATS, with family in tow.

The Yeats family twice sojourned at Bedford Park, living at 8 Woodstock Road from spring 1879 to late autumn 1881, and then at 3 Blenheim Road from March 24, 1888, to October 1902 (Yeats struck out on his own in October 1895, briefly living with ARTHUR SYMONS and then taking his own lodgings at WOBURN BUILDINGS). The family's rent for the house on Blenheim Road was £45 per year (*CL1* 56). Suggesting Bedford Park's hold on his youthful imagination, Yeats remembers feeling chagrined upon his family's return in 1888 because "the co-operative stores, with their little seventeenth-century panes, had lost the romance I saw there when I passed them still unfinished on my way to school; and because the public-house, called The Tabard after Chaucer's Inn, was so plainly a common public-house; and because the great sign of a trumpeter designed by Rooke, the Pre-Raphaelite artist, had been freshened by some inferior hand." Still, as Yeats says, Bedford Park "had some village characters and helped us to feel not wholly lost in the metropolis" (*Aut.* 113). Yeats's letters are less jaded. He wrote to KATHARINE TYNAN on March 14, 1888, that "Bedford Park is the least Londonish place hereabouts—a silent tree filled place where every thing is a little idyllic except the cockroaches that [abound] here. The quantity of new wood brings them—and the old wood brings a stray nightingale now and again, says rumour, & certainly thrushes and black birds in almost country plenty. I will have a study to myself with one of those white wooden balconies native to that part of the world" (*CL1* 56).

Bedford Park exposed Yeats to a rich and varied intellectual life, and most significantly, started him thinking about the theater. Among Bedford Park's many organizations was a dramatic club that each year produced three or four plays on a small stage attached to the community clubhouse. In May 1890, the club produced *A Sicilian Idyll,* an arcadian verse drama written by Todhunter at Yeats's urging. The production starred Bedford Park resident Heron Allen, a "solicitor, fiddler and popular writer on palmistry," and FLORENCE FARR, the sister-in-law of Henry Marriott Paget (*Aut.* 118). Though thinking little of the play as written (at least in retrospect), Yeats was enraptured by the actors' performance, discovering "for the first time that in the performance of all drama that depends for its effect upon beauty of language, poetical culture may be more important than professional experience" (118). Yeats contributed articles on the production to the *Boston Pilot* and to the *Providence Sunday Journal* (collected in *Letters to the New Island*). As his account in both his preface to *Letters to the New Island* and in AUTOBIOGRAPHIES makes clear, the performance—dreamy, poetic, ceremonial—was an intimation of his own future experiments in the theater. Farr, of course, later become one of his most important theatrical collaborators. Most notably, she directed the debut production *The LAND OF HEART'S DESIRE* (featuring her young niece Dorothy Paget as the fairy child) and shared in Yeats's experiments with the psaltery (see "SPEAKING TO THE PSALTERY").

Bibliography

Bolsterli, Margaret Jones. *The Early Community at Bedford Park: "Corporate Happiness" in the First Garden Community*; Yeats, W. B. *Autobiographies, The Collected Letters of W. B. Yeats* (vol. 1), *Letters to the New Island*.

Blake, William (1757–1827) No writer meant more to Yeats, early, middle, and late. Blake provided Yeats with nothing less than a sacred literature in which he could renew himself and in relationship to which he could orient himself as poet and thinker. Yeats found in Blake as well a source of condensed and ready wisdom: It may be that Yeats quoted no one more regularly and in more contexts than Blake. JOHN EGLINTON, remembering Yeats as a young man, ventures that Blake was "perhaps the only poet on whom he was really grounded" (*I&R,* I, 33). This discounts the crucial influence of SHELLEY (Harold Bloom views Shelley as even more influential than Blake) but makes the point that Blake was for Yeats completely primary (*Yeats* 68). In "A General Introduction for my Work," Yeats acknowledges that he owes his soul "to Shakespeare, to Spenser and to Blake, perhaps to WILLIAM MORRIS" (*LE* 212). In his lecture "Nationality and Literature," Yeats calls Blake his "master" (*UP1* 273). Yeats's devotion to Blake never waned, even as he shed other habiliments of the 1890s, including, to some extent, Shelley. In his essay "Swedenborg, Mediums, and the Desolate Places" (1920, written 1914), Yeats observes that Blake "grows always more exciting with every year of life" and "grows also more obscure" (*LE* 55). Virginia Moore comments that "from his twenty-fourth year to his death at nearly seventy-four—some fifty years—Yeats was a Blakean disciple: Blake's only disciple of genius" (*Unicorn* 26).

Yeats steeped himself in Blake during the years of his poetic apprenticeship. These studies, coupled with his occult studies, made an eccentric surrogate for the university education that he missed. In AUTOBIOGRAPHIES, he remembers that he started reading Blake when he was 15 or 16, encouraged by his father JOHN BUTLER YEATS (114). By 1889, Yeats had become a sufficiently knowledgeable and astute acolyte to join his father's friend, painter and poet Edwin John Ellis (1848–1916), in editing the three-volume *Works of William Blake, Poetic, Symbolic, and Critical*, published by Bernard Quaritch in 1893 (*CL1* 151). In addition to Blake's poems, the edition includes a stylish preface (see *P&I* 74–78), a 172-page memoir of Blake's life, an account of Blake's symbolic system, and an interpretive account of the poems. In *Autobiographies*, Yeats recollects that early in their acquaintance Ellis handed him "a scrap of notepaper" on which he had written an interpretation of "To the Jews," the preface to the second chapter of *Jerusalem*. "The four quarters of London represented Blake's four great mythological personages, the Zoas, and also the four elements," as Yeats remembered. "These few sentences were the foundation of all study of the philosophy of William Blake that requires an exact knowledge for its pursuit and that traces the connection between his system and

Portrait of William Blake, 1807, by Thomas Phillips (1770–1845). The painting is in the National Portrait Gallery, London. *(Library of Congress)*

that of Swedenborg or of Boehme. I recognized certain attributions, from what is sometimes called the Christian Cabbala, of which Ellis had never heard, and with this proof that his interpretation was more than fantasy he and I began our four years' work upon the 'Prophetic Books' of William Blake" (*Aut.* 144–145; see also *Mem.* 29; *P&I* 75). In his own copy of the edition, Yeats left a record of his working collaboration with Ellis: "The writing of this book is mainly Ellis's, the thinking is as much mine as his. The biography is by him. He rewrote and trebled in size a biography of mine. The greater part of the 'symbolic system' is my writing; the rest of the book was written by Ellis working over short accounts of the books by me, except in the case of the 'literary period' the account of the minor poems, & the account of Blake's art theories which are all his own except in so far as we discussed everything together" (*Biblio.* 241; see also *CL1* 224–227; *CL2* 469).

The edition represented an important reevaluation of Blake, for Yeats and Ellis struck a blow for the "solidity" and "wonderful coherence" of Blake's mystical system (*P&I* 74). "No one will ever call him mad again," Yeats wrote to JOHN O'LEARY on May 7, 1889 (*CL1* 163; see also 214; *CL2* 631). So too the edition unveiled Blake's unfinished and previously unpublished long poem *Vala, or the Four Zoas* (ca. 1797), which Yeats and Ellis had discovered while examining manuscripts belonging to the Linnell siblings, whose father, the landscape painter John Linnell (1792–1882), had been Blake's friend and patron. "Did I tell you that we have found a new long poem of Blakes," Yeats wrote in excitement to KATHARINE TYNAN on December 26, 1889. "Rossetti mentioned its name no more. We are the only people who ever read it. It is two thousand lines long or so and belongs to three old men & their sisters who live away at Red Hill in Surrey. Ellis & myself go from time to time and do a days copying out at it. The old men are very hospitable and bring out 30 year old port wine for us and when I am copying the oldest of the old men [John, 1821–1906] sits beside me with a penknife in his hand to point my pencil when it blunts" (*CL1* 202; see also *Aut.* 145).

The edition was less happily notable for the since discredited proposition that Blake was by heritage Irish, on the theory that his grandfather changed his name from O'Neil to evade financial and political difficulties (*CL1* 163–164, 183, 186; *Works*, I, 3–4). "The very manner of Blake's writing has an Irish flavour," opines Yeats, "a lofty extravagance of invention and epithet, recalling the *Tain Bo Cuilane* and other old Irish epics, and his mythology brings often to mind the tumultuous vastness of the ancient tales of god and demon that have come to us from the dawn of mystic tradition in what may fairly be called his fatherland" (*Works*, I, 3–4). Among the mockers of this theory was the poet Swinburne (*CL4* 434–435; see also 449–450). Equally suspicious was the inference from what seemed Rosicrucian elements in his work that Blake had been an initiate of "The Hermetic Students of the G.D.," evidently a precursor of the HERMETIC ORDER OF THE GOLDEN DAWN. Yeats himself, however, admitted that "this conjecture is not suscep-

tible of proof" (*Works*, I, 24). Clearly Yeats sought in Blake a lineal sanction for his own identity and own activities, sought not only to locate himself in Blake's tradition but more daringly to locate Blake in his own tradition.

For his four years of labor on what he called "truly a biggish book" Yeats received as payment "13 large paper copies" of the printed volume (*CL1* 179, 227). Touched by Yeats's zeal, the Linnells presented the young scholar-poet with Blake's series of seven engravings illustrating *The Divine Comedy.* These hung on the walls of WOBURN BUILDINGS along with two drawings by Blake and an engraving of Blake's head (*Unicorn* 87). In 1894, Yeats attempted to arrange publication of Blake's 102 designs and seven engravings inspired by Dante's masterwork, but nothing came of his effort (*CL1* 406).

Before many years had passed Yeats developed misgivings about the Blake edition. In November 1899, he wrote in Lady GREGORY's copy that the work gave him "no particular pleasure." He judged it "substantially correct in its interpretations," but full of misprints, and "its description of the doctrine of more ancient mystics than Blake are inadequate, & in one or two cases where I have tried to read Blake in their light I have blundered through not having enough light [. . .]" (*CL2* 468–469). In May 1900, Yeats noted in the flyleaf of his own copy the preponderance of misprints and acknowledged that some of his own "constructive symbolism is put with too much confidence. It is mainly right but parts should be used rather as an interpretive hypothesis than as a certainty" (*Biblio.* 241). Yeats was not being unduly modest. Bloom finds the edition replete with "some gorgeous nonsense and much more plain nonsense," and he catalogs at length Yeats's self-revealing misinterpretations of Blake (*Yeats* 69–82). He adds that Yeats and Ellis "make so many score of mistakes in recounting the narratives [of Blake's long poems] that any literate student with a little patience could do better" (80). Even Yeats's prose is "remarkably uninteresting, particularly when we recall that Yeats is one of the prose masters of the language" (75). While acknowledging that Yeats sometimes "followed false clues with misleading results," Kathleen Raine, on the other hand, judges that "Ellis and Yeats's work comes near to the underlying principles and intention of Blake's symbolic thought." In her opinion, Blake himself "would have condoned its mistakes, and probably set about adding to his all-embracing mythology whatever elements in the knowledge of Ellis and Yeats he had not already made his own" (*Yeats the Initiate* 95).

Yeats's passionate defense of Blake continued through the 1890s. In addition to *The Works of William Blake*, 1893 saw the publication of *The Poems of William Blake*, a single-volume selection of poetry edited and introduced by Yeats (for Yeats's preface, see *P&I* 79–101). Yeats's introduction—a lengthy and detailed biographical sketch—repeats the theory that Blake's paternal grandfather began life as John O'Neil (79). There followed two important essays distinguished by the fineness of their style: "William Blake and his Illustrations to the *Divine Comedy*" and "William Blake and the Imagination," which respectively appeared in the SAVOY (July–September 1896) and the *Academy* (June 19, 1897). In the latter essay, Yeats compresses and summarizes what he takes to be Blake's essential teaching: that "imagination was the first emanation of divinity," and that reason "binds us to mortality because it binds us to the senses, and divides us from each other by showing us our clashing interests; but imagination divides us from mortality by the immortality of beauty, and binds us to each other by opening the secret doors of all hearts. He cried again and again that everything that lives is holy, and that nothing is unholy except things that do not live—lethargies, and cruelties, and timidities, and that denial of imagination which is the root they grew from in old times. Passions, because most living, are most holy—and this was a scandalous paradox in his time—and man shall enter eternity borne upon their wings" (*E&I* 112–113; cf. *P&I* 77–78, 91–92). In a revealing apology, Yeats adds that Blake's confusing and obscure symbolism was forced upon him by historical circumstance, for modernity, unlike the 14th century of Dante, afforded no suitably coherent and encompassing mythology. Thus Blake was obliged to invent his own. Learning from Blake's dilemma, presumably, Yeats himself sought to root much of his own verse

and drama in the mythology of ancient Ireland (*E&I* 114). The long essay on Blake's Dante illustrations is, *The Works of William Blake* aside, Yeats's major statement on Blake, as well as a fine example of the sumptuous prose that was arguably Yeats's major achievement of the 1890s. Yeats begins by calling Blake the "first writer of modern times to preach the indissoluble marriage of all great art with symbol," and thus makes him the precursor of his own philosophy of symbolism (116). The second section gives a valuable account of Blake's cosmology and theology in an attempt to locate the keystones of Blake's thought and artistic practice.

During these years, as well, Yeats wrote two lesser pieces on Blake. "The Writings of William Blake" is an 1893 excoriation of Laurence Housman's *Selections from the Writings of William Blake*. It complains mightily about the kind of textual liberties and condescending treatment of Blake's mysticism that his own edition of Blake had been intended to correct once for all. "William Blake," an 1896 review of Richard Garnett's *William Blake*, issues much the same complaint about the treatment of Blake's mysticism, though a little more gently (see *UP1* 280–283, 400–403). On October 10, 1893, Yeats defended his review of Housman's book in a letter to Housman himself. As he admitted, his object had been to explode an entire school of Blake criticism by affirming the importance of Blake's mysticism, and that Housman had been merely "the outpost of the enemies army" (*CL1* 364).

Yeats's poetry mentions Blake in only two instances. In "An ACRE OF GRASS," Yeats beseeches for "an old man's frenzy" in order to remake himself as Timon and Lear or "that William Blake / Who beat upon the wall / Till truth obeyed his call. . . ." In "UNDER BEN BULBEN," he includes Blake, Calvert, Wilson, and Claude in the litany of artists who "prepared a rest for the people of God," as if in some expiring effort of religion before "confusion fell upon our thought." Additionally, Yeats chose an epigraph from Blake—"The stars are threshed, and the souls are threshed from their husks"—to head the group of early poems he assigned the title "Crossways" in 1895. The epigraph misquotes lines from Blake's *Vala*: "All the nations were threshed out & the stars threshed from their husks" (see "Night the Ninth," line 650).

Bibliography

Bloom, Harold. *Yeats*; Mikhail, E. H., ed. *W. B. Yeats: Interviews and Recollections* (vol. 1); Moore, Virginia. *The Unicorn: William Butler Yeats' Search for Reality*; Raine, Kathleen. *Yeats the Initiate: Essays on Certain Themes in the Work of W. B. Yeats*; Wade, Allan. *A Bibliography of the Writings of W. B. Yeats*; Yeats, W. B. *Autobiographies, The Collected Letters of W. B. Yeats* (vols. 1–2, 4), *Essays and Introductions, Later Essays, Memoirs, Prefaces and Introductions, Uncollected Prose by W. B. Yeats* (vols. 1–2), (ed. with Edwin John Ellis) *The Works of William Blake, Poetic, Symbolic, and Critical.*

Chatterjee, Mohini (1858–1936) An attorney and poet from Calcutta, Chatterjee became assistant secretary of the Bengal branch of the THEOSOPHICAL SOCIETY in 1882, and soon became, in R. F. Foster's phrase, "Theosophy's roving ambassador in Europe" (AM 47). Arrestingly handsome by all accounts, Chatterjee prompted OSCAR WILDE to quip that he had "never realized before what a mistake we make in being white" (*Madame Blavatsky* 307). Yeats met Chatterjee in April 1886 when the Indian guru visited Dublin as the guest of the local branch of the Theosophical Society (AM 552). Yeats was fascinated by Chatterjee, whom he remembers in AUTOBIOGRAPHIES as a "handsome young man with the typical face of Christ" (98). Of Chatterjee's doctrines Yeats recalls, "It was my first meeting with a philosophy that confirmed my vague speculations and seemed at once logical and boundless. Consciousness, he taught, does not merely spread out its surface but has, in vision and in contemplation, another motion and can change in height and in depth" (98). Yeats commemorates Chatterjee and his teachings on the circularity of life in two poems, "Kanva on Himself" (VP 723) and "MOHINI CHATTERJEE." The former poem appeared in *The Wanderings of Oisin and Other Poems* (1889), but Yeats did not choose to reprint it, feeling that his "clumsy verse" had marred Chatterjee's "beautiful words" on the subject of reincarnation (*Early Essays* 290).

Yeats additionally wrote a limpid prose reminiscence titled "The Way of Wisdom," which he published in the *Speaker* (December 14, 1900) and reprinted as "The Pathway" in *Discoveries* (1908). The essay recollects Chatterjee's stay among the Dublin theosophists in 1886, picturing him as he "sat there beautiful, as only an Eastern is beautiful, making little gestures with his delicate hands," his conversation seeming "a flight into the heart of truth" (289). From the vantage of 1900, Yeats says that he can no longer distinguish Chatterjee's doctrines from what he later made of them or from what he had learned in the "great ruined house" of BLAKE's Prophetic Books, but he does remember Chatterjee teaching "that those who die, in so far as they have imagined beauty or justice, are made a part of beauty or justice, and move through the minds of living men, as SHELLEY believed; and that mind overshadows mind even among the living, and by pathways that lie beyond the senses; and that he measured labour by this measure, and put the hermit above all other labourers, because, being the most silent and the most hidden, he lived nearer to the Eternal Powers, and showed their mastery of the world" (291). In September 1935, Yeats, having gotten Chatterjee's address from a friend, wrote him a kind note: "I write merely to tell you that you are vivid in my memory after all these years. That week of talk when you were in Dublin did much for my intellect, gave me indeed my first philosophical exposition of life. When I knew you, you were a very beautiful young man; I think you were twenty-seven years old, and astonished us all, learned and simple, by your dialectical powers. My wife tells me that I often quote you" (292).

Bibliography

Foster, R. F. *W. B. Yeats: A Life, I: The Apprentice Mage*; Meade, Marion. *Madame Blavatsky*; Yeats, W. B. *Autobiographies, The Collected Letters of W. B. Yeats* (vol. 1), *Early Essays, The Variorum Edition of the Poems of W. B. Yeats.*

Coleridge, Samuel Taylor (1772–1834) The great English romantic poet was an obscure but persistent influence on Yeats, as Matthew Gibson shows in his study *Coleridge, Yeats and the Romantic*

Sage. Prior to the 1930s, Yeats tended to conceive Coleridge as a type of the visionary artist dangerously caught up in his own vision, and thus as a herald of his own effort to "create once more the pure work" (*Aut.* 149). Yeats presents this notion of Coleridge in "William Blake and his Illustrations to *The Divine Comedy*" (1896), as well as in AUTOBIOGRAPHIES. In the latter, Yeats proposes that almost all poets "have had some propaganda or traditional doctrine to give companionship with their fellows. Had not Matthew Arnold his faith in what he described as the best thought of his generation, Browning his psychological curiosity, TENNYSON, as before him SHELLEY and WORDSWORTH, moral values that were not aesthetic values? But Coleridge of the 'Ancient Mariner', and 'Kubla Khan', and Rossetti in all his writings, made what Arnold has called that 'morbid effort', that search for 'perfection of thought and feeling, and to unite this to perfection of form', sought this new, pure beauty, and suffered in their lives because of it" (242). Thus understood, Coleridge was a spiritual precursor to the doomed poets of Yeats's "tragic generation."

Yeats's conception of Coleridge took a significant turn in "Pages from a Diary Written in Nineteen Hundred and Thirty" (see *Explorations*), in which he refers to Coleridge 18 times by name. Here Yeats is drawn not to the visionary poet of the 1790s, but to the transcendental idealist and political conservative who gathered a circle of young admirers while living at Highgate during the 1820s and set himself up as what Gibson calls a "romantic sage"—the "man of objective interests who yet desires the UNITY OF BEING usually desired by the artist" (43). This change of emphasis allowed Yeats to realign Coleridge with his late-arriving Anglo-Irish heroes, George Berkeley (1685–1753), Edmund Burke (1729–97), and JONATHAN SWIFT, who similarly epitomized the ideal of the romantic sage. In a diary entry of June 19, 1930, Yeats amplifies on his admiration of this type: "When I think of Swift, of Burke, of Coleridge, or Mallarmé, I remember that they spoke as it were sword in hand, that they played their part in a unique drama, but played it, as a politician cannot though he stand in the same ranks, with the whole soul" (*Expl.* 301).

Yeats attempted to follow this example in the 1920s and 1930s, devoting himself to the roles of public man and systematic thinker while striving to make "logic serve passion" (301).

Yeats's work, unsurprisingly, is suffused with echoes of Coleridge. To take only the most obvious and notable examples, there are discernible similarities between "Dejection: An Ode" (1802) and "LINES WRITTEN IN DEJECTION," "A PRAYER FOR MY DAUGHTER," and "VACILLATION"; between "Kubla Khan" (1816) and "ANCESTRAL HOUSES," "COOLE AND BALLYLEE, 1931," and "NEWS FOR THE DELPHIC ORACLE"; between "The Rime of the Ancient Mariner" (1798) and *The SHADOWY WATERS*.

Bibliography

Gibson, Matthew. *Yeats, Coleridge and the Romantic Sage*; Yeats, W. B. *Autobiographies, Explorations.*

Contemporary Club The Contemporary Club was founded in 1885 as a venue for weekly conversations on literary, artistic, social, and political topics. As a newly independent young woman who had just returned to Dublin, MAUD GONNE was invited to visit the club (probably in 1888) though it was "only later that a monthly ladies' night was arranged." She remembers a "cosy room, looking over College Green, where some twelve men were sitting smoking and drinking." The evening's debate topic was "some phase of the Land League," as Gonne recalls. "There were men of all shades of political opinion at the Club, even one or two Unionists, and the debate become very vehement" (SQ 89–90). The political economist Charles Hubert Oldham (1860–1926) founded the club and remained its "presiding genius" (in KATHARINE TYNAN's phrase) for 30-odd years (*Twenty-Five Years* 163–164). The club held its first meetings in Oldham's rooms at Trinity College, and then in November 1885 it acquired lodgings at 116 Grafton Street, Dublin (CL1 481). Yeats was brought to the club by his father early on and became a habitué, joining other regulars like the young poet and translator Douglas Hyde (1860–1949), the historian and novelist Standish James O'Grady (1846–1928), the poet and editor T. W. Rolleston (1857–1920), the barrister John F. Taylor (1850–1902), and the old

Fenian JOHN O'LEARY, whom Yeats revered as the last of the breed of "romantic Ireland" ("SEPTEMBER 1913"). Yeats regularly attended meetings of the club from 1885 until 1887, when his family moved to London, and he occasionally attended meetings of the club until at least 1908 (YC 116).

In AUTOBIOGRAPHIES, Yeats admits that he was drawn to the club not from any "natural liking" but from a "secret ambition" to become self-possessed and formidable in debate. He describes the tone of the meetings and his own somewhat callow role in the proceedings: "In Ireland harsh argument which had gone out of fashion in England was still the manner of our conversation, and at this club Unionist and Nationalist could interrupt one another and insult one another without the formal and traditional restraint of public speech. Sometimes they would change the subject and discuss Socialism, or a philosophical question, merely to discover their old passions under a new shape. I spoke easily and, I thought, well till some one was rude and then I would become silent or exaggerate my opinion to absurdity, or hesitate and grow confused, or be carried away myself by some party passion. I would spend hours afterwards going over my words and putting the wrong ones right (99).

The club was closely associated with the DUBLIN UNIVERSITY REVIEW, which Oldham and Rolleston edited. Yeats published his inaugural work in the review in 1885 and 1886.

Bibliography

Gonne, Maud. The Autobiography of Maud Gonne: A Servant of the Queen; Kelly, John S. A W. B. Yeats Chronology; Tynan, Katharine. Twenty-Five Years: Reminiscences; Yeats, W. B. Autobiographies, The Collected Letters of W. B. Yeats (vol. 1).

Coole Park "Certain woods at SLIGO [. . .] are so deep in my affections that I dream about them at night; and yet the woods at Coole, though they do not come into my dream, are so much more knitted to my thought that when I am dead they will have, I am persuaded, my longest visit." So writes Yeats in Autobiographies (283). Yeats first visited Coole Park, the Galway estate of the Gregory family, in August 1896. He and ARTHUR SYMONS were

guests at Tulira Castle, the Gothic manor of Lady GREGORY's neighbor EDWARD MARTYN, and Lady Gregory, whom Yeats had met briefly in London, invited the three writers to luncheon (Aut. 291; Lady Gregory 105). "E. Martyn had also poets with him, Symonds & Yeats," Lady Gregory recorded in her journal, "the latter full of charm & interest & the Celtic revival" (Lady Gregory's Diaries 118). In AUTOBIOGRAPHIES, Yeats admits that when he first saw Coole he was "so full of the mediaevalism of WILLIAM MORRIS" that he did not like "the gold frames, some deep and full of ornament, round the pictures in the drawing-room" and that it was only years later that he "came to understand the earlier nineteenth and later eighteenth century, and to love that house more than all other houses" (291). Yeats returned to Tulira the following summer in the company of GEORGE RUSSELL (AE). At the house of Count Florimond de Basterot (1836–1904), another Galway neighbor, Yeats and Lady Gregory sealed their friendship during a long afternoon talk, out of which came plans for an Irish theater (Lady Gregory's Diaries 152–153; see also Aut. 285; Mem. 117; Our Irish Theatre 19). Lady Gregory invited Yeats to spend the latter half of the summer at Coole, perceiving that his ineffectual pursuit of MAUD GONNE had left him broken down (Aut. 298; Lady Gregory's Diaries 118). Lady Gregory was convinced that open air and activity were the needed remedies, and she brought Yeats "from cottage to cottage collecting folk-lore" (Aut. 298; see also 283–284; Lady Gregory's Diaries 151–152). Setting down her impressions in her diary, Lady Gregory described her houseguest as a "most brilliant charming & lovable companion—never out of humour, simple, gentle—interested in all that went on—liking to do his work in the library in the midst of the coming & going, then if I was typing in the drawing room suddenly bursting in with some great new idea—& when it was expounded laughing & saying 'I treat you, as my father says, as an anvil, to beat out my ideas on'" (Lady Gregory's Diaries 150).

Until Lady Gregory's death in 1932, Yeats remained a household fixture, spending weeks or months as Lady Gregory's guest, an arrangement that did not necessarily delight the putative mas-

Coole Park, Yeats's spiritual home for 35 years. The house was demolished in 1941. The grounds are now a state-managed nature reserve. *(Fáilte Ireland)*

ter of the house, ROBERT GREGORY, and his wife, Margaret (AM 503). Amid the rooms, gardens, library, and woods, Yeats found beauty, comfort, companionship, rest, health ("the only place where I have ever had unbroken health"), and, most of all, an example of order and tradition that became one of his chief poetic inspirations (*Letters* 799). "This house has enriched my soul out of measure, because here life moves without restraint through spacious forms," Yeats wrote in an August 7, 1909, journal entry. "Here there has been no compelled labour, no poverty-thwarted impulse" (*Mem.* 226). Yeats's love of Coole undoubtedly had much to do with his decision to purchase THOOR BALLYLEE, an imposing but impractical stone tower that had once belonged to the Gregory estate (AP 84–85).

Robert Gregory (1727–1810), director and chairman of the East India Company and great-grandfather of Lady Gregory's husband Sir William Gregory (1817–92), purchased the estate in 1768 and built the manor house (*Lady Gregory* 49). The estate originally consisted of 600 acres, to which Robert Gregory added more than 1,000 acres that

had belonged to Lord Clanricarde's Ballylee estate (*Guide to Coole Park* 23). Yeats's Thoor Ballylee became part of the Coole demesne by the purchase. William Gregory sold two-thirds of this acreage in 1856 after incurring racing debts as a young man, but Thoor Ballylee was restored to the Coole demesne in the early 20th century, before passing to the Congested Districts Board (*Lady Gregory* 50; *Thoor Ballylee* 10). Edward Malins, in his preface to Lady Gregory's *Coole*, describes the Coole manor house as "neither grand nor imposing," but "very typically Irish, a simple three-storeyed cube of six bays on the east front, having a central theme window surmounting a tripartite Palladian window above a square porch." The Victorian bow windows in the drawing room and dining room looked down upon the lake, and "the view westwards towards the setting sun over the Burren, with the blue-shadowed Connemara hills in the distance was most beautiful as one approached along a wide drive through undulating parkland, before entering the gloom of the arched avenue of ilexes and limes" (*Coole* 8). Yeats describes the house as "plain and box-like, except on the side towards the lake, where somebody, probably Richard Gregory [1761–1839], had enlarged the drawing-room and dining-room with great bow windows" (*Aut.* 293). Lady Gregory calls it simply "a plain white house" (*Seventy Years* 24). The house was surrounded by the Seven Woods that Yeats came so much to love: Shanwalla (old homestead), Kyle Dortha (dark wood), Kyle-na-no (nut wood), Pairc-na-lee (calf field), Parc-na-carraig (rocky field), Pairc-na-tarav (bull field), and Inchy Wood (river meadow) (*Lady Gregory* 38; for a map of the woods, see *Guide to Coole Park* 39–40).

Lady Gregory became mistress of Coole in 1880, upon marrying her 63-year-old neighbor, a former governor of Ceylon. By then, the estate was less a going economic enterprise than a retreat from the expense of London, where Sir William spent most of his time (*Lady Gregory* 50–51). Sir William died in 1892, leaving the house in Lady Gregory's charge until their son Robert should come of age, but granting her the right to remain in the house until her death. Robert turned 21 on May 20, 1902, but Lady Gregory remained effective mistress of the estate, irremovable in her deep love of the house and in her implacable managerial competence. Lady Gregory's arrival at Coole coincided with the land reform movement and the demise of the great house as an Irish institution. She struggled tirelessly to preserve Coole for her son and grandson, but little by little the trend of society and history, coupled with the death of Robert in 1918, undid her efforts. Upon Robert's death, his widow Margaret inherited the estate. Lady Gregory managed to avert the outright sale of Coole only by agreeing to a hard bargain. In November 1920, most of the estate was sold to tenants at a price of £9,000, leaving only house, gardens, and 350 acres, with Lady Gregory responsible for all expenses and Margaret entitled to all income (266–268). On April 1, 1927, Margaret sold the house and remaining grounds to the Ministry of Lands and Agriculture. Lady Gregory managed to remain in the house until the end of her life only by leasing it from the ministry for £100 per year (*Lady Gregory's Journals*, II, 180). On March 24, 1927, with Coole in its very last days, Lady Gregory began writing "a sort

of farewell" to house and grounds (II, 178). The CUALA PRESS published her memoir in 1931 under the title *Coole*, with Yeats's poem "COOLE PARK, 1929"—then titled "Coole Park"—as preface. In a 1930 diary entry, Yeats imagined that Coole would wind up "an office and residence for foresters, a little cheap furniture in the great rooms, a few religious oleographs its only pictures," but even this glum vision was optimistic (*Expl.* 319). In 1941, the ministry sold the house to a building contractor who tore it down for its reusable stone (*Lady Gregory* 303).

Yeats found ceaseless poetic inspiration in the implicit values of Coole, and he commemorated the house in an abundance of verse. Poems explicitly set at Coole or touching on life at Coole include "An APPOINTMENT," "BEAUTIFUL LOFTY THINGS," "COOLE AND BALLYLEE, 1931," "Coole Park, 1929," "For Anne Gregory" (1932), "IN MEMORY OF MAJOR ROBERT GREGORY," "IN THE SEVEN WOODS," "An IRISH AIRMAN FORESEES HIS DEATH," "The MAN AND THE ECHO," "The MUNICIPAL GALLERY REVISITED," "The NEW FACES," the introductory lines to The SHADOWY WATERS, "Shepherd and Goatherd" (1919), "To a Squirrel at Kyle-na-no" (1917), "UPON A HOUSE SHAKEN BY THE LAND AGITATION," and "The WILD SWANS AT COOLE." While "A PRAYER FOR MY DAUGHTER" mentions only "Gregory's wood," its vision of a house "where all's accustomed, ceremonious" clearly pays homage to Coole, and may indeed be Yeats's supreme homage to Coole. In *Autobiographies*, meanwhile, Yeats gives a vivid picture of Coole and inventories the treasures of the house with a minuteness that suggests his attentive—almost proprietary—interest. He recalls "Mogul or Persian paintings," "great earthenware ewers and basins," "great silver bowls," the vast woods, the library full of "Greek and Roman Classics bound by famous French and English binders," the "mezzotints and engravings of the masters and friends of the old Gregorys," the "Persian helmets, Indian shields, Indian swords in elaborate sheaths, stuffed birds from various parts of the world" (292–293; he similarly describes the great house in PURGATORY and the fanciful Bell estate in *A VISION*). It was this rooted accretion of Coole that spoke most deeply to Yeats, who suf-

Coole from the rear. According to biographer Elizabeth Coxhead: "The left-hand bay was the drawing-room, the right-hand the dining-room, with the library between them. The guest-room converted as a writing-room for Yeats was above the library; its window is concealed by the right-hand bay." *(Fáilte Ireland)*

fered always an anguished sense of his own root-lessness as an early exile from his native Sligo (cf. "UNDER SATURN").

Yeats's reverence for the house and all it repre-sented is reflected in an anecdote. A "queer Dub-lin sculptor dressed like a workman and in filthy clothes" arrived at Coole on the day following Lady Gregory's death in order to pay his respects, Yeats told OLIVIA SHAKESPEAR. "He walked from room to room and then stood where hang the mezzotints and engravings of those under or with whom [. . .] the Gregorys have served, Fox, Burke and so on, and after standing silent said 'All the nobility of earth.' I felt he did not mean it for that room alone but for lost tradition. How much of my own verse has not been but the repetition of those words" (*Letters* 795–796).

Bibliography

Foster, R. F. *W. B. Yeats: A Life, I: The Apprentice Mage, II: The Arch-Poet*; Gregory, Lady. *Coole, Lady Gregory's Diaries 1892–1902, Lady Gregory's Jour-nals* (vol. 2, ed. Daniel J. Murphy), *Seventy Years: Being the Autobiography of Lady Gregory, Our Irish Theatre*; Hanley, Mary, and Liam Miller. *Thoor Bal-lylee: Home of William Butler Yeats*; Kohfeldt, Mary Lou. *Lady Gregory: The Woman Behind the Irish Renaissance*; Smythe, Colin. *A Guide to Coole Park, Co. Galway: Home of Lady Gregory*; Yeats, W. B. *Autobiographies, Explorations, The Letters of W. B. Yeats, Memoirs.*

Cuala Press In July 1908, Yeats's sisters, Lily (1866–1949) and Lolly (1868–1940), severed their ties with Dun Emer Industries and founded Cuala Industries, an arts and crafts manufactory on the pattern of its predecessor. The new concern was housed in a four-room cottage in Churchtown, near the village of Dundrum, County Dublin. As Liam Miller explains, the name "Cuala" was "taken from the Irish placename of the South County Dublin Barony in which the new premises were located" (*Dun Emer Press* 50). As had been the case at Dun

Emer, Lily was in charge of embroidery and Lolly in charge of printing and publishing. The DUN EMER PRESS became the Cuala Press, but all of the Dun Emer trademarks—small print runs, the use of 14-point Caslon type, the use of red ink to highlight headings and colophons—were maintained. In his continuing role of literary editor, Yeats remained responsible for soliciting and vetting manuscripts. "W. B. is editor of the Cuala Press," Lolly wrote ARTHUR SYMONS in March 1926, "in the sense that *I can not* print any book he does not *agree to my doing* [. . .] my brother is most helpful & I could not run the Press at all without him. He doesn't in any way supervise the work here—merely gets in the books—but *that is a very important part of it*." Yeats and his sister periodically clashed over editorial control, but as Lolly told Symons, putting a positive face on a tense relationship, "brothers and sisters often have these storms—I too am hot—& they bear no malice ever" (*AP 303*). It also fell to Yeats periodically to bail the industries out of financial trouble. In 1925, Yeats estimated that over the previous 20 years Cuala had run an average annual deficit of £135. He had made up much of this deficit, despite his own often straitened finances (*BG 334*).

Cuala Industries followed a steady if not lucrative course until 1923, when what seemed to be tuberculosis (actually retrosternal goiter) forced Lily to take a leave of absence. The concern relocated to the basement of Yeats's new house at 82 Merrion Square in Dublin (*BG 328–329*; *Dun Emer Press 80*). Yeats's wife, GEORGE YEATS, assumed Lily's duties as supervisor of embroidery, thus beginning the hands-on involvement with Cuala that was to continue for the remaining 45 years of her life (*Dun Emer Press 80*). On August 18, 1923, Yeats wrote of the change to T. STURGE MOORE: "My wife is full of energy of mind and body and will I think greatly improve the work. She knows what people wear and has seen modern art. My sister's work had become too sere, a ghost of long past colours and forms. I look forward to living in a house where there is so much going on" (*WBY&TSM 49*). In February 1925, Cuala moved to a leased showroom and workshop at 133 Lower Baggot Street, Dublin, which remained its lodgings for the next 17 years.

After her breakdown of 1923, Lily never entirely recovered her health, and the embroidery department closed in 1931 (*BG 447*). From 1938, the Cuala Press was governed by a board of directors, chaired by George. After Lolly died in January 1940, the press fell entirely into her hands, and she kept it alive, if only on a limited basis, until her death (*555, 585*). The war hampered Cuala's export business, and George was once again obliged to open her domestic door to the family business. The concern relocated to her house at 46 Palmerston Road, Dublin, in January 1942, and there it remained until her death in August 1968. Though it continued to issue prints and greeting cards, Cuala Press suspended book publication in 1946 (*593*). The press underwent a renaissance in 1969. Under the direction of Anne Yeats, Michael B. Yeats, Thomas Kinsella, and Liam Miller, it returned to book publishing and moved to new quarters at 116 Lower Baggot Street (*Dun Emer Press 119*).

Under the direction of Lolly and George, the Cuala Press issued 66 books by a roster of eminences that includes EDWARD DOWDEN, Lord Dunsany (1878–1957), Oliver St John Gogarty (1878–1957), Lady GREGORY, Douglas Hyde (1860–1949), John Masefield (1878–1967), Frank O'Connor (1903–66), EZRA POUND, GEORGE RUSSELL (AE), J. M. SYNGE, Rabindranath Tagore (1861–1941), and JOHN BUTLER YEATS. Yeats, of course, dominated the list. Between 1908 and 1944, Cuala published 27 works by Yeats in editions numbering between 250 and 500 copies. Typically, the Cuala editions of Yeats's work were followed by editions published by larger commercial firms. Yeats additionally wrote prefaces to eight publications by other writers.

Bibliography
Foster, R. F. *W. B. Yeats: A Life, II: The Arch-Poet*; Miller, Liam. *The Dun Emer Press, Later the Cuala Press*; Saddlemyer, Ann. *Becoming George: The Life of Mrs W. B. Yeats*; Yeats, W. B. *W. B. Yeats and T. Sturge Moore: Their Correspondence 1901–1937*.

Cuchulain   The warrior hero of Irish legend—his name pronounced "koo' hoo' lin"—recurs throughout Yeats's verse and drama (*YD 40*; *VPl. 420*). In Yeats's conceptualization, Cuchulain is the archetype of the solitary man in his pride and restless strength, his life expressive of what Yeats called "creative joy separated from fear" (*Letters* 913; *LOP* 184). Yeats was drawn to Cuchulain as to his own "antiself," defined as the mask that "delineates a being in all things the opposite" to one's own "natural state" (*Aut.* 200). If Yeats was imprisoned by the "definitions of the analytic mind" ("THE PEOPLE") or caught in the "cold snows of a dream" ("The ROAD AT MY DOOR"), Cuchulain represents the mind and body united, unfettered by self-consciousness, possessed of the "purity of a natural force" ("The People").

Yeats's version of the Cuchulain legend derives from diverse sources. As a young man, Yeats had been stirred by the treatment of Cuchulain in Standish James O'Grady's (1846–1928) two-volume *History of Ireland* (1878, 1880) and *The Coming of Cuculain* (1894). He included *The Heroic Period* (the first volume of O'Grady's history) and *The Coming of Cuculain* in the list of the 30 best Irish books that he published in the *Daily Express* in February 1895 (*CL1* 440–445), and he included the *History of Ireland* in the similar list he submitted to the *Bookman* in October 1895 (*UP1* 382–387). In his introduction to FIGHTING THE WAVES, Yeats writes that O'Grady, steeped in Homer, re-created Cuchulain "in the image of Achilles" and took up his legend "that he might bring back an heroic ideal." Though his retelling of the Cuchulain legend "founded modern Irish literature," his work, at least in Yeats's mature estimation, was "hasty and ill-constructed" and his style "marred by imitation of Carlyle" (*Expl.* 371; *VPl.* 567, 572; see also *Aut.* 296). A more decisive revelation was Lady GREGORY's *Cuchulain of Muirthemne* (1902). Braving inevitable accusations of logrolling, Yeats called it "a book to set beside the *Morte d'Arthur* and the *Mabinogion*" (*E&I* 188) and trumpeted it as the best Irish book of his time (*Expl.* 3). In his introduction to the volume, Yeats reveals the magnitude of the aspiration bound up in such myth-mongering. Only by retelling the legendary tales, he writes, will the land "begin again to be a Holy Land, as it was before men gave their hearts to Greece and Rome and Judea" (*Expl.* 12–13; *P&I* 123). Yeats's treatment of the most iconic scene in the Cuchulain cycle—the hero's maddened fight with the sea—additionally owes something to Jeremiah Curtin's 1890 volume *Myth and Folk-Lore of Ireland*, as Yeats acknowledges in a note to his early poem "CUCHULAIN'S FIGHT WITH THE SEA" (*VP* 799; on Curtin see *CL1* 269, 339).

Yeats instructively anatomizes his own vision of Cuchulain in a 1904 letter to his theatrical colleague Frank Fay (1870–1931), who was to play the hero in the debut production of ON BAILE'S STRAND at the ABBEY THEATRE on December 27, 1904. Intended as a dramatic prompt, the portrait is particularly revealing in its emphasis on Cuchulain's shedding of romantic "illusions & dreams," for Yeats, however much he strove to be coldly self-possessed, was incapable of precisely this disburdening. Cuchulain's character, says Yeats, includes "a shadow of something a little proud, barren & restless as if out of shere [sic] strength of heart or from accident he had put affection away." Yeats further specifies that Cuchulain is about 40, and that "one understands from his talk about women that he does not love like a young man. Probably his very strength of character made him put off illusions & dreams (that make young men a womans [sic] servant) & made him become quite early in life a deliberate lover, a man of pleasure who can never really surrender himself. He is a little hard, & leaves the people about him a little repelled [. . .]. The touch of something hard, repellent yet alluring, self assertive yet self immolating is not all but it must be there. He is the fool—wandering passion, houseless & and all but loveless. Concubar is reason that is blind because it can only reason because it is cold. Are they not the cold moon & the hot sun?" (*CL3* 527).

Cuchulain is the central figure in a cycle of plays that are themselves at the center of Yeats's dramatic canon and among his most successful. In order of publication, the plays are *On Baile's Strand*, *The* GREEN HELMET, AT THE HAWK'S WELL, *The ONLY JEALOUSY OF EMER*, *Fighting the Waves* (a rewriting of *The Only Jealousy of Emer*), and *The DEATH OF CUCHULAIN*. Yeats envisioned the cycle—originally intended as a cycle of poems—as early as 1897, and the idea of it preoccupied him to the very end of his life (*CL2* 75). DOROTHY WELLESLEY records that

Yeats struggled to make final corrections to *The Death of Cuchulain* upon his literal deathbed (*LOP* 195). Though he is primarily a creature of Yeats's drama, Cuchulain figures in a number of poems that span the decades of Yeats's career. These include "Alternative Song for the Severed Head in *The King of the Great Clock Tower*" (1934), "The Circus Animals' Desertion," "Crazy Jane on the Mountain," "Cuchulain Comforted" (1939), "Cuchulain's Fight with the Sea," "To the Rose upon the Rood of Time," "The Secret Rose," and "The Statues."

Bibliography

Conner, Lester I. *A Yeats Dictionary: Persons and Places in the Poetry of William Butler Yeats*; Yeats, W. B. *Autobiographies, The Collected Letters of W. B. Yeats* (vols. 1–3), *Essays and Introductions, Explorations, The Letters of W. B. Yeats, Letters on Poetry from W. B. Yeats to Dorothy Wellesley, Prefaces and Introductions, Uncollected Prose by W. B. Yeats* (vol. 1), *The Variorum Edition of the Plays of W. B. Yeats, The Variorum Edition of the Poems of W. B. Yeats*.

Dowden, Edward (1843–1913) Perhaps the most prominent Irish literary critic during the late 19th century, Dowden was the son of a Cork linen draper. He had been the bosom friend of John Butler Yeats while both were at Trinity College in Dublin during the late 1850s and early 1860s, and the two remained close for the rest of their lives despite temperamental and philosophical differences (*PF* 40). Dowden deferred his poetic aspirations in order to pursue an academic career. He became professor of literature at Trinity in 1867, and established his reputation with a series of literary studies: *Shakspere: A Critical Study of His Mind and Art* (1876), *Shakspere Primer* (1877), and *Studies in Literature* (1877). He later wrote an influential two-volume *Life of Percy Bysshe Shelley* (1886), and shorter biographies of Robert Southey (1879), Robert Browning (1904), and Montaigne (1905), as well as edited *The Poetical Works of William Wordsworth* (1892), *The Poetical Works of Percy Bysshe Shelley* (1893), and *Poems by Robert Southey* (1895). It was Dowden's seven-volume edition of Wordsworth published by Oxford University Press that

Yeats perseveringly read through in the winter of 1915 (see *Letters* 590). *Poems*—the only volume of verse Dowden published in his lifetime—appeared in 1876.

When Yeats began to stir as a writer, the elder Yeats naturally submitted his son's work to his old friend. Dowden was complimentary and encouraging, though not without private reservations (*AM* 38). "Willie Yeats is an interesting bow of hope in the clouds," he wrote to John Todhunter on July 23, 1885, "an interesting boy whether he turn out much of a poet or not. The sap in him is all so green and young that I cannot guess what his fibre may afterwards be. So I shall only prophesy that he is to be a great poet after the event" (*PF* 144). The following summer he reported to Todhunter that Yeats "hangs in the balance between genius and (to speak rudely) fool," adding, "I shall rejoice if it be the first. But it remains doubtful" (144).

Despite Dowden's mildness and charm, and the warm family connection, Yeats was eventually put off by his fundamental conventionality in politics and art, and by his lack of receptivity to the national literary movement that Yeats was attempting to galvanize. In early 1895, Yeats and Dowden were on opposite sides in a public controversy in which Yeats pulled few punches. Dowden was among the respondents to a lecture on Sir Samuel Ferguson written by Roden Noel and read by Emily H. Hickey on January 14, 1895, at Leinster Lecture Hall, Dublin. Resisting the prevailing mood of national enthusiasm, Dowden accused Irish poetry of being rhetorical, sentimental, and technically deficient (*CL1* 427). In Yeats's view, Dowden had "expressed scorn for the Irish Lit movement & Irish Lit generally for which he has been catching it from all the Dublin papers" (427). Yeats responded with a series of letters to the *Daily Express* that lambasted Dowden for failing to rally to the Irish cause (on the Dowden controversy, see *CL1* 427, 430–431, 433, 435–438, 440–446, 448–450; see also *UP2* 346–349, 351–353; cf. 88–89). In his letter of January 26, Yeats acknowledged that Irish literature has many faults but asked "whether we can best check these faults by carefully sifting out and expounding what is excellent [. . .] or by talking, like Professor Dowden, occasional vague generalities about rhetoric and sentimentality and bad technique" (*CL1* 430). Six years later Yeats gave Dowden another drubbing, this time on the subject of Shakespeare. In his essay "AT STRATFORD-ON-AVON" (1901), he rebukes Dowden—who was then "internationally recognized as the most outstanding contemporary authority on Shakespeare," according to one biographer—for the small-minded worship of the practical and the successful that colors his Shakespearean scholarship (*Edward Dowden* 149). "[Dowden] lived in Ireland, where everything has failed," writes Yeats, "and he meditated frequently upon the perfection of character which had, he thought, made England successful, for, as we say, 'cows beyond the water have long horns.'" Thus Dowden upheld Henry V as the "typical Anglo-Saxon" and the Shakespearean ideal, forgetting that England was made "by her adventurers, by her people of wildness and imagination and eccentricity" (*E&I* 104).

Yeats's most extensive comment on Dowden is section XXIV of "Reveries Over Childhood and Youth" (see AUTOBIOGRAPHIES). He recalls visiting Dowden's "orderly, prosperous house" in Rathgar after his family had returned to Dublin in 1882. The 17-year-old Yeats found Dowden an impressive figure, being struck by his "dark, romantic face" and believing on the basis of his poems that he had loved "unhappily and illicitly" (*Aut.* 94–95). For a time Yeats took Dowden as his "sage," but he was "chilled" when Dowden, one morning after breakfast, confessed that he had lost his enthusiasm for SHELLEY, and the spell was broken decisively after Yeats read George Eliot at Dowden's urging. Finding Eliot the enemy of "all in life that gives one a springing foot," Yeats worked himself into a "quarrel or half-quarrel" with Dowden (95). In the chapter of *Autobiographies* titled "Ireland after Parnell," Yeats diagnoses that Dowden had withered slowly in the "barren soil" of Dublin Unionism. In Yeats's estimation, Dowden was not without the capacity for passion and irreverence, and yet "he turned Shakespeare into a British Benthamite, flattered Shelley but to hide his own growing lack of sympathy, abandoned for like reason that study of Goethe that should have been his life-work, and at last cared but for Wordsworth, the one great

poet who, after brief blossom, was cut and sawn into planks of obvious utility" (193). During these years—the 1890s—Yeats would sometimes call on Dowden "out of gratitude for old encouragements" and because his house was "pleasant to the eye," but Yeats eventually came to feel that their differences made such visits uncomfortable (193).

In 1910, with Dowden ailing and mulling retirement, Yeats began political maneuvers to inherit his chair in literature at Trinity, which came with rooms and £600 per year (*AM* 430). "I am not very anxious one way or the other but would I think like the work and I know I would like rooms in College," Yeats wrote to his father on November 24 (*Letters* 555). Not surprisingly, Dowden was lukewarm about Yeats's candidacy. He wrote to John Butler Yeats that teaching is a "difficult and laborious trade, requiring a special training, constant vigilance, and perpetual study, and often of things that do not attract one"—the implication being that Yeats was not cut out for the job (*PF* 383). When Dowden died on April 3, 1913, Yeats once again tested the waters, but his hopes came to nothing (*AM* 484). Dowden's widow, meanwhile, approached Lolly Yeats (1868–1940) and proposed that the CUALA PRESS publish her husband's love poems. Yeats had not been informed of the negotiations and he was infuriated to be associated with the volume, which appeared anonymously in November 1913 as *A Woman's Reliquary*. Writing to Lolly on October 25, Yeats railed against the poems' "general flaccidity of technique" and demanded that the press's prospectus for the following year carry a disclaimer to the effect that the book had nothing to do with him (*PF* 408–409). A note in the press's 1914 prospectus duly states: "This book is not a part of the Cuala series arranged by W. B. Yeats" (*Dun Emer Press* 108).

In 1915, having completed a draft of his memoirs, Years wrote worriedly to his father, long relocated to New York, that he might "very much dislike" the unflattering portrait of Dowden. Yeats admitted that it was a "little harsh," but argued that it could not have been omitted. He explained that the book is a "history of the revolt, which perhaps unconsciously you taught me, against certain Victorian ideas. Dowden is the image of those ideals and has to stand for the whole structure in Dublin, Lord Chancellors and all the rest. They were ungracious realities and he was a gracious one and I do not think I have robbed him of the saving adjective" (*Letters* 602–603; see also 606). Yeats added, "Amiable as I have been, I wonder if Mrs. Smith, Dowden's daughter, whom I like [. . .] will invite me to any more séances at her house" (603).

Bibliography

Foster, R. F. *W. B. Yeats, A Life, I: The Apprentice Mage;* Ludwigson, Kathryn R. *Edward Dowden;* Miller, Liam. *The Dun Emer Press, Later the Cuala Press;* Murphy, William M. *Prodigal Father: The Life of John Butler Yeats (1839–1922);* Yeats, W. B. *Autobiographies, The Collected Letters of W. B. Yeats* (vol. 1), *Essays and Introductions, The Letters of W. B. Yeats, Uncollected Prose by W. B. Yeats* (vol. 2).

Dublin University Review   Founded in 1885, the *Dublin University Review* was a high-toned monthly magazine catering to a general readership. The review was edited by the political economist Charles Hubert Oldham (1860–1926), the leader of a "small group of intellectual Protestant Home Rulers in Trinity College" and the moving spirit behind the CONTEMPORARY CLUB (*W. B. Yeats* 45), and by the poet-journalist T. W. Rolleston (1857–1920), who would later become a member of the RHYMERS' CLUB and cofounder with Yeats of the Irish Literary Society of London (see NATIONAL LITERARY SOCIETY). Yeats's first published work began to appear in the review in 1885. In his AUTOBIOGRAPHIES, Yeats recalls having to perform a trial reading of his play *The* ISLAND OF STATUES before the editors of the review in Oldham's rooms at Trinity (98). Yeats's contributions to the review were as follows: "Song of the Fairies" and "Voices" (songs from *The Island of Statues,* the latter reprinted as "The Cloak, the Boat, and the Shoes"), March 1885; *The Island of Statues,* April–July 1885; "Love and Death," May 1885; *The* SEEKER, September 1885; "An Epilogue. To 'The Island of Statues' and 'The Seeker'" (later "The SONG OF THE HAPPY SHEPHERD"), October 1885; "In a Drawing-Room," January 1886; "Life," February 1886; "The Two Titans. A Political Poem," March 1886; "On Mr. Nettleship's Picture

at the Royal Hibernian Academy," April 1886; MOSADA, June 1886; "Miserrimus" (later "The SAD SHEPHERD") and "From the Book of Kauri the Indian—Section V. On the Nature of God" (later "The Indian upon God"), October 1886; "The Poetry of Sir Samuel Ferguson," November 1886; "An Indian Song" (later "The Indian to his Love"), December 1886. The poems and plays are reprinted in *The Variorum Edition of the Poems of W. B. Yeats,* while the essay on Ferguson is reprinted in the first volume of *Uncollected Prose by W. B. Yeats.*

Bibliography

Hone, Joseph. *W. B. Yeats;* Wade, Allan. *A Bibliography of the Writings of W. B. Yeats;* Yeats, W. B. *Autobiographies, Uncollected Prose by W. B. Yeats* (vol. 1), *The Variorum Edition of the Poems of W. B. Yeats.*

Dun Emer Press   The Dun Emer Industries, to which the Dun Emer Press belonged, were launched in 1902 by Evelyn Gleeson (1855–1944), the 46-year-old daughter of an Irish physician who abandoned medicine to found the Athlone Woolen Mills (*Dun Emer Press* 14). Inspired by WILLIAM MORRIS's craft movement and by the Irish Renaissance that was by then well under way, Gleeson sought to create a workshop that would assist the revival of Irish culture while providing young girls with employment and education in weaving, embroidery, and printing. Gleeson was familiar with Yeats's sisters, Lily Yeats (1866–1949) and Lolly Yeats (1868–1940), through the Irish Literary Society of London (see NATIONAL LITERARY SOCIETY), and she enlisted them as founding partners (*Yeats Sisters* 99). Their famous brother aside, they had much to recommend them. Lolly had published four primers for young painters (G. Philip and Son, London, 1895, 1898, 1899, 1900) and Lily had been an embroiderer with Morris and Company, working under Morris's daughter May from 1888 to 1894 (63–67). They had no capital to invest, but Gleeson's friend Augustine Henry, a botanist, came to the rescue. "Not only would he advance short-term loans towards the capital necessary for setting up the business," writes Joan Hardwick, "he would also guarantee in the form of a loan, a yearly income for Lily and Lolly should initial profits be insufficient to provide this. The loan was to be paid back from subsequent profits" (113). Lily was to be in charge of embroidery, and Lolly in charge of printing and publishing. The enterprise was called "Dun Emer" ("Emer's Fort") in honor of CUCHULAIN's wife, the legendary Emer, who was renowned for her domestic skills. In October 1902, JOHN BUTLER YEATS and his two daughters moved from BEDFORD PARK to a house called "Gurteen Dhas" ("pretty little meadow"), in the Dublin suburb of Churchtown, about five miles southwest of Dublin. From there it was a 35-minute walk to the leased house near the village of Dundrum that served as the Dun Emer workshop as well as Gleeson's residence (PF 241). By 1905, Dun Emer employed 30 young women (*Dun Emer Press* 15). As R. F. Foster notes, "Working at Dun Emer became a way-station, almost a rite of passage, for many young women involved in nationalist cultural enterprises: future writers, painters, Sinn Féin activists, and ABBEY actresses served their time there" (AM 275).

Lolly modeled the Dun Emer Press on Morris's Kelmscott Press. The Dun Emer publications were distinguished by fine paper (high rag-content paper from Saggart Mills, near Dublin) and elegant type (14-point Caslon Old Style). All printing was done on an 1853 model Demy Albion hand press (*Dun Emer Press* 103; *Yeats Sisters* 120). Headings, notes, and colophons were printed in red ink in what was to become a trademark of the press, and editions numbered between 200 and 500 copies. As one of the most renowned men of letters in Ireland, Yeats acted as literary adviser and editor, keeping the press supplied with his own work and with the work of his friends. It became customary that Yeats's work was published in small editions by his sisters and then in larger editions by commercial firms. Inevitably, Yeats and Lolly—the high-handed brother and the temperamental sister—quarreled about editorial decisions, and John Butler Yeats was frequently required to act as conciliator (PF 265, 304–307).

The press's maiden volume—a tour de force— was Yeats's collection of poems *In the Seven Woods*. It was sent to subscribers in August 1903. Yeats's inscription in a copy of the volume sent to JOHN QUINN indicates his satisfaction with the press's

Portrait of Lily Yeats, the poet's sister, circa 1877, by John Butler Yeats *(Dublin City Gallery The Hugh Lane)*

handiwork: "This is the first book of mine that is a pleasure to look at—a pleasure whether open or shut" (*Biblio.* 67; *Dun Emer Press* 33). Over the five-year career of the press there followed 10 further volumes: *The Nuts of Knowledge* by GEORGE RUSSELL (AE), December 1, 1903; *The Love Songs of Connacht* by Douglas Hyde (preface by Yeats), July 4, 1904; *Twenty-One Poems* by LIONEL JOHNSON (selected by Yeats), February 21, 1905; STORIES OF RED HANRAHAN, by Yeats, May 16, 1905; *Some Essays and Passages* by JOHN EGLINTON (selected by Yeats), August 25, 1905; *Sixteen Poems* by William Allingham (selected by Yeats), November 27, 1905; *A Book of Saints and Wonders* by Lady GREGORY, September 10, 1906; *By Still Waters: Lyrical Poems* by George Russell, December 14, 1906; *Twenty One Poems* by KATHARINE TYNAN (selected by Yeats), August 6, 1907; *Discoveries* by Yeats, December 15, 1907 (*Biblio.* 451–452; *Dun Emer Press* 105–107).

By 1904, relations with the difficult Gleeson were beginning to sour and the Yeats sisters were in financial difficulties, as they would be perpetually, with Yeats expected to come to the rescue (*CL3* 547–548). In an agreement arbitrated by George Russell on behalf of the sisters, the industries split into Gleeson's Dun Emer Guild and the sisters' Dun Emer Industries. The two entities operated independently though they remained under the same roof, with the sisters paying a third of the rent and a share of expenses (*Yeats Sisters* 131). In 1908, the sisters fully dissolved their partnership with Gleeson and struck out on their own, forming Cuala Industries on the model of its predecessor. Over subsequent decades the CUALA PRESS carried on the work of the Dun Emer Press.

Bibliography

Foster, R. F. *W. B. Yeats: A Life, I: The Apprentice Mage*; Hardwick, Joan. *The Yeats Sisters: A Biography of Susan and Elizabeth Yeats*; Murphy, William M. *Prodigal Father: The Life of John Butler Yeats (1839–1922)*; Miller, Liam. *The Dun Emer Press, Later the Cuala Press*; Wade, Allan. *A Bibliography of the Writings of W. B. Yeats*; Yeats, W. B. *The Collected Letters of W. B. Yeats* (vol. 3).

Easter Rising   The Easter Rising of 1916 catalyzed the final phase of the Irish struggle for independence and forced Yeats to recant "SEPTEMBER 1913'S" stinging assessment that "Romantic Ireland's dead and gone, / It's with O'LEARY in the grave." In light of the Easter Rising, Yeats could only conclude that "September 1913" had come to sound "old-fashioned" (*VP* 820). "EASTER 1916," Yeats's foremost statement on the Easter Rising, acknowledges romantic Ireland's resurrection and in the stunned admission of its most famous lines measures the momentousness of this development: "All changed, changed utterly: / A terrible beauty is born."

The rising commenced at noon on Easter Monday, April 24, when roughly 100 members of the Irish Volunteers and Citizen Army stormed the General Post Office on O'Connell Street (then Sackville Street). After clearing the building, the insurgents ran up a green flag bearing the emblem of a golden harp and the words "Irish Republic," as well as the green, white, and orange flag that became the national flag of Ireland in 1937. From the steps

of the building, Patrick Pearse (1879–1916), poet and schoolmaster, read a proclamation issued by the "provisional government of the Irish Republic," declaring an independent Irish state. The state was to be founded on principles of "religious and civil liberty, equal rights and equal opportunities to all its citizens" and was to "pursue the happiness and prosperity of the whole nation and of all its parts, cherishing all the children of the nation equally, and oblivious of the differences carefully fostered by an alien Government, which have divided a minority from the majority in the past." As F. S. L. Lyons notes, the proclamation was delivered to a "sparse and almost completely uncomprehending audience" (*Ireland Since the Famine* 368). Planned uprisings across Ireland were aborted, and those few that went forward sputtered, but in Dublin insurgents seized and tenaciously held some two dozen prominent buildings and central positions. British military reinforcements soon poured into the city, and it became only a matter of time before they suppressed the rebellion. Over the next five days, as historian Robert Kee writes, the Irish force "remained in most of the positions it had occupied on Easter Monday, inflicting what casualties it could—and these were sometimes substantial— on Irishmen and others in the British Army, who, backed by heavy artillery fire, inexorably closed in on them and eventually forced them to surrender" (*Bold Fenian Men* 255). For the citizens of Dublin, the Rising, in Lyons words, "began as a spectacle, became an inconvenience and ended as a tragedy. During the week that fighting continued the normal life of the city was paralyzed, communications were interrupted, food soon grew scarce and privations among the poor were especially severe" (*Ireland Since the Famine* 373). The self-declared Irish government issued a cease-fire order on Saturday, by which time substantial portions of the city were in ruins, 450 had been killed, and 2,614 had been wounded. As Lyons observes, however, the "chief casualty" of the violence was the "whole constitutional movement" by which Ireland had previously pursued its independence (374, 379).

Bent on crushing whatever remained of the revolutionary spirit, the British military arrested more than 3,000 putative rebels and executed 15

O'Connell Street, Dublin, in the aftermath of the Easter Rising *(National Library of Ireland)*

leaders of the rebellion, with the inevitable result that they were transformed into nationalist martyrs. Those executed were Pearse, Tom Clarke, and Thomas MacDonagh on May 3; Joseph Plunkett, Edward Daly, William Pearse, and Michael O'Hanrahan on May 4; John MacBride—MAUD GONNE's estranged husband—on May 5; Eamonn Ceannt, Michael Mallin, Con Colbert, and Sean Heuston on May 8; Thomas Kent on May 9; and James Connolly and Sean MacDermott on May 12 (376). Yeats knew several of the executed rebels, though not intimately. Richard Ellmann calls the roll: "Pearse whose school he had visited, MacDonagh whose poems he had read, Connolly who had joined him and Maud Gonne in the demonstrations against England and the Queen in the late 'nineties, MacBride, the 'drunken vainglorious lout' who had taken Maud Gonne away from him" (MM 217). On May 1, Yeats wrote to his sister Lolly, "I know most of the Sinn Fein leaders & the whole thing bewilders me for Connolly is an able man

& Thomas MacDonough [sic] both able & cultivated. Pearse I have long looked upon as a man made dangerous by the Vertigo of Self Sacrifice. He has moulded himself on Emmett" (AP 46)—that is, Robert Emmett whom the British executed in 1803 for his part in an abortive insurrection (see "September 1913"). In a diary entry of 1909, Yeats calls MacDonagh "a man with some literary faculty which will probably come to nothing though lack of culture and encouragement." Had he been born in England, Yeats continues, he "would have become remarkable in some way," but in Ireland he is "being crushed by the mechanical logic and commonplace eloquence which give power to the most empty mind, because, being 'something other than human life', they have no use for distinguished feeling or individual thought. I mean that within his own mind this mechanical thought is crushing as with an iron roller all that is organic" (Aut. 360; Mem. 177–178). Yeats's old acquaintance Constance Markiewicz (see "IN MEMORY OF EVA GORE-BOOTH

AND CON MARKIEWICZ") was likewise condemned to death, but her sentence was commuted to life imprisonment, and she was released from jail in 1917 ("ON A POLITICAL PRISONER" imagines Markiewicz during a subsequent stint in prison).

The execution of MacBride, of course, fell closest to home. On May 11, Gonne wrote to Yeats that her husband's sacrifice had given their son, Sean, a name to be proud of. "Those who die for Ireland are sacred," Gonne insisted. "Those who enter Eternity by the great door of Sacrifice atone for all—in one moment they do more than all our effort" (GY 375). MacBride's death made possible Yeats's final proposal of marriage to Gonne in July 1916. Consistent with the reproach of the political mindset expressed in "Easter 1916"—"Too long a sacrifice / Can make a stone of the heart"—Yeats made Gonne's retirement from politics a condition of their marriage, and his suit inevitably came to nothing (AP 56; W. B. Yeats 307–308).

Yeats received word of the Easter Rising while a guest at the Gloucestershire home of the British artist Sir William Rothenstein (1872–1945). He remained until April 26 and then returned to London. "I had no idea that any public event could so deeply move me," Yeats confessed in a May 11 letter to Lady GREGORY, "and I am very despondent about the future. At the moment I feel that all the work of years has been overturned, all the bringing together of classes, all the freeing of Irish literature and criticism from politics" (Letters 613). Yeats mentioned that he had begun a poem on "the men executed," and he quoted a version of the great refrain of "Easter 1916"—"terrible beauty has been born again." On May 23 he wrote to JOHN QUINN that the "Irish business has been a great grief. We have lost the ablest and most fine-natured of our young men. A world seems to have been swept away. I keep going over the past in my mind and wondering if I could have done anything to turn those young men in some other direction. At the moment I feel as if I shall return to Dublin to live, to begin building again" (614). Yeats wondered also whether he bore some distant responsibility for events. In "The MAN AND THE ECHO," he asks, referring to CATHLEEN NI HOULIHAN, his rabble-rousing drama of 1902, "Did that play of mine send out / Certain men the

English shot?" JOHN EGLINTON analogously wonders whether the "scornful refrain" of "September 1913" was not "the spark which fell upon the inflammable minds of the young Gaelic enthusiasts, poets most of them, and kindled their vague aspirations into a realistic purpose" (Irish Literary Portraits 33). Maud Gonne, too, detected Yeats's influence on events: "Without Yeats there would have been no Literary Revival in Ireland. Without the inspiration of that Revival and the glorification of beauty and heroic virtue, I doubt if there would have been an Easter Week" (Scattering Branches 27).

Yeats remained conflicted about the rising, finding it heroic and yet foolhardy, mythical and yet fanatical, romantic and yet blundering. The poles of Yeats's vacillation are implicit in a note to "September 1913" dated July 1916: "The late Dublin Rebellion, whatever one can say of its wisdom, will long be remembered for its heroism. 'They weighed so lightly what they gave,' and gave too in some cases without hope of success" (VP 820). Hugh Kenner attributes Yeats's reservations about the Rising at least in part to his offended elitism and sense of the seemly: "[Yeats] belonged to a club in Stephen's Green [see the opening stanza of "Easter 1916"], where you could warm your person by the fire and your companion's heart with a gibe at the current fire-eaters, the mobilized boy scouts (Fianna) Con Markievicz gave her heart to, the pale-faced drillers with their wooden rifles, the fervid ungrammatical Irish-speakers: none of them O'LEARY's kind of activist, and not an O'Leary among their leaders either: Catholic middle-class, most of them, counter-men, till-men" (Colder Eye 226).

Yeats made much of the rising in both verse and drama. In addition to "Easter 1916" and "The Man and the Echo," he took up the rising in The DEATH OF CUCHULAIN (see the final song), The DREAMING OF THE BONES, "The Ghost of Roger Casement" (1938), "The O'Rahilly" (1938), "Roger Casement" (1937), "The Rose Tree" (1920), "Sixteen Dead Men" (1920), "The STATUES," and "Three Songs to the One Burden" (1939). "The LEADERS OF THE CROWD," which follows an informal sequence of poems on the rising in the pages of both Michael Robartes and the Dancer (1921) and the collected poems, elaborates the critique of "On a Political

Prisoner" and reaffirms Yeats's commitment to values more fundamental than political values.

Bibliography

Eglinton, John. *Irish Literary Portraits*; Ellmann, Richard. *Yeats: The Man and the Masks*; Foster, R. F. *W. B. Yeats: A Life, II: The Arch-Poet*; Gwynn, Stephen, ed. *Scattering Branches: Tributes to the Memory of W. B. Yeats*; Hone, Joseph. *W. B. Yeats*; Kee, Robert. *The Green Flag, II: The Bold Fenian Men*; Kenner, Hugh. *A Colder Eye: The Modern Irish Writers*; Lyons, F. S. L. *Ireland since the Famine*; Yeats, W. B. *Autobiographies, The Letters of W. B. Yeats, The Gonne-Yeats Letters 1893–1938, Memoirs, The Variorum Edition of the Poems of W. B. Yeats*.

Eglinton, John (1868–1961) "John Eglinton" was the pen name of William Kirkpatrick Magee, an assistant librarian at the National Library from 1904 to 1921 and a literary critic who played a secondary part in the Irish Renaissance, frequently as a commentator and critic of Yeats. Most famous for his appearance in the "Scylla and Charybdis" chapter of Joyce's *Ulysses* (1922), in which, with "carping voice," he lengthily disputes with Stephen Dedalus on the subject of Shakespeare, Eglinton was the chief foil to Yeats in the literary debate on national drama that unfolded in the pages of the *Daily Express* during the autumn of 1898 (see Literary Ideals in Ireland).

Yeats and Eglinton first knew each other as fellow students at Erasmus Smith High School in Dublin. In his essay "Yeats and his Story," Eglinton recalls Yeats as a "yellow-skinned, lank, loose-coated figure" who "came and went as he pleased." He remembers also that Yeats, who oddly enough excelled in algebra and geometry, was always ready to shift his position so Eglinton could "cog" from his paper during an exam (*I&R*, I, 5; *Irish Literary Portraits* 20). Yeats introduced his schoolfellows to A. P. Sinnett's *Esoteric Buddhism* (1883), and both Eglinton and his older brother, among several others, were caught up in the sudden excitement about Eastern religion (*Irish Literary Portraits* 43). Eglinton joined the Dublin Hermetic Society, founded by Yeats and Charles Johnston (1867–1931) in 1885 (see *Aut.* 97–98), and later moved to the periphery of the Dublin branch of the Theosophical Society. Eglinton's brother, H. M. Magee, lived in the society's "lodge" at 3 Upper Ely Place, where he shared rooms with George Russell (AE). "I was not myself a Theosophist," recalls Eglinton, "but my friends were mostly of the faith, and I could hardly fail to know Russell, who at once took possession of me and always regarded me, I think, as a rather wayward spiritual disciple" (*Memoir of AE* 21). In 1887, Eglinton matriculated at Trinity College, Dublin. There he won the vice chancellor's prizes for verse in 1889 and 1890, and for prose in 1892 and 1893, with Yeats's family friend Edward Dowden acting as judge. It was Dowden, a library trustee, who later helped Eglinton secure his position at the National Library (*Oxford Dictionary of National Biography*).

Though always willing to admit Yeats's literary supremacy, and particularly attentive to Yeats's superlative ability as a prose stylist, Eglinton tended to distrust Yeats's aestheticism and his elevation of the folk and peasant culture. Despite being a "profound transcendentalist," as Yeats says, he refused to endorse Yeats's rejection of the world in its social, practical, modern, and reasoning dimensions (*UP2* 131). In the exchange of 1898, Yeats accuses Eglinton of promulgating "the poetry of the utilitarian and the theoretician and the sentimentalist and the popular journalists and the popular preacher," as against the poetry of the "seer" (130–131). In his "Philosophy of the Celtic Movement," collected in *Anglo-Irish Essays* (1918), Eglinton in turn worries, with Yeats in mind, that the modern poet shuns the "paths of actuality" in favor of "the twilight haunts of memory and shadows," and thereby makes himself something of a laughingstock with the "ordinary man" (45).

Yeats wrote two essays on Eglinton, "John Eglinton and Spiritual Art" (1898, an installment in the *Daily Express* controversy) and "John Eglinton" (1901), both of which appear in the second volume of *Uncollected Prose by W. B. Yeats*. He wrote a further essay, "The Autumn of the Body," that was provoked by Eglinton's critique of his aestheticism during the 1898 debate. Yeats furthermore edited *Some Essays and Passages* (1905), a collection of Eglinton's work published by the Dun Emer Press.

Bibliography

Eglinton, John. *Anglo-Irish Essays, Irish Literary Portraits, A Memoir of AE*; Lawrence, Goldman, ed. *Oxford Dictionary of National Biography*; Mikhail, E. H., ed. *W. B. Yeats: Interviews and Recollections* (vol. 1); Yeats, W. B. *Uncollected Prose by W. B. Yeats* (vol. 2).

Eliot, T. S. (1888–1965) Yeats and Eliot shared an important friend and colleague in EZRA POUND and inevitably crossed paths from time to time, beginning in late 1914 or early 1915 (*Letters of T. S. Eliot* 58, 95). According to Richard Ellmann, Pound brought Eliot to see Yeats on two or three occasions, and Eliot "allowed himself only to be bored," later complaining that Yeats's only topics of conversation at the time were "GEORGE MOORE and spooks" (*Eminent Domain* 90). The relationship remained cordial though not close, with both respect and ambivalence on both sides. Writing to Pound in October 1922, Eliot let drop that "Yeats does not particularly like me," though later in the year he told Ottoline Morrell (1873–1938), another mutual friend, that he had pleasantly lunched with Yeats at the Savile Club in London. "I enjoyed seeing him immensely," Eliot wrote. "I had not seen him for six or seven years and this was really the first time that I have ever talked to him for any length of time alone. He is really one of a very small number of people with whom one can talk profitably about poetry, and I found him altogether stimulating" (*Letters of T. S. Eliot* 585, 611). For his part, Yeats identified Eliot as the "most typical figure" of the reaction against Victorian poetic convention (*Letters* 792), but he took exception to something submerged and undemonstrative in Eliot's personality, and to a certain revaluation of romantic impulse as empty gesture or thwarted hope in his poetry. In a letter to DOROTHY WELLESLEY, Yeats wrote that the "worst language is Eliot's in all his early poems—a level flatness of rhythm" (*Letters* 846; *LOP* 44).

Despite his qualms, Yeats included seven of Eliot's poems in his edition of *The Oxford Book of Modern Verse* (1936). In his introduction to the volume, Yeats writes that Eliot has "produced his great effect upon his generation because he has described men and women that get out of bed or into it from mere habit; in describing this life that has lost heart his own art seems grey, cold, dry. He is an Alexander Pope, working without apparent imagination, producing his effects by a rejection of all rhythms and metaphors used by the more popular romantics rather than by the discovery of his own, this rejection giving his work an unexaggerated plainness that has the effect of novelty" (*LE* 190–191). Letting his temperamental aversion get the better of him, Yeats adds that he considers Eliot less a poet than a satirist (191).

Eliot's thoughtful essay on Yeats, delivered to the Friends of the Irish Academy at the ABBEY THEATRE in 1940 and reprinted in *On Poetry and Poets* (1957), wavers tactfully between criticism and appreciation. Eliot mildly denigrates Yeats's early poems as "only craftsman's work" and lampoons their vestigial PRE-RAPHAELITISM, but he acknowledges that in the poems of *In the Seven Woods* (1903) "something is coming through, and in beginning to speak as a particular man [Yeats] is beginning to speak for man" (300). He ends by calling Yeats "one of those few whose history is the history of their own time, who are part of the consciousness of an age which cannot be understood without them" (308). Eliot also comments on Yeats in his essay on "The Modern Mind" in *The Use of Poetry & The Use of Criticism* (1933), drolly chiding the Yeats of the early poetry: "He was very much fascinated by self-induced trance states, calculated symbolism, mediums, theosophy, crystal gazing, folklore and hobgoblins. Golden apples, archers, black pigs and such paraphernalia abounded. Often the verse has an hypnotic charm: but you cannot take heaven by magic, especially if you are, like Mr. Yeats, a very sane person." By "a great triumph of development," however, Yeats began to write and continues to write "some of the most beautiful poetry in the language, some of the clearest, simplest, most direct" (133). Eliot expresses much the same notion in *After Strange Gods* (1934). Ellmann proposes that the ghostly interlocutor of Eliot's "Little Gidding" (1946)—"some dead master"—is in fact Yeats, with whom Eliot has finally made his peace (*Eminent Domain* 94).

Bibliography

Eliot, T. S. *After Strange Gods: A Primer of Modern Heresy, The Letters of T. S. Eliot* (vol. 1), *On Poetry and Poets, The Use of Poetry & The Use of Criticism*; Ellmann, Richard. *Eminent Domain: Yeats among Wilde, Joyce, Pound, Eliot, and Auden*; Yeats, W. B. *Later Essays, The Letters of W. B. Yeats, Letters on Poetry from W. B. Yeats to Dorothy Wellesley*.

Farr, Florence Beatrice, married name Emery

(1860–1917)   Born and raised in the London suburb of Bromley, Kent, Florence Farr was the daughter of William Farr (1807–83), a respected medical reformer and social statistician who spent most of his career as an official in the General Register Office at Somerset House. Farr was a close protégé of Florence Nightingale, which most likely explains the choice of his daughter's name. In George Bernard Shaw's pithy account, "Florence had been born unexpectedly long after her mother had apparently ceased childbearing: she was possibly indulged as a welcome surprise on that account. Though Dr. Farr survived his wits and lost most of his means by senile speculations before his death in 1883, he left enough to enable Florence to live modestly without having to sell herself in any fashion, or do anything that was distasteful to her" (*FF, BS and WBY*, "Explanatory Word"). Upon completing her education at Cheltenham Ladies' College in Gloucestershire and Queen's College in London (*Florence Farr* 10, 19), Farr, whose inclinations were artistic and modern, took to the stage. She began her professional career in 1883. On December 31, 1884, she married her fellow actor Edward Emery (d. 1938), scion of a long-established theatrical family (21). In 1888, Emery emigrated to America, where he had a long and successful theatrical career (his son by a second marriage, John Emery, became a minor movie star, and, briefly, the husband of Tallulah Bankhead). In 1895, the couple divorced (23–24).

Farr is primarily remembered for her intimacy—professional and romantic—with Shaw and Yeats. The Yeats family moved to 3 Blenheim Road, BEDFORD PARK, in April 1888, where their neighbors included Farr's sister Henrietta Paget (b. 1852) and her brother-in-law Henry Marriott Paget (1856–1936). Yeats frequented Paget's studio and sat

for a portrait; dated April 6, 1889, the painting is now in the Belfast Museum and Art Gallery (32). Yeats may have met Farr through the Pagets, or, like Shaw, at the Hammersmith home of WILLIAM MORRIS, where, from 1889, Farr studied embroidery with Morris's daughter May, as did Yeats's sister Lily (1866–1949). On May 5, 1890, the physician-poet John Todhunter (1839–1916), a college friend of JOHN BUTLER YEATS, staged his Arcadian romance *A Sicilian Idyll* at the Bedford Park clubhouse, with Farr in a leading role and both Shaw and Yeats in the audience (39). Yeats puffed the play in the *Boston Pilot*, the *Providence Sunday Journal*, and *United Ireland* (see *Letters to the New Island* 31–39, 50–52, 98–101; *UP1* 190–194). He particularly praised Farr's performance: "Mrs. Edward Emery, who took the part of Amaryllis, won universal praise with her striking beauty and subtle gesture and fine delivery of the verse. Indeed her acting was the feature of the whole performance that struck one most, after the verse itself. I don't know that I have any word too strong to express my admiration for its grace and power" (*Letters to the New Island* 39). Both in his preface to *Letters to the New Island* and in AUTOBIOGRAPHIES, Yeats cites the play as an important influence in the later development of his own poetic drama (*Aut.* 118).

Yeats and Farr began their theatrical collaboration in 1894, when Farr arranged a dramatic program at the Avenue Theatre, London, with the financial backing of ANNIE HORNIMAN. Farr asked Yeats to write a one-act play that included a role for her young niece Dorothy Paget (1885–1974). The result was The LAND OF HEART'S DESIRE. Directed by Farr and featuring Paget as the fairy child, the play appeared on a bill with Todhunter's *The Comedy of Sighs* from March 29 to April 14. Yeats calls Todhunter's play a "rambling story told with a little paradoxical wit," while Shaw describes it as "inadequately cast and acted" (*Aut.* 220; *FF, BS and WBY*, "Explanatory Word"). After a catastrophic reception, Todhunter's play was replaced by Shaw's *Arms and the Man* starring Farr as Louka, and the reinvigorated bill—in retrospect, a watershed in modern drama—ran from April 21 to May 12. In Yeats's recollection, the original bill met with a response "almost as violent as that SYNGE met in January 1907," with much of the trouble of Farr's own making, "for always in revolt against her own poetical gift, which now seemed obsolete, and against her own Demeter-like face in the mirror, she had tried when interviewed by the Press to shock and startle; and yet, unsure of her own judgment, being out of her own trade, had feared to begin with Shaw's athletic wit; and now outraged convention saw its chance. For two hours and a half, pit and gallery drowned the voices of the players with boos and jeers [. . .]" (*Aut.* 220; see also *CL1* 385–386). Always prepared for pugilism, Shaw held his own. The audience began by laughing at the author, but "discovering that they themselves were being laughed at, sat there not converted—their hatred was too bitter for that—but dumbfounded, while the rest of the house cheered and laughed." When he took the stage, Shaw met with a single loud boo. "I assure the gentleman in the gallery that he and I are of exactly the same opinion," he readily retorted, "but what can we do against a whole house who are of the contrary opinion?" From that moment, Yeats writes, Shaw "became the most formidable man in modern letters, and even the most drunken of medical students knew it" (*Aut.* 221).

Yeats and Farr resumed their collaboration in May 1899, when Farr came to Dublin to direct the IRISH LITERARY THEATRE's controversial debut production of *The* COUNTESS CATHLEEN, as well as to play the role of Aleel. "Nothing satisfied me but Florence Farr's performance in the part of Aleel," Yeats recounts in *Autobiographies.* "Dublin talked of it for years, and after five-and-thirty years I keep among my unforgettable memories the sense of coming disaster she put into the words: '. . . but now / Two grey horned owls hooted above our heads'" (310). In 1894, Yeats introduced Farr to his future mistress OLIVIA SHAKESPEAR (*CL1* 397). Years later, the women cowrote two plays on Egyptian themes, *The Beloved of Hathor* and *The Shrine of the Golden Hawk.* The former debuted November 16, 1901, at the Victoria Hall in London, and the two plays shared a bill on January 20–21 and April 20–21, 1902, again at the Victoria Hall (*CL3* 121, 177). Despite fervent and even ecstatic performances by Farr and Dorothy

Paget, Yeats's review of the plays is equivocal. As with *The Sicilian Idyll,* however, he found an element in the performance that spoke to the future direction of his own art: "[The plays] are not only new in their subject, but in the rigorously decorative arrangements of the stage, which imitated the severe forms of Egyptian mural painting. The plays themselves are less plays than fragments of a ritual—the ritual of beautiful forgotten worship" (*UP2* 266).

Despite the best efforts of both Shaw and Yeats, Farr was inconsistent rather than consummate in her art. In *Autobiographies,* Yeats says that he formed with Farr "an enduring friendship that was an enduring exasperation." He complains: "She had three great gifts, a tranquil beauty like that of Demeter's image near the British Museum Reading-Room door, and an incomparable sense of rhythm and a beautiful voice, the seeming natural expression of the image," and yet "there was scarce another gift that she did not value above those three" (118–119). Her indiscipline drove Shaw, who was mentor as well as lover, to depths of despair and heights of invective: "I made desperate efforts to work up Florence's technique and capacity for hard professional work to the point needed for serious stage work; but her life had been too easy. I failed, and had to give up worrying and discouraging her. She found the friend she really needed in Yeats. What she called 'cantilating' for him was within her powers" (*FF, BS and WBY,* "Explanatory Word"). Vehemently opposed to cantilation, Shaw instead urged "athletic articulation"—clear and correct elocution—without which "cantilation can do nothing except intensify ordinary twaddling into nerve destroying crooning like the maunderings of an idiot-banshee" (*FF, BS and WBY* 20). Shaw's ridicule notwithstanding, Yeats and Farr began their experiments in "cantilation"—recitation to the accompaniment of the psaltery—in 1901, and they gave periodic public performances between 1901 and 1911 (*CL4* 885). The experiments were the most storied and involved aspect of their partnership, and the idea that poetry and music should be wed became a cornerstone of Yeats's aesthetic philosophy (see "SPEAKING TO THE PSALTERY").

In 1905 and 1906, Yeats and Farr dabbled in romance. Presumably repeating Yeats's own account, GEORGE YEATS mentions a "brief love affair" that ended when Farr became "bored" (FF, BS and WBY 43; see also AM 290–291; CL4 112–113, 160, 327–328). A letter of January 1906 finds Yeats writing to Farr in a distinctly romantic vein: "You cannot think what a pleasure it is to be fond of somebody to whom I can talk [. . .]. To be moved and talkative, unrestrained, one's own self, and to be this not because one has created some absurd delusion that it all is wisdom [. . .] but because one has found an equal, this is the best of life. All this means that I am looking forward to seeing you—that my spirits rise at the thought of it" (CL4 328; FF, BS and WBY 67). Having gotten over Yeats, presumably, Farr had a brief affair with JOHN QUINN during her three-month lecturing tour of AMERICA in early 1907 and thereafter remained his regular correspondent (CL4 630).

In addition to their theatrical and poetic collaborations, Yeats and Farr were fellow members of the HERMETIC ORDER OF THE GOLDEN DAWN (Florence Farr 72–73). With Yeats's encouragement, Farr joined the group by June 1890, and she played a leading role until resigning in 1902 to join the THEOSOPHICAL SOCIETY (91). Under the auspices of the latter, she first met Ponnambalam Ramanathan (1851–1930), a parliamentarian and, in Aleister Crowley's description, a "Yogi of the Shavite sect of Hindus" (92–93). In September 1912 Farr departed for Ceylon to become "lady principal" of Ramanathan's college for girls, which opened soon after Farr's arrival (190–191; Letters to W. B. Yeats, I, 254–255). Farr never returned to Europe, dying in Ceylon of breast cancer on April 29, 1917. In "ALL SOULS' NIGHT," Yeats's principal homage to his departed friend, Yeats proposes that Farr fled Europe to "hide her ageing beauty" (see also VPl. 1009). Yeats's portrait of Farr in Autobiographies (see "Four Years" I) has an addendum in EZRA POUND's poem "Portrait D'Une Femme" (1912). The lines "Great minds have sought you—lacking someone else. / You have been second always" suggest Gonne's irrevocable hold on Yeats. Additionally, Pound alludes to Farr's exile in Ceylon in Canto 28.

Bibliography

Finneran, Richard J., et al., eds. Letters to W. B. Yeats (vol. 1); Foster, R. F. W. B. Yeats: A Life, I: The Apprentice Mage; Johnson, Josephine. Florence Farr: Bernard Shaw's 'New Woman'; Yeats, W. B. Autobiographies, The Collected Letters of W. B. Yeats (vols. 1, 3–4), Florence Farr, Bernard Shaw and W. B. Yeats, Letters to the New Island, Uncollected Prose by W. B. Yeats (vols. 1–2), The Variorum Edition of the Plays of W. B. Yeats.

Golden Dawn   See HERMETIC ORDER OF THE GOLDEN DAWN.

Gonne, Iseult Lucille Germaine, married name Stuart (1894–1954)   MAUD GONNE's daughter, a fey beauty with intellectual and literary enthusiasms, cast a powerful spell on Yeats during his middle age. He proposed to Iseult twice (in 1916 and 1917) and wrote her into many of the poems of the period. Iseult was born in Paris, the illegitimate daughter of Gonne and Lucien Millevoye (1850–1918), a married lawyer, journalist, and politician allied to General Boulanger. In a deliberate attempt at reincarnation, her parents conceived her in the crypt containing the remains of their dead son Georges (1890–91). She grew up in France under emotionally difficult circumstances: Her mother and father were estranged from 1900 and she was frequently left in the care of nursemaids and governesses while her mother traveled abroad on political business. Even more trying, perhaps, was the permanent fiction that Iseult was Gonne's cousin or adopted daughter. Iseult referred to Gonne not as mother, but as "Moura," code for "amour." On February 21, 1903, Gonne married John MacBride (1865–1916), against Iseult's wishes. The marriage brought Iseult the company of a half brother, Sean (recipient of the Nobel Peace Prize in 1974), but MacBride left much to be desired as a stepfather. He was prone to drunkenness, licentiousness, and jealousy. His low moment came when he subjected Iseult to what Maud Gonne called an "indecent assault"; allegedly, he exposed himself to her (GY 231; see also CL4 7–8). In 1906, the French courts granted Gonne a legal separation on grounds of her husband's drunkenness (GY 232). Yeats did not learn of Iseult's existence until December 8,

1898, when Gonne confessed the details of her secret life overseas (*CL2* 314–315; *Mem.* 132–133). He was introduced to Iseult, then four years old, while visiting PARIS in February 1899, and upon his return to London he sent her books (*CL2* 369; *GY* 103). Yeats did not see Iseult again until he returned to Paris in June 1908. During this stay, the middle-aged poet and the young girl struck up a friendship that would endure until Yeats's death in 1939. Yeats made his first visit to Les Mouettes, Gonne's seaside house at Colleville-sur-Mer, in Calvados, Normandy, in April and May 1910, by which time the friendship between Yeats and Iseult had become tinged with romance, if only playful romance. Iseult in some manner proposed in 1910, but Yeats demurred because there was too much Mars in her horoscope (*Letters to WBY&EP*, XIV, 20; *Man and Poet* 190; *New Biography* 217).

By the time he had turned 50, Yeats urgently desired to be married. He proposed to Iseult in earnest in August 1916 and again in August 1917 while summering at Les Mouettes. Iseult sent an account of Yeats's first proposal to her cousin Thora Pilcher. She was excited and flattered ("he has proposed to me!!") but not tempted: "Thirty years difference is all the same a little too much, so of course I said *No* and it didn't seem to affect him much, he lost no appetite through this; so I came to the conviction that he had merely done it to follow a mad code of politeness which he had made for himself, he often told me: 'I think that a proposal is the myrrhe and the incense which every beautiful young women has the right to expect from every man who comes near her'" (*Letters to WBY&EP* 56). Yeats sent Lady GREGORY a detailed account of his second courtship (*Letters* 628–633), taking the blow in stride: "Iseult has always been something like a daughter to me and so I am less upset that I might have been—I am chiefly unhappy about her general prospects" (631). The marriage question was not definitely settled until mid-September, when the Gonnes returned with Yeats to London; there Iseult issued a final demurral in an ABC teashop (*New Biography* 220). Quickly shifting roles, Yeats performed the duties of a fond uncle, finding Iseult a position as a librarian at the School of Oriental Studies and later as secretary to EZRA POUND, with whom she had an affair in

1918 (see *Black List, Section H* 25–27). Yeats, meanwhile, immediately and somewhat guiltily turned his attention to Georgie Hyde-Lees, who became Mrs. W. B. Yeats on October 20, 1917. On the "emotional triangle of 1917," John Harwood comments, "Iseult Gonne had now assumed her mother's role, with Yeats picturing himself as the helpless and symbolically incapacitated devotee of beauty. The parallel between OLIVIA SHAKESPEAR and GEORGE YEATS is equally apparent: both, from his point of view, embodied the possibility of an equal, human love, as opposed to an unequal love with phantasmal overtones; both stood to lose Yeats because of their rivals' hold on his imagination" (*Olivia Shakespear and W. B. Yeats* 160).

On April 6, 1920, Iseult married Francis Stuart (1902–2000), an aspiring novelist and poet, then only 18, who had worshipped Yeats as a boy (*I&R*, II, 364). The marriage took place against the wishes and good judgment of Maud, who would later refer to Stuart as a "cur" (*GY* 412). The marriage was an immediate disaster. Maud's letters to Yeats in the months following the wedding allege horrifying abuse. Among other things, Stuart is said to have deprived Iseult of food and burned all of her clothes (*GY* 402–423; for Yeats's comments on the marriage, see *Letters* 800; see also *Black List, Section H* 31). In 1924, the couple moved to the countryside of County Wicklow, where Iseult remained for the rest of her life. The couple had three children—Dolores in 1921 (died in infancy of spinal meningitis), Ian in 1926, and Kay in 1931—before separating in 1939.

Yeats was briefly involved in the literary journal *To-morrow*, which Stuart, the artist Cecil Salkeld (1901–71), and the poet F. R. Higgins (1896–1941) launched in 1924. Yeats contributed the roistering inaugural editorial titled "To all Artists and Writers" (*UP2* 438–439) and "LEDA AND THE SWAN," which had appeared a month earlier in the *Dial*. Despite Yeats's high hopes, *To-morrow* appeared only twice (August and September). Yeats had dreamed of a "wild paper of the young which will make enemies everywhere and suffer suppression, I hope a number of times, with the logical assertion, with all fitting deductions, of the immortality of the soul" (*Letters* 706).

Iseult is not mentioned by name in Yeats's work, but she figures or conceivably figures in numerous poems, including "The DEATH OF THE HARE," "The DOUBLE VISION OF MICHAEL ROBARTES," "The LIVING BEAUTY," "LONG-LEGGED FLY," "Memory" (1916), "MEN IMPROVE WITH THE YEARS," "MICHAEL ROBARTES AND THE DANCER," "OWEN AHERNE AND HIS DANCERS," "PRESENCES," "A SONG," "TO A CHILD DANCING IN THE WIND," "TO A YOUNG BEAUTY," "TO A YOUNG GIRL," "TWO SONGS OF A FOOL," "Two Years Later" (see "To a Child Dancing in the Wind"), and "WHY SHOULD NOT OLD MEN BE MAD?" In "Two Songs of a Fool" (1919), Yeats relates his feeling of responsibility for both George Yeats (the "speckled cat") and Iseult (the "tame hare") and expresses the worry that Iseult would eventually take some tragic, wild leap (perhaps prescient in light of her marital troubles). In November 1918, Iseult wrote to reassure Yeats: "Why did you feel anxious about me, I mean anxious in that way? The hare seems to me a symbol of a personality—as helpless—but more active than mine, of one that both fears yet has to encounter danger, altogether a more dramatic personality. I don't really think I belong to that order of things. Sometimes I wish I did [. . .] but I doubt that it is in my destiny ever to meet directly with drama, unless it be the obscure drama of the mind in the hard process of sheding [sic] illusions" (*Letters to WBY&EP* 111).

Yeats additionally addressed to Iseult (known as "Maurice" to her intimates) the prologue of *PER AMICA SILENTIA LUNAE.* Yeats recalls that during the previous summer in Normandy the antics of her black cat Minnaloushe had interrupted a conversation upon his "convictions." After returning to London he could not rest until he had written down all that he had wanted to say: hence *Per Amica* (*LE* 1). "Minnaloushe and I are very grateful and honoured to have our names in your book," Iseult replied on June 6, 1917. "He is a little familiar divinity and well at his place in an occult work, as for me I am wholly undeserving, but none the less proud" (*Letters to WBY&EP* 84). Yeats's poem "THE CAT AND THE MOON" brought further fame to Minnaloushe.

Bibliography

Gonne, Iseult. *Letters to W. B. Yeats and Ezra Pound from Iseult Gonne*; Harwood, John. *Olivia Shake-spear and W. B. Yeats: After Long Silence*; A. Norman Jeffares, *W. B. Yeats: Man and Poet, W. B. Yeats: A New Biography*; Mikhail, E. H., ed. *W. B. Yeats: Interviews and Recollections* (vol. 2); Stuart, Francis. *Black List, Section H*; Yeats, W. B. *The Collected Letters of W. B. Yeats* (vols. 2, 4), *The Gonne-Yeats Letters 1893–1938, Later Essays, The Letters of W. B. Yeats, Memoirs, Uncollected Prose by W. B. Yeats* (vol. 2).

Gonne, Edith Maud, married name MacBride

(1866–1953)   The names of William Butler Yeats and Maud Gonne are as indissolubly joined in the annals of literature as the names of Dante and Beatrice. For 50 years, Gonne tormented and provoked Yeats; racked him with desire and struck him with awe; baffled and frustrated him; and inadvertently roused him to immense feats of art. Yeats thoroughly understood the fruitfulness of his obsession with Gonne and was perhaps in no hurry to overcome it. In "A DIALOGUE OF SELF AND SOUL" he speaks of the "folly that man does / Or must suffer, if he woos / A proud woman not kindred of his soul" as "that most fecund ditch of all." Gonne likewise understood this dynamic, and once told Yeats, rightly enough, "The world should thank me for not marrying you" (*SQ* 319). Yeats distilled the essence of their long and complicated symbiosis when he wrote, "She is my innocence and I her wisdom" (*Maud Gonne* 94).

Gonne was born on December 21, 1866, in Tongham, a village in Surrey. Her father Thomas Gonne, was a British army officer who came from a prosperous family of London wine merchants; her mother, Edith, was the granddaughter of a wealthy London drapery magnate (2). Maud's fateful connection to Ireland was established in 1868, when her father was posted to Curragh. The family lived first in a lodge near the Curragh military camp and then in Donnybrook, a Dublin suburb. After Gonne's mother died of tuberculosis in 1871, the Gonnes moved to Howth, where they remained until 1874 (4). Too old any longer to spend their days roaming the local cliffs and fields, Gonne and her sister, Kathleen (1868–1919), went to live with maternal relatives in London, and then with a governess in the south of France, while their father was

Maud Gonne, circa 1900. "A complexion like the blossom of apples," Yeats recalls in *Memoirs*, "and yet face and body had the beauty of lineaments which Blake calls the highest beauty because it changes least from youth to age, and a stature so great that she seemed of a divine race." *(Library of Congress)*

stationed in Vienna, Bosnia, India, and St. Petersburg (7). The Gonnes returned to Ireland in 1882. For the next four years, Gonne, by then a statuesque beauty, kept house for her father and made the social rounds as a debutante. On November

30, 1886, Tommy Gonne died of typhoid fever, and his daughters went to live with paternal relatives in London (12–13). In 1887, while recovering from a lung ailment at a spa in Royat, France, Gonne met Lucien Millevoye (1850–1918), a journalist and politician with close ties to General Georges Boulanger (1837–91), who was then jostling to assume the leadership of France (15). Gonne and Millevoye began a long relationship that was both romantic and political. Millevoye told her, "I will help you to free Ireland. You will help me to regain Alsace-Lorraine" (*SQ* 65). Upon coming of age in December 1887, Gonne inherited an income that maintained her comfortably but not lavishly for the rest of her life. With sufficient means at her disposal, she was able to abandon her nascent acting career for the cause closest to her heart: Irish independence.

In 1888, Gonne returned to Ireland and made her debut at the CONTEMPORARY CLUB, where she met many of Dublin's most interesting and influential cultural figures, including JOHN O'LEARY (*Maud Gonne* 18–21; *SQ* 89–92). On January 12, 1889, O'Leary's sister Ellen (1831–89), a minor poet (see *UP1* 256–288), wrote to Yeats, then in London, that she had given Gonne a letter of introduction to his father, JOHN BUTLER YEATS. "I'm sure she and you will like each other an artist and a poet could not fail to admire her," she said, rightly enough. "She is so charming, fine and handsome. Most of our male friends admire her" (*CL1* 134). On January 30, 1889, Gonne arrived at BEDFORD PARK, and the "troubling" of Yeats's life began (*Mem.* 40). In MEMOIRS, he remembers being instantly enraptured: "I had never thought to see in a living woman so great beauty. It belonged to famous pictures, to poetry, to some legendary past. A complexion like the blossom of apples, and yet face and body had the beauty of lineaments which BLAKE calls the highest beauty because it changes least from youth to age, and a stature so great that she seemed of a divine race" (40). Yeats could later remember nothing of the conversation except that she vexed John Butler Yeats with her "praise of war, for she too was of the Romantic movement and found those uncontrovertible Victorian reasons, that seemed to announce so prosperous a future, a little grey" (40; see also *Aut.*

119–120). Yeats and Gonne dined each night over the nine days of Gonne's stay in London. Gonne spoke of wanting to act in a suitable play, and Yeats promised to dramatize a story he had heard while compiling his 1888 volume *Fairy and Folk Tales of the Irish Peasantry* (*CL1* 154; *Mem.* 41; *SQ* 176). He duly began *The COUNTESS CATHLEEN* in February. In "The CIRCUS ANIMALS' DESERTION," Yeats suggests the psychological motives underlying the impulse to write the play: "I thought my dear must her own soul destroy, / So did fanaticism and hate enslave it, / And this brought forth a dream and soon enough / This dream itself had all my thought and love."

Yeats's letters of the following weeks show him fascinated, if not as suddenly and completely smitten as *AUTOBIOGRAPHIES* and *Memoirs* suggest. Writing to KATHARINE TYNAN on January 31, Yeats noncommittally described Gonne's initial visit to Bedford Park: "Miss Gone (you have heard of her no doubt) was here yesterday with introduction from the Olearys she says she cried over '[The] ISLAND OF STATUES' fragment but altogether favoured the Enchantress and hated Nachina" (*CL1* 134). By February 1, Yeats had warmed up. He wrote to John O'Leary after dining with Maud and her sister, Kathleen, that Gonne was "not only very handsome but very clever," though "her politics in European matters be a little sensational," and he predicted that she would make many converts to the Irish cause (137). By February 3, an effusive note had entered Yeats's correspondence. "Did I tell you how much I admire Miss Gonne?" he wrote to Ellen O'Leary. "She will make many converts to her political beleif [sic]. If she said the world was flat or the moon an old caubeen [i.e. cap] tossed up into the sky I would be proud to be of her party" (140–141). By March 21 he was obliged to deny rumors that he was in love with her. "Who told you that I am 'taken up with Miss Gonne,'" Yeats demanded of Tynan. "I think she is, 'very good looking' and that is all I think about her. What you say of her fondness for sensation is probably true. I sympathize with her love of the national idia [sic] rather than any secondary land movement but care not much for the kind of red Indian feathers in which she has trapped out that idea" (154).

Throughout the 1890s, Yeats and Gonne shared in mystical and political activities, though politics, as Yeats's earliest letters anticipate, would be a point of contention between them for the rest of their lives. In *Memoirs*, Yeats writes bluntly, "I came to hate her politics, my one visible rival" (63). In 1892, they collaborated in a NATIONAL LITERARY SOCIETY scheme to found rural libraries throughout Ireland (*Aut.* 189; *Mem.* 58–59). Later in the decade they threw themselves into the protest of Queen Victoria's Diamond Jubilee, a celebration of her 60th anniversary upon the throne, which took place on June 22, 1897 (*Aut.* 273–277; *CL2* 113–114; *Mem.* 111–114; *SQ* 214–221); and they helped organize events commemorating the 100th anniversary of the rebellion of 1798 (*Aut.* 267–268; *CL2* 695–707; *GY* 63–94; *Mem.* 108–111; *SQ* 259–265). On November 2, 1891, Gonne joined the HERMETIC ORDER OF THE GOLDEN DAWN, Yeats's beloved mystical society (*CL1* 266), but she found the initiates "the very essence of British middle-class dullness." Never enthusiastic, she resigned in December 1894 on the suspicion that the group was "an esoteric side of Masonry." She considered Freemasonry a British institution that "has always been used politically to support the British Empire" (*SQ* 210–212).

Yeats proposed marriage on August 3, 1891, but Gonne gently demurred, mentioning mysterious reasons why she could never marry (*Mem.* 46). Yeats did not receive an explanation until December 1898, when Gonne, contrite after having kissed Yeats for the first time with the "bodily mouth," confessed that she had been the mistress of Millevoye and had borne him two children, Georges (1890–91) and ISEULT GONNE (131–134). Yeats had known of Georges, but only as Gonne's adopted son (47). Though she and Millevoye had lived apart since the birth of Iseult in 1894, she remained "necessary to him," and the relationship continued until 1900, when Millevoye took up with another woman (*Maud Gonne* 64; *Mem.* 133). On December 8, Yeats wrote to Lady GREGORY, "MG is here & I understand everything now. I cannot say more than that if I am sorry for my self I am far more sorry for her & that I have come to understand her & admire her as I could not have done before. My life is a harder problem to me than it was yesterday" (*CL2* 314–315). On December 15, he added that Gonne had loved him for years, though for reasons that he could not mention she could never marry, and that he was "trying to see things more unselfishly & to live to make her life happier, content with just that manner of love which she will give me abundantly" (320). These revelations frayed Yeats's nerves and left him feeling "like a very battered ship with the masts broken off at the stump" (320). On December 18, on the eve of Gonne's departure for Paris, Yeats again "spoke of marriage," but Gonne said it was impossible, confessing "a horror and terror of physical love" (*Mem.* 134). In February 1899, Yeats joined Gonne in Paris and the revelations of her secret life continued in more detail, as Yeats reported to Lady Gregory (*CL2* 356–357). Yeats reiterated his marriage proposal, but with no success (*New Biography* 112–113).

In the years following this watershed, Yeats and Gonne settled into a "mystical marriage" that was emotionally but not physically intimate (*Maud Gonne* 56). Yeats's mood under this stricture, at once sad and tender, informs "ADAM'S CURSE," which records an evening Yeats spent with Maud and Kathleen in May 1902 (*SQ* 317–319). During these years there was an electrifying revival of Yeats and Gonne's public collaboration when Gonne played the role of Cathleen in the debut production of Yeats's CATHLEEN NI HOULIHAN in St. Teresa's Hall, Dublin, on April 2, 1902. She performed with such "weird power" (*Aut.* 332) that toward the end of his life Yeats was prompted to wonder, in "The MAN AND THE ECHO," "Did that play of mine send out / Certain men the English shot?"

The "troubling" of Yeats's life reached its climax in February 1903, when Gonne converted to Catholicism and married Major John MacBride (1865–1916), a nationalist hero who had fought against the British in the Boer War. MacBride was everything that Yeats was not: rugged, active, hard drinking, intrepid. Yeats received the news of Gonne's engagement on February 7, just before giving a lecture on "The Future of Irish Drama" (*AM* 284). In "RECONCILIATION," he describes being stricken deaf and blind as if by lightning. Accord-

ing to Richard Ellmann, Yeats "went through with his lecture, and afterwards members of the audience congratulated him on its excellence, but he could never remember a word of what he had said" (*MM* 159–160). In early February 1903 Yeats wrote Gonne four letters, only one of which survives, reminding her of their spiritual marriage and imploring her to reconsider her decision. "I know now that you have come to your moment of peril," Yeats warned. "If you carry out your purpose you will fall into a lower order & do great injury to the religeon [sic] of free souls that is growing up in Ireland, it may be to enlighten the whole world" (*CL3* 314–317; *GY* 164–168). Gonne pledged her continuing friendship but did not alter her marriage plans. She explained herself to her sister, Kathleen: "As for Willie Yeats I love him dearly as a friend, but I could not for one moment imagine marrying him. I think I will be happy with John. Our lives are exactly the same and he so fond and thoughtful that it makes life very easy when he is there and besides we have a vitality and joy in life which I used to have once, but which the hard life I have had wore out of me; with him I seem to get it back again a little" (*Maud Gonne* 76). In 1952, Gonne told Virginia Moore, "I never at any time considered marrying [Yeats]. I loved him, yes, but not in that way" (*Unicorn* 38).

The marriage went forward in Paris on February 21. Yeats's romantic dejection yielded two poems of 1905, "NEVER GIVE ALL THE HEART" and "O Do Not Love Too Long," while his lingering bitterness is apparent in an unpublished squib of 1909: "My dear is angry that of late / I cry all base blood down / As though she had not taught me hate / By kisses to a clown" (*Mem.* 145). The marriage produced a son, Sean MacBride, born on January 26, 1904, but otherwise it was an immediate fiasco. Gonne's biographer Margaret Ward summarizes that "MacBride was humiliated by Maud's comparative wealth, jealous of her past and suspicious of her friends. His solace was drink, which led to violence" (*Maud Gonne* 86). Yeats put the matter more succinctly, telling JOHN QUINN in January 1905 that MacBride suffered "eroto-mania from drink" (*CL4* 17). In her letters to Yeats, Gonne accused MacBride of drunkenness (*GY* 200–201, 204) and insane excesses of romantic jealousy (186). At one point, according to Gonne, he contemplated killing Yeats (GY 186; see also *CL4* 50). Most atrociously, he allegedly exposed himself to the 10-year-old Iseult (GY 231–232; *CL4* 7–8). Despite the obvious religious objection (*CL4* 9; GY 210–211), Gonne began divorce proceedings in January 1905. Due to the international complexion of the case, a Paris court granted only a legal separation (232). Yeats was an adviser and helpmate throughout the ordeal (see *CL4 passim*).

Yeats and Gonne renewed their "spiritual marriage" in July 1908, prompting him to write "Reconciliation" (GY 255–259). The evidence suggests that, in late 1908 or early 1909, Yeats and Gonne briefly became lovers (AM 393; *Maud Gonne* 94), which explains the sexually explicit reminiscence of "HIS MEMORIES." Citing an unpublished journal entry, Richard Ellmann writes that Yeats's love "found requital" somewhat earlier than this, in about 1907 (*Golden Codgers* 108). Despite their deep emotional intimacy, however, Yeats and Gonne remained divided by geography, religion, and politics, and by Gonne's only partially dissolved marriage.

On May 5, 1916, MacBride was executed for his part in the EASTER RISING and thereby redeemed in Gonne's eyes. "Major MacBride by his Death has left a name for [Sean] to be proud of," Gonne told Yeats. "Those who die for Ireland are sacred. Those who enter Eternity by the great door of Sacrifice atone for all—in one moment they do more than all our effort" (GY 375; see also 384). Yeats included MacBride in the martyrology of "EASTER 1916," though dubbing him a "drunken, vainglorious lout." Gonne repudiated the poem as insufficiently heroizing and mythologizing, though her own comment that "tragic dignity has returned to Ireland" apparently inspired its great refrain (see *Letters* 613). "No I don't like your poem," she wrote on November 8, 1916, "it isn't worthy of you & above all it isn't worthy of the subject—Though it reflects your present state of mind perhaps, it isn't quite sincere enough for you who have studied philosophy & know something of history know quite well that sacrifice has never yet turned a heart to stone though it has immortalised many & through

it alone mankind can rise to God—You recognise this in the line which was the original inspiration of your poem 'A terrible Beauty is born' but you let your present mood mar and confuse it till even some of the verses become unintelligible to many" (GY 384). MacBride's death renewed Yeats's marital hopes, but not burningly. He proposed for the last time in August 1916 while staying at Les Mouettes, Gonne's seaside home in Normandy. He stipulated that Gonne must renounce her political activities and was refused, apparently without much regret on either side (AP 56; *W. B. Yeats* 307–308). By this time, Yeats's romantic attention had turned to Iseult, then a 20-year-old beauty, willowy where her mother's beauty had been "like a tightened bow" ("NO SECOND TROY"). Yeats proposed in the summer of 1916 (AP 57–58; GY 382–383) and again in August 1917 (*Letters* 628–631), but, as Iseult told him in the second instance, she had "not the impulse" (628). Yeats's failed courtship of Iseult inspired numerous poems, most notably "The LIVING BEAUTY" and "MEN IMPROVE WITH THE YEARS."

In later years Yeats and Gonne grew apart and for a time "ceased to meet," though the pattern of friendship was too deep to be erased (*Scattering Branches* 25). As always, politics was the insurmountable divide. Gonne remained radical and Republican, while Yeats found "authoritative government" increasingly "interesting" and frowned upon political activism as unseemly and external to the soul (GY 437–439). On May 15, 1918, Gonne was arrested by the British government ostensibly in response to the spurious "German Plot" and was incarcerated for almost six months in Holloway Jail, London, before being released, with Yeats's help, on medical grounds (GY 393, 398–399; *Maud Gonne* 118–120). During her imprisonment Gonne shared quarters with Constance Markiewicz. Yeats's "ON A POLITICAL PRISONER" ponders Markiewicz's descent into political fanaticism, but, as Yeats wrote to his wife in 1918, he was only writing the poem "on Con to avoid writing one on Maud" (NCP 195). Gonne snuck back into Ireland and on November 24 presented herself at her house at 73 St. Stephen's Green, Dublin, which Yeats had been renting while Gonne stayed at WOBURN BUILDINGS in London.

With his wife pregnant and ill and there being the possibility of a raid, Yeats refused to admit her to her own home, causing the most bitter row of their long friendship (*Maud Gonne* 121–122). Yeats supported the treaty that ended the ANGLO-IRISH WAR and created the Irish Free State, and he served as an appointed senator from 1922 to 1928. Gonne opposed both the treaty (after tentatively supporting it at first) and the government. According to her son-in-law Francis Stuart (1902–2000), Gonne "violently disapproved" of Yeats's decision to serve as a senator (*I&R*, II, 370). During the ensuing IRISH CIVIL WAR, Gonne's house was ransacked by Free State soldiers and many of her papers, including letters from Yeats, were destroyed (*Maud Gonne* 137). She was briefly arrested by the Free State government in 1923—the same government that Yeats served as senator—and their relationship nearly foundered. "I cannot write any more as I have just learned that Maud Gonne has been arrested and I must write to Iseult and offer to help with the authorities in the matter of warm blankets," Yeats wrote OLIVIA SHAKESPEAR on January 5. "The day before her arrest she wrote to say that if I did not denounce the Government she renounced my society for ever. I am afraid my help in the matter of blankets, instead of her release (where I could do nothing), will not make her less resentful. She had to choose (perhaps all women must) between broomstick and distaff and she has chosen the broomstick—I mean the witches' hats" (*Letters* 697). On April 10, Gonne was again arrested; she was released only after a 20-day hunger strike (*Maud Gonne* 139–140). Gonne's later years were spent campaigning for prisoner's rights as president of the Women's Prisoner Defense League, which she formed in 1922, and protesting what she considered government repression.

This political activity struck Yeats as so much "intellectual hatred." Yeats's definitive comment on this "hatred" is "A PRAYER FOR MY DAUGHTER," which asks, "Have I not seen the loveliest woman born / Out of the mouth of Plenty's horn, / Because of her opinionated mind / Barter that horn and every good / By quiet natures understood / For an old bellows full of angry wind?" Upon reading Gonne's autobiography *A Servant of the Queen* in 1938, Yeats diagnosed what he considered Gonne's fundamental errancy: "Very much herself always—remarkable intellect at the service of the will, no will at the service of the intellect" (*BG* 553).

Though there were periodic fallings out, there was never a complete break between Yeats and Gonne. Of their last meeting, on August 26, 1938, Gonne wrote to Ethel Mannin in November 1945, "Politics had separated us for quite a long while, we got on each other's nerves over them & neither wanted to see the other, but at the last we had come together & the last time I saw him at RIVERSDALE he was planning things we would do together when he returned—but he seemed to me so ill, I felt unhappy for I didn't think we would meet again in this life" (*GY* 453; see also *Scattering Branches* 25).

Gonne pervades Yeats's work, and her presence particularly haunts the poems. In addition to those poems mentioned above, see, among others, "Against Unworthy Praise" (1910), "AMONG SCHOOL CHILDREN," "The ARROW," "BEAUTIFUL LOFTY THINGS," "BROKEN DREAMS," "A BRONZE HEAD," "A Deep-sworn Vow" (1917), "A Dream of Death" (1891), "FALLEN MAJESTY," "The FOLLY OF BEING COMFORTED," "FRIENDS," "The GREY ROCK" (lines 41–48), "He tells of a Valley full of Lovers" (1897), "HE THINKS OF THOSE WHO HAVE SPOKEN EVIL OF HIS BELOVED," "HE WISHES HIS BELOVED WERE DEAD," "Her Praise," "His Phoenix" (1916), "An IMAGE FROM A PAST LIFE," "The LOVER MOURNS FOR THE LOSS OF LOVE," "The LOVER TELLS OF THE ROSE IN HIS HEART," "A MAN YOUNG AND OLD," "Memory" (1916), "A MEMORY OF YOUTH," "OLD MEMORY," "PEACE," "The PEOPLE," "PRESENCES," "Quarrel in Old Age" (1932), "The SORROW OF LOVE," "That the Night Come" (1912), "A THOUGHT FROM PROPERTIUS," "TO A YOUNG GIRL," "The TWO TREES," "TWO YEARS LATER," "UNDER SATURN," "WHEN YOU ARE OLD," "The WHITE BIRDS," "A WOMAN HOMER SUNG," and "WORDS." "Beautiful Lofty Things" is the only poem that mentions Gonne by name. It is a psychological curiosity Gonne cited "The Two Trees" as her favorite among Yeats's poems (*Unicorn* 425). On another occasion, she more predictably and less interestingly cited "Red Hanrahan's Song about Ireland" (*New Biography* 88).

Bibliography

Ellmann, Richard. *Golden Codgers: Biographical Speculations, Yeats: The Man and the Masks*; Foster, R. F. *W. B. Yeats: A Life, I: The Apprentice Mage, II: The Arch-Poet*; Gonne, Iseult. *Letters to W. B. Yeats and Ezra Pound from Iseult Gonne*; Gonne, Maud. *The Autobiography of Maud Gonne: A Servant of the Queen*; Gwynn, Stephen, ed. *Scattering Branches: Tributes to the Memory of W. B. Yeats*; Hone, Joseph. *W. B. Yeats*; Jeffares, A. Norman. *A New Commentary on the Poems of W. B. Yeats, W. B. Yeats: A New Biography*; Mikhail, E. H. ed. *W. B. Yeats: Interviews and Recollections* (vol. 2); Moore, Virginia. *The Unicorn: William Butler Yeats' Search for Reality*; Saddlemyer, Ann. *Becoming George: The Life of Mrs W. B. Yeats*; Ward, Margaret. *Maud Gonne: A Life*; Yeats, W. B. *Autobiographies, The Collected Letters of W. B. Yeats* (vols. 1–4), *The Gonne-Yeats Letters 1893–1938, The Letters of W. B. Yeats, Memoirs, Uncollected Prose by W. B. Yeats* (vol. 1).

Gregory, Isabella Augusta, Lady (née Persse)

(1852–1932)   Of all the friends and colleagues who shared in Yeats's life, Lady Gregory was arguably the most important. Only MAUD GONNE and JOHN BUTLER YEATS exerted similar influence and occupied a comparable place in the depths of Yeats's emotion. Yeats's profound affection and plainly filial attachment is suggested by a diary entry of February 4, 1909. That morning, Yeats had received news that Lady Gregory had suffered a cerebral hemorrhage. The news brought on a momentary mental breakdown, as Yeats describes: "I thought my mother was ill and that my sister was asking me to come at once: then I remembered that my mother died years ago and that more than kin was at stake. She has been to me mother, friend, sister and brother. I cannot realize the world without her—she brought to my wavering thoughts steadfast nobility. All day the thought of losing her is like a conflagration in the rafters. Friendship is all the house I have" (*Aut.* 353; *Mem.* 160–161). If Lady Gregory provided Yeats with stability, haven, and a version of the maternal embrace, Yeats provided Lady Gregory with inspiration, purpose, and opportunity. He drew her into his own artistic circles and galvanized her middle-aged transformation, one of

The venerable Augusta Gregory. Yeats wrote of Lady Gregory in his 1909 diary, "She has been to me mother, friend, sister and brother. I cannot realize the world without her—she brought to my wavering thoughts steadfast nobility." *(Library of Congress)*

the most dramatic and unlikely in the annals of literature. Guided by the younger poet's example and encouragement, the rural dowager became a writer of lasting achievement and reputation and a leader of the Irish Renaissance. The debt, then, was mutual and immense, as both writers recognized. "I doubt I should have done much with my life but for her firmness and care," Yeats confesses in AUTOBIOGRAPHIES (283). Lady Gregory wrote to Yeats from her deathbed in similar terms: "I do think I have been of use to the country, & for that in great part I thank you" (*Theatre Business* 12). Gossip had it that Lady Gregory was secretly and quietly in love with Yeats—Maud Gonne hinted as much—but this is a matter of speculation (*SQ* 322; see also *Unicorn* 39). Elizabeth Coxhead, one of Lady Gregory's biographers, finds no justification for such rumors and proposes that the relationship between Lady Gregory and Yeats was essentially that of aunt and nephew (*Lady Gregory: A Literary Portrait* 49–51).

Lady Gregory's father, Dudley Persse, was the scion of an old Protestant family and the inheritor of the family estate, Roxborough, in County Galway. Lady Gregory was the 12th of his 16 children, and the ninth of 13 children who were the progeny of his second marriage to Frances Barrey. In his vivid cameo of Lady Gregory in *Autobiographies*, Yeats describes the Roxborough demesne as nine miles in circumference, with a surrounding wall that required the continuous care of three or four masons. The Persses themselves, writes Yeats, "had been soldiers, farmers, riders to hounds and, in the time of the Irish Parliament, politicians [. . .] but all had lacked intellectual curiosity until the downfall of their class had all but come" (294). This late family bloom produced not only Lady Gregory, but also her two nephews, HUGH LANE and John Shawe-Taylor (1866–1911) (see "COOLE PARK, 1929"). Plain, shy, and dutiful, Augusta was far from the center of attention amid the bustle of the massive family and the massive estate. Her life was taken up with the care of her four younger brothers; with books (Malory's *Morte d'Arthur* was her lifelong passion); and, following a Christian awakening at age 15, with charitable work among the tenants of the estate (*Lady Gregory* 14, 28–29). Her father died in 1878, leaving Roxborough to his eldest son. He provided only modestly for the 12 surviving children of his second marriage, leaving £10,000 to be divided among them (39). Augusta remained at Roxborough, but without bright prospects.

Lady Gregory's life took the first of its several unlikely turns on March 4, 1880, when she married Sir William Gregory (1817–92), a 63-year-old widower whom she had first met in 1877 at a cricket match at Roxborough (37). Gregory was a former member of Parliament for Dublin City (1842–47) and Galway County (1857–72), a former governor of Ceylon (1872–77), a trustee of the National Gallery in London (from 1867), and

a wealthy landowner whose estate, COOLE PARK, was seven miles from Roxborough. Notwithstanding the 35-year age difference between bride and groom, the marriage was a social triumph for the unprepossessing Augusta, and married life proved content enough. "She was intelligent, bright, eager to serve, and anxious to learn," writes biographer Mary Lou Kohfeldt. "He had had his great love, and she was not looking for hers" (40). Dividing her time between Coole and a house at Hyde Park Corner, London, Augusta spent the next 12 years performing the rounds appropriate to her station. She traveled widely, hosted the inevitable salon, dabbled in Middle Eastern politics, and took a lover, the poet Wilfred Scawen Blunt (1840–1922). In 1881, she bore a son, ROBERT GREGORY. Despite her fling with Blunt, Augusta was affectionately and admiringly attached to her husband; following his death in 1892, she wore mourning for the rest of her life. Sir William's will established Lady Gregory as mistress of Coole until Robert came of age and granted her the right to remain in the house until her death (91). Coole Park became one of the abiding attachments and enterprises of her life. Over the years of her stewardship she exerted herself mightily to maintain the house and clear its debts (which she managed to do by 1902). Even after Robert became titular master of Coole, Lady Gregory continued in her former role, ruling the house with a firm hand and playing hostess to the luminaries of the Irish Renaissance, as Yeats recalls in "Coole Park, 1929."

Lady Gregory's literary career began in 1894, when she edited and published her husband's life and letters. That same year she made a fateful entry in her diary. At the home of her old friend Sir Michael Morris, she had met "Yates," who looked "every inch a poet," though "his prose 'Celtic Twilight' is the best thing he has done" (*Lady Gregory's Diaries* 32). Their friendship did not begin to solidify, however, until August 1896, when Yeats and ARTHUR SYMONS were in the neighborhood as houseguests of EDWARD MARTYN (*CL2* 47–49; *Lady Gregory's Diaries* 118). Lady Gregory invited the three writers to lunch. She asked how she could assist the Irish movement, and Yeats told her, "If you get our books and watch what we are doing, you will soon find your work" (*Aut.* 291; *Lady Gregory* 105; *Mem.* 102). She saw Yeats in London during the winter, and the following summer the two began their active collaboration. In late June 1897, Yeats accompanied Martyn to lunch at the house of Count Florimond de Basterot (1836–1904), where he met Lady Gregory. The afternoon being wet and Martyn and the count having business to discuss, Lady Gregory and Yeats secluded themselves in the steward's office. The talk turned to plays. "I said it was a pity we had no Irish theatre where such plays could be given," Lady Gregory recalled. "Mr. Yeats said that had always been a dream of his, but he had of late thought it an impossible one, for it could not at first pay its way, and there was no money to be found for such a thing in Ireland. We went on talking about it, and things seemed to grow possible as we talked, and before the end of the afternoon we had made our plan" (*Our Irish Theatre* 19; see also *Aut.* 285; *Lady Gregory's Diaries* 152–153; *Mem.* 117). At Coole a few days later, Lady Gregory and Yeats typed a prospectus for their envisioned theatre (*CL2* 123–125). Thus the ground was laid for the IRISH LITERARY THEATRE, the IRISH NATIONAL THEATRE SOCIETY, and the ABBEY THEATRE; thus the Irish dramatic movement was born; thus the lifelong theatrical partnership between Lady Gregory and Yeats was begun.

Yeats returned to Coole with GEORGE RUSSELL (AE) on July 26. He remained for two months, the first of 20 consecutive summers spent at Coole (*Aut.* 304). His health and nerves shattered by years of frustrated love for Maud Gonne, he needed distraction and fresh air, as Lady Gregory saw. She took him folklore collecting among the local cottages, which was just the thing to calm and restore him (*Aut.* 283–284, 298; *CL1* 137; *Lady Gregory's Diaries* 148). Continuing her ministrations after both had returned to London in the fall, she outfitted Yeats's rooms in WOBURN BUILDINGS with curtains and a "great leather armchair"; sent care packages of fruit and wine; provided infusions of cash; and commissioned JOHN BUTLER YEATS to do pencil drawings of Yeats, AE, Horace Plunkett, and Douglas Hyde (*Aut.* 304; *CL2* 137, 155, 159, 162; *CL3* 140–141; *Lady Gregory* 121–122). Though straitened herself, Lady Gregory continued

to extend small loans for many years. In 1904, flush from his first tour of AMERICA, Yeats offered to repay the loans, but Lady Gregory refused to take his money until he had enough "to feel independent." When Lady Gregory finally consented to the repayment of the loans, Yeats was shocked to learn that he owed £500. He raised the amount by lecturing in America in 1914 (*AM* 517; *Aut.* 304).

Too talented, formidable, and ambitious to remain a mere patroness, Lady Gregory quickly evolved an artistic voice and a personal program. In October 1900, she began to translate the ancient Irish legends. The resulting works, *Cuchulain of Muirthemne* (1902) and *Gods and Fighting Men* (1904), made an enormous impression on Yeats. They confirmed his inclination to root his own drama in the ancient sagas and folklore of Ireland and provided him with copious source material to dramatize and versify in his own work. In his preface, Yeats extols *Cuchulain of Muirthemne* as the "best book that has ever come out of Ireland," for "the stories which it tells are a chief part of Ireland's gift to the imagination of the world—and it tells them perfectly for the first time." He adds that when Lady Gregory has completed "her translations from other cycles [of Irish folklore], she will have given Ireland its *Mabinogion*, its *Morte d'Arthur*, its *Nibelungenlied*" (*Expl.* 3–4). The extravagance of these encomiums inevitably met with raillery from James JOYCE and others (see *Ulysses* 9.1161–5).

As a dramatist, Lady Gregory was both prolific and popular. From 1901 to 1927 she authored 41 plays and translations of plays, making her a mainstay of the revitalized Irish stage. According to Joseph Holloway, the Abbey Theatre gave 600 performances of her plays between 1904 and 1912, compared to 245 performances of Yeats's plays and 182 performances of SYNGE's plays (*Joseph Holloway's Abbey Theatre* 283). Lady Gregory also made a direct contribution to Yeats's plays, for Yeats, by his own admission, could not "get down out of that high window of dramatic verse" and convincingly render the "country speech" (*VPl.* 232). Dedicating *Plays for an Irish Theater* (1903–07) to Lady Gregory, he acknowledged her ability in this regard: "One has to live among the people, like you, of whom an old man said in my hearing, 'She has been a serving maid among us,' before one can think the thoughts of the people and speak with their tongue'" (232). In a 1922 note to *The POT OF BROTH*, Yeats expresses his full debt: "I hardly know how much of the play is my work, for Lady Gregory helped me as she has helped in every play of mine where there is dialect, and sometimes where there is not. In those first years of the Theatre we all helped one another with plots, ideas, and dialogue, but certainly I was the most indebted as I had no mastery of speech that purported to be of real life. This play may be more Lady Gregory's than mine, for I remember once urging her to include it in her own work, and her refusing to do so" (254). He reiterates his debt in his preface to *Plays in Prose and Verse* (1922): "I have sometimes asked her help because I could not write dialect and sometimes because my construction had fallen into confusion. To the best of my belief 'The UNICORN FROM THE STARS,' but for fable and chief character, is wholly her work. 'The GREEN HELMET' and 'The PLAYER QUEEN' alone perhaps are wholly mine" (1306; see also 1292, 1295–1296, 1309). Lady Gregory made a similar editorial contribution to *STORIES OF RED HANRAHAN* (1905), as Yeats acknowledges in JOHN QUINN's copy of the book (*Biblio.* 74) and in a public dedication of 1925 (see Gould and Toomey, eds., *Mythologies* 139). In addition to his prefaces to her two volumes of ancient legend, Yeats, in turn, contributed notes and essays to Lady Gregory's *Visions and Beliefs in the West of Ireland* (1920), which was the final fruit of their folklore collecting among the local cottages years earlier.

Two tragedies of World War I further knit Yeats and Lady Gregory. On May 7, a German submarine sunk the *Lusitania* off the southern coast of Ireland. Lady Gregory's nephew Hugh Lane, director of the Irish National Gallery, died on board. Piqued by Dublin's refusal to build an adequate gallery for his paintings, Lane bequeathed 39 modern masterpieces to the National Gallery of London, but an unwitnessed—and hence unbinding—codicil restored the paintings to the Municipal Gallery in Dublin that Lane had founded in 1907. For the rest of her life, Lady Gregory, with Yeats loyally at her side, their pens blazing, fought to have the paintings restored to Ireland. In 1921, she published

Hugh Lane's Life and Achievement, a biography of her nephew as well as a full exposition of the case for the return of the paintings. Yeats's numerous articles on the controversy are collected in the second volume of *Uncollected Prose by W. B. Yeats*, and his Senate speech on the subject is included in *The Senate Speeches of W. B. Yeats*. Even more heartbreaking than the loss of Lane's paintings was the death of Robert Gregory, who had joined the Royal Flying Corps in 1916. On January 23, 1918, he was mistakenly shot down while returning from a mission in northern Italy. Providing what comfort he could, Yeats took on the duties of elegist, writing a prose reflection (*UP2* 429–431) and three poems— "IN MEMORY OF MAJOR ROBERT GREGORY," "An IRISH AIRMAN FORESEES HIS DEATH," "Shepherd and Goatherd" (1919)—in homage to Gregory. In a fourth poem touching on Gregory's death— "Reprisals"—Yeats asks Gregory to rise from his grave and to reconsider the British cause that he had served in light of the atrocities of the ANGLO-IRISH WAR. Lady Gregory considered the poem in poor taste and prevailed on Yeats to suppress it; it was finally published in 1948 (for the poem, see *VP* 791). She confided in her journal, "I cannot bear the dragging of R., from his grave to make what I think a not very sincere poem—for Yeats only knows by hearsay while our troubles go on—and he quoted words [George Bernard Shaw] told him and did not mean him to repeat—and which will give pain—I hardly know why it give me extraordinary pain [. . .]" (*Lady Gregory's Journals*, I, 207).

Lady Gregory underwent surgery for breast cancer in 1923, 1926, and 1929, and she spent her final years ailing. "COOLE AND BALLYLEE, 1931" records a poignant detail of her decline: "Sound of a stick upon the floor, a sound / From somebody that toils from chair to chair. . . ." During the winter of 1931 and the spring of 1932, Yeats largely resided at Coole and attended Lady Gregory with all the dutifulness of a son (*Letters* 783–797). In February 1932, Lady Gregory acknowledged this final act of gratitude and devotion: "I thank you also for these last months you have spent with me. Your presence made them pass quickly & happily in spite of bodily pain, as your friendship has made my last years—from first to last fruitful in work, in service" (*Theatre Business* 12). Lady Gregory died on May 22, 1932. As Yeats told OLIVIA SHAKESPEAR, she had been unwilling to take pain-killing medication unless "guaranteed not to contain morphia or to affect the mind"—in short, she had been "her indomitable self to the last" (*Letters* 794–795). Yeats meanwhile described himself, ensconced at RIVERSDALE, his new house in the Dublin suburb of Rathfarnham, as "heartbroken for Coole and its great woods" (795). The simultaneous loss of Lady Gregory and Coole ("the only place where I have ever had unbroken health") disordered Yeats's creative capacity for a time (*Letters* 797; *VPl.* 1309). In April 1933 he told Shakespear that he had written no verse in the year since Lady Gregory's death (*Letters* 808).

Yeats wrote prodigiously of Lady Gregory and Coole in both verse and prose. In verse, his tribute includes "BEAUTIFUL LOFTY THINGS," "Coole and Ballylee, 1931," "Coole Park, 1929," "The FOLLY OF BEING COMFORTED," "A FRIEND'S ILLNESS," "FRIENDS," "IN THE SEVEN WOODS," "The MUNICIPAL GALLERY REVISITED," "The NEW FACES," the prologue to The SHADOWY WATERS (see VP 217–218, 745–746), "These are the Clouds" (1910), "TO A FRIEND WHOSE WORK HAS COME TO NOTHING," "UPON A HOUSE SHAKEN BY THE LAND AGITATION," and "The WILD SWANS AT COOLE." Additionally, there are the four poems on Robert Gregory and "For Anne Gregory," a poem memorializing the golden hair of Lady Gregory's granddaughter Anne. The portrait of Lady Gregory and Coole is among the descriptive highlights of *Autobiographies*; appropriately enough, "Dramatis Personae" was originally titled "Lady Gregory" (see *Letters* 820). In A VISION, Yeats assigns Lady Gregory (as well as Queen Victoria and John Galsworthy) to Phase 24 in his lunar cycle. In what functions as a keen and unflinching psychological analysis of his friend, Yeats writes that this phase entails great pride and humility, and submission to a code of personal conduct "formed from social and historical tradition." There is "no philosophic capacity, no intellectual curiosity, but there is no dislike for either philosophy or science; they are a part of the world and that world is accepted. There may be great intolerance for all who break or resist the code, and great tolerance for all the evil

of the world that is clearly beyond it whether above it or below. The code must rule, and because that code cannot be an intellectual choice, it is always a tradition bound up with family, or office, or trade, always a part of history. It is always seemingly fated, for its subconscious purpose is to compel surrender of every personal ambition [. . .]" (169–170).

Lady Gregory, in turn, was a devoted chronicler of the Irish Renaissance. In her journals and several memoirs—*Our Irish Theatre* (1913), *Hugh Lane's Life and Achievement* (1921), *Coole* (1931), *Seventy Years* (1974)—she remembers Yeats and his milieu.

Bibliography

Coxhead, Elizabeth. *Lady Gregory: A Literary Portrait*; Foster, R. F. *W. B. Yeats: A Life, I: The Apprentice Mage*; Gonne, Maud. *The Autobiography of Maud Gonne: A Servant of the Queen*; Gregory, Lady. *Coole, Lady Gregory's Diaries 1892–1902*, *Lady Gregory's Journals* (vols. 1–2, ed. Daniel J. Murphy), *Our Irish Theatre*, *Sir Hugh Lane: His Life and Legacy*; Holloway, Joseph. *Joseph Holloway's Abbey Theatre: A Selection from His Unpublished Journal Impressions of a Dublin Playgoer*; Joyce, James. *Ulysses*; Kohfeldt, Mary Lou. *Lady Gregory: The Woman behind the Irish Renaissance*; Moore, Virginia. *The Unicorn: William Butler Yeats' Search for Reality*; Wade, Allan. *A Bibliography of the Writings of W. B. Yeats*; Yeats, W. B. *Autobiographies*, *The Collected Letters of W. B. Yeats* (vols. 1–3), *Explorations*, *The Letters of W. B. Yeats*, *Memoirs*, *Mythologies* (eds. Warwick Gould and Deirdre Toomey), *Theatre Business: The Correspondence of the first Abbey Theatre Directors: William Butler Yeats, Lady Gregory and J. M. Synge*, *Uncollected Prose by W. B. Yeats* (vol. 2), *The Variorum Edition of the Plays of W. B. Yeats*, *The Variorum Edition of the Poems of W. B. Yeats*, *A Vision*.

Gregory, William Robert (1881–1918) The only child of Sir William Gregory (1817–92) and Yeats's dearest friend AUGUSTA, LADY GREGORY, Robert Gregory was born and raised at COOLE PARK and educated at Harrow and New College, OXFORD. He excelled in boxing, cricket, and horsemanship, but he did not shine as a student.

In 1903, he entered the Slade School of Art in London with the ambition to become a painter. He married his fellow art student Margaret Parry (1884–1979) on September 26, 1907, and the couple had three children, Richard (b. 1909), Anne (b. 1911), and Catherine (b. 1913). Yeats playfully remembers Anne's blond hair in "For Anne Gregory" (1932). Gregory showed his work in London in 1912 and 1914. Commenting on the latter show, held at the Chenil Gallery, one newspaper critic identified Gregory's characteristic motifs of "storm-coloured hills, dun earth and purple rocks," and observed that there is "an extravagant loneliness about his landscapes. . . . Though Mr. Gregory's Ireland is distressful, it has poetry, and he is a master of decorative arrangement." Another critic commented, "Mr. Gregory, I feel certain, has felt the influence of two very different artists—Mr. Jack B. Yeats and Mr. [Augustus] John. . . . But if his work has been influenced by those two painters, it also reveals a very decided and original personality, and I look forward to seeing more of it" (*Robert Gregory* 40). John, in fact, served as best man at Gregory's wedding. He visited Coole prior

Portrait of Robert Gregory, 1905–1906, by Charles Shannon (1863–1937). Yeats alludes to the painting in "The Municipal Gallery Revisited." *(Dublin City Gallery The Hugh Lane)*

to the event; as Yeats told Florence Farr, Robert watched him "with ever visible admiration and discipleship" (*CL4* 726, 728). In addition to painting, Gregory occasionally labored in the trenches of the Irish dramatic movement. "I first came to understand his genius when, still almost a boy, he designed costumes and scenery for the Abbey Theatre," Yeats wrote in an obituary appreciation that appeared in the *Observer* on February 17, 1918. "Working for a theatre that could only afford a few pounds for the staging of a play, he designed for Lady Gregory's 'Kinkora' [sic] and her 'Image' and for my 'Shadowy Waters' and for Synge's 'Deirdre of the Sorrows' decorations which, obtaining their effect from the fewest possible lines and colours, had always the grave distinction of his own imagination" (*UP2* 430). He further designed costumes and scenery for the debut production of *The Hour-Glass* in 1903, scenery for a production of *On Baile's Strand* in 1906, and scenery for the debut production of *Deirdre* in 1906 (*AP* 289; *CL4* 384–385, 509). In 1907, Yeats dedicated *Deirdre* to Gregory in recognition of his beautiful designs for the play (*VPl.* 344).

Despite his astonishing versatility, Gregory seemed perpetually in danger of becoming an "idler," as both Yeats and Lady Gregory felt with some concern (*Lady Gregory* 163, 244). As "An Irish Airman Foresees his Death" and "Reprisals" (1948) suggest, he came into his own only after he joined the Royal Flying Corps in 1916. He received the Legion of Honor and the Military Cross in 1917, and he told George Bernard Shaw that his months as an aviator had been the happiest in his life (*UP2* 431). On January 23, 1918, he was killed in action when an Italian pilot accidentally shot down his plane over northern Italy (*Lady Gregory* 253–254).

Notwithstanding the lavish sentiment of "In Memory of Major Robert Gregory," Yeats and Gregory had an uneasy relationship. Yeats's willingness to make himself at home for months on end in Robert's house was the crux of the problem, but there was also Yeats's conviction that Robert had not lived up to his artistic potential or his birthright (*Lady Gregory* 204; *AM* 503). Yeats's most revealing and damning comment appears in a 1909 journal entry: "I thought of this house [Coole], slowly perfecting itself and the life within it in ever-increasing intensity of labour, and then of its probably sinking away through courteous incompetence, or rather sheer weakness of will, for ability has not failed in young Gregory. [. . .] Is it not always the tragedy of the great and the strong that they see before the end the small and the weak, in friendship or in enmity, pushing them from their place and marring what they have built, and doing one or the other in mere lightness of mind?" (*Mem.* 230). Yeats most likely had Gregory in mind when he wrote "ANCESTRAL HOUSES," a poem fraught with the anxiety of the great house "sinking away through courteous incompetence" ("And maybe the great-grandson of that house, / For all its bronze and marble, 's but a mouse"). Donald T. Torchiana maintains that Gregory, in turn, harbored a "vague animosity" toward Yeats, "twitting him on his scholarship, putting the gloves on with him at the Arts Club and then stretching him flat, mysteriously capsizing a boat with Yeats and himself in it" (*W. B. Yeats & Georgian Ireland* 66). It is possible to infer a submerged sibling rivalry between the two men, for Yeats undoubtedly found in Lady Gregory a maternal figure to fill the void left by his own mother's retreat into disappointment and invalidism (see *Mem.* 160–161). Adding to the strain of the situation, Yeats and Margaret Gregory tended to squabble, though Yeats had initially admired her (see *CL4* 736). As Yeats tells the story, she may have inadvertently facilitated the conception of his daughter Anne: "One night [. . .] she began at dinner to contradict as usual every thing I said & instead of avoiding reply as I had done hitherto I turned on her. I had come down to dinner in the highest of spirits with this wicked intention & at the end of dinner went up stairs in the highest of spirits. George told me I had behaved badly but had so much sympathy with me, that we omited [sic] our usual precaution against conception [. . .]" (*BG* 173).

Upon Robert Gregory's death Yeats assumed the role of elegist, discharging his duties with determination and technical genius if not with deep feeling. He wrote three poems in the months following Gregory's death, "In Memory of Major Robert Gregory," "An Irish Airman Foresees his Death," and "Shepherd and Goatherd" (1919), as well as the "note of appreciation" that appeared in the *Observer*. The latter—a delicate operation given Yeats's obligations to Lady Gregory—cloaks in philosophical abstraction the insinuation of dilettantism: "Though he often seemed led away from his work by some other gift, his attitude to life and art never lost intensity—he was never the amateur. I have noticed that men whose lives are to be an ever-growing absorption in subjective beauty [. . .] seek through some lesser gift, or through mere excitement, to strengthen that self which unites them to ordinary men. It is as though they hesitated before they plunged into the abyss" (*UP2* 430–431). In a letter of February 18, 1918, to JOHN QUINN, Yeats was less cagey and seems genuinely to endorse the encomiums of "In Memory of Major Robert Gregory": "I think [Gregory] had genius. Certainly no contemporary landscape moved me as much as two or three of his, except perhaps a certain landscape by [James Dickson] Innes, from whom he had learnt a great deal. His paintings had majesty and austerity, and at the same time sweetness. He was the most accomplished man I have ever known; I mean that he could do more things well than any other" (*Letters* 646).

In November 1920, Yeats sent Lady Gregory "Reprisals" (see *VP* 791), a fourth poem touching on Gregory's death (*YC* 213). The poem asks Gregory's shade to reconsider the cause it had served in light of British atrocities during the ANGLO-IRISH WAR. Lady Gregory prevailed on Yeats not to publish the poem. She wrote in her diary that she could not "bear the dragging of R., from his grave to make what I think a not very sincere poem—for Yeats only knows by hearsay while our troubles go on—and he quoted words [George Bernard Shaw] told him and did not mean him to repeat—and which will give pain—I hardly know why it give me extraordinary pain [. . .]" (*Lady Gregory's Journals,* I, 207). Yeats acceded to Lady Gregory's wishes and the poem did not appear until 1948. Yeats additionally includes Gregory in the roll call of "The MUNICIPAL GALLERY REVISITED"—his portrait having been painted by Yeats's friend Charles Shannon

(1863–1937)—but invokes him only as "Augusta Gregory's son."

Bibliography

Foster, R. F. *W. B. Yeats: A Life, I: The Apprentice Mage*; Gregory, Lady. *Lady Gregory's Journals* (vol. 1, ed. Daniel J. Murphy); Kelly, John S. *A W. B. Yeats Chronology*; Kohfeldt, Mary Lou. *Lady Gregory: The Woman behind the Irish Renaissance*; Saddlemyer, Ann. *Becoming George: The Life of Mrs W. B. Yeats*; Smythe, Colin, ed. *Robert Gregory 1881–1918: A Centenary Tribute with a Foreword by His Children*; Torchiana, Donald T. *W. B. Yeats & Georgian Ireland*; Yeats, W. B. *The Collected Letters of W. B. Yeats* (vol. 4), *The Letters of W. B. Yeats, Memoirs, Uncollected Prose by W. B. Yeats* (vol. 2), *The Variorum Edition of the Plays of W. B. Yeats, The Variorum Edition of the Poems of W. B. Yeats*.

Hermetic Order of the Golden Dawn Finding himself at odds with the orthodoxies of the THEOSOPHICAL SOCIETY—his official expulsion came in October 1890—Yeats cast his lot with the Hermetic Order of the Golden Dawn, a newly instituted occult society based in London, and maintained his affiliation for some 30 years. Explaining Yeats's extraordinary commitment to the order, George Mills Harper writes that "the search for meaning in the multiplicity and profusion and seeming chaos of nature required a framework, a system. The discipline of the [order's] magical examinations represented a search for truth, a striving for the union with the ideal in the invisible world. In the broadest sense all Yeats's creative energies were devoted to this religious quest" (*Yeats's Golden Dawn* 74). In *AUTOBIOGRAPHIES*, Yeats writes that he joined the Golden Dawn in "May or June 1887" (160) but his memory apparently deceived him. The actual date was March 7, 1890, and the place was the Isis-Urania Temple, No. 3, at 17 Fitzroy Street, London (*Unicorn* 134). In his study of the Golden Dawn, George Mills Harper speculates that in 1887 Yeats more accurately joined a group "associated with or an outgrowth of the Hermetic Society founded by Anna Kingsford and Edward Maitland which had withdrawn from the Theosophical Society, becoming an independent organization on 22 April 1884"

(*Yeats's Golden Dawn* 9). Harper theorizes that the Golden Dawn emerged to carry on the work of Kingsford (1846–88) after she died.

The Golden Dawn was born under mysterious—most would say dubious—circumstances. According to one story, the Rev. A. F. A. Woodford discovered a mysterious and seemingly ancient manuscript (the so-called "Cypher MS") on an old London bookstall in 1884. The manuscript included the "fragmentary outlines [. . .] of five mystical or pseudo-Masonic rituals," as well as the name and address of one Fräulein Sprengel of Stuttgart, Germany (*Magicians* 1). Woodford brought the manuscript to the attention of Dr. William Robert Woodman (born 1828) and Dr. William Wynn Westcott (1848–1925), members of the Societas Rosicruciana in Anglia, an organization devoted to the study of occultism, Cabbala, and Masonic symbolism (*Magicians* 8; *Yeats's Golden Dawn* 9). Westcott, a coroner, allegedly wrote to Fräulein Sprengel in Germany and received her authorization to found a branch of the Rosicrucian Order in England. Ellic Howe argues, however, that the five letters said to have come from Sprengel were most likely forged by Westcott, and that Sprengel was his own invention (*Magicians* 7). Whatever the veracity of its founding documents, the Isis-Urania Temple of the Order of the Golden Dawn came into being on March 1, 1888, under the leadership of Woodman, Westcott, and MACGREGOR MATHERS, who was likewise a member of the Societas Rosicruciana in Anglia. By 1896, the temple had inducted 189 initiates (49). Yeats brought several friends into the temple, the first of whom was FLORENCE FARR in July 1890. MAUD GONNE joined in November 1891, but found the initiates "the very essence of British middle-class dullness" and resigned in 1894 (*CL1* 266; *SQ* 210–212). Yeats's BEDFORD PARK neighbor John Todhunter (1839–1916) joined in February 1892, and his uncle GEORGE POLLEXFEN joined in December 1893 (51). ANNIE HORNIMAN, who would later bankroll the creation of the ABBEY THEATRE, slightly preceded Yeats in the organization; that they were soon brought together was perhaps the most significant serendipity of Yeats's occult involvement. Upon being initiated, Yeats took the initials DEDI, standing for the motto *Demon Est Deus Inversus* ("the devil is God inverted"). Madame Blavatsky's *Secret Doctrine* (1888) includes a disquisition on the meaning of the phrase (Book 1, Part II, Chapter XI) and undoubtedly inspired Yeats's choice.

In a document titled "The Historic Lecture for Neophytes," an introduction to the order for new initiates, the Golden Dawn laid claim to a "Doctrine and System of Theosophy and Hermetic Science" that had descended from the "Fratraes Rosae Crucis of Germany, which association was founded by one Christian Rosenkreuz about the year 1398"; the Rosicrucian teachings, in turn, were said to descend from the wisdom of the "Kabalistic Rabbis" and the ancient Egyptians (*Magicians* 22–23). Mathers was the Golden Dawn's "governing mind, a born teacher and organizer," according to Yeats, and it was he who developed the society's elaborate organization and ritual based on the contents of the Cypher MS (*Aut.* 160). The society was structured hierarchically, with 11 grades divided into three orders: $0°=0°$ (Neophyte, first order), $1°=10°$ (Zelator, first order), $2°=9°$ (Theoricus, first order), $3°=8°$ (Practicus, first order), $4°=7°$ (Philosophus, first order), $5°=6°$ (Adeptus Minor, second order), $6°=5°$ (Adeptus Major, second order), $7°=4°$ (Adeptus Exemptus, second order), $8°=3°$ (Magister Templi, third order), $9°=2°$ (Magus, third order), $10°=1°$ (Ipsissimus, third order) (*Magicians* 16). The second order was called the Inner Order of the Rose of Ruby and the Cross of Gold, otherwise known as "R.R. et A.C." The third order was considered attainable only by "Secret Chiefs" who inhabited the astral plane (17). Each grade had its own garb, instruction, and rituals. Advancement from grade to grade was governed by formal exams on occult subject matter.

From the early 1890s onward, the order's history was marked by near-continual factional quarreling and schism. Though he moved to PARIS in 1892 and founded a Parisian branch of the Golden Dawn—the Ahathoor Temple—in 1894, Mathers maintained his hold on the London order. High-handed and eccentric, Mathers was prone to provocation. In December 1896 he expelled Horniman on grounds of insubordination, and in March 1897, he finessed the departure of Westcott, apparently

by leaking word of his occult involvement and embarrassing his professional position (133–138, 165–166). In February 1900 open warfare broke out. In an angry letter to Farr, then the acting head of the London temple, Mathers took umbrage that his "private affairs" had been discussed at a meeting of the second order and charged that the correspondence between Westcott and the "Secret Chiefs of the Order" (i.e., Sprengel) had been forged. In a clear bid to shore up his own authority, he claimed that he alone had been in communication with the Secret Chiefs of the Order, and that "every atom of the knowledge of the order" had come through him (210). The climax of the power struggle came on April 17 when Aleister Crowley, Mathers's proxy, attempted to seize the society headquarters at 36 Blythe Road, London. Two days later, Yeats defended the property against a second attempt by Crowley, who was this time garbed flamboyantly in a black mask and full Highland dress (CL2 514–515). On April 21, the order expelled Mathers and reconstituted itself under a new executive council. "At last we have got a perfectly honest order, with no false mystery & no mystagogues of any kind," Yeats wrote to GEORGE RUSSELL (AE) on May 2, but his hopes for the order were to prove wildly optimistic (524). There were to follow three years of wrangling largely concerning the right of members to form subsidiary groups on their own authority. In 1902, following a rape trial in which the order's name had been aired, the Hermetic Order of the Golden Dawn became the Hermetic Society of the M.R., standing for *Morgenröthe* or "Golden Dawn" (*Magicians* 242). In 1903, further schism resulted in the founding of a new order, the Stella Matutina, with which Yeats remained loosely involved until 1922 (*Yeats's Golden Dawn* 124–125, 145).

Yeats's occult involvements have often been ridiculed, but their centrality to his thought and work cannot be questioned. Writing to JOHN O'LEARY on July 23, 1892, Yeats defended his occult involvement in self-conscious and sophisticated terms: "The mystical life is the centre of all that I do & all that I think & all that I write. It holds to my work the same relation that the philosophy of Godwin held to the work of SHELLEY & I have all-ways considered my self a voice of what I believe [sic] to be a greater renaisance [sic]—the revolt of the soul against the intellect—now begining [sic] in the world" (*CL1* 303). As this self-defense indicates, Yeats was engaged in no mere table-rapping or wand waving, but in a principled and self-conscious rebellion against the rationalism and scientific materialism of the modern world. With similar sophistication, Yeats theorizes the nature of magic in his 1901 essay "MAGIC," positing magician and poet as fellow-keepers of the secret by which symbols—"the greatest of all powers"—are evoked from the depths of ANIMA MUNDI (*E&I* 49–50). In his unpublished essay "Is the Order of R.R. & A.C. to Remain a Magical Order?" (1901), Yeats writes that the "central principle of all the Magic of power is that everything we formulate in the imagination, if we formulate it strongly enough, realises itself in the circumstances of life, acting either through our own souls, or through the spirits of nature" (*Yeats's Golden Dawn* 265). If this is magical doctrine, it is also romantic doctrine. WILLIAM BLAKE, in imaginative dialogue with Isaiah, says much the same thing in *The Marriage of Heaven and Hell* (written 1789–90): "Then I asked: 'Does a firm persuasion that a thing is so, make it so?' / He replied, 'All poets believe that it does, and in ages of imagination the firm persuasion removed mountains; but many are not capable of a firm persuasion of anything'" (Plate 12). That Yeats's doctrine of magic is so closely allied with romantic tradition and with his own poetic practice at the very least entitles it to thoughtful consideration.

Bibliography

Blavatsky, H. P. *The Secret Doctrine: A Facsimile of the Original Edition of 1888*; Gonne, Maud. *The Autobiography of Maud Gonne: A Servant of the Queen*; Harper, George Mills. *Yeats's Golden Dawn*; Howe, Ellic. *The Magicians of the Golden Dawn: A Documentary History of the Magical Order, 1887–1923*; Moore, Virginia. *The Unicorn: William Butler Yeats' Search for Reality*; Yeats, W. B. *Autobiographies*, *The Collected Letters of W. B. Yeats* (vols. 1–2), *Essays and Introductions*.

Horniman, Annie Elizabeth Fredericka (1860–1937)

The daughter and granddaughter of enormously successful British tea merchants, Annie Horniman was raised on a 15-acre estate in the London suburb of Forest Hill. There was much to stimulate her imagination, as her father, Frederick John Horniman, had amassed a vast collection of specimens and artifacts while traveling on behalf of the family firm, W.H. & F.J. Horniman & Co., producers of Horniman Tea (*Annie Horniman* 14–15). In 1889 he opened part of the family house as a public museum, with his daughter's occult protégé MACGREGOR MATHERS serving for a short time as caretaker. In 1898 he tore down the house to make way for a museum proper that flourishes to this day as the Horniman Museum (26). On the death of her grandfather in 1893, Horniman inherited £40,000, a fortune sizable enough to keep her in comfort for the rest of her life and subsidize her career as a patroness of the arts. Horniman was foremost a lover of the theater and wasted no time in putting her new wealth to use. She joined the HERMETIC ORDER OF THE GOLDEN DAWN in 1890 and became friends with her fellow initiates Yeats and FLORENCE FARR (5). In 1894, she subsidized a dramatic program featuring Yeats's *The LAND OF HEART'S DESIRE* and John Todhunter's *The Comedy of Sighs*, both of which were directed by Farr (9). She kept her patronage a closely guarded secret, as she feared that her parents would disapprove (*FF, BS, and WBY*, "Explanatory Word"). The plays debuted on March 29 at the Avenue Theatre, London. Todhunter's play—a "rambling story told with a little paradoxical wit"—met with a barrage of "boos and jeers" on opening night. George Bernard Shaw's *Arms and the Man* replaced it, and the renovated program ran for 11 weeks (*Aut.* 219–222).

Over the next 10 years, Horniman sporadically served as Yeats's unofficial secretary, in which capacity she took dictation, typed manuscripts, and attempted to keep his rooms neat (*Annie Horniman* 45). In 1903, with her long experience as a theatergoer and her training as a painter to recommend her, Horniman arrived in Dublin to design costumes for the fledgling IRISH NATIONAL THEATRE SOCIETY's production of Yeats's *The KING'S THRESHOLD* (*CL3* 442). Privately, Yeats acknowledged that her design work left something to be desired, but he predicted that with freedom to experiment, she would come into her own (528). Lacking Yeats's obvious ulterior motives, James Flannery describes Horniman's costumes for *The King's Threshold* as "stiff, graceless, illfitting and lacking in any sense of unity or style" (*Miss Annie F. Horniman* 15). She later designed costumes, with as little success, for the debut production of ON BAILE'S STRAND (CL3 687; *Joseph Holloway's Abbey Theatre* 49–50).

Exhilarated by her hands-on theatrical experience and won over by Yeats's ambitions, Horniman decided to provide the society with a theater of its own. She purchased the lease on the Mechanics' Institute on Abbey Street and an adjacent morgue on Marlborough Street and became the founding patroness of the ABBEY THEATRE (CL3 572–573). As an unevenly tempered Englishwoman with an "intense distaste" for Irish nationalism, Horniman was unpopular with the company that she subsidized (LTWBY, I, 167). She in turn cringed at the forward behavior of the young actresses and had much to say against what seemed to her the lax management style of William Fay (1872–1947). The antagonism between the two, according to Gerard Fay, amounted to civil war (*Cradle of Genius* 105). In Lady GREGORY's phrase, Horniman was like a "shilling in a tub of electrified water"—irresistible in her largesse, but punishing in her personality (FF, BS, and WBY 76). In 1907, Horniman purchased the Gaiety Theatre in Manchester and formed her own company, thus initiating the British repertory theater movement and distancing herself from the Irish dramatic movement.

The final rupture came in 1910, after manager Lennox Robinson neglected to cancel a Saturday matinee on the day after King Edward VII's death (*Annie Horniman* 138–141). Thin-skinned under the best of circumstances, Horniman construed the decision as a political statement and a deliberate affront, and she withdrew her subsidy. Yeats and Lady Gregory took legal action to recover the money. In the end, Horniman paid the £400 balance of her annual subsidy and relinquished the Abbey for £1,000 (148–149). On May 5, 1911, she sent a telegram to Yeats that indicates the extent of her bitterness: "You have shewn me that I do not matter in your eyes. The money [i.e., the remaining portion of the annual subsidy] is paid. Super-

men [i.e., Yeats] cannot associate with slaves. May time reawaken your sense of honour then you may find your friend again but repentance must come first" (149). As late as 1932, Horniman continued to grind the ax: "Lady Gregory actually published in a book [*Our Irish Theatre*] that she made the Abbey Theatre, but I did not contradict it; indeed, I only laughed at the time, as I fancied that she had come to believe it herself. [. . .] From the financial point of view, I have my old Dublin pass-books, which are clear evidence" (*Abbey Theatre: Interviews and Recollections* 29). Horniman had reason to feel underappreciated. Between 1904 and 1910, she contributed over £10,000 to the creation and upkeep of the theater. Horniman's annual income was £2,400 in 1910, which makes clear that her contribution to the Abbey was an amount large enough to mean something to her (*Miss Annie F. Horniman* 35). In his NOBEL PRIZE lecture, Yeats somewhat ungraciously refers to Horniman's "small subsidy" (Aut. 415).

With Horniman's departure, Yeats and Lady Gregory, as William M. Murphy puts it, "sat in lone splendor atop the dramatic edifice that so many hands had helped to build" (PF 375). Yeats and Horniman eventually reconciled, but they were never again intimate. The Gaiety Theatre, meanwhile, had a brilliant initial success that it could not sustain. Though well loved, the company disbanded in 1917, done in by wartime disruptions and mounting debt. Horniman sold the theater in 1921 and retired from public life.

In *A Servant of the Queen* (1938), MAUD GONNE archly characterizes the personal dynamics underlying the Abbey experiment: "I had been much amused in Dublin watching the rivalry between Lady Gregory and a rich English woman, Miss Horniman; both were interested in Willie and both were interested in the Irish theatre. Miss Horniman had the money and was willing to spend it, but Lady Gregory had the brains. They should have been allies for both stood for art for art's sake and deprecated the intrusion of politics, which meant Irish freedom; instead they were rivals; they both liked Willie too well" (SQ 322). More circumspectly, James W. Flannery describes on Horniman's part "a very strong emotional attachment for Yeats himself and the particular furtherance of his work" (*Miss Annie F. Horniman* 12). A. Norman Jeffares states bluntly that she "would obviously have been happy to marry him" (*New Biography* 141).

Bibliography

Fay, Gerard. *The Abbey Theatre: Cradle of Genius*; Finneran, Richard J., et al., eds. *Letters to W. B. Yeats* (vol. 1); Flannery, James W. *Miss Annie F. Horniman and the Abbey Theatre*; Gonne, Maud. *The Autobiography of Maud Gonne: A Servant of the Queen*; Gooddie, Sheila. *Annie Horniman: A Pioneer in the Theatre*; Holloway, Joseph. *Joseph Holloway's Abbey Theatre: A Selection from His Unpublished Journal* Impressions of a Dublin Playgoer; Jeffares, A. Norman. *W. B. Yeats: A New Biography*; Mikhail, E. H., ed. *The Abbey Theatre: Interviews and Recollections*; Murphy, William M. *Prodigal Father: The Life of John Butler Yeats (1839–1922)*; Yeats, W. B. *Autobiographies, The Collected Letters of W. B. Yeats* (vol. 3), *Florence Farr, Bernard Shaw, and W. B. Yeats*.

Horton, William Thomas (1864–1919)   A Belgian-born British artist of middling talent in the mystical tradition of BLAKE and Samuel Palmer (1805–81), Horton trained as an architect, but during the 1890s took up the life of struggling writer and illustrator, falling in with Yeats, ARTHUR SYMONS, and AUBREY BEARDSLEY, and contributing drawings to the SAVOY. Horton likely met Yeats in 1894, as George Mills Harper surmises in *W. B. Yeats and W. T. Horton* (4). The friendship was sealed after Horton joined the HERMETIC ORDER OF THE GOLDEN DAWN on March 21, 1896. Horton left the order a little more than a month later, being "fully convinced" that in his case the "only safe path is Jesus Christ & He alone" (95). All the same, the two disciples of Blake remained intermittent mystical confidants until Horton's death in 1919. With Yeats inclined to be blunt about the limitations of Horton's work, and Horton inclined to be sensitive, the friendship suffered many passing strains (27, 31). The most significant rift concerned Yeats's introduction to Horton's *Book of Images*, a collection of black-and-white prints on medieval and mystical themes that appeared in 1898. When

he republished his introduction as the essay "SYMBOLISM IN PAINTING" in 1903, Yeats omitted the third section, which dealt exclusively with Horton's work. In a 1903 letter, Yeats explained, not very comfortably, that it had always been his intention eventually to "detach the general statement from the rest," and that he had cut Horton's name from a list of illustrous symbolists in the second section on the grounds that his work, though interesting and beautiful, could not be named "with mature and elaborate talents like Mr. Whistler's and Mr. Ricketts'" (*CL3* 400). Far from being mollified, Horton was still smarting from this slight as late as 1917, when he confessed to Yeats that "from 1904 silently but ceaselessly a poison has been working" and that his confidence in his work had been undermined ever since (*W. B. Yeats and W. T. Horton* 132).

Yeats memorializes Horton in "ALL SOULS' NIGHT." The poem invokes Horton's shade with the recollection that he "loved strange thought," and with the more tender recollection that no words could provide "anodyne for his love" when "his lady died." Yeats alludes to the historian Amy Audrey Locke (born 1881), with whom Horton had a reputedly platonic love affair from 1912 or 1913 until her death from "ear and mastoid trouble" in 1916 (48). Harper quotes a 1915 notebook entry that suggests that Yeats himself had been attracted in some manner to Locke. Yeats mentions having had an "erotic dream of girl, who was like Miss Locke" and having been worried about the danger of an "amour." He had later decided, however, that Locke had not been the girl in his dream (48).

In his dedication of the 1925 edition of *A VISION* to MACGREGOR MATHERS's widow, Moina, Yeats writes that Horton "lived through that strange adventure, perhaps the strangest of all adventures—Platonic love. When he was a child his nurse said to him—'An Angel bent over your bed last night,' and in his seventeenth year he awoke to see the phantom of a beautiful woman at his bedside. Presently he gave himself up to all kinds of amorous adventures, until at last, in I think his fiftieth year but when he had still all his physical vigour, he thought 'I do not need women but God.' Then he and a very good, charming, young fellow-student fell in love with one another and though he could only keep down his passion with the most bitter struggle, they lived together platonically [. . .]." After Locke's death, Yeats continues, Horton endured "but a little time during which he saw her in apparition and attained through her certain of the traditional experiences of the saint" (*AV-1925* x). Yeats adds that he would have dedicated *A Vision* to Horton had he lived. Having come to believe in a "very simple piety," however, Horton would not have relished the architectonic ambition of the work (x).

Bibliography

Harper, George Mills. *W. B. Yeats and W. T. Horton: The Record of an Occult Friendship*; Horton, W. T. *A Book of Images*; Yeats, W. B. *The Collected Letters of W. B. Yeats* (vol. 3), *A Critical Edition of Yeats's A Vision (1925)*.

Irish Academy of Letters   The Irish Academy of Letters was Yeats's final organizational brainchild. On July 27, 1926, Yeats, GEORGE RUSSELL (AE), and Lennox Robinson (1886–1958) wrote to the president of the Royal Irish Academy and proposed that the academy incorporate an autonomous committee of 12 men of letters whose "principal function would probably be at first to crown certain books" every three years. In addition to themselves, the signatories proposed as founding members Douglas Hyde (1860–1949), St. John Ervine (1883–1971), Stephen MacKenna (1872–1934), Sean O'Casey (1880–1964), Forrest Reid (1875–1947), George Bernard Shaw (1856–1950), and James Stephens (1882–1950) (*Letters* 716–717). More than a year later, Yeats had received no response. Claiming that he had joined the academy only for the sake of his proposal, he duly resigned to organize an Irish Academy of Letters on his own terms (732). Attempting to cajole JAMES JOYCE to become a founding member, Yeats envisioned the academy as a "vigorous body capable of defending our interests, negotiating with Government, and I hope preventing the worst forms of censorship" (801).

On September 1, 1932, Yeats and Shaw, as the grand old men of Irish literature, sent a letter of invitation to prospective academicians (801–802). The academy held an organizational meeting on September 14. Shaw was to serve as president, Yeats as vice president. "Founding members" included, Austin Clarke (1896–1974), Padraic Colum (1881–1972), St. John Ervine, Oliver St John Gogarty (1878–1957), F. R. Higgins (1896–1941), Brinsley MacNamara (1890–1963), T. C. Murray (1873–1959), Frank O'Connor (1903–66), Peadar O'Donnell (1893–1986), Sean O'Faolain (1900–91), Liam O'Flaherty (1896–1984), Seumas O'Sullivan (1879–1958), Forrest Reid, Lennox Robinson, Russell, Edith Somerville (1858–1949), James Stephens, and Francis Stuart (1902–2000). "Associate members"—so designated, not without hurt feelings, because in some fashion "less Irish"—were JOHN EGLINTON, Stephen Gwynn (1864–1950), Joseph Hone (1882–1959), T. E. Lawrence (1888–1935), Walter Starkie (1894–1976), L. A. G. Strong (1896–1958), Eugene O'Neill (1888–1953), and Helen Waddell (1889–1965) (801; see also *AP* 448; *Irish Literature and Drama* 233–234; *W. B. Yeats* 431). As Yeats explained the distinction in membership to Joyce, "When we began talking over members we found we had to make this division or we should have been overrun with people from England or Scotland with a little Irish blood and a great desire to acquire a national character" (*Letters* 800).

Daniel Corkery (1878–1964), Douglas Hyde, Stephen MacKenna, GEORGE MOORE, and Sean O'Casey declined the offer of membership, as did Joyce, most disappointingly (*AP* 450–451; *Irish Literature and Drama* 234–235; *W. B. Yeats* 431). On October 5, 1932, Joyce responded to Yeats's generous invitation with his usual prickly independence: "I hope that the Academy of Irish Letters (if that is its title) which you are both forming will have the success it aims at. My case, however, being as it was and probably will be I see no reason why my name should have arisen at all in connection with such an academy: and I feel quite clearly that I have no right whatsoever to nominate myself as a member of it" (Joyce, *Letters*, I, 325).

In October 1932, Yeats departed for a tour of America in part to raise money for the new academy and to publicize its existence. In January 1933,

as his tour was coming to an end, he wrote to
OLIVIA SHAKESPEAR from New York that he had
raised £600 for himself and £600 for the academy. The money was primarily to underwrite the
academy's annual literary prizes (*Letters* 803). On
January 29, 1933, Yeats wrote to Shakespear with
a second account of his fund-raising success: "I
have brought GEORGE [YEATS] about £700 and the
Academy all the money it wants. It can now give
an annual prize of £50 to a young Irish writer or a
bi-annual prize of £100; a bronze medal, designed
by some famous sculptor, irrespective of age. I had
meant to lecture with these objects in London but
that is now unnecessary" (804). As Stephen Gwynn
notes, the academy gave four awards in Yeats's day:
the Harmsworth Award, for the year's best work of
"imaginative prose" (£100); the Casement Award,
for the year's best work of poetry and drama (£50);
the O'Growney Award, for the best "work of the
imagination published in Gaelic" (£50); and the
Gregory Medal, awarded every three years in
honor of Lady GREGORY (*Irish Literature and Drama*
235–236). Though it never formally dissolved, the
academy was effectively superseded by Aosdàna,
an organization of writers, artists, and musicians
founded by the Irish Arts Council in 1981 (*Dictionary of Irish Literature*, I, 579).

Bibliography

Foster, R. F. *W. B. Yeats: A Life, II: The Arch-Poet*;
  Gwynn, Stephen. *Irish Literature and Drama in the
  English Language: A Short History*; Hogan, Robert,
  ed. *Dictionary of Irish Literature* (vol. 1); Hone,
  Joseph. *W. B. Yeats*; Joyce, James. *Letters* (vol. 1);
  Yeats, W. B. *The Letters of W. B. Yeats*.

Irish Civil War   The Irish Civil War began in
June 1922 and ended in May 1923. All the more
bitter for dividing former comrades, the war was
fought by advocates and opponents of the treaty
that ended the ANGLO-IRISH WAR (1919–21). The
treaty, which had been arduously negotiated with
the Liberal ministry of Lloyd George, established
the Irish Free State, but it included provisions that
were anathema to the more ardent republicans in
the coalition that had forced the British to the
bargaining table. The treaty's controversial points

were the establishment of the Irish Free State as
a dominion within the British Commonwealth;
the British navy's right to use certain Irish ports;
Northern Ireland's right to remain within the
United Kingdom, its borders to be determined by
a Boundary Commission; and the requirement that
members of the Irish Dáil or parliament swear an
oath of allegiance to Britain. The Dáil approved
the treaty on January 7, 1922, by a vote of 64 to 57.
In protest, Eamon de Valera (1882–1975), leader
of the antitreaty contingent, resigned as president
of the republic, and Arthur Griffith (1871–1922)
was elected in his place (*Ireland Since the Famine*
447–449). The political rift steadily degenerated
into a military conflict, with the followers of de
Valera and dissident factions within the army (its
forces dubbed "Irregulars") making common cause
against the provisional government. In April, anti-
treaty forces seized the Four Courts (i.e., courts of
justice) in Dublin. In June, the government retook
the courts and arrested 400 (including MAUD
GONNE's son Sean MacBride), initiating 11 months
of intermittent assassinations, ambushes, executions, and house burnings (GY 428). The war cost
the lives of 800 government soldiers and, says R.
F. Foster, "far more Republicans" (*Modern Ireland*
512).

Yeats supported the Free State and served in
the new government as an appointed senator from
December 1922 to July 1928. Writing to OLIVIA
SHAKESPEAR in October 1922, Yeats gives the
impression of being startled by the war, which he
calls "very curious" and characterizes as a "revolt
against democracy" by the antitreaty forces. The
war struck Yeats as yet another confirmation that
modernity's tendency was essentially apocalyptic,
a matter of anarchy being loosed upon the world,
of things falling apart ("The SECOND COMING"),
with a pitiless conservative reaction waiting in
the wings. The ministers of the Free State, he told
Shakespear, "more and more seem too sober to
meet the wildness of these enemies; and everywhere one notices a drift towards Conservatism,
perhaps towards Autocracy. I always knew that it
would come, but not that it would come in this
tragic way. One wonders what prominent man will
live through it. One meets a minister at dinner,

passing his armed guard on the doorstep, and one feels no certainty that one will meet him again. We are entering on the final and most dreadful stage. Perhaps there is nothing so dangerous to a modern state, when politics takes the place of theology, as a bunch of martyrs. A bunch of martyrs (1916) were the bomb and we are living in the explosion"—this last an allusion to the EASTER RISING and its aftermath (*Letters* 690; see also 695; *WBY&TSM* 46).

Yeats remained in Ireland during the months of the civil war; its grit and confusion were neither distant nor abstract, as the atrocities of the Anglo-Irish War had been (Yeats knew these only by "hearsay" according to Lady GREGORY; see *Lady Gregory's Journals*, I, 207). In a note to his NOBEL PRIZE lecture "The Irish Dramatic Movement," Yeats describes firsthand the texture of daily life during the war: "I was in my Galway house during the first months of civil war, the railway bridges blown up and the roads blocked with stones and trees. For the first week there were no newspapers, no reliable news, we did not know who had won nor who had lost, and even after newspapers came, one never knew what was happening on the other side of the hill or of the line of trees. Ford cars passed the house from time to time with coffins standing upon end between the seats, and sometimes at night we heard an explosion, and once by day saw the smoke made by the burning of a great neighbouring house. Men must have lived so through many tumultuous centuries" (*Aut.* 522–523).

Yeats and his family had several close scrapes, but emerged unscathed. On August 19, 1922, Republican soldiers dynamited the bridge at THOOR BALLYLEE while the Yeats family took cover halfway up the stone tower, only a few feet away from the demolition (*AP* 214–215; *VP* 827). On October 30, a bomb exploded near Yeats's home at 82 Merrion Square, Dublin, shattering windows while one of Yeats's "Monday evenings" was underway (*AP* 225; *Letters* 692). On December 24, 1922, two bullets were fired through the window at Merrion Square (*AP* 230; *BG* 310; *Letters* 696). One of the bullets ended its flight in the nursery, where GEORGE YEATS was sitting with little Anne on her knee. Mother and daughter were showered with plaster, but they were otherwise uninjured. In light

of this danger, two armed guards were posted at 82 Merrion Square in 1922 and 1923. Sean O'Casey (1880–1964), for one, considered the posting of these sentinels melodramatic, for "the Republicans had as much idea of shooting Yeats as they had of shooting Lady Gregory or the Catholic Archbishop of Dublin" (*I&R*, I, 169–170). On August 18, 1923, Yeats reported to T. STURGE MOORE on the final damage at Ballylee: "Little harm has been done here, despite rumours in the press, and even in the neighbouring towns, except the windows and doors burst in and various traces of occupation by Irregulars, stray bullets, signs that a bed has been slept in and so on. The Irregulars took care of our property and even moved a Russian icon of my wife's from a dry wall to a dry shelf, but after they had gone the country people stole all the mirrors" (*WBY&TSM* 48). Nearby Roxborough House, the hereditary estate of the Persse family and the girlhood home of Lady Gregory, did not fare as well: marauders burned it down (*Homes* 77).

Many in Yeats's circle were also caught up in the turmoil of the war. On January 12, 1923, Oliver St John Gogarty (1878–1957), Yeats's friend and fellow senator, had to dive into the Liffey in order to evade assassins. Yeats relished the story of his friend's dashing escape and recounts it in his preface to Gogarty's *An Offering of Swans and Other Poems* (*P&I* 154–155), in his introduction to *The Oxford Book of Modern Verse* (*LE* 187), and in his essay "Modern Poetry" (*Expl.* 507; *LE* 100–101). In 1923, Maud Gonne and ISEULT GONNE were briefly imprisoned as Republican sympathizers: Maud in early January and again on April 10, Iseult in May (*Letters* 697; *GY* 429–430). "The day before [Maud Gonne's] arrest she wrote to say that if I did not denounce the Government she renounced my society forever," Yeats told Shakespear on January 5. "I am afraid my help in the matter of blankets, instead of her release (where I could do nothing), will not make her less resentful. She had to choose (perhaps all women must) between broomstick and distaff and she has chosen the broomstick—I mean the witches' hats" (*Letters* 697). Most disastrously, government soldiers raided Gonne's house in St. Stephen's Green, Dublin, and burnt her papers in the street, including many of her letters from

Yeats—a profound loss to the historical record of Yeats, Gonne, and their time (GY 44; *Maud Gonne* 137).

The war prompted some of Yeats's most profound poetry—namely the sequence "MEDITATIONS IN TIME OF CIVIL WAR," which Yeats began in June of 1922. "The ROAD AT MY DOOR" and "The STARE'S NEST BY MY WINDOW," the fifth and sixth poems in the sequence, touch overtly on the war. The sequence as a whole, however, is less concerned with the details of contemporary politics than with the antinomies of action and contemplation, hatred and love, evanescence and permanence, that govern human experience and that the war had set in relief.

Bibliography

Foster, R. F. *W. B. Yeats: A Life, II: The Arch-Poet, Modern Ireland, 1600–1972*; Gregory, Lady. *Lady Augusta's Journals* (vol. 1, ed. Daniel J. Murphy). Lyons, F. S. L. *Ireland Since the Famine*; Mikhail, E. H., ed. *W. B. Yeats: Interviews and Recollections* (vol. 1); Saddlemyer, Ann. *Becoming George: The Life of Mrs W. B. Yeats*; Walsh, Caroline. *The Homes of Irish Writers*; Ward, Margaret. *Maud Gonne: A Life*; Yeats, W. B. *Autobiographies, Explorations, The Gonne-Yeats Letters 1893–1938, Later Essays, The Letters of W. B. Yeats, Prefaces and Introductions, The Variorum Edition of the Poems of W. B. Yeats, W. B. Yeats and T. Sturge Moore: Their Correspondence 1901–1937*.

Irish Literary Society of London See National Literary Society.

Irish Literary Theatre Conceived in 1897, the Irish Literary Theatre was the first formal incarnation of the Irish dramatic movement. Yeats had long wanted to found a theater, but it was not until he allied himself with Lady GREGORY and EDWARD MARTYN that the idea gained momentum. He first broached the idea at a tea party given by Lady Gregory on February 23, 1897 (CL2 78). Lady Gregory describes the occasion in her diary: "[Yeats] is full of playwriting [. . .]. He with the aid of Miss FLORENCE FARR, an actress who thinks more of a romantic than of a paying play, is very keen about taking or building a little theatre somewhere in the suburbs to produce romantic drama, his own plays, Edward Martyn's, one of [Robert] Bridges', and he is trying to stir up Standish O'Grady and Fiona Macleod to write some. He believes there will be a reaction after the realism of Ibsen, and romance will have its turn" (*Our Irish Theatre* 17). These discussions came to fruition later in the year. In late June, Lady Gregory crossed paths with Yeats and Martyn at Duras, the home of Count Florimond de Basterot (1836–1904) in Galway. She was a summer houseguest; they came to lunch. As the count had private matters to discuss with Martyn, Lady Gregory and Yeats, who did not yet know each other well, secluded themselves in the office of the steward. Before long the idea of a theater had been born, as Lady Gregory relates: "We sat there through that wet afternoon, and though I had never been at all interested in theatres, our talk turned on plays. Mr. Martyn had written two, The *Heather Field* and *Maeve*. They had been offered to London managers, and now he thought of trying to have them produced in Germany where there seemed to be more room for new drama than in England. I said it was a pity we had no Irish theatre where such plays could be given. Mr. Yeats said that had always been a dream of his, but he had of late thought it an impossible one, for it could not at first pay its way, and there was no money to be found for such a thing in Ireland. We went on talking about it, and things seemed to grow possible as we talked, and before the end of the afternoon we had made our plan. We said we would collect money, or rather ask to have a certain sum of money guaranteed. We would then take a Dublin theatre and give a performance of Mr. Martyn's *Heather Field* and one of Mr. Yeats's own plays, The COUNTESS CATHLEEN. I offered the first guarantee of £25" (19)

Some days later Yeats visited Lady Gregory at COOLE PARK, which was just a few miles from Martyn's house, where he had been staying. The two composed a letter to potential guarantors of the new theater. The letter proposed a program of artistically ambitious Irish plays to be performed in Dublin each spring, in opposition to the "dramatic journalism" that has had "full possession of the stage in England for a century." Such a theater, the letter continues, would "show that Ireland is not the home of buffoonery and of easy sentiment, as it has been represented, but the home of an ancient idealism" (*CL2* 124). The letter sought guarantees totaling £300. Forty-five benefactors pledged the necessary amount, but in the event the money was not required, as the wealthy Martyn volunteered to meet any losses (*Ireland's Abbey Theatre* 3, 11). A legal obstacle soon cropped up: existing law permitted commercial performances in Dublin only in the three large theaters—the Gaiety, the Queen's, and the Theatre Royal—that were licensed by royal patent (*CL2* 223–224). With the help of W. E. H. Lecky (1838–1903), a member of Parliament as well as a guarantor of the new theater, this obstacle was overcome. In July 1898 the law was amended to allow performances "for charitable purpose or in aid of funds of any society instituted for the purpose of science, literature, or the fine arts exclusively" (*Our Irish Theater* 25). In January 1899, Yeats wrote to the *Daily Express*, the *Freeman's Journal*, and the *Irish Daily Independent* announcing the formation of the theater (*CL2* 338–340).

In its first season, the theater presented Yeats's *The COUNTESS CATHLEEN* and Martyn's *The Heather Field*, as originally planned. The plays respectively debuted on May 8 and 9, 1899, in the Antient Concert Rooms, Dublin, with further performances of Yeats's play on May 10, 12, and 13, and of Martyn's play on May 10 and 13. In the weeks leading up to the performance, *The Countess Cathleen* aroused furious allegations of heresy and national insult. Martyn, a devout Catholic, was so alarmed that he considered withdrawing his support from the theater. His scruples were allayed only after Yeats solicited the approval of two respected ecclesiasts (*Aut.* 308–309; *Our Irish Theatre* 25). The attack against the play was led by Frank Hugh O'Donnell (1848–1916), an erratic former MP and journalist—"half genius half sewer-rat" in Yeats's characterization—who circulated an acidic pamphlet titled *Souls for Gold! A Pseudo-Celtic Drama in Dublin* (for a minutely detailed account of the controversy, see *CL2* 669–680, 707–712). In the event, the debut performance of the play was interrupted. Joseph Holloway describes "an organized

claque of about twenty brainless, beardless, idiotic-looking youths" who did "all they knew to interfere with the progress of the play by their meaningless automatic hissing and senseless comments" (*Joseph Holloway's Abbey Theatre* 6; see also *Aut.* 308–309). Holloway calls the play itself "weirdly, fantastically, pathetically, or picturesquely effective by turns," and records that the play ended to "thunders of applause" (8). On May 11, the theater's inauguration was celebrated by a gala dinner hosted by Horace Plunkett and T. P. Gill of the *Daily Express.* Yeats recollects the evening in *AUTOBIOGRAPHIES* (313–315), as does GEORGE MOORE, with lavish comedy, in section four of *Ave* (*Hail and Farewell* 128–144).

In its second and third seasons, the Irish Literary Theatre engaged the Gaiety Theatre, Dublin. The second season saw performances of Martyn's *Maeve* and Alice Milligan's *The Last Feast of the Fianna* on February 19, 1900, and Moore's *The Bending of the Bough*, a reworking by Yeats and Moore of Martyn's failed *The Tale of a Town*, on February 20. The third season featured Yeats and Moore's *DIARMUID AND GRANIA* on October 21, 22, and 23, 1901, and Douglas Hyde's *Casadh an tSúgáin* (*The Twisting of the Rope*) on October 21. Throughout its three seasons the theater had drawn its actors from Britain, which did nothing for the theater's popularity in nationalist circles. *Casadh an tSúgáin*, by contrast, was performed in Gaelic by members of the Keating (Dublin) branch of the Gaelic League, with Hyde himself in the lead role. Reputedly the first play in Gaelic to be performed in a Dublin theater, Hyde's play, as Lennox Robinson writes, laid "the foundation-stone of the Gaelic Theatre" (*Ireland's Abbey Theatre* 23). Lady Gregory comments that "even to those who had no Irish, the performance was a delight, it was played with so much gaiety, ease, and charm" (*Our Irish Theatre* 29). The play was directed by William Fay (1872–1947), who would have a major role in the next phase of the Irish dramatic movement.

The Irish Literary Theatre disbanded after its third season. As Lady Gregory explains, "The time had come to play oftener and to train actors of our own" (29). Furthermore, Yeats recognized that Moore and Martyn—fractious and squeamish, respectively—could not serve as his permanent collaborators. The Irish Literary Theater was duly succeeded by the IRISH NATIONAL THEATRE SOCIETY.

Bibliography

Gregory, Lady. *Our Irish Theatre*; Holloway, Joseph. *Joseph Holloway's Abbey Theatre: A Selection from His Unpublished Journal* Impressions of a Dublin Playgoer; Moore, George. *Hail and Farewell*; Ritschel, Nelson O'Ceallaigh. *Productions of the Irish Theatre Movement, 1899–1916: A Checklist*; Robinson, Lennox. *Ireland's Abbey Theatre: A History, 1899–1951*; Yeats, W. B. *Autobiographies, The Collected Letters of W. B. Yeats* (vol. 2).

Irish National Theatre Society Following the breakup of the IRISH LITERARY THEATRE in October 1901 the torch of the dramatic movement passed to the Irish National Theatre Society. The new society differed from its predecessor chiefly in its aim of developing a repertory company of Irish actors (where the Irish Literary Theatre had depended on actors imported from Britain) and in the composition of its leadership. GEORGE MOORE and EDWARD MARTYN withdrew from the organization, while the brothers Frank Fay (1870–1931) and William Fay (1872–1947) provided new talent and energy, as well as significant practical experience as actors and directors. Robert Welch writes that the brothers offered Yeats "the possibility of creating something which the Irish Literary Theatre had failed to realize: a poetic drama, based upon Irish speech, that would work upon the nerves in the way Irish singing did" (*Abbey Theatre* 17).

The seeds of the society were sown in August 1901, when Yeats saw the Fays' production of Alice Milligan's *The Deliverance of Red Hugh* performed in the Antient Concert Rooms, Dublin. "I came away with my head on fire," Yeats recalls. "I wanted to hear my own unfinished ON BAILE'S STRAND, to hear Greek tragedy, spoken with a Dublin accent" (*Aut.* 331). The following year, the Irish Literary Theatre having run its course, Yeats let the Fays produce his incendiary CATHLEEN NI HOULIHAN. "W. G. Fay's Irish National Dramatic Company" staged the play to "continual applause" on April 2–4, 1902, in St. Teresa's Hall, Dublin, with MAUD GONNE in the role of Cathleen and William Fay in the role of Peter Gillane (see *CL3* 166–168). Sharing the bill was GEORGE RUSSELL's (AE) *Deirdre*. Keen to build on this success, the Fay brothers went forward with plans to form a permanent Irish repertory company. On August 8, 1902, the new society took possession of the Camden Street Hall for use as a workshop and rehearsal space at a cost of 10 shillings per week (715). The hall—dark, cramped, drafty, without dressing rooms and out of the way—remained the nerve center of the society until the advent of the ABBEY THEATRE in 1904 (*Ireland's Abbey Theatre* 28). An inaugural meeting was held the following day, at which Yeats (though not present) was elected president, and Gonne, AE, and Douglas Hyde (1860–1949) were elected vice presidents (*CL3* 219). Calling itself the "Irish National Dramatic Society," the group presented its inaugural program October 28–November 1, 1902, in the Antient Concert Rooms and gave an encore December 4–6 in the Camden Street Hall, the first and last time the venue would be used as a performance space. The season's program featured AE's *Deirdre* (October 28, 30), James Cousins's *The Sleep of the King* (October 29) and *The Racing Lug* (October 31), P. T. MacGinley's *Eilís agus an Bhean Déirce*, or *Lizzie and the Beggarwoman* (October 29, 31), Frederick Ryan's *The Laying of the Foundations* (October 29 and 31, November 1, December 4–6), and Yeats's *The POT OF BROTH* (October 31, November 1, December 4–6).

The society's evolution, however, was only just beginning. On February 15, 1903, the society reconstituted itself as a cooperative rather than commercial venture under the name of the Irish National Theatre Society. Meanwhile, squabbles arose about the fundamental direction of the society. Gonne, Hyde, and Russell maintained that the society's work should directly support the larger nationalist program, while Yeats was hostile to all mere political considerations. The society's fall program featured Yeats's *The KING'S THRESHOLD* and J. M. SYNGE's *In the Shadow of the Glen*. Debuting October 8, 1903, in Molesworth Hall, the double bill was Yeats's throwing down of the gauntlet in the ongoing power struggle. "These two plays seemed to turn aside from any form of Irish civic responsibility," Robert Welch writes. "*The King's Threshold*, with the hauteur of its hunger-striking poet, disdaining duty and the pressure to conform, was bad enough; but Synge's play, with its (then) shockingly frank depiction of adultery, greed, and moral cowardice amongst Irish country people, was seen as a calculated insult" (*Abbey Theatre* 25). There was an inevitable public controversy, and Yeats leapt to the defense of John MILLINGTON SYNGE's play (see *Aut.* 414; *CL3* 438–453; *Expl.* 114–123, 143–145; *UP2* 306–308, 331–338). Yeats's contribution to the 1903 edition of *Samhain*, the society's magazine, articulated the philosophy that informed *The King's Threshold* and that would increasingly govern the theater. He insisted that "beauty and truth are always justified of themselves, and that their creation is a greater service to our country than writing that compromises either in the seeming service of a cause" (*Expl.* 107; *IDM* 26). Alienated by Yeats's strident aestheticism and domineering managerial style, Hyde and Gonne resigned, while Russell resigned in April 1904 (*AM* 338; *GY* 176–178). Thus the way was opened for Yeats, Lady GREGORY, and Synge to become the society's ruling triumvirate.

The fall program was further important for making a convert of ANNIE HORNIMAN, heiress to a British tea fortune and member of the HERMETIC ORDER OF THE GOLDEN DAWN. She had arrived in Dublin to design costumes for *The King's Threshold* and was thrilled by the experience, effusing in an October letter to Yeats, "Do you realize that you have given me the right to call myself 'artist'? How I thank you'" (Welch, *Abbey Theatre* 27). Reassured by Yeats's stand against the politicization of the theater movement and stirred by his defense of artistic principle, she offered to provide the society with its own performance space. By April 1904, Horniman had committed to purchasing the lease of the Mechanics' Institute building on Abbey Street and an adjoining morgue on Marlborough Street. These were to be renovated and provided rent-free to the society (*CL3* 572–573). Thus was born the Abbey Theatre, upon whose boards the plays of Lady Gregory, Synge, and Yeats would be introduced to the world. Recalling the antenatal days of the Irish Literary Theatre, there was some difficulty in acquiring a royal patent for the Abbey, with opposition to the application coming from Dublin's three large commercial theaters. On August 20, the patent was granted in Lady Gregory's name on the condition that the Abbey restrict itself to plays on Irish themes or foreign works of artistic merit (Welch, *Abbey Theatre* 32; *CL3* 629–632; *Our Irish Theatre* 34–35). The new theater opened its doors on December 27 with performances of Yeats's *On Baile's Strand* and *Cathleen ni Houlihan* and Lady Gregory's *Spreading the News*. "There was not a vacant seat, all the notabilities of literary and artistic life in Dublin were present," writes Lennox Robinson, who calls the evening "an epoch-making event in the world of the theatre" (*Ireland's Abbey Theatre* 45–46).

Yeats orchestrated another reorganization of the society in 1905 in order to complete his consolidation of power. As he wrote to JOHN QUINN on September 16, "I think we have seen the end of the democracy in the Theatre which was Russell's doing, for I go to Dublin at the end of the week to preside at a meeting summoned to abolish it. If all goes well Synge and Lady Gregory and myself will have everything in our hands [. . .]. It has been a long fight, but the change could not be made until the old method had discredited itself and until three or four people had got some sort of natural leadership" (*CL4* 178). On September 22 the society agreed to become "The National Theatre Society Limited," a public limited company. The change was ratified on October 9. The overwhelming majority of shares—and hence votes—were allocated to Yeats, Synge, and Lady Gregory as unpaid members of a three-person "executive committee." After Synge's death in 1909 the third seat on the committee remained vacant for some 15 years; it was finally filled by Lennox Robinson (1886–1958) in 1924. The actors, meanwhile, were stripped of their previously held voting rights as members of the society and made full-time employees, with salaries guaranteed by Horniman to the extent of £400 per year (Hunt, *The Abbey* 65–66). The reorganization prompted the secession of several actors and aroused widespread bitterness, but at last Yeats had made the society an efficient vehicle for his own ambitions (Welch, *Abbey Theatre* 34).

The society had largely achieved mature form by 1905, but there were to be a number of important modifications and developments over the remaining years of Yeats's life. On February 13, 1908, the Fays departed in a huff. William Fay felt that his authority as theater manager was too often undermined by the directors, to the detriment of the company's discipline. After the directors rejected a five-point proposal that would have given him firmer control over the day-to-day operations of the theater, he resigned, taking his wife (the actress Brigid O'Dempsey) and his brother with him (*Cradle of Genius* 127, 132). He was replaced briefly by Norreys Connell (1874–1938), and then, in 1909, by Lennox Robinson, who remained at the theater in various managerial capacities until his death in 1958. In February 1910, the society acquired the Abbey for the price of £1,000. Horniman, who felt ill used and unappreciated, abandoned the Irish dramatic movement, having spent the enormous sum of £10,350 on the Abbey (*CL3* 713). In August 1925, the Irish government agreed to award the Abbey an annual subsidy (£850 in 1926), officially making it the "Irish National Theater."

Bibliography

Fay, Gerard. *The Abbey Theatre: Cradle of Genius*; Foster, R. F. *W. B. Yeats: A Life, I: The Apprentice Mage*; Gregory, Lady. *Our Irish Theatre*; Hunt, Hugh. *The Abbey: Ireland's National Theatre, 1904–1979*; Ritschel, Nelson O'Ceallaigh. *Productions of the Irish Theatre Movement, 1899–1916: A Checklist*; Robinson, Lennox. *Ireland's Abbey Theatre: A History, 1899–1951*; Welch, Robert. *The Abbey Theatre, 1899–1999*; Yeats, W. B. *Autobiographies, The Collected Letters of W. B. Yeats* (vols. 3–4), *Explorations, The Gonne-Yeats Letters 1893–1938, The Irish Dramatic Movement, Uncollected Prose by W. B. Yeats* (vol. 2).

Johnson, Lionel Pigot (1867–1902)   The foremost exhibit in Yeats's account of the "tragic generation," Johnson was an estimable poet of classical leanings and Catholic belief ruined by alcoholism. In the language of "Ego Dominus Tuus," which

Yeats applied to his case, Johnson was undone by the "dissipation and despair" that belongs to the artist who "has awakened from the common dream" (*Aut.* 241; cf. *LE* 8). In the end, he fell from a chair while drinking in a public house and died of his injuries (*CL3* 499). Johnson's hold upon Yeats is suggested by the company he keeps in the pages of *Autobiographies*: "Two men are always at my side, Lionel Johnson and John Synge, whom I was to meet a little later; but Johnson is to me the more vivid in memory, possibly because of the external finish, the clearly marked lineaments of his body, which seemed but to express the clarity of his mind" (241). Yeats found something that profoundly answered his own imagination in the "austere nobility" of Johnson's verse and in Johnson's mandarin disdain for the mere reality of the world. As Yeats mentions more than once, Johnson seemed to embody the spirit of the famous line from Villiers de l'Isle-Adam's *Axël* (1890)—"As for living, our servants will do that for us" (IV, ii; see *Aut.* 236; *E&I* 296; *LE* 33, 153; *P&I* 112, 156; *UP2* 117; *AV* 42).

Born in Broadstairs, Kent, Johnson belonged to a family of military men; being diminutive and bookish, he never entirely felt at ease. He arrived in London after graduating from New College, Oxford, in 1890. He was an active member of the Rhymers' Club and, proudly claiming Irish descent, of the London arm of the National Literary Society. In his essay "Modern Poetry" (1936), Yeats remembers that Johnson dominated the Rhymers' Club and shaped its most characteristic thought. Yeats summarizes the worldview that Johnson brought to the club: "Nothing of importance could be discovered, he would say, science must be confined to the kitchen or the workshop; only philosophy and religion could solve the great secret, and they said all their say years ago; a gentleman was a man who understood Greek" (*LE* 89). In those days, Yeats felt himself a "provincial, conscious of clumsiness and lack of self-possession," and he envied Johnson's sophistication and erudition (90). If he could not emulate Johnson's air, Yeats learned something from the "intellectual clearness" and "hard energy" of his verse, and Johnson's example was at least in part responsible for Yeats's emergence from the mists of the Celtic Twilight (*Aut.* 237–238, 241; *Mem.* 96).

Yeats observed Johnson's decline, which began in the mid-1890s, with horrified fascination (see *Aut.* 184–185, 238–240; *Mem.* 94–96). Eventually, Johnson's drinking brought an end to the friendship, which had been very close. Yeats explains in MEMOIRS that when Johnson called on him "he sat in gloomy silence if I refused him drink, and if I gave it became drunk, and if I went to see him got drunk as a matter of course. I felt that if I saw him I shared his responsibility, and once when I tried to get him to sign away his liberty in some Scottish institution he had said, 'I do not want to be cured'" (94–95). Yeats's candid account of Johnson's alcoholism apparently offended OLIVIA SHAKESPEAR, Johnson's cousin, when she read excerpts from his memoirs in the *London Mercury* in 1922. Yeats blamed the fact that the piece had been abridged, and explained that it "needs the wild mystical part to lift it out of gossip" (*Letters* 685).

Yeats's chief contributions to the memory of Johnson are *Autobiographies* and *Memoirs*. In addition, he favorably reviewed Johnson's *Ireland, with Other Poems* in 1898 (*UP2* 88–91); wrote an appreciation, "Mr. Lionel Johnson and Certain Irish Poets," which first appeared in the *Daily Express* in 1898 (*UP2* 115–118; *P&I* 111–112); and edited a selection of Johnson's verse, *Twenty One Poems*, which the DUN EMER PRESS published in 1905. In 1908, the CUALA PRESS brought out *Poetry and Ireland: Essays by W. B. Yeats and Lionel Johnson*. Yeats contributed the essay "Poetry and Patriotism" (see "Poetry and Tradition" in *E&I*); he also wrote a brief preface to Johnson's essay (see *P&I* 136). Yeats pays tribute to Johnson in two poems, "THE GREY ROCK" (lines 59–64) and "IN MEMORY OF MAJOR ROBERT GREGORY." In the description of the latter, Johnson, though "much falling," "Brooded upon sanctity / Till all his Greek and Latin learning seemed / A long blast upon the horn that brought / A little nearer to his thought / A measureless consummation that he dreamed."

Bibliography

Yeats, W. B. *Autobiographies, The Collected Letters of W. B. Yeats* (vol. 3), *Essays and Introductions, Later Essays, The Letters of W. B. Yeats, Memoirs, Prefaces and Introductions, Uncollected Prose by W. B. Yeats* (vol. 2), *A Vision.*

Joyce, James Augustine Aloysius (1882–1941)
Joyce readily acknowledged that Yeats was a writer of the highest gifts, yet he regarded him always warily, perhaps as one of the few who had the capacity to complicate or confuse his own struggle for artistic independence. Stanislaus Joyce recalls that as a young man his brother read "everything that Yeats had written in prose or verse, so far as it was procurable, and considered him, with [Clarence] Mangan, the only Irish poet worthy of that high title" (*My Brother's Keeper* 98; see also 180). Indeed, as Richard Ellmann suggests, Joyce's sense of Yeats's unchallengeable superiority in verse may have compelled him to adopt prose as his primary medium (*James Joyce* 83).

Yeats's and Joyce's entwinement in modernist myth begins with Yeats's controversial play *The* COUNTESS CATHLEEN, which inaugurated the IRISH LITERARY THEATRE. On May 8, 1899, Joyce attended the debut performance. The following day his fellow students at the Royal University circulated a letter protesting the play's representation of the Irish as a "loathsome brood of apostates" (86). Joyce, who had admired the play, refused to sign the letter, which was printed in the *Freeman's Journal* on May 10. Joyce was particularly moved by the lyric "WHO GOES WITH FERGUS?" (spoken by FLORENCE FARR in the role of Aleel). Joyce set the lyric to music, and Stephen Dedalus, in *Ulysses* (1922), sings the air to his dying mother (1.239–253). Stanislaus Joyce remembers Joyce in actual life singing the air to their dying brother, 14-year-old Georgie (*My Brother's Keeper* 134). By 1901, Joyce had begun the strategic work of distancing himself from Yeats. In his strongly worded essay "The Day of the Rabblement," Joyce criticizes Yeats's willingness as head of the Irish Literary Theatre to pander to the common taste of Dublin and refers to Yeats's "treacherous instinct of adaptability" (*Critical Writings* 71). His specific objection is that the theater had abandoned its initial promise to produce European masterpieces ("Ibsen,

Tolstoy or Hauptmann") in order to please the "rabblement" with Irish-themed plays (70).

Despite these misgivings, Joyce presented himself at the home of Yeats's oldest friend GEORGE RUSSELL (AE) late one night in the summer of 1902. Russell was impressed by Joyce's evident genius, but equally he sensed something of his prickly independence. He wrote perceptively to the artist Sarah Purser (1848–1943) on August 15 that he would not be Joyce's "Messiah for a thousand million pounds. He would be always criticizing the bad taste of his deity" (*James Joyce* 100). Russell arranged for Yeats and Joyce to meet in early November 1902. Again perceptively, Russell told Yeats that Joyce belonged to Yeats's "clan" more than to his own, and "still more to himself" (100). The two writers met in front of the National Library. In a nearby café, Joyce read some of his "Epiphanies." As Yeats tells the story in an abandoned introduction to *Ideas of Good and Evil* (1903), the conversation took an unexpected turn: "I praised his work but he said, 'I really don't care whether you like what I am doing or not. It won't make the least difference to me. Indeed I don't know why I am reading to you.' Then, putting down his book, he began to explain all his objections to everything I had ever done. Why had I concerned myself with politics, with folklore, with the historical setting of events, and so on? Above all why had I written about ideas, why had I condescended to make generalizations? These things were all the sign of the cooling of the iron, of the fading out of inspiration." Upon taking his leave, Joyce, with a sigh, made the famous comment, "I have met you too late. You are too old" (101–102; see also *I&R*, II, 307; *W. B. Yeats: A Memoir* 10). Stanislaus Joyce says that his brother "always denied the story" though Stanislaus himself credits its basic substance (*My Brother's Keeper* 179). What is certain, Stanislaus Joyce adds, is that Joyce told Yeats "how much he admired two stories of his, 'The TABLES OF THE LAW' and 'The ADORATION OF THE MAGI', and urged him to reprint them" (180). Yeats reissued the stories in 1904 and explained in a brief prefatory note that he had been urged to do so by a young man he had met "who liked them very much and nothing else that I have written" (234).

In *AUTOBIOGRAPHIES*, Yeats recollects Joyce as a young poet "who wrote excellently but had the worst manners" (148). Despite being slighted by the unknown writer 17 years his junior, Yeats attempted to assist Joyce by encouraging his literary ambitions, by introducing him to friends like ARTHUR SYMONS and Lady GREGORY, and by helping him find work as a reviewer. Yeats made further attempts to assist Joyce over the years. In 1915, Yeats was instrumental in procuring a disbursement of £75 from the Royal Literary Fund for the war-straitened Joyce (*James Joyce* 390–392; *Letters* 596–601). In 1932, he nominated Joyce as a founding member of the IRISH ACADEMY OF LETTERS (*Letters* 800–801). On October 5, 1932, Joyce responded to Yeats's generous invitation with his usual prickliness: "I hope that the Academy of Irish Letters (if that is its title) which you are both forming will have the success it aims at. My case, however, being as it was and probably will be I see no reason why my name should have arisen at all in connection with such an academy: and I feel quite clearly that I have no right whatsoever to nominate myself as a member of it" (Joyce, *Letters*, I, 325). On the other hand, Yeats was not able to assist Joyce in his ambition as a dramatist. In 1904, he rejected Joyce's translations of Gerhart Hauptmann's plays *Before Dawn* and *Michael Kramer* for production at the ABBEY THEATRE. He told Joyce that he had submitted the translations to a German scholar, whose verdict was unfavorable, and that in any case the theater had to build its audience "with Irish work" (*CL3* 657). In 1917, he rejected Joyce's play *Exiles* with the excuse that it was too far from the folk drama that was the Abbey's specialty (*James Joyce* 401).

Joyce's *A Portrait of the Artist as a Young Man* (1916) and *Ulysses* (1922) are suffused with both reverent and irreverent allusions to Yeats. Yeats fully appreciated the merit and importance of both novels. In a 1917 letter to EZRA POUND, he lauded *A Portrait* as "a very great book" (*James Joyce* 401), but his reaction to *Ulysses* was more equivocal. "His new story in the *Little Review* looks like becoming the best work he has done," Yeats wrote to JOHN QUINN on July 23, 1918. "It is an entirely new thing—neither what the eye sees nor the ear hears, but what the rambling mind thinks and imagines from moment to moment. He has certainly surpassed in intensity any novelist of our time [. . .]" (*Letters* 651). In the spring of 1922, Yeats was struggling with the full weight of Joyce's opus. "I hate it when I dip here and there but when I read it in the right order I am much impressed," he wrote to OLIVIA SHAKESPEAR on March 8. "However I have but read some thirty pages in that order. It has our Irish cruelty and also our kind of strength and the Martello Tower pages are full of beauty. A cruel playful mind like a great soft tiger cat—I hear, as I read, the report of the rebel sergeant in '98: 'O he was a fine fellow, a fine fellow. It was a pleasure to shoot him'" (679). The following summer, he wrote to Shakespear that he had invited Joyce to visit him in Dublin and would "have to use the utmost ingenuity to hide the fact that I have never finished *Ulysses*" (698). Addressing matters of copyright on the floor of the SENATE in 1927, Yeats confessed that he did not know whether *Ulysses* was a "great work of literature," but he affirmed that it was at the very least "the work of an heroic mind" (SS 148). Of the work that would become *Finnegans Wake*, Yeats wrote in his introduction to Joseph Hone and Mario M. Rossi's *Bishop Berkeley* (1931), "The romantic movement with its turbulent heroism, its self-assertion, is over, superseded by a new naturalism that leaves man helpless before the contents of his own mind. One thinks of Joyce's *Anna Livia Plurabelle*, Pound's *Cantos*, works of an heroic sincerity, the man, his active faculties in suspense, one finger beating time to a bell sounding and echoing in the depths of his own mind [. . .]" (LE 109). Yeats rejected this "new naturalism," being committed to the "active faculties," that is, to the passionate self-assertion of romanticism (109–110).

Upon Yeats's death in 1939, Joyce sent a funeral wreath to his grave at Roquebrune in the south of France, a gesture that suggests the esteem that was always at the back of his "cruel playful mind."

Bibliography

Ellmann, Richard. *James Joyce*; Gogarty, Oliver St John. *W. B. Yeats: A Memoir*; Joyce, James. *The Critical Writings, Letters* (vol. 1), *Ulysses*; Joyce, Stanislaus. My *Brother's Keeper: James Joyce's Early Years*; Mikhail, E. H., ed. *W. B. Yeats: Interviews and Recollections* (vol. 2); Yeats, W. B. *Autobiographies, The Collected Letters of W. B. Yeats* (vol. 3), *Later Essays, The Letters of W. B. Yeats, The Secret Rose: A Variorum Edition, The Senate Speeches of W. B. Yeats*.

Lane, Hugh Percy (1875–1915)   The nephew of Lady GREGORY, Lane was born of Irish parents and raised in England. He made his fortune as an art dealer and then became a museum administrator, serving as director of the National Gallery in Dublin from February 1914 until his death. His attempt to found a modern art gallery in Dublin having aroused suspicion and hostility rather than gratitude, Lane figures prominently in Yeats's mythology of "great Art beaten down" ("The FISHERMAN"). "In the thirty years or so during which I have been reading Irish newspapers, three public controversies have stirred my imagination," Yeats remarks in a note to *Responsibilities* (1914). "The first was the PARNELL controversy. There were reasons to justify a man's joining either party, but there were none to justify, on one side or on the other, lying accusations forgetful of past service, a frenzy of detraction. And another was the dispute over [J. M. SYNGE's *The Playboy of the Western World*]. There may have been reasons for opposing as for supporting that violent, laughing thing, though I can see the one side only, but there cannot have been any for the lies, for the unscrupulous rhetoric spread against it in Ireland, and from Ireland to America. The third prepared for the Corporation's refusal of a building for Sir Hugh Lane's famous collection of pictures. [. . .] These controversies, political, literary, and artistic, have showed that neither religion nor politics can of itself create minds with enough receptivity to become wise, or just and generous enough to make a nation" (VP 818).

Lane founded the Dublin Municipal Gallery in 1907 and opened the doors of the rented house on Harcourt Street on January 20, 1908 (*Images and Insights* 22). He put on display much of his own collection, including pictures by major continental artists like Corot, Daumier, Degas, Ingres, Manet, Monet, Pissarro, Renoir. The city had promised a £500 annual grant, but the money did not mate-

Portrait of Hugh Lane, ca. 1905, by Antonio Mancini
(1852–1930) *(Dublin City Gallery The Hugh Lane)*

rialize until 1911, and Lane largely supported the gallery with his own funds (*Sir Hugh Lane* 85). In the preface to the gallery's 1907 catalogue, Lane promised the so-called French pictures—there would eventually come to be 39—to Dublin on the condition that the city fund a suitable building to house them (84). In January 1913, the municipal council pledged £22,000 for construction of the new gallery, while a private committee was to secure a site and raise additional money toward the cost of the building (87). Yeats's "To A WEALTHY MAN WHO PROMISED A SECOND SUBSCRIPTION TO THE DUBLIN MUNICIPAL GALLERY IF IT WERE PROVED THE PEOPLE WANTED PICTURES" was an aggressive gambit in this fund-raising campaign.

Culturally conservative Dubliners were ambivalent about both the merits of the paintings and the expensive condition that attached to them. In his note to *Responsibilities*, Yeats recalls the groundswell of opposition to the proposed gallery: "One could respect the argument that Dublin, with much poverty and many slums, could not afford the £22,000 the building was to cost the city, but not the minds that used it. One frenzied man compared the pictures to Troy horse which 'destroyed a city,' and innumerable correspondents described Sir Hugh Lane and those who had subscribed many thousands to give Dublin paintings by Corot, Manet, Monet, Degas, and Renoir, as 'self-seekers,' 'self-advertisers,' 'picture-dealers,' 'log-rolling cranks and faddists,' and one clerical paper told 'picture-dealer Lane' to take himself and his pictures out of that. A member of the Corporation said there were Irish artists who could paint as good if they had a mind to, and another described a half-hour in the temporary gallery in Harcourt Street as the most dismal of his life" (*VP* 819). Yeats laid the heaviest blame on William Martin Murphy (1844–1919), transportation magnate and proprietor of the *Evening Herald* and the *Irish Independent* (see 819–820). Yeats derides Murphy as "old foul mouth" in "To A SHADE," and he most likely intends a dig at Murphy when he refers to one unashamed by his own lies in "To A FRIEND WHOSE WORK HAS COME TO NOTHING." Lane himself wrote to Lady Gregory on August 5, 1913: "If we had only one leader in Dublin with the energy and capacity (not to mention the unscrupulousness!) of Mr Murphy, the whole question would have been settled long ago" (*Sir Hugh Lane* 291).

In September 1913, the city rejected Edwin Lutyens's elegant design for a £45,000 gallery bridging the Liffey, at least in part because Lutyens was English (90, 100–101). In a will made on October 11, 1913, Lane, in his frustration, bequeathed the 39 French pictures to the National Gallery in London. His final wishes included the bitter hope that "this alteration from the Modern Gallery [in Dublin] to the National Gallery will be remembered by the Dublin Municipality & others as an example of its want of public spirit in the year 1913 & for the folly of such bodies assuming to decide on questions of Art instead of relying on expert opinion" (294). In late 1913, the National Gallery received the collection for exhibition but agreed to display only 15 of the paintings, while stipulating that Lane either present or bequeath the collection to the gallery (*Images and Insights* 28). Lane was indignant. On February 3, 1915, he wrote a codicil to his will leaving the paintings to Dublin after all, provided that a suitable gallery be built within five years of his death (*Sir Hugh Lane* 11–12). After Lane died aboard the *Lusitania* on May 7, 1915, the National Gallery refused to recognize the codicil on the grounds that it was not witnessed, thus sparking a squabble that persisted until 1959, when it was decided that the disputed paintings would be divided into two lots, and that the Municipal Gallery (which relocated to Charlemont House in 1933) and the National Gallery would trade lots every five years. The agreement was amended in 1979 and 1993. The 1993 agreement provided for a permanent display of 27 paintings at the Municipal Gallery, with eight of the paintings rotating between the two museums (*Images and Insights* 30).

The Lane controversy explains much of the bitterness that informs the poems of Yeats's middle period. Yeats's ire particularly pervades *Poems Written in Discouragement*—a "noble and indignant" volume, in Lady Gregory's phrase (*Sir Hugh Lane* 106). The CUALA PRESS published the volume in 1913 in an edition of only 50 copies; it includes "To a Wealthy Man," "SEPTEMBER 1913," "To a Friend whose Work has come to Nothing," "Paudeen," and "To a Shade" (*Biblio.* 114). Yeats less polemically alludes to Lane in "COOLE PARK, 1929" and in "The MUNICIPAL GALLERY REVISITED." Yeats's numerous public statements on the Lane controversy are collected in *The Senate Speeches of W. B. Yeats* and in *Uncollected Prose by W. B. Yeats* (vol. 2).

Bibliography

Gregory, Lady. *Sir Hugh Lane: His Life and Legacy*; Mayes, Elizabeth, and Paula Murphy, eds. *Images and Insights: Hugh Lane Municipal Gallery of Modern Art*; Wade, Allan. *A Bibliography of the Writings of W. B. Yeats*; Yeats, W. B. *The Variorum Edition of the Poems of W. B. Yeats*.

Martyn, Edward Joseph (1859–1923)   Scrupulously Catholic and compulsively anxious about the state of his soul, Edward Martyn was an unlikely participant in the Irish theatrical movement, but so he was, and from the very start. Martyn's family was enormously wealthy on both sides. His maternal grandfather had made a fortune purchasing land under the Encumbered Estates Act, while his father's family traced its wealth to the crusader Sir Oliver Martyn and resided in the imposing Tulira Castle, County Galway, which dates from the 12th century (*EM and the Irish Theatre* 11, 18). Martyn's father, John, died when Martyn was only a year old, and his mother dotingly raised Martyn and his brother in Galway, Dublin, and London. Martyn was educated at Belvedere College in Dublin and Beaumont College near Windsor, both Jesuit institutions, before matriculating at Christ Church, OXFORD. There he fared poorly as a student, and, as an Irish Catholic, struggled to fit in. He left after

Portrait of Edward Martyn, by Sarah Purser (1849–1943). Martyn, a Galway landowner turned playwright, founded the Irish Literary Theatre with Yeats and Lady Gregory. (*Dublin City Gallery The Hugh Lane*)

two years without a degree. "Moon-faced, podgy and flatfooted, awkward and shy," as his biographer describes him, "he was bereft of that charm that secured for Irishmen like [GEORGE] MOORE and WILDE a pass to any social circle" (*EM and the Irish Theatre* 17). Upon graduating, Martyn undertook a £20,000 renovation of Tulira, making it the monument of Victorian Gothicism that so impressed Yeats when he first visited in 1896. His mother desperately hoped that Martyn would marry, but he returned from Oxford "an uncompromising and incorrigible misogynist" (thus Denis Gwynn delicately broaches the matter of Martyn's sexual orientation) and a religious ascetic, living in a bare stone-floored room in one of Tulira's towers (49–50). Yeats, for his part, bluntly repeats Moore's accusation that Martyn possessed a "frustrated passion for his own sex" (*Mem.* 118–119; see also *I&R*, II, 334). Reading Irish history alone in his tower room, Martyn abandoned the unionist politics that were typical of his landowning class and became a fierce nationalist. Thus the ground was set for his otherwise unlikely involvement in the Irish theatrical movement (*EM and the Irish Revival* 107).

Yeats came to know Martyn in London through Martyn's impish cousin and boon companion, the novelist George Moore (*Mem.* 99). In August 1896, Yeats made his first stay at Tulira Castle. Though he was later to scoff at the sham Gothic of the renovated house (*Aut.* 289; *Mem.* 100), Yeats was at the time still in the throes of his youthful PRE-RAPHAELITISM and was clearly thrilled by the medieval effect. "This is a very curious Castle, part of very great antiquity with a secret stair & emmense [sic] walls & all of great beauty," he wrote to William Sharp. "While I write I hear my host playing medieval music on the organ in the great hall. He is a catholic ascetic & descended from Crusaders by a long line which has never lost for long, the ideal of the crusades" (*CL2* 49). While at Tulira, Yeats renewed his acquaintance with Lady GREGORY, whom he had met in 1894, and for the first time visited nearby COOLE PARK (*Aut.* 282). The following summer, Yeats was again a guest at Tulira. Martyn brought Yeats to lunch at the house of his neighbor, Count Florimond de Basterot (1836–1904), where Lady Gregory rounded out the party.

While the count and Martyn discussed business, Yeats and Lady Gregory secluded themselves in the steward's office and contrived the idea of founding an Irish theater (*Our Irish Theatre* 19). Yeats and Lady Gregory set about raising money (*CL2* 123–125), though in the end Martyn agreed to guarantee all expenses, and the IRISH LITERARY THEATRE was launched (*Mem.* 119). The theater was to open with productions of Yeats's COUNTESS CATHLEEN and Martyn's Ibsenite *Heather Field* (completed 1894, published with *Maeve* in 1899), but there was a last-minute crisis when religious objections were raised against Yeats's play. In order to appease Martyn, Yeats sent the play to two ecclesiastics, and the production went forward only after receiving a theological stamp of approval (*Aut.* 308–309; *CL2* 377–391; *Mem.* 119–120).

The Countess Cathleen premiered on May 8, 1899, and *The Heather Field* on May 9, both in the Antient Concert Rooms, Dublin. Despite protests against *The Countess Cathleen* in the press and in the theater (*CL2* 410–412; *Mem.* 119–123), the plays drew well and met with a generally positive critical response. The Irish Literary Theatre's second season included Martyn's *Maeve* and Moore's *The Bending of the Bough*, which respectively opened on February 19 and 20, 1900, at the Gaiety Theatre, Dublin. Moore was the credited author of *The Bending of the Bough*, but in fact the play represented Moore and Yeats's joint attempt to rescue Martyn's *The Tale of the Town*. Yeats and Lady Gregory had found *The Tale of the Town* "crude throughout, childish in parts, a play to make our movement and ourselves ridiculous," and Yeats denounced the play to Martyn's face at Tulira (*Aut.* 316–317; see also *Mem.* 122). Moore remembers Yeats that day as a "monk of literature, an inquisitor, a Torquemada," a description of which Yeats apparently approved, for he quoted the comparison to Torquemada in AUTOBIOGRAPHIES (*Hail and Farewell* 549; *Aut.* 316).

In early 1902, Martyn resigned from the Irish Literary Theatre (*CL3* 152). His understandably wounded feelings were one issue; his religious scruples were a second; artistic direction was a third. Loyal to the example of Ibsen, Martyn had no sympathy with the budding theater movement's emphasis on peasant plays. "If I could have written capable peasant plays, which I could not because they do not interest me, in that the peasant's mind is too crude for any sort of interesting complexity in treatment, I have no doubt I should have found my place naturally in the ABBEY THEATRE," Martyn wrote later (*EM and the Irish Revival* 158). Yeats offered a similar account in a letter of April 26, 1902, to the *United Irishman*: "Mr. Martyn likes a form of drama that is essentially modern, that needs for its production actors of what is called the 'natural school,' the dominant school of the modern stage. The more experience an actor has had of that stage the better he is for Mr. Martyn's purpose, and almost of a certainty the worse for mine" (*CL3* 178; *UP2* 292). Martyn was bitter over the split, as his satirical account of the Abbey's later success reveals: "The qualities by which Mr. Yeats has made the theatre are Napoleonic and consummate. A fine poet and subtle literary critic, [Yeats] has above all a weird appearance which is triumphant with middle-aged masculine women, and a dictatorial manner which is irresistible with the considerable bevy of female and male mediocrities interested in intellectual things" (*EM and the Irish Revival* 154–155). In 1906, after the Abbey was reorganized as a public limited company with power concentrated in the hands of Yeats, Lady Gregory, and J. M. SYNGE, secessionists formed an explicitly nationalist rival company, the Theatre of Ireland, with Martyn as president (*Abbey Theatre* 34–36). In 1914, Martyn cofounded the Irish Theatre, which dedicated itself to "the production of non-peasant plays, plays in the Irish language, and translations of Continental master-dramas" (*EM and the Irish Revival* 294).

Martyn figures prominently though not flatteringly in "Dramatis Personae," Yeats's memoir of the Irish Literary Theatre, which he first published in 1935 and soon after canonized in *Autobiographies*. Yeats was especially fascinated by the bizarre friendship between Martyn and Moore. He describes them as "cousins and inseparable friends, bound one to the other by mutual contempt," and as typical peasant types, the one a "peasant saint," the other a "peasant sinner" (*Aut.* 300). He caricatures their unlikely symbiosis in The CAT AND THE

MOON. The blind beggar tells of "the holy man in the big house at Laban"—i.e., Martyn—and incredulously contemplates his quirks: "What does he do but go knocking about the roads with an old lecher from the county of Mayo"—i.e., Moore—"and he a woman-hater from the day of his birth! And what do they talk of by candle-light and by daylight? The old lecher does be telling over all the sins he committed, or maybe never committed at all, and the man of Laban does be trying to head him off and quiet him down that he may quit telling them. [. . .] He wouldn't have him different, no, not if he was to get all Ireland. If he was different, what would they find to talk about, will you answer me that now?" (*VPl.* 797). Moore himself was even more a student and mordant celebrant of Martyn's personality. His great memoir *Hail and Farewell* (1912–14) has Martyn for its central character and chief comic relief (Martyn duly retaliated with his satirical play *The Dream Physician*). In one of uncountable *bons mots* at his cousin's expense, Moore epitomizes Martyn as a "great bulk of peasantry with a delicious strain of Palestrina running through it" (326). He says more generally of their relationship: "We had gone through life together, myself charging windmills, Edward holding up his hands in amazement" (372). And again: "There is no doubt that I owe a great deal of my happiness to Edward; all my life long he has been exquisite entertainment" (596).

Bibliography

Courtney, Marie-Thérèse. *Edward Martyn and the Irish Theatre*; Gregory, Lady. *Our Irish Theatre*; Gwynn, Denis. *Edward Martyn and the Irish Revival*; Mikhail, E. H., ed. *W. B. Yeats: Interviews and Recollections* (vol. 2); Moore, George. *Hail and Farewell*; Ritschel, Nelson O'Ceallaigh. *Productions of the Irish Theatre Movement, 1899–1916: A Checklist*; Welch, Robert. *The Abbey Theatre, 1899–1999*; Yeats, W. B. *Autobiographies, The Collected Letters of W. B. Yeats* (vols. 2–3), *Memoirs, Uncollected Prose by W. B. Yeats* (vol. 2), *The Variorum Edition of the Plays of W. B. Yeats*.

Mathers, Samuel Liddell "MacGregor" (1854–1918)

An eccentric even by the standards of the occultist demimonde in which for a time he reigned supreme, Mathers powerfully gripped the imagination of the young Yeats, demonstrating, like OSCAR WILDE, the dramatic potential of the constructed persona or mask. Mathers was, to say the least, colorful. Fancying himself the descendent of Ian MacGregor, comte de Glenstrae, Mathers assumed his ancestor's name and title and took to wearing full Highland dress. His obituarist, most likely A. E. Waite, described him as a "combination of Don Quixote and Hudibras" (*Magicians* 42). Yeats likewise makes the comparison to Quixote (*Aut.* 159).

Mathers was the son of a London clerk. After his father's death he was raised by his widowed mother in Bournemouth. From early youth he was seized with a fascination for the occult and the supernatural. In 1887, Mathers published *The Kabbalah Unveiled*, the most significant of his numerous books on occult subjects. As a member of the Societas Rosicruciana in Anglia during the 1880s, he became acquainted with Dr. William Robert Woodman (born 1828) and Dr. William Wynn Westcott (1848–1925), with whom, in March 1888, he founded the HERMETIC ORDER OF THE GOLDEN DAWN, an organization that in its various incarnations was to play a major part in Yeats's social and intellectual life for some three decades. Mathers, Yeats remembers, was the order's "governing mind, a born teacher and organizer" (160). During the early 1890s, a small circle of Golden Dawn initiates that included Yeats, FLORENCE FARR, and ANNIE HORNIMAN gathered around the romantic and charismatic Mathers. Yeats's essay "MAGIC" conveys the heady occult adventurism of those days as it recalls an evening of magical experimentation led by Mathers (*E&I* 28–36). Horniman had been intimate friends with Moina Bergson, sister of the French philosopher, while both were students at the Slade School of Art in London during the early 1880s. After Bergson and Mathers married in June 1890, Horniman became the couple's chief patron, supplying steady infusions of cash (until 1896, when she was expelled from the Golden Dawn) and setting up Mathers as caretaker at the Horniman Museum, her father's natural history museum in Forest Hill, a job he held during 1890 and 1891 (29). In May 1892, the Matherses moved to PARIS, where they founded the Ahathoor Temple, a sister branch of the Golden Dawn. Despite his permanent residency across the channel, Mathers retained leadership of the London temple until a series of quarrels largely brought on by his high-handedness resulted in his expulsion in 1900.

Yeats first encountered Mathers in the Reading Room of the British Museum. He recalls a "man of thirty-six, or thirty-seven, in a brown velveteen coat, with a gaunt resolute face, and an athletic body" whose only interests were "magic and the theory of war, for he believed himself a born commander" (*Aut.* 159). It was Mathers, Yeats says, who introduced him to "certain studies and experiences" that were to convince him that "images well up before the mind's eye from a deeper source than conscious or subconscious memory" (159). By 1900, however, Yeats had come to consider Mathers a "despot" and a "mystagogue" whose "fine nature" had gone to wrack (*CL2* 516, 524). Though he was free of any sharp animosity or visceral dislike, Yeats sided against Mathers in the Golden Dawn ruction of 1900, and the two became estranged.

Yeats's work is rife with allusions to Mathers. He unmistakably appears as "Samuel Maclagan" in the unfinished novel *The SPECKLED BIRD*, and he most likely lends something to the darkly romantic magus Michael Robartes, a central persona in Yeats's poetry and fiction. *The Trembling of the Veil*—later incorporated in AUTOBIOGRAPHIES—includes a vivid character study of Mathers in all his ardent strangeness (see "Four Years," XX, and "The Tragic Generation," XVIII). In perhaps his most shrewdly self-knowing comment on Mathers, Yeats writes that he was a "necessary extravagance," for he had "carried further than any one else a claim implicit in the romantic movement from the time of SHELLEY and of Goethe" (*Aut.* 162). Mathers's widow responded angrily in 1924, denouncing *The Trembling of the Veil* as an "awful book" and calling the account of Mathers a "caricature portrait" (*LTWBY*, II, 447–448). Yeats mollified her by offering to make slight revisions; the phrase "Mathers had learning but no scholarship," for example, became "Mathers had much learning but little scholarship" (*Yeats's Golden Dawn* 148). Sorry to have given offense where none was intended, Yeats warmly dedicated the 1925 edition of *A VISION* to

"Vestigia," as Moina Mathers was known within the Golden Dawn. "ALL SOULS' NIGHT"—the epilogue to *A Vision*—is Yeats's definitive commemoration of his old cohort. Though remembering Mathers as "half a lunatic, half knave," Yeats acknowledges his generosity, industry, and courage, and the ardor of his occult ambition.

Bibliography

Finneran, Richard J., et al., eds. *Letters to W. B. Yeats* (vol. 2); Harper, George Mills. *Yeats's Golden Dawn*; Howe, Ellic. *The Magicians of the Golden Dawn: A Documentary History of the Magical Order, 1887–1923*; Yeats, W. B. *Autobiographies, The Collected Letters of W. B. Yeats* (vol. 2), *Essays and Introductions, The Speckled Bird*.

Moore, George Augustus (1852–1933) Moore was the eldest son of a well-to-do Mayo landowner. In 1873, following the death of his father, Moore gave up plans to join the army and decamped to Paris, where he schooled himself in impressionism and naturalism, the chief aesthetic movements of the day. He frequented the Café Nouvelle Athènes, a haunt of writers and artists, and eventually became acquainted with many of the era's leading lights: Degas, Mallarmé, Manet, Monet, Pissarro, Renoir, Sisley, and Villiers de l'Isle-Adam. He had come to Paris with the idea of painting, but insufficient talent eventually obliged him to take up the pen. In 1880, he moved to London and began a career as a critic and a novelist. His hope, as he wrote in 1884, was to put "a dagger into the heart of the sentimental school" and to become "Zola's offshoot in England" (*Life of George Moore* 101). Moore established himself as a leading novelist with the publication of *Esther Waters* in 1894. By his own account, Moore first spotted Yeats prancing and preening in the dress-circle after a performance of his play *The* LAND OF HEART'S DESIRE at the Avenue Theatre, London, in the spring of 1894. That summer he and Yeats were brought together by their mutual friend, the painter John Nettleship (1841–1902), and thereafter they fell in with one another as the mutual friends of ARTHUR SYMONS (*Hail and Farewell* 78–83; see also *Aut.* 300–301). The first phase of the writers' friend-

Portrait of George Moore by John Butler Yeats. John Quinn commissioned the painting in August 1905. *(The National Gallery of Ireland)*

ship was marked by Moore's *Evelyn Innes* (1898). Moore dedicated the novel to Yeats, and the novel's romantic hero, Ulick Dean, was Yeats thinly disguised, though in a 1901 edition the character became more redolent of GEORGE RUSSELL (AE) (see *CL2* 308–310; *LTWBY*, I, 41–45).

The turn of the century found Moore disgusted with the English part in the Boer War and suddenly receptive to the siren call of the Irish Renaissance. The idea of an IRISH LITERARY THEATRE had been hatched by Yeats, Lady GREGORY, and Moore's cousin EDWARD MARTYN in 1897. In early 1899, Yeats and Martyn showed up at Moore's doorstep in London with the idea of involving him in their plans (*Hail and Farewell* 76). Moore lent a hand during the London rehearsals of Martyn's *The Heather Field* and Yeats's *The* COUNTESS CATHLEEN, which constituted the Irish Literary Theatre's inaugural program in May 1899. As Moore tells the story, however, the decisive event in his conversion to the Irish cause occurred in early 1901. He was walking in London when he heard a voice intoning "Go to Ireland!" Moore later wrote, "Of this I am sure—that the words Go to Ireland did not come from within, but from without" (257). Obeying this mystical injunction, Moore moved to Dublin in April 1901 and threw his weight behind the Irish movement.

During the 10 years of his residency in Dublin, Moore was both friend and nemesis to Yeats, their relationship a series of quarrels and semi-reconciliations. A June 1900 letter to Lady GREGORY records Yeats's ambivalence: "What a queer person he is. He is constantly so likable that one can beleive [sic] no evil of him & then in a moment a kind of devil takes hold of him & his voice changes & his look changes & he becomes perfectly hateful. [. . .] It is so hard not to trust him, & yet I am afraid he is quite untrustworthy. He has what Tallerand [sic] called 'the terrible gift of familiarity' & yet one must look upon him after all as only a mind that can be of service to ones [sic] cause" (CL2 536–537; see also *Aut.* 319). Yeats conducts involved and sometimes scathing analyses of Moore's character in both AUTOBIOGRAPHIES and MEMOIRS. The latter contains what may be his most incisive observation: "When logic is master and his personality is for the moment quiet, [Moore] has intellectual honesty and courage. These impersonal moods alternate with orgies of personal vanity during which he sees all the closed doors of the world and bangs them with his fist and shrieks at the windows. If his vanity had not made self-possession impossible, substituting a desire to startle and to shock for the solitude [which is] the first laborious creation of genius, he might have been a great writer, or at any rate as great a writer as a man of wholly external vision can be. That antithesis which I see in all artists between the artistic and the daily self was in his case too crude and simple, and the daily part too powerful, and his ignorance—and ignorance often helps external vision—deprived him of all discipline" (270).

Despite their temperamental incongruity, Yeats and Moore jointly authored the play DIARMUID AND GRANIA, on which they began work in 1899 (see *Aut.* 321–322; CL2 460–461). They planned a second dramatic collaboration, but the project

collapsed. Each claimed as his own the plot of the unwritten play, and a quarrel ensued, with Moore going so far as to threaten Yeats with a legal injunction (*Aut.* 334; *Life of George Moore* 241). Yeats prevailed in this squabble by dashing off WHERE THERE IS NOTHING and rushing it into print, but the damage to the friendship was done. As Yeats writes in *Autobiographies*, "Some months later an American friend, John Quinn [. . .] brought us together, but we were never cordial again; on my side distrust remained, on his disgust. I look back with some remorse. 'Yeats,' Moore had said, 'a man can only have one conscience, mine is artistic.' Had I abandoned my plot and made him write the novel, he might have put beside *Muslin* and *The Lake* a third masterpiece, but I was young, vain, self-righteous, and bent on proving myself a man of action" (334).

Moore's *Hail and Farewell*, a scabrous and monumental memoir that Joseph Hone calls "one of the world's great autobiographies," widened the breach between the two writers (*Life of George Moore* 471). It appeared in three parts: *Ave*, in 1911; *Salve*, in 1912; and *Vale*, in 1914. *Ave* did not excessively perturb Yeats (see *Letters* 564), but "Yeats, Lady Gregory, and Synge," an advance excerpt from *Vale* published in the January and February 1914 numbers of the *English Review*, put him in a rage, while Lady Gregory threatened a libel action (see section 7 of *Vale* for the offending passages). Moore's mockery of Yeats's aristocratic pretensions was particularly stinging. Moore recalls, for example, that in 1904 he had given a lecture on the French impressionists to rally support for an exhibition of paintings organized by HUGH LANE (the exhibition ran from November 21, 1904, to March 1905; see CL4 4–5, 324). As Moore tells the story, Yeats followed with an impromptu denunciation of the middle classes. "[We] could hardly believe our ears when, instead of talking to us as he used to about the old stories come down from generation to generation, he began to thunder like Ben Tillet himself against the middle classes, stamping his feet, working himself into a great passion, and all because the middle classes did not dip their hands into their pockets and give Lane the money he wanted for his exhibition. It is impossible to imagine the hatred which came into his voice when he spoke the words 'the middle classes'; one would have thought that he was speaking against a personal foe; but there are millions in the middle classes! And we looked round asking each other with our eyes where on earth our Willie Yeats had picked up such extraordinary ideas. He could hardly have gathered in the United States so ridiculous an idea that none but titled and carriage-folk can appreciate pictures. And we asked ourselves why Willie Yeats should feel himself called upon to denounce the class to which he himself belonged essentially [. . .] ("Yeats, Lady Gregory, and Synge," *English Review*, January 1914; see also *Hail and Farewell* 540). In a January 1914 diary entry (quoted in part above), Yeats responded with wounded venom, calling Moore "a born demagogue and in nothing more than in his love of the wealthy. He has always a passion for some crowd, is always deliberately inciting them against somebody. He shares the mob's materialism and the mob's hatred of any privilege which is an incommunicable gift. He can imagine himself rich, he cannot imagine himself with fine manners, and the mere thought of such manners gives him a longing to insult somebody. He looks at style, or the pursuit of it, in the same way" (*Mem.* 270).

The "INTRODUCTORY RHYMES" and "CLOSING RHYMES" to *Responsibilities* (1914) were the first volleys in Yeats's public response to Moore. *The CAT AND THE MOON* (1924), which lampoons Moore and Martyn as "typical peasants, the peasant sinner, the peasant saint," continued the campaign (*Aut.* 300). Yeats exacted full revenge only with the publication in 1935 of *Dramatis Personae* (see *Autobiographies*), a tit-for-tat riposte to *Hail and Farewell*. His account of Moore's early adulthood gives the tenor: "He had gone to Paris straight from his father's racing stables, from a house where there was no culture, as Symons and I understood that word, acquired copious inaccurate French, sat among art students, young writers about to become famous, in some café; a man carved out of a turnip, looking out of astonished eyes. I see him as that circle saw him, for I have in memory Manet's caricature [*Portrait of George Moore*, 1878 or 1879]. He spoke badly and much in a foreign tongue, read nothing, and was never to attain the discipline of style" (302). Yeats's nagging sense of grievance persisted even *in extremis*. While recovering from an illness he had expected to be fatal, Yeats told OLIVIA SHAKESPEAR in November 1927, "I have not had a moment's depression [. . .] yet I did hate leaving the last word to George Moore" (*Letters* 733).

Bibliography

Finneran, Richard J., et al., eds. *Letters to W. B. Yeats* (vol. 2); Hone, Joseph. *The Life of George Moore*; Moore, George. *Hail and Farewell*, "Yeats, Lady Gregory, and Synge" (in the *English Review*, January 1914); Yeats, W. B. *Autobiographies, The Collected Letters of W. B. Yeats* (vols. 2, 4), *The Letters of W. B. Yeats, Memoirs*.

Moore, Thomas Sturge (1870–1944)   The son of a Norwood physician and the brother of the Cambridge philosopher G. E. Moore (1873–1958), Moore attended Dulwich College (1879–1884), Croydon Art School, and Lambeth Art School, before commencing a distinguished career as poet, playwright, and engraver. Moore and Yeats were fast friends and devoted correspondents from the turn of the century until Yeats's death in 1939. In his essay "Modern Poetry" (1936), Yeats recalls first hearing word of Moore: "When 'The RHYMERS' CLUB' was breaking up I read enthusiastic reviews of the first book of Sturge Moore and grew jealous. He did not belong to 'The Rhymers' Club' and I wanted to believe that we had all the good poets; but one evening [the artist] Charles Ricketts brought me to a riverside house at Richmond and introduced me to Edith Cooper [a novelist who collaborated with her aunt under the pseudonym "Michael Field"]. She put into my unwilling hands Sturge Moore's book and made me read out and discuss certain poems. I surrendered. I took back all I had said against him. I was most moved by his poem called 'The Dying Swan'" (*E&I* 495–496; *LE* 92). In a note to "The TOWER," Yeats acknowledges that the third section of his monumental poem "unconsciously echoed" Moore's poem, which he calls "one of the loveliest lyrics of our time." He attributes the "theft" to the fact that he had often recited "The Dying Swan" during an American lecture tour (*VP* 826). Yeats naturally included the poem in his *Oxford Book of Modern Verse* (1936).

The two poets finally met in late 1900 through their mutual friend, the poet and art historian Robert Binyon (1869–1943). In a reminiscence of 1939, Moore recalled of this first interview, "His derision of the puritanical and scientific bases of my bringing up roused me to contend as much as his witty dream-soaked talk delighted me. He was nearly five years my senior and far better read, so that he held on his way with less and less gainsaying from me" (CL2 441). Moore belonged to a circle of aesthetes that included the artists Charles Ricketts (1866–1931) and Charles Shannon (1863–1937), and Yeats fell in comfortably. All were involved in the Literary Theatre Club (established July 30, 1901) and its successor The Masquers Society (established March 28, 1903). The shared hope was to found a "theatre of beauty" in London, but the groups' plans never fell into place (see CL3 721–725). Yeats would fare better in Dublin with the similarly intentioned ABBEY THEATRE.

In 1901, Yeats and Moore began to exchange letters and over the next several decades maintained a steady correspondence, collected in *W. B. Yeats and T. Sturge Moore: Their Correspondence 1901–1937* (1953). From the 1920s onward, the two poets engaged in a spirited debate on metaphysics and epistemology, with much discussion of Berkeley ("SWIFT'S *Epitaph* and Berkeley's *Commonplace Book* are the greatest works of modern Ireland," declared Yeats), Hegel, G. E. Moore (says Yeats of his friend's brother, "He has less gift of expression than any other able man who ever lived"), Plato, Plotinus, Bertrand Russell (Yeats's particular nemesis: a "peaky-nosed, bald-pated, pink-eyed harridan"), and Oswald Spengler. In Joseph Hone's summary of the poets' drawn-out disputation, Moore's "sympathies went out strongly to the contemporary British Realists, who doubt whether any philosophical question can be answered absolutely, and insist upon the reality of what we call nature as distinct from man. Yeats accuses this school of being mainly concerned, in its criticism of classical Idealism, to assert the prestige of science as a blind deity, invested with an infallible and objective authority" (*W. B. Yeats* 380). Says Virginia Moore, the exchange "shows a BLAKE-converted, Berkeley-encouraged Yeats scoffing at the theory that nature

with its primary and secondary qualities—Locke's intrinsic and extrinsic properties—exists independent of man's mind" (*Unicorn* 305–306). What the exchange lacks in rigor and precision ("metaphysics are no theme for a letter though the maledictions and beatitudes they inspire, being more compressed, are," wrote Yeats on April 9, 1929) it gains in amusing persiflage ("You are certainly quite wrong about my philosophy and I suspect you of being equally wrong about your own," wrote Moore on the same day). Then too there are flashes of Yeats's irrepressible intellectual originality. "Science is the criticism of Myth," he wrote on April 17, 1929, in his high oracular style. "There would be no Darwin had there been no Book of Genesis, no electron but for the Greek atomic myth; and when the criticism is finished there is not even a drift of ashes on the pyre. Sexual desire dies because every touch consumes the Myth, and yet a Myth that cannot be so consumed becomes a spectre."

Yeats valued Moore not only as a philosophical sounding board, but also as a working artist. He was responsible for the cover design of 12 books by Yeats: *Reveries Over Childhood and Youth* (1916), *Responsibilities* (1916), PER AMICA SILENTIA LUNAE (1918), *The Wild Swans at Coole* (1919), *The Cutting of an Agate* (1919), *Selected Poems* (1921), *Four Plays for Dancers* (1921), *Four Years* (1921), *The Tower* (1928), *The Winding Stair* (1933), *Letters to the New Island* (1934), and *Last Poems and Plays* (1940) (*WBY&TSM* 190–191). Yeats additionally commissioned Moore to design bookplates for himself (a candle upon the waves, flanked by figures evidently representing life and death or youth and age), for his wife (a unicorn bursting from a lightning-riven tower), and for his daughter (a girl "dancing in a single half-transparent garment in the light of a more than half moon on a rocky islet in an animated but not rough sea," in Moore's description); this last was never finished (90; for reproductions of the completed plates see 35, 39).

Bibliography

Joseph, Hone. *W. B. Yeats*; Moore, Virginia. *The Unicorn: William Butler Yeats' Search for Reality*; Yeats, W. B. *The Collected Letters of W. B. Yeats* (vols. 2–3), *Essays and Introductions, Later Essays, The Variorum*

Edition of the Poems of W. B. Yeats, W. B. Yeats and T. Sturge Moore: Their Correspondence 1901–1937.

Morris, William (1834–1896)   William Morris—novelist, poet, social thinker, painter, printer, and craftsman—exerted an enormous influence on Yeats during his early years; it may be that only BLAKE and SHELLEY did more to form the thought of the young poet. In "A General Introduction for my Work" (dated 1937), Yeats wrote that he owed his soul "to Shakespeare, to Spenser and to Blake, perhaps to William Morris," an expression of debt that he often repeated (*E&I* 519; *LE* 211; see also *AP* 458; *Letters* 872; *LOP* 111). In AUTOBIOGRA-PHIES, he extols Morris as his "chief of men" whose life, "poetry and all," he would choose above any other man's (131–132; see also *LE* 42). In an interview published in 1931, he calls himself "entirely devoted" to Morris, in whose work "you have all the great stories of the world greatly told" (*I&R,* II, 203).

Yeats's first brush with Morris came in April 1886, when he heard Morris speak on socialism in Dublin and met him at the CONTEMPORARY CLUB (*LE* 37–38; *P&I* 120; *YC* 8). During the late 1880s, Yeats frequented Kelmscott House, Morris's riverside home in the London borough of Hammersmith. There Morris held court surrounded by both workingmen and intellectuals (George Bernard Shaw and FLORENCE FARR among the latter). Yeats attended Sunday lectures on socialism, often staying to supper afterward (*Aut.* 130; *Mem.* 20). When his maiden volume, *The Wanderings of Oisin and Other Poems,* was published in January 1889, Yeats sent a copy to Morris's daughter May (1862–1938), hoping that Morris might read it. Bumping into Morris on the street sometime later, he received a fine compliment. "It is my kind of poetry," Morris pronounced. According to Yeats, Morris "would have said much more had he not caught sight of one of the decorated iron lamp-posts then recently, I believe, set up [by] the Corporation, and turned upon it with frenzy, waiving his umbrella" (*Mem.* 21; see also *Aut.* 135; *CL1* 128). Believing above all else in the war of the soul against the body, Yeats was repulsed by the materialism that prevailed among Morris's socialist aco-

William Morris, poet, novelist, artist, craftsman, and social theorist. As a young man, Yeats considered the Victorian titan his "chief of men." *(Library of Congress)*

lytes, as was LIONEL JOHNSON, who was moved to quip: "I wish those who deny the eternity of punishment could realize their unspeakable vulgarity" (*LE* 43). During one debate at Kelmscott House, Yeats "broke out [. . .] with all the arrogance of raging youth" and denounced this materialism, insisting that "there must be a change of heart and only religion could make it." Though Morris was not vexed, Yeats abandoned Kelmscott House from that moment forward (*Aut.* 136). Issues of religion and politics aside, a break was inevitable, for Yeats could fellow travel only so long with a man of such different temperament, a man who so utterly lacked what Yeats would later call the "Vision of Evil," the vision of the world as "continual conflict" (on the Vision of Evil, see *Aut.* 200, 217, 240, 251; *AV* 144–145).

Yeats almost immediately outgrew the socialism that he briefly borrowed from Morris (*Aut.* 135; *GY* 437; *Mem.* 20–21), but he fully absorbed

Morris's philosophy of culture, which emphasized beauty, community, and tradition, and looked to the Middle Ages as an abiding ideal and antidote to the mass production and industrialization of the modern age. Yeats's conception of "Unity of Culture" (see *Aut.* 165, 214–215, 229, 268, 273), which rules his thought from beginning to end, is largely indebted to Morris. His influence is palpable, for example, in Yeats's account of Byzantium in *A VISION* ("religious, aesthetic and practical life were one" while the "painter, the mosaic worker, the worker in gold and silver, the illuminator of sacred books, were almost impersonal, almost perhaps without the consciousness of individual design, absorbed in their subject-matter and that the vision of a whole people"); palpable as well in Yeats's account of the Stockholm City Hall in "The Bounty of Sweden" (*AV* 279–280; *Aut.* 407). Morris's poetic influence is harder to trace, though the general influence of PRE-RAPHAELITISM is apparent in Yeats's early verse. In T. S. ELIOT's view, "The Yeats of the Celtic Twilight—who seems to me to have been more the Yeats of the pre-Raphaelite twilight—uses Celtic folklore almost as William Morris uses Scandinavian folklore. His longer narrative poems bear the mark of Morris. Indeed, in the pre-Raphaelite phase, Yeats is by no means the least of the pre-Raphaelites. I may be mistaken, but the play, *The SHADOWY WATERS*, seems to me one of the most perfect expressions of the vague enchanted beauty of that school: yet it strikes me— this may be an impertinence on my part—as the western seas descried through the back window of a house in Kensington, an Irish myth for the Kelmscott Press [. . .]" (*On Poetry and Poets* 300). Yeats never expresses more than ambivalent enthusiasm for Morris's poems, but his prose romances—what would now be called "fantasy" novels—brought Yeats "so great a joy" that he deliberately read them slowly so he "might not come too quickly to the end" (*Aut.* 131).

Morris's influence on Yeats's sisters, Lily and Lolly, was if anything even greater than his influence on Yeats. Lily cut her teeth as an embroiderer with Morris and Company and worked under May Morris's direction from 1888 to 1894 (*CL1* 111, 120, 123; *Yeats Sisters* 63–67). The sisters self-

consciously modeled their later craft and printing enterprises on Morris's example. The sisters' DUN EMER PRESS and CUALA PRESS, which published much of Yeats's work in elegantly austere editions, represented the straightforward attempt to replicate the artisanal integrity, if not the elaborate artistry, of Morris's Kelmscott Press.

Yeats's principal reflections on Morris are to be found in *Autobiographies*; in his 1896 review of Morris's prose romance *The Well at the World's End* (*UP1* 418–420); in a 1929 letter to T. STURGE MOORE (*WBY&TSM* 154); and in his 1903 essay "The Happiest of the Poets." The latter essay— rendered in sumptuous prose, as appropriate to its subject—describes Morris as "the one perfectly happy and fortunate poet of modern times," for he was immune to the haunting anguish of the romantic tradition, the anguish of Rossetti and Shelley, of those who follow "the star of the Magi, the Morning and evening Star, the mother of impossible hope" (*E&I* 53). Morris wrote of "nothing but of the quest of the Grail"—was in this sense a romantic seeker in his own right—"but it was the Heathen Grail that gave every man his chosen food, and not the Grail of Malory or Wagner; and he came at last to praise, as other men have praised the martyrs of religion or of passion, men with lucky eyes and men whom all women love" (55). Yeats is careful to rescue the beauty of Morris's prophetic vision from the positivistic and materialistic taint of his leftist politics, and in effect to make Morris an honorary member of his own school—if not the school of infinite desire and impossible hope, at least the school of romantic imagination. Like that of all the great poets, his vision "is true because it is poetical, because we are a little happier when we are looking at it; and he knew as Shelley knew, by an act of faith, that the economists should take their measurements not from life as it is, but from the vision of men like him, from the vision of the world made perfect that is buried under all minds" (63).

Knowing his admiration for Morris, Yeats's friends made him a 40th birthday present of the Kelmscott edition of *The Works of Geoffrey Chaucer* (*CL4* 110, 125–126, 129, 140, 161–162, 166). Yeats called it "the most beautiful of all decorated books." Displayed on a lectern designed by ROBERT

GREGORY, it figured prominently in the décor of WOBURN BUILDINGS (166).

Bibliography

Eliot, T. S. *On Poetry and Poets*; Foster, R. F. *W. B. Yeats: A Life, II: The Arch-Poet*; Hardwick, Joan. *The Yeats Sisters: A Biography of Susan and Elizabeth Yeats*; Kelly, John S. *A W. B. Yeats Chronology*; Mikhail, E. H., ed. *W. B. Yeats: Interviews and Recollections* (vol. 2); Yeats, W. B. *Autobiographies, The Collected Letters of W. B. Yeats* (vols. 1, 4), *Essays and Introductions, The Gonne-Yeats Letters 1893–1938, Later Essays, The Letters of W. B. Yeats, Letters on Poetry from W. B. Yeats to Dorothy Wellesley, Prefaces and Introductions, Uncollected Prose by W. B. Yeats* (vol. 1), *A Vision, W. B. Yeats and T. Sturge Moore: Their Correspondence 1901–1937*.

National Literary Society   Yeats played a leading role in the founding of both the London-based Irish Literary Society (inaugural meeting on May 12, 1892) and the Dublin-based National Literary Society (inaugural meeting on August 16, 1892), as he describes in AUTOBIOGRAPHIES (169–175, 296). The analogous but independent organizations were intended to catalyze the nascent literary revival and to promote the traditions of Irish literature and culture. In *Autobiographies*, Yeats writes that the two societies "were necessary because their lectures must take the place of an educated popular Press, which we had not, and have not now, and create a standard of criticism" (170). Charles Gavan Duffy (1816–1903), with whom Yeats would soon clash over the NEW IRISH LIBRARY, was elected president of the London society, while Yeats served on a 14-man governing committee. Douglas Hyde (1860–1949) was elected president of the Dublin society (contrary to Yeats's assertion in *Autobiographies* that JOHN O'LEARY was president). Vice presidents were the Reverend Thomas Finlay (1848–1940), MAUD GONNE, Richard Ashe King (1839–1932), George Plunkett (1851–1948), George Sigerson (1836–1925), KATHARINE TYNAN, and Yeats (*CL1* 305).

Yeats's primary effort on behalf of the Dublin society was the attempt to establish a network of provincial libraries that would provide books on Irish subjects and host lecturers dispatched by the society (*Aut.* 189; *CL1* 317, 328, 342–343). With Yeats serving as secretary of the libraries subcommittee, the scheme began with a flourish—some 300 volumes had been distributed by June 1893—but ground to a halt after the society reproved the subcommittee's sloppy administration of the program (*CL1* 357–358). In Yeats's telling, "The trouble came from half a dozen obscure young men, who having nothing to do attended every meeting and were able to overturn a project that seemed my only bridge to other projects, including a travelling theatre. [. . .] The half a dozen young men, if a little jealous of me, were still more jealous of those country branches which were getting so much notice, and where there was so much of that peasant mind their schoolmasters had taught them to despise" (*Aut.* 189).

One of the most important outgrowths of the National Literary Society was the Gaelic League, which received its initial impetus from Hyde's presidential address, "The Necessity for De-Anglicizing Ireland," delivered on November 25, 1892 (see *Mem.* 58). The address, which called for the revival of the Irish language, put Yeats in an awkward position. As a cultural nationalist he could not denounce Hyde's campaign, but as an English-speaking poet in the tradition of BLAKE and SHELLEY he could not accept it. In a December letter to *United Ireland*, Yeats gingerly took exception to the gist of the address. While regretting the decline of Gaelic—a conveniently irreversible trend in Yeats's view—he questioned Hyde's notion that a national literature was incompatible with the English language. Yeats asked, anticipating his own literary program, whether it were not possible to impress English with "an indefinable Irish quality of rhythm and style" and to render in English the "histories and romances of the great Gaelic men of the past [. . .] until there has been made a golden bridge between the old and new" (*CL1* 338). The National Literary Society also played a role in the founding of the IRISH LITERARY THEATRE in 1899, sponsoring and to some extent legitimating the new organization as it attempted to get off the ground (*CL2* 340).

Neither society became the dominant institution that Yeats had hoped, but each carried on the work of sustaining interest in Irish literature and culture, primarily by sponsoring lectures. Yeats briefly resigned from the Irish Literary Society in March 1901 after GEORGE MOORE was blackballed, but he otherwise remained active in both societies (*Aut.* 320; *CL3* 49–51). According to John S. Kelly et al., the National Literary Society "continued to flourish in Dublin well into the next century," with a membership or more than 350 as of 1900, while the Irish Literary Society continues its work to this day (*CL1* 500, 496). In MEMOIRS, Yeats writes that the National Literary Society has come to afflict him "by its permanence and by its dullness, so changed it is from its fiery youth" (51).

Bibliography

Hyde, Douglas. *Language, Lore and Lyrics*; Yeats, W. B. *Autobiographies, The Collected Letters of W. B. Yeats* (vols. 1–3), *Memoirs*.

New Irish Library   Much of Yeats's attention during 1892 and 1893 was occupied by a sharp controversy over a prospective series of books on Irish subjects to be published under the auspices of the NATIONAL LITERARY SOCIETY. Yeats tells the story of the controversy in both AUTOBIOGRAPHIES and MEMOIRS, and both *The Collected Letters of W. B. Yeats* (vol. 1) and *Uncollected Prose by W. B. Yeats* (Vol. 1) record its progress. In *Autobiographies*, Yeats frames the controversy over the New Irish Library as his first public bout against the kind of narrow nationalist orthodoxy that conceives all history "as a melodrama with Ireland for blameless hero and poet." He continues: "It was all the harder to substitute for that melodrama a nobler form of art, because there really had been, however different in their form, villain and victim; yet fight that rancour I must, and if I had not made some headway against it in 1892 and 1893 it might have silenced in 1907 JOHN SYNGE, the greatest dramatic genius of Ireland" (173–174).

Yeats's chief adversary in this row was Sir Charles Gavan Duffy (1816–1903), a hero of the Young Ireland movement during the 1840s who emigrated to Australia in 1855 and served as prime minister of the state of Victoria in 1871 and 1872. He returned to Europe in 1888, residing in Nice

for health reasons but increasingly taking part in Irish cultural and political affairs (*CL1* 483–484). The library series was to be modeled on the popular 22-volume "Library of Ireland" that Duffy himself had edited in the 1840s (298). As early as February 1892, Yeats was busily making plans for the series, which he hoped to have published by the London firm of T. Fisher Unwin (280, 285–287). In July and August, however, Duffy effectively seized control of the publishing venture, proposing to form a new Irish National Publishing Company, with himself as chairman, to bring out the series (310–314). Sensing that the enterprise was slipping from his grasp, Yeats wrote to the *Freeman's Journal* in September expressing his reservations about Duffy's suitability as sole editor of the series, principally on the grounds that he had lived too long out of the country to be in touch with its "many needs and many interests" (310–311). In *Memoirs*, Yeats accuses Duffy of wanting to publish books "that by some chance had failed to find publication in his youth, the works of political associates or of friends long dead" (64). When the scheme to form a publishing company collapsed, Duffy pitched the series to T. Fisher Unwin. Yeats considered this co-option of negotiations that he had begun months earlier to be sheer duplicity; as he wrote to JOHN O'LEARY, it "simply means war" (*CL1* 331; see also *Aut.* 188). Yeats interceded with the publisher and in February 1893 forced a compromise: Duffy would edit the series with Douglas Hyde (1860–1949) and T. W. Rolleston (1857–1920) as subeditors respectively representing the National Literary Society in Dublin and the Irish Literary Society in London, while an advisory committee (on which Yeats wound up sitting) would recommend titles for publication (*CL1* 343–346; *Mem.* 64).

In the event, the series, titled "The New Irish Library," was a failure—killed, according to Yeats, by the stultifying first volume, Thomas Davis's *The Patriot Parliament of 1689* (*Aut.* 188; *CL1* 397–398). Yeats had his revenge in a scathing review of the series published in the August 1894 issue of the *Bookman* (see *UP1* 332–335). He wrote acidically of Davis's book, "Pages upon pages of Acts of Parliament may be popular literature on the planet Neptune, or chillier Uranus, but our quick-blooded globe has altogether different needs" (333). He was only a little kinder in a subsequent comment (339–340). Twelve volumes eventually appeared. In *Memoirs*, Yeats takes credit for pushing through Standish James O'Grady's *The Bog of Stars, and Other Stories and Sketches of Elizabethan Ireland* (1893) and Hyde's *The Story of Early Gaelic Literature* (1895), as well as lives of Oliver Goldsmith and JONATHAN SWIFT (64).

Bibliography

Yeats, W. B. *Autobiographies, The Collected Letters of W. B. Yeats* (vol. 1), *Memoirs, Uncollected Prose by W. B. Yeats* (vol. 1).

Nobel Prize in literature   Alfred Nobel, the Swedish industrial magnate and inventor of dynamite, died on December 10, 1896, leaving a will that provided for five prizes to recognize achievement in arts and science, with the prize in literature to be awarded by the decision of the Swedish Academy. First awarded in 1901, the Nobel Prize in literature was to become the most prestigious and richest prize of its type in the world. In 1922, Yeats had strongly contended for the prize, but the selection committee found Yeats's poetry "partly too obscure" and his drama lacking "the free, vigorous heartbeat that is surely essential to full-grown tragedy." There were also considerations concerning the "geographical distribution" of the prize. After carefully considering Yeats's merits, the academy awarded the prize to the Spanish dramatist Jacinto Benavente (*Nobel Prize* 48–50, 134). Kjell Espmark, a historian of the prize, comments that during the 1920s the prize committee's "predilection for a 'simple' kind of poetry approaching the nature of folk poetry made the committee quite incapable of appreciating the symbolist and modernist currents in twentieth-century poetry" (*Nobel Prize* 53–54).

The following year, however, Yeats's undeniable eminence overcame the committee's conservatism. On November 14, 1923, the committee announced that Yeats had won the 1923 prize for literature. Robert Maire Smyllie (1894–1954), assistant editor of the *Irish Times*, received word of the prize over the news wire and telephoned Yeats toward 11

o'clock in the evening. Yeats notoriously responded to word of the high honor, "How much, Smyllie, how much is it?" (*I&R*, II, 323–324). Ten minutes later Yeats received a telegram from the Swedish ambassador. The hubbub had died down by half past 12, and Yeats and his wife (see GEORGE YEATS) celebrated with wine and sausages (*Aut.* 393). On the following night, Yeats hosted a small celebratory dinner at the Shelbourne Hotel in Dublin. On November 23, Yeats wrote to T. STURGE MOORE that the prize "will be a great help to me in several ways. Here especially [i.e., in Dublin] it will help. I will find it easier to get the Government to listen to me on artistic things. I look upon it as a recognition of the Free State, and of Irish literature, and it is a very great help. People here are grateful because I have won them this recognition, and that is the distinction I want. If I thought it a tribute to my own capacity alone I, being a very social man, would be far less pleased" (*WBY&TSM* 51–52).

On December 6, Yeats and his wife departed for Stockholm. On December 10, Yeats formally received the prize ("for his always inspired poetry, which in a highly artistic form gives expression to the spirit of a whole nation") and delivered a speech at a banquet for the prizewinners at the Grand Hôtel (*Nobel Lectures* 199–200); on December 12, he attended a reception at the royal palace and found himself "moved as if by some religious ceremony, though to a different end, for here it is Life herself that is praised" (*Aut.* 399); on December 13, he delivered his Nobel lecture, titled "The Irish Dramatic Movement," to the Royal Academy of Sweden (see *Aut.* 410–418); on December 15 he attended a performance of CATHLEEN NI HOULIHAN and Oliver Goldsmith's *She Stoops to Conquer*; and on December 16, he set sail for England. In his brief banquet speech Yeats expressed his debt to the "Scandinavian nation," citing the influence of the Swedish mystic Emanuel Swedenborg (1688–1772) on his beloved BLAKE, and the influence of Norwegian playwright Henrik Ibsen (1828–1906) and the Swedish playwright August Strindberg (1849–1912) on the Irish dramatic movement (*Aut.* 398; on Yeats's slight acquaintance with Strindberg, see *LE* 32). The official annals of the Nobel Foundation, however, record that it was not Strindberg, but the Norwegian poet, novelist, and playwright Bjørnstjerne Bjørnson (1832–1910), recipient of the 1903 Nobel Prize, whom Yeats cited (*Nobel Lectures* 199; on Bjørnson, see *CL3* 120–121). "The Irish Dramatic Movement," one of Yeats's less inspired prose pieces, recounts the history and struggles of the movement in straightforward terms. It dwells generously on the contributions of fellow workers—the actress Molly Allgood (1887–1952), Lady GREGORY, ANNIE HORNIMAN, EDWARD MARTYN, the playwright and director Lennox Robinson (1886–1958), J. M. SYNGE—and grinds familiar political axes, remembering opposition to *The* COUNTESS CATHLEEN in 1899; to Synge's *In the Shadow of the Glen* in 1903; and to Synge's *The Playboy of the Western World* in 1907. The lecture ends, however, with a rustle of poignancy and a memorable silhouette of Lady Gregory and Synge: "[When] I received from the hands of your King the great honour your Academy has conferred upon me, I felt that a young man's ghost should have stood upon one side of me and at the other a living woman sinking into the infirmity of age" (*Aut.* 418).

Upon returning from Sweden, Yeats immediately set to work on "The Bounty of Sweden," a memoir of his days in Stockholm interlaced with cultural meditation. Yeats found in Stockholm—or perhaps projected upon Stockholm—a vision of the beauty of society in its traditional and aristocratic order. Yeats's ruminations culminate in his breathless account, the influence of WILLIAM MORRIS in full sail, of the Stockholm City Hall. The "myth-makers and mask-makers" who had constructed the building, Yeats enthuses, "worked as if they belonged to one family [. . .] all that multitude and unity, could hardly have been possible, had not love of Stockholm and belief in its future so filled men of different minds, classes, and occupations that they almost attained the supreme miracle, the dream that has haunted all religions, and loved one another. No work comparable in method or achievement has been accomplished since the Italian cities felt the excitement of the Renaissance, for in the midst of our individualistic anarchy, growing always, as it seemed, more violent, have arisen once more subordination, design, a sense of

human need" (*Aut.* 407). "The Bounty of Sweden" first appeared in the *Dial* and the *London Mercury* in September 1924, and subsequently appeared with "The Irish Dramatic Movement" in a small volume, *The Bounty of Sweden*, published by the CUALA PRESS in July 1925. Yeats later canonized both essays in AUTOBIOGRAPHIES.

The prize money about which Yeats had been so anxious was 114,935 kronor or the princely sum of £7,500. On January 13, Yeats made an accounting of the money to Lady Gregory: "I have invested £6,000 of the money, and kept £500 to go to pay off the debt on this house [82 Merrion Square], or pay [Lily Yeats's medical] expenses as the case may be. There was almost £400 which we have largely spent on our trip to Sweden and on completing the furnishing of this house—my bookcases, stair carpets, plates, dishes, knives and forks and something I have always longed for, a sufficient reference library—*Encyclo[pae]dia Britannica, Cambridge Medieval, Ancient,* and *Modern History* and a good edition of Gibbon and some art books" (*Letters* 701–702). As it happened, however, the Cuala Press's debts swallowed some £2,000, and Yeats invested only £3,500. He invested in railway stocks expecting a 5 percent annual return, but, as R. F. Foster notes, "within a few years the convulsions of the financial market would alter these prospects for the worse. Between the demands of Cuala and the effect of the depression, the financial security brought by the Nobel represented a brief interlude, not a settled future" (*AP* 347, 711).

Yeats was pleased to have made a good impression during his brief stay in Sweden. He wrote OLIVIA SHAKESPEAR in August 1934: "I had a Swedish compliment the other day, that has pleased me better than [any] I have ever had. Some Swede said to my wife 'Our Royal Family liked your husband better than any other Nobel prize winner. They said he has the manners of a Courtier'" (*Letters* 827). As a devotee of Castiglione's *The Book of the Courtier* (1528), Yeats knew precisely the nature of the compliment. He would later write that Castiglione's "admirable conversationalists knew that the old spontaneous life had gone, and what a man must do to retain UNITY OF BEING, mother-wit expressed in its perfection; he must know so many foreign tongues, know how to dance and sing, talk well, walk well, and be always in love" (*Expl.* 431; *LE* 234).

Bibliography

Espmark, Kjell. *The Nobel Prize in Literature: A Study of the Criteria behind the Choices*; Foster, R. F. *W. B. Yeats: A Life, II: The Arch-Poet*; Frenz, Horst, ed. *Nobel Lectures: Literature, 1901–1967*; Mikhail, E. H., ed. *W. B. Yeats: Interviews and Recollections* (vol. 2); Yeats, W. B. *Autobiographies, The Collected Letters of W. B. Yeats* (vol. 3), *Explorations, Later Essays, The Letters of W. B. Yeats, W. B. Yeats and T. Sturge Moore: Their Correspondence 1901–1937.*

O'Higgins, Kevin (1892–1927)   A conservative of Yeats's own stamp who has sometimes been called the "Irish Mussolini," Kevin O'Higgins was a friend and political comrade whose assassination came as both a painful shock and a source of poetic inspiration (*Yeats, Ireland and Fascism* 187). O'Higgins belonged to the inner circle of the Free State government from its inception. At the time of his death, he was minister of justice and external affairs, and vice president of the executive council (*Modern Ireland* 501). On July 10, 1927, three gunmen opened fire on O'Higgins while he was on his way to mass in Blackrock, a Dublin suburb (*Ireland Since the Famine* 492). The assailants were never identified or apprehended, though MAUD GONNE's son, Sean MacBride (1904–88), was erroneously arrested and eventually released in connection with the crime (*Maud Gonne* 144–145). During the IRISH CIVIL WAR, the Free State government executed 77 Republican prisoners, and O'Higgins's assassination was most likely a belated act of retribution and revenge (*AP* 340–342; *Ireland Since the Famine* 461–462). In a 1933 letter to OLIVIA SHAKESPEAR, Yeats mentions that O'Higgins had said, "Nobody can expect to live who has done what I have done" (*Letters* 809).

Yeats published a letter of condolence addressed to O'Higgins's widow in the *Irish Times* on July 14. "[The] country has lost the man it needed, its great builder of a nation," Yeats wrote. "When obscure men die in battle we say 'Their country will never forget them,' and it forgets them before daybreak; but a martyred intellect is the most powerful of all things. One remembers that when men write the history of this generation they will tell his life and know that all is told; one tries to find consolation in that thought, and then one remembers all that he had still to do" (*UP2* 476–477). Yeats similarly lamented O'Higgins in a heartfelt letter to Shakespear written soon after the assassination. "The murder of O'Higgins was no mere public event to us," he told his London confidante, speaking of himself and his wife. "He was our personal friend, as well as the one strong intellect in Irish public life and then too his pretty young wife was our friend. We got the news just when we reached the Gresham Hotel where we were to dine and we left without dining and walked about the streets till bed-time" (*Letters* 726–727).

Yeats memorializes O'Higgins in "The MUNICIPAL GALLERY REVISITED" and in "PARNELL'S FUNERAL." In *ON THE BOILER*, Yeats places him in his starriest pantheon of Irish heroes, proclaiming, "Berkeley, SWIFT, Burke, Grattan, PARNELL, AUGUSTA GREGORY, SYNGE, Kevin O'Higgins, are the true Irish people, and there is nothing too hard for such as these" (*Expl.* 442; *LE* 242). In a 1933 note to *The Winding Stair and Other Poems*, Yeats identifies O'Higgins's assassination as the catalyst of both "BLOOD AND THE MOON" and "DEATH," and he reiterates that O'Higgins was "the finest intellect in Irish public life" (*VP* 831).

Bibliography

Cullingford, Elizabeth. *Yeats, Ireland and Fascism*; Foster, R. F. *Modern Ireland, 1600–1927, W. B. Yeats: A Life, II: The Arch-Poet*; Lyons, F. S. L. *Ireland Since the Famine*; Ward, Margaret. *Maud Gonne: A Life*; Yeats, W. B. *Explorations, Later Essays, The Letters of W. B. Yeats, Uncollected Prose by W. B. Yeats* (vol. 2), *The Variorum Edition of the Poems of W. B. Yeats.*

O'Leary, John (1830–1907)   Among the numerous mentors of his youth, Yeats most revered John O'Leary, a Fenian exile who returned to Ireland in the immense dignity of his old age and became an inspirational figure to many of the younger generation. The son of a Tipperary shopkeeper, O'Leary briefly attended Trinity College, Dublin, and then studied medicine at the Queen's Colleges in Cork and Galway. He was inspired to take up nationalist politics by the poems of Thomas Davis (1814–45), as Yeats tells the tale of his conversion (*Aut.* 100, 175; *UP2* 37). In 1863, he became an editor of the *Irish People*. In the characterization of Robert Kee, the weekly Fenian newspaper flirted "continually with the language of violence" and maintained that "parliamentary agitation was a useless way of trying to achieve the Irish independence that was unequivocally its goal" (*Bold Fenian Men* 19). On September 14, 1865, the government raided the newspaper, and O'Leary was arrested with the rest of the editorial staff (*Recollections* 205–206). He was released from prison in 1871 on the condition that he serve the remainder of his 20-year sentence in exile. O'Leary accepted this condition and spent the next 15 years abroad, largely in PARIS. In 1885, O'Leary's sentence expired and he returned to Dublin. He set up house with his sister Ellen (1831–89), a minor poet (see *Letters to the New Island* 12; *UP1* 256–258), and busied himself with helping along the city's political and cultural ferment. Yeats crossed paths with O'Leary soon after his return to Dublin, and the two regularly met at meetings of the CONTEMPORARY CLUB from 1885 onward. Yeats soon fell under the spell of O'Leary's stoicism, integrity, and dignity, or what he later called O'Leary's "Roman virtue" and "Roman courage" (*Aut.* 177; *E&I* 247). Yeats, MAUD GONNE, the barrister John F. Taylor (1850–1902), and the writer T. W. Rolleston (1857–1920), among other fervently admiring young people, gathered about O'Leary, sometimes literally sitting at his feet, for he "had the moral genius that moves all young people and moves them the more if they are repelled by those who have strict opinions and yet have lived commonplace lives" (*Aut.* 100). Putting the same point another way, Yeats writes that O'Leary was "magnetic" to his generation because "he alone had personality, a point of view not made for the crowd's sake, but for self-expression" (176).

A collector of Irish books and a champion of Irish literature, O'Leary demonstrated a form of nationalism to which Yeats could commit while remaining true to his obvious literary calling. As Yeats wrote in 1889, "We of the younger genera-

tion owe a great deal to Mr. John O'Leary and his sister. What nationality is in the present literary movement in Ireland is largely owing to their influence—an influence all feel who come across them. The material for many a song and ballad has come from Mr. John O'Leary's fine collection of Irish books—the best I know. The whole house is full of them. One expects to find them bulging out of the windows. He, more clearly than any one, has seen that there is no fine nationality without literature, and seen the converse also, that there is no fine literature without nationality" (*Letters to the New Island* 12). Yeats naturally drew O'Leary into the literary movement that O'Leary had in part inspired. In 1892, O'Leary joined the 20-member governing council of the NATIONAL LITERARY SOCIETY (*CL1* 305–306). Yeats had expected O'Leary to be named president, but the position went to Douglas Hyde (1860–1949).

Amid this activity, Yeats and O'Leary drew closer as friends. In late 1892, they shared a "lodging full of old books and magazines, covered with dirt and dust" at Lonsdale House, St. Lawrence Road, Clontarf, Dublin (*Aut.* 175; *CL1* 324). In *Autobiographies*, Yeats ponders the unlikelihood of this friendship and wonders "why it was he who found almost all the subscribers for my *Wanderings of Oisin*, and why he now supported me in all I did, for how could he like verses that were all picture, all emotion, all association, all mythology? He could not have approved my criticism either, for I exalted Mask and Image above the eighteenth-century logic which he loved, and set experience before observation, emotion before fact." Yeats proposes in explanation that O'Leary "no more wished to strengthen Irish Nationalism by second-rate literature than by second-rate morality, and was content that we agreed in that. 'There are things a man must not do to save a nation', he had once told me, and when I asked what things, had said, 'To cry in public', and I think it probable that he would have added, if pressed, 'To write oratorical or insincere verse'" (178). Yeats, in turn, found in O'Leary sanction for a kind of nationalism unwilling to subordinate artistic and spiritual integrity to immediate political aims, a posture that Yeats scrupulously maintained for the rest of his life, though it divided him from Maud Gonne and others. When O'Leary died in 1907, Yeats could not bring himself to attend the funeral, for he "shrank from seeing about his grave so many whose Nationalism was different from anything he had taught or that I could share" (E&I 246).

Yeats's principal reflections on O'Leary are to be found in *Autobiographies* (see especially the fifth section of "Ireland after Parnell") and in his essay "Mr. John O'Leary" (UP2 35–38). "Mr. John O'Leary" was supposed to have been a review of O'Leary's autobiography *Recollections of Fenians and Fenianism* (1896), but, not liking the book, Yeats took refuge in an appreciation of the man. In *Autobiographies*, Yeats remembers O'Leary "taking immense trouble with every word and comma, for the great work must be a masterpiece of style," but the book wound up being "dry, abstract, and confused; no picture had ever passed before his mind's eye" (178). Yeats twice evokes his old friend in verse. "BEAUTIFUL LOFTY THINGS" includes O'Leary in its Olympian roll and remembers his "noble head" (cf. *Aut.* 100; *Mem.* 42), while the monumental refrain of "SEPTEMBER 1913"—"Romantic Ireland's dead and gone, / It's with O'Leary in the grave"—makes O'Leary the measure of Ireland's spiritual decline.

Bibliography

Kee, Robert. *The Green Flag, II: The Bold Fenian Men*; O'Leary, John. *Recollections of Fenians and Fenianism* (vols. 1–2); Yeats, W. B. *Autobiographies, The Collected Letters of W. B. Yeats* (vol. 1), *Essays and Introductions, Letters to the New Island, Memoirs, Uncollected Prose by W. B. Yeats* (vols. 1–2).

Oxford Soon after their marriage, Yeats and his wife were drawn to the venerable university town. They were attracted by its ancient beauty and ghostly accretion of history; by its splendid libraries and stimulating intellectual life; and by its distance from Irish and family entanglements (which GEORGE YEATS may have found daunting in the months after her marriage). Further, as Ann Saddlemyer proposes, there was the opportunity to participate "vicariously in student life," neither husband nor wife having attended university (BG 232). The couple took rooms at 45 Broad Street

on January 2, 1918, and remained until March. In October 1919, they moved into a 17th-century house at 4 Broad Street (since demolished), just opposite Balliol College, and more permanently set up house (YC 197, 205). Yeats approached Oxford with his usual intellectual and social zest. He served as honorary president of the Oxford Irish Society (AP 187); revived the "Monday evenings" that had been a mainstay of life at WOBURN BUILD-INGS (187); denounced British prosecution of the ANGLO-IRISH WAR in a passionate speech delivered before the Oxford Union (188–189); made himself available to undergraduates, "among whom he had a legendary status," according to the poet and novelist L. A. G. Strong (I&R, I, 147); conducted occult research at the Bodleian Library, the "most comfortable and friendly library in the world," in Yeats's estimation (*Letters* 646); and on weekends decamped to Lady Ottoline Morrell's nearby Garsington Manor, where he mingled in an atmosphere of glamorous Bohemian intellectualism (AP 158–160; BG 231–232). In *A VISION*, Yeats tells of constantly going to the chapel of All Souls College—"though never at service time"—and there thinking out his mystical philosophy (6–7).

Congenitally skeptical of the academic enterprise (as in "The SCHOLARS"), Yeats was out of his element among the dons. Strong, an undergraduate regular at Yeats's Monday evenings, recalls Yeats complaining of them, "No sooner does a period in which I have been seen to be harmless encourage them, and they decide that though I am an Irishman I have no plan to overthrow the British Empire, and their wives plan to ask my wife to tea, than the red heels of Lady Ottoline Morrell are seen gleaming upon my doorstep, and all shudder and retreat once more." The "liveliest" among the dons were not deterred, comments Strong, and "if the staider sort kept away, I think the poet's criticisms of university education perhaps had as much to do with it as the bizarre elegance of Lady Ottoline. Yeats in my hearing remarked to two English dons, 'I can't see what you think you are achieving. You seem to be busy with the propagation of second and third and fourth hand opinions upon literature. Culture does not consist in acquiring opinions, but in getting rid of them'" (I&R, I, 148). George Yeats found the academic culture no easier going. Yeats reported to JOHN QUINN on February 8, 1919, "My wife never knows which to be most surprised at, the hats or the minds of the dons' wives, and is convinced that if we live here every winter, which is possible, she will be given to great extravagance out of the desire for contrast" (*Letters* 645).

To economize, the Yeatses let 4 Broad Street and moved to Minchin's Cottage, Shillingford, in April 1921, and then to Cuttlebrook House, Thame, in June, both in the neighborhood of Oxford (*AP* 192, 198). They returned to Broad Street in the autumn, but by then Oxford was a dwindling enthusiasm. On March 1, 1922, Yeats wrote to OLIVIA SHAKESPEAR, "About two weeks [ago] George announced that she could stand Oxford no longer and was going at once to Dublin to get a house" (*Letters* 678). After summering at THOOR BALLYLEE, the Yeatses relocated to 82 Merrion Square, Dublin (see 689).

Oxford was tangential to the personal and national springs of Yeats's poetry, but it did yield one great poetic detail: the "great Christ Church Bell / And many a lesser bell" that sound at midnight through Yeats's room in the opening stanza of "ALL SOULS' NIGHT." In 1682, "Great Tom," the bell of Christ Church College, was removed from the college cathedral to a tower at the college entrance designed by Sir Christopher Wren. In his study *Oxford in English Literature*, John Dougill explains that Great Tom has always sounded—and still sounds—101 times each evening at five past nine o'clock, thus "warning errant students of the closing of the college gates and reinforcing the sense of university dominion" (32). Maurice Bowra (1898–1971), the eminent classicist and literary critic, calls "All Souls' Night" "probably the finest poem ever written in Oxford" (*I&R*, II, 401).

On May 26, 1931, Oxford University conferred on Yeats an honorary doctorate of letters. Bowra, a fellow of Wadham College from 1922, came to know Yeats during the Broad Street years and saw much of him during the 1920s, frequently at Garsington (*I&R*, II, 396). He nominated Yeats for the honorary degree and insisted that the university's executive council immediately vote on the matter, as he did not trust the council to act once

he had stepped down (398–400). Yeats's degree from Oxford was soon complemented by a degree from Cambridge, presented on June 8, 1933 (*Letters* 810–811).

Bibliography

Dougill, John. *Oxford in English Literature: The Making, and Undoing, of the 'English Athens'*; Foster, R. F. *W. B. Yeats: A Life, II: The Arch-Poet*; Kelly, John S. *A W. B. Yeats Chronology*; Mikhail, E. H., ed. *W. B. Yeats: Interviews and Recollections* (vols. 1–2); Saddlemyer, Ann. *Becoming George: The Life of Mrs W. B. Yeats*; Yeats, W. B. *The Letters of W. B. Yeats*, *A Vision*.

Paris Though his efforts to learn French came to nothing (*Aut.* 133; *CL1* 64; *Mem.* 20), Yeats was drawn to Paris. He visited twice in the mid-1890s with important consequences for his work and thought. He made his first excursion to the Continent in February 1894. He stayed at the house of his occult protégé MACGREGOR MATHERS at 1 Avenue Duquesne and called on his expatriate darling MAUD GONNE, but the chief excitement of the trip was his brush with the flourishing subculture of French symbolism. Yeats missed his chance to meet Stéphane Mallarmé (*CL1* 381), who was traveling in England, but he did manage to pay a memorable visit to PAUL VERLAINE, as Yeats recounts in both AUTOBIOGRAPHIES (261–262) and the essay "Verlaine in 1894," which was published in the April 1896 issue of the SAVOY (see *UP1* 397–399). On February 26, Yeats and Gonne attended a performance of Villiers de l'Isle-Adam's (1838–89) five-hour epic of experimental drama *Axël* at the Théâtre de la Gâité. The play made an enormous impression on Yeats, and the following April he published a review in the *Bookman* (see *UP1* 320–325). For years to come, Yeats quoted, as the epitome of lofty disdain for the subeternal, his favorite line from the play: "As for living, our servants will do that for us" (IV, ii; see *Aut.* 236; *E&I* 296; *LE* 33, 153; *P&I* 112, 156; *UP2* 117; *AV* 42).

Yeats's second visit to the Continent, from early December 1896 to mid-January 1897, was in part motivated by the need to gather color for his novel *The* SPECKLED BIRD, which was to be set in the ARAN ISLANDS and in Paris (*CL2* 63, 71). Yeats visited Mathers and Gonne and continued his symbolist education. Accompanied by ARTHUR SYMONS, his erstwhile roommate and mentor in all things French, Yeats attended a performance of Alfred Jarry's (1873–1907) *Ubu Roi* on December 12 at the Théâtre de l'Œuvre. Amid a fist-shaking ruckus, Yeats cheered the controversial play, feeling "bound to support the most spirited party," but he returned to his hotel in a dispirited mood, intuiting in the evening's performance a resurgence of "comedy" and "objectivity" (*Aut.* 265–266). Pondering the satirical tenor of the play, Yeats is moved to one of the most arresting flights of rhetoric in *Autobiographies*: "After Stéphane Mallarmé, after Paul Verlaine, after Gustave Moreau, after Puvis de Chavannes, after our own verse, after all our subtle colour and nervous rhythm, after the faint mixed tints of Conder, what more is possible? After us the Savage God" (266). Several days later, on the evening of December 17, Yeats and Symons ingested hashish pellets and then attended a gathering at the house of Symons's friend, the critic and translator Henry Davray (1873–1944), who had published translations of Yeats's poem "The Sad Shepherd" and his story-essay "The Untiring Ones" the previous July (*Biblio.* 433; *CL2* 13). There was wild talk and dancing. Yeats was "very anxious" to join in the dancing, but he could not remember any steps. He recalls sitting down and closing his eyes and hoping to experience a vision, but he experienced only "a sensation of some dark shadow which seemed to be telling me that some day I would go into a trance and so out of my body for a while, but not yet" (*E&I* 281; see also *Aut.* 264–265; *CL2* 66). It was Yeats's first drug experience but not his last. During the next two years he experimented occasionally with mescal and hashish (*AM* 178; *CL2* 66), and in March 1907 he offered to send Gonne an unidentified "wonderful powder" with hallucinogenic properties (*CL4* 637).

The most eventful incident of this second Parisian sojourn, however, was making the acquaintance of J. M. SYNGE on December 21 at the Hôtel Corneille, where both were lodging. Dismayed that the young Irishman was wasting his evident talent writing "morbid and melancholy verse," Yeats urged him to visit the ARAN ISLANDS, where he might "find a life that had never been expressed in literature" (*Aut.* 262–263; for different versions of the same anecdote see *E&I* 299, 325; *Mem.* 104–105). Synge eventually took Yeats's advice, with famous results.

Yeats's first two Parisian adventures confirmed his symbolist sympathies and helped lay the ground for symbolist-inspired plays like *The* SHADOWY WATERS and the symbolist-inspired essays that were to appear in *Ideas of Good and Evil* (1903). Yeats made numerous subsequent trips to France, but none as exhilarating and seminal as his first two.

Bibliography

Foster, R. F. *W. B. Yeats: A Life, I: The Apprentice Mage*; Wade, Allan. *A Bibliography of the Writings of W. B. Yeats*; Yeats, W. B. *Autobiographies, The Collected Letters of W. B. Yeats* (vols. 1–2, 4), *Essays and Introductions, Later Essays, Memoirs, Prefaces and Introductions, Uncollected Prose by W. B. Yeats* (vols. 1–2), *A Vision*.

Parnell, Charles Stewart (1846–1891) Champion of the Irish home rule movement until his fall from power and grace in 1890, Parnell was for Yeats an enduring symbol of the "subjective" personality type. Such men are solitary, proud, turbulent, tragic, and essentially aristocratic; they draw life from the "whole body" and make the closest possible approach to UNITY OF BEING (*Aut.* 167–168; *VP* 835). Their solitude, however, is inevitably an affront to the mobbism of the crowd. Born out of phase, they are "dragged" down ("PARNELL'S FUNERAL") or "beaten down" ("The FISHERMAN"). Yeats was haunted by Parnell's life and death, as imaginatively construed by himself, less as a chapter in Irish political history than as a parable of the subjective man sacrificed upon the altar of an objective age. At the same time, and with equal mythic resonance, Yeats conceived Parnell as the "last great figure" of Protestant Ireland, the last in a line descending from Edmund Burke (1729–97), Henry Grattan (1746–1820), and JONATHAN SWIFT, the heroes of Yeats's late-found Georgianism (*Aut.* 311; *Expl.* 336).

Parnell's father, John Henry Parnell (1811–59), was a Protestant landowner with a large if debt-

Charles Stewart Parnell, the "uncrowned king of Ireland," addressing a meeting of the Irish Land League, ca. 1881 *(Library of Congress)*

ridden estate in Wicklow; his mother, the former Delia Tudor (1816–96), was the daughter of an admiral in the American navy. According to one of his biographers, Parnell inherited from his father "an essentially decent reformist liberalism" and from his mother "a vague (and inconsistent) American republicanism" (*C. S. Parnell* 5). Parnell inherited the family estate, Avondale, upon his father's death in 1859. After being sent down from Cambridge for drunken brawling in 1869, he took up as a country squire, but a life of hunting, cricket, and estate management left him restless (*Charles Stewart Parnell* 83). Politics was the natural outlet for Parnell's energetic and practical nature. He commenced his political career in 1875 by winning a seat in Parliament for Meath (he held this seat until 1880, and was then elected for Cork city). With little delay, he assumed leadership of the home rule and land reform movements, becoming president of the Home Rule Confederation of Great Britain in 1877 and president of the Irish National Land League in 1879. In 1880 he assumed leadership of the Irish Parliamentary Party (the home rule delegation in Parliament) and came to be known as the "uncrowned king of Ireland" (*C. S. Parnell* 35–36).

In 1880, as well, Parnell met Katharine "Kitty" O'Shea (1845–1921), a 35-year-old Englishwoman who had been separated from her Irish husband, Captain William Henry O'Shea (1840–1905), since 1875. Parnell and O'Shea fell in love and remained devoted to each other until Parnell's death. Despite the risk to his reputation, Parnell made a second home at O'Shea's villa in Kent and fathered three children, two of whom survived infancy. Captain O'Shea, himself a member of Parliament, did not mind exploiting—even blackmailing—Parnell for his own benefit and turned a blind eye on his wife's liaison (77). Parnell's downfall began on Christmas Eve, 1889, when Captain O'Shea, no longer a member of Parliament and thus no longer in need of Parnell's patronage, filed for divorce. O'Shea's hand had been freed by the death of his wife's nonagenarian aunt in May 1889. He had long hoped for a share of his wife's inheritance, but in the end he was cut out of the will (110–111). The divorce suit named Parnell as "co-respondent" (i.e., formally charged him with adultery) and ignited a political scandal in both Britain and Ireland. Under pressure from Gladstone's Liberal Party, the Irish Parliamentary Party opened debate on Parnell's leadership at a meeting on December 1, 1890 (117–118). The debate turned acrimonious and the party split into bitterly opposed Parnellite and anti-Parnellite factions, with the latter in the majority. On December 3, the Catholic hierarchy called for the repudiation of Parnell, and there commenced a "frenzy of detraction," in Yeats's retrospective phrase (*VP* 818). On December 4, 1890, Yeats, who had not yet discerned in Parnell the stuff of myth, breezily commented on the unfolding controversy in a letter to John O'Leary: "This Parnell business is most exciting. Hope he will hold on, as it is he has driven up into dust & vacuum no end of insincerities. The whole matter of Irish politics will be the better of it" (*CL1* 237; see also 242).

Katharine O'Shea did not contest the suit, and her husband was granted a divorce on November 17, 1890. Parnell and O'Shea married on June 25, 1891, but by then Parnell's power had collapsed and his health was in decline. He died in Brighton on October 6 of kidney disease and heart failure. MAUD GONNE, as it happened, was on the boat that returned Parnell's body to Ireland. Yeats met the boat at Kingston Pier. Though he would make Parnell's funeral the subject of one his most ambitious late poems, Yeats did not attend, for in those days he had hated crowds and "what crowds implied" (*Mem.* 47; *VP* 834). That evening, however, Gonne brought news of the event (*VP* 834). Yeats wrote his sister Lily (1866–1949) on October 11 and relayed the substance of Gonne's report: "The Funeral is just over. The people are breathing fire & slaughter. The wreathes have such inscriptions as 'Murdered by the Priests' & a number of Wexford men were heard by man I know promising to remove a Bishop & seven priests before next sunday. Tomorrow will bring them cooler heads I doubt not" (*CL1* 265). In the days following Parnell's death, Yeats wrote a formal elegy titled "Mourn—And Then Onward," which appeared in *United Ireland* on October 10, 1891, and in the *Irish Weekly Independent* on May 20, 1893 (see *VP* 737–738). The poem was a "success," according to Yeats, but all the same he chose not to reprint it (*CL1* 265).

If Parnell's downfall was a tragedy, the nation's disillusioned and embittered recoil from parliamentary politics, according to Yeats, created an opportunity for a new kind of cultural expression and a new kind of nationalism (*Aut.* 410). As Yeats explains in his introduction to *The WORDS UPON THE WINDOW-PANE*, "The fall of Parnell had freed imagination from practical politics, from agrarian grievance and political enmity, and turned it to imaginative nationalism, to Gaelic, to the ancient stories, and at last to lyrical poetry and to drama" (*Expl.* 343; *VPl.* 957). Yeats similarly observes in his introduction to *FIGHTING THE WAVES* that when "Parnell was dragged down, his shattered party gave itself up to nine years' vituperation, and Irish imagination fled the sordid scene" (*Expl.* 372; *VPl.* 568; see also *UP2* 185–186, 321). Thus

began the wave of broadly cultural rather than explicitly political activity that coalesced as the Irish Renaissance.

Yeats's chief poetic testaments to Parnell are "Parnell's Funeral" and "TO A SHADE," the former a brilliantly dense synthesis of mythological, historical, political, and cultural theories, the latter at once a bitter broadside and a tender ministration. During the 1920s and 1930s, Yeats published a spate of poems in which Parnell figures: "Come Gather Round Me, Parnellites" (1937), "Parnell" (1938), "Three Marching Songs" (1939), "The Three Monuments" (1927), and "Three Songs to the Same Tune" (1934). Both "Come Gather Round Me, Parnellites" (1937) and the essay "Parnell" (1937) were written at the urging of Henry Harrison (1867–1954), an old acquaintance who paid Yeats a call at RIVERSDALE in 1936. As Yeats told DOROTHY WELLESLEY, Harrison had become an ardent follower of Parnell while an OXFORD undergraduate some 50 years earlier. He had written *Parnell Vindicated: The Lifting of the Veil* (1931) in defense of Parnell, but the Irish Catholic press had ignored the book, as it "preferred to think that the Protestant had deceived the Catholic husband" (*Letters* 864–865; *LOP* 93). Harrison begged Yeats to "write something in verse or prose to convince all Parnellites that Parnell had nothing to be ashamed of in [O'Shea's] love." Yeats's essay puffs Harrison's book and briefly catalogs the main facts of the divorce controversy. He lingers on Captain O'Shea, however, detecting "something interesting there" but unsure how to make sense of a man who had been both a blackmailer and "such a dashing figure that a Cabinet Minister considering a duel consults him upon the point of honour" (*E&I* 489; *LE* 87).

In *A VISION*, Yeats assigns Parnell to Phase 10 of the lunar cycle. A man of this phase suffers "a kind of burning restraint, a something that suggests a savage statue to which one offers sacrifice. This sacrifice is code, personality no longer perceived as power only. He seeks by its help to free the creative power from mass emotion, but never wholly succeeds, and so the life remains troubled, a conflict between pride and race, and passes from crisis to crisis" (123).

Bibliography

Bew, Paul. *C. S. Parnell*; Foster, R. F. *Charles Stewart Parnell: The Man and his Family*; Yeats, W. B. *Autobiographies, The Collected Letters of W. B. Yeats* (vol. 1), *Essays and Introductions, Explorations, Later Essays, The Letters of W. B. Yeats, Letters on Poetry from W. B. Yeats to Dorothy Wellesley, Memoirs, Uncollected Prose by W. B. Yeats* (vol. 2), *The Variorum Edition of the Plays of W. B. Yeats, The Variorum Edition of the Poems of W. B. Yeats, A Vision.*

Pollexfen, George (1839–1910)   The Yeats and the Pollexfen families were brought together by the schoolboy friendship of JOHN BUTLER YEATS and George Pollexfen. They met in 1851 while both were students at the Atholl Academy on the Isle of Man. "I had been extraordinarily fond of him at school where I was passive in his hands," the elder Yeats recalls in *Early Memories: Some Chapters of Autobiography* (1923). "I have sometimes an amused curiosity in thinking whether he cared for me at all, or how much he cared, but it has been only curiosity" (85). In September 1862, John Butler Yeats visited his old school friend at his home in SLIGO. There he met George's sister Susan, whom he would marry a year later (see SUSAN YEATS). In early life, Pollexfen was a renowned steeple-chaser and horseman, in later life a Freemason, astrologer, mystic, and hypochondriac. JBY remembers that "on a race-course, above all if mounted on a wild and splendid race-horse, [Pollexfen] was a transformed being. Puritanism was shattered, torn away, a mere rage of antidiluvianism" (18). A bachelor, Pollexfen worked for the family's shipping firm and became a partner in 1884 (AM 9). He returned to Sligo in 1882 after tending to the family interests in Ballina, and thereupon grew "sluggish and contemplative," as Yeats writes in "IN MEMORY OF MAJOR ROBERT GREGORY."

Though in later years they were estranged—the elder Yeats's chosen life of aesthetic vagabondism apparently at issue—JBY remained fascinated by his boyhood friend (*Early Memories* 97). To a curious degree *Early Memories* dwells on Pollexfen, drawing a fascinated, affectionate, interrogative portrait. Pollexfen, JBY recalls, "saw human nature sorrowfully, and with little hope. It only enhanced

his tenderness, which was like that of a nurse by the bedside of a sick man, and veritably there were times when thinking about this benighted and lost human nature he was like a tender mother with a fractious child: yet never did he lose his sense of proportion, or his sense of fact, or his mirthfulness" (14). JBY characterizes Pollexfen as a man free of the vulgarity of opinions, a type of the solitary man who nourishes himself "on the indwelling spirit of brooding truth." In this respect he was reminiscent of J. M. SYNGE and "the great Russian writers" (22). It was this saturnine and taciturn aspect of the Pollexfen personality that prompted JBY to exclaim over his son's first stirrings of poetic genius, "Behold I have given a tongue to the sea-cliffs" (20). And yet Pollexfen was afflicted with what JBY calls the family Puritanism, the "combination of selfishness and religion" that results in reverence for success and explains the pride and pleasure he took in his famous nephew. "An applauded poet is better after all than a rich trader, a more conspicuous success," the elder Yeats reflects. "He would have liked to have kept him always with him, that he might watch over him as he did over his race-horses" (98).

Like his father, the younger Yeats was a lifelong ponderer of Pollexfen's quirks and charms, which he chronicles in "IN MEMORY OF ALFRED POLLEXFEN" and "In Memory of Major Robert Gregory," as well as in AUTOBIOGRAPHIES. As a young man, Yeats regularly visited Sligo and found a second home under his uncle's roof. Yeats recalls that Pollexfen lived in a "little house" in town, and later in "a little house about a quarter of a mile into the country" (Thorn Hill), while during the summer he vacationed in a "little house" at nearby Rosses Point (*Aut.* 83, 206–207). Yeats's lengthiest stay stretched from October 1894 to May 1895. As he recalls in MEMOIRS, "It was during this long visit that my friendship with my uncle become very close. He never treated me quite as a grown man and had the selfishness of an old bachelor—I remember still with a little resentment that if there was but one kidney with the bacon at breakfast he always took it without apology—and he complained continually of his health. I took all this as part of [a] character I could not imagine different, and began to think of his house very much as one thinks of home" (79). Significantly, Pollexfen was the only relation who shared Yeats's occult and astrological interests, and in December 1893 he joined the HERMETIC ORDER OF THE GOLDEN DAWN (AM 104). In *Autobiographies*, Yeats remembers Pollexfen as the confidant of his "boyish freaks and reveries" and recounts their collaboration in various telekinetic experiments (84, 207–214).

Pollexfen died of stomach cancer in September 1910. He left an estate of £50,000, of which £920 went to Yeats (AM 432; *Letters* 551–554). Pollexfen's funeral is remembered in "In Memory of Alfred Pollexfen." The poem describes how "Masons drove from miles away / To scatter the Acacia spray / Upon a melancholy man / Who had ended where his breath began" (see also *Letters* 553). R. F. Foster comments on Pollexfen's demise, "With him went—for the Yeatses—the last vestige of Pollexfen Sligo" (AM 431).

Bibliography

Foster, R. F. *W. B. Yeats: A Life, I: The Apprentice Mage*; Yeats, John Butler. *Early Memories: Some Chapters of Autobiography*; Yeats, W. B. *Autobiographies, The Letters of W. B. Yeats, Memoirs*.

Pollexfen, William (1811–1892)   Yeats's maternal grandfather was from Brixham in Devonshire. He ran away to sea at age 12 and by 1833 owned his own ship (*Aut.* 43–44). He arrived in SLIGO in 1833 to visit his cousin Elizabeth (1798–1853), who had been left a widow after her husband, William Middleton (ca. 1770–1832), head of the Sligo Steam Navigation Company, died of cholera (43). In 1837, Pollexfen married Elizabeth's daughter (1819–92), who was also named Elizabeth, and took over the family firm with his brother-in-law William Middleton (1820–82). The shipping business was later augmented by a milling company called Middleton and Pollexfen. Yeats spent a good deal of his childhood at Merville, Pollexfen's large and elegant house in Sligo, making a six-month stay in 1869 and a two-year stay beginning in 1872. In AUTOBIOGRAPHIES, Yeats recalls that the "house was so big that there was always a room to hide in" (41). The opening pages of *Autobiographies* portray

Pollexfen as a romantic old sea-dog, replete with a "great scar" on his hand from a whaling hook. "He was never unkind," Yeats recalls, "and I cannot remember that he ever spoke harshly to me, but it was the custom to fear and admire him." Epitomizing his grandfather's rugged integrity, Yeats remembers that he "had great physical strength and had the reputation of never ordering a man to do anything he would not do himself," and he adds, "Even to-day when I read *King Lear* his image is always before me, and I often wonder if the delight in passionate men in my plays and in my poetry is more than his memory" (42–43). Yeats mentions Pollexfen in four poems: "ARE YOU CONTENT?," "IN MEMORY OF ALFRED POLLEXFEN," "INTRODUCTORY RHYMES" to *Responsibilities*, and "UNDER SATURN." In "Introductory Rhymes," Yeats, having reached middle age without perpetuating the family name, addresses his grandfather as "silent and fierce old man" and asks for his pardon "most of all," for his example had awoken Yeats's childhood fancy and prompted his realization that "only the wasteful virtues earn the sun."

Bibliography

Yeats, W. B. *Autobiographies*.

Pound, Ezra (1885–1972)   The expatriate American poet was many things to Yeats: a fellow architect of modernism; a fellow student of Asia; an amanuensis, housemate, and fencing partner; a standard bearer and a cautionary tale. Most of all, he was a provocateur whose unruly energy and omnivorous intellect were, for some three decades, a bracing challenge to Yeats's own thought and work. Twenty years Yeats's junior, Pound arrived in London on August 14, 1908, determined to meet Yeats, whom he adulated as the "greatest living poet" (*Selected Letters* 7–8). Pound had little to recommend him beyond bravado, but he rapidly gained a foothold in London literary circles as an attendee of the Poet's Club and the Irish Literary Society (see NATIONAL LITERARY SOCIETY). Yeats was then in Dublin, but Pound insinuated himself into his London circle, getting to know FLORENCE FARR, the publisher Elkin Matthews (1851–1921), T. STURGE MOORE, and most of the available alumni of the RHYMERS' CLUB (*Stone Cottage* 11). In January 1909, OLIVIA SHAKESPEAR, Yeats's erstwhile lover and his most intimate London friend, invited Pound to tea at her house in Kensington. Pound became a pet of both Shakespear and her daughter Dorothy (1886–1973), whom Pound married in 1914 with the grudging consent of her parents. In May, Shakespear brought Pound to meet Yeats at WOBURN BUILDINGS, and thereafter Pound was a bumptious and overbearing mainstay of Yeats's "Monday evenings" (*I&R*, I, 42; *Man and Poet* 167; *Serious Character* 119; *Stone Cottage* 11–12). In a December 1909 letter to Lady GREGORY, Yeats referred to "this queer creature Ezra Pound, who has become really a great authority on the troubadours, has I think got closer to the right sort of music for poetry than Mrs. Emery [Florence Farr]—it is more definitely music with strongly

Portrait of Ezra Pound, by Alvin Langdon Coburn (1882–1966). The photograph, taken on October 22, 1913, served as the frontispiece of Pound's *Lustra* (1916) and later appeared in Coburn's *More Men of Mark* (1922). *(New York Public Library)*

marked time and yet it is effective speech. However he can't sing as he has no voice. It is like something on a very bad phonograph" (*Letters* 543).

Yeats and Pound rapidly moved toward a collaborative relationship, each goading the other toward a style that was leaner and more concrete—in a word, more modern. In one dubious but commonplace version of the tale, Pound dispelled the lingering mists of the nineties and rescued Yeats for the 20th century. Yeats encouraged this impression by frequently acknowledging his dependence on Pound's modernist instinct (he liked the idea of young men in garrets outmoding the older generation, even when he represented the older generation). Yeats most famously puffed Pound's modernism at a 1914 banquet that *Poetry* (the Chicago magazine that Pound served as "foreign correspondent") gave in Yeats's honor. "We rebelled against rhetoric," Yeats remarked in his after-dinner speech, "and now there is a group of younger poets who dare to call us rhetorical. When I returned to London from Ireland, I had a young man go over all my work with me to eliminate the abstract. This was an American poet, Ezra Pound" (*UP2* 414). In a 1924 postscript to his essay "William Blake and his Illustrations to the *Divine Comedy*" (1896), Yeats gives a similar account: "Some seven or eight years ago I asked my friend Mr. Ezra Pound to point out everything in the language of my poems that he thought an abstraction, and I learned from him how much further the movement against abstraction had gone than my generation had thought possible" (*E&I* 145). He told Lady Gregory: "[Pound] is full of the middle ages and helps me get back to the definite and the concrete away from modern abstractions. To talk over a poem with him is like getting you to put a sentence into dialect. All becomes clear and natural." He added, however, that in his own work Pound "is very uncertain, often very bad though very interesting sometimes. He spoils himself by too many experiments and has more sound principles than taste" (*AM* 476; *Man and Poet* 167).

The notion that Pound made a modern poet of Yeats has much to do with an incident of 1912. Yeats sent five poems for publication in the December issue of *Poetry*, and Pound took it upon himself to alter three ("FALLEN MAJESTY," "The MOUNTAIN TOMB," "TO A CHILD DANCING IN THE WIND"). Most significantly, he excised the limp qualifier "as it were" in the final line of "Fallen Majesty"; before Pound salvaged its greatness, the line read: "Once walked a thing that seemed, as it were, a burning cloud" (AM 475; IY 131; *Serious Character* 191). Yeats was initially "furious," but he recognized Pound's good judgment and forgave his effrontery (*Serious Character* 191).

In a 1910 letter, Pound assessed the lines of influence this way: "Yeats has been doing some new lyrics—he has come out of the shadows & has declared for life—of course there is in that a tremendous uplift for me—for he and I are now as it were in one movement with *aims* very nearly identical. That is to say the movement of the '90'ies [nineties] for drugs & the shadows has worn itself out. There has been no 'influence'—Yeats has found within himself spirit of the new air which I by accident had touched before him" (*Stone Cottage* 17). Pound's claim to priority is questionable, however. Reviewing *Responsibilities* (1914), Pound lauded a new "hardness of outline" in poems like "The MAGI," "NO SECOND TROY," and "SEPTEMBER 1913," but Yeats had been in pursuit of this "hardness" long before Pound arrived in London (*Literary Essays* 379–380). Remarking on his essay collection *Ideas of Good and Evil* in a 1903 letter to JOHN QUINN, for example, Yeats announced his intention to remake his work: "The book is, I think, too lyrical, too full of aspirations after remote things, too full of desires. Whatever I do from this out will, I think, be more creative. I will express myself so far as I can express myself in criticism at all by that sort of thought that leads straight to action, straight to some form of craft" (*CL3* 372). In a note to *In the Seven Woods* (1904), Yeats similarly mentions a "change that may bring a less dream-burdened will" into his verse, while poems like "ADAM'S CURSE," "The FOLLY OF BEING COMFORTED," and "IN THE SEVEN WOODS" attest that this change was already afoot (VP 814). In a 1904 letter to GEORGE RUSSELL (AE), Yeats speaks of struggling to defeat his own tendency toward "sentament [sic] & sentimental sadness & a womanish introspection," and ends his spontaneous manifesto with a rallying cry:

"We possess nothing but the will & we must never let the children of vague desire breathe upon it nor the waters of sentiment rust the terrible mirror of its blade. [. . .] Let us have no emotions, however abstract, in which there is not an athletic joy" (*CL3* 577–578). Indeed, Yeats had begun to dispense with the "children of vague desires" before the "nineties" had even begun. In an 1888 letter to KATHARINE TYNAN, Yeats announced what amounts to a program of self-modernization: "I have noticed some things about my poetry [. . .] for instance that it is almost all a flight into fairy land, from the real world, and a summons to that flight. [. . .] That is not the poetry of insight and knowledge but of longing and complaint—the cry of the heart against necessity. I hope some day to alter that and write poetry of insight and knowledge" (*CL1* 54–55).

Despite Pound's impudent fiddling with his verse, Yeats did Pound two good turns the following year. In August 1913, he proposed that the CUALA PRESS publish a selection of JOHN BUTLER YEATS's letters (*Letters* 583) and chose Pound to edit the volume, which was warmly received when it appeared in 1917 as *Passages from the Letters of John Butler Yeats*. Explaining the decision to turn the project over to Pound, Yeats told his father that he himself was "too familiar with the thought," and that Pound's "approval, representing as he does the most aggressive contemporary school of the young, would be of greater value than my approval, which would seem perhaps but family feeling" (607). Yeats continued to plump for Pound when, in November, *Poetry* selected "The GREY ROCK" as the best poem to appear in its pages that year. The magazine awarded Yeats a $250 prize. In a public letter, Yeats said that he would use £10 to commission a book-plate by T. Sturge Moore and proposed that the magazine settle the remaining £40 on Pound. Yeats's impulse was generous, but his endorsement of Pound was less than ringing: "I suggest him to you because, although I do not really like with my whole soul the metrical experiments he has made for you, I think those experiments show a vigorous creative mind. He is certainly a creative personality of some sort, though it is too soon yet to say of what sort. His experiments are perhaps errors, I am not certain; but I would always sooner give the laurel to vigorous errors than to any orthodoxy not inspired" (584–585).

The period of the poets' closest collaboration began in 1913, when they spent two months (November 10, 1913–January 16, 1914) as tenants of Stone Cottage, a six-room house near Coleman's Hatch in Sussex, an hour's train-ride from London. Pound acted as a paid part-time secretary to Yeats, who had trouble with his eyes. On the eve of the Stone Cottage experiment, Pound wrote to his mother with perhaps a nervous affectation of nonchalance: "My stay in Stone Cottage will not be in the least profitable. I detest the country. Yeats will amuse me part of the time and bore me to death with psychical research the rest. I regard the visit as a duty to posterity" (*Selected Letters* 25). Upon arrival at the cottage, however, the two poets settled into a mutually agreeable routine. On December 19, Pound wrote to William Carlos Williams, "Yeats is much finer *intime* than seen spasmodically in the midst of the whirl. We are both, I think, very contented in Sussex"; and in January he wrote to his mother, "I believe Sussex agrees with me quite nicely" (27, 30). The cooking was done for them. In Canto 83, Pound remembers that Yeats "would not eat ham for dinner / because peasants eat ham for dinner / despite the excellent quality / and the pleasure of having it hot"; he remembers too Yeats testing and shaping phrases as he was composing "The PEACOCK."

The poets kept themselves busy with reading and writing. Pound had just begun his exploration of China and Japan, with far-reaching consequences for both himself and Yeats. He arrived at Stone Cottage recently having received the papers of the American Orientalist Ernest Fenollosa (1853–1908), who had been a curator at the Boston Museum of Fine Arts. During his first winter in Stone Cottage Pound translated three Noh plays from Fenollosa's notes; improved on the translation of several Chinese poems he found in H. A. Giles's *History of Chinese Literature*; and read Confucius (*Stone Cottage* 39–42, 44–48). None of this activity was lost on Yeats, who would found his own mature drama on the Noh, following Pound's example. In his introduction to Pound's 1916 volume of Noh

translations, *Certain Noble Plays of Japan*, he writes, "I have written a little play [AT THE HAWK'S WELL] that can be played in a room for so little money that forty or fifty readers of poetry can pay the price. There will be no scenery, for three musicians, whose seeming sunburned faces will, I hope, suggest that they have wandered from village to village in some country of our dreams, can describe place and weather, and at moments action and accompany it all by drum and gong or flute and dulcimer. Instead of the players working themselves into a violence of passion indecorous in our sitting-room, the music, the beauty of form and voice all come to climax in pantomimic dance. In fact, with the help of Japanese plays 'translated by Ernest Fenollosa and finished by Ezra Pound,' I have invented a form of drama, distinguished, indirect, and symbolic, and having no need of mob or Press to pay its way—an aristocratic form" (*E&I* 221).

Yeats and Pound spent two further winters secluded in Stone Cottage (January 6 to March 1, 1915, and December 21, 1915, to March 6, 1916). Rounding out the cenacle was Dorothy Shakespear, whom Pound married on April 20, 1914. Yeats welcomed the presence of the young woman, writing to John Quinn in December 1915 that Pound "has a beautiful young wife who does the housekeeping & both treat me with the respect due to my years and so make me feel that it is agreeable to grow old" (*Stone Cottage* 184). Much of the second stay at Stone Cottage was devoted to reading EDWARD DOWDEN's seven-volume edition of WORDSWORTH (*Letters* 590), while much of the third stay was devoted to reading Walter Savage Landor (*Selected Letters* 89). In Canto 83, Pound remembers Yeats "hearing nearly all Wordsworth / for the sake of his conscience but / preferring Ennemosor on Witches"—a reference to Joseph Ennemoser's *The History of Magic* (1854). The poets' eclectic reading came to literary fruition in Pound's "Three Cantos" (1917) and Yeats's *PER AMICA SILENTIA LUNAE*. James Longenbach proposes these works "as the culmination and synthesis of three winters of collaborative research. Their range of reference is remarkably similar: Noh drama and Renaissance Neoplatonism figure largely in both, and each work contains passing references to most of the authors in the Stone Cottage curriculum—Doughty, Landor, Wordsworth, Browning, and Homer filtered through John Heydon or Henry More" (*Stone Cottage* 247). "Doughty" is Charles Doughty (1843–1926), whose *Travels in Arabia Deserta* (1888) gave color and detail to the fictional frame of *A VISION*; John Heydon (b. 1629) was an astrologer, alchemist, and occultist; Henry More (1614–87) was a Neoplatonic theologian and philosopher associated with the Cambridge Platonists (see ANIMA MUNDI).

Pound moved to PARIS in 1921 and to Rapallo, Italy, in late 1924. Hoping to recover his health, Yeats visited Rapallo several times during the late 1920s and early 1930s (February–March 1928, October 1928–April 1929, November 1929–July 1930, June 1934) and the poets remained entwined in each other's intellectual lives. "I see Ezra daily," Yeats wrote to Lady Gregory during his second stay. "We disagree about everything, but if we have not met for 24 hours he calls full of gloomy and almost dumb oppression" (*Serious Character* 463). *A Packet for Ezra Pound*, which Yeats finished in August 1929, reflects Yeats's renewed friendship with Pound (*Letters* 748). It consists of "Rapallo," an evocation of life in the Italian seaside village, with descriptions of Pound attempting to explain the scheme of *The Cantos* and feeding the neighborhood cats; two poems titled "Meditations on Death" (later titled "AT ALGECIRAS—A MEDITATION UPON DEATH" and "MOHINI CHATTERJEE"); "Introduction to 'A Vision,'" an account of the automatic writing sessions that gave rise to *A Vision*; and a letter to Pound, in which Yeats urges his friend to keep out of politics (the province of bankers, lawyers, and businessmen) and moots the central ideas of *A Vision*. The "packet" was published by the Cuala Press in August 1929, and republished (minus section VI of "Rapallo" and the two poems) as a preface to *A Vision* in October 1937. In "Rapallo" Yeats describes Pound as a man "whose art is the opposite of mine, whose criticism commends what I most condemn, a man with whom I should quarrel more than with anyone else if we were not united by affection" (*AV* 3). Yeats does not explain why Pound is the recipient of his "packet," but his teasing account of Pound trying to explain *The Cantos'* "mathematical structure" provides a hint. Where Pound had apparently failed in his effort to bring all experience within the single structure of a great fugue, Yeats would succeed, creating "a stylistic arrangement of experience" that allows him "to hold in a single thought reality and justice" (25). Pound did not appreciate Yeats's account; he thundered to a correspondent on April 14, 1936, "CONFOUND uncle Bill YEATS' paragraph on fuge [sic] blighter never knew WHAT a fugue was anyhow. More wasted ink due to his 'explanation', that you cd. mop up with a moose hide" (*BG* 419). He was still thundering in February 1939: "God damn Yeats's bloody paragraph. Done more to prevent people reading Cantos for what is *on the page* than any other one smoke screen" (*Selected Letters* 321).

Despite their shared enterprise as modernist rebels against the bankruptcy of the 20th century and the philistinism of the middle classes, Yeats and Pound were far from reflexive admirers of each other's work. Pound acknowledged Yeats as "the greatest living poet" as a matter of course, but in later life he could be an irascible and eccentric critic. In a September 1920 letter to William Carlos Williams, Pound dismissed Yeats as "faded," a bizarre judgment given the recent triumph of *The Wild Swans at Coole* (*Selected Letters* 158). During his 1934 visit to Rapallo, Yeats asked Pound to read the manuscript of *The KING OF THE GREAT CLOCK TOWER*. Pound gave his verdict in a single word: "Putrid" (*VPl.* 1310). The incident seems to have dispirited rather than angered Yeats. He could no longer ignore that he and Pound had fundamentally diverged. R. F. Foster suggests that this incident "marked the effective end of a long literary association and to a certain extent a personal friendship too" (*AP* 501). Yeats, in turn, never entirely reconciled himself to Pound's poetry. He admired *Hugh Selwyn Mauberly* (1920), which borrowed from his own tales of the 1890s (*AP* 381; *Stone Cottage* 171), but he had lasting qualms about *The Cantos*, the epochal poetic sequence that was Pound's lifework from 1915 onward. Yeats's introduction to *The Oxford Book of Modern Verse* (1936) includes his fullest comment on *The Cantos*. "Like other readers I discover at present merely exquisite or grotesque fragments," Yeats confesses. "[Pound] hopes to give the impression that all is living, that there are no edges, no convexities, nothing to check the flow; but can such a poem have a mathematical structure? Can impressions that are in part visual, in part metrical, be related like the notes of a symphony; has the author been carried beyond reason by a theoretical conception? His belief in his own conception is so great that since the appearance of the first Canto I have tried to suspend judgement" (LE 192–193; see also 109) Assessing Pound's work as a whole, Yeats finds "more style than form; at moments more style, more deliberate nobility and the means to convey it than in any contemporary poet known to me, but it is constantly interrupted, broken, twisted into nothing by its direct opposite, nervous obsession, nightmare, stammering confusion; he is an economist, poet, politician, raging at malignants with inexplicable characters and motives, grotesque figures out of a child's book of beasts. [. . .] Even where there is no interruption he is often content, if certain verses and lines have style, to leave unbridged transitions, unexplained ejaculations, that make his meaning unintelligible" (193). In his introduction to the anthology, Yeats notes that Pound, like Kipling, is "inadequately represented because too expensive even for an anthologist with the ample means the Oxford University Press puts at his disposal" (291). Yeats may not have minded. "I am tired," he wrote to DOROTHY WELLESLEY in September 1935. "I have spent the day reading Ezra Pound for the Anthology—a single strained attitude instead of passion, the sexless American professor for all his violence" (LOP 23).

Yeats was equally ambivalent about Pound's highly strung and sometimes incoherent right-wing politics, though he obviously shared Pound's reactionary impulse. In an April 1928 letter to Lady Gregory, Yeats reflected that Pound has "most of MAUD GONNE's opinions (political and economic) about the world in general, being what [Wyndham] Lewis calls 'the revolutionary simpleton.' The chief difference is that he hates Palgrave's Golden Treasury as she does the Free State Government, and thinks even worse of its editor than she does of President Cosgrave. He has even her passion for

cats and large numbers wait for him every night at a certain street corner knowing that his pocket is full of meat bones or chicken bones. They belong to the oppressed races" (Letters 739; cf. AV 5–6). The 1934 break between Yeats and Pound was undoubtedly a matter of wounded literary pride on both sides, but Yeats's account of the contretemps in his preface to The King of the Great Clock Tower suggests that politics played a part in his dismay. Yeats describes being taken aback as Pound violently denounced all modern statesmen except "Mussolini and that hysterical imitator of his Hitler" and pronounced Dublin a "reactionary hole" (VP 1310). Pound was equally and similarly dismissive of Yeats's occult preoccupations. He told John Quinn that Yeats "will be quite sensible till some question of ghosts or occultism comes up, then he is subject to a curious excitement, twists everything to his theory, usual quality of mind goes" (Selected Letters 141). Pound added that Maud Gonne was much the same way on matters of politics. The two poets agreed at least that Gonne's politics were the benchmark of incoherent fanaticism.

As a relatively late entrant in Yeats's life, Pound did not enter into Yeats's personal mythology as so many other protégés and friends did, whether in capacious retrospectives like "ALL SOULS' NIGHT," "COOLE PARK, 1929," "IN MEMORY OF MAJOR ROBERT GREGORY," and "The MUNICIPAL GALLERY REVISITED," or in Yeats's prose memoirs. Certainly Pound would have made a colorful addition. Yeats does not mention Pound in his poetry, and, A Packet for Ezra Pound aside, only occasionally in his prose.

Bibliography

Carpenter, Humphrey. A Serious Character: The Life of Ezra Pound; Ellmann, Richard. The Identity of Yeats; Foster, R. F. W. B. Yeats: A Life, I: The Apprentice Mage, II: The Arch-Poet; Jeffares, A. Norman. W. B. Yeats: Man and Poet; Longenbach, James. Stone Cottage: Pound, Yeats, and Modernism; Mikhail, E. H., ed. W. B. Yeats Interviews and Recollections (vol. 1); Pound, Ezra. Literary Essays of Ezra Pound, The Selected Letters of Ezra Pound, 1907–1941; Saddlemyer, Ann. Becoming George: The Life of Mrs W. B. Yeats; Yeats, W. B. The Collected Letters of W. B.

Yeats (vols. 1, 3), *Essays and Introductions, Later Essays, The Letters of W. B. Yeats, Letters on Poetry from W. B. Yeats to Dorothy Wellesley, Uncollected Prose by W. B. Yeats* (vol. 2), *The Variorum Edition of the Plays of W. B. Yeats, The Variorum Edition of the Poems of W. B. Yeats, A Vision.*

Pre-Raphaelitism   Pre-Raphaelitism was a principal expression of the romantic medievalism that flourished throughout the 19th century. Wearing on its sleeve its many inspirations—Arthurian legend, 14th- and 15th-century Italian painting, Dante, Keats, TENNYSON, John Ruskin—Pre-Raphaelitism spurned Victorian utilitarianism and academicism and strove to create an art of ceremonial beauty and spiritual vision.

Pre-Raphaelitism coalesced in 1848 with the founding of the Pre-Raphaelite Brotherhood, a coterie of like-minded artists that included William Holman Hunt (1827–1910), John Everett Millais (1829–96), and Dante Gabriel Rossetti (1828–82), and more peripherally James Collinson (1825–81), William Michael Rossetti (1829–1919, the group's only nonartist), Frederick George Stephens (1828–1907), and Thomas Woolner (1825–92). The group's name emphasized its opposition to Raphael and his followers, who, in the brotherhood's view, had corrupted the tradition of medieval art with their artificiality and extravagance. Imagining the brotherhood's first meeting in Millais's studio, Timothy Hilton suggests the intellectual temper of the group: "We can [. . .] be sure that the Brothers laid claim to some kind of bond between themselves and the Italian painters of the Quattrocento [15th century], in purpose if not in technique; and that they determined to approach nature with a freshness and directness of technique that was absent from academic painting of a conventional sort. They would have discussed their dislike of the classical and baroque traditions. Hunt would surely have talked about the principles behind [Ruskin's] *Modern Painters*. Rossetti would have talked of the poetic content of painting, and perhaps of the Nazarene-derived ideas he had learnt from [painter Ford Madox] Brown. They might—*might*—have talked of some moral and religious purpose" (*Pre-Raphaelites* 33). Despite initial resistance from the Royal

Academy and the press, the movement flourished. It added to its ranks painters like Edward Burne-Jones (1833–98), Arthur Hughes (1832–1915), Frederick Sandys (1829–1904), and J. W. Waterhouse (1849–1917), and, largely due to the prodigious enterprise of WILLIAM MORRIS, extended its influence to the full panoply of domestic and decorative art. Though foremost a movement in the visual arts, Pre-Raphaelitism also had an important literary dimension, as poets like Morris, Christina Rossetti (1830–94), and Dante Gabriel Rossetti attempted to achieve in print much the same intricate archaic beauty that had been achieved on canvas.

As an essentially reactionary, arch-romantic rebellion against modernity in its positivistic, materialistic, and naturalistic manifestations, Pre-Raphaelitism was an irresistible inspiration to the young Yeats. While studying painting at the Dublin Metropolitan School of Art and the Royal Hibernian Academy during the mid-1880s, Yeats was put off by the naturalistic philosophy that prevailed, longing instead for "pattern, for Pre-Raphaelitism, for an art allied to poetry" but he was too timid or uncertain to break with the schools or with the example of his father, the talented portrait artist JOHN BUTLER YEATS, who had turned away from the Pre-Raphaelitism of his own youth (*Aut.* 91). Yeats recalls that he sometimes remonstrated with his father, having "come to think the philosophy of his fellow-artists and himself [i.e., naturalism] a misunderstanding created by Victorian science" and hating science "with a monkish hate." However, he made little headway in these arguments: "[In] a moment I would unsay what I had said and pretend that I did not really believe it. My father was painting many fine portraits, Dublin leaders of the bar, college notabilities, or chance comers whom he would paint for nothing if he liked their heads; but all displeased me. In my heart I thought that only beautiful things should be painted, and that only ancient things and the stuff of dreams were beautiful. And I almost quarrelled with my father when he made a large water-colour, one of his finest pictures and now lost, of a consumptive beggar-girl" (92). In "Art and Ideas" (1914), Yeats remembers thinking as a young man that he "would be content to paint, like Burne-Jones and Morris under Rossetti's rule, the Union at OXFORD, to set up there the traditional images most moving to young men while the adventure of uncommitted life can still change all to romance, even though I should know that what I painted must fade from the walls" (*E&I* 347). Yeats's enthusiasm for Pre-Raphaelitism continued unabated well into his maturity. As he confesses in an introduction to a never-published edition of his work: "When I was thirty I thought the best of modern pictures were four or five portraits by Watts [. . .]; four or five pictures by Madox Brown; four or five early Millais; four or five Rossettis where there are several figures engaged in some dramatic action; and an indefinite number of engravings by WILLIAM BLAKE who was my particular study" (*E&I* vii; *LE* 217; see also *E&I* 346–347).

Yeats did not long endure as a painter, but Pre-Raphaelitism became a pervasive influence on his early poetry, and especially on the poetry of *The Wind Among the Reeds* (1899). Poems like "HE REMEMBERS FORGOTTEN BEAUTY" and "The Lover asks Forgiveness because of his Many Moods" (1895) strike the unmistakable Pre-Raphaelite note, combining archaic detail ("marble cities loud with tabors of old") and a mood of sensuous languor—"drugged melancholy" is the phrase Hilton uses to describe Rossetti's portraits of Jane Morris (*Pre-Raphaelites* 185). Yeats's allusions throughout the volume to the "dim heavy hair" of his beloved may borrow specifically from the later paintings of Rossetti, which delight in Jane Morris's luxuriant tresses. T. S. ELIOT comments that the "Yeats of the Celtic Twilight" was more accurately the "Yeats of the pre-Raphaelite twilight," and that Yeats was "by no means the least of the pre-Raphaelites." He calls *The SHADOWY WATERS* "one of the most perfect expressions of the vague enchanted beauty of that school: yet it strikes me—this may be an impertinence on my part—as the western seas descried through the back window of a house in Kensington, an Irish myth for [Morris's] Kelmscott Press" (*On Poetry and Poets* 300).

Bibliography

Eliot, T. S. *On Poetry and Poets*; Hilton, Timothy. *The Pre-Raphaelites*; Yeats, W. B. *Autobiographies, Essays and Introductions, Later Essays*.

Quinn, John (1870–1924) The eldest son of Irish immigrant proprietors of a flourishing bakery in Fostoria, Ohio, Quinn studied law at Georgetown and Harvard before embarking on a legal career in New York. Even as a teenager, Quinn had an improbable love for the literature and art of the avant-garde, and from roughly the turn of the century he devoted his keen mind, vast energy, and considerable salary to the cause of literary and artistic modernism. Biographer B. L. Reid writes that Quinn was "at once an authentic original, very much himself, self-made, and a representative of a species, perhaps a peculiarly American species: the driving, pragmatical, 'successful' man of affairs who finds that not enough, yearns for 'culture,' finds that not enough, yearns to make 'art' but has to content himself with a lesser order of usefulness, with knowing and having rather than making—the artist *manqué*" (*Man from New York* ix). As friend, patron, and collector, Quinn made himself indispensable to a panoply of major writers and artists that included, among many others, Joseph Conrad, T. S. ELIOT, Lady GREGORY, JAMES JOYCE, EZRA POUND, GEORGE RUSSELL (AE), ARTHUR SYMONS, JOHN BUTLER YEATS, and W. B. Yeats. Quinn was also a man of interesting romantic involvements; his intimates included FLORENCE FARR (see *CL4* 630), Lady Gregory, and May Morris (1862–1938), daughter of WILLIAM MORRIS.

Quinn's services took numerous forms: He secured American copyrights, arranged lectures and tours, provided legal and medical advice, negotiated with publishers, and provided those passing through New York with social introductions and comfortable accommodation in his apartments, first at 1 West 87th Street and later at 79 Central Park West. Even more important, he provided sometimes lifesaving infusions of cash in the process of assembling a monumental collection of contemporary manuscripts and paintings that was regrettably sold at auction, the manuscripts in 1923 and 1924, the paintings after Quinn's death. Quinn was one of the earliest, most discerning, and most courageous collectors of modern art, as he had to be, given his ample but not inexhaustible income as a self-employed lawyer. His 2,500-item collection, in which he invested some half a million dollars,

Yeats and John Quinn. Arnold Genthe (1869–1942) photographed the old friends in 1914, while Yeats was in New York. *(Library of Congress)*

would have made for a small but superlative modern museum (*Man from New York* 652, 661). His taste, as Reid writes, evolved over the course of his collecting career, moving "from the first basically literary impulse in the portraits of the writers, to the genetic and parochial affection for Irish painters and subjects, to Augustus John and the English, to the first tentative braveries of the Armory Show pictures [Quinn helped organize the famous 1913 exhibition], and then the swift settling upon the real love of Quinn's life, the School of PARIS, along with the effort to secure representative examples of the ancestors of that school" (652). Quinn's was one of the world's finest private collections of modern art; it was particularly well stocked with the work of Constantin Brancusi, André Derain, Raymond Duchamp-Villon, Jacob Epstein, Henry Gaudier-Brzeska, Augustus John, Gwen John, Walt Kuhn, Ernest Lawson, Henri Matisse, Pablo Picasso, Maurice Prendergast, Pierre Puvis de Chavannes, Odilon Redon, Georges Rouault, Henry Rousseau, George Russell, André Dunoyer de Segonzac, Georges Seurat, Jack B. Yeats, and John Butler Yeats. Masterpieces by Cézanne, Gauguin, and Van Gogh crowned the collection (653; for an illustrated catalog of Quinn's collection, see the 1926 memorial volume *John Quinn, 1870–1925, Collection of Paintings, Water Colors, Drawings & Sculpture*). Quinn's book and manuscript collection was a lesser love, but was no less prescient and discerning. It included, in draft, several modernist monuments—Eliot's *The Waste Land*, Joyce's *Ulysses*, SYNGE's *The Playboy of the Western World*— as well as nearly all of the work of Joseph Conrad and numerous works by Yeats. Between November 1923 and March 1924, Quinn auctioned his library item by item. A total of 12,096 items—including 272 items by Yeats—fetched $226,351.85 (see *The Complete Catalogue of the Library of John Quinn*).

Quinn made his first trip to Ireland in the summer of 1902, having already read Yeats's poetry and become interested in the Irish Renaissance. Before his arrival he had queried John Butler Yeats and Jack Yeats about the availability of their work and had sent Yeats, by way of self-introduction, a copy of William James's *Human Immortality* (CL3 119–120, 140; *Man from New York* 8). While in Dublin, Quinn purchased nearly a dozen paintings by Jack Yeats and a portrait of W. B. Yeats by John Butler Yeats. He additionally commissioned the elder Yeats to paint Douglas Hyde (1860–1949), JOHN O'LEARY, and AE. Recommended by his formidable intelligence and ready cash, Quinn met most of the leading figures of the movement, and he struck up genuine and lifelong friendships with the entire Yeats family, with Lady Gregory, and with AE (*Man from New York* 8). After returning to New York in mid-September, Quinn sent Yeats Alexander Tille's 1899 translation of *Thus Spake Zarathustra* (CL3 239; *Letters of John Quinn* 40). The gift set Yeats on the Nietzschean path and helped retire the Celtic Twilight. Yeats's appreciative response prompted a further gift of the first four volumes of *The Works of Friederick Nietzsche* in an edition edited by Tille and published by T. Fisher Unwin (313, 335). Yeats wrote to Quinn on March 20, 1903, "[Nietzsche] has been of particularly great service to me just now, because I am setting out to try & re-create an heroical ideal in manhood—in plays of old Irish life—" (335).

Quinn solidified his friendships on return visits to Dublin in August 1903 and October 1904, and he made his apartment available to Yeats as he came and went on his first lecture tour of AMERICA, which Quinn had proposed and arranged, from November 1903 to March 1904. Yeats felt at home in Quinn's apartment, for, as he wrote to Lady Gregory, "Jacks pictures & Russells & my fathers portrait of me pretty well cover the walls & look very well" (468). Quinn's relations with the Yeats family became quasi-familial when, in 1907, John Butler Yeats, aged 70, decided to try his luck in America. For the next 15 years Quinn performed a plainly filial role, seeing to the elder Yeats's domestic needs, escorting him about town, drumming up commissions, regularly reporting back to friends and family in Ireland, and, finally, attending to his deathbed. In addition, Quinn and the elder Yeats kept up a steady exchange of letters on artistic and philosophical topics.

Despite their shared solicitude for John Butler Yeats, Quinn and Yeats maintained an icy silence from 1909 to 1914, the only interruption in their warm if sometimes grumbling friendship. The contretemps concerned Quinn's mistress Dorothy Coates. "When Dorothy Coates had visited Paris," writes William F. Murphy, "she and Willie had become warm friends, and Willie had apparently carried his tales of conquest to Dublin. Miss Coates gave a different, self-serving account to Quinn, depicting Willie as the aggressor and would-be seducer and herself as a staunch pillar of mistressly fidelity" (PF 348). Yeats's diary entry for August 11, 1909, alludes to the rift. A letter from MAUD GONNE brought the news that "Quinn is offended at something I said or am said to have said to or about some friend of Quinn's. I do not think I can have said the things he complains of, whatever they are, but I know myself to be utterly indiscreet." The drama continues to unfold in an entry of August 19: "Have been to Dublin—saw Quinn and had whole thing out. Various incautious sayings of mine to a friend of his in Paris have been

made the foundation for an architecture of lies. As usual [. . .] I accepted the worst case possible against myself and did years' work of repentance in ten minutes. Quinn is between a bad woman and a good one and the bad can control nothing in her nature, least of all her imagination and her speech" (Mem. 227–228). Yeats returned to America in February 1914. Acting on the wishes of Coates, then deathly ill, Quinn immediately sent a note in which he offered to "let by-gones be by-gones" and the two old friends reconciled (Letters of John Quinn 135). By the following month Yeats was once again ensconced in Quinn's apartment. Later in the year Yeats and Quinn came to an arrangement for the upkeep of the elder Yeats, who was as blithely destitute as ever. It was agreed that Quinn would buy Yeats's manuscripts, and that Yeats would use the proceeds to support his father. In this manner, as Murphy writes, Quinn "acquired most WBY's original literary papers" (PF 433).

Quinn performed his most dramatic service on behalf of the Irish Renaissance when he rushed to the defense of the ABBEY THEATRE players after they were arrested in Philadelphia on January 18, 1912, in the middle of their first tour of America. The charges were performing an "immoral or indecent play"—specifically, The Playboy of the Western World. In Lady Gregory's telling, Quinn made a dramatic entrance in the middle of the trial and made mincemeat of several complainants, eliciting from one witness the declaration that a "theatre is no place for a sense of humour" (Our Irish Theatre 123–124). During this tour, as well, Quinn and Lady Gregory began their discrete autumnal romance, which continued to flicker during Lady Gregory's return visit to America in 1913 and her two visits in 1915. She and Quinn never saw each other again, but they maintained a fond friendship and regularly corresponded (Lady Gregory 229–233, 246, 248).

Yeats's published work mentions Quinn only briefly and passingly, but the dedication of The Trembling of the Veil (1922), the second installment in what would become AUTOBIOGRAPHIES, is to the point: "To John Quinn / My Friend and Helper / And Friend and Helper of Certain People / Mentioned in this Book" (Aut. 110; see also Letters 682;

Letters of John Quinn 280). Upon Quinn's death from liver cancer in 1924, Yeats sent an informal eulogy to the poet and journalist Jeanne Robert Foster, who had been Quinn's companion from 1918: "I have known no other man so full to overflowing with energy & benevolence & these always arising out of his nature like a fountain & having the quality of his nature. I mean his benevolence expressed him as a work of art expresses the artist. I, as you know, have great cause for gratitude to him on my own & on my fathers [sic] account. The lecture tour he arranged for me many years ago brought me the first substantial sum I ever earned. To that tour he must have given daily thought for weeks or rather months. All this week [of the Tailteann Games] I have been wishing that he had seen Dublin with all its flags, & the joyous crowds (war & civil war put away at last) as it has been for the last few days. He did his share to bring it all about" (AP 276).

Quinn's correspondence is collected in *The Letters of John Quinn to William Butler Yeats* (1983), *Too Long a Sacrifice: The Letters of Maud Gonne and John Quinn* (1999), and *On Poetry, Painting, and Politics: The Letters of May Morris and John Quinn* (1997). Quinn and Morris conducted a long-distance romance between 1910 and 1917. Morris clearly hoped for marriage, but Quinn, wed to his comfortable bachelorhood, kept her at a distance and, as she frankly admitted, broke her heart (*On Poetry, Painting and Politics* 82, 166).

Bibliography

Foster, R. F. *W. B. Yeats: A Life, II: The Arch-Poet*; Gonne, Maud, and John Quinn. *Too Long a Sacrifice: The Letters of Maud Gonne and John Quinn*; Gregory, Lady. *Our Irish Theatre*; Kohfeldt, Mary Lou. *Lady Gregory: The Woman behind the Irish Renaissance*; Morris, May, and John Quinn. *On Poetry, Painting, and Politics: The Letters of May Morris and John Quinn*; Murphy, William M. *Prodigal Father: The Life of John Butler Yeats (1839–1922)*; Quinn, John. *The Letters of John Quinn to William Butler Yeats*, "Introduction" in *Complete Catalogue of the Library of John Quinn Sold by Auction in Five Parts (with Printed Prices)* (vols. 1–2); Reid, B. L. *The Man from New York: John Quinn and His Friends*; Watson, Forbes. "Introduction" in *John Quinn, 1870–1925, Collection of Paintings, Water Colors, Drawings & Sculpture*; Yeats, W. B. *Autobiographies*, *The Collected Letters of W. B. Yeats* (vols. 3–4), *The Letters of W. B. Yeats*, *Memoirs*.

realism   Yeats's prose adverts constantly to the opposition between realism (or naturalism) and traditions of imagination, whether embodied in Asian art and drama, philosophical idealism of the kind theorized by George Berkeley (1685–1753), romanticism, symbolism, or PRE-RAPHAELITISM. In a 1937 note that became the introduction to *Essays and Introductions* (1961), Yeats associates this tradition with a "table of values, heroic joy always, intellectual curiosity and so on—and a public theme: in Japan the mountain scenery of China; in Greece its cyclic tales; in Europe the Christian mythology," while realism is "always topical" and has "for public theme the public itself" (*E&I* viii–ix). In "Certain Noble Plays of Japan" (1916) he says of realism that it "is created for the common people and was always their peculiar delight, and it is the delight to-day of all those whose minds, educated by schoolmasters and newspapers, are without the memory of beauty and emotional subtlety" (227). He was particularly hostile to realism in its theatrical manifestations, as it touched on the affairs of his own theater. In *A VISION*, he complains in the fictive voice of Daniel O'Leary that "a few years before the Great War the realists drove the last remnants of rhythmical speech out of the theatre." During a performance of *Romeo and Juliet* rendered in "kitchen gabble," O'Leary throws his boots at the actors, a protest with much of Yeats's own sentiment in it (33–34; cf. *UP1* 322–323).

With varying degrees of hostility, Yeats leveled the charge of realism against a wide array of writers and artists, including Arnold Bennett (1867–1931), John Galsworthy (1867–1933), Thomas Hardy (1840–1928), Henrik Ibsen (1828–1906), GEORGE MOORE, George Bernard Shaw (1856–1950), H. G. Wells (1866–1946), and Emile Zola (1840–1902). In *AUTOBIOGRAPHIES*, Yeats makes the French painters Carolus Duran (1837–1917) and Jules Bastien-Lepage (1848–84) his recurrent symbols of flaccid naturalism. In later life, he associated realism with fellow modernists like JAMES JOYCE, EZRA POUND, and Marcel Proust (1871–1922), who attempted to represent consciousness with the same meticulous fidelity that more conventional realists had brought to the representation of the social and natural worlds, though Yeats acknowledges that a writer like Joyce "differs from Arnold Bennett and Galsworthy, let us say, because he can isolate the human mind and its vices as if in eternity" (*Expl.* 333; see also *E&I* 405). Yeats's most fraught antagonism was directed against his own father, JOHN BUTLER YEATS, a talented portrait artist. In *AUTOBIOGRAPHIES*, Yeats describes his anguish after his father turned away from the Pre-Raphaelitism of his younger days: "My father was painting many fine portraits, Dublin leaders of the bar, college notabilities, or chance comers whom he would paint for nothing if he liked their heads; but all displeased me. In my heart I thought that only beautiful things should be painted, and that only ancient things and the stuff of dreams were beautiful. And I almost quarrelled with my father when he made a large water-colour, one of his finest pictures and now lost, of a consumptive beggar-girl" (92; see also 114).

Yeats theorizes his critique of realism in "Pages from a Diary Written in Nineteen Hundred and Thirty" (1944), writing that he would "found literature on the three things which Kant thought we must postulate to make life livable—Freedom, God, Immortality. The fading of these three before 'Bacon, Newton, Locke' has made literature decadent. Because Freedom is gone we have Stendhal's 'mirror dawdling down a lane'; because God has gone we have realism, the accidental, because Immortality is gone we can no longer write those tragedies which have always seemed to me alone legitimate—those that are a joy to the man who dies" (*Expl.* 332–333). In the system of *A Vision*, Yeats associates realism with Phase 22 of his lunar cycle. In Yeats's characterization of this phase, "There is no longer a desired object, as distinct from thought itself, no longer a *Will*, as distinct from the process of nature seen as fact; and so thought itself, seeing that it can neither begin nor end, is stationary. Intellect knows itself as its own object of desire; and the *Will* knows itself to be the

world; there is neither change nor desire of change. For the moment the desire for a form has ceased and an absolute realism becomes possible" (163).

Yeats's fine short poem "The REALISTS" ironically articulates the spiritual defeatism of the realistic school.

Bibliography
Yeats, W. B. *Autobiographies, Essays and Introductions, Explorations, Uncollected Prose by W. B. Yeats* (vol. 1), *A Vision*.

Red Hanrahan   See STORIES OF RED HANRAHAN.

Rhymers' Club   Made legendary by Yeats's reminiscences in *AUTOBIOGRAPHIES*, the Rhymers' Club was a clique of young writers and poets who met for weekly poetry reading, discussion, and debate, from early 1890 to 1894, in an upper room at the Old Cheshire Cheese, a pub in Wine Office Court off Fleet Street in London (CL1 217). "[Our] rule was to sup downstairs then climb to a smoking-room at the top of the house, which we looked upon as the Club sanctum," Ernest Rhys recalls. "There

Ye Olde Cheshire Cheese, ca. 1914. The Fleet Street pub was the haunt on the Rhymers' Club during the 1890s. *(Library of Congress)*

we smoked long clays or churchwardens, and cigarettes, and every man had a lyric or piece of verse in his pocket, which he read out, and we criticized afterwards" (I&R, I, 36). In *Autobiographies,* Yeats remembers that the meetings were "decorous and often dull," and that the members criticized each other's work "too politely for the criticism to have great value" (233). He mentions as regular attendees John Davidson (1857–1909), Ernest Dowson (1867–1900), Edwin Ellis (1848–1916), Selwyn Image (1849–1930), LIONEL JOHNSON, Richard Le Gallienne (1866–1947), Victor Plarr (1863–1929), Ernest Radford (1857–1919), Ernest Rhys (1859–1946), T. W. Rolleston (1857–1920), and John Todhunter (1839–1916), while Herbert Horne (1864–1916) and ARTHUR SYMONS attended less regularly, and OSCAR WILDE would sometimes attend when the group met in a private house, as he hated the Bohemian setting of the Cheshire Cheese (147; see also *Mem.* 36–37). The members of the club, several Irish or otherwise Celtic-leaning, shared an allegiance to aestheticism and decadence under the influence of the PRE-RAPHAELITES (especially Dante Gabriel Rossetti) and Walter Pater (*Aut.* 149, 235), and they contributed to the notorious fin de siècle reviews in the *Yellow Book* and the SAVOY.

In a 1892 newspaper article titled "Hopes and Fears for Irish Literature," Yeats describes the tenor of the club and indicates his own misgivings about its leanings: "I well remember the irritated silence that fell upon a noted gathering of the younger English imaginative writers once, when I tried to explain a philosophy of poetry in which I was profoundly interested, and to show the dependence, as I conceived it, of all great art and literature upon conviction and upon heroic life. To them literature had ceased to be the handmaid of humanity, and become instead a terrible queen, in whose services the stars rose and set, and for whose pleasure life stumbles along in the darkness" (UP1 248). Yeats gives his most extensive and darkly romantic account of the club in *Autobiographies,* famously dubbing its members "the tragic generation" and recounting their various lines of descent into madness, despair, dissipation, and early death. Yeats writes that he has never found a satisfactory explanation as to why the club broke up in tragedy:

"[Sometimes] I have remembered that, unlike the Victorian poets, almost all were poor men, and had made it a matter of conscience to turn from every kind of money-making that prevented good writing, and that poverty meant strain, and, for the most part, a refusal of domestic life. Then I have remembered that Johnson had private means, and that others who came to tragic ends had wives and families. Another day I think that perhaps our form of lyric, our insistence upon emotion which has no relation to any public interest, gathered together overwrought, unstable men; and remember, the moment after, that the first to go out of his mind had no lyrical gift, and that we valued him mainly because he seemed a witty man of the world; and that a little later another who seemed, alike as man and writer, dull and formless, went out of his mind, first burning poems which I cannot believe would have proved him, as the one man who saw them claims, a man of genius" (233). Reminiscing in the company of L. A. G. Strong, Yeats tallied the fallen: Radford, Arthur Cecil Hillier (b. 1858), and Symons had gone mad, while Dowson and Johnson had died of drink (I&R, I, 149–150). Yeats did not mention Wilde's spectacular demise, but he might have done so. He might also have mentioned John Davidson, who, suffering from depression, likely took his own life in 1909.

Yeats further discusses the Rhymers in the 1892 article "The Rhymers' Club" (see *Letters to the New Island*), in the 1936 essay "Modern Poetry" (see *E&I* 491–495; *LE* 89–92), and in MEMOIRS. Yeats addressed his long poem "The GREY ROCK" to the memory of his old "tavern comrades," whom he extols in a long parenthetical comment: "You had to face your ends when young—/ 'Twas wine or women, or some curse—/ But never made a poorer song / That you might have a heavier purse, / Nor gave loud service to a cause / That you might have a troop of friends. / You kept the Muses' sterner laws, / And unrepenting faced your ends, / And therefore earned the right—and yet / Dowson and Johnson most I praise—/ To troop with those the world's forgot, / And copy their proud steady gaze." The poem implicitly contrasts Aoife's mortal lover and the Rhymers: while he preserves his worldly honor at the cost of divine fellowship, they kept faith with the "holy shades that rove / The grey rock and the windy light."

The club produced two anthologies, *The Book of the Rhymers' Club* (1892) and *The Second Book of the Rhymers' Club* (1894). To the first anthology, Yeats contributed, in order of appearance, "The MAN WHO DREAMED OF FAIRYLAND," "Father Gilligan" (later "The Ballad of Father Gilligan"), "Dedication of 'Irish Tales'" (later "The Dedication to a Book of Stories selected from the Irish Novelists"), "A Fairy Song," "The LAKE ISLE OF INNISFREE," and "An Epitaph" (later "A Dream of Death"). To the second anthology, he contributed "The Rose in my Heart" (later "The LOVER TELLS OF THE ROSE IN HIS HEART"), "The Folk of the Air" (later "The Host of the Air"), "The Fiddler of Dooney," "A Mystical Prayer to the Masters of the Elements—Finvarra, Feacra, and Caolte" (later "The Poet pleads with the Elemental Powers"), "The Cap and Bells," and "The Song of the Old Mother" (*Biblio.* 281–284).

Yeats's comment on the second book in a June 1894 letter to JOHN O'LEARY suggests his estimation of the club's members. He writes that "everybody is tolerably good except the Trinity College men, Rolleston, Hillier, Todhunter & Greene who are intollerably [sic] bad as was to be expected—Todhunter is of course skillful enough with more matter of fact themes & quite admits the dreadful burden of the TCD tradition—& some are exceeding good notably Plar [sic], Dowson & Le Galliene" (*CL1* 391). "Greene" is George Arthur Greene (1853–1921), who served as vice chairman of the Irish Literary Society of London (see NATIONAL LITERARY SOCIETY).

Bibliography

Mikhail, E. H., ed. *W. B. Yeats: Interviews and Recollections* (vol. 1); Wade, Allan. *A Bibliography of the Writings of W. B. Yeats*; Yeats, W. B. *Autobiographies, The Collected Letters of W. B. Yeats* (vol. 1), *Essays and Introductions, Later Essays, Letters to the New Island, Memoirs, Uncollected Prose by W. B. Yeats* (vol. 1).

Riversdale Yeats's final home was a leased 18th-century farmhouse called Riversdale. The four-acre property was on the outskirts of the village of Rathfarnham, about four miles southwest of central Dublin. It included a stable and summer house, as well as croquet, tennis, and bowling lawns. The house itself was small-roomed and boxy, but surrounded by charming gardens (*AP* 446–447; *BG* 451–452). The Yeats family moved to Riversdale from 42 Fitzwilliam Square, Dublin, in July 1932, and remained until soon after Yeats's death. "There apple trees, cherry trees, roses, smooth lawns and no long climb upstairs," Yeats wrote to OLIVIA SHAKESPEAR, explaining the appeal of the new house on the eve of the move (*Letters* 798).

Riversdale, like Yeats's Ballylee, Oxford, and Merrion Square homes, made a poetic—even stylized—backdrop. The "creeper-covered farmhouse" was like a "Calvert wood-cut," as Yeats had it, and its pastoral seclusion suited a poet's final meditative solitude (799). Not incidentally, he had envisioned just such a farmhouse in PER AMICA SILENTIA LUNAE: "A poet, when he is growing old, will ask himself if he cannot keep his mask and his vision without new bitterness, new disappointment. [. . .] He will buy perhaps some small old house where like Ariosto he can dig his garden, and think that in the return of birds and leaves, or moon and sun, and in the evening flight of the rooks he may discover rhythm and pattern like those in sleep and so never awake out of vision" The poet will remember, however, "WORDSWORTH withering into eighty years, honoured and empty-witted, and climb to some waste room and find, forgotten there by youth, some bitter crust" (*LE* 15–16). "An ACRE OF GRASS," Yeats's only poem set identifiably at Riversdale, embodies the same dynamic, as Yeats shakes himself awake from the sleepiness of his shuffling rounds in the garden and musters his old *antithetical* rage.

Riversdale was both a painful reminder of and a potential surrogate for COOLE PARK, the beloved second home that Yeats had lost upon the death of Lady GREGORY on May 22, 1932. In this respect, Riversdale belongs with DOROTHY WELLESLEY's Penns in the Rocks and Edith Shackleton Heald's Chantry House, both in Sussex, which were similarly bound up with Yeats's sense of loss. Yeats told Shakespear on May 31, "[Riversdale] has the most beautiful gardens I have seen round a small house, and all well stocked. I shall step out from my study into the front garden—but as I write the words I know that I am heartbroken for Coole and its great woods" (*Letters* 795). On July 8, he wrote to Shakespear in a more optimistic mood: "I hope I shall there re-create in some measure the routine that was my life at Coole, the only place where I have ever had unbroken health." He went on to enumerate the advantages and charms of Riversdale: "I am just too far from Dublin to go there without good reason and too far, I hope, for most interviewers and the less determined travelling bores. I shall have a big old fruit garden all to myself—the study opens into it and it is shut off from the flower garden and the croquet and tennis lawns and from the bowling-green. George is painting my walls lemon yellow and the doors green and black. We have a lease for but thirteen years but that will see me out of life" (799). Writing on July 25, Yeats told Shakespear, "At first I was unhappy, for everything made me remember the great rooms and the great trees at Coole, my home for nearly forty years, but now that the pictures are up I feel more content" (799).

Yeats's letters minutely render both bedroom and study at Riversdale. Writing from his bed to Wellesley in November 1936, Yeats described the room: "In front of me, over the mantelpiece, is a large lithograph by Shannon, boys bathing, the most conspicuous boy drawn with voluptuous pleasure in back and flank, as always with Shannon. Under it a charcoal study by Burne Jones of sirens luring a ship to its doom, the sirens tall, unvoluptuous, faint, vague forms flitting here and there. On the other wall are drawings, paintings or photographs of friends and relatives, and three reproductions of pictures, Botticelli's 'Spring,' Gustave Moreau's "Women and Unicorns,' Fragonard's 'Cup of Life' [. . .]. To right and left are windows, one opening on to a walled garden full of fruit, one on a flower garden, a field and trees" (*Letters* 865; *LOP* 109). T. R. Henn identifies the Fragonard as "La Fontaine d'Amour" and cites Moreau's painting as the source of imagery in "I SEE PHANTOMS OF HATRED AND OF THE HEART'S FULLNESS AND OF THE COMING EMPTINESS" (*Lonely Tower* 255). In a November 1937 letter to Heald (1885–1976), Yeats offered a similar catalog: "All round the study walls are book-

cases but some stop half way up and over them are pictures by my brother, my father, by ROBERT GREGORY. On each side of the window into flower garden are two great Chinese pictures (Dulac's gift) and in the window into the greenhouse hangs a most lovely Burne-Jones window (Ricketts's gift). Through the glass door into the flower garden I see the bare boughs of apple trees and a few last flowers [. . .]" (*Letters* 901; see also 802).

Following Yeats's death on January 28, 1939, GEORGE YEATS found Riversdale, with its extensive gardens, too costly to keep up. On July 26, 1939, she moved to 46 Palmerston Road, Rathmines, Dublin (*BG* 578–579).

Bibliography

Foster, R. F. *W. B. Yeats: A Life, II: The Arch-Poet*; Henn, T. R. *The Lonely Tower: Studies in the Poetry of W. B. Yeats*; Saddlemyer, Ann. *Becoming George: The Life of Mrs W. B. Yeats*; Yeats, W. B. *Later Essays, The Letters of W. B. Yeats, Letters on Poetry from W. B. Yeats to Dorothy Wellesley.*

rose The rose is a central symbol in many of Yeats's poems of the 1890s. It figures with varying significance in "The Blessed" (1897), "HE BIDS HIS BELOVED BE AT PEACE," "The LOVER TELLS OF THE ROSE IN HIS HEART," "The Poet pleads with the Elemental Powers" (1892), "The ROSE OF BATTLE" (1892), "The Rose of Peace" (1892), "The Rose of the World" (1892), "The SECRET ROSE" (1896), "The Song of the Rosy Cross" (1895; see *VP* 744), "TO IRELAND IN THE COMING TIMES," "TO THE ROSE UPON THE ROOD OF TIME," "The TRAVAIL OF PASSION," and "The WHITE BIRDS." With the publication of his collected *Poems* in 1895, Yeats placed poems originally published in *The Countess Kathleen and Other Poems* (1892) under the heading "The Rose," in which arrangement they remain enshrined in the standard edition of Yeats's work. The rose additionally gives its name to the prose volume *The SECRET ROSE* (1897), which includes the stories "Out of the Rose" (1893), "The Rose of Shadow" (1894), and "ROSA ALCHEMICA." With the turn of the century, Yeats largely abandoned the rose as a mystic symbol; it recurs in only two later poems, "The MOUNTAIN TOMB" and

"MY HOUSE." The latter refers to the "symbolic rose" in lowly lowercase, signifying a self-conscious detachment from the ardent "rosolatry"—Richard Ellmann's word—of the 1890s (*IY* 75). "The Rose Tree" (1920) employs the image as well, though not obviously with mystic implication.

In a 1915 letter, Yeats explained to an inquirer that he found authority for his symbolic use of the rose in the "medieval mystics," whom he had studied since 1887. He mentions Johannes Valentine Andreae (1586–1654), a German theologian who reputedly authored *The Chymical Marriage of Christian Rosencreutz,* one of the founding documents of Rosicrucianism (*Letters* 592). In a 1901 manuscript entry, Yeats indicates the rose's meaning within the Rosicrucian symbolic system: "I woke up [from a dream] saying that father Rosy Cross was the first who [proclaimed] that beauty was holiness and all that is ugly unholiness. I thought between waking and sleeping, 'He set the rose upon the cross and thereby united religion and beauty, the spirit and nature, and the universe of spirit and of nature in magic" (*IY* 66). Analyzing the cover design of *The Secret Rose*—a rose and cross efflorescing as the tree of life—by Yeats's friend Althea Gyles (1868–1949), Ellmann elaborates the more specific aspects of this meaning. He specifies that the four petals of the rose represent the four elements, while the conjunction of rose and cross "suggests the fifth element or quintessence" that is "the central myth of Rosicrucianism." In the Rosicrucian tradition, this conjunction "is often referred to as a 'mystic marriage', as the transfiguring ecstasy which occurs when the adept, after the long pain and self-sacrifice of the quest in this world, a world in which opposites are for ever quarrelling, finds his cross—the symbol of that struggle and opposition—suddenly blossom with the rose of love, harmony, and beauty" (64). Additionally, says Ellmann, the conjunction of cross and rose represents the union of male and female.

In a note to *The Wind Among the Reeds* (1899), Yeats writes that the Rose has "been for many centuries a symbol of spiritual love and supreme beauty," while in the Irish tradition it is a "religious symbol," the symbol of the nation, and the symbol of female beauty (*VP* 811–812; see also 798, 842).

Yeats most often speaks of the rose as the symbol—or even the living mystical embodiment—of this "spiritual love and supreme beauty." In his preface to the 1895 edition of *Poems,* he writes that he has placed his poems under the heading of "The Rose" because "in them he has found, he believes, the only pathway whereon he can hope to see with his own eyes the Eternal Rose of Beauty and of Peace" (*VP* 846). In *AUTOBIOGRAPHIES,* Yeats characterizes "To the Rose upon the Rood of Time" as a prayer to "the Red Rose, to Intellectual Beauty," an evident allusion to SHELLEY's "Hymn to Intellectual Beauty" (1817). The suggestion is that the rose, like Shelley's analogous conception of Intellectual Beauty, is a kind of supernal reality or presiding deity (205). In a note dated 1925, Yeats comments that "the quality symbolised as The Rose differs from the Intellectual Beauty of Shelley and of Spenser in that I have imagined it as suffering with man and not as something pursued and seen from afar" (*VP* 842). In his 1908 essay "Poetry and Tradition," Yeats associates the rose with the culminating moments of the highest tragic art, the moment of resolved antinomies. Reiterating the Rosicrucian conception of "To the Rose upon the Rood of Time," he writes that the "nobleness of the arts is in the mingling of contraries, the extremity of sorrow, the extremity of joy, perfection of personality, the perfection of its surrender, overflowing turbulent energy, and marmorean stillness; and its red rose opens at the meeting of the two beams of the cross, and at the trysting-place of mortal and immortal, time and eternity" (*E&I* 255).

Despite its Rosicrucian underpinnings, the rose is multivocal to the point of ambiguity in Yeats's work. Harold Bloom comments that, in addition to representing the universal spirit of beauty and peace, the rose "was MAUD GONNE, Ireland (Dark Rosaleen), a central symbol of the Rosicrucian Order of the Golden Dawn, a sexual emblem, the sun, and much else," and that "it is not a coherent image." Bloom nonetheless hazards the notion that the rose is most fundamentally a "displacement of the Muse herself," and that it is "in itself not a mystical entity but simply all of beauty that is apprehended beyond the range of the senses" (*Yeats* 114).

Bibliography

Bloom, Harold. *Yeats*; Ellmann, Richard. *The Identity of Yeats*; Yeats, W. B. *Autobiographies, Essays and Introductions, The Letters of W. B. Yeats, The Variorum Edition of the Poems of W. B. Yeats*.

Ruddock, Margot, married name Collis (1907–1951)

Margot Ruddock, a British actress and poet whose artistic career was cut short by mental illness, belonged to a line of women in Yeats's life who were at once collaborators, pupils, muses, and love interests. FLORENCE FARR, ISEULT GONNE, and GEORGE YEATS had earlier filled this role, and DOROTHY WELLESLEY to some extent filled it coextensively with Ruddock.

In his introduction to Yeats and Ruddock's correspondence, *Ah, Sweet Dancer*, Roger McHugh sketches Ruddock's adult life. While still in her teens she married her brother's Cambridge friend Jack Hollis. They divorced, and their son, Michael, was raised by his father. In May 1932, she married the promising actor Raymond Lovell while both belonged to the Terence Byron Company at Bradford. They had a daughter, Simone, in February 1934. Hoping to found a poets' theater in London, Ruddock wrote to Yeats in the autumn of 1934 and requested his advice. They arranged to meet in London on October 4 (*Sweet Dancer* 9, 19). Yeats, then 69, was smitten with the beautiful 27-year-old actress, and they soon began an affair of sorts carried on in a London flat that Yeats had taken on Ruddock's advice (21). In late November, Yeats mentions being thrown into an "utter black gloom" by the fear that his "nervous inhibition" had not left him: the implication seems to be that Yeats had tried but failed to consummate the relationship (*AP* 509; *Sweet Dancer* 30–31). Yeats enjoyed the frisson of Ruddock's beauty, youth, and tempestuousness, while he provided Ruddock with aesthetic counsel and the inspiration of his living example. He also provided her with a professional leg up. He emended her poems; campaigned aggressively to land her the lead role of Decima in a production of *The* PLAYER QUEEN staged at the Little Theatre in London in October 1935, though in the end she wound up with the supporting role of the queen (*AP* 532–533; *Sweet Dancer* 56–57); rewrote *The* KING OF THE GREAT CLOCK TOWER as *A* FULL MOON IN MARCH at least in part for her to act the role of the queen (*Sweet Dancer* 23); included seven of her poems in his *Oxford Book of Modern Verse* (1936); wrote an introduction to a selection of her poems in the July 1936 issue of the *London Mercury* (see *UP2* 501–505); expanded his introduction for inclusion in her 1937 volume of poems *The Lemon Tree* (see *P&I* 186–190); and had her participate in his BBC radio broadcasts on April 22, July 3, and October 29, 1937 (*Biblio.* 472–474; *Sweet Dancer* 117). In his introduction to *The Lemon Tree*, Yeats tells that upon first meeting Ruddock he had divined in her a "frustrated tragic genius." There was "something hard, tight, screwed-up, in her," he perceived, "but were that dissolved by success she might be a great actress, for she possessed a quality rare upon the stage or, if found there, left unemployed—intellectual passion" (*P&I* 186). He calls her poems, meanwhile, "passionate, incoherent improvisations, power struggling with that ignorance of books and of arts which has made the modern theatre what it is" (187)

The brief relationship added one permanent anecdote to the lore of Yeats. In May 1936 Ruddock suffered a psychotic episode that presaged her permanent breakdown the following year. She chronicles her misadventures in brief prose memoir titled "Almost I Tasted Ecstasy" that appeared in *The Lemon Tree* (see also *Sweet Dancer* 91–98). Yeats gives his own account of the episode in a letter of May 22, 1936, to OLIVIA SHAKESPEAR (*Letters* 856) and in his introduction to *The Lemon Tree* (see also *AP* 542–545). Unhinged by domestic pressures, financial pressures, professional impasse, and incipient schizophrenia, she contemplated suicide, but decided that if she were a good poet she had "the right to live" (*Sweet Dancer* 91). Believing that Yeats could tell her whether or not she was a good poet, she showed up unexpectedly at Majorca (ca. May 12), where Yeats was convalescing. Ruddock remembers telling Yeats that she must die if she could not "write a poem that would live." Unyielding in his standards even under the unusual circumstances, Yeats told her that she must "work at each until it was perfect" (93). While Yeats reviewed her poems, she slipped outside and "went slowly down to the shore through the rain." As she remembers: "I thought, 'if I am to die something will help me', I stood on the rocks and could not go into the sea because there was so much in life I loved, then I was so happy at not having to die I danced" (93). Yeats borrowed the image of Ruddock dancing by the sea in two poems, "A CRAZED GIRL" (titled "At Barcelona" when it first appeared in *The Lemon Tree*) and "Sweet Dancer" (1938).

The next evening Ruddock went to see friends in Barcelona with money and slippers borrowed from the Indian guru Shree Purohit Swami (1882–1941), who was staying at a nearby pension and collaborating with Yeats on a translation that would be published in 1937 as *The Ten Principal Upanishads*. In Barcelona, Ruddock's psychosis deepened. After she became lost in the streets, her well-meaning friends locked her in a room while they made arrangements for her. She attempted to escape by jumping from a window and plunged through the roof of a barber's shop, breaking her knee, as Yeats mentions in "A Crazed Girl" (*Sweet Dancer* 95–98). The Yeatses rushed to Barcelona and arranged for Ruddock to return to England in the company of a nurse (98). Yeats told Shakespear, "It was impossible to get adequate money out of her family, so I accepted financial responsibility and she was despatched to England and now I won't be able to afford new clothes for a year. When her husband wrote it had not been to send money, but to congratulate her on the magnificent publicity" (*Letters* 856). After having done his part, Yeats tried to disentangle himself, telling Shakespear, "When I am in London I shall probably hide because the husband may send me journalists and because I want to keep a distance from a tragedy where I can be no further help" (856). Ruddock's breakdown in Majorca was followed by a final breakdown the following year. She was permanently institutionalized in late 1937.

In addition to "A Crazed Girl" and "Sweet Dancer," Yeats wrote a third poem, "Margot," that echoes the far superior poems of desire shackled by age—"The LIVING BEAUTY," "MEN IMPROVE WITH THE YEARS"—that Iseult Gonne had inspired years earlier. Otherwise unpublished, the poem appears in Yeats's correspondence with Ruddock (*Sweet*

Dancer 33). A fourth poem, "The MAN AND THE ECHO," alludes to Ruddock's breakdown. After posing the more famous question—"Did that play of mine send out / Certain men the English shot?"—Yeats asks, "Did words of mine put too great strain / On that woman's reeling brain?" Yeats most likely refers to the exacting artistic standard he imposed on Ruddock. She complained in an April 1936 letter: "Do you know that you have made poetry, my solace and my joy, a bloody grind I hate! If we are in our natural state we write like the Swami (in his native). 52 poems of sheer *ecstasy* in a day. I loathe poetry, I loathe working at it for given grammar and words (of which I have not enough), poetry should *not* be worked at. Scrub floors and sweat in offices but do not sweat at poetry which is spiritual sweat! And to make it physical sweat as well is to condemn it with all other earthly things" (*Sweet Dancer* 88; see also 81; *P&I* 187).

Bibliography

Foster, R. F. *W. B. Yeats: A Life, II: The Arch-Poet*; Wade, Allan. *A Bibliography of the Writings of W. B. Yeats*; Yeats, W. B. *Ah, Sweet Dancer: W. B. Yeats and Margot Ruddock*, *The Letters of W. B. Yeats*, *Prefaces and Introductions*, *Uncollected Prose by W. B. Yeats* (vol. 2).

Russell, George William (AE) (1867–1935)

For some 50 years Yeats and Russell were fellow workers in the cause of national and spiritual revival. Though their early friendship permanently bound them to each other almost as brothers are bound—buckled to each other's hearts, in Yeats's phrase—they were on opposite sides of fundamental questions and never shared the kind of collaborative bond that Yeats enjoyed with Lady GREGORY and J. M. SYNGE (*E&I* 412; *LE* 113). Russell was amazed and fascinated by Yeats's energy and originality, but he kept always a certain wary distance. In a letter congratulating Yeats on his 70th birthday, Russell surmised that Yeats would "be the pivot round which Ireland will turn from its surfaces to more central depths," and then summarized the lifelong dilemma of his relations with Yeats: "There are deeps in the Irish character to be sounded. I could not sound them. I could only find

Portrait of George Russell, better known as AE, by Casimir Markiewicz (1874–1932), ca. 1903. *(Dublin City Gallery The Hugh Lane)*

intermittently access to some spiritual nature which is not more Irish than Hindu, but to find access to that however intermittently was the only thing I really cared about in life & it is the reason why so often I could not or would not be with you in your work or policies for I dreaded that a nature more formidable and powerful than my own would lead me away from my own will & centre" (*LTWBY*, II, 574). In turn, Yeats was often frustrated by what he considered Russell's genial amateurism as a painter and a poet. "He has the religious genius, and it is the essence of that genius that all souls are equal in its eyes," Yeats writes in MEMOIRS. "Queen or apple woman, it is all one, seeing that none can be more than an immortal soul. Whereas I have been concerned with men's capacities, with all [that] divides man from man. I seem to him harsh, hypercritical, overbearing even, and he seems to encourage in all the arts the spirit of the amateur" (130; see also *CL4* 290, 488–490). Frank O'Connor, touching on this deep temperamental difference, contrasts Yeats's "pin-point awareness" and Rus-

sell's "dim benevolence." Where Yeats "was subtle, casuistical, elegant, mannered; a diplomatist who had flattered rich and brilliant women into serving his cause, a man of the world who had been the friend of artists and bohemians," Russell was "guileless, untravelled, full of universal benevolence but with a nonconformist conscience that occasionally gave out the shrill notes of the 'Old Orange Flute'" (*I&R*, II, 262–263).

Russell was born on April 10, 1867, the youngest of three children, in the small market town of Lurgan, County Armagh. His father was a bookkeeper for a cambric manufacturer and his mother worked in a general shop. Both belonged to the Church of Ireland, though their Protestantism had an evangelical streak (*Myriad-Minded Man* 3). In 1878, Russell's father joined an accounting firm, and the family moved to Dublin. From 1880 to 1885, Russell intermittently took classes at the Metropolitan School of Art, Kildare Street. Yeats enrolled in May 1884, and the two art students became boon companions. "He did not paint the model as we tried to," Yeats remembers of Russell's days as an art student, "for some other image rose always before his eyes (a Saint John in the Desert I remember), and already he spoke to us of his visions. One day he announced that he was leaving the art schools because his will was weak and the arts or any other emotional pursuit could but weaken it further" (*Aut.* 90). Russell in those days "seemed incapable of coherent thought," according to Yeats, and he struck his fellow students as "sacred, as the fool is sacred in the East," though his painting showed a remarkable facility (196–197). From 1885 to 1887, Russell attended evening classes at the painting school affiliated with the Royal Hibernian Academy (*Myriad-Minded Man* 11), but his genuine education was the youthful symposium he and Yeats shared and the visionary experience that was his peculiar gift and resource. In 1885, Yeats and Russell, along with Yeats's school friends Charles Johnston (1867–1931) and JOHN EGLINTON, discovered Eastern religion in the pages of A. P. Sinnett's *Esoteric Buddhism* (1883). Yeats and Johnston formed the Dublin Hermetic Society (*Aut.* 97–98), but Russell did not join, most likely because, as Peter Kuch writes, "he did not approve of the constraints that organizations placed on spiritual enquiry" (*Yeats and A.E.* 15). Johnston next founded a Dublin Lodge of the THEOSOPHICAL SOCIETY. Though Theosophy would later become his guiding system of thought, Russell declined to become a member.

In May 1887, the Yeats family moved to London, and the two friends saw less of each other for the time being. During the years of Yeats's absence, Russell lived with his parents in the suburb of Rathmines, took odd jobs, schooled himself in the sacred literature of India, and cultivated both his art and his vision. This was vision in the literal sense; as Yeats writes, "If he sat silent for a while on the Two Rock Mountain [near Dublin], or any spot where man was absent, the scene would change; unknown, beautiful people would move among the rocks and trees; but his vision, unlike that of Swedenborg, remained always what seemed an unexplained, external, sensuous panorama" (*E&I* 413; *LE* 113–114). Despite his unwillingness to join Johnston's lodge, Russell became increasingly absorbed in Theosophy. In 1889, he formally joined the Theosophical Society. In 1891, he moved to 3 Upper Ely Place, a dormitory for young acolytes as well as the headquarters of the society's Dublin lodge, and he remained a resident of the "Household," as it was called, for the next six years (*Myriad-Minded Man* 29, 31, 33). AUTOBI-OGRAPHIES includes a mildly patronizing account of the Household, in which Yeats describes Russell as the "saint and genius" of the eccentric little community (195). By day, Russell earned his keep as a clerk at Pim Brothers, a large Dublin drapery store. Spiritually rich if otherwise unexceptional, these days were the happiest of Russell's life (*Myriad-Minded Man* 34).

In June 1894, Russell published his first volume of verse, *Homeward: Songs by the Way*, under the name "AE," a nom de plume he had first used in the Theosophist magazine *Lucifer* in 1888 (*Myriad-Minded Man* 31). The name derives from a mystical experience, as Russell explained in an 1886 letter: "I was thinking of what would be the sound for the most primeval thought I could think and the word 'aön' passed into my head. I was afterwards surprised at finding out that the Gnostics of the

Christian Era called the first created things 'Æons' and that the Indian word for the commencement of all things is Aom" (14). According to Eglinton, Russell meant to call himself "Aeon," but a compositor working on one of his articles misrendered the word as "AE" (*Memoir of AE* 27). Russell accepted this accident and thereafter called himself "Æ." He preferred the diphthong, but the typical rendering is "AE" or "A.E." Determined to bring Russell into his own literary movement, Yeats reviewed *Homeward: Songs by the Way* in the August 1894 issue of the *Bookman* (*UP1* 335–339) and then noticed the American edition and second British edition in the May 1895 issue (356–358). While acknowledging "faults in plenty"—"certain rhymes are repeated too often, the longer lines stumble now and again, and here and there a stanza is needlessly obscure"—Yeats called the volume "the most haunting book I have seen these many days" (339). Russell's next volume of verse, *The Earth Breath and Other Poems*, appeared in 1897. Dedicated to Yeats, the volume seemed a step in Yeats's direction, for, as Henry Summerfield writes, "Celtic faery lore has displaced the Indian words and names of the earlier collection" (*Myriad-Minded Man* 81). Yeats reviewed the volume on April 6, 1898, in the *Sketch*, and ended with an effusion: "Many verses in this little book have so much high thought and they sing it so sweetly and tenderly that I cannot but think them immortal verses" (*UP2* 113). Yeats further plumped for Russell in the December 1897 issue of the *Irish Homestead* (70–73) and in the September 3, 1898, issue of the *Daily Express* (*P&I* 113–115; *UP2* 121–124). In 1895, Yeats dedicated the "Crossways" section of his *Poems* to Russell, and in 1897 he dedicated *The Secret Rose* to him, calling him the "one poet of modern Ireland who has moulded a spiritual ecstasy into verse" (*CL2* 59–60). This was the second book that Yeats had dedicated to Russell: nine years earlier he had inscribed *Fairy and Folk Tales of the Irish Peasantry* to "my mystical friend, G.R." Russell, however, was not so easily lassoed into Yeats's movement, for he remained skeptical of Yeats's aestheticism, and he disapproved of Yeats's more *outré* artistic involvements. Most memorably, he sent Yeats a letter denouncing the *SAVOY* as "the Organ of the Incubi and the Succubi" (*Aut.* 252; *Mem.* 91).

Toward the end of the 1890s, Russell established the pattern of his mature life. In February 1897, he left the Household. In November, he ended his seven-year tenure at Pim Brothers and took a job as a rural organizer with Horace Plunkett's Irish Agricultural Organisation Society (I.A.O.S.). Founded in 1894, the I.A.O.S. aimed to alleviate the plight of farmers and rural communities by helping organize cooperative societies. Russell's initial assignment was to organize cooperative banks whose function was to secure and administer loans from commercial banks (*Myriad-Minded Man* 89). As a mystic and Theosophist, Russell was an unlikely agrarian organizer and man of business, but he soon excelled in his work, being dedicated, pragmatic, and immensely likable, and bringing to the job, as Yeats writes, his "impassioned versatility" (*Aut.* 197). Yeats encouraged and facilitated Russell's career move, believing that he would benefit from immersion in rural Ireland and that the work would "take him out of the narrow groove of theosophical opinion" (*CL2* 145). In *Memoirs*, Yeats describes a degree of arm twisting: "He had at first refused Horace Plunkett's offer, though it more than trebled his income in the large shop where he was accountant, because his [Theosophical] followers had need of him. He only consented when I brought them in deputation to say—the thought and wording were their own—that they were becoming his shadows, and would find themselves, perhaps, if he went away" (*Mem.* 130; see also *CL2* 146–147, 175–177). In April 1898, Russell conveyed the tenor of his new life in a letter to Yeats: "Look what you have drawn me into. [. . .] Today I dine with a Bishop. I give evidence before a money-lending Commission; I am asked to enquire the price of pigs; I have been forced to learn the different properties of manures; I have lived in country hotels, and been a thing apart from the 'wholesome cheerful life of men', because I won't get drunk" (*Letters from AE* 28–29).

Watershed changes continued in 1898. In March, Russell resigned from the Theosophical Society ostensibly on doctrinal grounds, but more fundamentally because he found his spiritual and intellectual freedom impinged by all formal structures. Eglinton quips that Russell's Theosophy had a distinctly Protestant aspect (*Memoir of AE* 52). He remained loyal to Theosophy as a guiding idea, however. In June 1898, he married his fellow Theosophist Violet North (1869–1932). The couple had three sons and a daughter, though only the two younger sons survived infancy. Writing to Lady Gregory on June 13, Yeats described himself as "not very pleased" with Russell's "aerial Theosophical marriage": "Mrs Russell is a person who sees visions & is well bred & pleasant enough; but I suppose I would never think anybody quite good enough for Russell. She has, as I have noticed, been in love with him for years. He has got into the habit of looking after her. She is consumptive & has some literary power" (*CL2* 236–237). In a letter of the following day, Yeats called the marriage "shere philanthropy" (237). Of Russell's later married life, Eglinton comments that Russell "could hardly be called a domestic man, and he always seemed as much disengaged from family ties as Socrates amongst the young men of Athens" (*Memoir of AE* 47; see also 74).

The couple's house in the Dublin suburb of Rathmines became a meeting place for young writers and Theosophists and a hub of the Irish Renaissance. Yeats sometimes attended Sunday evenings at Russell's house, but he did not belong to the circle that gathered there, as he tells in *Autobiographies*: "Five or six years earlier [Russell] had published his lovely *Homeward; Songs by the Way*, and because of those poems and what he was in himself, writers or would-be writers, among them James Stephens, who has all my admiration to-day, gathered at his house upon Sunday nights, making it a chief centre of literary life in Dublin." Yeats considered Russell's circle for the most part made up by "barren rascals" and felt that it led "the opposition, not the violent attacks, but the sapping and mining" (331; see also *Mem.* 222–223). In 1904, Russell edited *New Songs*, an anthology of poems by eight poets—Padraic Colum (1881–1972), Eva Gore-Booth (1870–1926), Thomas Keohler (1874–1942), Alice Milligan (1866–1953), Susan Mitchell (1866–1926), Seumas O'Sullivan (1879–1958), George Roberts (1873–1953), and Ella Young

(1867–1956)—who belonged to his circle. Yeats's poems "A COAT" and "TO A POET, WHO WOULD HAVE ME PRAISE CERTAIN BAD POETS, IMITATORS OF HIS AND MINE" express his low estimate of Russell's acolytes (see also *CL3* 576–578; *CL4* 488).

Between 1905 and 1913, Yeats and Russell were estranged. As so often in Yeats's life, theater business was the bone of contention. Russell had been involved in the Irish dramatic movement almost from the start. In April 1902, his only play, *Deirdre*, was produced by W. G. Fay's Irish National Dramatic Society, along with Yeats's CATHLEEN NI HOULIHAN. In *Autobiographies*, Yeats describes *Deirdre* as a "protest" against his own DIARMUID AND GRANIA, which "had made mere men out of heroes." He calls *Deirdre* well constructed, but objects that "all its male characters resembled Lord TENNYSON's King Arthur" (331; see also *UP2* 291–293), while in private conversation he was apparently brutally dismissive (see *GY* 256). In February 1903, Yeats founded the IRISH NATIONAL THEATRE SOCIETY, with himself as president, and MAUD GONNE, Douglas Hyde (1860–1949), and Russell as vice presidents. Yeats and Russell were never in agreement about the aims of the theater. As Peter Kuch writes, Russell wanted a "small, amateur theatre that would encourage local talent and that would provide sixpence-worth of wholesome, informative, Irish entertainment," while Yeats wanted "a fully professional theatre that would be the equal of the best experimental theatres in England, Norway, France, and Germany" (*Yeats and A.E.* 172; see also *CL4* 488–490). In April 1904, Yeats and Russell quarreled after Russell gave a group of actors who had resigned from the society permission to perform *Deirdre* at an exposition in St. Louis, Missouri (*CL3* 566–567, 575–576; *Yeats and A.E.* 220–221). Russell resigned from the society, but there was more grief to come. In September 1905, Russell, acting at Yeats's behest, mediated a reorganization of the society that would transform it into a limited liability company and concentrate power in a directorate consisting of Lady Gregory, Synge, and Yeats (*CL4 passim*). With his usual tact, efficiency, and good will, Russell accomplished the task, but, along with many of the actors, he was disgusted by Yeats's dictatorial manner. In December 1905, Russell sent

Yeats a long and bitter letter of complaint and the 20-year friendship seemed at an end (*CL4* 292–298; *LTWBY*, I, 151–155; for Yeats's response, see *CL4* 290). In a letter to Lady Gregory, Russell said, "Every time I meet W.B.Y. I feel inclined to throw him out of the window when he talks business. He has no talent for anything but writing and literature or literary discussions. Outside that he should be fined every time he opens his mouth" (*AM* 340). Yeats and Russell resumed their friendship in 1913, after they found themselves on the same side of a bitter labor crisis involving a lock-out of the Irish Transport and General Workers' Union (see *Letters from AE* 85–88, 91–94; *UP2* 405–407).

In 1905, Russell became the editor of the I.A.O.S.'s weekly journal, the *Irish Homestead*, and his voice became consequential. Plunkett, as Eglinton writes, "had set AE his theme of rural co-operation, and AE's journalism rose like a song out of the bitter newspaper press of Ireland, building up Plunkett's ideal kingdom. People who looked into the *Irish Homestead* to see how AE would write about pigs and poultry shrugged their shoulders when they found perfectly readable discourses, with glints of science, metaphysics and the lore of the East, and hints of AE's peculiar doctrines [. . .]" (*Memoir of AE* 72). He continued at the *Irish Homestead* until September 1923, when he became editor of its successor, Plunkett's *Irish Statesman*. The weekly journal allowed Russell to continue his hydra-headed journalistic effort on a broader footing. As Eglinton comments, "In a single number we find (all written by himself) well-informed notes on current topics, home and foreign; at least one brilliant leading article; a literary or philosophical 'causerie'; a poem; book-reviews; besides that part of the paper which continued the work of the *Irish Homestead*" (150–151). As for its place in the culture, the paper was "the organ in which the return of the Lane Pictures [see HUGH LANE] could be advocated, or in which the new censorship could be resisted; it was the organ of those who, interested chiefly in the ideas animating literature, politics and social science, are called nowadays in each country its 'Intellectuals'" (191). Russell remained at the *Irish Statesmen* until it succumbed to financial difficulties in April 1930 (*Myriad-Minded Man*

250–251). Yeats told Russell that he regretted the journal's demise "on public grounds—it leaves us 'sheep without a shepherd when the snow shuts out the day'—but not on private for you can now write books" (*Letters* 774). Yeats soon had the book he desired: Russell's *Song and its Fountains,* an account of his visionary experience. Yeats reviewed the volume in the April 9, 1932, issue of the *Spectator* and reprinted the review in his 1937 volume *Essays* (see *Expl.* 412–418; *LE* 113–117). Yeats writes that he "began by hating the book for its language," but "came to love the book for its thought."

In *A VISION,* Yeats places Russell in Phase 25 of his lunar cycle, where he keeps company with Cardinal Newman, Luther, Calvin, and the poet George Herbert (1593–1633). A man of this phase, writes Yeats, is "strong, full of initiative, full of social intellect; absorption has scarce begun; but his object is to limit and bind, to make men better, by making it impossible that they should be otherwise, to so arrange prohibitions and habits that men may be naturally good, as they are naturally black, or white, or yellow" (173). Poets of this phase, like Russell and Herbert, "are always stirred to an imaginative intensity by some form of propaganda." Though Russell was undoubtedly of this phase, the "signs are obscured by the influence upon his early years of poets and painters of middle *antithetical* phases. Neither Russell's visionary painting nor his visions of 'nature spirits' are, upon this supposition, true to phase. Every poem, where he is moved to write by some form of philosophical propaganda, is precise, delicate and original, while in his visionary painting one discovers the influence of other men, Gustave Moreau, for instance" (175–176; see also *Aut.* 200–201). Russell respectfully reviewed the 1925 edition of *A Vision* and pronounced himself "a little uncomfortable" with some of his "fellow-prisoners" in Phase 25: "I welcome George Herbert, but am startled to find myself along with Calvin, Luther and Cardinal Newman, as no doubt the last three would be incredulous of their own affinities to associate pilgrim souls" (*Critical Heritage* 271). Following Russell's death in 1935, Yeats offered a more intimate summarizing comment in a letter to DOROTHY WELLESLEY: "All is well with AE. His ghost will not walk. He had no passionate human

relationships to draw him back. My wife said the other night 'AE was the nearest to a saint you or I will ever meet. You are a better poet but no saint. I suppose one has to choose.' [. . .] A.E. was my oldest friend—we began our work together. I constantly quarrelled with him but he never bore malice and in his last letter, a month before his death, he said that generally when he differed from me it was that he feared to be absorbed by my personality [see above]. He had no passions, but as a young man had to struggle against his senses. He gave up writing poetry for a time because it stirred his senses. He wanted always to be free" (*Letters* 838; *LOP* 11–12).

Bibliography
Eglinton, John. *A Memoir of AE*; Finneran, Richard J., et al., eds. *Letters to W. B. Yeats* (vols. 1–2); Foster, R. F. *W. B. Yeats: A Life, I: The Apprentice Mage*; Jeffares, A. Norman, ed. *W. B. Yeats: The Critical Heritage*; Kuch, Peter. *Yeats and A.E.: 'The antagonism that unites dear friends'*; Mikhail, E. H., ed. *W. B. Yeats: Interviews and Recollections* (vol. 2); Russell, George. *Letters from AE*; Summerfield, Henry. *That Myriad-Minded Man: A Biography of George Russell, "A.E.," 1867–1935*; Yeats, W. B. *Autobiographies, The Collected Letters of W. B. Yeats* (vols. 2–4), *Essays and Introductions, Explorations, The Gonne-Yeats Letters 1893–1938, Later Essays, The Letters of W. B. Yeats, Letters on Poetry from W. B. Yeats to Dorothy Wellesley, Memoirs, Prefaces and Introductions, Uncollected Prose by W. B. Yeats* (vols. 1–2), *A Vision*.

Savoy   Though it appeared a mere eight times, the *Savoy,* in conjunction with the *Yellow Book,* defined the "decadence" and aestheticism of the 1890s. The magazine took its name from the glamorous and louche London hotel, which had opened in 1889 and become notorious as the scene of OSCAR WILDE's trysts (in a draft of *The Importance of Being Ernest,* Algernon is dunned for a debt of £762 14s 2d run up at the Savoy—a comically vast sum). The magazine was the brainchild of Leonard Smithers (1861–1907), a publisher of erotica whom Yeats detested (see *CL2* 473–474). In the summer of 1895 he enlisted as editor Yeats's friend and future flatmate ARTHUR SYMONS, who in turn enlisted as art editor AUBREY BEARDSLEY (*Aut* 248–249; *Mem.* 90–92). In addition to Yeats, Symons, and Beardsley, contributors included Max Beerbohm, Joseph Conrad, Ernest Dowson, Havelock Ellis, Edmund Gosse, W. T. HORTON, Ford Madox Hueffer (later Ford Madox Ford), GEORGE MOORE, OLIVIA SHAKESPEAR, and George Bernard Shaw. In the introduction to his anthology *The Savoy: Nineties Experiment*, Stanley Weintraub notes that 14 of the 35 writers who contributed to the *Savoy* had previously contributed to the *Yellow Book* (xvii) and suggests that the *Savoy* was largely conceived in response to the *Yellow Book*'s retreat into respectability (xv). Yeats puts a finer point on the matter, noting that Beardsley's dismissal from the *Yellow Book* on charges of immorality (he was associated in the public mind with Wilde) roused his circle to "fury" (*Mem.* 90). Yeats describes the magazine's contributors as "outlaws" and the magazine itself as a campaign of "warfare on the British public at a time when we had all against us" (90). The "hated name" of Beardsley particularly marked the *Savoy* as an object of mainstream scorn and mistrust (*Aut.* 250). Less romantically, the magazine provided Yeats with a respectable income—an estimated total of more than £100—making it possible for him to take lodgings at 18 WOBURN BUILDINGS and pursue his affair with Shakespear (*CL2* 722).

The magazine's eight numbers appeared in January, April, July, August, September, October, November, and December 1896. In an epilogue published in the final number of the magazine, Symons diagnoses the causes of the *Savoy*'s downfall: "Our first mistake was in giving so much for so little money; our second, in abandoning a quarterly for a monthly issue. The action of Messrs. Smith and Son in refusing to place 'The Savoy' on their bookstalls, on account of the reproduction of a drawing by BLAKE, was another misfortune. And then, worst of all, we assumed that there were very many people in the world who really cared for art, and really for art's sake" (*Savoy* 276). The contretemps with W. H. Smith was particularly damaging, as the bookseller had exclusive rights to operate the all-important bookstalls at train stations (*CL2* 721). The offending image was a reproduction of

Blake's "Antaeus setting Virgil and Dante upon the verge of Cocytus," which accompanied Yeats's article "William Blake and his Illustrations to the *Divine Comedy*" (*Aut.* 249; *CL2* 40, 721). The painting, now held by the National Gallery of Victoria, Melbourne, shows Antaeus in the nude.

Yeats contributed poems, stories, and essays to the *Savoy* as follows: "The Shadowy Horses" (January, later "HE BIDS HIS BELOVED BE AT PEACE"), "The TRAVAIL OF PASSION" (January), "The Binding of the Hair" (January), "ROSA ALCHEMICA" (April), "A Cradle Song" (April), "The VALLEY OF THE BLACK PIG" (April), "Verlaine in 1894" (April), "O'Sullivan Rua to Mary Lavell" (July, later "HE REMEMBERS FORGOTTEN BEAUTY"), "William Blake and his Illustrations to the *Divine Comedy*" (July, August, September), "O'Sullivan Rua to the Secret Rose" (September, later "The SECRET ROSE"), "O'Sullivan Rua to the Curlew" (November, later "HE REPROVES THE CURLEW"), "Out of the Old Days" (November, later "TO HIS HEART, BIDDING IT HAVE NO FEAR"), and "The TABLES OF THE LAW" (November) (*Biblio.* 348–351).

Bibliography

Wade, Allan. *A Bibliography of the Writings of W. B. Yeats*; Weintraub, Stanley, ed. *The Savoy: Nineties Experiment*; Yeats, W. B. *Autobiographies, The Collected Letters of W. B. Yeats* (vol. 2), *Memoirs*.

Senate Yeats ceaselessly denounced politics as incompatible with "intellectual innocence"—the "delight in what is unforeseen, and in the mere spectacle of the world, the mere drifting hither and thither that must come before all true thought and emotion"—and yet eagerly joined the political fray at nearly every opportunity (*E&I* 314). During the 1890s Yeats threw himself into nationalist politics, often in alliance with MAUD GONNE. Galvanized by the opposition to *The* COUNTESS CATHLEEN in 1899, he subsequently became Dublin's self-appointed defender of aesthetic autonomy, and, in a series of bitter skirmishes, turned against many who had been former allies—in short, engaged in a slashing variety of antipolitics that was yet overtly political. By the 1920s, Yeats had adopted a pose of aristocratic Georgianism founded in part on the example of statesman Edmund Burke—"A PRAYER FOR MY DAUGHTER" is emblematic—and he did not hesitate to accept appointed membership in the Irish Senate in December 1922, despite the dangers of serving while the IRISH CIVIL WAR continued to rage (see SS 50). The position came with a substantial salary; when his term expired in 1928, Yeats more than anything regretted the loss of £360 per year (*Letters* 745).

The constitution of the newly formed Irish Free State established two legislative bodies, the Dáil and the Senate. "As originally designed," writes Donald R. Pierce, editor of *The Senate Speeches of W. B. Yeats*, "the Senate numbered sixty members, thirty of whom were elected for a period of three years by the Dáil, and thirty appointed for six years by the President of the Executive Council in consultation with certain legal and commercial groups." The Senate "could initiate legislation on all matters excepting finance, but could reject no proposal that had been passed by the Dáil" (SS 13). Given his expertise in cultural matters and the luster of his great name, Yeats was a natural candidate for membership in the new body. His friend and fellow senator Oliver St John Gogarty (1878–1957) is said to have taken up the cudgels and pushed his name through, declaring before a skeptical nominating committee, "If it had not been for W. B. Yeats there would be no Irish Free State!" (15). Ernest Blythe (1889–1975), minister for finance (1922–32) during Yeats's Senate tenure and later managing director of the ABBEY THEATRE (1941–67), attributes Yeats's nomination to the advocacy of cabinet member Desmond Fitzgerald (1888–1947), a man of literary interests who "ascribed his national feelings and convictions to the influence of Yeats's poetry" and was set on Yeats's membership "from the moment proposals for a Senate took definite shape" (*I&R*, II, 392). It may have helped that Yeats had interceded on Fitzgerald's behalf after he was arrested in early 1921 (*Free State* 56–57). According to Blythe, Yeats's nomination "encountered no opposition in the Cabinet" (*I&R*, II, 392).

On December 18, 1922, seven days after he took office, Yeats wrote to OLIVIA SHAKESPEAR in evident excitement about his new position: "My work on the Senate interests me, a new technique which I am learning [is] silence—I have only spoken once and then but six sentences and shall not speak again perhaps till I am (if I shall ever be) at ease with it. [. . .] At the Senate house I have for near neighbours two senators, one of whom has had his house bombed for being a senator, and one is under sentence of death because he owns the *Freeman's Journal*. For all that we are a dull (and as President Cosgrave has pointed out with evident content) well-dressed crowd. I shall speak very little but probably intrigue a great deal to get some old projects into action. On Wednesday next I get a D.Litt from Trinity College, and feel that I have become a personage" (*Letters* 694–695). Blythe remembers that Yeats "allied himself with what has generally been described as the ex-Unionist group, though it included James Douglas, Mrs. Alice Stopford Green, the historian, and Sam Brown, K.C., none of them Unionists. Its leader, however, if it could rightly be said to have had a leader, was Andrew Jameson [1855–1941, head of the famous distillery and a director of the Bank of Ireland, as well as an old friend of JOHN BUTLER YEATS]. He had been head of the Irish Unionist Alliance and a redoubtable opponent of Home Rule, but he became a contented loyal citizen of the Free State on its establishment. It was natural that Yeats, back again for the first time for many years in active politics, should drift to this so-called ex-Unionist group. Most of its members were personally distinguished by reason of talent or influence and Yeats's romantic longing for aristocratic and authoritarian ways and standards made him feel at home in the circle which they formed. I would not say that his opinion carried great weight amongst them on general issues. But when he was on his ground he could, of course, bring the majority with him" (*I&R*, II, 392–393).

During his Senate tenure, Yeats served on the Irish Manuscript Committee (1923–24), which was to devise a plan for the preservation and promotion of the Gaelic language (SS 42–45, 68–77); the Coinage Committee (1926–28), which was to oversee the design of a new Irish currency (105, 161–167); and the Committee for the "Federation of the Arts," which was to oversee the creation of a national academy of the arts (18). Recognizing his limited expertise, Yeats for the most part addressed matters of art and culture. He voiced opinions on the Irish language, the HUGH LANE pictures, film censorship, the preservation of ancient monuments, the stained glass industry, the design of a new coinage (see *P&I* 166–171), the design of Irish lace (see *Letters* 704), the condition and funding of schools, copyright protection, and judges' attire. For the most part, he made an effort to be practical and soft-spoken, as if deliberately repressing the imperiousness that he brought to theater business and voiced in much of his poetry. Only a motion to proscribe the right to divorce (by requiring that private bills of divorce "must be read a first time in each House before they are further proceeded with in the Senate") roused Yeats to his grand manner (*SS* 90). Having already published an "undelivered speech" on divorce in the *Irish Statesman* on March 14 (see *UP2* 449–52), he took the Senate floor on June 11, 1925, and made an impassioned plea for the separation of church and state, for the rights of Ireland's Protestant minority, and for what he considered humane common sense, invoking with superb arrogance the Protestant tradition that he felt to be under attack. The speech, which had offended his own typist to tears (*Letters* 709), includes Yeats's most famous invocation of the Protestant tradition with which he identified himself: "We against whom you have done this thing are no petty people. We are one of the great stocks of Europe. We are the people of Burke; we are the people of Grattan; we are the people of SWIFT, the people of Emmet, the people of PARNELL. We have created the most of the modern literature of this country. We have created the best of its political intelligence" (*SS* 99). Joseph Hone calls Yeats's speech on divorce "perhaps the most remarkable witnessed in the Irish Senate during its existence" (*W. B. Yeats* 373). If the speech was a deliberate provocation, its aim was of the highest; as Donald T. Torchiana writes, "Not snobbery but pride, not two nations but possibly one in a future that would see the defeat of bigotry, not rudeness but a high inspired appeal in the midst of despair for a coming intellectual transformation—these were Yeats's lonely intentions" (*W. B. Yeats & Georgian Ireland*

150). The speech expressed no mere passing political opinion but found the formula for an entire order of values and commitments, and Yeats redeployed the language of the speech to great effect in "The TOWER," which he began that summer (see lines 126–133).

Yeats's most substantive policy interest was education. In 1925 GEORGE YEATS found a copy of Giovanni Gentile's (1875–1944) *La Reforma dell'educazione* while browsing a bookstall in Rome and translated it for her husband (*BG* 342). Thereafter Yeats counted himself a disciple of the Italian minister of education and idealist philosopher. As he states in his 1925 essay "The Child and the State," Yeats believed, under Gentile's influence, that the "whole curriculum of a school should be as it were one lesson and not a mass of unrelated topics," a notion consistent with his adherence to the ideal of UNITY OF BEING (*SS* 173; *UP2* 459). Surprisingly, given that artistic controversies had so often made an anticleric of him, Yeats avows that he "would have each religion, Catholic or Protestant, so taught that it permeates the whole school life." He explains that every child "in growing from infancy to maturity should pass in imagination through the history of its own race and through something of the history of the world, and the most powerful part in that history is played by religion. Let the child go its own way when maturity comes, but it is our business that it has something of that whole inheritance, and not as a mere thought, an abstract thing like those Graeco-Roman casts upon the shelves in the art-schools, but as a part of its emotional life" (*SS* 173–174; *UP2* 459–460). As a would-be philosopher of education, Yeats toured primary schools in 1925 and 1926. His most consequential visit was to the Montessorian St. Otteran's School in Waterford on March 21–22, 1926, which inspired "AMONG SCHOOL CHILDREN." Whatever Yeats's legislative accomplishments or political realizations, this poem was the most important result of his term in the Senate. Yeats commences with the image himself as a "sixty-year-old smiling public man," but this senatorial guise is almost immediately shed as the poem deepens into reverie, implying that the senator left off precisely where the poet—by far the more rich and fundamental identity—began.

Ailing, Yeats declined to seek a second term and resigned his Senate seat on September 28, 1928 (*BG* 403; *Letters* 737, 745–746). In later years, Yeats neither mythologized nor excessively dwelled upon his term in the Senate. His principal comments are to be found in "A Packet for Ezra Pound" (see *A VISION*), in *ON THE BOILER*, and in the essay "Ireland, 1921–1931" (*UP2* 486–490). "Do not be elected to the Senate of your country," Yeats advises POUND in "A Packet for Ezra Pound." Experience had taught Yeats that poets cannot "match those old lawyers, old bankers, old business men, who, because all habit and memory, have begun to govern the world. They lean over the chair in front and talk as if to half a dozen of their kind at some board-meeting, and, whether they carry their point or not, retain moral ascendancy" (*AV* 26). In this polished company, Yeats was conscious of his inexperience and, to a surprising degree given his eminence, fell prey to insecurity and anxiety. He paints a picture of his discomfort for Pound: "[The] group you belong to will invite you to one of those private meetings where the real work of legislation is done, and the ten minutes they can grant you, after discussing the next Bill upon the agenda for two hours with unperturbed lucidity, will outlast your self-confidence. [. . .] Whenever I stood up to speak, no matter how long I had pondered my words, unless I spoke of something that concerned the arts, or upon something that depended not upon precise knowledge but upon public opinion [. . .] I was ashamed until shame turned at last, even if I spoke but a few words—my body being somewhat battered by time—into physical pain" (27). In *On the Boiler*, Yeats's comments have an anti-democratic undercurrent. He remembers the original class of 30 senators whom President Cosgrave appointed as "plainly the most able and the most educated," while the "few able men among the elected Senators had been nominated for election by Ministers. As the nominated element began to die out—almost all were old men—the Senate declined in ability and prestige. In its early days some old banker or lawyer would dominate the House, leaning upon the back of the chair in front, always speaking with undisturbed self-possession as at some table in a board-room. My imagination sets up against him

some typical elected man, emotional as a youthful chimpanzee, hot and vague, always disturbed, always hating something or other" (*Expl.* 412–413; *LE* 224). The ministers, on the other hand, "seemed men of skill and mother-wit, men who had survived hatred. But their minds knew no play that my mind could play at; I felt that I could never know them. One of the most notable said he had long wanted to meet me. We met, but my conversation shocked and embarrassed him. No, neither Gogarty nor I, with our habit of outrageous conversation, could get near those men" (*Expl.* 413; *LE* 224).

Bibliography

Hone, Joseph. *W. B. Yeats*; Krimm, Bernard G. *W. B. Yeats and the Emergence of the Irish Free State, 1918–1939: Living in the Explosion*; Mikhail, E. H., ed. *W. B. Yeats: Interviews and Recollections* (vol. 2); Saddlemyer, Ann. *Becoming George: The Life of Mrs W. B. Yeats*; Torchiana, Donald T. *W. B. Yeats & Georgian Ireland*; Yeats, W. B. *Essays and Introductions, Explorations, Later Essays, The Letters of W. B. Yeats, Prefaces and Introductions, The Senate Speeches of W. B. Yeats, Uncollected Prose by W. B. Yeats* (vol. 2), *A Vision*.

Shakespear, Olivia (née Tucker) (1863–1938) A minor novelist and well-known figure in London artistic circles from the 1890s, Shakespear is primarily remembered in relation to the more famous and the more talented. In addition to being the quondam lover and lifelong confidante of Yeats, she was the cousin of LIONEL JOHNSON, the mother-in-law of EZRA POUND, and the step-aunt of GEORGE YEATS (Olivia's brother Henry Tucker married George's mother, the widowed Edith Ellen "Nelly" Hyde-Lees, in February 1911). It was through Shakespear that Yeats first came to know both his most estimable literary acolyte and his future wife. On May 10, 1909, Shakespear brought Pound to one of Yeats's "Monday Evenings," and in 1910 or 1911, over tea, she introduced Yeats to Georgie Hyde-Lees, who was then her daughter Dorothy's closest friend (*Olivia Shakespear and W. B. Yeats* 132, 141).

Shakespear was the daughter of Major-General Henry Hod Tucker (1808–96), a retired Anglo-Indian officer of comfortable means and kindly disposition, and Harriet Maria Johnson (1821–1900), whose large family was also military. Shakespear grew up in Sussex and, from 1877, in London. She received no formal education but read widely and voraciously; in MEMOIRS, Yeats credits her with "profound culture" and "a knowledge of French, English and Italian literature" (74). She was close to her cousin Lionel Johnson, the one family member who shared her literary interests. Despite these interests, Olivia married Henry Hope Shakespear (1849–1923), a conventional and middlingly successful London solicitor 14 years her senior, on December 8, 1885. Yeats describes Hope Shakespear "as a little heavy, a little without life," and recalls Olivia's complaint that her husband "ceased to pay court" to her from the day they were married (*Mem.* 74, 88). The couple had one child: Dorothy Shakespear—the future Mrs. Ezra Pound—was born on September 14, 1886. During the early 1890s, Shakespear became known in London literary society, most likely with the help of her cousin. She published her first novel, *Love on a Mortal Lease*, in June 1894. There followed five further novels: *The Journey of High Honour* (November 1894), *The False Laurel* (June 1896), *Rupert Armstrong* (January 1899), *The Devotees* (June 1904), and *Uncle Hilary* (April 1910), as well as the novella "Beauty's Hour" (published in the August and September 1896 numbers of the SAVOY), and two Egyptian-themed plays, *The Beloved of Hathor* and *The Shrine of the Golden Hawk*, that she wrote and produced in collaboration with FLORENCE FARR. Yeats's letters frankly comment on Shakespear's work (CL1 397–397, 414–416, 463–464; CL2 649–651; CL3 628–629, 633–634), and he wrote a mixed review of the Egyptian plays (UP2 265–267).

Shakespear and Yeats first laid eye on each other on April 16, 1894, at a dinner celebrating the publication of the *Yellow Book. Memoirs* records Yeats's first impression of Shakespear, who had arrived in the company of the novelist and playwright Pearl Craigie (1867–1906) and GEORGE MOORE: "At a literary dinner where there were some fifty or sixty guests I noticed opposite me, between celebrated novelists, a woman of great beauty. Her face had a perfectly Greek regularity, though her skin was a little darker than a Greek's would have been and

her hair was very dark. She was exquisitely dressed with what seemed to me very old lace over her breast, and had the same sensitive look of distinction I had admired in Eva Gore-Booth. She was, it seemed, about my own age, but suggested to me an incomparable distinction. I was not introduced to her, but found that she was related to a member of the RHYMERS' CLUB [Johnson] and had asked my name" (72). Intrigued by the darkly handsome young poet, Shakespear made a point of seeing Yeats's The LAND OF HEART'S DESIRE performed at the Avenue Theatre and resolved to introduce herself (74). With Johnson acting as chaperone, Yeats visited Shakespear at home in May 1894 (*Olivia Shakespear and W. B. Yeats* 37). The friendship solidified, and Yeats remained a faithful correspondent while staying with his uncle GEORGE POLLEXFEN in SLIGO from October 1894 to May 1895, writing what Shakespear later called "unconscious love-letters" (*Mem.* 85).

Upon Yeats's return to London, the friendship deepened into an affair. The would-be lovers contemplated running away together, but agreed to delay their elopement until Shakespear's mother died (86). Limiting themselves to kisses—the first of which left Yeats "startled and a little shocked"—the couple met for nearly a year in "railway carriages and at picture galleries and occasionally at her house" (86). Shakespear eventually asked her husband for a separation, but he became ill with distress, and the illicit couple decided it would be "kinder to deceive him" (88). Richard Ellmann speculates that with MAUD GONNE a continuing preoccupation Yeats most likely had a "strong half-conscious repulsion to the elopement" (MM 159). In those days, as well, Yeats was sexually inexperienced and timid in bedroom matters; an elopement may have seemed like a distressing plunge into the unknown.

In February 1896, Yeats took rooms at WOBURN BUILDINGS and the couple consummated their relationship. The virginal Yeats was at first "impotent from nervous excitement" (*Mem.* 88; cf. AV 43). Shakespear returned to his rooms a week later. Yeats remembers that his "nervous excitement was so painful that it seemed best but to sit over our tea and talk. I do not think we kissed each other except at the moment of her leaving. She understood instead of, as another would, changing liking for dislike—was only troubled by my trouble. My nervousness did not return again and we had many days of happiness" (*Mem.* 88). The affair lasted until March or April 1897, when Gonne returned to London and Yeats fell into his old torment. "And at last one morning instead of reading much love poetry, as my way was to bring the right mood round, I wrote letters," Yeats recalls. "My friend found my mood did not answer hers and burst into tears. 'There is someone else in your heart,' she said. It was the breaking between us for many years" (89). The breakup became the stuff of poetry in "The LOVER MOURNS FOR THE LOSS OF LOVE." Shakespear and Yeats reestablished their friendship in 1900 (*CL2* 529) and possibly resumed their affair in 1903 and in 1911 or 1912 (*Olivia Shakespear and W. B. Yeats* 118, 136).

Hope Shakespear died on July 5, 1923. Olivia's widowhood, in biographer John Harwood's description, was a pleasant and stimulating round of "frequent visitors, regular outings to the theatre, concerts and art galleries, and frequent visits to friends out of London, most of them people she had already known for fifteen or more years" (*Olivia Shakespear and W. B. Yeats* 169). Additionally, she brought up her grandchild Omar Pound, while Ezra and Dorothy resided in Italy. Omar was born on September 10, 1926; two weeks later Yeats wrote to Olivia, "I divine that you have already adopted the grandchild" (*Letters* 718). The boy lived in the Sussex village of Felpham with the "retired superintendent of a Norland 'nanny' training institution," but he went to his grandmother on vacations and generally fell under her supervisory eye (*Serious Character* 455–456). During these years Yeats was largely in Ireland and abroad, but the two old friends maintained an affectionate, chatty correspondence (see *Letters passim*). Shakespear died on October 3, 1938, of complications arising from what she called "gall bladder trouble" (*Olivia Shakespear and W. B. Yeats* 192). Yeats wrote to DOROTHY WELLESLEY on October 8, "For more than forty years she has been the centre of my life in London and during all that time we have never had a quarrel, sadness sometimes but never a difference. When I first

met her she was in her late twenties but in looks a lovely young girl. When she died she was a lovely old woman. [. . .] She was not more lovely than distinguished—no matter what happened she never lost her solitude. She was Lionel Johnson's cousin and felt and thought as he did. For the moment I cannot bear the thought of London. I will find her memory everywhere" (*Letters* 916).

Shakespear's image—and especially the image of her luxuriant and embowering hair—dominates the poems of *The Wind Among the Reeds* (1899). The image of embowering hair may also have been helped along by Villiers de l'Isle-Adam's symbolist drama *Axël* (1890), which Yeats saw in PARIS in 1894. In his introduction to a 1925 edition of the play, Yeats quotes a line that had stuck with him for 30 years: "O to veil you with my hair where you will breathe the spirit of dead roses" (*P&I* 156). In Harwood's estimation, Shakespear inspired "HE BIDS HIS BELOVED BE AT PEACE," "HE GIVES HIS BELOVED CERTAIN RHYMES" (disputable), "HE REMEMBERS FORGOTTEN BEAUTY," "HE REPROVES THE CURLEW," "The Lover asks Forgiveness because of his Many Moods," "The Lover mourns for the Loss of Love," "A Poet to his Beloved," and "The TRAVAIL OF PASSION" (*Olivia Shakespear and W. B. Yeats* 71). Harwood writes, "In the 'Olivia Shakespear' poems, the iconography centres on imagery of hair, and the beloved is clearly mortal, whereas in the 'Maud Gonne' poems the emphasis falls upon eyes and eyelids, and the beloved becomes a quasi-immortal being, with absolute power over the poet. The distinction only exists during the years 1895–1897, after which [apart from "The Lover mourns for the Loss of Love"] Olivia Shakespear is no longer represented in the poems, and imagery of hair reverts to Maud Gonne" (73–74). R. F. Foster detects in the poems of *The Wind Among the Reeds* a similar division: "One group, usually featuring [Michael] Robartes, inevitably suggests the doomed affair with Olivia Shakespear and conveys the regrets of a lover who cannot quite convince himself, nor lose himself in love [. . .]. Another group of poems strikes a note of desperation, and the longing for total possession in death. These were inspired by 'Aedh's' commitment to Gonne, and include 'AEDH [HE] WISHES HIS BELOVED WERE DEAD', 'AEDH [HE] HEARS THE

CRY OF THE SEDGE' and 'MONGAN [HE] THINKS OF HIS PAST GREATNESS'" (AM 215). Among Yeats's later poems, Shakespear figures in "AFTER LONG SILENCE" and "FRIENDS," both of which attest to Yeats's unwavering attachment.

Bibliography

Carpenter, Humphrey. *A Serious Character: The Life of Ezra Pound*; Ellmann, Richard. *Yeats: The Man and the Masks*; Foster, R. F. *W. B. Yeats: A Life, I: The Apprentice Mage*; Harwood, John. *Olivia Shakespear and W. B. Yeats: After Long Silence*; Yeats, W. B. *The Collected Letters of W. B. Yeats* (vols. 1–3), *The Letters of W. B. Yeats, Memoirs, Prefaces and Introductions, Uncollected Prose by W. B. Yeats* (vol. 2), *A Vision*.

Shelley, Percy Bysshe (1792–1822) The great romantic poet was one of the few most important influences—if not the most important influence—on Yeats's poetic and intellectual development. In AUTOBIOGRAPHIES Yeats recalls his late teenage penchant for Shelley: "I had many idols, and as I climbed along the narrow ledge I was now [Byron's] Manfred on his glacier, and now [Shelley's] Prince Athanase with his solitary lamp, but I soon chose [Shelley's] Alastor for my chief of men and longed to share his melancholy, and maybe at last disappear from everybody's sight as he disappeared drifting in a boat along some slow-moving river between great trees" (80). Yeats recalls also how the women of his fantasies were like Cythna in *The Revolt of Islam,* and accompanied "their lovers through all manner of wild places, lawless women without homes and without children"; how he had made Shelley's *Prometheus Unbound*—which his father would read aloud during breakfast at his Dublin studio—his "sacred book"; how he had given himself to "Shelley's dream of a young man [Athanase], his hair blanched with sorrow, studying philosophy in some lonely tower, or of his old man [Ahasuerus], master of all human knowledge, hidden from human sight in some shell-strewn cavern on the Mediterranean shore"; and how a long passage from "Hellas"—an account of Ahasuerus—"ran perpetually" in his ears (80, 95, 151). In his late essay "PROMETHEUS UNBOUND," Yeats

describes coming to the middle-aged realization that Shelley, even more than BLAKE, had shaped his life (E&I 424; LE 121–122).

Shelley's influence on Yeats's poetry—especially the early poetry—is pervasive. From Shelley, George Bornstein summarizes, the early Yeats "extrapolated a world where melancholy lovers seek their ladies with varying success, often in exotic settings presided over by a symbolic star, where esoteric wisdom and magic spells either frustrate or complete the search," though as Bornstein notes, "what he found in Shelley did not always coincide with what was there to be found" (*Yeats and Shelley* 14). From Shelley, as well, Yeats at least in part derived the images of swan, fountain, cave, and tower, and the motif of the soul-allegorizing journey upon sea or river (Yeats frequently acknowledges the precedent of Shelley's symbol language; see for example "BLOOD AND THE MOON"; E&I 235; VP 831). From Shelley's life—perhaps also from the lives of Blake and COLERIDGE—Yeats derived the notion of the poet as visionary outcast tragically at odds with "the noisy set / Of Bankers, schoolmasters, and clergymen / The martyrs call the world" ("ADAM'S CURSE"), a notion Yeats institutionalized in his account of the "tragic generation" in AUTOBIOGRAPHIES.

Particularly seminal was "Alastor" (1816), which gave Yeats the particulars of the quest paradigm that recurs throughout his work. Its image of the solitary poet-magician-visionary crossing the sea in pursuit of immortal essence or beauty informs poems like "SAILING TO BYZANTIUM," *The SHADOWY WATERS,* and "The WANDERINGS OF OISIN"; its conception of the visionary enterprise as a withering process of estrangement from the natural order informs poems like "ALL SOULS' NIGHT," "The CHOICE," "FERGUS AND THE DRUID," "The MAN WHO DREAMED OF FAERYLAND," "The SONG OF WANDERING AENGUS" (an "Irish *Alastor* in miniature," as Bornstein calls it), and "TO THE ROSE UPON THE ROOD OF TIME," as well as Yeats's account of "the tragic generation" in *Autobiographies*; and its notion of a tormenting and finally destructive romantic attachment informs much of Yeats's figuration of his own attachment to MAUD GONNE, as for example in "FIRST LOVE," which commences "A MAN YOUNG

AND OLD." From the fragments of "Prince Atha-nase," which present in broken outline a Platoniz-ing version of the Alastor-poet, Yeats extrapolated a model of hermetic solitude and occult wisdom, an influence detectable in poems like "EGO DOMI-NUS TUUS," "The LEADERS OF THE CROWD," "MY HOUSE," and "The PHASES OF THE MOON." From the figure of Cythna in *The Revolt of Islam* (1818), as Harold Bloom notes, Yeats derived "the heroic conception of Maud Gonne as a rebel against all established order" (*Yeats* 57). Shelley's essay "A Defence of Poetry" (1840) confirmed Yeats's sense that poets are the "unacknowledged legislators of the World." Yeats all but paraphrases Shelley's famed words in his 1903 essay "The Happiest of the Poets" (WILLIAM MORRIS "knew as Shelley knew, by an act of faith, that the economists should take their measurements not from life as it is, but from the vision of men like him, from the vision of the world made perfect that is buried under all minds") and in *Autobiographies* (Yeats remembers propos-ing that "whatever the great poets had affirmed in their finest moments was the nearest we could come to an authoritative religion, and that their mythology, their spirits of water and wind, were but literal truth"), and he explicitly proclaims the preeminence of the poet in his stage polemic *The KING'S THRESHOLD* (*E&I* 63; *Aut.* 97). Shelley's "Hymn to Intellectual Beauty" (1817), finally, models the posture of supplication in the several poems of the 1890s that address the mystic ROSE. In *AUTOBIOGRAPHIES*, Yeats characterizes "To the Rose upon the Rood of Time" as a prayer to "the Red Rose, to Intellectual Beauty," an evident allu-sion to the Shelleyan conception, while in a 1925 note he comments that "the quality symbolised as The Rose differs from the Intellectual Beauty of Shelley and of Spenser in that I have imagined it as suffering with man and not as something pursued and seen from afar" (*Aut.* 205; *VP* 842).

Yeats's Shelleyism became more measured and qualified in his later life. His attempt during the early years of the 20th century to evolve a more vigorous and austere STYLE—a style premised on "athletic joy"—partially involved shedding some-thing of Shelley's influence (*CL3* 577–578). In his 1901 essay "Ireland and the Arts," Yeats writes that

it had taken years to rid himself of "Shelley's Italian light" and thus find his own style, and in his 1902 essay "What is 'Popular Poetry'?" he remembers the struggle to disentangle his style from Shelley's: "I had a conviction, which indeed I have still, that one's verses should hold, as in a mirror, the colours of one's own climate and scenery in their right pro-portion; and, when I found my verses too full of the reds and yellows Shelley gathered in Italy, I thought for two days of setting things right, not as I should now by making my rhythms faint and nervous and filling my images with a certain coldness, a certain wintry wildness, but by eating little and sleeping upon a board" (*E&I* 5). So too Yeats became intol-erant of Shelley's political sympathies, placing him in the implicitly disreputable company of Browning, TENNYSON, and WORDSWORTH, all of whom upheld "moral values that were not aesthetic values" (*Aut.* 242; cf. 148–149). In Yeats's view, Shelley's politics were essentially an attempt to evade the poetic burden, a species of "the chief temptation of the artist, creation without toil" (171). In 1924, Lady GREGORY recorded Yeats's mature assessment of Shelley's achievement. "Very little of Shelley will last for say 400 years," Yeats pronounced. "I know, for I was reading him the other day. There are about twenty pages of exquisite beauty that will live for ever. [. . .] I remember my father telling me Keats was a better poet than Shelley. I didn't believe him then but I know what he meant now, though I care more for Shelley" (*Lady Gregory's Journals*, I, 603–604).

In *A VISION*, Yeats assigns Shelley to the desir-able 17th lunar phase, the phase of Dante, the admired Walter Savage Landor (1775–1864), and Yeats himself. This is the phase of the "daimonic man," for whom "UNITY OF BEING, and consequent expression of *Daimonic* thought, is now more easy than at any other phase" (*AV* 141; on Yeats as a man of Phase 17, see *Making of Yeats's 'A Vision*,' II, 116). Yeats's involved discussion of Shelley ends, however, with an unfavorable comparison to Dante. For all his tribulations and partisanship, Dante attained Unity of Being and thus "as a poet saw all things set in order." Shelley, on the other hand, only partially attained Unity of Being, and thus "found compensation for his 'loss', for the taking away of his children, for his quarrel with his first wife, for later sexual disappointment, for his exile, for his obloquy—there were but some three or four persons, he said, who did not consider him a monster of iniquity—in his hopes for the future of mankind." Yeats concludes with the critical insight that Shelley "lacked the Vision of Evil, could not conceive of the world as a continual conflict, so, though great poet he certainly was, he was not of the greatest kind. Dante suffering injustice and the loss of Beatrice, found divine justice and the heavenly Beatrice, but the justice of *Prometheus Unbound* is a vague propagandist emotion and the women that await its coming are but clouds" (AV 143–144; see also *Aut.* 251). The debatable notion that Shelley lacked the Vision of Evil (and thus in Yeats's view fell prey to a facile utopian eschatology in both politics and poetry) marks the limit of Yeats's identification with Shelley. In the end, Yeats's insistence on the Vision of Evil as a necessary and even desirable precondition of tragic joy situated him in the camp of Blake rather than the camp of Shelley, at least as Yeats himself saw matters. Harold Bloom, however, detects a deeper affinity than Yeats was comfortable admitting to himself. Despite himself, says Bloom, Yeats "remained always a poet of autobiographical self-recognition, in the solitary tradition that Shelley had founded upon Wordsworth. Yeats's subject, again despite his own will, tended to be his relation as poet to his own vision, in Shelley's mode rather than Blake's, for Blake largely centered on the content of the poetic vision itself"; thus "the idea of the Yeatsian lyric is Shelley's idea, powerfully modified, but still recognizable" (*Yeats* 63).

In addition to the commentary of *A Vision*, Yeats's fullest discussions of Shelley are his two essays, "The PHILOSOPHY OF SHELLEY'S POETRY" and "PROMETHEUS UNBOUND." The former ends with a purple flourish that sets Blake and Shelley, the two writers who meant most to Yeats, in symbolic and clarifying contrast: "In ancient times, it seems to me that Blake, who for all his protest was glad to be alive, and ever spoke of his gladness, would have worshipped in some chapel of the Sun, but that Shelley, who hated life because he sought 'more in life than any understood,' would have wandered,

lost in a ceaseless reverie, in some chapel of the Star of infinite desire" (*E&I* 94).

Bibliography

Bloom, Harold. *Yeats*; Bornstein, George. *Yeats and Shelley*; Gregory, Lady. *Lady Gregory's Journals* (vol. 1, ed. Daniel J. Murphy); Harper, George Mills. *The Making of Yeats's 'A Vision': A Study of the Automatic Script* (vol. 2); Yeats, W. B. *Autobiographies, The Collected Letters of W. B. Yeats* (vol. 3), *Essays and Introductions, Later Essays, The Variorum Edition of the Poems of W. B. Yeats, A Vision.*

Sligo   "Cut him anywhere," Virginia Moore says of Yeats, "and he bled Sligo" (*Unicorn* 42). The small shipping town nestled in Sligo Bay on the west coast of Ireland was the closest thing Yeats possessed to a spiritual home. His connection was through his maternal family. In 1833, his grandfather WILLIAM POLLEXFEN arrived in town to assist his distant cousin Elizabeth Middleton, who was struggling to sustain the shipping and milling concern that had been left by her late husband (AM 4). Pollexfen married Elizabeth Middleton's daughter, also named Elizabeth, and entered the family business in partnership with his brother-in-law William. The firm of Middleton and Pollexfen prospered, helping make Sligo, as Joseph Hone writes, "the busy little town which it became in the latter part of the nineteenth century" (*W. B. Yeats* 15). In part due to his father's perpetual financial straits, Yeats spent much of his boyhood in Sligo, summering there in 1868, 1869 (remaining until December), 1870, and 1876, and making a longer stay from July 1872 to October 1874. During these sojourns the family resided at Merville, William Pollexfen's 60-acre estate southwest of town. According to Hone, the house contained "fourteen bedrooms, a stone kitchen, offices, a glorious laundry redolent of soap, and a storeroom like a village shop, with windows and fireplaces, shelves and drawers and a strong smell of ground coffee" (15). Yeats recollects, "The house was so big that there was always a room to hide in, and I had a red pony and a garden where I could wander [. . .]" (*Aut.* 41). Yeats also had the run of his great uncle William Middleton's two homes—Elsinore Lodge at Rosses Point in summers

O'Connell Street, Sligo, in the late 19th century *(National Library of Ireland)*

and Avena House at Ballisodare in winters—both of which were within a few miles of Sligo (*Aut.* 48; *Yeats Country* 36–37). The lodge had been a smuggler's house a century earlier, according to Yeats, and "sometimes three loud raps would come upon the drawing-room window at sundown, setting all the dogs barking: some dead smuggler giving his accustomed signal" (*Aut.* 48). Yeats heard his first fairy stories in the cottages surrounding the Middleton properties (48).

Yeats gives the impression that Sligo was an ideal nursing ground for a young boy: abundant in natural beauty and open space, thickly peopled with family, touched by the romance of the sea and the wonder of ancient legends. He confesses in AUTOBIOGRA-PHIES that he was brokenhearted to leave: "Years afterwards, when I was ten or twelve years old in London, I would remember Sligo with tears, and when I began to write, it was there I hoped to find my audience" (49). Yeats's most famous poem of Sligo, "The LAKE ISLE OF INNISFREE," immortalizes this ache of homesick longing. As an adult, Yeats returned to Sligo to visit his grandparents (who died in 1892) and his uncle GEORGE POLLEXFEN (who died in 1910). After his uncle died, Yeats's ties to Sligo were essentially severed. In "UNDER SATURN," he recalls returning to town with GEORGE YEATS and growing saturnine as he remembered "a child's vow sworn in vain / Never to leave that valley his fathers called their home."

Yeats's work is suffused with references to Sligo and its environs. Among the sites that figured prominently in Yeats's imagination are Ben Bulben, a mountain just north of Sligo, said to be the location of Diarmuid's fateful battle with the wild boar (see "Alternative Song for the Severed Head in *The King of the Great Clock Tower*," DIARMUID AND GRANIA, "ON A POLITICAL PRISONER," "Towards Break of Day," "The TOWER," "UNDER BEN BULBEN"); Drumcliff, a village north of Sligo, where Yeats's great-grandfather John Yeats (1774–1846) served as parish rector, and where Yeats himself is buried (see "ARE YOU CONTENT?" and "Under Ben Bulben"); Glen-Car, a valley with lake and waterfall northeast of Sligo (see "Towards Break of Day" and "The STOLEN CHILD"); Innisfree, an island in Lough Gill, west of Sligo (see "The Lake Isle of Innisfree"); Kilmacowen, a townland south of Sligo (where The LAND OF HEART'S DESIRE is set); Knocknarea, a mountain southwest of Sligo, said to be the resting place of the legendary Queen Maeve (see "Alternative Song for the Severed Head," The COUNTESS CATHLEEN [II, 305–306], "The Ballad of Father Hart," "The HOSTING OF THE SIDHE," "The MAN AND THE ECHO," "Red Hanrahan's Song about Ireland"); Lissadell, the estate of the Gore-Booth family, northwest of Sligo (see "IN MEMORY OF EVA GORE-BOOTH AND CON MARKIEWICZ" and "The MAN WHO DREAMED OF FAERYLAND"); Lugnagall, a mountain northeast of Sligo (see "The Man who Dreamed of Faeryland"); Rosses Point, a village on a promontory at the mouth of Sligo Harbour, northwest of Sligo, which Yeats describes as a "little sea-dividing, sandy plain covered with short grass, like a green tablecloth, and lying in the foam midway between the round cairn-headed Knocknarea" and Ben Bulben (*Myth.* 88; see "Alternative Song for the Severed Head," "AT ALGECIRAS—A MEDITATION UPON DEATH," "Three Songs to the One Burden," "The Stolen Child"); and Sleuth Wood, a forest on the south shore of Lough Gill (see "The Stolen Child"). Sligo also features in the poems "The Fiddler of Dooney," "IN MEMORY OF ALFRED POLLEXFEN," and "The MEDITATION OF THE OLD FISHERMAN." The title of Yeats's prose polemic ON THE BOILER derives from a scrap of Sligo recollection: a painted sign announcing that "the great McCoy will speak on the old boiler." Yeats well knew the boiler—"very big, very high, the top far out of reach, and all red rust"—and learned then or later that McCoy was a "mad ship's carpenter" (*Expl.* 407; *LE* 220). No less

than his poems and plays, Yeats's memoirs, stories, and folkloric accounts are saturated with local references, settings, and recollections. He gives much local folklore in his 1889 prose piece "Drumcliff and Rosses" (*Myth.* 88–94).

Bibliography

Conner, Lester I. *A Yeats Dictionary: Persons and Places in the Poetry of William Butler Yeats*; Foster, R. F. *W. B. Yeats: A Life, I: The Apprentice Mage*; Hone, Joseph. *W. B. Yeats*; Kirby, Sheelah. *The Yeats Country: A guide to the Sligo district and other places in the West of Ireland associated with the life and work of W. B. Yeats*; Moore, Virginia. *The Unicorn: William Butler Yeats' Search for Reality*; Yeats, W. B. *Autobiographies, Explorations, Later Essays, Mythologies*.

Sophocles (ca. 496–406 B.C.)   Yeats considered the Greek tragedian a byword of arch-canonical greatness and repeatedly mentioned him in the same breath as Homer and Shakespeare (see *Expl.* 196; *UP1* 284, 322; *UP2* 293, 438–439, 470). In *A VISION*, Yeats presents him as Shakespeare's only rival and imaginably even his superior: "Perhaps secular intellect, setting itself free after five hundred years of struggle, has made [Shakespeare] the greatest of dramatists, and yet because an *antithetical* age alone could confer upon an art like his the unity of a painting or of a temple pediment, we might, had the total works of Sophocles survived, [. . .] not think him greatest" (294). Yeats found in Sophocles a folklore rooted in the common life of the people and in the symbol-language of the ANIMA MUNDI and mounting always toward tragic joy. "No tragedy is legitimate unless it leads some great character to his final joy," Yeats writes in ON THE BOILER. "Polonius may go out wretchedly, but I can hear the dance music in 'Absent thee from felicity awhile', or in Hamlet's speech over the dead Ophelia, and what of Cleopatra's last farewells, Lear's rage under the lightning, Oedipus sinking down at the story's end into an earth 'riven' by love?" (*Expl.* 448–449; *LE* 247). It was Sophocles as much as anyone whom Yeats had in mind as he sought to re-create the modern stage. "You and I and SYNGE, not understanding the clock, set out to bring again the theatre of Shakespeare or rather perhaps of Sophocles," Yeats writes in "A People's Theatre," addressing Lady GREGORY (*Expl.* 252; see also *Letters* 610; *VPl.* 572).

Yeats associates Sophocles, like Shakespeare, with the breakup of racial consciousness and the birth of individuality. In "Nationality and Literature" (1893), he writes that while Homer describes "great racial or national movements and events, and sings of the Greek race rather than of any particular member of it," Aeschylus and Sophocles "subdivide these great movements and events into the characters who lived and wrought in them. The Siege of Troy is now no longer the theme, for Agamemnon and Clytemnestra and Oedipus dominate the stage" (*UP1* 269). In his introduction to *The Holy Mountain* (1934), Yeats proposes the related notion that Sophocles brought into the world a new humanism: "Greece, [Hegel] explained, first delivered mankind from nature; the Egyptian Sphinx, for all its human face, was Asiatic and animal; but when Oedipus answered the riddle, that Sphinx was compelled to leap into the abyss; the riddle, 'What goes first on four legs, then upon two, then upon three?' called up man" (*E&I* 466; *LE* 151; cf. *AV* 202–203). In *A Vision*, Yeats describes Aeschylus and Sophocles as "Phidian men," which says more than it seems to (*AV* 269). An Athenian sculptor whom Yeats exalts in "NINETEEN HUNDRED AND NINETEEN," "THE STATUES," and "UNDER BEN BULBEN," Phidias (ca. 490–430 B.C.) defines Greek civilization's 15th lunar phase, the phase of "complete beauty" (135). Though none of Phidias's work survives, Yeats hazards that in Phidias "Ionic and Doric influence unite [. . .] and all is transformed by the full moon, and all abounds and flows" (270).

Yeats's creative work first registers Sophocles in "Life," a poem that appeared in the February 1886 issue of the *DUBLIN UNIVERSITY REVIEW*. Lines 1–4 and 17–20, which Yeats correctly identified as the strongest in the poem, were subsequently incorporated in "Quatrains and Aphorisms," which appeared in *The Wanderings of Oisin and Other Poems* (1889) but otherwise fell by the wayside (see *VP* 686, 735). Already present is an embryonic notion of Sophoclean tragic joy: "'I laughed upon the lips of Sophocles, / I go as soft as folly; I am

Fate.' / This heard I where among the apple trees, / Wild indolence and music have no date."

Yeats returned to Sophocles almost 20 years later. While visiting the University of Notre Dame in January 1904 (see *CL3* 518–522), he learned that the students had produced *Oedipus Rex*, and he decided to translate and stage Sophocles himself. The play had been censored in England for its theme of incest, Yeats recalls in a 1933 note, and he thought that a successful performance in Ireland, where the play was not censored, "might make her proud of her freedom" (*Letters* 537; see also *Expl.* 131–132; *IDM* 45). Having no Greek, Yeats collaborated with his friend Oliver St John Gogarty (1878–1957), as he recollects in his note: "When I got back to Dublin [from AMERICA] I found a young Greek scholar who, unlike myself, had not forgotten his Greek, took out of a pigeonhole at the theatre a manuscript translation of *Oedipus* too complicated in its syntax for the stage, bought Jebb's translation and a translation published at a few pence for dishonest schoolboys. Whenever I could not understand the precise thoughts behind the translators' half Latin, half Victorian dignity, I got a bald translation from my Greek scholar. I spoke out every sentence, very often from the stage, with one sole object, that the words should sound natural and fall in their natural order, that every sentence should be a spoken, not a written sentence" (*Letters* 537). Midway through this work, the English censor withdrew the ban and Yeats lost interest in the project (537). In early 1905 Yeats asked the classicist Gilbert Murray (1866–1957) to translate the play so it might be produced at the ABBEY THEATRE. Murray declined to translate the play and urged Yeats not to produce it on the grounds that it has "nothing Irish about it" (*CL4* 22–24; *LTWBY*, I, 145–146; *W. B. Yeats* 260). In 1909 and 1910, Yeats revived the idea of producing the play, but nothing came of it (*Letters* 537, 546). In 1911 and 1912, according to Joseph Hone, Yeats was once again busily at work on his own translation: "Dr. Rynd of the Norwich Cathedral Chapter, who was on a visit to Dublin, stood over him with the Greek text while he turned Jebb into speakable English with rough unrhymed verse for

Chorus." This translation, too, was eventually set aside (259–260).

Yeats returned to his Sophoclean endeavors in 1926. Working from his old manuscripts, he finally completed translations that were later published as *Sophocles' 'King Oedipus'* (1928) and *Sophocles' 'Oedipus at Colonus'* (1934). When Yeats had a full draft of the former, he and Lady GREGORY "went through it all, altering every sentence that might not be intelligible on the Blasket Islands" (*Letters* 537). Even so, Yeats told OLIVIA SHAKESPEAR in December 1926 that he was shocked at his own "moderation" and that he had become bolder in his work on *Oedipus at Colonus*, which was to be "less literal and more idiomatic and more modern" (721). The plays respectively debuted at the Abbey Theatre on December 7, 1926, and September 12, 1927. Both were directed by Lennox Robinson (1886–1958) and featured F. J. McCormick (1884–1947) as Oedipus, in what the *Evening Herald* described as a "masterly" turn (*The Abbey* 141). Yeats wrote to Shakespear on the day that *King Oedipus* was to be first performed, "I think my shaping of the speech will prove powerful on the stage, for I have made it bare, hard and natural like a saga, and that it will be well, though not greatly, acted—it is all too new to our people." On the envelope Yeats added ex post facto, "*Oedipus* great success. Critics and audience enthusiastic" (*Letters* 720). Abbey historian Robert Welch suggests that Oedipus's tale resonated with the Abbey's Dublin audience because it "spoke pointedly to a deep sense of trouble about the nature of Irish society in the aftermath of independence. [. . .] Oedipus answers the riddle of the oppressive sphinx only to find himself all the more completely entangled in a fate that is ineluctable. The Irish, it would appear, had found some kind of release from the dominion of England, only to realize also that the freedom gained was a kind of plague, a torment of impossible choices, treacherous alliances, moral recrimination, and murder. Yeats here raised questions as to what consequences may flow from violent acts, even if those acts are committed in impetuous good faith or on understandable impulse" (*Abbey Theatre* 101).

Yeats's poetic canon includes three extracts from Sophocles. "Colonus' Praise (From 'Oedipus at Colonus')" first appeared in *The Tower* (1928). "FROM 'OEDIPUS AT COLONUS'" also appeared in *The Tower*, and subsequently became the 11th and final poem in the sequence "A MAN YOUNG AND OLD." Both of these choral speeches appear unchanged in the text of Yeats's translated play (see *VPl.* 887, 872–873). "From the 'Antigone,'" the 11th and final poem in the sequence "A WOMAN YOUNG AND OLD," first appeared in *The Winding Stair* (1929).

Bibliography

Finneran, Richard J. et al., eds. *Letters to W. B. Yeats* (vol. 1); Hone, Joseph. *W. B. Yeats*; Hunt, Hugh. *The Abbey: Ireland's National Theatre, 1904–1978*; Welch, Robert. *The Abbey Theatre, 1899–1999*; Yeats, W. B. *The Collected Letters of W. B. Yeats* (vols. 3–4), *Essays and Introductions, Explorations, The Irish Dramatic Movement, Later Essays, The Letters of W. B. Yeats, Uncollected Prose by W. B. Yeats* (vols. 1–2), *The Variorum Edition of the Plays of W. B. Yeats, The Variorum Edition of the Poems of W. B. Yeats, A Vision*.

style   It is a scholarly truism that Yeats's stylistic development underwent a conspicuous revolution during the first years of the 20th century, resulting in a necessary distinction between "the early Yeats" and "the later Yeats" (a distinction that is sometimes messy, for the later Yeats frequently imposed himself on the early Yeats by means of revision). The characteristic notion is that the fey, visionary, PRE-RAPHAELITE lyricism of the early poems gave way to an austere discipline and dramatic tension, a change first noticeable in poems like "ADAM'S CURSE" and "The FOLLY OF BEING COMFORTED" from *In the Seven Woods* (1903), and reaching fruition with the appearance of *The Green Helmet and Other Poems* (1910) and *Responsibilities* (1914). T. S. ELIOT epitomizes this notion in his essay on "The Modern Mind" in *The Use of Poetry & The Use of Criticism* (1933): "[The early Yeats] was very much fascinated by self-induced trance states, calculated symbolism, mediums, theosophy, crystal gazing, folklore and hobgoblins. Golden apples, archers, black pigs and such paraphernalia abounded. Often the verse has an hypnotic charm: but you cannot take heaven by magic, especially if you are, like Mr. Yeats, a very sane person. Then, by a great triumph of development, Mr. Yeats began to write and is still writing some of the most beautiful poetry in the language, some of the clearest, simplest, most direct" (133). EZRA POUND expresses a similar notion in his review of *Responsibilities*, complimenting the "hard light" of Yeats's recent poetry in contrast to the "romantically Celtic" quality of his earlier work (*Literary Essays* 380). In a May 1913 letter to JOHN BUTLER YEATS, Yeats put this change in his own words: "Of recent years instead of 'vision' [. . .] I have tried for more self portraiture. I have tried to make my work convincing with a speech so natural and dramatic that the hearer would feel the presence of a man thinking and feeling" (*Letters* 583).

Yeats's stylistic development is often explained by the influence of others; in chronological order, plausible influences include LIONEL JOHNSON, J. M. SYNGE, Nietzsche (whom Yeats first read in 1902 and 1903), and Castiglione (whom Yeats first read in 1903). Pound is typically cited as *the* crucial influence on Yeats's later development, a notion generously promoted by Yeats himself. Speaking at a 1914 banquet hosted by *Poetry*, the Chicago magazine that Pound served as "foreign correspondent," Yeats described Pound as his late-arriving tutor in the ways of modernism. "We rebelled against rhetoric," Yeats said of his own generation of poets, "and now there is a group of younger poets who dare to call us rhetorical. When I returned to London from Ireland, I had a young man go over all my work with me to eliminate the abstract. This was an American poet, Ezra Pound" (UP2 414). In a 1913 letter to Lady GREGORY, Yeats wrote that Pound "is full of the middle ages and helps me get back to the definite and the concrete away from modern abstractions" (AM 476; *Man and Poet* 167). Pound made at least one editorial suggestion for which he deserves the world's thanks, eliminating the needless hiccup "as it were" from the final line of "FALLEN MAJESTY" (IY 131). There is reason to think, however, that Pound merely helped Yeats culminate a process that had begun in the early 1890s as a reaction against the most obvious forms of Victorian verbosity and sentimentality. As Richard Ellmann observes, there is a discernable ten-

dency toward simplicity and directness in even the 1892 version of *The* COUNTESS CATHLEEN (120). Obviously, as well, the watershed poems of *In the Seven Woods* predate Yeats's involvement with Pound by six or more years (the two poets first met in the spring of 1909). As early as 1904, writing to GEORGE RUSSELL (AE), Yeats speaks of struggling to defeat his own tendency toward "sentament [sic] & sentimental sadness & a womanish introspection," and calls for a literature founded upon "an athletic joy" (CL3 577–578).

Following the lead of Eliot, Pound, and Yeats himself, critics, reasonably enough, have tended to conceive Yeats's stylistic development as a steady process of change for the better. This conception has at least one formidable detractor in Harold Bloom: "One of our slogans is that Middle Yeats is superior to Early Yeats, while Late Yeats [. . .] improved with every year. This is nonsense, no matter how many academic critics repeat it. *The Wind Among the Reeds* is a better volume of poetry than Yeats was to write until *The Wild Swans at Coole,* and the poems collected in the *Crossways* and *The Rose* groupings are better than all but seven or eight of the poems of the whole middle period" (*Yeats* 162).

Bibliography

Bloom, Harold. *Yeats*; Eliot, T. S. *The Uses of Poetry & The Uses of Criticism*; Ellmann, Richard. *The Identity of Yeats*; Foster, R. F. *W. B. Yeats: A Life, I: The Apprentice Mage*; Jeffares, A. Norman. *W. B. Yeats: Man and Poet*; Pound, Ezra. *The Literary Essays of Ezra Pound*; Yeats, W. B. *The Collected Letters of W. B. Yeats* (vol. 3), *The Letters of W. B. Yeats, Uncollected Prose by W. B. Yeats* (vol. 2).

Swift, Jonathan (1667–1745) Yeats saw in the Irish 18th century a formula of passion and personality wed to discipline and tradition, of spiritual solitude wed to public service, and as he entered middle age he increasingly took his stand with those he considered the emblematic figures of this flickering Renaissance moment in Irish history: George Berkeley (1685–1753), Edmund Burke (1729–97), and most especially Jonathan Swift. Explaining his immersion in the work of the great

Georgians, Yeats wrote in 1930, "I collect materials for my thought and work, for some identification of my beliefs with the nation itself, I seek an image of the modern mind's discovery of itself, of its own permanent form, in that one Irish century that escaped from darkness and confusion" (*Expl.* 344–345; *VPl.* 957–958). Yeats was unperturbed by the irony that Swift, though born in Dublin and a clergyman of the Church of Ireland, relished his role as a maneuverer and string-puller in Tory political circles and regarded his exile in Ireland as a perpetual frustration and disappointment. Upon being named dean of St. Patrick's Cathedral in 1713, Swift, as biographer David Nokes writes, felt himself "bundled unceremoniously back to oblivion" (*Jonathan Swift* 182). Swift himself complained to a correspondent, "I reckon no man is thoroughly miserable unless he be condemned to live in Ireland" (111). Swift's ambivalence notwithstanding, Yeats included his name when he called the roll of those who had created the best of the national tradition: "Berkeley, Swift, Burke, Grattan, Parnell, Augusta Gregory, Synge, Kevin O'Higgins, are the true Irish people, and there is nothing too hard for such as these," Yeats declared in ON THE BOILER (*Expl.* 442; *LE* 242). In his defiant contribution to the SENATE's debate on divorce in 1925, he similarly declared, proudly brandishing the inclusive pronoun, "We are the people of Burke; we are the people of Grattan; we are the people of Swift, the people of Emmet, the people of Parnell. We have created the most of the modern literature of this country. We have created the best of its political intelligence" (*SS* 99).

During the 1890s, Yeats's allegiance was to the romantic poets and the folk traditions of Ireland; by his own admission, he knew little of Swift, whom he regarded as no more than nominally Irish (*Mem.* 68). In May 1904, for example, Yeats wrote that Swift, Burke, and Oliver Goldsmith (1728–74) "hardly seem to me to have come out of Ireland at all," and that he would trade "all those great geniuses" for Lady GREGORY's *Cuchulain of Muirthemne* (1902), the first book to retell "the old epic fragments in a style so full at once of dignity and simplicity and lyric ecstasy, that I can read them with entire delight" (*CL3* 592–593; *UP2*

328). In his introduction to *The WORDS UPON THE WINDOW-PANE*, Yeats remembers that in those days he "turned from Goldsmith and from Burke because they had come to seem a part of the English system, from Swift because I acknowledged, being a romantic, no verse between Cowley and Smart's *Song to David*, no prose between Sir Thomas Browne and the *Conversations* of Landor" (*Expl.* 344; *VPl.* 957). By 1912, Yeats was willing to admit that although Swift had "little or no Irish blood" he had been brought up as an "Irish product" and that in his bitterness, hostility, and sarcasm he represented a distinct Irish type (*UP2* 403–404).

During the early 1920s, Yeats experienced a revolutionary change of opinion and embraced Swift with the zeal of a convert, coming to regard him as nothing less than the central figure in the central era of Irish achievement. In his 1932 essay "Ireland, 1921–1931," Yeats recounted the happenstance that set him reading the Irish Georgians with new eyes: "An Irish Free State soldier, engaged in dangerous service for his Government, said to me that all the philosophy a man needed was in Berkeley. Stirred by those words I began to read *The Dialogues of Hylas and Philonus*." Berkeley led to Swift, and Yeats, seeking an Irish lineage to explain and justify himself, never looked back (*UP2* 489). By the end of the decade, Yeats was prepared to pronounce Swift's epitaph and Berkeley's *Commonplace Book* "the greatest works of modern Ireland," and Swift himself "the last passion of the Renaissance" (*WBY&TSM* 141; *Letters* 773). In November 1930, he told Joseph Hone that he wanted "Protestant Ireland to base some vital part of its culture upon Burke, Swift and Berkeley" (*Letters* 779). In his introduction to *The Words upon the Window-pane*, he states simply, "Swift haunts me; he is always just round the next corner" (*Expl.* 345; *VPl.* 958).

Swift was important to Yeats less as a lampooner of human folly than as an antagonist of modernity and therefore a forerunner of Yeats's own enterprise of opposition. *On the Boiler* defines the nature of Swift's—and Yeats's own—reaction: "Instead of hierarchical society, where all men are different, came democracy; instead of a science which had re-discovered ANIMA MUNDI, its experiments and observations confirming the speculations of Henry

More, came materialism: all that Whiggish world Swift stared on till he became a raging man" (*Expl.* 435; *LE* 237; see also *LE* 106–107). In their different ways, Yeats's four poems concerning Swift—"BLOOD AND THE MOON," "PARNELL'S FUNERAL," "The SEVEN SAGES," and "SWIFT'S EPITAPH"—share this understanding; they make Swift a standard-bearer of righteous indignation and proud estrangement, as well as a symbol of the passionate integrity and personality that the modern age had sacrificed to logical order and material progress. "The Seven Sages" leaves least to interpretation. It straightforwardly champions Berkeley, Burke, Goldsmith, and Swift as the enemies of "Whiggery," defined as a "levelling, rancorous, rational sort of mind / That never looked out of the eye of a saint / Or out of drunkard's eye" and meant as a catchphrase for the spiritual decadence of the modern world.

In 1930, Yeats immersed himself in Swift. Writing from Italy in June 1930, he told OLIVIA SHAKESPEAR that he read Swift "constantly" (*Letters* 776). This reading prompted the numerous reflections on Swift in "Pages from a Diary Written in Nineteen Hundred and Thirty" (see *Explorations*) and the thorough consideration of Swift in *The Words upon the Window-pane*. Yeats finished the play in October 1930, and it debuted at the ABBEY THEATRE on November 17. Soon after, Yeats began a lengthy "introduction" (see *Explorations* and *The Variorum Edition of the Plays of W. B. Yeats*). Play and essay represent Yeats's most concerted attempt to come to terms with Swift's life and thought, and particularly with the mystery of his relations with "Stella" and "Vanessa," the two women who loved Swift and whom in his way Swift loved, while always maintaining his distance. Yeats airs a tentative theory toward the end of his play: "Swift was the chief representative of the intellect of his epoch, that arrogant intellect free at last from superstition. He foresaw its collapse. He foresaw Democracy, he must have dreaded the future. Did he refuse to beget children because of that dread? Was Swift mad? Or was it the intellect itself that was mad?" (*VPl.* 955; cf. 967; *Expl.* 363).

In a 1933 letter to Mario M. Rossi, author of *Swift; or, The egotist* (1934), Yeats theorizes Swift's life as the baffled tragedy of the man out of his torical phase: "Swift's absorption in the useful (the contemporary decline of common sense), all that made him write *The Tale of a Tub*, compelled his nature to become coarse. The man who ignores the poetry of sex, let us say, finds the bare facts written up on the walls of a privy, or is himself compelled to write them there. But all this seems to me of his time, his mere inheritance. When a [man] of Swift's sort is born into such dryness, is he not in the Catholic sense of the word its *victim*? A French Catholic priest once told me of certain holy women. One was victim for a whole country, another for such and such a village. Is not Swift the human soul in that dryness, is not that his tragedy and his genius? Perhaps every historical phase may have its victims—its poisoned rat in a hole . . ." (*Letters* 819; on the priest, see *Aut.* 253; *LE* 256).

Bibliography

Nokes, David. *Jonathan Swift, A Hypocrite Reversed: A Critical Biography*; Yeats, W. B. *Autobiographies, The Collected Letters of W. B. Yeats* (vol. 3), *Explorations, Later Essays, The Letters of W. B. Yeats, Memoirs, The Senate Speeches of W. B. Yeats, Uncollected Prose by W. B. Yeats* (vol. 2), *The Variorum Edition of the Plays of W. B. Yeats, W. B. Yeats and T. Sturge Moore: Their Correspondence 1901–1937*.

Symons, Arthur William (1865–1945) Of Yeats's numerous London cronies of the 1890s, Symons was probably the closest and most important. The son of a Wesleyan minister, Symons grew up in a series of rural towns and villages in Wales, Devon, Cornwall, and Northumberland. In 1882, he left school and embarked on a career as a poet and critic, publishing his first volume, *An Introduction to the Study of Browning*, in 1886. Symons fell in with the RHYMERS' CLUB in early 1890 and thus made the acquaintance of Yeats, one the club's founders. Yeats recalls that he was at first "repelled" by Symons, who, following Walter Pater's *Marius the Epicurean* (1885), conceived literature as a "series of impressions" and deliberately chose "a life of music halls and amorous adventure" that he "might have vivid impressions for his verse" (*Mem.* 36). Yeats, by contrast, "sought passion, religious passion above all, as the greatest good of life, and

Portrait of Arthur Symons, 1895, by Jacques-Emile Blanche (1861–1942). The painting was reproduced in the November 1896 number of the *Savoy,* of which Symons was the editor. It now resides in the Tate Gallery, London. *(Library of Congress)*

always cherished the secret hope of some mysterious initiation" (36). By the middle of the decade, however, Symons had become Yeats's "most intimate friend" and trusted artistic confidant, taking the place of LIONEL JOHNSON, who had succumbed to drink (*Aut.* 246; *Mem.* 97). In October 1895, Yeats moved into two empty rooms in Symons's lodgings in Fountain Court, The Temple, London, and remained until the following February or March, when he moved into WOBURN BUILDINGS. During this time as well Yeats and Symons were brought together by their involvement in the SAVOY, which Symons edited.

As the foremost student of French symbolism in England, Symons exposed Yeats to the work of Stéphane Mallarmé (1842–98), PAUL VERLAINE, Philippe-Auguste Villiers de l'Isle-Adam (1838–89), and others of the same school. In AUTOBIOGRA-PHIES, Yeats recalls that during this period Symons

"was making those translations from Mallarmé and from Verlaine, from Calderón, from Saint John of the Cross, which are the most accomplished metrical translations of our time, and I think that those from Mallarmé may have given elaborate form to my verses of those years, to the latter poems of *The Wind Among the Reeds,* to The SHADOWY WATERS, while Villiers de l'Isle-Adam had shaped whatever in my ROSA ALCHEMICA Pater had not shaped" (247). Symons's translation of a portion of Mallarmé's verse drama *Hérodiade,* published in the December 1896 issue of the *Savoy* and quoted by Yeats in *Autobiographies* (247), was particularly influential. Like some ancient MAUD GONNE, the heroine of Mallarmé's drama burns in the frigid ecstasy of her celibacy, and in her apotheosis of pride and renunciation envisions herself as a kind of carven goddess. Yeats went to school in the hieratic tone and inorganic imagery of Symons's translation, and his late play A FULL MOON IN MARCH closely paraphrases it (*VPl.* 982). Symons, in turn, dedicated his groundbreaking 1899 volume *The Symbolist Movement in Literature* to Yeats, calling him the "chief representative" of the symbolist movement in England (the 1919 edition of the study omits this dedication; by then Symons and Yeats had grown apart). Yeats responded with "The SYMBOLISM OF POETRY," an essay that continued Symons's effort to clarify the meaning of symbolism.

In September 1908, while traveling in Italy, Symons suffered a mental breakdown that completely incapacitated him for two years and from which he never completely recovered (see *Arthur Symons: Selected Letters* 197–198; *Memoirs of Arthur Symons* 234–253). He spent more than a year as an inmate of the Brooke House asylum in East London, where Yeats visited him several times in late 1908 and early 1909 (*Aut.* 374, 382; *Letters* 523, 529; *Mem.* 199, 214). In January 1909, Yeats found Symons writing a "mad rigmarole" of a play about "Teig the Fool," a character in Yeats's own play *The* HOUR-GLASS whom Symons believed to be God (*Letters* 523). Yeats explained Symons's breakdown as a symptom of overwork, to which he was driven by his immoderate wife Rhoda. Thereafter Yeats kept his distance, seeing his old friend only four times over the ensuing decades (*Arthur*

Symons: A Life 264). Karl Beckson, Symons's biographer, speculates that Yeats distanced himself as a defense against the painful spectacle of his friend's decline (264).

Yeats warmly reviewed Symons's collections of verse, *London Nights* (1895) and *Amoris Victima* (1897) (see *UP1* 373–375; *UP2* 38–42), and later enshrined him as a representative figure of the "tragic generation" in *Autobiographies* and MEMOIRS. In the latter, Yeats theorizes Symons's decline: "After he was shut off by marriage [in 1901] from the old resorts, his work lost in curiosity and animation. His poetry was only charming when a criticism or the emotion of a learned connoisseur, and I doubt if mere life ever moved him deeply. He alone of all that circle, if indeed he wrecked himself, did so from no passionate need but, as it were, casually" (*Mem.* 98). Yeats's version of their shared history sat well with Symons, for he called *The Trembling of the Veil* (1921–22), which includes Yeats's account of the tragic generation, "an absolute masterpiece: far & away the best thing he has ever done" (*Arthur Symons: A Life* 304).

Bibliography

Beckson, Karl. *Arthur Symons: A Life*; Symons, Arthur. *Arthur Symons: Selected Letters, 1880–1935, The Memoirs of Arthur Symons*; Yeats, W. B. *Autobiographies, The Letters of W. B. Yeats, Memoirs, Uncollected Prose by W. B. Yeats* (vols. 1–2), *The Variorum Edition of the Plays of W. B. Yeats*.

Synge, John Millington (1871–1909)   "Being young you have not known / The fool's triumph, nor yet / Love lost as soon as won, / Nor the best labourer dead / And all the sheaves to bind." Thus Yeats writes in "TO A CHILD DANCING IN THE WIND." The "best labourer" refers of course to the playwright J. M. Synge, who more than anybody else stood with Yeats as an artistic near-equal in the daily work of manufacturing the Irish Renaissance. In his NOBEL PRIZE address of 1923, Yeats said, referring to the Irish dramatic movement, "Two events brought us victory: a friend gave us a theatre, and we found a strange man of genius, John Synge" (*Aut.* 415). Synge died in 1909, and for the next 30 years Yeats lamented, eulogized,

and inveighed, never forgetting the life that meant so much to him and—had people only realized it—to the culture of Ireland. In the hierarchy of Yeats's personal mythology, Synge stands as a figure of importance below only MAUD GONNE and Lady GREGORY.

Synge was a Dublin Protestant. His father, a barrister, died of smallpox when Synge was one year old and left the family with "enough landed income to live quietly but comfortably," as Ann Saddlemyer writes (*Collected Letters of JMS*, I, 3). Synge grew up in the Dublin suburb of Rathgar in a household that included his widowed mother, his widowed maternal grandmother, three older brothers, and an older sister. He was an indifferent student at Trinity College, Dublin, from 1888 to 1892, where he devoted himself to music, with the idea of becoming a professional violinist. Literary inclinations led him to PARIS and studies at the Sorbonne. He first met Yeats on December 21, 1896, at the Hôtel Corneille, where both were staying. Yeats recalls that Synge spent his time reading

J. M. Synge, whom Yeats, in *Autobiographies*, calls the "greatest dramatic genius of Ireland" *(Fáilte Ireland)*

Mackerel drying on a cottage roof, Aran Islands, County Galway. On the Aran Islands, according to Yeats, J. M. Synge "found among forgotten people a mirror for his bitterness." *(Fáilte Ireland)*

French literature—"Racine mostly"—and "hoped to live by writing articles upon it in English papers" (*Mem.* 104; see also *Aut.* 262–263, 415; *E&I* 298). Yeats drew Synge into a Young Ireland Society that he and Gonne were organizing in Paris (*CL2* 69–70; *Mem.* 106–107), but having no real sympathy for revolutionary expatriate politics—"unfitted to think a political thought," as Yeats later maintained—he quit the organization on April 6 (*Collected Letters of JMS*, I, 47; *E&I* 319). More significantly, Yeats encouraged Synge to throw off the factitious influence of French literature and immerse himself in the fundament of Irish culture: "I persuaded him that [ARTHUR] SYMONS would always be a better critic [of French literature], and that he should go to Ireland—[he] knew Irish; I told him of Aran where I had just been—and find expression for a life that lacked it" (*Mem.* 104–105; see also *Aut.* 416; *E&I* 298–299).

Though he did not sever his ties to Paris until March 1903, Synge took Yeats's advice and thereby made his literary career. Synge first visited the ARAN ISLANDS from May 10 to June 25, 1898, and on his return to the mainland first visited Lady Gregory's COOLE PARK. He made further visits to the islands in 1899, 1900, 1901, and 1902. According to Yeats, "Synge fled to the Aran Islands to escape 'the squalor of the poor and the nullity of the rich,' and found among forgotten people a mirror for his bitterness" (*Expl.* 418; *LE* 227). Synge published *The Aran Islands*, an account of his sojourns, in 1907, but his plays were the more important legacy of this experience. On his second trip to the islands, as W. J. McCormack writes, Synge "picked up the basic ingredients of three plays—the story of the father-killer protected by local people (*The Playboy of the Western World*, 1907), the legends of a miraculous well (ironically exploited in *The Well of the Saints*, 1905), and the stoical expressive grief of women robbed of their menfolk by Atlantic storms (*Riders to the Sea*, 1904)" (*Oxford Dictionary of National Biography*).

Synge wrote drafts of *Riders to the Sea* and *In the Shadow of the Glen* in the summer of 1902. Lennox Robinson remembers that they "seem to have arrived by the same post" (*Ireland's Abbey Theatre* 36). By December, Yeats was attempting to involve Synge in the fledgling IRISH NATIONAL

THEATRE SOCIETY, though he had not yet read Synge's plays (CL3 483). On March 20, 1903, he wrote to JOHN QUINN that the society "had just received two wonderful prose peasant plays" by Synge, and that Symons "has the greatest admiration for these plays" (334). *In the Shadow of the Glen* debuted on October 8, 1903, in Molesworth Hall, Dublin, to much controversy—a foretaste of controversies to come (438–453; see also *Aut.* 414; *Expl.* 114–123, 143–145; *UP2* 306–308, 331–338). Maud Gonne left the theater during the opening performance, and afterward resigned as vice president of the society along with Douglas Hyde. As Gonne complained on September 25, "Nationalists are fighting a hard up-hill fight against overwhelming odds. It is somewhat hard to see an instrument we fashioned at considerable sacrifice of time & money [i.e., the theater society] quietly taken possession of for another purpose by people who to say the least of it are not *militantly* national" (GY 177–178). The sticking point, as Lennox Robinson puts it, was the "idea of a young wife parting from her elderly husband"; this, in the words of the *Daily Independent and Nation,* was "nothing more or less than a farcical libel on the character of the average decently reared Irish peasant woman" (*Ireland's Abbey Theatre* 36).

Riders to the Sea debuted on February 25, 1904, while Yeats was touring AMERICA. The critical response was ambivalent. Subsequently, as Yeats says, *Riders to the Sea* "grew into great popularity in Dublin, partly because, with the tactical instinct of an Irish mob, demonstrators against *The Playboy* both in the Press and in the theatre [. . .] selected it for applause. It is now what SHELLEY's *Cloud* was for many years, a comfort to those who do not like to deny altogether the genius they cannot understand" (*E&I* 337). Yeats hailed Synge's next play, *The Well of the Saints,* as a "masterpiece" (CL3 586, 594, 624–625), but when it was first performed, on February 4, 1905, it was "coldly received," according to Robinson (*Ireland's Abbey Theatre* 52). Synge followed with *The Tinker's Wedding,* which was completed by 1904 but not performed until after Synge's death by the Afternoon Theatre Company, London, on November 11, 1909, in a production arranged by Harry Stephens (1856–1935), Synge's

brother-in-law (*Collected Letters of JMS,* I, 73; *Mem.* 217–218). Yeats found the performance "disgraceful," and left the theater in a rage after the first act (*Letters* 538–539).

In 1905, the Irish National Theatre Society underwent a series of reorganizations and schisms, leaving Yeats, Lady Gregory, and Synge firmly in control of the organization as its new directors. The three directors made an iron-fisted triumvirate in the practical matter of the theater's governance, but they were linked as well in all of Yeats's subsequent thought. He never doubted that he, Lady Gregory, and Synge had all but exclusively created modern Irish theater and to a large extent modern Irish culture. "The MUNICIPAL GALLERY REVISITED" asserts as much in its provocative use of the phrase "we three alone" (cf. *Mem.* 251), and Yeats included his fellow directors, alone of all his theatrical and literary protégés, in his roll call of the great Irish: "Berkeley, SWIFT, Burke, Grattan, PARNELL, Augusta Gregory, Synge, KEVIN O'HIGGINS, are the true Irish people, and there is nothing too hard for such as these" (*Expl.* 442; *LE* 242).

Synge's next play, *The Playboy of the Western World,* was his masterpiece. In his Nobel Prize address, Yeats called it "[p]icturesque, poetical, fantastical, a masterpiece of style and of music, the supreme work of our dialect theatre" (*Aut.* 417). It set the stage for the defining political and cultural battle of Yeats's career. Ever since his own COUNTESS CATHLEEN had aroused Catholic ire in 1899 (*Mem.* 121), Yeats had been stewing for a fight against the moralizing and politicizing enemies of the ABBEY THEATRE's aestheticism. Writing on the eve of the controversy over *In the Shadow of the Glen,* Maud Gonne drew the battle lines: "[With] me the National Ideal is a religion, & a Theatre Co unless it serves the National cause seems to me of little importance. I know your answer, Beyreuth, Christiana theatre etc., serve their Nation though not propaganda but the circumstances are so different. We are in a life & death struggle with England [. . .] & have not time & energy for purely literary & artistic movements unless they can be made to serve directly & immediately the National cause" (GY 178). *The Playboy of the Western World* set these differing notions about the nature and purpose of art on a collision course, creating a controversy that was, for Yeats, symbolic of everything he stood for and against, both in art and in public life.

Synge had written a draft of *The Playboy* by September 1904 and Yeats declared himself "delighted" (*CL3* 674). The play debuted at the Abbey Theatre on January 26, 1907. Despite much agonized revision and last-minute expurgation, it was greeted by interruption and riot (*Our Irish Theatre* 80). Lady Gregory famously telegrammed to Yeats, who was in Scotland at the time, that the audience had broken up at the word "shift," that is, at the mention of feminine undergarments (*E&I* 311). As the *Freeman's Journal* described the contretemps, "It was mere dumbshow as far as the artistes were concerned. Not a syllable they spoke could be heard. At last the curtain descended on the conclusion of the first section of the production, amidst howls, cheers and the singing of national songs" (*Cradle of Genius* 116). There were disturbances, though of decreasing intensity, as the play continued its weeklong run (*CL4* 618), and the police were called in to keep the peace (619). Gerard Fay comments that "the Dublin Metropolitan Police were regarded, just as much as the Royal Irish Constabulary as instruments of British oppression and calling them in to the National Theatre was giving the Nationalists a powerful weapon of propaganda against the Abbey" (*Cradle of Genius* 118). Yeats hosted a public debate on the "freedom of the stage" at the Abbey Theatre on February 4 and clearly reveled in the duel of ideas (*CL4* 627; for his remarks, see *Expl.* 226–228; *IDM* 110–112; *UP2* 348–354). JOHN BUTLER YEATS was among the defenders of the play. Yeats counts his father's speech among his resplendent memories in "BEAUTIFUL LOFTY THINGS."

Yeats was exhilarated by the long-awaited outbreak of open hostilities between the "intellectual element" of Dublin and "the more brainless patriotic element" (*CL4* 627). He wrote to Quinn on February 18, "It has been the first real defeat to the mob here, and may be the start of a party of intellect in the Arts" (627). Synge, on the other hand, was in Yeats's view "much shaken by the *Playboy* riot, on the first night confused and excited, knowing not what to do, and ill before many days," though "it made no difference in his work. He

neither exaggerated out of defiance nor softened out of timidity" (*E&I* 329). The *Playboy* provoked another major spasm of controversy in 1912, when the Abbey players made their first tour of America. Irish-American nationalists disrupted the play, and the entire cast was arrested in Philadelphia on charges of immorality and indecency (*Our Irish Theatre* 121).

If Synge's indelicate representation of Irish womanhood and the Irish peasantry was the nominal cause of the *Playboy* controversy, the more fundamental issue was the affront of his unwillingness to sentimentalize or pander (*E&I* 311). In Yeats's estimation, "The outcry against *The Playboy* was an outcry against its style, against its way of seeing; and when the audience called Synge 'decadent'—a favourite reproach from the objective everywhere—it was but troubled by the stench of its own burnt cakes. How could they that dreaded solitude love that which solitude had made?" (*Expl.* 253; *IDM* 13–1). Elsewhere he theorizes that the controversy over Synge's play "was really a controversy between two Irelands, the normal Ireland of the crowd and the antithetical Ireland of the proud, personal, solitary intellect" (*I&R*, I, 122).

On March 24, 1909, Synge died of Hodgkin's disease, for which he had first undergone surgery in 1897. Taking a page from Shelley's mythologization of Keats's death in "Adonais" (1821), Yeats wondered whether Synge might have lived "if he had not had his long, bitter misunderstanding with the wreckage of Young Irelandism. Even a successful performance of one of his plays seems to have made him ill" (*Mem.* 154; see also *LE* 5). Synge left his final play, *Deirdre of the Sorrows*, unfinished. He had wished to put Yeats in charge of his literary estate, but his family raised objections and Harry Stephens was reluctant to cede control (*Letters* 528–529; *Mem.* 217–221). On April 22, 1909, Yeats finally received *Deirdre of the Sorrows* in manuscript, but found it "full of mistakes and confusion" (*Mem.* 221). Yeats and Lady Gregory "took infinite trouble to bring the versions together," but, as Lady Gregory writes, "it needed the writer's hand" (*Our Irish Theatre* 82). Yeats thought the play "would have been a masterpiece if Synge had lived long enough to do about a month more work. He put into it all his hatred of death as well as his own acceptance of it. There is wonderful writing" (*Letters* 529). In a brief preface to the published play, Yeats reiterated that *Deirdre* "would have been [Synge's] masterwork, so much beauty is there in its course, and such wild nobleness in its end, and so poignant is an emotion and wisdom that were his preparation for death" (*P&I* 137). The Abbey Theatre performed the play on January 13, 1910, with Molly Allgood (1887–1952), who had been Synge's fiancée, in the role of Deirdre (*Mem.* 239–240). Synge's death dominated Yeats's journal for many months afterward. Yeats published these journal entries as *The Death of Synge and Other Passages from an Old Diary* (1928) and later added them to the canon of his AUTOBIOGRAPHIES under the title "The Death of Synge." They appear also in MEMOIRS (186–260).

Yeats's commentary on Synge as both man and writer is profuse. Most significant are his 1905 preface to *The Well of the Saints* (*E&I* 298–305), his 1909 preface to Synge's *Poems and Translations* (306–310), and his 1911 essay "J. M. Synge and the Ireland of his Time" (311–342). In his preface to *Poems and Translations*, Yeats states what were, for him, Synge's essential lineaments: "He was a solitary, undemonstrative man, never asking pity, nor complaining, nor seeking sympathy but in this book's momentary cries: all folded up in brooding intellect, knowing nothing of new books and newspapers, reading the great masters alone; and he was but the more hated because he gave his country what it needed, an unmoved mind where there is a perpetual Last Day, a trumpeting, and coming up to judgment" (*E&I* 310). "J. M. Synge and the Ireland of his Time," a philosophic and stylistic tour de force, is Yeats's principal argument against the political mindset that Gonne was so willing to voice, as well as one of his most sustained discussions of a fellow writer. "COOLE PARK, 1929," "IN MEMORY OF MAJOR ROBERT GREGORY," "The Municipal Gallery Revisited," and "ON THOSE THAT HATED 'THE PLAYBOY OF THE WESTERN WORLD', 1907" comprise Yeats's poetic testament to Synge.

Bibliography

Fay, Gerard. *The Abbey Theatre: Cradle of Genius*; Gregory, Lady. *Our Irish Theatre*; Hone, Joseph. *W. B. Yeats*; Goldman, Lawrence, ed. *Oxford Dictionary of National Biography*; Mikhail, E. H. ed. *W. B. Yeats: Interviews and Recollections* (vol. 1); Robinson, Lennox. *Ireland's Abbey Theatre: A History, 1899–1951*; Synge, J. M. *The Collected Letters of John Millington Synge* (vols. 1–2); Yeats, W. B. *Autobiographies, The Collected Letters of W. B. Yeats* (vols. 2–4), *Essays and Introductions, Explorations, The Gonne-Yeats Letters 1893–1938, The Irish Dramatic Movement, Later Essays, The Letters of W. B. Yeats, Memoirs, Prefaces and Introductions, Uncollected Prose by W. B. Yeats* (vol. 2).

Tennyson, Alfred, Lord (1809–1892)   Britain's preeminent Victorian poet was an important but uncomfortable influence on Yeats. Tennyson was too elaborately gifted and culturally central to be lightly dismissed, but too ambivalent in his romanticism and transcendentalism to be warmly embraced. Yeats saw Tennyson, like WORDSWORTH, as a cautionary example of imperfect commitment to the visionary instinct. Yeats was furthermore put off by Tennyson's all-encompassing air of Englishness. In Yeats's own description, Tennyson was the "most English writer of the century," a status that did not especially recommend him (*CL2* 197). JOHN EGLINTON remembers Yeats repudiating Tennyson as "brainless" (*I&R*, I, 32).

As AUTOBIOGRAPHIES suggests, Tennyson pervaded the intellectual climate in which Yeats was reared by his father, JOHN BUTLER YEATS (91, 93). David R. Clark observes that Tennyson's *Idylls of the King*—and especially "Merlin and Vivien"—is the dominant influence on the two-act play *Vivien and Time*, which Yeats wrote between the ages of 17 and 19 (*Desolate Reality* 71–74). Late in life, according to biographer Joseph Hone, Yeats was asked which poet he most venerated as a young man. His immediate and surprising answer was "Tennyson" (*W. B. Yeats* 34). By the time his literary career was under way, however, Yeats understood that Tennyson would not serve his own aspirations, and that the modern movement, then beginning to coalesce, would have to debunk his example. Recalling a crucial realization of the early 1890s, Yeats writes, "I saw [. . .] that Swinburne in one way, Browning in another, and Tennyson in a third, had filled their work with what I called 'impurities', curiosities about politics, about science, about history, about religion; and that we must create once more the pure work" (*Aut.* 148–149; see also 242). Yeats was still sounding this theme in his introduction to *The Oxford Book of Modern Verse* (1936): "The revolt against Victorianism meant to the young poet a revolt against irrelevant descriptions of nature, the scientific and moral discursiveness of *In Memoriam* [. . .] the political eloquence of Swinburne, the psychological curiosity of Browning, and the poetical diction of everybody" (*LE* 183). In 1894, Yeats made his first visit to PARIS and was confirmed in his misgivings about Tennyson by PAUL VERLAINE, who issued a shrewd *pensée* on the subject of *In Memoriam* (1850): "Tennyson was too noble, too *Anglais*, and when he should have been broken-hearted, he had many reminiscences." Yeats clearly found this an essential insight into Tennyson's failure, and he repeatedly quoted the comment (see *Aut.* 261; *E&I* 270; *LE* 91–92, 183; *UP1* 399; *UP2* 413). Harold Bloom goes so far as to suggest that the "school of Lionel Johnson and Yeats was founded upon what they took to be an anti-Wordsworthian, anti-Tennysonian thesis: against recollection" (*Yeats* 30). In opposition to Tennyson's defeated impulse of "recollection," Yeats was to undertake a brazen enterprise of temporal transcendence, as embodied in a poem like "SAILING TO BYZANTIUM."

After Tennyson died in October 1892, Yeats wrote a long letter to the *Bookman* on the subject of the poet laureateship. He argued that "the ending of any so venerable and honourable a thing as the Laureateship should be out of all question" but that the laureate must be granted a wider and freer scope, as life no longer "displays itself under the best conditions in royalties and nobilities" (*CL1* 325). For this reason, Yeats continues, Tennyson's dedication of *Idylls of the King* to Prince Albert and Queen Victoria—in fact, the volume is dedicated to Albert—has "a little lessened the significance of the great imaginative types of Arthur and Guinevere, and cast round the greatest romantic poem of the century a ring of absurdity" (325; for another version of this critique see *UP1* 95). Even so, Yeats acknowledges Tennyson as a "supreme artist" (*CL1* 325). Yeats's most extensive, complimentary,

and insightful observations on Tennyson come in an 1892 review of the laureate's final volume, *The Death of Oenone, Akbar's Dream, and Other Poems*. While finding fault with some of the verse, Yeats recognizes Tennyson's thwarted kinship with BLAKE and SHELLEY, and credits him with having learned later in life to "base his dreams alone upon the regeneration of the heart of man" (*UP1* 252). He continues, "As years passed over him the poet grew not less and the man grew incomparably greater, and this growth was accompanied ever by a shedding off of hopes based upon mere mechanical change and mere scientific or political inventiveness, until at the last his soul came near to standing, as the soul of the poet should, naked under the heavens" (251–252). An interview published in 1931 makes clear that Yeats's relations with the great Victorian remained fraught even late in life. "[If] I live another ten years I shall admire Tennyson again," he told his interlocutor, though it is unclear whether this reconciliation depended upon a final senility, calm, or wisdom (*I&R*, II, 203).

Though ambivalent about Tennyson, Yeats was unreserved in his admiration for Arthur Henry Hallam (1811–33), Tennyson's bosom friend, whose sudden death in Vienna from a brain aneurysm occasioned the laureate's great elegy *In Memoriam* (1850). Yeats frequently and approvingly quoted from Hallam's essay "On Some of the Characteristics of Modern Poetry and on the Lyrical Poems of Alfred Tennyson" (1831), which he had read in *The Poems of Arthur Henry Hallam* (1893), edited by his RHYMERS' CLUB friend Richard Le Gallienne (1866–1947). Yeats called the essay "one of the most profound criticisms in the English language" (*UP2* 130; see also *Aut.* 358, 361; *E&I* 347–349; *UP1* 276–277; *UP2* 34, 88–89). In an anticipation of Yeats's own principal conviction, Hallam lays down as his first principle that the mind of the artist must not allow itself to be occupied by "any other predominant motive than the desire of beauty" (*Writings of Arthur Hallam* 184). On this basis, Hallam contrasts "poets of reflection" like Wordsworth, who attempt to convince, with "poets of sensation" like Shelley and Keats, who attempt to enrapture (185). Hallam champions the latter school's "powerful tendency of imagination to a life of immediate sympathy with the external universe," while acknowledging that poets of such high-pitched sensitivity were "especially liable to moral temptations" and were doomed to be unpopular, for their "senses told them a richer and ampler tale than most men could understand" (186–187). The public inevitably derided such poets as visionaries and "gibbeted *in terrorem* those inaccuracies of diction occasioned sometimes by the speed of their conceptions, sometimes by the inadequacy of language to their peculiar conditions of thought" (187; cf. "RIBH IN ECSTASY"). Yeats discerned in Hallam's defense of the poetry of sensation a precedent for his own defense of symbolism, aestheticism, and modernism, and for his own analysis of the difficulties that beset the "tragic generation." Ironically, Yeats turned Hallam's critical apparatus against Tennyson, whom it was meant to promote. While Hallam championed the young Tennyson as the standard-bearer of sensation among the poets of the younger generation, Yeats, with the benefit of hindsight, placed him in the camp of reflection.

Bibliography

Bloom, Harold. *Yeats*; Clark, David R., with Rosalind Clark, *W. B. Yeats and the Theatre of Desolate Reality* (expanded edition); Hallam, Arthur. *The Writings of Arthur Henry Hallam*; Hone, Joseph. *W. B. Yeats*; Mikhail, E. H., ed. *W. B. Yeats: Interviews and Recollections* (vols. 1–2); Yeats, W. B. *Autobiographies, The Collected Letters of W. B. Yeats* (vols. 1–2), *Essays and Introductions, Later Essays, Uncollected Prose by W. B. Yeats* (vols. 1–2).

Theosophical Society Before he embarked on his decades-long involvement with the HERMETIC ORDER OF THE GOLDEN DAWN, Yeats spent a brief but lively season as a member of the Theosophical Society, an occult organization founded in New York in 1875 by the flamboyant Russia émigré Helena Blavatsky (1831–91) and the American lawyer manqué Henry Olcott (1832–1907). In 1878, the two decamped to India, and made Adyar, Madras, the capital of what was soon to be a flourishing if controversial global movement. Equally a brilliant, imaginative intellect and an outright charlatan, Blavatsky claimed to have received her mystical philosophy from a pair of secretive Tibetan "mahatmas" named Koot Hoomi and Morya who communicated either telepathically or by means of handwritten notes. These latter would dramatically materialize—in many instances, flutter earthward from the ceiling—to the amazement of whomever Blavatsky wished to amaze. In December 1884, an investigator from the British Society for Psychical Research arrived in India and discovered evidence of rampant miracle rigging (*Madame Blavatsky* 335). Fearing legal action, Blavatsky fled to Europe in March 1885 (346–347). She drifted about Europe for two years and was then invited to London in the hope that she could reinvigorate the local Theosophical community. In May 1887, she arrived in London and began the most successful phase of her career. Though a Theosophical lodge had existed in London since 1878 (181), her young acolytes established a new "Blavatsky Lodge" in her honor and the following September enthroned her in a pleasant house at 17 Lansdowne Road, fronting Holland Park.

Yeats's involvement with Theosophy began in 1884 when his aunt, Isabella Pollexfen Varley, sent him a copy of Alfred Sinnett's *Esoteric Buddhism* (1883), which outlines the doctrines of Theosophy (AM 45). Yeats and his high school friend Charles Johnston (later to marry Blavatsky's niece) soon drew together a small circle of budding mystics and Theosophists that included GEORGE RUSSELL (AE) and JOHN EGLINTON (AM 47; *Aut.* 97; *CL1* 101, 104). The circle constituted itself first as the Dublin Hermetic Society, founded June 16, 1885, and then as the Dublin Theosophical Society, founded April 1886, though Yeats did not officially join the latter organization (AM 47, 552; *CL1* 514). "A little body of young men hired a room in York street, some dozen years ago, and began to read papers to one another on the Vedas, and the Upanishads, and the Neoplatonists, and on modern mystics and spiritualists," Yeats recalls of the Hermetic Society in an 1898 article on Russell. "They had no scholarship, and they spoke and wrote badly, but they discussed great problems ardently and simply and unconventionally as men, perhaps, discussed great problems in the mediaeval Universities" (*UP2* 121). It was under the auspices of the Theosophical

Society, in April 1886, that Yeats met the exotic and charismatic Bengali guru MOHINI CHATTERJEE (*Aut.* 98; *CL1* 514).

In April 1887 the Yeats family returned to London after a six-year sojourn in Ireland. In May, Yeats first called upon Blavatsky, then temporarily lodging in the suburb of Upper Norwood. It was a stilted encounter. An apparently broken cuckoo clock hooted at Yeats. To his hostess's dismay, Yeats tried to examine the clock, suggesting that his mindset was not entirely credulous; as he mentions in MEMOIRS, he had read "with care" the Society for Psychical Research's report on "fraudulent miracle-working" (*Aut.* 153; *Mem.* 24). All the same, Yeats joined the newly formed "Blavatsky Lodge" and became a regular at Blavatsky's house at 17 Lansdowne Road. There Blavatsky tempestuously and mirthfully held court among an eccentric menagerie of disciples, a scene vividly rendered in AUTOBIOGRAPHIES (153–159). On November 30, 1888, Yeats joined the more exclusive Esoteric Section of the lodge. Membership required abstention from meat, alcohol, and sex, as well as complete obedience to Blavatsky and profession of belief in the mahatmas (*Madame Blavatsky* 408). Yeats balked at this last stricture, and it was loosened to allow a tolerable freedom of conscience (*Mem.* Appendix A). Membership in the Esoteric Section, according to Richard Ellmann, brought Yeats a "system of arcane correspondences and symbols, establishing interrelationships between parts of the body, seasons, colors, elements, and the like, giving the naked universe a garment at once mystical and personal" (*MM* 64).

Although he never ceased to be fascinated by Blavatsky, whom he called the "most human person alive," Yeats was not long for the Theosophical Society (*CL1* 164). Having learned "from BLAKE to hate all abstraction," Yeats proposed to put the society's magical teachings to the test of empirical experimentation (*Aut.* 158). With Blavatsky's permission, Yeats established a paranormal research committee and conducted several experiments, the most colorful of which was an attempt to raise the ghost of a burned flower by placing it under a glass bell in the moonlight (*Aut.* 158; *Mem.* 23; *Madame Blavatsky* 439). In October 1890, Blavatsky's deputy, George Mead, informed Yeats that he was

"causing discussion and disturbance" and asked him to leave the society (*Aut.* 159; *Madame Blavatsky* 439). Contradicting both *Autobiographies* and *Memoirs*, Yeats's letters suggest that the immediate cause of the break was less his occult experimentation than an article published in the *Weekly Review* (now lost) in which Yeats criticized the society's magazine *Lucifer* (*CL1* 234). Yeats explained the contretemps in a November 1890 letter to JOHN O'LEARY: "They wanted me to promise to criticize them never again in same fashion. I refused because I looked upon request as undue claim to control right of individual to think as best pleased him. I may join them again later on. We are of course good friends & allies—except in this matter & except that I told them they were turning a good philosophy into a bad religion. The latter remark has not been well taken by some of the feircer [sic] sort. Relations have been getting strained for about a year—on these points" (234).

Blavatsky presents the metaphysics of Theosophy in her lengthy tomes *Isis Unveiled* (1877) and *The Secret Doctrine* (1888), both of which she claimed to have written at the dictation of her secret mahatmas. The 1,500-page *Secret Doctrine* may have been a jumble of misunderstood Hindu and Buddhist doctrines, as learned critics have alleged, but its metaphysical premises—that there is an "omnipresent and eternal reality" that is beyond all apprehension and speculation; that the universe is governed by "an absolute law of periodicity, of flux and reflux, ebb and flow"; that the individual soul is a microcosm of the universal soul; that the individual soul must pass through a cycle of incarnations—long resonated with Yeats (*Madame Blavatsky* 413, 417). In the words of Ellmann, "Theosophy had furnished him with shield and sword, and he went forth like Don Quixote, though with some hesitancy, to tilt at the windmills of modern life" (*MM* 69).

See also Yeats's reflections on Blavatsky in an 1893 interview given to the *Irish Theosophist* (*UP1* 298–302).

Bibliography

Ellmann, Richard. *Yeats: The Man and the Masks*; Foster, R. F. *W. B. Yeats: A Life, I: The Apprentice Mage*;

Meade, Marion. *Madame Blavatsky*; Yeats, W. B. *Autobiographies*, *The Collected Letters of W. B. Yeats* (vol. 1), *Memoirs*, *Uncollected Prose by W. B. Yeats* (vols. 1–2).

Thoor Ballylee ("Ballylee Tower")   Of all the images and symbols that parade through Yeats's poetry, the austere tower that Yeats made his intermittent summer home is the most iconic, as it was meant to be. As he writes in "BLOOD AND THE MOON," mincing no words, "I declare this tower is my symbol; I declare / This winding, gyring, spiring treadmill of a stair is my ancestral stair. . . ." In T. R. Henn's catalogue of resonances, the tower, dominating the cottages around it, is a symbol of aristocracy; so too "an emblem of the night of war, of violence, of man's aspirations to philosophy, of the decay of civilization, of ancient ceremony, disintegrating in the face of the world"; finally, it is "astronomical, the departure-point for man's thought facing the universe" (*Lonely Tower* 132, 134). The poet in his tower, meanwhile, "is part hermit, part sage, part fool, inheriting the empty attributes of the man of action, conscious of the past, yet powerless" (132; cf. *E&I* 290–291). JOHN BUTLER YEATS wrote in November 1916 to congratulate his son on his impending land ownership and knowingly glossed the symbolism of the tower in this way: "It is all a symbol of the poetical life, a thirst for the soil, and you have it to the centre of the earth. It is in Ireland, another thirst instinctive, and therefore of the poet. And it is old, therefore again a poet's desire. The poet, who is always *conservative* and attached to the legendary—and it is away off by itself and of a fashion no one will want to imitate. The poet is lonely and quiet and silent and obstinately averse to change. So he has been, so he will be, and so he is. And your old castle is all this. And it is reached by an old bridge. The last is best of all though it escapes analysis" (*LTWBY*, II, 328).

Thoor Ballylee (pronounced *tor*) is located by the side of the Cloon River in the townland of Ballyllee, County Galway, roughly three miles east of COOLE PARK and three miles northeast of the town of Gort, which in Yeats's day had a population of about 1,000. The castle is variously dated. R. F. Foster cautiously remarks that the "tower is probably sixteenth century, though its origins may go back to the fourteenth century" (*AP* 84). The tower became part of the Gregory estate after Robert Gregory (1727–1810), director and chairman of the East India Company and great-grandfather of Lady GREGORY's husband, Sir William Gregory (1817–92), purchased more than 1,000 acres that had belonged to Lord Clanricarde's Ballylee estate (*Guide to Coole Park* 23). William Gregory sold two-thirds of this acreage in 1856, but Thoor Ballylee was restored to the Coole demesne in 1902 (*BG* 165; *Lady Gregory* 50; *Thoor Ballylee* 10, 12). As part of a land distribution plan, the Congested Districts Board assumed control of the property in 1916 (*Thoor Ballylee* 12). Deciding that the time had come to "set a powerful emblem up" ("Blood and the Moon"), Yeats negotiated the purchase of the tower for the modest sum of £35 and signed the sale contract on June 30, 1917 (*AP* 85). At age 52, then, Yeats for the first time became the owner of home and property.

Thoor Ballylee, County Galway. The tower was Yeats's summer home during the 1920s and his most fecund poetic symbol. In the description of "My House": "An ancient bridge, and a more ancient tower, / A farmhouse that is sheltered by its wall, / An acre of stony ground, / Where the symbolic rose can break in flower . . ." *(Fáilte Ireland)*

At the time of Yeats's purchase, the tower, as Mary Hanley and Liam Miller write, "consisted of four floors with one room on each, connected by a spiral stone stairway built into the seven-foot thickness of the massive outer wall. Each floor had a window overlooking the river which flowed alongside. At the top there was a flat roof reached by a final steep flight of steps from the floor below." There was an adjacent cottage that had been built in the 19th century; this "connected to the original entrance door of the Tower by a porch, which Yeats had extended to form an entrance to a second cottage which he had built behind, and parallel to the first. A walled cottage adjoined the cottage, and across the road which passed Ballylee a grove of trees surrounded another plot of land on which a small outhouse was later built as a garage" (*Thoor Ballylee* 13; see also *Letters* 625–626, 682–683). In a 1930 letter, GEORGE YEATS summarized the primitive discomforts of the property: there was "no indoor 'accomodation' [sic] except one earth closet"; bath water had to be fetched from the river in a wheeled carrier; the nearest drinking water was "either half a mile or a mile according to flood or drought"; and the "two cottages and the dining room (tower) and garage flood roughly 12–18 inches" (*BG* 407).

William A. Scott, professor of architecture at the National University of Ireland and in Yeats's description a "drunken man of genius," oversaw the renovation and designed the furniture, while Thomas Rafferty, a local builder, and Patrick Connolly, a local joiner, carried out the work; both Scott and Rafferty are mentioned in the draft of "To be Carved on a Stone at Thoor Ballylee" (1921) that Yeats sent to JOHN QUINN on July 23, 1918 (*Letters* 651). "I dream of making a house that may encourage people to avoid ugly manufactured things—an ideal poor man's house," Yeats wrote to MAUD GONNE in May 1918 (*GY* 393–394). Scott died of pneumonia in 1921, and, as Ann Saddlemyer writes, designs for a "magnificent wrought-iron floor candelabrum, great oak hall table, and other furnishings were never executed" (*BG* 170). Renovation of the largely dilapidated property went on through 1917 and 1918. In the summer of 1919 the Yeats family—

poet, wife, and infant daughter—finally moved in. Yeats's letters of the next several years are filled with descriptions of the tower and progress reports on the continuing renovation work, though the family was in residence only intermittently. In the midst of the IRISH CIVIL WAR, the bridge at Thoor Ballylee was blown up by Republican forces on August 19, 1922 (*AP* 214–215; *VP* 827), but otherwise the property came through the war more or less unscathed, as Yeats reported to T. STURGE MOORE: "Little harm has been done here, despite rumours in the press, and even in the neighbouring towns, except the windows and doors burst in and various traces of occupation by Irregulars, stray bullets, signs that a bed has been slept in and so on. The Irregulars took care of our property and even moved a Russian icon of my wife's from a dry wall to a dry shelf, but after they had gone the country people stole all the mirrors" (*WBY&TSM* 48). In October 1928, with his health beginning to fail, Yeats abandoned Thoor Ballylee as a residence (*AP* 377). The property remained in the ownership of the family until 1963, when it passed into the hands of a preservation trust. Today it is a popular tourist attraction.

Yeats made no secret of the mythic and symbolic motives underlying his purchase of a property that was otherwise impractical and inconvenient. He explained his attraction to the tower in a July 1918 letter to Quinn: "I am making a setting for my old age, a place to influence lawless youth, with its severity and antiquity. If I had this tower when JOYCE began I might have been of use, have got him to meet those who might have helped him" (*Letters* 651). Writing to Quinn the following July, Yeats referred to the tower as "a fitting monument and symbol," and in September 1927 he told T. Sturge Moore that he liked "to think of that building as a permanent symbol of my work plainly visible to the passer-by. As you know, all my art theories depend upon just this—rooting of mythology in the earth" (*Letters* 659; *WBY&TSM* 114). In a note to *The Winding Stair* (1933), Yeats writes that he has "used towers, and one tower in particular, as symbols and have compared their winding stairs to the philosophical gyres, but it is hardly necessary to interpret what comes from the main track of thought and expression. SHELLEY uses towers constantly as symbols, and there are gyres in Swedenborg, and in Thomas Aquinas and certain classical authors. Part of the symbolism of 'Blood and the Moon' was suggested by the fact that Thoor Ballylee has a waste room at the top and that butterflies come in through the loopholes and die against the window-panes" (VP 831; see also 830). Yeats discusses Shelley's pervasive use of the tower in "The PHILOSOPHY OF SHELLEY'S POETRY," calling it an image of the "mind looking outward upon men and things" (E&I 87). In "The PHASES OF THE MOON," Yeats acknowledges that he may have chosen Thoor Ballylee as his home under the spell of Milton's "Il Penseroso" (1632) and Shelley's "Prince Athanase" (1817). George Bornstein goes farther, writing that Yeats made Thoor Ballylee his home "partly to become Athanase at last" (Yeats and Shelley xi; see also 72, 90). Byron's Manfred—like Athanase, an idol of Yeats's youthful imagination—was likewise a solitary tower-dweller (Aut. 80). A final influence on Yeats's "turriphilia" (Theodore Ziolkowski's word) was Villiers de l'Isle-Adam's symbolist drama Axël (1890), which Yeats saw in PARIS in 1894 (View from the Tower 6). In his introduction to a 1925 edition of the play, Yeats comments, "Even those strange sentences so much in the manner of my time—'as to living, our servants will do that for us'; 'O to veil you with my hair where you will breathe the spirit of dead roses'—did not seem so important as the symbols: the forest castle, the treasure, the lamp that had burned before Solomon. Now that I have read it all again [. . .] and recalled that first impression, I can see how those symbols became a part of me, and for years to come dominated my imagination, and when I point out this fault or that [. . .] I but discover there is no escape, that I am still dominated. Is it only because I opened the book for the first time when I had the vivid senses of youth that I must see that tower room always, and hear always that thunder?" (P&I 156).

If the flood-prone Thoor Ballylee was a failure as a home, it was an inspired conception as a poetic symbol, and it became one of the chief symbols of Yeats's mature work. When he published what may be his most ambitious and consummate collection of poems in 1928, Yeats called both the volume and the title poem The Tower. For good measure, the cover of the volume featured the image of Thoor Ballylee in gaunt outline, in a design by T. Sturge Moore. In February 1928, Yeats congratulated Moore on the engraving: "Your cover for The Tower is a most rich, grave and beautiful design, admirably like the place, and I am all the more grateful because I may see but little of that place henceforth" (WBY&TSM 123; for Moore's design, see 125). Yeats called his next collection The Winding Stair, an allusion to the tower's spiraling inner staircase; once again Moore provided the relevant cover design (163; for Moore's design, see 179). Thoor Ballylee figures prominently in numerous poems of Yeats's middle and late years. In addition to "Blood and the Moon," "The Phases of the Moon," "To be Carved on a Stone at Thoor Ballylee," and "The TOWER," Yeats's poems of Thoor Ballylee include "COOLE AND BALLYLEE, 1931," "A DIALOGUE OF SELF AND SOUL," "EGO DOMINUS TUUS," "IN MEMORY OF MAJOR ROBERT GREGORY," "I SEE PHANTOMS OF HATRED AND OF THE HEART'S FULLNESS AND OF THE COMING EMPTINESS," "MY DESCENDANTS," "MY HOUSE," "A PRAYER FOR MY DAUGHTER," "A PRAYER ON GOING INTO MY HOUSE," "The ROAD AT MY DOOR," and "The STARE'S NEST BY MY WINDOW." Yeats's deathbed poem, "The Black Tower" (1939), is a final deployment of the tower symbol though not obviously a poem of Thoor Ballylee, while "The STATUES" is obliquely a poem of the tower ("We Irish, born into that ancient sect / But thrown upon this filthy modern tide / And by its formless, spawning, fury wrecked / Climb to our proper dark"). Yeats's first allusion to Thoor Ballylee appears in "Dust hath closed Helen's Eye" (1899), a chronicle of the blind poet Anthony Raftery (1779–1835) and the famed local beauty Mary Hynes (cf. "The Tower"). Revisiting the scene of their legend, Yeats mentions "the old square castle, Ballylee, inhabited by a farmer [Patrick Spellman] and his wife, and a cottage where their daughter and their son-in-law live, and a little mill with an old miller, and old ash-trees throwing green shadows upon a little river and great stepping-stones" (Myth. 22).

Bibliography

Bornstein, George. *Yeats and Shelley*; Finneran, Richard J., et al., eds. *Letters to W. B. Yeats* (vol. 2); Foster, R. F. *W. B. Yeats: A Life, II: The Arch-Poet*; Hanley, Mary, and Liam Miller, *Thoor Ballylee: Home of William Butler Yeats*; Henn, T. R. *The Lonely Tower: Studies in the Poetry of W. B. Yeats*; Kohfeldt, Mary Lou. *Lady Gregory: The Woman behind the Irish Renaissance*; Saddlemyer, Ann. *Becoming George: The Life of Mrs W. B. Yeats*; Smythe, Colin. *A Guide to Coole Park, Co. Galway: Home of Lady Gregory*; Yeats, W. B. *Autobiographies, Essays and Introductions, The Gonne-Yeats Letters 1893–1938, The Letters of W. B. Yeats, Mythologies, Prefaces and Introductions, The Variorum Edition of the Poems of W. B. Yeats, W. B. Yeats and T. Sturge Moore: Their Correspondence 1901–1937*; Ziolkowski, Theodore. *The View from the Tower: Origins of an Antimodernist Image.*

Tynan, Katharine (1859–1931) The daughter of a successful Clondalkin farmer, Tynan was a hugely prolific though minor poet, novelist, and critic, and one of Yeats's closest colleagues and confidantes during the early years of his career. The two young writers first met in June 1885, when they were brought together by Charles Hubert Oldham (1860–1926), editor of the DUBLIN UNIVERSITY REVIEW, to which they both contributed. In her memoir *Twenty-Five Years* (1913), Tynan describes the youthful Yeats as gentle, docile, and wholly preoccupied by his poetic musings. "Certainly he had not a trace of bitterness when I first knew him, nor for long afterwards," she writes. "He was beautiful to look at with his dark face, its touch of vivid colouring, the night-black hair, the eager dark eyes. [. . .] I must acknowledge that in those days we all bullied Willie Yeats, I myself not excepted. I believe it was because *we* did not want to live, breathe, eat, drink, and sleep poetry: and he would have you do all those things if you allowed him. But then and always I knew that he was that precious thing to the race and the world, a genius" (166–167). They maintained a copious correspondence over the next several years, the highlight of which is a preliminary version of "The LAKE ISLE OF INNISFREE" that Yeats sent by way of Christmas greeting in December 1888 (CL1 120–121).

In MEMOIRS, Yeats acknowledges that there was an element of romance in the early phase of their friendship: "I wrote many letters to Katharine Tynan, a very plain woman, and one day I overheard somebody say that she was the kind of woman who might make herself very unhappy about a man. I began to wonder if she was in love with me and if it was my duty to marry her." The plausibility of such a marriage increased when Yeats was safely in London, but whenever in Tynan's company he felt that such a marriage was "impossible" (*Mem.* 32). In a letter written around 1930, Tynan's sister presents a different recollection: during an evening of cards and poetry (in late 1887 or early 1888) Yeats proposed marriage and was rejected, though he did not seem to take it too much amiss after the fact (AM 72). Writing to Tynan on March 21, 1888, after having met MAUD GONNE, Yeats tried to quell rumors, with a telling defensiveness, that he had fallen in love. "Who told you that I am 'taken up with Miss Gonne,'" Yeats demanded of Tynan. "I

Portrait of the writer Katharine Tynan, 1887, by John Butler Yeats *(Dublin City Gallery The Hugh Lane)*

think she is, 'very good looking' and that is all I think about her" (*CL1* 154). In 1893, Tynan married Henry Albert Hinkson (1865–1919), a classical scholar, novelist, and magistrate, with whom she had three surviving children. Hinkson had been Yeats's high school classmate in 1881 and 1882, though Yeats apparently did not remember him (258). By the mid 1890s, Yeats had come to recognize Tynan's limitations and their relationship waned into cordial and distant regard.

Yeats patterned Mary Carton, the maternal but less than enrapturing love interest in JOHN SHERMAN, on Tynan, while he patterned the "strong farmer" in the story "A Knight of the Sheep" on Tynan's father (*Twenty-Five Years* 294; for the story, see *Myth.* 31–33). Yeats's early criticism frequently refers to Tynan, whom he considered a fellow laborer in the work of the Irish Renaissance. He warmly noticed the second and third of Tynan's 27 poetry collections: his review of *Shamrocks* (1887) appeared in the July 9, 1887, number of the *Irish Fireside*, and his review of *Ballads and Lyrics* (1891) in the January 2, 1892, number of the *Evening Herald* (see *UP1* 119–122; *UP2* 511–514). Yeats was less solicitous in his response to *Dublin Verses. By members of Trinity College* (1895), a collection edited by Henry Hinkson. "Year after year the graduates and undergraduates of Trinity College compose vacant verses, and how vacant their best are can be seen from a recent anthology," Yeats complained in an article on "the best Irish books," thus straining relations with his old friend; perhaps mitigating his offense, Yeats's included Tynan's *Ballads and Lyrics* and her edited volume *Irish Love Songs* in his list (*UP1* 384, 387). In 1907, Yeats edited a selection of Tynan's verse, *Twenty One Poems*, for publication by his sisters' DUN EMER PRESS.

Tynan's *Twenty-Five Years: Reminiscences* appeared in 1913. It included much recollection of Yeats and a selection of passages from his early letters. Yeats approved of the book, but he was mildly annoyed that Tynan had not asked permission to reproduce his letters. Ever the compulsive reviser, he asked to see any further letters she intended to publish, as he might—"in defiance of all right conduct"—choose to improve on them (*Letters* 585–586).

Bibliography
Foster, R. F. *W. B. Yeats: A Life, I: The Apprentice Mage*; Tynan, Katharine. *Twenty-Five Years: Reminiscences*; Yeats, W. B. *The Collected Letters of W. B. Yeats* (vol. 1), *The Letters of W. B. Yeats, Memoirs, Mythologies, Uncollected Prose by W. B. Yeats* (vols. 1–2).

Unity of Being   Yeats made "Unity of Being" not only an aspiration of his own life, but also a "cardinal principle" of his late doctrine (*Letters* 667). Yeats means by Unity of Being something like a passionately achieved self-identity freed from self-division and self-consciousness. Perhaps heeding the voice in the climactic fourth act of SHELLEY's *Prometheus Unbound* (1820) that issues the single mighty injunction "Unite!," Yeats had from the very start made an ideal of unity, whether aesthetic, cultural, or personal. In 1898, he wrote to GEORGE RUSSELL (AE), who had recently become a rural organizer for the Irish Agricultural Organisation Society (I.A.O.S.), "You are face to face with the herterogenous [sic], and the test of one's harmony is ones [sic] power to absorb it & make it harmonius [sic]" (*CL2* 175). In his essay "If I were Four-and-Twenty," published August 23 and 30, 1919, Yeats recalls that the conception of "unity" as a governing ideal came to him suddenly and mysteriously in the manner of revelation: "One day when I was twenty-three or twenty-four this sentence seemed to form in my head, without my willing it, much as sentences form when we are half-asleep: 'Hammer your thoughts into unity.' For days I could think of nothing else, and for years I tested all I did by that sentence" (*Expl.* 263; *LE* 34). The essay ends with Yeats's first public reference to Unity of Being. If he were "not four-and-fifty, with no settled habit but the writing of verse, rheumatic, indolent, discouraged, and about to move to the Far East," Yeats would "begin another epoch by recommending to the Nation a new doctrine, that of unity of being" (*Expl.* 280; *LE* 46).

Yeats again invoked Unity of Being in his essay "A People's Theatre," published November 29 and December 6, 1919, and for the first time associated the idea with Dante's *Il Convivio* or *Convito* ("The Banquet," written 1304–07). Perceiving in Dante something of the temper that he would bring to the

Irish theater, Yeats writes that "his study was unity of being, the subordination of all parts to the whole as in a perfectly proportioned human body—his own definition of beauty—and not, as with those I have described, the unity of things in the world [. . .]" (*Expl.* 250; on Dante's formulation of Unity of Being, see also 356; *LE* 162, 179, 210; *AV* 82, 258, 291). George Bornstein notes that Dante does not in fact compare Unity of Being to the "perfectly proportioned human body" in the *Convito,* and he calls it a mystery that Yeats "should repeatedly err in citing a source for one of his principal doctrines." He speculates that Yeats misremembered two passages from Dante's Third Treatise, which he quotes in Elizabeth Price Sayer's 1887 translation: 1) "Man is the most wonderful, considering how in one form the Divine Power joined three natures; and in such a form how subtly harmonized his body must be. It is organized for all his distinct powers; wherefore, because of the great concord there must be, among so many organs, to secure their perfect response to each other," 2) "The beauty of the body is the result of its members in proportion as they are fitly ordered" (*Poetic Remaking* 89).

In AUTOBIOGRAPHIES, Yeats elaborates the idea of Unity of Being in its historical dimension: as unity and disunity define individuals, so they define eras and cultures. Yeats describes his younger self as tormented by the conviction that the world had become a "bundle of fragments," and he remembers that he delighted "in every age where poet and artist confined themselves gladly to some inherited subject-matter known to the whole people, for I thought that in man and race alike there is something called 'Unity of Being', using that term as Dante used it when he compared beauty in the *Convito* to a perfectly proportioned human body. My father, from whom I had learned the term, preferred a comparison to a musical instrument so strung that if we touch a string all the strings murmur faintly" (163–164). It followed that "there could be no aim for poet or artist except expression of a 'Unity of Being' like that of a 'perfectly proportioned human body'" (200). Elsewhere in *Autobiographies,* Yeats describes Western modernity as a fall from precisely this unity: "Somewhere about 1450 [. . .] men attained to personality in great num-

bers, 'Unity of Being', and became like 'a perfectly proportioned human body', and as men so fashioned held places of power, their nations had it too, prince and ploughman sharing that thought and feeling. What afterwards showed for rifts and cracks were there already, but imperious impulse held all together. Then the scattering came, the seeding of the poppy, bursting of pea-pod [. . .]" (227; see also *Expl.* 431; *LE* 234). Yeats's political conservatism and cultural nationalism largely derive from his yearning to recover this unity, which functions in the scheme of his desire as a surrogate for the mythic golden age or for "supernal Eden" (*E&I* 297). In an attempt to regain this unity, he would undo or forestall modernity's dispersion and multiplicity: "If Chaucer's personages had disengaged themselves from Chaucer's crowd, forgot their common goal and shrine, and after sundry magnifications became each in turn the centre of some Elizabethan play, and had after split into their elements and so given birth to romantic poetry, must I reverse the cinematograph?" (*Aut.* 166). MEMOIRS opens with a vision of such a reversal, as Yeats recalls walking the oppressively ugly streets of London as a young man and seeing in his "mind's eye a London full of moss and grass, and a sort of preaching friar far off among fields," and saying to himself, "the right voice could empty London again" (20). Ireland, he thought, was particularly primed for such a restoration of unity, as it had been only partially brought within the modern industrial and scientific order and had never entirely accepted it (cf. "The STATUES").

As applied both to individuals and to cultures, Unity of Being is one of the ruling ideas of *A VISION.* Yeats associates it with the 15th phase of the lunar cycle—the phase of the full moon, of "perfect beauty"—and with the phases clustered around the 15th phase. At Phase Thirteen there is "a possible complete intellectual unity, Unity of Being apprehended through the images of the mind"; at Phase Seventeen—the phase of Dante, SHELLEY, Walter Savage Landor (1775–1864), and Yeats himself—"Unity of Being, and consequent expression of *Daimonic* thought, is now more easy than at any other phase"; at Phase Nineteen, Unity of Being ceases to be possible, as "the being is compelled to live in a fragment of itself and to dramatise that fragment" (129, 141, 148). Historically, Yeats associates Unity of Being with ancient Greece (ca. 500 B.C.), Byzantium (ca. A.D. 500) and Renaissance Europe (1450–1550).

Yeats's poetry does not include the phrase "Unity of Being" or even the word "unity," but it pervasively expresses the condition of this unity. The concept informs the image of the dancer in both "AMONG SCHOOL CHILDREN" and "THE DOUBLE VISION OF MICHAEL ROBARTES," and it explicitly informs Michael Robartes's theory in "MICHAEL ROBARTES AND THE DANCER" that "blest souls are not composite, / And that all beautiful women may / Live in uncomposite blessedness, / And lead us to the like—if they / Will banish every thought. . . ." "SAILING TO BYZANTIUM" envisions and pines for Byzantium in its moment of unity, the era, as Yeats writes in *A Vision*, "a little before Justinian opened St. Sophia and closed the Academy of Plato" when "religious, aesthetic and practical life were one" (279).

Bibliography

Bornstein, George. *Poetic Remaking: The Art of Browning, Yeats, and Pound*; Yeats, W. B. *Autobiographies, The Collected Letters of W. B. Yeats* (vol. 2), *Essays and Introductions, Explorations, Later Essays, The Letters of W. B. Yeats, Memoirs, A Vision*.

Verlaine, Paul (1844–1896) ARTHUR SYMONS introduced Yeats to the work of the great French symbolist poet and then introduced him to the poet himself (*Aut.* 246). An early student of French symbolism and later the movement's most influential English critic and promoter, Symons first met Verlaine on April 29, 1890, at the Café François Premier in Paris, and he remained ever after a devoted follower of the poet. In 1893, Symons arranged for Verlaine to give a series of lectures in London and provided the poet with a bed in his rooms at Fountain Court, the Temple (*Arthur Symons* 92–95). Verlaine describes the visit in his essay "My Visit to London," which appeared in the November 1893 number of the SAVOY. Suffering from a cold in Dublin (YC 31), Yeats missed the chance to meet Verlaine. The following year he visited PARIS

with a letter of introduction from Symons (*Arthur Symons* 103; *CL1* 378–379). Invited to partake of "coffee and cigarettes plentifully," Yeats called on Verlaine in the top floor of a "tenement house" in February 1894. He pictures the meeting in his essay "Verlaine in 1894," published in the April 1896 issue of the *Savoy* (see *UP1* 397–399) and later revised for inclusion in AUTOBIOGRAPHIES (261–262). The essay recalls Verlaine talking of Shakespeare, Maeterlinck, Victor Hugo, and Villiers de l'Isle-Adam, and issuing a shrewd *pensée* on the subject of *In Memoriam* (1850): "TENNYSON was too noble, too *Anglais*, and when he should have been broken-hearted, he had many reminiscences" (*UP1* 399). Verlaine's comment crystallized an aspect of Yeats's own reservations about Tennyson, and Yeats frequently quoted it (see *Aut.* 261; *E&I* 270; *LE* 91–92, 183; *UP2* 413). The spectacle of the ailing, impoverished poet reminded Yeats of the Hebrew maxim, "He who sees Jehovah dies," which anticipates his diagnosis of the "tragic generation" in *Autobiographies* (*UP1* 399). Yeats never again met Verlaine, but ever after he expressed his admiration. In "SYMBOLISM IN PAINTING," Yeats places Verlaine in the pantheon of modern artists who take "all the Divine Intellect, its anger and its pity, its waking and its sleep, its love and its lust, for the substance of their art" (*E&I* 149). In 1906, having descended from the transcendentalism of the 1890s, Yeats lauded Verlaine's "feeling for his own personality, his delight in singing his own life, even more than that life itself" (270–271).

Bibliography

Beckson, Karl. *Arthur Symons: A Life*; Kelly, John S. *A W. B. Yeats Chronology*; Yeats, W. B. *Autobiographies, The Collected Letters of W. B. Yeats* (vol. 1), *Essays and Introductions, Later Essays, Uncollected Prose by W. B. Yeats* (vols. 1–2).

Wellesley, Dorothy Violet (née Ashton) (1889–1956) Dorothy Wellesley, duchess of Wellington from 1943, was Yeats's closest aesthetic confidante and one of his most habitual correspondents from 1935 until his death. In some sense, Penns in the Rocks, Wellesley's manorial home in Withyham, Sussex, came to replace Lady GREGORY's estate,

COOLE PARK, as a country refuge, but even more as a touchstone of the aristocratic values that Yeats attempted to embody in his verse. Yeats called it the "perfect country house" and extolled its "lettered peace" (*LOP* 38). On May 22, 1936, he wrote to Wellesley that he longed for her "intellect & sanity," adding, most revealingly, "Hitherto I have never found these anywhere but at Coole" (63). Wellesley married Lord Gerald Wellesley (1885–1972), a secretary in the diplomatic service and later an architect, in 1914, but the couple lived apart and led separate lives; the correspondence between Yeats and Wellesley does not mention her husband, nor for the most part does Wellesley's autobiography *Far Have I Travelled* (1952). "Married or not," R. F. Foster writes, "Dorothy Wellesley's life was closely woven into the tangled web of upper-class lesbian intrigue spun around the glamorous Vita Sackville West," with whom she had a love affair (*AP* 528).

Surveying recent verse for inclusion in his *Oxford Book of Modern Verse* (1936), Yeats came across Wellesley's poems "Walled Garden" and "Horses" in J. C. Squire's anthology *Younger Poets of To-day* (1932). He was intrigued and wanted to meet the author (*LOP* 1; *P&I* 182). Lady Ottoline Morrell (1873–1938), a friend of both poets, arranged a get-together. On June 3, 1935, she drove Yeats to Penns in the Rocks for an overnight stay. Yeats told Wellesley the visit had been "delightful and exciting" (*LOP* 1–2). In August, Yeats returned to Penns in the Rocks for a two-week visit. He and Wellesley spent much time discussing the make-up of his anthology, and Yeats proposed that Wellesley prepare a volume of her own selected poems, with an introduction by himself. The book was published in June 1936 as *Selections from the Poems of Dorothy Wellesley*. In his fulsome introduction—his prose eclipsing extracts from Wellesley's poetry—Yeats encapsulates what he considered the strong point of Wellesley's work: "Face to face with the problem that has perplexed us all, she can unite a modern subject and vocabulary with traditional richness" (*P&I* 183).

When it appeared in November 1936, *The Oxford Book of Modern Verse* included eight poems by Wellesley (as opposed to seven by T. S. ELIOT)

and an introduction that is almost perversely complimentary. Toward the end of his long essay, Yeats writes, "[Though] the concentration of philosophy and social passion of the school of [Cecil] Day Lewis and in [Louis] MacNeice lay beyond my desire, I would, but for a failure of talent, have been in that of [Walter James] Turner and Dorothy Wellesley" (*LE* 203). MacNeice himself considered this statement "astonishing." In Turner and Wellesley, he observes, Yeats "found two things he looked for—faith and an elegance of phrase," and on this basis he allowed himself to overlook limitations in craft. "Yeats as a critic of poetry was partisan," he adds, "as is patent from his anthology" (*Poetry of W. B. Yeats* 207–208).

Unflinching in the role of poetic mentor, Yeats insisted on correcting Wellesley's poems, as she was the first to acknowledge. "W.B.Y. is for ever trying to revise my poems," she complains in a note on her friendship with Yeats. "We have quarreled about this. I say to him: 'I prefer bad poems written by myself to good poems written by you under my name.' When he has made a suggestion for altering a certain line in my verses and I demur saying: 'I shall make a note saying this line was altered by W.B.Y. otherwise I am cheating', he says, 'No! it has always been done in a company of poets', which is true" (*LOP* 46). Yeats's editorial instincts are fully on display in a letter of July 3, 1938, in which he proposed replacing "What a chorus was the stars!" with the subtly more mellifluous line "What an audience were the stars" (169). In the case of "The THREE BUSHES," based on a ballad by Wellesley, Yeats's editorial hand became so heavy that he wound up appropriating Wellesley's poem as his own.

Yeats and Wellesley were artistic collaborators foremost, but their relationship had an odd romantic and sexual dimension, despite Wellesley's sexual orientation and Yeats's advanced age (*AP* 546). On October 29, 1936, Yeats wrote, "O my dear I thank you for that spectacle of personified sunlight. I can never while I live forget your movement across the room just before I left, the movement made to draw attention to the boy in yourself." He added cryptically, "Also [for "Alas"?] that so long must pass before we meet—at last an intimate understanding is possible" (*Letters* 864; *LOP* 99). The following month a discussion of "The Chambermaid's First Song" and "The Chambermaid's Second Song" (see "The Three Bushes") led Yeats back to the vision of Wellesley, apparently in explanation of the poems' sexual understanding. "My dear, my dear—when you crossed the room with that boyish movement, it was no man who looked at you, it was the woman in me. It seems that I can make a woman express herself as never before. I have looked out of her eyes. I have shared her desire" (*Letters* 868; *LOP* 108; see also 113).

In addition to his introduction to *Selections from the Poems of Dorothy Wellesley*, Yeats paid Wellesley the tribute of a striking poem, "To Dorothy Wellesley," which bids her to her cloistral library, there to await communion with the proud, torch-bearing furies, muses of heroic passion. Wellesley called the poem "wonderful," and it was to her "lasting joy" that it immortalized Brutus, her beloved Great Dane (*LOP* 87, 145–146). Yeats and Wellesley's correspondence is collected in *Letters on Poetry from W. B. Yeats to Dorothy Wellesley*, which appeared in 1940, edited and annotated by Wellesley herself.

Wellesley went to France in December 1938 and took a villa near the hotel in Cap Martin where Yeats spent his final weeks. *Letters on Poetry* ends with her account of Yeats's decline, death, and burial. She attests that Yeats died "murmuring poetry to the last gasp" (195–196).

Bibliography

Foster, R. F. *W. B. Yeats: A Life, II: The Arch-Poet*; MacNeice, Louis. *The Poetry of W. B. Yeats*; Wellesley, Dorothy. *Far Have I Travelled*; Yeats, W. B. *Later Essays*, *The Letters of W. B. Yeats*, *Letters on Poetry from W. B. Yeats to Dorothy Wellesley*, *Prefaces and Introductions*.

Wilde, Oscar (Oscar Fingal O'Flahertie Wills Wilde) (1856–1900)

Yeats and Wilde were men and writers of largely incompatible temperament and outlook, but Richard Ellmann, an eminent scholar of both, suggests that they had at least one crucial commonality: a predilection for the mask, an instinct for the "tension between the pose and

Oscar Wilde, ca. 1882. Yeats writes in *Memoirs*: "I had always felt the man in him and that his wit was . . . but the sword of the swashbuckler." *(Library of Congress)*

the real self" (MM 72). The two Anglo-Irish writers came to know one another at the Sunday evening gatherings held by editor and poet W. E. Henley (1849–1903) at his home in Chiswick, a 15-minute walk from Bedford Park (*Aut.* 120; *Mem.* 39). Yeats's first encounter with Wilde, most likely in September 1888, was an "astonishment," as he had "never before heard a man talking with perfect sentences, as if he had written them all overnight with labour and yet all spontaneous" (*Aut.* 124). By December 1888, the two writers were on sufficiently friendly terms that Wilde asked Yeats to have Christmas dinner with his family in Chelsea, an occasion recounted in *Autobiographies* and *Memoirs*. Yeats remembers the interior of Wilde's house as a meticulous study in white, reminiscent of Whistler, and he recalls thinking that "the perfect harmony of his life there, with his beautiful wife and his two young children, suggested some deliberate artistic composition" (*Aut.* 127; see also *Mem.* 21–22). After dinner Wilde read excerpts from the proofs of his essay "The Decay of Lying" (1889). In the substitution of the word *melancholy* for *sad*, Yeats found evidence of the "vague impressiveness" that spoiled Wilde's writing for him, but the essay's central thesis that art constructs rather than reflects life—that "Truth is entirely and absolutely a matter of style"—must have aroused his sympathy and interest (*Aut.* 128). The two writers subsequently traded reviews of each other's work: Wilde cordially reviewed *Fairy and Folk Tales of the Irish Peasantry* (*Woman's World*, February 1889) and *The Wanderings of Oisin and Other Poems* (*Woman's World*, March 1889; *Pall Mall Gazette*, July 12, 1889), while Yeats less enthusiastically reviewed *Lord Arthur Savile's Crime and Other Stories* and *A Woman of No Importance* (*Critical Heritage* 72–73; *UP1* 202–205, 354–355). Much later—in 1923—Yeats wrote an introduction to Wilde's *The Happy Prince and Other Fairy Tales*, the third volume in an edition of Wilde's complete works (see *P&I* 147–151). During the early 1890s, Wilde occasionally attended meetings of the RHYMERS' CLUB, but never when they were held at the Cheshire Cheese, as Wilde "hated Bohemia" (*Aut.* 147; *Mem.* 37). The two writers met for the last time in the spring of 1894 following a performance of Yeats's *The LAND OF HEART'S DESIRE* (*Aut.* 224).

When Wilde's life spectacularly combusted in 1895, Yeats, unlike so many others, refused to turn on him. In advance of Wilde's trial for indecency and sodomy, which began on May 22, Yeats solicited and delivered letters of support from various Irish writers, with only EDWARD DOWDEN refusing to offer a sympathetic word (*Aut.* 224–225; *CL1* 465–466). R. F. Foster surmises that Yeats's loyalty to Wilde was "compounded of gratitude to someone who had helped him, solidarity with an avant-garde Irish writer, and a cosmopolitan determination not to be shocked" (*AM* 154). Ultimately, Wilde joined CHARLES STEWART PARNELL and J. M. SYNGE in Yeats's pantheon of Irish heroes broken by the mob. "When the verdict was announced," Yeats writes, referring to Wilde's conviction, "the harlots

in the streets outside danced upon the pavement" (*Aut.* 227). The *SAVOY*, a notoriously advanced literary journal with which Yeats was closely associated during its brief run in 1896, was named after the London hotel where Wilde engaged in many of his trysts. The name was presumably a gesture of daring and defiance directed at British conventionality in the wake of Wilde's fall.

In *Autobiographies*, Yeats ponders the intricate and obscure problem of Wilde's personality at great length, suggesting Wilde's grip on Yeats's imagination. Out of these reminiscences comes the shard of a definite theory: As the moon rounds through its late phases, "men who belong by nature to the nights near to the full are still born, a tragic minority, and how shall they do their work when too ambitious for a private station, except as Wilde of the nineteenth Phase, as my symbolism has it, did his work? He understood his weakness, true personality was impossible, for that is born in solitude, and at his moon one is not solitary; he must project himself before the eyes of others, and, having great ambition, before some great crowd of eyes; but there is no longer any great crowd that cares for his true thought. He must humour and cajole and pose, take worn-out stage situations, for he knows that he may be as romantic as he please, so long as he does not believe in his romance [. . .]" (228–229). In *A VISION*, Yeats indeed assigns Wilde to the 19th lunar phase, along with Byron, Gabriele D'Annunzio ("perhaps") and a "certain actress" (Mrs. Patrick Campbell; see *LE* 5). He describes this phase as "the beginning of the artificial, the abstract, the fragmentary, and the dramatic. UNITY OF BEING is no longer possible, for the being is compelled to live in a fragment of itself and to dramatise that fragment" (148).

Yeats had an entirely independent acquaintance with and interest in Wilde's mother, Lady Jane Francesca Wilde (1821–96). During the 1840s, Lady Wilde, writing as "Speranza," had contributed fiercely nationalist poems to the *Nation*; later she became well known as a folklorist and hostess. Provided with an introduction by KATHARINE TYNAN, Yeats called on Lady Wilde on July 28, 1888, and thereafter attended Saturday gatherings at her home in Chelsea (*CL1* 87). Yeats remembers that she received her guests "with blinds drawn and shutters closed that none might see her withered face" and offers that "she longed always, perhaps, though certainly amid much self-mockery, for some impossible splendour of character and circumstance" (*Aut.* 129). Both Lady Wilde and her son, in turn, were briefly and peripherally involved in Yeats's London-based Irish Literary Society (see NATIONAL LITERARY SOCIETY). Lady Wilde resigned in July 1893 due to ill health (*CL1* 360; *Oscar Wilde* 126). Yeats's *Fairy and Folk Tales of the Irish Peasantry* (1888) included four excerpts from Lady Wilde's *Ancient Legends, Mystic Charms, and Superstitions of Ireland* (1887), while his play *The* KING'S THRESHOLD borrowed elements from "Seanchan the Bard and the King of the Cats," a traditional tale retold by Lady Wilde in *Ancient Legends.* Yeats further reviewed her folkloric collection *Ancient Cures, Charms, and Usages of Ireland* (1890) in Henley's *Scots Observer* on March 1, 1890 (*UP1* 169–173).

Bibliography

Ellmann, Richard. *Oscar Wilde, Yeats: The Man and the Masks*; Foster, R. F. *W. B. Yeats: A Life, I: The Apprentice Mage*; Jeffares, A. Norman, ed. *W. B. Yeats: The Critical Heritage*; Yeats, W. B. *Autobiographies, The Collected Letters of W. B. Yeats* (vol. 1), *Later Essays, Memoirs, Prefaces and Introductions, Uncollected Prose by W. B. Yeats* (vol. 1), *A Vision.*

Woburn Buildings   In February 1896, following a six-month stint as ARTHUR SYMONS's roommate at Fountain Court, the Temple, Yeats took lodgings of his own at 18 Woburn Buildings (now 5 Woburn Walk) in north Bloomsbury, just south of St. Pancras' Church. In the definitive account of Yeats's association with Woburn Buildings, John Kelly et al. describe the address as an "unsalubrious alley, a slum in the shadow of three great railway terminals" that had the advantage of being "adjacent to Euston Station (from which the Irish Mail ran), and close enough to the British Museum. It was also discreet, and allowed a poor man to walk to most locations in central London" (*CL2* 725). John Masefield (1878–1967), who first visited in 1900, remembers "a kind of blackguard beauty" about

Woburn Buildings. "The houses had come down in the world, and as it were gone on the streets. They seemed to screen discreet vice and secret crime. The court was quiet enough, behind drawn blinds and curtains; but in a street at the eastern end there were nightly rows and singings, and the children seemed never to go to bed. Yeats was known there as the 'toff what lives in the Buildings'. He was said to be the only man in the street who ever received letters" (*I&R*, I, 47; *Some Memories* 13–14). Upon entering, "you went along the hall to the stair, which led inwards, then curved, and brought you to the landing on which he lived. On this, the second floor, he had a biggish front sitting-room and a small back kitchen. On the floor above, he had corresponding rooms, in which he slept" (*Some Memories* 5). Clifford Bax (1886–1962), poet and dramatist, remembers going up some "narrow and ancient stairs" to find rooms that resembled a "square black cave," with a candle that "threw an exaggerated chiaroscuro about the scene," and dim figures moving about in the shadows (*I&R*, I, 43).

In AUTOBIOGRAPHIES, Yeats himself recalls the specifics of his living arrangement: "On the Ground floor at Woburn Buildings lived a shoemaker; on the first floor a workman and his family; I on the second floor; in the attic an old pedlar, who painted a little in watercolours" (304). The cleaning and some of the cooking was done by the wife of the landlord, Mrs. Sarah Old (1855–1939), who had been Symons's housekeeper at Fountain Court (*AM* 160). In a letter written soon after moving in, Yeats described the lodging as "very cheap"; Yeats's initial rent is unknown, but comparable apartments on the street rented for an amount between five shillings, six pence and seven shillings, six pence (*CL2* 9–10). He paid an additional amount for meals and housekeeping. The furnishings were equally cheap, but as the rooms evolved they achieved a Bohemian éclat. As Masefield recalls, the walls featured engravings by BLAKE, a BEARDSLEY poster advertising the debut production of *The* LAND OF HEART'S DESIRE, the fine water-color *Memory Harbour* by Jack Yeats, a pencil drawing of Yeats by his father, a pencil drawing by Cecil French showing a woman with a rose, and two watercolors by Yeats himself depicting the lake and hills of Coole (*Some*

Memories 6). Upon a lectern, from 1905, was displayed the Kelmscott Chaucer that Yeats received as a 40th birthday present from his friends (*CL4* 110, 125–126, 129, 140, 161–162, 166).

Not least, the rooms were a private haven in which Yeats hoped to consummate his relationship with the married OLIVIA SHAKESPEAR. In MEMOIRS Yeats recounts furniture shopping with her: "She came with me to make every purchase, and I remember an embarrassed conversation in the presence of some Tottenham Court shop man upon the width of the bed—every inch increased the expense" (88). The rooms allowed Yeats to extend his social life in other ways as well. Within days of his arrival at Woburn Buildings he had arranged the first of the Monday evening gatherings that were to be a mainstay of his years in London. These typically went from eight until two or three in the morning, as Masefield remembers. "Tea & whiskey & no dress," Yeats specified in his inaugural invitation to Ernest Rhys (1859–1946), suggesting that talk was to be the main attraction (*CL2* 8). During the early days of this weekly institution, as the painter Sir William Rothenstein (1872–1945) remembers, Yeats would hold forth on "fairies and magic, the cabala, and the philosopher's stone," while FLORENCE FARR would sometimes "croon" to the strains of the psaltery (*I&R*, I, 48).

In the early 1900s, Yeats extended his demesne by taking over the attic, and in 1916 he took over the lower floor, giving him a total of five rooms, for which he paid £50 per year (*CL2* 729–31). In January 1918, Yeats, by then married, took up residence in OXFORD. He sublet the apartment before giving up the lease in June 1919.

Though Yeats spent more than two decades as an inhabitant, Woburn Buildings figure only obliquely in a single poem. "PRESENCES" describes a delegation of uncanny female visitants who climbed the "creaking stair" and "stood in the door and stood between / My great wood lectern and the fire / Till I could hear their hearts beating."

Bibliography

Foster, R. F. *W. B. Yeats: A Life, I: The Apprentice Mage*; Masefield, John. *Some Memories of W. B. Yeats*; Mikhail, E. H., ed. *W. B. Yeats: Interviews and Recollections* (vol. 1); Yeats, W. B. *Autobiographies, The Collected Letters of W. B. Yeats* (vols. 2, 4), *Memoirs*.

Wordsworth,   William (1770–1850)   Though Wordsworth was the paterfamilias of English romanticism, Yeats, like SHELLEY, was at best ambivalent about his example. In general terms, Yeats objected to Wordsworth's intermittent sentimentality and didacticism, his sensitivity to the mere outward forms of nature, and the spiritual defeat implicit in his nostalgia for the days of his youthful communion with nature. JOHN EGLINTON remembers Yeats as a young man saying that Wordsworth was "too much of the rural dean," and something of this notion remained with him (*I&R*, I, 33). Harold Bloom goes so far as to assert that the "school of LIONEL JOHNSON and Yeats was founded upon what they took to be an anti-Wordsworthian, anti-Tennysonian thesis: against recollection" (*Yeats* 30).

Yeats's prose is rife with the denigration of Wordsworth. In "The AUTUMN OF THE BODY," Yeats cites Goethe, Wordsworth, and Browning as examples of the degenerate modern conception of poetry as a mere criticism of life and interpretation of "things as they are" (*E&I* 192). AUTOBIOGRAPHIES includes several astute epigrams at Wordsworth's expense. Yeats calls Wordsworth "the one great poet who, after brief blossom, was cut and sawn into planks of obvious utility"; he notes that Wordsworth is "often flat and heavy, partly because his moral sense has no theatrical element, it is an obedience to a discipline which he has not created"; and following the distinction made by TENNYSON's friend Arthur Henry Hallam (1811–33), he brands Wordsworth a type of the "impure artist" who brings "popular morality" into his work, in contrast to "pure artists" like Keats and Shelley (193, 347, 361; on Wordsworth's lack of theatrical element, see also *LE* 10; *Mem.* 151). Yeats offers a version of Hallam's distinction in his 1897 essay "William Blake and the Imagination," in which he unfavorably compares Wordsworth to BLAKE: "Sometimes one feels, even when one is reading poets of a better time—Tennyson or Wordsworth, let us say—that they have troubled the energy and simplicity of their imaginative passions by asking whether they were for the helping or for the hindrance of the world, instead of believing that all beautiful things have 'lain burningly on the Divine hand'" (*E&I* 113). In his 1914 essay "Art and Ideas," he cites Wordsworth as an example of the poet who "condescended to moral maxims, or some received philosophy" and calls him "a little disreputable" (347–348; see also 351). In PER AMICA SILENTIA LUNAE, Yeats finds a spur to renewed visionary endeavor in the spectacle of Wordsworth's slack old age: "Surely, [the poet] may think, now that I have found vision and mask I need not suffer any longer. He will buy perhaps some small old house where like Ariosto he can dig his garden, and think that in the return of birds and leaves, or moon and sun, and in the evening flight of the rooks he may discover rhythm and pattern like those in sleep and so never awake out of vision. Then he will remember Wordsworth withering into eighty years, honoured and empty-witted, and climb to some waste room and find, forgotten there by youth, some bitter crust" (*LE* 16).

During their second winter at Stone Cottage (January 6 to March 1, 1915), Yeats and EZRA POUND read deeply in EDWARD DOWDEN's seven-volume edition of Wordsworth's poetry (1892–93). On January 18, 1915, Yeats wrote to his father, JOHN BUTLER YEATS, "[Wordsworth] strikes me as always destroying his poetic experience, which was of course of incomparable value, by his reflective power. His intellect was commonplace, and unfortunately he has been taught to respect nothing else. He thinks of his poetical experience not as incomparable in itself but as an engine that may be yoked to his intellect. He is full of a sort of utilitarianism and that is perhaps the reason why in later life he is continually looking back upon a lost vision, a lost happiness" (*Letters* 590). In Canto 83, Pound remembers Yeats "hearing nearly all Wordsworth / for the sake of his conscience but / preferring Ennemosor on Witches"—a reference to Joseph Ennemoser's *The History of Magic* (1854).

Whatever his misgivings, Yeats's work shows inevitable traces of Wordsworth's influence. "The LAKE ISLE OF INNISFREE," for example, is unmistakably indebted to the famous lines in "Tintern Abbey" (1798) in which Wordsworth describes the solace provided by memories of nature: "But oft, in lonely rooms, and 'mid the din / Of town and cities, I have owed to them / In hours of weariness, sensations sweet, / Felt in the blood, and felt along the heart. . . ." It might be said that Yeats's many poems of defiant age (and his few poems of defeated or acquiescent age) implicitly respond to Wordsworth's formulation of the elemental romantic dilemma: the attenuation and enervation wrought by the passing years.

Bibliography

Bloom, Harold. *Yeats*; Mikhail, E. H., ed. *W. B. Yeats: Interviews and Recollections* (vol. 1); Yeats, W. B. *Autobiographies, Essays and Introductions, Later Essays, The Letters of W. B. Yeats, Memoirs*.

Yeats, Bertha Georgie ("George") (née Hyde Lees) (1892–1968)   Mrs. W. B. Yeats, the second child and only daughter of William Gilbert Hyde Lees (1865–1909) and the former Edith Ellen ("Nelly") Woodmass (1868–1942), grew up in the comfortable and fashionable upper-middle-class world of late Victorian London, a life made possible by the trickling down to her father of family money that originated in the manufacture of cotton (*BG* 14). Her father briefly entertained a military career, but from 1896 onward led the life of a gentleman alcoholic (24–25). Georgie's girlhood involved intermittent schooling and frequent foreign travel; her genuine education was provided by the literate and cultured milieu in which her family moved and by her voracious and eclectic reading in English, French, German, Italian, and Spanish. Nelly Hyde Lees was a fixture in London's artistic and occult salons. During the first years of the century she entered the social orbit of the novelist OLIVIA SHAKESPEAR and thus became acquainted with Yeats. Georgie's parents separated in 1907 or 1908, and her father died on November 18, 1909, possibly from syphilis (31). On February 1, 1911, Nelly married Shakespear's genial brother Harry Tucker, whose chief interests were art collecting and golf. The couple settled at 16 Montpelier Square, Knightsbridge (29–30). Bound by artistic interests as well as new family ties, Georgie and Olivia's daughter Dorothy became fast friends, even though Dorothy was older by six years (32–33). From February 1911 to January 1912, Georgie studied at the Heatherley School of Art, where JOHN BUTLER YEATS had been a student some 40 years earlier (31). During the prewar years Georgie and Dorothy were frequently together, both home and abroad, as novice artists busy at sketching and gallery touring. EZRA POUND fell in with Shakespear's circle in 1909 and married Dorothy in 1914. Under Pound's tutelage, the young women developed modernist leanings in art and literature (36–39).

Yeats and George made each other's acquaintance over tea at Olivia Shakespear's house in May 1911 (BG 41; Unicorn 229). Yeats became friendlier with the Tuckers in the following years. In October 1912, he vacationed with the Tuckers and Shakespears in Devon; in March 1913 he again joined the Tuckers in Devon; and in August 1913 he spent 10 days with the Tuckers in a house near Coleman's Hatch in Sussex, a stay that inspired his return to the neighborhood the following winter with Pound, the first of three winters passed at Stone Cottage (BG 41, 47–48). At least in part due to Yeats's influence, Georgie immersed herself in astrology, mysticism, occultism, and spiritualism, and with her usual application became well versed in these traditions. She also began to cast horoscopes and to frequent séances, sometimes in Yeats's company. After discussing the matter with Yeats and receiving his sponsorship, Georgie joined the HERMETIC ORDER OF THE GOLDEN DAWN on July 24, 1914 (65–66). In mid-November 1915,

Yeats with his wife, George, and his children, Anne and Michael, in the garden at Thoor Ballylee, 1929 (Private Collection/The Bridgeman Art Library)

Georgie told a cousin that she had become secretly engaged to marry Yeats, while Yeats referred two years later to their "talk alone" (80, 92–93). Whatever transpired between them—whether their talk was substantive, tentative, or merely playful—Yeats clearly did not consider himself bound, for in 1916 and 1917 he pursued marriage with both MAUD GONNE and ISEULT GONNE.

After his pursuit of Iseult ground to a halt in the autumn of 1917, Yeats turned to Georgie with a plodding determination to marry. In a letter to Lady GREGORY, Yeats acknowledged that his plans might seem "strangely cold & calculating" and admitted to a certain romantic ennui: "I certainly feel very tired & have a great longing for order, for routine and shall be content if I find a friendly serviceable woman. I merely know—we had our talk alone two years ago—that I think [this] girl both friendly, serviceable & very able. After all I want quiet more than any other thing & with me quiet & habit create great affection" (91–92). Yeats proposed on September 26 and was immediately accepted, though not without reservations on Nelly Tucker's part having to do with Iseult. Worried that Yeats's heart was divided, Nelly on second thought tried to quash the engagement in a letter of September 30 to Lady Gregory, warning that if Georgie "had an inkling of the real state of affairs she would never consent to see him again, if she realised it after her marriage to him she would leave him at once" (93). Far from naïve or unobservant, Georgie almost certainly possessed such an "inkling," but even so the marriage remained on track: Lady Gregory reassured the anxious mother, Maud and Iseult inspected and approved the bride, and Yeats attempted to play the part of enthusiastic groom, though he experienced moments of "wild misery" in which he was sure that his proposal had been an attempt to "end by a kind of suicide an emotional strain"—his courtship of Iseult—"that had become unendurable" (98). Despite misgivings on all sides, the marriage went forward, unspectacularly, on October 20, at the Harrow Road Registry Office, with Nelly Tucker and Pound in attendance.

Yeats and his bride spent their honeymoon at the Ashdown Forest Hotel, near Stone Cottage. Convinced that he had mistaken himself and betrayed his bride, Yeats became despondent (*Letters* 633). In this condition, he wrote "OWEN AHERNE AND HIS DANCERS," a bride's nightmare of an epithalamium. The poem makes no secret of Yeats's continuing obsession with Iseult; it unflatteringly deems Georgie a "cage bird" in contrast to Iseult's "wild bird," and acknowledges that it would break Georgie's heart to know that his thoughts were so far away. With remarkable aplomb and psychological shrewdness, Georgie managed to rescue the fast degenerating situation. Hoping to distract and reassure Yeats by a display of "automatic writing," she began to scribble on a page, as if conveying a message from the spirit world. She wrote that "with the bird"—Iseult—"all is well at heart. Your action was right for both but in London you mistook its meaning" (633). As she told Virginia Moore, George initially intended a bit of well-meaning fakery but suddenly felt her hand genuinely gripped by a controlling force and continued to write (BG 102–103; *Unicorn* 253). Yeats describes the miraculous or semimiraculous honeymoon intervention in A VISION: "On the afternoon of October 24th 1917, four days after my marriage, my wife surprised me by attempting automatic writing. What came in disjointed sentences, in almost illegible writing, was so exciting, sometimes so profound, that I persuaded her to give an hour or two day after day to the unknown writer, and after some half-dozen such hours offered to spend what remained of life explaining and piecing together those scattered sentences. 'No,' was the answer, 'we have come to give you metaphors for poetry'" (8). On October 29, Yeats wrote to Lady Gregory reporting the advent of the automatic writing sessions and announcing that they had entirely dispelled his gloom and uncertainty: "The strange thing was that within half an hour after writing of this message my rheumatic pains and my neuralgia and my fatigue had gone and I was very happy. From being more miserable than I ever remember being since Maud Gonne's marriage I became extremely happy. That sense of happiness has lasted ever since" (*Letters* 633). By the following month Georgie had shed her long disliked name. "We have abolished Georgie—she is now George," Yeats wrote to Lady Gregory on November 25, with

a proud air of complicity and possession (BG 143). Ann Saddlemyer, George's outstanding biographer, remarks that the change reflects "the purposefulness with which she embraced her new career" (143). By mid-December, Yeats's postmarital jitters were a distant memory. "My wife is a perfect wife, kind, wise, and unselfish," he effused in a December 16 letter to Lady Gregory. "I think you were such another young girl once. She has made my life serene and full or order" (*Letters* 634).

Within two weeks of their marriage, as Saddlemyer writes, the newlyweds "began to look upon George's script as an ongoing record of revelation which should be properly annotated and preserved" (BG 105). It was the usual arrangement that Yeats asked questions and George, in a hypnotic trance, translated responses from various controls, or as Yeats called them, "instructors." The first four years of the marriage saw a burst of activity: 450 automatic writing sessions yielded 3,627 pages of preserved script. The automatic writing sessions were complemented by "philosophical sleeps," in which George communicated verbally while asleep or hypnotized; 164 such sessions between 1920 and 1924 yielded another 270 pages of preserved script (AV-1925 xix–xxi). Though mediumistic activities became less frequent after 1922, they continued intermittently until 1937 (BG 124, 246, 405). Whether or not George's performance was a triumph of psychic or subconscious power, her mind proved remarkably intricate and fecund. It was no small feat to rivet the attention of Yeats's massive intellect for so many years; the analogy to Scheherazade has occurred to many commentators. As R. F. Foster observes, "What remains astonishing is the depth, ingenuity, and oracular confidence of the bizarre wisdom she imparted" (AP 111). The automatic writing sessions gradually yielded the doctrines of A Vision, which was first published in 1925. It was a work in the truest sense collaborative, though George was embarrassed and aggrieved that Yeats revealed the nature of her contribution in the revised version of 1937.

Throughout the 1920s the marriage was busy and contented. The order and serenity of which Yeats spoke to Lady Gregory was at least in part responsible for his monumental literary achievements of the

1920s and early 1930s. George proved an energetic and efficient helpmate, acting not only as muse and medium, but also as nurse, secretary, and housekeeper (*BG* 143). To these duties George added the duties of mother, which she dispatched with equally brisk efficiency—Anne Butler Yeats was born on February 26, 1919, and William Michael Butler Yeats was born on August 22, 1921. During these years, George began her lifelong involvement with the Cuala industries (see CUALA PRESS), which Yeats's sisters Lily (1866–1949) and Lolly (1868–1940) had founded on the example of WILLIAM MORRIS's craft enterprise. After Lily's health began to fail in 1923, the industries moved to the ground floor of the Yeatses' house at 82 Merrion Square, where it remained until a suitable showroom at 133 Lower Baggot was procured in February 1925. George temporarily oversaw the embroidery section and remained involved until the embroidery department closed in 1931 (331). "My wife is full of energy of mind and body and will I think greatly improve the work," Yeats crowed in a letter to T. STURGE MOORE on August 18, 1923. "She knows what people wear and has seen modern art. My sister's work had become too sere, a ghost of long past colours and forms. I look forward to living in a house where there is so much going on" (*WBY&TSM* 49). From 1938, the Cuala Press was governed by a board of directors, chaired by George. After Lolly died in January 1940, the press fell entirely into her hands, and she kept it alive, if only on a limited basis, until her death (*BG* 555, 585).

Though it was prolific in all regards, the marriage showed signs of strain from the late 1920s. Yeats was often ill and George wearied of her perpetual nursing and secretarial duties, though she was never slack in fulfilling them. The couple's sexual life diminished in the early 1930s, leaving Yeats "puzzled and hurt," according to Edith Shackleton Heald, and the relationship settled into a collaborative routine that was essentially practical (474, 477, 538). In 1935, Yeats told Iseult that "everything was terrible," and that George had become "a mother rather than a wife" (474). Mutual respect and underlying affection prevented any ugliness, however, and there was nothing in the way of a rupture. During the 1930s, Yeats revitalized himself by carrying on amours with MARGOT RUDDOCK, Ethel Mannin (1900–84), and Edith Shackleton Heald (1885–1976). He also became intimate, intellectually and emotionally if not physically, with DOROTHY WELLESLEY. George turned a blind eye on Yeats's liaisons, welcoming, as Saddlemyer writes, "the additional support in keeping her husband physically well and intellectually stimulated" (530). Upon Yeats's death in 1939, George became her husband's literary executor and, with mixed feelings, devoted much of her remaining time and energy to overseeing the "Yeats industry," as she called the postwar boom in Yeats scholarship. Ensconced at 46 Palmerston Road, Rathmines, from July 1939, she answered questions, received visitors, and granted access to manuscript materials as she saw fit. George tried at one point to write a memoir of her years as the poet's wife but, regrettably, she later burned the manuscript (641).

Maud Gonne, Iseult Gonne, and Lady Gregory pervade Yeats's work as iconic and even mythic figures, but less so George. She figures in relatively few poems, none of which are central expressions of Yeats's thought and experience. These include "The GIFT OF HARUN AL-RASHID," "AN IMAGE FROM A PAST LIFE," "MY DESCENDANTS," "Owen Aherne and his Dancers," "A Prayer for my Son" (1922), "SOLOMON AND THE WITCH," "Solomon to Sheba" (1918), "To be Carved on a Stone at Thoor Ballylee" (1921), "Two Songs of a Fool" (1919), and "UNDER SATURN." Yeats wrote a third poem on Solomon and Sheba, "On Woman," but, unlike "Solomon and the Witch" and "Solomon to Sheba," it does not pay homage to George. Yeats finished the poem in May 1914 (*YC* 174), indicating that the motif of the biblical lovers was less prompted than fulfilled by the experience of marriage. Though it derives from Irish legend, *The* ONLY JEALOUSY OF EMER is Yeats's most overt and concerted attempt to negotiate his conflicted romantic attractions; as Yeats himself construed the play, Emer represents George, Eithne represents Iseult, and Fand represents Maud (*BG* 118).

Bibliography

Foster, R. F. *W. B. Yeats: A Life, II: The Arch-Poet*; Kelly, John S. *A W. B. Yeats Chronology*; Moore, Virginia.

The Unicorn: William Butler Yeats' Search for Reality; Saddlemyer, Ann. *Becoming George: The Life of Mrs W. B. Yeats*; Yeats, W. B. *A Critical Edition of Yeats's A Vision (1925), The Letters of W. B. Yeats, A Vision, W. B. Yeats and T. Sturge Moore: Their Correspondence 1901–1937.*

Yeats, John Butler (1839–1922)   The poet's father was a gifted painter, prose stylist, and conversationalist whose career was fatally hobbled by a deficit of practicality, discipline, and initiative. He was raised in comfortable circumstances: his own father, the Reverend William Butler Yeats, was rector in the parish of Tullyish, County Down, and the owner of modest properties in Dublin and Thomastown, County Kildare. In 1851, JBY was sent to school at the Atholl Academy on the Isle of Man, and there fell in with Charles and GEORGE POLLEXFEN, scions of a SLIGO family that had built up a flourishing milling and shipping concern. Though JBY did not know it at the time, his friendship with the Pollexfen brothers represented a fateful turn in his life. In 1857, JBY matriculated at Trinity College, Dublin, but the culture of the university in those days was not likely to appeal to a young man with a passionate intellectual enthusiasm; he found "the Trinity College intellects noisy and monotonous, without ideas or any curiosity about ideas, and without any sense of mystery, everything sacrificed to mental efficiency" (PF 33). JBY graduated in the spring of 1862 and the following September paid a visit to his old friend George Pollexfen in Sligo. He became enamored of his friend's younger sister, Susan Mary, and by the end of his two-week visit the couple was engaged. They were married on September 10, 1863, but their profoundly differing temperaments almost immediately began to set them at odds. Like all of the Pollexfens, SUSAN YEATS was self-contained, stolid, and solemn, and she could not comprehend much less countenance her husband's ebullient impracticality.

JBY, meanwhile, had embarked on a career as a solicitor. He was admitted to the bar in January 1866 and seemed poised for a promising career. To the dismay and astonishment of his wife and in-laws, he threw off the yoke of respectability the following year and pledged himself to art. The subsequent

four decades, spent shifting between London and Dublin, comprise a long tale of ineffectuality and missed opportunities. JBY developed into a formidable artist and became the court portraitist of the Irish Renaissance, but he was otherwise a model of inefficiency: a self-defeating perfectionist, a hopeless procrastinator, and an inept businessman. He had no heart for the practical aspects of his profession—drumming up commissions, restricting himself to saleable work—nor for the management of his patrimony. In 1862, upon the death of his father, JBY inherited property valued at £10,000 pounds; rents declined and the property was gradually sold, with the meager proceeds largely swallowed by debts (AM 63; PF 109, 150–151, 159). In consequence of these peccadilloes, the Yeats family lived in constant financial crisis, and JBY's daughters, Lily Yeats (1866–1949) and Lolly Yeats (1868–1940), were obliged to make their living as artisans (see DUN EMER PRESS and CUALA PRESS).

During the 1870s and 1880s, JBY oversaw the vital components of his eldest son's education, introducing him to BLAKE, Keats, Shakespeare, and SHELLEY, and exposing him to the stimulating talk of his inner circle, which included literary critic EDWARD DOWDEN, poet and painter Edwin Ellis (1848–1916), painter John Nettleship (1841–1902), and physician, playwright, and poet John Todhunter (1839–1916). Most important, perhaps,

Artists' Evening (1916), by George Bellows (1882–1925). John Butler Yeats, white-bearded, holds court in the dining room of the Petitpas boarding house, New York. *(Library of Congress)*

JBY bequeathed to his eldest son a faith in the preeminence of the artist and the need for entire commitment to the artistic calling. "My father's influence upon my thoughts was at its height," Yeats recalls of his teenage years in AUTOBIOGRA-PHIES. "We went to Dublin by train every morning [from Howth], breakfasting in his studio. He had taken a large room with a beautiful eighteenth-century mantelpiece in a York Street tenement-house [44 York Street], and at breakfast he read passages from the poets, and always from the play or poem at its most passionate moment. He never read me a passage because of its speculative interest, and indeed did not care at all for poetry where there was generalization or abstraction however impassioned" (80). Yeats's high school friend, Charles Johnston (1867–1931), remembers the "long room, with its skylight, the walls of pale green, frames and canvasses massed along them; a sofa and a big armchair or two; the stout iron stove with its tube; and filling the whole with his spirit, the artist stepping forward along a strip of carpet to touch his work with tentative brush [. . .] and now and then breaking into talk on the second part of 'Faust,' or the Hesperian apples, or the relation of villainy to genius" (I&R, I, 10).

Yeats's apprenticeship in JBY's studio was crucially stimulating, but it was also intellectually oppressive. In his aborted autobiographical novel *The* SPECKLED BIRD, Yeats projects his own dilemma onto his hero Michael Hearne: "His father's thoughts and words filled the world for him, and to disobey his father was like disobeying God; every thought he had, almost every feeling he had, was but a shadow of some thought or of some feeling of his father's" (80). Inevitably, Yeats rebelled in the interest of his own imaginative autonomy, abandoning his nascent career as a painter and turning to occultism in opposition to his father's Victorian positivism. "It was only when I began to study psychical research and mystical philosophy that I broke away from my father's influence," Yeats writes in *Autobiographies.* "He had been a follower of John Stuart Mill and so had never shared Rossetti's conviction that it mattered to nobody whether the sun went round the earth or the earth round the sun" (96). So too Yeats rebelled against the

capable naturalism of his father's art. "My father was painting many fine portraits," Yeats remembers, "Dublin leaders of the bar, college notabilities, or chance comers whom he would paint for nothing if he liked their heads; but all displeased me. In my heart I thought that only beautiful things should be painted, and that only ancient things and the stuff of dreams were beautiful. And I almost quarrelled with my father when he made a large water-colour, one of his finest pictures and now lost, of a consumptive beggar-girl" (92). On occasion, at least, Yeats *did* quarrel with his father. In ON THE BOILER, he recalls a youthful scene that suggests the difficult crosscurrents of his filial tie: "When I was in my 'teens I admired my father above all men; from him I learnt to admire Balzac and to set certain passages in Shakespeare above all else in literature, but when I was twenty-three or twenty-four I read Ruskin's *Unto This Last,* of which I do not remember a word, and we began to quarrel, for he was John Stuart Mill's disciple. Once he threw me against a picture with such violence that I broke the glass with the back of my head" (*Expl.* 417; *LE* 226; see also *PF* 161).

Susan Yeats suffered a pair of strokes during the late 1880s and finally died in 1900, thus freeing JBY to spring his final surprise on the world. On December 21, 1907—at age 68—he sailed for New York with Lily. The visit was supposed to have been brief, but JBY refused to accompany his daughter when she sailed for home the following June. JBY's life in New York, much like his life in Dublin and London, was a charming if embarrassed idyll, involving erratic labor, ceaseless talk, and mounting debt. New York, in GEORGE YEATS's view, allowed JBY "to give his clothes away, eat when he chose, sleep when he chose, come and go as he liked" (BG 251). He made his home in a cheap boardinghouse on West 29th Street run by a trio of French sisters named Petitpas. Holding forth each night at the head of the table in the communal dining room, he attracted a circle of young admirers that included literary critic Van Wyck Brooks (1886–1963), poet Conrad Aiken (1889–1973), and painter John Sloan (1871–1951). Brooks's admiring reminiscence "Yeats at Petitpas'" preserves the talk and atmosphere of the boardinghouse (see his 1954 volume *Scenes and Portraits: Memoirs of Childhood and Youth*). Over the ensuing years he stubbornly resisted pressure from friends and family to return to Dublin and spent the rest of his life in New York. His emigration was at least in part a bid to evade financial responsibilities and family cares. As he wrote to Lily in April 1919, "I have always dreaded returning to Dublin when I thought I could not help you while sharing all your anxieties" (*PF* 492; see also 435).

In 1914, Yeats and JOHN QUINN devised a scheme for JBY's maintenance: Quinn would purchase Yeats's literary manuscripts, and Yeats would use the money to pay his father's debts. This arrangement saw JBY through the rest of his life (*PF* 417, 432–433). JBY did not find artistic success in New York, but he eventually enjoyed a modicum of literary success. In 1917, the CUALA PRESS published *Passages from the Letters of John Butler Yeats*, a selection of letters edited by EZRA POUND (see *Letters* 583, 607). The volume was widely and positively reviewed (by T. S. ELIOT, among others). It was followed in 1918 by *Essays Irish and American* and in 1920 by *Further Letters of John Butler Yeats*, both of which matched the success of the first volume. His engaging if fragmentary memoir, *Early Memories*, appeared posthumously in 1923, with a short preface by his son (see *P&I* 152–153). T. Fisher Unwin in London and Talbot Press in Dublin copublished *Essays Irish and American*, while his daughters' Cuala Press published *Further Letters* and *Early Memories*.

The relationship between JBY and his renowned son was fraught with complicated tensions, both intellectual and practical. In a letter of September 30, 1921, to Quinn, Yeats points to what was perhaps the fundamental tension: "It is this infirmity of will which has prevented him from finishing his picture and ruined his career. He even hates the signs of will in others [. . .]. The qualities which I thought necessary to success in art or in life seemed to him 'egotism' or 'selfishness' or 'brutality.' I had to escape this family drifting, innocent and helpless, and the need for that drew me to dominating men like [W. E.] Henley and MORRIS, and estranged me from his friends" (*PF* 162). In *The Speckled Bird*, the painter-landlord John Hearne, a saturnine version

of JBY, ventriloquizes Yeats's own filial critique: "I have not painted for years now. There was a little fellow at Davray's [a studio] who used to say I was too fond of pleasure to come to anything" (6). Hearne articulates also what Yeats may have taken to be his father's essential understanding: "The chief way to be happy is to be interested in everything and everybody. If one is, it does not matter who one sees or where one lives or what one does. When one has learned to live in the present, in the present scene and the present time, life has nothing more to teach one" (7). For his part, JBY was both thrilled and shamed to be so thoroughly upstaged by his son. Upon being asked by a young man whether he was the father of the "great Yeats," JBY retorted, "*I* am the great Yeats," a wounded reaction that suggests the difficulty of his position (*PF* 364). For all their differences and disagreements, however, Yeats abided by his father's most fundamental teachings. Upon his father's belief in the freedom of the soul to discover and express its own reality Yeats built the entire structure of his thought. While at work on a series of lectures in February 1910 ("a plea for uniting literature once more to personality"), Yeats wrote to his father: "It has made me realize with some surprise how fully my philosophy of life has been inherited from you in all but its details and applications" (*Letters* 548–549).

Bibliography

Foster, R. F. *W. B. Yeats: A Life, I: The Apprentice Mage*; Mikhail, E. H., ed. *W. B. Yeats: Interviews and Recollections* (vol. 1); Murphy, William M. *Prodigal Father: The Life of John Butler Yeats (1839–1922)*; Saddlemyer, Anne. *Becoming George: The Life of Mrs W. B. Yeats*; Yeats, W. B. *Autobiographies, Explorations, Later Essays, The Letters of W. B. Yeats, Prefaces and Introductions, The Speckled Bird*.

Yeats, Susan Mary (1841–1900) Yeats's mother played a strangely marginal role in his life. She was born Susan Mary Pollexfen, the daughter of WILLIAM POLLEXFEN, head of a successful shipping firm based in SLIGO. On September 10, 1863, she married JOHN BUTLER YEATS, the old school friend of her brothers Charles and GEORGE POLLEXFEN. The

Portrait of Susan Mary Yeats, ca. 1875, by John Butler Yeats *(The National Gallery of Ireland)*

marriage proved unfortunate in all except its offspring. JBY was mercurial, Susan Yeats saturnine; he freethinking and nonobservant, she conventionally Protestant; he thrived amid the bustle of Dublin and London, she preferred the settled rituals of Sligo and the Irish countryside. Exacerbating the inevitable domestic tensions, JBY abandoned his law career for art in 1867, plunging the family into a permanent condition of financial distress. In a 1915 letter attempting to account for his misalliance, JBY told JOHN QUINN that he had wanted to submit himself to the Pollexfen family's genius "for being dismal," explaining, "I thought I would place myself under prison rule and learn all the virtues" (*PF* 37). Perhaps getting at the nature of his father's initial attraction to his mother, Yeats remembers him saying that "she pretended to nothing she did not feel," and that she had "intensity," which was his "chief word of praise" (*Aut.* 78). A veritable philosopher of the Pollexfen temperament, John Butler Yeats later theorized his marriage as a kind of necessary synthesis: "Among my friends and in their type of civilization we made enjoyment of first

importance, and for that reason we were eager for art and poetry, which are all made of enjoyment. Yet it was bound to come to nothing, because we had not that deep sincerity, which is another name for what may be indifferently called human force or, better still, genius. Inarticulate as the sea cliffs were the Pollexfen heart and brain, lying buried under mountains of silence. They were released from bondage by contact with the joyous amiability of my family, of my bringing up, and so all my four children are articulate, and yet with the Pollexfen force" (*Early Memories* 92; see also *Aut.* 52). In his famous son, John Butler Yeats observed "a good deal of his mother." As he wrote to Quinn, "She was not sympathetic. The feelings of people about her did not concern her. She was not aware of them. She was always in an island of her own. Yet had you penetrated to her inner mind you would have found it all occupied with thoughts of other people and of how to help them. [. . .] I used to tell her that if I had been lost for years and then suddenly presented myself she would have merely asked, 'Have you had your dinner?' All this very like Willie" (*Man from New York* 425–426).

Susan Yeats has no place in the poems of her son, but AUTOBIOGRAPHIES includes a tender remembrance of his mother as the keeper of Sligo memory after the family moved to London in 1874. "She would spend hours listening to stories or telling stories of the pilots and fishing-people of Rosses Point, or of her own Sligo girlhood, and it was always assumed between her and us that Sligo was more beautiful than other places," Yeats recalls. "I can see now that she had great depth of feeling, that she was her father's daughter. My memory of what she was like in those days has grown very dim, but I think her sense of personality, her desire of any life of her own, had disappeared in her care for us and in much anxiety about money. I always see her sewing or knitting in spectacles and wearing some plain dress. Yet ten years ago when I was in San Francisco, an old cripple came to see me who had left Sligo before her marriage; he came to tell me, he said, that my mother 'had been the most beautiful girl in Sligo'" (58). From 1881 to 1883, the family lived at Howth, a seaside village on a promontory overlooking Dublin Bay. There Susan Yeats was more in her element than she had been in London, and she found a measure of happiness. Something of this happiness informs Yeats's governing memory of his mother: "When I think of her, I almost always see her talking over a cup of tea in the kitchen with our servant, the fisherman's wife, on the only themes outside our house that seemed of interest—the fishing-people of Howth, or the pilots and fishing-people of Rosses Point [near Sligo]. She read no books, but she and the fisherman's wife would tell each other stories that Homer might have told, pleased with any moment of sudden intensity and laughing together over any point of satire" (78).

Susan Yeats suffered a stroke on August 11, 1887, and a second stroke on December 11. In a January 31, 1889, letter to KATHARINE TYNAN, Yeats reported that his mother "is as usual, that is to say feable [sic] and unable to go out of doors, or move about much" (CL1 136). In a July 1, 1890, letter to Tynan, he describes his mother as "better in actual health than she used to be but feable [sic] as to nervous power & memory" (222). In Autobiographies, Yeats says that "her mind had gone in a stroke of paralysis and she had found, liberated at last from financial worry, perfect happiness feeding the birds at a London window" (78). After years of incapacitation, she died suddenly on January 3, 1900, at the age of 58 (CL2 485–489).

Bibliography

Murphy, William M. Prodigal Father: The Life of John Butler Yeats (1839–1922); Reid, B. L. The Man from New York: John Quinn and His Friends; Yeats, John Butler. Early Memories: Some Chapters of Autobiography; Yeats, W. B. Autobiographies, The Collected Letters of W. B. Yeats (vols. 1–2).

PART IV

Appendices

CHRONOLOGY OF YEATS'S LIFE

For the chronology of Yeats's published work, see Appendix 2. For the definitive chronology of Yeats's life, see John S. Kelly's *A W. B. Yeats Chronology* (2003).

1863

September 10. Yeats's parents John Butler Yeats and Susan Mary Pollexfen marry at St. John's Church, Sligo.

1865

June 13. William Butler Yeats is born at 10:40 P.M. at 1 George's Ville, Dublin (subsequently 5 Sandymount Avenue).

1866

January. John Butler Yeats is admitted to the bar.

Summer. Family visits Sligo.

August 25. Yeats's sister Susan Mary ("Lily") Yeats is born at Enniscrone, near Sligo.

December 21. Maud Gonne is born, Tongham Manor, Farnham, Surrey.

1867

Late February or Early March. Resolved to give up the law and become an artist, John Butler Yeats departs for London, where he lodges at 10 Gloucester Street. He enrolls at Heatherley's Art School and hunts for a new family home.

Late July. Family moves to 23 Fitzroy Road, Regent's Park, London, taking a six-year lease.

1868

March 11. Yeats's sister Elizabeth Corbet ("Lolly") Yeats is born at Fitzroy Road.

Summer. Family visits Sligo.

1869

Summer. Family visits Sligo. The children remain until December.

1870

March 27. Yeats's brother Robert Corbet Yeats is born at Fitzroy Road.

Summer. Family visits Sligo.

1871

August 29. Yeats's brother John Butler ("Jack") Yeats is born at Fitzroy Road.

September. Family visits Sligo.

1872

July. Susan Yeats and children begin two-year sojourn in Sligo.

1873

March 3. Robert Corbet Yeats dies of croup, age two, at Sligo.

July. The lease on the house at Fitzroy Road expires. William M. Murphy writes, "What is known is that JBY had no fixed residence outside Merville [the Pollexfen family home in Sligo] until the family's return to England more than a year later" (PF 85).

1874

October. Family moves to 14 Edith Villas, North End, Fulham, London.

1875

August 29. Yeats's sister Jane Grace Yeats is born at Edith Villas.

1876

June 6. Jane Grace Yeats dies, age one, of bronchial pneumonia.

1877

January. Enrolls at Godolphin School, Iffley Road, Hammersmith, London.

1879

Spring. Family moves to 8 Woodstock Road, Bedford Park, Turnham Green, London.

1880

March 4. Augusta Persse marries Sir William Gregory (1817–92) and becomes mistress of Coole Park.

1881

Spring. Leaves Godolphin School.

May 20. Robert Gregory is born in London.

Autumn. Family moves to Balscaddan Cottage, Howth, just north of Dublin. Yeats enters Erasmus Smith High School, Harcourt Street, Dublin.

1882

Spring. Family moves to Island View, Harbour Road, Howth.

1883

December. Leaves Erasmus Smith High School.

1884

Spring. Family moves to 10 Ashfield Terrace, Terenure, Dublin.

May. Enrolls at Metropolitan School of Art, Kildare Street, Dublin, where he becomes friends with George Russell (AE).

1885

March. "Song of the Faeries" and "Voices"—Yeats's first published poems—appear in the *Dublin University Review* (for the poems, see VP 69–70, 643–644). Yeats's earliest poetry steadily appears in the review through late 1886.

June. Yeats and his high school friend Charles Johnston (1867–1931) found the Dublin Hermetic Society. Meets the poet Katharine Tynan, who becomes for a time an artistic confidante as well as the object of ambivalent romantic feelings.

November. Charles Hubert Oldham (1860–1926) founds the Contemporary Club. As a regular attendee, Yeats begins to make a name for himself in Dublin intellectual circles. John O'Leary, whom Yeats had met earlier in the year, makes an indelible impression.

1886

April. Leaves the Metropolitan School of Art.

October. Sealy, Bryers, & Walker, Dublin, prints *Mosada*, Yeats's first book. The dramatic poem had appeared in the June issue of the *Dublin University Review*.

1887

May. Family moves to Eardley Crescent, South Kensington, London. Yeats meets Madame Blavatsky (1831–91), co-founder of the Theosophical Society.

June. Begins to frequent William Morris's Kelmscott House in Hammersmith.

August 11. Susan Yeats has first stroke.

December 11. Susan Yeats has second stroke.

1888

March 24. Family moves to 3 Blenheim Road, Bedford Park.

August. Meets the poet and editor W. E. Henley (1849–1903), who would become an early mentor.

September. Meets Oscar Wilde through Henley.

November. Joins the Esoteric Section of the Theosophical Society.

December 25. Celebrates Christmas with Oscar Wilde's family.

1889

January 30. Meets Maud Gonne, who calls at Bedford Park with an introduction from John O'Leary.

1890

January. With Ernest Rhys (1859–1946), whom he had met at Kelmscott House in 1887, Yeats founds the Rhymers' Club.

March 7. Initiated as a member of the Hermetic Order of the Golden Dawn.

October. Expelled from the Theosophical Society (see CL1 234–235).

1891

August 3. Proposes marriage to Maud Gonne. She says she can never marry, but asks for Yeats's friendship. The next day the couple walks the cliffs of Howth (see "Beautiful Lofty Things").

October 6. Charles Stewart Parnell dies. He is buried on October 11 in Glasnevin cemetery, Dublin (see "Parnell's Funeral").

November 2. Maud Gonne joins the Hermetic Order of the Golden Dawn (she resigns in December 1894).

1892

March 6. Sir William Gregory dies. Lady Gregory, widowed, is free to pursue the arts.

May 12. Inaugural meeting of the London-based Irish Literary Society.

August 16. Inaugural meeting of the Dublin-based National Literary Society.

October 17. Bertha Georgie Hyde Lees (see George Yeats) is born in London.

1894

February. Visits Paris for the first time. He meets the poet Paul Verlaine. With Maud Gonne, he attends a performance of Villiers de l'Isle-Adam's *Axël*, February 26.

March 29. The Land of Hearts Desire debuts at the Avenue Theatre, London. This is the first stage production of a play by Yeats.

April 14. Meets Lady Gregory at the London home of Sir Michael Morris.

April 16. Meets Olivia Shakespear at a dinner celebrating the *Yellow Book.*

August 6. Iseult Gonne is born in Paris.

1895

October. Moves to Fountain Court, the Temple, London, rooming with Arthur Symons.

1896

January 22. Attends the inaugural dinner of the *Savoy.* The magazine begins its yearlong run in January.

February. Moves to 18 Woburn Buildings.

August. Yeats and Arthur Symons spend the month as guests at Edward Martyn's Tulira Castle, Galway. They visit the Aran Islands, August 5–7. Yeats pays his first visit to nearby Coole Park as the lunch guest of Lady Gregory.

December. Visits Paris from early December to mid-January. Meets J. M. Synge on December 21.

1897

February. Yeats becomes involved in preparations to commemorate the centennial of the 1798 rebellion, serving as chairman of the London organizing committee. He remains busily engaged in this work for more than a year.

Spring. Romantic relationship with Olivia Shakespear ends (see "The Lover mourns for the Loss of Love").

Late June. Yeats and Lady Gregory conceive the Irish Literary Theatre following luncheon at the home of Count Florimond de Basterot (1836–1904), Lady Gregory's Galway neighbor.

July–September. Yeats spends the first of many summers at Coole Park, where he collects folklore and recovers his health.

1898

May 10–June 25. J. M. Synge makes the first of five visits to the Aran Islands.

August 15. The commemoration of the 1798 rebellion culminates in a mass demonstration in Dublin. Yeats addresses the crowd.

December 8. Maud Gonne confesses to Yeats that she had been the mistress of the French journalist and politician Lucien Millevoye (1850–1918) and that she had borne two children, Georges (1890–91) and Iseult Gonne.

1899

January 31–February 16. Visits Paris, where he proposes for the second time to Maud Gonne.

May 8. The Countess Cathleen debuts at the Antient Concert Rooms, Dublin, thus inaugurating the Irish Literary Theatre.

1900

January 3. Yeats's mother, Susan Mary Yeats, dies at age 58 of complications from stroke.

April 21. The membership of the Hermetic Order of the Golden Dawn suspends MacGregor Mathers, climaxing a long power struggle.

December 8. Yeats and Florence Farr give their first public exhibition of chanted verse (see *CL2* 597).

1901

October 21. Diarmuid and Grania debuts at the Gaiety Theatre, Dublin. It is the final production of the Irish Literary Theatre.

1902

July. In partnership with Evelyn Gleeson, the Yeats sisters found Dun Emer Industries.

April. John Murray publishes Lady Gregory's *Cuchulain of Muirthemne.* Yeats would continually draw on the volume for material and inspiration.

April 2. Cathleen ni Houlihan debuts at St. Teresa's Hall, Dublin. Maud Gonne electrifies in the lead role.

August. The Irish National Theatre Society coalesces. Yeats is elected president of the new society (see *CL3* 219).

October 1. John Butler Yeats and the Yeats sisters move from Bedford Park to "Gurteen Dhas," Churchtown, outside of Dublin. It is a 35-minute walk to the Dun Emer quarters in Dundrum.

October 4. Lionel Johnson dies.

October 30. The Pot of Broth debuts at the Antient Concert Rooms, Dublin.

Early November. Meets James Joyce.

1903

February. Receives word that Maud Gonne plans to marry Major John MacBride (1865–1916), February 7. Dispatches letters pleading with her to reconsider, February 8–10.

February 21. Maud Gonne marries Major John MacBride in Paris.

March 14. The Hour-Glass debuts at Molesworth Hall, Dublin.

May 4. Maud Gonne confesses her marital troubles (see *CL3* 356–357).

August. The Dun Emer Press issues its first book, Yeats's *In the Seven Woods: Being Poems Chiefly of the Irish Heroic Age.*

October 8. The King's Threshold debuts at Molesworth Hall, Dublin.

November 4. Departs on a four-month lecture tour of America, where he solidifies his friendship with the New York lawyer and art collector John Quinn.

1904

January 14. The Shadowy Waters debuts at Molesworth Hall, Dublin.

January 26. Maud Gonne's son Sean MacBride (1904–88) is born in Paris.

March 9. Departs New York for London.

May 11. The Irish National Theatre Society formally accepts Annie Horniman's offer to secure "a permanent Theatre in Abbey Street" (*CL3* 596). Thus the Abbey Theatre is born.

June 26. Where There is Nothing debuts at the Royal Court Theatre, London.

December 27. The Abbey Theatre opens with performances of *Cathleen ni Houlihan, On Baile's Strand,* and Lady Gregory's *Spreading the News.*

1905

Early January. Learns that Maud Gonne's marriage has collapsed and that she wishes to divorce (*CL4* 6–9).

June 13. Turns 40. His friends raise £40 and present him with a copy of the Kelmscott Chaucer (see William Morris).

August 9. A French court grants Maud Gonne a legal separation from her husband.

September. The Irish National Theatre Society reorganizes as a limited liability company.

1906

November 24. Deirdre debuts at the Abbey Theatre.

1907

January 26. J. M. Synge's *The Playboy of the Western World* opens at the Abbey Theatre. Lady Gregory wires Yeats in Scotland: "AUDIENCE BROKE UP IN DISORDER AT THE WORD SHIFT." The play's seven-night run is marked by disturbances and arrests.

February 4. Hosts a public debate on *The Playboy.*

March 16. John O'Leary dies.

April. Departs for Italy, April 10, where he joins Lady Gregory and Robert Gregory. He remains abroad until May 22.

November 21. The Unicorn from the Stars debuts at the Abbey Theatre, Dublin.

December 21. John Butler Yeats and Lily Yeats sail for New York. Lily departs for home on June 6, 1908, but John Butler Yeats refuses to accompany her. He remains abroad until his death in 1922.

1908

January. Frank and Willie Fay, who had been instrumental in creating and nurturing the Abbey Theatre, leave the company.

January 20. Hugh Lane's Municipal Gallery of Modern Art opens at 17 Harcourt Street, Dublin.

March 19. The Golden Helmet—a preliminary version of *The Green Helmet*—debuts at the Abbey Theatre.

Late March. Begins a protracted romantic relationship—"primarily physical," in A. Norman Jeffares's description—with Mabel Dickinson, a masseuse (*New Biography* 163).

June. Visits Maud Gonne in Paris.

July. Lily and Lolly Yeats sever their ties with Dun Emer Industries and found Cuala Industries. The work of the Dun Emer Press is carried on by the Cuala Press.

September. Arthur Symons suffers a mental breakdown in Italy.

December. Visits Maud Gonne in PARIS.

1909

February 3. Lady Gregory suffers a cerebral hemorrhage and nearly dies. Yeats sends her "A Friend's Illness" on February 8.

March 24. J. M. Synge, age 38, dies of Hodgkin's disease.

May. Olivia Shakespear introduces Yeats to Ezra Pound, who had arrived in London on August 14, 1908. Pound attends his first "Monday Evening" at Woburn Buildings, May 10.

August. Gossip concerning Yeats and John Quinn's mistress Dorothy Coates leads to a quarrel. Yeats and Quinn remain estranged until 1914.

1910

February 10. The Green Helmet debuts at the Abbey Theatre.

April 28–May 16. Visits Maud Gonne and Iseult Gonne in Normandy.

May 7. The Abbey Theatre remains open following the death of Edward VII, bringing to a climax long-strained relations with Annie Horniman and precipitating her withdrawal from the theater.

Early August. Receives a Civil List Pension of £150 per year, roughly doubling his income.

September 25. George Pollexfen dies in Sligo. Yeats attends his funeral, September 28.

1911

May (?). Meets Georgie Hyde Lees (the future Mrs. W. B. Yeats) in Olivia Shakespear's drawing room (the date of this meeting is uncertain; see BG 41, 670).

September 13. The Abbey Theatre departs on its first tour of America, remaining abroad for four months. Yeats accompanies the players during the first month of the tour.

October 18. Yeats departs for London.

October–March. Under the chaperonage of Lady Gregory, the Abbey Theatre players remain in America until March 6, 1912. J. M. Synge's *Playboy of the Western World* again arouses controversy, and the players are arrested in Philadelphia on charges of immorality, January 18, 1912. Lady Gregory and John Quinn have a "brief, passionate affair," in A. Norman Jeffares's phrase (*New Biography* 181).

1912

August. Visits Maud Gonne and Iseult Gonne at their home in Normandy.

September 5. Florence Farr departs for Ceylon, where she is to teach at a girl's school.

November 29. A "Citizens Provisional Committee" is formed to raise money for a gallery to house Hugh Lane's collection of paintings. (In 1907, Lane had pledged to donate his collection of pictures to Dublin on the condition that the city construct a suitable gallery). Yeats rebukes diffident philanthropists in "To a Wealthy Man who promised a Second Subscription to the Dublin Municipal Gallery if it were proved the People wanted Pictures."

1913

January 5. Pays his first visit to the hospital room of Mabel Beardsley, who is dying of cancer (see "Upon a Dying Lady").

January 20. The Dublin municipal council pledges £22,000 for construction of a new gallery to house Hugh Lane's collection of paintings, provided the Citizens Provisional Committee can supply a site and raise £3,000 from private sources. The ongoing controversy arouses Yeats's bitterest passion.

June–July. Yeats's relationship with Mabel Dickinson ends after a pregnancy scare.

September 8. The Dublin municipal council rejects Edwin Lutyens's £45,000 design for a gallery bridging the Liffey.

October 11. In frustration, Hugh Lane bequeaths his 39 French pictures to the National Gallery in London. A codicil dated February 3, 1915— unwitnessed and therefore legally invalid— reverses this decision.

November 10. Arrives at Stone Cottage, Coleman's Hatch, Sussex, where he is to spend the winter with Ezra Pound acting as his paid secretary.

1914

January–February. George Moore's memoir "Yeats, Lady Gregory, and Synge" appears in the January and February issues of the *English Review*. Moore's brilliant lampoon infuriates Yeats (see "Closing Rhymes" to *Responsibilities*).

January 16. Leaves Stone Cottage.

January 31. Departs on a lecture tour of America.

February 9. John Quinn writes and offers to reconcile. Yeats is delighted to end their five-year estrangement.

April 2. Departs America for London.

April 20. Ezra Pound marries Dorothy Shakespear in London, with Yeats as best man.

May 8–27. Visits Paris.

July 24. Georgie Hyde Lees joins the Hermetic Order of the Golden Dawn, with Yeats's sponsorship.

1915

January 6. Arrives at Stone Cottage, where he spends the winter with Ezra and Dorothy Pound.

March 1. Leaves Stone Cottage.

May 7. A German submarine sinks the *Lusitania*, en route from New York to Liverpool, off the southern coast of Ireland. Hugh Lane dies on board. The Trustees of the National Gallery in London refuse to recognize the codicil to Lane's will, initiating a protracted controversy about the ownership of his French pictures. In the years to come, Yeats leads the effort to repatriate the paintings.

December 21. Returns to Stone Cottage, where he spends the winter with Ezra Pound and Dorothy Pound.

1916

March 6. Leaves Stone Cottage.

April 2. At the Hawk's Well debuts in Lady Cunard's drawing-room, Cavendish Square, London.

April 24–29. The Easter Rising convulses Dublin (see "Easter 1916"). Yeats is far removed from the conflict as a houseguest of the artist William Rothenstein (1872–1945) in Gloucestershire. He returns to London on April 26.

May 5. John MacBride is executed for his part in the Easter Rising.

May 8. Mabel Beardsley dies of cancer (see "Upon a Dying Lady").

July–August. Visits Maud Gonne and Iseult Gonne in Normandy. He proposes to the widowed Maud on July 1. He proposes to Iseult in mid-August.

1917

Spring. Negotiates the purchase of Thoor Ballylee.

April 29. Florence Farr dies of breast cancer in Ceylon.

June 30. Signs the deed of sale and becomes owner of Thoor Ballylee.

August 7–September 17. Visits Maud Gonne and Iseult Gonne in Normandy, where he again proposes to Iseult.

September 26. Proposes to Georgie Hyde Lees.

October 20. Marries Georgie Hyde Lees at the Harrow Road Registry Office, London, with Ezra Pound as best man.

October 22–November 2. The couple honeymoon at the Ashdown Forest Hotel in Forest Row, Sussex. Georgie alleviates Yeats's anxiety and unhappiness with a display of automatic writing, October 24. Hundreds of automatic writing sessions follow during the first years of the marriage.

November–December. The Yeatses begin married life peripatetically, shifting between London, Stone Cottage, and Ashdown Cottage, Forest Row. "Georgie" decides that she will be called "George."

1918

January 2. The Yeatses move to 45 Broad Street, Oxford. They spend the following spring and summer in Ireland.

January 23. Robert Gregory, Lady Gregory's son, is killed in action when his plane is mistakenly shot down by an Italian pilot over northern Italy (see "An Irish Airman Foresees his Death" and "In Memory of Major Robert Gregory").

May–October. Charged with conspiring in the spurious "German plot," Maud Gonne is imprisoned in Holloway Jail, London. Yeats helps secure her release on medical grounds.

September 12–October 8. The Yeatses make their first stay at Thoor Ballylee, occupying the cottage attached to the still unfinished tower.

October 5. The Yeatses move to 73 Stephen's Green, renting the house from Maud Gonne. Gonne flouts the terms of her prison release by returning to Ireland and arrives at her own doorstep on November 24. Worried that Gonne will attract the police, and protective of his dangerously ill and pregnant wife, Yeats refuses to admit her. This results in the most serious quarrel of their long relationship.

Mid-December. The Yeatses move to 96 Stephen's Green.

1919

January 21. The Anglo-Irish War begins (see "Nineteen Hundred and Nineteen").

February 22. The Yeatses leave 96 Stephen's Green.

February 26. Anne Butler Yeats is born in a Dublin nursing home (see "A Prayer for my Daughter").

March 19–late April. The Yeatses rent lodgings in Dundrum.

May 25. *The Player Queen* debuts at King's Hall, Covent Garden, London.

June 25. Yeats ends his 23-year tenancy at Woburn Buildings.

Summer. The Yeatses reside at Thoor Ballylee.

October. The Yeatses move to 4 Broad Street, Oxford.

1920

January 13. The Yeatses depart on a lecture tour of America, leaving Anne in the care of Lily and Lolly Yeats.

January 24. George Yeats is introduced to John Butler Yeats at the Petitpas boardinghouse in New York. They immediately take to one another.

March 20. In Portland, Oregon, Junzo Sato presents Yeats with an ancient family sword (see "A Dialogue of Self and Soul" and "My Table").

May 29. The Yeatses depart Montreal for England.

July 12. After stopping in London, the Yeatses return to 4 Broad Street, Oxford.

1921

February 17. Speaking before the Oxford Union, Yeats condemns Britain's prosecution of the Anglo-Irish War.

April 2. The Yeatses move to Minchin's Cottage, Shillingford, Berkshire.

June 29. The Yeatses move to Cuttlebrook House, Thame.

July 11. The Anglo-Irish War halts in a truce.

August 22. Michael Butler Yeats is born in Thame (see "A Prayer for my Son").

September 30. The Yeatses return to Oxford.

December 6. Britain and Ireland sign the Anglo-Irish Treaty ending the Anglo-Irish War. The treaty establishes the Irish Free State as a partially autonomous dominion of the British Empire. The Dáil Éireann ratifies the treaty on January 7.

1922

January 18–26. The Yeatses visit Paris.

February 3. John Butler Yeats, age 82, dies in New York.

April 2. *The Only Jealousy of Emer* debuts (in translation) in Amsterdam.

April–September. The Yeatses reside at Thoor Ballylee.

June 28. The Irish Civil War begins as Free State forces attempt to recapture the Four Courts, which the Republicans have occupied since April 13 (see "Meditations in Time of Civil War").

Late September. The Yeatses move to 82 Merrion Square, Dublin.

December 7. The Free State government appoints Yeats to a six-year term in the Senate.

December 20. Receives an honorary doctorate from Trinity College, Dublin.

1923

January 5. The Free State government arrests Maud Gonne. She is released following a 20-day hunger strike.

April 27. The Irish Civil War halts in a cease-fire.

May 24. The Republican leadership issues the order to lay down arms, and the Irish Civil War ends.

June 2. Lady Gregory undergoes the first of three operations for breast cancer. She convalesces at 82 Merrion Square from June 8 to June 15. Yeats escorts her back to Coole Park.

August. With Lily Yeats ailing, Cuala Industries relocates to 82 Merrion Square.

November 15. Receives the Nobel Prize in literature.

December 8. The Yeatses arrive in Stockholm for a week of ceremonies and cultural activities.

December 10. King Gustav V presents Yeats with the Nobel medal. The prize recognizes Yeats "for his always inspired poetry, which in a highly artistic form gives expression to the spirit of a whole nation."

December 13. Delivers his Nobel lecture, "The Irish Dramatic Movement," before the Royal Academy of Sweden (see *Autobiographies*).

December 16. Departs Stockholm for London.

1924

July 10. Receives an honorary degree from Aberdeen University.

July 29. John Quinn, age 54, dies of liver cancer in New York.

1925

Early January–late February. The Yeatses travel in Italy. They join Ezra Pound and Dorothy Pound in Sicily. Parting ways with the Pounds, they continue on to Naples, Capri, and Rome.

February 25. Cuala Industries moves from 82 Merrion Square to 133 Lower Baggot Street.

April 22. Yeats finishes *A Vision*, which has been some eight years in the making.

June 11. In his most famous Senate speech, Yeats defends the right to divorce and champions the Anglo-Irish tradition (SS 99).

July–October. The Yeatses intermittently reside at Thoor Ballylee.

1926

March 21–22. The Yeatses visit the St. Otteran's School in Waterford (see "Among School Children").

May 9. *The Only Jealousy of Emer* and *The Cat and the Moon* debut at the Abbey Theatre, Dublin.

The former play had been given in Dutch in April 1922.

December 7. Yeats's translation of SOPHOCLES' *King Oedipus* debuts at the Abbey Theatre, Dublin.

1927

April 1. Lady Gregory's Coole Park is sold to the Ministry of Lands and Agriculture. Lady Gregory leases house and gardens for £100 per year.

July 10. Kevin O'Higgins is assassinated in Dublin (see "Death" and "Blood and the Moon").

September 12. Yeats's translation of Sophocles' *Oedipus at Colonus* debuts at the Abbey Theatre, Dublin.

October. Severely ill with pneumonia and "general nervous breakdown." Wintering abroad becomes imperative.

November 4. The Yeatses depart for Gibraltar.

November 14. The Yeatses proceed to Seville. Yeats's condition worsens.

November 23. The Yeatses proceed to Cannes.

1928

February 17. The Yeatses arrive in Rapallo, Italy, where Pound has lived since late 1924. They take rooms at a hotel.

Early March. Having decided to give up 82 Merrion Square on the assumption that Yeats will continue to require winters abroad, the Yeatses take a five-year lease on a new and as yet unfinished apartment at Via Americhe 12–8, Rapallo.

April. The Yeatses return to Dublin.

May 24. The Yeatses sell 82 Merrion Square and vacate the house in July.

Early August. The Yeatses move to 42 Fitzwilliam Square, Dublin.

September. Yeats's term in the Senate expires.

October 31. The Yeatses depart London for Rapallo, arriving November 3. They move into their new apartment at Via Americhe 12–8 in late November.

1929

Early January. The Yeatses spend a week in Rome.

August 13. *Fighting the Waves* debuts at the Abbey Theatre, Dublin.

April 29. After their long sojourn in Rapallo, the Yeatses arrive in London.

November 21. The Yeatses depart London for Rapallo. In Rapallo, Yeats contracts Malta fever and remains seriously ill throughout the winter.

1930

March. Remains weak, but the worst of his illness is behind him.

April. The Yeatses move to a hotel in nearby Portofino, returning to Rapallo toward the middle of the month. Yeats is immersed in Jonathan Swift.

July. The Yeatses depart Italy on July 3 and arrive in London on July 9. George Yeats returns to Dublin while Yeats returns on July 17.

November 17. *The Words upon the Window-pane*— the fruit of Yeats's immersion in Swift—debuts at the Abbey Theatre, Dublin.

1931

May 26. Receives an honorary degree from Oxford University.

Early June. T. Sturge Moore introduces Yeats to Shree Purohit Swami (1882–1941). The two would later collaborate on *The Ten Principal Upanishads* (1937).

July. Lady Gregory has begun her final decline. Yeats primarily resides at Coole Park between July and May 1932, when Lady Gregory succumbs to her cancer.

September 8. Participates in a BBC radio broadcast (see *Biblio.* 468).

December 6. *The Dreaming of the Bones* debuts at the Abbey Theatre, Dublin.

1932

May 22. Lady Gregory, age 80, dies of breast cancer. Emotionally shattered by her death, Yeats writes no verse until April 1933 (see *Letters* 808).

April 10. Participates in a BBC radio broadcast, reading several poems about women (see *Biblio.* 468–469).

July. Having signed a 13-year lease in May, the Yeatses move to Riversdale in the village of Rathfarnham, four miles southwest of Dublin. This is Yeats's final home.

September 1. Yeats and George Bernard Shaw send a letter of invitation to prospective members of a new Irish Academy of Letters (see *Letters* 801–802).

September 14. The Irish Academy of Letters takes form at an organizational meeting. Shaw is to serve as president, Yeats as vice president.

October 21. Departs England for America. Yeats's final lecture tour is to raise money for the Irish Academy of Letters.

1933

January 22. Departs New York for England, arriving in Southampton on January 27.

June 8. Receives an honorary degree from Cambridge University.

July 17. Eoin O'Duffy (1892–1944), leader of the fascist Blue Shirt movement, calls on Yeats at Riversdale. Yeats had been enthusiastic about the movement, but he is unimpressed by O'Duffy and thereafter tends to distance himself (see *Letters* 812–813).

1934

March 17. Participates in a BBC radio broadcast (see *Biblio.* 469).

April 5. Yeats undergoes the so-called Steinach operation at Beaumont House Hospital, London. The operation—a vasectomy—restores Yeats's sexual vitality and renews his creativity.

July 30. *The Resurrection* and *The King of the Great Clock Tower* debut at the Abbey Theatre, Dublin.

October 4. Meets Margot Ruddock, a 27-year-old British actress and poet, with whom he begins an affair.

October 7–16. Visits Rome as a guest of the Italian government to attend the fourth congress of the Alessandro Volta Foundation. The conference is devoted to drama.

Late December. Meets Ethel Mannin (1900–84) at a dinner party hosted by Dr. Norman Haire, who had performed the Steinach operation. Mannin plans to seduce Yeats to test the efficacy of the operation, and the two become lovers.

1935

June 3–4. Meets the poet Dorothy Wellesley, staying overnight at her Sussex manor, Penns in the Rocks. Yeats and Wellesley immediately become friends and collaborators (see "To Dorothy Wellesley").

June 13. Turns 70. Participates in a BBC radio broadcast "on the occasion of his 70th birthday" (see *Biblio.* 470).

July 5. Receives a Chinese scene sculpted in a piece of lapis lazuli from Harry Clifton (see "Lapis Lazuli").

July 17. George Russell (AE), Yeats's oldest friend, dies in Bournemouth.

November 30. Departs Liverpool for Majorca, where he and Shree Purohit Swami are to translate the principal Upanishads.

1936

Late January. Falls seriously ill. George Yeats arrives to care for him, February 2. Gradually recovers, but he is not entirely well until April.

May 15. Margot Ruddock arrives unannounced in a psychotic state (see "A Crazed Girl"). She flees to Barcelona, where she falls from a window and breaks her knee. The Yeatses follow her to Barcelona and arrange her return to England.

May 26. The Yeatses depart Majorca for London, arriving June 2.

October 11. Participates in a BBC radio broadcast. Reads poems by numerous modern authors and delivers the talk printed as "Modern Poetry" (see *Biblio.* 470–471; *LE* 89–102).

1937

April. Edmund Dulac (1882–1953) introduces Yeats to the journalist Edith Shackleton Heald (1885–1976), who is to be the last of his romantic interests. Her house in Steyning, Sussex, becomes a country retreat to complement Penns in the Rocks.

April 2. Participates in a BBC radio broadcast (see *Biblio.* 471).

April 22. Participates in a BBC radio broadcast (see *Biblio.* 472).

July 3. Participates in a BBC radio broadcast (see *Biblio.* 473).

October 29. Participates in a BBC radio broadcast (see *Biblio.* 473–474).

1938 and 1939

January 7. Departs London for Monte Carlo, where he is to vacation with Edith Shackleton Heald, arriving on January 9. He moves to Menton on January 22.

February 4. George Yeats arrives in Menton. Edith Shackleton Heald departs for Paris.

March 4. The Yeatses relocate to the Hôtel Idéal-Séjour in Cap-Martin.

March 23. The Yeatses return to London.

August. Sensing his approaching end, Yeats arranges to be buried in the church cemetery at Drumcliff, just north of Sligo, and composes a fitting epitaph: "Cast a cold eye / On life, on death. / Horseman, pass by!" (see *Letters* 914).

August 10. Purgatory debuts at the Abbey Theatre, Dublin.

August 26. Maud Gonne comes to tea at Riversdale. This is to be their last meeting and they part with affection.

October 3. Olivia Shakespear, age 75, dies at her home in London from gall bladder complications (see *Letters* 916).

Late November. The Yeatses depart for the south of France, settling at the Hôtel Idéal-Séjour in Cap-Martin, where they had stayed the previous March.

December–January. Yeats sees much of Dorothy Wellesley, who is staying nearby. She later gives a detailed account of Yeats's decline and death (see *LOP* 192–196).

December 22–January 15. Michael Yeats visits.

January 24. Yeats is not well enough to join a farewell party for the poet W. J. Turner and his wife. He begins his final decline.

January 27. Slips into a coma.

January 28. Dies at 2:30 P.M.

January 30. Buried at the cemetery at Roquebrune. Due to the war, he was not interred in the Drumcliff churchyard until September 17, 1948.

SOURCES: Foster, R. F. *W. B. Yeats: A Life, I: The Apprentice Mage, II: The Arch-Poet*; Gonne, Iseult. *Letters from Iseult Gonne to W. B. Yeats and Ezra Pound from Iseult Gonne*; Hardwick, Joan. *The Yeats Sisters: The Biography of Susan and Elizabeth Yeats*; Hone, Joseph. *W. B. Yeats*; Jeffares, A. Norman. *A New Biography*; Kelly, John S. *A W. B. Yeats Chronology*; Macardle, Dorothy. *The Irish Republic*; Murphy, William M. *Prodigal Father: The Life of John Butler Yeats (1839–1922)*; Saddlemyer, Ann. *Becoming George: The Life of Mrs W. B. Yeats*; Wade, Allan. *A Bibliography of the Writings of W. B. Yeats*; Yeats, W. B. *Ah, Sweet Dancer: W. B. Yeats and Margot Ruddock, Autobiographies, The Collected Letters of W. B. Yeats* (vols. 1–4), *The Gonne-Yeats Letters 1893–1938, Later Essays, The Letters of W. B. Yeats, Letters on Poetry from W. B. Yeats to Dorothy Wellesley, Memoirs, The Senate Speeches of W. B. Yeats*.

Books Published or Prepared for Publication during Yeats's Lifetime

For a comprehensive and detailed account of Yeats's publications, see Allan Wade's *A Bibliography of the Writings of W. B. Yeats*, third edition, 1968. This chronology conforms to Wade's bibliography, but it does not reproduce it fully. Intended to serve as a preliminary rather than a final and definitive resource, it cites books that Yeats authored, coauthored, edited, and translated, but it does not cite pamphlets and periodicals, books to which Yeats merely contributed, books for which Yeats wrote prefaces, translations of Yeats's work, and certain relatively obscure editions that are mentioned but do not have their own headings in Wade's bibliography. The "Wade Number" of each publication appears in parentheses. Vertical lines indicate where subtitles are set off by line breaks or fleurons rather than by punctuation marks in the original title pages.

1886
Mosada. A Dramatic Poem, Dublin: Sealy, Bryers, and Walker, October (?) 1886. (#1)

1888
(*ed.*) *Fairy and Folk Tales of the Irish Peasantry,* London: Walter Scott, New York: Thomas Whittaker, Toronto: W. J. Gage and Co., 1888. (#212)

1889
The Wanderings of Oisin and Other Poems, London: Kegan Paul, Trench & Co., January 1889. (#2)

(*ed.*) *Stories from Carleton,* London: Walter Scott, New York and Toronto: W. J. Gage & Co., August 1889. (#214)

1891
John Sherman and Dhoya, London: T. Fisher Unwin, November 1891. Published under the pseudonym "Ganconagh." (#4)

John Sherman and Dhoya, New York: Cassell Publishing Company, 1891. Published under the pseudonym "Ganconagh." (#5)

(*ed.*) *Representative Irish Tales,* 2 vols., New York and London: G. P Putnam's Sons, Knickerbocker Press, March 1891. (#215)

(*ed.*) *Irish Tales,* New York and London: G. P Putnam's Sons, Knickerbocker Press, no date. (#215a)

1892
The Wanderings of Oisin | Dramatic Sketches | Ballads & Lyrics, London: T. Fisher Unwin, May 1892. (#3)

The Countess Kathleen and Various Legends and Lyrics, London: T. Fisher Unwin, September 1892. (#6)

The Countess Kathleen and Various Legends and Lyrics, Boston: Roberts Bros., London: T. Fisher Unwin, 1892. (#7)

(*ed.*) *Irish Fairy Tales,* London: T. Fisher Unwin, 1892. (#216)

(*ed.*) *Irish Fairy Tales,* New York: Cassell Publishing Company, 1892. (#217)

1893

The Celtic Twilight. Men and Women, Dhouls and Faeries, London: Lawrence and Bullen, December 1893. (#8)

(*ed.*) *The Works of William Blake | Poetic, Symbolic, and Critical,* 3 vols., London: Bernard Quaritch, February 1893. Coedited with Edwin John Ellis. (#218)

(*ed.*) *The Poems of William Blake,* London: Lawrence & Bullen, New York: Charles Scribner's Sons, 1893. (#219)

(*ed.*) *The Poems of William Blake,* London: Lawrence & Bullen, 1893. (#220)

(*ed.*) *Irish Fairy and Folk Tales,* London: Walter Scott, October 1893. (#223)

(*ed.*) *Irish Fairy Tales,* London: Walter Scott. (#223a)

1894

The Celtic Twilight. Men and Women, Dhouls and Faeries, New York: Macmillan and Co., 1894. (#9)

The Land of Heart's Desire, London: T. Fisher Unwin, April 1894. (#10)

The Land of Heart's Desire, Chicago: Stone & Kimball, 1894. (#11)

1895

Poems, London: T. Fisher Unwin, October 1895. (#15)

Poems, London: T. Fisher Unwin, Boston: Copeland and Day, 1895. (#16)

(*ed.*) *Irish Fairy and Folk Tales,* London: Walter Scott, New York: Charles Scribner's Sons, 1895. (#224)

(*ed.*) *A Book of Irish Verse Selected from Modern Writers,* London: Methuen and Co., March 1895. (#225)

1897

The Secret Rose, London: Lawrence & Bullen, April 1897. (#21)

The Secret Rose, New York: Dodd, Mead & Company, London: Lawrence & Bullen, 1897. (#22)

The Tables of the Law. The Adoration of the Magi, London: privately printed, June 1897. Wade

notes that the book, though "privately printed," was offered for sale in the catalogue of Lawrence and Bullen. (#24)

1899

Poems, London: T. Fisher Unwin, May 1899. (#17)

The Wind Among the Reeds, London: Elkin Mathews, April 1899. (#27)

The Wind Among the Reeds, New York and London: John Lane: The Bodley Head, 1899. (#28)

Literary Ideals in Ireland, London: T. Fisher Unwin, Dublin: The Daily Express, May 1899. Coauthored with John Eglinton, George Russell (AE), and William Larminie. (#297)

1900

The Wind Among the Reeds, London: Elkin Mathews, 1900. (#29)

The Shadowy Waters, London: Hodder and Stoughton, December 1900. (#30)

1901

Poems, London: T. Fisher Unwin, April 1901. (#18)

The Shadowy Waters, New York: Dodd, Mead and Company, 1901. (#31)

The Shadowy Waters, New York: Dodd, Mead & Company, autumn 1901. (#32)

1902

The Celtic Twilight, London: A.H. Bullen, July 1902. (#35)

The Celtic Twilight, Macmillan Company, no date. (#36).

Cathleen ni Hoolihan | A Play in One Act and in Prose, London: A.H. Bullen, October 1902. (#40)

Where There is Nothing: A Play in Five Acts, a supplement to the *United Irishman,* November 1, 1902. (#41)

Where There is Nothing | A Drama in Five Acts, John Lane, 1902. (#42)

Where There is Nothing | A Drama in Five Acts, privately printed, 1902. (#43)

(*ed.*) *Irish Fairy and Folk Tales,* New York: A.L. Burt Company, 1902. (#212a) *(ed.) Irish Fairy and Folk Tales,* New York: Carlton House, no date. (#212b)

1903

The Land of Heart's Desire, Portland, Maine: privately printed, July 1903. (#12)

The Land of Heart's Desire, Portland, Maine: Thomas B. Mosher, October 1903. (#13)

Where There is Nothing: Being Volume One of Plays for an Irish Theatre, London: A.H. Bullen, May 1903. (#44)

Where There is Nothing | Being Volume One of Plays for An Irish Theatre, New York: Macmillan Company, London: Macmillan & Co., May 13, 1903. (#45)

Ideas of Good and Evil, London: A.H. Bullen, May 1903. (#46)

Ideas of Good and Evil, New York: Macmillan Company, 1903. (#47)

In the Seven Woods: Being Poems Chiefly of the Irish Heroic Age, Dundrum: Dun Emer Press, August 1903. (#49)

In the Seven Woods | Being Poems Chiefly of the Irish Heroic Age, New York: Macmillan Company, London: Macmillan & Co., August 25, 1903. (#50)

The Hour-Glass | A Morality, London: Wm. Heinemann, 1903. (#51)

1904

Poems, London: T. Fisher Unwin, June 1904. (#19)

The Tables of the Law and The Adoration of the Magi, London: Elkin Mathews, June 1904. (#25)

The Hour-Glass and Other Plays | Being Volume Two of Plays for an Irish Theatre, New York: Macmillan Company, London: Macmillan & Co., January 13, 1904. (#52).

The Hour-Glass, Cathleen ni Houlihan, The Pot of Broth: Being Volume Two of Plays for an Irish Theatre, London: A.H. Bullen, March 1904. (#53)

The King's Threshold, New York: privately printed, 1904. (#55)

The King's Threshold: and On Baile's Strand: Being Volume Three of Plays for an Irish Theatre, London: A.H. Bullen, March 1904. (#56)

1905

The Secret Rose, Dublin: Maunsel and Co., August 1905. (#23)

The Celtic Twilight, Dublin: Maunsel and Co., August 1905. (#37)

Ideas of Good and Evil, Dublin: Maunsel and Co., August 1905. (#48)

The Hour-Glass, Cathleen ni Houlihan, The Pot of Broth, Dublin: Maunsel and Co., 1905. (#54)

The King's Threshold, Dublin: Maunsel and Co., 1905. (#57)

On Baile's Strand, Dublin: Maunsel and Co., 1905. (#58)

Stories of Red Hanrahan, Dundrum: Dun Emer Press, May 16, 1905. (#59)

The Pot of Broth, London: A.H. Bullen, 1905. (#60)

(ed.) Poems of William Blake, London: George Routledge & Sons, New York: E.P. Dutton Co., June 1905. (#221)

(ed.) Poems of William Blake, New York: Modern Library, no date. (#222)

(ed.) Twenty One Poems Written by Lionel Johnson, Dundrum: Dun Emer Press, February 21, 1905. (#231)

(ed.) Some Essays and Passages by John Eglinton, Dundrum: Dun Emer Press, August 25, 1905. (#232)

(ed.) Sixteen Poems by William Allingham, Dundrum: Dun Emer Press, November 27, 1905. (#234)

1906

Cathleen ni Houlihan, London: A.H. Bullen, 1906. (#62)

Poems, 1899–1905, London: A.H. Bullen, Dublin: Maunsel & Co., October 1906. (#64)

The Poetical Works of William B. Yeats in Two Volumes | Volume 1 | Lyrical Poems, New York: Macmillan Company, London: Macmillan & Co., November 27, 1906. (#65).

(ed.) Poems of Spenser, Edinburgh: T.C. & E.C. Jack, October 1906. (#235)

1907

The Shadowy Waters. Acting Version, As First Played at the Abbey Theatre, December 8th, 1906, London: A.H. Bullen, 1907. (#66)

The Hour-Glass: A Morality, London: A.H. Bullen, 1907. (#67)

On Baile's Strand, London: A.H. Bullen, 1907. (#68)

Deirdre | Being Volume Five of Plays for an Irish Theatre, London: A.H. Bullen, Dublin: Maunsel & Co., August 1907. (#69)

The Poetical Works of William B. Yeats in Two Volumes | Volume II | Dramatical Poems, New York: Macmillan Company, London: Macmillan & Co, July 8, 1907. (#71)

Discoveries; A Volume of Essays, Dundrum: Dun Emer Press, December 15, 1907. (#72)

(ed.) Twenty One Poems by Katharine Tynan, Dundrum: Dun Emer Press, August 6, 1907. (#238)

1908

Poems, London: T. Fisher Unwin, 1908. (#20)

The Unicorn from the Stars, New York: Macmillan Company, 1908. Lady Gregory is credited as coauthor. (#72a)

The Unicorn from the Stars and Other Plays, New York: Macmillan Company, May 13, 1908. Lady Gregory is credited as coauthor. (#73)

The Golden Helmet, New York: John Quinn, 1908. (#74)

Poems Lyrical and Narrative | Being the First Volume of the Collected Works in Verse and Prose of William Butler Yeats, Stratford-on-Avon: Shakespeare Head Press, September 1908. (#75)

The King's Threshold. On Baile's Strand. Deirdre. Shadowy Waters | Being the Second Volume of the Collected Works in Verse & Prose of William Butler Yeats, Stratford-on-Avon: Shakespeare Head Press, September 1908. (#76)

The Countess Cathleen. The Land of Heart's Desire. The Unicorn from the Stars | Being the Third Volume of the Collected Works in Verse and Prose of William Butler Yeats, Stratford-on-Avon: Shakespeare Head Press, October 1908. (#77)

The Hour-Glass. Cathleen ni Houlihan. The Golden Helmet. The Irish Dramatic Movement | Being the Fourth Volume of the Collected Works in Verse & Prose of William Butler Yeats, Stratford-on-Avon: Shakespeare Head Press, October 1908. (#78)

The Celtic Twilight and Stories of Red Hanrahan | Being the Fifth Volume of the Collected Works in Verse & Prose of William Butler Yeats, Stratford-on-Avon: Shakespeare Head Press, November 1908. (#79)

Ideas of Good and Evil | Being the Sixth Volume of the Collected Works in Verse & Prose of William Butler Yeats, Stratford-on-Avon: Shakespeare Head Press, November 1908. (#80)

The Secret Rose. Rose Alchemica. The Tables of the Law. The Adoration of the Magi. John Sherman and Dhoya | Being the Seventh Volume of the Collected Works in Verse & Prose of William Butler Yeats, Stratford-on-Avon: Shakespeare Head Press, December 1908. (#81)

Discoveries. Edmund Spenser. Poetry and Tradition; & Other Essays | Being the Eighth Volume of the Collected Works in Verse & Prose of William Butler Yeats, Stratford-on-Avon: Shakespeare Head Press, December 1908. (#82)

(ed.) Poetry and Ireland: Essays by W. B. Yeats and Lionel Johnson, Churchtown, Dundrum: Cuala Press, December 1, 1908. (#242)

1909

The Land of Heart's Desire, Portland, Maine: Thomas B. Mosher, 1909. (#13a)

The Land of Heart's Desire, New York: Dodd, Mead & Company, October 30, 1909. (#14)

Cathleen ni Houlihan, London: A.H. Bullen, 1909. (#63)

(ed.) Poems and Translations by John M. Synge, Churchtown, Dundrum: Cuala Press, July 5, 1909. (#243)

(ed.) Poems and Translations by John M. Synge, New York: privately printed for John Quinn, 1909. (#244)

1910

Poems: Second Series | The Wind Among the Reeds | The Old Age of Queen Maeve | Baile and Aillinn | In the Seven Woods | Songs from Deirdre | The Shadowy Waters, London and

Stratford-on-Avon: A.H. Bullen, March 1910 (the title page is dated 1909). (#83)

The Green Helmet and Other Poems, Churchtown, Dundrum: Cuala Press, December 1910. (#84)

(ed.) *Deirdre of the Sorrows: A Play by John M. Synge,* Churchtown, Dundrum: Cuala Press, July 5, 1910. (#245)

(ed.) *Deirdre of the Sorrows: A Play by John M. Synge,* New York: privately printed for John Quinn, 1910. (#246)

1911

The Celtic Twilight, London and Stratford-on-Avon: A.H. Bullen, December 1911. (#38)

The Pot of Broth, London: A.H. Bullen, November 1911. (#61)

Cathleen ni Houlihan, Stratford-on-Avon: Shakespeare Head Press, 1911. (#63)

The Green Helmet and Other Poems, New York: R. Harold Paget, 1911. (#85)

Deirdre, Stratford-upon-Avon: Shakespeare Head Press, July 1911. (#86)

Synge and the Ireland of his Time, Churchtown, Dundrum: Cuala Press, July 26, 1911. (#88)

The Green Helmet | An Heroic Farce, Stratford-on-Avon: Shakespeare Head Press, November 1911. (#89)

The King's Threshold, Stratford-upon-Avon: Shakespeare Head Press, November 1911. (#90)

Plays for an Irish Theatre | Deirdre | The Green Helmet | On Baile's Strand | The King's Threshold | The Shadowy Waters | The Hour-Glass | Cathleen ni Houlihan, London and Stratford-upon-Avon: A.H. Bullen, December 1911. (#92)

1912

The Countess Cathleen, London: T. Fisher Unwin, June 1912. (#93)

The Land of Heart's Desire, London: T. Fisher Unwin, June 1912. (#94)

The Poetical Works of William B. Yeats in Two Volumes | Volume II | Dramatic Poems, New York: Macmillan Company, London: Macmillan & Co., August 7, 1912. (#98)

Poems, London: T. Fisher Unwin, September 1912. (#99)

The Green Helmet and Other Poems, New York: Macmillan Company, London: Macmillan & Co., October 23, 1912. (#101)

The Cutting of an Agate, New York: Macmillan Company, November 13, 1912. (#102)

(ed.) *Selections from the Writings of Lord Dunsany,* Churchtown, Dundrum: Cuala Press, October 1912. (#247)

1913

Poems, London: T. Fisher Unwin, 1913. (#100)

A Selection from the Poetry of W. B. Yeats, Leipzig: Bernhard Tauchnitz, 1913. (#103)

Stories of Red Hanrahan: The Secret Rose: Rosa Alchemica, London and Stratford-upon-Avon: A.H. Bullen, March 1913. (#104)

A Selection from the Love Poetry of William Butler Yeats, Churchtown, Dundrum: Cuala Press, July 25, 1913. (#106)

Poems Written in Discouragement, Dundrum: Cuala Press, October 1913. (#107)

1914

The Tables of the Law; & The Adoration of the Magi, Stratford-upon-Avon: Shakespeare Head Press, 1914. (#26)

Deirdre, Stratford-upon-Avon: Shakespeare Head Press, 1914. (#87)

Stories of Red Hanrahan | The Secret Rose | Rosa Alchemica, New York: Macmillan Company, April 1, 1914. (#105)

The Hour Glass, privately printed by the Cuala Press, January 1914. (#108)

Nine Poems Chosen from the Works of William Butler Yeats, New York: privately printed for John Quinn and his friends, April 1, 1914. (#109)

Responsibilities: Poems and a Play, Churchtown, Dundrum: Cuala Press, May 25, 1914. (#110)

1915

The King's Threshold, Stratford-upon-Avon: Shakespeare Head Press, 1915. (#91)

1916

Reveries over Childhood and Youth, Churchtown, Dundrum: Cuala Press, March 20, 1916. (#111)

Reveries over Childhood and Youth, New York: Macmillan Company, April 26, 1916. (#112)

Reveries over Childhood & Youth, London: Macmillan and Co., October 10, 1916. (#113)

Eight Poems, London: "Form" at the Morland Press, April 1916. (#114)

Responsibilities and Other Poems, London: Macmillan and Co., October 10, 1916. (#115)

Responsibilities and Other Poems, New York: Macmillan Company, November 1, 1916. (#116)

Easter, 1916, London: privately printed by Clement Shorter, 1916. (#117)

The Well of Immortality, no publisher or date. The play is a version of *At the Hawk's Well.* (#119)

1917

The Wild Swans at Coole, Other Verses and a Play in Verse, Churchtown, Dundrum: Cuala Press, November 17, 1917. (#118)

1918

Per Amica Silentia Lunae, London: Macmillan and Co., January 18, 1918. (#120)

Per Amica Silentia Lunae, New York: Macmillan Company, January 18, 1918. (#121)

Nine Poems, London: privately printed by Clement Shorter, October 1918. (#122)

(ed.) Irish Fairy and Folk Tales, New York: Boni and Liveright, 1918. (#213)

1919

Two Plays for Dancers, Churchtown, Dundrum: Cuala Press, January 1919. (#123)

The Wild Swans at Coole, London: Macmillan and Co., March 11, 1919. (#124)

The Wild Swans at Coole, New York: Macmillan Company, March 11, 1919. (#125)

The Cutting of an Agate, London: Macmillan and Co., April 8, 1919. (#126)

1921

Michael Robartes and the Dancer, Churchtown, Dundrum: Cuala Press, February 1921. (#127)

Selected Poems, New York: Macmillan Company, June 28, 1921. (#128)

Four Plays for Dancers, London: Macmillan and Co., October 28, 1921. (#129)

Four Plays for Dancers, New York: Macmillan Company, October 28, 1921. (#130)

Four Years, Churchtown, Dundrum: Cuala Press, December 1921. (#131)

1922

The Land of Heart's Desire, Boston: Walter H. Baker & Co., 1922. (#96)

Seven Poems and a Fragment, Churchtown, Dundrum: Cuala Press, June 1922. (#132)

The Trembling of the Veil, London: privately printed for subscribers only by T. Werner Laurie, issued to subscribers in October 1922. (#133)

Later Poems, London: Macmillan and Co., November 3, 1922. (#134)

Plays in Prose and Verse | Written for an Irish Theatre, and Generally with the Help of a Friend, London: Macmillan and Co., November 3, 1922. (#136)

The Player Queen, London: Macmillan and Co., November 21, 1922. (#138)

1923

Plays and Controversies, London: Macmillan and Co., November 27, 1923. (#139)

1924

The Countess Cathleen, London: T. Fisher Unwin, 1924. The volume includes *The Land of Heart's Desire.* (#95)

Later Poems, New York: Macmillan Company, April 8, 1924. (#135)

Plays in Prose and Verse | Written for an Irish Theatre, and Generally with the Help of a Friend, New York: Macmillan Company, April 8, 1924. (#137)

Plays and Controversies, New York: Macmillan Company, September 16, 1924. (#140)

Essays, London: Macmillan and Co., May 6, 1924. (#141)

Essays, New York: Macmillan Company, October 14, 1924. (#142)

The Irish Dramatic Movement | Lecture Delivered to the Royal Academy of Sweden, Stockholm: P.A. Norstedt & Fils, 1924. (#144)

The Cat and the Moon and Certain Poems, Dublin: Cuala Press, July 1924. (#145)

1925

The Land of Heart's Desire | The Countess Cathleen, London: T. Fisher Unwin, 1925. (#95)

The Bounty of Sweden: A Meditation, and a Lecture Delivered before the Royal Swedish Academy and Certain Notes, Dublin: Cuala Press, July 1925. (#146)

Early Poems and Stories, London: Macmillan and Co., September 22, 1925. (#147)

Early Poems and Stories, New York: Macmillan Company, November 17, 1925. (#148)

A Vision | An Explanation of Life Founded upon the Writings of Giraldus and upon Certain Doctrines Attributed to Kusta Ben Luka, London: privately printed for subscribers only by T. Werner Laurie, 1925. Issued to subscribers on January 15, 1926. (#149)

1926

The Land of Heart's Desire, San Francisco: Windsor Press, 1926. (#97)

Estrangement: Being Some Fifty Thoughts from a Diary Kept by William Butler Yeats in the Year Nineteen Hundred and Nine, Dublin: Cuala Press, August 1926. (#150)

Autobiographies: Reveries over Childhood and Youth and The Trembling of the Veil, London: Macmillan and Co., November 5, 1926. (#151)

1927

Autobiographies: Reveries over Childhood and Youth and The Trembling of the Veil, New York: Macmillan Company, February 8, 1927. (#152)

Poems, London: T. Fisher Unwin Limited (Ernest Benn Limited), February 1927. (#153)

The Augustan Books of English Poetry, Second Series, Number Four, London: Ernest Benn Ltd., April 1927. (#155)

October Blast, Dublin: Cuala Press, August 1927. (#156)

Stories of Red Hanrahan and The Secret Rose, London: Macmillan and Co., November 11, 1927. (#157)

1928

The Tower, London: Macmillan and Co., February 14, 1928. (#158)

The Tower, New York: Macmillan Company, May 22, 1928. (#159)

Sophocles' King Oedipus | A Version for the Modern Stage, London: Macmillan and Co., March 27, 1928. (#160)

Sophocles' King Oedipus | A Version for the Modern Stage, New York: Macmillan Company, July 3, 1928. (#161)

The Death of Synge, and Other Passages from an Old Diary, Dublin: Cuala Press, June 1928. (#162)

1929

Poems, London: Ernest Benn Limited, May 10, 1929. (#154)

A Packet for Ezra Pound, Dublin: Cuala Press, August 1929. (#163)

The Winding Stair, New York: Fountain Press, 1929. (#164)

Selected Poems | Lyrical and Narrative, London: Macmillan and Co., October 8, 1929. (#165)

Three Things, London: Faber and Faber, October 9, 1929. (#166)

1932

Stories of Michael Robartes and his Friends: An Extract from a Record Made by his Pupils: And a Play in Prose, Dublin: Cuala Press, March 1932. (#167)

Words for Music Perhaps and Other Poems, Dublin: Cuala Press, November 14, 1932. (#168)

1933

The Winding Stair and Other Poems, London: Macmillan and Co., September 19, 1933. (#169)

The Winding Stair and Other Poems, New York: Macmillan Company, October 1933. (#170)

The Collected Poems of W. B. Yeats, New York: Macmillan Company, November 14, 1933. (#171)

The Collected Poems of W. B. Yeats, London: Macmillan and Co., November 28, 1933. (#172)

1934

Letters to the New Island, Cambridge: Harvard University Press, January 24, 1934. (#173)

The Words upon the Window Pane: A Play in One Act, with Notes upon the Play and its Subject, Dublin: Cuala Press, April 1934. (#174)

Wheels and Butterflies, London: Macmillan and Co., November 13, 1934. (#175)

The Collected Plays of W. B. Yeats, London: Macmillan and Co., November 30, 1934. (#177)

The King of the Great Clock Tower, Commentaries and Poems, Dublin: Cuala Press, December 14, 1934. (#179)

The Singing Head and the Lady, Bryn Mawr: privately printed by Frederic Prokosch, Christmas, 1934. (#180)

1935

Wheels and Butterflies, New York: Macmillan Company, February 19, 1935. (#176)

The Collected Plays of W. B. Yeats, New York: Macmillan Company, August 27, 1935. (#178)

The King of the Great Clock Tower, Commentaries and Poems, New York: Macmillan Company, May 1935. (#179a)

The Irish National Theatre | Estratto Dagli Atti Del IV Convegno Della "Fondazione Alessandro Volta" | Tema: Il Teatro Drammatico | Roma 8–14 Ottobre 1934–XII, Rome: Reale Accademia d'Italia, 1935. (#181)

A Full Moon in March, London: Macmillan and Co., November 22, 1935. (#182)

Dramatis Personæ, Dublin: Cuala Press, December 9, 1935. (#183)

Poems, Dublin: privately printed by Cuala Press, 1935. (#184)

Leda and the Swan, Florence: privately printed by Frederic Prokosch, Christmas, 1935. (#185)

1936

Dramatis Personae 1896–1902 | Estrangement | The Death of Synge | The Bounty of Sweden, New York: Macmillan Company, May 12, 1936. (#186)

Dramatis Personae 1896–1902 | Estrangement | The Death of Synge | The Bounty of Sweden, London: Macmillan and Co., May 15, 1936. (#187)

Modern Poetry | The Eighteenth of the Broadcast National Lectures Delivered on 11 October 1936, London: British Broadcasting Corporation, December 1936. (#188)

(*ed.*) *The Oxford Book of Modern Verse | 1892–1935,* Oxford: Clarendon Press, November 19, 1936. (#250)

(*ed.*) *The Oxford Book of Modern Verse | 1892–1935,* New York: Oxford University Press, November 1936. (#251)

1937

The King's Threshold, London: Macmillan and Co., March 25, 1937. (#189)

Nine One-Act Plays, London: Macmillan and Co., June 8, 1937. (#190)

A Vision, London: Macmillan & Co., October 7, 1937. (#191)

A Speech and Two Poems, Dublin: privately printed, December 1937. (#193)

Essays | 1931 to 1936, Dublin: Cuala Press, December 14, 1937. (#194)

(*ed.*) *The Ten Principal Upanishads,* London: Faber and Faber, April 1937. Edited and translated with Shree Purohit Swami. (#252)

(*ed.*) *The Ten Principal Upanishads,* New York: Macmillan Company, 1937. Edited and translated with Shree Purohit Swami. (#253)

1938

A Vision, New York: Macmillan Company, February 23, 1938. (#192)

The Herne's Egg | A Stage Play, London: Macmillan and Co., January 21, 1938. (#195)

The Herne's Egg and Other Plays, New York: Macmillan Company, April 12, 1938. (#196)

New Poems, Dublin: Cuala Press, May 18, 1938. (#197)

The Autobiography of William Butler | Yeats Consisting of Reveries over Childhood and Youth | The Trembling of the Veil and Dramatis Personae, New York: Macmillan Company, August 30, 1938. (#198)

1939

Selected Poems of W. B. Yeats, Amsterdam: A.A. Balkema, 1939. (#199)

Last Poems and Two Plays, Dublin: Cuala Press, July 10, 1939. (#200)

On the Boiler, Dublin: Cuala Press. (#201)

On the Boiler, Dublin: Cuala Press, autumn 1939. (#202)

1940

Last Poems & Plays, London: Macmillan & Co., January 1940. (#203)

Last Poems & Plays, New York: Macmillan Company, May 14, 1940. (#204)

Some Significant Posthumous Publications (first editions only)

1939

If I were Four-and-Twenty, Dublin: Cuala Press, September 28, 1940. (#205)

1940

Letters on Poetry from W. B. Yeats to Dorothy Wellesley, London, New York, and Toronto: Oxford University Press, June 1940. (#325 and #325a)

1944

Pages from a Diary Written in Nineteen Hundred and Thirty, Dublin: Cuala Press, November 1944. (#207)

1953

W. B. Yeats and T. Sturge Moore | Their Correspondence | 1901–1937, edited by Ursula Bridge, London: Routledge & Kegan Paul, September 25, 1953. New York: Oxford University Press, 1953. (#340 and #341)

1954

The Letters of W. B. Yeats, edited by Allan Wade, London: Rupert Hart-Davis, September 24, 1954. (#211j)

1957

The Variorum Edition of the Poems of W. B. Yeats, edited by Peter Allt and Russell K. Alspach,

New York: Macmillan Company, October 29, 1957. (#211n)

1959

Mythologies, London: Macmillan & Co., March 12, 1959. (#211p)

1960

The Senate Speeches of W. B. Yeats, edited by Donald R. Pearce, Bloomington: Indiana University Press, 1960. (#211r)

1961

Essays and Introductions, London: Macmillan & Co., February 16, 1961. (#211t)

1962

Explorations, London: Macmillan & Co., July 23, 1962. (211y)

1966

A Variorum Edition of the Plays of W. B. Yeats, edited by Russell K. Alspach, London, Melbourne, Toronto: Macmillan, January 1966. (#211ee)

1970

Ah, Sweet Dancer | A Correspondence Edited by Roger McHugh, London: Macmillan, New York: Collier-Macmillan, 1970. Coauthored with Margot Ruddock.

1972

Memoirs: Autobiography (first draft) | Journal, edited by Denis Donoghue, London: Macmillan, 1972.

1978

A Critical Edition of Yeats's A Vision (1925), edited by George Mills Harper and Walter Kelly Hood, London: Macmillan, Atlantic Highlands, New Jersey: Humanities Press, 1978.

1981

The Secret Rose: Stories by W. B. Yeats: A Variorum Edition, edited by Phillip L. Marcus, Warwick Gould, and Michael J. Sidnell, Ithaca and London: Cornell University Press, 1981.

1986

The Collected Letters of W. B. Yeats, vol. 1, edited by John Kelly and Eric Domville, Oxford: Clarendon Press, 1986.

1988

Prefaces and Introductions: Uncollected Prefaces and Introductions by Yeats to Works by Other Authors and to Anthologies Edited by Yeats, edited by William H. O'Donnell, New York and Basingstoke: Macmillan, 1988. *The Collected Works of W. B. Yeats,* vol. 6.

1989

Letters to the New Island, edited by George Bornstein and Hugh Witemeyer, New York and Basingstoke: Macmillan, 1989. *The Collected Works of W. B. Yeats,* vol. 7.

The Poems, edited by Richard J. Finneran, New York: Scribner, Macmillan, 1989. *The Collected Works of W. B. Yeats,* vol. 1.

1991

John Sherman and Dhoya, edited by Richard J. Finneran, New York: Macmillan, 1991. *The Collected Works of W. B. Yeats,* vol. 12.

1992

The Gonne-Yeats Letters 1893–1938: always your friend, edited by Anna MacBride White and A. Norman Jeffares, London: Hutchinson, Pimlico, 1992.

1994

The Collected Letters of W. B. Yeats, vol. 3, edited by John Kelly and Ronald Schuchard, Oxford: Clarendon Press, 1994.

Later Essays, edited by William H. O'Donnell, New York and London: Charles Scribner's Sons, 1994. *The Collected Works of W. B. Yeats,* vol. 5.

1997

The Collected Letters of W. B. Yeats, vol. 2, edited by Warwick Gould, John Kelly, and Deirdre Toomey, Oxford: Clarendon Press, 1997.

1999

Autobiographies, edited by William H. O'Donnell and Douglas N. Archibald, New York: Scribner, 1999. *The Collected Works of W. B. Yeats,* vol. 3.

2000

Later Articles and Reviews: Uncollected Articles, Reviews, and Radio Broadcasts Written after 1900, edited by Colton Johnson, New York: Scribner, 2000. *The Collected Works of W. B. Yeats,* vol. 10.

2001

The Plays, edited by David R. Clark and Rosalind E. Clark, New York: Scribner, Basingstoke: Palgrave, 2001. *The Collected Works of W. B. Yeats,* vol. 2.

2003

The Speckled Bird: An Autobiographical Novel with Variant Versions, edited by William H. O'Donnell, Basingstoke: Palgrave Macmillan, 2003.

The Irish Dramatic Movement, edited by Mary FitzGerald and Richard J. Finneran, New York: Scribner, Basingstoke: Palgrave Macmillan, 2003. *The Collected Works of W. B. Yeats,* vol. 8.

2004

Early Articles and Reviews: Uncollected Articles and Reviews Written between 1886 and 1900, edited by John P. Frayne and Madeleine Marchaterre, New York: Scribner, Basingstoke: Palgrave Macmillan, 2004. *The Collected Works of W. B. Yeats,* vol. 9.

2005

The Collected Letters of W. B. Yeats, vol. 4, edited by John Kelly and Ronald Schuchard, Oxford: Oxford University Press, 2005.

Mythologies, edited by Warwick Gould and Deirdre Toomey, Basingstoke: Palgrave Macmillan, 2005.

2007

Early Essays, edited by Richard J. Finneran and George Bornstein, New York: Scribner, 2007, Palgrave Macmillan, 2007. *The Collected Works of W. B. Yeats,* vol. 4.

SOURCES: Wade, Allan. *A Bibliography of the Writings of W. B. Yeats,* 3d edition, revised and edited by Russell K. Alspach, London: Rupert Hart-Davis, 1968.

ELECTRONIC SOURCES: *WorldCat,* Dublin, Ohio: OCLC, 1971–Present.

Further Reading: A Selection of Essential Books by and about Yeats

More than most authors, Yeats has been exceptionally well served by his commentators and critics. A. Norman Jeffares, Richard Ellmann, and Virginia Moore were among the first to begin sifting the meaning of Yeats's achievement, and their intelligence, sensitivity, and determination set an enduring precedent for what became "the Yeats industry." Most important, perhaps, was their willingness to give Yeats the benefit of the doubt, to suspend the modem impulse to insist upon its own assumptions. W. H. Auden famously called Yeats "silly like us"; modern Yeats criticism began with the entirely constructive working hypothesis that Yeats was not silly at all.

More than a half century later, the student of Yeats faces a dilemma of abundance. K. P. S. Jochum's bibliography of Yeats criticism runs to 1,176 pages and includes some 12,000 items, and even this massive tally, last revised in 1990, falls well short of the present reality. Every conceivable angle of approach—Irish, romantic, modernist, occult, political, theatrical, to name only the most obvious—has its cadre of scholars and theorists. There are immense rafts of material on themes, motifs, symbols, and patterns; intellectual influences; cultural, historical, and literary background; personal connections and friendships; manuscript materials and textual revision. To recommend "a single shelf of Yeats" is not to deny the many mutually exclusive lifetimes of reading that might be undertaken; it is merely to suggest a means of initial orientation.

Yeats has been the subject of numerous biographies, and nearly all of his colleagues, friends, and close relatives have received biographical attention. This material constitutes a vast play of perspective that cumulatively reveals Yeats in rich dimensionality. Those with a solid month to spare should begin with R. F. Foster's two-volume leviathan, *W. B. Yeats: A Life* (1997, 2003), a monument of modern literary biography. Foremost a historian of Ireland, Foster has a particular gift for placing Yeats's life in a detailed context of society, culture, and history. Additionally, Foster has a muscular, sometimes mordant narrative voice that is well matched to Yeats's muscular, sometimes mordant life. The most serviceable of the shorter biographies are A. Norman Jeffares's *W. B. Yeats: A New Biography* (1988) and Terence Brown's *The Life of W. B. Yeats* (1999), while Joseph Hone's *W. B. Yeats, 1865–1939* (1942) and Richard Ellmann's *Yeats: The Man and the Masks* (1948) are graceful and intelligent if now somewhat antiquated. E. H. Mikhail's *W. B. Yeats: Interviews and Recollections* (1977) collects the impressions and reminiscences of contemporaries and nicely supplements the formal biographical material. John S. Kelly's *A W. B. Yeats Chronology* (2003) records Yeats's daily movements and functions as an extremely handy reference. Of the dozens of biographies that intersect with Yeats's own biography, the most valuable for the student of Yeats are William M. Murphy's *Prodigal Father: The Life of John Butler Yeats (1839–1922)* (1978) and Ann Saddlemyer's *Becoming George: The Life of Mrs*

W. B. Yeats (2002). Like Foster's biography, these are significant examples of the biographer's art.

The standard bibliography of Yeats's work is Allan Wade's *A Bibliography of the Writings of W. B. Yeats* (third edition, 1968). At more than 500 pages, it is the indispensable tool for making sense of Yeats's massive and scrambled oeuvre. K. P. S. Jochum's *W. B. Yeats: A Classified Bibliography of Criticism* (second edition, 1990) is the most complete guide to secondary literature, while Edward O'Shea's *A Descriptive Catalog of W. B. Yeats's Library* (1985) lends an evidentiary basis to the discussion of Yeats's influences.

There are a number of helpful reference works available. Sam McCready's *A William Butler Yeats Encyclopedia* (1997) is an all-purpose source of concise factual information about Yeats's life and work. Sheelah Kirby's *The Yeats Country* (1962) and James P. McGarry's *Places in the Writings of William Butler Yeats* (1976) clarify the Irish geography that informs so much of Yeats's work. Lester I. Conner's *A Yeats Dictionary: Persons and Places in the Poetry of William Butler Yeats* (1998) makes sense of the persons and places mentioned in its title. A. Norman Jeffares's *A New Commentary on the Poems of W. B. Yeats* (1983) and Jeffares and A. S. Knowland's *A Commentary on the Collected Plays of W. B. Yeats* (1975) are less commentaries—that is, interpretive narratives—than sourcebooks of explanatory information and relevant prose material. All but the most erudite scholars will want to keep these volumes within reach.

To recommend a selection of critical and interpretive studies is to court controversy and even contention. Preferences in criticism, of course, speak to a host of underlying issues: notions of the purpose and proper method of criticism, notions of what is most valuable in Yeats's work, notions of what is most interesting and important in Yeats's life. Certain books, however, have won wide approval and might be recommended as expert and for the most part accessible introductions to the primary facets of Yeats's identity.

T. R. Henn's *The Lonely Tower* (1950) and Richard Ellmann's *The Identity of Yeats* (1954) are arguably the best general introductions to Yeats's poetry. Fifty years on, their elegance and insight

continue to stand above all mere trends. Donald T. Torchiana's *W. B. Yeats and Georgian Ireland* (1966) is a classic exploration of Yeats's political and spiritual affinity with the Protestant culture of 18th-century Ireland. Harold Bloom's *Yeats* (1970) is a sweeping—and some might say idiosyncratic—commentary on Yeats's work from the perspective of romantic tradition. It may be the most extensive and intellectually ambitious study of Yeats's work ever undertaken; at the very least, it is a dazzling display of mental power. Frank Kermode's *Romantic Image* (1957) less expansively but no less acutely places Yeats in the romantic lineage. Phillip L. Marcus's *Yeats and the Beginning of the Irish Renaissance* (1970, revised 1987) gives a straightforward account of Yeats's early literary career. George Mills Harper's *Yeats's Golden Dawn* (1974) is the best guide to Yeats's long and potentially baffling association with the Hermetic Order of the Golden Dawn, the London occult society that was so important to him from 1890 onward. Elizabeth Cullingford's *Yeats, Ireland and Fascism* (1980) addresses the most delicate of all subject matter—Yeats's political evolution—and gives a lucid, comprehensive, and judicious account. Also valuable are Paul Scott Stanfield's *Yeats and Politics in the 1930s* (1988) and *Yeats's Political Identities* (1996), an anthology of essays edited by Jonathan Allison. Mary Helen Thuente's *W. B. Yeats and Irish Folklore* (1980) definitively discusses Yeats's immersion in and expropriation of Irish folklore. Elizabeth Bergmann Loizeaux's *Yeats and the Visual Arts* (1986) details Yeats's continual recourse to painting as both inspiration and theme. James Longenbach's *Stone Cottage: Pound, Yeats, and Modernism* (1988) is a quasi-biographical account of the crucial Yeats-Pound alliance. Unlike so many academic tomes, *Stone Cottage* is full of vivid detail and lively anecdote. It represents academic storytelling at its best. *Yeats and Women* (1992, second edition 1997), an eminent anthology of essays edited by Deirdre Toomey, addresses its theme from a variety of illuminating perspectives. John Harwood's *Olivia Shakespear and W. B. Yeats: After Long Silence* (1989) focuses on the specific relationship, but at the same time sheds light on Yeats's romantic and sexual attitudes and his approach to women generally. The formal aspects of Yeats's poetry have received relatively passing and scattered attention. Helen Vendler's substantial study *Our Secret Discipline: Yeats and Lyric Form* (2007) is a major corrective. Notable studies in this vein also include Marjorie Perloff's *Rhyme and Meaning in the Poetry of Yeats* (1970) and Adelyn Dougherty's *A Study of Rhythmic Structure in the Verse of William Butler Yeats* (1973).

Yeats's theatrical career was perhaps too long and varied, too split between the practical and the imaginative, to be encapsulated in a single work. Readers might preliminarily consult James W. Flannery's *W. B. Yeats and the Idea of a Theatre: The Early Abbey Theatre in Theory and Practice* (1976) and Liam Miller's *The Noble Drama of W. B. Yeats* (1977). For closer textual analysis of the plays, readers might consult Peter Ure's *Yeats the Playwright: A Commentary on Character and Design in the Major Plays* (1963), Helen Vendler's *Yeats's Vision and the Later Plays* (1963), and David R. Clark's *W. B. Yeats and the Theatre of Desolate Reality* (1965, revised 1993).

The most daunting and perilous aspect of Yeats's thought—the philosophy underlying *A Vision*—has tended to defeat would-be exegetes. There are a number of useful studies that set *A Vision* in literary relation—Vendler's study of the later plays comes to mind—but there is no fully satisfactory analysis of the text itself. Hazard Adams's *The Book of Yeats's Vision: Romantic Modernism and Antithetical Tradition* (1995) is an attempt at this analysis, but it is self-protectively slim, in many ways declining to rise to the bait of the text's sprawling difficulty and maddening intricacy. Adams's book, in any case, is the obvious place to begin an inquiry into the mechanics of Yeats's visionary philoso-

phy. It might be complemented by Morton Irving Seiden's *William Butler Yeats: The Poet as a Mythmaker, 1865–1939* (1962), a more general discussion of *A Vision* and *Vision*-related themes. George Mills Harper's two-volume *The Making of Yeats's 'A Vision': A Study of the Automatic Script* (1987) and Margaret Mills Harper's *Wisdom of Two: The Spiritual and Literary Collaboration of George and W. B. Yeats* (2006) take a different approach, focusing with great knowledge on the automatic writing sessions from which *A Vision* emerged.

Yeats's own writings are in the process of being enshrined in brilliantly annotated standard editions that will replace all previous editions. *The Collected Works of W. B. Yeats* (1989–present), published under the general editorship of George Bornstein, George Mills Harper, and Richard J. Finneran, now runs to 12 volumes and will eventually run to 14. The edition is meticulous and nearly exhaustive; the student and common reader need supplement it only with *The Variorum Edition of the Poems of W. B. Yeats* (1957) and *The Variorum Edition of the Plays of W. B. Yeats* (1966), which trace textual revisions, and with *Memoirs* (1972), which includes Yeats's candid autobiographical fragment and journal. *The Collected Letters of W. B. Yeats* (1986–present), published under the general editorship of John S. Kelly, now runs to four volumes, spanning the period 1865–1907. Its apparatus of annotation is awesome in its microscopic detail and comprehensive knowledge, and the completed edition will surely be recognized as one of the age's great scholarly achievements. In the meantime, Yeats's later correspondence remains scattered (see LETTERS). Allan Wade's *The Letters of W. B. Yeats* (1954), though a mere smattering, continues to be the standard resource.

Works Cited and Consulted

Note: Yeats's several collaborative works are listed with Yeats as lead author; cited as sources in the body of the text, they are given under Yeats's name.

Adams, Hazard. *The Book of Yeats's Poems.* Tallahassee: Florida State University Press, 1990.

———. *The Book of Yeats's Vision: Romantic Modernism and Antithetical Tradition.* Ann Arbor: University of Michigan Press, 1995.

Antheil, George. *Bad Boy of Music.* Garden City, N.Y.: Doubleday, Doran & Company, 1945.

Beckson, Karl. *Arthur Symons: A Life.* Oxford: Clarendon Press, 1987.

———. *The Oscar Wilde Encyclopedia.* New York: AMS Press, 1988.

Bence-Jones, Mark. *A Guide to Irish Country Houses.* Rev. ed. London: Constable, 1988.

Bennett, Douglas. *The Encyclopedia of Dublin.* Dublin: Gill and Macmillan, 2005.

Bew, Paul. *C. S. Parnell.* Dublin: Gill and Macmillan, 1980.

Bjersby, Birgit. *The Interpretation of the Cuchulain Legend in the Works of W. B. Yeats.* Uppsala: A.-B. Lundequistka Bokhandeln, 1950.

Blake, William. *The Complete Poems.* 2d ed. Edited by W. H. Stevenson. London and New York: Longman, 1989.

———. *The Complete Poetry and Prose of William Blake.* Rev. ed. Edited by David V. Erdman. New York: Anchor Press, 1988.

Blavatsky, H. P. *The Secret Doctrine: A Facsimile of the Original Edition of 1888.* Los Angeles: Theosophy Company, 1947.

Bloom, Harold. *Shelley's Mythmaking.* New Haven: Yale University Press, 1959.

———. *Yeats.* New York: Oxford University Press, 1972.

Bolsterli, Margaret Jones. *The Early Community at Bedford Park: "Corporate Happiness" in the First Garden Community.* Athens: Ohio University Press, 1977.

Bornstein, George. *Poetic Remaking: The Art of Browning, Yeats, and Pound.* University Park: Pennsylvania State University Press, 1988.

———. *Yeats and Shelley.* Chicago and London: University of Chicago Press, 1970.

Bradford, Curtis. *Yeats at Work.* Carbondale and Edwardsville: Southern Illinois University Press, 1965.

Brodetsky, Selig. *Sir Isaac Newton: A Brief Account of His Life and Work.* London: Methuen and Co., 1927.

Brooks, Van Wyck. *Scenes and Portraits: Memories of Childhood and Youth.* New York: E.P. Dutton & Co., 1954.

Campbell, Margaret. *Dolmetsch: The Man and His Work.* Seattle: University of Washington Press, 1975.

Carpenter, Humphrey. *A Serious Character: The Life of Ezra Pound.* Boston: Houghton Mifflin Company, 1988.

Castiglione, Baldesar. *The Book of the Courtier.* Edited by Daniel Javitch. Translated by Charles Singleton. New York and London: W. W. Norton & Company, 2002.

Clark, David R., with Rosalind Clark. *W. B. Yeats & the Theatre of Desolate Reality.* Washington, D.C.: Catholic University of America Press, 1993.

Conner, Lester I. *A Yeats Dictionary: Persons and Places in the Poetry of William Butler Yeats.* Syracuse, N.Y.: Syracuse University Press, 1998.

Connolly, S. J., ed. *The Oxford Companion to Irish History.* Oxford: Oxford University Press, 1998.

Courtney, Marie-Thérèse. *Edward Martyn and the Irish Theatre.* New York: Vantage Press, 1956.

Coxhead, Elizabeth. *Lady Gregory: A Literary Portrait.* London: Macmillan & Co., 1961.

Cullingford, Elizabeth. *Yeats, Ireland and Fascism.* New York: New York University Press, 1981.

Curtin, Jeremiah. *Myths and folk-lore of Ireland.* Detroit: Singing Tree Press, 1968.

Dante Alighieri, *The Convivio of Dante Alighieri.* Translated by Philip H. Wicksteed. London: J.M. Dent, 1909.

———. *The Divine Comedy.* Translated by John Ciardi. New York: W.W. Norton & Company, 1977.

———. *La Vita Nuova.* Translated by Dante Gabriel Rossetti. Mineola, N.Y.: Dover, 2001.

Delaney, J. G. P. *Charles Ricketts: A Biography.* Oxford: Clarendon Press, New York: Oxford University Press, 1990.

Dougill, John. *Oxford in English Literature: The Making, and Undoing, of the 'English Athens'.* Ann Arbor: University of Michigan Press, 1998.

Egan, Maurice Francis. *Recollections of a Happy Life.* New York: George H. Doran, 1924.

Eglinton, John. *Anglo-Irish Essays.* New York: John Lane Company, 1918.

———. *Irish Literary Portraits.* Freeport, N.Y.: Books for Libraries Press, 1967.

———. *A Memoir of AE.* London: Macmillan & Co., 1937.

———. *Some Essays and Passages by John Eglinton: Selected by William Butler Yeats.* Shannon: Irish University Press, 1971.

Eliot, T. S., *After Strange Gods: A Primer of Modern Heresy.* New York: Harcourt, Brace and Company, 1934.

———. *The Letters of T. S. Eliot.* Vol. 1. Edited by Valerie Eliot. San Diego: Harcourt Brace Jovanovich, 1988.

———. *On Poetry and Poets.* New York: Farrar, Straus and Cudahy, 1957.

———. *The Use of Poetry & The Use of Criticism.* Cambridge, Mass.: Harvard University Press, 1986.

Ellmann, Richard. *Eminent Domain: Yeats among Wilde, Joyce, Pound, Eliot and Auden.* London and New York: Oxford University Press, 1970.

———. *Golden Codgers: Biographical Speculations.* London and New York: Oxford University Press, 1973.

———. *The Identity of Yeats.* London: Faber and Faber, 1983.

———. *James Joyce.* New York: Oxford University Press, 1982.

———. *Oscar Wilde.* New York: Alfred A. Knopf, 1988.

———. *W. B. Yeats's Second Puberty: A lecture delivered at the Library of Congress on April 2, 1984.* Washington, D.C.: Library of Congress, 1985.

———. *Yeats: The Man and the Masks.* New York: E.P. Dutton & Co., 1973.

Engelberg, Edward. *The Vast Design: Patterns in W. B. Yeats's Aesthetic.* Toronto: University of Toronto Press, 1974.

Espmark, Kjell. *The Nobel Prize in Literature: A Study of the Criteria behind the Choices.* Boston: G.K. Hall & Co., 1991.

Faulkner, Peter. *William Morris and W. B. Yeats.* Dublin: Dolmen Press, 1962.

Fay, Gerard. *The Abbey Theatre: Cradle of Genius.* London: Hollis & Carter, 1958.

Finneran, Richard J., George Mills Harper, and William M. Murphy, eds. *Letters to W. B. Yeats.* 2 vols. New York: Columbia University Press, 1977.

Flannery, James W. *Miss Annie F. Horniman and the Abbey Theatre.* Dublin: Dolmen Press, 1970.

Foster, R. F. *Charles Stewart Parnell: The Man and His Family.* Hassocks, Sussex: Harvester Press Limited, 1976.

———. *Modern Ireland, 1600–1972.* London: Allen Lane, Penguin Press, 1988.

———. *W. B. Yeats: A Life.* Vol. 1, *The Apprentice Mage, 1865–1914.* Oxford and New York: Oxford University Press, 1997.

———. *W. B. Yeats: A Life.* Vol. 2, *The Arch-Poet, 1915–1939.* Oxford and New York: Oxford University Press, 2003.

Frazer, James George. *The Golden Bough: The Roots of Religion and Folklore.* New York: Avenel Books, 1981. This reprints the first edition of 1890.

———. *The Golden Bough: A Study in Magic and Religion.* Part IV, Vol. 1, the Palgrave Archive Edition.

Basingstoke, England: Palgrave, 2002. This reprints the third edition of 1915.

Frenz, Horst, ed. *Nobel Lectures: Literature, 1901–1967*. Amsterdam and New York: Elsevier Publishing Company, 1969.

Frye, Northrop. *Spiritus Mundi: Essays on Literature, Myth, and Society*. Bloomington: Indiana University Press, 1983.

Gibson, Matthew. *Yeats, Coleridge and the Romantic Sage*. London: Macmillan, 2000.

Gifford, Don. *Joyce Annotated: Notes for* Dubliners *and* A Portrait of the Artist as a Young Man. 2d ed. Berkeley: University of California Press, 1982.

———. *Ulysses Annotated: Notes for James Joyce's* Ulysses. 2d ed. Berkeley: University of California Press, 1988.

Gogarty, Oliver St John. *W. B. Yeats: A Memoir*. Dublin: Dolmen Press, 1963.

Gonne, Iseult. *Letters to W. B. Yeats and Ezra Pound from Iseult Gonne: a girl that knew all Dante once*. Edited by A. Norman Jeffares, Anna MacBride White, and Christina Bridgwater. Basingstoke and New York: Palgrave Macmillan, 2004.

Gonne, Maud. *The Autobiography of Maud Gonne: A Servant of the Queen*. Edited by A. Norman Jeffares and Anna MacBride White. Chicago: University of Chicago Press, 1995.

Gonne, Maud, and John Quinn. *Too Long a Sacrifice: The Letters of Maud Gonne and John Quinn*. Edited by Janis and Richard Londraville. Selinsgrove, Pa.: Susquehanna University Press, 1999.

Gooddie, Sheila. *Annie Horniman: A Pioneer in the Theatre*. London: Methuen, 1990.

Grant, Michael. *Greek and Latin Authors, 800 B.C.–A.D. 1000*. New York: H. W. Wilson Company, 1980.

Graves, Robert. *The Greek Myths*. London and New York: Penguin Books, 1992.

Gregory, Anne. *Me and Nu: Childhood at Coole*. Gerrards Cross, England: Colin Smythe, 1970.

Gregory, Augusta. *Coole*. Edited by Colin Smythe. Dublin: Dolmen Press, 1971.

———. *Cuchulain of Muirthemne: The Story of the Men of the Red Branch of Ulster Arranged and Put into English by Lady Gregory*. New York: Oxford University Press, 1970.

———. *Gods and Fighting Men: The Story of the Tuatha De Danaan and of the Fianna of Ireland, Arranged and Put into English by Lady Gregory*. Gerrards Cross, England: Colin Smythe, 1976.

———. *The Kiltartan Books: Comprising the Kiltartan Poetry, History and Wonder Books*. Gerrards Cross: Colin Smythe, 1971.

———. *Lady Gregory's Diaries, 1892–1902*. Edited by James Pethica. Gerrards Cross, England: Colin Smythe, 1996.

———. *Lady Gregory's Journals*. Vol. 1. Edited by Daniel J. Murphy. New York: Oxford University Press, 1978.

———. *Lady Gregory's Journals*. Vol. 2. Edited by Daniel J. Murphy. New York: Oxford University Press, 1987.

———. *Lady Gregory's Journals, 1916–1930*. Edited by Lennox Robinson. New York: Macmillan Company, 1947.

———. *Our Irish Theatre: A Chapter of Autobiography*. New York: Oxford University Press, 1972.

———. *Poets and Dreamers: Studies and Translations from the Irish by Lady Gregory Including Nine Plays by Douglas Hyde*. New York: Oxford University Press, 1974.

———. *Seventy Years: Being the Autobiography of Lady Gregory*. Gerrards Cross, England: Colin Smythe, 1974.

———. *Sir Hugh Lane: His Life and Legacy*. New York: Oxford University Press, 1973.

———. *Visions & Beliefs in the West of Ireland*. Gerrards Cross, England: Colin Smythe, 1976.

Gwynn, Denis. *Edward Martyn and the Irish Revival*. New York: Lemma Publishing, 1974.

Gwynn, Stephen. *Irish Literature and Drama in the English Language: A Short History*. London and New York: Thomas Nelson and Sons, 1936.

———, ed. *Scattering Branches: Tributes to the Memory of W. B. Yeats*. New York: Macmillan Company, 1940.

Hallam, Arthur. *The Writings of Arthur Hallam*. Edited by T. H. Vail Motter. New York: Modern Language Association of America, 1943.

Hanley, Mary, and Liam Miller. *Thoor Ballylee: Home of William Butler Yeats*. Mountrath, Ireland: Dolmen Press, 1984.

Hardwick, Joan. *The Yeats Sisters: A Biography of Susan and Elizabeth Yeats*. London: Pandora, 1996.

Harper, George Mills. *The Making of Yeats's 'A Vision': A Study of the Automatic Script*. 2 vols. Carbondale and Edwardsville: Southern Illinois University Press, 1987.

———. *W. B. Yeats and W. T. Horton: The Record of an Occult Friendship.* Atlantic Highlands, N.J.: Humanities Press, 1980.

———. *Yeats's Golden Dawn.* New York: Barnes & Noble, 1974.

Harwood, John. *Olivia Shakespear and W. B. Yeats: After Long Silence.* Basingstoke, England: Macmillan, 1989.

Henn, T. R. *The Lonely Tower: Studies in the Poetry of W. B. Yeats.* London: Methuen, 1966.

Herbermann, Charles G., Edward A. Pace, Condé B. Pallen, Thomas J. Shahan, John J. Wynne, eds. *The Catholic Encyclopedia: An International Work of Reference on the Constitution, Doctrine, Discipline, and History of the Catholic Church.* New York: Encyclopedia Press, 1913–1914.

Hilton, Timothy. *The Pre-Raphaelites.* New York: Harry N. Abrams, 1971.

Hogan, Robert, ed. *Dictionary of Irish Literature.* 2 vols. Westport, Conn.: Greenwood Press, 1996.

Holloway, Joseph. *Joseph Holloway's Abbey Theatre: A Selection from His Unpublished Journal* Impressions of a Dublin Playgoer. Edited by Robert Hogan and Michael J. O'Neill. Carbondale and Edwardsville: Southern Illinois University Press, 1967.

Hone, Joseph. *The Life of George Moore.* London: Victor Gollancz, 1936.

———. *W. B. Yeats.* Harmondsworth, England: Penguin, 1971.

Horton, W. T. *A Book of Images.* London: Unicorn Press, 1898.

Hough, Graham. *The Last Romantics.* London: Methuen, New York: Barnes & Noble, 1961.

Howe, Ellic. *The Magicians of the Golden Dawn: A Documentary History of a Magical Order, 1887–1923.* London: Routledge & Kegan Paul, 1972.

Hunt, Hugh. *The Abbey: Ireland's National Theatre, 1904–1978.* New York: Columbia University Press, 1979.

Hyde, Douglas. *Language, Lore and Lyrics: Essays and Lectures.* Blackrock, County Dublin: Irish Academic Press, 1986.

Ishibashi, Hiro. *Yeats and the Noh: Types of Japanese Beauty and Their Reflection in Yeats's Plays.* Edited

by Anthony Kerrigan. Dublin: Dolmen Press, 1966.

Jeffares, A. Norman. *A New Commentary on the Poems of W. B. Yeats.* Stanford, Calif.: Stanford University Press, 1984.

———, ed. *W. B. Yeats: The Critical Heritage.* London and Boston: Routledge & Kegan Paul, 1977.

———. *W. B. Yeats: Man and Poet.* New York: Barnes & Noble, 1966.

———. *W. B. Yeats: A New Biography.* London: Hutchinson, 1988.

Jeffares, A. Norman, and K. G. W. Cross, eds. *In Excited Reverie: A Centenary Tribute to William Butler Yeats 1865–1939.* London: Macmillan; New York: St. Martin's Press, 1965.

Jeffares, A. Norman, and A. S. Knowland. *A Commentary on the Collected Plays of W. B. Yeats.* London and Basingstoke: Macmillan Press, 1975.

Jochum, K. P. S. *A Classified Bibliography of Criticism.* 2d ed. Urbana: University of Illinois Press, 1990.

Johnson, Josephine. *Florence Farr: Barnard Shaw's 'New Woman'.* Totowa, N.J.: Rowman and Littlefield, 1975.

Joyce, James. *The Critical Writings.* Edited by Ellsworth Mason and Richard Ellmann. New York: Viking Press, 1964.

———. *Letters.* Vol. 1. Edited by Stuart Gilbert. New York: Viking Press, 1966.

———. *Letters.* Vols. 2–3. Edited by Richard Ellmann. New York: Viking Press, 1966.

———. *A Portrait of the Artist as a Young Man.* Edited by Chester G. Anderson. New York: Viking Press, 1968.

———. *Ulysses.* Edited by Hans Walter Gabler. London: Bodley Head, 1993.

Joyce, Stanislaus. *My Brother's Keeper: James Joyce's Early Years.* New York: Viking Press, 1958.

Keats, John. *The Complete Poems.* Edited by Miriam Allot. London and New York: Longman, 1972.

Kee, Robert. *The Green Flag.* Vol. 1, *The Most Distressful Country.* Harmondsworth, England: Penguin, 1989.

———. *The Green Flag.* Vol. 2, *The Bold Fenian Men.* Harmondsworth, England: Penguin, 1989.

———. *The Green Flag.* Vol. 3, *Ourselves Alone.* Harmondsworth, England: Penguin, 1989.

Kelly, John S. *A W. B. Yeats Chronology.* Basingstoke and New York: Palgrave Macmillan, 2003.

Kenner, Hugh. *A Colder Eye: The Modern Irish Writers*. New York: Penguin, 1984.

———. *The Pound Era*. Berkeley and Los Angeles: University of California Press, 1973.

Kermode, Frank. *Romantic Image*. London: Routledge, 2002.

Kiely, Kevin. *Francis Stuart: Artist and Outcast*. Dublin: Liffey Press, 2007.

King, Francis. *The Rites of Modern Occult Magic*. New York: Macmillan Company, 1971.

Kirby, Sheelah. *Yeats Country: A Guide to the Sligo District and Other Places in the West of Ireland Associated with the Life and Work of W. B. Yeats*. Atlantic Highlands, N.J.: Humanities Press, 1977.

Kohfeldt, Mary Lou. *Lady Gregory: The Woman behind the Irish Renaissance*. New York: Atheneum, 1985.

Knight, G. Wilson. *The Starlit Dome: Studies in the Poetry of Vision*. New York: Barnes & Noble, 1960.

Krimm, Bernard G. *W. B. Yeats and the Emergence of the Irish Free State, 1918–1939: Living in the Explosion*. Troy, N.Y.: Whitston Publishing Company, 1981.

Kuch, Peter. *Yeats and A.E.: 'The antagonism that unites dear friends'*. Gerrards Cross: Colin Smythe; Totowa, N.J.: Barnes & Noble, 1986.

Lewis, Samuel. *A Topographical Dictionary of Ireland*. 2 vols. Baltimore: Genealogical Publishing Company, 1984.

Loizeaux, Elizabeth Bergmann. *W. B. Yeats and the Visual Arts*. New Brunswick. N.J.: Rutgers University Press, 1986.

Longenbach, James. *Stone Cottage: Pound, Yeats, and Modernism*. New York: Oxford University Press, 1988.

Ludwigson, Kathryn R. *Edward Dowden*. New York: Twayne Publishers, 1973.

Lyons, F. S. L. *Ireland Since the Famine*. London: Weidenfeld and Nicolson, 1971.

Macardle, Dorothy. *The Irish Republic: A Documented Chronicle of the Anglo-Irish Conflict and the Partitioning of Ireland, with a Detailed Account of the Period 1916–1923*. London: Corgi, 1968.

MacCarthy, Fiona. *William Morris: A Life for Our Time*. London: Faber and Faber, 1994.

MacNeice, Louis. *The Poetry of W. B. Yeats*. New York: Oxford University Press, 1941.

Malins, Edward. *Yeats and the Easter Rising*. Dublin: Dolmen Press, 1965.

Mannin, Ethel. *Young in the Twenties: A Chapter of Autobiography*. London: Hutchinson, 1971.

Masefield, John. *Some Memories of W. B. Yeats*. Shannon: Irish University Press, 1971.

Mathers, Powys, trans. *The Book of the Thousand Nights and One Night: Rendered into English from the Literal and Complete French Translation of Dr J. C. Mardrus*. 4 vols. London and New York: Routledge, 1996.

Mayes, Elizabeth, and Paula Murphy, eds. *Images and Insights*. Dublin: Hugh Lane Municipal Gallery of Modern Art, 1993.

McCoole, Sinéad. *Hazel: A Life of Lady Lavery, 1880–1935*. Dublin: Lilliput Press, 1996.

McGarry, James P. *Place Names in the Writings of William Butler Yeats*. Edited by Edward Malins. Gerrards Cross, England: Colin Smythe, 1976.

Meade, Marion. *Madame Blavatsky: The Woman behind the Myth*. New York: G.P. Putnam, 1980.

Melchiori, Giorgio. *The Whole Mystery of Art: Pattern into Poetry in the Work of W. B. Yeats*. Westport, Conn.: Greenwood Press, 1979.

Mikhail, E. H., ed. *The Abbey Theatre: Interviews and Recollections*. Totowa, N.J.: Barnes & Noble Books, 1988.

———. ed., *Lady Gregory: Interviews and Recollections*. Totowa, N.J.: Rowman and Littlefield, 1977.

———. ed., *W. B. Yeats: Interviews and Recollections*. 2 vols. New York: Barnes & Noble, 1977.

Miller, Liam. *The Dun Emer Press, Later the Cuala Press*. Dublin: Dolmen Press, 1973.

———. *The Noble Drama of W. B. Yeats*. Atlantic Highlands, N.J.: Humanities Press, 1977.

Moore, George. *Hail and Farewell*. Edited by Richard Cave. Toronto: Macmillan of Canada, 1976.

———. "Yeats, Lady Gregory, and Synge," *The English Review*, January 1914, pgs. 167–180, and February 1914, pgs. 350–364.

More, Henry. *The Immortality of the Soul*. Edited by Alexander Jacob. Dordrecht, Netherlands: Martinus Nijhoff Publishers, 1987.

Morris, May, and John Quinn. *On Poetry, Painting, and Politics: The Letters of May Morris and John Quinn*. Selinsgrove, Pa.: Susquehanna University Press, 1997.

Murphy, Frank Hughes. *Yeats's Early Poetry: The Quest for Reconciliation*. Baton Rouge: Louisiana State University Press, 1975.

Murphy, William M. *Family Secrets: William Butler Yeats and His Relatives.* Syracuse: Syracuse University Press, 1995.

———. *Prodigal Father: The Life of John Butler Yeats (1839–1922).* Ithaca and London: Cornell University Press, 1978.

Nokes, David. *Jonathan Swift, A Hypocrite Reversed: A Critical Biography.* Oxford: Oxford University Press, 1985.

Norman, Diana. *Terrible Beauty: A Life of Constance Markiewicz.* Dublin: Poolbeg Press, 1988.

O'Connor, Patrick. Introduction. *Municipal Art Gallery.* Dublin: Corporation of Dublin, 1958. An illustrated catalogue of the gallery's collection.

O'Connor, Ulick. *Oliver St John Gogarty: A Poet and His Times.* London: Jonathan Cape, 1964.

O'Grady, Standish James. *History of Ireland.* Vol. 1, *The Heroic Period*; vol. 2, *Cuculain and His Contemporaries.* New York: Lemma Publishing, 1970.

O'Leary, John. *Recollections of Fenians and Fenianism.* London: Downey and Co., 1896.

Oram, Hugh. *The Newspaper Book: A History of Newspapers in Ireland, 1649–1983.* Dublin: MO Books, 1983.

O'Shea, Edward. *A Descriptive Catalog of W. B. Yeats's Library.* New York; London: Garland Publishing, 1985.

Pater, Walter. *The Renaissance: Studies in Art and Poetry.* Edited by Donald L. Hill. Berkeley, Los Angeles, and London: University of California Press, 1980.

Plato. *The Collected Dialogues.* Edited by Edith Hamilton and Huntington Cairns. Princeton: Princeton University Press, 1987.

Plotinus. *The Enneads.* Translated by Stephen MacKenna. London: Faber and Faber, 1969.

Pound, Ezra. *The Cantos.* London: Faber and Faber, 1987.

———. *Literary Essays of Ezra Pound.* Edited by T. S. Eliot. London: Faber and Faber, 1985.

———. *Personae: The Collected Shorter Poems of Ezra Pound.* New York: James Laughlin, 1971.

———. *Selected Letters of Ezra Pound, 1907–1941.* New York: New Directions, 1971.

Pyle, Hilary. *Yeats: Portrait of an Artistic Family.* London: Merrell Holberton, 1997.

Quinn, John. Introduction. *Complete Catalogue of the Library of John Quinn Sold by Auction in Five Parts (with Printed Prices).* 2 vols. New York: Lemma Publishing, 1969.

———. *The Letters of John Quinn to William Butler Yeats.* Edited by Alan Himber. Ann Arbor: University of Michigan Research Press, 1983.

Raine, Kathleen. *Yeats the Initiate: Essays on Certain Themes in the Work of W. B. Yeats.* Mountrath, Ireland: Dolmen Press, London: George Allen & Unwin, 1986.

Reid, B. L. *The Man from New York: John Quinn and His Friends.* New York: Oxford University Press, 1968.

Ritschel, Nelson O'Ceallaigh. *Productions of the Irish Theatre Movement, 1899–1916: A Checklist.* Westport, Conn.: Greenwood Press, 2001.

Robinson, Lennox. *Ireland's Abbey Theatre: A History, 1899–1951.* London: Sidgwick and Jackson, 1951.

Robinson, Lennox, and Micheál Ó hAodha. *Pictures at the Abbey: The Collection of the Irish National Theatre with a Conversation Piece by Lennox Robinson.* Mountrath, Portlaoise: Dolmen Press, 1983.

Russell, George. *Letters from AE.* Edited by Alan Denson. London, New York, and Toronto: Abelard-Schuman, 1961.

———. *Some Passages from the Letters of Æ to W. B. Yeats.* Shannon: Irish University Press, 1971.

Saddlemyer, Ann. *Becoming George: The Life of Mrs W. B. Yeats.* Oxford and New York: Oxford University Press, 2002.

Salvadori, Corinna. *Yeats and Castiglione: Poet and Courtier.* Dublin: Allen Figgis, 1965.

Savoy, The (periodical). Edited by Arthur Symons, Nos. 1–8. London: Leonard Smithers, 1896.

Shelley, Percy Bysshe. *The Complete Poems of Percy Bysshe Shelley.* New York: Modern Library, 1994.

———. *Shelley's Poetry and Prose.* 2d ed. Edited by Donald H. Reiman and Neil Fraistat. New York and London: W.W. Norton & Company, 2002.

Shovlin, Frank. *The Irish Literary Periodical 1923–1958.* Oxford: Clarendon Press, 2003.

Skene, Reg. *The Cuchulain Plays of W. B. Yeats: A Study.* New York: Columbia University Press, 1974.

Smythe, Colin. *A Guide to Coole Park, Co. Galway: Home of Lady Gregory.* Gerrards Cross, England: Colin Smythe, 1973.

———. ed. *Robert Gregory 1881–1918: A Centenary Tribute with a Foreword by His Children.* Gerrards Cross, England: Colin Smythe, 1981.

Stallworthy, John. *Between the Lines: Yeats's Poetry in the Making.* Oxford, England: Clarendon Press, 1963.

———. *Vision and Revision in Yeats's Last Poems.* Oxford, England: Clarendon Press, 1969.

———, ed. *Yeats: Last Poems.* Nashville: Aurora Publishers, 1970.

Stevenson, Robert Louis. *The Letters of Robert Louis Stevenson.* Vol. 8. Edited by Bradford A. Booth and Ernest Mehew. New Haven and London: Yale University Press, 1995.

Stuart, Francis. *Black List, Section H.* Carbondale and Edwardsville: Southern Illinois University Press, 1971.

Summerfield, Henry. *That Myriad-Minded Man: A Biography of George William Russell, "A.E.," 1867–1935.* Totowa, N.J.: Rowman and Littlefield, 1975.

Symons, Arthur. *Arthur Symons: Selected Letters, 1880–1935.* Edited by Karl Beckson and John M. Munro. Basingstoke, England: Macmillan, 1989.

———. *Cities and Sea-Coasts and Islands.* Evanston, Ill.: Marlboro Press/Northwestern University Press, 1998.

———. *Dramatis Personae.* London: Faber & Gwyer, 1925.

———. *The Memoirs of Arthur Symons: Life and Art in the 1890s.* Edited by Karl Beckson. University Park and London: Pennsylvania State University Press, 1977.

———. *Poems by Arthur Symons.* 2 vols. London: William Heinemann, 1924.

———. *The Symbolist Movement in Literature.* New York: E.P. Dutton and Co., 1958.

Synge, J. M. *The Collected Letters of John Millington Synge.* Edited by Ann Saddlemyer. 2 vols. Oxford: Clarendon Press, 1983–1984.

———. *Collected Plays and Poems and The Aran Islands.* Edited by Alison Smith. London: J.M. Dent, Rutland, Vt.: Charles E. Tuttle, 1996.

Terrell, Carroll F. *A Companion to The Cantos of Ezra Pound.* Berkeley: University of California Press, 1993.

Thuente, Mary Helen. *W. B. Yeats and Irish Folklore.* Totowa, N.J.: Barnes & Noble, 1981.

Torchiana, Donald T. *W. B. Yeats and Georgian Ireland.* Washington, D.C.: Catholic University of America Press, 1992.

Tynan, Katharine. *Twenty-Five Years: Reminiscences.* New York: Devin-Adair Company, 1913.

Unterecker, John. *A Reader's Guide to William Butler Yeats.* New York: Noonday Press, 1959.

Ure, Peter. *Yeats and Anglo-Irish Literature.* Edited by C. J. Rawson. Liverpool: Liverpool University Press, 1974.

———. *Yeats the Playwright: A Commentary on Character and Design in the Major Plays.* New York: Barnes & Noble, 1963.

Ussher, Arland. Introduction. *Yeats at the Municipal Gallery.* Dublin: Charlemont House, 1959.

Vendler, Helen Hennessy. *Yeats's Vision and the Later Plays.* Cambridge, Mass.: Harvard University Press, 1963.

Vickery, John B. *The Literary Impact of The Golden Bough.* Princeton, N.J.: Princeton University Press, 1973.

Villiers de l'Isle-Adam, Philippe-Auguste. *Axel.* Translated by Marilyn Gaddis Rose. Dublin: Dolmen Press, 1970.

Virgil. *The Aeneid.* Translated by Robert Fitzgerald. New York: Vintage Books, 1985.

Wade, Allan. *A Bibliography of the Writings of W. B. Yeats.* 3d ed. Revised and edited by Russell K. Alspach. London: Rupert Hart-Davis, 1968.

Walsh, Caroline. *The Homes of Irish Writers.* Dublin: Anvil Books, 1982.

Ward, Margaret. *Maud Gonne: A Life.* London: Pandora, 1993.

Watson, Forbes. Introduction. *John Quinn, 1870–1925, Collection of Paintings, Water Colors, Drawings & Sculpture.* Huntington, N.Y.: Pidgeon Hill Press, 1926.

Weintraub, Stanley. *Beardsley.* New York: George Braziller, 1967.

———. *The Savoy: Nineties Experiment.* University Park: Pennsylvania State University Press, 1966.

Welch, Robert. *The Abbey Theatre, 1899–1999.* Oxford: Oxford University Press, 1999.

Wellesley, Dorothy. *Far Have I Travelled.* London: James Barrie, 1952.

Whitaker, Thomas R. *Swan and Shadow: Yeats's Dialogue with History.* Chapel Hill: University of North Carolina Press, 1964.

Wilson, F. A. C. *W. B. Yeats and Tradition.* New York: Macmillan Company, 1958.

———. *Yeats's Iconography*. London: Victor Gollancz, 1960.

Winters, Yvor. *The Poetry of W. B. Yeats*. Denver, Colo.: Alan Swallow, 1960.

Yeats, John Butler. *Early Memories: Some Chapters of Autobiography*. Shannon: Irish University Press, 1971.

———. *Further Letters of John Butler Yeats: Selected by Lennox Robinson*. Shannon: Irish University Press, 1971.

———. *Letters to his Son W. B. Yeats and Others, 1869–1922*. Edited by Joseph Hone, abridged by John McGahern. London: Faber and Faber, 1999.

———. *Passages from the Letters of John Butler Yeats: Selected by Ezra Pound*. Shannon: Irish University Press, 1971.

Yeats, W. B. *Autobiographies*. Edited by William H. O'Donnell and Douglas N. Archibald. The Collected Works of W. B. Yeats, vol. 3. New York: Scribner, 1999.

———. *The Collected Letters of W. B. Yeats*. Vol. 1. Edited by John Kelly and Eric Domville. Oxford: Clarendon Press, 1986.

———. *The Collected Letters of W. B. Yeats*. Vol. 2. Edited by Warwick Gould, John Kelly, and Deirdre Toomey. Oxford: Clarendon Press, 1997.

———. *The Collected Letters of W. B. Yeats*. Vol. 3. Edited by John Kelly and Ronald Schuchard. Oxford: Clarendon Press, 1994.

———. *The Collected Letters of W. B. Yeats*. Vol. 4. Edited by John Kelly and Ronald Schuchard. Oxford: Oxford University Press, 2005.

———. *A Critical Edition of Yeats's A Vision (1925)*. Edited by George Mills Harper and Walter Kelly Hood. London: Macmillan, 1978.

———. *Early Articles and Reviews: Uncollected Articles and Reviews Written between 1886 and 1900*. Edited by John P. Frayne and Madeleine Marchaterre. The Collected Works of W. B. Yeats, vol. 9. New York: Scribner, 2004.

———. *Early Essays*. Edited by Richard J. Finneran and George Bornstein. The Collected Works of W. B. Yeats. vol. 4. New York: Scribner, 2007.

———. *Essays and Introductions*. New York: Macmillan Company, 1961.

———. *Explorations*. London: Macmillan & Co., 1962.

———. *The Irish Dramatic Movement*. Edited by Mary FitzGerald and Richard J. Finneran. The Collected Works of W. B. Yeats, vol. 8. New York: Scribner, 2003.

———. *John Sherman and Dhoya*. Edited by Richard J. Finneran. The Collected Works of W. B. Yeats, vol. 12. New York: Macmillan Publishing Company, 1991.

———. *Later Articles and Reviews: Uncollected Articles, Reviews, and Radio Broadcasts Written after 1900*. Edited by Colton Johnson. The Collected Works of W. B. Yeats, vol. 10. New York: Scribner, 2000.

———. *Later Essays*. Edited by William H. O'Donnell. The Collected Works of W. B. Yeats, vol. 5. New York: Charles Scribner's Sons, 1994.

———. *The Letters of W. B. Yeats*. Edited by Allan Wade. New York: Macmillan Company, 1955.

———. *Letters to the New Island*. Edited by George Bornstein and Hugh Witemeyer. The Collected Works of W. B. Yeats, vol. 7. N.Y.: Macmillan Publishing Company, 1989.

———. *Literatim Transcription of the Manuscript of William Butler Yeats's The Speckled Bird*. Edited by William H. O'Donnell. Delmar, New York: Scholars' Facsimiles & Reprints, 1976.

———. *Memoirs*. Edited by Denis Donoghue. New York: Macmillan Company, 1973.

———. *Mythologies*. London: Macmillan, 1982.

———. *Mythologies*. Edited by Warwick Gould and Deirdre Toomey. Basingstoke, England: Palgrave Macmillan, 2005.

———. *The Plays*. Edited by David R. Clark and Rosalind E. Clark. The Collected Works of W. B. Yeats, vol. 2. New York: Scribner, 2001.

———. *The Poems*. Edited by Richard J. Finneran. The Collected Works of W. B. Yeats, vol. 1. Basingstoke, England: Macmillan, 1991.

———. *Prefaces and Introductions: Uncollected Prefaces and Introductions by Yeats to Works by Other Authors and to Anthologies Edited by Yeats*. Edited by William H. O'Donnell. The Collected Works of W. B. Yeats, vol. 6. New York: Macmillan Publishing Company, 1989.

———. *The Secret Rose, Stories by W. B. Yeats: A Variorum Edition*. Edited by Phillip L. Marcus, Warwick Gould, and Michael J. Sidnell. Ithaca and London: Cornell University Press, 1981.

————. *The Senate Speeches of W. B. Yeats.* Edited by Donald R. Pearce. Bloomington: Indiana University Press, 1960.

————. *The Speckled Bird.* Edited by William H. O'Donnell. Dublin: Cuala Press, 1973–1974.

————. *The Speckled Bird.* Edited by William H. O'Donnell. Toronto: McClelland and Stewart, 1976.

————. *The Speckled Bird: An Autobiographical Novel with Variant Versions.* Edited by William H. O'Donnell. Basingstoke, England: Palgrave Macmillan, 2003.

————. *Uncollected Prose by W. B. Yeats.* Vol. 1. Edited by John P. Frayne. New York: Columbia University Press, 1970.

————. *Uncollected Prose by W. B. Yeats.* Vol. 2. Edited by John P. Frayne and Colton Johnson. New York: Columbia University Press, 1976.

————. *The Variorum Edition of the Plays of W. B. Yeats.* Edited by Russell K. Alspach. New York: Macmillan Company, 1966.

————. *The Variorum Edition of the Poems of W. B. Yeats.* Edited by Peter Allt and Russell K. Alspach. New York: Macmillan Company, 1968.

————. *A Vision.* London: Macmillan, 1981.

————. *Yeats's Poems.* Edited by A. Norman Jeffares. Basingstoke, England: Macmillan, 1996.

————, ed. *A Book of Irish Verse.* Mineola, N.Y.: Dover, 2001.

————, ed. *Fairy and Folk Tales of Ireland.* Gerrards Cross, England: Colin Smythe, 1988. Encompasses *Fairy and Folk Tales of the Irish Peasantry* (1888) and *Irish Fairy Tales* (1892).

————, ed. *The Oxford Book of Modern Verse 1892–1935.* New York: Oxford University Press, 1936.

————, ed. *Representative Irish Tales.* Gerrards Cross, England: Colin Smythe, 1979.

————, ed. *Stories from Carleton.* New York: Lemma Publishing, 1973.

Yeats, W. B., and John Eglinton, A. E., and W. Larminie. *Literary Ideals in Ireland.* New York: Lemma Publishing Corporation, 1973.

Yeats, W. B., Florence Farr, and Bernard Shaw, *Florence Farr, Bernard Shaw, and W. B. Yeats.* Edited by Clifford Bax. Shannon: Irish University Press, 1971.

Yeats, W. B., and Maud Gonne. *The Gonne-Yeats Letters 1893–1938.* Edited by Anna MacBride White and A. Norman Jeffares. Syracuse, N.Y.: Syracuse University Press, 1994.

Yeats, W. B., Lady Gregory, and J. M. Synge. *Theatre Business: The Correspondence of the First Abbey Theatre Directors: William Butler Yeats, Lady Gregory and J. M. Synge.* Edited by Ann Saddlemyer. Gerrards Cross, England: Colin Smythe, 1982.

Yeats, W. B., and Lionel Johnson. *Poetry and Ireland: Essays by W. B. Yeats and Lionel Johnson.* Shannon: Irish University Press, 1970.

Yeats, W. B., and T. Sturge Moore. *W. B. Yeats and T. Sturge Moore: Their Correspondence 1901–1937.* Edited by Ursula Bridge. New York: Oxford University Press, 1953.

Yeats, W. B., and Margot Ruddock. *Ah, Sweet Dancer: W. B. Yeats and Margaret Ruddock.* New York: Macmillan Company, 1971.

Yeats, W. B., and Dorothy Wellesley. *Letters on Poetry from W. B. Yeats to Dorothy Wellesley.* London and New York: Oxford University Press, 1964.

Yeats, W. B., and Edwin John Ellis, eds. *The Works of William Blake, Poetic, Symbolic, and Critical.* 3 vols. London: B. Quaritch, 1893.

Yeats, W. B., and Shree Purohit Swāmi, trans. *The Ten Principal Upanishads.* New York: Macmillan Publishing Co., 1975.

Ziolkowski, Theodore. *The View from the Tower: Origins of an Antimodernist Image.* Princeton, N.J.: Princeton University Press, 1998.

Online Sources

Oxford Art Online (Oxford: Oxford University Press, 1998–Present). Provides access to the entire text of *The Dictionary of Art* (1996, 34 vols.) and several other reference works, with the continuous addition of new and updated articles. URL: www.oxfordartonline.com.

Oxford Dictionary of National Biography. Online edition, edited by Lawrence Goldman (Oxford and New York: Oxford University Press, 2004–Present). URL: www.oxforddnb.com.

Oxford English Dictionary. Online edition (Oxford: Oxford University Press, 2000–Present). "A complete text of the 2nd. ed. of the Oxford English dictionary with quarterly updates, including revisions not available in any other form." URL: www.oed.com.

The W. B. Yeats Collection. Editorial adviser Richard J. Finneran (Alexandria, Virginia: Chadwyck-Healey, 1999–Present). "*The W. B. Yeats Collection* contains the major work of W. B. Yeats in all genres, including poetry, plays, criticism and fiction, collected in 22 volumes."

WorldCat (Dublin, Ohio: OCLC, 1971–Present). An electronic database providing access to 110 million bibliographic records held by participating institutions. URL: www.oclc.org/worldcat.

INDEX

This index does not include every reference, but every reference likely to interest the reader. Trivial and incidental references are not indexed, as, for example, the reference to Lady Gregory in a sentence such as, "He told Lady Gregory that the god of the new age would be a Buddha or Sphinx." or the reference to *Autobiographies* in a sentence such as, "In *Autobiographies*, Yeats extravagantly compares Gonne to the statue of Artemisia in the British Museum." Prose works are indexed where they are the subject of discussion or analysis, but not where they are merely quoted, as in the sentence above. References found in the bibliographies at the end of entries and in the appendixes at the end of the book are not indexed. For the most part, legendary figures, fictive characters, peripheral historical figures, and peripheral place-names are not indexed.

References to literary works, excepting those by Yeats, are indexed under the author's name. Literary works are indexed by their final titles and retain their original capitalization. Superseded titles are not indexed. Stories and poems associated with Red Hanrahan are indexed under Red Hanrahan. Places and landmarks in County Sligo (Ben Bulben, Lissadell, etc.) are indexed under Sligo. Doctrines associated with *Per Amica Silentia Lunae* (anti-self, etc.) and *A Vision* (gyre, etc.) are indexed under these works. Installments of Yeats's autobiography are indexed under *Autobiographies*.

Pages containing images are identified as such. Page numbers in boldface indicate the principal discussion of a subject. Readers should consult these pages before turning elsewhere.